Fodor's 97

New England

" "When it comes to information on regional history, what to see and do, and shopping, these guides are exhaustive."

—*USAir Magazine*

"Usable, sophisticated restaurant coverage, with an emphasis on good value."

—Andy Birsh, *Gourmet Magazine* columnist

"Valuable because of their comprehensiveness."

—*Minneapolis Star-Tribune*

"Fodor's always delivers high quality...thoughtfully presented...thorough."

—*Houston Post*

"An excellent choice for those who want everything under one cover."

—*Washington Post* "

Fodor's Travel Publications, Inc.
New York • Toronto • London • Sydney • Auckland
http://www.fodors.com/

Fodor's New England

Editor: Anastasia Redmond Mills

Contributors: Jonathon Alsop, Craig Altschul, Steven K. Amsterdam, Robert Andrews, Dorothy Antczak, Marty Basch, David Brown, Anthony Chase, Andrew Collins, Jeanne Cooper, Laura Cronin, Audra Epstein, Robert Fisher, Paula Flanders, Mary Frakes, Tara Hamilton, Katherine Imbrie, Anne Merewood, Rebecca Miller, Dale Northrup, Tracy Patruno, Anne Peracca, Heidi Sarna, William G. Scheller, Helayne Schiff, Stephanie Schorow, Mary Ellen Schultz, M. T. Schwartzman, (Gold Guide editor), Peggi F. Simmons, Dinah Spritzer.

Creative Director: Fabrizio La Rocca

Cartographer: David Lindroth

Cover Photograph: David W. Hamilton/Image Bank

Text Design: Between the Covers

Copyright

ISBN 0–679–03261–4

Special Sales

Fodor's Travel Publications are available at special discounts for bulk purchases for sales promotions or premiums. Special editions, including personalized covers, excerpts of existing guides, and corporate imprints, can be created in large quantities for special needs. For more information, contact your local bookseller or write to Special Markets, Fodor's Travel Publications, 201 East 50th Street, New York, NY 10022. Inquiries from Canada should be directed to your local Canadian bookseller or sent to Random House of Canada, Ltd., Marketing Department, 1265 Aerowood Drive, Mississauga, Ontario L4W 1B9. Inquiries from the United Kingdom should be sent to Fodor's Travel Publications, 20 Vauxhall Bridge Road, London, England SW1V 2SA.

PRINTED IN THE UNITED STATES OF AMERICA

10 9 8 7 6 5 4 3 2 1

CONTENTS

ON THE ROAD WITH FODOR'S

WE'RE ALWAYS THRILLED to get letters from readers, especially one like this:

It took us an hour to decide what book to buy and we now know we picked the best one. Your book was wonderful, easy to follow, very accurate, and good on pointing out eating places, informal as well as formal. When we saw other people using your book, we would look at each other and smile.

Our editors and writers are deeply committed to making every Fodor's guide "the best one"—not only accurate but always charming, brimming with sound recommendations and solid ideas, right on the mark in describing restaurants and hotels, and full of fascinating facts that make you view what you've traveled to see in a rich new light.

About Our Writers

Our success in achieving our goals—and in helping to make your trip the best of all possible vacations—is a credit to the hard work of our extraordinary writers and editors.

A contributing editor to *National Geographic Traveler,* **William G. Scheller** writes frequently on travel. His books include *New Hampshire: Portrait of the Land and Its People* and *New Hampshire Backroads.* Not surprisingly perhaps, Scheller wrote the introduction to the New Hampshire chapter as well as the introductions to the Rhode Island, Vermont, and Maine chapters.

Originally from Maine, **Paula J. Flanders** has lived in New Hampshire for 15 years—ever since she married a New Hampshire native who refused to move. Flanders, who has a reporter's instincts and an eye for detail, writes a monthly travel feature for the *Portsmouth Sunday Herald* that focuses on lesser known destinations, and teaches writing at the University of New Hampshire.

Katherine Imbrie has been a staff writer at the *Providence Journal* since 1981. Her "leisure beat" ensures she's the first to know about great new restaurants, attractions, and B&Bs.

Anne Merewood has updated the bulk of the Massachusetts chapter (which she wrote) since 1989. Merewood has contributed travel and health articles to numerous magazines including *Islands, Vogue,* and *Child.* We Yankees don't hold her English accent against her.

Dorothy Antczak vacationed in Provincetown, Massachusetts one year and never left. From her perch on the fist of the arm that is the Cape, Antczak updates the *Cape Cod, Martha's Vineyard, Nantucket* Fodor's guide, and the same regions of this guide.

Our Beantown sightseeing savior, **Stephanie Schorow,** has yet to drop her "r"'s despite six happy years residing in the Boston area. A former Associated Press reporter and editor for TAB Newspapers, she now claims the title of assistant lifestyles editor for the *Boston Herald.* A former Cantabrigian, she refuses to divulge her closely guarded secret for finding a parking spot in Harvard Square.

Laura Cronin, who wrote our introductions to New England and to Massachusetts, has a master's degree in American history; she was raised in Connecticut, and both her grandmother and great-grandmother were Vermonters.

After many Maine summers, **Anastasia Mills,** editor, developed her tolerance for swimming in cold water ("You move around a little and you warm up"). Although she has sampled the pleasures of 47 states, Mills is determined never to venture too far from the topography, architecture, and change of seasons of her native New England. She believes that a year without making snow angels and crunching on brilliantly colored leaves is a year spent in purgatory.

New This Year

This year we've reformatted our guides to make them easier to use. Each chapter of *New England '97* begins with brand-new recommended itineraries to help you decide what to see in the time you have; a section called When to Tour points out the optimal time of day, day of the week, and season for your journey. You may also notice our fresh graphics, new in 1996. More readable and more helpful than ever? We think so—and we hope you do, too.

On the Web

Also check out Fodor's Web site (http://www.fodors.com/), where you'll find travel information on major destinations around the world and an ever-changing array of travel-savvy interactive features.

Let Us Do Your Booking

Our writers have scoured New England to come up with a well-balanced list of the best B&Bs, inns, resorts, and hotels, both small and large, new and old. But you don't have to beat the bushes for a reservation. Now that we've teamed up with an established hotel-booking service, reserving a room at the property of your choice is easy. It's fast and free, and confirmation is guaranteed. If your first choice is booked, the operators can recommend others. Call 1–800/FODORS–1 or 1–800/363–6771 (0800–89–1030 in Great Britain; 0014–800–12–8271 in Australia; 1–800/55–9101 in Ireland).

How to Use This Book

Organization

Up front is the **Gold Guide.** Its first section, **Important Contacts A to Z,** gives addresses and telephone numbers of organizations and companies that offer destination-related services and detailed information and publications. **Smart Travel Tips A to Z,** the Gold Guide's second section, gives specific information on how to accomplish what you need to in New England as well as tips on savvy traveling. Both sections are in alphabetical order by topic.

Chapters in *New England '97* are arranged by state, moving from south to north. Each state chapter is divided by region; within each region, towns are covered in logical geographical order, and attractive stretches of road and minor points of interest between them are indicated by the designation *En Route*. Throughout, Off the Beaten Path sights appear after the places from which they are most easily accessible. And within town sections, all restaurants and lodgings are grouped together. Boston, however, is treated differently, due to its size. Boston begins with an Exploring section, which is subdivided by neighborhood; each subsection lists sights in alphabetical order.

To help you decide what to visit in the time you have, all chapters begin with recommended **itineraries**; you can mix and match those from several chapters to create a complete vacation. There are also themed itineraries in Chapter 1 that cross state lines. The **A to Z section** that ends each state chapter covers getting there, getting around, and helpful contacts and resources.

At the end of the book you'll find **Portraits,** with a wonderful essay about walking Cape Cod's beaches that was originally published in *Condé Nast Traveler*. This is followed by suggestions for pretrip reading, both fiction and nonfiction, and movies on tape with New England as a backdrop.

Icons and Symbols

★   Our special recommendations
✕   Restaurant
🏠   Lodging establishment
✕🏠   Lodging establishment whose restaurant warrants a detour
⚠   Campground
☺   Rubber duckie (good for kids)
☞   Sends you to another section of the guide for more info
✉   Address
☏   Telephone number
☉   Opening and closing times
💲   Admission prices (those we give apply only to adults; substantially reduced fees are almost always available for children, students, and senior citizens)

Numbers in white and black circles—②and ❷, for example—that appear on the maps, in the margins, and within the tours correspond to one another.

Dining and Lodging

The restaurants and lodgings we list are the cream of the crop in each price range. Price charts appear in the Pleasures and Pastimes section that follows each chapter introduction.

Hotel Facilities

We always list the facilities that are available—but we don't specify whether they cost extra: When pricing accommodations, always ask what's included.

Assume that hotels operate on the **European Plan** (EP, with no meals) unless we note that they use the **American Plan** (AP, with all meals), the **Modified American Plan** (MAP, with breakfast and dinner daily), or the **Continental Plan** (CP, with a Continental breakfast daily).

Restaurant Reservations and Dress Codes

Reservations are always a good idea; we note only when they're essential or when they are not accepted. Book as far ahead as you can, and reconfirm when you get to town. Unless otherwise noted, the restaurants listed are open daily for lunch and dinner. We mention dress only when men are required to wear a jacket or a jacket and tie. Look for an overview of local habits in the Packing for New England section of Smart Travel Tips A to Z in the Gold Guide.

Credit Cards

The following abbreviations are used: **AE**, American Express; **D**, Discover; **DC**, Diners Club; **MC**, MasterCard; and **V**, Visa.

Please Write to Us

You can use this book in the confidence that all prices and opening times are based on information supplied to us at press time; Fodor's cannot accept responsibility for any errors. Time inevitably brings changes, so always confirm information when it matters—especially if you're making a detour to visit a specific place. In addition, when making reservations be sure to mention if you have a disability or are traveling with children, if you prefer a private bath or a certain type of bed, or if you have specific dietary needs or any other concerns.

Were the restaurants we recommended as described? Did our hotel picks exceed your expectations? Did you find a museum we recommended a waste of time? If you have complaints, we'll look into them and revise our entries when the facts warrant it. If you've discovered a special place that we haven't included, we'll pass the information along to our correspondents and have them check it out. So send your feedback, positive *and* negative, to the New England Editor at 201 East 50th Street, New York, New York 10022—and have a wonderful trip!

Karen Cure
Editorial Director

New England

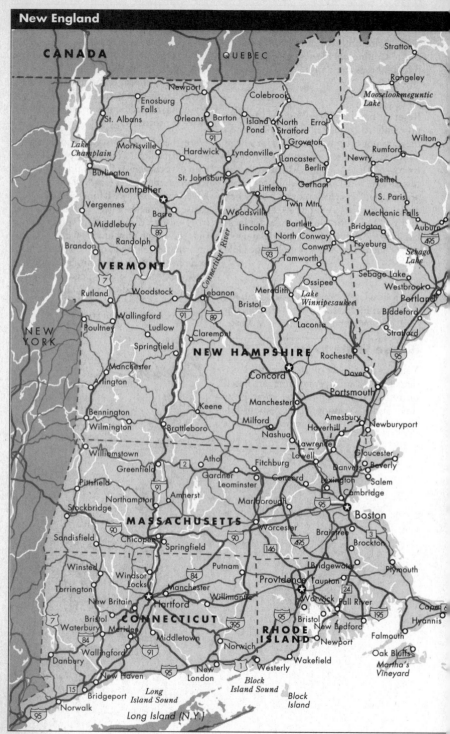

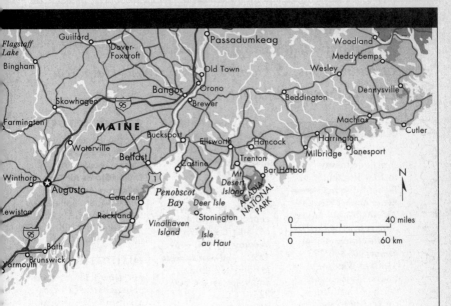

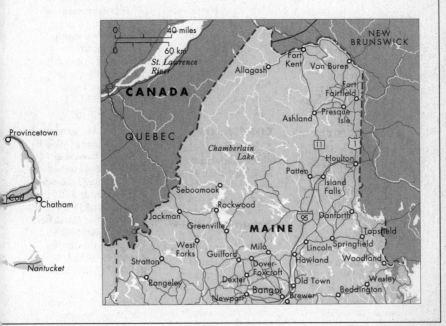

IMPORTANT CONTACTS A TO Z

An Alphabetical Listing of Publications, Organizations, & Companies That Will Help You Before, During, & After Your Trip

A

AIR TRAVEL

A major gateway to New England is Boston's **Logan International Airport** (☎ 800/235–6426), the largest airport in New England. **Bradley International Airport** (☎ 860/293–3300),in Windsor Locks, Connecticut, north of Hartford, is convenient to southern Massachusetts and all of Connecticut. **Theodore Francis Green State Airport** (☎ 401/737–4000), just outside Providence, Rhode Island, is another major airport. Additional New England airports served by major carriers include those in Manchester, New Hampshire; Portland and Bangor, Maine; Burlington, Vermont; and Hyannis and Worcester, Massachusetts.

FLYING TIME

Flying time is 1 hour from New York, 2 hours and 15 minutes from Chicago, 6 hours from Los Angeles, and 4 hours from Dallas.

CARRIERS

Airlines that fly to New England include: **American** (☎ 800/433–7300), **Carnival Airlines** (☎ 800/824–7386), **Continental** (☎ 800/525–0280), **Delta** (800/221–1212), **Northwest** (☎ 800/225–2525), **TWA** (☎ 800/221–

2000), **United** (☎ 800/722–5243), **USAir** (☎ 800/428–4322), and **Value Jet** (☎ 800/825–8538).

LOW-COST➤ For inexpensive, no-frills flights, contact **Carnival Airlines** (☎ 800/824–7386), **Midway** (☎ 800/446–4392), **Midwest Express** (☎ 800/452–2022), and **Value Jet** (☎ 800/825–8538).

FROM THE U.K.➤ Four airlines fly direct to Boston. **British Airways** (☎ 0181/897–4000; outside London, 0345/222–111) and **American** (☎ 0345/789–789) depart from Heathrow. **Northwest** (☎ 01293/561–000) and **Virgin Atlantic** (☎ 01293/747–747) fly from Gatwick. Northwest also flies from Glasgow. Flight time is approximately eight hours.

COMPLAINTS

To register complaints about charter and scheduled airlines, contact the U.S. Department of Transportation's **Aviation Consumer Protection Division** (☒ C-75, Washington, DC 20590, ☎ 202/366–2220). Complaints about lost baggage or ticketing problems and safety concerns may also be logged with the **Federal Aviation Administration (FAA) Consumer Hotline** (☎ 800/322–7873).

CONSOLIDATORS

For the names of reputable air-ticket consolidators, contact the **United States Air Consolidators Association** (☒ 925 L St., Suite 220, Sacramento, CA 95814, ☎ 916/441–4166, FAX 916/441–3520).

PUBLICATIONS

For general information about charter carriers, ask for the Department of Transportation's free brochure **"Plane Talk: Public Charter Flights"** (☒ Aviation Consumer Protection Division, C-75, Washington, DC 20590, ☎ 202/366–2220). The Department of Transportation also publishes a 58-page booklet, **"Fly Rights,"** available from the Consumer Information Center (☒ Supt. of Documents, Dept. 136C, Pueblo, CO 81009; $1.75).

For other tips, consult the Consumers Union's monthly **"Consumer Reports Travel Letter"** (☒ Box 53629, Boulder, CO 80322, ☎ 800/234–1970; $39 1st year) and the newsletter **"Travel Smart"** (☒ 40 Beechdale Rd., Dobbs Ferry, NY 10522, ☎ 800/327–3633; $37 per year).

Some worthwhile publications on the subject are *The Official Frequent Flyer Guidebook,* by Randy Petersen (☒ Airpress, 4715-C Town

Center Dr., Colorado Springs, CO 80916, ☎ 719/597–8899 or 800/487–8893; $14.99 plus $3 shipping); *Airfare Secrets Exposed,* by Sharon Tyler and Matthew Wunder (✉ Studio 4 Productions, Box 280400, Northridge, CA 91328, ☎ 818/700–2522 or 800/408–7369; $16.95 plus $2.50 shipping); *202 Tips Even the Best Business Travelers May Not Know,* by Christopher McGinnis (✉ Irwin Professional Publishing, 1333 Burr Ridge Pkwy., Burr Ridge, IL 60521, ☎ 800/634–3966; $11 plus $3.25 shipping); and *Travel Rights,* by Charles Leocha (✉ World Leisure Corporation, 177 Paris St., Boston, MA 02128, ☎ 800/444–2524; $7.95 plus $3.95 shipping).

Travelers who experience motion sickness or ear problems in flight should get the brochures **"Ears, Altitude, and Airplane Travel"** and **"What You Can Do for Dizziness & Motion Sickness"** from the American Academy of Otolaryngology (✉ 1 Prince St., Alexandria, VA 22314, ☎ 703/836–4444, FAX 703/683–5100, TTY 703/519–1585).

B
BETTER BUSINESS BUREAU

For local contacts, consult the **Council of Better Business Bureaus** (✉ 4200 Wilson Blvd., Suite 800, Arlington, VA 22203, ☎ 703/276–0100, FAX 703/525–8277).

BUS TRAVEL

Greyhound Lines (☎ 800/231–2222) provides bus service to Boston and other major cities and towns in New England. **Peter Pan Bus Lines** (☎ 800/237–8747) serves Massachusetts and southern Connecticut. **Concord Trailways** (☎ 800/639–3317) connects Boston with Portland, Bangor, and coastal Maine in addition to New Hampshire. **Bonanza** (☎ 800/556–3815) serves Connecticut, Massachusetts, and Rhode Island with connecting service to Vermont, New Hampshire, and Maine.

C
CAR RENTAL

The major car-rental companies represented in New England are **Alamo** (☎ 800/327–9633; in the U.K., 0800/272–2000), **Avis** (☎ 800/331–1212; in Canada, 800/879–2847), **Budget** (☎ 800/527–0700; in the U.K., 0800/181181), **Dollar** (known as Eurodollar outside North America, ☎ 800/800–4000; in the U.K., 0990/565–656), **Hertz** (☎ 800/654–3131; in Canada, 800/263–0600; in the U.K., 0345/555–888), and **National InterRent** (☎ 800/227–7368; in the U.K., where National is known as Europcar InterRent, 01345/222525). Rates in New England begin at $33 a day and $144 a week for an economy car with unlimited mileage. This does not include tax on car rentals, which is 5%.

RENTAL WHOLESALERS

Contact **Auto Europe** (☎ 207/828–2525 or 800/223–5555).

CHILDREN & TRAVEL

DISCOUNT PASS

The **American Lung Association**'s (☎ 800/458–6472) "Children's Fun Pass" costs $15 annually and gives a child free admission to more than 115 of New England's top attractions, including ski areas, with the purchase of an adult admission.

FLYING

Look into **"Flying with Baby"** (✉ Third Street Press, Box 261250, Littleton, CO 80163, ☎ 303/595–5959; $4.95 includes shipping), cowritten by a flight attendant. Every two years the February issue of *Family Travel Times* (☞ Know-How, *below*) details children's services on three dozen airlines.

KNOW-HOW

Family Travel Times, published quarterly by Travel with Your Children (✉ TWYCH, 40 5th Ave., New York, NY 10011, ☎ 212/477–5524; $40 per year), covers destinations, types of vacations, and modes of travel.

The *Family Travel Guides* catalog (✉ Carousel Press, Box 6061, Albany, CA 94706, ☎ 510/527–5849; $1 postage) lists about 200 books and articles on traveling with children. Also check *Take Your Baby and Go! A Guide for Traveling with Babies,*

Toddlers and Young Children, by Sheri Andrews, Judy Bordeaux, and Vivian Vasquez (✉ Bear Creek Publications, 2507 Minor Ave. E, Seattle, WA 98102, ☎ 206/322–7604 or 800/326–6566; $5.95 plus $1.50 shipping).

LOCAL INFORMATION

Consult Fodor's lively by-parents, for-parents ***Where Should We Take the Kids? Northeast*** (available in bookstores, or ☎ 800/533–6478; $17).

TOUR OPERATORS

Contact **Grandtravel** (✉ 6900 Wisconsin Ave., Suite 706, Chevy Chase, MD 20815, ☎ 301/986–0790 or 800/247–7651), which has tours for people traveling with grandchildren ages 7–17; or **Rascals in Paradise** (✉ 650 5th St., Suite 505, San Francisco, CA 94107, ☎ 415/978–9800 or 800/872–7225).

CUSTOMS

CANADIANS

Contact **Revenue Canada** (✉ 2265 St. Laurent Blvd. S, Ottawa, Ontario K1G 4K3, ☎ 613/993–0534) for a copy of the free brochure **"I Declare/Je Déclare"** and for details on duty-free limits. For recorded information (within Canada only), call 800/461–9999.

U.K. CITIZENS

HM Customs and Excise (✉ Dorset House, Stamford St., London SE1 9NG, ☎ 0171/202–4227) can answer questions about U.K. customs regulations and publishes a free pamphlet, **"A Guide for Travellers,"** detailing standard procedures and import rules.

D

DISABILITIES & ACCESSIBILITY

COMPLAINTS

To register complaints under the provisions of the Americans with Disabilities Act, contact the U.S. Department of Justice's **Disability Rights Section** (✉ Box 66738, Washington, DC 20035, ☎ 202/514–0301 or 800/514–0301, FAX 202/307–1198, TTY 202/514–0383 or 800/514–0383). For airline-related problems, contact the U.S. Department of Transportation's **Aviation Consumer Protection Division** (☞ Air Travel, *above*). For complaints about surface transportation, contact the Department of Transportation's **Civil Rights Office** (☎ 202/366–4648).

ORGANIZATIONS

TRAVELERS WITH HEARING IMPAIRMENTS➢ The **American Academy of Otolaryngology** (✉ 1 Prince St., Alexandria, VA 22314, ☎ 703/836–4444, FAX 703/683–5100, TTY 703/519–1585) publishes a brochure, "Travel Tips for Hearing Impaired People."

TRAVELERS WITH MOBILITY PROBLEMS➢ Contact the **Information Center for Individuals with Disabilities** (✉ Box 256, Boston, MA 02117, ☎ 617/450–9888; in MA, 800/462–5015; TTY 617/424–6855); **Mobility International USA** (✉ Box 10767, Eugene, OR 97440, ☎ and TTY 541/343–1284, FAX 541/343–6812), the U.S. branch of a Belgium-based organization (☞ *below*) with affiliates in 30 countries; **MossRehab Hospital Travel Information Service** (☎ 215/456–9600, TTY 215/456–9602), a telephone information resource for travelers with physical disabilities; the **Society for the Advancement of Travel for the Handicapped** (✉ 347 5th Ave., Suite 610, New York, NY 10016, ☎ 212/447–7284, FAX 212/725–8253; membership $45); and **Travelin' Talk** (✉ Box 3534, Clarksville, TN 37043, ☎ 615/552–6670, FAX 615/552–1182) which provides local contacts worldwide for travelers with disabilities.

TRAVELERS WITH VISION IMPAIRMENTS➢ Contact the **American Council of the Blind** (✉ 1155 15th St. NW, Suite 720, Washington, DC 20005, ☎ 202/467–5081, FAX 202/467–5085) for a list of travelers' resources or the **American Foundation for the Blind** (✉ 11 Penn Plaza, Suite 300, New York, NY 10001, ☎ 212/502–7600 or 800/232–5463, TTY 212/502–7662), which provides general advice and publishes "Access to Art" ($19.95), a directory of museums that accommodate travelers with vision impairments.

IN THE U.K.

Contact the **Royal Association for Disability and Rehabilitation**

(⊠ RADAR, 12 City Forum, 250 City Rd., London EC1V 8AF, ☎ 0171/250–3222) or **Mobility International** (⊠ rue de Manchester 25, B-1080 Brussels, Belgium, ☎ 00–322–410–6297, FAX 00–322–410–6874), an international travel-information clearing-house for people with disabilities.

PUBLICATIONS

The brochure **"MBTA: ACCESS"** outlines Boston's transportation options (⊠ MBTA, Office for Transportation Access, 10 Boylston Pl., Boston, 02116, ☎ 617/722–5123, TTY 617/722–5415). Those visiting Cape Cod can get accessibility ratings from the publications, **"Visitor's Guide"** and **"Resort Directory,"** available from the Cape Cod Chamber of Commerce (⊠ Rtes. 6 and 132, Hyannis, 02601, ☎ 508/362–3225), and from the Seashore's publication, **"Cape Cod National Seashore Accessibility"** (⊠ South Wellfleet, 02663, ☎ 508/349–3785). The New Hampshire Office of Vacation Travel publishes the **"New Hampshire Guide Book,"** which includes accessibility ratings for hotels, restaurants, and attractions.

Fodor's **Great American Vacations for Travelers with Disabilities** (available in bookstores, or ☎ 800/533–6478; $18) details accessible attractions, restaurants, and hotels in U.S. destinations. The 500-page **Travelin' Talk Directory** (⊠ Box 3534, Clarksville, TN 37043,

☎ 615/552–6670, FAX 615/552–1182; $35) lists people and organizations who help travelers with disabilities. For travel agents worldwide, consult the **Directory of Travel Agencies for the Disabled** (⊠ Twin Peaks Press, Box 129, Vancouver, WA 98666, ☎ 360/694–2462 or 800/637–2256, FAX 360/696–3210; $19.95 plus $3 shipping). The Sierra Club publishes **Easy Access to National Parks** (⊠ Sierra Club Store, 730 Polk St., San Francisco, CA 94109, ☎ 415/776–2211 or 800/935–1056; $16 plus $3 shipping).

TRAVEL AGENCIES, TOUR OPERATORS

The Americans with Disabilities Act requires that all travel firms serve the needs of all travelers. That said, you should note that some agencies and operators specialize in making travel arrangements for individuals and groups with disabilities, among them **Access Adventures** (⊠ 206 Chestnut Ridge Rd., Rochester, NY 14624, ☎ 716/889–9096), run by a former physical-rehab counselor.

TRAVELERS WITH MOBILITY PROBLEMS➤ Contact **Hinsdale Travel Service** (⊠ 201 E. Ogden Ave., Suite 100, Hinsdale, IL 60521, ☎ 708/325–1335 or 800/303–5521), a travel agency that benefits from the advice of wheelchair traveler Janice Perkins; and **Wheelchair Journeys** (⊠ 16979 Redmond Way, Redmond, WA 98052, ☎ 206/

885–2210 or 800/313–4751), which can handle arrangements worldwide.

TRAVELERS WITH DEVELOPMENTAL DISABILITIES➤ Contact the nonprofit **New Directions** (⊠ 5276 Hollister Ave., Suite 207, Santa Barbara, CA 93111, ☎ 805/967–2841) and **Sprout** (⊠ 893 Amsterdam Ave., New York, NY 10025, ☎ 212/222–9575), which specializes in custom-designed itineraries for groups but also books vacations for individual travelers.

TRAVEL GEAR

The **Magellan's** catalog (☎ 800/962–4943, FAX 805/568–5406), includes a range of products designed for travelers with disabilities.

DISCOUNTS & DEALS

AIRFARES

For the lowest airfares to New England, call 800/FLY–4–LESS. Also try 800/FLY–ASAP.

CLUBS

Contact **Entertainment Travel Editions** (⊠ Box 1068, Trumbull, CT 06611, ☎ 800/445–4137; $28–$53, depending on destination), **Great American Traveler** (⊠ Box 27965, Salt Lake City, UT 84127, ☎ 800/548–2812; $49.95 per year), **Moment's Notice Discount Travel Club** (⊠ 163 Amsterdam Ave., Suite 137, New York, NY 10023, ☎ 212/486–0500; $25 per year, single or family), **Privilege Card** (⊠ 3391 Peachtree Rd. NE, Suite 110, Atlanta, GA

30326, ☎ 404/262–0222 or 800/236–9732; $74.95 per year), **Travelers Advantage** (✉ CUC Travel Service, 49 Music Sq. W, Nashville, TN 37203, ☎ 800/548–1116 or 800/648–4037; $49 per year, single or family), or **Worldwide Discount Travel Club** (✉ 1674 Meridian Ave., Miami Beach, FL 33139, ☎ 305/534–2082; $50 per year for family, $40 single).

HOTEL ROOMS

For discounts on hotel rates in Boston, contact the **Hotel Reservations Network** (☎ 800/964–6835) or **Quickbook** (☎ 800/789–9887).

STUDENTS

Members of Hostelling International–American Youth Hostels (☞ Students, *below*) are eligible for discounts on car rentals, admissions to attractions, and other selected travel expenses.

PUBLICATIONS

Consult *The Frugal Globetrotter,* by Bruce Northam (✉ Fulcrum Publishing, 350 Indiana St., Suite 350, Golden, CO 80401, ☎ 800/992–2908; $15.95). For publications that tell how to find the lowest prices on plane tickets, *see* Air Travel, *above.*

G

GAY & LESBIAN TRAVEL

ORGANIZATIONS

The **International Gay Travel Association** (✉ Box 4974, Key West, FL 33041, ☎ 800/448–8550, FAX 305/296–6633), a consortium of more than 1,000 travel

companies, can supply names of gay-friendly travel agents, tour operators, and accommodations.

PUBLICATIONS

The premier international travel magazine for gays and lesbians is *Our World* (✉ 1104 N. Nova Rd., Suite 251, Daytona Beach, FL 32117, ☎ 904/441–5367, FAX 904/441–5604; $35 for 10 issues). The 16-page monthly *"Out & About"* (☎ 212/645–6922 or 800/929–2268, FAX 800/929–2215; $49 for 10 issues and quarterly calendar) covers gay-friendly resorts, hotels, cruise lines, and airlines.

TOUR OPERATORS

Cruises and resort vacations for gays are handled by **R.S.V.P. Travel Productions** (✉ 2800 University Ave. SE, Minneapolis, MN 55414, ☎ 612/379–4697 or 800/328–7787). **Toto Tours** (✉ 1326 W. Albion St., Suite 3W, Chicago, IL 60626, ☎ 312/274–8686 or 800/565–1241) offers group tours to worldwide destinations.

TRAVEL AGENCIES

The largest agencies serving gay travelers are **Advance Travel** (✉ 10700 Northwest Fwy., Suite 160, Houston, TX 77092, ☎ 713/682–2002 or 800/695–0880), **Islanders/Kennedy Travel** (✉ 183 W. 10th St., New York, NY 10014, ☎ 212/242–3222 or 800/988–1181), **Now Voyager** (✉ 4406 18th St., San Francisco, CA 94114, ☎ 415/626–1169 or

800/255–6951), and **Yellowbrick Road** (✉ 1500 W. Balmoral Ave., Chicago, IL 60640, ☎ 312/561–1800 or 800/642–2488). **Skylink Women's Travel** (✉ 3577 Moorland Ave., Santa Rosa, CA 95407, ☎ 707/588–9961 or 800/225–5759) serves lesbian travelers.

I

INSURANCE

IN CANADA

Contact **Mutual of Omaha** (✉ Travel Division, 500 University Ave., Toronto, Ontario M5G 1V8, ☎ 800/268–8825 or 416/598-4321).

IN THE U.S.

Travel insurance covering baggage, health, and trip cancellation or interruptions is available from **Access America** (✉ Box 90315, Richmond, VA 23286, ☎ 804/285–3300 or 800/284–8300), **Carefree Travel Insurance** (✉ Box 9366, 100 Garden City Plaza, Garden City, NY 11530, ☎ 516/294–0220 or 800/323–3149), **Near Travel Services** (✉ Box 1339, Calumet City, IL 60409, ☎ 708/868–6700 or 800/654–6700), **Tele-Trip** (✉ Mutual of Omaha Plaza, Box 31716, Omaha, NE 68131, ☎ 800/228–9792), **Travel Guard International** (✉ 1145 Clark St., Stevens Point, WI 54481, ☎ 715/345–0505 or 800/826–1300), **Travel Insured International** (✉ Box 280568, East Hartford, CT 06128, ☎ 203/528–7663 or 800/243–3174), and **Wallach &**

Company (⊠ 107 W. Federal St., Box 480, Middleburg, VA 22117, ☎ 703/687–3166 or 800/237–6615).

IN THE U.K.

The **Association of British Insurers** (⊠ 51 Gresham St., London EC2V 7HQ, ☎ 0171/600–3333) gives advice by phone and publishes the free pamphlet "Holiday Insurance," which sets out typical policy provisions and costs.

L
LODGING

For information on hotel consolidators, *see* Discounts & Deals, *above*.

APARTMENT & VILLA RENTAL

Among the companies to contact are **Property Rentals International** (⊠ 1008 Mansfield Crossing Rd., Richmond, VA 23236, ☎ 804/378–6054 or 800/220–3332, FAX 804/379–2073), **Rent-a-Home International** (⊠ 7200 34th Ave. NW, Seattle, WA 98117, ☎ 206/789–9377 or 800/488–7368, FAX 206/789–9379), and **Vacation Home Rentals Worldwide** (⊠ 235 Kensington Ave., Norwood, NJ 07648, ☎ 201/767–9393 or 800/633–3284, FAX 201/767–5510). Members of the travel club **Hideaways International** (⊠ 767 Islington St., Portsmouth, NH 03801, ☎ 603/430–4433 or 800/843–4433, FAX 603/430–4444; $99 per year) receive two annual guides plus quarterly newsletters and arrange rentals among themselves.

HOME EXCHANGE

Some of the principal clearinghouses are **HomeLink International/Vacation Exchange Club** (⊠ Box 650, Key West, FL 33041, ☎ 305/294–1448 or 800/638–3841, FAX 305/294–1148; $70 per year), which sends members three annual directories, with a listing in one, plus updates; and **Intervac International** (⊠ Box 590504, San Francisco, CA 94159, ☎ 415/435–3497, FAX 415/435–7440; $65 per year), which publishes four annual directories.

M
MONEY MATTERS

ATMS

For specific **Cirrus** locations in the United States and Canada, call 800/424–7787. For U.S. **Plus** locations, call 800/843–7587 and enter the area code and first three digits of the number from which you're calling (or of the calling area in which you want to locate an ATM).

WIRING FUNDS

Funds can be wired via **MoneyGram℠** (for locations and information in the U.S. and Canada, ☎ 800/926–9400) or **Western Union** (for agent locations or to send money using MasterCard or Visa, ☎ 800/325–6000; in Canada, 800/321–2923; in the U.K., 0800/833833; or visit the Western Union office at the nearest major post office).

N
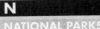
NATIONAL PARKS

A variety of passes is available for senior citizens, travelers with disabilities, and frequent visitors. The passes can be purchased at any park that charges admission or obtained by mail from the **National Park Service** (⊠ Dept. of the Interior, Washington, DC 20240).

P
PACKING

For strategies on packing light, get a copy of *The Packing Book,* by Judith Gilford (⊠ Ten Speed Press, Box 7123, Berkeley, CA 94707, ☎ 510/559–1600 or 800/841–2665, FAX 510/524–4588; $7.95).

PASSPORTS & VISAS

U.K. CITIZENS

For fees, documentation requirements, and to request an emergency passport, call the **London Passport Office** (☎ 0990/210–410). For U.S. visa information, call the **U.S. Embassy Visa Information Line** (☎ 01891/200–290; calls cost 49p per minute or 39p per minute cheap rate) or send a self-addressed, stamped envelope to the **U.S. Embassy Visa Branch** (⊠ 5 Upper Grosvenor St., London W1A 2JB). If you live in Northern Ireland, write to the **U.S. Consulate General** (⊠ Queen's House, Queen St., Belfast BTI 6EO).

PHOTO HELP

The **Kodak Information Center** (☎ 800/242–2424) answers consumer questions about film and photography. The **Kodak Guide to Shooting Great Travel Pictures** (available in bookstores; or contact Fodor's Travel Publications, ☎ 800/533–6478; $16.50) explains how to take expert travel photographs.

S

SAFETY

"Trouble-Free Travel," from the AAA, is a booklet of tips for protecting yourself and your belongings when away from home. Send a stamped, self-addressed, legal-size envelope to Trouble-Free Travel (✉ Mail Stop 75, 1000 AAA Dr., Heathrow, FL 32746).

SENIOR CITIZENS

EDUCATIONAL TRAVEL

The nonprofit **Elderhostel** (✉ 75 Federal St., 3rd Floor, Boston, MA 02110, ☎ 617/426–7788), for people 60 and older, has offered inexpensive study programs since 1975. Courses cover everything from marine science to Greek mythology and cowboy poetry. Fees for programs in the United States and Canada, which usually last one week, run about $300, not including transportation.

ORGANIZATIONS

Contact the **American Association of Retired Persons** (✉ AARP, 601 E St. NW, Washington, DC 20049, ☎ 202/434–2277; annual dues $8 per person or couple). Its Purchase Privilege Program secures discounts for members on lodging, car rentals, and sightseeing, and the AARP Motoring Plan (☎ 800/334–3300) furnishes domestic trip-routing information and emergency road-service aid for an annual fee of $39.95 ($59.95 for a premium version). Senior citizen travelers can also join the AAA for emergency road service and other travel benefits (☞ Driving, *and* Discounts & Deals *in* Smart Travel Tips A to Z).

Additional sources for discounts on lodgings, car rentals, and other travel expenses, as well as helpful magazines and newsletters, are the **National Council of Senior Citizens** (✉ 1331 F St. NW, Washington, DC 20004, ☎ 202/347–8800; annual membership $12) and Sears's **Mature Outlook** (✉ Box 10448, Des Moines, IA 50306, ☎ 800/336–6330; annual membership $9.95).

PUBLICATIONS

The 50+ Traveler's Guidebook: Where to Go, Where to Stay, What to Do, by Anita Williams and Merrimac Dillon (✉ St. Martin's Press, 175 5th Ave., New York, NY 10010, ☎ 212/674–5151 or 800/288–2131; $13.95), offers many useful tips. **"The Mature Traveler"** (✉ Box 50400, Reno, NV 89513, ☎ 702/786–7419; $29.95), a monthly newsletter, covers all sorts of travel deals.

SPORTS

BIKING

Free information on biking trails is available from the Maine Publicity Bureau and the Vermont Travel Division; other sources include **Maine Sport** (✉ Rte. 1, Rockport, 04856, ☎ 207/236–8797 or 800/722–0826) and **Vermont Bicycle Touring** (✉ Box 711, Bristol, 05443, ☎ 802/453–4811 or 800/245–3868).

FISHING

Freshwater-lake fishing, surf-casting, deep-sea fishing, angling, and trout fishing are among the offerings in New England. Contact Connecticut's **Department of Environmental Protection** (✉ 79 Elm St., Fisheries Division, Hartford, 06106, ☎ 203/424–3434); the **Maine Department of Inland Fisheries and Wildlife** (✉ 284 State St., State House Station 41, Augusta, ME 04333, ☎ 207/827–3616); the **Massachusetts Division of Fisheries and Wildlife** (✉ 100 Cambridge St., Room 1902, Boston, MA 02202, ☎ 617/727–3151); the **New Hampshire Fish and Game Department** (✉ 2 Hazen Dr., Concord, NH 03301, ☎ 603/271–3421); Rhode Island's **Department of Environmental Management, Division of Fish and Wildlife** (✉ 4808 Tower Hill Rd., Wakefield, RI 02879, ☎ 401/789–3094); or the **Vermont Fish and Wildlife Department** (✉ 103 S. Main St., Waterbury, VT 05676, ☎ 802/241–3700).

HIKING

For free information on hiking the Appalachian Trail contact the **Appalachian Mountain Club** (⊠ Box 298, Gorham, NH 03581, ☎ 603/466–2725), and the **White Mountains National Forest** (⊠ 719 North Main St., Laconia, NH 03246, ☎ 603/528–8721). The **Audubon Society of New Hampshire** (⊠ 3 Silk Farm Rd., Concord, NH 03301, ☎ 603/224–9909) maintains marked trails for hikers in parks throughout the region.

STUDENTS

GROUPS

A major tour operator specializing in student travel is **Contiki Holidays** (⊠ 300 Plaza Alicante, Suite 900, Garden Grove, CA 92640, ☎ 714/740–0808 or 800/466–0610).

HOSTELING

In the United States, contact **Hostelling International–American Youth Hostels** (⊠ 733 15th St. NW, Suite 840, Washington, DC 20005, ☎ 202/783–6161 or 800/444–6111 for reservations at selected hostels, FAX 202/783–6171); in Canada, **Hostelling International–Canada** (⊠ 205 Catherine St., Suite 400, Ottawa, Ontario K2P 1C3, ☎ 613/237–7884); and in the United Kingdom, the **Youth Hostel Association of England and Wales** (⊠ Trevelyan House, 8 St. Stephen's Hill, St. Albans, Hertfordshire AL1 2DY, ☎ 01727/855215 or 01727/845047). Membership (in the U.S., $25; in Canada, C$26.75; in the U.K., £9.30) gives you access to 5,000 hostels in 77 countries that charge $5–$30 per person per night.

I.D. CARDS

To be eligible for discounts on transportation and admissions, get either the **International Student Identity Card,** if you're a bona fide student, or the **GO 25: International Youth Travel Card,** if you're not a student but under age 26. Each includes basic travel-accident and illness coverage, plus a toll-free travel hot line. In the United States, either card costs $18; apply through the Council on International Educational Exchange (☞ Organizations, *below*). In Canada, cards are available for $15 each ($16 by mail) from Travel Cuts (☞ Organizations, *below*), and in the United Kingdom for £5 each at student unions and student travel companies.

ORGANIZATIONS

A major contact is the **Council on International Educational Exchange** (⊠ mail orders only: CIEE, 205 E. 42nd St., 16th Floor, New York, NY 10017, ☎ 212/661–1450), with walk-in locations in Boston (⊠ 729 Boylston St., 02116, ☎ 617/266–1926), Miami (⊠ 9100 S. Dadeland Blvd., 33156, ☎ 305/670–9261), Los Angeles (⊠ 10904 Lindbrook Dr., 90024, ☎ 310/208–3551), 43 other college towns in the U.S., and in the United Kingdom (⊠ 28A Poland St., London W1V 3DB, ☎ 0171/437–7767). Twice per year, it publishes *Student Travels* magazine. The CIEE's Council Travel Service is the exclusive U.S. agent for several student discount cards.

The **Educational Travel Centre** (⊠ 438 N. Frances St., Madison, WI 53703, ☎ 608/256–5551 or 800/747–5551, FAX 608/256–2042) offers rail passes and low-cost airline tickets, mostly for flights that depart from Chicago.

In Canada, also contact **Travel Cuts** (⊠ 187 College St., Toronto, Ontario M5T 1P7, ☎ 416/979–2406 or 800/667–2887).

T

TOUR OPERATORS

Among the companies that sell tours and packages to New England, the following are nationally known, have a proven reputation, and offer plenty of options.

GROUP TOURS

DELUXE➤ **Globus** (⊠ 5301 S. Federal Circle, Littleton, CO 80123-2980, ☎ 303/797–2800 or 800/221–0090, FAX 303/795–0962), **Maupintour** (⊠ Box 807, Lawrence, KS 66047, ☎ 913/843–1211 or 800/255–4266, FAX 913/843–8351), and **Tauck Tours** (⊠ Box 5027, 276 Post Rd. W, Westport, CT 06881, ☎ 203/226–6911 or 800/468–2825, FAX 203/221–6828).

THE GOLD GUIDE / IMPORTANT CONTACTS

FIRST CLASS➤ **Brendan Tours** (✉ 15137 Califa St., Van Nuys, CA 91411, ☎ 818/785–9696 or 800/421–8446, FAX 818/902–9876), **Caravan Tours** (✉ 401 N. Michigan Ave., Chicago, IL 60611, ☎ 312/321–9800 or 800/227–2826), **Collette Tours** (✉ 162 Middle St., Pawtucket, RI 02860, ☎ 401/728–3805 or 800/832–4656, FAX 401/728–1380), **Gadabout Tours** (✉ 700 E. Tahquitz Canyon Way, Palm Springs, CA 92262, ☎ 619/325–5556 or 800/952–5068), and **Mayflower Tours** (✉ Box 490, 1225 Warren Ave., Downers Grove, IL 60515, ☎ 708/960–3430 or 800/323–7064).

BUDGET➤ **Cosmos** (☞ Globus, *above*).

FROM THE U.K.➤ Tour operators offering packages to Boston include **American Vacations Ltd.** (✉ Morley House, 320 Regent St., London W1R 5AD, ☎ 0171/637–7853), **Jetsave** (✉ Sussex House, London Rd., East Grinstead, West Sussex RH19 1LD, ☎ 01342/312–033), **Key to America** (✉ 1–3 Station Rd., Ashford, Middlesex TW15 2UW, ☎ 01784/248–777), **Kuoni Travel** (✉ Kuoni House, Deepdene Ave., Dorking, Surrey RH5 4AZ, ☎ 01306/742–222), and **Trailfinders** (✉ 42–50 Earls Court Rd., London W8 6FT, ☎ 0171/937–5400; ✉ 58 Deansgate, Manchester M3 2FF, ☎ 0161/839–6969).

PACKAGES

Independent vacation packages including airfare, car rental, accommodations and sightseeing are available from **Delta Dream Vacations** (☎ 800/872–7786) and **United Vacations** (☎ 800/328–6877). For packages to Boston, try **SuperCities** (✉ 139 Main St., Cambridge, MA 02142, ☎ 617/621–0099 or 800/333–1234). For rail packages that combine air, hotel and tour options, contact **Amtrak's Great American Vacations** (☎ 800/321–8684).

Also contact **Amtrak**'s Great American Vacations (☎ 800/321–8684).

FROM THE U.K.

Some of the tour operators that offer packages to New England are **British Airways Holidays** (✉ Astral Towers, Betts Way, London Rd., Crawley, West Sussex RH10 2XA, ☎ 01293/518–022), **Kuoni Travel** (✉ Kuoni House, Dorking, Surrey RH5 4AZ, ☎ 01306/742–222), **Americana Vacations Ltd.** (✉ Morley House, 320 Regent St., London W1R 5AD, ☎ 0171/637–7853), and **Key to America** (✉ 1–3 Station Rd., Ashford, Middlesex TW15 2UW, ☎ 01784/248–777).

Independent travelers should contact **Trailfinders** (✉ 42–50 Earls Court Rd., London W8 7RG, ☎ 0171/937–5400; 58 Deansgate, Manchester M3 2FF, ☎ 0161/839–6969). Two travel agencies that offer cheap fares to Chicago are **Travel Cuts**

(✉ 295a Regent St., London W1R 7YA, ☎ 0171/637–3161) and **Flightfile** (✉ 49 Tottenham Court Rd., London W1P 9RE, ☎ 0171/700–2722).

THEME TRIPS

BICYCLING➤ For two-wheeled travel between New England inns and campsites, contact **Backroads** (✉ 1516 5th St., Berkeley, CA 94710-1740, ☎ 510/527–1555 or 800/462–2848, FAX 510-527-1444) or, for those on a more limited budget, **Cycle America** (✉ Box 485, Cannon Falls, MN 55009, ☎ 507/263–2665 or 800/245–3263). For bicycle tours of Martha's Vineyard, Nantucket, and Block Island, try **Bike Riders** (✉ Box 254, Boston, MA 02113, ☎ 617/723–2354 or 800/473–7040), FAX 617/723–2355).

HIKING➤ Look into **Hiking Holidays** (✉ Box 750-AN Bristol, VT 05443, ☎ 802/453–4816), **Hike Inn to Inn** (✉ RR 3, Box 3115, Brandon, VT 05733, ☎ 802/247–3300), and **New England Hiking Holidays** (✉ Box 1648, North Conway, NH 03860, ☎ 800/869–0949) for backcountry hiking and stays at inns with character.

HORSEBACK RIDING➤ **FITS Equestrian** (✉ 685 Lateen Rd., Solvang, CA 93463, ☎ 805/688–9494 or 800/666–3487, FAX 805/688–2943) has several New England programs.

INN-HOPPING➤ **Winding Roads Tours** (☎ 800/240–4363) customizes tours throughout New

England for fans of charming and historic inns.

LEARNING➤ **Earthwatch** (✉ Box 403, 680 Mount Auburn St., Watertown, MA 02272, ☎ 617/926–8200 or 800/776–0188, FAX 617/926–8532) recruits volunteers to serve in its EarthCorps as short-term assistants to scientists on research expeditions. Also contact **Oceanic Society Expeditions** (✉ Fort Mason Center, Bldg. E, San Francisco, CA 94123-1394, ☎ 415/441–1106 or 800/326–7491, FAX 415/474–3395) for natural history tours.

WALKING➤ **Backroads** (☞ Bicycling, *above*) and **Country Walkers** (✉ Box 180, Waterbury, VT 05676-0180, ☎ 802/244–1387 or 800/464–9255, FAX 802/244–5661) lead 2- to 13-day jaunts through New England.

WHALE-WATCHING➤ **Oceanic Society Expeditions** (✉ Fort Mason Center, Bldg. E, San Francisco, CA 04123, ☎ 415/441–1106 or 800/326–7491) cruises the New England coastline searching for whales.

YACHT CHARTERS➤ For crewed or bareboat sailing off the New England coast, try **Huntley Yacht Vacations** (✉ 210 Preston Rd., Wernersville, PA 19565, ☎ 610/678–2628 or 800/322–9224, FAX 610/670–1767), **Lynn Jachney Charters** (✉ Box 302, Marblehead, MA 01945, 617/639–0787 or 800/223–2050, FAX 617/639–0216), **Nichol-**

son Yacht Charters (✉ 78 Bolton St., Cambridge, MA 02140-3321, ☎ 617/225–0555 or 800/662–6066, FAX 617/661–0554), **Ocean Voyages** (✉ 1709 Bridgeway, Sausalito, CA 94965, ☎ 415/332–4681, FAX 415/332–7460), and **Russell Yacht Charters** (✉ 404 Hulls Hwy., #175, Southport, CT 06490, ☎ 203/255–2783 or 800/635–8895).

ORGANIZATIONS

The **National Tour Association** (✉ NTA, 546 E. Main St., Lexington, KY 40508, ☎ 606/226–4444 or 800/755–8687) and the **United States Tour Operators Association** (✉ USTOA, 211 E. 51st St., Suite 12B, New York, NY 10022, ☎ 212/750–7371) can provide lists of members and information on booking tours.

PUBLICATIONS

Contact the USTOA (☞ Organizations, *above*) for its **"Smart Traveler's Planning Kit."** Pamphlets in the kit include the "Worldwide Tour and Vacation Package Finder," "How to Select a Tour or Vacation Package," and information on the organization's consumer protection plan. Also get copy of the Better Business Bureau's **"Tips on Travel Packages"** (✉ Publication 24-195, 4200 Wilson Blvd., Arlington, VA 22203; $2). The National Tour Association will send you **"On Tour,"** a listing of its member operators, and a personalized package

of information on group travel in North America.

Amtrak (☎ 800/872–7245) offers frequent daily service along its Northeast Corridor route from Washington and New York to Boston.

The **Massachusetts Bay Transportation Authority** (☎ 617/722–5000) connects Boston with outlying areas on the north and south shores of the state. Canada's **VIA Rail** (☎ 800/561–9181) crosses Maine, providing its only rail service.

TRAVEL AGENCIES

For names of reputable agencies in your area, contact the **American Society of Travel Agents** (✉ ASTA, 1101 King St., Suite 200, Alexandria, VA 22314, ☎ 703/739–2782), the **Association of Canadian Travel Agents** (✉ Suite 201, 1729 Bank St., Ottawa, Ontario K1V 7Z5, ☎ 613/521–0474, FAX 613/521–0805) or the **Association of British Travel Agents** (✉ 55-57 Newman St., London W1P 4AH, ☎ 0171/637–2444, FAX 0171/637–0713).

TRAVEL GEAR

For travel apparel, appliances, personal-care items, and other travel necessities, get a free catalog from **Magellan's** (☎ 800/962–4943, FAX 805/568–5406), **Orvis Travel** (☎ 800/541–3541, FAX 703/343–7053), or **TravelSmith** (☎ 800/950–1600, FAX 415/455–0554).

V

VISITOR INFORMATION

Connecticut Department of Economic Development (✉ 865 Brook St., Rocky Hill, CT 06067, ☎ 203/258–4355 or 800/282–6863).

Maine Publicity Bureau (✉ 325-B Water St., Box 2300, Hallowell, ME 04347, ☎ 207/623–0363 or 800/533–9595).

Maine Innkeepers Association (✉ 305 Commercial St., Portland, ME 04101, ☎ 207/773–7670).

Massachusetts Office of Travel and Tourism (✉ 100 Cambridge St., Boston, MA 02202, ☎ 617/727–3201 or 800/447–6277).

New Hampshire Office of Travel and Tourism Development (✉ Box 856, Concord, NH 03302, ☎ 603/271–2343, for a recorded message about seasonal events 800/258–3608).

Rhode Island Department of Economic Development, Tourism Division (✉ 7 Jackson Walkway, Providence, RI 02903, ☎ 401/277–2601 or 800/556–2484).

Vermont Travel Division (✉ 134 State St., Montpelier, VT 05602, ☎ 802/828–3236, for a brochure 800/837–6668).

Vermont Chamber of Commerce, Department of Travel and Tourism (✉ Box 37, Montpelier, VT 05601, ☎ 802/223–3443).

In the United Kingdom, also contact ☎ 0173/274–2777, FAX 0173/371–6902.

W

WEATHER

For current conditions and forecasts, plus the local time and helpful travel tips, call the **Weather Channel Connection** (☎ 900/932–8437; 95¢ per minute) from a Touch-Tone phone.

The *International Traveler's Weather Guide* (✉ Weather Press, Box 660606, Sacramento, CA 95866, ☎ 916/974–0201 or 800/972–0201; $10.95 includes shipping), written by two meteorologists, provides month-by-month information on temperature, humidity, and precipitation in more than 175 cities worldwide.

SMART TRAVEL TIPS A TO Z

*Basic Information on Traveling in New England &
Savvy Tips to Make Your Trip a Breeze*

A
AIR TRAVEL

If time is an issue, **always look for nonstop flights,** which require no change of plane. If possible, **avoid connecting flights,** which stop at least once and can involve a change of plane, even though the flight number remains the same; if the first leg is late, the second waits.

For better service, **fly smaller or regional carriers,** which often have higher passenger satisfaction ratings. Sometimes they have such in-flight amenities as leather seats or greater leg room and they often have better food.

CUTTING COSTS

The Sunday travel section of most newspapers is a good place to look for deals.

MAJOR AIRLINES➤ The least-expensive airfares from the major airlines are priced for round-trip travel and are subject to restrictions. Usually, you must **book in advance and buy the ticket within 24 hours** to get cheaper fares, and you may have to **stay over a Saturday night.** The lowest fare is subject to availability, and only a small percentage of the plane's total seats is sold at that price. It's smart to **call a number of airlines, and when you are quoted a good price,**

book it on the spot—the same fare may not be available on the same flight the next day. Airlines generally allow you to change your return date for a $25 to $50 fee. If you don't use your ticket, you can apply the cost toward the purchase of a new ticket, again for a small charge. However, most low-fare tickets are nonrefundable. To get the lowest airfare, **check different routings.** If your destination has more than one gateway, **compare prices to different airports.**

FROM THE U.K.➤ To save money on flights, **look into an APEX or Super-Pex ticket.** APEX tickets must be booked in advance and have certain restrictions. Super-PEX tickets can be purchased right at the airport.

CONSOLIDATORS➤ Consolidators buy tickets for scheduled flights at reduced rates from the airlines, then sell them at prices below the lowest available from the airlines directly—usually without advance restrictions. Sometimes you can even get your money back if you need to return the ticket. Carefully read the fine print detailing penalties for changes and cancellations. If you doubt the reliability of a consolidator, **confirm your reservation with the airline.**

ALOFT

AIRLINE FOOD➤ If you hate airline food, **ask for special meals when booking.** These can be vegetarian, low-cholesterol, or kosher, for example; commonly prepared to order in smaller quantities than standard fare, they can be tastier.

SMOKING➤ Smoking is banned on all flights of less than six hours' duration within the United States and on all Canadian flights; the ban also applies to domestic segments of international flights aboard U.S. and foreign carriers. Delta has banned smoking system-wide.

C
CAMERAS, CAMCORDERS, & COMPUTERS

LAPTOPS

Before you depart, **check your portable computer's battery;** at security you may be asked to turn on the computer to prove that it is what it appears to be. At the airport, you may prefer to **request a manual inspection,** although security X-rays do not harm hard-disk or floppy-disk storage.

PHOTOGRAPHY

If your camera is new or if you haven't used it for a while, **shoot and develop a few rolls of film** before you leave. Always **store film in a**

THE GOLD GUIDE / SMART TRAVEL TIPS

cool, dry place—never in your car's glove compartment or on the shelf under the rear window.

Select the right film for your purpose—use print film if you plan to frame or display your pictures, but use slide film if you hope to publish your shots. Also, consider black-and-white film for different and dramatic images. For best results, **use a custom lab** for processing; use a one-hour lab only if time is a factor.

The chances of your film growing cloudy increase with each pass through an X-ray machine. To protect against this, carry it in a clear plastic bag and **ask for hand inspection at security.** Such requests are virtually always honored at U.S. airports. Don't depend on a lead-lined bag to protect film in checked luggage—the airline may increase the radiation to see what's inside.

Keep a skylight or haze filter on your camera at all times to protect the expensive (and delicate) lens glass from scratches. Better yet, **use an 81B warming filter,** which—unlike skylight or haze filters—really works in overcast conditions and will pump up those sunrises and sunsets.

VIDEO

Before your trip, **test your camcorder, invest in a skylight filter to protect the lens, and charge the batteries.** (Airport security personnel may ask you to turn on the camcorder

to prove that it's what it appears to be.)

Videotape is not damaged by X-rays, but it may be harmed by the magnetic field of a walk-through metal detector, so **ask that videotapes be hand-checked.**

CAR RENTAL

CUTTING COSTS

To get the best deal, **book through a travel agent who is willing to shop around.** When pricing cars, **ask where the rental lot is located.** Some off-airport locations offer lower rates—even though their lots are only minutes away from the terminal via complimentary shuttle. You also may want to **price local car-rental companies,** whose rates may be lower still, although service and maintenance standards may not be as high as those of a national firm. Ask your agent to **look for fly-drive packages,** which also save you money, and **ask if local taxes are included** in the rental or fly-drive price. These can be as high as 20% in some destinations. Don't forget to find out about required deposits, cancellation penalties, drop-off charges, and the cost of any required insurance coverage.

Also **ask your travel agent about a company's customer-service record.** How has it responded to late plane arrivals and vehicle mishaps? Are there often lines at the rental counter, and—if you're traveling during a holiday period—does a

confirmed reservation guarantee you a car?

INSURANCE

When driving a rented car, you are generally responsible for any damage to or loss of the rental vehicle, as well as any property damage or personal injury that you cause. Before you rent, **see what coverage you already have** under the terms of your personal auto insurance policy and credit cards.

For about $14 a day, rental companies sell protection, known as a collision- or loss-damage waiver (CDW or LDW), that eliminates your liability for damage to the car; it's always optional and should never be automatically added to your bill.

In most states, the renter's personal auto insurance or other liability insurance covers damage to third parties. Only when the damage exceeds the renter's own insurance coverage does the car-rental company pay. However, companies renting cars in Massachusetts have the initial responsibility for damage caused to third parties, after which the renter's personal auto or other liability insurance covers the loss. This may seem like unlimited protection for the renter, but state law caps the amount that the car-rental company must pay. If you do not have auto insurance or an umbrella insurance policy that covers damage to third parties, purchasing CDW or LDW is highly recommended.

U.K. CITIZENS

In the United States you must be 21 to rent a car; rates may be higher if you're under 25. You'll pay extra for child seats (about $3 per day), compulsory for children under five, and for additional drivers (about $2 per day). To pick up your reserved car you will need the reservation voucher, a passport, a U.K. driver's license, and a travel policy that covers each driver.

SURCHARGES

Before you pick up a car in one city and leave it in another, **ask about drop-off charges or one-way service fees,** which can be substantial. Note, too, that some rental agencies charge extra if you return the car before the time specified on your contract. To avoid a hefty refueling fee, **fill the tank just before you turn in the car**—but be aware that gas stations near the rental outlet may overcharge.

CHILDREN & TRAVEL

When traveling with children, **plan ahead** and **involve your youngsters** as you outline your trip. When packing, **include a supply of things to keep them busy** en route. On sightseeing days, try to **schedule activities of special interest to your children,** like a trip to a zoo or a playground. If you **plan your itinerary around seasonal festivals,** you'll never lack for things to do. In addition, **check local newspapers for special events** mounted by

public libraries, museums, and parks.

In New England, there's no shortage of things to do with children. Major museums have children's sections, and there are children's museums in cities large and small. Children love the roadside attractions found in many tourist areas, and miniature golf courses are easy to come by. Attractions such as beaches and boat rides, parks and planetariums, lighthouses and llama treks are fun for youngsters as are special events, such as crafts fairs and food festivals.

BABY-SITTING

Innkeepers, concierges, and desk clerks can usually recommend baby-sitters or baby-sitting services.

DINING

As for restaurants, you don't have to stick with fast food. Asking around will turn up family-oriented restaurants that specialize in pizza or pasta and come equipped with Trivial Pursuit cards, pull toys, fish tanks, and other families traveling with children—sure-fire entertainment for the interval between ordering and eating. A New England–based restaurant chain known for its legendary ice cream desserts, Friendly's is particularly family-friendly: In some, you'll find crayons on the tables and a rack of children's books not far from the stack of booster seats. Like many restaurants in the region, Friendly's has a children's menu and an

array of special deals for families.

DRIVING

If you are renting a car, don't forget to **arrange for a car seat when you reserve.** Sometimes they're free.

FLYING

On domestic flights, children under 2 not occupying a seat travel free, and older children are charged at the lowest applicable adult rate.

BAGGAGE➤ In general, the adult baggage allowance applies to children paying half or more of the adult fare.

SAFETY SEATS➤ According to the FAA, it's a good idea to **use safety seats aloft** for children weighing less than 40 pounds. Airline policies vary. U.S. carriers allow FAA-approved models but usually require that you buy a ticket, even if your child would otherwise ride free, since the seats must be strapped into regular seats.

FACILITIES➤ When making your reservation, **request for children's meals or freestanding bassinets** if you need them; the latter are available only to those seated at the bulkhead, where there's enough legroom. If you don't need a bassinet, **think twice before requesting bulkhead seats**—the only storage space for in-flight necessities is in inconveniently distant overhead bins.

LODGING

Chain hotels and motels welcome children, and New England has

Smart Travel Tips A to Z

THE GOLD GUIDE / SMART TRAVEL TIPS

many family-oriented resorts with lively children's programs. You'll also find family farms that accept guests and that are lots of fun for children; the Vermont Travel Division (☞ Visitor Information, in *in* Important Contacts A to Z) publishes a directory. Rental houses and apartments abound, particularly around ski areas; off-season, these can be economical as well as comfortable touring bases. Some country inns, especially those with a quiet, romantic atmosphere and those furnished with antiques, are less enthusiastic about small fries, so **be up front about your traveling companions** when you reserve.

Most hotels allow children under a certain age to stay in their parents' room at no extra charge; others charge them as extra adults. Be sure to **ask about the cutoff age.**

CUSTOMS & DUTIES

IN CANADA

If you've been out of Canada for at least seven days, you may bring in C$500 worth of goods duty-free. If you've been away for fewer than seven days but for more than 48 hours, the duty-free allowance drops to C$200; if your trip lasts between 24 and 48 hours, the allowance is C$50. You cannot pool allowances with family members. Goods claimed under the C$500 exemption may follow you by mail;

those claimed under the lesser exemptions must accompany you.

Alcohol and tobacco products may be included in the seven-day and 48-hour exemptions but not in the 24-hour exemption. If you meet the age requirements of the province or territory through which you reenter Canada, you may bring in, duty-free, 1.14 liters (40 imperial ounces) of wine or liquor *or* 24 12-ounce cans or bottles of beer or ale. If you are 16 or older, you may bring in, duty-free, 200 cigarettes, 50 cigars or cigarillos, and 400 tobacco sticks or 400 grams of manufactured tobacco. Alcohol and tobacco must accompany you on your return.

An unlimited number of gifts with a value of up to C$60 each may be mailed to Canada duty-free. These do not affect your duty-free allowance on your return. Label the package "Unsolicited Gift—Value Under $60." Alcohol and tobacco are excluded.

IN THE U.K.

From countries outside the EU, including the United States, you may import, duty-free, 200 cigarettes, 100 cigarillos, 50 cigars, or 250 grams of tobacco; 1 liter of spirits or 2 liters of fortified or sparkling wine or liqueurs; 2 liters of still table wine; 60 milliliters of perfume; 250 milliliters of toilet water; plus £136 worth of other goods, including gifts and souvenirs.

D

DISABILITIES & ACCESSIBILITY

In Boston, many sidewalks are brick or cobblestone and may be uneven or sloping; many have curbs cut at one end and not the other. To make matters worse, Boston drivers are notorious for running yellow lights and ignoring pedestrians. Back Bay has flat, well-paved streets; older Beacon Hill is steep and difficult; Quincy Market's cobblestone and brick malls are criss-crossed with smooth, tarred paths. The downtown financial district and Chinatown are accessible, while areas such as South Boston and the Italian North End may prove more problematic for people who use wheelchairs. In Cape Cod, a number of towns such as Wellfleet, Hyannis, and Chatham have wide streets with curb cuts; and the Cape Cod National Seashore has several accessible trails. In Kennebunkport, as in many of Maine's coastal towns south of Portland, travelers with mobility impairments will have to cope with crowds as well as with narrow, uneven steps, and sporadic curb cuts. L.L. Bean's outlet in Freeport is fully accessible, and Acadia National Park has some 50 accessible miles of carriage roads that are closed to motor vehicles. In New Hampshire, many of Franconia Notch's natural attractions are accessible.

When discussing accessibility with an operator or reservationist, **ask hard questions.** Are there any stairs, inside *or* out? Are there grab bars next to the toilet *and* in the shower/tub? How wide is the doorway to the room? To the bathroom? For the most extensive facilities, meeting the latest legal specifications, **opt for newer accommodations,** which more often have been designed with access in mind. Older properties or ships must usually be retrofitted and may offer more limited facilities as a result. Be sure to **discuss your needs before booking.**

DISCOUNTS & DEALS

LOOK IN YOUR WALLET

When you **use your credit card to make travel purchases,** you may get free travel-accident insurance, collision damage insurance, medical or legal assistance, depending on the card and bank that issued it. Visa and MasterCard provide one or more of these services, so **get a copy of your card's travel benefits.** If you are a member of the AAA or an oil-company-sponsored road-assistance plan, always **ask hotel or car-rental reservationists for auto-club discounts.** Some clubs offer additional discounts on tours, cruises, or admission to attractions. And don't forget that auto-club membership entitles you to free maps and trip-planning services.

SENIOR CITIZENS & STUDENTS

As a senior-citizen traveler, you may be eligible for special rates, but you should mention your senior-citizen status up front. If you're a student or under 26, you can also get discounts, especially if you have an official ID card (☞ Senior-Citizen Discounts *and* Students on the Road, *below*).

DIAL FOR DOLLARS

To save money, **look into "1-800" discount reservations services,** which often have lower rates. These services use their buying power to get a better price on hotels, airline tickets, and sometimes even car rentals. When booking a room, always **call the hotel's local toll-free number** (if one is available) rather than the central reservations number—you'll often get a better price. Ask the reservationist about special packages or corporate rates, which are usually available even if you're not traveling on business.

JOIN A CLUB?

Discount clubs can be a legitimate source of savings, but you must use the participating hotels and visit the participating attractions in order to realize any benefits. Remember, too, that you have to pay a fee to join, so **determine if you'll save enough to warrant your membership fee.** Before booking with a club, **make sure the hotel or other supplier isn't offering a better deal.**

DRIVING

A car is the most convenient means of travel, but driving is not without its frustrations; traffic can be heavy on coastal routes and beach-access highways on weekends and in midsummer, and Newport in summer and Boston all year long are inhospitable to automobiles. Each of the states makes available, free on request, an official state map that has directories, mileage, and other useful information in addition to routings. The speed limit in much of New England is 65 miles per hour (55 in more populated areas).

H
HEALTH CONCERNS

LYME DISEASE

Use insect repellent; recent outbreaks of Lyme disease all over the East Coast make it imperative (even in urban areas) that you protect yourself from ticks from early spring through the summer. Wear light-colored clothing, tuck pant legs into socks, and look for black ticks about the size of a pin head around hairlines and the warmest parts of the body. **If you have been bitten, consult a physician,** especially if you see the telltale bull's-eye bite pattern. Influenza-like symptoms often accompany a Lyme infection. Early treatment is always the best bet.

THE GOLD GUIDE / SMART TRAVEL TIPS

THE GOLD GUIDE / SMART TRAVEL TIPS

I
INSURANCE

BAGGAGE

Airline liability for baggage is limited to $1,250 per person on domestic flights. On international flights, it amounts to $9.07 per pound or $20 per kilogram for checked baggage (roughly $640 per 70-pound bag) and $400 per passenger for unchecked baggage. Insurance for losses exceeding the terms of your airline ticket can be bought directly from the airline at check-in for about $10 per $1,000 of coverage; note that it excludes a rather extensive list of items, shown on your airline ticket.

COMPREHENSIVE

Comprehensive insurance policies include all the coverages described above plus some that may not be available in more specific policies. If you have purchased an expensive vacation, especially one that involves travel abroad, comprehensive insurance is a must; **look for policies that include trip delay insurance,** which will protect you in the event that weather problems cause you to miss your flight, tour, or cruise. A few insurers will also sell you a waiver for preexisting medical conditions. Some of the companies that offer both these features are Access America, Carefree Travel, Travel Insured International, and TravelGuard (☞ Insurance *in* Important Contacts A to Z).

FLIGHT

You should **think twice before buying flight insurance.** Often purchased as a last-minute impulse at the airport, it pays a lump sum when a plane crashes, either to a beneficiary if the insured dies or sometimes to a surviving passenger who loses his or her eyesight or a limb. Supplementing the airlines' coverage described in the limits-of-liability paragraphs on your ticket, it's expensive and basically unnecessary. Charging an airline ticket to a major credit card often automatically provides you with coverage that may also extend to travel by bus, train, and ship.

U.K. TRAVELERS

According to the Association of British Insurers, a trade association representing 450 insurance companies, it's wise to **buy extra medical coverage when you visit the United States.** You can buy an annual travel insurance policy valid for most vacations during the year in which it's purchased. If you are pregnant or have a preexisting medical condition make sure you're covered before buying such a policy.

TRIP

Without insurance, you will lose all or most of your money if you cancel your trip regardless of the reason. Especially if your airline ticket, cruise, or package tour is nonrefundable and cannot be changed, it's essential that you **buy trip-cancellation-and-inter-**ruption insurance. When considering how much coverage you need, look for a policy that will cover the cost of your trip plus the nondiscounted price of a one-way airline ticket should you need to return home early. Read the fine print carefully, especially sections that define "family member" and "preexisting medical conditions." Also **consider default or bankruptcy insurance,** which protects you against a supplier's failure to deliver. Be aware, however, that if you buy such a policy from a travel agency, tour operator, airline, or cruise line, it may not cover default by the firm in question.

L
LODGING

Hotel and motel chains provide standard rooms and amenities in major cities and at or near traditional vacation destinations. At small inns, where each room is different and amenities vary in number and quality, price isn't always a reliable indicator; fortunately, when you call to make reservations, most hosts will be happy to give all manner of details about their properties, down to the color scheme of the handmade quilts—so **ask all your questions before you book.** Don't expect telephone, TV, or honor bar in your room; you might even have to share a bathroom. Most inns offer breakfast—hence the name bed-and-breakfast—yet this formula varies, too; at one B&B you may be served muffins and coffee, at another a multicourse feast with fresh flowers on the table. Many inns prohibit smoking, which is a fire hazard in older buildings, and some are wary of children. Almost all say no to pets.

APARTMENT & VILLA RENTAL

If you want a home base that's roomy enough for a family and comes with cooking facilities, **consider taking a furnished rental.** This can also save you money, but not always—some rentals are luxury properties (economical only when your party is large). Home-exchange directories list rentals—often second homes owned by prospective house swappers—and some services search for a house or apartment for you (even a castle if that's your fancy) and handle the paperwork. Some send an illustrated catalog; others send photographs only of specific properties, sometimes at a charge; up-front registration fees may apply.

HOME EXCHANGE

If you would like to find a house, an apartment, or some other type of vacation property to exchange for your own while on holiday, **become a member of a home-exchange organization,** which will send you its updated listings of available exchanges for a year, and will include your own listing in at least one of them. Arrangements for the actual exchange are made by the two parties involved, not by the organization.

M
MONEY & EXPENSES

ATMS

CASH ADVANCES➣ Chances are that you can **use your bank card, MasterCard, or Visa at ATMs** to withdraw money from an account or get a cash advance. Before leaving home, **check on frequency limits** for withdrawals and cash advances.

TRANSACTION FEES➣ On credit-card cash advances you are charged interest from the day you receive the money, whether from a teller or an ATM. Transaction fees for ATM withdrawals outside your local area may be higher than those charged for withdrawals at home.

TRAVELER'S CHECKS

Whether or not to buy traveler's checks depends on where you are headed; **take cash to rural areas and small towns, traveler's checks to cities.** The most widely recognized checks are issued by American Express, Citicorp, Thomas Cook, and Visa. These are sold by major commercial banks for 1%–3% of the checks' face value—it pays to **shop around.** Both American Express and Thomas Cook issue checks that can be countersigned and used by either you or your traveling companion. Before leaving home, **contact your issuer for information on where to**

cash your checks without a incurring a transaction fee. Record the numbers of all your checks, and keep this listing in a separate place, crossing off the numbers of checks you have cashed.

WIRING MONEY

For a fee of 3%–10%, depending on the amount of the transaction, you can have money sent to you from home through Money-Gram^{SM} or Western Union (☞ Money Matters *in* Important Contacts A to Z). The transferred funds and the service fee can be charged to a Master-Card or Visa account.

N
NATIONAL PARKS

If you are a frequent visitor, senior citizen, or traveler with a disability, you can **save money on park entrance fees** by getting a discount pass. The Golden Eagle Pass can be a good deal if you plan to visit several parks during your travels. Priced at $25, it entitles you and your companions to free admission to *all* parks for a year. It does not cover additional park fees such as those for camping or parking. Both the Golden Age Passport, for U.S. citizens or permanent residents 62 or older, and the Golden Access Passport, for travelers with disabilities, entitle holders to free entry to all national parks plus 50% off fees for the use of all park facilities and services except those run by private concessionaires. Both passports are free; you must show proof of age and U.S. citizenship or permanent residency (such as a U.S. passport, driver's license, or birth certificate) or proof of disability. All three passes are available at all national park entrances.

P

PACKING FOR NEW ENGLAND

The principal rule on weather in New England is that there are no rules. A cold, foggy morning can and often does become a bright, 60-degree afternoon. A summer breeze can suddenly turn chilly, and rain often appears with little warning. Thus, the best advice on how to dress is to **layer your clothing** so that you can peel off or add garments as needed for comfort. Showers are frequent, so **pack a raincoat and umbrella.** Even in summer you should bring long pants, a sweater or two, and a waterproof windbreaker, for evenings are often chilly and the sea spray can make things cool.

Casual sportswear— walking shoes and jeans—will take you almost everywhere, but swimsuits and bare feet will not: Shirts and shoes are required attire at even the most casual venues. Dress in restaurants is generally casual, except at some of the distinguished restaurants of Boston, Newport, Maine coast towns such as Kennebunkport, a number of inns in the Berkshires, and in Litchfield and

Fairfield counties in Connecticut.

In summer, bring a hat and sunscreen. Remember also to **pack insect repellent;** to prevent Lyme disease you'll need to guard against ticks from early spring through the summer (☞ Health Concerns, *above*).

Bring an extra pair of eyeglasses or contact lenses in your carry-on luggage, and if you have a health problem, **pack enough medication** to last the trip. It's important that you **don't put prescription drugs or valuables in luggage to be checked,** for it could go astray. To avoid problems with customs officials, carry medications in the original packaging. Also, don't forget the addresses of offices that handle refunds of lost traveler's checks.

LUGGAGE

Airline baggage allowances depend on the airline, the route, and the class of your ticket; ask in advance. In general, on domestic flights you are entitled to check two bags. A third piece may be brought on board, but it must fit easily under the seat in front of you or in the overhead compartment. In the United States, the FAA gives airlines broad latitude regarding carry-on allowances, and they tend to tailor them to different aircraft and operational conditions. Charges for excess, oversize, or overweight pieces vary.

SAFEGUARDING YOUR LUGGAGE➣ Before

leaving home, **itemize your bags' contents** and their worth, and label them with your name, address, and phone number. (If you use your home address, cover it so that potential thieves can't see it readily.) Inside each bag, **pack a copy of your itinerary.** At check-in, **make sure that each bag is correctly tagged** with the destination airport's three-letter code. If your bags arrive damaged—or fail to arrive at all—file a written report with the airline before leaving the airport.

PASSPORTS & VISAS

CANADIANS

No passport is necessary to enter the United States.

U.K. CITIZENS

British citizens need a valid passport to enter the United States. If you are staying for fewer than 90 days and traveling on a vacation, with a return or onward ticket, you probably will not need a visa. However, you will need to fill out the Visa Waiver Form, 1-94W, supplied by the airline.

It is advisable that you **leave one photocopy of your passport's data page** with someone at home and keep another with you, separated from your passport, while traveling. If you lose your passport, promptly call the nearest embassy or consulate and the local police; having the data page information can speed replacement.

S

SENIOR-CITIZEN DISCOUNTS

To qualify for age-related discounts, **mention your senior-citizen status up front** when booking hotel reservations, not when checking out, and before you're seated in restaurants, not when paying the bill. Note that discounts may be limited to certain menus, days, or hours. When renting a car, **ask about promotional car-rental discounts**—they can net even lower costs than your senior-citizen discount.

STUDENTS ON THE ROAD

To save money, **look into deals available through student-oriented travel agencies.** To qualify, you'll need to have a bona fide student ID card. Members of international student groups are also eligible (☞ Students *in* Important Contacts A to Z).

T

TELEPHONES

LONG-DISTANCE

The long-distance services of AT&T, MCI, and Sprint make calling home relatively convenient and let you avoid hotel surcharges; typically, you dial an 800 number in the United States.

TOUR OPERATORS

Firms that sell tours and packages reserve airline seats, hotel rooms, and rental cars in bulk and pass some of the savings on to you. In addition, the best operators have local representatives available to help you at your destination.

A GOOD DEAL?

The more your package or tour includes, the better you can predict the ultimate cost of your vacation. Make sure you know exactly what is covered, and **beware of hidden costs.** Are taxes, tips, and service charges included? Transfers and baggage handling? Entertainment and excursions? These can add up.

Most packages and tours are rated deluxe, first-class superior, first class, tourist, or budget. The key difference is usually accommodations. If the package or tour you are considering is priced lower than in your wildest dreams, **be skeptical.** Also, **make sure your travel agent knows the accommodations** and other services. Ask about the hotel's location, room size, beds, and whether it has a pool, room service, or programs for children, if you care about these. Has your agent been there in person or sent others you can contact?

BUYER BEWARE

Each year a number of consumers are stranded or lose their money when operators—even very large ones with excellent reputations—go out of business. To avoid becoming one of them, take the time to **check out the operator**—find out how long the company has been in business and ask several agents about its reputation. Next, **don't book unless the firm has a consumer-protection program.** Members of the USTOA and the NTA are required to set aside funds for the sole purpose of covering your payments and travel arrangements in case of default. Nonmember operators may instead carry insurance; look for the details in the operator's brochure—and for the name of an underwriter with a solid reputation. Note: When it comes to tour operators, **don't trust escrow accounts.** Although there are laws governing those of charter-flight operators, no governmental body prevents tour operators from raiding the till.

Next, **contact your local Better Business Bureau and the attorney general's offices** in both your own state and the operator's; have any complaints been filed? Finally, **pay with a major credit card.** Then you can cancel payment, provided that you can document your complaint. Always **consider trip-cancellation insurance** (☞ Insurance, *in* Important Contacts A to Z).

BIG VS. SMALL➤ Operators that handle several hundred thousand travelers per year can use their purchasing power to give you a good price. Their high volume may also indicate financial stability. But some small companies provide more personalized service; because they tend to specialize, they may also be more knowledgeable about a given area.

USING AN AGENT

Travel agents are excellent resources. In fact, large operators accept bookings made only through travel agents. But it's good to **collect brochures from several agencies** because some agents' suggestions may be skewed by promotional relationships with tour and package firms that reward them for volume sales. If you have a special interest, **find an agent with expertise in that area**; ASTA can provide leads in the United States. (Don't rely solely on your agent, though; agents may be unaware of small-niche operators, and some special-interest travel companies only sell direct.)

SINGLE TRAVELERS

Prices are usually quoted per person, based on two sharing a room. If traveling solo, you may be required to pay the full double-occupancy rate. Some operators eliminate this surcharge if you agree to be matched up with a roommate of the same sex, even if one is not found by departure time.

W
WHEN TO GO

All six New England states are largely year-round destinations. While summer is a favored time all over New England, fall is balmy and idyllically colorful, and winter's snow makes for great skiing. The only times vacationers might want to stay away are during mud season in April and black-fly season in the last two weeks of May. Note that many smaller museums and attractions are open only from Memorial Day to mid-October, at other times by appointment only.

Memorial Day is the start of the migration to the beaches and the mountains, and summer begins in earnest on July 4. Those who are driving to Cape Cod in July or August should know that Friday and Sunday are the days weekenders clog the overburdened Route 6; a better time to visit the beach areas and the islands may be after Labor Day.

Fall is the most colorful season in New England, a time when many inns and hotels are booked months in advance by foliage-viewing visitors. The first scarlet and gold colors emerge in mid-September in northern areas; "peak" color occurs at different times from year to year. Generally, it is best to visit the northern reaches in early October and then move southward as the month progresses.

All leaves are off the trees by Halloween, and hotel rates fall as the leaves do, dropping significantly until ski season begins. November and early December are hunting season in much of New England; those who venture into the woods then should wear bright orange clothing.

Winter is the time for downhill and cross-country skiing. New England's major ski resorts, having seen dark days in years when snowfall was meager, now have snowmaking equipment.

In spring, despite mud season, maple sugaring goes on in Maine, New Hampshire, and Vermont, and the fragrant scent of lilacs is never far behind.

CLIMATE

What follows are average daily maximum and minimum temperatures for some major cities in New England.

Climate in New England

HARTFORD, CT

Jan.	36F	2C	May	70F	21C	Sept.	74F	23C
	20	− 7		47	8		52	11
Feb.	38F	3C	June	81F	27C	Oct.	65F	18C
	20	− 7		56	13		43	6
Mar.	45F	7C	July	85F	29C	Nov.	52F	11C
	27	− 3		63	17		32	0
Apr.	59F	15C	Aug.	83F	28C	Dec.	38F	3C
	38	3		61	16		22	− 6

BOSTON, MA

Jan.	36F	2C	May	67F	19C	Sept.	72F	22C
	20	− 7		49	9		56	13
Feb.	38F	3C	June	76F	24C	Oct.	63F	17C
	22	− 6		58	14		47	8
Mar.	43F	6C	July	81F	27C	Nov.	49F	9C
	29	− 2		63	17		36	2
Apr.	54F	12C	Aug.	79F	26C	Dec.	40F	4C
	38	3		63	17		25	− 4

BURLINGTON, VT

Jan.	29F	− 2C	May	67F	19C	Sept.	74F	23C
	11	−12		45	7		50	10
Feb.	31F	− 1C	June	77F	25C	Oct.	59F	15C
	11	−12		56	13		40	4
Mar.	40F	4C	July	83F	28C	Nov.	45F	7C
	22	− 6		59	15		31	− 1
Apr.	54F	12C	Aug.	79F	26C	Dec.	31F	− 1C
	34	1		58	14		16	− 9

PORTLAND, ME

Jan.	31F	− 1C	May	61F	16C	Sept.	68F	20C
	16	− 9		47	8		52	11
Feb.	32F	0C	June	72F	22C	Oct.	58F	14C
	16	− 9		54	15		43	6
Mar.	40F	4C	July	76F	24C	Nov.	45F	7C
	27	− 3		61	16		32	0
Apr.	50F	10C	Aug.	74F	23C	Dec.	34F	1C
	36	2		59	15		22	− 6

THE GOLD GUIDE / SMART TRAVEL TIPS

1 Destination: New England

A NEW ENGLAND PAUL REVERE WOULD RECOGNIZE

JUST 20 YEARS after the Declaration of Independence, the Reverend Timothy Dwight, President of Yale College and grandson of the fiery Puritan preacher Jonathan Edwards, set out on the first of a series of annual rambles through his native New England. In his journal, Dwight declared, "A succession of New England villages, composed of neat houses, surrounding neat schoolhouses and churches, adorned with gardens, meadows, and orchards, and exhibiting the universally easy circumstances of the inhabitants, is . . . one of the most delightful prospects which this world can afford." Two hundred years after Dwight's first tour, the graceful small towns he described remain intact: Clapboard farmhouses, weather-beaten barns, lovely old churches, and some of the nation's best schools still line the rural routes in all six New England states.

The difference, from Dwight's day to our own, is that a whole world of cities and suburbs has grown up around these rural villages. New England's first cities—Portland, Boston, Providence, Newport, New London, New Haven—began as harbor towns. In the 17th century, English Puritans, fleeing religious persecution and civil war, were the first Europeans to make their fortunes in these harbors. Merchants, fishermen, and shipbuilders from all over the world thrived here in the years before the American Revolution.

Even as their cities expanded, New Englanders protected their natural resources. The most famous pioneer of conservation and outdoor recreation is poet and naturalist Henry David Thoreau, who led the way in the 1840s with his famous pilgrimages to Walden Pond in Massachusetts and Mount Katahdin in Maine. In the years after the Civil War, middle class New Englanders flocked to the mountains and the seashore seeking relief from the pressures of city life. Nature lovers and amateur mountaineers cut hiking trails and built rustic shelters in the White Mountains of New Hampshire; Massachusetts families camped and tramped in

the rolling Berkshire hills; in Maine, Harvard President Charles W. Eliot and his fellow "rusticators" conserved craggy cliffs, rocky beaches, and pine forests for future generations by donating land to establish Acadia National Park. By 1910, Vermont hikers had begun work on the 265-mile "Long Trail" that connects the Green Mountain summits from Canada to the Massachusetts border. During the Great Depression, conservationists rescued the trail from highway planners who would have paved this favorite mountain footpath.

New England's tangle of turnpikes and highways originated with the first settlers' footpaths. The Pocumtucks, Nehantics, Nipmucks, Wampanoags, Pequots, Mohegans, Kennebecs, Penobscots, and Narragansetts created paths with skills that modern engineers might envy. This vast trail network extended over rolling hills, through dense woodlands, along riverbanks and the Atlantic coast. The Mohawk Trail—Route 2 on your Massachusetts road map—ran east to west through the Deerfield and Connecticut River valleys to the Hudson River. Seasonal feasts and athletic competitions were held along this route for hundreds of years.

Like well-worn Indian byways, the familiar ingredients of the New England diet have been around since before the Mayflower: clams, cranberries, pumpkins, corn-on-the-cob, squash, beans, blueberries, cod, and lobster. Clambakes and baked beans were also Native American specialties.

Another New England specialty is education: There are sixty-five institutions of higher learning in the greater Boston area alone. Dedication to the life of the mind is fostered at Harvard, Yale, and hundreds of excellent secondary schools, colleges, and universities throughout the region.

When it comes to weather, variety is New England's great virtue: All four seasons get full play here. September and October are dazzling as the dying leaves turn color. Foliage fans take to the rural roads and country inns to observe the way in which warm sunny days and cool autumn nights work together to paint the treetops crimson and gold. Winter usually brings plenty of snow, but if Mother Nature fails to satisfy skiers, resort owners rely on high-tech Yankee know-how to make up the difference. Spring brings crocuses, muddy boots, and maple syrup—sugaring begins when the days are warm and the nights are still below freezing. Summer is the season to enjoy New England's lakes, beaches, and ocean resorts, from Cape Cod to Bar Harbor. Although they may not agree on matters of state, both George Bush and Bill Clinton concede that New England is a great place for a summer vacation: President Clinton is a regular guest on Martha's Vineyard and former President Bush is a longtime summer resident of Kennebunkport, Maine.

At the turn of the century, summer visitors briefly turned their backs on New England's rustic charms in favor of imported Old World grandeur. Rhode Island—once the refuge of that purest of Puritans, Roger Williams—became the summer home of the nation's most conspicuous consumers. In Newport, gilded halls with magnificent ocean views were built to house wealthy families with princely appetites. For a short period, before World War I, New Englanders discovered that being counted by Mrs. Astor as fit for fashionable society—one of "The Four Hundred"—was a struggle on par with their ancestors' quest for eternal salvation among the Puritan elect.

THE STREETS OF BOSTON, New England's largest city, provide a crash course in the early political history of the United States. The red line of the Freedom Trail begins at Boston Common, America's oldest public park, and winds past a dozen Revolutionary-era memorials, including: the Granary Burial Ground where the victims of the Boston Massacre were laid to rest; Faneuil Hall, the meeting house and marketplace that earned the name "the Cradle of Liberty"; Old North Church, immortalized in Longfellow's poem, "Paul Revere's Ride"; and the obelisk commemorating the Battle of Bunker Hill. Monuments to 18th-century glory stand alongside glass office towers in the busy financial district; and

in the North End, the house where midnight rider Paul Revere lived is just around the corner from some of the best Italian restaurants in town.

The story of the preservation of Boston's most elegant neighborhood gives us clues about the New England character that we know incompletely from novels, films, and history books. The Boston Brahmin, the ingenious Yankee, the doom-laden Puritan, and the straitlaced reformer have contributed as much to our sense of the place as have New England's snug harbors, salt sea air, stone walls, and pine forests. In 1947, Beacon Hill matrons, dressed in felt hats and furs, conducted a sit-in to save the brick sidewalks of this historic neighborhood, which is known architecturally for its gaslights, cast-iron fences, and sturdy brownstones. With true New England spirit, these earnest women let their opinions be known. Such a polished group of protesters was impossible to resist. Tradition was properly preserved.

These days prominent people with roots in New England are a diverse crowd. The traditional monikers—"Yankee," "Puritan," and "Brahmin"—no longer quite fit. New England luminaries include: consumer advocate Ralph Nader; movie idols and "foodie" philanthropists Paul Newman and Joanne Woodward; actresses Katharine Hepburn, Glenn Close, Meg Ryan, and Geena Davis; actor James Spader; disco diva Donna Summer; rockers Aerosmith and Talking Heads; baby-care guru Dr. Benjamin Spock; *Star Trek's* Mr. Spock, Leonard Nimoy; painter Frank Stella; media exec Sumner Redstone; Supreme Court Justice David Souter; conservative pundit John McLaughlin; novelist John Irving; and late-night talk show host Conan O'Brien.

Despite two hundred years of growth and change–and several large cities notwithstanding–the Reverend Dwight would still recognize his beloved New England. And he'd be delighted you've decided to visit.

—*Laura E. Cronin*

WHAT'S WHERE

Connecticut

Southwestern Connecticut, the richest part of the richest state, is home to commuters, celebrities, and others who enjoy both its privacy and rusticity and its convenience to New York City. Far less touristy than other parts of the state, the Connecticut River Valley is an unspectacular stretch of small river villages and uncrowded state parks punctuated by a few small cities and one large one: Hartford. The Litchfield Hills has grand old inns, rolling farmlands, and plenty of forests and rivers. People escape here from New York City; now, people are escaping the Litchfield Hills, in the northwestern part of the state, for The Quiet Corner, a string of sparsely populated towns in the northeast. New Haven is home to Yale and several fine museums. Along the southeastern coast, there are quiet shoreline villages and, a bit inland, Foxwoods Casino draws droves of gamblers to the Mashantucket Pequots' reservation in Ledyard.

Rhode Island

Just about everyone knows that Rhode Island is the smallest of the 50 states. What is less known is that the state boasts 20% of the country's National Historic Landmarks and has more restored Colonial and Victorian buildings than any other destination in the United States. Founded in 1635, the state's capital, Providence, is home to both Brown University and the Rhode Island School of Design, and has colorful Italian, Portuguese, and Jewish communities. The state's other well-known city is Newport, one of the great sailing capitals of the world and host to world-class music festivals; its over-the-top "cottages" were built in the 19th century as summer residences for the likes of Astors and Vanderbilts. South County has rolling farmland, sparsely populated beaches, and wilderness to explore; Block Island, 11 square miles in area, has one village and 365 ponds.

Massachusetts

New England's largest and most important city, Boston has buildings that are national icons and a lively population of students, artists, academics, and young professionals. Plymouth is on the South Shore, a region that's not as prosperous or as picturesque as other areas of Massachusetts. Martha's Vineyard is much less developed than Cape Cod, yet more diverse and cosmopolitan than neighboring Nantucket. Salem and Gloucester are on the North Shore, which extends past grimy docklands to the picturesque Cape Ann region. The Pioneer Valley is a string of historic settlements, and the Berkshires, in the western end of the state, live up to the storybook image of rural New England.

Vermont

Southern Vermont has farms, freshly starched New England towns, quiet back roads, bustling ski resorts, and strip-mall sprawl. Central Vermont's trademarks include famed marble quarries, just north of Rutland, and large dairy herds and pastures that create the quilted patchwork of the Champlain Valley. The heart of the area is the Green Mountains, and the surrounding wilderness of the Green Mountain National Forest. Both the state's largest city (Burlington) and the nation's smallest state capital (Montpelier) are in northern Vermont, as are some of the most rural and remote areas of New England. Much of the state's logging, dairy farming, and skiing take place here. With Montréal only an hour from the border, the Canadian influence is strong, and Canadian accents and currency common.

New Hampshire

Portsmouth, the star of New Hampshire's 18-mile coastline, has great shopping, restaurants, music, theater, and one of the best historic districts in the nation; Exeter is New Hampshire's enclave of Revolutionary War history. The lakes region, rich with historic landmarks, also has good restaurants, several golf courses, hiking trails, and antiquing. People come to the White Mountains to hike and climb, to photograph the dramatic vistas and the vibrant sea of foliage, and to ski. More than a mile high, Mt. Washington's peak claims the harshest winds and lowest temperatures ever recorded. Western and central New Hampshire is the unspoiled heart of the state: This region has managed to keep the water slides and the outlet malls at bay. Beyond the museums and picture-perfect greens, this area offers Lake Sunapee and Mt. Monadnock, the second-most-climbed mountain in the world. It is also an informal artists' colony where people come to write, paint, and weave in solitude.

Maine

Maine is by far the largest state in New England. At its extremes it measures 300 miles by 200 miles; all other New England states could fit within its perimeters. Due to overdevelopment, Maine's southernmost coastal towns won't give you the rugged, "downeast" experience, but the Kennebunks will: classic townscapes, rocky shorelines punctuated by sandy beaches, quaint downtown districts. Purists hold that the Maine coast begins at Penobscot Bay, where the vistas over the water are wider and bluer, the shore a jumble of granite boulders. Acadia National Park is Maine's principal tourist attraction; and in Freeport, a bewildering assortment of outlets has sprung up around the famous outfitter L. L. Bean. The vast north woods is a destination for outdoors enthusiasts. Tourism has supplanted fishing, logging, and potato farming as Maine's number-one industry: The visitor seeking an untouched fishing village with locals gathered around a potbellied stove in the general store may be sadly disappointed; that innocent age has passed in all but the most remote of villages.

PLEASURES AND PASTIMES

Beaches

Long, wide beaches edge the New England coast from southern Maine to southern Connecticut; the most popular are on Cape Cod, Martha's Vineyard, Nantucket, and the shore areas north and south of Boston; on Maine's York County Coast; Long Island Sound in Rhode Island; and the coastal region of New Hampshire. Many are maintained by state and local governments and have lifeguards on duty; they may have picnic facilities, rest rooms, changing facilities, and concession stands. Depending on the locale, you may need a parking sticker to use the lot. The waters are at their warmest in August, though they're cold even at the height of summer along much of the Maine coast. Inland, there are small lake beaches, most notably in New Hampshire and Vermont.

Biking

Cape Cod has miles of bike trails, some paralleling the National Seashore, most on level terrain. On either side of the Cape Cod Canal is an easy 7-mile straight trail offering a view of the bridges and canal traffic. Other favorite areas for bicycling are the Massachusetts Berkshires, the New Hampshire lakes region, and Vermont's Northeast Kingdom. Biking in Maine is especially scenic in and around Kennebunkport, Camden, and Deer Isle; the carriage paths in Acadia National Park are ideal.

Boating

In most lakeside and coastal resorts, sailboats and powerboats can be rented at a local marina. Newport, Rhode Island, and Maine's Penobscot Bay are famous sailing areas. Lakes in New Hampshire and Vermont are splendid for all kinds of boating. The Connecticut River in the Pioneer Valley and the Housatonic River in the Berkshires are popular for canoeing.

Dining

Seafood is king throughout New England. Clams, quahogs, lobster, and scrod are prepared here in an infinite number of ways, some fancy and expensive, others simple and moderately priced. One of the best ways to enjoy seafood is in the rough—off paper plates on a picnic table at a clam boil or clambake—or at one of the many shacklike eating places along the coast, where you can smell the salt air.

At inland resorts and inns, traditional fare dominates the menu. Among the quintessentially New England dishes are Indian pudding, clam chowder, fried clams, and cranberry anything. You can also find multicultural variations on themes, such as Portuguese *chouriço* (a spicy red sausage that transforms a clamboil into something heavenly) and the mincemeat pie made with pork in the tradition of the French Canadians who populate the northern regions.

Fishing

Anglers will find sport aplenty throughout the region—surf-casting along the shore, deep-sea fishing in the Atlantic on party and charter boats, fishing for trout in rivers, and angling for bass, landlocked salmon, and other fish in freshwater lakes; Maine's Moosehead Lake is a draw for serious fisherfolk. Sporting goods stores and bait-and-tackle shops are reliable sources for licenses—necessary in fresh waters—and for leads to the nearest hot spots.

Hiking

Probably the most famous trails are the 255-mile Long Trail, which runs north–south through the center of Vermont, and the Maine-to-Georgia Appalachian Trail, which runs through New England on both private and public land. You'll find good hiking in many state parks throughout the region.

National and State Parks and Forests

National and state parks offer a broad range of visitor facilities, including campgrounds, picnic grounds, hiking trails, boating, and ranger programs. State forests are usually somewhat less developed. For more information on any of these, contact the state tourism offices or parks departments (☞ Visitor Information, *in* the Gold Guide).

CONNECTICUT➤ The Litchfield Hills has a strong concentration of wilderness areas, of which the best include: Kent Falls State Park, Mt. Tom, Dennis Hill, Haystack Mountain, Campbell Falls, Housatonic Meadows, and Burr Pond. Elsewhere in the state, Rocky Neck State Park in Niantic has one of the finest beaches on Long Island Sound; the 15,652-acre Cockaponset in Haddam has 60-foot cascades; Wadsworth Falls, near Wesleyan University, also has a beautiful waterfall and 285 acres of forest; and Dinosaur State Park, north of Middletown in Rocky Hill, has dinosaur tracks dating from the Jurassic period. There's excellent hiking and picnicking at the state's leading oddity, Gillette Castle State Park, an outrageous hilltop castle on 117 acres.

RHODE ISLAND➤ With 19 preserves, state parks, beaches, and forest areas, including Charlestown's Burlingame State Park and Ninigret National Wildlife Refuge, South County is a region that respects the concept of wilderness. Fifteen state parks throughout the state permit camping.

MASSACHUSETTS➤ Cape Cod National Seashore, a 40-mile stretch of the Cape between Eastham and Provincetown, offers excellent swimming, bike riding, bird-watching, and nature walks.

Some of the newest parks in Massachusetts have been created by the Urban Heritage State Park Program, which celebrates the Industrial Revolution, in Lowell, Gardner, North Adams, Holyoke, Lawrence, Lynn, Roxbury, and Fall River.

VERMONT➤ The 275,000-acre Green Mountain National Forest extends south from the center of the state to the Massachusetts border. Hikers treasure the miles of trails; canoeists work its white waters; and campers and anglers find plenty to keep them happy. Among the most popular spots are the Falls of Lana and Silver Lake near Middlebury; Hapgood Pond between Manchester and Peru; and Chittenden Brook near Rochester.

NEW HAMPSHIRE➤ The White Mountain National Forest covers 770,000 acres of northern New Hampshire. New Hampshire parklands vary widely, even within a region. Major recreation parks are at Franconia Notch, Crawford Notch, and Mt. Sunapee. Rhododendron State Park (Monadnock) has a singular collection of wild rhododendrons; Mt. Washington Park (White Mountains) is on top of the highest mountain in the Northeast.

MAINE➤ Acadia National Park, which preserves fine stretches of shoreline and high mountains, covers much of Mount Desert Island and more than half of Isle au Haut and Schoodic Point on the mainland.

Baxter State Park comprises more than 200,000 acres of wilderness surrounding Katahdin, Maine's highest mountain. Hiking and moose-watching are major activities. The Allagash Wilderness Waterway is a 92-mile corridor of lakes and rivers surrounded by vast commercial forest property.

Shopping

Antiques, crafts, maple syrup and sugar, fresh produce, and the greatly varied offerings of the factory outlets lure shoppers to New England's outlet stores, flea markets, shopping malls, bazaars, yard sales, country stores, and farmers' markets. Connecticut sales tax is 6%; Rhode Island, 7%; Massachusetts, 5% (except clothing purchases under $150, which are not taxed); Vermont, 5%; and Maine, 6%. New Hampshire has no sales tax.

ANTIQUES➤ Best bets for antiquing in Connecticut include: Route 7, Deep River,

New Preston and Putnam, Woodbury and Southbury, and the area of West Cornwall just over the covered bridge. Antiques stores are plentiful in Newport, but are a specialty of Rhode Island's South County: The best places to browse are Wickford, Charlestown, and Watch Hill. In Massachusetts, there's a large concentration of antiques stores on the North Shore around Essex, but there are also plenty sprinkled throughout Salem and Cape Ann. Also try the Berkshires around Great Barrington, South Egremont, and Sheffield. People sometimes joke that New Hampshire's two cash crops are fudge and antiques. Particularly in the Monadnock region, dealers abound in barns and home stores that are strung along back roads. Best antiquing concentrations are in North Conway; along Route 119, from Fitzwilliam to Hinsdale; Route 101, from Marlborough to Wilton; and the towns of Hopkinton, Hollis, and Amherst. In Maine, antiques shops are clustered in Searsport and along Route 1 between Kittery and Scarborough.

CRAFTS➤ Try Washington Street in South Norwalk, Connecticut, and in Massachusetts, Boston, Cape Cod, and the Berkshires. In Vermont, Burlington and Putney are crafts centers. On Maine's Deer Isle, Haystack Mountain School of Crafts attracts internationally renowned craftspeople to its summer institute.

OUTLET STORES➤ In Connecticut, try Norwalk and Mystic; in Massachusetts, the area around New Bedford; in Maine shop along the coast, in Kittery, Freeport, Kennebunkport, Wells, and Ellsworth; in New Hampshire, North Conway; and Manchester, in Vermont.

PRODUCE➤ Opportunities abound for obtaining fresh farm produce from the source; some farms allow you to pick your own strawberries, raspberries, blueberries, and apples. October in Maine is prime time for pumpkins and potatoes. There are maple-syrup producers who demonstrate the process to visitors, most noticeably in Vermont. Maple syrup is available in different grades; light amber is the most refined; many Vermonters prefer grade C, the richest in flavor and the one most often used in cooking. A sugarhouse can be the most or the least expensive place to shop, depending on how tourist-oriented it is. Small grocery stores are often a good source of less-expensive syrup.

Skiing

The softly rounded peaks of New England have been attracting skiers for a full century.

LIFT TICKETS➤ A good bet is that the bigger and more famous the resort, the higher the lift ticket's price. Although lift tickets come in many configurations, most people make the mistake of listing the single-day, weekend-holiday adult lift pass as the "guidepost." It is always the highest price; astute skiers look for off-site purchase locations, senior discounts and junior pricing, and package rates, multiple days, stretch weekends (a weekend that usually includes a Monday or Friday), frequent-skier programs and season-ticket plans to save their skiing dollars.

On the positive side of things, skiing remains one of the more inexpensive sports, even at resorts that demand top-of-the-line rates. Divide six hours of skiing time into $45 (for a high-end full-day lift ticket), and the price is $7.50 per hour.

LODGING➤ Lodging is among the most important considerations for skiers who plan more than a day trip. While some of the ski areas described in this book are small and draw only day trippers, most offer a variety of accommodations—lodges, condominiums, hotels, motels, inns, bed-and-breakfasts—close to or at a short distance from the action. Because of the general state of the New England economy, some prices have dropped a bit to lure skiers back to the hills. There might be a pleasant surprise or two awaiting your pocketbook.

For a longer vacation, you should request and study the resort area's accommodations brochure. For stays of three days or more, a package rate may offer the best deal. Packages vary in composition, price, and availability throughout the season; their components may include a room, meals, lift tickets, ski lessons, rental equipment, transfers to the mountain, parties, races, and use of a sports center, tips, and taxes.

EQUIPMENT RENTAL➤ Rental equipment is available at all ski areas, at ski shops around resorts, and even in cities far from ski areas. Shop personnel will advise customers on the appropriate equipment for an individual's size and ability and on how to operate the equipment. Good skiers should ask to "demo," or test, premium equipment.

8

Vermont
Ascutney Mountain Resort, **11**
Bolton Valley Resort, **4**
Bromley Mountain, **13**
Jay Peak, **1**
Killington, **9**
Mad River Glen, **7**
Mt. Snow/Haystack Ski Resort, **15**
Northern Star, **5**
Okemo Mountain, **12**
Pico Ski Resort, **8**
Smugglers' Notch Resort, **3**
Stowe Mountain Resort, **2**
Stratton Mountain, **14**
Sugarbush, **6**
Suicide Six, **10**

New Hampshire
Attitash Bear Peak, **22**
Balsams/ Wilderness, **16**
Black Mountain, **20**
Bretton Woods, **17**
Cannon Mountain, **19**
Gunstock, **26**
King Pine Ski Area at Purity Spring Resort, **25**
Loon Mountain, **21**
Mt. Cranmore, **23**
Mt. Sunapee, **27**
Pats Peak, **28**
Waterville Valley, **24**
Wildcat Mountain, **18**

Maine
Big Squaw Mountain Resort, **29**
Camden Snowbowl, **35**
Saddleback Ski and Summer Lake Preserve, **31**
Shawnee Peak, **34**
Ski Mt. Abram, **33**
Sugarloaf/USA, **30**
Sunday River, **32**

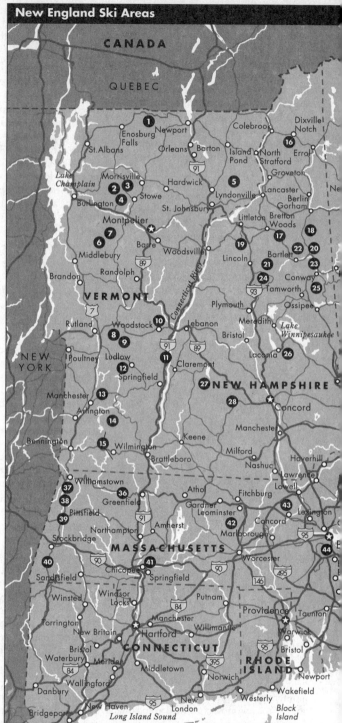

New England Ski Areas

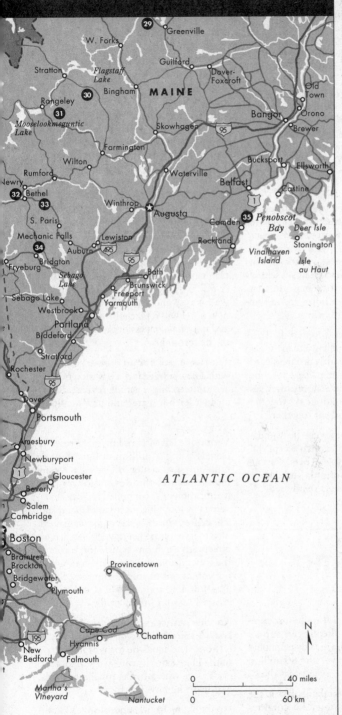

TRAIL RATING➤ Ski areas have devised standards for rating and marking trails and slopes that offer fairly accurate guides. Trails are rated Easier (green circle), More Difficult (blue square), Most Difficult (black diamond), and Expert (double diamond). Keep in mind that trail difficulty is measured relative to other trails *at the same ski area,* not to those of an area down the road, in another state, or in another part of the country; a black-diamond trail at one area may rate only a blue square at a neighboring area. Yet the trail-marking system throughout New England is remarkably consistent and reliable.

LESSONS➤ Within the United States, the Professional Ski Instructors of America (PSIA) have devised a progressive teaching system that is used with relatively little variation at most ski schools. This allows skiers to take lessons at ski schools in different ski areas and still improve. Class lessons usually last 1½–2 hours and are limited in size to 10 participants.

Most ski schools have adopted the PSIA teaching system for children, and many also use SKIwee, which awards progress cards and applies other standardized teaching approaches. Many ski schools offer sessions in which the children ski together with an instructor and eat together.

CHILD CARE➤ Nurseries can be found at virtually all ski areas, and often accept children aged 6 weeks to 6 years. Parents must usually supply formula and diapers for infants; reservations are advised.

NEW AND NOTEWORTHY

Connecticut

A $350 million dollar, 1.4-million-square-foot expansion of the already gargantuan **Foxwoods Resort Casino** in Ledyard should come to fruition by 1997; an $80 million expansion was underway at press time.

An **area code change** is taking place in the northern half of the state. All counties except New Haven and Fairfield (including Bethlehem and Woodbury, excluding Sherman) are changing their area codes from 203 to 860.

The **Dinosaur State Park** in Rocky Hill has once again opened the doors of its geodesic dome and exhibit hall after several years of renovation.

By 1997, **Hartford's** contribution to urban renewal, the ambitious **Riverfront Recapture,** should be in place. Plans call for a 6-mile river walk, with benches, art, sculpture, and an amphitheater. The river walk will span both sides of the river, from about Wethersfield to Windsor.

Massachusetts

The major changes are in Boston where the **"big dig"** continues. The Ted Williams Tunnel, which at press time was scheduled to open by December 1996, will connect Boston and Logan Airport/East Boston, considerably easing traffic. Logan itself is undergoing expansion; construction is planned to end by the year 2000. A 5,700-space parking garage, moving walkways, and gates are being buit; a new hotel will replace the airport Hilton; and national concessions are being added to the terminals.

The **cleanup of Boston Harbor** continues, with a new sewage facility. Boston beaches are undergoing a small revival due to cleaner harbor water and new facilities.

Vermont

Vermont's Division of Historic Preservation is using a million-dollar grant to build a visitor center in Orwell at **Mount Independence,** the Revolutionary War fortification once connected to Fort Ticonderoga by footbridge over Lake Champlain. The center, which at press time was scheduled to have opened in July 1996, will have interpretive exhibits on the fort's role in the Revolution and the living and working conditions of soldiers on the Mount. The 400-acre archaeological site is crisscrossed by four hiking trails.

Another new attraction, **Lake Champlain Basin Science Center,** is on Burlington's waterfront. The hands-on focus of the Secrets of the Lake exhibit will have you looking eye-to-eye with a turtle, touching fossils, and learning how fish move.

On the skiing front, **Sugarbush**'s $28 million capitol improvement plan is well underway—Slide Brook Express is now operational, finally uniting the North and South mountains. Mad River Glen makes ski history by becoming the first cooperatively owned ski area.

New Hampshire

The opening of the **Museum of New Hampshire History,** in Concord's Eagle Square, means that New Hampshire finally has a state museum in the state's capital. Elsewhere in the state, work continues to widen Route 101 between Manchester and Hampton. With each passing year, the highway link between the state's largest city and the popular seacoast comes closer to being a reality.

Maine

Portland is the proud new home of both a baseball and hockey team. The new stadium at Hadlock Field is the site of home games for the **Portland Seadogs,** the farm team of the Florida Marlins. During their initial year in Portland the team received unprecedented support and sells out nearly all its 71 homes games in advance. The season runs mid-April to Labor Day.

The **Portland Pirates,** the farm team of the Washington Capitals, play 40 home games at the Cumberland County Civic Center, beginning in October and running into April.

FODOR'S CHOICE

Sights

★**Long Island Sound from the tip of Water Street in Stonington Village, CT.** Wander past the historic buildings, which line the town green and border both sides of Water Street, to the imposing Old Lighthouse Museum, which you can climb for a spectacular view.

★**The mansions of Bellevue Avenue, Newport, RI.** Magnificent mansions with pillars, mosaics, and marble are set on grounds with fountains, formal gardens, and broad lawns that roll to the ocean.

★**Bright purple cranberries floating on the flooded bogs just before the fall harvest on Cape Cod and Nantucket.** Cape Cod's Rail Trail passes salt marshes, cranberry bogs, and ponds; on Nantucket, visit the 205-acre Windswept Cranberry Bog.

★**The candy-color Victorian cottages of the Oak Bluffs Camp Ground on Martha's Vineyard.** More than 300 Carpenter Gothic Victorian cottages, gaily painted in pastels and trimmed in lacy filigree, are tightly packed on a warren of streets.

★**The nearly frozen-in-time town of Nantucket, whose cobblestone streets and antique houses evoke whaling days.** Settled in the mid-17th century, Nantucket has a town center that remains remarkably unchanged, thanks to a strict building code.

★**The view from Appalachian Gap on Route 17, VT.** Views from the top and on the way down this panoramic mountain pass toward the quiet town of Bristol are a just reward for the challenging drive.

★**Early October on the Kancamagus Highway between Lincoln and Conway, NH.** This 34-mile trek with classic White Mountains vistas erupts into fiery color each fall.

★**Sunrise from the top of Cadillac Mountain on Mt. Desert Island, ME; sunset over Moosehead Lake from the Lily Bay Road in Greenville, ME.** From the summit of Cadillac Mountain you have a 360° view of the ocean, islands, jagged coastline, woods, and lakes; Lily Bay Road passes through Greenville, the largest town on Moosehead Lake, as well as outposts with populations of "not many."

★**Yacht-filled Camden Harbor, ME, from the summit of Mt. Battie.** Mt. Battie may not be very tall, but it has a lovely vista over Camden Harbor, which has the nation's largest fleet of windjammers.

Ski Resorts

★**Smugglers' Notch, VT, for learning to ski.** Smugglers' third mountain, Morse (1,150-foot vertical), specializes in beginner trails.

★**Jay Peak, VT, for the international ambience.** Because of its proximity to Québec, Jay Peak, which receives the most natural snow of any ski area in the East, attracts Montréalers.

★**Mad River Glen, VT, for challenging terrain.** Rugged individualists come here for less-polished terrain: The apt area motto is "Ski It If You Can."

★**Sugarbush, VT, for an overall great place to ski.** Sugarbush has formidable steeps, beginner runs, and intermediate cruisers; there's a with-it attitude, but everyone feels comfortable.

⭐ **Waterville Valley, NH, for vacation packages.** The bulk of the 53 trails are intermediate, but no one will be bored.

⭐ **Saddleback, ME, for scenic wilderness views.** A down-home, laid-back atmosphere prevails at Saddleback, where the quiet and the absence of crowds, even on busy weekends, draw return visitors.

⭐ **Sugarloaf, ME, for the East's only above-treeline skiing.** With a vertical of 2,820 feet, Sugarloaf is taller than any other New England ski peak except Killington.

Country Inns and Bed-and-Breakfasts

⭐ **Boulders Inn, New Preston, CT.** This idyllic and prestigious inn on Lake Waramaung has panoramic views and an outstanding window-lined, stone-wall dining room. $$$$

⭐ **Manor House, Norfolk, CT.** Among the house's remarkable features are 20 stained-glass windows designed and given by Louis Tiffany. $$–$$$

⭐ **Weekapaug Inn, Weekapaug, RI.** Perched on a peninsula surrounded by water, this inn has large, bright guest rooms, with wide windows offering impressive views. $$$$

⭐ **Charlotte Inn, Edgartown, MA.** Rooms here, in one of the finest inns in New England, are elegantly furnished, and the beautifully landscaped grounds include an English garden. $$$$

⭐ **Captain's House Inn, Chatham, MA.** You will find finely preserved architectural details, tasteful decor, delicious baked goods, and an overall feeling of warmth and quiet comfort here. $$$–$$$$

⭐ **The Inn at Shelburne Farms, Shelburne VT.** This is storybook land: A tudor-style inn built for William Seward and Lila Vanderbilt Webb that sits on the edge of Lake Champlain and has outstanding views of the Adirondack Mountains. $$$–$$$$

⭐ **Clark Currier Inn, Newburyport, MA.** Guest rooms are spacious and furnished with antiques in this 1803 Federal mansion that has been restored with care, taste, imagination, and enthusiasm. $$–$$$

⭐ **Historic Merrell Inn, South Lee, MA.** Built as a stagecoach stopover around

1792, this inn has an authentic, unfussy style that makes it stand out among its peers. $$–$$$

⭐ **West Mountain Inn, Arlington, VT.** This former farmhouse of the 1840s has a llama ranch on the property and sits on 150 acres that provide glorious views. $$$–$$$$

⭐ **Snowvillage Inn, Snowville, NH.** Innkeepers of this 18-room abode take guests on gourmet-picnic hikes; cuisine is dueling Continental: The Austrian chef has a French assistant. $$–$$$

⭐ **Inn at Sunrise Point, Camden/Lincolnville Beach, ME.** For luxury and location, you can't beat this elegant B&B perched on the water's edge, with magnificent views over Penobscot Bay. $$$$

⭐ **Bufflehead Cove, Kennebunkport, ME.** On the Kennebunk River at the end of a winding dirt road, this friendly bed-and-breakfast with dollhouse-pretty guest rooms affords the quiet of country fields and apple trees only five minutes from Dock Square. $$$–$$$$

Places to Eat

⭐ **The Golden Lamb Buttery, Brooklyn, CT.** This is Connecticut's most unusual—and magical—dining experience. Eating here is a social and gastronomical event. $$$$

⭐ **Abbott's Lobster in the Rough, Noank, CT.** This unassuming seaside lobster shack with a magnificent view serves some of the state's best lobster, mussels, crab, and clams. $$–$$$

⭐ **Al Forno, Providence, RI.** Cementing Providence's reputation as a culinary center in New England, this restaurant serves Italian dishes that make the most of New England's fresh produce. $$$$

⭐ **Chillingsworth, Brewster, MA.** This dramatically orchestrated, elegant spot has award-winning French and nouvelle cuisine and an outstanding wine cellar. $$$$

⭐ **Lambert's Cove Country Inn, West Tisbury, MA.** President and Mrs. Clinton dined in this romantic gourmet restaurant, set in an elegant 1790 farmhouse surrounded by pine woods and an apple orchard. $$$

⭐ **Biba, Boston, MA.** Boston's overwhelmingly favorite place to see and be seen, Biba serves gutsy fare that mixes flavors from five continents. $$$$

★**Yankee Pedlar Inn, Holyoke, MA.** Try baked Boston scrod or prime rib of beef in this dining room with exposed beams, antique wood paneling, and candle chandeliers. $$–$$$

★**Georgio's, Waitsfield, VT.** This restaurant with a warm Mediterranean feel in the Tucker Hill Lodge, serves dishes like stone-seared scallops, and fondue, pasta, and pizza. $$–$$$

★**Inn at Montpelier, Montpelier, VT.** This spacious inn with elegant guest rooms and a wide wraparound Colonial Revival porch has an outstanding restaurant. $$–$$$

★**Balsams Grand Resort Hotel, Dixville Notch, NH.** In summer the buffet lunch is heaped upon a 100-foot-long table; stunning dinners might include chilled strawberry soup spiked with Grand Marnier and poached fillet of salmon with caviar sauce. $$$$

★**Hurricane, Ogunquit, ME.** Don't let its weather-beaten exterior deter you—this small, seafood bar-and-grill offers first-rate cooking and spectacular views of the crashing surf. $$–$$$

★**Jessica's, Rockland, ME.** The Swiss chef at this European bistro in a Victorian home whips up delicious creations such as paella, and pork Portofino. $$

GREAT ITINERARIES

Scenic Coastal Tour

From southwestern Connecticut through Rhode Island and Massachusetts to Maine, New England's coastline is a picturesque succession of rocky headlands, sand-rimmed coves, and small towns built around shipbuilding, fishing, and other seaside trades. For more detailed information, follow the tours entitled "The Coast" in individual state chapters.

Duration: Six to 10 days

One to two nights: Travel through such classic Connecticut towns as Old Lyme and Mystic, passing through Rhode Island's South County to end up in Newport, with its magnificent turn-of-the-century mansions open for tours.

One to three nights: Stop off in the historic whaling port of New Bedford, Massachusetts, then head for one of the charming summer resort towns of Cape Cod.

One night: Drive north to Boston, one of the country's oldest thriving port cities.

One night: Head north through such historic North Shore fishing towns as Marblehead, Gloucester, and Rockport; visit sea captains' mansions in Newburyport.

Two to three nights: Swing through the Kennebunks and Portland to the small towns and islands around Penobscot Bay.

Historical Preservations

Although they appear to be simply villages that time forgot, these meticulously preserved hamlets are the products of years of research and painstaking restoration, providing a living lesson in American history that's surprisingly free of commercial gloss. Tour escorts are likely to be immensely learned, and costumed interpreters on site give the eerie impression of having just stepped out of a time machine.

Duration: Four to six days

Two nights: From a base in Boston, venture south on Route 3 to Plimouth Plantation for a glimpse of the lives of the first Puritan settlers. Then refresh your sense of Colonial history by following the Freedom Trail, a route of fine historic sites in the middle of busy modern Boston.

One night: Head west on the Massachusetts Turnpike to Old Sturbridge Village, which brings to life a prosperous farm town of the 1830s.

One night: I–395 will take you south to Mystic, Connecticut, and Mystic Seaport, a large, lively restoration that focuses on the whaling and shipbuilding industries of the mid- and late 19th century.

One night: A half-day's drive to Hartford and then up I–91 into western Massachusetts will take you to Old Deerfield, a tranquil pre-Revolutionary settlement preserved as a National Historic District.

One night: Take either the Massachusetts Turnpike or the more scenic Mohawk Trail (Route 2) west, then take Route 7 to Hancock, Massachusetts, where the Hancock Shaker Village offers a historic glimpse of a way of life that has always stood apart from America's mainstream.

College Towns

As one of the first settled areas in the United States, New England was the site of some of the nation's first colleges and universities. As those fine institutions were joined by others over the years, they enshrined in the American imagination an image of imposing ivy-clad buildings on green, shady campuses. College towns have an added attraction in that they usually offer excellent bookstores and museums, inexpensive restaurants, and plenty of friendly, casual street life.

Duration: Five to ten days

One to three nights: In the greater Boston area, perhaps the premier "college town" in the United States, visit the Cambridge campuses of Harvard University and the Massachusetts Institute of Technology and the busy urban campus of Boston University, centered on Kenmore Square. Head to the suburbs to visit Tufts University (Medford), Brandeis University (Waltham), Boston College (Newton), or Wellesley College (Wellesley).

One to two nights: Drive west to the five-college region of the Pioneer Valley, where you can visit Amherst College, Hampshire College, and the University of Massachusetts in Amherst; Mount Holyoke College in the quaint village of South Hadley; and Smith College in the bustling county seat of Northampton.

One to two nights: Head west to Williamstown, home of Williams College, in the Berkshires. Then swing north on Route 7 into Vermont to Bennington, where you'll find Bennington College.

One to two nights: Travel east on Route 9 to Keene State College, in Keene, New Hampshire, a well-kept college town with one of the widest main streets in the world. Head southeast through Worcester, Massachusetts, where Holy Cross is the most well known of several colleges in town, and on to Providence, Rhode Island, where Brown University and the Rhode Island School of Design share a fine hillside site.

One night: A westward drive along I-95 will take you to New Haven, Connecticut, the home of Yale University, with its gothic-style quadrangles of gray stone.

Kancamagus Trail

This circuit takes in some of the most spectacular parts of the White and Green mountains, along with the upper Connecticut River Valley. In this area the antiques hunting is exemplary and the traffic is often almost nonexistent. The scenery evokes the spirit of Currier & Ives.

Duration: Three to six days

One to three days: From the New Hampshire coast, head northwest to Wolfeboro, perhaps detouring to explore around Lake Winnipesaukee. Take Route 16 north to Conway, then follow Route 112 west along the scenic Kancamagus Pass through the White Mountains to the Vermont border.

One to two days: Head south on Route 10 along the Connecticut River, past scenic Hanover, New Hampshire, home of Dartmouth College. At White River Junction, cross into Vermont. You may want to follow Route 4 through the lovely town of Woodstock to Killington, then travel along Route 100 and I-89 to complete the loop back to White River Junction. Otherwise, simply proceed south along I-91, with stops at such pleasant Vermont towns as Putney and Brattleboro.

One to two days: Take Route 119 east to Rhododendron State Park in Fitzwilliam, New Hampshire. Nearby is Mt. Monadnock, the most-climbed mountain in the United States; in Jaffrey take the trail to the top. Dawdle along back roads to visit the preserved villages of Harrisville, Dublin, and Hancock, then continue east along Route 101 to return to the coast.

Cape Cod and the Islands

Cape Cod, Martha's Vineyard, and Nantucket are favorite resort areas in and out of season. Because the Cape is only some 70 miles from end to end, day trips from a single base are easily managed. A visit to Martha's Vineyard or Nantucket takes about two hours each way from Hyannis (and it's only 45 minutes to the Vineyard from Woods Hole), so you may want to plan to stay overnight on an island, though a day trip is certainly feasible.

Duration: Three to five days

One day: Drive east on Route 6A to experience old Cape Cod, sampling some of the Cape's best antiques and crafts shops and looking into historic sites and museums. Here, too, are charming restaurants and intimate bed-and-breakfasts. A stop at Scargo Hill Tower in Dennis allows a view of the lake, the bay, and the village below.

One day: Take Route 6 east to Provincetown. Do a whale-watch in the morning, spend the afternoon browsing the shops and galleries of the main street, and at sunset go for a Jeep or horseback ride through the dunes of the Province Lands. Try one of Provincetown's fine restaurants—or drive south to Chatham for dinner and theater.

One day: Take Route 6 to the Salt Pond Visitor Center in Eastham and choose your activity: swimming or surf-fishing at Coast Guard or Nauset Light Beach, wandering the bike path, taking a self-guided nature walk, or joining in one of the National Seashore programs. On the way there, you might look into some of the galleries or crafts shops in Wellfleet.

Four to five days: From Hyannis, take a ferry to either Martha's Vineyard or Nantucket. If you choose the Vineyard, visit the Camp Meeting Grounds and the old carousel in Oak Bluffs, then head for the sunset at Gay Head Cliffs before returning on the evening ferry; if you stay over, explore a nature preserve or the historic streets of Edgartown the next day. In Nantucket, you might explore the Whaling Museum, the mansions, and the shops; if you stay over, bike or take a bus to 'Sconset for a stroll around this village of rose-covered cottages and perhaps a swim at a fairly uncrowded beach.

FESTIVALS AND SEASONAL EVENTS

WINTER

DECEMBER➤ History buffs will want to attend the **reenactment of the Boston Tea Party,** which occurs on the *Beaver II* in Boston Harbor. In Arlington (VT), the **St. Lucia Pageant** is a "Festival of Lights" that celebrates the winter solstice. Christmas celebrations are plentiful throughout New England: In **Nantucket** (RI), the first weekend of the month sees an early Christmas celebration with elaborate decorations, costumed carolers, theatrical performances, art exhibits, and a tour of historic homes. In **Newport** (RI), several Bellevue Avenue mansions open for the holidays, and there are crafts fairs, holiday concerts, and candlelight tours of Colonial homes throughout the month. At **Mystic Seaport** (CT), costumed guides escort visitors to holiday activities. **Old Saybrook** (CT) has a Christmas Torchlight Parade and Muster of Ancient Fife and Drum Corps, which ends with a carol sing at the Church Green. Historic **Strawbery Banke** (NH) has a Christmas Stroll, with carolers, through nine historic homes decorated for the season. The final day of the year is observed with festivals, entertainment, and food in many locations during **First Night Celebrations.** Some of the major cities hosting such events are Burlington (VT), Providence (RI), Boston, and, in Connecti-

cut, Danbury, Hartford, and Stamford.

JANUARY➤ Stowe's (VT) **Winter Carnival** heats up around mid-month; it's among the country's oldest such celebrations. Brookfield (VT) holds its **Ice Harvest Festival,** one of New England's largest.

FEBRUARY➤ The **Brattleboro Winter Carnival,** held weekends throughout the month, features jazz concerts and an ice fishing derby. The **Mad River Valley Winter Carnival** (VT) is a week of winter festivities including dogsled races and a masquerade ball; Burlington's **Vermont Mozart Festival** showcases the Winter Chamber Music Series. The **New England Boat Show** is held in Boston's Bayside Expo Center.

SPRING

MARCH➤ This is a boon time for **maple-sugaring festivals and events:** Throughout the month and into April, the sugarhouses of Maine, New Hampshire, Massachusetts, and Vermont demonstrate procedures from maple-tree tapping to sap boiling. Many offer tastings of various grades of syrup, sugar-on-snow, traditional unsweetened doughnuts, and pickles. Maine's Moosehead Lake has a renowned **Ice-Fishing Derby,** and Rangeley's **New England Sled Dog Races** attract more than 100 teams from throughout the Northeast

and Canada. Stratton Mountain (VT) hosts the **U.S. Open Snowboarding Championships.** March 17 is traditionally a major event in Boston: Its **St. Patrick's Day Parade** is one of the nation's largest.

APRIL➤ Early blooms are the draw of Bristol's (RI) **Annual Spring Bulb Display,** which takes place at Blithewolde Gardens and Arboretum, and of Nantucket's **Daffodil Festival,** which celebrates spring with a flower show, elaborate shop-window displays, and a procession of antique cars along roadsides bursting with daffodils. You can gorge on sea grub at Boothbay Harbor's (ME) **Fishermen's Festival** the third weekend in April. Dedicated runners draw huge crowds to the **Boston Marathon,** run each year on Patriot's Day (the Monday nearest April 19).

MAY➤ You know all those Holsteins you see grazing in fields alongside Vermont's windy roads? Well, the Enosburg Falls **Vermont Dairy Festival** is just the place to celebrate the delicious fruits (or cheeses, rather) of their labor. Or, if you're a sheep fancier, stop by the **New Hampshire Sheep and Wool Festival** in New Boston, where shearing, carding, and spinning are demonstrated. Rhode Island's **May breakfasts** have been a tradition since 1867: Johnnycakes and other native dishes are served statewide at bird sanctuaries, churches, grange halls, yacht clubs, schools, and veterans posts. **Lobster Weekend** kicks off Mystic Seaport's (CT) summer of festivities with live entertainment and plenty of good food; down the coast, Bridgeport's (CT) **Barnum Festival** culminates in an enormous parade through downtown. Holyoke's (MA) **Shad Fishing Derby** is said to be the largest freshwater fishing derby in North America.

SUMMER

JUNE➤ In Vermont, you can listen to jazz at Burlington's **Discover Jazz Festival** or folk at Warren's **Ben & Jerry's One World One Heart Festival,** which is held at Sugarbush. **Jacob's Pillow Dance Festival** at Becket (MA) in the Berkshires hosts performers of various dance traditions from June through September. The spring thaw calls for a number of boating celebrations, including the *Vermont Canoe and Kayak Festival* at Waterbury State Park; the **Yale–Harvard Regatta** along New London's (CT) Thames River, the oldest intercollegiate athletic event in the country; the **Boothbay Harbor Windjammer Days,** which starts the high season for Maine's boating set; and the **Blessing of the Fleet** in Provincetown, which culminates a weekend of festivities—a quahog feed, a public dance, a crafts show, a parade. Young ones are the stars of Somersworth's (NH) **International Children's Festival,** where games, activities, and crafts keep everybody busy. **A Taste of**

Hartford lets you eat your way through the capital city while enjoying outdoor music, dance, comedy, and magic. You can visit Providence's (RI) stately homes, some by candlelight, on one of the **Providence Preservation Society's tours.** Major **crafts and antiques fairs** are held in Farmington (CT) and Springfield (MA).

JULY➤ **Fourth of July** parties and parades kick off throughout New England; Bristol's (RI) parade is the nation's senior Independence Day parade. Concerts, family entertainment, an art show, a parade, and fireworks are held in Bath (ME). Exeter (NH) celebrates with 18th-century Revolutionary War battle reenactments, period crafts and antiques, and a visit from George Washington himself at the American Independence Museum. And the **Mashpee Powwow** (MA) brings together Native Americans from North and South America for three days of dance contests, drumming, a fireball game, and a clambake; Native American food and crafts are sold. Some of the better music festivals include the **Marlboro Music Festival** of classical music, held at Marlboro College (VT); Newport's (RI) **Music Festival,** which brings together celebrated musicians for a two-week schedule of concerts in Newport mansions; the **Bar Harbor Festival** (ME), which hosts classical, jazz, and popular music concerts into August; and the **Tanglewood Music Festival** at Lenox (MA), which shifts into high gear with performances by the

Boston Symphony Orchestra and a slew of major entertainers. Shoppers can rummage through major **antiques fairs** in Wolfeboro (NH) and Dorset (VT). Or you can simply admire the furnishings of homes during **Open House Tours** in Litchfield (CT) and Camden (ME). Boaters and the men and women who love them flock to the **Sail Festival** at New London's (CT) City Pier to watch sail races, outdoor concerts, fireworks, and the Ugliest Dog Contest. In nearby Mystic, enthusiasts can view vintage powerboats and sailboats at the **Antique and Classic Boat Rendezvous.** The **Great Schooner Race** (ME), which runs from Penobscot Bay to Rockland, features replicas and relics of the age of sail. Two of the region's most popular **country fairs** are held in Bangor (ME) and on Cape Cod in Barnstable (MA).

AUGUST➤ The music festivals continue—in Newport (RI) with **Ben & Jerry's Newport Folk Festival** and **JVC's Jazz Festival** and in Essex (CT) with the **Great Connecticut Traditional Jazz Festival.** Stowe (VT) hosts a popular **Antique and Classic Car Rally.** Popular arts, crafts, and antiques festivals are held at **Haystack Mountain** (VT), at the **Southern Vermont Crafts Fair** in Manchester (VT), at the **Outdoor Arts Festival** in Mystic (CT), at the **Maine Antiques Festival** in Union, and at the **Fair of the League of New Hampshire Craftsmen** at Mt. Sunapee State Park in Newbury—the nation's oldest crafts fair. Foodies should bring their appetites to Maine's **Lobster Festival** in Rockland and **Blueberry Festival** in Rangeley Lake. A few general summer fairs include the **Woodstock Fair** (CT), which has livestock shows, Colonial crafts, puppet shows, and food; the **Hyannis Street Festival** (MA), a three-day weekend of Main Street shopping, food, and entertainment; and the **Martha's Vineyard Agricultural Fair** (MA), which includes contests, animal shows, a carnival, and evening entertainment.

AUTUMN

SEPTEMBER➤ Summer's close is met with dozens of Labor Day fairs including the **Vermont State Fair** in Rutland, with agricultural exhibits and entertainment; the **Providence Waterfront Festival** (RI), a weekend of arts, crafts, ethnic foods, musical entertainment, and boat races; the **International Seaplane Fly-In Weekend,** which sets Moosehead Lake (ME) buzzing; and Burlington's (VT) **Champlain Valley Exposition,**

which has all the features of a large county fair. Foot stomping and guitar strumming are the activities of choice at several musical events: the **Cajun & Bluegrass Music-Dance-Food Festival** at Stepping Stone Ranch in Escoheag (RI), the **National Traditional Old-Time Fiddler's Contest** in Barre (VT), the **Bluegrass Festival** in Brunswick (ME), and the **Rockport Folk Festival** in Rockport (ME). In Stratton (VT), artists and performers gather for the **Stratton Arts Festival.** One of the best and oldest **antiques shows** in New England occurs in New Haven (CT). Providence (RI) shows off its diversity during its **Annual Heritage Festival.**

Agricultural fairs not to be missed are **the Common Ground Country Fair** in Windsor (ME), an organic farmer's delight; the **Deerfield Fair** (NH), one of New England's oldest; and the **Eastern States Exposition** in Springfield (MA), New England's largest. Autumn is ushered in at the **Northeast Kingdom Fall Foliage Festival** (VT), a weeklong affair hosted by the six small towns of Walden, Cabot, Plainfield, Peacham, Barnet, and Groton. Fish lovers show up in schools to attend the

Bourne Scallopfest in Buzzards Bay (MA), where there's crafts, entertainment, and buckets of fried scallops; the **Martha's Vineyard Striped Bass and Bluefish Derby,** one of the East Coast's premier fishing contests; and the **Annual Seafood Festival** in Hampton Beach, where you can sample the seafood specialties of more than 50 local restaurants, dance to live bands, and watch fireworks explode over the ocean.

OCTOBER➤ In Maine, the **Fryeburg Fair** features agricultural exhibits, harness racing, an iron-skillet-throwing contest, and a pig scramble. The **Nantucket Cranberry Harvest** is a three-day celebration including bog and inn tours and a crafts fair.

NOVEMBER➤ In Vermont there are two major events in this otherwise quiet month: The **International Film Festival** presents films dealing with environmental, human rights, and political issues for a week in Burlington, and the **Bradford Wild Game Supper** draws thousands to taste a variety of large and small game animals and birds.

2 Connecticut

Southwestern Connecticut is home to commuters, celebrities, and others who enjoy its privacy and convenience to New York City. Far less touristy than other parts of the state, the Connecticut River Valley is an unspectacular stretch of small river villages punctuated by a few small cities. The Litchfield Hills have grand old inns and rolling farmlands. New Haven is home to Yale and several fine museums, and along the southeastern coast are quiet shoreline villages. A string of sparsely populated towns in the northeast comprises the Quiet Corner.

By Andrew
Collins

Updated by
Rebecca Miller

ONNECTICUT HAS VERY FEW SIDEWALKS. Except for a dozen midsize metropolises, Connecticut's towns and villages exist without those concrete emblems of urbanity—the brackets that crisscross much of America at right angles, defying nature's alluvial and undulating boundaries: the rivers and ridges, mountains and meadows. In such a densely populated state—only three states have more residents per square mile—visitors are typically taken aback by the seeming wealth of space and the seeming distance and inaccessibility between the homes of neighbors.

Nearly every Connecticut town is anchored by a glorious elm-shaded town green, a throwback to a forgotten era but evidence that today's "Nutmeggers" still hold precious the ever-elusive commodity of elbowroom and the rich and verdant gifts of nature. Zoning laws in most towns forbid abutting edifices—at least in residential neighborhoods—and 2-acre zoning is the norm in many towns.

This is not to say Connecticut Yankees are unfriendly, or even aloof. It is a state of decidedly civilized and proper persons. But glowing behind this somewhat frosty veneer is a hospitable, if not garrulous, soul. If we rely on the trusty measure of how well Connecticutters respond to distressed drivers seeking directions, the state scores well. Not only will you be told how to get where you're going, but you will also endure the presentation of a complicated but scenic shortcut, the enactment of which is executed with hand gestures, furrowed brows, and ponderous gazes.

People here are inventive, particular, and quirky: History has seen the manufacture of locks, clocks, guns, hats, submarines, bicycle spokes, and numerous tools and innovative mechanisms. There was a time when scheming merchants whittled blocks of wood to resemble rounds of nutmeg and sold them as such to unsuspecting buyers.

Of course, the aforementioned stereotypes speak mostly of the state's natives—and this fraction of the population is dwindling rapidly. Remember the state motto: "He who transplanted still sustains." Outsiders move here, often to build or renovate their dream house in the sticks, and as in any proud land, locals generally resent the throngs of city-dwellers invading the countryside like locusts. Starting in the southwest corner and fanning out a little farther every year, urban sprawl is attacking. Hillside after hillside is taken, stripped of its flora and fauna, and developed. And even with all those zoning laws, things are getting a bit crowded. Some developments even have sidewalks. The immigration is not without its financial advantages, but most natives would gladly trade wealth, which many already have, for privacy.

Connecticut *is* the richest state in the country. A troublesome aspect of this wealth is its uneven distribution. From the top of Yale University's ivory-like Harkness Tower, you can look in no direction without seeing evidence of a deeply troubled city, New Haven, too much of which trudges along below the poverty level. Winding country roads flow arterially from Connecticut's struggling cities into prosperous satellite communities. Many fear that if out of disrespect we allow our once-vibrant cities to fall away in disrepair, the lifeblood of every small thriving town will cease to flow, and the state as a whole will suffer. The notions of ethnic integration and urban renewal are hotly discussed at town meetings these days, as residents find ways to keep Connecticut a desirable gateway to New England.

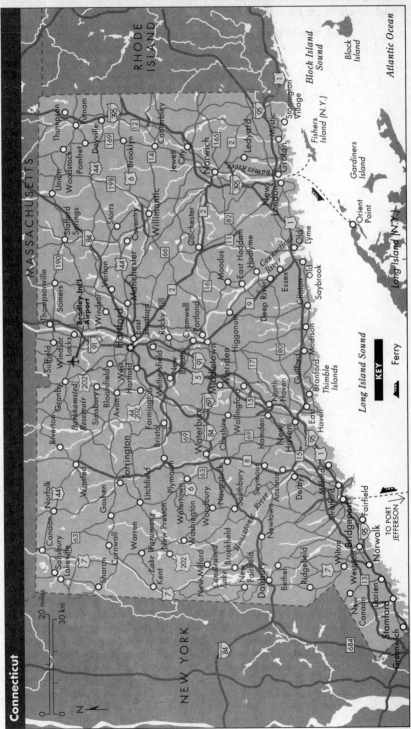

Connecticut

Pleasures and Pastimes

Antiquing

Although you'll find everything from chic boutiques to vast outlet malls in Connecticut, the state is an antiquer's paradise—antiques dealers are virtually everywhere. The Litchfield Hills region, in the state's northwest corner, is the heart of antiques country. Woodbury, once the capital of it all, still has a number of shops, many in converted 18th- and 19th-century houses. Today you'll find plenty of wares, from 18th-century French furniture to American folk art, along the main street of nearly every town here, including New Preston, Kent, and Litchfield. In the Quiet Corner, east of the Litchfield Hills, there are more than 400 dealers in the towns of Pomfret, Woodstock, and Putnam, which has two large, well-stocked multidealer shops. Also, Mystic, Old Saybrook, and other towns south along the coast are filled with markets, galleries, and shops, many specializing in antique prints, maps, books, and collectibles.

Dining

Call it the fennel factor. Or the arugula influx. Or the prosciutto preponderance. However you wish to characterize it, southern New England has witnessed a gastronomic revolution in recent years. Preparation and ingredients now reflect the culinary trends of nearby Manhattan and Boston. And although a few traditional favorites remain, such as New England clam chowder, Yankee pot roast, and grilled haddock, Grand Marnier is now favored on ice cream over hot fudge sauce, duck is often served boneless minus its rich, gooey orange glaze, and wilted field greens and grilled seasonal vegetables now complement meat dishes. In cities you'll find a burgeoning selection of Indian, Vietnamese, Thai, Japanese, and Mexican restaurants. Perhaps most astounding is the renaissance of the once thick and greasy pizza pie, something for which Connecticut has long been known. Traditional deep-pan Grecian-style pizzas are being slowly eclipsed in popularity by thin, crispy, gourmet pies, topped by, you guessed it, fennel, arugula, prosciutto, and the like. The drawback of this turn in cuisine is that finding an under-$10 entrée (or even under-$10 14″ pizza) is proving difficult.

CATEGORY	COST*
$$$$	over $40
$$$	$25–$40
$$	$15–$25
$	under $15

average cost of a three-course dinner, per person, excluding drinks, service, and 6% sales tax

Fishing

Anglers will find Connecticut teeming with possibilities, from deep-sea fishing in coastal waters to fly-fishing in one of the state's many streams. Try the Litchfield Hills region for freshwater fish: If you're just a beginner, don't fret, you'll be catching trout or bass in the Housatonic River in no time—fly-fishing instruction is readily available. Southeastern Connecticut is the charter- and party-boat capital of New England. Charter fishing boats take passengers out on Long Island Sound for half-day, full-day, and overnight trips. Party fishing boats are open to the public on a first-come basis.

Hiking

Connecticut, of which 60 percent is forested, has much to entice the hiker—rolling hills, green meadows, dense woods, and hardwood- and hemlock-covered mountains. There are many nature centers—the Connecticut Audubon Society in Fairfield, the Audubon Center of Greenwich—throughout southwestern Connecticut, with miles of marked trails through woods and wetlands. In the Litchfield Hills area, trails seem to skirt every stream. The highest peak in the state—Bear Mountain—is here in Salisbury. Trails are especially spectacular around the cool, clear water at Lake Waramaug State Park and the 200-foot-high waterfall at Kent Falls State Park. Further east in the Hanging Hills of Meridien are some of the most stunning views in the state—rich hues of green in summer and an array of oranges and reds in autumn. At Gillette Castle State Park near East Haddam there are several trails, some on former railroad beds.

Lodging

Connecticut offers a variety of accommodations. Where major chain hotels are concerned, we've tried to mention the best and the most popular, but many are nondescript, located in busy cities, and appealing mostly to business travelers. We pay more attention to those unusual inns, resorts, bed-and-breakfasts, and country hotels you might not spy from the fast lane of I–95. You'll pay dearly for rooms in summer on the coast and in autumn in the hills, where thousands peek at the peaking foliage. In winter, rates are lowest, but so is the windchill factor—leaving verdant spring as the best time for bargain seekers unwilling to dress in wool and mufflers.

CATEGORY	COST*
$$$$	over $170
$$$	$120–$170
$$	$70–$120
$	under $70

All prices are for a standard double room during peak season, with no meals unless noted, and excluding service charge and 12% state lodging tax.

Exploring Connecticut

Connecticut can basically be divided into five geographical regions. The southernmost region is southwestern Connecticut, with its wealthy, coastal communities. Moving east along the coast (in most states you usually travel north or south along the coast; however, in Connecticut you actually travel east or west), you'll come to New Haven and the southeastern coast, which is broken by many small bays and inlets. The third region, bordered by Rhode Island to the east and Massachusetts to the north, is the Quiet Corner, where you'll find rolling hills and tranquil countryside. To the west is the fertile farmland of the Connecticut River Valley and the state's capital, Hartford. Finally, in the mid- and northwestern parts of the state is the Litchfield Hills area, covered with miles of forests, lakes, and rivers.

Great Itineraries

Because of Connecticut's size—it's the third-smallest state in the union—most everything in the state is within a few hours' drive. In addition, the roads are extremely easy to navigate. So, for example, you could begin your day in the museums and galleries of New Haven, and easily spend the night in a quaint bed-and-breakfast in the quiet countryside of Litchfield Hills. Although you can see some of the state's highlights in one day, five days will give you enough time to leisurely explore the diversity of Connecticut.

Numbers in the text correspond to numbers in the margin and on the maps.

IF YOU HAVE 1 DAY

Begin in **New Preston** ㊳, a charming town on the Aspetuck River, and then head for Lake Waramaug. Next, stop in **West Cornwall** ㊶ to see the state's largest covered bridge. Working your way north, stop in **Lakeville** ㊸ and then, perhaps for lunch, **Salisbury** ㊹, home to the state's highest mountain—Bear Mountain. Next, spend a couple of hours in **Litchfield** ㊿, where you can visit its historic houses. Lastly, head south via **Bethlehem** ㊾ to **Woodbury** ㊽ to see what it's best known for: its churches and antiques shops. This is also a good place to conclude your day as there are some great choices for dinner.

IF YOU HAVE 3 DAYS

Greenwich ①, a wealthy community with grand homes and great restaurants, makes a good starting point. From here head toward **Stamford** ②, where you can visit the Whitney Museum of American Art at Champion or go malling across the street. Traveling east along the coast, stop in **Norwalk** ④, with its SoNo commercial district and popular Maritime Center; and hit **Westport** ⑪ for dinner. Overnight in ⛺ **Ridgefield** ⑦, where you may want to spend an hour or two the next day. Then head for **New Preston** ㊳. From here drive north via **West Cornwall** ㊶ to **Norfolk** ㊻, one of the best preserved villages in the northeast. Next spend a couple of hours in **Litchfield** ㊿, where you may want to conclude your day. If not, travel a little farther south to overnight in the charming town of ⛺ **Washington** ㊾. The next day, start in **Woodbury** ㊽, perhaps browsing in its many antiques shops. From here travel to **New Haven** ㊾, home to Yale and its museums. Near campus, there are many great shops and restaurants.

IF YOU HAVE 5 DAYS

In this amount of time, you will be able to get a good feel for nearly the entire state. Spend the morning in **Hartford** ㉕–㉜ and begin your afternoon in **West Hartford** ㉝, home to the Science Museum of Connecticut. Spend the remainder of your afternoon in the towns of ⛺ **Farmington** ㉞, which has two excellent house museums as well as the prestigious Miss Porter's School, and ⛺ **Simsbury** ㉟, where you can visit Massacoh Plantation. Both these towns are good spots to spend the night. On your second day, head west to **Woodbury** ㊽ and then spend a few hours in **Litchfield** ㊿. Next, visit **Kent** ㊴, which has a charming downtown and Kent Falls State Park nearby. From here you can overnight in either ⛺ **Washington** ㊾ or ⛺ **Ridgefield** ⑦. On your third day, explore Fairfield County, which is in southwestern Connecticut. Begin your day in **Greenwich** ① and then stop in **Stamford** ②, **Westport** ⑪, and **Bridgeport** ⑭. Spend the remainder of your afternoon in ⛺ **New Haven** ㊾, where you can also stay for the night. Your fourth day will include some of the Connecticut River Valley. Start in **Essex** ⑯ and visit the Connecticut River Museum. Farther along Route 9 is **Deep River** ⑱, and across the river is Gillette Castle State Park, where you can tour the hilltop castle built by the actor William Gillette, best known for his role as Sherlock Holmes. From here, backtrack to the coastal town of **Old Saybrook** ㊽ and then cross the river to ⛺ **Old Lyme** ㊽, a former art colony and home of the Florence Griswold Museum. Spend the last day of your tour along the coast, starting in either **New London** ㊿ or **Groton** ㊿, and heading east toward **Mystic** ㊿. Take time to visit Mystic Seaport, the nation's largest maritime museum. You may also want to visit the Mystic Marinelife Aquarium. Your last stop is the little village of **Stonington** ㊿, your final peek at Connecticut's coastline.

When to Tour Connecticut

Although Connecticut is lovely year-round, fall and spring are the best times to visit. A drive along the rolling hills of the state's back roads (and even the Merritt Parkway) in fall is a memorable experience, as your surroundings come to life. You can experience exactly what fall should be: foliage in an array of warm colors, long hikes, apple-picking and hot cider, and football on the town green. However, the state blooms in springtime, too. The landscape is freshly verdant, town greens are painted with daffodils and tulips, and roads are punctuated with trees in bloom. The scent of flower blossoms is in the air, especially in Fairfield, which holds an annual Dogwood Festival. Many attractions that are closed in winter reopen in March or April.

SOUTHWESTERN CONNECTICUT

In terms of both money and personality, southwestern Connecticut, just 50 miles outside of midtown Manhattan, is a rich swirl of old New England and new New York. Encompassing all of Fairfield County, it consistently registers the highest cost of living and most expensive homes of any community in the country. Its bedroom communities are home primarily to white-collar executives; some still make the nearly two-hour mad dash to and from Gotham, but most enjoy a more civilized morning drive to Stamford, which is reputed to have more corporate headquarters per square mile than any other U.S. city. Strict zoning has preserved a certain privacy and rusticity uncommon in other such densely populated areas, and numerous celebrities—Paul Newman, David Letterman, Ron Howard, Ivan Lendl, and Dustin Hoffman among them—call Fairfield County home. The combination of drivers, winding roads, and heavily wooded countryside has resulted in at least one major problem: According to a survey in central Fairfield County, nearly 50% of area drivers have struck a deer.

Venture away from the wealthy communities, and you'll discover four cities in different stages of urban renewal: Stamford, Norwalk, Bridgeport, and Danbury. The cities do have some of the region's best cultural and shopping opportunities, but the economic disparity between Connecticut's tony towns and troubled cities is perhaps nowhere more visible than in Fairfield County.

Numbers in the margin correspond to points of interest on the Southwestern Connecticut map.

Greenwich

❶ *28 mi northeast of New York City, 64 mi southwest of Hartford.*

Greenwich is the first home to many of New York's CEOs who retreat here for the area's accessibility, beauty, and sophistication. You'll have no trouble believing that Greenwich is one of the wealthiest towns in the United States, if not the world, when you drive along Route 1 (a.k.a. West Putnam Avenue, East Putnam Avenue, and the Post Road, among others), where the streets are lined with ritzy car dealers, Euro-chic clothing shops, and other posh emporia.

You'll probably want to start your visit to Greenwich by buying a Ferrari or Aston Martin at **Miller Motor Cars** (✉ 275 W. Putnam Ave., ☎ 203/629–8830). But if you can't plunk down $200,000 (the going rate for a low-end Aston Martin), you can inspect the walls of the sales room, which are covered with a terrific collection of sepia-tone prints of classic autos.

🦢 Make it a point to see the **Bruce Museum.** It now devotes a section to environmental history, which includes a wigwam, a spectacular mineral collection, a marine touch tank, and a 16th-century-era woodland diorama. Still popular in the original section is the small but worthwhile collection of American Impressionist paintings. ✉ *1 Mu-*

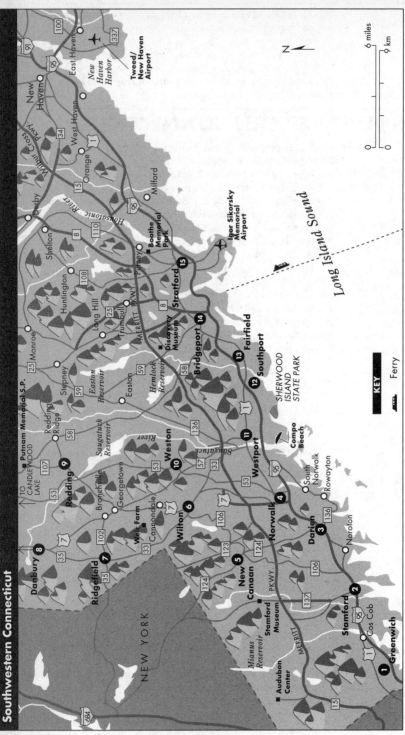

Southwestern Connecticut

KEY

Ferry

seum Dr. (Exit 3 off I–95), ☎ *203/869–0376.* 🖾 *$3.50, free on Tues.* ☉ *Tues.–Sat. 10–5, Sun. 2–5.*

The small, barn-red **Putnam Cottage,** built in 1690 and operated as Knapp's Tavern during the Revolutionary War, was a frequent meeting place of Revolutionary War hero General Israel Putnam. Today you can meander through a lush herb garden and examine the cottage's Colonial furnishings and prominent fieldstone fireplace. 🖾 *243 E. Putnam Ave. (Rte. 1),* ☎ *203/869–9697.* ☉ *Wed., Fri., Sun. 1–4. Group tours available.*

The 1732 **Bush–Holley House,** a handsome central-chimney saltbox, houses a wonderful collection of artwork by sculptor John Rogers, potter Leon Volkmar, and painters Childe Hassam, Elmer Livingstone MacRae, and John Twachtman. It was run as a boardinghouse during the early 20th century, and Hassam, Twachtman, Willa Cather, Lincoln Steffens, and other famous personages spent time here. 🖾 *39 Strickland Rd., Cos Cob,* ☎ *203/869–6899.* 🖾 *$4.* ☉ *Feb.–late Dec., Tues.–Fri. noon–4, Sun. 1–4.*

Dining and Lodging

$$$$ ✕ **Bertrand.** The spectacular brick vaulting in this former bank build-
★ ing on the town's main street sets the scene for classic and nouvelle French cuisine. Owner-chef Christian Bertrand was sous-chef at Lutèce, one of Manhattan's best French restaurants. The confit of duck with sorrel sauce and the salmon in a pastry crust seem more at home here than stacks of money bags, and financial matters are forgotten with the arrival of the nougat ice cream—until the check comes. 🖾 *253 Greenwich Ave.,* ☎ *203/661–4618. Jacket and tie. AE, DC, MC, V. No lunch Sat. Closed Sun.*

$$$$ ✕ **Restaurant Jean-Louis.** Roses, Villeroy & Boch china, and crisp, white
★ tablecloths with lace underskirts complement extraordinary food, carefully served. Specialties include quail-and-vegetable ragout with foie gras sauce, scaloppine of salmon on a bed of leeks with fresh herb sauce, and, for dessert, lemon and pear gratin. 🖾 *61 Lewis St.,* ☎ *203/622–8450. Jacket and tie. AE, D, DC, MC, V. No lunch. Closed Sun.*

$$$ ✕ **64 Greenwich Avenue.** The somewhat country yet contemporary American decor at this elegant spot has got lots of flair, as does the well-turned-out nouvelle American cuisine. You might start with a small plate (as appetizers are called here) of grilled portobello mushrooms with brie and apple puree. For your entrée, you may try marinated breast of Muscovy duck with pumpkin polenta, rutabaga, and cinnamon jus, or perhaps a simple steamed vegetable platter. Don't miss the desserts— they all earn kudos—particularly the gingerbread with apples, warm cider-caramel sauce, and cinnamon-walnut ice cream. 🖾 *64 Greenwich Ave.,* ☎ *203/861–6400. AE, DC, MC, V.*

$–$$ ✕ **Pasta Vera.** The small, plain white dining space of this shop-cum-restaurant belies the splendor of its many variations on simple pasta. Try the wild mushroom ravioli or the deliciously imaginative *pesto torte* (layers of zucchini pesto in puff pastry topped with tomato sauce). Fettuccine, linguine, and angel hair pasta are available with 18 different preparations. 🖾 *48 Greenwich Ave.,* ☎ *203/661–9705. Reservations not accepted. AE, MC, V.*

$$$–$$$$ ✕🏠 **Homestead Inn.** This enormous Italianate wood-frame house, in a posh residential neighborhood not far from the water, is an architectural treasure with its cupola, ornate bracketed eaves, and enclosed wraparound Victorian porch. Rooms are decorated individually with antiques and period reproductions. But it's for Jacques Thiebeult's cuisine that the Homestead is best known: The appetizers mostly involve

exquisitely prepared shellfish; and such entrées as veal kidney finished with brandy, cream, and mustard represent some of the best French cuisine in the area. The staff can be a bit uppity. ⊠ *420 Field Point Rd., 06830,* ☎ FAX *203/869–7500. 17 rooms with bath, 6 suites. Restaurant (jacket required). CP. AE, D, DC, MC, V.*

$$–$$$$ ✕▥ **Greenwich Harbor Inn.** Rooms at this informal harborside inn have soft colors, floral bedspreads, and reproductions of 18th-century antiques. This is more like an upscale chain hotel, however, than a rambling inn. It's clean and within walking distance of the railroad station and the Greenwich Avenue boutiques. The Atlantis Restaurant, which has an outdoor deck overlooking the harbor, serves such seafood dishes as Mediterranean shellfish stew and yellowtail snapper with roast tomatoes and fennel. ⊠ *500 Steamboat Rd., 06830,* ☎ *203/661–9800,* FAX *203/629–4431. 91 rooms, 2 suites. Restaurant, pub, dock, meeting rooms. AE, DC, MC, V.*

$$–$$$ ▥ **Stanton House Inn.** The original structure of this large, Federal-style mansion, within walking distance of downtown, was built in 1840. In 1899, under architect Stanford White's supervision, the house was enlarged to its present size. The interior has been carefully decorated with a mixture of antiques and tasteful reproductions; several rooms have working fireplaces. Breakfast includes fresh fruits, oatmeal, bagels, and other homemade goodies. ⊠ *76 Maple Ave., 06830,* ☎ *203/869–2110,* FAX *203/629–2116. 24 rooms, 2 share bath. CP. AE, D, MC, V.*

$$ ▥ **Hyatt Regency Greenwich.** At one time the Condé Nast publishing
★   empire was ruled from the four-story turreted tower of this modern edifice. Inside, a vast but comfortable atrium contains a flourishing lawn and abundant flora. The rooms are spacious, with all the amenities, including modem-compatible telephones. The pleasant Winfield's restaurant serves interesting renditions of classic dishes. ⊠ *1800 E. Putnam Ave., 06870,* ☎ *203/637–1234 or 800/233–1234,* FAX *203/637–2940. 349 rooms with bath, 4 suites. 2 restaurants, bar, indoor pool, sauna, health club, AE, D, DC, MC, V.*

Outdoor Activities and Sports

HIKING

In northern Greenwich is the 485-acre **Audubon Center** (⊠ 613 Riversville Rd., ☎ 203/869–5272. ☉ Tues.–Sun.9–5), with 8 miles of hiking trails and exhibits about the local environment. More than 1,000 species of flora and fauna have been recorded at the center. There is also an environmental book and gift shop.

Shopping

Greenwich Avenue, an abridged version of New York's Madison Avenue, is renowned for its swank brand-name stores and boutiques.

Stamford

❷   *6 mi northeast of Greenwich, 38 mi southwest of New Haven, 33 mi northeast of New York City.*

Glitzy office buildings, chain hotels, and major department stores have revitalized much of Stamford and made it the most dynamic city on the southwestern shore. Having finally weathered the late-'80s recession and worked out a few growing pains, the downtown is taking back its streets and historic buildings—properly harnessing the region's affluence and the desire of suburbanites to spend an exciting night on the town without having to brave New York City. Restaurants, nightclubs, and shops are opening rapidly along Atlantic and lower Summer streets: The city now envisions itself as the model that might spur other decaying Connecticut cities to splendor.

Stamford's top cultural attraction, the **Whitney Museum of American Art at Champion,** displays primarily 20th-century American painting and photography. The exhibits change every 10 to 12 weeks and have included works by the likes of Hopper, Calder, O'Keeffe, and other artists shown in the Whitney's permanent New York City collection. ⊠ *Atlantic St. and Tresser Blvd.,* ☎ *203/358–7630.* ☜ *Free.* ☉ *Tues.–Sat. 11–5.*

One of the country's most unusual churches is the fish-shaped **First Presbyterian Church.** It has beautiful stained-glass windows and an enormous mechanical-action pipe organ. ⊠ *1101 Bedford St.,* ☎ *203/324–9522.* ☉ *Weekdays 9–5.*

ℭ The 118-acre **Stamford Museum and Nature Center,** in the quieter northern half of Stamford, has five galleries with changing exhibits on natural history, art, and early American artifacts, as well as a permanent exhibit on Native American life. It's all centered around a re-created Colonial-era farm, complete with animals and period farm tools. Plenty of visitors come to walk along the many nature trails. The best time to come is during either the spring harvest or the maple sugaring—call for exact dates. A new addition to the center is Nature's Playground for children, with large birds' nests that kids can climb into, a treehouse, and plenty of slides. ⊠ *39 Scofieldtown Rd. (Rte. 137),* ☎ *203/322–1646.* ☜ *Grounds $4, planetarium an additional $2, observatory $3 (but no grounds fee charged).* ☉ *Grounds Mon.–Sat. 9–5, Sun. 1–5; planetarium shows Sun. at 3; observatory Fri. 8–10 PM.*

The **Bartlett Arboretum,** owned by the Horticultural College of the University of Connecticut, has 63 acres of natural woodlands, cultivated gardens, and a greenhouse and gift shop. There are marked ecology trails, a swamp walk, and a pond. Trail maps are available at the information desk. The wildflower garden is stunning in the spring. ⊠ *151 Brookdale Rd., off High Ridge Rd. (Exit 35 Meritt Pkwy.),* ☎ *203/322–6971.* ☜ *Free.* ☉ *Daily 8:30–sunset.*

Dining and Lodging

$$$–$$$$ ✕ **Amadeus.** Folks from the countrified environs drive to this stretch of Summer Street for a great meal at one of about a dozen nearby restaurants—Amadeus leads the pack. Both the food and the decor are Continental, with decadent Viennese flare. The dining room overflows with elegant dried-flower arrangements, and lavishly framed prints dot the walls. For dinner, try the Marseille fish and shellfish soup, followed by the trademark Vienna schnitzel, served with golden pan-fried potatoes. Forget your waistline! ⊠ *201 Summer St.,* ☎ *203/348–7775. AE, DC, MC, V. No lunch weekends.*

$$–$$$ ✕ **Fjord Fisheries.** Stamford's best fish house—decorated with Scandinavian touches (a Swedish flag hangs outside the door)—is in a truly unappealing concrete building adjacent to the Sportsplex Health Club. It's about five minutes from Exit 6 on I–95; call for directions. Inside, however, is a casual eatery that warrants the high prices charged. You won't find fish in this area any fresher—trucks coming from northern New England, carrying the latest catches, make drops here before heading to Manhattan's Fulton Fish Market. There are dozens of varieties and preparations of fish, including grouper, halibut, salmon, and trout, as well as a mean filet mignon. A chatty yuppied bar up front serves a limited menu. ⊠ *49 Brownhouse Rd.,* ☎ *203/325–0255. Reservations essential. AE, DC, MC, V. No lunch. Closed Mon.*

$$–$$$ ✕ **Kathleen's.** Helping to cultivate the new, chic look Stamford is striving for these days is this dimly lit streetside bistro, within walking distance of downtown clubs, theaters, and shopping. Behind a striking facade of black with cornflower blue trim lurks this wonderful, uncharacteristically quiet, little eatery. The menu features hearty

interpretations of popular regional American victuals: pan-seared yellowfin tuna with white- and black-bean sauces, veal with country ham stuffing, and many pastas. Save room for the apple pie or Kathleen's famous chocolate cake. ⊠ *25 Bank St.,* ☎ *203/323–7785. AE, DC, MC, V. No lunch Sat. Closed Sun.*

$$–$$$ × **Restaurant Michael Michael on Long Ridge.** A meal at Michael
★   Michael, a restaurant in a rustic red barn by the New York border, is filled with sparkle, enthusiasm, and whimsy. Starters such as andouille sausage with caramelized onion and whole grain mustard ($4.91) awaken the taste buds. Entrées include creative pizzas and seared herb-crusted tuna with basmati rice and soy-ginger vinaigrette ($18.76). The ingredients are fun, the staff is a blast, and even the prices are offbeat (never rounded). The Sunday gospel brunch (reserve well ahead) features international gospel sensations Jean Cheek and Faces. As you listen, sample delicacies from the southern-style buffet. ⊠ *2635 Long Ridge Rd.,* ☎ *203/322–2953. AE, MC, V. No lunch.*

$$ × **Hacienda Don Emilio.** The decor of this Mexican restaurant is more
★   upscale Spanish than Americanized south-of-the-border—there are no streamers here. Imaginative and authentic cuisine includes *pollo en mole poblano* (chicken mole), a favorite not to be confused with the bland version of the dish you usually find around the state; and *tacos pibil,* a Yucatán specialty consisting of shredded pork marinated in a delicious roasted-tomato salsa. ⊠ *222 Summer St.,* ☎ *203/324–0577. AE, D, DC, MC, V. No lunch Sun.*

$$$ 🏨 **Stamford Marriott.** The Marriott stands out for its convenience to trains and airport buses and for its up-to-date facilities. Furnishings throughout are modern and comfortable, if unmemorable. The large, busy lobby is a favorite meeting place of the city's movers and shakers, who frequently head for one of several meeting rooms or to Windows on the Sound, the state's only revolving rooftop restaurant. ⊠ *2 Stamford Forum, 06901,* ☎ *203/357–9555 or 800/228–9290,* FAX *203/358–0157. 501 rooms with bath, 7 suites. 3 restaurants, bar, indoor-outdoor pool, health club, jogging, racquetball, nightclub. AE, D, DC, MC, V.*

$$$ 🏨 **Stamford Sheraton.** The drive leading to the ultramodern entrance of this downtown luxury hotel should prepare you for the dramatic atrium lobby inside, with its brass-and-glass-enclosed gazebo. Attractive, contemporary furnishings in the rooms are complemented by spacious bathrooms. ⊠ *1 First Stamford Pl., 06901,* ☎ *203/967–2222 or 800/325–3535,* FAX *203/967–3475. 451 rooms with bath, 23 suites. Restaurant, indoor pool, 2 tennis courts, health club, meeting rooms. AE, D, DC, MC, V.*

$–$$ 🏨 **Stamford Super 8 Motel.** The furnishings in this link of the national hotel chain are modern but nondescript. The property is clean and convenient to all local attractions. ⊠ *32 Grenhart Rd., 06902,* ☎ *203/324–8887 or 800/843–1991. 97 rooms, 1 suite. AE, D, DC, MC, V.*

Nightlife and the Arts

NIGHTLIFE

For alternative dance music try the **Art Bar** (⊠ 84 W. Park Pl., ☎ 203/973–0300), which is gay and lesbian on Sunday nights. For a collegiate crowd, cheap drinks, and straightforward rock and roll, head to **Boppers** (⊠ 220 Atlantic St., ☎ 203/357–0300). The **Terrace Club** (⊠ 1938 W. Main St., ☎ 203/961–9770) books famed music stars of yesteryear and musicians on today's cutting edge.

THE ARTS
The **Stamford Center for the Arts** (⊠ 307 Atlantic St., ☎ 203/325–4466) offers everything from one-act plays, comedy shows, and musicals to film festivals and a young-audience series. Stamford's **Palace Theatre** (⊠ 61 Atlantic St., ☎ 203/325–4466) presents the **Stamford Symphony Orchestra** (☎ 203/325–1407), the **Connecticut Grand Opera and Orchestra** (☎ 203/327–2867), and other fine musical performances.

Outdoor Activities and Sports
The 18-hole **Sterling Farms Golf Course** (⊠ 1349 Newfield Ave., ☎ 203/461–9090) offers winter golfing.

Shopping
Our World Gallery (⊠ The Stone Studio, 82 Erskine Rd., Stamford, ☎ 203/322–7018) shows the work of international and local painters and sculptors. At northern Stamford's **United House Wrecking** (⊠ 535 Hope St., ☎ 203/348–5371), acres of architectural artifacts, decorative accessories, antiques, nautical items, lawn and garden furnishings, and other less valuable but certainly unusual items await you. The nine-story **Stamford Town Center** (⊠ 100 Greyrock Pl., ☎ 203/356–9700), which houses 130 shops, is one of the chic malls in which Woody Allen and Bette Midler's on-screen marriage crumbled in the film *Scenes from a Mall.*

Darien

❸ *9 mi northeast of Stamford, 37 mi northeast of New York City.*

A drive through Darien may leave you thinking the entire town is one enormous country club. The small downtown area on Route 1, in and around the train station, has a variety of little shops and restaurants.

The small yachting enclave of **Rowayton,** south of Darien via Route 136, is a village that retains the low-key blue-blood atmosphere you expect to find on Nantucket or eastern Long Island. Not dissimilar from Rowayton is **Noroton.** The Noroton Bay Yacht Club has produced a number of America's Cup contenders (crew as well as boat designers).

Dining
$$$ ✕ **Black Goose Grill.** The Black Goose serves good, dependable bistro fare in a classy little dining room on Route 1 just south of the railbridge, in the heart of downtown. It's a tan brick building with black and white awnings over each window, through which models of carved black geese are visible from the outside. A couple of the better dishes are grilled pork chops with pan gravy, braised cabbage, and fried sweet potatoes and Dijon-glazed lamb with squash and wild rice. ⊠ *972 Post Rd.,* ☎ *203/655–7107. AE, MC, V.*

Norwalk

❹ *5 mi northeast of Darien, 42 mi northeast of New York City, 16 mi southwest of Bridgeport.*

Norwalk is the home of Yankee Doodle Dandies: In 1756, Colonel Thomas Fitch threw together a motley crew of Norwalk soldiers and led them off to fight at Fort Crailo, near Albany. Supposedly, Norwalk's women gathered feathers for the men to wear as plumes in their caps in an effort to give them some appearance of military decorum. Upon the arrival of these shoddily clad warriors, one of the British officers sarcastically dubbed them "Macaronis"—slang for fops or dandies. The saying caught on, and so did the song.

In the 19th century, Norwalk became a major New England port and manufactured pottery, clocks, watches, shingle nails, and paper. It then fell into a state of neglect, in which it remained for much of this century. During the past decade, however, its coastal business district has been the focus of a major redevelopment project.

The **SoNo** (short for South Norwalk) **commercial district** is an avenue with art galleries, restaurants, and trendy boutiques. The cornerstone of the SoNo district is the **Maritime Center.** Built within a restored 1860 redbrick ironworks factory on the west bank of the Norwalk River, the 5-acre waterfront center brings to life the ecology and history of Long Island Sound. A huge aquarium competes for attention with such actual marine vessels as the 56-foot oyster sloop *Hope.* Harbor study cruises—the Winter Creature Cruise and the Marine Life Cruise in summer—are run several days a week. The screen of the 340-seat IMAX theater is 60 feet high by 80 feet wide. Although not as popular as Mystic Seaport, the Maritime Center is one of the state's most worthwhile attractions—especially for families. ⊠ *10 N. Water St.,* ☎ *203/852–0700.* 🎟 *$7.50, IMAX theater $6, combined $11.75.* ◷ *Daily 10–5 (July–Labor Day, until 6).*

Restoration continues at the **Lockwood-Matthews Mansion Museum,** an ornate tribute to Victorian decorating—it's hard not to be impressed by the octagonal rotunda and 50 rooms of gilt, fresco, marble, woodwork, and etched glass. ⊠ *295 West Ave.,* ☎ *203/838–1434.* 🎟 *$5.* ◷ *Mar.–mid-Dec.*

Dining and Lodging

$$–$$$ ✕ **Meson Galicia.** Good Spanish restaurants are rare in this region; but the tapas served in this restored trolley barn in downtown Norwalk are extraordinary, inventive, and electrifying to the taste buds: Ingredients include sweetbreads, capers, asparagus, chorizo . . . the list goes on. Come with an empty stomach and an open mind, and let the enthusiastic staff spoil you. No greasy paellas here. ⊠ *10 Wall St.,* ☎ *203/866–8800. AE, D, DC, MC, V. No lunch weekends. Closed Mon.*

$–$$ ✕ **Sunrise Pizza.** Across the drawbridge from SoNo is this tiny, store-
★   front pizza place where there's always a long wait on weekends. Sit on green wooden benches at varnished-wood tables and ogle the amazing list of toppings, including ricotta, leeks, zucchini, Greek olives, apples, clams, andouille sausage, and fine herbs. There's a great variety of salads, too. If in Stamford, try the branch on Long Ridge Road (☎ 203/348–3433). ⊠ *211 Liberty Square,* ☎ *203/838–0166. Reservations not accepted. AE, DC, MC, V.*

$$–$$$ ✕🏠 **Silvermine Tavern.** The rooms above the tavern (circa 1775) and
★   the separate country store are among the better values in the region. Each of the cozy rooms is configured and furnished differently, with hooked rugs and antiques as well as some modern touches. The large, low-ceiling dining room is romantic, with its Colonial decor and numerous windows overlooking a waterfall. Traditional New England favorites are given some new slants—semi-boneless duckling is served in lingonberry sauce. The lobster pie and Yankee pot roast, however, are traditional favorites, and the preparation of the filet mignon and salmon changes seasonally. Sunday brunch is a local tradition. ⊠ *194 Perry Ave., 06850,* ☎ *203/847–4558,* 📠 *203/847–9171. 10 rooms with bath. Restaurant. CP. AE, DC, MC, V. Closed Tues.*

$–$$ 🏠 **Days Inn.** This well-kept, late-'80s motel is next door to the Marriott. The small lobby is efficient, if not cheery, and rooms contain modern furnishings in soft colors. Pick any room—all the views are equally blah. ⊠ *426 Main Ave., 06851,* ☎ *203/849–9828 or 800/325–2525,* FAX *203/846–6925. 119 rooms with bath. Restaurant, bar, exercise room, coin laundry. AE, D, DC, MC, V.*

Nightlife

Bars are plentiful around these parts, and most have a tavernlike atmosphere. The best are in the SoNo district of South Norwalk.

Outdoor Activities and Sports

FISHING

Fishing boats can be chartered from **Tigra Boat Charters** (☎ 203/259–7719) at **Norwalk Cove Marina** (⊠ Exit 16 off I–95, Norwalk, ☎ 203/838–2326).

SAILING

For charters, half-day rentals, lessons, or even advice on buying a boat, contact the **Sound Sailing Center** (⊠ 160 Water St., ☎ 203/838–1110, FAX 203/838–0377). The center is a member of the American Sailing Association and U.S. Sailing.

Shopping

The **Barter Shop** (⊠ 140 Main St., ☎ 203/846–1242) has several buildings chock-full of bric-a-brac and furniture, both antique and reproduction. **Washington Street** in South Norwalk (SoNo) has excellent galleries and crafts dealerships.

The **Factory Outlets at Norwalk** (⊠ 230 East Ave., ☎ 203/838–1349), with 20 brand-name outlet shops, including Carter's Childrenswear, is near the East Norwalk train station. **Decker's** (⊠ 666 West Ave., ☎ 203/866–5593) sells Polo clothing, along with several other fashionable labels, at discount prices.

New Canaan

⑤ *5 mi northwest of Norwalk, 33 mi southwest of New Haven.*

New Canaan is an even neater, inland version of Darien. So rich and elegant is the landscape that you may want to invest in a local street map and spend the afternoon driving around the estate-studded countryside.

The **Historical Society,** one of the best in Connecticut, operates several buildings on its property, including the town house in which it's based, the John Rogers Sculpture Studio, a Colonial schoolhouse, a tool museum, a print shop, and a restored Georgian Colonial home. ⊠ *13 Oenoke Ridge,* ☎ *203/966–1776.* ☉ *Main building Tues.–Sat. 10–noon and 2–4; other buildings Wed., Thurs., Sun. 2–4. Call for extended hrs.*

There are more than 40 acres of woods and habitats at the **New Canaan Nature Center.** You can take part in the hands-on natural science exhibits at the Discovery Center in the main building or walk along the many nature trails. In fall, you can see live demonstrations at the cider house and, in spring, at the maple sugar shed. ⊠ *144 Oenoke Ridge,* ☎ *203/966–9577,* ▣ *Donation suggested for museum.* ☉ *Grounds daily, dawn–dusk; museum Tues.–Sat. 9–4, Sun. noon–4.*

Lodging

$$$–$$$$ 🏨 **Maples Inn.** This white-trim, yellow-clapboard structure—which is just a short drive from downtown—has 13 gables, most of which are veiled by a canopy of aged maples. Bedrooms are furnished with antiques and queen-size canopy beds. Mahogany chests, gilt frames, and brass lamps gleam with energetic polishing, and the imaginative use of fabrics and paper fans is an education in design. ⊠ *179 Oenoke*

Ridge, 06840, ☎ *203/966–2927,* FAX *203/966–5003. 6 double rooms with bath, 4 suites, 9 apartments. CP. AE, MC, V.*

Shopping
Main Street in New Canaan is loaded with trendy, upscale shops.

Wilton

❻ *6 mi east of New Canaan, 35 mi southwest of New Haven.*

Wilton, with rolling hills and wooded countryside, is a dapper community on a par with New Canaan.

Wilton is home to Connecticut's first National Historic Site, **Weir Farm.** It's also the first property of its kind dedicated to the legacy of an American painter, J. Alden Weir. Hikers and picnickers will enjoy the property's 60 heavily wooded acres. Tours of Weir's former studios are offered; there is also a self-guided tour of Weir's painting sites. ⊠ *735 Nod Hill Rd. (off Rte. 33),* ☎ *203/834–1896.* ☞ *Free.* ☉ *Visitor center Apr.–Nov., daily 8:30–5; Dec.–Mar., weekdays 8:30–5.*

The Arts
The **Wilton Playshop** (⊠ Lovers La., Box 363, ☎ 203/762–7629) dates to 1937, when townsfolk were looking for a creative outlet. Today, this community theater has five major productions a year, from musicals to mysteries.

Dining
$$–$$$ ✕ **Mediterranean.** The owners of Norwalk's popular Meson Galicia have opened this stylish dining room in an otherwise dull Colonial-style shopping center. Like Meson Galicia, Mediterranean is a tribute to all things Spanish—trendy Spanish that is. Appetizers range from grilled shrimp on a generous bed of spinach and white beans to crêpes stuffed with salmon. An added bonus are samplings from other Mediterranean lands, including Morocco, Greece, and Italy. The dishes are expertly prepared; the portions huge. ⊠ *5 River Rd. (Wilton Center),* ☎ *203/762–8484. No lunch weekends. Closed Mon. AE, D, MC, V.*

Outdoor Activities and Sports
NATURE CENTER
Spanning 146 acres of forest and wetlands, the **Woodcock Nature Center** (⊠ 56 Deer Run Rd., ☎ 203/762–7280) is in both Wilton and Ridgefield. Activities include botany walks, birding and geology lectures, and hikes on 2 miles of trails and swamp boardwalk.

Shopping
Route 7, which runs through Wilton, has dozens of fine antiques sheds and boutiques. Of particular note is **Cannon Crossing** (⊠ Just off Rte. 7, Cannondale, ☎ 203/762–2233), a pre–Civil War farm village–turned–shopping complex with antiques shops, restaurants, and galleries.

Ridgefield

❼ *8 mi north of Wilton, 43 mi west of New Haven.*

New Yorkers have been known to stay at one of the rambling inns in Ridgefield rather than drive all the way to comparatively remote Litchfield County, 40 miles north. In Ridgefield, you'll find northwestern Connecticut's atmosphere within an hour of Manhattan. The town center, which you approach from Wilton on Route 33, is still a largely residential sweep of lawns and majestic homes.

An outstanding sculpture garden is the major draw of the **Aldrich Museum of Contemporary Art,** a first-rate collection of contemporary artwork that rivals any small collection in New York. ✉ *258 Main St.,* ☎ *203/438–4519.* 🎫 *$3.* ⊘ *Tues.–Sun. 1–5.*

A British cannonball is lodged in the wall of the **Keeler Tavern Museum,** a historic inn and the former home of architect Cass Gilbert. Tours of this museum, filled with furniture and Revolutionary War memorabilia, are given by guides dressed in Colonial costumes. ✉ *132 Main St.,* ☎ *203/438–5485.* ⊘ *Feb.–Dec., weekends and Wed. 1–4.*

Dining and Lodging

$$$–$$$$ ✕🏠 **Stonehenge Inn.** When this famous 18th-century inn burned to the ground a few years ago, everybody wondered if a rebuilt Stonehenge could ever equal the original. Alas, much of the old charm is lost. Although this white-clapboard imposter is lavishly decorated, it feels more like a luxury hotel than a cozy and characterful inn. One thing that has improved is the restaurant, which presents a solid but pricey menu of Continental classics, including Long Island duck with plum wine sauce and beef Wellington—there are no surprises here. ✉ *Stonehenge Rd. off Rte. 7, 06877,* ☎ *203/438–6511,* 📠 *203/438–2478. 14 rooms with bath, 2 suites. Restaurant (jacket and tie). CP. AE, MC, V.*

$$–$$$ ✕🏠 **The Elms Inn.** The best rooms are in the impressive frame house, built by a Colonial cabinetmaker in 1760, near the site of the Battle of Ridgefield; rooms in the adjacent 1850 building are nondescript. With its mix of antiques, reproductions, and modern fixtures, the inn is a comfortable stopping-off place. The restaurant is bright and churns out dependable Provence-influenced cuisine, including local game specialties and, in January, wild boar. Breakfast is served in your room. ✉ *500 Main St., 06877,* ☎ *203/438–2541. 16 rooms with bath, 4 suites. Restaurant, pub, meeting rooms. CP. AE, DC, MC, V.*

Outdoor Activities and Sports

Ridgefield Golf Club (✉ Ridgebury Rd., ☎ 203/748–7008) has an 18-hole course.

Shopping

The **Hay Day Market** (✉ 21 Governor St., ☎ 203/431–4400) stocks hard-to-find fresh produce, mouth-watering locally made sauces and salads, jams, cheeses, fresh baked goods, flowers, and much more.

Danbury

❽ *9 mi north of Ridgefield, 20 mi northwest of Bridgeport.*

Now a middle-class slice of suburbia, Danbury was the hat capital of America for nearly 200 years—until the mid-1950s. Rumors persist that the term "mad as a hatter" originated here. Hat makers suffered widely from the injurious effects of mercury poisoning, a fact that is said to explain the resultant "madness" of veteran hatters.

You can learn a great deal about Danbury's hat-making history by visiting the **Scott-Fanton Museum,** a complex that includes a re-created hat shop and a house decorated in Federal-period decor. ✉ *43 Main St.,* ☎ *203/743–5200.* 🎫 *Donation suggested.* ⊘ *Wed.–Sun. 2–5.*

Outdoor Activities and Sports

Golf Digest rates Danbury's **Richter Park Golf Course** (✉ 100 Aunt Hack Rd., ☎ 203/792–2550) one of the top 25 public courses in the country.

Shopping

The **Danbury Fair Mall** (✉ Intersection of Rte. 7 and I–84, ☎ 203/743–3247) has scores of shops ranging from discount to mainstream.

Stew Leonard's Dairy (✉ 99 Federal Rd., ☎ 203/790–1571), the self-billed "Disneyland of Supermarkets," is a great place to take children. It has a petting zoo and animated characters such as a cow, a chicken, and a walking banana wandering throughout the store.

Redding

⑨ *11 mi east of Danbury, 35 mi southwest of Waterbury.*

Redding was once the home of Mark Twain's estate, Stormfield. Little has changed since Twain described the area as "one of the loveliest spots in America."

In the winter of 1778–79, three brigades of Continental Army soldiers, under the command of General Israel Putnam, made their winter encampment at the site of **Putnam Memorial State Park** (✉ Junction of Rtes. 58 and 107, West Redding, ☎ 203/938–2285), then known as "Connecticut's Valley Forge." It is now a superb place for hiking and cross-country skiing.

En Route From Redding to Weston, take Route 53 south along the picturesque Saugatuck Reservoir.

Weston

⑩ *6 mi south of Redding, 36 mi southwest of New Haven.*

The heavily wooded town of Weston is the home of more artists and entertainers (e.g., Erica Jong, Keith Richards, Robert Redford, and Elizabeth Ashley) than you can shake a stick at.

Outdoor Activities and Sports

HIKING

More than 1,660 acres of woodlands, wetlands, and rock ledges await intrepid hikers at **Devil's Den Nature Preserve** (✉ 33 Pent Rd., ☎ 203/226–4991; from Rte. 57, turn onto Godrey Rd.; after ½ mile, turn left onto Pent Rd., which ends in the park's main parking area). Trail maps are available in the parking lot registration area. There are no rest room facilities.

Westport

⑪ *7 mi south of Weston, 47 mi northeast of New York City.*

Westport, an artists' mecca since the turn of the century, continues to attract artists. Even today, despite commuters and corporations, Westport remains more arty and cultured than its neighbors: If the rest of Fairfield County is stylistically five years behind Manhattan, Westport lags by just five months. The celebrity feel you may sense here is no illusion: Paul Newman and Joanne Woodward have their home here, as does America's homemaking and entertaining guru, Martha Stewart.

The Arts

The **Westport Playhouse** (✉ 25 Powers Ct., ☎ 203/227–4177) is a summer theater. Summer musical performances are given at the outdoor **Levitt Pavilion** (✉ Off Jesup Green, ☎ 203/226–7600) in Westport.

Beaches

In summer, visitors to Westport congregate at **Sherwood Island State Park** (✉ I–95, Exit 18, ☎ 203/226–6983). In addition to its long sweep of sandy beach, it has two water's-edge picnic groves and several food concessions. Sunbathing, swimming, and fishing are the chief attractions.

Dining and Lodging

$$$ ✕ **Cafe Christina.** One of the more recent reasons Westport now rivals
★   Greenwich as Connecticut's culinary capital is this outstanding take on American-Mediterranean cooking. Installed in a former library built at the turn of the century, it is bright and colorful, with faux columns and other trompe l'oeil touches. You might start with baked polenta or an arugula-and-portobello mushroom risotto fritter. The striped bass with stewed tomatoes stars among the entrées, which change every week but always include filling pasta dishes. ⊠ *1 Main St.,* ☎ *203/221–7950. Reservations essential on weekends. AE, DC, MC, V.*

$$–$$$ ✕ **The Mansion Clam House.** Here, the nautical atmosphere is casual, the service is friendly, and the oysters are outstanding (several seasonal varieties are usually featured). Louisiana crawfish tails and steamed Maine mussels in Chardonnay, garlic, tomato, and herb broth are among the other standouts. Seafood standards are also available—fried scallops, shrimp scampi, broiled sole, lobster—and there are a few chicken and steak entrées on the menu for the crustacean-shy. ⊠ *541 Riverside Ave.,* ☎ *203/454–7979. AE, MC, V.*

$$$–$$$$ ✕⊡ **Inn at National Hall.** The self-important name belies the whimsi-
★   cal and exotic interior of this towering redbrick Italianate on the downtown banks of the Saugatuck River. Each room is a study in innovative restoration, wall-stenciling, and decorative design. The furniture collection is exceptional, from the 300-year-old Swedish grandfather clock in the lobby to the chandelier in the conference room, which once hung in London's Savoy Hotel. Rooms and suites are magnificent—some with sleeping lofts and 18-foot windows. With its Corinthian columns and tasseled curtain swags, Restaurant Zanghi, on the lushly decorated first floor, sets the stage for venison, rabbit, oysters, and peanut-and-sesame-crusted calves' liver with sweet-and-sour caramelized onion sauce. ⊠ *2 Post Rd. W, 06880,* ☎ *203/221– 1351 or 800/628–4255,* FAX *203/221–0276. 8 rooms, 7 suites. Restaurant (*☎ *203/221–7572, reservations essential), refrigerators, in-room VCRs, meeting rooms. CP. AE, DC, MC, V.*

$$$$ ⊡ **Cotswold Inn.** Honeymooners often nest at this elegant cottage in the heart of downtown Westport's chic shopping area. Though the steep gabled roof and stone porches recall England's Cotswold region, rooms capture the essence of 18th-century Connecticut, with reproduction Chippendale and Queen Anne furnishings—highboys, mule chests, wing chairs. Two rooms have canopy beds; one has a fireplace. It's more museumlike than it is homey. ⊠ *76 Myrtle Ave., 06880,* ☎ *203/226–3766,* FAX *203/221–0098. 3 rooms with bath, 1 suite. CP. AE, MC, V.*

$$–$$$ ⊡ **Westport Inn.** Bedrooms in this upscale motor lodge have been refurbished with attractive contemporary furniture. Rooms surrounding the large indoor pool are set back nicely and are slightly larger than the rest. Several excellent restaurants are within walking distance. ⊠ *1595 Post Rd. E, 06880,* ☎ *203/259–5236 or 800/446–8997,* FAX *203/254–8439. 114 rooms with bath, 2 suites. Restaurant, indoor pool, health club. AE, D, DC, MC, V.*

Outdoor Activities and Sports

NATURE CENTER
Several trails traverse the 62-acre **Nature Center for Environmental Activities.** You'll discover woods, fields, streams, and wetlands at this peaceful sanctuary. And inside, there is a natural history museum, an

Aquarium Room, a live Animal Hall, and a Discovery Room with hands-on exhibits. ⊠ *10 Woodside La.,* ☎ *203/227–7253.* ⌑ *$1.* ☺ *Grounds dawn–dusk; Nature Center building Mon.–Sat. 9–5, Sun. 1–4.*

WATER SPORTS

You can rent sailboats at the **Longshore Sailing School** (⊠ Longshore Club Park, 260 S. Compo Rd., ☎ 203/226–4646).

Shopping

The outdoor equivalent to the upscale Stamford Town Center is Main Street in Westport, with **J Crew, Barney's, Ann Taylor, Eddie Bauer,** and dozens of other fashionable shops.

En Route   For a scenic route from Westport to Southport, get back onto Route 1 and follow signs to Sherwood Island State Park. Make a left onto Greens Farms Road, following it east along what's commonly dubbed Connecticut's Gold Coast.

Southport

⑫ *5 mi east of Westport, 23 mi southwest of New Haven.*

The village of Southport, on the Pequot River, is an enclave of sailing enthusiasts and old money. Here, and elsewhere along Greens Farms Road, hiding behind creeper-covered fortress walls of varying sizes and colors, are Gatsbyesque mansions (F. Scott Fitzgerald summered here in the early '20s), whose architectural inconsistencies are jarring—one compound is even hot pink.

Fairfield

⑬ *4 mi east of Southport, 33 mi south of Waterbury.*

Fairfield, a town that was settled well before Westport, still has many old Dutch and postmedieval English Colonials on the network of quaint, winding roads north of Route 1.

Each May the **Greenfield Hill** historic area hosts the annual Dogwood Festival, which has been going strong for more than 60 years.

The Arts

The **Gateway's Candlewood Playhouse** (⊠ Rte. 37 at Rte. 39, New Fairfield, ☎ 203/746–4441) stages plays between April and December. The **Fairfield Symphony Orchestra** (☎ 203/831–6020) performs at various county locales.

Beaches

New Fairfield's **Squantz Pond State Park** (⊠ Western shore of Candlewood Lake, Rte. 39, ☎ 203/797–4165) is crowded in summer but still pretty; it has boat and canoe rentals, fishing and bait shops, picnicking, and hiking trails.

Outdoor Activities and Sports

GOLF

The **H. Smith Richardson Golf Course** (⊠ 2425 Morehouse Hwy., ☎ 203/255–7300) is an 18-hole town municipal golf course with dining facilities.

HIKING

The **Connecticut Audubon Society** (⊠ 2325 Burr St., ☎ 203/259–6305) maintains a 160-acre wildlife sanctuary that includes 6 miles of rugged hiking trails and special walks for people with visual impairments and mobility problems.

NATURE CENTER

The Connecticut Audubon Society operates the **Birdcraft Sanctuary** (⊠ 314 Unquowa Rd., ☎ 203/259–0416), which has a children's activity corner, 6 acres of trails, and a pond that attracts waterfowl during their spring and fall migrations.

Bridgeport

⓮ *5 mi east of Fairfield, 28 mi south of Waterbury, 63 mi west of New London.*

Bridgeport, a city that has fallen on hard times, is unsafe at night and rather unappealing by day. It does, however have three interesting attractions.

The **Barnum Museum,** associated with past resident and former mayor P. T. Barnum, has exhibits depicting the great showman's career, which feature such characters as General Tom Thumb and Jenny Lind, the Swedish Nightingale. You can also tour a scaled-down model of Barnum's legendary three-ring circus. This is one of the most visited attractions in the state. ⊠ *820 Main St.,* ☎ *203/331–1104.* ⌧ *$5.* ☉ *Tues.–Sat. 10–4:30, Sun. noon–4:30.*

☾ **Beardsley Park and Zoological Gardens,** north of downtown Bridgeport, is an extremely pleasant surprise. Connecticut's largest zoo is contained within the grounds, which sprawl over 30 acres. Its indoor walk-through South American rain forest, the only one in New England, alone justifies a visit. In the rest of the zoo you'll find 350 species of animals. A smaller children's zoo offers pony rides. ⊠ *Noble Ave.,* ☎ *203/576–8082.* ⌧ *Zoo $4, grounds and park (per car) $5 out-of-state visitors, $3 CT residents.* ☉ *Daily 9–4.*

☾ Among the many installations at the **Discovery Museum** is an eclectic collection of art from the Renaissance to contemporary times, a planetarium, several hands-on science exhibits, a computer-art exhibit, the Challenger learning center with a simulated space flight, and a children's museum. ⊠ *4450 Park Ave.,* ☎ *203/372–3521.* ⌧ *$6.* ☉ *Tues.–Sat. 10–5, Sun. noon–5.*

The Arts

The **Downtown Cabaret Theatre** (⊠ 263 Golden Hill St., Bridgeport, ☎ 203/576–1636), is still shining with top-notch talent. Anything goes at this dinner theater where you can bring your own food—try Chinese takeout or a gourmet picnic.

Stratford

⓯ *3 mi east of Bridgeport, midway between Boston and New York City, 15 mi southwest of New Haven.*

Stratford, named after the English town, Stratford-upon-Avon, has more than 150 historic homes, many of which are on the Sound. Academy Hill, with its quaint streets, is a good area in which to stroll.

Boothe Memorial Park, a complex with several unusual buildings, includes a blacksmith shop, carriage and tool barns, and a museum that traces the history of the trolley. There's also a beautiful rose garden and a children's playground. ⊠ *Main St., Putney, (Rte. 110),* ☎ *203/381–2046.* ⌧ *Free.* ☉ *Park year-round, dawn–dusk; museum June–Oct., Tues.–Fri. 11–1, weekends 1–4.*

Outdoor Activities and Sports

BOATING

Bareboats and crewed boats are available at the **Brewer Yacht Sales and Charters** at Stratford Marina (⊠ Broad St., ☎ 203/377–1281).

Shopping

The **Stratford Antique Center** (⊠ 400 Honeyspot Rd., ☎ 203/378–7754) shows the wares of about 120 dealers.

Southwestern Connecticut A to Z

Getting Around

BY CAR

Merritt Parkway and the coastal I–95 are the region's main arteries; both are subject to harrowing rush-hour snarls. Route 7 is the main road between Norwalk and Danbury, a 40-minute proposition when traffic is behaving. But the best way to see the region is via back roads, so grab a good map and dig around. Travel time from Greenwich to Bridgeport is roughly 35 minutes, Greenwich to New Haven an hour.

Contacts and Resources

EMERGENCIES

Norwalk Hospital (⊠ 34 Maple St., Norwalk, ☎ 203/852–2000).

PHARMACY

CVS Pharmacy (⊠ 235 Main St., Norwalk, ☎ 203/847–6057) is open 24 hours.

VISITOR INFORMATION

Housatonic Valley Tourism Commission (⊠ Box 406, Danbury 06813, ☎ 203/743–0546 or 800/841–4488). **Coastal Fairfield County Convention and Visitors Bureau** (⊠ 297 West Ave., The Gate Lodge–Matthews Park, Norwalk 06850, ☎ 203/854–7825 or 800/866–9255).

THE CONNECTICUT RIVER VALLEY

It was along the meandering Connecticut River that westward expansion in the New World began. Dutch explorer Adrian Block first checked things out in 1614, and in 1633 a trading post was set up in what is now Hartford. Within five years, throngs of restive Bay colonists had settled in this fertile valley. What followed was more than three centuries of barque building, shad hauling, and river trading with ports as far away as the West Indies and the Mediterranean.

Far less touristy than the coast and northwest hills, the Connecticut River Valley is an unspectacular stretch of small river villages and uncrowded state parks punctuated by a few small cities and one large one: Hartford. Of all the regions in Connecticut, this is the one seemingly designed for travelers just passing through—it's seldom the goal of a journey. Hartford, the Connecticut River's major port, is known to most as the insurance capital of America. Its small but lively downtown and dramatic skyline of distinctive office towers belie what is actually just an enormous suburban settlement that continues to outgrow itself. To the south, with the exception of industrial Middletown, a slew of genuinely quaint hamlets vie for a share of Connecticut's tourist crop, offering antiques shops, scenic drives, trendy restaurants, and museums—most of the latter with only local appeal.

Numbers in the margin correspond to points of interest on the Connecticut River Valley and Downtown Hartford maps.

Essex

🔟 *29 mi east of New Haven.*

Essex looks much as it did in the mid-19th century, at the height of its shipbuilding prosperity. So important to a young America was Essex's

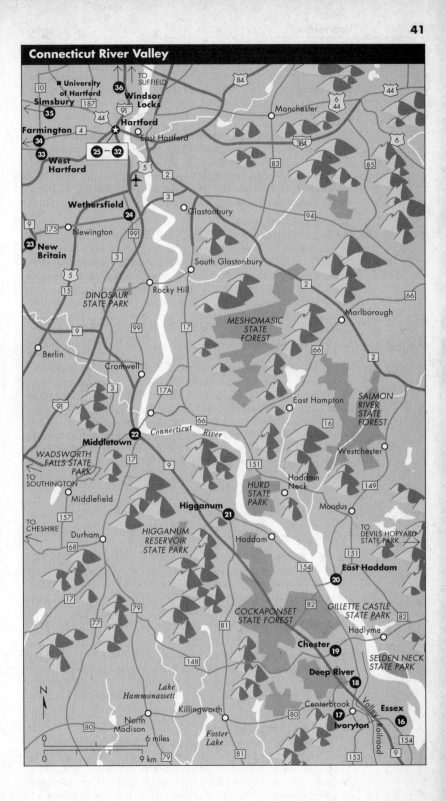

Connecticut River Valley

boat manufacturing, that the British burned more than 40 ships here during the War of 1812. Gone are the days of steady trade with the West Indies, when the aroma of imported rum, molasses, and spices hung heavy in the air. Now its main street is lined with charming whitewashed houses—many the former roosts of weary sea captains—and shops selling clothing, antiques, paintings and prints, and sweets.

On the river in Essex are wood- and aluminum-mast yachts, and the **Connecticut River Museum.** In addition to pre-Colonial artifacts and displays, the museum has a full-size reproduction of the world's first submarine, the *American Turtle;* the original was built by David Bushnell in 1775. ⊠ *67 Main St., Steamboat Dock,* ☎ *860/767–8269.* ⌨ *$4.* ⊙ *Tues.–Sun. 10–5.*

Dining and Lodging

$$–$$$ ✕ **Steve's Centerbrook Café.** This Victorian mansion, complete with latticework and a touch of gingerbread trim, was formerly known as Fine Bouche, one of the best French restaurants in the state. The owners have now transformed it into a bright, healthful bistro. The interior is light, with peaches and whites. The menu, although still listing some French classics, is composed mainly of grilled chicken, fish, and steak, creative pastas, and intriguing main-dish salads. It's packed on weekends. ⊠ *78 Main St., Centerbrook,* ☎ *860/767–1277. AE, MC, V. No lunch. Closed Mon.*

$$–$$$ ✕⌨ **Griswold Inn.** The Gris, which has been offering rooms since 1776, sometimes goes overboard in its efforts to sustain its nautical character. Bedrooms have original beam ceilings, antique and reproduction furnishings—and push-button telephones (but no TVs or radios). With its worn floorboard and exposed ceiling beams, the dining room is probably the most Colonial. The restaurant serves no-frills, traditional American fare such as fried oysters, roast duckling, baked stuffed shrimp, and ribs; portions are hearty. ⊠ *36 Main St., 06426,* ☎ *860/767–1776,* ⌨ *860/767–0481. 14 rooms with bath, 13 suites. Dining room, taproom, library. AE, MC, V.*

Ivoryton

⑰ *4 mi west of Essex.*

Ivoryton was named for its steady import of elephant tusks from Kenya and Zanzibar during the 19th century. What was Ivoryton's leading *export* during this time? Piano keys. At one time, the Comstock-Cheney piano manufacturers processed so much ivory that Japan regularly purchased Ivoryton's surplus, using the scraps to make souvenirs. The Depression closed the lid on Ivoryton's pianos, and what remains is a sleepy, shady hamlet.

The **Museum of Fife and Drum** on Main Street has a lively collection of martial sheet music, instruments, and uniforms chronicling America's history of parades, from the Revolutionary War to the present. Live performances are given Tuesday nights in summer. ⊠ *62 N. Main St.,* ☎ *860/767–2237.* ⊙ *By appointment.*

Dining and Lodging

$$$–$$$$ ✕⌨ **Copper Beech Inn.** A magnificent copper beech tree shades the imposing main building of this Victorian inn, which is furnished in period pieces. Each of the four guest rooms in the main house has an old-fashioned tub; the nine rooms in the Carriage House are more modern and have private decks. Seven acres of wooded grounds and groomed terraced gardens create an atmosphere of privileged seclusion. Highlights of the distinctive country French menu in the romantic din-

ing room are the country pâté and game dishes. Save room for the great white-chocolate mousse. ⊠ *46 Main St., 06442,* ☎ *860/767–0330. 13 rooms with bath. 3 dining rooms (reservations essential; jacket and tie; closed Mon. and Jan.–Mar., Tues.), bar. CP. AE, DC, MC, V.*

Deep River

⑱ *3 mi north of Ivoryton, 44 mi southeast of Waterbury.*

Deep River, like its neighbor Essex, has a small main street lined with antiques shops. It, too, was famous for many years as a manufacturer of piano keys. Its antiques stores are the town's main draw.

Shopping
Deep River seems like an enormous antiques fair, with its concentration of dealers on **Main Street** and at the **intersection of Routes 80 and 145.** One store worth noting is the **Great American Trading Company Factory Outlet Store** (⊠ 39 Main St., 860/526–4335), which sells wooden games, toys, and boxes at a discount. Some of the seconds they sell may have small defects, but the artisanship is still gorgeous.

Chester

⑲ *3 mi north of Deep River, 24 mi northwest of New London.*

Although upscale and arty, Chester remains charming. Shopping is a favorite pastime in this small community, and the National Theatre of the Deaf is active here.

Just across the river from Chester, perched high on a cliff, is the state's leading oddity, **Gillette Castle State Park.** The outrageous (some might say tacky) 24-room, oak-and-granite hilltop castle was built by the eccentric actor William Gillette between 1914 and 1919; he modeled it after the medieval castles of the Rhineland. You can tour the castle and hike on trails near the remains of the 3-mile private railroad that chugged about the property until the owner's death in 1937. Gillette, in his will, demanded that the castle not fall into the hands of "some blithering saphead who has no conception of where he is or with what surrounded." To that end, the castle and 117-acre grounds were designated a state park—it's an excellent spot for hiking and picnicking. ⊠ *67 River Rd. (off Rte. 82), Hadlyme,* ☎ *860/526–2336.* ▭ *$4.* ☺ *Castle: Memorial Day weekend–Columbus Day, daily 10–5; Columbus Day–mid-Dec, weekends 10–4; grounds year-round 8 AM–dusk.*

The Arts
The Goodspeed at Chester presents new works or works in progress at the **Norma Terris Theatre** (⊠ N. Main St., Rte. 82, ☎ 860/873–8668). The **National Theatre of the Deaf** (⊠ 5 W. Main St., ☎ 860/526–4971), originates here the spectacular productions it takes on tour throughout the country.

Dining
$$$–$$$$ ✕ **Restaurant du Village.** A black wrought-iron gate beckons you away from the tony antiquaries of Chester's quaint Main Street and an off-white awning draws you through the door of this classic little Colonial storefront, painted in historic Newport blue and adorned with flower boxes. Here you can sample exquisite classic French cuisine— escargots in puff pastry, filet mignon—while recapping the day's shopping coups. ⊠ *59 Main St.,* ☎ *860/526–5301. AE, MC, V.*

$$$ ✕ **Inn at Chester.** This hulking gambrel-roof inn, about 5 miles west of downtown Chester, successfully captures that warm-and-cozy atmosphere for which New England hostelries are known. There are several dining rooms—the largest inside a rebuilt 19th-century barn with

chandeliers and original beams, another in a glassed-in porch with a flagstone floor. The food is far tastier than is suggested by its nondescript monikers (goat cheese salad, pork medallions). ⊠ *318 W. Main St. (Rte. 148),* ☎ *860/526–9541. AE, MC, V.*

$$–$$$ ✕ **Fiddler's.** Purists may scoff at the location (20 miles inland), but where freshness and preparation are concerned, Fiddler's is as fine a fish house as exists. House specialties are the rich bouillabaisse and the lobster with peaches, shallots, mushrooms, peach brandy, and cream sauce. Blond bentwood chairs, lacy stenciling on the walls, prints of famous schooners, and the amber glow of oil lamps lend a gentrified air—further confounding those purists. ⊠ *4 Water St.,* ☎ *860/526–3210. MC, V. No lunch Sun. Closed Mon.*

Outdoor Activities and Sports
STATE FOREST

The 15,652-acre **Cockaponset** (⊠ Cedar Lake Rd., off Rte. 148, ☎ 860/345–8521) is Connecticut's second-largest state forest.

Shopping
Chester's **The Artisans** (⊠ 1 Spring St., ☎ 860/526–5575), a crafts gallery cooperative, makes and sells one-of-a-kind works including fine pottery, jewelry, and folk art.

East Haddam

② *7 mi north of Chester, 28 mi southeast of Hartford.*

East Haddam, a former fishing, shipping, and musket-making concern, is the only town in the state that occupies both banks of the Connecticut River.

The upper floors of the 1876 gingerbread **Goodspeed Opera House** have served as a venue for theatrical performances for more than 100 years. From 1960 to 1963 the Goodspeed underwent a restoration that included the stage area, the Victorian bar, the sitting room, and the drinking parlor. More than 14 Goodspeed productions have gone on to Broadway, including *Annie* and *Man of La Mancha.* ⊠ *Rte. 82,* ☎ *860/873–8668.* ☞ *Tour $2.* ☉ *Tours Memorial Day–Columbus Day; performances Apr.–Dec.*

The folks at **St. Stephen's Church** believe that the belfry, which is fitted with a 9th-century Spanish bell, is the oldest in the Western Hemisphere. The **schoolhouse** where Nathan Hale taught from 1773 to 1774 displays some of his possessions and other items of local history. ⊠ *Rte. 149 (rear of St. Stephen's Church),* ☎ *860/873–9547.* ☞ *Donation suggested.* ☉ *Memorial Day–Labor Day, weekends 2–4.*

Lodging
$$–$$$ ☒ **Bishopsgate Inn.** This Federal inn around the bend from the landmark Goodspeed Opera House is filled with pictures of guests who have graced the Goodspeed stage. The rooms are cozy and inviting, furnished with period reproductions, a smattering of antiques, and crisp curtains; some have a fireplace. Elaborate candlelight dinners can be served in your room. ⊠ *7 Norwich Rd., Rte. 82, 06423,* ☎ *860/873–1677,* ℻ *860/873–3898. 5 rooms with bath, 1 suite. Full breakfast included. MC, V.*

Outdoor Activities and Sports
CANOEING

Down River Canoes (⊠ Rte. 154, Haddam 06438, ☎ 860/345–8355; Mar.–Nov.) rents canoes.

Hurd State Park (✉ Rte. 151, Haddam Neck, no phone), which sits high on the east bank of the Connecticut River, has excellent views in spring and summer. Sixty-foot cascades flow down Chapman Falls at the 860-acre **Devil's Hopyard** (✉ 3 mi north of the junction of Rtes. 82 and 156, ☎ 860/873–8566). The park, which has 20 campsites, is open mid-April–September.

Higganum

🟤 *15 mi north of East Haddam.*

Higganum's name is a variation on the Native American word *higganumpus* (fishing place). Indeed, it was the home for many years to several important shad fisheries.

The 1970 restoration of **Sundial Herb Garden,** a Colonial farmstead, led to the development of its three unusual gardens—a knot garden of interlocking hedges, a typical 18th-century geometric garden with central sundial, and a topiary garden. In the barn shop you'll find herbs, books, and gourmet items. Call ahead for information on the Sunday afternoon teas held at the farm throughout the year. To get here, take Route 9 to Route 81, then follow it for 3 miles and turn right onto Brault Hill Road; follow signs from there. ✉ *59 Hidden Lake Rd.,* ☎ *860/345–4290.* 🎫 *$2.* ☉ *Jan.–Oct., weekends 10–5; Nov.–Dec. 24, daily 10–5. Closed Dec. 25–Jan. 1.*

Camping

🏕 **Markham Meadows Campground.** ✉ *7 Markham Rd., East Hampton,* ☎ *860/267–9738.*

🏕 **Nelson's Family Compound.** This campground has 285 campsites and is open mid–April through Columbus Day. ✉ *71 Mott Hill Rd., East Hampton,* ☎ *860/267–4561.*

Middletown

🟤 *14 mi north of Higganum, 24 mi northeast of New Haven.*

Middletown, once a bustling river city, was named for its location halfway between Hartford and Long Island Sound. Interestingly enough, it's also halfway between New York City and Boston. From about 1750 to 1800, Middletown was the wealthiest town in the state. Unfortunately, for a variety of reasons, it's fallen further and further downhill in years since.

The imposing campus of **Wesleyan University** (☎ 860/685–2000), founded here in 1831, is traversed prominently by **High Street,** which Charles Dickens once called the loveliest Main Street in America—even though Middletown's actual Main Street runs parallel to it a few blocks east. It is an impressive and architecturally eclectic thoroughfare. Note the massive, fluted Corinthian columns of the Greek Revival Russell House (circa 1828) at the corner of Washington Street, near the pink Mediterranean-style Davison Arts Center, built just 15 years later; farther on are gingerbreads, towering brownstones, Tudors, and Queen Annes. A few hundred yards up Church Street, which intersects High Street, is the impressive Olin Library. Designed in 1928 by Lincoln Memorial architect Henry Bacon, the building was later ingeniously enlarged to allow the original structure to remain intact within the walls of the addition.

The Federal **General Mansfield House** has 18th- and 19th-century decorative arts, Civil War memorabilia and firearms, and local artifacts.

⊠ *151 Main St.,* ☎ *860/346–0746.* ▭ *$2.* ☉ *Sun. 2–4:30, Mon.
1–4, and by appointment.*

You can pick your own fruits and vegetables at **Lyman Orchards** (⊠
Rtes. 147 and 157, Middlefield, ☎ 860/349–3673), just south of
Middletown, from June through October—berries, peaches, pears,
apples, even sweet corn.

The Arts

Wesleyan University's **Center for the Arts** (⊠ Between Washington
Terr. and Wyllys Ave., ☎ 860/685–3355) is the frequent host of concerts, theater, films, and art exhibits.

Dining

$ ✕ **O'Rourke's Diner.** For a university town, Middletown has surpris-
ingly few worthy eateries. This stainless-steel greasy-spoon, which has
a line at the door most weekend mornings, is a cut above any of the
"real" restaurants, despite the fact that it serves only breakfast and lunch.
The usual diner fare is featured, along with such regional delicacies as
steamed cheeseburgers (not served on weekends); it's all unusually good.
The weekend breakfast menu is quite extensive with five full pages of
options. It opens at 4:30 AM. ⊠ *728 Main St.,* ☎ *860/346–6101. No
credit cards. No dinner.*

Outdoor Activities and Sports

STATE PARK

Dinosaur State Park, north of Middletown in Rocky Hill, is roughly
where dinosaurs once roamed. Tracks dating from the Jurassic period,
200 million years ago, are preserved under a giant geodesic dome
here, and in summer, you can make plaster casts of them. It's a great
place for hiking—the park has nature trails that run through woods,
along a ridge, and through swamps on a boardwalk. ⊠ *West St.,
Rocky Hill,* ☎ *860/529–8423.* ▭ *Fee charged.* ☉ *Exhibits Tues.–Sun.
9–4:30; trails daily 9–4.*

Shopping

The **Wesleyan Potters** (⊠ 350 S. Main St., ☎ 860/347–5925) has pottery and weaving studios that you can tour if arranged in advance;
all of the products, such as jewelry, baskets, pottery, and weavings are
for sale.

Skiing

Powder Ridge. The trails here drop straight down from the 500-foot-
high ridge for which it's named. There is nightly night-skiing. ⊠ Powder Hill Rd., Middlefield, ☎ 860/349–3454

New Britain

㉓   *13 mi northwest of Middletown, 10 mi southwest of Hartford.*

New Britain got its manufacturing start producing sleigh bells. From
these modest beginnings, it soon became known as the "Hardware City,"
distributing builders' tools, ball bearings, locks, and other hardware
items to the world. Now no longer a factory town, New Britain is home
to the Central Connecticut State College campus and a lively performing arts community.

New Britain's **Museum of American Art** is the oldest museum collection devoted to American works. Among the 3,000 pieces are murals
by Thomas Hart Benton, western bronzes by Solon Borglum, and the
Sanford Low Memorial collection of American Illustration. ⊠ *56 Lexington St.,* ☎ *860/229–0257.* ▭ *Free.* ☉ *Tues.–Sun. 1–5.*

Outdoor Activities and Sports

From April to September, you might see the next Kirby Puckett at a game of the **Hardware City Rock Cats** (✉ S. Main St., Willow Brook Park, ☎ 860/224–8383), the Minnesota Twins double-A farm club.

Wethersfield

㉔ *7 mi northeast of New Britain, 32 mi northeast of New Haven.*

Wethersfield, a vast Hartford suburb, dates from 1634. As was the case throughout early Connecticut, the Native Americans indigenous to these lands fought the arriving English with a vengeance; here their struggles culminated in the 1637 Wethersfield Massacre, when Pequot Indians killed nine settlers. Three years later, the citizens held a public election, America's first defiance of British rule, for which they were fined £5.

The Joseph Webb House, Silas Deane House, and Isaac Stevens House, all built in the mid- to late 1700s, jointly form one of the state's best historic house-museums, the **Webb-Deane-Stevens Museum.** The houses are well-preserved examples of Georgian and Federal architecture, and they reflect their individual owners' lifestyles as a merchant, a diplomat, and a tradesman, respectively. The Webb House was the site of the strategy conference between Washington and Rochambeau that led to the British defeat at Yorktown. ✉ *211 Main St. (Exit 26 off I–91),* ☎ *860/529–0612.* ➳ *$6.* ☉ *May–Oct., Wed.–Mon. 10–4; Nov.–Apr., weekends only 10–4.*

The **Buttolph-Williams House,** built in 1692, has a remarkable hand-hewn overhanging eave and small casement windows that suggest English Colonial architecture. The kitchen is one of the best preserved in New England. ✉ *249 Broad St.,* ☎ *860/529–0460.* ➳ *$2.* ☉ *May–Oct., Wed.–Mon. 10–4.*

Dining

$$$ ✕ **Ruth's Chris Steak House.** True satisfaction is biting into a juicy T-bone steak—such as is found at this branch of the national chain with the harsh discordant name. The dark-shingle roadhouse exterior and location on the ticky-tacky Berlin Turnpike belie the excellent renditions of good red meat to be found inside: Every steak comes precisely as specified, sizzling on a stainless platter and dripping with flavorful butter. ✉ *2513 Berlin Turnpike, Newington,* ☎ *860/666–2202. No lunch. AE, D, DC, MC, V.*

Hartford

4 mi north of Wethersfield, 45 mi northwest of New London, 81 mi northeast of Stamford.

Hartford, the so-called Insurance City, at the intersection of I–84 and I–91, is where America's insurance industry was born in 1810—largely in an effort to protect the Connecticut River Valley's tremendously important shipping interests. Throughout the 19th century, insurance companies expanded their coverage to include fires, accidents, life, and in 1898, automobiles. At that time, the premium on a $5,000–$10,000 policy was $11.25—how times have changed. Through the years, Hartford industries have included the inspection and packing of the northern river valley's once prominent tobacco industry and the manufacture of everything from bed springs to artificial limbs to pool tables to coffins. Today, 50,000 Connecticutters are employed by the headquarters of more than 40 insurance companies. For the most part, it's a dull city of uninspired office blocks and tenements, made bear-

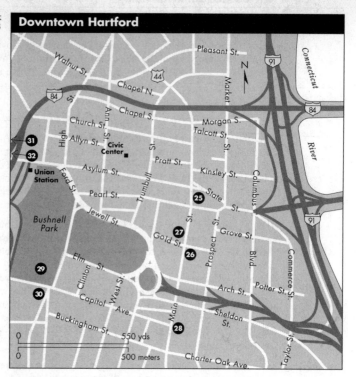

Downtown Hartford

able by a few outstanding cultural, historic, and architectural offerings: Hartford's individual parts are of far greater interest than the city as a whole.

㉕ The Federal **Old State House,** a distinctive building with an elaborate cupola and roof-balustrade, was designed by Charles Bulfinch, architect of the U.S. Capitol, and occupied by the state legislature from 1796 to 1878. The restored Senate chamber contains a Gilbert Stuart portrait of George Washington that remains in its commissioned location. ⊠ *800 Main St.,* ☎ *860/522–6766.* ⊠ *Free.* ☉ *Mon.–Sat. 10–5, Sun. noon–5.*

The hallmark of Hartford's skyline, the **Travelers Insurance Tower,** was once the tallest building in New England. This 527-foot beacon, capped by a pyramidal roof and gold-leafed cupola looms nearby the Old State House. ⊠ *1 Tower Sq.,* ☎ *860/277–0111.* ☉ *Tours May–mid-Oct.*

㉖ The first public art museum in the country, the **Wadsworth Atheneum,** has a 40,000-item collection that spans 5,000 years. The museum's holdings include paintings from the Hudson River School (it's the largest such collection in the country), the Impressionists, and 20th-century painters. The Atheneum also mounts changing exhibits of contemporary art and has an estimable collection of Pilgrim-era furnishings. The Fleet Gallery of African-American Art has one of the nation's best collections. ⊠ *600 Main St.,* ☎ *860/278–2670.* ⊠ *$5; free Sat. 11–noon and Thurs.* ☉ *Tues.–Sun. 11–5; 1st Thurs. of each month until 8 PM.*

㉗ The **Center Church and Ancient Burying Ground,** built in 1807 and patterned after London's Church of St. Martin-in-the-Fields—though the parish itself dates to 1632—was founded by Thomas Hooker. Five of the stained-glass windows were created by Louis Tiffany. The Burying Ground is filled with granite and brownstone headstones, some dating to the 1600s. ⊠ *Main and Gold Sts.,* ☏ *860/249–5631.* ⊗ *Mid-Apr.–mid-Dec., Wed. and Fri. 11–2 or by appointment.*

㉘ The Federal **Butler-McCook Homestead** was built in 1782 and was occupied continuously by the same family until 1971. Its furnishings show the evolution of tastes over time, with the Victorian era predominating. There's also an extensive collection of East Asian artifacts. ⊠ *396 Main St.,* ☏ *860/522–1806 or 860/247–8996.* 🎟 *$4.* ⊗ *Mid-May–mid-Oct., Tues.–Thurs. noon–4.*

Bushnell Park, which fans out from the State Capitol building, was the first public space in the country with natural landscaping rather than with a traditional village green. The park was created by the firm of Frederick Law Olmsted, the Hartford landscape architect who designed New York City's Central Park. On Bushnell's 40 acres you'll find 150 varieties of trees as well as such landmarks as the 100-foot-tall, 30-foot-wide medieval-style **Soldiers and Sailors Memorial Arch,** dedicated to Civil War soldiers.

㉙ Rising above Bushnell Park and visible citywide is the grandiose **State Capitol,** a colossal edifice composed of wholly disparate architectural elements. Built in 1879 of marble and granite—to a tune of $2.5 million—this gilt-dome wonder is replete with crockets, finials, and pointed arches. It currently houses the governor's office and legislative chambers and displays historic murals, statuary, flags, and furnishings. ⊠ *210 Capitol Ave.,* ☏ *860/240–0222.* 🎟 *Free.* ⊗ *Weekdays 9–3; tours weekdays 9:15–1:15 and Apr.–Oct., Sat. 10:15–2:15.*

㉚ The **Raymond E. Baldwin Museum of Connecticut History,** has a large collection of artifacts of Connecticut military, industrial, and political history, including the state's original Colonial charter and a vast assemblage of Samuel Colt firearms—the so-called Arm of Law and Order was first manufactured in Hartford. ⊠ *231 Capitol Ave.,* ☏ *860/566–3056.* 🎟 *Free.* ⊗ *Weekdays 9:30–4.*

Nook Farm, a late 19th-century neighborhood, was home to several prominent families. Here, Samuel Langhorne Clemens, better known as Mark Twain, built his Victorian mansion in 1874. During his resi-**㉛** dency at the **Mark Twain House,** he published seven major novels, including *Tom Sawyer, Huckleberry Finn,* and *The Prince and the Pauper.* Personal memorabilia and original furnishings are on display. One-hour guided tours of the house, including information on its architecture and interior, as well as Twain's personal and family life, are given. ⊠ *351 Farmington Ave. (intersection with Forest St.),* ☏ *860/493–6411.* 🎟 *$7.50.* ⊗ *Mon.–Sat. 9:30–5 (except Tues., June–early Oct.), Sun. noon–5; last tour at 4.*

㉜ The **Harriet Beecher Stowe House,** which was erected in 1871, stands as a tribute to the author of one of 19th-century America's most popular novels, *Uncle Tom's Cabin.* Inside are the author's personal writing table and effects, several of her paintings, a period pinewood kitchen, and a terrarium of native ferns, mosses, and wildflowers. ⊠ *71 Forest St.,* ☏ *860/525–9317.* 🎟 *$6.50.* ⊗ *Mon.–Sat. 9:30–4, Sun. noon–4. Closed Mon., Columbus Day–Memorial Day.*

Dining and Lodging

$$$–$$$$ ✕ **Chez Pierre.** This outstanding classic French restaurant in Strafford Springs, about 24 miles from Hartford, is worth the drive. The formal dining room, in a glorious white Victorian with red trim, serves such memorable dishes as cassoulet with garlic sausage, duck preserve, and beans and fillet of beef with green peppercorns, cognac, and cream.

✉ *111 W. Main St. (Rte. 190), Strafford Springs,* ☎ *860/684–5826. AE, D, MC, V. No lunch. Closed Sun.–Tues.*

$$–$$$$ ✗ **Cavey's.** The 20 minutes it takes to get here from Hartford is time well spent. Downstairs is a formal French restaurant decorated with priceless antiques; the cuisine is classic all the way, and dishes such as squab and herb-crusted roast bass are hallmarks. Upstairs is a casual Italian dining room with Palladian windows, rush-seated wooden chairs, and contemporary art; the mixed grill with chicken and sausage, spinach, potato, and taleggio cheese is popular, as is the straw-and-hay pasta with arugula sauce. ✉ *45 E. Center St., Manchester* ☎ *860/643– 2751. AE, MC, V.*

$$–$$$ ✗ **Blue Star Cafe.** The Blue Star's eclectic menu is a great asset to Hartford's expanding dining scene. It's a lively place to be seen in, with a focus on live music, dancing, and chatting. It's easy to make a meal of reasonably priced appetizers such as the Middle Eastern sampler with hummus, tabouleh, eggplant salad, and grilled flatbread with basil oil. Entrées are huge, so come hungry. The pan-seared yellow-fin tuna with papaya and coriander crust and vegetable nori rolls is superb. ✉ *26 Trumbull St.,* ☎ *860/527–4557. AE, D, DC, MC, V. No lunch Sat. Closed Sun., Mon.*

$$–$$$ ✗ **Max on Main.** Calamari and carpaccio come with spicy touches here, and the designer pizzas are mouth-watering: Try the version with smoked chicken, pancetta, sweet peppers, scallions, and Monterey Jack cheese (a favorite of the late-night crowd); or the one topped with shrimp, sun-dried tomatoes, pesto, calamata olives, and two cheeses. There's a great oyster bar. ✉ *205 Main St.,* ☎ *860/522–2530. AE, DC, MC, V. Closed Sun.*

$$–$$$ ✗ **Peppercorns Grill.** This trendy storefront bistro pulses with energy.
★ Tubes of neon snake about the ceiling and windows like swirls of dayglo paint, and funky wood-and-glass chairs encircle tables laid with traditional white linen. The decor and boisterous crowds make for a vibrant though noisy dining experience. The Continental cuisine reflects current trends—lots of designer pizzas, creatively adorned pastas, and chicken and fish dishes. ✉ *357 Main St.,* ☎ *860/547–1714. AE, DC, MC, V. No lunch Sat. Closed Sun.*

$ ✗ **First and Last Tavern.** What looks to be a simple neighborhood joint
★ is actually one of the state's most hallowed pizza grounds. The long, old-fashioned wooden bar in one room is jammed most evenings with suburbia-bound daily-grinders shaking off their suits; the main dining room is just as noisy, its brick outer wall covered with the requisite array of celebrity photos. Pie toppings are refreshingly untrendy. It's a few miles south of downtown. ✉ *939 Maple Ave.,* ☎ *860/956–6000. Reservations not accepted. AE, D, DC, MC, V.*

$$–$$$$ ✗🏨 **Goodwin Hotel.** The only truly grand city hotel in Connecticut,
★ this establishment looks a little odd in the downtown business district— its dark red, ornate classical facade is dwarfed by the Civic Center. Considering its stately exterior, rooms are nondescript, yet they are large and tastefully decorated—and they're the best in town. This 1881 registered historical landmark has Italian marble baths. The clubby, mahogany-panel Pierpont's Restaurant serves commendable new American fare. Along with an unsurprising selection of steak, chicken, and fish entrées, you can order unusual side dishes, such as celery-root chips. ✉ *1 Haynes St., 06103,* ☎ *860/246–7500 or 800/922–5006,* FAX *860/247–4576. 124 rooms with bath, 11 suites. Restaurant, exercise room, meeting rooms. AE, D, DC, MC, V.*

$$–$$$ ✗🏨 **Sheraton-Hartford.** At 15 stories, this is the city's largest hotel. It's not sumptuous, but there are touches of elegance, such as the street-level lobby abloom with fresh flowers. Connected to the Civic

Center by an enclosed bridge, it's within easy walking distance of the downtown area. ✉ *315 Trumbull St. (at the Civic Center Plaza), 06103,* ☎ *860/728–5151 or 800/325–3535,* FAX *860/240–7247. 378 rooms with bath, 8 suites. Restaurant, bar, indoor pool, health club. AE, D, DC, MC, V.*

$–$$ ✕🏨 **Ramada Inn.** Just beside Bushnell Park, the Ramada has an unobstructed view of the Capitol. However, rooms facing the rear overlook the train station around the corner, a parking lot, and a busy highway. Its new restaurant, Sharky's, serves traditional American fare such as hamburgers and steaks. ✉ *440 Asylum St., 06103,* ☎ *860/246–6591 or 800/228–2828,* FAX *860/728–1382. 96 rooms with bath. Restaurant. CP. AE, D, DC, MC, V.*

Nightlife and the Arts

NIGHTLIFE

Hartford offers the most varied options of nightlife in the area. **Brown Thomson's Last Laugh Club** (✉ 942 Main St., ☎ 860/525–1600) showcases comics from Boston and New York on weekend evenings. **Bourbon Street North** (✉ 70 Union Pl., ☎ 860/525–1014) has a large dance floor and tunes ranging from New Orleans jazz to Motown. **The 880 Club** (✉ 880 Maple Ave., ☎ 860/956–2428), the oldest jazz club in Hartford, presents live acts in an intimate atmosphere. **The Russian Lady Cafe** (✉ 191 Ann St., ☎ 860/525–3003) swings into the wee hours with rock, R&B, and pop music. **The Arch Street Tavern** (✉ 85 Arch St., ☎ 860/246–7610) hosts local rock bands.

THE ARTS

In Hartford, the Tony Award–winning **Hartford Stage Company** (✉ 50 Church St., ☎ 860/527–5151) turns out plenty of future Broadway hits, innovative productions of the classics, and new plays. **Theatreworks** (✉ 233 Pearl St., ☎ 860/527–7838), the Hartford equivalent of Off Broadway, presents a series that includes experimental new dramas. The **Hartford Ballet** (✉ 166 Capitol Ave., ☎ 860/525–9396) stages classical and contemporary productions, including a holiday presentation of the *Nutcracker*. The Hartford Symphony and tours of major musicals headline at **The Bushnell** (✉ 166 Capitol Ave., ☎ 860/246–6807). **Chamber Music Plus** (☎ 860/278–7148), one of Connecticut's better chamber groups, performs at **Cathedral Theatre** (✉ 45 Church St.). **Hartford Camerata Conservatory** (✉ 834 Asylum Ave., ☎ 860/246–2588) has numerous performances throughout the year, usually more traditional works. The **Real Art Ways Music Series** (☎ 860/232–1006) presents mostly modern and experimental recitals. The **Little Theater of Manchester** (✉ 177 Hartford Rd., Manchester, ☎ 860/645–6743), built in 1867, is the state's oldest theater and, though drawing on local talents, is highly professional.

Outdoor Activities and Sports

ICE HOCKEY

The NHL's **Hartford Whalers** (☎ 860/728–6637) play at the Civic Center.

Shopping

In Hartford, the **Civic Center** (✉ 1 Civic Center Plaza, ☎ 860/275–6100) has more than 60 shops as well as a 16,500-seat sports and performing-arts arena. The **Richardson Mall** (✉ 942 Main St., ☎ 860/525–9711) has more than 40 shops selling everything from hats to video games. The art deco–style **Pavilion** (✉ State House Sq., ☎ 860/241–0100) has 25 shops. About 7 miles west is **Westfarms Mall** (✉ I-84, Exit 40, ☎ 860/561–3024), with 140 shops.

Skiing

Mt. Southington. This mountain, an easy drive from Hartford, has night skiing and racing camps. The 12 trails off the 425 feet of vertical range from basic beginner to low intermediate, with a bit of steeper stuff here and there. ☎ 860/628–0954.

West Hartford

㉝ *5 mi west of Hartford, 33 mi of northeast of Woodbury.*

West Hartford, with almost every square inch developed and landscaped, has some great urban qualities. Not as white-bread as much of the state, West Hartford has ethnic communities that ensure your finding Japanese pickled cabbage or pounds of Indian spices at the many ethnic grocery stores. You'll also hear a variety of languages, from Russian to Spanish, spoken here.

The **Science Center of Connecticut** has an aquarium with a tank you can reach into, a mini-zoo, and a planetarium. You're greeted at the museum's entrance by a life-size, walk-through replica of a 60-foot sperm whale. There are daily animal and planetarium shows plus changing exhibits on subjects ranging from the human heart to computers. ⊠ *950 Trout Brook Dr.,* ☎ *860/231–2824.* ☞ *$5; laser and planetarium shows $2.* ☉ *Weekdays 10–4, Sat. 10–5, Sun. noon–5. Closed Mon., Sept.–June.*

The **Noah Webster House and Museum** is the birthplace of the famed author of the *Blue-Backed Speller* and the *American Dictionary.* An 18th-century farmhouse, it contains Webster memorabilia and period furnishings along with changing exhibits. ⊠ *227 S. Main St.,* ☎ *860/521–5362.*

The Arts

Varied shows are staged at the **Saltbox and Clubhouse Gallery** (⊠ 37 Buena Vista Rd., ☎ 860/521–3732).

Dining

$–$$$ ✗ **Butterfly Chinese Restaurant.** The live piano entertainment suggests that this is not your ordinary order-by-number Chinese restaurant; indeed, the food is authentic, the staff gracious and outgoing. Entrées are mostly Cantonese with some Szechuan; specialties—and there are 140 to choose from—include Peking duck and shrimp with walnuts. ⊠ *831 Farmington Ave.,* ☎ *860/236–2816. AE, MC, V.*

Farmington

㉞ *5 mi southwest of West Hartford, 67 mi northeast of New Canaan.*

Proximity to Hartford has transformed the town of Farmington into a somewhat busy suburb. Incorporated in 1645, it is a classic river town with lovely estates, a perfectly preserved main street, and the prestigious **Miss Porter's School** (⊠ 60 Main St., 06032, ☎ 860/677–1321), Jacqueline Kennedy Onassis's alma mater. You'll also find several antiques shops around the intersection of Routes 4 and 10, and some excellent house museums.

The **Hill-Stead Museum** was converted from a private home into a museum by its unusual owner, Theodate Pope, the woman who helped Stanford White design it. A Colonial-Revival farmhouse, it contains a superb collection of Impressionist art. Its drawing room is the only one in America with Monet haystacks at either end and Manet's *The Guitar Player* in the middle. ⊠ *35 Mountain Rd.,* ☎ *860/677–4787.* ☞ *$6.* ☉ *May–Oct., Tues.–Sun. 10-5; Nov.–Apr., Tues.–Sun. 11–4.*

Dating to 1720, the **Stanley-Whitman House** has been a museum since the 1930s. The house is characterized by a massive central chimney and an excellent collection of 18th-century furnishings. ⊠ *37 High St.,* ☎ *860/677–9222.* ⊘ *Mar.–Dec. (by appointment).*

Dining and Lodging

$–$$$$ ✕ **Ann Howard's Apricots.** Several miles west of Miss Porter's, almost in the tiny village of Unionville, is the area's best—though somewhat overpriced—eatery. Apricots is in a white Colonial with dozens of windows looking out over gardens and the Farmington River. Fine new American cuisine is presented in the quiet and cozy formal dining room (the array of inventive salads is a hallmark); less expensive fare is available in the convivial pub. ⊠ *1593 Farmington Ave.,* ☎ *860/673–5903. AE, DC, MC, V. No lunch Sun.*

$$–$$$ ▥ **Farmington Inn.** This modern alternative to the Barney House has an ill-chosen white-painted brick exterior, but the rooms are generous in size and appointed tastefully with antiques and reproductions. It's much nicer than a chain hotel and very close to Miss Porter's and the area museums. ⊠ *827 Farmington Ave., 06032,* ☎ *860/677–2821 or 800/648–9804,* ℻ *860/677–8332. 72 rooms with bath, 13 suites. Business services, meeting rooms. CP. AE, D, DC, MC, V.*

$$ ▥ **Barney House.** This thriving B&B on a quiet street is set amid 4½ acres of formal gardens. Spacious guest rooms mix modern furnishings with antiques; baths are oversize. ⊠ *11 Mountain Spring Rd., 06032,* ☎ *860/674–2796,* ℻ *860/677–7259. 6 rooms with bath. Pool, tennis courts. CP. AE, MC, V.*

Simsbury

㉟   *12 mi north of Farmington; from Farmington, follow Route 10 through Avon.*

Simsbury closely resembles the tony bedroom communities of Fairfield County, with its neat Colonial-style shopping centers, smattering of antiques shops, and proliferation of insurance-industry executives commuting daily to Hartford. Followers of the increasingly popular sport of figure skating will recognize Simsbury as the home and training ground for world-class Olympic athletes Oksana Baiul and Viktor Petrenko.

Run by the Historical Society, **Massacoh Plantation** tells the town's 300-year history. Included on the property are a Victorian carriage house (circa 1880), a 1795 cottage and herb garden, a 1740 schoolhouse, and a 1771 Colonial home. Tours are mandatory. ⊠ *800 Hopmeadow St.,* ☎ *860/658–2500.* ▧ *$5.* ⊘ *Tours May–Oct., Sun.–Fri. hourly 1–3.*

Dining and Lodging

$$–$$$ ✕▥ **Avon Old Farms Hotel.** This 20-acre compound is set into the Avon countryside at the foot of Talcott Mountain, about midway between Farmington and Simsbury. It consists of several redbrick, Georgian-style buildings, and though it is immense and caters largely to business travelers, the rooms retain a warm, elegant ambience. The restaurant, one of the 20 oldest in America, churns out traditional American dishes in a setting of spinning wheels, antique guns, stained glass, and country hearths. One of the dining rooms is a converted blacksmith shop whose horse stalls have been transformed into booths. ⊠ *Rtes. 10 and 44, 06001,* ☎ *860/677–1651,* ℻ *860/677–0364. 150 rooms with bath. Restaurant (*☎ *860/677–6352). Pool, meeting rooms. AE, D, DC, MC, V.*

$$–$$$ ✕⊞ **Simsbury 1820 House.** Perched on a hillside above the main road through town is this classic country inn—a two-story brick mansion built in 1820, with an 1890 addition on its west side. It's a homey, pleasant inn that's neither luxurious nor pretentious. The bedrooms vary in configuration, with a judicious mix of antiques and modern furnishings. Each has its special feature—a fireplace, a balcony, a patio, a wet bar, a dormer with a cozy window seat. The restaurant, with its fireplace and white napery with fine china, is recognized for its outstanding traditional American cuisine. ⊠ *731 Hopmeadow St., 06070,* ☎ *860/658–7658 or 800/879–1820,* FAX *860/651–0724. 34 rooms with bath. Restaurant. CP. AE, D, DC, MC, V.*

Outdoor Activities and Sports
STATE PARK

Talcott Mountain (⊠ Rte. 185, ☎ 860/242–1158) offers views of four states from the 165-foot Heublein Tower, a former private home that's just a 1-mile hike from the parking lot.

Shopping
Arts Exclusive Gallery (⊠ 690 Hopmeadow St., ☎ 860/651–5824) represents 35 contemporary artists who work in different mediums. The **Farmington Valley Arts Center** (⊠ 25 Arts Center La., Avon, ☎ 860/678–1867) shows the works of nationally known artists.

Windsor Locks

36 *13 mi northeast of Simsbury, 94 mi northeast of Greenwich, 48 mi northeast of New Haven, 56 mi northwest of New London.*

Windsor Locks was named for the locks of a canal built to bypass falls in the Connecticut River in 1833; in 1844, the canal closed to make way for a railroad line. Today, the town is home to Bradley International Airport.

The largest air museum in the Northeast, the **New England Air Museum** has more than 80 aircraft, the earliest dating to 1909. World War II's P-47 Thunderbolt and B-29 Superfortress are on display in addition to other vintage fighters and bombers. ⊠ *Next to Bradley International Airport, Rte. 75,* ☎ 860/623–3305. ⊠ *$6.50.* ☉ *Daily 10–5.*

The **Connecticut Trolley Museum** has more than 50 trolleys and a 3-mile antique-trolley ride. A special "Electric Sleigh" ride is offered each Christmas, during which the trolley rolls through a colorful tunnel of Christmas lights. ⊠ *58 North Rd., East Windsor,* ☎ 860/627–6540. ⊠ *$6.* ☉ *Mar.–Memorial Day and Labor Day–Dec., weekends 11–5; Memorial Day–Labor Day, daily 11–5. Closed Jan. and Feb.*

The **Hatheway House** is one of the finest architectural specimens in New England. The walls of its neoclassical north wing (1794) display their original 18th-century French hand-blocked wallpaper. The main house (1761) is typical of Connecticut Valley homes with its double-front doors and gambrel roof. An ornate picket fence fronts the property. It's 20 miles north of Hartford and 7 miles from Windsor Locks. ⊠ *55 S. Main St., Suffield,* ☎ 860/247–8996. ⊠ *$4.* ☉ *Mid-May–mid-Oct., Wed. and weekends 1–4; July–Aug., Wed.–Sun. 1–4.*

Connecticut River Valley A to Z

Getting Around
BY BUS AND TRAIN

Hartford's attractively renovated **Union Station** (⊠ 1 Union Pl., ☎ 860/727–1777) is the main terminus for **Amtrak** (☎ 800/872–7245) trains as well as **Greyhound** (☎ 800/231–2222) and **Peter Pan Bus Lines**

(☎ 800/237–8747) buses. Bus and train service is available to most major northeastern cities.

BY CAR

I–84, I–91, Route 2, Route 202, and Route 44 intersect in Hartford. The major road through the valley is Route 9, which extends from just south of Hartford at I–91 to I–95 at Old Saybrook. Farmington is reached from Hartford on Route 4.

Contacts and Resources

EMERGENCIES

Hartford Hospital (⊠ 80 Seymour St., ☎ 860/545–5555). **Middlesex Hospital** (⊠ 28 Crescent St., Middletown, ☎ 860/347–9471).

GUIDED TOURS

Heritage Trails (⊠ Box 138, Farmington 06034, ☎ 860/677–8867) runs daily city tours and candlelight dinner tours of Hartford, and it sells self-guided driving tours on tape for $9.95. **Chester Charter** (⊠ Chester Airport, 61 Winthrop Rd., Chester, ☎ 860/526–4321) makes 15-minute scenic flights over the lower Connecticut River Valley, weather permitting. The cost is $20. The **Greater Hartford Architecture Conservancy** (⊠ 278 Farmington Ave., ☎ 860/525–0279) sponsors "Hartford on Tour," one- and two-hour walking tours of historic sights (in the fall only, by appointment), and sells tape tours for $7.

The **Valley Railroad** carries you along the Connecticut River and lower valley; if you wish to continue, a riverboat can take you up the river. The train trip lasts an hour; the riverboat ride, 90 minutes. ⊠ *Exit 3 off Rte. 9, Essex,* ☎ *860/767–0103.* ◪ *Train fare $10; combined train–boat fare $14.* ☉ *May 6–June 9, Wed.–Fri.; June 10–Sept. 3, weekends (special schedules for July 4 and Labor Day); Sept. 6–Oct. 30, Wed.–Sun.; Nov. 4–Dec. 22, Fri.–Sun. (special schedules Dec. 18–21).*

LATE-NIGHT PHARMACIES

CVS (⊠ 1099 New Britain Ave., West Hartford, ☎ 860/236–6181). **Community Pharmacy** (⊠ 197 Main St., Deep River, ☎ 860/526–5379).

VISITOR INFORMATION

Connecticut River Valley and Shoreline Visitors Council (⊠ 393 Main St., Middletown 06457, ☎ 860/347–0028 or 800/486–3346). **Greater Hartford Tourism District** (⊠ 1 Civic Center Plaza, Hartford 06103, ☎ 860/520–4480 or 800/793–4480).

THE LITCHFIELD HILLS

Two scenic highways, I–84 and Route 8, form the southern and eastern boundaries of the region. New York, to the west, and Massachusetts, to the north, complete the rectangle. Here, in the foothills of the Berkshires, is some of the most spectacular and unspoiled scenery in the state. Grand old inns—most of them fairly expensive—are plentiful, as are surprisingly sophisticated eateries. Rolling farmlands abut thick forests, and engaging trails traverse the state parks and forests. Two rivers, the Housatonic and the Farmington, attract anglers and canoeing enthusiasts, and there are two sizable lakes, Waramaug and Bantam. Towns such as Litchfield, New Milford, and Sharon are anchored by sweeping town greens and stately homes; Kent, New Preston, and Woodbury draw avid antiquers; and Washington, Salisbury, and Norfolk offer a glimpse of quiet, New England village life as it might have existed two centuries ago.

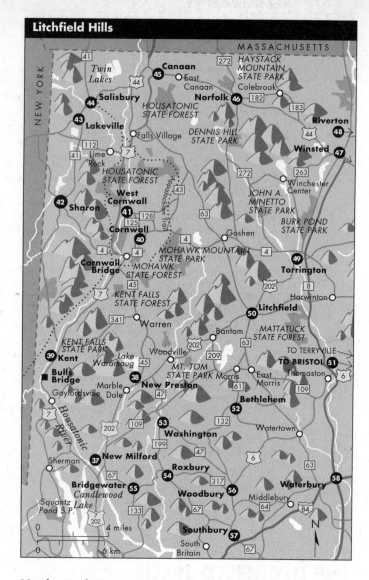

Litchfield Hills

Numbers in the margin correspond to points of interest on the Litch-field Hills map.

New Milford

37 *28 mi east of Waterbury.*

New Milford is a practical starting point to begin a tour of the Litch-field Hills as it's one of the southernmost towns in the area and near Route 7. It was also a starting point of sorts for a young cobbler named Roger Sherman, who, in 1743, opened his shop where Main and Church streets meet. A Declaration of Independence signatory, Sherman also helped draft the Constitution and the Articles of Confederation.

Route 7/202 is, up to its junction with Route 67, a dull stretch of shop-ping centers and consistently ugly storefronts. But where the road crosses the Housatonic River, you'll find old shops, galleries, and eateries all within a short stroll of New Milford green—one of the longest in New England.

OFF THE
BEATEN PATH **THE SILO –** New Yorkers who miss Zabar's and Balducci's feel right at home in this silo and barn packed with objets de cookery and crafts; the array of gourmet goodies and sauces is unbelievable. Band leader Skitch Henderson and his wife, Ruth, own and operate this bazaar, whose success proves there's a great desire for sophisticated, urbane ingredients, even under the elms. It's north of the New Milford green 4 miles on Route 202. ⊠ *44 Upland Road,* ☎ *860/355-0300.*

Dining and Lodging

$$–$$$ ✕ **Bistro Café.** Copper pots hang about and vintage black-and-white
★ photos are on the walls of this café in a redbrick corner building. An excellent array of regional American dishes changes weekly. You might try the tender grilled swordfish with whipped potatoes, veggies, and a chive aioli one week, the oven-roasted duck with pecans and cranberry coulis the next. For something new and different, sample buffalo, moose, antelope, kangaroo, alligator, or northern black bear—they're all farm-raised and low in cholesterol. Upstairs is a taproom, where you can chill out with a bottle of wine or feast from the same menu as downstairs. The dessert list is frighteningly long. ⊠ *31 Bank St.,* ☎ *860/355–3266. AE, MC, V.*

$$ ⬚ **Homestead Inn.** High on a hill overlooking New Milford's town green,
★ the Homestead was built in 1853 and opened as an inn in 1928. Life is casual here, and the owners, Rolf and Peggy Hammer, are always game for a leisurely chat. The extensive breakfast is served in a large, cheery living room, where you can sit by the fire or admire the Steinway piano. The eight rooms in the main house have more personality than those in the motel-style structure next door. ⊠ *5 Elm St., 06776,* ☎ *860/354–4080,* ⅨⅩ *860/354–7046. 14 rooms with bath. CP. AE, D, DC, MC, V.*

Nightlife

In most of the northwest corner of the state, after-dark entertainment means listening to the bug-zapper on the front porch, but in New Milford there's **Poor Henry's** (⊠ 65 Bank St., ☎ 860/355–2274), which has live jazz and other music nightly.

New Preston

㊳ *4 mi north of New Milford.*

The one-horse village of New Preston, perched on the Aspetuck River, has a little town center that's packed with antiques shops, many specializing in folk furniture and fine prints.

Lake Waramaug, just north of New Preston on Route 45, is an area that reminds many of Austria and Switzerland—though it's actually named for Chief Waramaug, one of the most revered figures in Connecticut's Native American history. Drive completely around the lake (8 miles), admiring the beautiful homes and inns—a few of which serve delicious Continental food. The state park of the same name, at the northwest tip, is an idyllic 75-acre spread, great for picnicking.

Dining and Lodging

$$–$$$ ✕ **Doc's Restaurant.** Though in a small nondescript house across from
★ Lake Waramaug, this place with mismatched chairs and tables covered with butcher's paper serves sophisticated Northern Italian food. The designer pizzas are predictable, but everything else is delicious. Try one

of the fresh pastas, the tomato braised lamb shank with Chianti and barley risotto, or sautéed salmon and tuna with sun-dried tomatoes, roasted peppers, leeks, and lemon. ⊠ *Rte. 45 and Flirtation Ave.,* ☎ *860/868–9415. Reservations essential. No credit cards. BYOB. No lunch Wed. Closed Mon., Tues.*

$$$–$$$$ ✕⊞ **Boulders Inn.** This is the most idyllic and prestigious of the inns
★ along Lake Waramaug's uneven shoreline. The Boulders opened in 1940 but still looks like the private home it was at the turn of the last century. Apart from the main house, a carriage house and several guest houses command panoramic views of the countryside and the lake. Rooms contain Victorian antiques and interesting odds and ends. The Boulders's window-lined, stone-wall dining room is outstanding. The exquisite menu includes grilled tuna with a crispy noddle cake and wasabi horseradish cream and marinated duck breast with warm black bean salad. ⊠ *E. Shore Rd. (Rte. 45), 06777,* ☎ *860/868–0541 or 800/552–6853,* FAX *860/868–1925. 15 rooms with bath, 3 suites. Restaurant (no lunch; closed Mon.–Wed. in winter), lake, tennis courts, boating. MAP. AE, MC, V.*

$$$–$$$$ ✕⊞ **Inn on Lake Waramaug.** From many of the antiques-filled bedrooms—some with working fireplaces—you can see Lake Waramaug sparkling through a grove of century-old sugar maples. In the candlelit dining room, new American accents are given to the likes of breast of pheasant and grilled New York strip steak. ⊠ *107 North Shore Rd., 06777,* ☎ *860/868–0563 or 800/525–3466,* FAX *860/868–9173. 23 rooms with bath. Restaurant, indoor pool, tennis courts, recreation room. MAP. AE, MC, V.*

$$–$$$ ✕⊞ **Hopkins Inn.** This grand Victorian, built in 1847 on a hill over-
★ looking Lake Waramaug, is one of the best bargains in the Hills. Rooms have plain white bedspreads, simple antiques, and pastel floral wallpaper. In winter, the whole inn smells of burning firewood; year-round, it is redolent of the aromas coming from the rambling dining rooms, which serve outstanding Swiss and Austrian dishes—calves' brains in black butter, wiener schnitzel, sweetbreads Viennese. When the weather is kind, you can dine on the terrace overlooking the lake. ⊠ *22 Hopkins Rd. (1 mi off Rte. 45), 06777,* ☎ *860/868–7295,* FAX *860/868–7464. 8 rooms with bath, 2 rooms share bath, 1 suite. Restaurant. No credit cards.*

Shopping
Black Swan Antiques (⊠ Main St., ☎ 860/868–2788) sells 17th- and 18th-century English country furniture. **J. Seitz & Co.** (⊠ 9 E. Shore Rd., ☎ 860/868–0119) is known for southwestern antiques and reproduction painted furniture.

Kent

🟢 *12 mi northwest of New Preston; reached from New Milford on Route 7 or from New Preston on Route 341.*

Kent has the area's greatest concentration of art galleries, some nationally renowned. Kent is also home to a prep school of the same name, a long history of ironworks, and the Schaghticoke Indian Reservation. During the Revolutionary War, 100 Schaghticokes helped defend the Colonies: They transmitted messages of army intelligence from the Litchfield Hills to Long Island Sound, along the hilltops, by way of shouts and tom-tom beats. Today, these prominent ridges tower above downtown Kent's bookshops, bakeries, and antiques shops.

One of the state's two covered bridges, **Bulls Bridge,** is still open to cars. Bulls Bridge is said to be where George Washington's horse slipped on a rotted plank and tumbled into the roaring river. It's a few miles south of Kent on Route 7.

The **Sloane–Stanley Museum** was built by the author and artist Eric Sloane, whose work celebrates Early American woodworking and craftsmanship. Iron tools and implements, many from the 17th century, are on display. ⊠ *Rte. 7,* ☎ *860/927–3849 or 860/566–3005.* ☽ *Mid-May–Oct., Wed.–Sun. 10–4.*

Outdoor Activities and Sports

STATE PARK

Macedonia Brook (⊠ Rte. 341), in addition to other activities, has hiking and cross-country ski trails.

Shopping

Pauline's Place (⊠ 79 N. Main St., ☎ 860/927–4475) specializes in Victorian, Georgian, Art Deco, Edwardian, and contemporary jewelry. The **Bachelier-Cardonsky Gallery** (⊠ Main St., ☎ 860/927–3129), one of the foremost galleries in the Northeast, specializes in contemporary works. The **Paris–New York–Kent Gallery** (⊠ Kent Station, off Rte. 7, ☎ 860/927–4152) exhibits contemporary works by local and world-famous artists.

En Route Heading north on Route 7 from Kent toward Cornwall Bridge, you'll pass the entrance to **Kent Falls State Park,** where you can hike a short way to one of the most impressive waterfalls in the state.

Cornwall

40 *12 mi north of Kent.*

Here in Cornwall, among the virgin pines and thick forest, fleeting pockets of civilization came and went throughout the 18th and 19th centuries. Starvation and cold took the lives of most who settled here in the eerily named communities of Mast Swamp, Wildcat, Great Hollow, Crooked Esses, and Ballyhack.

Mohawk Mountain State Park is a great spot for a picnic. The view at the top of Mohawk Mountain (1,683 feet) is breathtaking; the hike up is 2½ miles long. A severe tornado ripped through Cornwall in 1989, and most of the pines snapped like matchsticks—the devastation can still be seen here. The park is off of Route 4, a mile from Cornwall.

Skiing

Mohawk Mountain. This mountain is a busy place midweek, with junior racing programs and special discount days; weekends attract families from nearby metropolitan areas. The 23 trails, ranged down 660 vertical feet, include a lot of terrain for beginners and intermediates, and there are a few steeper sections toward the top of the mountain. ⊠ *Off Rte. 4,* ☎ *860/672–6100 or, for conditions, 860/672–6464.*

West Cornwall

41 *3 mi northwest of Cornwall.*

Oddly, Connecticut's most romantic covered bridge, called Cornwall Bridge, is not in the town of the same name, but several miles up Route 7 in West Cornwall. (The covered bridge in Cornwall Bridge smashed to bits during the great flood of 1936.)

The wooden, barn-red, one-lane **Cornwall Bridge** was built in 1841 and has since carried travelers into the small village of West Cornwall, the site of a few notable crafts shops and restaurants. The bridge, which won national recognition for its superb restoration, incorporates strut techniques that were copied by bridge builders around the country.

Dining

$$–$$$ ✕ **Brookside Bistro.** The softly lighted, airy dining room of this charming spot is within view of the historic covered bridge that spans the Housatonic River. In warm weather, you can dine on a deck overlooking a waterfall. It's cozy in winter, too, with a fire almost always burning in the stone hearth. French country food is the bill of fare here; choose from the likes of coq au vin, escargots, and a great endive salad. ✉ *Rte. 128 (off Rte. 7, just over bridge),* ☎ *860/672–6601. MC, V. Closed Tues., Wed.*

Outdoor Activities and Sports

BOATING

Clarke Outdoors (✉ Rte. 7, ☎ 860/672–6365) offers canoe and kayak rentals as well as 10-mile trips from Falls Village to Housatonic Meadow State Park.

Shopping

Cornwall Bridge Pottery Store (✉ Rte. 128, ☎ 860/672–6545) sells pottery, glass by Simon Pearce, and fine Shaker-style furniture. **Ian Ingersoll Cabinetmakers** (✉ Main St., by the Covered Bridge, ☎ 860/672–6334) offers reproduction Shaker-style rockers and chairs.

Sharon

42 *17 mi west of Cornwall, 24 mi northwest of Litchfield.*

The well-preserved Colonial town of Sharon has a history of Colonial manufacturing—everything from munitions and oxbows to wooden mousetraps was made here. There was even an attempt to introduce the silkworm; it failed because of New England's unwelcoming climate, but the mulberry trees that were planted as part of the experiment still line Main Street. Perhaps the strangest sight in town is the elaborate **Hotchkiss Clock Tower,** which looms importantly above the intersection of Routes 4 and 41. It was built in 1885 of native gray granite as a memorial to town son and inventor of the Hotchkiss explosive shell, Benjamin Berkeley Hotchkiss.

One of the best places to hike in Connecticut is the **Sharon Audubon Center.** In addition to various trails and nature walks, the 684-acre sanctuary is home to many types of birds, a shop, and a library. ✉ *325 Rte. 4,* ☎ *860/364–0520.* ➣ *$3.* ✇ *Mon.–Sat. 9–5, Sun. 1–5; trails dawn–dusk.*

Camping

🏕 **Housatonic Meadows.** This state park offers camping. ✉ *Rte. 7, Sharon.*

Lakeville

43 *9 mi north of Sharon.*

You can usually spot an original Colonial home in Lakeville by looking for the grapevine design cut into the frieze above the front door. It's the apparent trademark of whoever built the town's first homes. Although tradition remains, signs of urban invasion are visible here—fancy inns and restaurants, chic shops.

The lake of Lakeville is **Lake Wononscopomuc,** whose shoreline is lined with attractive weekend homes, well hidden in the foliage. Here and there, as you drive along Routes 44 or 41, you catch a glimpse of its sparkling waters.

The **Holley-Williams House,** an early Classical Revival and Federal mansion that dates to 1808, contains fine furniture, Colonial art, and exquisite glass, silver, and china. John Milton Holley made his money running the Mt. Riga Iron Furnace and later founded the Holley Manufacturing Company, which was the nation's first pocketknife factory. ⊠ *Milllerton Rd., Rte. 44,* ☎ *860/435–2878.* ☉ *Memorial Day–Labor Day.*

The Arts

Music Mountain (⊠ Falls Village, ☎ 860/824–7126) presents chamber music concerts on weekends, with such distinguished guest artists as the Manhattan String Quartet, from mid-June to mid-September.

Outdoor Activities and Sports

AUTO RACING

Lime Rock Park (⊠ Rte. 112, ☎ 860/435–2571 or 860/435–0896) has been home to the best road racing in the Northeast for nearly four decades. Races take place on Saturday and holiday Mondays, late April through mid-October; amphitheater-style lawn seating allows for great views all around.

CANOEING

Riverrunning Expeditions (⊠ Main St., Falls Village, ☎ 860/824–5579) offers canoe rentals, instruction, guides, and trips that begin in Falls Village and end at Cornwall Bridge.

HORSEBACK RIDING

Rustling Wind Stables (⊠ Mountain Rd., Falls Village, ☎ 860/824–7634) gives lessons and takes riders along the beautiful trails of Canaan Mountain.

Salisbury

🟤 *6 mi north of Lakeville.*

Salisbury, were it not for the obsolescence of its ironworks, might today be the largest city in Connecticut. Instead, it settles for having both the state's highest mountain, Bear Mountain (2,355 feet), and its highest point, the shoulder of Mount Frissel (2,380 feet)—whose peak is actually in Massachusetts. There's a spot on Mt. Frissel where you can place various limbs in Connecticut, Massachusetts, and New York.

Iron was discovered here in 1732, and for the next century, the slopes of Salisbury's Mount Riga produced the finest iron in America—Swiss and Russian immigrants, and later Hessian deserters from the British army, worked the great furnaces. These dark, mysterious people inbred and lived in tiny hillside cabins in these parts until well into the 20th century, long after the last forge cast a glow in 1847. "Raggies," as they were known, are cloaked in a legend of black magic and suspicion, and are believed to be responsible for various mishaps and ghostly sightings. As for the ironworks, the spread of rail transport opened up better and more accessible sources of ore, the region's lumber supply was eventually depleted, and the Bessemer process of steel manufacturing—partially invented by Salisbury native Alexander Holley—was introduced. Most signs of cinder heaps and slag dumps are long gone, replaced by grand summer homes and gardens.

NEED A BREAK?

No trip through the region is complete without a brief stop at **Chaiwalla** tea house (⊠ 1 Main St., ☎ 860/435-9758; closed Mon., Tues., and Mar.), just across from the grand White Hart Inn. Choose from more than 20 different kinds of tea and try owner Mary O'Brien's tasty soups, light fare, and scrumptious desserts.

Dining and Lodging

$$–$$$$ ✕🅣 **White Hart Inn.** This celebrated 1815 country inn is furnished
★ throughout with Chippendale reproductions and country pine pieces.
There are three wonderful restaurants here: The Tap Room is a pub-
like space where you can quaff a pint of Guinness while dining on cre-
ative cuisine befitting far fancier restaurants; the Garden Court Room
works off the same menu, but has a brightly lighted, traditional Colo-
nial ambience; and the cushy, elegant Julie's New American Sea Grill
serves such expertly prepared dishes as tea-smoked lobster with red
pepper flan and onion-and-horseradish-crusted salmon. ✉ *The Village
Green, 06068,* ☎ *860/435–0030,* ℻ *860/435–0040. 23 rooms with
bath, 3 suites. 3 restaurants, meeting rooms. AE, DC, MC, V.*

$$$ ✕🅣 **Under Mountain Inn.** The nearest neighbors of this white-clapboard
farmhouse are the horses grazing in the field across the road. There
are antiques, knickknacks, and objets d'art in every corner; chess and
checkers games are set up by the fireplace. The hospitality has a pronounced British flavor; dinner, too, recalls Britain, with a variety of
authentic game dishes and hearty steak-and-kidney pie. ✉ *482 Under
Mountain Rd. (Rte. 41), 06068,* ☎ *860/435–0242,* ℻ *860/435–
2379. 7 rooms with bath. Restaurant (open to public Fri.–Sat., by reservation only), pub, hiking. MC, V.*

$$ ✕🅣 **Ragamont Inn.** The tall white pillars of the 165-year-old down-
town edifice signal a cozy country inn and restaurant. Seven rooms are
furnished in the Colonial style with assorted antiques; three contem-
porary rooms in the annex have king-size beds, color TVs, and air-con-
ditioning; a small suite has a charming sitting room with a fireplace.
✉ *Main St., 06068,* ☎ *860/435–2372. 9 rooms with bath, 1 suite.
Restaurant. No credit cards. Closed Nov.–Apr.*

Shopping

Salisbury Antiques Center (✉ 46 Library St., off Rte. 44, ☎ 860/435–
0424) is one of the largest shops in the region, with a varied collection
of American and English pieces. The center is only open Friday, Sat-
urday, and Sunday from January through March.

Canaan

㊺ *10 mi northeast of Salisbury, 84 mi northeast of Stamford, 42 mi
northwest of Hartford.*

Canaan is one of the more developed towns in the Litchfield region:
It has a McDonald's. Canaan was the site of some important late
18th-century industry, including a gun-barrel factory and a paper mill,
and it's also the home of Captain Gershom Hewitt, who's credited with
securing the plans of Fort Ticonderoga for Ethan Allen.

Canaan Union Station (✉ Rtes. 44 and 7, ☎ 860/824–0339) was built
in 1871 as a train station and now houses a pub-style restaurant and
a few shops. It's one of the oldest train stations in the United States.

Camping

🏕 **Lone Oak Campsites.** This campground has more than 500 sites,
and is open mid-April to mid-October. ✉ *Rte. 44, East Canaan,* ☎
860/824–7051.

Dining

$$–$$$ ✕ **Cannery Cafe.** This quaint, storefront dining room is a chic Amer-
★ ican bistro. Eggshell-color walls are painted with a pattern of gleam-
ing gold stars, and elegant brass fixtures reflect the room's muted
lighting. All is crisp and clean, the service chatty but refined. Smoked-
chicken pot pie, cashew-crusted salmon, and shrimp risotto headline

a regularly retooled menu. ✉ *85 Main St. (Rtes. 44 and 7),* ☎ *860/824–7333. DC, MC, V. Closed Tues.*

Shopping

The **Connecticut Woodcarvers Gallery** (✉ Rte. 44, East Canaan, ☎ 860/824–0883) specializes in the work of professional woodcarvers and stocks Colonial-style eagles, pineapples, birds, clocks, and mirrors.

Norfolk

46 *12 mi east of Canaan, 59 mi north of New Haven.*

Norfolk, thanks to its severe climate and terrain, is one of the best pre-served villages in the Northeast. Notable industrialists have been sum-mering here for two centuries, and several enormous homesteads still exist. At the junction of Routes 182 and 44 is the striking town green. At its southern corner is a fountain—designed by Augustus Saint-Gau-dens and executed by Stanford White—a memorial to Joseph Battell, who turned this town into a major trading center 200 years ago.

The northwest corner of the Norfolk green is anchored by the Music Shed on the grounds of the magnificent Ellen Battell Stoeckel Estate, which is the site of the **Norfolk Chamber Music Festival.**

No gardeners worth their weight in topsoil should miss **Hillside Gar-dens,** one of the foremost nurseries and perennial gardens in the North-east. The garden's 5 acres, surrounded by stone walls and punctuated with a 1780s farmhouse, are a few miles south of the town green and glow from May through September with daffodils, lilies, foxgloves, chrysanthemums, and ornamental grasses. You can purchase most of what you see, and you can picnic on the verdant grounds of adjacent Dennis Hill State Park. ✉ *515 Litchfield Rd. (Rte. 272),* ☎ *860/542–5345,* ✉ *Free.* ☉ *May–mid-Sept., 9–5.*

The Arts

The **Yale School of Music and Art** summer session students and the **Nor-folk Chamber Music Festival** (☎ 203/432–1966 Sept.–May or 860/542–3000 June–Aug.) perform Friday and Saturday evenings and some Sunday afternoons at the Music Shed on the Ellen Battell Stoeckel Es-tate, which is at the convergence of Routes 44 and 272.

Dining and Lodging

$–$$ ✕ **The Pub.** Norfolk lacked a proper dining venue until a few years ago,
★   when a former owner of Ridgefield's Stonehenge, David Davis, bought the town pub and magically reinvented it as a tavern where visiting antiques hunters mingle merrily—if warily—with local deer hunters. The restaurant, on the ground floor of a redbrick Victorian near the town green, still has plenty of cheap everyday grub and a down-to-earth pubby atmosphere, where trendy beer bottles line the shelves. In addition to the burgers and pizzas, however, are such upscale or un-usual listings as strip steak and lamb curry. This is a real melting pot. ✉ *Rte. 44,* ☎ *860/542–5716. AE, MC, V. Closed Mon.*

$$$$ ▦ **Greenwoods Gate.** This neatly preserved Colonial is possibly the
★   state's foremost romantic hideaway. In each of the four suites, beds are covered in starched white linens. The Levi Thompson Suite is the most interesting: A short flight of stairs leads to a small sitting area with a cathedral ceiling; from here, two additional staircases, which have solid cherry hand-tapered railings, lead to either side of an enor-mous master bed. A spacious two-bedroom suite with its own den and library is the inn's most popular accommodation, so reserve well

ahead. ⊠ *105 Greenwoods Rd. E (Rte. 44), 06058,* ☎ *860/542–5439.*
4 suites. Full breakfast included. No credit cards.

$$–$$$ 🖵 **Manor House.** This unusual Bavarian Tudor residence, built and de-
   ★   signed in 1898 by the architect of London's subway system, Charles
Spofford, is one of the most charming bed-and-breakfasts in the state.
Innkeepers Diane and Hank Tremblay run a first-rate establishment
and always take time to get to know their guests. Among the house's
remarkable features are 20 stained-glass windows designed and given
by Louis Tiffany; one room with its own private wood-paneled elevator; and an extensive array of characterful bibelots, mirrors, carpets,
antique beds, and prints. ⊠ *Box 447, Maple Ave., 06058,* ☎ FAX
860/542–5690. 7 rooms with bath, 1 suite. Full breakfast included.
AE, D, MC, V.

Outdoor Activities and Sports

HORSE-AND-CARRIAGE RIDES

The **Loon Meadow Farm Horse & Carriage Livery Service** (⊠ Loon
Meadow Dr., ☎ 860/542–6085) gives horse-drawn sleigh, hay, and
carriage rides.

STATE PARKS

Dennis Hill (⊠ Rte. 272) has picnic facilities. You'll find plenty of hiking trails at **Haystack Mountain** (⊠ Rte. 272).

Shopping

Artisans Guild (⊠ Greenwoods Rd. E, ☎ 860/542–5487) carries local
crafts—from personalized enameled eggs to unique arrangements of
wild and cultivated flowers.

Winsted

🔢 *9 southeast of Norfolk, 28 mi north of Waterbury, 25 mi northwest*
of Hartford.

Winsted still looks a bit like the set of a Frank Capra movie, with its
rows of old homes and businesses seemingly untouched since the
1940s. Although far less fashionable than its neighbor Norfolk to the
west, it's still worth a brief stop. Here you can contemplate the devastation wreaked upon the town in 1955, when a major flood destroyed
many homes and took lives. Or you can drive around the hills and alongside the reservoirs, hoping to glimpse the notorious "Winsted Wild Man,"
who has been described during sightings that span a couple centuries
as possessing everything from cloven feet to an upright, eight-foot and
hairy, 300-pound frame. Authorities explain away these stories as
black bear sightings, but you never know.

The more than 500 hanging and standing kerosene-powered lamps date
mostly from 1852 to 1880 at the **Kerosene Lamp Museum,** which occupies a former gristmill. ⊠ *100 Old Waterbury Turnpike (Rte. 263),*
Winchester Center (4 mi from Winchester), ☎ *860/379–2612.* 🖼
Free. ☉ *Daily 9:30–4.*

Camping

⛺ **White Pines Campground.** There are 206 sites and swimming, hiking, and fishing on the premises of this campground. ⊠ *232 Old*
North Rd., ☎ *860/379–0124.*

Nightlife

Winsted's downtown has a few bars. The **Gilson Cafe and Cinema** (⊠
354 Main St., ☎ 860/379–6069), a refurbished Art Deco movie house,
serves food and drinks unobtrusively during the movie, evenings Tuesday through Sunday. You must be 21 or older.

Outdoor Activities and Sports

CANOEING

Main Stream Canoe Corp. (⊠ Rte. 44, New Hartford, ☎ 860/693–6791) does flatwater and whitewater day trips on the Farmington River and moonlight trips on summer evenings. Equipment rentals are available March through November, weekends only.

TUBING

North American Canoe Tours (⊠ Rte. 44, Satan's Kingdom State Recreation Area, New Hartford, ☎ 860/739–0791) offers exhila_____g self-guided tubing tours along the Farmington River from Me_____al Day through June on weekends only and daily from June throu____abor Day.

Shopping

Folkcraft Instruments (⊠ Corner of High and Whee_____ts., ☎ 860/379–9857) crafts harps and psalteries on the premi_____and is a great place to learn to play the dulcimer.

Skiing

Ski Sundown. This area has some neat_____hes—a sundeck on the mountain and a Mountaineers social clu____ skiers 57 and older—as well as excellent facilities and equipmen_____he mountain is impressive for Connecticut. The vertical drop is 6____eet, and most trails (15 lighted at night) are for beginners and inter_____ates; there's one advanced run. ⊠ *New Hartford,* ☎ *860/379–9___1, or, for conditions, 860/379–7669.*

Riverton

48 *6 mi north of_____sted.*

Almost eve____New Englander has sat in a Hitchcock chair, and visitors still____ve up to Riverton (formerly Hitchcockville) to see where Lamb____Hitchcock built the first one in 1826. The Farmington and Stil____vers meet in this tiny hamlet, and it's one of the more unspoiled ____ons in the Hills—great for hiking and driving.

The **Hitchcock Museum** is in the gray granite Union Church; the nearby Hitchcock furniture shop (☎ 860/379–4826) is open daily, year-round. ⊠ *Rte. 20,* ☎ *860/738–4950.* ▨ *Donation suggested.* ☉ *Apr.–Dec., Thurs.–Sun. noon–4.*

Dining and Lodging

$$ ✕▥ **Old Riverton Inn.** This rickety blue inn, built in 1796 and overlooking the Still River and the Hitchcock Chair Factory, is a wonderfully peaceful weekend retreat. Rooms are small—except for the fireplace suite—and the decorating is ordinary, but the inn always delivers warm hospitality. The inviting dining room serves ordinary traditional New England fare. ⊠ *Rte. 20, 06065,* ☎ *860/379–8678 or 800/378–1796,* FAX *860/379–1006. 11 rooms with bath, 1 suite. Restaurant. AE, D, DC, MC, V.*

Torrington

49 *14 mi south of Riverton.*

The raggedly industrial city of Torrington is birthplace of abolitionist John Brown and of Gail Borden, who developed the first successful method for the production of evaporated milk. Torrington's pines were for years used for shipbuilding, and factories produced brass kettles, needles, pins, and bicycle spokes. Its heyday was largely prior to World War II; nowadays it seems as though most of the attractive homes here are funeral parlors, and strip malls are the only sign of progress.

The **Hotchkiss-Fyler House,** a turn-of-the-century Victorian, is one of the better house-museums in the state, containing 16 rooms of elegant mahogany period pieces and hand-stenciled walls. ⊠ *192 Main St.,* ☎ *860/482–8260.* ☉ *Tours Apr.–Dec., weekdays 9–4, Sat. 10–3.*

OFF THE BEATEN PATH

GOSHEN – Five miles west of Torrington, Goshen was once a dairy farming center. On Labor Day weekend it has one of the best agricultural fairs in the Northeast.

The Arts

The **Warner Theatre** (⊠ 68 Main St., ☎ 860/489–7180), a former Art Deco movie palace, presents live Broadway musicals, ballet, and concerts by touring pop and classical musicians.

Lodging

$$–$$$ ⊡ **Yankee Peddlar Inn.** This brick-trim century-old inn, in the heart of a somewhat glum little city has rooms that are now modern and even characterful, if a little musty. It's nothing fancy, but it's a good value and is run by friendly folks. ⊠ *93 Main St., 06790,* ☎ *860/489–9226 or 800/777–1891,* FAX *860/482–7851. 58 rooms with bath, 2 suites. Restaurant, bar. Full breakfast included. AE, D, DC, MC, V.*

Outdoor Activities and Sports

STATE PARK

Burr Pond (⊠ Rte. 8) offers many facilities, from canoe rentals to wheelchair-accessible picnic shelters.

Litchfield

50 *5 mi south of Torrington, 48 mi north of Bridgeport, 34 mi west of Hartford.*

Litchfield Hills' wealthiest and most noteworthy town is Litchfield. Everything here seems to exist on a larger scale than in neighboring towns: Enormous white Colonials line broad, majestic elm-shaded streets.

Litchfield Green is surrounded by old shops and restaurants and is the most impressive green for miles around. This is the town where Aaron Burr, Horace Mann, John C. Calhoun, and Noah Webster earned law degrees. It's also where Harriet Beecher Stowe and Henry Ward Stowe were born and raised, and where, during the infamous Stove Wars of the late 18th century, worshipers vehemently debated the burning issue of whether a church would retain its sanctity if heated by a stove. By 1790, with a population exceeding 20,000, Litchfield had become the third most populous town in America.

Near the village green is the **Tapping Reeve House,** America's first law school, which was founded in 1773 and is now a museum. In addition to the prominent graduates listed above, alums include six U.S. cabinet members, 26 U.S. senators, more than 100 congressmen, and dozens of Supreme Court justices, governors, and college presidents. ⊠ *82 South St.,* ☎ *860/567–4501.* ⊡ *Combined ticket to Litchfield Historical Society Museum (☞ below) and Reeve House $3.* ☉ *Mid-May–mid-Oct., Tues.–Sat. 11–5, Sun. 1–5.*

The **Litchfield Historical Society Museum** has several well-organized galleries exhibiting decorative arts, paintings, and antique furnishings, as well as an extensive reference library. You can also find information on the town's many historic buildings, including Harriet Beecher Stowe's birthplace; the Sheldon Tavern, where George Washington slept on several occasions; and the Pierce Academy, America's first school for girls. ⊠ *Rtes. 63 and 118, 7 South St.* ☎ *860/567–4501.* ⊡ *Com-*

bined ticket to Reeve House (☞ above) and Historical Society Museum $3. ☺ Mid-Apr.–mid-Nov.

Whether to buy or to browse, a stroll through the grounds of **White Flower Farm** is a pleasure for any gardening lover. It's the home base of a mail-order operation where much of America buys its perennials and bulbs. ☒ *Rte. 63 (3 mi south of Litchfield),* ☎ *860/567–8789. ☺ Oct.–Mar., daily 10–5; Apr.–Sept., daily 9–5:30.*

Haight Vineyard and Winery flourishes despite the town's severe climate. Stop in for vineyard walks, winery tours, and tastings. ☒ *Chestnut Hill Rd., Rte. 118 (1 mi east of Litchfield),* ☎ *860/567–4045. ▨ Free. ☺ Mon.–Sat. 10:30–5, Sun. noon–5.*

Lourdes of Litchfield Shrine was built and is operated by the Montfort Missionaries. The 35-acre complex contains a replica of the famous grotto at Lourdes, France, and during pilgrimage season, May through mid-October, outdoor mass is held Sundays at 11:30; Holy Hour is at 3. Picnickers are welcome any time. It's a short drive from the village green. ☒ *Rte. 118,* ☎ *860/567–1041. ☺ Grounds year-round.*

The state's largest nature center and wildlife sanctuary is the 4,000-acre **White Memorial Foundation.** Besides 35 miles of hiking, cross-country skiing, and horseback-riding trails, the sanctuary has fishing areas, bird-watching platforms, two self-guided nature trails, and several boardwalks. The main conservation center has natural history exhibits and a gift shop. ☒ *Rte. 202 (2 mi west of village green),* ☎ *860/567–0857. ▨ Grounds free; conservation center $2. ☺ Grounds daily; conservation center spring–fall, Mon.–Sat. 9–5, Sun. noon–4, and winter, Mon.–Sat. 8:30–4:30, Sun. noon–4.*

OFF THE
BEATEN PATH

BANTAM – A small, not especially picturesque village 4 miles southwest of Litchfield, Bantam has some good antiques and crafts shops and boutiques. **Gilyard's Antiques** (☒ Rte. 202, ☎ 860/567–4204) sells 18th- and 19th-century country furniture and decorative items. **Gooseboro Brook Antiques** (☒ 38 Old Turnpike Rd., ☎ 860/567–5245) carries antique furniture, baskets, quilts, stoneware, and collectibles.

LOCK MUSEUM OF AMERICA – There are some 20,000 items displayed at the nation's largest collection of locks, keys, and ornate hardware. ☒ 130 Main St. (Rte. 6), Terryville (13 mi southeast of Litchfield), ☎ 203/66589-6359. ▨ $2. ☺ May–Oct., daily 1:30–4:30.

Dining and Lodging

$$$ ✕ **West Street Grill.** The creative chef here, Fredrick Favoux, and the
★ friendly staff are always roving about, making sure their customers are not just satisfied, but enraptured. This small, unpretentious dining room on Litchfield's quaint shopping street is the favorite of local glitterati, but all are warmly welcomed. If you start off with the grilled peasant breads topped with roasted tomatoes and goat cheese or a Parmesan aioli, you'll have a tough time making room for one of the imaginative grilled fish, poultry, and lamb dishes, served with fresh vegetables. ☒ *43 West St. (Rte. 202),* ☎ *203/567–3885. AE, MC, V.*

$–$$$ ✕ **Village Restaurant.** The folks who run this storefront eatery in a charming redbrick town house serve food as tasty as any in town—inexpensive pub grub in one room, so-called new New England cuisine in the other. Whether you order burgers or polenta with wild mushrooms, you'll get plenty to eat. ☒ *25 West St.,* ☎ *860/567–8307. AE, MC, V.*

$–$$ ✕ **Grappa.** Yet another branch has sprouted from the tree that began as James O'Shea's beloved West Street Grill. O'Shea and his partner, Charles Kafferman, have dreamt up a small, intimate pizza-and-pasta café with cute upholstered booths, creamy yellow and white walls, and plenty of indirect lighting and mirrors. The pizzas are the star of the show: One is dappled with chévre, fresh veggies, and generous doses of roasted garlic. If you're especially hungry, the starter salad of white beans and roasted eggplant is delicious. ⊠ *Litchfield Common,* ☎ *860/567–1616. AE, MC, V. No lunch. Closed Mon., Tues.*

$$$–$$$$ ✕▥ **Tollgate Hill Inn and Restaurant.** The 250-year-old Tollgate, formerly a way station for weary Colonials stagecoaching between Hartford and Albany, retains a romantic tavern atmosphere. The menu, however, is clearly contemporary: Grilled salmon roulade with citrus-cilantro pesto and walnut-crusted roast rack of lamb with apple-dried cherry chutney are likely choices. Rooms in the main building, in a nearby schoolhouse, and in a modern building are decorated Colonial-style; many have canopy beds and working fireplaces. The only drawback is being a few miles from the town center on an extremely busy road. Still, the road is not visible through the dense evergreens surrounding the property. ⊠ *Rte. 202 (2 mi east of Litchfield Center),* ☎ *860/567–4545* ℻ *860/567–8397. 15 rooms with bath, 5 suites. Restaurant (closed Mon. and Tues., Jan.–Mar.). CP. AE, D, DC.*

Outdoor Activities and Sports
FISHING

Trout season runs from mid-April through February; a license is required. Pick up some gear at **Bantam Sportsman** (⊠ Lake Rd., ☎ 860/567–8517).

HORSEBACK RIDING

Lee's Riding Stables (⊠ 57 E. Litchfield Rd., ☎ 860/567–0785) gives trail and pony rides.

STATE PARK

Mt. Tom (⊠ Rte. 202) has boating in fishing in summer and ice-skating in winter.

Shopping

The **P. S. Gallery** (⊠ On-the-Green, ☎ 860/567–1059) is an excellent general fine-arts gallery.

Bristol

🖲 *17 mi southeast of Litchfield.*

There were some 275 clockmakers in and around Bristol during the late 1800s, and it is said that by the turn of the century just about every household in America told time to a Connecticut clock. Eli Terry (for which nearby Terryville is named) first mass-produced clocks in the mid-19th century, and Seth Thomas (for which nearby Thomaston is named) learned under Terry and carried on the tradition.

You can see examples of more than 1,800 New England–made clocks and watches at the **American Clock and Watch Museum,** one of the most interesting and charming museums in the state. Try to arrive on the hour, when 300 clocks strike in close succession. ⊠ *100 Maple St., south of Rte. 6,* ☎ *860/583–6070.* ☞ *$3.50.* ☉ *Apr.–Nov., daily 10–5.*

Bethlehem

🖲 *16 mi west of Bristol.*

Of course, come Christmas, Bethlehem is the most popular town in Connecticut. Cynics say that towns such as Canaan, Goshen, and

Bethlehem were named primarily with the hope of attracting prospective residents and not truly out of religious deference. In any case, the local post office has its hands full postmarking the 220,000 pieces of holiday greetings mailed here every December.

In mid-December, the **Bethlehem Christmas Town Festival** (☎ 203/266–5702) draws quite a crowd, and yes, there's even a **Christmas Shop** (✉ 18 East St., ☎ 203/266–7048) that hawks the trimmings and trappings of happy holidays year-round.

Washington

53 *11 mi west of Bethlehem.*

Washington is one of the best-preserved Colonial towns in the state. The beautiful buildings of the Gunnery prep school mingle with stately Colonials and churches, all set together on a sunny mound of old New England money. The Mayflower Inn, just south of the Gunnery on Route 47, attracts an exclusive clientele. Washington was settled in 1734, and in 1779 became the first town in our young nation to be named for our heroic statesman and general.

NEED A BREAK?
Past the Gunnery, at the intersection of Routes 47 and 109, you'll discover one of the best bookstores in the region, the **Hickory Stick Bookshop** (✉ Titus Sq., ☎ 860/868–0525), and behind it a small clapboard deli called simply **The Pantry** (☎ 860/868–0258), where you can find all the makings of a gourmet picnic lunch.

Dining and Lodging

$$–$$$ ✕ **Bee Brook.** You'll find delightful variations on new American cuisine here: Many dishes are served with Asian influences such as lemongrass, ginger, wasabi paste, and *nori* (a Japanese seaweed). The dining room is simple, cleanly defined, and well lighted—not the least bit jarring as so many trendy new eateries are today. In summer, lunch on the outdoor patio or deck overlooking the Shepaug River is a good way to spend the afternoon. ✉ *Rte. 47, Washington Depot,* ☎ *860/868–6633. AE, MC, V. Closed Tues.*

$$$$ ✕▦ **Mayflower Inn.** Though certain suites at this inn will set you back $495 a night, the place is always booked well ahead (and with guests who are only a tad livelier than the Joshua Reynolds portrait in the living room). Streams and trails crisscross the 28-acre grounds. The inn is impeccably decorated: Guest rooms have fine antiques and four-poster canopied beds. The mouth-watering cuisine of chef Christopher Freeman includes New York strip steak and Maine shellfish risotto. Many weekends from August through October are sold out as early as one year ahead. ✉ *118 Woodbury Rd. (Rte. 47), 06793,* ☎ *860/868–9466, ⅢX 860/868–1497. 17 rooms with bath, 8 suites. Restaurant, pool, tennis courts, health club, meeting rooms. AE, MC, V.*

En Route
The **Institute for American Studies,** between Roxbury and Washington, is an excellent and thoughtfully arranged collection of exhibits and displays that details the history of the state's Native Americans. Highlights include a replicated longhouse inside and nature trails on the grounds. The Institute is at the end of a forested residential road (just follow the signs). ✉ *Curtiss Rd. (off Rte. 199),* ☎ *860/868–0518. ▣ $4. ⊙ Apr.–Dec., Mon.–Sat. 10–5, Sun. noon–5. Closed Jan.–Mar., Mon. and Tues.*

Roxbury

54 *7 mi south of Washington.*

There's really not a whole lot to do or see in Roxbury. But you can drive around hoping to spot one of this artist colony's prestigious residents, who include Richard Widmark, William Styron, Arthur Miller, Walter Matthau, and Philip Roth. A couple of centuries ago, you might have bumped into a Revolutionary hero or two, including the likes of Ethan Allen, Seth Warner, and the not-easily-forgotten Remember Baker. If you don't happen to brush with fame, you'll at least spot several outstanding examples of Colonial architecture, mostly around the intersections of Routes 317, 67, and 199.

Bridgewater

55 *5 mi southwest of Roxbury, 7 mi southeast of New Milford.*

Architecture buffs will want to visit this tiny hamlet to see its dozens of restored Colonial homes. Bridgewater is best known as the home of Charles B. Thompson, father of the mail-order business. In the late 18th century, Thompson began selling dolls, toys, housewares, and lotions out of his home, a novel practice that soon caused the town's diminutive post office to burst at the seams from the ensuing flood of orders. Today, the ornately Victorian general store and post office out of which Thompson's store was run is an architectural landmark. Locals still remember the days when a dungaree-clad Marilyn Monroe, then married to Arthur Miller, bought her groceries here.

Woodbury

56 *12 mi east of Bridgewater.*

Woodbury is known these days for two things: its antiques and its churches. There may very well be more antiques shops in this quickly growing town than in the rest of the Litchfield Hills combined. The five magnificent **churches** and the Greek Revival **King Solomon's Temple,** formerly a Masonic lodge, line Route 6; they represent some of the finest preserved examples of Colonial religious architecture in New England.

The **Glebe House** is the large gambrel-roofed Colonial in which Dr. Samuel Seabury was elected America's first Episcopal bishop in 1783. Inside is an excellent collection of antiques; outside is a noteworthy garden, designed by renowned horticulturist Gertrude Jekyll. ✉ *Hollow Rd.,* ☎ *203/263–2855.* ✆ *Apr.–Nov.*

Dining and Lodging

$$–$$$ ✕ **Good News Cafe.** Carole Peck is a kitchenhold name in these parts,
★ and her decision to open a restaurant in Woodbury was met with cheers by all. The emphasis is on healthful, innovative fare: buffalo steak and onion skewers with ale sauce and gnocchi; wok-seared shrimp with new potatoes, grilled green beans, and a garlic aioli. Or, you can just bounce in for cappuccino and munchies—there's a separate room just for this purpose, decorated with a fascinating collection of vintage radios. Prices are extremely fair for such tasty creations, and sharing is encouraged for only a nominal fee. ✉ *694 Main St. S,* ☎ *203/266–4663. AE, MC, V. Closed Tues.*

$–$$ ✕ **Charcoal Chef.** Sprung straight from the 1950s, this classic American grilled-food eatery is the real thing. Within its knotty pine–paneled walls, feast on charcoal-grilled halibut, chicken, steak, or burgers, served with a baked potato or fries and coleslaw. It's just the kind of honest place to go after a day in the country—and the bartender pours generous drinks. ✉ *670 Main St. N (Rte. 6 on the way to Watertown),* ☎ *203/263–2538. No credit cards.*

$ ✕🍴 **Curtis House.** Connecticut's oldest inn (1754), at the foot of Woodbury's antiques row, may also be its cheapest. If you arrive with modest expectations, you should have a great time. The inn has seen dozens of alterations and renovations over the years, but the floorboards still creak like whoopie cushions, and the TVs in some rooms look to be from the Ed Sullivan era. A fireplace roars downstairs and the furnishings vary from genuinely antique to just plain old. The restaurant serves heavy and filling steak-and-potato-type dishes in an ancient dining room. ✉ *506 Main St. (Rte. 6), 06798,* ☎ *203/263–2101. 8 rooms with bath, 6 rooms share 3 baths. Restaurant. MC, V.*

$–$$$ 🍴 **Tucker Hill Inn.** This is not truly an inn but a proper, contemporary
★   bed-and-breakfast run out of the 1923 Colonial-style clapboard home of Susan Cebelenski. Spacious rooms come with cable TV and VCR and country-style furnishings. The location is great—about 40 minutes from both New Haven and Hartford in the Litchfield foothills. ✉ *96 Tucker Hill Rd., Middlebury 06762,* ☎ *203/758–8334,* FAX *203/598–0652. 2 rooms with bath, 2 rooms share bath. Full breakfast included. AE, MC, V.*

Shopping

British Country Antiques (✉ 50 Main St. N, ☎ 203/263–5100) imports polished pine and country furniture from England and France. **Country Loft Antiques** (✉ 555 Main St. S, ☎ 203/266–4500) sells 18th- and 19th-century French furniture and accessories. **David Dunton** (✉ Rte. 132 off Rte. 47, ☎ 203/263–5355) is one of the foremost dealers of formal antiques in the country. **Mill House Antiques** (✉ 1068 Main St. N, ☎ 203/263–3446), closed on Tuesday, has formal and country English and French furniture and the state's largest collection of Welsh dressers. **Monique Shay** (✉ 920 Main St. S, ☎ 203/263–3186) carries French-Canadian country antiques.

Southbury

57   *6 mi south of Woodbury, 36 mi south of Winsted, 18 mi northwest of New Haven.*

Southbury has a number of well-preserved Colonial homes and quite a few antiques shops. Unfortunately, you'll also find that this former agricultural community has been heavily developed and, like New Milford to the west, the town now acts as the bridge between southern Connecticut's modern suburbia and the Litchfield Hills' pre-20th-century charm.

Lodging

$$–$$$ 🍴 **Heritage Inn.** You may be disappointed if you come here expecting to find a quaint country inn—rooms and public areas have a contrived rusticity about them. Still, as far as resorts go, the Heritage has plenty to offer. The inn has several meal plans that are a good value. ✉ *Heritage Village, 06488,* ☎ *203/264–8200 or 800/932–3466,* FAX *203/264–5035. 160 rooms, 3 suites. Restaurant, bar, golf, tennis courts, recreation room. AE, D, DC, MC, V.*

Outdoor Activities and Sports

HORSE-AND-CARRIAGE RIDES
Gems Morgan (✉ 75 N. Poverty Rd., ☎ 203/264–6196) gives horse-drawn hay and carriage rides using registered Morgan Horses.

Rides above the Hills are offered year-round by **Steppin' Up Balloons** (☎ 203/264–0013).

Shopping

The **Beaux-Arts Gallery** (✉ 348 Main St., ☎ 203/264–9911) has the work of many regionally and nationally recognized artists.

Waterbury

58 *15 mi northeast of Southbury, 28 mi southwest of Hartford and 28 mi north of Bridgeport.*

Waterbury, today one of America's gloomiest cities, is nevertheless home to a large and diverse historic district. The 60-acre downtown district, which flourished around the turn of the century as the cradle of the U.S. brass industry, comprises nearly 50 important buildings. The dramatic 240-foot **Clock Tower** (✉ 389 Meadow St.) was modeled after the city hall tower in Siena, Italy.

Pick up literature at the **Waterbury Region Convention and Visitors Bureau** (✉ 83 Bank St., 06721, ☎ 203/597–9527) to take a self-guided walking tour of the town. The tour is detailed and fascinating—even if you aren't an architecture buff. It starts from the Mattatuck Museum at 144 W. Main Street.

The **Mattatuck Museum** has a fine collection of 19th- and 20th-century Connecticut art and memorabilia documenting the state's rich industrial history. ✉ *144 W. Main St.,* ☎ *203/753–0381,* 🎫 *Free.* ☉ *Tues.–Sat. 10–5, Sun. noon–5 (except July–Aug.).*

Dining

$$$ ✕ **Diorio Restaurant and Bar.** During its heyday as America's brass cap-
★   ital, Waterbury had a downtown notable for its dining and nightlife. Neglected for several decades following World War II, the city is now being resuscitated. One major cog in the urban renewal machine was the re-opening of Diorio, which had been for a half-century the premier fine Italian restaurant in Waterbury. The dining room retains its original mahogany bankers' booth, marble brass bar, high tin ceilings, exposed brick, and white-tile floors. Any dish off the long, impressive menu is expertly prepared, from the juicy shrimp scampi to the dozens of pastas, chicken, veal, and seafood plates. ✉ *231 Bank St.,* ☎ *203/754–5111. AE, DC, MC, V. No lunch Sat. Closed Sun.*

Outdoor Activities and Sports

Rides above the Litchfield Hills are offered year-round by **Watershed Balloons** (✉ Watertown, ☎ 860/274–2010).

Litchfield Hills A to Z

Getting Around

Northwestern Connecticut is a Sunday driver's paradise. Narrow roads wind over precarious ridges, past antiques shops and soup-and-sandwich pantries, and through the occasional covered bridge. From New York, take I–684 to I–84, from which Exits 7 through 18 lead you northward into the Hills. From Hartford, it's most direct to follow Routes 44 west and 6 south. Favorite roads for admiring fall foliage and sprawling farmsteads are Route 7, from New Milford through Kent and West Cornwall to Canaan; Routes 41 to 4 from Salisbury through Lakeville, Sharon, Cornwall Bridge, and Goshen to Torrington; and Routes 47 to 202 to 341 from Woodbury through Washington, New

Preston, Lake Waramaug, and Warren to Kent. Roads and intersections are well marked, but a good map is helpful.

Contacts and Resources

EMERGENCIES

New Milford Hospital (✉ 21 Elm St., ☎ 860/355–2611). **Sharon Hospital** (✉ 50 Hospital Hill Rd., ☎ 860/364–4141). **Winsted Memorial Hospital** (✉ 115 Spencer St., ☎ 860/738–6600).

LATE-NIGHT PHARMACY

CVS Pharmacy (✉ 627 Farmington Ave., Bristol, ☎ 860/583–8351) is open 24 hours.

STATE PARKS

For detailed information on any parks mentioned in this section, contact the **State Parks Division Bureau of Outdoor Recreation** (✉ 79 Elm St., Hartford 06106, ☎ 860/424–3200).

VISITOR INFORMATION

Litchfield Hills Travel Council (✉ Box 968, Litchfield 06759, ☎ 860/567–4506).

NEW HAVEN AND THE SOUTHEASTERN COAST

As you drive east along I–95, culturally rich New Haven is the final urban obstacle between southwestern Connecticut's overdeveloped coast and southeastern Connecticut's quieter shoreline villages. The remainder of the jagged coast, which stretches all the way to the Rhode Island border, consists of small coastal villages, quiet hamlets, and undisturbed beaches. Along this mostly undeveloped seashore, the only interruptions are the industry and piers of New London and Groton. Mystic, Stonington, Old Saybrook, and Guilford claim the bulk of antiques and boutiques aficionados. North of Groton, in the heretofore seldom-visited town of Ledyard, the Mashantucket Pequots Reservation owns and operates Foxwoods, the controversial casino that has quickly become the East Coast's greatest gaming facility outside of Atlantic City.

Numbers in the margin correspond to points of interest on the Southeastern Connecticut map.

New Haven

🟡 *46 mi northeast of Greenwich, 36 mi south of Hartford, 59 mi southeast of Norfolk.*

New Haven is a city of extremes: Although the historic area surrounding Yale University and the shops, museums, theaters, and restaurants on nearby **Chapel Street** prosper, roughly 20% of the city's residents live below the poverty level. Stay near the campus and city common, especially at night, and get a good map.

New Haven is a manufacturing center dating to the 19th century, but the city owes its fame to Elihu Yale. In 1718, a donation by wealthy Yale enabled the Collegiate School, founded in 1701, to settle in New Haven, where it changed its name to **Yale University** to honor its benefactor. The university provides knowledgeable guides for one-hour walking tours that include Connecticut Hall in the Old Campus, which once housed the young Nathan Hale, William Howard Taft, and Noah Webster, not to mention George Bush and Bill and Hilary Clinton. ✉ *344 College St., Phelps Gateway,* ☎ *203/432–2300.* ⊘ *Tours week-*

Southeastern Connecticut

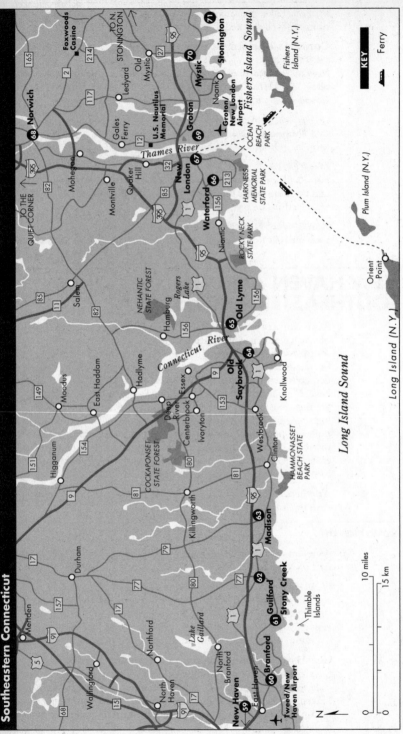

KEY

⚓ Ferry

Long Island Sound

Fishers Island Sound

Long Island (N.Y.)

Fishers Island (N.Y.)

Plum Island (N.Y.)

Orient Point

TO N. STONINGTON

71 Stonington

70 Mystic

Foxwoods Casino

Noank

Groton/New London Airport

Groton

69 New London

67

66 Waterford

Niantic

213

HARKNESS MEMORIAL STATE PARK

OCEAN BEACH PARK

ROCKY NECK STATE PARK

Old Mystic

Ledyard

Gales Ferry

U.S. Nautilus Memorial

Thames River

Quaker Hill

Mohegan

Montville

Norwich 68

TO THE QUIET CORNER

Salem

NEHANTIC STATE FOREST

Rogers Lake

Hamburg

65 Old Lyme

Connecticut River

Moodus

East Haddam

Hadlyme

156

64 Old Saybrook

Knollwood

Higganum

Deep River

Essex

Centerbrook

Ivoryton

Westbrook

Clinton

HAMMONASSET BEACH STATE PARK

COCKAPONSET STATE FOREST

Durham

Killingworth

63 Madison

Northford

Lake Gaillard

Stony Creek 62

Thimble Islands

Guilford 61

Wallingford

North Branford

North Haven

Branford 60

59 New Haven

East Haven

Tweed/New Haven Airport

Meriden

10 miles

15 km

N

days at 10:30 and 2, weekends at 1:30. Tours start from 149 Elm St. on north side of New Haven Green.

James Gamble Rogers, an American architect, designed many buildings for Yale, his alma mater, including the **Sterling Memorial Library** (✉ 120 High St., ☎ 203/432–2798), which he built to be "a cathedral of knowledge and a temple of learning." This is evident in the major interior area, which resembles a Gothic cathedral. The **Beinecke Rare Book Library** (✉ 121 Wall St., ☎ 203/432–2977) houses major collections, including a Gutenberg Bible, illuminated manuscripts, and original Audubon bird prints. The **Yale Art Gallery,** the country's oldest college art museum, contains American, African, and Near and Far Eastern art, as well as Renaissance paintings and European art of the 20th century. Don't miss the remarkable reconstruction of a Mithraic shrine. ✉ *1111 Chapel St.,* ☎ *203/432–0600.* 🎟 *Free.* ☉ *Tues.–Sat. 10–4:45, Sun. 2–4:45.*

☾ The **Peabody Museum of Natural History** opened in 1876; it has amassed more than 9 million specimens and grown into one of the largest natural history museums in the nation. Some of the best exhibits cover dinosaurs, meteorites, and Andean, Mesoamerican, and Pacific cultures. ✉ *170 Whitney Ave.,* ☎ *203/432–5050.* 🎟 *$5.* ☉ *Mon.–Sat. 10–4:45, Sun. 12–4:45.*

The **Yale Center for British Art** has probably the best collection of British art outside of Britain itself. The center's skylit galleries, designed by Louis I. Kahn, are graced by original works by Constable, Hogarth, Gainesborough, Reynolds, and Turner, to name but a few. You'll also find rare books and paintings documenting English history from the 16th century to the present. ✉ *1080 Chapel St.,* ☎ *203/432–2800.* 🎟 *Free.* ☉ *Tues.–Sat. 10–5, Sun. noon–5.*

NEED A
BREAK?

The cheerful **Atticus Bookstore-Cafe** (✉ 1082 Chapel St., ☎ 203/776–4040), adjacent to the Yale Center for British Art, is a funky hangout for hungry bookworms and cappuccino lovers—and it's open daily 8 AM until midnight. Lower of brow but far higher of culinary significance, **Louis' Lunch** (✉ Crowne St., between High and College Sts., ☎ 203/562–5507. ☉ Mon.–Wed. 11 AM–4 PM, Thurs.–Sat. 11 AM–2 AM. Closed Sunday), a minuscule redbrick box with batten doors, looks as if it might house some secret Yale society; in fact, it is the birthplace of America's beloved hamburger.

The most notable example of the Yale campus's traditional university-style neo-Gothic architecture is the **Harkness Tower** (✉ High St.), with its famous motto, sometimes described as the world's greatest anticlimax: "For God, for country, and for Yale." Bordered by the Yale campus on one side, the **New Haven Green** (✉ Between Church and College Sts.) offers impressive architecture as well as a superb example of urban planning. As early as 1638, village elders set aside the 16-acre plot as a town common. Three early 19th-century churches—the Gothic-style **Trinity Episcopal Church,** the Georgian-style **Center Congregational Church,** and the predominantly Federal **United Church**—contribute to its present appeal.

Dining and Lodging

$$–$$$ ✗ **Leon's.** It was in 1938 that the enthusiastic, down-to-earth Varipapa
★ family started this traditional Italian restaurant, which has red-vinyl booths and rough-plaster walls. They've been running it in the same location ever since and have garnered countless awards from critics and local newspaper polls; it has also become a hangout of celebs and hot-

shots. The extensive menu includes 10 varieties of veal and a number of specialties you won't find anywhere else outside of Italy. Portions are enormous and most of the appetizers are meals in themselves. ⊠ *321 Washington St.,* ☎ *203/777–5366. AE, DC, MC, V. No lunch Sat. Closed Mon.*

$$–$$$ ✕ **Saigon City.** Vietnamese cuisine incorporates some of the best ingredients of Chinese, Thai, and Indian cultures, and Saigon City does it as well as any. Try charbroiled jumbo shrimp, mushrooms sautéed with chicken, or spicy beef curry. ⊠ *Corner of Chapel and Park Sts.,* ☎ *203/865–5033. AE, MC, V. Closed Mon.*

$$–$$$ ✕ **Union League Cafe.** The French country cuisine served here has twists like smoked salmon terrine with pesto sauce. Dishes such as roast duck with sautéed green apples and green peppercorn sauce and Black Angus steak with paprika béarnaise sauce are delectable. There is a prix-fixe menu on Sunday. ⊠ *1032 Chapel St.,* ☎ *203/562–4299. AE, MC, V. No lunch weekends.*

$$ ✕ **Caffé Adulis.** The combination of light, high ceilings and exposed brick gives this trendy Eritrean restaurant a comfortable, contemporary feel. Try *tsebhes,* a dish of chicken, lamb, or vegetables simmered with tomatoes and *berbere* (hot peppers). It's served over *injera* (a sourdough crepe), and eating it with your right hand is de rigueur. Another northeast African specialty is *tibsies,* a fajita-like entrée. There are several vegetarian dishes including fragrant stews and fresh greens. ⊠ *228 College St.,* ☎ *203/777–5081. Reservations not accepted. AE, MC, V. No lunch weekends.*

$ ✕ **Frank Pepe's.** Is this really the best pizza in the world—as critics
★ from all over have been known to say? Of course not, but it's darn close, and it's the only thing on the menu, which is actually just a chalkboard on the wall. So don't ask for garlic bread, or one of the smart-mouthed waitresses will groan at you. However, if you order a Sicilian pizza—a white pizza with clams and Canadian bacon (which is not on the menu)—they'll definitely think you're in the know. Expect to wait an hour or more for a table—or, on weekend evenings, go after 10. ⊠ *157 Wooster St.,* ☎ *203/865–5762. Reservations not accepted. No credit cards. No lunch Mon., Wed., Thurs. Closed Tues.*

$$–$$$ ✕▥ **Colony Inn.** The lobby of this inn in the center of the Chapel Street hotel district is eclectic, with an ornate chandelier that's part grand Baroque, part Victorian. Guest rooms have Colonial reproductions and attractive modern baths; some overlook the Yale campus. ⊠ *1157 Chapel St., 06511,* ☎ *203/776–1234 or 800/458–8810,* ℻ *203/772–3929. 80 rooms with bath, 6 suites. Restaurant, bar. AE, DC, MC, V.*

$$$$ ▥ **Three Chimneys Inn.** Despite its bordering a questionable neigh-
★ borhood, this 1847 Victorian mansion is one of the most polished small inns in the state. The rooms are furnished individually, in styles ranging from Victorian to country home to contemporary; all are luxurious. Both the breakfast and sitting rooms, each with two fireplaces, are comfy. ⊠ *1201 Chapel St., 06511,* ☎ *203/789–1201,* ℻ *203/789–0234. 10 rooms with bath. Continental breakfast and afternoon refreshments included. AE, D, DC, MC, V.*

$$–$$$ ▥ **New Haven Hotel.** One of the best kept secrets in town, this quiet hotel is right in the heart of the city. You may feel as if you're at a small, exclusive hotel, yet the amenities here are those of a large one. The freshly decorated rooms are comfortable and modern. Templeton's, the hotel's restaurant, serves innovative American cuisine. ⊠ *229 George St., 06510,* ☎ *203/498–3100,* ℻ *203/498–3190. 92 rooms with bath. Restaurant, bar, indoor lap pool, hot tub, business services, meeting rooms. AE, D, DC, MC, V.*

Nightlife and the Arts

NIGHTLIFE

Toad's Place (⊠ 300 York St., ☎ 203/624–8263) has been drawing crowds for years to hear both alternative and traditional rock bands.

THE ARTS

New Haven is where many shows work out the kinks before heading to Broadway. The **Long Wharf Theatre** (⊠ 222 Sargent Dr., ☎ 203/787–4282) is known for its fresh and imaginative revivals of neglected classics as well as the production of works by new writers. The **Yale Repertory Theatre** (⊠ Chapel and York Sts., ☎ 203/432–1234) stages major star-studded dramas year-round. The **Shubert Performing Arts Center** (⊠ 247 College St., ☎ 203/562–5666) presents an array of musical, operatic, and dramatic performances, usually following their run in the Big Apple. For show and ticket information, call Protix at 800/955–5566.

Yale School of Music (☎ 203/432–4157) presents an impressive roster of performers, from classical to jazz. **Yale University's Woolsey Hall** (⊠ College and Grove Sts.) hosts the **New Haven Symphony Orchestra** (☎ 203/865–0831). The orchestra was founded more than 100 years ago and has been presenting its delightful Young People's Concerts—the country's leading music program for children—for 62 years.

Outdoor Activities and Sports

The 88-acre **Lighthouse Point Park** (⊠ Lighthouse Rd., ☎ 203/946–8005), in southeastern New Haven, has a public beach, nature trails, and an antique carousel in a turn-of-the-century beach pavilion.

Shopping

True bibliophiles will head for the **Arethusa Book Shop** (⊠ 87 Audubon St., ☎ 203/624–1848) and its large selection of out-of-print and used books and its early and first editions. Here you can also get a handy guide to the many new and used bookstores that thrive in this university town. The **Chapel Square Mall** (⊠ 900 Chapel St., ☎ 203/777–6661), opposite the New Haven Green, has 63 shops. New Haven's **Broadway** is an avenue of great little shops and eateries.Dr/d The **Yale Co-op** (☎ 203/772–2200), an enormous campus bookstore, carries Yale goods and a vast stock of books.

En Route   More than 100 classic trolleys are housed at the **Shoreline Trolley Museum,** among them, the oldest rapid-transit car and the world's first electric freight locomotive. Admission includes a 3-mile ride aboard a vintage trolley. ⊠ *17 River St., East Haven (midway between New Haven and Branford),* ☎ *203/467–6927.* ⊡ *$5.* ☉ *Memorial Day–Labor Day, daily 11–5; May, Sept.–Oct., and Dec., weekends 11–5; Apr. and Nov., Sun. 11–5.*

Branford

⑥⓪   *8 mi east of New Haven.*

Founded in 1644, Branford was once a prosperous port and the site of a salt works that, during the Revolutionary War, provided salt to preserve food for the Continental Army. Today, visitors are attracted to this residential town for its historic buildings.

The **Nathaniel Harrison House,** a restored classic Colonial saltbox, was built in the early 18th century. The only historic house open to the public in Branford, it displays archives and photographs of the town as well as period furnishings. Outside, there is a fragrant herb garden. ⊠

124 S. Main St., ☎ 203/488–4828. 🖂 Donation suggested. ⊘ June–Oct., Thurs.–Sat. 2–5, or by appointment.

Dining

$$–$$$ ✕ **Riviera Cafe.** This tiny but tony eatery, by the Long Island Sound
★ community of Indian Neck, serves Continental food with Mediterranean
flair—lots of capers, garlic, and black olives. There are exceptions,
though, such as sole and shrimp française (with basil, orange, and pig-
noli nuts). The usual meat and seafood grills, many dusted with generous pinches of *herbes de Provence,* are transformed into works of
art, and after feasting here, you may expect to stumble out the door
onto a pebbly beach in Nice. 🖂 *3 Linden Ave., ☎ 203/481–7011. MC,
V. No lunch. Closed Mon. in winter.*

Outdoor Activities and Sports

WATER SPORTS

Surfboards and sailboards can be rented from **Action Sports** (🖂 324
W. Main St., ☎ 203/481–5511).

Shopping

Branford Craft Village (🖂 779 E. Main St., ☎ 203/488–4689; closed
Mon.), on the 150-year-old 85-acre Bittersweet Farm, has 25 crafts shops
and studios in a village setting as well as a small play area and a café.

Stony Creek

🖢 *3 mi south of Branford's town center. Go east on Route 1 to Leetes
Island Road; turn right and follow it to Stony Creek's small harbor.*

The small village of Stony Creek, with a few tackle shops, a general
store, and a marina, is very picturesque. It's also the departure point
for cruises to the **Thimble Islands.** This group of 365 tiny islands was
named for their abundance of thimbleberries, which are similar to goose-
berries. Legend has it that Captain Kidd buried pirate gold on one island. Two sightseeing vessels vie for your patronage, the *Volsunga III*
(☎ 203/481–3345 or 203/488–9978) and the *Sea Mist* (☎ 203/481–
4841 or 203/488–8905). Both offer trips daily between 10 and 4, early
May through Columbus Day only. Both depart from Stony Creek
Dock, at the end of Thimble Island Road.

The Arts

In Stony Creek, **Puppet House Theatre** (🖂 128 Thimble Island Rd., ☎
203/488–5752) has a lively season of comedy, drama, and musical productions by three companies. **East Haven Cultural Arts Council** produces
a concert series at the East Haven Community Center (🖂 91 Taylor
Ave., ☎ 203/468–2963).

Guilford

🖢 *5 mi east of Stony Creek, 37 mi west of New London.*

Guilford is home to nearly 500 historic buildings and sites and one of
the largest and oldest town greens in New England.

The **Whitfield House Museum,** New England's oldest stone house, is
right on Guilford's village green. It was built by the Reverend Henry
Whitfield, an English vicar who settled here in 1639. The late medieval–style building has 17th-century furnishings. 🖂 *Old Whitfield
St., ☎ 203/453–2457. ⊘ Feb.–mid-Dec., Wed.–Sun. 10–4:30.*

Dining

$–$$$ ✕ **Stone House.** This friendly waterside establishment sparkles with
floral-print table linens, red-tile floors, and wicker or striped rush-seated
chairs. Seafood and pasta dishes make up the bulk of the menu, though

grilled pizzas and a few chicken entrées are offered, too. ⊠ *506 Whitfield St.,* ☎ *203/458–1311. Reservations not accepted. AE, MC, V.*

En Route   Route 146 from Guilford to Madison is a scenic country road surrounded by salt marshes, tall, willowy reeds, and tidal ponds.

Madison

63   *5 mi east of Guilford, 62 mi northeast of Greenwich.*

The shoreline community of Madison, with 2 miles of white, sandy beach, has understated charm. Route 1, the town's main street, is filled with quirky gift boutiques, ice cream parlors, antiques stores, and a couple of good bookshops.

The **Allis–Bushnell House and Museum,** built about 1785, has an early furnished doctor's office, along with period rooms containing antique furnishings and costumes. Original telegrams from President Abraham Lincoln to Cornelius Bushnell are also on display. ⊠ *853 Boston Post Rd.,* ☎ *203/245–4567 or 203/245–1368.* ☉ *Memorial Day–Labor Day, or by appointment throughout yr.*

Beach
Hammonasset Beach State Park (⊠ I–95, Exit 62, ☎ 203/245–2785), the largest of the state's shoreline sanctuaries, has a 2-mile beach.

Dining, Lodging, and Camping
$$–$$$$ ✕⊞ **The Inn at Café Lafayette.** In an 1830's converted church, this charming inn has a light and airy interior accented with skylights, painted murals, and handcrafted woodwork. The rooms may be small for the price, but the decoration is immaculate, with beautiful fabrics and reproduction 17th- and 18th-century antique furniture. The modern marble baths have telephones. Even if you don't stay at the inn, the restaurant is a must; the nouvelle American cuisine is prepared with many local ingredients. Sunday brunch includes scrambled eggs with lobster, pumpkin bisque, and shaved fennel and gravlax salad. ⊠ *725 Boston Post Rd., 06443,* ☎ *203/245–7773,* ℻ *203/245–6256. 5 rooms with bath. Restaurant, bar, business services. AE, DC, MC, V.*

⚲ **Riverdale Farm Campsites.** This campground is open mid-April through mid-October and has 222 campsites. ⊠ *111 River Rd., Clinton,* ☎ *860/669–5388.*

⚲ **River Road Campground.** There are 55 campsites here. ⊠ *13 River Rd., Clinton,* ☎ *860/669–2238.*

Shopping
R. J. Julia Booksellers (⊠ 768 Boston Post Rd., ☎ 203/245–3959) has been named bookseller of the year by *Publishers Weekly.*

En Route   The Marquis de Lafayette stayed at the **Stanton House** in 1824, in a bed still displayed in its original surroundings. Built about 1790, the house was once a general store and now exhibits items it might have sold back then as well as a large collection of antique American and Staffordshire dinnerware. ⊠ *63 E. Main St., Clinton (9 mi from Madison),* ☎ *860/669–2132.* ☉ *June–Sept., Tues.–Sun. 2–5.*

Old Saybrook

64   *9 mi east of Madison, 29 mi east of New Haven.*

Old Saybrook, once a lively shipbuilding and fishing town, bustles today mostly from its many summer vacationers.

The Georgian **General William Hart House,** once the residence of a prosperous merchant and politician, was built about 1767 and contains period furnishings. ⊠ *350 Main St.,* ☎ *860/388–2622.* ☺ *Mid-June–mid-Sept. and late-Nov.–mid-Dec.*

Dining and Lodging

\$\$–\$\$\$ ✕ **Aleia's.** This large, late 18th-century house between Clinton and Old
★   Saybrook looks quite ordinary from the outside but is surprisingly el-
egant inside, with dark wainscoting and bentwood chairs, classic dark
green-and-white color scheme, and walls painted with images of plants.
The eclectic menu has several nouvelle-inspired pasta, veal, pork, and
poultry dishes, such as tenderloin of pork wrapped in prosciutto with
dried-cranberry port sauce and roasted winter vegetables. ⊠ *1353 Boston
Post Rd., Westbrook* ☎ *860/399–5050. AE, MC, V. No lunch in win-
ter. Closed Mon.*

\$\$\$\$ ✕🖼 **Saybrook Point Inn.** This establishment feels more like a small hotel
than an inn. Rooms are furnished with traditional British reproduc-
tions, floral-print spreads, and Impressionist- and classical-style art.
The health club and pools overlook the inn's marina and the Connecticut
River. The Terra Mar Grille dishes up elegant northern Italian cuisine,
including Dijon-and-pistachio crusted lamb with pear compote. ⊠ *2
Bridge St., 06475,* ☎ *860/395–2000,* ℻ *860/388–1504. 55 rooms,
7 suites. Restaurant (☎ 860/388–1111), indoor and outdoor pools,
spa, health club, meeting rooms. AE, D, DC, MC, V.*

\$\$\$–\$\$\$\$ ✕🖼 **Water's Edge Inn.** With its spectacular setting on Long Island Sound
★   in Westbrook, this traditional weathered gray-shingle compound is one
of the Connecticut shore's premier resorts. The main building has
warm and bright public rooms furnished with antiques and repro-
ductions, and its upstairs bedrooms, with wall-to-wall carpeting and
clean, modern bathrooms, afford priceless Sound views. Suites in the
surrounding outbuildings are not as nicely kept and lack the fine views.
⊠ *1525 Boston Post Rd., 06498,* ☎ *860/399–5901 or 800/222–5901,*
℻ *860/399–6172. 100 rooms and suites. Restaurant, bar, indoor and
outdoor pools, tennis courts, volleyball, beach, meeting rooms. AE,
D, DC, MC, V.*

Outdoor Activities and Sports

BOATING
Private charter boats, whose rentals range from \$275 to \$375 for a
half day, to \$450 and up for a full day, are available in Westbrook at
Brewer Yacht Sales (☎ 860/399–6213). Boats can be rented or char-
tered (sailboat rentals start at about \$150 per day) from **Colvin Yachts**
(⊠ Hammock Rd. S, Westbrook–Old Saybrook, ☎ 860/399–9300).

FISHING
Deep-sea fishing and private charter boats, whose rentals range from
\$400 for a half day, to \$500 and up for a full day, are available in Clin-
ton at **Sea Sprite Charters** (⊠ 113 Harbor Pkwy., ☎ 860/669–9613).
Charters leave from Old Saybrook Point.

WATER SPORTS
The **Sunset Bay Surf Shop** (⊠ 192 Boston Post Rd., Westbrook, ☎
860/669–7873) rents surfboards and sailboards.

Shopping
The **Antiques Village** (⊠ Box 411, 345 Middlesex Turnpike, 06475,
☎ 860/388–0689) has more than 125 dealers.

Old Lyme

⑥⑤ *4 mi east of Old Saybrook, 40 mi south of Hartford.*

Old Lyme, on the other side of the Connecticut River from Old Say-brook, is renowned among art lovers throughout the world for its history as America's foremost Impressionist art colony.

Central to Old Lyme's artistic reputation is the **Florence Griswold Museum,** the former home of a great patron of the arts, which is set on 6 beautifully landscaped acres. Built in 1817, the well-preserved Federal mansion housed an art colony that included Willard Metcalfe, Clark Voorhees, and Childe Hassam. Many of their works are still on display here, along with early furnishings and decorative items. A turn-of-the-century artist's studio, was purchased and moved here from another part of town. ⊠ 96 Lyme St., ☎ 860/434–5542. ☜ $4. ☉ Jan.–May, Wed.–Sun. 1–5; June–Dec., Tues.–Sat. 10–5, Sun. 1–5.

The **Lyme Academy of Fine Arts** is in a former private Federal home built in 1817. Today it's a popular gallery with works by contemporary artists. ⊠ 84 Lyme St., ☎ 860/434–5232. ☜ $2 donation suggested. ☉ Tues.–Sat. 10–4, Sun. 1–4.

Dining and Lodging

$$$–$$$$ ✕🏨 **Old Lyme Inn.** This gray-clapboard farmhouse, built in the 1850s, serves the best American cuisine in the area. Innkeeper, local historian, and antiques collector Diane Field Atwood has filled the spacious bedrooms with Empire and Victorian furnishings, including canopy beds and Rococo Revival settees; bathrooms are contemporary. Some of her collection is also on display in the bright and airy common rooms and in the restaurant, where you might sample Irish smoked salmon, sweetbreads, rack of lamb, and sliced loin of venison or antelope. ⊠ 85 Lyme St. (just north of I–95), Box 787, 06371, ☎ 860/434–2600 or 800/434–5352, ℻ 860/434–5352. 5 rooms with bath, 8 suites. Restaurant. CP. AE, D, DC, MC, V. Closed 1st 2 wks in Jan.

$$–$$$$ ✕🏨 **Bee & Thistle Inn.** This establishment just down the street from
★   the Old Lyme Inn is a bit homier than its neighbor; it's also farther out of the shadows of I–95. Innkeepers Bob and Penny Nelson have furnished this two-story 1756 Colonial on the Lieutenant River with period antiques and plenty of warm touches. Most bedrooms have canopy or four-poster beds and private baths. The outstanding American cuisine has some French touches, and is served in one of the most romantic dining rooms around. ⊠ 100 Lyme St., 06371, ☎ 860/434–1667 or 800/622–4946, ℻ 860/434–3402. 11 rooms, 9 with bath; cottage. Restaurant (closed Tues. and 1st 2 wks in Jan.). AE, DC, MC, V.

Waterford

🚌 13 mi east of Old Lyme.

Waterford has a great state park, and the nearby town of Niantic, has a spectacular shoreline.

☾ The **Children's Museum of Southeastern Connecticut,** about 4 miles from Waterford, is an excellent museum that uses a hands-on approach to engage kids in the fields of science, math, and current events. Rotating exhibits and special programs are planned throughout the year. ⊠ 409 Main St., Niantic, ☎ 860/691–1255. ☜ $3. ☉ Memorial Day–Labor Day, Mon.–Sat. 9–4, Sun. noon–4; Labor Day–Memorial Day, Tues.–Sat. 9–4, Sun. noon–4.

The mile-long crescent-shape strand at **Rocky Neck State Park** (⊠ Rte. 156, Niantic, ☎ 860/739–5471) is one of the finest beaches on Long Island Sound.

Outdoor Activities and Sports

FISHING

Southeastern Connecticut is the charter- and party-boat capital of New England. Charter fishing boats take passengers for half-day, full-day, and some overnight trips at fees from $20 to $35 per person; tuna-fishing trips may cost as much as $100 a day. Party fishing boats, which are open to the public on a first-come basis, include the **Sunbeam Express** (⌧ 15 1st St., ☎ 860/443–7259). **Captain John's Dock** (☎ 860/443–7259) has boat charters.

STATE PARK

Harkness Memorial State Park (⌧ 275 Great Neck Rd., Rte. 213, ☎ 860/443–5725), a former summer estate, has formal gardens, picnic areas, a beach for strolling and fishing (not swimming), and the Italian villa–style mansion, Eolia. Come for the summer music festival (☎ 860/442–9199) in July and August that features classical, pop, and jazz.

WILDLIFE-WATCHING

Spend the day here spotting whales, seals, or eagles aboard the 100-foot *Sunbeam Express*. Naturalists from Mystic Aquarium sail with you and answer questions. Contact **Captain John's Sports Fishing** (⌧ 15 1st St., ☎ 203/443–7259).

New London

67 *3 mi east of Waterford, 46 mi east of New Haven.*

New London is home to both **Connecticut College** (⌧ 270 Mohegan Ave., ☎ 860/447–1911) and the **U.S. Coast Guard Academy.** The Academy's 100-acre cluster of traditional redbrick buildings includes a museum and visitors' pavilion with a gift shop. The three-masted training bark, the USCGC *Eagle* (☎ 860/444–8595), may be boarded when in port. ⌧ 15 Mohegan Ave., ☎ 860/444–8270. ▣ Free. ☉ *Academy daily 9–5; museum weekdays 9–4:30, Sat. 10–4:30, Sun. noon–5.*

The **Lyman Allyn Art Museum,** at the southern end of the Connecticut College campus, displays a small collection of art and antiques—including an impressive array of dolls, dollhouses, miniature furniture, and toys—dating from the 18th and 19th centuries. You can also see decorative arts from Africa, India, China, and Japan. The American collection of furniture and paintings is especially popular. ⌧ 625 Williams St., ☎ 860/443–2545. ▣ $3. ☉ *Tues.–Sun. 1–5.*

The **Hempsted Houses** showcase Early American life. The **Joshua House,** built in 1678, is one of the oldest documented houses in the nation. Nearly a century later in 1758, Nathaniel Hempsted built the nearby **Stone House.** You may see an open-hearth cooking demonstration in the house's stone beehive bake oven. ⌧ 11 Hempstead St., ☎ 860/443–7949 or 860/247–8996. ▣ $4. ☉ *Mid-May–mid-Oct., Thurs.–Sun. noon–5.*

The **Monte Cristo Cottage** was the boyhood home of playwright Eugene O'Neill and was named for the literary count, his actor-father's greatest role. The setting figures in two of O'Neill's landmark plays, *Ah, Wilderness!* and *Long Day's Journey into Night.* ⌧ 325 Pequot Ave., ☎ 860/443–0051. ☉ *Apr.–mid-Dec.* ▣ $3.

Dining and Lodging

$ ✕ **Recovery Room.** It's a favorite game of Connecticut pizza parlors to declare: "We're as good as Pepe's"—a reference to the famed godfather of the pizza pie in New Haven. But this white Colonial storefront eatery, presided over by the friendly Cash family, lives up to its claim. Plenty of "boutique" toppings are available, but be advised not to ruin a great pizza with too many flavors. Perfection is realized by the three-cheese 'za with grated Parmesan, Romano, and gorgonzola. ⊠ *445 Ocean Ave.,* ☎ *860/443–2619. MC, V. No lunch weekends.*

$$–$$$ 🛏 **Queen Anne Inne.** For those interested in visiting Foxwoods Casino, this inn is only 25 minutes from Ledyard. The turreted, three-story mansion has floral-patterned wallpaper, stained-glass windows, fireplaces, and furniture that dates from the inn's founding in 1903. A hot tub is available to all guests. Delicious baked goods are served at afternoon tea. ⊠ *265 Williams St., 06320,* ☎ *860/447–2600 or 800/347–8818. 10 rooms, 8 with bath. Full breakfast and afternoon tea included. AE, D, DC, MC, V.*

$$–$$$ 🛏 **Radisson Hotel.** A downtown location makes this property convenient to State Street, I–95, and the Amtrak station. Rooms have nondescript modern furnishings but are quiet and spacious. ⊠ *35 Gov. Winthrop Blvd., 06320,* ☎ *860/443–7000 or 800/333–3333,* FAX *860/443–1239. 116 rooms with bath, 4 suites. Restaurant, bar, indoor pool. AE, D, DC, MC, V.*

Nightlife and the Arts

NIGHTLIFE

The **El 'n' Gee Club** (⊠ 86 Golden St., ☎ 860/437–3800) has different programs nightly—heavy metal, reggae, local bands, and occasionally nationally known acts.

THE ARTS

Connecticut College's **Palmer Auditorium** (⊠ Mohegan Ave., ☎ 860/ 439–2787) presents both dance and theater programs. The **Garde Arts Center** (⊠ 325 State St., ☎ 860/444–6766) hosts the Eastern Connecticut Symphony Orchestra, a theater series, innovative dance programs, and a number of well-known performers. **Shoreline Alliance for the Arts** (☎ 860/453–3890) sponsors concerts throughout the western part of the region.

Outdoor Activities and Sports

FISHING

Private charter boats, whose rentals range from $275 to $375 for a half day, to $450 and up for a full day, are available at the **City Pier** (☎ 860/442–1777). Also try **Burr's Yacht Haven** (☎ 860/443–8457) for charters.

WATER SPORTS

Ocean Beach Park (⊠ Ocean Ave., ☎ 860/447–3031) has an Olympic-size outdoor pool with a triple water slide; the park also has miniature golf and an amusement park.

Norwich

 15 mi north of New London, 37 mi southeast of Hartford.

Norwich has some outstanding examples of Georgian and Victorian architecture around the triangular town green and downtown by the river, and a couple of house museums. The Connecticut Trust for Historic Preservation and the state Department of Economic Development are working on renovating this former bustling mill town—here's hoping for a prosperous rebound.

Businessman Christopher Leffingwell built the **Leffingwell Inn** in 1675. It later served as a meeting point for patriots during the revolution. ⊠ *348 Washington St.,* ☎ *860/889–9440.* 🕐 *May–Oct.* 🎟 *$3.*

OFF THE
BEATEN PATH

FOXWOODS CASINO – On the Mashantucket Indian Reservation, 15 miles from Norwich near Ledyard, is the state's first—and New England's largest—gambling operation. It's open daily around the clock. This surprisingly attractive skylit Colonial-style compound draws more than 45,000 visitors daily to its slot machines, 3,000-seat bingo parlor, poker rooms, keno station, and Racebook room, which has 12′ × 50′ screens for race viewing. This monstrous complex includes the Foxwoods Resort Hotel and Two Trees Inn, which have more than 500 rooms combined, a retail concourse, a food court, and more than 10 casual restaurants. For kids there is a virtual reality ride that takes you beneath the sea; Cinedrome 360, a movie theater in-the-round; and Turbo Ride, with specially engineered seats that let you feel all the takeoffs and G-forces of action films. ⊠ Rte. 2, Box 410, Ledyard, ☎ 203/885–3000 or 800/752–9244; hotel reservations 800/369–9663.

Dining and Lodging

$$$–$$$$ ⛤ **Norwich Inn and Spa.** This Georgian-style inn on 40 acres high on a bluff a few hundred yards from the Thames River, is the state's only true spa. And though the quaint, Colonial ambience is a bit forced with regard to the lobby and bedroom decor, this is an efficiently and cheerfully run property. Many fitness classes and spa treatments are available. The Prince of Wales restaurant serves American contemporary spa cuisine that's much more than carrot and celery sticks—you certainly don't have to be on a diet to enjoy this spot. ⊠ 607 W. Thames St. (Rte. 32), ☎ 860/886–2401 or 800/275–4772, FAX 860/886–4492. 65 rooms with bath, 70 villas. Restaurant, indoor pool, spa, golf, health club. AE, D, DC, MC, V.

$$$$ ✕⛤ **Foxwoods Resort Hotel.** You never have to step outside the gaming rooms to reach this hotel at the humongous Foxwoods complex. Standard rooms are spacious, and facilities will occupy those who aren't interested in gambling. ⊠ Rte. 2, Box 410, Ledyard, ☎ 800/369–9663. 312 rooms. Restaurant, indoor pool, beauty salon, health club, shops, meeting rooms.

Groton

🄾🄽   15 mi south of Norwich, 6 mi south of Ledyard.

Groton is submarine country. There's no escaping the impact of the **U.S. submarine base** on the area.

The world's first nuclear-powered submarine, the Nautilus, launched from Groton in 1954, is now permanently berthed at the **U.S. Nautilus Submarine Force Library and Museum;** you're welcome to climb aboard. The adjacent library-museum contains submarine memorabilia, artifacts, and displays, including working periscopes and controls. The museum is just outside the entrance to the submarine base. ⊠ Crystal Lake Rd., ☎ 860/449–3174 or 860/449–3558. ☜ Free. ⊙ Wed.–Mon. 9–4 (until 5, mid-Apr.–mid-Oct.).

Ft. Griswold Battlefield State Park (⊠ Monument St. and Park Ave., ☎ 860/445–1729) has battle emplacements and historic displays marking the site of the massacre of American defenders by Benedict Arnold's British troops in 1781. From the top of the memorial tower you get a sweeping view of the shoreline.

Outdoor Activities and Sports

FISHING

The *Hel-Cat II* (⊠ 181 Thames St., ☎ 203/445–5991) is a party fishing boat open to the public on a first-come basis.

Mystic

⑦ *8 mi east of Groton.*

The town of Mystic has tried with dedication to recapture (albeit with excessive commercialism) the spirit of the 18th and 19th centuries.

Some people think the name of the town is **Mystic Seaport,** and it very well might be, given the lure of the museum that goes by that name. It is the nation's largest maritime museum, and its 17 riverfront acres have authentic 19th-century sailing vessels you can board, a maritime village with historic homes, working craftspeople who give demonstrations, steamboat cruises, small-boat rentals, shops, restaurants, art exhibits, and special events in keeping with the seasons. ⊠ *75 Greenmanville Ave.,* ☎ *860/572–0711.* ☞ *$16.* ☉ *May–June and Sept.–Oct., 9–5; July–Aug., 9–7; Nov.–Apr., 9–4.*

The **Mystic Marinelife Aquarium,** with more than 6,000 specimens and 50 live exhibits of sea life, includes Seal Island, a 2½-acre outdoor exhibit, which shows off seals and sea lions from around the world. At the Marine Theater, dolphins and sea lions perform every hour on the half hour. Don't miss the Penguin Pavilion. ⊠ *55 Coogan Blvd.,* ☎ *860/536–3323 or 860/536–9631.* ☞ *$9.50.* ☉ *Daily 9–5.*

Dining and Lodging

$$–$$$ ✕ **Abbott's Lobster in the Rough.** If you want some of the state's best
★ lobster, mussels, crab, or clams on the half shell, grab a bottle of wine and slip down to this unassuming seaside lobster shack in sleepy Noank. Seating is outdoors or on the dock, and views are magnificent. ⊠ *117 Pearl St., Noank,* ☎ *860/536–7719.* ☉ *Memorial Day–Labor Day, daily; Labor Day–Columbus Day, weekends. BYOB. MC, V.*

$ ✕ **Mystic Pizza.** It's hard to say who benefited most from the success of the 1988 sleeper film *Mystic Pizza:* then budding actress Julia Roberts or the pizza parlor on which the film is based (none of the scenes was actually filmed here). This joint does serve terrific, inexpensive pizza, garlic bread, and grinders, but beware of seething summertime crowds. ⊠ *56 W. Main St.,* ☎ *860/536–3700.*

$$–$$$$ ✕🏠 **Inn at Mystic.** The highlight of this inn, which sprawls over 15 hill-
★ top acres and overlooks picturesque Pequotsepos Cove, is the five-bedroom, Georgian Colonial mansion in which Lauren Bacall and Humphrey Bogart honeymooned. Almost as impressive are the rambling four-bedroom gatehouse and the unusually attractive motor lodge. The Floodtide Restaurant has a convivial, sun-filled dining room and specializes in New England fare. Brunchaholics flock here on Sunday. ⊠ *Rtes. 1 and 27, 06355,* ☎ *860/536–9604 or 800/237–2415,* ℻ *860/572–1635. 68 rooms with bath. Restaurant (☎ 860/536–8140), pool, tennis courts, dock, boating. AE, D, DC, MC, V.*

$$–$$$ ✕🏠 **Whaler's Inn and Motor Court.** On the Mystic River, this is the perfect compromise between a chain motel and a country inn. The public rooms are furnished with lovely antiques. The restaurant, Bravo Bravo, has delicious nouvelle Italian food: fettuccine comes with grilled scallops, roasted apples, sun-dried tomatoes, and a gorgonzola cream sauce. There's also a terrific bagel shop. ⊠ *20 E. Main St., 06355,* ☎ *860/536–1506 or 800/243–2588,* ℻ *860/572–1250. 41 rooms with bath. 3 restaurants, meeting rooms. AE, D, MC, V.*

$$$-$$$$ ⊞ **Steamboat Inn.** This establishment, with rooms named after famous
Mystic schooners, is no creaky old Connecticut inn. Six rooms have
wood-burning fireplaces, all have whirlpool baths, and most have dra-
matic river views and look as though they're posing for the cover of
House Beautiful. Despite the inn's busy downtown location (within
earshot of the eerie hoot of the Bascule Drawbridge and the chatter of
tourists), its rooms are the most luxurious and romantic in town. ⊠
*73 Steamboat Wharf (off W. Main St.), 06355, ☎ 860/536–8300. 10
rooms with bath. AE, D, MC, V.*

$$-$$$$ ⊞ **Red Brook Inn.** The 1770 center-chimney Crary Homestead is one
  ★   of the few first-rate New England bed-and-breakfasts in the area.
Innkeeper Ruth Keyes has furnished the house with period furnishings,
many of them quite rare. Most rooms have fireplaces, and two rooms
have whirlpool tubs. The inn is midway between the Foxwoods Casino
and Mystic Seaport. ⊠ *Gold Star Hwy. (Rte. 184), Box 237, 06372,
☎ FAX 860/572–0349. 10 rooms with bath. Recreation room. Full breakfast included. AE, MC, V.*

$$-$$$$ ⊞ **Taber Inn and Townhouses.** This is a popular complex for visitors
to Stonington and Mystic; the variety of accommodations is great for
families and couples traveling together. The Taber has everything from
two-bedroom townhouses to single-occupancy motel units. The town-
house rooms and one-bedroom units are luxuriously appointed with
fireplaces, hot tubs, balconies, and terrific water views. The award-win-
ning gardens are beautiful. Guests have access to the Williams Beach
indoor swimming pool, tennis, sauna, and aerobics. ⊠ *66 Williams
Ave., 06355, ☎ 860/536–4904, FAX 860/572–9140. 16 rooms with bath;
3 townhouses and 16 1-bedrooms with hot tubs and fireplaces. AE,
MC, V.*

Outdoor Activities and Sports

Private charter boats are available in Noank at **Noank Village Boat-
yard** (☎ 860/536–1770). **Shaffer's Boat Livery** (⊠ 106 Mason's Is-
land Rd., ☎ 860/536–8713) rents and charters boats.

Shopping

Downtown Mystic has an interesting collection of boutiques and gal-
leries, as well as factory-outlet stores. **Tradewinds Gallery** (⊠ 20 W.
Main St., ☎ 860/536–0119) represents some New England artists, but
specializes in antique maps and prints. **Framers of the Lost Art Gallery**
(⊠ 48 W. Main St., ☎ 860/536–8339) has nautical prints and other
rare artwork. At the **Mystic Factory Outlets** (⊠ 12 Coogan Blvd.),
nearly two dozen stores offer discounts on famous-name clothing and
other merchandise. **Olde Mistick Village** (⊠ Exit 90, I–95, ☎ 860/536–
1641), a re-creation of what an American village might have looked
like about 1720, is at once hokey and picturesque. Here stores sell crafts,
clothing, souvenirs, and food.

Stonington

❼ *7 mi east of Mystic, 57 mi east of New Haven.*

The little village of Stonington is your final (some say the most mem-
orable) peek at Connecticut's coastline. Poking into Fishers Island
Sound, Stonington remains a quiet fishing community clustered around
white-spired churches and is far less commercial than neighboring
Mystic. Wander around the historic buildings that line the town green
and border both sides of Water Street until you reach the imposing Old
Lighthouse Museum.

The **Old Lighthouse Museum** was built in 1823, and was moved not
long afterward to higher ground, where it remains today, displaying a

wealth of shipping, whaling, and early village artifacts. Climb to the top of the tower for a spectacular view of the sound, the Atlantic Ocean, and Fishers Island. ⊠ *7 Water St.,* ☎ *860/535–1440.* ☞ *$3.* ☉ *July–Aug., daily 11–5; May–June and Sept.–Oct., Tues.–Sun. 11–5, or by appointment.*

The **Stonington Vineyards,** a small coastal winery, has grown premium vinifera and French hybrid grape varieties since 1979. Picnicking is encouraged—the grounds are a terrific spot for it. ⊠ *Taugwonk Rd.,* ☎ *860/535–1222.* ☞ *Free.* ☉ *Daily 11–5; tours at 2.*

Dining and Lodging

$ ✕ **Kitchen Little.** A great place for breakfast, this offbeat restaurant serves up delicious eggs dishes, including the Portuguese Fisherman with scrambled eggs, chorizo, linguiça, onions, peppers, and jalapeño cheese. This spot is small, so anticipate a wait. ⊠ *Highway 27 off I–95,* ☎ *860/536–2122. No credit cards. No dinner Sun.–Wed.*

$$–$$$$ ✕▣ **Randall's Ordinary.** This inn is famed for its open-hearth cook-
★ ing. Arrive by 7 PM; then watch preparations before sitting down at simple old wood tables. The prix-fixe menu changes daily; choices might include loin of pork or Nantucket scallops. Waiters dress in Colonial garb. The 17th-century John Randall House provides bare, simple accommodations. The Jacob Terpenning Barn has wonderfully irregular guest rooms, all with authentic, early Colonial decor. ⊠ *Rte. 2, Box 243, North Stonington 06359,* ☎ *860/599–4540,* ℻ *860/599–3308. 14 rooms with bath, 1 suite. Restaurant (reservations essential for dinner). CP. AE, MC, V.*

$$$–$$$$ ▣ **Antiques & Accommodations.** The English influence is evident in the
★ Georgian formality of this Victorian country home, built about 1861. Exquisite furniture and accessories, many of them for sale, decorate all the rooms. An 1820 house has a similarly furnished three-bedroom suite. Aromatic candles and fresh flowers create a warm and inviting atmosphere. ⊠ *32 Main St., North Stonington 06359,* ☎ *860/535– 1736 or 800/554–7829. 3 rooms with bath, 2 suites, 1 3-bedroom house. Full breakfast included. MC, V.*

$$ ▣ **Lasbury's Guest House.** In the heart of the village and within walking distance of many elegant restaurants, this modest establishment occupies a frame house and the small, red Colonial building a few steps behind it. It's on a quiet side street, disturbed only by the occasional speeding Amtrak train, with a salt marsh to the rear. A nautical theme, along with framed posters for the annual Stonington Fair, provides the decoration. ⊠ *24 Orchard St., 06378,* ☎ *860/535–2681. 3 rooms share 2 baths. No credit cards.*

Outdoor Activities and Sports

GOLF

Elmridge Golf Course (⊠ Elmridge Rd., Pawcatuck, ☎ 860/599–2248).

HAYRIDE

Davis Farm (⊠ 568 Greenhaven Rd., Pawcatuck, ☎ 860/599–5859) offers hayrides in horse-drawn wagons along the Pawcatuck River.

WATER SPORTS

Dodson Boat Yard (⊠ 194 Water St., ☎ 860/535–1507) rents and charters boats. Sailboat rentals start at about $300 per day.

New Haven and the Southeastern Coast A to Z

Getting Around

BY BUS

Southeastern Area Transit (☎ 203/886–2631) has local bus service between East Lyme and Stonington.

BY CAR

From New Haven to the Rhode Island border, I–95 and Route 1, which run mostly parallel but sometimes intertwine, are the principal routes through the coastal area.

BY FERRY

From New London, **Cross Sound Ferry** (☎ 860/443–5281; runs year-round) has passenger and car service to and from Orient Point, Long Island, New York. **Fishers Island Ferry** (☎ 860/443–6851) has passenger and car service to and from Fishers Island, New York.

BY TAXI

Metro Taxi (☎ 203/777–7777) serves New Haven and environs.

BY TRAIN

Connecticut Department of Transportation (☎ 860/594–2000 or 800/842–8299 in CT) has commuter rail service (weekdays, westbound in the morning, eastbound in the evening) connecting the towns from Old Saybrook to New Haven. **Amtrak** (☎ 800/872–7245) makes stops in New London and Mystic.

Contacts and Resources

EMERGENCIES

Lawrence & Memorial Hospital (✉ 365 Montauk Ave., New London, ☎ 860/442–0711). **Yale–New Haven Hospital** (✉ 20 York St., ☎ 203/785–2222).

LATE-NIGHT PHARMACY

CVS (✉ 1168 Whalley Ave., New Haven, ☎ 203/389–4714) is open until 10 on weeknights, 9 on weekends.

VISITOR INFORMATION

Connecticut River Valley and Shoreline Visitors Council (✉ 393 Main St., Middletown 06457, ☎ 860/347–0028 or 800/486–3346). **Connecticut's Mystic and More** (✉ 470 Bank St., Box 89, New London 06320, ☎ 860/444–2206 or 800/863–6569). **Greater New Haven Convention and Visitors District** (✉ 1 Long Wharf Dr., Suite. 7, New Haven, CT 06511, ☎ 203/777–8550 or 800/332–7829).

THE QUIET CORNER

Few visitors to Connecticut leave versed in the old-fashioned ways of Connecticut's "Quiet Corner," a vast patch of sparsely populated towns that looks today much as Litchfield County did 15 years ago. The Quiet Corner has a reclusive allure: People used to leave New York City for the Litchfield Hills; now people are leaving the Litchfield Hills, in the northwestern part of the state, for northeastern Connecticut.

Its cultural capital is Putnam, a small mill city on the Quinebaug River, whose formerly industrial town center has been transformed into a year-round antiques mart of sorts. Smaller jewels in and around the Putnam area are Brooklyn, Pomfret, Thompson, and Woodstock—four towns where authentic Colonial homesteads still seem to outnumber the contemporary, charmless clones that are springing up rapidly across the state.

Brooklyn

45 mi east of Hartford.

The village of Brooklyn (⊠ Rtes. 6 and 169) bears no resemblance to the more famous borough that carries the same name. Here is the stuff of white picket fences and beautifully restored Colonial homes.

The **New England Center for Contemporary Art** (⊠ Rte. 169, ☎ 860/774–8899) is a four-story pre-Revolutionary barn with regularly changing 20th-century art presentations.

Dining

$$$$ ✕ **Golden Lamb Buttery.** Connecticut's most unusual—and magical—
★ dining experience has achieved almost legendary status; this restaurant celebrates its 35th anniversary in 1997. Eating here is far more than a chance to enjoy good food: It's a social and gastronomical event. There is one seating each for both lunch and dinner in this converted barn. Owners Bob and Virginia "Jimmie" Booth have a vintage Jaguar roadster and a hay wagon that guests can ride in. Choose from one of three daily soups and one of four entrées, which might include duck à l'orange or pan-fried beef tenderloin. ⊠ *Bush Hill Rd. (off Rte. 169),* ☎ *860/774–4423. No credit cards. Closed Jan.–late May and Sun.–Mon. No dinner Tues.–Thurs.*

Pomfret

6 mi north of Brooklyn.

Pomfret is one of the grandest towns in the region and was once called the "Inland Newport." The hilltop campus of the Pomfret School offers some of Connecticut's loveliest views.

Dining and Lodging

$ ✕ **Vanilla Bean Cafe.** This tan Colonial-style house is the perfect lunch stop, where salads and hearty sandwiches served on fresh home-baked breads are served in an informal dining room. Dinner entrées such as lobster ravioli and roast pork with winter vegetables are served until 8. From May to October, fare from the outside grill is served on the patio till 9. The fresh-baked desserts are a treat. ⊠ *450 Deerfield Rd. (Rtes. 44, 97, and 169),* ☎ *860/928–1562. No credit cards.*

$$ ⊡ **Karinn Bed and Breakfast.** Thanks to its lovely manager, Karen Schirack, and grand Victorian furnishings, Karinn's is the nicest of the area's many moderately priced B&Bs. Behind the brown cedar-shake facade near Pomfret's town center are several antiques-filled rooms that, 100 years ago, were part of Miss Vinton's School for Girls. Ricotta cheese pie and Belgian waffles are two breakfast dishes on the long menu. ⊠ *330 Pomfret St.,* ☎ *860/928–5492. 4 rooms with bath. Full breakfast included. No credit cards.*

Putnam

10 mi northeast of Pomfret.

Putnam, which became, following the Depression, a neglected mill town not unlike Norwich, to the south, has been reinvented in recent years by the ambitions of antiques dealers. The town is peopled with a blend of working-class locals and shoppers visiting from all over: The closest New England capital isn't Hartford; Providence is just 30 miles east.

Shopping

Putnam's downtown is the heart of the region's antiquing. **Antiques Marketplace** (⊠ 109 Main St., ☎ 860/928–0442), is a 20,000-square-foot shop in a Victorian department store. The **Putnam Antique Exchange** (⊠ 75–83 Main St., ☎ 860/928–1905), is 30,000 square feet of 18th-century to Deco paintings, stained-glass, architectural elements, and fine furnishings.

Thompson

7 mi north of Putnam, 50 mi north of Groton.

Thompson, like Pomfret, has 19th-century estates and restored Colonial homes. One particularly impressive stretch is along Route 200, from Thompson Center to where it crosses I–395.

Dining and Lodging

$$–$$$ ✕ **Vernon Stiles Inn.** This rambling white Colonial is a New England tavern as it might have appeared 150 years ago. The staff is friendly, the dining room unfancy. The Continental menu includes shrimp Provençal and veal Tuscano with asparagus, pimentos, Parmesan cheese, and Marsala wine. ⊠ *351 Thompson Rd. (Rtes. 193 and 200),* ☎ *203/923–9571. AE, DC, MC, V. Closed Tues. No lunch Mon. or Sat.*

$$ ⊞ **Lord Thompson Manor.** Down a ½-mile potholed driveway is this
★   stunning bed-and-breakfast inn that could be in England's Devonshire countryside. The 30-room mansion has African marble fireplaces and parquet floors; the sprawling grounds were laid out by Frederick Law Olmsted. ⊠ *Rte. 200, Box 428, 06277,* ☎ *860/923–3886,* FAX *860/923–9310. 4 rooms with 2 baths, 4 suites. Meeting rooms. Full breakfast included. MC, V.*

Woodstock

10 mi west of Thompson.

The landscape of this enchanting town is splendid in every season— the gently rolling hills seem to stretch for miles.

Roseland Cottage (⊠ Rte. 169, ☎ 860/928–4074) is probably the region's most notable historic home. This brilliant rose-hued, board-and-batten Gothic Revival home was built in 1846 by New York publisher and merchant Henry Bowen. The pride of its grounds is an 1850s boxwood parterre garden, through which four presidents—Grant, Hayes, Harrison, and McKinley—have strolled. The neighboring barn contains what may be the oldest indoor bowling alley in the country.

Dining and Lodging

$$$ ✕ **Inn at Woodstock Hill.** This classic country inn, high on a hill overlooking the verdant countryside, has sumptuous rooms with antiques, four-poster beds, fireplaces, pitched ceilings, and timber beams. The restaurant next door serves excellent Continental and American shrimp, veal, and chicken dishes. ⊠ *94 Plaine Hill Rd., South Woodstock 06267,* ☎ *860/928–0528,* FAX *860/928–3236. 22 rooms with bath. Restaurant, meeting rooms. D, MC, V.*

Shopping

Woodstock is a haven of crafts shops and boutiques. The **Christmas Barn** (⊠ 835 Rte. 169, ☎ 860/928–7652) has 12 rooms of country and Christmas goods. **Cornucopia Crafts** (⊠ 197 Dugg Hill Rd., ☎ 860/928–4931) specializes in basketry. **Scranton's Shops** (⊠ 300 Rte. 169, ☎ 860/928–3738) shows off the wares of 90 local artisans. And **Windy Acres Florist** (⊠ Rte. 171, ☎ 860/928–0554) is a country shop overflowing with dried floral arrangements, baskets, pottery, and other collectibles.

Coventry

27 mi south of Woodstock.

Coventry is the birthplace of the legendary Revolutionary War hero Captain Nathan Hale, who was hanged in 1776 as a spy by the British. It was Hale who spoke the immortal last words, "I only regret that I have but one life to lose for my country."

The **Nathan Hale Homestead** was built by Deacon Richard Hale, father to Nathan, in 1776. Here, ten Hale children were raised, six of whom served in the Revolutionary War. Family artifacts still remain in the completely furnished house. The grounds include a corn crib, an 18th-century barn, and a maple sugar farm. ⊠ 2299 South St.,☏ 860/742–6917. ☉ *Mid-May–mid-Oct., daily 1–5 or by appointment.*

Coventry's **Caprilands Herb Farm** (⊠ 534 Silver St., ☏ 860/742–7244) draws thousands of visitors annually to 38 gardens, containing more than 300 varieties of herbs. There's a noon luncheon lecture program, and tea is held on the weekends (phone for reservations).

Quiet Corner A to Z

Getting Around

You'll need a car both to reach and to explore the area. Many Nutmeggers live their entire lives without even noticing I–395, let alone driving on it, but this is the main highway connecting Worcester, Massachusetts, with New London—and it passes right through the Quiet Corner. From Hartford take I–84 east to Route 44 east, and from Providence, Rhode Island, take either Routes 44 or 6 west.

Contacts and Resources

Northeast Connecticut Visitors District (⊠ Box 598, Putnam 06260, ☏ 860/928–1228).

CONNECTICUT A TO Z

Arriving and Departing

By Bus

Greyhound (☏ 800/231–2222) joins Connecticut with most major cities in the United States. **Bonanza Bus Lines** (☏ 800/556–3815) connects Hartford, Middletown, New London, Stamford, Bridgeport, New Haven, and smaller towns with Boston and New York. **Peter Pan Bus Lines** (☏ 800/237–8747) serves the eastern seaboard, including many New England cities.

By Car

From New York City, head north on I–95, which hugs the Connecticut shoreline into Rhode Island or, to reach the Litchfield Hills and Hartford, head north on I–684, then east on I–84. From Springfield, Massachusetts, go south on I–91, which bisects I–84 in Hartford and I–95 in New Haven. From Boston, take I–95 south through Providence or take the Massachusetts Turnpike west to I–84. I–395 runs north–south from southeastern Connecticut to Massachusetts.

By Plane

Bradley International Airport (☏ 860/627–3000), 12 miles north of Hartford and New England's second-largest airport, has scheduled daily flights by most major U.S. airlines. **Igor Sikorsky Memorial Airport** (☏

203/576–7498), 4 miles south of Stratford, is served by Delta, Northwest, and USAir. **Tweed/New Haven Airport** (☎ 203/946–8283), 5 miles southeast of the city, is served by Continental, USAir, and United.

Connecticut Limo (☎ 800/472–5466) has bus and van service between Connecticut and the New York airports. The **Airport Connection** (☎ 860/627–3400) has scheduled service from Bradley to the Hartford Bus Station, as well as door-to-door service.

By Train
Amtrak (☎ 800/872–7245) runs from New York to Boston, stopping in Greenwich, Stamford, Bridgeport, and New Haven before heading either north to Hartford or east to New London. **Metro North** (☎ 212/532–4900 or 800/638–7646 in CT) stops locally between Greenwich and New Haven, and a few trains head inland to New Canaan, Danbury, and Waterbury.

Getting Around
By Car
The interstates are quickest but they are busy and ugly. If time allows, skip them in favor of the historic, winding Merritt Parkway (Rte. 15), which runs between Greenwich and Middletown; Routes 7 and 8, extending between I–95 and the Litchfield Hills; and Route 9, which heads south from Hartford through the Connecticut River Valley to Old Saybrook. State maps are available free from the **Connecticut Department of Tourism** (☞ Visitor Information, *below*).

Guided Tours
Classics Limited (✉ 855 Ridge Rd., Wethersfield 06109, ☎ 860/563–0848 or 860/257–9161) offers individual and group tours throughout Connecticut and Southern New England by private car, limousine, van, and coach.

Unique Auto Tours (✉ Box 879, Canton 06019, ☎ 860/693–0007; tours available June–Oct.) helps you design a four- or seven-day itinerary through New England, then sends you and a pal off in an antique Rolls-Royce or '50s Cadillac. The cost ranges from $1,600 to $2,100.

Contacts and Resources
Reservation Services
Covered Bridge B&B Reservation Service (☎ 860/542–5944). **Nutmeg B&B Agency** (☎ 860/236–6698). **B&B, Ltd.** (☎ 203/469–3260).

Visitor Information
Connecticut Department of Tourism (✉ 865 Brook St., Rocky Hill 06067, ☎ 860/258–4355 or, for a brochure, 800/282–6863).

3 Rhode Island

Founded in 1635, Rhode Island's capital, Providence, is home to Brown University and Rhode Island School of Design, and has colorful Italian, Portuguese, and Hispanic communities. The state's other well-known city is Newport, one of the great sailing capitals of the world and host to first-class music festivals; its over-the-top "cottages" were built in the 19th century as summer residences for the likes of Astors and Vanderbilts. South County has rolling farmland, beaches, and wilderness to explore; Block Island, 11 square miles in area, has one village and 365 ponds.

By Deborah
Kovacs and
Marjorie Ingall,
with an
introduction by
William G.
Scheller

Updated by
Katherine
Imbrie

HODE ISLAND, which shares with New Jersey the distinction of being one of the two most densely populated states in the Union, has at least one other characteristic in common with the Garden State: All too often it is a place people pass through on their way to somewhere else. The culprit in both cases is I–95, but for Rhode Island the problem is compounded by its size. With dimensions of 48 by 37 miles, the state can come and go without being noticed by someone who is humming along to the car radio. Just about everyone knows Rhode Island is the smallest of the 50 states. What is less known is that the state is home to 20% of the country's National Historic Landmarks and has more restored Colonial and Victorian buildings than any other destination in the United States.

To experience Rhode Island as an end rather than a means, stay off the interstate. Traveling the city streets and blacktop roads reveals a place where changes in landscape and character come abruptly.

Take the 5 miles or so of Route 1 just above Wickford. On the face of it, this is a crass and tacky example of modern strip-mall Americana. But if you turn off the highway onto a discreetly marked drive in North Kingstown, you'll pass through a grove of trees and enter the 17th-century world of Smith's Castle, a beautifully preserved saltbox plantation house on the quiet shore of an arm of Narragansett Bay. Little appears to have changed here since Richard Smith built his "castle" after buying the surrounding property from Rhode Island's founder, Roger Williams, in 1651. Follow Route 1 a bit farther south to Route 1A, and the scene will change once again: The bay-side town of Wickford is the kind of almost-too-perfect, salty New England period piece that is usually conjured up only in books and movies—and, in fact, this was John Updike's model for the New England of his novel *The Witches of Eastwick.*

So there it is: a run of tawdry highway development, a restored relic of a house that was once the seat of a 17,000-acre plantation, and a picture-perfect seacoast town that suggested the locale for a novel of contemporary witchcraft. Pick the Rhode Island you want; all are cheek by jowl and none is visible from I–95. Nor is the 2,600-acre Great Swamp south of Kingston, the Victorian shore resort of Watch Hill, or the exquisite desolation of Block Island, 13 miles out in the Atlantic.

Pleasures and Pastimes

Beaches

Rhode Island has 400 miles of shoreline with more than 100 salt and freshwater beaches concentrated in and around the resort communities of Narragansett, Watch Hill, Newport, and Block Island. The south coast of Rhode Island has miles of beautiful ocean beaches, many of which are open to the public. The beaches are sandy, for the most part, and their water is clear and clean—in some places, the water takes on the turquoise color of the Caribbean Sea. There are several good beaches in and around Newport: There's a beautiful view of Newport's harbor from Ft. Adams State Park's beach; Middletown has a sandy beach adjacent to a bird sanctuary; and Portsmouth's Sandy Point Beach has calm surf. Being an island, Block Island has miles of shoreline, some of it quite rocky. But the Frederick J. Benson Town Beach, in the middle of the several-mile-long Crescent Beach, is patrolled by lifeguards and is good for a swim.

Rhode Island

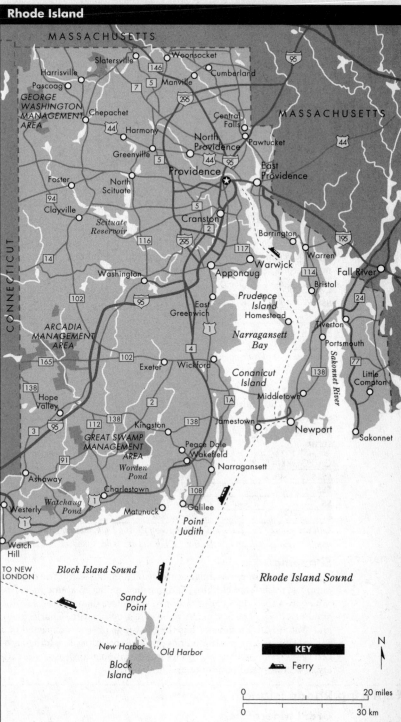

MASSACHUSETTS

Slatersville
Woonsocket
Harrisville
146
Cumberland
Pascoag
7 5
Manville
GEORGE
WASHINGTON
MANAGEMENT
AREA
Chepachet
295
MASSACHUSETTS
Central
Falls
44
44
Harmony
North
Providence
Greenville
5
Pawtucket
44
Providence
East
Providence
Foster
5
95
North
Scituate
94
Cranston
195
Clayville
5
2
Scituate
Reservoir
Barrington
116
Warren
Fall River
CONNECTICUT
14
295
117
Warwick
114
Bristol
Washington
Apponaug
102
Prudence
Island
95
24
East
Greenwich
Homestead
ARCADIA
MANAGEMENT
AREA
1
Narragansett
Bay
Tiverton
165
102
4
Portsmouth
77
Exeter
Wickford
Conanicut
Island
Little
Compton
138
1A
138
Hope
Valley
2
Middletown
112
138
3
95
Kingston
138
Jamestown
Newport
91
GREAT SWAMP
MANAGEMENT
AREA
Peace Dale
Sakonnet
Ashaway
Worden
Pond
Wakefield
Narragansett
Charlestown
108
Westerly
Watchaug
Pond
Matunuck
Galilee
1
Watch
Hill
Point
Judith

TO NEW
LONDON
Block Island Sound
Rhode Island Sound

Sandy
Point

New Harbor
Old Harbor
N

Block
Island

KEY
Ferry

0   20 miles
0   30 km

Boating

Newport is one of the great sailing cities of the world. Historically, as an accessible port, it prospered from shipbuilding and trade. Today, it's the headquarters of several sailing schools, and the beginning or endpoint of several important sailing races. A new emphasis on Providence's waterfront has resulted in a riverfront park, Waterplace, where boating outfitters vie for your business. Paddleboats meander around Roger Williams Park, and boating is also available on the Seekonk River and in Narragansett Bay. Many tidal rivers and large salt ponds in South County are perfect for canoeing and kayaking.

Dining

Rhode Island is home to much traditional regional fare. Johnnycakes are a sort of corn cake cooked on a griddle, and the native clam, the quahog (pronounced *ko*-hog), is served in chowder, as stuffed clams, fried clams, and even clam pie. Particularly popular are "shore dinners," which include clam chowder, steamers, clam cakes, sausage, corn-on-the-cob, lobster, watermelon, and Indian pudding (a steamed pudding made with cornmeal and molasses). Providence restaurants are less expensive than those of Boston and Manhattan, and the city's many ethnic groups are well represented.

CATEGORY	COST*
$$$$	over $35
$$$	$25–$35
$$	$15–$25
$	under $15

average cost of a three-course dinner, per person, excluding drinks, service, and 7% sales tax

Lodging

Although the major chain hotels are represented in Rhode Island, smaller inns and B&Bs offer more color. Rates are very much seasonal; in Newport, for example, winter rates are often half those of summer.

CATEGORY	COST*
$$$$	over $150
$$$	$100–$150
$$	$60–$100
$	under $60

All prices are for a standard double room during peak season, with no meals unless noted, and excluding 12% hotel and sales taxes.

Shopping

Newport is a shopper's—but not a bargain hunter's—city. You can find antiques, traditional clothing, and marine supplies in abundance. Antiques are a specialty of South County, with more than 30 stores within an hour's drive. The best places to browse are Wickford, Charlestown, and Watch Hill. Providence has the full range of stores expected of a capital city. Its ethnic communities produce specialties like Italian groceries and Hmong clothes, and its student population ensures a variety of second-hand boutiques and funky shops.

Exploring Rhode Island

Great Itineraries

Less than a week is enough to get a good feel for this small state and to take in its many charms.

Numbers in the text correspond to numbers in the margin and on the maps.

IF YOU HAVE 1 DAY
Spend it in 🚗 **Newport** ㉕–㊽, the highlight of most visitors' first trip to Rhode Island. This seaport community has an unbeatable combination of restaurants, shops, and beaches, all geared to please tourists.

IF YOU HAVE 3 DAYS
Spend a day and a half in 🚗 **Newport** ㉕–㊽, then make the 40-minute drive north to the capital, 🚗 **Providence** ①–⑯. While this city's attractions are less packaged than Newport's, they include sophisticated restaurants, lovely historic districts, and the academic environments of Brown University and Rhode Island School of Design.

IF YOU HAVE 5 DAYS
Spend the first three in 🚗 **Newport** ㉕–㊽ and 🚗 **Providence** ①–⑯, then take two days to explore South County, with its splendid beaches and a kick-your-shoes-off-and-relax atmosphere that's just right for summer. Shop and soak up 🚗 **Watch Hill**'s ⑱, turn-of-the-century elegance, then spend a day beaching it in **Charlestown** ⑳ or **South Kingston.** 🚗 **Narragansett** ㉓, with its great beaches and numerous bed-and-breakfasts, is one option for a second South County night—or you might pop over on the ferry to unspoiled **Block Island** ㊾–㊼.

When to Tour Rhode Island

May through October are the best months to visit Rhode Island, when Providence and Newport are at their prettiest. In summer, Newport hosts several high-profile music festivals that are magnets for large numbers of tourists. Block Island and the beach towns of South County are also geared for summer, but don't get nearly as crowded as Newport.

PROVIDENCE

50 mi from Boston, 30 mi from Newport, 190 mi from New York City.

Founded by Roger Williams in October 1635 as a refuge for freethinkers and religious dissenters, Providence remains a community that tolerates difference and fosters cultural inquiry and diversity. Brown University, Rhode Island School of Design (RISD), and Trinity Square Repertory Company are major forces in New England's intellectual and cultural life.

After Roger Williams, the most significant name in Providence history may be Brown. Four Brown brothers played a major part in the city's development in the 18th century. John Brown traded in slaves, opened trade with China, and aided the American Revolution; his mansion on the East Side is a must-see. Joseph Brown's designs—including his brother's mansion and the First Baptist Meeting House—changed the face of the city. Moses Brown, an abolitionist and a pacifist, founded the Quaker School that bears his name. Nicholas Brown rescued the failing Rhode Island College—known today as Brown University.

Although Providence suffered in the 1940s and '50s with the decline of its two main industries, textiles and costume jewelry (the city was once the nation's chief producer of the glittering baubles), downtown is coming back to life: Historic buildings are being renovated, and a convention center and downtown river-walk park, Waterplace, have opened in the last few years. Surrounding the center city are diverse neighborhoods attractive for strolling: Fox Point's Portuguese community, Federal Hill's Italian section, the historically Yankee East Side, and the young and hip College Hill. Providence is also a culinary center and home to the prestigious Johnson and Wales University Culinary Institute. Local restaurants include several that have won national recognition and quite a few that reflect the panoply of cuisines of the

city's ethnic populations. Many residents will argue that it is this eth-
nicity that makes Providence special.

Exploring

*Numbers in the margin correspond to points of interest on the Cen-
tral Providence map.*

❶ Founded in 1764, **Brown University** is the country's seventh oldest college. At the admissions office (✉ 45 Prospect St., ☎ 401/863–2378),
you can orient yourself to the history and layout of the university and
even join a tour of the National Historic Landmark campus, dominated
by Gothic and Beaux Arts structures. A walk on Thayer Street will ac-
quaint you with the campus's principal commercial thoroughfare.

NEED A   **Ocean Coffee Roasters** (✉ 110 Waterman Ave., ☎ 401/331–5282) is
BREAK?   a comforting café that sells tempting varieties of fresh-brewed coffee and
             rich homemade pastries. Here you can sit and watch the students de-
             bate esoteric points of academia.

❷ The 1910 **John Hay Library,** named for Abe Lincoln's secretary, houses
11,000 items related to the 16th president. The library also has American drama and poetry collections, 500,000 pieces of American sheet
music, the Webster Knight Stamp Collection, the letters of the early
horror and science-fiction writer H. P. Lovecraft, military prints, and
a world-class collection of toy soldiers. ✉ *20 Prospect St.,* ☎ *401/863–
2146.* 🆓 *Free.* ⌚ *Weekdays 9–5.*

★ **❸** The **Providence Athenaeum,** housed in an imposing 1838 Greek Revival, was established in 1753 and is among the oldest lending libraries in the world. Here Edgar Allan Poe, visiting Providence to lecture
at Brown, met and courted Sarah Helen Whitman, who was said to
be the inspiration for his poem "Annabel Lee." The library has a collection of Rhode Island art and artifacts, as well as an original set of
elephant folio *Birds of America* prints by John J. Audubon. ✉ *251 Benefit St.,* ☎ *401/421–6970.* 🆓 *Free.* ⌚ *June–Labor Day, weekdays 8:30–
5:30; Labor Day–May, weekdays 8:30–5:30 (until 8:30 Wed.), Sat.
9:30–5:30, Sun. 1–5.*

❹ The small **Rhode Island School of Design Museum of Art** is amazingly
comprehensive. In addition to about 25 exhibitions that change annually, many involving textiles (a longstanding native industry), the permanent holdings contain the Abby Aldrich Rockefeller collection of
Japanese prints, Paul Revere silver, 18th-century porcelain, and French
Impressionist paintings. Especially popular with kids are the 10-foot
statue of Buddha and the mummy from the Ptolemaic period (circa 300
BC). The RISD Museum of Art is connected to **Pendleton House,** a replica
of an early 19th-century Providence house, with period furnishings.
✉ *224 Benefit St.,* ☎ *401/454–6100.* 🆓 *$2; free Sat.* ⌚ *Summer,
Wed.–Sat. noon–5; fall–spring, Tues.–Wed., Fri.–Sat. 10:30–5, Thurs.
noon–8, Sun. 2–5.*

❺ **Market House** (✉ Market Sq., South Main St.), designed by Joseph
Brown, was central to Colonial Providence's trading economy. Tea was
burned here in March 1775, and the upper floors were used as a bar-
racks during the Revolutionary War. Afterward Market House was the
seat of city government from 1832 to 1878. A plaque shows the height
reached by floodwaters during the Great Hurricane of 1938.

❻ The 1828 **Arcade,** America's very first indoor shopping mall, is now
a National Historic Landmark. The graceful Greek Revival building
has cast-iron railings, a facade with six gigantic Ionic columns, and three

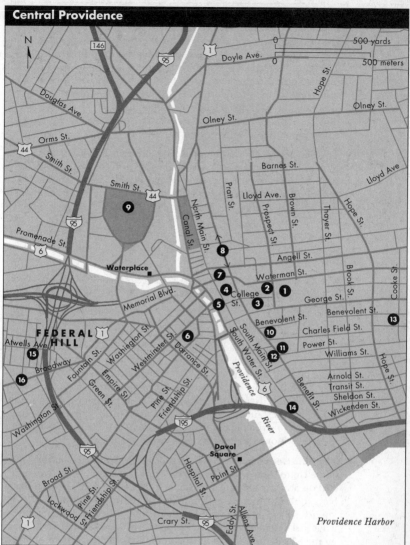

Central Providence

Ambrose Burnside's
House, **12**

Arcade, **6**

Benefit Street, **8**

Broadway, **16**

Brown University, **1**

Federal Hill, **15**

First Baptist Church
in America, **7**

First Unitarian
Church of
Providence, **10**

Fox Point, **14**

John Brown
House, **11**

John Hay Library, **2**

Market House, **5**

Museum of Rhode
Island History,
Aldrich House, **13**

Providence
Athenaeum, **3**

Rhode Island School
of Design Museum of
Art, **4**

State House, **9**

tiers of shops: The shops on the upper levels have clothing, furnishings, jewelry (be sure to stop in the eclectic Copacetic Rudely Elegant Jewelry), paper goods, and toys. The Weybosset Street and Westminster Street facades differ—one has a pediment, the other stone panels. The reason for this discrepancy is that the man who owned only half the land on which his arcade was to be built could not agree with the other owners on an architect, so they hired two—each of whom insisted on carrying out his own conception. ⊠ *65 Weybosset St.,* ☎ *401/272–2340.* ☉ *Jan.–Nov., Mon.–Sat. 10–6; Thanksgiving–Dec. 25, weekdays 10–8, Sat. 10–6, Sun. noon–5.*

❼ The **First Baptist Church in America** was designed by Joseph Brown and built in 1775 for a congregation established in 1638 by Roger Williams and his fellow dissenters. The church has a carved wood interior, a Waterford crystal chandelier, and graceful but austere Ionic columns. It was rebuilt by ships' carpenters in 1775, and so it survived the Gale of 1875 and the 1938 hurricane. ⊠ *75 N. Main St.,* ☎ *401/751–2266.* ☞ *Free; donations accepted.* ☉ *Weekdays 9–4, guided tours 10–3; Sun. guided tours at 10:45 (July–Aug.), 12:15 (Sept.–June); Sat. guided tours by appointment.*

❽ The centerpiece of any visit to Providence is **Benefit Street,** the "Mile of History." A bumpy cobblestone sidewalk leads past a long row of early Federal and 19th-century candy-color houses, crammed shoulder-to-shoulder, on a steep hill overlooking downtown Providence. Here is a reminder of the wealth brought to Rhode Island by the triangular trade of slaves, rum, and molasses in Colonial times—and also a reminder that neighborhoods long thought past their prime can be brought back to fashion, given a timely influx of ambitious "rehabbers." Throughout the 1980s, much of Providence beyond Benefit Street was discovered by erstwhile Bostonians looking for drastically cheaper real estate even though it meant enduring an hour-plus commute. Try to stroll here at dusk, when there is still some daylight but the old-fashioned streetlights have already lit up.

❾ The **State House,** built in 1900, has the first unsupported marble dome in the United States (also one of the world's largest), which was modeled on St. Peter's Basilica in Rome. The ornate white Georgian marble exterior is topped by the gilded statue *Independent Man.* The interior's focal point is a full-length portrait of George Washington by Rhode Islander Gilbert Stuart, the same artist who created the likeness on the $1 bill. You'll also see the original parchment charter granted by King Charles to the colony of Rhode Island in 1663 and military accoutrements of Nathanael Greene, Washington's second-in-command during the Revolutionary War. ⊠ *82 Smith St.,* ☎ *401/277–2357.* ☉ *Weekdays 8:30–4:30; tours given 9:30–3:30.*

Just below the State House is Providence's river-walk park, **Waterplace.** The city opened Waterplace in 1994, hoping to attract street entertainers and their admirers to the amphitheater and pleasure boaters for trips along the riverfront.

❿ The **First Unitarian Church of Providence,** on the corner of Benefit and Benevolent streets, was built in 1816. The bell tower houses the largest bell ever cast in Paul Revere's foundry, a 2,500-pounder. ⊠ *1 Benevolent St.,* ☎ *401/421–7970.* ☞ *Free.* ☉ *By appointment; Sun. service at 10:30.*

★ ⓫ The **John Brown House,** designed by Joseph Brown for his brother in 1786, is a three-story Georgian mansion whose opulence suggests that the slave trade was good business. John Quincy Adams called this house "the most magnificent and elegant mansion that I have ever seen on this continent." Abolitionist brother Moses wasn't impressed; through his organization, the Anti-Slavery Society, Moses brought charges against John for illegally engaging in the buying and selling of human lives. In addition to opening trade with China, John is famous for his role in the burning of the British customs ship *Gaspee*. George Washington slept here—and he probably found it lovely: The house is replete with elaborate woodwork and filled with examples of decorative arts, furniture, silver, pewter, glass, linens, and Chinese porcelain from the late 18th and early 19th centuries. Children may enjoy the antique doll collection. ⊠ *52 Power St.,* ☏ *401/331–8575.* ⌨ *$5.* ⊘ *Mar.–Dec., Tues.–Sat. 11–4, Sun. 1–4; Jan.–Feb. by appointment.*

⓬ Ambrose Burnside's House, a now rather dilapidated 1866 redbrick Victorian with a turret, is across the street from the John Brown House. Burnside was the Civil War general who led the Rhode Island army in defense of Washington and who later became governor. Today he is best remembered for his facial hair: Sideburns are named after him. ⊠ *314 Benefit St. Not open to the public.*

⓭ The **Museum of Rhode Island History, Aldrich House,** has no permanent collection but presents two to five exhibits a year on the history, culture, architecture, and crafts of Rhode Island. ⊠ *110 Benevolent St.,* ☏ *401/331–8575.* ⌨ *$2.* ⊘ *Tues.–Fri. 9–5, weekends for special exhibitions.*

⓮ Fox Point used to be a lower-class Portuguese neighborhood, but gentrification is rapidly changing its character, and Wickenden Street is now chockablock with antiques stores, galleries, and trendy cafés. Nonetheless, many of the houses along Wickenden, Transit, Gano, and neighboring streets are painted the pastel colors of Portuguese homes, and people still sit out on their stoops on hot summer evenings.

⓯ The Italian community is vital to Providence's culture and sense of self, and **Federal Hill** is its center. Entering the neighborhood via Atwells Avenue might make you think you're walking down a main street in a small Italian town: You're as likely to hear Italian as English. The stripe down the middle of the avenue is repainted each year in red, white, and green, and a huge *pigna* (pinecone), an Italian symbol of abundance, hangs on an arch soaring over the street and also adorns a decorative fountain. The hardware shops may sell boccie sets and the corner store may sell little china statues of saints, but the "Avenue," as locals call it, isn't cutesy. The St. Joseph's and Columbus Day seasonal celebrations, with music, street food, and parades, are not to be missed.

NEED A BREAK? | **Pastiche** (⊠ 92 Spruce St., ☏ 401/861–5190), on a quiet side street of Federal Hill, is an intimate, European-style dessert café where patrons can take their *caffé latte* (one-quarter espresso, three-quarters milk) or espresso with fine pastries. Heavenly treats include chocolate-hazelnut torte, pumpkin cheesecake, and fresh fruit tarts. If you want more than a snack, visit the **Grotta Azzura** (⊠ 210 Atwells Ave., ☏ 401/272–9030), a great Old World restaurant, and **Plaza Grille** (⊠ 64 DePasquale Ave., ☏ 401/274–8684), on a side street off the avenue, first. The former is for more formal dining; the latter serves bistro-style burgers and omelets in a cozy, pink, exposed-brick setting.

⓰ Broadway is a Victorian boulevard first developed in the 1830s by Irish immigrants. They built the large, rambling gingerbread houses frosted with external bric-a-brac and such details as porticoes, turrets, towers, and small stained-glass windows. Toward the turn of the century, Broadway gradually turned Italian, like neighboring Federal Hill. "Barnaby's Castle," the huge mansion at No. 229—adorned with a four-story, 12-sided tower—was owned by J. B. Barnaby, "The Rhode Island Clothing Prince." Barnaby's wife was the victim in a famous murder, which came to trial in 1891; her doctor had sent her a New Year's present of whiskey laced with arsenic. Other particularly stunning houses are at No. 514 and No. 78. The houses vary in style from Greek Revival to Italianate to Queen Anne to Gothic Revival; there's even a row of brownstones (rare in Providence).

OFF THE
BEATEN PATH
Roger Williams Park and Zoo is popular with children and dogs. With 430 acres, there's plenty of room to run, tumble, and shriek. Have a picnic, take out a paddleboat, feed the ducks in the lakes, take a pony ride. There's even tennis in warmer months. At the zoo you can see giraffes and elephants, watch the penguins, and pet the animals in the petting zoo (but do not feed Norton and Trixie, the polar bears). At nearby Carousel Village, kids can ride the vintage carousel or a miniature train, explore the playground, then mellow out with the family in the restful Japanese Garden. The museum on the grounds has exhibits on local history, wildlife, and Narragansett Bay. ⊠ *Elmwood Ave.,* ☎ *401/785–3510.* ▨ *$3.50.* ☉ *Zoo: summer, daily 9–5; winter, daily 9–4; museum Tues.–Fri. 10–4, weekends noon–4.*

Dining and Lodging

$$$$ ✕ **Al Forno.** This restaurant cemented Providence's reputation as a culi-
★   nary center in New England. George Germon and Johanne Killeen's combined talents draw upon Italian recipes to make the most of New England's fresh produce. Wood-grilled pizza could be your appetizer, followed by a clam roast with spicy sausage served in a tomato broth or charcoal-seared tournedos with mashed potatoes and onion rings. Desserts range from crepes with apricot purée and crème anglaise to fresh cranberry tart with walnuts and brown sugar. ⊠ *577 S. Main St.,* ☎ *401/273–9760. Reservations not accepted. AE, MC, V. Closed Sun., Mon.*

$$$$ ✕ **Capital Grille.** This is the place to go in Rhode Island for a truly great
★   steak. Beef is the star of the menu (fine cuts are dry-aged for maximum flavor), but lobster appears as well, and side dishes such as mashed potatoes, cottage fries, and Caesar salad are served in portions large enough to sate the heartiest appetite. Lots of leather and brass, along with oil portraits on the walls and stock prices ticking over by the bar, give the place the feeling of a tony men's club. ⊠ *1 Cookson Pl.,* ☎ *401/521–5600. AE, D, DC, MC, V. No lunch weekends.*

$$$$ ✕ **L'Epicureo.** Now one of the most elegant restaurants in Providence, L'Epicureo began life as half of a Federal Hill butcher shop called Joe's. Joe's daughter Rozann and son-in-law Tom have turned the former market into a marvel of an upscale Italian bistro, winning the highest marks from satisfied reviewers for their wood-grilled steaks and veal chops and well-turned out pasta such as fettuccine tossed with arugula, garlic, and lemon. ⊠ *238 Atwells Ave.,* ☎ *401/454–8430. Reservations not accepted. AE, D, DC, MC, V. Closed Sun. and Mon.*

$$$ ✕ **Bluepoint Oyster Bar.** This tiny, handsome place at the base of College Hill near Providence's river-walk park, has one of the area's best wine lists and offers a changing menu of fresh, well-prepared seafood, including a sampler plate of succulent oysters from New England waters. ⊠ *99 N. Main St.,* ☎ *401/272–6145. AE, DC, MC, V.*

$$$ ✕ **Rue de l'Espoir.** This eclectic menu blends ethnic preparations into such tempting appetizers as chicken-and-cashew spring rolls or fried calamari with hot-pepper relish. Follow with roasted pork crusted with mustard and pepper, or any of the creative pastas. Breakfast is

served beginning at 7:30 (brunch on weekends). Eye-pleasing art, including a great mural, and homey decor add to the appeal. The crusty bread from Palmieri's is a local institution. ✉ *99 Hope St.,* ☎ *401/751–8890. AE, D, DC, MC, V. Closed Mon.*

$$–$$$ ✕ **Leon's on the West Side.** Leon's is a lively, artsy spot for creative,
★ light entrées and salads. Known for its inventive pizzas and create-your-own pasta dishes (you pick your pasta and sauce), Leon's also has a wildly popular weekend brunch. Blackboard specials are good bets. ✉ *166 Broadway,* ☎ *401/273–1055. AE, D, MC, V. Closed Mon.*

$$ ✕ **Casa Christine.** Family-run Christine's is a find on Federal Hill for
★ its zesty pastas and other Italian entrées of chicken, veal, and seafood. Be sure to check the board for specials. ✉ *145 Spruce St.,* ☎ *401/453–6255. No credit cards. BYOB. Closed Sun. and Mon.*

$ ✕ **Angelo's Civita Farnese.** On Federal Hill in the heart of Little Italy, Angelo's is a family-run place with Old World charm. This is a local favorite for fresh and simply prepared pasta, where the portions are large and the noise level is high. ✉ *141 Atwells Ave.,* ☎ *401/621–8171. Reservations not accepted. No credit cards.*

$ ✕ **Kabob 'n' Curry.** This attractive, small restaurant with an elevated view of the collegiate bustle of Thayer Street from its glass-enclosed porch specializes in the flamboyant cuisine of northern India. Particular favorites are chicken tikka masala, lamb shajahani, and vegetable curry. ✉ *261 Thayer St.,* ☎ *401/273–8844. AE, D, DC, MC, V.*

$ ✕ **Little Chopsticks.** The spicy, intense dishes of the Szechuan and Hunan regions are specialties in this clean, modern restaurant. Try the spicy shredded pork in garlic sauce or Strange Flavor Chicken. ✉ *495 Smith St.,* ☎ *401/351–4290. D, DC, MC, V.*

$$$ 🏨 **Marriott Hotel.** Although it lacks the Biltmore's old-fashioned elegance, you may prefer the Marriott's larger size and modern conveniences. Rooms are modern and are decorated in tones of peach, green, and jade. ✉ *Charles and Orms Sts., near Exit 23 off I–95,* ☎ FAX *401/272–2400 or 800/937–7768. 339 rooms with bath, 6 suites. Restaurant, indoor and outdoor pools, sauna, health club, meeting rooms, free parking. AE, D, DC, MC, V.*

$$$ 🏨 **Old Court Bed & Breakfast.** On historic Benefit Street, this three-story Italianate inn was built in 1863 as a rectory. Elegant antique furniture, chandeliers, richly colored wallpaper, and memorabilia throughout the house reflect the best of 19th-century decor. Rooms are generally large with high ceilings; several have nonworking marble fireplaces, and some have views of the state house and downtown. A few of the well-worn rugs could be replaced, but overall there's a sedate, elegant atmosphere. ✉ *144 Benefit St.,* ☎ *401/751–2002. 10 rooms with bath, 1 suite. Free parking. CP. AE, MC, V.*

$$$ 🏨 **Biltmore Hotel.** The Biltmore, completed in 1922, has a sleek Art
★ Deco exterior, Old World charm, and an external glass elevator that allows delightful views of Providence at night. The personal attentiveness of its staff, the downtown location, and modern amenities make this hotel the best base from which to explore the city. ✉ *Kennedy Plaza,* ☎ *401/421–0700 or 800/843–6664,* FAX *401/421–0210. 217 rooms with bath, 21 suites. Restaurant, café, health club, meeting rooms, parking. AE, D, DC, MC, V.*

$$$ 🏨 **Westin Hotel.** Opened in November 1994, the multiturreted Westin towers over Providence's compact downtown, connected by a skywalk to the city's gleaming convention center. The 25-story brick Westin is another link in the city's effort to become a major convention destination. ✉ *1 West Exchange St.,* ☎ *401/598–8000 or 800/228–*

3000, FAX *401/598–8200. 363 rooms with bath. Restaurant, health club, meeting rooms, parking. AE, D, DC, MC, V.*

$$ 🏨 **C. C. Ledbetter's.** The unmarked, somber green exterior of C. C.'s Benefit Street home belies its vibrant interior—the place is filled with lively art, books, photographs, quilts, a homey blend of contemporary furnishings and antiques, and two English springer spaniels. A well-located (across the street from the John Brown House) bargain (about half the price of the Old Court Bed & Breakfast), this B&B is the hostel of choice for parents of Brown University students. ⊠ *326 Benefit St.,* ☎ FAX *401/351–4699. 1 room with bath, 4 rooms share 2 baths. Free parking. CP. No credit cards.*

$$ 🏨 **Days Hotel on the Harbor.** Despite its small lobby (modern, with marble floors and ficus trees), this plain but comfortable hotel affords a sense of openness: You can even watch the chef at work. Guest rooms have contemporary furnishings in pastel colors; half the rooms have harbor views, while the other half overlook speeding traffic on I–95. A few rooms have their own whirlpool bath. ⊠ *220 India St.,* ☎ FAX *401/272–5577, ext. 199. 136 rooms with bath. Restaurant, hot tub, exercise room, meeting rooms, airport shuttle, free parking. AE, D, DC, MC, V.*

$$ 🏨 **Holiday Inn.** This high-rise hotel, attractively remodeled in 1995, is conveniently close to Exit 21 off I–95, the Providence Civic Center, and the Rhode Island Convention Center. The comfortable lounge (Early American decor with nautical overtones) encourages relaxed conversation. Spacious rooms with great city views are decorated in shades of green and purple, with highly polished Colonial furniture, and have all the amenities (room service, phones, cable TV) endemic to good chain hotels. ⊠ *21 Atwells Ave.,* ☎ *401/831–3900 or 800/465–4329,* FAX *401/751–0007. 274 rooms with bath. Restaurant, bar, indoor pool, hot tub, exercise room, meeting rooms, airport shuttle, free parking. AE, D, DC, MC, V.*

$$ 🏨 **State House Inn.** Beautifully restored rooms of this classy, conve-
★ nient inn are furnished with Shaker or Colonial-style pieces, and some have canopy beds and working fireplaces. In addition, all have phones and TVs: Frank and Monica Hopton, who renovated the large 1880s house in 1990, have done a fine job of combining Old World style with the conveniences that befit a city inn just a few blocks from the state house. Some rooms are on the small side, but that's the only caveat about this inviting inn. Breakfast is served in a country-style dining room with wide-plank floors, a brick fireplace, and a carved mantel. ⊠ *43 Jewett St.,* ☎ *401/785–1235. 9 rooms with bath. Breakfast room, free parking. Full breakfast included. AE, MC, V.*

$ 🏨 **Lansing House.** This bed-and-breakfast is in a quiet neighborhood, a short bus ride or a very long walk from downtown. The pink three-story house with gambrel roof was built in 1904, and the current owner "derenovated" the '50s interior when she bought it—uncovering large brick fireplaces and reinstating a floor-to-ceiling wooden sideboard, which was languishing in the basement. The staircase has an art nouveau stained-glass oriel window; guest rooms have Laura Ashley wallpaper and Victorian antiques. Three rooms share a gloriously old-fashioned bathroom with the original pedestal sink, stolid tub, and enormous faucets. ⊠ *Box 2441 (call for physical address),* ☎ *401/421–7194. 3 rooms share 1½ baths. CP. AE, MC, V.*

Nightlife and the Arts

See the *Providence Journal,* the *Providence Phoenix* (free in restaurants and bookstores; extensive rock/funk/blues coverage), and *Rhode Island Monthly* magazine. Look for free speaking events and performances at Brown and RISD.

Nightlife

The Hot Club (✉ 575 S. Water St., ☎ 401/861–9007; live jazz Sun. and Wed.) is just that, a hip place—with plants, a jukebox, and nice lighting—that was an early entry in the movement to revive nightlife on the city's waterfront. **Oliver's** (✉ 83 Benevolent St., ☎ 401/272–8795), with a pool table, bar, and jukebox upstairs as well as good pub food, booths, and brass downstairs, is a hangout for Brown students.

Sh-Booms (✉ 108 N. Main St., ☎ 401/751–1200) has a 1950s theme, good dance music, a pink Cadillac as part of the decor, and some hairy chests and chains. **AS220** (✉ 111 Empire St., ☎ 401/831–9327), a gallery and performance space, features paintings, plays, and performance art primarily for the young at heart. Musical styles run the gamut from techno-pop, hip-hop, and jazz to traditional Hmong folk music and dance. **Lupo's Heartbreak Hotel** (✉ 239 Westminster St., ☎ 401/272–5876), **Met Café** (✉ 130 Union St., ☎ 401/861–2142), and **The Call** (✉ 15 Elbow St., ☎ 401/421–7170) are all good spots for rock and rhythm-and-blues in funky, youthful settings. **Desperado's Contemporary Country Night Club** (✉ 180 Pine St., ☎ 401/751–4263) has country-and-western music, dancing, and country-dancing lessons. **Gerardo's** (✉ 1 Franklin Sq., ☎ 401/274–5560) is a popular gay and lesbian disco.

The Arts

Kind of seedy, kind of musty, the **Cable Car Cinema** is a relic from another time. Sit on old couches, munch popcorn, and watch low-budget, foreign, and cult films. Before the show, watch the street-theater artists perform. ✉ 204 S. Main St., ☎ 401/272–3970. 🎟 $6.

Providence Civic Center (✉ 1 LaSalle Sq., ☎ 401/331–6700) has 14,500 seats and hosts touring rock groups. **Providence Performing Arts Center** (✉ 220 Weybosset St., ☎ 401/421–2787) is a 3,200-seat hall that is home to touring Broadway shows, concerts, and other large-scale happenings. Opened in 1928, its lavish interior is filled with painted frescoes, Art Deco chandeliers, gilt, bronze moldings, and marble floors. The **Rhode Island Philharmonic** (✉ 222 Richmond St., ☎ 401/831–3123) presents 10 concerts at the Providence Performing Arts Center between October and May. **Veterans Memorial Auditorium** (✉ Brownell St., ☎ 401/277–3150) hosts concerts, children's theater, and ballet—both traveling productions and short-run performances.

Trinity Square Repertory Company (✉ 201 Washington St., ☎ 401/351–4242) has become nationally known for Tony Award–winning plays. In the renovated old Majestic movie house downtown, the Rep generally offers a varied season: classics, foreign plays, new works. Audiences from all over New England support the repertory actors in what can be unusual and risky works. **Alias Stage** (✉ 31 Elbow St., ☎ 401/831–2919), an ambitious offshoot of Trinity, presents original works. **Brown University** (✉ Leeds Theatre, 77 Waterman St., ☎ 401/863–2838) mounts productions that range from contemporary works to classics to avant-garde and student pieces. **New Gate Theatre** (✉ 134 Mathewson St., ☎ 401/421–9680) has a season that runs September through May. Although the company specializes in producing new plays, it also stages Broadway musicals and a popular Christmas cabaret.

Outdoor Activities and Sports

Baseball

The Pawtucket Red Sox, the Boston Red Sox triple-A farm team, plays spring–fall at McCoy Stadium (⊠ Pawtucket, I–95S to Exit 2A; follow Newport Ave. for 2 mi, then turn right onto Columbus at light, ☎ 401/724–7300).

Basketball

The **Providence College Friars** play Big East basketball at the Providence Civic Center (⊠ 1 LaSalle Sq., ☎ 401/331–6700). The **Boston Celtics** (basketball) play exhibition games at the Civic Center.

Biking

The best biking from Providence is along the 14½-mile **East Bay Bicycle Path,** which hugs the Narragansett Bay shore from India Point Park, through four towns, to Independence Park in Bristol.

Boating

In addition to the Roger Williams Park paddleboats, boating is available on the Seekonk River and in Narragansett Bay. For more information, contact the **Narragansett Boat Club** (⊠ River Rd., Providence, ☎ 401/272–1838). **Baer's River Workshop** (⊠ 222 South Water St., Providence, ☎ 401/453–1633) rents canoes and kayaks.

Football

Brown's mediocre but enthusiastic team plays at **Brown Stadium** (⊠ Elmgrove and Sessions Sts., Providence, ☎ 401/863–2236). The NFL Patriots train in July and August at **Bryant College** (Smithfield, ☎ 401/232–6070).

Hockey

The **Providence Bruins,** a farm team for the Boston Bruins, play a regular schedule at the Civic Center.

Jogging

Try the 3-mile tree-and-bench-lined Blackstone Boulevard, where Brown's track team works out.

Shopping

Antiques

Wickenden Street has the greatest concentration of antiques stores, as well as several art galleries. **The Cat's Pajamas** (⊠ 227 Wickenden St., ☎ 401/751–8440) specializes in 1920s–1960s jewelry, linens, housewares, accessories, and small furnishings. **CAV Coffee House** (⊠ 14 Imperial Pl., ☎ 401/751–9164) brings together an eclectic blend of fine rugs, tapestries, prints, portraits, and antiques in a coffeehouse located in a restored factory. A nice place to relax and listen, from time to time, to local music. **Tilden-Thurber** (⊠ 292 Westminster St., ☎ 401/272–3200) has high-end Colonial- and Victorian-era furniture and other antiques. **Roxy Deluxe** (⊠ 286 Thayer St., ☎ 401/861–4606) sells such glamorous antique duds as beaded sweaters from the 1950s, Edwardian gowns, and men's vests, hats, and overcoats.

Art

The Alaimo Gallery (⊠ 301 Wickenden St., ☎ 401/421–5360) specializes in ephemera: antique posters, hand-colored engravings, magazine and playbill covers, political cartoons, antique prints, book pages, and box labels. The gallery is run by the former director of the picture collection of the library at RISD. **JRS Fine Art** (⊠ 218 Wickenden St., ☎ 401/331–4380) sells contemporary jewelry, paintings, and sculpture, including some Southwest-inspired work. **The Peaceable**

Kingdom and Black Crow (✉ 116 Ives St., ☎ 401/351–3472) offers folk art, with strengths in Native American jewelry and crafts, kilims, and brilliantly colored, finely detailed, embroidered Hmong story cloths. (Rhode Island has a large Hmong community, and Joan Ritchie, the owner of the store, has written about the cloths made by these people from Laos.)

Foods

Roma Gourmet Foods (✉ 285 Atwells Ave., ☎ 401/331–8620) on Federal Hill sells homemade pasta, bread, pizza, pastries, and a large selection of cheeses. Gourmands will enjoy **Tony's Colonial** (✉ 311 Atwells Ave., ☎ 401/621–8675), a neighborhood grocery store that has dried pasta of every conceivable shape, color, and size; Abruzzese sausage; Parma ham; extra-virgin olive oil; fresh mozzarella; and a wide assortment of such freshly prepared foods as stuffed peppers, eggplant parmigiana, and chicken cacciatore. You can create your own Italian feast at home if you stop by **Venda's** (✉ 265 Atwells Ave., ☎ 401/421–9105) to take out some fresh, homemade ravioli or gnocchi.

Jewelry

Copacetic Rudely Elegant Jewelry (✉ the Arcade, 65 Weybosset St., ☎ 401/273–0470) sells the work of a group of diverse artists. Expect the unusual, and you will not be disappointed—anything from glass to precious metal and from holograms to computer-designed jewelry may be on display.

Maps

The Map Center (✉ 671 N. Main St., ☎ 401/421–2184) has an extensive selection of wall maps, world maps, U.S. topographical maps, nautical charts, road and street maps, and U.S. and foreign atlases.

Men's Clothing

Harvey Ltd. (✉ 114 Waterman St., ☎ 401/331–5950) sells upscale men's clothing including the Polo line. **Hillhouse Ltd.** (✉ 135 Thayer St., ☎ 401/421–8620) is preppy–traditional—the store where many a Brown student bought his first good suit.

Toys

The Game Keeper (✉ The Arcade, 65 Weybosset St., ☎ 401/351–0362), on the third floor of the Arcade, sells board games, puzzles, and many little spur-of-the-moment gadgets.

Women's Clothing

Urban Cargo (✉ 224 Thayer St., ☎ 401/421–7179), smack in the middle of collegeland, features young, casual, and moderately priced clothing and a selection of costume jewelry.

Side Trips

🖐 The **Children's Museum of Rhode Island** is a "please touch" museum. Great-Grandmother's Kitchen encourages children to rifle through cabinets filled with Victorian utensils, letting them see what cooking was like long ago; they can also explore "our house," which is a small replica of the museum, play in the shape-lab math exhibit, and visit a room-size map of Rhode Island. ✉ *58 Walcott St., Pawtucket,* ☎ *401/726–2590. 🎟 $3.50; free 1st Sun. of each month. 🕐 Tues.–Sat. 9:30–5, Sun. 1–5.*

🖐 **Slater Mill Historic Site,** the first factory in America to successfully produce cotton yarn from water-powered machines, was built in 1793 by Samuel Slater and two Providence merchants, William Almy and Smith Brown. The mill now houses classrooms, a theater with a slide show, and machinery used to illustrate the conversion of raw cotton to finished cloth. Marvel at the 16,000-pound waterwheel that powers the operating 19th-century mill, and visit the worker's cottage, built in 1758. The mill offers such classes as weaving, chair caning, and basketry. ✉ *727 Roosevelt Ave., Pawtucket,* ☎ *401/725–8638.* 🎟 *$4.* ☉ *June–Labor Day, Tues.–Sat. 10–5, Sun. 1–5; Mar.–May and Labor Day–Dec. 21, weekends 1–5.*

Providence A to Z

Getting Around

BY BUS

Rhode Island Public Transit Authority (☎ 401/781–9400 or, in RI, 800/244–0444; TDD 401/461–9400) runs around town, as well as out to the airport; the fare is 85¢–$2.50. A free trolley (painted green and orange) circles the downtown area from 11 AM to 2 PM weekdays, making a loop every 15 minutes between Davol Square and the State House, and calling also at Kennedy Plaza, where most of the city's other bus lines begin.

BY CAR

Overnight parking is not allowed on Providence's streets, and the gaping potholes and countless diversions of ongoing urban renewal render downtown driving a nightmare. Providence is small, so try to find a central lodging with parking, forget your car, and walk or take buses. On the plus side, I–95 cuts right through the city, so access is easy.

BY TAXI

Try **Airport Taxi** (☎ 401/737–2868), **Checker Cab** (☎ 401/273–2222), **East Side Taxi Service** (☎ 401/521–4200), and **Yellow Cab** (☎ 401/941–1122). Fare is $1.20 at the flag drop, then $1.60 per mile. The ride from the airport takes about 15 minutes and costs about $20.

Contacts and Resources

EMERGENCIES

Rhode Island Hospital (✉ 593 Eddy St., ☎ 401/444–4000).

GUIDED TOURS

Providence Preservation Society (✉ 21 Meeting St., ☎ 401/831–7440) offers two 90-minute cassette tours, one of College Hill (including Brown University and Rhode Island School of Design), and one of the downtown area. The society runs popular Historic Houses tours the first week of June, which allow visitors to explore stunningly furnished private homes. Three additional tours visit historic houses with architecture ranging from pre-Revolutionary to Federal, Greek Revival to Victorian.

24-HOUR PHARMACY

CVS (✉ 681 Reservoir Ave., Cranston, ☎ 401/943–7186) has branches throughout the Providence region.

VISITOR INFORMATION

Greater Providence Convention and Visitors Bureau (✉ 30 Exchange Terr., 02903, ☎ 401/274–1636; ☉ Weekdays 8:30–5.)

SOUTH COUNTY

When the principal interstate traffic shifted from the coastal Route 1 to the new I–95, coastal Rhode Island—known within the state as South County—was left behind in time, largely escaping the advance of malls and tract-housing developments that has overtaken other, more accessible areas. More popular with visitors today than in recent years, this region of rolling farmland is still undervisited compared to other parts of New England; its vast stretches of sandy beaches, wilderness, and colorful historic sites escape the crush of tourists.

With 19 preserves, state parks, beaches, and forest areas, including Charlestown's Burlingame State Park and Ninigret National Wildlife Refuge, South County is a region that respects the concept of wilderness.

Numbers in the margin correspond to points of interest on the Rhode Island Coast map.

Westerly

⑰ *50 mi from Providence, 100 mi from Boston, 140 mi from New York City.*

Westerly is a busy little railway town that grew up in the late 19th century around a major station on what is now the New York–Boston Amtrak corridor. Victorian and Greek Revival mansions line many streets just off the town center. **Wilcox Park** (⊠ 71½ High St., ☎ 401/596–8590), designed in 1898 by Warren Manning, an associate of Frederick Law Olmsted and Calvert Vaux, is an 18-acre park in the heart of town with a garden designed for people with visual impairments and other disabilities. Here signs in Braille identify the plantings of carnations, mint, chives, thyme, bay leaves—as well as coconut-, apple-, lemon-, and rose-scented geraniums—to touch, smell, and taste.

Dining and Lodging

$$$ ✕🏠 **Shelter Harbor Inn.** In a quiet rural setting not far from the beach
★   (the inn provides van service), this inn begs a romantic weekend getaway ruled by simple comforts and privacy. The original 19th-century house has been renovated, as have several outbuildings. Several rooms have both a working fireplace and a deck, and there's another deck, with a barbecue and a hot tub, on the roof. The corner room, No. 9, is a particular favorite. At the excellent restaurant, the frequently changing menu might include smoked scallops and capellini or pecan-crusted duck breast. The wine list is extensive, and a bowl of warm, buttery Indian pudding makes a solid finish to any dinner. Breakfast is good any day, but Sunday brunch is legendary. Although the address is Westerly, the inn is about 6 miles east of downtown. ⊠ *Rte. 1, 02892,* ☎ *401/322–8883. 24 rooms with bath. Restaurant, hot tub, croquet, paddle tennis. Full breakfast included. AE, DC, MC, V.*

Nightlife and the Arts

NIGHTLIFE
The **Windjammer** (⊠ Atlantic Ave., Westerly, ☎ 401/322–0271) offers oceanfront dining and dancing to rock bands in a room that holds 1,500.

THE ARTS
The Chorus of Westerly (⊠ 119 High St., Westerly, ☎ 401/596–8663) performs a variety of choral works year-round. **Colonial Theatre** (⊠ 1 Granite St., Westerly, ☎ 401/596–0810) presents professional musicals, comedies, and dramas throughout the year.

Shopping

Sun-Up Gallery (⊠ 95 Watch Hill Rd., ☎ 401/596–0800) sells fine American crafts, clothing, and jewelry.

Watch Hill

★ **⑱** *A part of Westerly, Watch Hill is 5 mi from Westerly's downtown.*

Watch Hill, a pretty Victorian-era resort town, has miles of beautiful beaches; it's a good place to shop for jewelry, summer clothing, and

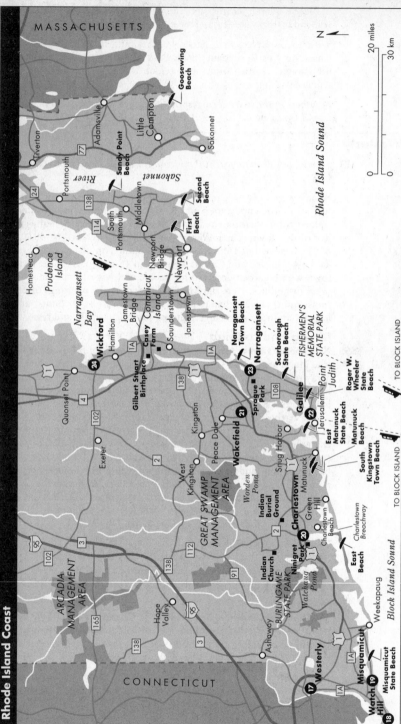

Rhode Island Coast

antiques. On Bay Street you'll be greeted by the **statue of Ninigret,** a chief of the Niantics. The model for this 19th-century statue was part of Buffalo Bill Cody's "Wild West Review."

The **Flying Horse Carousel,** at the beach end of Bay Street, is the oldest merry-go-round in America. It was built by the Charles W. F. Dare Co. of New York in about 1867. The horses, suspended from a center frame, swing out when in motion. Each is hand-carved from a single piece of wood and embellished with real horse hair, leather saddle, and agate eyes. ⊠ *Bay St.* 🎫 *50¢.* ⏱ *June 15–Labor Day, weekdays 1–9, weekends and holidays 11–9. Children only.*

The immensity of the **Ocean House** (⊠ 2 Bluff Ave., ☎ 401/348–8161), a yellow-clapboard Victorian hotel, will just about take your breath away. Built by George Nash in 1868, this was one of the grand hotels that helped earn Watch Hill its fame as a 19th-century resort. It's looking a bit down at the heels today, but it still offers unparalleled views of the Atlantic.

The **U.S. Coast Guard Light Station** has great views of the ocean and of Fishers Island, New York. There's a tiny museum here with exhibits about the light. ⊠ *Lighthouse Road, no phone.* 🎫 *Free.* ⏱ *May–Sept., Tues. and Thurs. 1–3.*

Napatree Point offers one of the best long beach walks in the state. A sandy spit lying between Watch Hill's Little Narragansett Bay and the ocean, Napatree Point is a protected conservation area teeming with wildlife. There's no admission fee, no phone, and no parking at Napatree; but there's municipal parking (for a fee) nearby.

Dining and Lodging

$$$ ✕ **Olympia Tea Room.** Step back in time to a small restaurant, first opened in 1916, where the soda fountain has a long marble counter and there are varnished wood booths. Try a marshmallow sundae—or an orangeade. For dinner sample ginger chicken or mussels steamed in white wine. On the dessert menu, the "world famous Avondale swan" is a fantasy of ice cream, whipped cream, chocolate sauce, and puff pastry. ⊠ *30 Bay St.,* ☎ *401/348–8211. Reservations not accepted. AE, MC, V. Closed Dec.–Easter.*

$$$ 🏨 **Ocean House.** Although a bit down-at-the-heels, this enormous grand old lady has one of the best seaside porches in New England. Casual, relaxing, and quiet, the inn has a reassuring if faded elegance. The furniture could be called "maple eclectic," with oldish mattresses, blankets, and sheets; those considerations pale next to the beautiful ocean view (ask for a good one). The porch offers great sunset views, and a set of splintery stairs leads to an excellent private beach. The restaurant here serves three meals a day. ⊠ *2 Bluff Ave., 02891,* ☎ *401/348–8161. 59 rooms with bath. Restaurant, lobby lounge, beach. MAP available. MC, V. Closed Sept.–June.*

Shopping

ANTIQUES
Book and Tackle Shop (⊠ 7 Bay St., Watch Hill, ☎ 401/596–0700) buys, sells, and appraises old and rare books, prints, autographs, and photographs.

CHILDREN'S CLOTHING
Gabrielle's Originals (⊠ 1 Fort Rd., Watch Hill, ☎ 401/348–8986) sells better-quality cotton goods, locally produced hand-knit sweaters, and Mousefeather clothing.

Puffins of Watch Hill (⌧ 84 Bay St., ☎ 401/596–1140) offers Halcyon Days enamels, Perthshire paperweights, Arthurcourt Designs, Seagull pewter, garden statuary and fountains, and handcrafted jewelry and gifts.

Misquamicut

⑲ *2 mi east of Watch Hill.*

In Misquamicut, Victorian hotels cede graciously to legions of 20th-century strip motels. In their midst lies **Atlantic Beach Park** (☎ 401/322–0504), a mile-long beach with an amusement park, giant water slide, carousel, miniature golf, and fast-food stands. Kids from 2 to 92 will love it. The beach is accessible year-round, but most amusements close by late September, leaving an eerie, abandoned atmosphere off-season.

Beach

A haven for young people, the lively stretch of sand from Atlantic Beach Park to Misquamicut State Beach draws crowds in the summer.

Dining and Lodging

$$ ✕ **Paddy's Seafood Restaurant.** Leather booths line the walls of the big square dining room of this beachside restaurant. It's a friendly, family-style, no-frills place, as befits its setting, but the food is good and portions are generous. Seafood dishes rule the menu—lobster, scrod, stuffed shrimp, and grilled tuna—but there's also pasta, a choice of salads, and an extensive children's menu. ⌧ *159 Atlantic Ave., Misquamicut Beach,* ☎ *401/596–2610. AE, D, MC, V. Closed Jan.–Apr.; Oct.–Dec., Tues.–Wed.*

$$$$ ✕⊞ **Weekapaug Inn.** This inn, with a peaked roof, stone foundation, and huge wraparound porch, is perched on a peninsula surrounded on ★ three sides by salty Quonochontaug Pond; just beyond a barrier beach is Block Island Sound. As if a set from "Father Knows Best," there's a comfy tidiness about the furnishings, where every surface looks freshly painted, waxed, or varnished. Room decor is cheerful, if not particularly remarkable, and most rooms are big and bright, with wide windows offering impressive views. Many guests are regulars—some for as long as 50 years. Restaurant standards are very high; a new menu every day emphasizes seafood and lists four to six entrées; a full-time baker makes all the desserts, breads, and rolls. Thursday-night cook-outs feature swordfish, steak, and chicken. ⌧ *15 Spring Ave., 02892,* ☎ *401/322–0301. 54 rooms with bath. Restaurant. No credit cards.*

$$ ✕⊞ **Grandview Bed and Breakfast.** This large home on a rise above Route 1A has clean, comfortable rooms at moderate prices. Guest rooms are simply but attractively furnished; front rooms have ocean views, and there's a small guest sitting room with TV and VCR. Breakfast is served on the porch in summer or in the family dining room out of season. It's friendly, relaxed, and affordable—just like the original British version of a B&B. Although the mailing address is Westerly, it's closer to Weekapaug. ⌧ *212 Shore Rd., Westerly, 02891,* ☎ *401/596–6384. 10 rooms, 6 with bath. AE, MC, V.*

$$$ ⊞ **Breezeway Motel.** The roads around Misquamicut are thick with strip motels—this is probably the best. The Bellone family takes great pride in its business and offers a variety of accommodations: villas with fireplaces and hot tubs, suites, efficiencies, and standard rooms. The decor varies from room to room: "Junior suites" are resplendent in dark green and white with king-size beds. The grounds have a swing set, shuffleboard, and a couple of floodlit fountains. ⌧ *Box 1368, 70*

Winnapaug Rd., 02891, ☎ 401/348–8953 or 800/462–8872, FAX 401/596–3207. 44 rooms with bath, 8 suites, 2 villas. Refrigerators, pool, game room. CP. AE, D, DC, MC, V. Closed Nov.–Apr.

Charlestown

㉒ *10 mi east of Misquamicut.*

Charlestown, which straggles along the Old Post Road and is bisected by Route 1, has a posse of motels and summer chalets. Most visitors come here for the excellent beaches, though a couple of large parks offer a chance to sample the inland outdoors. **Burlingame State Park** (☎ 401/322–7337 or 401/322–7994) is a 2,100-acre park offering fresh-water swimming, camping, and picnic areas, as well as boating and fishing on Watchaug Pond. **Ninigret Park** (☎ 401/365–1222) is a 172-acre park with picnic grounds, ball fields, a bike path, tennis, nature trails, and the Frosty Drew Observatory and Nature Center (☎ 401/364–9508), which runs nature and astronomy programs on Friday evenings.

Long before the first Europeans showed up, the region was inhabited by the Narragansett, a powerful Native American tribe that occupied the lands and islands of Narragansett Bay. The Niantics, ruled by Chief Ninigret, were one branch of this tribe. Many Narragansetts still live in the Charlestown area, but their historical sites are unmarked and easy to miss. The **Indian Burial Ground,** resting place of sachems (chiefs), is on the left side of Narrow Lane just north of Route 1: You'll recognize it by the tall fences, but there's no sign and it's not open for visits. Visitors are, however, welcome during the annual Narragansett meeting, usually the second Sunday in August, when tribal members from around the nation convene for costumed dancing and rituals.

Beaches

Charlestown Town Beach (✉ Charlestown Beach Rd.) can have high waves. **East Beach** (✉ East Beach Rd.) comprises two miles of dunes backed by the crystal-clear waters of Ninigret Pond, making this beach a treasure, especially for the adventurous beachgoer willing to hike a distance from the car. Lovely **Blue Shutters Town Beach** is family oriented. Beyond Charlestown, Route 1 barrels eastward again for a few miles to the next major "beach exit," which leads to fun-loving **Matunuck Beach,** with its popular roadhouse, large trailer park, and good surf.

Dining and Lodging

$$–$$$ ✕🏠 **The General Stanton Inn.** For helping pay the ransom of an Indian princess in 1655, the Narragansetts rewarded Thomas Stanton with the land where this inn now stands. Stanton, a trader from England, first ran it as a schoolhouse for African and Native American children. It was an inn and was operated as such since the 18th century, offering dining and lodging in an authentic Colonial atmosphere. Guest rooms have low ceilings, uneven floorboards, small windows, and period antiques and wallpapers; some have nonworking fireplaces. The restaurant dining rooms have brick fireplaces, beams, and wooden floors, and the menu offers traditional New England fare—steaks, lobster, scrod, rack of lamb—as well as pasta and salads. ✉ *Old Post Rd. (Rte. 1A), 02813, ☎ 401/364–0100, FAX 401/364–5021. 16 rooms with bath. Restaurant, bar. Full breakfast included. MC, V.*

Outdoor Activities and Sports

CANOEING AND KAYAKING

A Charlestown outfitter that offers rentals and advice is **Narragansett Kayak Co.** (✉ 2144 Matunuck Schoolhouse Rd., ☎ 401/364–2000).

FISHING

Ocean House Marina (⊠ 60 Town Dock Rd., ☎ 401/364–6040) is a tackle shop.

WATER SPORTS

Ocean House Marina, Inc. (⊠ 60 Town Dock Rd., ☎ 401/364–6060) is a full service marina.

WILDLIFE REFUGE

Ninigret National Wildlife Refuge is a 400-acre park that borders Ninigret Pond, Rhode Island's largest salt pond (separated from Block Island Sound by a long barrier of sand dunes) and home to many species of waterfowl. The refuge has about 2½ miles of trails from which dozens of species of birds have been sighted. Walking along the outer barrier of the pond is advised only at low tide, and then only with sturdy shoes. ⊠ Charlestown, ☎ 401/364–9124. ☉ Daily, dawn–dusk.

Shopping

ANTIQUES

Artists Guild and Gallery (⊠ 5429 Post Rd., Rte. 1, ☎ 401/322–0506) exhibits 19th- and 20th-century art, and the staff will help with conservation, frame repair, and gilding. **Fox Run Country Antiques** (⊠ Rtes. 1 and 2, Crossland Park, Charlestown, ☎ 401/364–3160 or 401/377–2581) has for years sold old jewelry, lighting devices, Orientalia, country primitives, and a large selection of china and glassware.

CRAFTS

At **The Fantastic Umbrella Factory** (⊠ Rte. 1A, Charlestown, ☎ 401/364–6616) three rustic shops are built around a spectacular wild garden in which peacocks, pheasants, and chickens parade; the factory sells its own hardy perennials and unusual daylilies as well as greeting cards, kites, crafts, and other wares. An outdoor café serves organic food in the summer.

Wakefield

㉑ 8 mi from Charlestown.

Wakefield, a small mill town (like its northern England namesake), is home to several big shopping centers, as well as the old **Washington County Jail.** Built in 1792, it now houses the Pettaquamscutt Historical Society. Here you can see jail cells and rooms from the Colonial period, a Colonial garden, and changing exhibits that depict South County life during the last 300 years. ⊠ 1348 Kingstown Rd., ☎ 401/783–1328. ☒ Free. ☉ May–Oct., Tues., Thurs., and Sat. 1–4.

Dining and Lodging

$$$ ✕ **Larchwood Inn.** The owners call this "a country inn with a Scottish flavor." More than 150 years old, the original building is set in a grove of larch trees. Ask for a table near the fireplace in winter, and try for a patio spot under the larch trees in summer. On the menu are halibut stuffed with scallops as well as seafood, chicken, beef, and veal. ⊠ 521 Main St., ☎ 401/783–5454. AE, D, DC, MC, V. No lunch Sun.

$$$ ✕ **South Shore Grille.** This restaurant is notable for its wood-fired grill
★   and waterfront views: One wall, overlooking upper Point Judith Pond, is all windows. Favorites on the constantly changing menu include crispy fried chicken, herb-grilled swordfish, and fillet of beef. In summer, the patio deck opens for an informal lunch and snacks from noon to dusk. ⊠ 210 Salt Pond Rd., ☎ 401/782–4780. MC, V. Closed Mon.–Wed. Jan.–Mar.

$$–$$$ 🏨 **Admiral Dewey Inn.** Listed on the National Register of Historic Places, the building was constructed as a seaside hotel in 1898. Rooms are furnished with Victorian antiques; some have views of the ocean, others are tucked cozily under the eaves. The inn is part of a summer community just across the road from Matunuck Beach. Smoking is permitted only on the wraparound veranda, which is filled with old-fashioned rocking chairs. ⊠ *668 Matunuck Beach Rd., 02881,* ☎ *401/783–2090. 8 rooms with bath, 2 rooms share bath. CP. MC, V.*

Outdoor Activities and Sports

HIKING

Great Swamp (near West Kingston), a temporary home to migrating waterfowl, has a network of trails; pick up a map from park headquarters (☎ 401/789–0281).

WATER SPORTS

The Watershed (⊠ 396 Main St., ☎ 401/789–3399) rents surfboards, Windsurfers, body boards, and wet suits. Owner Peter Pan offers lessons at Narragansett Town Beach.

Shopping

ANTIQUES

Dove and Distaff Antiques (⊠ 365 Main St., ☎ 401/783–514) is a good spot for Early American furniture and accessories; restoration, refinishing, and upholstery and drapery workshops are held here, too. **Peter Pots Authentic Americana** (⊠ 494 Glen Rock Rd., West Kingston, ☎ 401/783—2350) sells stoneware, period furniture, and collectibles.

ART GALLERIES

Hera Gallery (⊠ 327 Main St., ☎ 401/789–1488), established as a women's art cooperative in 1974, exhibits the work of emerging local artists, often dealing with ethnic or other provocative themes.

Galilee

22 *5 mi from Wakefield.*

Galilee is a busy, workaday fishing port, offering visitors whale-watching and fishing trips, good seafood restaurants, plenty of fish, and, as one local put it, "the smell," which may or may not be your idea of heaven. The only year-round **ferry to Block Island,** run by the Interstate Navigation Company (⊠ Galilee State Pier, Point Judith, ☎ 401/783–4613) leaves from Galilee. From the port it's a short drive to the **Point Judith Lighthouse** and a beautiful ocean view. ⊠ *1460 Ocean Rd.,* ☎ *401/789–0444.* ☉ *Daylight hours.*

Beaches

Matunuck beaches are closest to Galilee. **East Matunuck State Beach** (Succotash Rd.) is popular with the college crowd for its white sand, picnic areas, and bathhouse. Unpredictable high waves make **Matunuck Beach** (Matunuck Beach Rd.) a good spot for surfing and raft-riding. **Roy Carpenter's Beach** (Matunuck Beach Rd.) is part of a cottage-colony of seasonal renters, but is open to the public for a fee. **South Kingstown Town Beach** (Matunuck Beach Rd.) draws many families.

Dining and Lodging

$ ✕ **Aunt Carrie's.** This tremendously popular, family-owned place has been serving up traditional Rhode Island shore dinners, clam cakes and chowder, and meat dinners for more than 60 years. At the height of the season you may find a line; one alternative is to order from the take-out window and picnic on the grass nearby. Try the enormous but light clam cakes or the squid burger, served on homemade bread. Indian pudding à la mode is a favorite dessert. ⊠ *Rte. 108 and Ocean Rd., Point*

Judith, ☎ *401/783–7930. Reservations not accepted. No credit cards. Closed Labor Day–Memorial Day.*

$ ✕ **Champlin's Seafood.** Come to this casual, self-service restaurant for
★ the best fried scallops in South County. Other possibilities are boiled lobster, fried oysters, and snail salad. Take a seat out on the oceanfront deck and look down on the fishing trawlers tied to the docks below, or sit at one of the wood tables inside. Take-out service is offered. ⊠ *Port of Galilee,* ☎ *401/783–3152. Reservations not accepted. MC, V.*

$ ✕ **George's of Galilee.** The lines around the building on summer Saturday nights baffle local residents, who speculate that it might be because of the location at the end of a spit of land in a busy fishing harbor. They insist that it's certainly not the atmosphere (frantic and noisy) or the food (much better, they say, elsewhere in Galilee). Yet it's hard to argue with success, and George's has been a "must" for tourists since 1948. The restaurant serves several chowders and hosts barbecues on the beach on summer weekends. ⊠ *Port of Galilee,* ☎ *401/783–2306. Reservations not accepted. D, MC, V. Closed Nov.–Dec.; weekdays, Jan.–Feb.*

$$$ ▤ **Dutch Inn by the Sea.** A windmill, a tropical terrace, talking par-
★ rots, and a fountain in the lobby—kinda crazy, but the kids will love this stellar motel. The large indoor pool has a slide and is surrounded by palm trees and tropical birds; there are also pool tables, pinball machines, and outdoor tennis. Some rooms overlook the pool, and many have been refurbished luxuriously with deep green carpeting, white furniture, and king-size beds; others are in beige and brown. The motel, which has a large, family-oriented restaurant, is across the street from the Block Island Ferry Terminal and is open year-round. ⊠ *Port of Galilee, Narragansett, 02882,* ☎ *401/789–9341 or 800/336–6662,* ℻ *401/789–1590. 100 rooms with bath. Restaurant, bar, indoor pool, sauna, tennis, exercise room. AE, D, DC, MC, V.*

Nightlife and the Arts

Ocean Mist (⊠ 145 Matunuck Beach Rd., Matunuck, ☎ 401/782–3740) is a lively beachfront nightspot. The barn-style **Theatre-by-the-Sea** (⊠ Cards Pond Rd., off Rte. 1, Matunuck, ☎ 401/782–8587), built in 1933 and listed on the National Register of Historic Places, presents musicals and plays in summer.

Outdoor Activities and Sports

FISHING

The Frances Fleet (⊠ 2 State St., ☎ 401/783–4988 or 800/662–2824) offers day and overnight fishing trips. **Snug Harbor Marina** (⊠ Snug Harbor, Gooseberry Rd., ☎ 401/783–7766) can put you in touch with captains who skipper fishing boats.

WHALE-WATCHING

The Frances Fleet offers whale-watching aboard the **Lady Frances,** leaving Point Judith at 1 PM and returning at 6 PM. ⊠ *2 State St.,* ☎ *401/783–4988 or 800/662–2824.* ▣ *$30.* ☉ *July–Sept., Mon., Tues., and Thurs.–Sat.*

Narragansett

㉓ *5 mi from Galilee.*

The town of Narragansett takes in the peninsula east of Point Judith Pond and the Pettaquamscutt River as well as the two villages of Galilee and Jerusalem.

Narragansett, which locals sometimes refer to as "the Pier" for a now-demolished amusement wharf, is now a languid little town, but at the turn of this century it was a posh resort linked by rail with New York and Boston and was a major stop on the New York–Newport steamboat line. The well-to-do traveled in from those cities and beyond, and many of them headed for the Narragansett Pier Casino. Designed by McKim, Mead, and White in 1885, the casino was the center of social activity, with bowling, billiards, tennis, a rifle gallery, a theater, and a ballroom. The great structure, and a six-story Victorian hotel nearby, burned to the ground in September 1900. Now only the **Towers** (☎ 401/783–7121), the grand stone-turreted entrance to the former casino, remains, spanning the road and housing the Narragansett Chamber of Commerce.

In **Sprague Park** (✉ Kingstown Rd. and Strathmore St.) you can see the **Narragansett Indian Monument.** Donated to the town by the sculptor Peter Toth, the 23-foot monument weighs 10,000 pounds and is made from a single piece of wood, the trunk of a giant Douglas fir. To create the sculpture, Toth worked with hammer and chisel 12 hours a day for two months, then applied 100 coats of preservative.

☺ **Adventureland in Narragansett** has bumper boats, minigolf, and other games and rides. ✉ *Rte. 108,* ☎ *401/789–0030.* ✍ *Combination tickets: $1.50–$9.50.* ☉ *June 15–Labor Day, daily 10–10; Labor Day–Oct. and Apr. 15–May 30, weekends 10–10.*

☺ **The South County Museum,** on the grounds of Canonchet Farm, has reconstructions of typical New England buildings. Exhibits include a general store, a cobbler's shop, a tack shop, a print shop, a children's nursery, and vintage vehicles. The museum hosts special events throughout the season. ✉ *Canonchet Farm, Strathmore St.,* ☎ *401/783–5400.* ✍ *$2.50.* ☉ *May–Oct., Wed.–Sun. 11–4.*

The Gilbert Stuart Birthplace, built in 1751, was the home of America's foremost portraitist of George Washington. The adjacent 18th-century snuff mill was the first in America. ☎ *401/294–3001.* ✍ *$2.* ☉ *Apr.–Oct., Sat.–Thurs. 11–4:30.*

Beaches

Narragansett Town Beach (✉ Rte. 1A) has good surf, and is within walking distance of many Narragansett hotels and guest houses. Its pavilion has changing rooms, showers, and concessions. **Roger W. Wheeler State Beach** (✉ Sand Hill Cove Rd.) has picnic areas, a playground, mild surf, and swimming lessons. It's near Galilee. With surf, a bathhouse, and concessions, **Scarborough State Beach** (✉ Ocean Rd.) becomes crowded with teenagers on weekends. Still, many consider Scarborough the jewel of Ocean State beaches.

Dining and Lodging

$$$–$$$$ ✕ **Basil's.** Basil's, within walking distance of the Towers, serves French and Continental cuisine in an intimate setting. Dark, floral wallpaper and fresh flowers decorate the small dining room. The specialty is milk-fed baby veal topped with a light cream and mushroom sauce; other dishes include fine fresh fish dishes and duck à l'orange. Desserts are homemade. ✉ *22 Kingstown Rd.,* ☎ *401/789–3743. AE, DC, MC, V. No lunch. Closed Mon. and, Oct.–June, Tues.*

$$$ ✕ **Coast Guard House.** This restaurant, which dates to 1888 and which
★ served for 50 years as a life-saving station, displays interesting photos of bygone Narragansett Pier and the casino. Tables are candlelit and picture windows on three sides allow views of the ocean. The menu offers a range of typical American fare—seafood, pasta, veal, steak, and lamb entrées. On Friday and Saturday nights there's live enter-

tainment in the Oak Room and a DJ in the upstairs lounge. ⊠ *40 Ocean Rd.,* ☎ *401/789–0700. AE, D, DC, MC, V.*

$$$ ✕ **Spain Restaurant.** South County's only true Spanish restaurant is appropriately dark and atmospheric, the air pungent with garlic and spices. Enjoy such appetizers as shrimp in garlic sauce, stuffed mushrooms, and Spanish sausages; the main courses are variations on lobster, steak, paella and mariscada, and other meat dishes. ⊠ *1144 Ocean Rd.,* ☎ *401/783–9770. AE, D, DC, MC, V.*

$$–$$$ ▥ **The Richards.** Imposing and magnificent, this English manor–style mansion has a broodingly Gothic mystique that is almost the antithesis of a summer house. From the wood-panel common rooms downstairs, French windows allow views of a lush landscape, with a grand swamp oak the centerpiece of a handsome garden. A fire crackles in the library fireplace on chilly afternoons. Some rooms have 19th-century English antiques, floral-upholstered furniture, and fireplaces. Breakfast consists of fresh fruit and baked goods as well as such main courses as eggs Florentine and oven pancakes. ⊠ *144 Gibson Ave., 02882,* ☎ *401/789–7746. 2 rooms with bath, 2 rooms share bath, 1 2-bedroom suite. Full breakfast included. No credit cards.*

$$–$$$ ▥ **Stone Lea.** This spacious house is more than 100 years old and is filled with period furniture collected by the owners. The atmosphere is rather stiff and stilted, but the location is wonderful and it has lawns that roll down to the sea. Ocean-facing rooms have panoramic views, the most striking in Nos. 1 and 7. ⊠ *40 Newton Ave., 02882,* ☎ *401/783–9546. 6 rooms with bath, 1 suite. Full breakfast included. Bar, billiards, piano. MC, V.*

En Route The **Silas Casey Farm,** between Narragansett and Wickford, still functions much as it has since the 18th century. The farmhouse contains original furniture, prints, paintings, and political and military documents from the 18th to 20th centuries. The 360-acre farmstead is surrounded by nearly 30 miles of stone walls and has many barns. ⊠ *Boston Neck Rd., Rte. 1A, Saunderstown,* ☎ *401/295–1030.* ⌑ *$3.* ☾ *June–Oct., Tues.–Thurs. 1–5, Sun. 1–5.*

Wickford

★ ㉔ *10 mi north of Narragansett, 15 mi south of Providence.*

The Colonial village of Wickford has an attractive little harbor, dozens of 18th- and 19th-century homes, and a tempting assortment of antiques, furniture, and curiosity shops. Wickford's **Old Narragansett Church,** built in 1707, is one of the oldest Episcopal churches in America. ☎ *401/294–4357.* ☾ *Mid-June–Labor Day, Fri. 11–5, Sat. 10–5, Sun. worship, and by appointment.*

NEED A   **Wickford Gourmet Foods** (⊠ 21 W. Main St., ☎ 401/295–8190) prof-
BREAK?   fers homemade and specialty foods to eat in its comfortable loft, outside on the patio, or to take for a picnic. It's only a short walk down historic Brown Street to the Municipal Wharf, where beaches and lawns provide a lovely view of the harbor and its fishing activities.

Smith's Castle, built in 1678 by Richard Smith, Jr., was the site of many orations by Roger Williams, Rhode Island's most famed historical figure. A major restoration project is underway, but modified tours are offered May through September. Call for updated information. ⊠ *55 Richard Smith Dr., N. Kingstown,* ☎ *401/294–3521.* ⌑ *$3.* ☾ *May and Sept., Fri.–Sun. noon–4; June–Aug., Thurs.–Mon. noon–4.*

Nightlife and the Arts

South County isn't exactly famous for nightlife—the area around Misquamicut and Atlantic Beach Park is about the liveliest for summer visitors. There are a few nightclubs in Wakefield, and in nearby Narragansett you can find weekend entertainment, including live bands. **South County Players Children's Theater** (⊠ South Kingstown High School, ☎ 401/783–6110) gives performances by children for children.

Outdoor Activities and Sports

For fishing, canoeing, and kayaking supplies and rentals, head for **Quaker Lane Bait and Tackle** (⊠ 4019 Quaker La., North Kingstown, ☎ 401/294–9642).

Shopping

ANTIQUES

Mentor Antiques (⊠ 7512 Post Rd., Rte. 1, ☎ 401/294–9412) receives monthly shipments of English furniture—mahogany, pine, and oak—and has an extensive inventory of armoires. **Wickford Antiques Center I** (⊠ 16 Main St., ☎ 401/295–2966) vends wooden kitchen utensils and crocks, country furniture, china, glass, linens, and jewelry. **Wickford Antiques Center II** (⊠ 93 Brown St., ☎ 401/295–2966) sells antique furniture from many periods and fine art.

CRAFTS

Needlepoint pillows, fabric-bound books, Florentine leather books, lamps, and woven throws are just a few of the elegant gifts and home furnishings you'll find at **Askham & Telham Inc.** (⊠ 12 Main St., ☎ 401/295–0891).

South County A to Z

Getting Around

BY CAR

I–95 passes just north of Westerly before heading inland toward Providence. Routes 1 and 1A follow the coastline up into Narragansett Bay and are the more scenic coastal routes.

Contacts and Resources

EMERGENCIES

South County Hospital (⊠ 100 Kenyon Ave., Wakefield, ☎ 401/782–8000). **Westerly Hospital** (⊠ Wells St., Westerly, ☎ 401/596–6000).

24-HOUR PHARMACY

Granite Drug (⊠ Granite Shopping Center, Westerly, ☎ 401/596–0306).

VISITOR INFORMATION

South County Tourism Council (⊠ 4808 Tower Hill Rd., Wakefield 02879, ☎ 401/789–4422 or 800/548–4662). **Charlestown Chamber of Commerce** (⊠ Old Post Rd., Charlestown, ☎ 401/364–3878; ⊙ Memorial Day–Columbus Day, daily 9–5; rest of yr, weekdays 9 AM–11:30 AM). **Greater Westerly Chamber of Commerce** (⊠ 74 Post Rd., Rte. 1, Westerly, ☎ 401/596–7761 or 800/732–7636; ⊙ May–Oct., weekdays 9–5, weekends 9–2). **Narragansett Chamber of Commerce** (⊠ The Towers, Rte. 1A, Narragansett, ☎ 401/783–7121; ⊙ May–Sept., daily 9–4; Oct.–Apr., weekdays 9–3). **Visitor Information Center** (⊠ I–95 at the CT border; ⊙ Daily 8:30–4:30; Memorial Day–Columbus Day until 6:30).

NEWPORT

30 mi from Providence, 80 mi from Boston.

Perched gloriously on the southern tip of Aquidneck Island and bounded on three sides by water, Newport is one of the great sailing cities of the world and the host to world-class jazz, blues, folk, and classical music festivals.

Newport's first age of prosperity was in the late 1700s, when it was a major port city almost on a par with Boston and New York. Dozens of Colonial homes still stand today, most of them restored, in the historic "Point District."

By the 19th century Newport became a summer playground for the wealthiest families in America. These riches were not made in Rhode Island but imported by the titans of the Gilded Age and translated into the fabulous "cottages" overlooking the Atlantic. The masters and mistresses of such estates as Marble House and the Breakers lived in luxury that would be unimaginable even to New York developers today; ironically, the same sorts of local citizens whom one society matron once referred to as "footstools" weathered the days of ersatz feudalism and now earn a good deal of their tourism income from visitors to the palaces by the sea.

Newport in summer can be exasperating, its streets jammed with visitors and the traffic slowed by the procession of air-conditioned sightseeing buses. Yet the quality of Newport's arts festivals persuades many people to brave the crowds. In fall, winter, and spring, you stand a much better chance of soaking in Newport's merits without the migraine of standing in long lines. The weather is pleasant well into November, and the city goes all out to attract visitors in December with the many "Christmas in Newport" activities.

Exploring

Numbers in the margin correspond to points of interest on the Downtown Newport and Greater Newport maps.

㉕ A walk around Colonial Newport should give you a good idea of what the town was like in Revolutionary times. The **Hunter House** (circa 1748) is on the outskirts of the historic Point District. Notice the carved pineapple over the doorway; throughout Colonial America the pineapple was a symbol of hospitality, from the days when a seaman's wife placed a fresh pineapple at the front door to announce that her husband had returned from the sea. The elliptical arch in the central hall is a typical Newport detail. Much of the house is furnished with pieces made by Newport craftsmen Townsend and Goddard. ⊠ *54 Washington St.,* ☎ *401/847–1000.* ⌨ *$6.* ☉ *May–Sept., daily 10–5; Apr. and Oct., weekends 10–5.*

㉖ Farewell Street is lined with historic cemeteries. The oldest is the 18th-century **Common Burial Ground,** with tombstones that are fine examples of Colonial stone carving, much of it the work of John Stevens.

㉗ The **Brick Market,** built in 1760, was designed by Peter Harrison, who was also responsible for the Touro Synagogue and the Redwood Library. It was used as both a theater and a town hall, and today it's surrounded by some 40 shops and curio stores that make up the Brick Market Place. The original market building, once used for slave trading, is now the **Museum of Newport History,** a multimedia exhibit with

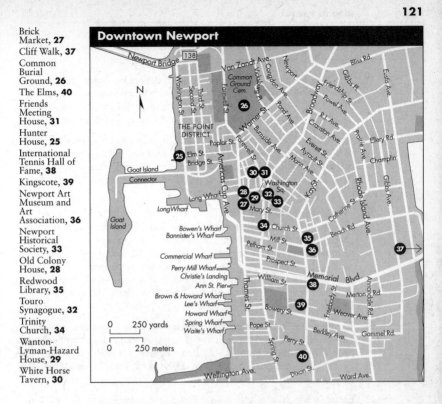

audiovisual programs exploring Newport's past. ✉ *Thames St.,* ☎ *401/841–8770.* 🎟 *$5.* ☉ *Wed.–Mon. 10–5.*

❷❽ The **Old Colony House,** built in 1739, was the headquarters of the Colonial and state governments. It was from the balcony of this building that the succession of George III was announced and the Declaration of Independence read to Newporters. George Washington met here with General Rochambeau. ✉ *Washington Sq.,* ☎ *401/846–2980 or 401/277–2669. Tours by appointment.*

❷❾ Newport's oldest house, the **Wanton-Lyman-Hazard House,** displays a "two-room" plan typical of the Colonial era. Dating from before 1700, this dark red house with steep-pitched roof was the site of the city's Stamp Act riot in 1765. ✉ *17 Broadway,* ☎ *401/846–0813.* 🎟 *$4.* ☉ *Mid-June–Sept., Thurs.–Sun. Call for hrs.*

❸⓪ The **White Horse Tavern** (✉ Corner of Marlborough and Farewell Sts., ☎ 401/849–3600) has been in operation since 1687, making it the oldest tavern in America. Its low, dark-beam ceiling, cavernous fireplaces, uneven plank floors, and cozy, yet elegant, tables epitomize Newport's Colonial charm.

❸❶ The **Friends Meeting House,** built in 1699, is the oldest Quaker meetinghouse in America. With its wide-plank floors, simple benches, balcony, and beam ceiling (considered lofty by Colonial standards), this two-story, shingle structure reflects the elegance, quiet reserve, and steadfast faith of Colonial Quakers. ✉ *29 Farewell St.,* ☎ *401/846–0813. Tours by appointment.*

❸❷ The oldest surviving synagogue in the country, **Touro Synagogue,** was designed by Peter Harrison and dedicated in 1763. Although very simple on the outside, the building has an elaborate interior. Notice the way its design combines the ornate columns and moldings of the Georgian style with Jewish ritualistic requirements. ✉ *85 Touro St.,* ☎ *401/847–4794.* ⛬ *Free.* ⊙ *Guided tours on ½ hr in summer, Sun.–Fri. 10–4; fall–spring, Sun. 1–2:30 or by appointment.*

㉝ The **Newport Historical Society** is the departure point for walking tours of Newport. The building is also a museum featuring a large collection of Newport memorabilia, furniture, and maritime items. ✉ *82 Touro St.,* ☎ *401/846–0813.* ⛬ *Free.* ⊙ *Tues.–Fri. 9:30–4:30.*

㉞ **Trinity Church** is a Colonial beauty built in 1724 and modeled after many of Sir Christopher Wren's churches in London. A special feature of the interior is the three-tier wineglass pulpit, the only one of its kind in America. ✉ *Queen Anne Sq.,* ☎ *401/846–0660.* ⛬ *Free.* ⊙ *June–Oct., daily 10–4; Nov.–May, daily 10–1.*

㉟ The **Redwood Library,** built in 1748, is the nation's oldest library in continuous use. Another magnificent example of the architecture of Peter Harrison, the building, although made of wood, was designed to look like a Roman temple, the original exterior paint mixed with sand to resemble stone. The library houses a wonderful collection of paintings by such important Early American artists as Gilbert Stuart and Rembrandt Peale. ✉ *50 Bellevue Ave.,* ☎ *401/847–0292.* ⛬ *Free.* ⊙ *Mon.–Sat. 9:30–5:30.*

㊱ The **Newport Art Museum and Art Association** displays contemporary art by New England artists in a stick-style Victorian building designed by Richard Morris Hunt. ✉ *76 Bellevue Ave.,* ☎ *401/848–8200.* ⛬ *$4.* ⊙ *Memorial Day–Labor Day, daily 10–5; Labor Day–Memorial Day, Tues.–Sat. 10–4, Sun. 1–5.*

★ **㊲** Easton's Beach (also called First Beach) is the beginning of the 3-mile **Cliff Walk,** which runs south along Newport's cliffs to Bailey's Beach and offers a water view of many Newport mansions. This is a challenging walk, not recommended for the infirm or for children under six, but it promises breathtaking vistas.

㊳ The **International Tennis Hall of Fame and Tennis Museum,** in a magnificent building by Stanford White, displays photographs and other tennis memorabilia. ✉ *Newport Casino, 194 Bellevue Ave.,* ☎ *401/849–3990.* ⛬ *$6.* ⊙ *Daily 10–5.*

It is hard to imagine the sums of money possessed by the wealthy elite who made Newport their summer playground in the late 1800s and early 1900s. The "cottages" they built are almost obscenely grand, laden with ornate rococo detail and designed with a determined one-upmanship.

Six Newport mansions are maintained by the **Preservation Society of Newport County** (☎ 401/847–1000). A combination ticket—available at any of the society's properties or at the visitors bureau—gives you a discount. Each mansion provides a guided tour that lasts about an hour.

㊴ **Kingscote** was built in 1839 for George Nòble Jones, a Savannah, Georgia, plantation owner. (Newport was popular with Southerners before the Civil War.) Today it is furnished with antique furniture, glass, and Asian art. It also has a number of Tiffany windows. ✉ *Bowery St., off Bellevue Ave.* ⛬ *$6.* ⊙ *May–Sept., daily 10–5; Apr. and Oct., weekends 10–5.*

㊵ **The Elms,** one of Newport's most gracious mansions, pays homage to the classical design, broad lawn, fountains, and formal gardens of the Château d'Asnières near Paris; it was built for Edward Julius Berwind, a bituminous-coal baron, at the turn of the century. ✉ *Bellevue Ave.* ⛬ *$7.* ⊙ *May–Oct., daily 10–5; Apr., weekends 10–4.*

41 **Chateau-sur-mer,** the first of Bellevue Avenue's stone mansions, was built in 1852 and enlarged for William S. Wetmore, a China-trade tycoon. The mansion houses a toy collection. Compared to the more opulent homes built during the 1890s, this one seems rather modest today. A December visit will find the home decorated for a Victorian Christmas. ⊠ *Bellevue Ave.* 🎟 *$6.* ⊙ *May–Oct., daily 10–5; Nov.–Apr., weekends 10–4.*

★ **42** It's easy to understand why it took more than 2,500 workers two years to create the **Breakers,** the most magnificent of the Newport mansions. Built in 1893 for Cornelius Vanderbilt II and his small family, the Breakers has 70 rooms and required 40 servants to keep it running. Just a few of the marvels within the four-story limestone villa are a gold-ceiling music room, a blue marble fireplace, rose alabaster pillars in the dining room, and a porch whose mosaic ceiling took Italian artisans six months, lying on their backs, to install. If it were possible to build the Breakers today, it could cost $400 million. ⊠ *Ochre Point Ave.* 🎟 *$7.50.* ⊙ *May–Oct., daily 10–5; Nov.–Apr., weekends 10–4.*

43 **Rosecliff,** Newport's most romantic mansion, was built for Mrs. Hermann Oelrichs in 1902. Modeled after the Grand Trianon at Versailles, the 40-room home includes the Court of Love (inspired by a similar room at Versailles) and a heart-shape staircase designed by Stanford White. It has appeared in several movies, including *The Great Gatsby.* ⊠ *Bellevue Ave.* 🎟 *$6.* ⊙ *Apr.–Oct., daily 10–5.*

44 At the **Astors' Beechwood,** actors in period costume play the Astor family (including Mrs. Astor, the belle of New York and Newport society), servants, and household guests. The guides involve visitors in much banter, such as noticing a woman's knee-length skirt and asking, "Do your clothes have a shrinkage problem?"! ⊠ *580 Bellevue Ave.,* ☎ *401/846–3772.* 🎟 *$7.75.* ⊙ *May–mid-Dec., daily 10–5; Feb.–Apr., Fri.–Sun. 10–4.*

45 **Marble House,** with its extravagant gold ballroom, was the gift of William Vanderbilt to his wife, Alva, in 1892. Alva divorced William in 1895 and married Oliver Perry Belmont to become the lady of Belcourt Castle (just down the road). When Oliver died in 1908, she returned to Marble House. Mrs. Belmont was involved with the suffragist movement and spent much of her time campaigning for women's rights. In the kitchen you'll see plates marked Votes for Women. The lovely Chinese teahouse behind the estate was built in 1913 by Mrs. Belmont. ⊠ *Bellevue Ave.* 🎟 *$6.* ⊙ *Apr.–Oct., daily 10–5; Jan.–Mar., weekends 10–4.*

46 **Belcourt Castle,** designed by Richard Morris Hunt based on Louis XIII's hunting lodge, contains an enormous collection of European and Oriental treasures. Sip tea and admire the stained glass and carved wood, and don't miss the Golden Coronation Coach. ⊠ *Bellevue Ave.,* ☎ *401/846–0669 or 401/849–1566.* 🎟 *$6.50.* ⊙ *Apr.–Oct., daily 10–5; Nov.–Dec. and Feb.–Mar., daily 10–4; Jan., weekends 10–3.*

....

NEED A
BREAK?

Ocean Drive takes you along Newport's rocky, surf-washed south coast to **Brenton Point State Park.** One of the most scenic spots in the state, the park is an ideal spot for a picnic.

....

47 **Hammersmith Farm** was the childhood summer home of Jacqueline Bouvier Kennedy Onassis, the site of her wedding to John F. Kennedy, and a summer White House during the Kennedy Administration. It is also the only working farm in Newport. Loaded with Bouvier and Kennedy memorabilia, the house is so comfortable that it seems as though its owners have just stepped out of the room. The elaborate gardens were

124

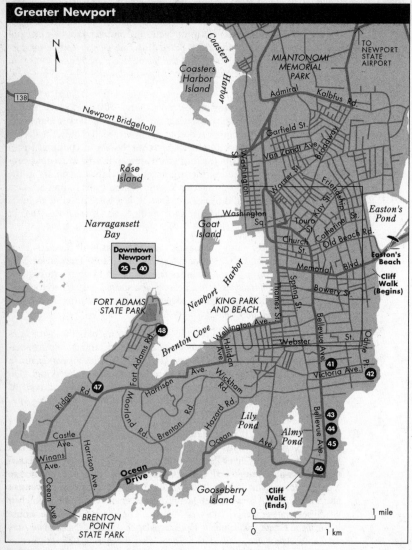

Greater Newport

The Astors'
Beechwood, **44**

Belcourt Castle, **46**

The Breakers, **42**

Chateau-sur-mer, **41**

Hammersmith
Farm, **47**

Marble House, **45**

Museum of
Yachting, **48**

Rosecliff, **43**

designed by Frederick Law Olmsted, and there are breathtaking views of the ocean. ⊠ *Ocean Dr., near Ft. Adams,* ☎ *401/846–7346.* ⏏ *$6.50.* ☯ *Memorial Day–Labor Day, daily 10–7; Mar.–Memorial Day and Labor Day–mid-Nov., daily 10–5. Closed mid-Nov.–Feb., with special openings around Christmas.*

48 The **Museum of Yachting** has four galleries of pictures: Mansions and Yachts, Small Craft, America's Cup, and the Hall of Fame for Single-handed Sailors. ⊠ *Ft. Adams, Ocean Dr.,* ☎ *401/847–1018.* ⏏ *$2.50.* ☯ *May–Oct., daily 10–5.*

OFF THE
BEATEN PATH

NORMAN BIRD SANCTUARY – The 450-acre sanctuary has nature trails, guided tours, and a small natural history museum. ⊠ *583 Third Beach Rd., Middletown,* ☎ *401/846-2577.* ⏏ *$2.* ☯ *Tues.–Sun. 9-5.*

Beaches

Newport

Easton's Beach (⊠ Memorial Blvd.), also known as First Beach, is popular for its carousel for the kids. **Ft. Adams State Park** (⊠ Ocean Dr.), a small beach with a picnic area and lifeguards during the summer, has beautiful views of Newport Harbor.

Middletown

Sachuest Beach, or Second Beach (⊠ Sachuest Point area), is a beautiful sandy beach adjacent to the Norman Bird Sanctuary. Dunes and a campground make it popular with singles and surfers. **Third Beach** (⊠ Sachuest Point area), on the Sakonnet River, with a boat ramp, is a favorite of windsurfers.

Dining and Lodging

$$$$ ✕ **The Black Pearl.** At this popular waterfront restaurant with a nau-
★ tical decor, diners choose between the casual tavern and the very formal Commodore's Room. The latter offers such appetizers as black-and-blue tuna with red pepper sauce and entrées such as swordfish with Dutch pepper butter and duck breast with green peppercorn sauce. ⊠ *Bannister's Wharf,* ☎ *401/846–5264. Commodore Room: Reservations essential and jacket required. AE, MC, V.*

$$$$ ✕ **Clarke Cooke House.** Formal dining is on the upper level; its timber-ceiling room has water views, dark green latticework, richly patterned pillows, and wood model hulls, which combine to pay homage to Colonial, nautical, and Gilded Era Newport. The upstairs menu is sophisticated Tuscan; a similar but less expensive menu is offered downstairs. The Candy Store is the bar area, which looks down to the bustling pedestrian traffic of the wharf. ⊠ *Bannister's Wharf,* ☎ *401/849–2900. Reservations required in summer. Jacket required upstairs. AE, D, DC, MC, V.*

$$$$ ✕ **La Petite Auberge.** In this romantic Colonial home, diners are served exquisite French cuisine in intimate rooms with lace tablecloths; in summer, you can dine on the patio. The colorful owner-chef (once the maître d' for General de Gaulle) prepares such delicacies as trout with almonds, duck flambé with orange sauce, and medallions of beef with goose liver pâté. ⊠ *19 Charles St.,* ☎ *401/849–6669. AE, MC, V.*

$$$$ ✕ **White Horse Tavern.** The nation's oldest operating tavern, the White
★ Horse offers a setting conducive to intimate dining. Lobster and beef Wellington are served here, along with more exotic entrées such as honey-and-cinnamon roast duckling and Thai poached shrimp. The food is fine—but what you're really paying for is the historical ambience of the tavern. On Sunday there's a champagne brunch. ⊠ *Marlborough*

and Farewell Sts., ☎ *401/849–3600. Reservations essential. Jacket required. AE, D, DC, MC, V. No lunch Tues.*

$$$ ✕ **Scales & Shells.** Check the blackboard menu here for seafood specials prepared with zest over a wood grill. Lobster fra diavolo and mesquite-grilled shrimp are especially good. But this informal place gets busy on summer evenings, so it's best to go early. ⊠ *527 Thames St.,* ☎ *401/846–3474. Reservations not accepted. No credit cards.*

$$–$$$ ✕ **The Mooring.** In fine weather, dine on the enclosed patio overlooking the yachts moored in the harbor; on chilly winter evenings take advantage of the open fire in the sunken interior room. The menu ranges from meats to seafood, and lobster lovers find this crustacean delectable and reasonably priced. ⊠ *Sayer's Wharf,* ☎ *401/846–2260. AE, D, DC, MC, V.*

$$ ✕ **Anthony's Shore Dinner Hall.** The large, light room with the panoramic views of Newport Harbor is famous for lobsters, fried clams, fish-and-chips, and other seafood at reasonable prices. Families find the atmosphere congenial. The adjoining seafood shop sells fresh specialties. ⊠ *Lower Thames St., at Waite's Wharf,* ☎ *401/848–5058. Reservations not accepted. AE, MC, V. Closed Dec.–Mar.; and Mon.–Wed., Oct–Nov.*

$$ ✕ **Puerini's.** The aroma of garlic and basil greets you as soon as you
★ enter this friendly neighborhood restaurant with lace curtains and soft-pink walls covered with black-and-white photographs of Italy. The long and intriguing menu presents such selections as green noodles with chicken in marsala wine sauce, tortellini with seafood, and cavatelli in four cheeses. Smoking is not allowed. ⊠ *24 Memorial Blvd.,* ☎ *401/847–5506. Reservations not accepted. No credit cards. No lunch. Closed Mon. in winter.*

$$ ✕ **Salas'.** Movie posters, red-and-white plastic tablecloths, and lines of waiting customers create a lively, good-natured waterfront dining spot that is great for families. Pastas, lobster, clams, and corn-on-the-cob are the principal fare. Spaghetti and macaroni are served by the ¼, ½, and full pound. In the summer there's a raw bar. ⊠ *345 Thames St.,* ☎ *401/846–8772. Reservations not accepted. AE, DC, MC, V.*

$ ✕ **Ocean Coffee Roasters.** Known around here as the Wave Café, this place attracts coffee aficionados, who come for the fresh-roasted coffee (the restaurant will ship its blends) and gladly indulge in the fresh-baked muffins and bagels, salads, and homemade Italian soups. For late risers, breakfast is served until 3 PM. ⊠ *22 Washington Sq.,* ☎ *401/846–6060. Reservations not accepted. MC, V.*

$$$$ ▥ **Cliffside Inn.** Near Newport's Cliff Walk and downtown, on a quiet,
★ tree-lined street, this elegant 1880 Victorian home offers an atmosphere of grandeur and comfort. The wide front porch has a view of the lawn, the foyer is welcoming and dramatic, and the tastefully appointed rooms—all with Victorian antiques and some with bay windows—are light and airy. One suite has a two-sided fireplace; whirlpool bath; king-size, four-poster bed; and an antique, brass, bird-cage shower. Seven other rooms also have whirlpool baths, and five have working fireplaces. ⊠ *2 Seaview Ave., 02840,* ☎ *401/847–1811 or 800/845–1811. 12 rooms with bath. Meeting room. Full breakfast included. AE, D, DC, MC, V.*

$$$$ ▥ **The Francis Malbone House.** The design of this stately buff-painted
★ brick 1760 house is attributed to the architect responsible for the Touro Synagogue and the Redwood Library. Beautifully restored with highly polished original wide-plank flooring, the inn has period reproductions. All guest rooms are large corner rooms (with two windows) and face either the garden or across the street to the harbor; six rooms have working fireplaces. The suite is on the ground floor with its own entrance from Thames Street and from the garden. For lounging, guests have three salons. Breakfast is served in a country-style kitchen.

⊠ *392 Thames St., 02840,* ☎ *401/846–0392. 8 rooms with bath, 1 suite. Full breakfast and afternoon tea included. AE, MC, V.*

$$$$ ⊞ **The Inn at Castle Hill.** Perched on an oceanside cliff 3 miles from
★ the center of Newport and close to the Bellevue mansions, this rambling inn was built as a summer home in 1874, and much of the original furniture remains. Despite some recent refurbishments and an enthusiastic staff, the inn remains a bit shabby. Nevertheless, bookings well in advance are necessary. The public areas have tremendous charm, and the views over the bay are enthralling. The inn is famous for its Sunday brunches—be sure to reserve ahead. ⊠ *Ocean Dr., 02840,* ☎ *401/849–3800. 10 rooms, 7 with bath. Restaurant (closed Nov.–Mar.), 3 private beaches. CP. AE, MC, V.*

$$$$ ⊞ **The Marriott.** This luxury hotel on the harbor at Long Wharf has an atrium lobby with marble floors and a gazebo. Rooms, bordering the atrium or overlooking the skyline or the water, are decorated in mauve and seafoam, with either a king-size bed or two double beds. Fifth-floor rooms facing the harbor have sliding French windows opening onto a large deck. Rates vary greatly according to season and to whether your room has a harbor view. The visitors bureau is right next door. ⊠ *25 America's Cup Ave., 02840,* ☎ *401/849–1000 or 800/228–9290,* FAX *401/849–3422. 307 rooms with bath, 12 suites. Restaurant, bar, indoor pool, hot tub, sauna, health club, racquetball, dance club, meeting rooms, parking. AE, D, DC, MC, V.*

$$$$ ⊞ **Newport Islander Doubletree Hotel.** On Goat Island, just across from the Colonial Point District, the Doubletree has great views of the harbor and Newport Bridge. Most rooms have water views. There's free parking, and although it's a 15-minute walk to Newport's center, bike and moped rentals are nearby. All rooms have oak furnishings and multicolor jewel-tone fabrics. ⊠ *Goat Island, 02840,* ☎ *401/849–2600 or 800/528–0444,* FAX *401/846–7210. 250 rooms. 2 restaurants, indoor and outdoor pools, beauty salon, sauna, tennis, health club, racquetball, boating, meeting rooms. AE, D, DC, MC, V.*

$$$ ⊞ **The Inntowne.** This small town-house hotel is in the center of Newport and 1½ blocks from the harbor. Another plus is the staff's personal attention; they greet you warmly on your arrival and are on hand throughout the day to give sightseeing advice. The neatly appointed rooms are decorated in floral motifs with low-hung pictures; light sleepers may prefer rooms on the upper floors, which let in less traffic noise. ⊠ *6 Mary St., 02840,* ☎ *401/846–9200 or 800/457–7803,* FAX *401/846–1534. 26 rooms, 25 with bath. Parking (fee). Continental breakfast and afternoon tea included. AE, MC, V.*

$$$ ⊞ **Ivy Lodge.** The only B&B in the mansion district, this grand Vic-
★ torian (small by Newport's standards but mansionesque anywhere else) has gables and a Gothic turret. Rooms are large, lovely, and private, but even the brass and four poster beds, claw-foot tubs, window seats, and glorious antiques pale beside the home's greatest feature: a 33-foot gothic paneled oak entry with a three-story turned baluster staircase. A fire burns brightly on fall and winter afternoons in the huge brick fireplace shaped like a Moorish arch. ⊠ *12 Clay St., 02840,* ☎ *401/849–6865. 10 rooms, 8 with bath. Parking. Full breakfast included. AE, MC, V.*

$$$ ⊞ **Victorian Ladies.** This B&B is sumptuously decorated with Victorian antiques and is within walking distance of Newport's shops. Bedrooms have either antique or reproduction beds—all with down quilts. Windows are trimmed with lace curtains and balloon shades. Most rooms have pedestal sinks. The house's insulation muffles the city's sounds significantly. ⊠ *63 Memorial Blvd., 02840,* ☎ *401/849–9960. 11 rooms with bath. Parking. Full breakfast included. MC, V.*

$ 🏠 **Harbor Base Pineapple Inn.** This basic motel is the least expensive
lodging in Newport. All rooms, decorated in shades of blue, contain
two double beds; some also have kitchenettes. Close to the Navy base
and jai alai, it's a five-minute drive from downtown. ⊠ *372 Coddington
Hwy., 02840,* ☎ *401/847–2600. 48 rooms. AE, D, DC, MC, V.*

Nightlife and the Arts

Newport County Convention and Visitors Bureau (⊠ 23 America's Cup
Ave., ☎ 401/849–8048 or 800/326–6030) has listings of concerts,
shows, and special events, as do the Newport and Providence newspapers.

Nightlife

To sample Newport's lively nightlife, you need only stroll down Thames
Street after dark. For a classy bar, try the **Candy Store** in the Clarke
Cooke House restaurant (⊠ Bannister's Wharf, ☎ 401/849–2900).
Thames Street Station (⊠ 337 America's Cup Ave., ☎ 401/849–9480)
plays high-energy dance music and videos and offers live progressive
rock bands Monday through Thursday in summer. **David's** (⊠ 28
Prospect Hill St., ☎ 401/847–9698) is a mainly gay bar with a DJ daily
in season and weekends in winter. **One Pelham East** (⊠ 270 Thames
St., ☎ 401/847–9460) draws a young crowd for progressive rock, reggae, and R&B.

The Arts

Murder-mystery plays are performed Thursday evening July–October
at the **Astors' Beechwood mansion** (⊠ 580 Bellevue Ave., ☎ 401/846–
3772). **Stage 3** (☎ 401/849–7892) performs plays that combine classical and contemporary elements at several spaces in Newport. **Newport
Children's Theatre** (⊠ Box 144, ☎ 401/848–0266) puts on several major
productions for children each year.

Outdoor Activities and Sports

Biking

Ten Speed Spokes (⊠ 18 Elm Street, ☎ 401/847–5609) and **Firehouse
Bicycle** (⊠ 25 Mill St., ☎ 401/847–5700) lease bikes for $20 per day.
Fun Rentals (⊠ 1 Commercial Wharf and Goat Island, ☎ 401/846–
4374) offers Rollerblades at $10 for two hours, bikes at $16 per day,
and mountain bikes and mopeds for $40–$50 per day. The 15-mile
swing down Bellevue Avenue and along Ocean Drive and back is a great
route to ride your rented wheels. For a long country ride, cycle across
the bridge over the Sakonnet River and through the small villages of
Tiverton and Little Compton.

Boating

Oldport Marine Services (⊠ Sayer's Wharf, ☎ 401/847–9109) offers
harbor tours, daily and weekly yacht charters, and rides on a harbor
ferry. **Sight Sailing of Newport** (⊠ Bowen's Wharf, ☎ 401/849–3333)
organizes one-and two-hour sailing tours of Newport Harbor in a six-
passenger sailboat with a U.S. Coast Guard–licensed captain; they
also run a sailing school and charter captained yachts for longer periods. **Sail Newport** (⊠ Ft. Adams State Park, ☎ 401/846–1983) rents
sailboats by the hour.

Fishing

No license is required for saltwater fishing, although anglers should
check with local bait shops, such as **Sam's Bait** (⊠ 936 Aquidneck Ave.,
☎ 401/848–5909), **Edwards Bait** (⊠ 36 Aquidneck Ave., ☎ 401/846–
4521), and **Beachfront Bait Shop** (⊠ 103 Wellington Ave., ☎ 401/849–
4665) for minimum size requirements. Charter fishing boats depart daily

from Newport, spring–fall. For information, call the Newport County Convention and Visitor's Bureau (☞ Visitor Information, *in* Newport A to Z).

Jai Alai
Newport Jai Alai (⊠ 150 Admiral Kalbfus Rd., ☎ 401/849–5000) has its season from May to mid-October.

Shopping

Many of Newport's arts and antiques shops are on Thames Street or near the waterfront; others are on Spring Street, Franklin Street, and at Bowen's and Bannister's wharves. The Brick Market area—between Thames Street and America's Cup Avenue—has more than 40 shops.

Antiques
Aardvark Antiques (⊠ 475 Thames St., ☎ 401/849–7233) has architectural pieces: mantels, doors, garden ornaments, and stained glass. **John Gidley House** (⊠ 22 Franklin St., ☎ 401/846–8303) sells Continental furnishings from the 18th and 19th centuries. The store's own chandeliers and marble are a reminder of what Newport was like in the Gilded Age. **The Nautical Nook** (⊠ 86 Spring St., ☎ 401/846–6810) stocks an unusual combination of antiques and collectibles related to ships: maps, navigational instruments, model boats, and ships in bottles. **The Old Fashion Shop** (⊠ 38 Pelham St., ☎ 401/847–2692) sells American furniture and accessories, including elegant china, kitchenware, quilts, and glass—and Orientalia.

Art
The Liberty Tree (⊠ 104 Spring St., ☎ 401/847–5925) has contemporary folk art, furniture, carvings, and paintings. **MacDowell Pottery** (⊠ 220 Spring St., ☎ 401/846–6313) is a studio/shop where you can not only purchase the wares of many New England potters, but also see a potter's wheel in use. **Thames Glass** (⊠ 688 Thames St., ☎ 401/846–0576) sells delicate and dramatic blown-glass gifts, designed by Matthew Buechner and handmade in the adjacent studio. Don't miss the selection of slight imperfects. **William Vareika Fine Arts** (⊠ 212 Bellevue Ave., ☎ 401/849–6149) exhibits and sells American paintings and prints from the 18th through 20th centuries and offers appraisal and consulting.

Books
Anchor & Dolphin Books (⊠ 30 Franklin St., ☎ 401/846–6890) buys, sells, and appraises rare books, libraries, and collections. The store is especially rich in garden history, architecture, and design. **The Armchair Sailor** (⊠ 543 Thames St., ☎ 401/847–4252) stocks marine and travel books, charts, and maps.

Clothing
Explorer's Club (⊠ 138 Spring St., ☎ 401/846–8465) specializes in quality outdoor sportswear with British and American labels. **JT's Ship Chandlery** (⊠ 364 Thames St., ☎ 401/846–7256) is a major supplier of clothing, marine hardware, and equipment. **Tropical Gangsters** (⊠ 375 Thames St., ☎ 401/847–9113) has very hip clothes for men and women. **World View Graphics** (⊠ 11 Christie's Landing, ☎ 401/847–8120) displays hand-painted T-shirts in vibrant colors; its wares illustrate nautical, environmental, and pop-culture themes.

Crafts
Kelly & Gillis (⊠ 29 America's Cup Ave., ☎ 401/849–7380) has an interesting selection of offbeat and artsy American crafts.

Department Stores

Ley's (⊠ Long Wharf Mall, opposite Gateway Center, ☎ 401/846–2100), America's oldest department store (established in 1796), sells clothing, linens, home furnishings, and souvenirs. **Josephson's Clothing** (⊠ 1 Bannister's Wharf, ☎ 401/847–0303) sells Polo, leather, cashmere, and silk fashions for men and women.

Side Trips

Portsmouth

In Portsmouth, 4 miles north of Newport, **Sandy Point Beach** is a choice spot for families and beginning windsurfers because of the calm surf of the Sakonnet River. On a Victorian estate, with toy collections and a plant shop, **Green Animals Topiary Gardens,** is filled with plants sculpted to look like an elephant, a camel, a giraffe, and even a teddy bear. ⊠ Cory La. (off Rte. 114), ☎ 401/847–1000. ☞ $6. ☺ May–Oct., daily 10–5.

Tiverton

In Tiverton, a couple of miles from Portsmouth via the Sakonnet River Bridge, are the remains of **Ft. Barton.** Named for Colonel William Barton, who captured Newport's British commander during the Revolutionary War, the fort has a fine view of Aquidneck Island.

Little Compton

Main Road (Route 77) in Little Compton, 12 miles south of Tiverton and 5 miles from Newport, is lined with fruit and vegetable stands, poultry farms, and a vineyard. The town green, known as **Little Compton Commons,** is overlooked by the lofty United Congregational Church, built in 1832. The Commons burial ground, laid out in 1675, includes the grave of Benjamin Church, who was prominent in the Indian conflict called King Philip's War. At **Sakonnet Point,** there's a lovely view over the bay to Newport.

Newport A to Z

Arriving and Departing

BY PLANE

Newport State Airport (☎ 401/846–2200), 3 miles northeast of the city, has connecting flights by charter companies to Theodore Francis Green State Airport in Warwick. **Cozy Cab** (☎ 401/846–2500) runs a frequent shuttle service ($15) between the airport and the visitors bureau downtown, and some Newport hotels provide free airport shuttle service to guests.

Getting Around

BY BUS

Rhode Island Public Transit Authority (☎ 401/847–0209 or, in RI, 800/221–3797) serves the Newport area.

BY CAR

With the exception of Ocean Drive and Bellevue Avenue, Newport is a walker's city. A car is a liability in summer, when traffic thickens on the city's narrow one-way streets. Once in town, it's worth parking in one of the many pay lots and forgetting about your car for the rest of your stay. However, you may find a car useful in covering the considerable distances between the grand homes, for you'll have plenty of walking to do inside the mansions themselves, and free parking is available at each site.

Contacts and Resources

Newport Hospital (⊠ Friendship St., Newport, ☎ 401/846–6400).

GUIDED TOURS
Old Colony & Newport Railway follows an 8-mile route along Narragansett Bay from Newport to Portsmouth's Green Animals Topiary Gardens. The round-trip takes a little over three hours, with a 1¼-hour stop at the garden. ⊠ *19 America's Cup Ave.,* ☎ *401/624–6951.* ⚑ *$6.* ☉ *Departs May–mid-June and mid-Sept.–mid-Nov., Sun. 12:30; mid-June–mid-Sept., weekends 12:30.*

The Spirit of Newport (☎ 401/849–3575) gives one-hour minicruises of Newport Harbor and Narragansett Bay, departing from the Newport Harbor Hotel (America's Cup Ave.) every 90 minutes from June through Labor Day and less frequently out of season.

Viking Bus and Boat Tours of Newport (⊠ Gateway Center, 23 America's Cup Ave., ☎ 401/847–6921) runs Newport tours on air-conditioned buses and one-hour cruises of Narragansett Bay.

Walking Tours: The **Newport Freedom Trail** makes a loop through the downtown area, beginning at the Historical Society on Touro Street and finishing at the Automobile Museum. **Newport Historical Society** (⊠ 82 Touro St., ☎ 401/846–0813) sponsors walking tours on Friday and Saturday in summer. **Newport on Foot** (⊠ Box 1042, ☎ 401/846–5391) organizes mile-long walks through Colonial Newport.

PHARMACY
Douglas Drug (⊠ 7 E. Main Rd., Middletown, ☎ 401/849–4600) is open until 9 PM.

VISITOR INFORMATION
Newport County Convention and Visitors Bureau (⊠ Gateway Center, 23 America's Cup Ave., ☎ 401/849–8048 or 800/326–6030; ☉ May–Sept., daily 9–7, Oct.–Apr., daily 9–5.), one of the best centers of its kind, shows an orientation film and provides maps, cassette tours, and advice.

BLOCK ISLAND

13 mi from Galilee.

Situated 13 miles off the coast, Block Island's 11-square-mile area has been a popular tourist destination since the 19th century. Despite the large number of visitors who come here each summer, the island's beauty and privacy have been preserved; its 365 freshwater ponds make it a haven for more than 150 species of migrating birds.

Block Island's original inhabitants were the Native Americans who called it Manisses, or Isle of the Little God. In 1524 Verrazano renamed it Claudia, after the mother of the French king. Revisited in 1614 by the Dutch explorer Adrian Block, the island was given the name Adrian's Eyelant, which later became Block Island. In 1661 the island was settled by Colonists seeking religious freedom; they established a farming and fishing community that still exists today.

Most tourism here occurs between May and September—at other times, the majority of restaurants, inns, stores, and visitor services close down.

Exploring

Numbers in the margin correspond to points of interest on the Block Island map.

Block Island has two harbors, Old Harbor and New Harbor. The Old Harbor commercial district extends along Water and Dodge streets. Approaching Block Island by sea from Newport or Point Judith, you'll see the Old Harbor and its group of Victorian hotels.

The Old Harbor area is the island's only village. A concentration of shops, boutiques, restaurants, inns, and hotels, it's a short walk from the ferry landing and near most of the interesting sights.

49 At the **Block Island Historical Society,** permanent and special exhibits describe the island's farming and maritime past. You'll be given a short introduction to the house (an 1850 structure with a mansard roof, furnished with many original pieces), and then you may look around on your own; the house is well worth a visit. ✉ *Old Town Rd.,* ☎ *401/466–2481 or 401/466–5009.* 🖅 *$2.* ☉ *July–Aug., daily 10–4; June and Sept., weekends 10–4.*

The **Frederick J. Benson Town Beach,** in the middle of several-mile-
★ **50** long **Crescent Beach,** is patrolled by lifeguards and is good for a swim.
51 The **Clay Head Nature Trail** meanders along oceanside cliffs. Explore side trails for the best ocean views and wildlife spotting. Guided tours are available in summer.

52 **Settler's Rock,** on the shores of Chagum Pond, lists the names of the original settlers and marks the spot where they first landed in 1661. On this narrow strip of land straddling the pond and Rhode Island Sound, there's a sense of openness and quietness.

53 **North Light** is a lighthouse on the northernmost tip of Block Island. Built in 1867 of Connecticut granite hauled across the island to the site by oxen, it was restored and opened as a maritime museum in 1993. 🖅 *$2.* ☉ *July–Aug., daily 10–4; June and Sept., weekends 10–4.*

54 **New Harbor,** on the inland side of the Great Salt Pond, provides safe anchor for the many small craft that call at Block Island and is the arrival and departure point for the ferry from Montauk. The harbor also has a few shops and marina facilities.

55 The **Block Island Historical Cemetery** contains the remains of island residents since the 1700s. Not only will you recognize the names of quite a few longstanding Block Island families (Ball, Rose, Champlin) at this well-maintained, sprawling cemetery, you'll also get a wonderful view of New Harbor and Great Salt Pond.

56 **Rodman's Hollow,** a ravine formed by a glacier, is one of Block Island's five wildlife refuges and a natural wonder. You can follow the deep cleft in the hills along many winding paths all the way down to the ocean; then have a picnic on the rocky beach, beneath sandstone cliffs, as you watch the boats go by.

57 From the top of **Mohegan Bluffs,** you'll get dramatic ocean views, and you'll see the **Southeast Light,** an 1873 redbrick building with ginger-bread detail. Originally surrounded by fields, the lighthouse was repositioned by erosion and sat precariously close to the edge of a 200-foot cliff until 1993, when it was moved to a safer location away from the precipice.

☍ The owners of the 1661 Inn and Hotel Manisses run a small **Animal Farm,** with a collection of llamas, emus, cows, goats, ducks, and the like coexisting happily in a large meadow next to the hotel. Visitors are free to view and pet the animals. ✉ *Spring St.,* ☎ *401/466–2063.* 🖅 *Free.* ☉ *Dawn–dusk.*

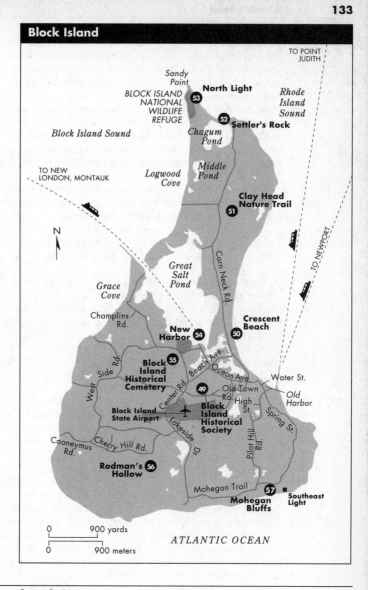

Block Island

Dining and Lodging

$$$$ ✕ **Manisses.** Dine inside by the long oak bar, under the canopy on the
★ outdoor deck, or in the glassed-in garden terrace. Try the smoked fish
or meats from the smokehouse, or enjoy the raw bar for an appetizer.
Main courses include local seafood and light fare such as gourmet pizzas and littleneck clams Dijonnaise. Vegetables are grown in the hotel's
garden, and delicious homemade desserts are prepared by the pastry
chef. ⊠ *Spring St.,* ☎ *401/466–2421. AE, MC, V. Closed Nov.–mid-
May, Mon.–Thurs. No lunch.*

$$ ✕ **Ballard's Inn.** The place to go for lobster, Italian food, or family-
★ style dinners, this noisy, lively spot caters especially to the boating crowd.
The enormous dining room has flags from around the world hanging
from the wood rafters, and the waiters are just as informal and quirky
as the decor. Come here if you're looking for a place to polka. ⊠ *Old
Harbor,* ☎ *401/466–2231. MC, V. Closed mid-Oct.–May.*

$$ ✕ **Finn's Seafood Bar.** Eat inside or out on the deck, which offers a panoramic view of the harbor. The smoked bluefish pâté is wonderful. A popular lunch order is the Workman's Special platter—a burger, coleslaw, and french fries. Take-out is also available. ✉ *Ferry Landing,* ☎ *401/466–2473. Reservations not accepted. AE, MC, V. Closed mid-Oct.–May.*

$$ ✕ **Harborside Inn.** This cheerful and noisy restaurant in the heart of town features excellent, fresh native seafood, as well as steaks, and an extensive salad bar. Order the scallops sautéed in butter or the lobster, swordfish, or steak, and enjoy the view of the harbor from the pleasant, bustling outdoor terrace. ✉ *Water St.,* ☎ *401/466–5504. MC, V. Closed Nov.–Apr.*

$ ✕ **The BeacHead.** This is a favorite local spot where you can play pool, catch up on local gossip, or sit at the bar and stare out at the sea. Food and service are unpretentious—burgers come on paper plates with potato chips and pickles—but the food is satisfying, the price is right, and you won't feel like a tourist. The spicy chili is also a good bet. ✉ *Corn Neck Rd.,* ☎ *401/466–2249. Reservations not accepted. No credit cards. No dinner in winter.*

$ ✕ **Old Harbor Take-out.** This is a great place to stop for lunch or a snack when taking a break from the beach or exploring the Old Harbor area. Orders are placed at the roadside shanty, and seating is outdoors, overlooking the ferry dock, at blue picnic tables with big blue umbrellas. The light, fresh sandwiches are a cut above the usual take-out fare, and the clam chowder is packed with big chunks of juicy clams. This place offers the best value in the Old Harbor district. ✉ *Water St.,* ☎ *401/466–2935. No reservations. No credit cards. Closed Oct.–May.*

$$$–$$$$ ⊞ **Atlantic Inn.** Built in 1879, this is a long, white, classic, Victorian resort that bravely fronts the elements on a hill above the ocean (and that is duly rewarded with panoramic views). Big windows, high ceilings, and a sweeping staircase contribute to the breezy atmosphere. Guest rooms are lined up on long hallways. The generally austere feel is softened by pastel colors. The inn welcomes children and has a wooden swing set. ✉ *Box 188, High St., 02807,* ☎ *401/466–5883,* ☎ *401/466–5678. 21 rooms with bath. Restaurant, tennis courts, croquet, playground, meeting rooms. CP. AE, MC, V. Closed Nov.–Easter.*

$$$–$$$$ ⊞ **Hotel Manisses.** Many of the rooms in this 1870 mansion are filled with unusual Victorian pieces, and intriguing knickknacks occupy every available bit of space. Some small rooms are almost overpowered by the furniture—if you prefer light and airy to dark and formal, stay at the nearby 1661 Inn (☞ *below*). The many extras include afternoon tea in a romantic parlor overlooking the garden, a copious buffet breakfast (served at the 1661 Inn), picnic baskets, gourmet cooking, and an animal farm with llamas and emus. Some rooms have hot tubs. ✉ *Box 1, Spring St., 02807,* ☎ *401/466–2063,* ☎ *401/466–2858. 17 rooms with bath. Restaurant, fans. Full breakfast and afternoon tea included. AE, MC, V.*

$$$–$$$$ ⊞ **1661 Inn and Guest House.** If you're celebrating a special occasion, ★ choose the 1661 Inn and splurge for the Edwards Room, an enormous, split-level suite with a hot tub in the loft, a king-size canopy bed, and a huge private terrace with spectacular views of marshes, swans, and the sea beyond. This is one of New England's loveliest inns, and all the guest rooms are exquisite. Decorated in pastel shades with thick carpets, they contain Victorian antiques and four-poster or canopy beds; some are huge and have decks or hot tubs. A sumptuous buffet breakfast—bluefish, Boston baked beans, and Belgian waffles—is served in the dining room or outdoors on a canopied deck. ✉ *Spring St., 02807,* ☎ *401/466–2421,* ☎ *401/466–2858. 21 rooms, 19 with bath. Play-*

ground, parking. AE, MC, V. Full breakfast and afternoon tea included. Inn closed mid-Nov.–mid-Apr.; guest house and cottage open year-round.

$$–$$$ ⊞ **Blue Dory Inn.** This hotel, with three small additional houses, is decorated with Victorian-era antiques. Rooms are not large, but each is tastefully furnished and has either an ocean or a harbor view. There's a small, cozy living room, and breakfast is served each morning in a homey kitchen facing the ocean. The inn is open year-round. ⊠ *Box 488, Dodge St., 02807,* ☎ *401/466–2254 or 800/992–7290. 14 rooms with bath. CP. AE, MC, V.*

$$–$$$ ⊞ **Rose Farm Inn.** Just outside the village of Old Harbor, next to the Atlantic Inn, Rose Farm is convenient to downtown and the beaches. The wallpapered rooms are furnished with antiques, and all have views. Porch and sundeck offer society and relaxation. The owners also run the Captain Rose House across the driveway: It has nine more rooms, four with a hot tub. ⊠ *Box E, Roslyn Rd., 02807,* ☎ *401/466–2021,* ⅢⅩ *401/466–2053. 17 rooms with bath, 2 share bath. Breakfast room. Buffet breakfast included. AE, MC, V. Closed mid-Oct.–Apr.*

$$–$$$ ⊞ **Surf Hotel.** This hotel seems to have changed very little since it first opened in 1876. The lobby, a study in cheerful chaos, has a birdcage with chirping residents. Rooms are simply furnished with Victorian antiques and ceiling fans, and, with Crescent Beach at the back door, back rooms have terrific ocean views (front rooms have harbor views). There's a spacious front porch with rockers and a back deck. ⊠ *Box C, Dodge St., 02807,* ☎ *401/466–2241. 38 rooms, 3 with bath. Breakfast room. CP. MC, V. Closed mid-Oct.–Apr.*

Nightlife

The National Hotel (⊠ Water St., ☎ 401/466–2901) has live music in the bar every evening in summer and Saturday nights off-season. **McGovern's Yellow Kittens Tavern** (⊠ Corn Neck Rd., ☎ 401/466–5855), established in 1876, has live music, with reggae, rock, and R&B bands every night in season.

Outdoor Activities and Sports

Boating
Block Island Boat Basin (☎ 401/466–2631) offers charters. **Oceans & Ponds** (☎ 401/466–5131) rents and sells kayaks and canoes. **Twin Maples** (☎ 401/466–5547) rents rowboats.

Fishing
Oceans & Ponds (☎ 401/466–5131) offers charters. Shellfishing without a license is illegal; licenses may be obtained at the police station.

Water Sports
Sailboard rentals and lessons are available from **Island Moped** (☎ 401/466–2700) and **Oceans & Ponds** (☎ 401/466–5131).

Shopping

Art and Crafts
Block Island Blue Pottery (⊠ Dodge St., ☎ 401/466–2945; closed winter), true to its name, sells handmade bowls, mugs, pins, and wind chimes—mostly in blue. The shop is housed in a 1790 building with a central brick chimney. **Ragged Sailor** (⊠ Water St., ☎ 401/466–7704) shows paintings, crafts, porcelain, folk art, and photographs. **The Red Herring** (⊠ Water St., ☎ 401/466–2540), on the second floor of **The Shoreline,** sells distinctive folk art and crafts—pottery, jewelry, home furnishings.

Scarlet Begonia (⊠ Dodge St., ☏ 401/466–5024; closed winter) offers unusual jewelry and crafts, including place mats and handmade quilts. **Spring Street Gallery** (⊠ Spring St., ☏ 401/466–5374), an artist's cooperative, shows and sells hand-knit baby clothing, stained glass, serigraphs, and other work of island artists and artisans.

Books

The Book Nook (⊠ Water St., ☏ 401/466–2993) stocks paperbacks (mostly beach reading, plus a rack of classics and a children's section), posters, magazines, and newspapers.

Water-Sports Gear

Block Island Boatworks & Block Island Kite Co. (⊠ Corn Neck Rd., ☏ 401/466–2033) occupies two buildings, one filled with boogie boards and kites, the other with snorkeling gear, bathing suits, casual clothing, and fine garden furniture.

Women's Clothing

The Shoreline (⊠ Water St., ☏ 401/466–2541; ⊠ Fish Head Bldg., Ocean Ave., ☏ 401/466–5800) has contemporary clothing by Patagonia and Esprit. The branch in the Fish Head Building stocks sportswear and surfboards. (Both closed weekdays, Oct.–Apr.)

Block Island A to Z

Arriving and Departing

BY CAR AND FERRY

Interstate Navigation Co. (⊠ Galilee State Pier, Point Judith, ☏ 401/783–4613) has ferry service from Galilee (1 hr, 10 min; make auto reservations well in advance) and passenger boats from Providence via Newport. Passengers cannot make reservations but should arrive 45 minutes ahead in high season as the boats fill up.

From Montauk, Long Island (NY), the **Jigger III** (☏ 516/668–2214) has passenger ferry service (2 hrs), June–September, and **Viking Ferry Lines** (☏ 516/668–5709) has passenger and bicycle service (1 hr, 45 min), mid-May–mid-October.

Nelseco Navigation (☏ 203/442–7891) runs an auto ferry from New London, Connecticut (2 hrs), in summer; reservations are advised.

BY PLANE

New England Airlines (☏ 401/596–2460 or 800/243–2460) flies from Westerly State Airport to Block Island. **Action Air** (☏ 203/448–1646 or 800/243–8623) has flights from Groton, Connecticut, to Block Island from June through October. Several hotels run courtesy vans from the airport. Taxis are also available (☞ By Taxi, *below*).

Getting Around

BY BICYCLE AND MOPED

The best way to cover the island effectively *and* make the most of its natural beauty is by bicycle or moped. **The Sea Crest Inn** (☏ 401/466–2882; bikes only), **Esta's at Old Harbor** (☏ 401/466–2651), **Old Harbor Bike Shop** (☏ 401/466–2029), **Block Island Boat Basin** (☏ 401/466–2631), and **Moped Man** (☏ 401/466–5011) have rentals: Bikes cost about $15 per day, mopeds about $40, and most places have child seats for bikes. Most rental places close at summer's end; Moped Man is open through October. Operating a motorcycle between midnight and 6 AM is forbidden, and mopeds are prohibited on dirt roads.

BY CAR

Because most inns, restaurants, and shops are in or near the Old Harbor area, and bicycling to any point on the island is a joy, there's no need to have a car. If you do want to rent one, try **Block Island Car Rental** (☎ 401/466–2297).

BY TAXI
Taxis are plentiful at both the Old Harbor and New Harbor ferry landings. The island's dispatch services include **O. J. Berlin** (☎ 401/782–5826), **A. Ernst Taxi** (☎ 401/466–7739), and **Wolfie's Taxi** (☎ 401/466–5550).

Contacts and Resources

HIKING
One of the best trail guides for the region is the *AMC Massachusetts and Rhode Island Trail Guide*, available at local outdoors shops or from the Appalachian Mountain Club (✉ 5 Joy St., Boston, MA 02114, ☎ 617/523–0636). The **Rhode Island Audubon Society** (✉ 12 Sanderson Rd., Smithfield 02917, ☎ 401/949–5454) leads interesting hikes and field expeditions. The **Sierra Club** (✉ 3 Joy St., Boston, MA 02114, ☎ 617/227–5339) and the **Appalachian Mountain Club** both have active groups in Rhode Island.

VISITOR INFORMATION
Block Island Chamber of Commerce (✉ Drawer D, Water St., 02807, ☎ 401/466–2982; ⊙ Apr.–mid-Oct., daily 10–5; mid-Oct.–Mar., Mon.–Sat. 10–4). A second tourist information booth at Old Harbor opens for ferry arrivals.

RHODE ISLAND A TO Z

Arriving and Departing

By Bus
Greyhound Lines (☎ 800/231–2222) and **Bonanza Bus Lines** (☎ 800/556–3815) link cities of the northeastern United States with the **Providence Bus Terminal** (✉ Bonanza Way, off Exit 25 from I–95, ☎ 401/751–8800). A shuttle service connects the terminal with Kennedy Plaza in downtown Providence. Bonanza also runs a bus from Boston's Logan Airport to Providence. **Peter Pan Bus Lines** (☎ 800/237–8747), in association with other bus lines, serves Providence from across the United States.

By Car
I–95 cuts diagonally across the state, the fastest route to Providence from Boston, coastal Connecticut, and New York City. I–195 links Providence with New Bedford and Cape Cod. Route 146 links Providence with Worcester and I–90. Route 1 follows much of the Rhode Island coast east from Connecticut before turning north to Providence.

By Plane
Theodore Francis Green State Airport (☎ 401/737–4000), in Warwick, has scheduled daily flights by seven major U.S. airlines and additional service by regional carriers.

By Train
Amtrak (☎ 800/872–7245) service between New York City and Boston makes stops at Westerly, Kingston, and Providence's **Union Station** (✉ 100 Gaspee St.). **MBTA commuter rail service** (☎ 617/722–3200) connects Boston and Providence during weekday morning and evening rush hours at about half the cost of Amtrak.

Getting Around

By Bus

Rhode Island Public Transit Authority (☎ 401/781–9400) has service within and between the state's major cities.

By Car

Get a free official state map from the Rhode Island Department of Economic Development (☞ *below*).

By Ferry

Ferries leave Providence for Newport and Block Island from the **India Street Pier** (☎ 401/483–4613). Ferries from Point Judith to Block Island depart from **Galilee State Pier** (☎ 401/783–4613). Reservations are required for cars, and service is curtailed in the off-season.

Contacts and Resources

Guided Tours

Stumpf Balloons (✉ Box 913, Bristol, ☎ 401/253–0111) offers fall foliage tours of Rhode Island by balloon—with champagne.

Reservation Service

Bed and Breakfast of Rhode Island, Inc. (✉ Box 3291, Newport 02840, ☎ 401/849–1298).

Visitor Information

Rhode Island Department of Economic Development, Tourism Division (✉ 7 Jackson Walkway, Providence 02903, ☎ 401/277–2601 or 800/556–2484).

4 Massachusetts

Boston has a lively population of students, artists, and academics. Martha's Vineyard is less developed than Cape Cod, yet more cosmopolitan than neighboring Nantucket. Salem and Gloucester are on the North Shore, which extends past grimy docklands to the scenic Cape Ann region. The Pioneer Valley is a string of historic settlements, and the Berkshires, to the west, embody the storybook image of rural New England.

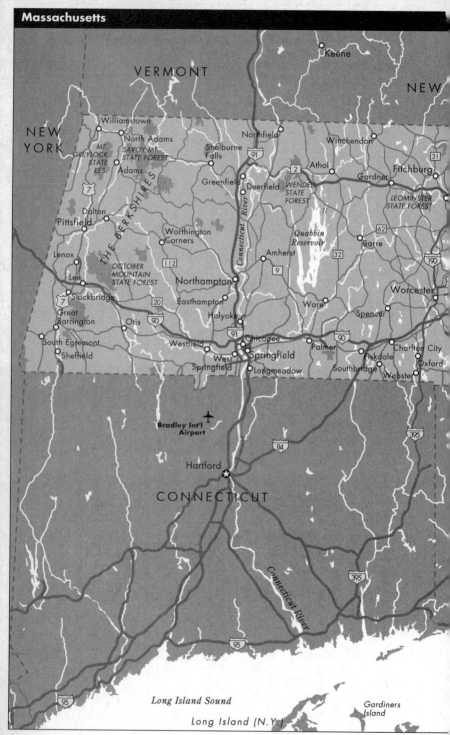

VERMONT

NEW

Keene

NEW
YORK

Williamstown

North Adams
SAVOY MT.
STATE FOREST

MT.
GREYLOCK
STATE
RES.

Adams

Shelburne
Falls

Northfield

91

Winchendon

Fitchburg

31

Athol

2

Gardner

LEOMINSTER
STATE FOREST

Greenfield

Deerfield

WENDELL
STATE
FOREST

Dalton

Pittsfield

THE BERKSHIRES

7

Worthington
Corners

Quabbin
Reservoir

Barre

62

190

Lenox

112

OCTOBER
MOUNTAIN
STATE FOREST

Amherst

32

Lee

9

Northampton

Worcester

Stockbridge

20

Easthampton

Ware

Spencer

7

Great
Barrington

Otis

90

Holyoke

91

Charlton City

South Egremont

Westfield

Chicopee

Palmer

Fiskdale

Sheffield

West
Springfield

Springfield

Longmeadow

Southbridge

Oxford

Webster

Bradley Int'l
Airport

84

Hartford

395

CONNECTICUT

Connecticut River

395

Connecticut River

95

95

Long Island Sound

Gardiners
Island

Long Island (N.Y.)

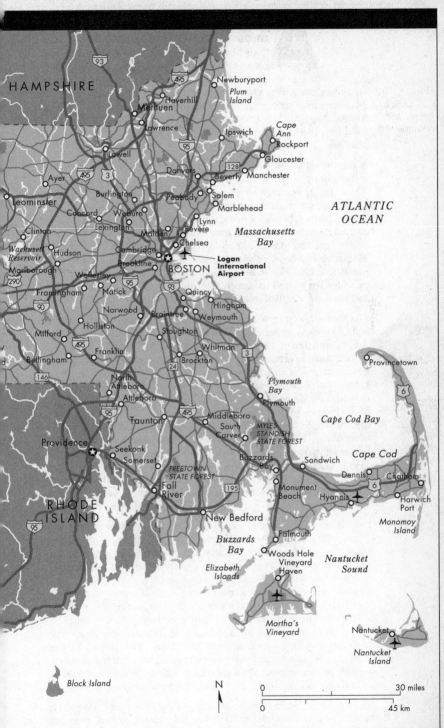

HAMPSHIRE

Newburyport
Plum
Island
Haverhill
Methuen
Lawrence
Ipswich
Cape
Ann
Rockport
Lowell
Gloucester
Ayer
Danvers
Beverly
Manchester
Leominster
Burlington
Peabody
Salem
Concord
Woburn
Marblehead
Clinton
Lexington
Lynn
Massachusetts
Bay
Wachusett
Reservoir
Hudson
Cambridge
Malden
Revere
Chelsea
Marlborough
Brookline
BOSTON
Logan
International
Airport
Wellesley
Framingham
Natick
Quincy
Norwood
Hingham
Holliston
Braintree
Weymouth
Milford
Stoughton
Franklin
Whitman
Bellingham
Brockton
ATLANTIC
OCEAN
North
Attleboro
Plymouth
Bay
Attleboro
Plymouth
Provincetown
Taunton
Middleboro
South
Carver
MYLES
STANDISH
STATE FOREST
Cape Cod Bay
Providence
Seekonk
Somerset
FREETOWN
STATE FOREST
Buzzards
Bay
Sandwich
Cape Cod
Fall
River
Monument
Beach
Dennis
Chatham
RHODE
ISLAND
New Bedford
Hyannis
Harwich
Port
Falmouth
Monomoy
Island
Buzzards
Bay
Woods Hole
Vineyard
Haven
Nantucket
Sound
Elizabeth
Islands
Martha's
Vineyard
Nantucket
Nantucket
Island
Block Island
N
0   30 miles
0   45 km

By Anne
Merewood
and Candice
Gianetti, with
an introduction
by Laura E.
Cronin

ALTHOUGH ONLY A HALF-DOZEN STATES are smaller than Massachusetts, few have had greater influence on American commerce, culture, and politics. As succeeding generations of Bay State merchants, industrialists, and computer executives charted the course for the national economy, Massachusetts writers, artists, and intellectuals enriched American life. As for politics, the good people of Massachusetts are a contentious lot. From the meeting house to the White House, Bay State opinion has fueled the national debate.

Massachusetts seaboard towns—from Newburyport to Provincetown—were built before the Revolution, in the heyday of American shipping. These quaint coastal villages evoke a bygone world of clipper ships, robust fisherman, and sturdy sailors bound for distant Cathay, while Lowell, on the Merrimack River, was the first American city to be planned around manufacturing. This textile town introduced the rest of the nation to the routines of the industrial revolution. In our own time, Massachusetts has set the pace with the high-tech firms along suburban Route 128: The business communities of Boston and Cambridge provided the capital to launch this information-age boom while MIT and Harvard supplied intellectual heft to deliver it to the wider world.

The Massachusetts town meeting set the tone for politics in the 13 original Colonies. A century later, Boston was a hotbed of rebellion—Samuel Adams and James Otis, the "Sons of Liberty," started a war with words, creating crucial support for the American Revolution with patriotic pamphlets and fiery speeches at Faneuil Hall. Twentieth-century heirs to Sam Adams's independent rhetoric include Boston's flashy four-time mayor, James Michael Curley; Tip O'Neill, the popular Speaker of the House; and, of course, the Kennedys. In 1961, the young senator from the Boston suburb of Brookline, John F. Kennedy, became President of the United States. JFK's service to Massachusetts was family tradition: In the years before World War I, Kennedy's grandfather, John "Honey Fitz" Fitzgerald, served in Congress and as mayor of Boston. But political families are nothing new here—don't forget President John Adams and President John Quincy Adams; Massachusetts is the only state that has ever sent both a father and son to live in the White House.

Despite its compact size, Massachusetts has an extensive system of parks, protected forests, beaches, and nature preserves. Like medieval pilgrims, readers of *Walden* come to Concord to visit the place where Thoreau wrote his prophetic essay. Thoreau's disciples can be found hiking to the top of the state's highest peak, Mt. Greylock, shopping for organic produce in an unpretentious college burg like Williamstown, or strolling the sandy beaches of Martha's Vineyard and Nantucket. For those who prefer the hills to the ocean, the rolling Berkshire terrain defines the landscape from North Adams to Great Barrington in the western part of the state. A favorite vacation spot since the 19th century, the Berkshires has been called an "Inland Newport" in honor of the grand summer residences of its wealthiest visitors. This area continues to attract vacationers seeking superb scenery and food and an active cultural scene.

The list of Bay State writers, artists, and musicians who have shaped American culture is long indeed. The state has produced great poets in every generation: Anne Bradstreet, Phillis Wheatley, Emily Dickinson, Henry Wadsworth Longfellow, William Cullen Bryant, e.e. cummings, Robert Lowell, Elizabeth Bishop, Sylvia Plath, and Anne Sexton. Massachusetts writers include: Louisa May Alcott, author of the enduring classic, *Little Women*; Nathaniel Hawthorne, who re-created the Salem of his Puritan ancestors in *The Scarlet Letter*; Herman Melville, who wrote *Moby-Dick* in a house at the foot of Mount Greylock; Eugene O'Neill, whose early plays were produced at a makeshift theater in Provincetown on Cape Cod; Jack Kerouac, author of *On the Road*; and John Cheever, chronicler of suburban angst. Painters Winslow Homer and James McNeill Whistler both hailed from the commonwealth. Norman Rockwell, quintessential American illustrator, lived and worked in Stockbridge. The celebrated composer and Boston native, Leonard Bernstein, was the first American to conduct the New York Philharmonic. Joan Baez got her start singing songs in Harvard Square, and contemporary Boston singer-songwriter Tracy Chapman picked up the beat with folk songs for the new age.

Sailors and cyberpunks, poets and presidents, vegetarians and venture capitalists—they're all here in Massachusetts.

Pleasures and Pastimes

Beaches

Massachusetts has many excellent beaches, especially on Cape Cod, where Bostonians go for weekends and summer vacations. Beaches on Cape Cod Bay generally have colder water and gentle waves. Southside beaches, on Nantucket Sound, have rolling surf and are warmer. Open-ocean beaches on the Cape Cod National Seashore are cold and have serious surf. Parking lots fill up by 10 AM. Those beaches not restricted to residents charge parking fees; for weekly or seasonal passes, contact the local town hall.

Bostonians head for wide sweeps of sand along the North Shore (beware of biting blackflies in late May and early June). Try Singing Beach in Manchester or Good Harbor beach in Gloucester. Boston's city beaches are not particularly attractive, but are improving, due to the ongoing cleanup of Boston Harbor. The Atlantic waters tend to be cold until late July, but lingeringly warm into September.

Boating

Cape Cod and the North Shore are centers for ocean-going pleasure craft, with public mooring available in many towns. Sea kayaking is popular along the marshy coastline of the North Shore, where freshwater canoeing is also an option. Inland, the Connecticut River in the Pioneer Valley is navigable by all types of craft between the Turners Falls Dam, just north of Greenfield, and the Holyoke Dam. The large dams control the water level daily, so you will notice a tidal effect; those with larger craft should beware of sandbanks. Canoes can also travel north of Turners Falls beyond the Vermont border, and canoeing is popular in lakes and small rivers of the Berkshires.

Dining

Apart from the seafood specialties that the state shares with other New England regions, Massachusetts claims fame for inventing the fried clam, a revolutionary event that apparently took place in Essex. Fried clams, therefore, appear on many North Shore menus, especially around the salt marshes of Essex and Ipswich, and on Cape Cod, where clam chowder—New England style with no tomatoes—is another specialty. Eating seafood "in the rough" (from paper plates in shacklike wooden buildings dominated by deep-fryers) is a revered local custom.

Not all regional cuisine focuses on seafood. Some spots pride themselves on hefty, traditional New England "dinners" strongly reminiscent of old England: Double-cut pork chops, rack of lamb, game, Boston baked beans, Indian pudding, and the dubiously glorified "New England boiled dinner" are popular with country inns in the Berkshires

and the Pioneer Valley. And on the Cape, you can find ethnic specialties such as Portuguese kale soup or linguiça.

Nantucket has plenty of first-rate gourmet restaurants (with price tags
to match), as does, for example, Brewster, on the Cape. In the off-season many Cape restaurants advertise early-bird specials and Sunday
brunches, often with musical accompaniment. On the North Shore,
Rockport is a "dry" town, though you can almost always take your
own alcohol into restaurants; most places charge a nominal corking
fee. This law leads to early closing hours—many Rockport dining establishments are shut by 9 PM. Martha's Vineyard also has dry towns.

CATEGORY	COST*
$$$$	over $40
$$$	$25–$40
$$	$15–$25
$	under $15

*average cost of a three-course dinner, per person, excluding drinks, service,
and 5% sales tax*

Fishing
You can take deep-sea fishing trips from Boston, Cape Cod, and the
South and North shores, and surf casting is particularly popular on
the North Shore. The rivers, lakes, and streams of the Pioneer Valley
and Berkshire County abound with fish—bass, pike, and perch, to name
but a few. Stocked trout waters include the Hoosic River (south branch),
near Cheshire; Green River, Great Barrington; Notch Brook and Hoosic
River (north branch), North Adams; Goose Pond and Hop Brook, Lee;
and Williams River, West Stockbridge.

Lodging
You can stay in a hotel or a motel anywhere in the United States, and
Massachusetts is no exception. But particular to the region is the increasingly popular country inn, and in the Berkshires, where many magnificent mansions have been converted into accommodations, the inns
reach a very grand scale indeed. Coastal inns have their own oceanside characteristics. Less extravagant and less expensive are bed-and-
breakfast establishments, many of them located in private homes. On
Cape Cod, where many people take extended vacations, rental homes
are widely available, in everything from modern condominiums on the
golf course to seaside estates with private beaches.

CATEGORY	BOSTON, THE CAPE, AND THE ISLANDS*	OTHER AREAS*
$$$$	over $150	over $100
$$$	$95–$150	$70–$100
$$	$70–$95	$40–$70
$	under $70	under $40

*All prices are for a standard double room during peak season and do not in-
clude tax or gratuities. Some inns add a 15% service charge. The state tax on
lodging is 5.7%; individual towns can impose an extra tax of up to 10%
more.*

Shopping
Boston, of course, has many high-quality shops, especially in the Newbury Street and Beacon Hill neighborhoods, and most suburban communities have at least a couple of main street stores selling stylish old
furniture and collectibles. On the South Shore, antiques stores are centered around Plymouth, while Essex, Newburyport, and Salem are antiquing capitals on the North Shore. Antiques abound in the northern
towns of the Pioneer Valley—try Amherst or Deerfield—and are every-

where in the Berkshires, with particularly rich hunting grounds around Sheffield and Great Barrington.

On Cape Cod, Provincetown has a history as an art colony and remains an important art center. Wellfleet has emerged as a vibrant center for art and crafts as well, without Provincetown's crowds. Hyannis's Main Street—the Cape's longest—is lined with bookshops, gift shops, jewelers, and clothing stores. Chatham's Main Street is a pretty shopping area, with generally more upscale and conservative merchandise. Falmouth and Orleans also have a large number of shops.

Skiing

Ski areas in Massachusetts have become expert at providing quality snowmaking, and when conditions are marginal farther north in New England, skiing in-state is a good idea. The Massachusetts Berkshires are, in fact, foothills of the Green Mountains of Vermont, and many of the ski areas here have significant vertical drops of just over 1,000 feet, usually on gentle beginner-to-intermediate terrain. These ski areas attract a mix of people—beginners, families, and bus groups—and provide excellent opportunities for learning the sport.

In the Boston and Springfield areas the hills may be smaller, but the numbers of skiers tend to rival those in the Berkshires.

Whale Watching

This is a must for visitors to Massachusetts in the summer and early fall. Boats leave Boston, Cape Cod, and Cape Ann two or more times a day to observe the gentle giants feeding a few miles offshore, and it's extremely rare—almost unheard of—not to see several whales, most of them extremely close up. If you have even the remotest interest in wildlife, this is one attraction you mustn't miss.

Exploring Massachusetts

Most people come to Massachusetts for Boston, the beach, or the Berkshires, three very different aspects of this small and varied state. Boston has the museums, the history, the shopping, and the traffic; Cape Cod and the North and South shores have beaches, more history, more shopping, and plenty of traffic. In the Berkshires and the Pioneer Valley you'll find historic towns, antiques shopping, green hills, and a little less traffic.

Great Itineraries

Numbers in the text correspond to numbers in the margin and on the maps.

IF YOU HAVE 3 DAYS

Spend two days and nights in ⊞ **Boston.** If the third day (preferably a weekday to avoid crowds) falls in July or August, head for a beach on either Cape Cod or the North Shore or go whale watching (☞ Pleasures and Pastimes, *above*). In fall, take a drive to enjoy the foliage—either to western Massachusetts and **Old Sturbridge Village** ⑧ or to **Plimoth Plantation** on the South Shore.

IF YOU HAVE 6 DAYS

Spend three nights in ⊞ **Boston.** If you're a beach lover, head for the Cape on day four, taking in **Plymouth** and Plimoth Plantation en route—you'll need a good half day to see them properly. At the Sagamore Bridge rotary, follow the signs to Bourne Bridge and Route 28, which traces the shore of the Cape. Stop at a beach for sunning and swimming or continue to **Woods Hole** ① to visit the Woods Hole Oceanographic Institution. Overnight in ⊞ **Falmouth** ②. Start day five with a walk around Falmouth's village green, then head to **Hyannis** ③ where you can shop in the bustling downtown area or take a narrated tour of the harbor. Cross over to Route 6 for **Chatham** ⑥. Birdwatchers and nature lovers should take an excursion to **Monomoy Island.** Stop at the Marconi Station in **South Welfleet** and take the 45-minute walk through the White Cedar Swamp, on of the Cape's most beautiful trails. Spend the rest of the day biking or hiking through the National Seashore or relaxing at a beach. Take a sunset cruise out of **Provincetown**'s ⑰ MacMillan Wharf or an auto tour though the dunes. Start day six with a whale watching trip. Head back up along Route 6 and switch to Route 6A in Orleans; antique shops, historical sights, and beautiful beaches line this route. Stop in **Sandwich** ⑨ at the Heritage Plantation. Then head toward Route 6 and cross to Bourne Bridge, perhaps stopping in Onset for a Cape Cod Canal cruise.

Visitors who aren't up for the beach should take the Massachusetts Turnpike (I–90) out of Boston on day four and make a half day stop at **Old Sturbridge Village** ㊽, about an hour's drive from Boston. Afterward, continue west and then north for an overnight stay in the college town of **Amherst** ㊸, surrounded by antiques stores and pretty countryside. Spend the next morning in **Deerfield** ㊷, taking lunch at the marvelous Deerfield Inn, before continuing west to the Berkshires, where you should take time to stroll around archetypal New England villages. Make your overnight headquarters **Lenox** (54), a picturesque town with an excellent choice of country inns and restaurants. For the essential Berkshires flavor visit a "summer cottage"—Edith Wharton's "The Mount," in Lenox, is a good choice. Other nearby highlights include the Norman Rockwell Museum in **Stockbridge** (56) and the Hancock Shaker Village near **Pittsfield** (53).

IF YOU HAVE 8 DAYS

Spend three nights in **Boston.** On day four drive north for a half day visit to **Salem** ㉝ with its witchcraft, glamorous maritime history, and tourist-friendly modern shops and restaurants. Continue north and take your pick of North Shore towns for an overnight stay—**Rockport** ㊱ is a good choice. On day five, take Route 128 south, then Route 2 west, and stop for a couple of hours and lunch at **Lexington** and **Concord** to explore the Revolutionary sites and museums. Continue west as far as I–91, then head south for **Deerfield** ㊷ and an overnight stay in the Pioneer Valley. After visiting Historic Deerfield, continue west for a spectacular drive (mountains and fall foliage) on Route 2 as far as **Williamstown** ㊿ at the head of the Berkshires. Williamstown is an unusually grandiose small college town, with a couple of good art museums. Route 7 south takes you through Pittsfield into the heart of Berkshire County to **Lenox** (54) for another overnight stay. After exploring the Berkshires (☞ *above*), take I–90 east, then Route 495 south (about 3½ hours' drive) to spend your last night on Cape Cod. Take the Cape Cod Scenic Railroad dinner train, beginning and ending in **Hyannis** ③, or a moonlight cruise out of **Falmouth** ②.

When to Tour Massachusetts

Fall is the best time to visit western Massachusetts, and it's the perfect season to see Boston as well. Everyone else knows this too, of course, so be sure to make fall reservations well in advance. Summer is ideal for visitors to the Cape and beaches, but Boston itself can be unbearably hot and humid in July and August. Winters are harsh and snowy throughout the state, which makes driving vacations unappealing but family-oriented ski trips attractive.

BOSTON

Updated by
Jeanne
Cooper, Anne
Merewood,
and Stephanie
Schorow

New England's largest and most important city, the cradle of American independence, Boston is more than 360 years old, far older than the republic it helped to create. Its most famous buildings are not merely civic landmarks but national icons; its great citizens are not the political and financial leaders of today but the Adamses, Reveres, and Hancocks, who live at the crossroads of history and myth.

At the same time, Boston is a contemporary center of high finance and higher technology, a place of granite and glass towers rising along what once were rutted village lanes. Its enormous population of students, artists, academics, and young professionals has made the town a haven for the arts, international cinema, late-night bookstores, squash, Thai food, alternative music, and unconventional local politics.

Best of all, Boston is meant for walking. Most of its historical and architectural attractions are in compact areas, and its varied and distinctive neighborhoods reveal their character and design to visitors who take the time to stroll through them.

Numbers in the margin correspond to points of interest on the Boston map.

Beacon Hill and Boston Common

Enclave of Old Money grandees—all of whom have at least one ancestor who berthed on the Mayflower—contender for the "Most Beautiful" award among the city's neighborhoods, and hallowed address for many of its literary lights, Beacon Hill remains Boston at its most Bostonian. As if with a flick of a Wellsian time-machine, the redbrick elegance of its narrow, cobbled streets wafts visitors back to the 19th century. But make no mistake: Beacon Hill is no Williamsburg clone; here, people aren't living *in* the past, but *with* it. From the gold-topped splendor of the State House to the Neoclassical panache of its mansions, Beacon Hill exudes power, prestige, and a calm yet palpable undercurrent of history.

Beacon Hill is bounded by Cambridge Street to the north, Beacon Street to the south, the Charles River Esplanade to the west, and Bowdoin Street to the east. In contrast to Beacon Hill, the Boston Common, the country's oldest public park, exudes an attitude that is for, by, and of the people. Beginning with its use as public land for cattle grazing, the Common has always accommodated the needs and desires of its citizens. Public hangings, however, have gone the way of the Puritans.

A good place to begin an exploration of the Common or Beacon Hill is at the **Visitor Information Center** on Tremont Street just east of the Park Street Station. The facility, which includes public rest rooms, is well supplied with stacks of free pamphlets about Boston. *Center takes no incoming calls; for general Boston information* ☎ *617/536–4100 or 800/374–7400.* ☻ *Mon.–Sat. 8:30–5, Sun. 9–5.*

Here, too, you can pick up a free map of Boston's **Freedom Trail** or buy a more extensive guide for $5. The red line of the trail begins just outside in Parkman Plaza with its 1950s bronze monuments extolling religion, industry, and learning. Note that ranger-led tours leave frequently from the **National Park Visitor Center** (☎ 617/242–5642) on State Street in spring, summer, and fall. The 16 sites begin with the State House and Boston Common and end at the Bunker Hill Monument; it's a self-guiding stroll, although a map/brochure (free at the Tremont Street Visitor Center) is recommended.

Sights to See

Acorn Street. Surely the most photographed street in the city, Acorn is Ye Olde Colonial Boston at its best. Almost toylike row houses line one side, and on the other are the doors to Mt. Vernon Street's hidden gardens. Nineteenth-century artisans and small tradesmen once called these row houses home.

㉟ African Meeting House. Built in 1806 and centerpiece of the historic Smith Court African-American community, the African Meeting House is the oldest black church building still standing in the United States. In 1832 the New England Anti-Slavery Society was formed here under the leadership of William Lloyd Garrison. Tours are offered by employees of the National Park Service (☞ Black Heritage Trail, *below*). ⊠ *8 Smith Ct. (off Joy St., between Cambridge and Myrtle Sts.)*, ☜ *$3.* ⊙ *Memorial Day–Labor Day, daily 10–4; rest of yr, weekdays 10–4. T stop, Park St.*

Beacon Street. One of the city's most famous thoroughfares, Beacon Street epitomizes Boston. From the magnificent State House to the stately patrician mansions, it's lined with architectural treasures. The ☞ **Boston Athenaeum** is on this street as are the **Appleton Mansions,** at Nos. 39 and 40. Be sure to note their celebrated purple panes; only a few buildings have them, and they are as valuable as an ancestor in the China Trade. Their amethystine mauve color was the result of the action of sunlight on the imperfections in a shipment of glass sent to Boston around 1820. The mansions are not open to the public. Further along, you'll find some of the most important buildings of Charles Bulfinch—the ultimate designer of the Federal style in America—and dozens of elegant bowfront row town houses.

Black Heritage Trail. First established in the late 1960s, the 1.6-mile Black Heritage Trail celebrates the heritage of Boston's African-American community by stitching together 14 sites. National Park Service guided tours of the trail start out from the Shaw Memorial on the Beacon Street side of the Boston Common; a self-guided version can be done by brochure (available from the National Park Service Visitor Center). ⊠ *National Park Service Visitor Center, 15 State St. or 46 Joy St.,* ☏ *617/742–5415.* ⊙ *Tours Memorial Day–Labor Day, daily at 10 AM, noon, and 2 PM (reservations advised); rest of yr, by appointment. For self-guided tours, obtain brochure at NPS visitor centers.*

㉓ Boston Athenaeum. Visitors will delight in one of the most marvelous sights in Boston world of academe, the fifth-floor Reading Room. Founded in 1807, it moved to its present imposing quarters—modeled after Palladio's Palazzo da Porta Festa in Vicenza, Italy—in 1849. Occasional exhibitions are open to the public. ⊠ *10½ Beacon St.,* ☏ *617/227–0270.* ☜ *Free.* ⊙ *Mon. 9–8, Tues.–Fri. 9–5:30; Sept.–May, Sat. 9–4.* ⊙ *Free guided tours Tues. and Thurs. at 3 PM, by appointment 24 hrs ahead. Closed holidays and Bunker Hill Day (June 17). T stop, Park St.*

⑲ Boston Common. Nothing is more central to Boston than Boston Common, the oldest public park in the United States and undoubtedly the largest and most famous of the town commons around which New England settlements were traditionally arranged. It is as old (dating to 1634) as the city around it.

Within Boston Common are two intriguing sights. The **Central Burying Ground** is the final resting place of Tories and Patriots alike, as well as many British casualties of the Battle of Bunker Hill. On the Beacon Street side of the Common sits the splendidly restored **Robert Gould Shaw Memorial,** executed in deep-relief bronze by Augustus

Saint-Gaudens in 1897. It commemorate~~~
Regiment, the first Civil War unit made up of~~~
young Robert Gould Shaw, a stirring saga that~~~
movie *Glory*.

16 **Bull & Finch Pub.** If the entrance to this pub looks strangely fa~~~
you might find yourself humming the words, ". . .where everybo~~~
knows your name." Yes, this is the watering hole that inspired the long-
running NBC sit-com *Cheers*, as evidenced by the yellow *Cheers* flag
and the (usually) long line of tourists outside. The interior, however,
has merely a passing resemblance to its TV counterpart. ⊠ *84 Beacon
St.* ☎ *617/227–9605. T stop, Arlington.*

NEED A
BREAK?
For a good cappuccino, take your pick of coffee shops along Charles
Street. **Rebecca's Bakery** (⊠ 119 Mt. Vernon St., ☎ 617/742–9542)
has one of the more historic locations as it's on the ground floor of the
Charles Street Meeting House, once an anti-slavery stronghold and,
after the Civil War, a prominent black church.

Chestnut Street. Chestnut and Mt. Vernon are two of the loveliest
streets in the city. Here, delicacy and grace characterize virtually every
structure, from the fanlights above the entryways to the wrought-iron
boot scrapers on the steps. In particular, note the **Swan Houses,** at Nos.
13, 15, and 17—complete with Adam-style entrances, marble colum-
nettes, and recessed arches—commissioned from Charles Bulfinch.

14 **Esplanade.** At the northern end of Charles Street is one of several foot-
bridges crossing Storrow Drive to the Esplanade, one of the nicest places
in the city for jogging, picnicking, and watching the sailboats along
the Charles River. For the almost nightly entertainment in the summer,
Bostonians haul chairs and blankets to the lawn in front of the **Hatch
Memorial Shell.**

18 **Louisburg Square.** One of the quaintest corners in a neighborhood that
epitomizes quaint, Louisburg Square is the very heart of Beacon Hill.
Its houses—many built in the 1840s—have seen their share of famous
tenants, incuding the Alcotts at No. 10 (Louisa May not only lived but
died here, on the day of her father's funeral). In 1852 the singer Jenny
Lind was married in the parlor of No. 20, residence of Samuel Ward,
brother of Julia Ward Howe.

Mt. Vernon Street. With Chestnut Street, Mt. Vernon has some of Beacon Hill's most distinguished addresses. Mt. Vernon is the grander of
the two streets, with houses set back farther and rising taller; it even
has a freestanding mansion, the Second Harrison Gray Otis House, at
No. 87. Henry James once wrote that this was "the only respectable
street in America," and he must have known, since he lived with his
brother William at No. 131 in the 1860s.

21 **Museum of Afro-American History.** Ever since Crispus Attucks became
one of the legendary victims of the Boston Massacre of 1770, the
African-American community of Boston has played an important part
in the city's history. Throughout the century, abolition became the cause
célèbre for Boston's intellectual elite. To study up on this fascinating
history, head for this museum, which occupies a charming schoolhouse
of the 1830s—the first grammar school for black children in Boston.
⊠ *46 Joy St.* ☎ *617/742–1854.* ☉ *Weekdays 10–4; Memorial
Day–Labor Day, daily 10–4.* 🎟 *Free; suggested donation $3.* ☉ *Tours
at 10, noon, and 2. T stop, Park St.*

15 **Museum of Science.** With 15-foot lightning bolts in the Theater of Electricity and a 20-foot-high T. Rex model, this is just the place to ignite

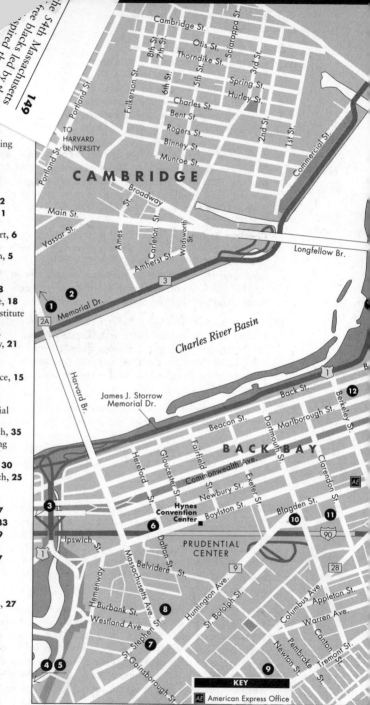

KEY

AE American Express Office

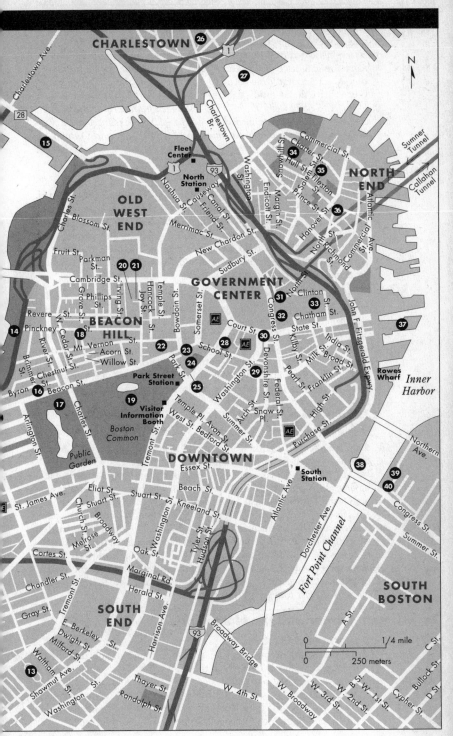

N

CHARLESTOWN ㉖
㉗
1

CHARLESTOWN AVE.
㉘
㉕

Fleet
Center
North
Station
Charlestown Br.

Sumner
Tunnel

Callahan
Tunnel

NORTH
END

㉞ Commercial St.
㉟
㊱

OLD
WEST
END

Nashua St.
Causeway St.
Friend St.
Canal St.
Merrimac St.

Washington St.

Charles St.
Blossom St.
Fruit St.
Parkman St.
Cambridge St.
Grove St.
Phillips St.
Irving St.
Temple St.
Hancock St.
Joy St.

New Chardon St.
Sudbury St.

GOVERNMENT
CENTER

Clinton St.
Congress St.
North St.
Chatham St.
State St.
㉛
㉜
㉝
㊲

Hanover St.
North St.
Richmond St.
Prince St.
Salem St.
Hull St.
Snow Hill St.
Tileston St.
Margin St.
Endicott St.
Charter St.

Atlantic Ave.
Commercial St.

John F. Fitzgerald Expwy.

Rowes
Wharf

Inner
Harbor

㊳
㊴
㊵

BEACON
HILL
㉒
㉓
㉔
㉕

Revere St.
Pinckney
W. Cedar St.
Mt. Vernon St.
Acorn St.
Willow St.
Park St.
School St.
Court St.
Devonshire St.
Kilby St.
Milk St.
Broad St.
Pearl St.
Franklin St.
High St.
India St.
㉘
㉙
㉚

Park Street
Station

Visitor
Information
Booth

Boston
Common

Public
Garden

Arlington St.
Charles St.
Tremont St.
Beacon St.
Chestnut St.
Byron St.
Brimmer St.
River St.

Washington St.
Temple Pl.
West St. Bedford St.
Avon St.
Summer St.
Arch
Snow Pl.

DOWNTOWN

Essex St.
Beach St.

South
Station

Atlantic Ave.
Purchase St.
Dorchester Ave.

Congress St.
Summer St.
Northern Ave.

Fort Point Channel

SOUTH
BOSTON

St. James Ave.
Eliot St.
Stuart St.
Broadway
Melrose St.
Cortes St.
Church St.
Chandler St.
Gray St.
Tremont St.
E. Berkeley St.
Dwight St.
Milford St.
Waltham St.
Shawmut Ave.
Washington St.

SOUTH
END

Stuart St.
Kneeland St.
Tyler St.
Hudson St.
Oak St.
Marginal Rd.
Herald St.
Harrison Ave.
Washington St.

Broadway Bridge
Thayer St.
Randolph St.
W. 4th St.
W. Broadway
W. 3rd St.
W. 2nd St.
W. 1st St.
A St.
B St.
C St.
D St.
Bullock St.
Cypher St.

0   1/4 mile
0   250 meters

any child's Jurassic spark. The museum sits astride the Charles River Dam and has three restaurants, a gift shop, a planetarium, and a theater you can visit separately. The **Charles Hayden Planetarium,** with its sophisticated multi-image system, produces exciting programs on astronomical discoveries. The **Mugar Omni Theater** has a four-story domed screen that wraps around and over you, and 27,000 watts of power drive the 84 loudspeakers. ⊠ *Science Park at the Charles River Dam,* ☎ *617/723–2500, 617/523–6664 for planetarium and theater.* 🎫 *Museum $8, planetarium and theater $7.50 each; reduced price combination tickets available for museum, planetarium, and Omni Theater.* ☉ *Sat.–Thurs. 9–5, Fri. 9–9; extended hrs July 5–Sept. 5. Closed Thanksgiving, Dec. 25. T stop, Science Park.*

㉔ **Old Granary Burial Ground.** "It is a fine thing to die in Boston," A. C. Lyons once remarked—alluding to Boston's cemeteries, among the most picturesque and historic in America. If you found a resting-place here at the Old Granary (just to the right of ☞ **Park Street Church**), chances are your headstone would have been eloquently ornamented and your neighbors would have been mighty eloquent, too: Samuel Adams, John Hancock, Paul Revere, and "Mother" Goose. ⊠ *Tremont St. near Bosworth St.* ☉ *Daily 8–4:30. T stop, Park St.*

㉕ **Park Street Church.** If the Congregationalist Park Street Church—at the corner of Tremont and Park streets—could talk, what a joyful noise it would make. Inside the church, which was designed by Peter Banner and completed in 1810, Samuel Smith's hymn "America" was first sung on July 4, 1831. Here, also, in 1829 William Lloyd Garrison began his long public campaign for the abolition of slavery. The church— called "the most impressive mass of brick and mortar in America" by Henry James—is landmarked by its steeple, considered by many critics to be the most beautiful in New England. ⊠ *1 Park St.* ☎ *617/523– 3383.* ☉ *Tours mid-June–mid-Aug., Tues.–Sat. 9:30–3:30. Sun. services at 9, 10:45, and 6:30. Closed July 4. T stop, Park St.*

㉒ **State House.** At the corner of Park and Beacon streets stands Charles Bulfinch's magnificent State House, one of the greatest works of classical architecture in America. It is so striking that it hardly suffers for having been appendaged in three directions by bureaucrats and lesser architects. The neoclassical design is poised between Georgian and Federal; its finest features are the delicate Corinthian columns of the portico, the graceful pediment and window arches, and the vast yet visually weightless dome. The dome is sheathed in copper from the foundry of Paul Revere; the gilding was added in 1874. During World War II, the dome was painted gray so that it would not reflect moonlight during blackouts. ⊠ *Beacon St.,* ☎ *617/727–3676.* 🎫 *Free.* ☉ *Tours weekdays 10–4, last tour at 3:15. T stop, Park St.*

Government Center and the North End

Government Center

This is the section of town Bostonians love to hate. Not only does Government Center house that which they can't fight—City Hall—it also features some of the bleakest-design architecture since the advent of poured concrete. The sweeping brick plaza that marks City Hall and the twin towers of the John F. Kennedy Federal Office Building begins at the junction in which Cambridge becomes Tremont Street.

Separating the North End from the Government Center area is the Fitzgerald Expressway, due to be replaced with an underground highway. In the meantime, calling the area a mess is putting it mildly. Driver alert: The rerouting of traffic and shifts in one-way signs have changed what was once a conquerable maze into a nearly impenetrable puzzle. Trust no maps.

SIGHTS TO SEE

Blackstone Block. Landmarked by the ☞ **Union Oyster House,** the Blackstone Block is the city's oldest commercial block, for decades dominated by the butcher trade. Today, the block is Boston at its time-machine best, with more than three centuries of architecture on view.

32 **Faneuil Hall.** Faneuil Hall was erected in 1742 to serve as both a place for town meetings and a public market. Inside is the great mural *Webster's Reply to Hayne,* Gilbert Stuart's portrait of Washington at Dorchester Heights, and, on the top floors, the headquarters and museum of the Ancient and Honorable Artillery Company of Massachusetts, the oldest militia in the nation (1638). ⊠ *Faneuil Hall Square.* ☎ *Free.* ⊙ *Daily 9–5. Closed Thanksgiving, Dec. 25, Jan 1. T stop, Government Center or Aquarium.*

Haymarket. Centered around the relentlessly picturesque ☞ **Blackstone Block,** this is an exuberant maze of a marketplace, packed with loudly self-promoting vendors who fill Marshall and Blackstone streets on Friday and Saturday from 7 AM until mid-afternoon.

33 **Quincy Market.** Also known as Faneuil Hall Marketplace, this pioneer effort at urban recycling set the tone for many similar projects throughout America. The market consists of three block-long annexes: Quincy, North, and South markets, each 535 feet long, built to the 1826 design of Alexander Parris. There may be more restaurants in Quincy Market than existed in all of downtown Boston before World War II. Abundance and variety have been the watchwords of Quincy Market since its reopening in 1976. Some people consider it hopelessly trendy; another 50,000 or so visitors a day rather enjoy the extravaganza. At the east end of Quincy Market, the newer **Marketplace Center** is also filled with temptations for those with itchy credit cards. ⊠ *Off State St.,* ☎ *617/338–2323.* ⊙ *Mon.–Sat. 10–9, Sun. noon–6. Restaurants and bars generally open daily 11 AM–2 AM; food stalls open earlier. T stop, Haymarket, Government Center, State, or Aquarium.*

31 **Union Oyster House.** Centerpiece of the historic ☞ **Blackstone Block,** this is the city's oldest restaurant. Daniel Webster downed an occasional brandy and ate oysters by the dozens here in the 1830s; John F. Kennedy was among its contemporary patrons. ⊠ *41 Union St.,* ☎ *617/227– 2750.* ⊙ *Sun.–Thurs. 11 AM–9:30 PM, Fri.–Sat. 11 AM–10 PM; oyster bar nightly until midnight. T stop, Haymarket.*

The North End

Opposite the pedestrian tunnel beneath the Fitzgerald Expressway is the oldest neighborhood in Boston and one of the oldest in the New World. Men and women walked these narrow byways when Shakespeare was not yet 20 years buried and Louis XIV was new to the throne of France. In the 17th century the North End *was* Boston, for much of the rest of the peninsula was still under water or had yet to be cleared.

Today's North End is almost entirely a creation of the late 19th century, when brick tenements began to fill up with European immigrants—first the Irish, then Eastern European Jews, then the Portuguese, and finally the Italians. For more than 60 years the North End attracted an Italian population base, so much so that one wonders whether wandering Puritan shades might scowl at the concentration of Mediterranean verve, volubility, and Roman Catholicism here. This is not only Boston's haven for Italian restaurants (there are dozens) but of

Italian groceries, bakeries, churches, social clubs, cafés, street-corner debates over home-team soccer games, and encroaching gentrification.

SIGHTS TO SEE

34 Copp's Hill Burying Ground. An ancient and melancholy air hovers over this Colonial-era burial ground like a fine mist. Many headstones were chipped by practice shots fired by British soldiers during the occupation of Boston, and a number of musketball pockmarks can still be seen. ⊠ *Snowhill St.* ☼ *Daily 9–4. T stop, North Station.*

NEED A BREAK?   **Caffe Vittoria** (⊠ 296 Hanover St., ☎ 617/227-7606) specializes in cappuccino and other coffee drinks; its Old World café ambience makes it a great spot at any hour. Next door, **Mike's Pastry** (⊠ 300 Hanover St., ☎ 617/742-3050) has fresh ricotta, cannoli, and Italian pastries.

35 Old North Church. This church is famous not only for being the oldest one in Boston (1723), but for the two lanterns that glimmered from its steeple on the night of April 18, 1775. This is Christ Church, or the Old North, where a middle-aged silversmith named Paul Revere and a young sexton named Robert Newman managed that night to signal the departure by water to Lexington and Concord of the British regulars. (Longfellow's poem aside, the lanterns were not a signal *to* Revere but *from* him to the citizens of Charlestown across the harbor.) The church was designed by William Price from a study of Christopher Wren's London churches. ⊠ *193 Salem St.,* ☎ *617/523-6676.* ☼ *Daily 9–5. Sun. services at 9, 11, and 4. Closed Thanksgiving, Dec. 25. T stop, Haymarket or North Station.*

☙ **36 Paul Revere House.** It is an interesting coincidence that the oldest house standing in downtown Boston should also have been the home of Paul Revere, patriot activist and silversmith. And it *is* a coincidence, since many homes of famous Bostonians have burned or been demolished over the years, and the Revere House could easily have become one of them back when it was just another makeshift tenement in the heyday of European immigration. It was saved from oblivion in 1905 and restored, lovingly though not quite scientifically, to an approximation of its original 17th-century appearance.

The house was built nearly a hundred years before Revere's 1775 midnight ride through Middlesex County. Few of Revere's furnishings are on display here, but just gazing at Paul's own toddy-warmer brings the great man alive. Many special events are scheduled here through the year for children. ⊠ *19 North Sq.,* ☎ *617/523-1676.* 🎫 *$2.50.* ☼ *Daily 9:30–4:15; Apr. 15–Nov. 1 until 5:15 PM. Closed holidays and Mon., Jan.–Mar. T stop, Haymarket.*

Charlestown

Boston started here. Charlestown was a thriving settlement a year before Colonials headed across the Charles River to found the city proper. Today, the district lures visitors with two of the most visible—and vertical—monuments in Boston's history: the Bunker Hill Monument and the USS *Constitution.*

To get to Charlestown, you may take Bus 93 from Haymarket Square, Boston, which stops three blocks from the Navy Yard entrance. A more interesting way to get here is to take the MBTA water shuttle (☎ 617/227-4320) from Long Wharf in downtown Boston, which runs every 15 or 30 minutes year-round.

Sights to See

26 Bunker Hill Monument. Three classic misnomers surround this famous monument. First, the Battle of Bunker Hill was actually fought on Breed's Hill, which is where the monument sits today. Second, Americans actually lost the battle in a Pyrrhic victory for the British Redcoats, who relinquished nearly half of their 2,200 soldiers; American casualties numbered 500 to 600. And third: The famous war cry, "Don't fire until you see the whites of their eyes," may not have been uttered by American Colonel William Prescott, but if he did shout it, he was quoting an old Prussian command. No matter. The Americans did employ a deadly delayed action strategy on June 17, 1775, and conclusively proved themselves worthy fighters.

The monument's zenith is reached by a flight of 294 steps. There is no elevator, but the views from the observatory are worth the effort of the arduous climb. In the lodge at the base, dioramas tell the story of the battle; and ranger programs are conducted hourly. If you are in Boston on June 17, go to the hill to see a reenactment of the battle; it's quite a splendid production. ☎ 617/242–5641. ⚃ *Free.* ☉ *Lodge daily 9– 5, monument daily 9–4:30. Closed Thanksgiving, Dec. 25, Jan. 1. T stop, Community College.*

A multimedia Bunker Hill presentation, **"Whites of Their Eyes,"** is shown in the Bunker Hill Pavilion near the Navy Yard entrance. ⊠ *55 Constitution Rd.,* ☎ *617/241–7576.* ⚃ *$3.* ☉ *Apr.–Nov. 9:30–4; July–Aug. 9:30–5; shows every ½ hr.*

27 USS Constitution. Better known as "Old Ironsides," the USS *Constitution* is at the **Charlestown Navy Yard.** The oldest commissioned ship in the U.S. fleet is a battlewagon of the old school, of the days of "wooden ships and iron men"—when she and her crew of 200 asserted the sovereignty of an improbable new nation. Her principal service was in the War of 1812. Of her 42 engagements, her record was 42–0. Once a year, on July 4th, she is towed out into Boston harbor. The venerable craft celebrates her 200th birthday in 1997. ⊠ *Constitution Wharf,* ☎ *617/426–1812 museum, 617/242–5670 ship.* ⚃ Constitution *free; museum $4.* ☉ *Museum: summer, daily 9–6; fall and spring, daily 10– 5. Ship: daily 9:30–sunset; 20-min tours, last at 3:50 PM. T stop, Haymarket; then MBTA Bus 92 or 93 to Charlestown City Sq. or Boston Harbor Cruise water shuttle from Long Wharf.*

NEED A
BREAK?
Stop for a drink or some food with an international twist at the **Warren Tavern** (⊠ 2 Pleasant St., ☎ 617/241-8142). Built in 1780, this is a restored Colonial neighborhood pub once frequented by George Washington and Paul Revere. It was the first building reconstructed after the Battle of Bunker Hill, which leveled the town.

Downtown Boston

The financial district—what Bostonians usually refer to as "downtown"—is off the beaten track for visitors who are concentrating on following the Freedom Trail, yet there is much to see in a walk of an hour or two. There is little logic to the streets here; they were, after all, village lanes that only now happen to be lined with 40-story office towers. The area may be confusing, but it is mercifully small.

Downtown is home to some of Boston's most idiosyncratic neighborhoods. The old Leather District directly abuts Chinatown, which is also bordered by the Theater District, farther west (and the buildings of the

Tufts New England Medical Center), while to the south, the red light of the once brazen and now decaying Combat Zone flickers weakly.

Sights to See

㊳ Beaver II. A faithful replica of one of the ships forcibly boarded and unloaded the night Boston Harbor became a teapot bobs in the Fort Point Channel at the Congress Street Bridge. Visitors receive a complimentary cup of tea, and when there are enough people, kids may be pressed into donning feathers and warpaint to reenact the tea drop. The site of the actual tea party is marked by a plaque on Pearl Street and Atlantic Avenue. ⊠ *Congress St. Bridge,* ☎ *617/338–1773.* ✆ *$6.50.* ☺ *Memorial Day–Labor Day, daily 9–6; Labor Day–Dec. and Mar.–Memorial Day, 9–5. Closed Thanksgiving and Dec.–Apr. T stop, South Station.*

㊵ Children's Museum. Just across the Congress Street Bridge is Museum Wharf, home of the ever-popular Children's Museum (not for kids only). Hands-on exhibits include computers, video cameras, and displays designed to help children understand cultural diversity, their own bodies, and the nature of disabilities. Don't miss Grandmother's Attic, where children can dress up in old clothing. ⊠ *300 Congress St.,* ☎ *617/426–6500 or 617/426–8855 for recorded information.* ✆ *$7; $1 on Fri. 5–9.* ☺ *Tues.–Sun. 10–5, Fri. 10–9. Closed Mon., Thanksgiving, Dec. 25, Jan. 1. T stop, South Station.*

Chinatown. Boston's Chinatown may be geographically small in the scheme of the city yet it is home to one of the larger concentrations of Chinese-Americans in the United States. Today, the many Chinese restaurants—most along Beach and Tyler streets and Harrison Avenue—are interspersed with a handful of Vietnamese eateries, a reflection of the latest wave of immigration. *T stop, Chinatown.*

NEED A
BREAK?

It's a special treat to sample the Chinese baked goods in shops along **Beach Street,** such as Hing Sing Pastry at No. 67. Many visitors familiar with Cantonese and even Szechuan cuisine will still be surprised and delighted with moon cakes—steamed cakes made with rice flour—and other sweets that seldom turn up on restaurant menus.

㊳ Computer Museum. At the Computer Museum you can learn about the thinking machines running our lives in a user-friendly setting both you and your kids will enjoy. Conveniently located next to the ☞ **Children's Museum,** the Computer Museum has more than 75 exhibits, including the two-story, Walk-Through Computer™. ⊠ *300 Congress St.,* ☎ *617/426–2800 or 617/423–6758 for talking computer.* ✆ *$7; ½ price Sun. 3–5.* ☺ *Tues.–Sun. 10–5. Closed Mon., holidays, and Fri. evenings in winter. T stop, South Station.*

㉘ King's Chapel. Both somber and dramatic, King's Chapel, built in 1754, looms over the corner of Tremont and School streets. Its distinctive shape was not achieved entirely by design; for lack of funds it was never topped with the steeple that architect Peter Harrison had planned. The interior is a masterpiece of elegant proportion and Georgian calm. The chapel's bell is Paul Revere's largest and, in his judgment, was his sweetest-sounding. Take the path to the right from the entrance of the **King's Chapel Burying Ground,** the oldest cemetery in the city. On the left is the gravestone (1704) of Elizabeth Pain, the model for Hester Prynne in Hawthorne's *The Scarlet Letter.* Elsewhere, you'll find the graves of the first Massachusetts governor, John Winthrop, and several generations of his descendants. ⊠ *58 Tremont St.,* ☎ *617/227–2155.* ☺ *June–Oct., Mon.–Sat. 9:30–4, Sun. noon–4; Nov.–May, Tues.–Wed.*

11–1, Sat. 10–4. Sun. service at 11. Music program Tues. 12:15–12:45.
T stop, Park St. or Government Center.

㊲ New England Aquarium. This aquarium is one of Boston's most popular attractions. Inside you'll find penguins, jellyfish, sharks—more than 2,000 species in all. ✉ *Central Wharf (between Central and Milk Sts.).* ☎ *617/973–5200 or 617/973–5277 for whale-watching information.* 🎫 *$8.50; $1 off Thurs. after 4 PM.* ☉ *Weekdays 9–5, Thurs. 9–8, weekends and holidays 9–6. Closed Thanksgiving, Dec. 25. T Stop, Aquarium.*

㉙ Old South Meeting House. Some of the fieriest of the town meetings that led to the Revolution were held here, culminating in the tumultuous gathering of December 16, 1773, which was called by Samuel Adams to address the question concerning some dutiable tea that activists wanted returned to England. The Old South is closed for renovations until the spring of 1997. *T stop, State or Downtown Crossing.*

㉚ Old State House. This Colonial-era landmark has one of the most elegant facades in Boston, with its State Street gable adorned by a brightly gilded lion and unicorn, symbols of British imperial power. This was the seat of the Colonial government from 1713 until the Revolution, and after the evacuation of the British from Boston in 1776 it served the independent Commonwealth until its replacement on Beacon Hill was completed. The permanent collection traces Boston's Revolutionary War history, while changing exhibits address such contemporary issues as "Urban Renewal and Boston's West End."

Immediately outside the Old State House at 15 State Street is a visitor's center run by the National Park Service; there is an abundance of free brochures and rest rooms. ✉ *206 Washington St.,* ☎ *617/720–3290.* 🎫 *$3.* ☉ *Daily 9:30–5. Closed Thanksgiving, Dec. 25, Jan. 1. T stop, State.*

Rowes Wharf. This 15-story Skidmore, Owings, and Merrill extravaganza is one of the more welcome additions to the Boston Harbor skyline, and the site of the Boston Harbor Hotel and the Rowes Wharf Restaurant. From under the complex's gateway six-story arch, there are great views of Boston Harbor and the luxurious yachts parked in the marina. Water shuttles pull up here from Logan Airport—the most spectacular way to enter the city. *T Stop, Aquarium.*

The Back Bay

In the folklore of American neighborhoods, the Back Bay stands with New York's Park Avenue and San Francisco's Nob Hill as a symbol of propriety and high social standing. This is one of Boston's newer neighborhoods—before the 1850s, it was a bay, a tidal flat that formed the south bank of a distended Charles River. Bostonians began to fill in the shallows in 1858, using gravel brought from West Needham by railroad at a rate of up to 3,500 carloads per day. By 1900 the area was the smartest and most desirable in all Boston.

The main east-west streets—Beacon Street, Marlborough Street, Commonwealth Avenue, Newbury Street, and Boylston Street—were bisected by eight streets named in alphabetical order from Arlington to Hereford. The Back Bay remains a living museum of urban Victorian residential architecture. A walk through the Public Garden is a good way to begin a Back Bay tour.

Sights to See

Boylston Street. This broad thoroughfare is the southern commercial spine of the Back Bay. It has a variety of interesting shops and restaurants, the Hynes Convention Center, and an F.A.O. Schwarz store with a huge teddy bear sculpture on the sidewalk in front.

8 **Christian Science Church.** The world headquarters of the Christian Science faith combines an Old-World basilica with a sleek office complex designed by I. M. Pei. This church was established here by Mary Baker Eddy in 1879. Mrs. Eddy's original granite First Church of Christ, Scientist (1894), has since been enveloped by a domed Renaissance basilica, added to the site in 1906. In the publishing society's lobby is the fascinating **Maparium,** a huge stained-glass globe that allows visitors to traverse its 30-foot diameter thanks to a glass bridge. There's also a 670-foot reflecting pool. ⊠ *175 Huntington Ave.,* ☎ *617/450–3790.* ⊙ *Mother church, Mon.–Sat. 10–4, Sun. 11:15–2, free 30-min tours. On Mon. only original edifice open for tours. Sun. services at 10 AM and 7 PM. Closed Labor Day, Dec. 25. Maparium: Mon.–Sat. 10–4, closed Sun. T stop, Prudential.*

10 **Copley Place.** An upscale, glass and brass urban mall, Copley Place is comprised of two major hotels, shops, restaurants, and offices attractively grouped around bright, open indoor spaces. ⊙ *Shopping galleries: Mon.–Sat. 10–7, Sun. noon–5. T stop, Copley.*

12 **Gibson House.** One of the first Back Bay residences (1859), the Gibson House has been preserved with all its Victorian fixtures and furniture intact; a conservative family scion lived here until the 1950s and left things as they had always been. ⊠ *137 Beacon St.,* ☎ *617/267–6338.* ☞ *$3.* ⊙ *Tours May–Oct., Wed.–Sun. at 1, 2, and 3; Nov.–Apr., weekends at 1, 2, and 3. T stop, Arlington.*

6 **Institute of Contemporary Art.** The fact that a 1989 exhibition of Mapplethorpe photographs hardly raised an eyebrow here demonstrates how cutting edge this small showcase has become. In a historical 19th-century police station and firehouse, the ICA has no permanent collection, it instead hosts temporary exhibitions. ⊠ *955 Boylston St.,* ☎ *617/266–5152.* ☞ *$5.25; free Thurs. 5–9.* ⊙ *Wed.–Sun. noon–5, Thurs. noon–9. Tours weekends at 1 and 3. T stop, Hynes Convention Center.*

11 **John Hancock Tower.** The tallest building in New England is this stark and graceful reflective blue rhomboid tower, designed by I. M. Pei. The 60th-floor observatory makes one of the three best vantage points in the city, and the "Boston 1775" exhibit shows what the city looked like before the great hill-leveling and landfill operations commenced. ⊠ *Observatory ticket office, Trinity Pl. and St. James Ave.,* ☎ *617/247–1977.* ☞ *$3.75.* ⊙ *Mon.–Sat. 9 AM–10 PM, Sun. noon–10. Closed Thanksgiving, Dec. 25. T stop, Copley.*

Newbury Street. The eight blocks of Newbury Street have been compared to New York's Fifth Avenue, and certainly this is the city's poshest shopping mecca. But here the pricey boutiques are more intimate than grand, and people actually live above the trendy restaurants and hair salons. Toward the Massachusetts Avenue end, cafés proliferate and the stores get funkier.

☝ **17** **Public Garden.** A walk through the Back Bay properly begins with the Public Garden, the oldest botanical garden in the United States. The park's pond has been famous since 1877 for its foot pedal–powered **Swan Boats,** which make leisurely cruises during warm months. They were invented by Robert Paget who was inspired by the popularity of swan boats made fashionable by Wagner's opera, *Lohengrin.* Paget descendants still run the boats, which have carried luminaries ranging from Shirley Temple to Ted Danson.

Follow the kids quack-quacking along the pathway between the pond and the park entrance at Charles and Beacon streets to the *Make Way for Ducklings* bronze statues. Jack, Kack, Lack, Mack, Nack, Ouack, Pack, and Quack comprise Mrs. Mallard's pack—made famous in the 1941 classic children's story (set along Beacon Street and within the Public Garden). ☎ *617/635–4505.* ⊘ *Dawn–10 PM; not recommended for strolling after dark. Swan boats: mid-Apr.–late Sept., daily 10–4.* 🎫 *Swan boats $1.50. T stop, Arlington.*

❼ **Symphony Hall.** Symphony Hall, since 1900 the home of the Boston Symphony Orchestra, was another contribution of McKim, Mead, and White to the Boston landscape, but acoustics, rather than exterior design, make this a special place for performers and concert goers. ⊠ *301 Massachusetts Ave.,* ☎ *617/266–1492, box office 800/274–8499.* ⊘ *Tours by appointment with volunteer office (wk ahead suggested). T stop, Symphony.*

Trinity Church. In his 1877 masterpiece, architect Henry Hobson Richardson brought his Romanesque Revival style to maturity; all the aesthetic elements for which he was famous—bold masonry, careful arrangement of masses, sumptuously carved interior woodwork—come together magnificently. The church remains the centerpiece of Copley Square. ⊠ *206 Clarendon St.,* ☎ *617/536–0944.* ⊘ *Daily 8–6. Sun. services at 8, 9, 11, and 6. T stop, Copley.*

The South End

History has come full circle in the South End. Once a fashionable neighborhood created with landfill in the mid-19th century, it was deserted by the well-to-do for the Back Bay toward the end of the century. Solidly back in fashion, today it is a polyglot of upscale eateries and ethnic enclaves adorned by redbrick row houses, in refurbished splendor or elegant decay. An observation often made is that the Back Bay is French-inspired while the South End is English. The houses, too, are different. In one sense they continue the pattern established on Beacon Hill (in a uniformly bowfront style), yet they also aspire to a much more florid standard of decoration.

There is a substantial black presence in the South End, particularly along Columbus Avenue and Massachusetts Avenue, which marks the beginning of the predominantly black neighborhood of Roxbury. You are likely to hear Spanish spoken along Tremont, and there are Middle Eastern groceries along Shawmut Avenue. At the north end of the South End, Harrison Avenue and Washington Street lead to Chinatown, and consequently there is a growing Asian influence, evidenced by a huge Chinese supermarket on Washington Street on the South End side. Along East Berkeley Street, neighbors have created a lush community garden. Also, Boston's gay community has a large presence in the South End.

Sights to See

Bay Village. This neighborhood is a pocket of early 19th-century brick row houses that appears to be almost a toylike replication of Beacon Hill. Edgar Allan Poe once lived here. It seems improbable that so fine and serene a neighborhood can exist in the shadow of busy Park Square—a 1950s developer might easily have leveled these blocks in an afternoon–yet here it is, another Boston surprise. To get here, follow Columbus avenue almost into Park Square, turn right on Arlington Street, then left onto one of the narrow streets of this neighborhood.

9 **Rutland Square** (between Columbus Avenue and Tremont Street) and
13 **Union Park** (between Tremont Street and Shawmut Avenue) are elliptical, shady havens, bordered by rows of bowhouses. Both reflect a time
in which the South End was the most prestigious Boston address.

The Fens

The marshland known as the Back Bay Fens gave this section of Boston
its name, but two quirky institutions give it its character: Fenway
Park, where hope for another World Series pennant springs eternal,
and the Isabella Stewart Gardner Museum, the legacy of a bon vivant
Brahmin. Kenmore Square, a favorite haunt for college students, adds
a bit of funky flavor to the mix.

The Fens mark the beginning of Boston's Emerald Necklace, a loosely
connected chain of parks designed by Olmsted that extends along the
Fenway, Riverway, and Jamaicaway to Jamaica Pond, the Arnold Arboretum, and Franklin Park.

Sights to See

3 **Fenway Park.** While Fenway may be one of the smallest parks in the
major leagues (capacity 34,000), it is one of the most loved. Since its
construction in 1912, there has been no shortage of heroics: Babe
Ruth pitched here when the place was new; Ted Williams and Carl Yas-
trzemski slugged out their entire careers here. ☎ *607/267–8661 or
617/267–1700 for tickets.*

5 **Isabella Stewart Gardner Museum.** A spirited young society woman,
Isabella Stewart came from New York in 1860 to marry John Lowell
Gardner. When it came time to finally house the Old Master paintings
and Medici treasures she and her husband had acquired in Europe, she
decided to build the Venetian palazzo of her dreams along Commonwealth Avenue—today, a monument to one woman's extraordinary taste.

Despite the loss of a few masterpieces in a daring 1990 robbery, there
is much to see: a trove of spectacular paintings—including such masterpieces as Titian's *Rape of Europa,* Giorgione's *Christ Bearing the
Cross,* Piero della Francesca's *Hercules,* and John Singer Sargent's *El
Jaleo*—rooms bought outright from great European houses, Spanish
leather panels, Renaissance hooded fireplaces, and Gothic tapestries.
An intimate restaurant overlooks the courtyard, and in the spring and
summer tables and chairs spill outside. To fully conjure up the spirit
of days past, attend one of the concerts held in the elegant Music Room.
✉ *280 The Fenway,* ☎ *617/566–1401, 617/566–1088 for café.*
$7. ☉ *Tues.–Sun. 11–5. T stop, Museum.*

Kenmore Square. Kenmore Square is home to fast-food parlors, rock-
and-roll clubs, an abundance of university students, and an enormous
sign advertising Citgo gasoline. The red, white, and blue neon sign put
up in 1965 is so thoroughly identified with the area that historic
preservationists have fought, successfully, to save it—proof that Bostonians are an open-minded lot who do not insist that their landmarks
be identified with the American Revolution.

4 **Museum of Fine Arts.** The M.F.A.'s holdings of American art surpass
those of all but two or three U.S. museums. There are more than 50
works by John Singleton Copley—Colonial Boston's most celebrated
portraitist—alone; plus major paintings by Winslow Homer, John
Singer Sargent, and Edward Hopper.

The museum also has the most extensive collection in the world of Asi-
atic art and a fine Egyptian collection. French Impressionists abound;
there are 43 Monets, the largest collection of his work outside Paris.

The museum has a gift shop, a good restaurant, and a cafeteria serving light snacks; all are in the West Wing. ⊠ *465 Huntington Ave.,* ☎ *617/267–9300.* ☞ *$8; voluntary admission Wed. 4–9:45.* ☉ *Entire museum: Tues.–Sun. 10–4:45, Wed. until 9:45. West Wing: Thurs. and Fri. until 9:45, with admission reduced by $1. 1-hr tours available Tues.–Fri. Closed Mon. (except holidays). T stop, Museum.*

On the Fenway Park side of the Museum of Fine Arts, **Tenshin Garden,** the "garden at the heart of heaven," allows visitors to experience landscape as a work of art. A combination of Japanese and American trees and shrubs fuse the concept of the Japanese garden with elements of the New England landscape.

Cambridge

Pronounced with either prideful satisfaction or the occasional smirk, the nickname "The People's Republic of Cambridge" sums up this independent city of 95,000 west of Boston. Cambridge not only houses two of the country's greatest educational institutions—Harvard University and the Massachusetts Institute of Technology—it has a long history as a haven for freethinkers, writers, activists, and iconoclasts of every stamp. Once a center for publishing, Cambridge has become a high-tech mecca; more than a few MIT students launched software companies even before they graduated. The more than 30,000 students insure a cornucopia of cafés, record stores, music clubs, street-chic boutiques, and bookstores that stay open until the wee hours.

Cambridge, just minutes from Boston by MBTA, is easily reached on the Red Line train to Harvard Square. The area is notorious for limited parking. If you insist on driving into Cambridge, you may want to avoid the local circling ritual by pulling into a garage.

Sights to See

Cambridge Discovery Information Booth. At this kiosk, just outside the MBTA Cambridge station entrance, you will find maps, brochures, and information about the entire city. Cambridge Discovery also gives a rewarding tour of Old Cambridge conducted by a corps of well-trained high school students. ⊠ *Cambridge Discovery, Inc., Box 1987, Harvard Sq., Cambridge 02238,* ☎ *617/497–1630.* ☉ *Winter, daily 9–5; summer, daily 9–6.*

Fogg Art Museum. Harvard's most famous art museum owns 80,000 works of art from every major period and from every corner of the world. Behind Harvard Yard on Quincy Street, the Fogg was founded in 1895; its collection focuses primarily on European, American, and Far Eastern works, with notable collections of 19th-century French Impressionist and medieval Italian paintings. Special exhibits change monthly. ⊠ *32 Quincy St.,* ☎ *617/495–9400.* ☞ *$5; free Sat. 10–noon.* ☉ *Mon.–Sat. 10–5, Sun. 1–5.*

A ticket to the Fogg also gains admission to Harvard's **Busch–Reisinger Museum** (☎ 617/495–9400), in the Werner Otto Hall entered through the Fogg. From the serenity of the Fogg's old masters, you step into the jarring and mesmerizing world of German Expressionists and other 20th-century artists. The same ticket also allows you to visit the **Arthur M. Sackler Museum** (☎ 617/495–9400), across the street, which has important scholarly collections of Chinese, Japanese, ancient Greek, Egyptian, Roman, Buddhist, and Islamic works. Hours for both museums are the same as at the Fogg.

Harvard Museums of Cultural and Natural History. Many museums promise something for every member of the family; the Harvard museum complex actually delivers. There are four museums here, all accessible through one admission fee. The most famous exhibit is the display of glass flowers in the **Botanical Museum** (✉ 26 Oxford St., ☎ 617/495–3045), which were created as teaching tools. The **Peabody Museum of Archaeology and Ethnology** (✉ 11 Divinity Ave., ☎ 617/495–2248) holds one of the world's outstanding anthropological collections; exhibits focus on Native American and Central and South American cultures. Animal and dinosaur lovers will enjoy the **Museum of Comparative Zoology** (✉ 26 Oxford St., ☎ 617/495–3045), which traces the evolution of animals and humans. Jewelry lovers will lust over the oversized garnets and crystals in the **Mineralogical and Geological Museum,** (✉ 24 Oxford St., ☎ 617/495–4758) which also has an extensive collection of meteorites. ✱ *$4; free Sat. 9–11.* ☉ *Mon.–Sat. 9–4:30, Sun. 1–4:30. Closed major holidays.*

❶ Harvard Square. Gaggles of students, buskers, homeless, end-of-the-world preachers, and political-cause proponents make for a nonstop pedestrian flow at this most celebrated of Cambridge crossroads. Sharing the peninsula is the Out-of-Town newsstand, a local institution that occupies the restored 1928 kiosk that used to be the entrance to the MBTA station.

Harvard University. In 1636 the Great and General Court of the Massachusetts Bay Colony established the country's first college here. Named in 1638 for John Harvard, a young Charlestown clergyman who died that year, leaving the college his entire library and half his estate, Harvard remained the only college in the New World until 1693, by which time it was firmly established as a respected center of learning. The **Harvard University Information Office** is run by students and offers maps of the university area and a free hour-long walking tour of Harvard Yard (during the academic year, weekdays at 10 and 2, Sat. at 2; mid-June–Aug., Mon.–Sat. at 10, 11:15, 2, and 3:15, Sun. at 1:30 and 3:30). ✉ *Holyoke Center, 1350 Massachusetts Ave.* ☎ *617/495–1573.*

Longfellow National Historic Site. Once home to Henry Wadsworth Longfellow—the poet whose stirring renditions of "Miles Standish," The Village Blacksmith, "Evangeline," "Hiawatha," and "Paul Revere's Midnight Ride," thrilled 19th-century America—this elegant mansion was a wedding gift for the poet in 1843. He filled it with the exuberant spirit of his own work and that of his literary circle, which included Emerson, Thoreau, and Holmes. ✉ *105 Brattle St.,* ☎ *617/876–4491.* ✱ *$2.* ☉ *Mid-May–Oct., daily 10–4:30 for guided tours only; last tour departs at 4.*

❷ Massachusetts Institute of Technology. MIT occupies 135 acres 1½ miles southeast of Harvard, bordering the Charles River. The West Campus has some extraordinary buildings: The Kresge Auditorium, designed by Eero Saarinen with a curving roof and unusual thrust, rests on three, instead of four, points; the nondenominational MIT Chapel is a circular Saarinen design. The **MIT Information Center** gives free tours of the campus weekdays at 10 and 2. ✉ *Building 7, 77 Massachusetts Ave.,* ☎ *617/253–4795.* ☉ *Weekdays 9–5.*

☺ Sports Museum of New England. Filled with sports memorabilia, life-size models of sports heroes, and interactive exhibits, the Sports Museum is on the first level of Cambridge's shopping mall, near the ☞ **Museum of Science.** Kids can feel what it's like to catch a pitch from Roger Clemens or test their sports-trivia knowledge. The museum has announced plans to move; at press time, the new location was not yet determined. ✉ *CambridgeSide Galleria, 100 Cambridgeside Pl.,* ☎ *617/577–7678.* ☉ *Mon.–Sat. 10–9:30, Sun. 11–7. T Stop, Lechmere on*

Green Line or Kendall Square on Red Line. The Gall...
tle bus from Kendall Square.

Dining

Updated by
Jonathon Alsop

To understand exactly how far the restaurant scene in Bosto...
it's important to give a little thought to how it all began...
Pilgrims and watered-down beer and boiled fish—and marv...
as lively and experimental as it is. Out-of-towners invariabl...
Boston as a city with a lobster pound on every corner, and a...
seafood is naturally a huge part of the cuisine mix, local che...
to traditional New England produce and meat, as well as seafoo...
inspiration.

Except for very few exceptions, avoid all tourist destinations, wh...
in a nutshell means Faneuil Hall and the waterfront. This is certain...
not a condemnation of all downtown restaurants, but if you want...
taste of the authentic Boston, seek out the growing number of bistros
and trattorias that serve splendidly fresh fare, usually in cozy local storefronts tucked here and there.

Back Bay

$$$$ ✕ **Ambrosia.** An outstanding new addition to Boston's restaurant
scene, Ambrosia specializes in out-of-this-world, 3-D architectural
food sculptures, many of which are so towering they could put an eye
out. The fare is French Provincial with an Asian influence. Service is
excellent, and the decor is dramatic. ⊠ *116 Huntington Ave. (Copley
Place),* ☎ *617/247–2400. AE, MC, V.*

$$$$ ✕ **Aujourd'hui.** This large, formal dining room of the Four Seasons Hotel
is one of the city's power rooms. The food reflects an inventive approach
to regional ingredients and new American cuisine. Some entrées, such
as rack of Colorado meadow lamb with layered potato and lasagna,
can be extremely rich, but the seasonal menu also offers healthy "alternative cuisine." The extraordinary vegetarian tasting menu, with dishes
such as roast acorn squash risotto with cinnamon oil, and parsnip ravioli with truffle broth and root vegetables, is exquisitely presented on
Villeroy and Boch plates. Window tables overlook the Public Garden.
⊠ *200 Boylston St.,* ☎ *617/451–1392. Reservations essential. Jacket
and tie. AE, DC, MC, V.*

$$$$ ✕ **Biba.** Everything about Biba makes it Boston's overwhelmingly fa-
★ vorite place to see and be seen, from the vividness of the dining room's
rambling mural to the huge street-level windows of the downstairs bar.
The menu encourages inventive, inexpensive combinations, and the gutsy
fare mixes flavors from five continents. Dishes include pan-fried oysters on semolina *blinis* (small, thick pancakes) and grilled sirloin with
English Stilton. Allow plenty of time for dining; service can be slow.
⊠ *272 Boylston St.,* ☎ *617/426–7878. DC, MC, V.*

$$$$ ✕ **L'Espalier.** This special restaurant is one of America's very best.
★ Fresh native ingredients dominate the daily menu of contemporary French
and American cuisine. All dinners are prix fixe; $56 for the regular menu
and $72 for the seven-course tasting menu. Specialties include roast
partridge with chanterelles and cappuccino chanterelle soup. The wine
list is excellent and the three intimate but elegant dining rooms have
well-spaced tables. ⊠ *30 Gloucester St.,* ☎ *617/262–3023. Reservations essential. Jacket and tie. AE, D, MC, V. No lunch. Closed Sun.*

$$$ ✕ **Mirabelle.** Few places compete with Newbury Street when it comes
★ to ogling the beautiful people, and the outdoor café at Mirabelle pro-
vides ringside seating. Inside, the dining room is on two levels, and it
has a soft and elegant feel. Granted, the kitchen has had its ups and
downs, but the sauces are always rich and the pâté is always *formidable.*

eria runs a shut-

...has come,
—with the
...el that it's
... picture
... although
... look
..d, for

...ch
...y

CAMBRIDGE

Cambridge St.

Otis St.

Thorndike St.

8th St.
7th St.

Sciarappa St.

3rd St.

Spring St.

Hurley St.

Charles St.

Bent St.

Rogers St.

Binney St.

Munroe St.

Portland St.

Fulkerson St.

6th St.

5th St.

2nd St.

1st St.

Commercial St.

42

41

50

Broadway

43–48

Main St.

Ames St.

Carleton St.

Wadsworth St.

Athenaeum St.

49

Vassar St.

Amherst St.

Longfellow Br.

Memorial Dr.

3

2A

Charles River Basin

Harvard Br.

James J. Storrow
Memorial Dr.

1

Back St.

Beacon St.

Marlborough St.

Berkeley St.

62

BACK BAY

Fairfield

Gloucester St.

Commonwealth Ave.

Dartmouth St.

Clarendon St.

60

Hereford

Newbury St.

Exeter St.

Blagden St.

52 **53**

Boylston St.

56

57

59

51

90

Ipswich

PRUDENTIAL
CENTER

58

1

Dalton St.

Belvidere

9

28

Hemenway

Massachusetts Ave.

Huntington Ave.

St. Botolph St.

Columbus Ave.

Appleton St.

Burbank St.

Westland Ave.

54

Warren Ave.

Pembroke St.

Canton St.

Tremont St.

St. Stephen St.

Newton St.

St. Gainsborough St.

Claremont St.

55

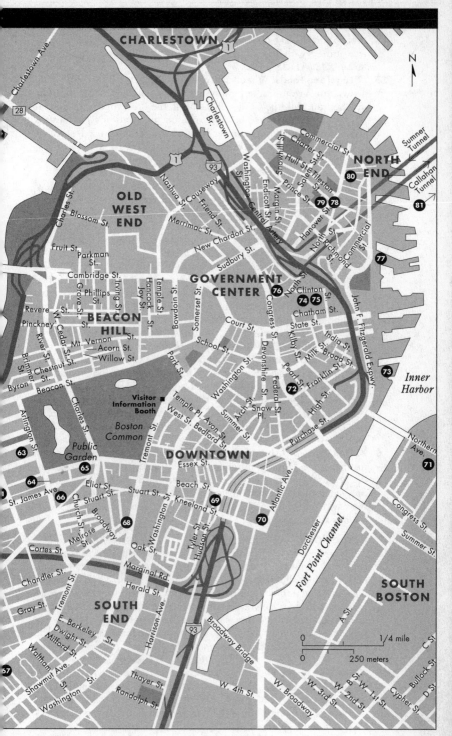

CHARLESTOWN

NORTH END

OLD WEST END

GOVERNMENT CENTER

BEACON HILL

Visitor Information Booth

Boston Common

Public Garden

DOWNTOWN

SOUTH END

SOUTH BOSTON

Inner Harbor

Fort Point Channel

Sumner Tunnel

Callahan Tunnel

Charlestown Ave.

Charlestown Br.

Nashua St.

Causeway St.

Friend St.

Merrimac St.

New Chardon St.

Sudbury St.

Washington St. Central Artery

Endicott St.

Margin St.

Prince St.

Hanover St.

Commercial St.

Charter St.

Hull St.

Snowhill St.

Friston St.

North St.

Richmond St.

Commercial St.

Fruit St.

Parkman St.

Blossom St.

Charles St.

Cambridge St.

Phillips St.

Grove St.

Irving St.

Hancock St.

Temple St.

Joy St.

Bowdoin St.

Somerset St.

Revere St.

Pinckney St.

Cedar St.

Mt. Vernon St.

Acorn St.

Willow St.

River St.

Brimmer St.

Byron St.

Chestnut St.

Beacon St.

Arlington St.

Charles St.

Court St.

School St.

Park St.

Tremont St.

Temple Pl.

West St. Bedford St.

Avon St.

Washington St.

Summer St.

Arch St.

Snow Pl.

Devonshire St.

Federal St.

Clinton St.

Chatham St.

State St.

Kilby St.

Milk St.

India St.

Broad St.

Pearl St.

Franklin St.

High St.

Purchase St.

John F. Fitzgerald Expwy.

Congress St.

Essex St.

Beach St.

Eliot St.

Stuart St.

Church St.

Broadway

Melrose St.

Kneeland St.

Washington St.

Tyler St.

Hudson St.

Oak St.

Atlantic Ave.

Dorchester

Northern Ave.

Congress St.

Summer St.

Cortes St.

Chandler St.

Gray St.

Tremont St.

E. Berkeley St.

Dwight St.

Milford St.

Waltham St.

Shawmut Ave.

Washington St.

Thayer St.

Randolph St.

Marginal Rd.

Herald St.

Harrison Ave.

Broadway Bridge

W. 4th St.

W. Broadway

W. 3rd St.

W. 2nd St.

B. St.

W. 1st St.

A. St.

Bullock St.

Cypher St.

C St.

D St.

St. James Ave.

63 64 65 66 68 69 70 71 72 73 74 75 76 77 78 79 80 81 57

0 — 1/4 mile

0 — 250 meters

The interior features soft goldenrod-color walls and smooth, rounded woodwork. The menu is seasonal; especially tasty are the grilled portobello and shiitake mushroom appetizer and the roasted veal chop entrée stuffed with prosciutto and sage. ⊠ *85 Newbury St.,* ☎ *617/ 859–4848. AE, DC, MC, V.*

$$$ ✕ **Legal Sea Foods.** What began as a tiny adjunct to a fish market has
★ grown into a restaurant of important status, with additional locations in Chestnut Hill, the Copley Place Mall, the Prudential, and Kendall Square in Cambridge. The style of food preparation is, as always, straightforward: You can order seafood raw, broiled, fried, steamed, or baked; fancy sauces and elaborate presentations are rare. ⊠ *35 Columbus Ave., next to Park Plaza Hotel,* ☎ *617/426–4444. Reservations not accepted. AE, D, DC, MC, V.*

$$ ✕ **Miyako.** This ambitious little restaurant in a bilevel space on Newbury Street serves some of the most exotic sushi in town. Among its estimable hot dishes are *age-shumai* (shrimp fritters), *hamachi teriyaki* (yellowtail teriyaki), and *agedashi* (fried bean curd). The waitresses are uncommonly personable, too. Tatami seating is available. ⊠ *297A Newbury St.,* ☎ *617/236–0222. AE, DC, MC, V.*

$$ ✕ **Small Planet.** This world-beat bistro blends global peasant cuisine
★ with new American motifs for an interesting mix of intriguing food and exotic atmosphere. The dining room is colorful with a lively bar scene, eccentric animal sculptures, and a waterfall. Specials include pizzas, homemade pastas and curries, paella, fresh grilled fish, and quesadillas. ⊠ *565 Boylston St.,* ☎ *617/536–4477. Reservations not accepted. AE, D, DC, MC, V. No lunch Sun. and Mon.*

$ ✕ **Cottonwood Cafe.** This is Tex-Mex pushed to the next dimension. The atmosphere is Nuevo-Wavo, with kinky architectural touches and rustic Southwestern details. Best of all is the Snake Bite appetizer: deep-fried jalapeños stuffed with shrimp and cheese—impossible to resist yet nearly too hot to eat. ⊠ *222 Berkeley St.,* ☎ *617/247–2225. AE, D, DC, MC, V. Cambridge branch:* ⊠ *1815 Massachusetts Ave.,* ☎ *617/661–7440.*

$ ✕ **Thai Cuisine.** Dishes can be very spicy, but the kitchen will make adjustments. The food is not merely exotica; it is well cooked, and the kitchen uses first-rate ingredients. A main course of half a duck is the only single-size entrée on the menu; the rest are the kind you order and share with two or three. ⊠ *14A Westland Ave.,* ☎ *617/262–1485. Reservations not accepted. AE, DC, MC, V. No lunch Sun.*

Cambridge

$$$$ ✕ **Salamander.** Critics with a soft spot for fusion cuisine say that this
★ is the best dining spot in town—and if you taste Salamander's striped bass in chili-shallot vinaigrette, you'll probably agree. The atrium seating is airy and intimate, the main dining room expansive and gorgeous, filled with aromas of wood and spice. Favorite entrées are the wood-grilled squid with coconut sauce and the pepper tenderloin over a ragout of wild mushrooms. For dessert, the banana wontons are deliciously indescribable. ⊠ *1 Athenaeum St. (lobby of former Carter Ink Bldg.),* ☎ *617/225–2121. AE, DC, MC, V. Closed Sun.*

$$$ ✕ **The Blue Room.** Hip, funky, and Cambridge, the Blue Room blends a world of ethnic cuisines. The emphasis is on grilled and smoked fare and an eclectic blend of spices and savory ingredients. Dishes here focus on flavor rather than formality: Recommended are the smoked duck leg and hominy appetizer, and the Latin Trio—a large platter of assorted specialties, such as chili-glazed shrimp, garlic and chicken chorizo, pork loin with spices, cornbread salad, black beans, flour tortillas, and salsa. ⊠ *1 Kendall Sq.,* ☎ *617/494–9034. AE, D, MC, V.*

$$$ ✕ **Harvest.** The menu changes nightly; favorites include oven-roasted
★ pheasant with wild rice and wild mushrooms, pan-roasted salmon
with oats and maple-saffron sauce, and the outstanding roasted-gar-
lic risotto. The ambience is bright, open, and airy. ✉ *44 Brattle St.,*
☎ *617/492–1115. Reservations essential. AE, D, DC, MC, V.*

$$ ✕ **Iruna.** After July 4th, when the weather in Boston starts to get hot,
★ sitting outside for lunch or an early dinner at Iruna captures the spirit
of Spain, if only temporarily. Popular with students for years, Iruna
specializes in paellas and seafoods and has great salads. The wine list
is good, but after July 4th, go straight for the sangria. ✉ *56 JFK St.,*
☎ *617/868–5633. AE, D, MC, V. Closed Sun.*

Downtown

$$$$ ✕ **Julien.** For empty-your-wallet luxury food, this is one of Boston's
top spots, ranked right up there with L'Espalier and Aujourd'hui. In
particular, the kitchen has a way with denizens of the briny deep: Oriental poached oysters and the velouté of New England clams will have
your taste buds begging for mercy. The food is delicious, but the decor
is even more so. ✉ *Le Meridien Hotel, 250 Franklin St.,* ☎ *617/451–
1900, ext. 7120. Reservations essential. Jacket and tie. AE, D, DC,
MC, V. Closed Sun.*

$$ ✕ **Blue Diner.** Boston's favorite diner gets rave reviews for such orig-
inals as pork loin stuffed with Granny Smith apples and homemade
corned beef hash. Tuesday through Saturday, it's one of the few places
in town that's open 24 hours; it closes only briefly from midnight Sun-
day till 11:30 AM Monday. ✉ *150 Kneeland St.,* ☎ *617/695–0087.
Reservations not accepted. AE, D, DC, MC, V.*

$ ✕ **Ho Yuen Ting.** Every night a line forms outside this Chinatown
★ hole-in-the-wall. The reason is simple: Ho Yuen Ting serves some of
the best seafood in town. The house specialty is a sole and vegetable
stir-fry presented in a spectacular whole, crisply fried fish. Come with
friends so you can also enjoy the clams with black bean sauce, lobster
with ginger and scallion, and steamed bass. ✉ *13A Hudson St.,* ☎
617/426–2316. No credit cards.

Faneuil Hall

$$$ ✕ **Cornucopia on the Wharf.** This restaurant is best when it takes such
★ liberties as pan-roasted monkfish with lobster saffron risotto, and
bouillabaisse in tomato saffron broth. Lunch is reasonable, and the views
are beautiful. ✉ *100 Atlantic Ave.,* ☎ *617/367–0300. AE, D, DC,
MC, V. No lunch Sat.*

$$$ ✕ **Seasons.** Popular with businesspeople and politicians (City Hall is
just a block away), this solarium-like restaurant on the fourth floor of
the Bostonian Hotel overlooks Faneuil Hall Marketplace and is a good
place to entertain when you want to impress. The cuisine of chef Peter
McCarthy is American with international influences. Entrées include
steamed halibut with Oriental spices and apple paper, and for dessert,
macadamia nut and coconut flan with mango sorbet. The wine list is
exclusively American. ✉ *Bostonian Hotel, North and Blackstone Sts.,*
☎ *617/523–3600. AE, DC, MC, V. No lunch Sat.*

$$ ✕ **Durgin-Park.** Diners here should be hungry for enormous portions,
yet not so hungry that they can't tolerate the inevitably long wait. Dur-
gin-Park was serving its same hearty New England fare (Indian pudding, baked beans, and huge prime rib) back when Faneuil Hall was
a working market instead of a tourist attraction. The atmosphere is
uniquely Old Boston, brusque bordering on rude bordering on good-
natured. ✉ *340 Faneuil Hall Marketplace (North Market Bldg.),* ☎
617/227–2038. AE, D, DC MC, V.

$$ ✕ **Union Oyster House.** Established in 1826, the Union Oyster House is Boston's oldest restaurant. Its best feature is a first-floor raw bar. The rooms at the top of the narrow staircase are dark and have low ceilings—very Ye Olde New England. ⊠ *41 Union St.,* ☎ *617/227–2750. AE, D, DC, MC, V. No lunch Sun.*

North End

$$ ✕ **Daily Catch.** You've just got to love this shoulder-crowding place,
★   for the noise, for the intimacy, and, above all, for the food. There's something about a big skillet full of linguine and calamari that would be less than perfect served on a plate. Lobster fra diavolo is a favorite that turns up the hot and spicy valve a notch. Because it's almost always crowded, a second restaurant has opened at 261 Northern Avenue, across from Jimmy's Harborside, and a third in Brookline at 441 Harvard Street. Hours of operation vary greatly; call for times. ⊠ *323 Hanover St.,* ☎ *617/523–8567. Reservations not accepted. No credit cards.*

$$ ✕ **Pomodoro.** This restaurant is right next door to the Daily Catch, so couples often split up—one person on line for seafood and another on line for Pomodoro's fine Italian cuisine—to see who gets to the mâitre d' first. This tiny trattoria serves excellent rustic-style entrées. Try the clam and tomato stew with herbed flat bread, and a bottle of Vernaccia. ⊠ *319 Hanover St.,* ☎ *617/367–4348. No credit cards.*

$$ ✕ **Ristorante Lucia.** Some aficionados consider Lucia's the best Italian restaurant in the North End. Its specialties from the Abruzzi region include batter-fried artichoke hearts as an appetizer and chicken *alla Lucia* (sautéed in wine, herbs, and ingredients that the restaurant keeps secret) as an entrée. Check out the upstairs bar, with its pink marble and its takeoff on the Sistine Chapel ceiling. ⊠ *415 Hanover St.,* ☎ *617/523–9148. AE, D, MC, V. No lunch Mon.–Thurs.*

South End

$$$ ✕ **Hamersley's Bistro.** This restaurant has a full bar, a café area with
★   10 tables for walk-ins, and a larger dining room that's a little more formal and decorative than the bar and café, though nowhere near stuffy. Specialties that have a permanent place on the daily menu include a garlic and mushroom sandwich (served as an appetizer) and roast chicken with garlic, lemon, and parsley. ⊠ *553 Tremont St.,* ☎ *617/423–2700. Reservations essential. AE, D, DC, MC, V.*

Waterfront

$$ ✕ **Jimmy's Harborside.** This popular seafood establishment enjoys a
★   solid reputation. The bright, three-tier main dining room was designed to ensure that every table has an unobstructed view of the harbor. Try the scampi Luciana, a bouillabaisse made with white wine, cream, and fresh fish and shrimp. ⊠ *242 Northern Ave.,* ☎ *617/423–1000. AE, DC, MC, V. No lunch Sun.*

Lodging

If your biggest dilemma is deciding whether to spend $300 per night on either old-fashioned elegance or extravagant modernity, you've come to the right city. The bulk of Boston's accommodations are not cheap; however, visitors with limited cash will find abundant choices among the smaller, older establishments, modern motels, or—perhaps the best option (if you can take early-morning small talk)—the bed-and-breakfast inn. Less expensive than most hotels, and more stylish than most HoJos (which kids will prefer), B&Bs are becoming increasingly popular in the Boston area and give visitors the chance to experience Boston's famous neighborhoods, from the trendy South End to the hallowed, gaslit streets of Beacon Hill.

Back Bay

$$$$ ⊞ **The Copley Plaza—A Wyndham Hotel.** This stately classic among
★ Boston hotels, built in 1912, retains its grande dame elegance with an
ornate, marble-pillared lobby, painted ceilings, golden lions, and crystal chandeliers. Guest rooms have carpeting from England, furniture
from Italy, and bathroom fixtures surrounded by marble tile. The
piano in the Plaza Bar, rich in mahogany, is often shrouded in smoke.
⊠ *138 St. James Ave., 02116,* ☏ *617/267–5300 or 800/996–3426,*
𝖥𝖠𝖷 *617/267–7668. 373 rooms, 51 suites. 2 restaurants, 2 bars, beauty
salon, barbershop. AE, D, DC, MC, V.*

$$$$ ⊞ **Four Seasons.** The only hotel (other than the Ritz-Carlton) to over-
★ look the Public Garden, the newer eight-story Four Seasons specializes in luxurious personal service, discretion, elegance, and comfort.
Thoughtful touches for children include toys and elfin white terry
robes; pets get a room-service menu, beds, and attentive walkers. A
room overlooking the garden is worth the extra money. Stunning floral arrangements punctuate the public rooms, which literally sparkle.
A cozy piano lounge has a fireplace and Aujourd'hui is a fine restaurant, serving new American cuisine. ⊠ *200 Boylston St., 02116,* ☏
617/338–4400 or 800/332–3442, 𝖥𝖠𝖷 *617/423–0154. 288 rooms, including 80 suites. Restaurant, bar, room service, indoor pool, sauna,
exercise room, concierge, parking (fee). AE, D, DC, MC, V.*

$$$$ ⊞ **Ritz-Carlton.** Since 1927, this hotel overlooking the Public Garden
★ has been one of the most luxurious and elegant places to stay in Boston.
Its reputation for quality and service (there are two staff members for
every guest) continues. The most coveted rooms are the suites in the
older section, which have working fireplaces and the best views of the
Public Garden. The three top floors have a private club and butlers on
hand. Public rooms include the elegant café, with a window on chic
Newbury Street; the sumptuous dining room; the sedate bar; and The
Lounge. ⊠ *Arlington and Newbury Sts., 02117,* ☏ *617/536–5700 or
800/241–3333,* 𝖥𝖠𝖷 *617/536–1335. 278 rooms, including 42 suites.
Restaurant, bar, room service, refrigerators, beauty salon, exercise
room, baby-sitting, laundry service, concierge, parking (fee). AE, D,
DC, MC, V.*

$$$ ⊞ **Copley Square Hotel.** One of Boston's oldest hotels (1891), the
Copley Square is one of the best values in the city. Quirky, friendly,
Continental in flavor, and well managed, the place is popular with Eu-
ropeans. Rooms of various shapes and sizes are strung along cir-
cuitously laid out corridors and have voice mail, modems, windows
you can open, hair dryers, and coffeemakers. If you want quiet, ask
for a room on the top floor, overlooking the courtyard. The popular
Hungarian-cuisine restaurant, Cafe Budapest, is downstairs. ⊠ *47
Huntington Ave., 02116,* ☏ *617/536–9000 or 800/225–7062,* 𝖥𝖠𝖷
*617/267–3547. 143 rooms, 12 suites. Restaurant, bar, coffee shop,
air-conditioning, parking (fee). AE, D, DC, MC, V.*

$$$ ⊞ **Eliot Hotel.** An ambitious renovation has transformed the Eliot into
★ a luxurious, all-suite, European-style hotel. Guest rooms, on nine
floors, have Italian-marble bathrooms, living rooms with period furnishings, and up-to-date kitchenettes; all suites have air-conditioning
and two cable-TV sets. The split-level, marble-clad lobby contains
writing desks and a huge chandelier. You can eat a big breakfast for a
small charge in the stylish breakfast room; drinks and bar meals are
available in the popular Eliot Lounge. ⊠ *370 Commonwealth Ave.,
02215,* ☏ *617/267–1607 or 800/443–5468,* 𝖥𝖠𝖷 *617/536–9114. 91
suites. Lounge, parking (fee). AE, D, DC, MC, V.*

$$ ⊞ **Lenox Hotel.** Extensive renovations (due to be completed in March
★ 1997) have transformed the conveniently located Lenox, built in 1900,
into a charming home away from home with low-key elegance. The

first 10 floors have Early American furnishings, while the top floor is decorated in the French provincial style; all renovated rooms have marble bathrooms with hair dryers. Corner rooms are particularly spacious; some have working fireplaces. The Upstairs Grille serves lamb, steaks, and seafood in an upscale pub-like atmosphere, while the Samuel Adams Brewhouse offers true pub fare in a small and lively space. ⊠ *710 Boylston St., 02116, ☎ 617/536–5300 or 800/225–7676, FAX 617/266–7905. 214 rooms, 3 suites. Restaurant, pub, barbershop, exercise room, baby-sitting, concierge, parking (fee). AE, DC, MC, V.*

$ 🏨 **Boston International Hostel.** Guests sleep in dormitories for three to five persons and must provide their own linens or sleep sacks (sleeping bags are not permitted) in this hostel near the Museum of Fine Arts. Five family rooms are available by reservation. The maximum stay is three nights in summer, seven nights off-season. Doors close at 2 AM. Preference is given to AYH members in high season; contact the Greater Boston Council of American Youth Hostels (⊠ 1020 Commonwealth Ave., Boston 02215, ☎ 617/731–5430) for information. ⊠ *12 Hemenway St., 02115, ☎ 617/536–9455, FAX 617/424–6558. Capacity 190 in summer, 100 in winter. MC, V.*

Cambridge

$$$$ 🏨 **The Charles Hotel.** Set around a brick plaza facing the Charles River, close to Harvard Square, the Charles Hotel has spare and modern architecture that is softened by New England antiques and paintings by local artists. Guest rooms have quilts, TV in the bathrooms, and an honor bar. A Sunday brunch is served buffet-style in the Bennett Street Cafe; the Rialto, a Mediterranean-style restaurant is one of Cambridge's trendiest; and the Regattabar is one of the city's hottest spots for jazz. ⊠ *1 Bennett St., 02138, ☎ 617/864–1200 or 800/882–1818, FAX 617/864–5715. 296 rooms, 44 suites. Room service, pool, spa. AE, D, DC, MC, V.*

$$$ 🏨 **The Inn at Harvard.** This understated four-story property sits on a
★ pedestrian island in the heart of Harvard Square. Guest rooms that are generally modern, with sandy tones and geometric-patterned fabrics, but cherry-wood headboards, brass lamps, and well-crafted wooden desks recall 18th-century America. Walls are decorated with original 17th- and 18th-century sketches, on loan from the nearby Fogg Art Museum, as well as with contemporary watercolors. Many rooms have tiny balconies; all have oversize windows with views of Harvard Square or Harvard Yard. ⊠ *1201 Massachusetts Ave., Cambridge 02138, ☎ 617/491–2222 or 800/222–8733, FAX 617/491–6520. 113 rooms. Dry cleaning, laundry service, business services, meeting rooms, parking (fee). AE, D, DC, MC, V.*

$$$ 🏨 **Royal Sonesta Hotel.** There are superb views of Beacon Hill across
★ the Charles River from this high-rise building, which is near the Museum of Science. An impressive collection of modern art is displayed throughout the hotel. There are superb family excursion packages that include boat rides, ice cream, and bicycles. ⊠ *5 Cambridge Pkwy., 02142, ☎ 617/491–3600 or 800/766–3782, FAX 617/661–5956. 400 rooms, 28 suites. 2 restaurants, indoor pool, air-conditioning, business services, baby-sitting. AE, DC, MC, V.*

$$ 🏨 **Cambridge House Bed and Breakfast.** A gracious 1892 Greek Re-
★ vival home listed on the National Register of Historic Places, Cambridge House is convenient to the T. It has 16 antiques-filled guest rooms, most with private baths. ⊠ *2218 Massachusetts Ave., 02140, ☎ 617/491–6300 or 800/232–9989, FAX 617/868–2848. AE, MC, V. Full breakfast and afternoon tea and sherry included.*

$$ 🏨 **Sheraton Commander.** Many rooms in this nicely maintained, older hotel on Cambridge Common have four-poster beds; some have kitch-

enettes. ⊠ *16 Garden St., 02238,* ☎ *617/547–4800 or 800/325–3535,* 𝕗𝕒𝕩 *617/868–8322. 176 rooms, 20 suites. Restaurant, exercise room, concierge, air-conditioning, business services, free parking. AE, D, DC, MC, V.*

$ 🏨 **Susse Chalet Inn.** This is a typical Susse Chalet: clean, economical, and spare. It is isolated from most shopping and attractions, being a 10-minute drive from Harvard Square, but it is within walking distance of the Red Line T terminus. ⊠ *211 Concord Turnpike, 02140,* ☎ *617/661–7800 or 800/258–1980,* 𝕗𝕒𝕩 *617/868–8153. 78 rooms. Air-conditioning, free parking. CP. AE, D, DC, MC, V.*

Downtown

$$$$ 🏨 **Boston Harbor Hotel at Rowes Wharf.** Possibly the most exciting
★ place to stay in Boston, this elegant, conveniently located harborside hotel provides a dramatic entryway into the city for travelers arriving from Logan Airport via water shuttle, which docks right at the door amid a slew of yachts. The hotel is part of a modern, 15-story development at Rowes Wharf, which includes a dramatic 80-foot arch and Foster's Rotunda, an observatory with striking views of the harbor and city. Guest rooms have either city or water views, and some have balconies. Rowes Wharf Restaurant offers seafood and American regional cuisine, a spectacular if expensive Sunday brunch, and sweeping harbor views. ⊠ *70 Rowes Wharf, 02110,* ☎ *617/439–7000 or 800/752–7077,* 𝕗𝕒𝕩 *617/330–9450. 230 rooms, 24 suites. Restaurant, bar, outdoor café, indoor lap pool, beauty salon, health club, concierge, business services, parking (fee). AE, D, DC, MC, V.*

$$$$ 🏨 **Bostonian.** Enter the gateway into the Bostonian and you see a
★ small rotary teeming with pink and purple impatiens and ringed with sleek, black limos. This exciting, small hotel is quintessentially Bostonian, successfully combining the best of the old with the aggressively modern. The Harkness Wing, constructed as a warehouse in 1824, contains suites with working fireplaces, exposed-beam ceilings, and brick walls, while rooms in the contemporary wing, with its glass-and-steel atrium, are quietly opulent: cream and pink furnishings, spacious dressing rooms, and oversize bathtubs. Service is attentive, and the highly regarded Seasons restaurant is in a glass-enclosed penthouse overlooking the marketplace. ⊠ *Faneuil Hall Marketplace, 02109,* ☎ *617/523–3600 or 800/343–0922,* 𝕗𝕒𝕩 *617/523–2454. 152 rooms, 16 suites. Room service, parking (fee). AE, D, DC, MC, V.*

$$$$ 🏨 **Le Meridien Hotel.** The respected French chain refurbished the old
★ Federal Reserve Building, a landmark Renaissance Revival structure, to create this exclusive hotel in the financial district. Everything about it, from the stiff marble lobby to the uncomfortable couches, breathes high-class city business, and if you're not wearing a suit, your first inclination might be to turn around and tiptoe out (does anyone *ever* stay here with kids?). Julien is one of the city's finest French restaurants; Café Fleuri is more informal. ⊠ *250 Franklin St., 02110,* ☎ *617/451–1900 or 800/543–4300,* 𝕗𝕒𝕩 *617/423–2844. 326 rooms, 22 suites. Restaurant, 2 bars, no-smoking floor, room service, indoor pool, health club, concierge, parking (fee). AE, D, DC, MC, V.*

Logan Airport

$$$$ 🏨 **Harborside Hyatt Conference Center and Hotel.** At Logan Airport, across the harbor from downtown, the city's newest hotel looks like a gigantic glass lighthouse. The best rooms face across the harbor toward the skyline or look out to sea. Guests can obtain discount rates on the Logan Airport water shuttle, which crosses the harbor from the hotel to downtown every half hour. ⊠ *101 Harborside Dr., 02128,* ☎ *617/568–1234 or 800/233–1234,* 𝕗𝕒𝕩 *617/567–8856. 270 rooms, 11* *suites. Pool, sauna, health club, jogging, business services, parking (fee). AE, D, DC, MC, V.*

Theater District

$$ 🏨 **Tremont House.** Built as national headquarters for the Elks Club organization in 1925, this hotel has a rather grand lobby, with high ceilings, marble columns, a marble stairway, and lots of gold leaf. Guest rooms (and bathrooms) tend to be small, but all have cable TV and are furnished with 18th-century reproductions (but note the authentic Elks Club brass doorknobs) and prints from the Museum of Fine Arts. The Tremont is across from the Wang Center and is surrounded on all sides by Boston theaters. ⊠ *275 Tremont St., 02116,* ☎ *617/426–1400 or 800/331–9998,* 𝔽𝔸𝕏 *617/338–7881. 281 rooms, 34 suites. 2 no-smoking floors, room service, nightclub, laundry service, concierge, valet parking. AE, D, DC, MC, V.*

Nightlife and the Arts

Nightlife

The **Quincy Market** area may be the center of the city's tourist nightlife; it has been thronged with visitors from the day the restoration opened in 1976. Here you'll find international cuisine and singles bars among the specialty shops and boutiques. **Copley Square** is the hub of another major entertainment area. **Kenmore Square,** near the Boston University campus, has clubs and discos devoted to rock and alternative groups.

Thursday's *Boston Globe* Calendar, a schedule of events for the upcoming week, includes an extensive listing of live entertainment in the "Nightlife" section. The weekly *Boston Phoenix* (also published on Thursday) is another excellent source for entertainment. The monthly *Boston* magazine, although a bit less current, is a good source of information.

BARS AND LOUNGES

Boston Beer Works (⊠ 61 Brookline Ave., ☎ 617/536–2337) is a brewery, with all the works exposed—the tanks, pipes, and gleaming stainless steel and copper kettles used in producing beer. Other brews that change with the season are also draws for students and young adults. The menu has pastas and pub fare.

The **Bull and Finch Pub** (⊠ 84 Beacon St., at the Hampshire House, ☎ 617/227–9605) was dismantled in England and reassembled here, an obvious success. This was the inspiration for the TV series *Cheers.* You will generally find an international crowd of tourists and students; there is often a line out the door. Karaoke and live bands add to the hubbub Thursday–Saturday.

Copley's (⊠ Copley Plaza Hotel, 138 St. James Ave., ☎ 617/267–5300) is a small, high-ceilinged room with marble-top tables, caricatures on the wall, and globular chandeliers on each side of the bar. An older business crowd gathers here.

The Custom House (⊠ 60 State St., ☎ 617/723–1666), by day a private club, is an enchanted spot at night where you sip a drink, look out on the panorama of Boston Harbor, and enjoy live music and dancing. It is closed Sunday. The restaurant, the Bay Tower Room (jacket required) serves New England fare.

Daisy Buchanan's (⊠ 240a Newbury St., ☎ 617/247–8516) is a favorite hangout of athletes and young professionals; you might run into Cam Neely or Mike Greenwell at the bar. The jukebox is loud in the simply adorned room at basement level, with pinball and video games in the rear. Free hot dogs are served weekends, which helps explain the overflowing crowd; no credit cards.

The Mercury Bar (⊠ 11 Boylston St., ☎ 617/482–7799) has a long sleek bar facing a row of raised, semicircular booths and a more private dining room off to the side, with the kitchen in view. Bar patrons may order from the extensive *tapas* menu. The bar is popular among well-heeled young professionals and theatergoers.

The Middle East (⊠ 472 Massachusetts Ave., Cambridge, ☎ 617/354–8238) is one of Boston's best—and most eclectic—clubs for jazz, world music, and rock, and it serves good ethnic cuisine. Three beats under one roof and a coffeehouse make it the choice for discerning listeners. There's usually a different cover charge for each part of the club.

The Plaza Bar (⊠ Copley Plaza Hotel, 31 St. James Ave. off Copley Sq., ☎ 617/267–6495) is Boston's answer to New York's Oak Room. The high, ornately decorated wood-paneled ceilings, the rich fabrics of the settees, and the elegant bar somehow create a warm, intimate ambience. The well-to-do and the simply well-dressed mingle and sing along here.

BLUES/R&B CLUBS

House of Blues (⊠ 96 Winthrop St., Cambridge, ☎ 617/491—2583) has the best sax in town. Co-owned by Dan Aykroyd and other celebrity investors, the place opened in 1992 (thanks to plenty of faux decor, it looks like it's been around forever). There's a museum, store, restaurant, and recording facility in the compact space.

Marketplace Cafe (⊠ 300 Faneuil Hall, ☎ 617/227–9660) is a "no cover" treasure in the North Market building amid the bustle of Faneuil Hall. It offers a blues/jazz format, with music every night from 9, and nouvelle American cuisine.

CAFÉS AND COFFEEHOUSES

Blacksmith House (⊠ 56 Brattle St., Cambridge), the original 18th-century house where Longfellow's blacksmith lived, is now operated by the Cambridge Center for Adult Education (☎ 617/547–6789). It houses an excellent German bakery (☎ 617/534–3036) with indoor tables and a warm-weather streetside café. Poetry readings, concerts, and plays are staged in the Spiegel Performance Center, at the rear of the building.

Passim's (⊠ 47 Palmer St., Cambridge, ☎ 617/492–7679), one of the country's first and most famous venues for live folk music, is by day a quiet basement setting for a light lunch or a coffee break. By night it's a gathering place for folk and bluegrass music or poetry readings.

The Daily Grind (⊠ 168 Cambridge St., ☎ 617/367–3233) is a welcome bit of funkiness on the edge of Beacon Hill. Patrons enjoy the well-prepared coffee drinks, fresh pastries, and the small but intriguing selection of sandwiches and other lunch fare. The regular coffee is served in huge mugs, and the prices are low. It's open till 9 PM weeknights (8 in summer) and till 4 PM weekends. No credit cards.

COMEDY

Comedy Connection (⊠ Faneuil Hall Marketplace, ☎ 617/248—9700) offers a mix of local and nationally known acts, seven nights a week (two shows Friday and Saturday), with a cover charge.

Nick's Comedy Stop (⊠ 100 Warrenton St., ☎ 617/482–0930) presents local comics every night except Monday, and occasionally a well-known comedian pops in. Reservations advised on weekends, since it's in the heart of the theater and bar district; cover charge varies.

DISCO

Axis (⊠ 13 Lansdowne St., ☎ 617/262–2424) is one of Boston's largest clubs. Near Kenmore Square, it features high-energy disco and a giant dance floor that can accommodate more than 1,000 people. Sunday night is gay night, when it combines with Avalon, next door, and dancers can circulate between the two.

At **Joy** (⊠ 533 Washington St., ☎ 617/338–6999), two levels of wealthy international students and their well-dressed companions move to a techno or acid jazz beat, once they make it out of the line to get in.

Quest (⊠ 1270 Boylston St., ☎ 617/424–7747) is a four-floor club with a roof deck playing high-energy and house music. A straight crowd comes Thursday, Friday, and Sunday; a gay crowd on Monday and Saturday.

JAZZ

Some top names in jazz perform at **Regattabar** (⊠ Bennett and Eliot Sts., Cambridge, ☎ 617/864–1200), a spacious and elegant club in the Charles Hotel. The **Boston Jazz Line** (☎ 617/787–9700) reports jazz happenings.

Scullers (⊠ DoubleTree Suites Hotel, 400 Soldiers Field Rd., ☎ 617/783–0811) has made a very strong name for itself by hosting such well-knowns as Herb Pomeroy and the Victor Mendoza Quintet.

Top of the Hub (⊠ Prudential Center, ☎ 617/536–1775) has a wonderful view over the entire city; that and the sounds of hip jazz make the pricey drinks worth it. At press time, the lounge was undergoing renovation and expansion. Hours and entertainment may vary; call before you go.

Turner Fisheries Bar (⊠ Westin Hotel, 10 Huntington Ave., ☎ 617/262–9600, ext. 7425) has live jazz nightly from 8 till midnight. A pianist plays Sunday through Wednesday; Thursday through Saturday a jazz trio backs varying soloists, and plays till 1 AM. The sleek but comfortable room with modern-art overtones is adjacent to a handsome oyster bar.

ROCK

The Paradise (⊠ 967 Commonwealth Ave., ☎ 617/254–2052 or 617/254–2053) is known for big-name talent. Rock, jazz, folk, blues, alternative pop/rock, and country all take turns on stage here, and the audience varies with the entertainment. This is a good venue for live shows; artists play here for the intimate setting.

SINGLES

Frogg Lane Bar and Grille (⊠ Faneuil Hall Marketplace, ☎ 617/720–0610) is a popular spot with tourists and singles in the heart of the swinging Quincy Market. The jukebox is very loud.

Il Panino (⊠ 295 Franklin St., ☎ 617/338–1000) is where a non-student, more mature and upscale crowd comes. The first two floors offer informal and formal dining, the third has a jazz bar, and the top two are dance floors.

Sonsie (⊠ 327 Newbury St., ☎ 617/351-2500) has no music except a stereo system that diners at the hip restaurant often drown out. The bar crowd, which spills into the sidewalk cafe, is full of trendy, cosmopolitan professionals.

The Arts

Boston is a paradise for patrons of all the arts, from the symphony orchestra to experimental theater and dance. Good sources of information are Thursday's *Boston Globe* calendar and the weekly *Boston Phoenix* (published on Thursday). *Boston* magazine's "On the Town" section gives a somewhat less detailed but useful monthly overview.

BosTix is Boston's official entertainment information center and the largest ticket agency in the city. In addition to being a full-price Ticketmaster outlet, half-price tickets are sold here beginning at 11 AM for the same day's performances; the "menu board" in front of the booth announces the available events. Only cash and traveler's checks are accepted. People often begin queuing well before the agency opens. ⊠ *Faneuil Hall Marketplace,* ☎ *617/723–5181 (recorded message).* ☉ *Tues.–Sat. 10–6, Sun. 11–4. Copley Sq., near corner of Boylston and Dartmouth Sts.* ☉ *Mon.–Sat. 10–6, Sun. 11–4. Both booths closed major holidays.*

Call *concertcharge* (☎ 617/497–1118; ☉ Weekdays 9–6, Sat. 9–5:30) or **Ticketmaster** (☎ 617/931–2000; ☉ Weekdays 9 AM–10 PM, weekends 9–8) for tickets.

DANCE

Boston Ballet (⊠ 19 Clarendon St., ☎ 617/695–6950), the city's premier dance company, performs at the Wang Center for the Performing Arts. **Dance Umbrella** (⊠ 380 Green St., Cambridge, ☎ 617/492–7578) is one of New England's largest presenters of contemporary dance. Performances are scheduled in theaters throughout Boston. The Umbrella also offers information on all dance performances in the Boston area.

FILM

Cambridge is the best place in New England for finding classic, foreign, and nostalgia films. **The Brattle Theater** (⊠ 40 Brattle St., Cambridge, ☎ 617/876–6837) is a recently restored landmark cinema for classic-movie buffs. **Harvard Film Archive** (⊠ Carpenter Center for the Visual Arts, 24 Quincy St., Cambridge, ☎ 617/495–4700) programs the work of directors not usually shown at commercial cinemas; two or more screenings daily.

MUSIC

For its size, Boston is the most musical city in America, unsurpassed in the variety and caliber of its musical life. Of the many contributing factors, perhaps the most significant is the abundance of universities and other institutions of learning. Boston's churches also offer outstanding, often free, music programs; check the Thursday and Saturday listings in the *Boston Globe.* Early music, choral groups, and chamber music also thrive.

Symphony Hall (⊠ 301 Massachusetts Ave., ☎ 617/266–1492 or 800/274–8499) is one of the world's most perfect acoustical settings, home to conductor Seiji Ozawa, the Boston Symphony Orchestra, and the Boston Pops.

OPERA

The **Boston Lyric Opera Company** (⊠ 114 State St., ☎ 617/248–8660) presents three productions each season. They always include a 20th-century work in their repertoire.

THEATER

First-rate Broadway tryout theaters are clustered in the theater district (near the intersection of Tremont and Stuart Sts.) and include the Colonial, the Shubert, the Wang Center for the Performing Arts, and the Wilbur. Local theater companies all over the city thrive as well.

The city-sponsored arts and culture complex **Boston Center for the Arts** (⊠ 539 Tremont St. ☎ 617/426–5000), also known as the Cyclorama Building, houses three small theaters, the Mills Gallery, and studio space for some 60 artists. The **Loeb Drama Center** (⊠ 64 Brattle St., ☎ 617/495–2668) has two theaters, the main one an experimental stage. This is the home of the American Repertory Theater, the long-established resident professional repertory. The highly respected ART produces both classic and experimental works. **Emerson Majestic Theatre** (⊠ 219 Tremont St., ☎ 617/578–8727), at Emerson College, the nation's only private institution devoted exclusively to communications and performing arts, has undertaken the extensive multimillion-dollar job of restoring this 1903 Beaux Arts building. The Majestic hosts professional productions from all walks of Boston's cultural scene, from avant-garde dance to drama to classical concerts. The **Huntington Theatre Company** (⊠ 264 Huntington Ave., ☎ 617/266–0800), under the auspices of Boston University, is Boston's largest professional resident theater company, performing five plays annually, a mix of established 20th-century plays and classics.

Outdoor Activities and Sports

Participant Sports

The mania for physical fitness is big in Boston. Most public recreational facilities, including the many skating rinks and tennis courts, are operated by the Metropolitan District Commission (MDC; ☎ 617/727–5114, ext. 555).

BIKING

The **Dr. Paul Dudley White Bikeway,** approximately 18 miles long, runs along both sides of the Charles River. **The Bicycle Workshop** (⊠ 259 Massachusetts Ave., Cambridge, ☎ 617/876–6555) rents bicycles, fixes flat tires (while you wait), and delivers bicycles to your hotel.

GOLFING

The **Massachusetts Golf Association** (⊠ 175 Highland Ave., Needham, ☎ 617/449–3300) provides information on courses open to the public and equipment rentals.

JOGGING

Both sides of the Charles River are popular with joggers. Many hotels have printed maps of nearby routes.

SKIING

Blue Hills. Just 30 minutes south of downtown Boston, Blue Hills is a day and night option for suburban skiers, and a good place for kids to make their first outing. Evenings attract a cross-section of skiers; weekends see mostly families. The vertical drop is only 365 feet, but the terrain is surprisingly varied. Most of the slopes are easy; a double chairlift and three surface lifts carry skiers. ⊠ *Blue Hills Reservations, Washington St., Canton, Exit 2B from Rte. 128, 02186, ☎ 617/828–7490, ski school 617/828–5090, snow conditions 617/828–5070.*

Nashoba Valley. This area attracts suburban families for day and night skiing. Package instruction programs are offered to adults in the morning and evening, and to children on afternoons and weekend mornings. There are 15 ski trails of mostly novice–intermediate terrain and a 300-foot half-pipe for snowboarders. Two double chairlifts, two triple chairlifts, and five surface lifts provide transport. Though the hill is short, each year it's host to a major slalom race, as part of the U.S. Pro Ski Tour. ⊠ *Power Rd., Westford 01886, ☎ 508/692–3033.*

Wachusett Mountain. One hour west of Boston, Wachusett offers a good-size mountain and a large base lodge with facilities usually found only at bigger resorts. Skiing is available daily until 10 PM. Wachusett has two peaks, the higher with a vertical drop of 1,000 feet. The more difficult terrain is toward the top of the higher peak; most of the rest is intermediate. Beginner slopes are separated from the main traffic. The area has a detachable high-speed quad that whisks skiers to the summit in 3½ minutes, in addition to one triple chair, a double chairlift, surface lift, and a poma. There are 18 trails; the longest is 1 mile. Steep trails such as 10th Mountain and Smith Walton, plus 10 or so blue cruisers, keep skiers coming back. Twenty-five kilometers (16 mi) of cross-country ski trails circle the mountain. There are full-day SKIwee lessons on weekends for children 3–12. ⊠ *99 Mountain Rd., Princeton 01541,* ☎ *508/464–2300, snow conditions 800/754–1234.*

Spectator Sports

Sports are as much a part of Boston as are codfish and Democrats. Everything you may have heard about the zeal of Boston fans is true, and out-of-towners wishing to experience it firsthand have several choices.

The **Boston Red Sox,** American League (☎ 617/267–8661 or 617/267–1700 for tickets), play at Fenway Park.

The **Boston Celtics,** NBA (☎ 617/624–1000 or Ticketmaster, ☎ 617/931–2000 for tickets), shoot hoops at the FleetCenter.

The **New England Patriots,** NFL (☎ 800/543–1776), play football at Sullivan Stadium in Foxboro, 45 minutes south of the city.

The **Boston Bruins,** NHL (☎ 617/624–1000 or Ticketmaster, ☎ 617/931–2000 for tickets), are now on the ice at the FleetCenter—skating, for the first time, on a regulation-size rink.

Shopping

Boston's shops and stores are generally open Monday–Saturday from 9 or 9:30 until 6 or 7; many stay open until 8 late in the week. Some stores, particularly those in malls or tourist areas, are open Sunday from noon until 5. The state sales tax of 5% does not apply to clothing or food (except food bought in restaurants and for purchases of more than $300). Boston's two daily newspapers, the *Globe* and the *Herald,* are the best places to learn about sales; Sunday's *Globe* often announces sales for later in the week.

Shopping Districts

Most of Boston's stores and shops are in the area bounded by Quincy Market, the Back Bay, downtown, and Copley Square. There are few outlet stores in the area, but there are plenty of bargains, particularly in the world-famous Filene's Basement and Chinatown's fabric district. Charles Street in Beacon Hill is a mecca for antiques lovers from all over the country.

BOSTON
Copley Place (☎ 617/375–4400), an indoor shopping mall connecting the Westin and Marriott hotels, has 87 stores, restaurants, and cinemas that blend the elegant, the glitzy, and the overpriced. **Downtown Crossing,** Boston's downtown shopping area at Summer and Washington streets, is a pedestrian mall with outdoor merchandise kiosks, street performers, and benches for people-watchers. Here are the city's two largest department stores, Macy's (a.k.a. Jordan Marsh—in 1995 the Federated chain renamed this beloved New England institution) and Filene's. **Faneuil Hall Marketplace** (☎ 617/338–2323) has small shops, kiosks of every description, street performers, and one of the great food

experiences, Quincy Market. The intrepid shopper must cope with crowds of people, particularly on weekends. **Marketplace Center,** where 33 stores on two levels ring a central plaza, is adjacent to Faneuil Hall Marketplace and smack in the middle of the "Walkway to the Sea" from Government Center to Boston's waterfront. **Newbury Street,** Boston's version of New York's Fifth Avenue, is where the trendy gives way to the chic and the expensive.

CAMBRIDGE

Cambridgeside Galleria (⌧ 100 Cambridgeside Pl., ☎ 617/621–8666), in East Cambridge, is a three-story mall accessible by the Green Line's Lechmere T stop. It encompasses more than 100 shops, including the anchor stores of Filene's, Lechmere, and Sears. **Harvard Square** in Cambridge has more than 150 stores within a few blocks. In addition to the surprising range of items sold in the square, Cambridge is a book lover's paradise.

Department Stores

Filene's (⌧ 426 Washington St., ☎ 617/357–2100), a full-service department store, is known for its two-level bargain basement (☎ 617/542–2011), where items are automatically reduced in price according to the number of days they've been on the rack. The competition can be stiff for the great values on discontinued, overstocked, or slightly irregular items. The **Harvard Coop Society** (⌧ 1400 Massachusetts Ave., ☎ 617/499–2000; at MIT, 3 Cambridge Center, ☎ 617/499–3200), begun in 1882 as a nonprofit service for students and faculty and now run by Barnes & Noble, is known for its extensive selection of records and books.

Food Markets

Every Friday and Saturday, **Haymarket** (near Faneuil Hall Marketplace) is a crowded jumble of outdoor fruit and vegetable vendors, meat markets, and fishmongers. The fruit sold here is often very ripe, and you may have to discard some of it, but you will still end up with more for your money.

Specialty Stores

ANTIQUES

Charles Street in Beacon Hill is a mecca for antiques lovers. **River Street,** parallel to Charles, is also an excellent source for chipped Chippendale and age-old bibelots. The **Boston Antique Center** (⌧ 54 Canal St., ☎ 617/742–1400) has 20,000 square feet filled with antiques and furniture in a restored warehouse close to North Station. The **Boston Antique Co-op** (⌧ 119 Charles St., ☎ 617/227–9810) is a collection of 14 dealers that occupies two floors, carrying everything from vintage photos and paintings to porcelain, silver, bronzes, and furniture.

CLOTHING

Shop at **Alan Bilzerian** (⌧ 34 Newbury St., ☎ 617/536–1001) for avant-garde and au courant men's and women's clothing. **Ann Taylor** (⌧ 18 Newbury St., ☎ 617/262–0763, and Faneuil Hall Marketplace, ☎ 617/742–0031) sells high-quality fashions for both classic and trendy dressers. **Brooks Brothers** (⌧ 46 Newbury St., ☎ 617/267–2600; 75 State St., ☎ 617/261–9990) offers traditional formal and casual clothing. Basically Brooks is Brooks, correct and durable through the ages. **Louis, Boston** (⌧ 234 Berkeley St., ☎ 617/262–6100) carries elegantly tailored designs and a wide selection of imported clothing and accessories, including many of the more daring Italian styles. The ultrapricey store for men and women, similar to Barneys New York, also has subtly updated classics in everything from linen to tweed.

ICE CREAM

Herrell's (⊠ 15 Dunster St., Cambridge, ☎ 617/497–2179) was founded by the original creator of Steve's Ice Cream, Steve Herrell, who, selling his business (along with his first name), decided to get back in the ice-cream business. Nondairy ice cream and frozen yogurt complement the extensive variety of flavors, of which chocolate pudding is one of the more intense.

JEWELRY

Shreve, Crump & Low (⊠ 330 Boylston St., ☎ 617/267–9100) sells the finest jewelry, china, crystal, and silver and an extensive collection of clocks and watches. One of Boston's oldest and most respected stores, this is where generations of Brahmin brides have registered their china selections.

SPORTING GOODS

Eastern Mountain Sports (⊠ 1041 Commonwealth Ave., Brighton, ☎ 617/254–4250) offers New England's best selection of gear for the backpacker, camper, climber, or skier.

TOBACCONISTS

L. J. Peretti Company (⊠ 2½ Park Square, corner of Boylston and Charles Sts., ☎ 617/482–0218) is one of the few places that still makes pipes. A Boston institution since 1870, Peretti sells a large selection of tobacco, including its own blends, and handmade imported cigars.

TOYS

F.A.O. Schwarz (⊠ 440 Boylston St., ☎ 617/266–5101), a branch of the famed New York toy emporium, offers the highest quality (and the highest-priced) toys.

Side Trip: Lexington and Concord

The events of April 19, 1775, the first military encounters of the American Revolution, are very much a part of present-day Lexington and Concord. In these two quintessential New England towns, rich in literary and political history, one finds the true beginning of America's Freedom Trail on the very sites where a Colonial people began their fight for freedom and a new nation.

Lexington

The town of Lexington comes alive each **Patriot's Day** (the Monday nearest April 19) to celebrate and re-create the events of April 19, 1775, beginning at 6 AM, when "Paul Revere" rides down Massachusetts Avenue shouting "The British are coming! The British are coming!"

As the Redcoats retreated from Concord on April 19, 1775, the Minutemen peppered them with musket fire from behind low stone walls and tall pine trees before marching to the safety of Charlestown's hills. "The bloodiest half-mile of Battle Road," now Massachusetts Avenue in Arlington, began in front of the **Jason Russell House,** a Colonial farmhouse. Bullet holes are still visible. Adjoining the Russell House, a much newer, barn-shape building (circa late 1970s) houses the **George Abbot Smith History Museum,** offering a contemporary look at American historical and cultural phenomena. Changing exhibits have included such varied topics as evolution of the Barbie Doll and early Jewish communities in the New World. ⊠ 7 Jason St., Arlington, ☎ 617/648–4300. ≊ $2. ⊙ Weekdays 1–5, weekends by appointment. 30-min tours available.

In the Arlington Heights section of Lexington, near the intersection of Lowell Street and Massachusetts Avenue, the Battle of the Foot of the Rocks was waged. Not far from this site, you'll find the Old Schwamb

Mill (✉ 17 Mill La., ☎ 617/643–0554). In this restored mill, artisans produce and sell reproductions of Shaker furniture, baskets, and boxes. At East Lexington (take Massachusetts Ave. through its intersection with Route 2A), the **Museum of Our National Heritage** (✉ 33 Marrett Rd., ☎ 617/861–6559) houses changing exhibitions that focus on America's history and culture.

NEED A
BREAK?
Head for the **Munroe Tavern** (✉ 1332 Massachusetts Ave., ☎ 617/674–9238), a 1635 pub. Here, dazed and demoralized British troops regrouped on their retreat back to Boston.

The centerpiece of the town is **Lexington Green.** On this 2-acre, triangular piece of land, the Minuteman Captain John Parker assembled his men to await the arrival of the British, who marched from Boston to Concord to "teach rebels a lesson" on the morning of April 19. Henry Hudson Kitson's renowned statue of Parker, the **Minuteman Statue,** stands at the tip of the Green, facing downtown Lexington. ✉ *Visitors Center (Lexington Chamber of Commerce), 1875 Massachusetts Ave., Lexington 02173,* ☎ *617/862–1450.* ✆ *June–Oct., daily 9–5; Nov.–Dec. and Mar.–Apr., daily 9–3; Jan.–Feb., daily 10–2.*

On the right side of Lexington Green is **Buckman Tavern,** built in 1690, where the Minutemen gathered initially to wait for the British on April 19. A 40-minute tour visits the tavern's seven rooms. ✉ *1 Bedford St.,* ☎ *617/862–5598.* ✆ *$3.* ✆ *Weekend nearest Apr. 1– Oct., Mon.–Sat. 10–5, Sun. 1–5.*

A quarter-mile north of Lexington Green stands the eight-room **Hancock-Clarke House,** a parsonage built in 1698. Here the patriots John Hancock and Samuel Adams were roused from their sleep by Paul Revere, who had ridden out from Boston to "spread the alarm through every Middlesex village and farm" that the British were marching to Concord. A 20-minute tour is offered. ✉ *36 Hancock St.,* ☎ *617/861– 0928.* ✆ *$3. The Lexington Historical Society offers a $7 combination ticket for the Munroe Tavern, the Buckman Tavern, and the Hancock-Clarke House.* ✆ *Weekend nearest Apr. 19–Oct., Mon.–Sat. 10–5, Sun. 1–5.*

DINING

$$$$ ✕ **Versailles.** An intimate French restaurant, Versailles serves such specialties as brie with caviar baked in puff pastry and quiche Lorraine for lunch, rack of lamb and veal Oscar for dinner. ✉ *1777 Massachusetts Ave.,* ☎ *617/861–1711. AE, DC, MC, V. No lunch Sun.*

$ ✕ **Bertucci's.** This popular restaurant chain began in Boston and is spreading through the area because of its great food, reasonable prices, and family friendly atmosphere. Specialties include chicken and mushroom ravioli (in a sauce to die for), gnocchi, and a wide range of brick-oven-baked pizzas and calzones. ✉ *1777 Massachusetts Ave.,* ☎ *617/860–9000. AE, D, MC, V.*

GETTING TO LEXINGTON

To reach Lexington by **car** from Boston, cross the Charles River at the Massachusetts Avenue Bridge and proceed through Cambridge, bearing right for Arlington at Harvard Square. Continue through Arlington Center on Massachusetts Avenue to the first traffic light, turn left onto Jason Street, and begin your tour. Travel time is 25 minutes one-way.

The **MBTA** (☎ 617/722–3200) operates buses to Lexington and Boston's western suburbs from Alewife Station in Cambridge. Travel time is about one hour.

Concord

To reach Concord from Lexington, take Routes 4/225 through Bedford and Route 62 west to Concord; or better, backtrack on Massachusetts Avenue to pick up Route 2A west at the Museum of Our National Heritage. The latter route will take you through parts of **Minute Man National Historical Park,** whose more than 750 acres commemorate the events of April 19; it includes Fiske Hill and the **Battle Road Visitors Center,** approximately 1 mile from the Battle Green on the right off Route 2A. ☎ 617/862–7753. ✉ Free. ☉ Mid-Apr.–Dec., daily 8:30–5. Audiovisual programs, printed material, lectures in summer.

Near the center of Concord—just take a short drive from Monument Square on Main Street to Thoreau Street, then left onto Belknap Street—the **Thoreau Lyceum** houses survey maps, letters, and other memorabilia of Henry David Thoreau, Concord's eminent writer and naturalist. The most fascinating item is an exact replica—down to the caned bed and writing desk—of Thoreau's Walden Pond cabin. ✉ 156 Belknap St., ☎ 508/369–5912. ✉ $2. ☉ Feb., Sat. 10–5, Sun. 2–5; Mar.–Dec., Mon.–Sat. 10–5, Sun. 2–5.

At the **Old North Bridge,** a half-mile from Concord Center, Minutemen from Concord and surrounding towns fired "the shot heard round the world," signaling the start of the American Revolution. Here, Daniel Chester French's *Minuteman* statue (1875) honors the country's first freedom fighters. The National Historical Park's North Bridge Visitors Center is ½ mile down Monument Street. ✉ 174 Liberty St., ☎ 508/369–6993. ☉ Daily 9–4. Lectures Apr.–Oct.

Within sight of the Old North Bridge is the **Old Manse,** built from 1769 to 1770, where Nathaniel Hawthorne and Ralph Waldo Emerson lived at different times. The house is filled with memorabilia from the Emerson family's more than 160 years here and Hawthorne's brief 3½-year stay. ✉ Monument St., ☎ 508/369–3909. ✉ $5. ☉ Mid-Apr.–late Oct., Mon. and Wed.–Sat. 10–4:30; Sun. 1–4:30.

When Hawthorne returned to Concord in 1852, he bought a rambling structure called **The Wayside,** where visitors can now see his tower study. ✉ 455 Lexington Rd. (Rte. 2A), ☎ 508/369–6975. ✉ $2. ☉ Mid-Apr.–Oct. 31, Tues.–Sun. 10–5:30 (last tour leaves promptly at 5).

Louisa May Alcott's **Orchard House** is so named for the apple orchard that once surrounded it. A stone's throw from Hawthorne's Wayside, this lovely house is where she wrote *Little Women.* Nothing is roped off here so visitors can get a good sense of what life was like for the Alcotts. ✉ 399 Lexington Rd., ☎ 508/369–4118. ✉ $5.50. ☉ Apr.–Oct., Mon.–Sat. 10–4:30, Sun. 1–4:30; Nov.–Mar., weekdays 11–3, Sat. 10–4:30, Sun. 1–4:30. Closed Jan. 1–15.

On the other side of the Wayside, the yard of **Grapevine Cottage** (✉ 491 Lexington Rd.; not open to the public) has the original Concord grapevine, the grape that the Welch's jams and jellies company made famous.

After leaving the Old Manse, Emerson moved to what we know as the **Ralph Waldo Emerson House** at 28 Cambridge Turnpike. Here he wrote the famous *Essays* ("To be great is to be misunderstood"; "A foolish consistency is the hobgoblin of little minds, adored by little statesmen and philosophers and divines"). Furnishings are pretty much as Emerson left them, even down to his hat on the banister newel post. ✉ 28 Cambridge Turnpike, on Rte. 2A, ☎ 508/369–2236. ✉ $3.50. ☉ Mid-Apr.–mid-Oct., Thurs.–Sat. 10–4:30, Sun. 2–4:30. 30-min tours.

The original contents of Emerson's private study and 15 period rooms are in the **Concord Museum,** ½ mile southeast of Emerson's House on Route 2A heading into Concord. ⊠ *200 Lexington Rd.,* ☎ *508/369–9609.* ▨ *$6.* ☺ *Mon.–Sat. 10–5, Sun. 1–5.*

For many, the highlight of a trip to Concord is a visit—or should we say, pilgrimage—to **Walden Pond,** Henry David Thoreau's most famous residence. Here, in 1845, when he was 28, Thoreau moved into a one-room cabin—built for $28.12½ cents—on the shore of this 100-foot-deep "kettle hole," formed 12,000 years ago by the retreat of the New England glacier. Far from civilization, he discovered that solitude is not solitude and came to truly appreciate the beauties of nature. "Thank God they can't cut down the clouds," he once remarked; such sentiments—so effectively seeded at Walden—made him into the philosophical godfather of the 20th-century ecological movement. Thoreau later published *Walden* (1854), a collection of essays on observations he made while living there over a 15-month period. The site of that first cabin—only discovered a few decades ago—is staked out in stone. A full-size, authentically furnished replica of the cabin stands about a half mile from the original site, near the parking lot for the Walden Pond State Reservation.

Walden Pond has excellent water quality, a result of the absence of shoreline development and the presence of tributary streams. Conservationists have fought long and hard, as did Thoreau, to keep commercial development at bay. It's a popular place to swim in the summer; you can also row in the pond and fish, and hike in the woods around Walden, all popular for recreational activities since Thoreau's time. The indigenous vegetation has been allowed to grow back and today resembles what it was in his day. Walden Pond is once again Edenic and picnickers—rightly so—never dare to litter. ⊠ *Rte. 126, (parking across from pond),* ☎ *508/369–3254.* ▨ *Free.* ☺ *Daily until approximately ½ hr after sunset.*

DINING AND LODGING

$–$$ ✕ **Walden Station.** A casual restaurant situated in an old brick firehouse, Walden Station prepares American cuisine such as fresh seafood and beef fillets. The fresh desserts are made on premises. ⊠ *24 Walden St.,* ☎ *508/371–2233. AE, D, DC, MC, V.*

$$$ ✕▥ **Colonial Inn.** Traditional fare—from prime rib to scallops—is served in the gracious dining room of this 1716 inn. Lighter fare is offered in the lounge. Overnight accommodations are available in 49 rooms. ⊠ *48 Monument Sq.,* ☎ *508/369–9200 or 800/370–9200,* ℻ *508/369–2170. AE, D, DC, MC, V.*

Side Trip: Plymouth

If you have time to visit just one South Shore destination, make it Plymouth, a historic seaside town of narrow streets and clapboard mansions. Plymouth, 41 miles south of Boston, is known across the nation as "America's home town" because of the 102 weary Pilgrims who disembarked here in December 1620.

★   **Plimoth Plantation** is a reconstruction of the original Pilgrim settlement, where actors in period costume speak Jacobean English and carry on the daily life of the 17th century. In the furnished homes, "residents" demonstrate such household skills as soapmaking; you can also tour a meetinghouse, crafts center, and the vegetable gardens. ⊠ *Warren Ave. (Rte. 3A),* ☎ *508/746–1622.* ▨ *$18.50 (includes entry to Mayflower II); plantation only $15.* ☺ *Apr.–Nov., daily 9–5.*

The **Mayflower II,** an exact replica of the 1620 *Mayflower,* is moored at Plymouth's picturesque waterfront. This second version was built in England and sailed across the Atlantic in 1957; it is staffed by costumed "Pilgrims" who regale visitors with tales of their trying journey. ⊠ *State Pier,* ☎ *508/746–1622.* ☞ *$5.75.* ☼ *Apr.–Nov., daily 9–5; July–Aug., 9–7.*

Plymouth Rock, popularly believed to have been the Pilgrims' stepping stone when they left the *Mayflower,* is protected and obscured by an enormous (some would say ugly) pillared monument near the water. There's a $20 million renovation of the surrounding area underway: The plan is to turn the Plymouth waterfront into a park, with the rock as a centerpiece, and to dismantle the monument at the same time.

Cole's Hill, across the street from Plymouth Rock, is where the Pilgrims buried their dead (at night, so the Native Americans could not count the dwindling numbers of survivors). The **Plymouth National Wax Museum,** on top of Cole's Hill, displays 26 scenes with life-size models that tell the Pilgrims' story. ⊠ *16 Carver St.,* ☎ *508/746–6468.* ☞ *$5.50.* ☼ *Mar.–Nov., daily 9–5; July–Aug., daily 9–9.*

The **Pilgrim Hall Museum,** away from the waterfront, exhibits a sizable collection of household goods, books, weapons, and furniture used by the Pilgrims. ⊠ *75 Court St. (Rte. 3A),* ☎ *508/746–1620.* ☞ *$5.* ☼ *Daily 9:30–4:30. Closed Jan.*

Cranberry World, operated by Ocean Spray, tells the story of this state's local crop with displays on harvesting, an outdoor working cranberry bog, and information about the natural inhabitants of the wetlands. The best time to visit is in early October when the cranberry harvest takes place. ⊠ *225 Water St.,* ☎ *508/747–2350.* ☞ *Free.* ☼ *May–Nov., daily 9:30–5.*

Dining and Lodging

$$$ ✕ **Isaac's.** Every table has an ocean view at this modern, second floor
★ restaurant, which has shiny glass and brass interiors and picture windows overlooking Plymouth harbor. Seafood and lobster dishes are the specialties: try baked stuffed scrod, stuffed shrimp, or bouillabaisse. ⊠ *114 Water St.,* ☎ *508/830–0001. AE, D, DC, MC, V.*

$ ✕ **The Lobster Hut.** This casual oceanside restaurant is known for its
★ great value. Order as you enter, then eat either in the small, bright dining room with modern, fast food–style furnishings, or at stone picnic tables on a deck overlooking the harbor. Best bets are fried lobster, clam chowder, fish-and-chips, and fried clams. Chicken and burgers are among the nonseafood items served. ⊠ *Town Wharf,* ☎ *508/746–2270. MC, V. Closed Dec. 20–Jan. 31.*

$$–$$$ ▦ **Pilgrim Sands Motel.** Although it's a couple of miles south of down-
★ town Plymouth, on Route 3A, this A-one motel is opposite Plimoth Plantation and has its own private beach. Choose a room with an ocean view—the sea practically laps against the walls. Second-floor ocean-view rooms have balconies and deck chairs. Some rooms have refrigerators. ⊠ *150 Warren Ave., 02360,* ☎ *508/747–0900,* 𝖥𝖠𝖷 *508/746–8066. 64 rooms, 2 suites. Bar, coffee shop, indoor and outdoor pools, hot tub. AE, D, DC, MC, V.*

$$ ▦ **The Mabbett House.** This airy, gracious bed-and-breakfast offers classy,
★ peaceful accommodation on a quiet side street just a couple of minutes' walk from Plymouth harbor. Owners Bill and Judy Stevens are well-traveled diplomats who have brought home an amazing array of

European antiques. In guest rooms you can find a high, brass four-poster French bed, writing desks, and even antique clothing. Breakfast is served on the large screened porch in summer. ⊠ *7 Cushman St., 02360,* ☎ *800/572–7829,* FAX *508/830–1911. Full breakfast included. AE, MC, V.*

Shopping

Most of the antiques stores on the South Shore are close to Plymouth. For a brochure, contact **Southeastern New England Antiques Dealers Association** (⊠ Box 4416, East Providence, RI 02914, ☎ 401/781–7222 or 508/993–4944). **Cordage Park** (⊠ Court St., Rte. 3A, ☎ 508/746–7707), a restored 19th-century rope mill, now contains 15 stores, several of which are factory outlets.

Plymouth A to Z

GETTING AROUND

By Bus: From Boston, the **Plymouth and Brockton Street Railway Co.** (☎ 508/746–0378), which is actually a bus company, calls at Plymouth en route to Cape Cod.

By Car: Interstate–93 connects Boston with Quincy; from here Route 3 is the quickest way to Plymouth.

GUIDED TOURS

Colonial Lantern Tours (⊠ Box 3541, ☎ 508/747–4161 or 800/698–5636, FAX 508/747–4284) runs 90-minute, lantern-lit strolls around Plymouth after dark, which take in Brewster Gardens, Plymouth Rock, and the site of the original Plimoth Plantation (not the re-created version). Tours ($7) leave at 7:30 PM from the office at 98 Water St., or the John Carver Inn (⊠ 25 Summer St.; Apr. and May, Fri.–Sun.; June–Thanksgiving, daily).

Plymouth Rock Trolley Co. (☎ 508/747–3419) leads narrated trolley tours of Plymouth, making 40 stops including Plimoth Plantation, the *Mayflower II,* and Plymouth Harbor. A one-day ticket ($7) allows unlimited reboarding; trolleys run every 20 minutes May–late November.

Captain John Boats (⊠ 117 Standish Ave., ☎ 508/746–2643 or 800/242–2469) operates whale-watching cruises from Plymouth in spring, summer, and early fall; it also runs daily 45-minute tours of Plymouth Harbor, June through September. All tours depart from either State Pier or the nearby Town Wharf.

VISITOR INFORMATION

Plymouth County Development Council (⊠ Box 1620, Pembroke 02359, ☎ 617/826–3136). **Plymouth Visitor Information** (⊠ Exit 5 off Rte. 3, Plymouth, ☎ 508/746–1150; ☉ May–Oct., daily 9–5; Nov.–Apr., daily 8–4:30).

Boston A to Z

Arriving and Departing

FROM THE AIRPORT

Only 3 miles—and Boston Harbor—separate Logan International Airport from downtown, yet it can seem like 20 miles when you're caught in one of the many daily traffic jams at the two tunnels that go under the harbor. Boston traffic is almost always heavy, and the worst conditions prevail during the morning (6:30–9) and evening (3:30–7) rush hours. For 24-hour information on parking, bicycle access, and bus, subway, and water shuttle transport, call Logan's **Ground Transportation Desk** (☎ 800/235–6426).

Cab fare into the city is about $15, including tip; call **MASSPORT** (☎ 617/561–1751) for information. The **Airport Water Shuttle** (☎ 800/235–6426) crosses Boston Harbor in about seven minutes, running between Logan Airport and Rowes Wharf (a free shuttle bus operates between the ferry dock and airline terminals). The **MBTA Blue Line** to Airport Station is one of the fastest ways to reach downtown from the airport (free shuttle buses connect the subway station with all airline terminals; ☎ 800/235–6426). **City Transportation** (☎ 617/561–9000) is a scheduled van service that runs between Logan Airport and area hotels. If you are driving from Logan to downtown, take the Sumner Tunnel; if that's not passable, try Route 1A north to Route 16, then to the Tobin Bridge and into Boston.

Getting Around

BY BUS

Bus, trolley, and subway service is provided by the Massachusetts Bay Transportation Authority (MBTA). The MBTA bus routes crisscross the metropolitan area and extend farther into the suburbs than those of the subways and trolleys. Fares on MBTA local buses are 60¢ for adults, 30¢ children 5–11; longer suburban bus trips cost more. For general travel information, call 617/722–3200 or 800/392–6100 (TTY 617/722–5146), weekdays 6:30 AM–11 PM, weekends 9–6; for 24-hour recorded service information, call 617/722–5050.

Visitor passes are available for three- or seven-day periods. The fares are $9 for a three-day pass and $18 for a seven-day pass. The passes are good for unlimited travel on city buses and subways. These passes are not sold at every station, so call 617/722–3200 for a nearby location.

A free map of the entire public transportation system is available at the Park Street Station information stand (street level), open daily 7 AM–10 PM.

BY CAR

Those who cannot avoid bringing a car into Boston should be able to minimize their frustration by keeping to the main thoroughfares and by parking in lots—no matter how expensive—rather than on the street. Parking on Boston streets is a tricky business.

The major public parking lots are at Government Center and Quincy Market; beneath Boston Common (entrance on Charles Street); beneath Post Office Square; at the Prudential Center; at Copley Place; and off Clarendon Street near the John Hancock Tower. Smaller lots are scattered through the downtown area. Most are expensive, especially the small outdoor lots; a few city garages are a bargain at about $6–$10 a day.

BY SUBWAY AND TROLLEY

The MBTA, or "T," operates subways, elevated trains, and trolleys along four connecting lines. The **Red Line** has points of origin at Braintree and Mattapan to the south; the routes join near South Boston and proceed to Harvard and to suburban Arlington. The **Green Line** is a combined underground and elevated surface line, originating at Cambridge's Lechmere and heading south through Park Street to divide into four major routes: Boston College (Commonwealth Avenue), Cleveland Circle (Beacon Street), Riverside, and Arborway. Green Line trains are actually trolleys that travel major streets south and west of Kenmore Square and operate underground in the central city. The **Blue Line** runs from Bowdoin Square (near Government Center) to the Wonderland Racetrack in Revere, north of Boston. The **Orange Line** runs from Oak Grove in north suburban Malden to Forest Hills near the Arnold Ar-

boretum. Trains operate from about 5:30 AM to about 12:30 AM. The
fare is 85¢ for adults, 40¢ for children 5–11. An extra fare is required
for the distant Green and Red Line stops.

BY TAXI

Cabs are not easily hailed on the street, except at the airport; if you
need to get somewhere in a hurry, use a hotel taxi stand or telephone
for a cab. Companies offering 24-hour service include **Checker** (☎
617/536–7000), **Independent Taxi Operators Association** or ITOA
(☎ 617/426–8700), **Green Cab Association** (☎ 617/628–0600), **Town
Taxi** (☎ 617/536–5000), and, in Cambridge, **Cambridge Taxi** (☎
617/547–3000). The current rate is about $1.60 per mile.

Contacts and Resources

BED AND BREAKFAST RESERVATION SERVICE

A Bed and Breakfast Reservation Agency of Boston (✉ 47 Commercial Wharf, 02110, ☎ 617/720–3540, 800/248–9262, or 0800/895128
in the U.K.) can book a variety of accommodation ranging from historic B&Bs to modern condominiums.

EMERGENCIES

Police, fire, ambulance (☎ 911). **Massachusetts General Hospital** (☎
617/726–2000). **Dental emergency** (☎ 508/651–3521). **Poison control** (☎ 617/232–2120).

GUIDED TOURS

ORIENTATION: Beantown Trolleys (✉ 435 High St., Randolph, ☎
617/236–2148) covers the Freedom Trail among its many stops. One
ticket allows you to get on and off at will all day long. The narration
runs 1½ hours total. Fare is $16 adults, $11 senior citizens, $5 chil-
dren 5–11; trolleys run every 15 minutes, 9 AM–dark. **Brush Hill/Gray
Line** (✉ 39 Dalton Ave., ☎ 617/236–2148) has buses leaving from several downtown hotels twice daily from March to November for 3½-
hour tours of Boston and Cambridge. **Old Town Trolley** (✉ 329 W.
2nd St., ☎ 617/269–7010) takes you on a 1½-hour narrated tour of
Boston or an hour-long tour of Cambridge. You can catch it at major
hotels, Boston Common, Copley Place, or in front of the New England
Aquarium on Atlantic Avenue.

Boston Harbor Cruises (✉ 1 Long Wharf, ☎ 617/227–4320) has tours
from mid-April through October. The **Charles River Boat Co.** (✉ 100
Cambridgeside Pl., Cambridge, ☎ 617/621–3001) offers a 50-minute
narrated tour of the Charles River Basin. It departs from the Galleria
and Museum of Science dock on the hour from noon to 5 daily,
June–September, and on weekends in April, May, and October.

Boston Duck Tours (✉ 64 Long Wharf, ☎ 617/723–3825) uses a fleet
of restored World War II amphibious landing vehicles (DUKWS), to
take passengers on an 80-minute tour of the city that includes all the
usual landmarks and a half-hour ride on the Charles River.

WALKING TOURS: The **Black Heritage Trail** (☎ 617/742–5415), a 90-
minute walk exploring the history of Boston's 19th-century black
community, passes 14 sites of historical importance on Beacon Hill.
Guided tours are available by appointment in the winter, and from April
to October at 10, noon, and 2 daily from the Shaw Memorial in front
of the State House on Beacon Street. Maps and brochures can be obtained for self-guided tours.

The 2½-mile **Freedom Trail** (☎ 617/242–5642) is marked in the sidewalk by a red line that winds its way past 16 of Boston's most important
historic sites. The walk begins at the Freedom Trail Information Cen-

ter on the Tremont Street side of Boston Common, not far from the MBTA Park Street Station. Sites include the State House, Park Street Church, Old State House, Boston Massacre Site, Paul Revere House, and Old North Church.

WHALE-WATCHING: The **Bay State Cruise Company** (✉ 67 Long Wharf, ☎ 617/723–7800) offers whale-watch cruises Saturday and Sunday from late April to mid-June, Saturday during the summer.

LATE-NIGHT PHARMACY

Phillips Drug Store (✉ 155 Charles St., ☎ 617/523–1028 or 617/523–4372).

VISITOR INFORMATION

For general information and brochures, contact the **Greater Boston Convention and Visitors Bureau** (✉ Box 490, Prudential Tower, 02199, ☎ 617/536–4100 or 800/888–5515; ⊙ Weekdays 8:30–5) or the **Boston Welcome Center** (✉ 140 Tremont St., 02111, ☎ 617/451–2227; open daily 9–5, with longer hours in effect during peak summer season). The latter has a second office at the Park Street subway station.

CAPE COD

Updated by
Dorothy
Antczak

Formed by glacial deposits of rock and sand, the Cape has been shaped and reshaped by ocean currents and wind erosion. Separated from the Massachusetts "mainland" by the 17.4-mile Cape Cod Canal, the Cape is likened in form to an outstretched arm bent at the elbow.

The natural beauty of the Cape is astounding: long beaches backed by rolling sand dunes; forests of beech, birch, and oak; crimson- colored bogs; grassy marshlands studded with cattails. Only about 70 miles from end to end, much of the area is protected by the Cape Cod National Seashore, and by historical preservation commissions.

The area is steeped in history—several towns were settled nearly 100 years before the American Revolution. Visitors continue to enjoy the Cape's charming old New England villages of weathered-shingle houses and white steepled churches, symbols that testify to over 300 years of historical tradition.

In 1602, Bartholomew Gosnold was the first known European explorer to set foot on these shores; he named the peninsula Cape Cod after the bounty of codfish in the surrounding waters, and went on to claim Martha's Vineyard for the British crown. Eighteen years later, the *Mayflower* sailed into what is now Provincetown Harbor. The Pilgrims explored the area for a month, then traveled on to Plymouth. Before they left, they took the time to sign the *Mayflower Compact,* which established the basis for the government of the Commonwealth of Massachusetts. Later, Colonists fleeing persecution by the Massachusetts Bay Colony migrated to Cape Cod. As the soil proved unsuitable for farming, these seaboard settlers turned to fishing and whaling to make their fortunes. Many Cape homes were once stately captain's mansions or refurbished fish shanties.

Though the fishing industry has dwindled, Cape Cod still has a fascination with all things nautical, from museums that preserve artifacts from the whaling era, to shipwrecks, to maritime ceremonies like "The Blessing of the Fleet." The sea provides an outlet for sport, study, and solace, attracting sailors, scientists, and artists.

The Cape is for relaxing—swimming and sunning, fishing and boating, playing golf and tennis, attending theater (summer stock theater

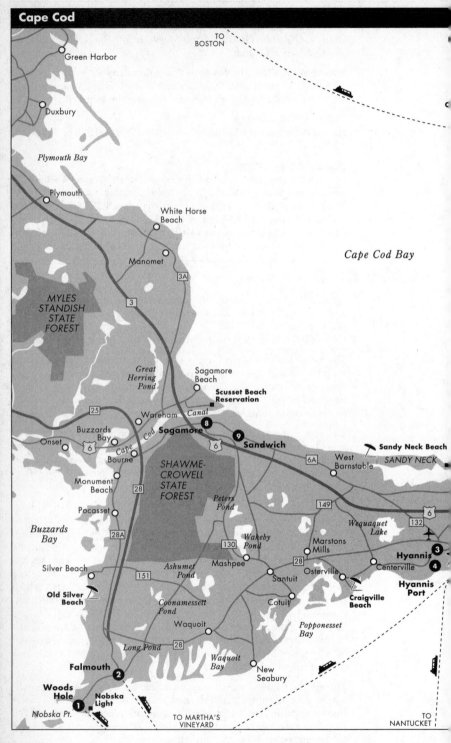

TO
BOSTON

Green Harbor

Duxbury

Plymouth Bay

Plymouth

White Horse
Beach

Cape Cod Bay

Manomet

3A

MYLES
STANDISH
STATE
FOREST

3

*Great
Herring
Pond*

Sagamore
Beach

**Scusset Beach
Reservation**

25

Wareham   *Canal*

Buzzards
Bay   **Sagamore**   8

Onset   6   *Cape*   9   **Sandwich**

Bourne   *Cod*   6A

Sandy Neck Beach
West   *SANDY NECK*
Barnstable

Monument
Beach

28

SHAWME-
CROWELL
STATE
FOREST

*Peters
Pond*

149

*Wequaquet
Lake*

6

132

Pocasset

*Buzzards
Bay*

28A

Silver Beach

151

*Ashumet
Pond*

130   *Wakeby
Pond*

Mashpee   28

Marstons
Mills

Osterville

Hyannis   3

Centerville   4

**Hyannis
Port**

**Old Silver
Beach**

*Coonamessett
Pond*

Santuit

Cotuit

**Craigville
Beach**

Waquoit

*Popponesset
Bay*

Falmouth   2

Long Pond   28

*Waquoit
Bay*

New
Seabury

**Woods
Hole**

**Nobska
Light**

Nobska Pt.   1

TO MARTHA'S
VINEYARD

TO
NANTUCKET

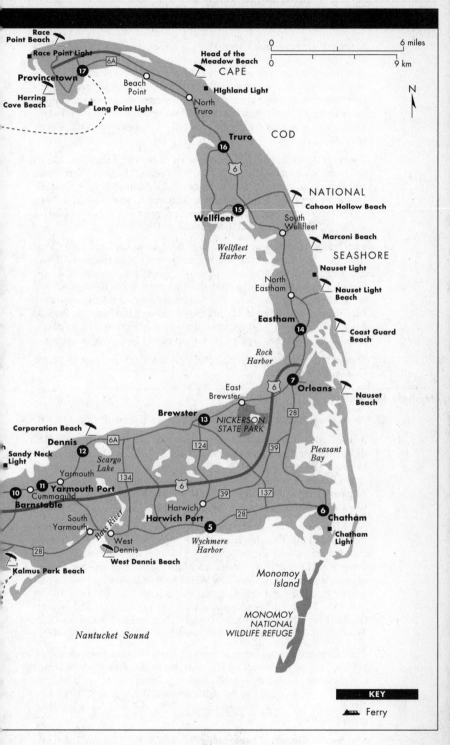

Race Point Beach

Race Point Light

Provincetown

Herring Cove Beach

Long Point Light

Beach Point

North Truro

Head of the Meadow Beach

CAPE

Highland Light

Truro

COD

NATIONAL

Cahoon Hollow Beach

Wellfleet

South Wellfleet

SEASHORE

Wellfleet Harbor

Marconi Beach

Nauset Light

North Eastham

Nauset Light Beach

Eastham

Coast Guard Beach

Rock Harbor

East Brewster

Orleans

Nauset Beach

Brewster

NICKERSON STATE PARK

Pleasant Bay

Corporation Beach

Dennis

Sandy Neck Light

Scargo Lake

Yarmouth

Yarmouth Port

Cummaquid

Barnstable

South Yarmouth

Harwich

Harwich Port

Chatham

Chatham Light

West Dennis

West Dennis Beach

Wychmere Harbor

Kalmus Park Beach

Bass River

Monomoy Island

Nantucket Sound

MONOMOY NATIONAL WILDLIFE REFUGE

0   6 miles

0   9 km

N

KEY

Ferry

is popular) and hunting antiques. Despite summer crowds and overde-velopment, much remains unspoiled.

Memorial Day through Labor Day (in some cases, Columbus Day) is high season on Cape Cod; you'll find good beach weather then, but high prices and crowds as well. Spring and fall are best for bird-watch-ing, nature hikes, country drives, and lower prices at inns and specials at restaurants. In winter, many museums, shops, restaurants, and lodg-ing places are closed; the intimate bed-and-breakfasts and inns that re-main open—their tariffs greatly reduced—can make romantic winter retreats.

The term Upper Cape refers to the towns of Bourne, Falmouth, Mash-pee, and Sandwich; Mid-Cape, to Barnstable, Hyannis, Yarmouth, and Dennis; and Lower Cape, to Harwich, Chatham, Brewster, Orleans, Eastham, Wellfleet, Truro, and Provincetown. Most towns are broken up into villages, which may or may not progress in a logical order (for example, West Dennis is actually south of Dennis).

Two bridges, the Bourne and the Sagamore, cross the Cape Cod Canal from the "mainland." The south shore of the Cape, traced by Route 28, is heavily populated and the major center for tourism. Route 6, the Mid-Cape Highway, passes through the relatively unpopulated center of the Cape, characterized by a landscape of scrub pine and oak. Paralleling Route 6 but following the north coast is Route 6A, the Old King's Highway, in most sections a winding country road that passes through some of the Cape's best-preserved old New England towns.

Numbers in the margin correspond to points of interest on the Cape Cod map.

Woods Hole

❶ *76 mi from Boston, 12½ mi southwest of the Bourne Bridge.*

At the Cape's extreme southwest corner is Woods Hole, where ferries depart for Martha's Vineyard. As parking is difficult in summer, the Whoosh Trolley (☎ 800/352–7155), which runs from Falmouth Mall down Route 28 to the Woods Hole National Marine Fisheries Service Aquarium, is recommended. It leaves every half hour and makes seven stops, June–September, daily 10–9. The fare is 50¢.

An international center for marine research, Woods Hole is home to the Woods Hole Oceanographic Institution (WHOI), whose staff led the successful search for the *Titanic* in 1985; the Marine Biological Lab-oratory (MBL); and the National Marine Fisheries Service, among other scientific institutions. The **WHOI Exhibit Center** has videos and other exhibits on the institute and its projects. ⊠ *15 School St.,* ☎ *508/289–2663.* ⬚ *Suggested donation: $1 individuals, $10 groups.* ◷ *Mid-May–Oct., Tues.–Sat. 10–4:30, Sun. noon–4:30; Nov.–Dec., Fri.–Sat. 10–4:30, Sun. noon–4:30; mid-Mar.–Apr., Fri.–Sat. 10–4:30.*

☾ The National Marine Fisheries Service has a public **aquarium** with a pool for rescued and recovering seals, tanks displaying regional fish and shellfish, plus hands-on tanks and magnifying glasses and dissecting scopes for children. ⊠ *Corner Albatross and Water Sts.,* ☎ *508/548–7684.* ⬚ *Free.* ◷ *Late June–mid-Sept., daily 10–4; mid-Sept.–late June, weekdays 9–4.*

The **Marine Biological Laboratory** (☎ 508/289–7623; call for reser-vations and meeting instructions; children 10 and older only) offers 1½-hour tours of its facilities, led by retired scientists, on weekdays, mid-June–August.

A free walking tour of the village is conducted one afternoon a week in July and August by guides from the **Woods Hole Historical Collection,** which houses various exhibits, including native small crafts and a model village of Woods Hole, circa 1895. ⊠ *Bradley House Museum, 573 Woods Hole Rd.,* ☎ *508/548–7270.* ▧ *Free.* ☉ *July–Aug., Tues.–Sat. 10–4.*

Falmouth

❷ *3 mi northeast of Woods Hole.*

The **village green** in Falmouth was used as a military training field in the 18th century. Today it is the center of a considerable shopping district, flanked by attractive old homes, some fine inns, and the 1856 **First Congregational Church,** with a bell cast by Paul Revere.

The Falmouth Historical Society conducts free, docent-guided walking tours of the town in season. It also maintains two museums. The 1790 **Julia Wood House** has fine period architectural details (wide-board floors, leaded-glass windows, Colonial kitchen with wide hearth), plus embroideries, baby shoes and clothes, toys and dolls, and furniture. The **Conant House** next door, a 1794 half-Cape, has military memorabilia, whaling items, scrimshaw, sailors' valentines, silver, glass, and china. The complex includes a barn filled with period kitchen and farm equipment, and a Colonial garden. ⊠ *Palmer Ave. at the Village Green,* ☎ *508/548–4857.* ▧ *$2.* ☉ *Mid-June–mid-Sept., weekdays 2–5.*

Outside town is the **Ashumet Holly and Wildlife Sanctuary,** a 45-acre tract of woods, ponds, meadows, and hiking trails. The 1,000 holly trees include American, Oriental, and European varieties. ⊠ *286 Ashumet Rd., off Rte. 151, East Falmouth,* ☎ *508/563–6390.* ▧ *$3.* ☉ *Daily sunrise–sunset.*

The Arts

The **College Light Opera Company** (⊠ Highfield Theatre, Depot Ave. Ext., ☎ 508/548–0668) is college music majors who perform operettas and musical comedies.

Beach

Old Silver Beach, a beautiful white crescent in North Falmouth, is especially good for small children because a sandbar keeps it shallow at one end and makes tidal pools with crabs and minnows. There are lifeguards, rest rooms, showers, and food.

Dining and Lodging

$$$ ⨉ **Regatta of Falmouth-by-the-Sea.** One of the Cape's best dining rooms
★ has beautiful ocean views and an intimate, romantic atmosphere. Continental and Asian cuisines have been colliding on the menu lately, resulting in more than one delicious sauce rendering, especially the sautéed shellfish sampler: scallops, mussels, lobster, and shrimp with a sensational curried lobster sauce over Asian greens. Three menus are served each night: lighter fare, regular fare, and a three-course early dinner menu. ⊠ *Clinton Ave., Falmouth harbor,* ☎ *508/548–5400. Reservations essential. AE, MC, V. Closed Oct.–Memorial Day. No lunch Sat.*

$$$ ⨉▥ **Coonamessett Inn.** Built in 1796, this classic inn provides fine din-
★ ing and gracious accommodations in a tranquil country setting. The dining rooms have lots of old-fashioned charm. The regional American menu focuses on fresh fish and seafood—it's famed for the 1½-pound seafood-stuffed lobsters. One- or two-bedroom suites are located in five buildings arranged around a landscaped lawn that spills down to a scenic wooded pond. Rooms are casually decorated, with bleached

wood or pine paneling, New England antiques or reproductions, up-holstered chairs, couches, and TVs. ⊠ *Jones Rd. and Gifford St., Box 707, 02541,* ☏ *508/548–2300,* FAX *508/540–9831. 25 suites, 1 cottage. 2 restaurants (closed Mon., Nov.–Dec.; closed weekdays, Jan.–Mar.), bar. AE, DC, MC, V.*

\$\$\$ 🏨 **Mostly Hall.** Set in a landscaped, park-like yard far back from the
★   street, this 1849 house is imposing, with a wraparound porch and a dramatic cupola. Accommodations in corner rooms afford leafy views through large shuttered windows; reading areas, antique pieces and reproduction canopy queen beds, pretty floral wallpapers, Oriental accent rugs, and central air-conditioning create an atmosphere of elegant comfort. Inviting common areas include a TV room in the cupola, a fireplaced parlor, and a backyard gazebo. There is no smoking here. ⊠ *27 Main St., 02540,* ☏ *508/548–3786 or 800/682–0565. 6 rooms. Lawn games, bicycles, library. Full breakfast included. AE, D, MC, V. Closed Jan.–mid-Feb.*

Outdoor Activities and Sports

BIKING

The **Shining Sea Bikeway** is a nice-and-easy 3½-mile coastal route between Locust Street, Falmouth, and the Woods Hole ferry parking lot.

FISHING

Fishing licenses and tackle rentals are available from **Eastman's Sport & Tackle** (⊠ 150 Main St., ☏ 508/548–6900).

Deep-sea fishing trips are operated on a walk-on basis by **Patriot Party Boats** (⊠ Falmouth Harbor, ☏ 508/548–2626 or 800/734–0088 in MA), which also offers sailing and sightseeing excursions, as well as a 24-hour water taxi service to Martha's Vineyard.

GOLF

Not far from Falmouth is the semiprivate **New Seabury Country Club** (⊠ Shore Dr. W, New Seabury, ☏ 508/477–9110) with 36 excellent holes.

HORSEBACK RIDING

Haland Stables (⊠ Rte. 28A, West Falmouth, ☏ 508/540–2552) offers lessons and trail rides.

Shopping

Falmouth Mall (⊠ Rte. 28, ☏ 508/540–8329) has Bradlees, T. J. Maxx, and 30 other shops. **Maxwell & Co.**(⊠ 200 Main St., ☏ 508/540–8752) sells traditional men's and women's clothing, hand-made French shoes and boots, and leather goods and accessories.

Hyannis

❸   *17½ mi northeast of Falmouth.*

Hyannis is the Cape's year-round commercial hub that came to be popular during the Kennedy era. On its bustling Main Street, housed in the redbrick Old Town Hall, is the **John F. Kennedy Hyannis Museum,** which focuses on JFK's ties to the Cape through videos and artifacts from the presidential years. ⊠ *397 Main St.,* ☏ *508/775–2201.* ☜ *$2.* ☉ *June–Aug., Mon.–Sat. 10–4, Sun. 1–4. Call for reduced off-season hrs and admission.*

Beach

Craigville Beach, a long, wide strip of beach near Hyannis, is extremely popular, especially with the roving and volleyball-playing young (hence the nickname "Muscle Beach"). It has lifeguards and a bathhouse, and food shops across the road.

Dining and Lodging

$$$ ✕ **Up the Creek.** The name is fun-loving and delightfully impetuous,
★ and it nicely captures the spirit of this casual little spot. The fresh-from-
the-ocean seafood—certainly not creek raised—is sometimes tradi-
tional, sometimes inventive. The broiled seafood platter is one of the
better seafood samplers anywhere on the Cape. Baked stuffed lobster
is also a favorite. ⊠ *36 Old Colony Rd.,* ☎ *508/771–7866. AE, D,
DC, MC, V. Closed some weekdays off-season.*

$$–$$$ ✕ **The Paddock.** For years, the Paddock has been synonymous with
★ excellent, formal dining on the Cape—authentically Victorian with sump-
tuous upholstery in the main dining room, and old-style wicker on the
preferable, breezy summer porch. A Continental menu looks to New
England for ingredients. For a real treat, pick out a brawny red wine
from the award-winning wine list and put it together with the steak
au poivre, encrusted in crushed peppercorns with a cognac glaze. ⊠
W. Main St. Rotary (next to Melody Tent), ☎ *508/775–7677. AE, DC,
MC, V. Closed mid-Nov.–Mar.*

$$ ✕ **Baxter's Fish N' Chips.** Fried seafood being the Cape staple that it
★ is, you may want to plan ahead for a trip to the undisputed king of
the fry-o-lator. Fried clams are delicious and generous, cooked up hot
to order with french fries and homemade tartar sauce. Outside, a number of picnic tables allow you to lose no time in the sun with lobster,
burgers, or something from the excellent raw bar. Indoors, Baxter's Boat
House Club serves the same menu, but with a number of very good
specials as well. The restaurant is right on Lewis Bay, and it's always
been a favorite of boaters and bathers alike. ⊠ *Pleasant St.,* ☎
*508/775–4490. Reservations not accepted. MC, V. Closed Oct.–Apr.
and weekdays Labor Day–Columbus Day.*

$$$–$$$$ ▥ **Tara Hyannis Hotel & Resort.** For its central-Cape location, beauti-
★ ful landscaping, extensive services, and superior resort facilities, it's hard
to beat the Tara. The lobby is elegant, but room decor is a bit dull,
with pale colors and standard contemporary furnishings. Each room
has a TV, a phone, and a private patio. Rooms overlooking the golf
greens or the courtyard garden have the best views. ⊠ *West End Cir-
cle, 02601,* ☎ *508/775–7775 or 800/843–8272,* ℻ *508/778–6039.
224 rooms, 8 suites. Restaurants, bar, pools, beauty salon, golf course,
tennis courts, health club, business services, children's program. AE,
D, DC, MC, V.*

$$$ ▥ **Capt. Gosnold Village.** An easy walk to the beach and town, this
colony of efficiency units and motel rooms is ideal for families. Ac-
commodations range from simple motel-style rooms to three-bed-
room, three-bath units with kitchens and living rooms. All but motel
rooms have gas grills, phones, and decks; all rooms have TVs. ⊠ *230
Gosnold St., 02601,* ☎ *508/775–9111. 40 units in 18 buildings. Pool,
playground. MC, V. Closed Nov.–mid-Apr.*

Nightlife and the Arts

NIGHTLIFE

In summer **Guido Murphy's** (⊠ 615 Main St., ☎ 508/775–7242)
draws a young crowd, with dancing to live and DJ music. **Bud's Country Lounge** (⊠ Bearse's Way and Rte. 132, ☎ 508/771–2505) has pool
tables, keno, and live entertainment year-round.

THE ARTS

Cape Cod Melody Tent (⊠ 21 W. Main St., ☎ 508/775–9100) presents
such top musical and comedy performers as Willie Nelson and Joan
Rivers in summer theater-in-the-round under a tent.

Outdoor Activities and Sports

Deep-sea fishing trips are operated on a walk-on basis by **Hy-Line** (⊠ Ocean St. dock, ☎ 508/790–0696).

Shopping

The **Cape Cod Mall** (⊠ Rtes. 132 and 28, ☎ 508/771–0200), the Cape's largest, is where everyone congregates on rainy days. Its 90 shops include Jordan Marsh, Filene's, The Gap, Victoria's Secret, Sears, and restaurants.

Hyannis Port

❹ *1½ mi south of Hyannis.*

The quietly posh village of Hyannis Port is where JFK spent his summers. The **John F. Kennedy Memorial Park,** on Ocean Street next to Veterans Beach, has a plaque and fountain pool in memory of the president. **The Kennedy family compound**—best viewed from the Hy-Line cruise—became the summer White House during the JFK administration.

Harwich Port

❺ *12½ mi west of Hyannis Port.*

Harwich Port is a quaint, scenic little town on Nantucket Sound. Harbor Road will take you to beautiful **Wychmere Harbor.**

Nightlife

Bishop's Terrace restaurant (⊠ Rte. 28, West Harwich, ☎ 508/432–0253) has dancing to jazz nearly year-round.

Outdoor Activities and Sports

GOLF

Cranberry Valley Golf Course (⊠ 183 Oak St., Harwich, ☎ 508/430–7560) has 18 holes.

HORSEBACK RIDING

Deer Meadow Riding Stables (⊠ Rte. 137, East Harwich, ☎ 508/432–6580) offers trail rides.

TENNIS

Melrose Tennis Center (⊠ 792 Main St., ☎ 508/430–7012; ⊙ Memorial Day–Sept.) has three Omni and six Har-Tru courts, a pro shop, private and group lessons, and round robins.

WATER SPORTS

Cape Water Sports (⊠ Rte. 28, ☎ 508/432–7079) has locations on several beaches for sailboat and sailboard rentals and lessons, and canoe and powerboat rentals.

Chatham

❻ *7 mi east of Harwich Port.*

Chatham is a seaside town that is relatively free of the development and commercialism found elsewhere on the Cape. Wandering its tidy, attractive Main Street, which is lined with traditional clothing, crafts, and antiques shops, is a pleasant way to while away the afternoon.

The **Old Atwood House and Museums** includes a furnished 1752 house museum, the old turret and lens from the Chatham Light, collections of seashells, Sandwich glass, Parian ware, and antique dolls and toys. ⊠ *347 Stage Harbor Rd.,* ☎ *508/945–2493.* ⊡ *$3.* ⊙ *Mid-June–Sept., Tues.–Fri. 1–4.*

The view from the grounds of **Chatham Light** (✉ Main St.)—of the harbor, the sandbars, and the sea beyond—is spectacular.

MONOMOY NATIONAL WILDLIFE REFUGE – Monomoy Island, just south of Chatham, was created during a fierce storm in 1958. A fragile barrier-beach area with dunes, it is protected as the Monomoy National Wildlife Refuge. The island provides nesting and resting grounds for 285 bird species. ✉ *Visitor Center: Morris Island, Chatham,* ☎ *508/ 945-0594. Ferry service is available from Morris Island mid-June–mid-Sept.; contact the Monomoy Island Ferry,* ☎ *508/945-5450, or Stage Harbor Marine,* ☎ *508/945-1850.*

Dining and Lodging

$$ ✕ **The Impudent Oyster.** Just barely off the beaten path in downtown Chatham, the Impudent Oyster offers an alternative to strictly traditional seafood, with world-beat seafood interpretations. The most popular menu item is barbecued tuna, made with orange juice, soy sauce, vinegar, and cumin. In summer, bouillabaisse and seafood fra Diavolo are added to the menu. ✉ *15 Chatham Bars Ave.,* ☎ *508/945–3545. Reservations essential in summer. AE, MC, V.*

$$$$ ★ **Chatham Bars Inn.** High above the beach on a commanding bluff, the Chatham Bars Inn enjoys a wondrous view of the ocean through massive floor-to-ceiling windows. This old, gracious hotel has diversified its menu and serves lunch and dinner in the North Beach Tavern and breakfast and lunch down by the water at the Beach House Bar and Grille in season. The main dining room's menu leans on modern American motifs with favorites like a very rich seared foie gras, and steamed swordfish with clams. You can stay in the main building or in 26 one- to eight-bedroom cottages on the inn's 20 landscaped acres. Some rooms have private ocean-view porches; all have TVs, traditional furnishings, and either wall-to-wall carpeting or hardwood floors with antique Oriental rugs. Service is attentive and extensive. ✉ *Shore Rd., 02633,* ☎ *508/945–0096 or 800/527–4884,* FAX *508/945–5491. 130 rooms, 20 suites, 26 cottages. 3 restaurants (reservations essential; no lunch; no dinner Sun.–Thurs., except holiday weekends, Nov.–Mar.), bar, pool, beach, tennis courts, children's programs (July and Aug.). MAP available. AE, DC, MC, V.*

$$$–$$$$ ★ **Captain's House Inn.** Finely preserved architectural details, tasteful decor, delicious baked goods, and an overall feeling of warmth and quiet comfort are just part of what makes this one of the Cape's very best inns. Every room in each of the three inn buildings has its own personality; some have fireplaces. The decor is mostly Williamsburg-style; one lovely, large room in the Carriage House has a rustic, Cape Cod look. ✉ *371 Old Harbor Rd., Chatham 02633,* ☎ *508/945–0127,* FAX *508/945–0866. 14 rooms, 2 suites. Full breakfast and afternoon tea included. AE, MC, V. Closed Jan.–mid-Feb.*

Nightlife and the Arts

NIGHTLIFE

The **Chatham Squire** (✉ 487 Main St., ☎ 508/945–0945) is a rollicking place, with four bars open in season.

THE ARTS

The Ohio University Players present a different play each week during their summer tenure at the **Monomoy Theatre** (✉ 776 Main St., ☎ 508/945–1589).

The **Monomoy Chamber Ensemble** plays a week of concerts at the end of July (Monomoy Theatre, ✉ 776 Main St., ☎ 508/945–1589).

Outdoor Activities and Sports
GOLF

Chatham Seaside Links (☎ 508/945–4774) is, with nine holes, a good beginner's course. Now town-owned, this was formerly the Chatham Bars Inn course.

Shopping
The Spyglass (✉ 618 Main St., ☎ 508/945–9686) carries telescopes, barometers, writing boxes, and antique maps.

Orleans

7 *11 mi north of Chatham.*

Orleans is the busy commercial center of the Lower Cape. Rock Harbor Road, a winding street lined with gray-shingle Cape houses, white picket fences, and neat gardens leads to the harbor, a former packet landing and today the base for a fishing fleet (both commercial and charter). Main Street leads east to Nauset Beach, which begins a virtually unbroken 30-mile stretch of barrier beach extending to Provincetown (☞ "A Solo Sojourn on Cape Cod's Beaches" *in* Chapter 8).

The Arts
The **Cape & Islands Chamber Music Festival** (✉ Box 2721, Orleans 02653, ☎ 508/349–7709) presents three weeks of top-caliber performances and master classes in August.

Beach
Nauset Beach is open to off-road vehicles. A 10-mile stretch of sandy beach with low dunes and waves big enough for body or board surfing, Nauset offers lifeguards, rest rooms, showers, and food.

Dining
$ ✕ **Land Ho!** Walk in, grab a newspaper from the rack, take a seat, and
★   relax: Land Ho! has been making folks feel right at home since 1969. This casual spot serves kale soup that has been noted by *Gourmet* magazine, plus burgers, hearty sandwiches, grilled fish in summer, and very good chicken wings, chowder, and fish and chips. ✉ *Rte. 6A and Cove Rd.,* ☎ *508/255–5165. Reservations not accepted. MC, V.*

Outdoor Activities and Sports
FISHING

Charters for deep-sea fishing are available at **Rock Harbor** (☎ 508/255–9757 or, in MA, 800/287–1771).

SAILING

Arey's Pond Boat Yard (✉ Off Rte. 28, South Orleans, ☎ 508/255–0994) has a sailing school with individual and group lessons.

Shopping
Hannah (✉ 47 Main St., ☎ 508/255–8234) has upscale women's fashions in unusual styles. **Tree's Place** (✉ Rte. 6A at Rte. 28, ☎ 508/255–1330), one of the Cape's most original shops, has handcrafted kaleidoscopes, art glass, hand-painted porcelain and pottery, handblown stemware, Russian lacquer boxes, imported tiles, and jewelry, as well as fine art.

Sagamore

8 *3½ mi northwest of Sandwich.*

Sagamore, on the north-shore of the Cape, is where you'll find a factory-outlet mall and a large Christmas Tree Shop, a fun place to browse for both secular and Christmas-related bric-a-brac. At **Pairpoint Crys-**

tal you can watch colored lead crystal being hand-blown (weekdays 9—4:30), as it has been for 150 years, and buy the finished wares. ⊠ *Rte. 6A, Sagamore,* ☎ *508/888–2344.* ⊙ *Daily 8:30–6.*

Not far from Sagamore, before crossing the bridge from the "mainland," **Water Wizz Water Park** is a great treat for kids and young-at-heart adults. There's a 50-foot-high water slide, a river ride, a six-story tube ride, a kiddie water park, an arcade, volleyball, miniature golf, food concessions, and a cabana area here. A highlight is the enclosed Black Wizard slide that descends 75 feet in darkness. ⊠ *Rtes. 6 and 28, Wareham,* ☎ *508/295–3255.* ⊠ *$16.* ⊙ *Memorial Day–mid-June, weekends 11–4; mid-June–Labor Day, daily 10–6:30.*

OFF THE BEATEN PATH

At the 22,000-acre **Massachusetts Military Reservation** (known as Otis Air Base) in Bourne, an Air National Guard tour includes a film, a look into F–15 fighter planes, a tour of the aircraft museum, and, sometimes, observation of flying drills. Reservations for group tours, which last approximately 1½ hours, must be made well in advance. Call the Air National Guard (☎ 508/968-4090) or the Army National Guard (☎ 508/968-5975) for more information. The Cape Cod Air Show, on the first weekend in August, spotlights precision-flying teams, a military band, and static displays (☎ 508/968-4090 or 508/968-4003).

Dining

$$ ✕ **The Bridge.** The Yankee pot roast is the star of the eclectic menu, ★ which also includes *bijoux de la mer* (lobster, scallops, and shrimp with lemon and tarragon on pasta with a smoky mushroom-cream sauce). The several small dining rooms have recessed lighting and linen tablecloths. ⊠ *Rte. 6A,* ☎ *508/888–8144. D, DC, MC, V.*

Shopping

Cape Cod Factory Outlet Mall (⊠ Factory Outlet Rd., Exit 1 off Rte. 6, ☎ 508/888–8417) has more than 20 outlets. **Christmas Tree Shops** (⊠ Exit 1 off Rte. 6, ☎ 508/888–7010; 6 other locations) are a Cape Cod tradition. Fun, not fancy, they offer discounted secular and Christmas-related "stuff" of all kinds: paper goods, candles, home furnishings, kitchen items.

Sandwich

❾ *16 mi west of Barnstable.*

Founded in 1637, Sandwich is the oldest town on the Cape, and one of the most charming. It remains famous for the striking colored glass that was produced here at the Boston & Sandwich Glass Co. from 1825 until 1888, when competition with glassmakers in the Midwest closed the factory. The **Sandwich Glass Museum** contains artifacts of the early history of the town, as well as an outstanding collection of Sandwich glass. ⊠ *129 Main St., Rte. 130,* ☎ *508/888–0251.* ⊠ *$3.50.* ⊙ *Apr.–Oct., daily 9:30–4:30; Nov.–Dec. and Feb.–Mar., Wed.–Sun. 9:30–4.*

The **Hoxie House** is a restored shingle saltbox virtually unaltered since it was built in 1675. Overlooking Shawme Pond and the waterwheel-operated gristmill, it has been furnished authentically to reflect the Colonial period and has a collection of antique textile machines. ⊠ *Rte. 130,* ☎ *508/888–1173.* ⊠ *$1.50.* ⊙ *Mid-June–mid-Oct., Mon.–Sat. 10–5, Sun. 1–5.*

Heritage Plantation, on 76 beautifully landscaped acres, is a complex of several museum buildings and gardens, including an extensive rhododendron grove. Its Shaker Round Barn showcases classic and historic cars. The Military Museum exhibits miniature soldiers and antique firearms. The Art Museum has Currier & Ives prints and an outstanding collection of Elmer Crowell carvings. ⊠ *Grove and Pine Sts.,* ☎ *508/888–3300.* ☜ *$8.* ☉ *Mid-May–Oct., daily 10–5.*

Ⓒ The kids will enjoy **Green Briar Nature Center and Jam Kitchen.** It has changing exhibits on natural history, a full summer program of nature classes, self-guided walks through 52 acres of Sandwich Conservation land, and weekday tours of the Jam Kitchen. ⊠ *6 Discovery Hill Rd., off Rte. 6A, East Sandwich,* ☎ *508/888–6870.*

North of Sandwich center (take Jarves St. past the train depot, turn left onto Factory Street, then right onto Harbor St.), the **Sandwich Boardwalk** provides a breathtaking walk over marsh, creek, and low dunes, ending at Town Neck Beach, a rocky beach with a sandy strip near the dunes. After Mother Nature took out the old boardwalk, town residents and businesses donated planks and volunteers rebuilt the walk. Inscribed on the planks are donors' names, jokes, thoughts, and memorials to lovers, grandparents, and boats. From the platform at the end, there's a very nice view (especially at sunset) of a long sweep of bay in both directions, the white cliffs beyond Sagamore, Sandy Neck, stone jetties, dunes and waving grasses, and the entrance to the canal. If you have a canoe, the creeks running through the salt marsh would make for great paddling.

Dining and Lodging

$ ✕ **Marshland Restaurant and Bakery.** If you eat out every meal, vacation dining can get very expensive. This tiny coffee shop is the sure antidote to overspending. Entrées are consistently delicious, and daily specials are very good, especially prime rib (eat your heart out!) and a chicken stir fry. For breakfast, try an Italian omelet, a rich mix of Italian sausage, fresh vegetables, and cheese. ⊠ *Rte. 6A,* ☎ *508/888–9824.* ☉ *Tues.–Sat; breakfast only Sun.; no dinner Mon. No credit cards.*

$$–$$$ ✕▥ **Dan'l Webster Inn.** This classy, traditional inn has an excellent
★ restaurant. The glassed-in conservatory displays luxuriant greenery while the main dining rooms, one with a working fireplace, have a traditional Colonial look; the fourth dining room is Victorian. Expect to be just as delighted with the bread presented before dinner as with such dishes as striped bass crusted with cashews and macadamia nuts, accompanied by mango sauce. The inn also prepares hearty and elegant breakfasts and Sunday brunches. Full of friendliness and warmth, this inn may look old, but it was in fact built in 1971. Guest rooms are decorated with fine reproduction furnishings, including some canopy beds. All rooms have cable TV, phones, and air-conditioning; some suites have fireplaces or whirlpools. ⊠ *149 Main St., 02563,* ☎ *508/888–3622 or 800/444–3566,* ⅃ⅨⅩ *508/888–5156. 37 rooms, 9 suites. Restaurant, bar, pool, golf privileges. AE, D, DC, MC, V.*

$–$$ ▥ **Captain Ezra Nye House.** Staying with Elaine and Harry Dickson is as much a pleasure as is this B&B's heart-of-town location. Whether informing you of their house or town's history, serving delicious breakfasts, or suggesting activities day or night, the Dicksons will make a difference in your stay in Sandwich. The house isn't crammed with state-of-the-period pieces or overly precious from a museum-like restoration. Instead, it is brimming with the kind of hospitality for which there is no substitute. ⊠ *152 Main St.,* ☎ *508/888–6142. 6 rooms, 2 suites. Full breakfast included. No smoking. No pets.*

$–$$ ▥ **Earl of Sandwich Motor Manor.** Single-story Tudor-style buildings form a U around a wooded lawn with a duck pond. The decor is a bit somber—dark paneled walls, exposed beams on white ceilings, olive leatherette wing chairs, Oriental throw rugs on slate or carpeted floors—but rooms are a good size, with large Tudor-style windows, small tiled baths, color cable TV, and telephones. Most have air-conditioning. ⊠ *378 Rte. 6A, East Sandwich 02537,* ☎ *508/888–1415 or 800/442–3275. 24 rooms. CP. AE, D, DC, MC, V.*

Shopping

H. Richard Strand (⊠ Town Hall Sq., ☎ 508/888–3230), in an 1800 home, displays fine pre-1840 and Victorian antique furniture, paintings, American glass, and more. **Titcomb's Bookshop** (⊠ 432 Rte. 6A, East Sandwich, ☎ 508/888–2331) has used, rare, and new books, including a large collection of Cape and nautical titles and an extensive collection of children's books.

State Forest and Reservation

Scusset Beach Reservation (⊠ In Sandwich, off Rte. 3; mailing address: 140 Scusset Beach Rd., Buzzards Bay 02532, ☎ 508/888–0859), attracting primarily RV campers, comprises 490 acres near the canal, with a long beach on the bay. Its pier is a popular fishing spot; biking, hiking, picnicking, and swimming are also popular.

Activities at **Shawme-Crowell State Forest** (⊠ Rte. 130, 02563, ☎ 508/888–0351), on 742 acres near the canal, include wooded tent and RV camping, biking, hiking, and swimming at Scusset Beach.

Barnstable

⑩ *2 mi west of Yarmouth Port.*

The town of Barnstable comprises several "villages" including West Barnstable, Centerville, Cotuit, Hyannis, Hyannis Port, Osterville, Marston's Mills, Mashpee, and Barnstable Village. The area is scenic with lovely old homes and historical properties. The listings below include sites found in these different villages; not all are central to Barnstable Village itself and may require a bit of traveling.

Beach

Sandy Neck Beach in West Barnstable, a 6-mile barrier beach between the bay and marshland, is one of the Cape's most beautiful: a wide swath of pebbly sand backed by grassy dunes extending forever in both directions.

Dining and Lodging

$$$ ✕ **East Bay Lodge.** This casually elegant restaurant with an outstand-
★ ing waitstaff is set in an 1880 summer house with a glassed-in veranda. Favorites like wild mushroom tart and chilled poached salmon seem inspired every time. Chateaubriand Boquetière, the kitchen's signature dish, is perfectly prepared and is accompanied by an outstanding side plate of potato gratin, tomato confit, and asparagus with Bordelaise sauce. Sunday there's a lavish brunch buffet. The renowned Eddie Perkins jazz trio entertains evenings in the lounge. ⊠ *199 East Bay Rd., Osterville,* ☎ *508/428–5200. AE, D, DC, MC, V. Dinner and Sun. brunch only.*

$$$ ✕ **The Regatta of Cotuit.** Just like its sister restaurant in Falmouth, the
★ Regatta serves elegant American interpretations of local foods in an equally elegant setting. In a restored antique Colonial stagecoach inn, the restaurant is decorated with original wood and brass, and Oriental carpets. The original taproom is a cozy place for a rainy evening or for an early dinner from their more modest menu. In the dining room, classic yet original cuisine comes in the form of pâtés of rabbit, veal, and venison, and a signature seared loin of lamb with cabernet sauce,

surrounded by chèvre, spinach, and pine nuts. Three menus are served each night: lighter fare, regular fare, and a three-course early dinner menu. ⊠ *Rte. 28, Cotuit,* ☎ *508/428–5715. AE, D, MC, V. No lunch.*

$$ ✕ **The Flume.** This clean, plain fish house, decorated only with a few Native American artifacts and crafts (the owner is a Wampanoag chief), offers a small menu of simple, traditional dishes guaranteed to satisfy. The chowder is outstanding, perhaps the Cape's best. Other specialties are fried clams, Indian pudding, roast duck, and fresh broiled fish. ⊠ *Lake Ave. (off Rte. 130), Mashpee,* ☎ *508/477–1456. MC, V. Closed Dec.–Mar.*

$$$–$$$$ 🏠 **Ashley Manor.** This charming country inn, which has a relaxed and
   ★ homey atmosphere, dates to 1699. Large, well-appointed rooms have private baths, working fireplaces, and pencil-post or canopy beds; the Garden Cottage has an efficiency kitchen. In the sitting room are a large fireplace, piano, antiques, Oriental rugs, handsome country furniture, and a view of the brick terrace, lovely grounds, and a fountain garden. ⊠ *Box 856, 3660 Olde King's Hwy. (Rte. 6A), Barnstable 02630,* ☎ *508/362–8044. 2 rooms, 3 suites, 1 cottage. Tennis courts. Full breakfast included. AE, MC. V.*

$$$ 🏠 **The Inn at Fernbrook.** The inn's grounds, originally landscaped by
   ★ Frederick Law Olmsted, are striking. Paths wind past duck ponds blooming with water lilies, a heart-shaped sweetheart rose garden, and a windmill. The house itself, an 1881 Queen Anne Victorian mansion, is a beauty, from the turreted exterior to the fine woodwork and furnishings within. Some rooms have garden views; some have bay-window sitting areas and/or canopy beds, pastel Oriental carpets, and working fireplaces. ⊠ *481 Main St., Centerville 02632,* ☎ *508/775–4334,* 🆔 *508/778–4455. 4 rooms, 1 suite, 1 cottage. Full breakfast and afternoon beverages included. AE, D, MC, V.*

Outdoor Activities and Sports

FISHING

At **Barnstable Harbor** (☎ 508/362–3908), charters are available for deep-sea fishing.

WHALE-WATCHING

Out of Barnstable Harbor, **Hyannis Whale Watcher Cruises** (☎ 508/362–6088 or 800/287–0374; tours Apr.–Oct.), narrates cruises to the whales' feeding grounds via Cape Cod Bay.

Shopping

Eldred Wheeler (⊠ 866 Main St., Box 90, Osterville 02655, ☎ 508/428–9049) is well-known for handcrafting fine 18th-century furniture reproductions. **The Blacks Handweaving Shop** (⊠ 597 Rte. 6A, West Barnstable, ☎ 508/362–3955), in a barnlike building with looms upstairs and down, makes and sells beautiful shawls, scarves, throws, and more, in traditional and jacquard weaves.

Yarmouth Port

   ⑪ *5 mi southwest of Dennis.*

In Yarmouth Port, **Hallet's Store** (⊠ Rte. 6A, ☎ 508/362–3362), a country drugstore and soda fountain, is preserved as it was over a century ago; upstairs houses a collection of local artifacts and memorabilia (call for hours). Follow signs to Gray's Beach, where the **Bass Hole Boardwalk** extends out over a marshy creek.

   ☙ Yarmouth Port has a couple of fun places especially for kids. **ZooQuarium** has sea lion shows, a petting zoo with native wildlife, pony rides (in summer), aquariums, and a children's discovery center. ⊠ *Rte. 28,*

West Yarmouth, ☎ *508/775–8883.* ⌖ *$7.50.* ⊘ *Mid-Feb.–late Nov., daily 9:30–5; July–Aug. until 8.*

☾ **Pirate's Cove** is the most elaborate of the Cape's many miniature-golf emporiums. Two 18-hole courses designed by former Disney animation specialists have waterfalls and mountain caves. ⊠ *728 Main St. (Rte. 28), South Yarmouth,* ☎ *508/394–6200.* ⌖ *$6.* ⊘ *Summer, daily 9 AM–11 PM; spring and fall, daily 10–7:30 or 8.*

Dining and Lodging

$$–$$$ ✕ **Abbicci.** Unassuming to a fault from outside, the interior of Abbicci
★ tells an entirely different story, with stunning modern decor, explosions of color, and a compelling black slate bar. The menu finely tunes contemporary Italian, with a very light oil and fat content but rich and full tasting food. One of the latest, most pleasing dishes is braised rabbit with fresh green beans and tiny onions over garlic mashed potatoes. In summer, a dozen elegant pasta dishes and a few Continental favorites, such as rack of lamb, are on the menu, but the emphasis is on fish. ⊠ *43 Main St. (Rte. 6A), Yarmouth Port,* ☎ *508/362–3501. AE, D, DC, MC, V.*

$$$ ▦ **Wedgewood Inn.** A handsome 1812 Greek Revival building houses
★ this exceptional inn. The sophisticated country decor includes fine antiques, cherry pencil-post beds with antique quilts, period wallpapers, large Stobart sporting prints, and Oriental and hand-hooked rugs on wide-board floors. Rooms are large and air-conditioned, with (mostly) large baths. The suites have canopy beds, fireplaces, and porches. A gazebo enhances the gardens. ⊠ *83 Main St. (Rte. 6A), Yarmouth Port 02675,* ☎ *508/362–5157 or 508/362–9178. 4 rooms, 2 suites. Full breakfast and afternoon tea included. AE, DC, MC, V.*

Nightlife and the Arts

NIGHTLIFE

Oliver's restaurant (⊠ Rte. 6A, Yarmouth Port, ☎ 508/362–6062) has live guitar music weekends in its lounge. **The Compass** (⊠ Rte. 28, South Yarmouth, ☎ 508/394–4450) is a large nightclub with dancing to country western, rock, and Top 40 tunes, plus laser light shows and a 24-foot video screen. The **Mill Hill Club** (⊠ 164 Rte. 28, West Yarmouth, ☎ 508/775–2580) has live entertainment and DJ music, plus large-screen satellite sports and videos.

THE ARTS

The 100-member **Cape Cod Symphony** (⊠ Mattacheese Middle School, Higgins-Crowell Rd., West Yarmouth, ☎ 508/362–1111) gives regular and children's concerts, with guest artists, October through May.

Outdoor Activities and Sports

FISHING

Fishing licenses and rental gear are available at **Truman's** (⊠ Rte. 28, West Yarmouth, ☎ 508/771–3470).

TENNIS

Mid-Cape Racquet Club (⊠ 193 White's Path, South Yarmouth, ☎ 508/394–3511) has one outdoor all-weather and nine indoor tennis courts, two racquetball and two squash courts, and full health-club facilities.

Shopping

Cummaquid Fine Arts (⊠ 4275 Rte. 6A, Cummaquid, ☎ 508/362–2593) has works by Cape Cod and New England artists, plus decorative antiques, beautifully displayed in an old home. **Parnassus Book Service** (⊠ Rte. 6A, Yarmouth Port, ☎ 508/362–6420) offers a huge

selection—including Cape Cod, maritime, and antiquarian books—
housed in an 1840 former general store.

Dennis

⑫ *7 mi west of Brewster.*

In Dennis, **Scargo Hill,** the highest spot in the area at 160 feet, offers
a fine view of Scargo Lake and Cape Cod Bay.

Beach

West Dennis Beach is a long, wide, sandy beach on the warm south
shore, across from marshland and Bass River, offering windsurfer
rentals, all services, and lots of parking.

Dining

$$-$$$ ✕ **Red Pheasant Inn.** The main dining room is pleasantly intimate and
★   rustic, with antique pine floors, exposed beams, and two fireplaces.
The American regional cuisine has a refreshingly creative spin (tuna
pastrami, for example). Lamb, seafood, game, and pastas are always
on the long menu, and there's an award-winning, extensive wine list.
✉ *905 Main St. (Rte. 6A),* ☎ *508/385–2133. D, MC, V. No lunch.*

Nightlife and the Arts

NIGHTLIFE
Clancy's (✉ 8 Upper County Rd., Dennisport, ☎ 508/394–6661 and
175 Rte. 28, West Yarmouth ☎ 508/775–3332) features jazz piano.
Sundancer's (✉ 116 Rte. 28, West Dennis, ☎ 508/394–1600) has dancing to a DJ and live bands.

THE ARTS
Broadway-style shows and children's plays are performed at the **Cape
Playhouse** (✉ Off Rte. 6A, ☎ 508/385–3911).

Outdoor Activities and Sports

BIKING
Cape Cod Rail Trail, the paved right-of-way of the old Penn Central Railroad, is the Cape's premier bike path. Running 20 miles, from Dennis
to Eastham (with an extension underway), it passes salt marshes, cranberry bogs, and ponds, and cuts through Nickerson State Park. The
terrain is easy to moderate. The Butterworth Company (✉ 38 Rte. 134,
South Dennis 02660, ☎ 508/760–2000) sells a guide to the trail.

WATER SPORTS
Rental powerboats, sailboats, and canoes are available from **Cape Cod
Boats** (✉ Rte. 28 at Bass River Bridge, West Dennis, ☎ 508/394–9268).

Shopping

Eldred's (✉ 1483 Rte. 6A, Box 796, East Dennis 02641, ☎ 508/385–
3116), open year-round, auctions top-quality antiques and art as well
as "general antiques and accessories" (less-expensive wares). **Scargo
Pottery** (✉ Off Rte 6A on Dr. Lord's Rd. S, ☎ 508/385–3894) has
been a Cape favorite since 1953. In a pine forest, Harry Holl's unusual
wares—such as his signature castle bird feeders—are displayed on tree
stumps and hanging from branches. More pottery and the workshop
and kiln are indoors. With luck you'll catch a potter at the wheel; watching is encouraged.

Brewster

⑬ *6 mi west of Orleans.*

Brewster, in the early 1800s the terminus of a packet cargo service from
Boston, was home to many seafaring families. Many of the stately man-

sions built for sea captains remain today, and quite a few have been turned into bed-and-breakfasts.

The **Cape Cod Museum of Natural History** has environmental and marine exhibits, guided field walks, and self-guided trails through 80 acres rich in wildlife. ⊠ *Rte. 6A,* ☎ *508/896–3867.* ☞ *$4.* ☉ *Mon.–Sat. 9:30–4:30, Sun. 12:30–4:30.*

☾ **Bassett Wild Animal Farm** has lions, tigers, birds, monkeys, and llamas on 20 acres, plus hayrides, pony rides, a petting zoo, and a picnic area. ⊠ *Tubman Rd., between Rtes. 124 and 137,* ☎ *508/896–3224.* ☞ *$5.75.* ☉ *Mid-May–mid-Sept., daily 10–5.*

Dining and Lodging

$$$$ ✕ **Chillingsworth.** This is surely the crown jewel of Cape Cod restau-
★ rants, extremely formal, terribly pricey, and outstanding in every way. The menu and wine cellar continue to win award after award, and the classic French cuisine is tops. Every night, the seven-course table d'hôte menu ($40–$56) changes, cycling through an assortment of appetizers, entrées and "amusements." Recent favorites are caramelized sea scallops and roast lobster. At dinner, a more modest bistro menu is served in the Garden Room. ⊠ *2449 Main St. (Rte. 6A),* ☎ *508/896–3640. AE, DC, MC, V. Closed Mon., mid-June–mid-Oct.; closed weekdays Memorial Day–mid-June and mid-Oct.–Thanksgiving; closed Thanks-giving–Memorial Day.*

$$$ ✕ **High Brewster.** A romantic country inn overlooking a pond, this restored farmhouse with dark exposed beams, wide paneling, gilt-frame oil paintings, and Oriental carpeting serves seasonal four-course prix-fixe meals; a fall menu might include pumpkin-and-sage bisque and tenderloin medallions with chives and cheese sauce. ⊠ *964 Satucket Rd.,* ☎ *508/896–3636. Reservations essential. AE, MC, V. No lunch. Call for off-season hrs, mid-Sept.–mid-June.*

$$–$$$ 🏠 **Captain Freeman Inn.** The ground floor of this 1866 Victorian is
★ impressive, with 12-foot ceilings and windows, ornate plaster ceiling medallions, and seating around a marble fireplace. Common areas include the wraparound veranda, a screened porch, and a backyard bordered in wild grapes and berries. Guest rooms have high ceilings, grand windows, and antiques and Victorian reproductions. "Luxury suites" offer queen canopy beds, fireplaces, cable TVs and VCRs, minifridges, and enclosed balconies with private hot tubs. No smoking. ⊠ *15 Breakwater Rd., 02631,* ☎ *508/896–7481 or 800/843–4664,* 🖷 *508/896–5618. 12 rooms (3 share bath). In-room VCRs, pool, badminton, croquet, health club, bicycles. Full breakfast and afternoon tea included. AE, MC, V.*

Outdoor Activities and Sports

Brewster has some fine golf courses. **Ocean Edge Golf Course** (832 Villages Dr., ☎ 508/896–5911) is the top championship course, with 18 holes. **Captain's Golf Course** (⊠ 1000 Freeman's Way, ☎ 508/896–5100), also has 18 holes.

Shopping

Kingsland Manor (⊠ 440 Main St., Rte. 6A, West Brewster, ☎ 508/385–9741) is like a fairyland, with ivy covering the facade, fountains in the courtyard, and everything "from tin to Tiffany" from end to end. **The Spectrum** (⊠ 369 Rte. 6A, Brewster, ☎ 508/385–3322; 342 Main St., Hyannis, ☎ 508/771–4554) showcases imaginative American arts and crafts, including pottery, jewelry, stained glass, art glass, and more. **Sydenstricker Galleries** (⊠ Rte. 6A, ☎ 508/385–3272) sells glassware handcrafted by a unique process, which you can watch in progress at the studio on the premises.

State Park

Nickerson State Park (⊠ 3488 Main St., 02631-1521, ☎ 508/896–3491; map available on-site) is almost 2,000 acres of forest with eight freshwater kettle ponds stocked with trout for fishing. Other recreational options are camping, biking, canoeing, sailing, motorboating, bird-watching, and cross-country skiing in winter.

Eastham

⑭ *2½ mi north of Orleans.*

Just beyond the village of Eastham is the headquarters of the **Cape Cod National Seashore,** established in 1961 to preserve the Lower Cape's natural and historic resources. Within the Seashore are superb ocean beaches; great rolling dunes; forests, swamps, marshes, and wetlands; scrub and grasslands; and all kinds of wildlife.

The **Salt Pond Visitor Center** has displays, literature, and an auditorium for nature films. ⊠ *Off Rte. 6,* ☎ *508/255–3421.* ⊙ *Mar.–Dec., daily 9–4:30 (until 6 July–Aug.); Jan.–Feb., weekends 9–4:30.*

From the Visitor Center, roads and bicycle trails lead to **Coast Guard Beach, Nauset Light Beach,** and the **Nauset Light.** You can hike to a marsh and to Salt Pond. From Memorial Day to Labor Day, park guides lead daily nature walks and lectures.

Lodging

$$$–$$$$ ☆ **Whalewalk Inn.** This stately Georgian inn, one of the best in the
★ Eastern United States, dates to when Maine was just beginning to break away from Massachusetts. Period antiques successfully blend with designer fabrics in a light and breezy manor atypical of Cape Cod. Rooms are sumptuous and romantic, the hospitality is genuine, and the gourmet breakfasts are divine. There are accommodations in several structures on the property, including a barn and a saltbox. ⊠ *220 Bridge Rd., 02642,* ☎ *508/255–0617. 12 rooms and suites. MC, V. Full breakfast included. Closed Dec.–Mar.*

Outdoor Activities and Sports

BIKING

The **Cape Cod National Seashore** maintains three bicycle trails. (A brochure with maps is available at visitor centers.) **Nauset Trail** is 1.6 miles, from Salt Pond Visitor Center in Eastham to Coast Guard Beach.

CAMPING

Camping is not permitted within the National Seashore, however there are many private campgrounds throughout the Cape. Nickerson State Park is a favorite tent and RV camping spot for its setting and wildlife, and Shawme-Crowell State Forest has tent, trailer, and motor-home sites on 742 acres.

Wellfleet

⑮ *10 mi north of Eastham.*

Wellfleet was once the site of a large oyster industry and, along with Truro to the north, a Colonial whaling and codfishing port. It is one of the more tastefully developed Cape resort towns, with fine restaurants, historic homes, and art and crafts galleries.

At the Seashore's **Marconi Station** is a model of the first transatlantic wireless station erected on the U.S. mainland. From here, Guglielmo

Marconi sent the first American wireless message to Europe on January 18, 1903. ⊠ *Off Rte. 6, South Wellfleet,* ☎ *508/349–3785.* ☉ *Weekdays 8–4:30.*

🖑 **Wellfleet Bay Wildlife Sanctuary** is a 1,000-acre haven for more than 250 species of birds, attracted by the varied habitats found here. Hiking trails lead through woods, past moors and salt marshes that rim Cape Cod Bay—where you can take in beautiful sunsets any time of year. Many activities, such as guided birding, day camp for children, marsh cruises, canoe and kayak trips, and evening bat watches are offered; a schedule is available on-site, or write for one. A nature center has aquariums and other exhibits, plus a gift shop. ⊠ *Off Rte. 6 (Box 236), South Wellfleet 02663,* ☎ *508/349–2615.* 🎫 *$3.* ☉ *Daily 8 AM–dusk.*

Dining

$$$ ✗ **Aesop's Tables.** A worthy choice for a special dinner, Aesop's specializes in delightful seafood entrées, and appetizers that often take the local Wellfleet oyster to new heights. Aim for a table on the porch of this antique 19th-century home, overlooking the center of town. The signature dish is an exotic bouillabaisse, with mounds of seafood and a hot saffron broth. Death by Chocolate, a heavy mousse cake, is as splendid as everyone says. On Thursday night in summer, there's live jazz in the tavern, where the mood and the menu are more casual. ⊠ *316 Main St.,* ☎ *508/349–6450. AE, DC, MC, V. Closed Columbus Day–Mother's Day. No lunch.*

$ ✗ **Flying Fish Cafe.** An anytime breakfast spot like this is a welcome discovery. Great omelets, "green eggs and ham," (green veggies, ham, and cheese), and something called "risky home fries," (home fries with cheese and veggies)—you'll probably end up at the Flying Fish more than once. Lunch and dinner are also served, and the owners are planning to have take-out barbecue. ⊠ *Briar La. east of Main,* ☎ *508/349–3100. Reservations not accepted. MC, V. Closed mid-Oct.–mid-Apr.*

Nightlife and the Arts

NIGHTLIFE

Beachcomber (⊠ Cahoon Hollow Beach, off Rte. 6, ☎ 508/349–6055) is a beachfront restaurant and dance club, open day and night for live rock and reggae in summer.

THE ARTS

May–October, **Wellfleet Harbor Actors Theatre** (⊠ Wellfleet town pier, ☎ 508/349–6835) performs mostly serious drama, but also stages farce and satire.

Shopping

Blue Heron Gallery (⊠ Bank St., ☎ 508/349–6724) is one of the Cape's best, with representational contemporary art by regional and nationally recognized artists. **Hannah** (⊠ Main St., ☎ 508/349–9884) has upscale women's fashions in unusual styles. **The Wellfleet Drive-In Theatre** (⊠ Rte. 6, Eastham–Wellfleet line, ☎ 508/349–2520) is the site of a giant flea market (mid-Apr.–Oct., weekends and Mon. holidays 8–4; July–Aug., also Wed. and Thurs.). The drive-in theater shows movies throughout the summer; a four-screen indoor cinema screens films year-round.

Truro

🔞 *5 mi north of Wellfleet.*

Truro is popular with writers and artists for its high dunes and virtual lack of development. The most prominent painter to have lived here was Edward Hopper, who found the Cape's light ideal for his austere brand of realism.

Follow signs to the **Pilgrim Heights Area** of the National Seashore. *Mayflower* passengers explored this area for weeks before settling in Plymouth; a short walking trail leads to the spring where a Pilgrim party stopped to refill its casks.

Outdoor Activities and Sports

BIKING

Head of the Meadow Trail is 2 miles of easy cycling between sand dunes and salt marshes from High Head Road, off Route 6A in North Truro, to the Head of the Meadow Beach parking lot. The **Cape Cod National Seashore** maintains three bicycle trails; a brochure with maps is available at visitor centers.

Provincetown

⑰ *12 mi northwest of Truro.*

Provincetown has spectacular beaches and dunes, as well as first-rate shops and galleries, lots of nightlife, and a wide variety of restaurants. Portuguese and American fisherfolk mix with painters, poets, writers, whale-watching tourists, and a steady nesting of gays and lesbians. During the early 1900s Provincetown became known as Greenwich Village North. Inexpensive summer lodgings close to the beaches attracted young rebels and artists, including John Reed, Sinclair Lewis, and Eugene O'Neill. Some of O'Neill's early plays were presented first in Provincetown. More recent glitterati include Norman Mailer and Pulitzer Prize–winning poet Stanley Kunitz. The Historical Society publishes a series of walking-tour pamphlets, available for less than $1 each at many shops in town, with maps and information on the history of many buildings and the famous folk who have occupied them.

The Seashore's **Province Lands Area** comprises Race Point and Herring Cove beaches, a picnic area, and bike, horse, and nature trails through forest and vast duneland. The visitor center has films and exhibits. ☎ *508/487–1256.* ☉ *Mid-Apr.–Nov., daily 9–5 (until 6 July–Aug.)*

Provincetown's main tourist attraction is the **Pilgrim Monument,** on a hill above the town center, commemorating the landing of the Pilgrims in 1620. From atop the 252-foot-high granite tower, there's a panoramic view of the entire Cape. At the base, a historical museum houses a diorama of the *Mayflower* and exhibits on whaling, shipwrecks, and more. ☎ *508/487–1310.* ☞ *$5.* ☉ *Apr.–Nov., daily 9–5.*

MacMillan Wharf is a center for whale-watching and fishing excursion boats. Plans are underway to open a museum on the wharf to house and conserve the items recovered from the shipwreck of the *Whydah,* a pirate ship loaded with treasure that sunk off the coast of Wellfleet in 1717.

Beach

Beaches surround Provincetown—harbor beaches, bay beaches, and open ocean beaches. All of the Atlantic Ocean beaches on the **National Seashore** are superior—wide, long, sandy, dune-backed, with great views. They're also contiguous: you can walk from Eastham to Provincetown almost without leaving sand. **Race Point Beach** and **Herring Cove** both have lifeguards and rest rooms; only Herring Cove has food.

Dining and Lodging

$$$ ✕ **Ciro's and Sal's.** Opened in 1950, this stage-set Italian restaurant—
★   raffia-covered Chianti bottles hanging from the rafters, walls of plaster and brick, strains of Italian opera in the air—plays out its role with the confidence of years on the boards. Scampi alla Griglia is grilled shrimp

in lemon, parsley, garlic, butter, leeks, and shallots; veal and pasta dishes are specialties. ✉ *4 Kiley Court,* ☎ *508/487–0049. Reservations essential in summer and Sat. yr-round. MC, V. Closed Mon.–Thurs. Nov.–Memorial Day. No lunch.*

$$–$$$ ✕ **Cafe Edwige.** Delicious contemporary food, interesting fellow diners, relaxed and friendly service, a tastefully homey and eclectic upstairs setting—it's hard to argue with the good feeling of a night at Cafe Edwige. Consider lobster and Wellfleet scallops over pasta with a wild mushroom, Asiago, and tomato broth, or planked local codfish with roasted corn and shiitakes. Don't pass on wonderful desserts, and remember that the café is open for a very tasty breakfast. ✉ *333 Commercial St., upstairs,* ☎ *508/487–2008. AE, MC, V. Closed late Oct.–Mar.*

$$–$$$ ✕ **Front Street.** In the cellar of a Victorian mansion, this intimate,
★ bistro-like restaurant is easy to miss . . . but don't! The herb-crusted rack of lamb, topped with cloves of roasted garlic, is the best on the Cape, and is always offered in addition to a diverse Continental menu that changes every Friday. The wine list is extensive and award-winning. ✉ *230 Commercial St.,* ☎ *508/487–9715. AE, MC, V. Closed Jan.–Apr.*

$$ ✕ **Gloria's.** Authentically Portuguese with a couple of Italian selections on the menu, this busy place serves hearty helpings in a bustling atmosphere. Gloria is famous for her kale soup. Her specialty, *mariscada,* is a big pot of fresh seafood stew with lobster, shrimp, scallops, and Gloria's special sauce. Arrive early to avoid a long wait. ✉ *269 Commercial St.,* ☎ *508/487–0015. Reservations not accepted. D, MC, V.*

$$$ 🏠 **Hargood House.** This apartment complex on the water is a great option for longer stays and families. Most of the individually decorated units have decks and large water-view windows; all have kitchens and modern baths. Apartment 8 is on the water, with three glass walls, cathedral ceilings, and private deck; apartment 7 is its mirror image, on the ground floor. Rental is mostly by the week in season; two-night minimum off-season. ✉ *493 Commercial St., 02657,* ☎ FAX *508/487–9133. 19 apartments. Beach. AE, MC, V.*

$$ 🏠 **The Fairbanks Inn.** Just one block from Provincetown's busy Commercial Street, this comfortable inn has cozy rooms filled with antique and reproduction furnishings. Rooms in the 1776 main house have four-poster or canopy beds and Oriental rugs. All rooms have cable TV and air-conditioning; some have kitchens or working fireplaces. ✉ *90 Bradford St., 02657,* ☎ *508/487–0386. 13 rooms, 1 efficiency, 1 2-bedroom apartment. CP. AE, D, MC, V.*

Nightlife

Club Euro (✉ 258 Commercial St., ☎ 508/487–2505) has world-music concerts weekends in season, plus blues and Sunday reggae in a funky room painted as an underwater dreamscape.

Outdoor Activities and Sports

BIKING

Province Lands Trail is a 5¼-mile loop off the Beech Forest parking lot, with spurs to Herring Cove and Race Point beaches and Bennett Pond. A brochure with maps is available at visitor centers.

FISHING

Deep-sea fishing trips are operated on a walk-on basis by **Cap'n Bill & Cee Jay** (✉ MacMillan Wharf, ☎ 508/487–4330 or 800/675–6723).

HORSEBACK RIDING

The **Province Lands Horse Trails** meander to the beaches through or past dunes, cranberry bogs, forests, and ponds. **Nelson's Riding Stables** (✉ 43 Race Point Rd., ☎ 508/487–1112) gives trail rides.

Bissell's Tennis Courts (✉ Bradford St. at Herring Cove Beach Rd., ☎ 508/487–9512; ⊙ Memorial Day–Sept.) has five clay courts and offers lessons.

Flyer's (✉ 131A Commercial St., ☎ 508/487–0898) rents sailboats, Sunfish, canoes, outboards, and rowboats, and teaches sailing.

Provincetown is close to the feeding grounds at Stellwagen Bank, 6 miles to the north. Several operators offer whale-watch tours from April through October, with morning, afternoon, or sunset cruises lasting three to four hours. Tickets are available at booths on MacMillan Wharf. **Dolphin Fleet** (☎ 508/349–1900 or 800/826–9300) tours are accompanied by scientists from Provincetown's Center for Coastal Studies, who provide commentary while collecting data on the whale population they've been monitoring for years.

Shopping

Remembrances of Things Past (✉ 376 Commercial St., ☎ 508/487–9443) deals in Bakelite jewelry, photographs, neon, telephones, and other articles dating from the 1920s to the 1960s. **Long Point Gallery** (✉ 492 Commercial St., ☎ 508/487–1795) is a cooperative of several well-established artists, including Robert Motherwell.

UFO Gallery (✉ 424 Commercial St., ☎ 508/487–4424) has 20th-century and contemporary master prints, Picasso ceramics, and features artists from the Provincetown, Boston, and New York region. **Provincetown Art Association and Museum** (✉ 460 Commercial St., ☎ 508/487–1750) has a gift shop with many books on Provincetown and its artists.

Cape Cod A to Z

Arriving and Departing

The **Cape Cod Regional Transit Authority** (☎ 508/385–8326 or 800/352–7155 in MA) offers its Sea Line service between Barnstable Village and Woods Hole, with stops at popular destinations; the buses can be flagged along the route. **Plymouth & Brockton Street Railway** (☎ 508/746–0378 or 508/775–5524) has service from Boston and Logan Airport to Hyannis, and from Hyannis to Provincetown, with stops at many towns in between. **Bonanza** (☎ 508/548–7588 or 800/556–3815) serves Bourne, Falmouth, Woods Hole, and Hyannis. All service is year-round.

From Boston (60 mi), take Route 3 south to the Sagamore Bridge. From New York (220 mi), take I–95 north to Providence; change to I–195 and follow signs for the Cape to the Bourne Bridge. Both roads connect to Route 6, running the length of the Cape. In summer, avoid arriving at the bridges in late afternoon, especially on holidays: All the major roads are heavily congested eastbound on Friday night and westbound on Sunday afternoon.

Getting Around

The Cape will satisfy both the avid and the occasional cyclist. The terrain is fairly flat, and there are several bike trails. Rentals are available at **Arnold's** (✉ 329 Commercial St., Provincetown, ☎ 508/487–0844), **Cascade Motor Lodge** (✉ 201 Main St., one block from the Nantucket ferry, near the bus and train station, Hyannis, ☎

508/775–9717), **Idle Times** (✉ Off the RailTrail in Nickerson State Park, Rte. 6A, Brewster; Bracket Rd. in N. Eastham; Rte. 6 at Wellfleet; and main office on Rte. 6 at N. Eastham, ☎ 508/255–8281), **The Little Capistrano** (✉ Across from Salt Pond Visitor Center, Rte. 6, Eastham, ☎ 508/255–6515), **Outdoor Shop** (✉ 50 Long Pond Dr., South Yarmouth, ☎ 508/394–3819), and **P&M Cycles** (✉ Across from canal path, 29 Main St., Buzzards Bay, ☎ 508/759–2830).

BY TROLLEY
Trolley service to transport passengers from town to town is in the works, and should be available by 1997.

Contacts and Resources

CAR RENTALS
Avis (☎ 508/775–2888). **Budget** (☎ 508/771–2744). **Hertz** (☎ 508/775–5825). **National** (☎ 508/771–4353).

EMERGENCIES
Cape Cod Hospital (✉ 27 Park St., Hyannis, ☎ 508/771–1800). **Falmouth Hospital** (✉ 100 Ter Heun Dr., Falmouth, ☎ 508/548–5300).

FISHING
Charter boats and party boats (per-head fees, rather than charters' group rates) take you offshore for tuna, marlin, and mako and blue sharks. The Cape Cod Chamber of Commerce's *Fresh and Saltwater Fishing Guide* has lots of useful information.

GUIDED TOURS
Cape Cod Canal Cruises (two or three hours, narrated) leave from Onset, just northwest of the Bourne Bridge. A Sunday jazz cruise, sunset cocktail cruises, and Friday and Saturday evening dance cruises are available. ✉ *Onset Bay Town Pier,* ☎ *508/295–3883.* ⊠ *$6.50–$12.* ☾ *Tours May–mid-Oct.*

Hy-Line narrates one-hour tours of Hyannis Harbor (including a view of the Kennedy compound), sunset and evening cocktail cruises. ✉ *Ocean St. dock, Pier 1, Hyannis,* ☎ *508/778–2600.* ⊠ *$8.* ☾ *Tours mid-May–mid-Oct.*

Capt. John Boats offers excursions to Provincetown from Plymouth. ✉ *State Pier, Plymouth,* ☎ *508/747–2400 or 800/242–2469 in MA.* ⊠ *Round-trip $22.* ☾ *Tours Memorial Day–Sept.*

Art's Dune Tours (✉ Commercial St. at Standish, ☎ 508/487–1950 or 800/894–1951) gives hour-long narrated auto tours through the National Seashore and dunes around Provincetown, mid-April–late October.

The **Massachusetts Audubon Society** (contact Wellfleet Bay Wildlife Sanctuary, ✉ *Box 236, South Wellfleet 02663,* ☎ *508/349–2615) sponsors year-round, naturalist-led wildlife tours, including trips to Monomoy Island, cruises in Nauset Marsh and Pleasant Bay, and popular marine-life cruises in Cape Cod Bay.*

The **Cape Cod Museum of Natural History** (✉ Box 1710, Brewster, MA 02631, ☎ 508/896–3867) offers year-round naturalist-led walks, including summer nature walks in Chatham's Monomoy National Wildlife Refuge and an overnight in the island lighthouse. For a relaxing afternoon, take a two-hour boat ride through Nauset Marsh, or try canoeing on one of the Cape's ponds or rivers.

Sightseeing tours by air are offered by **Hyannis Air Service** (Barnstable airport, ☎ 508/775–8171), **Cape Cod Flying Service** (✉ Cape Cod Airport, Rte. 149 at 1000 Race La., Marstons Mills, ☎ 508/428–8732), and **Cape Air** (✉ Provincetown airport, ☎ 508/487–0241 or 800/352–

0714). Cape Air also gives rides in a 1930 Stinson; Cape Cod Flying Service has a 1938 biplane replica.

Cape Cod Scenic Railroad runs 1¾-hour excursions between Sagamore and Hyannis with a stop in Sandwich. The train passes ponds, cranberry bogs, and marshes. A dinner run is also offered some evenings; call for schedule. ⊠ *Main and Center Sts., Hyannis,* ☎ *508/771–3788.* 🎫 *$11.50.* ☉ *Several departures daily (except Mon.) in each direction mid–June–Oct.*

PHARMACY

Most of the Cape's 20 **CVS** stores, such as the one in the Cape Cod Mall in Hyannis (☎ 508/771–1774), are open daily until 9 PM.

RESERVATION AGENCIES

B&B reservations services include **House Guests Cape Cod and the Islands** (⊠ Box 1881, Orleans 02653, ☎ 508/896–7053 or 800/666–4678) and **Bed and Breakfast Cape Cod** (⊠ Box 341, West Hyannis Port 02672–0341,☎ 508/775–2772, 508/775–2884). **DestINNations** (☎ 800/333–4667) will arrange any and all details of a visit. **Provincetown Reservations System** (☎ 508/487–2400 or 800/648–0364) is a full-service travel agency that makes reservations year-round for accommodations, shows, restaurants, transportation, and condos. In summer, lodgings should be booked as far in advance as possible—several months for the most popular cottages and bed-and-breakfasts. Assistance with last-minute reservations is available at the **Cape Cod Chamber of Commerce information booths** by the two bridges in season.

SHOPPING

Write for a free "Provincetown Gallery Guide" (Provincetown Gallery Guild, Box 242, Provincetown 02657) or a free walking map of Wellfleet's art galleries and restaurants (Wellfleet Art Galleries Assoc., Box 916, Wellfleet 02667).

VISITOR INFORMATION

The main source of information on the Cape is the **Cape Cod Chamber of Commerce** (⊠ Rtes. 6 and 132, Hyannis 02601, ☎ 508/362–3225; ☉ Weekdays 8:30–5 and, Memorial Day–Columbus Day, weekends 9–4). Information booths are open daily 9–4, Memorial Day through Columbus Day, at the Sagamore Bridge rotary (☎ 508/888–2438) and just over the Bourne Bridge on Route 28 (☎ 508/759–3814) heading toward Falmouth.

MARTHA'S VINEYARD

Updated by
Dorothy
Antczak

Much less developed than Cape Cod, yet more diverse and cosmopolitan than neighboring Nantucket, Martha's Vineyard has a split personality. From Memorial Day through Labor Day this island southeast of Woods Hole is a vibrant, star-studded event. Seekers of chic descend in droves on the boutiques of Edgartown and the main port of Vineyard Haven. Summer regulars return, including such celebrities as William Styron, Art Buchwald, Walter Cronkite, and Carly Simon.

But in the off-season the island becomes a place of peace and simple beauty. The beaches, always lovely, can now be appreciated in private. Free from the throng of other cars, bikes, and mopeds, there's time to linger over pastoral views on drives along country lanes. Though the pace is slower, cultural and recreational events continue, and a number of inns, shops, and restaurants remain open (only Edgartown and Oak Bluffs allow the sale of liquor; in the "dry" towns restaurants are glad to provide setups).

The island's maximum distances are about 20 miles east to west and 10 miles north to south. Aside from the three main towns, much of its 130 square miles is undeveloped.

Numbers in the margin correspond to points of interest on the Martha's Vineyard map.

Vineyard Haven

⑱ *6 mi northwest of Edgartown.*

Most visitors to Martha's Vineyard arrive by ferry at Vineyard Haven (officially named Tisbury), the year-round commercial center of the island. **Main Street,** lined with shops and eating places, is just up the hill from the steamship terminal. The next block up from Main is **William Street,** a quiet, pretty stretch of white picket fences and Greek Revival houses, many of them built for prosperous sea captains. Now part of a National Historic District, the street was spared during the Great Fire of 1883, which claimed most of the old whaling and fishing town.

☾ Children can visit with llamas and miniature donkeys at **Takemmy Farm.** ⊠ *State Rd., North Tisbury,* ☎ *508/693–2486,* ⊡ *$3 per car.* ☉ *Mon.–Sat. 1–5.*

Dining and Lodging

$$$–$$$$ ★ ✕ **Le Grenier.** It's hard to picture a genuinely fine French restaurant in a dry town, but Le Grenier bears the standard with classic French preparations like *moules à la marinière* (mussels steamed in white wine), steak au poivre, and lobster Normande (flambéed with Calvados and served with fresh apples and cream sauce). Candlelight, fresh flowers, and a second-floor dining room—a mix of garret and garden room, with a slanted, slatted ceiling, and a screened porch where painted vine tendrils climb posts to the roof—overlooking the main street of Vineyard Haven add to the Continental feeling. The owners also operate Borderlands, the patisserie downstairs, which serves breakfast, lunch, and dinner with a southwestern flair. ⊠ *Upper Main St.,* ☎ *508/693–4906. AE, DC, MC, V. BYOB. No lunch.*

$$$ ✕ **Black Dog Tavern.** This Vineyard landmark sells more Black Dog T-shirts, coffee mugs, doodads, and hoo-has than anything else these days, but the food is surprisingly good. You can get a basic chowder and burger meal, as well as slightly pricey entrées such as grilled yellowfin tuna, baked stuffed squid, and baked cod with shrimp and leeks. Waiting for a table is something of a tradition. The decor is nautical and the glassed-in porch, lighted by ships' lanterns, looks directly out on the harbor. For a snack, try the Black Dog Bakery on Water Street, where you can buy the little loaves served with dinner as well as desserts and T-shirts. Some locals love an early breakfast at the restaurant. ⊠ *Beach St. Ext.,* ☎ *508/693–9223. Reservations not accepted. AE, D, MC, V. BYOB. No smoking.*

$$$–$$$$ ★ 🏠 **Thorncroft Inn.** Set on 3½ acres of woods about a mile from the ferry, the 1918 Craftsman bungalow is furnished with very fine Colonial and richly carved Renaissance Revival antiques and tasteful reproductions. The atmosphere is somewhat formal but not fussy. All rooms have air-conditioning, cable TV, telephones, and amenities such as bathrobes and hairdryers; some have wood-burning fireplaces, whirlpools, canopy beds, or minirefrigerators; and two have private, screened porches with hot tubs. Breakfast is a gourmet, sit-down affair conducive to chatting. ⊠ *278 Main St., Box 1022, 02568,* ☎ *508/693–3333 or 800/332–1236,* 𝖥𝖠𝖷 *508/693–5419. 13 rooms. Full breakfast (or Continental breakfast in bed) and afternoon tea included. AE, D, DC, MC, V.*

Martha's Vineyard

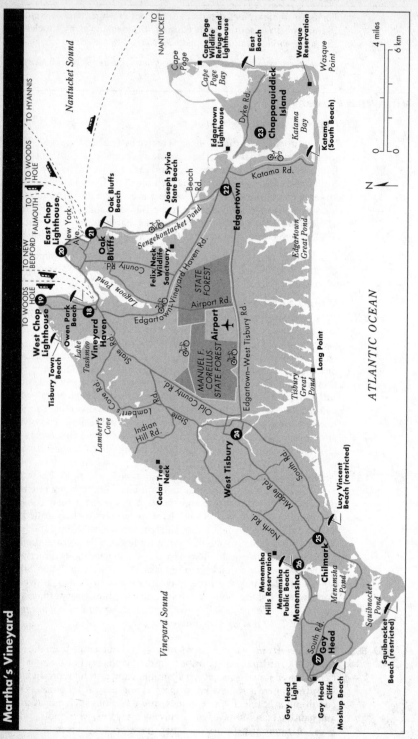

Nantucket Sound

TO HYANNIS

TO NANTUCKET

TO WOODS HOLE

TO FALMOUTH

TO NEW BEDFORD

TO WOODS HOLE

Vineyard Sound

Cape Poge

Cape Poge Wildlife Refuge and Lighthouse

East Beach

Wasque Reservation

Cape Poge Bay

Wasque Point

Edgartown Lighthouse

Katama Bay

Chappaquiddick Island

Dyke Rd.

23

Katama (South Beach)

Joseph Sylvia State Beach

Beach Rd.

Katama Rd.

22

Oak Bluffs Beach

New York Ave.

21

Oak Bluffs

20

East Chop Lighthouse

Felix Neck Wildlife Sanctuary

County Rd.

Sengekontacket Pond

Edgartown–Vineyard Haven Rd.

Edgartown

Edgartown Great Pond

STATE FOREST

Airport Rd.

MANUEL F. CORELLUS STATE FOREST

Vineyard Haven Airport

Long Point

ATLANTIC OCEAN

19

West Chop Lighthouse

Tisbury Town Beach

Owen Park Beach

Lake Tashmoo

18

State Rd.

Lagoon Pond

Edgartown–West Tisbury Rd.

Tisbury Great Pond

Lambert's Cove

Lambert's Cove Rd.

Indian Hill Rd.

Cedar Tree Neck

State Rd.

Old County Rd.

24

West Tisbury

North Rd.

Middle Rd.

South Rd.

Lucy Vincent Beach (restricted)

25

Chilmark

Menemsha Hills Reservation

Menemsha Public Beach

26

Menemsha

Menemsha Pond

Squibnocket Pond

Squibnocket Beach (restricted)

South Rd.

27

Gay Head

Gay Head Light

Gay Head Cliffs

Moshup Beach

N

4 miles

6 km

0

$$$ 🏠 **Captain Dexter House.** This 1843 sea captain's house has a historical appeal, with period-style wallpapers, velvet wing chairs, and 18th-century antiques and reproductions. The small guest rooms are tastefully and comfortably furnished, some with four-poster canopy beds and hand-sewn quilts; the Captain Harding room has a fireplace and a claw-foot tub. The innkeepers are delightful and know wonderful anecdotes about the history of the house. ✉ *100 Main St., Box 2457, 02568,* ☎ *508/693–6564. 7 rooms, 1 suite. Continental breakfast and afternoon tea included. AE, MC, V.*

Nightlife and the Arts

NIGHTLIFE

Wintertide Coffeehouse (✉ Five Corners, ☎ 508/693–8830) was voted by *Billboard* magazine as one of America's top 10 coffeehouses. It has a rustic, hearty lunch and dinner menu and live music—mostly folk and blues, but there's jazz on Wednesday and Saturday nights and musical improv on Tuesday.

THE ARTS

The **Vineyard Playhouse** (✉ 10 Church St., ☎ 508/693–6450), the island's only professional theater company, offers a full summer season, including outdoor Shakespeare, as well as a winter season, the Spring Short Play Festival in May, and an October reading series of award-winning New England plays. The Playhouse also runs a weekly art and theater camp for kids in summer and improvisation workshops for teens year-round.

Outdoor Activities and Sports

BIKING

Paths run along the coast road from Oak Bluffs to Edgartown, inland from Vineyard Haven to Edgartown, and from Edgartown to South Beach; all connect with scenic paths that weave through the State Forest. Rent bikes in Vineyard Haven at **Martha's Vineyard Scooter and Bike Rental** (✉ By the steamship terminal, ☎ 508/693–0782).

GOLF

The public **Mink Meadows Golf Course** (✉ off Franklin St., Vineyard Haven, ☎ 508/693–0600), on elite West Chop, has nine holes.

WATER SPORTS

Windsurfing and sailing lessons and rentals are offered at **Wind's Up!** (✉ 95 Beach Rd., ☎ 508/693–4252) on the lagoon. Also available are kayak and canoe rentals, plus an invaluable brochure on windsurfing, including best locations and safety tips.

Shopping

The **Bunch of Grapes Bookstore** (✉ 68 Main St., ☎ 508/693–2291) carries new books, including many island-related titles. **Bramhall & Dunn** (✉ Main St., ☎ 508/693–6437) has superb hand-knit sweaters, as well as fine English country pine antiques, crafts, linens, and housewares. **Island Children** (✉ 94 Main St., ☎ 508/693–6130) has hand-block-printed children's and women's clothing in 100% cotton. **Murray's of the Vineyard** (✉ Main St., ☎ 508/693–2640) sells classic designer fashions and accessories. **Sioux Eagle Designs** (✉ Main St., ☎ 508/693–6537) sells handcrafted jewelry in exotic designs. **Brickman's** (✉ Main St., Vineyard Haven, ☎ 508/693–0047; Main St., Edgartown, ☎ 508/627–4700) has sports and surfer-type clothes, major-label footwear and sports equipment. **Wind's Up!** (✉ 95 Beach Rd., ☎ 508/693–4340) sells swimwear, windsurfing and sailing equipment, and other outdoor gear.

West Chop Lighthouse

⑲ *2 mi from downtown Vineyard Haven.*

An elite extension of Vineyard Haven, about 2 miles out on Main Street, is **West Chop,** which has an 85-acre conservation area, West Chop Woods (entrance on Franklin Street), and a scenic overlook at the West Chop Lighthouse. Built in 1881 and moved back twice from the eroding bluff, the lighthouse is one of a pair guarding the entrance to Vineyard Haven harbor—in the 19th century, one of the world's busiest.

East Chop Lighthouse

⑳ *4¾ mi east of West Chop Lighthouse.*

The 1876 East Chop Lighthouse affords spectacular views of Nantucket Sound and a look at the expansive bluff-top summer "cottages" built in the breezy, porch-wrapped shingle style by the Boston and Newport rich in the late 19th and early 20th centuries.

Oak Bluffs

㉑ *3 mi east of Vineyard Haven.*

A favorite with the young crowd, Oak Bluffs was a popular summer resort for the wealthy more than 100 years ago. Once the setting for a number of grand hotels—the **Wesley Hotel** (1879) on Lake Avenue is the last of them—the busy and colorful Oak Bluffs harbor now has guest houses and minimalls hawking fast food and souvenirs.

Two attractions on Oak Bluffs Avenue are fun for kids: a 75-game arcade, **The Game Room** and **Flying Horses Carousel,** a National Historic Landmark. *Game Room* ☎ *508/693–5163, Carousel* ☎ *508/693–9481.* ▦ *Rides $1 each or $8 for book of 10.* ☉ *Mid-June–Labor Day, daily 10–10; spring and fall, weekends only.*

Circuit Avenue is the center of the action, with most of the town's shops, ★ bars, and restaurants. Here you'll find the entrance to the **Oak Bluffs Camp Ground,** a warren of streets tightly packed with more than 300 Carpenter Gothic Victorian cottages, gaily painted in pastels and trimmed in lacy filigree. Methodist summer camp meetings have been held here since 1835; as the site's popularity grew, the original nine tents gave way to 500 tiny cottages by 1880. This development was compounded by an influx of fashionable folk who came on steamers from New Bedford, New York, and Boston for the bathing and sea air, creating a resort town known as Cottage City (now Oak Bluffs). Visitors are invited to a community sing held Wednesday at 8 PM, in season, at the **Tabernacle,** an impressive open-air structure at the center of the campground.

Beach

At **Joseph A. Sylvia State Beach,** between Oak Bluffs and Edgartown, you can see Cape Cod across Nantucket Sound. The mile-long sandy beach is popular with families for its calm, warm water.

Dining and Lodging

$$$-$$$$ ✕ **Oyster Bar.** The hottest dining spot on the Vineyard, the Oyster Bar ★ rocks with celebrities and beautiful people. The Oyster Bar (named for its 35-foot mahogany raw bar) has a sophisticated art-deco look, with faux-marble columns, tropical greenery, and a line of pink neon along the walls. The standard veal chop is revamped with porcini mushroom custard, black truffle juice, and light veal stock, and the wood-rotisseried suckling pig is tempting. ✉ *162 Circuit Ave.,* ☎ *508/693–*

3300. *Reservations essential. AE, MC, V. Closed Dec.–mid-May, Tues.–Wed. in May and Oct.–Nov. No lunch.*

$$ ✕ **Giordano's.** Bountiful portions of simply prepared Italian food (pizzas, pastas, cacciatores, cutlets) and fried fish and other seafood at excellent prices keep Giordano's—run by the Giordano clan since 1930—a family favorite. The ambience suits the clientele—hearty, noisy, and cheerful—with sturdy booths, bright green-topped wood tables, and hanging greenery. Lines wrap around the corner. ⊠ *107 Circuit Ave.,* ☎ *508/693–0184. Reservations not accepted. No credit cards. Closed late Sept.–early June.*

$$ ✕ **Zapotec.** Serving authentic and creative Mexican dishes with chunky,
★ coriander-flecked salsa, Zapotec is an intimate place with heart and style. Highly recommended is the lobster quesadilla, crispy and flavorful with chunks of lobster. ⊠ *10 Kennebec Ave.,* ☎ *508/693–6800. Reservations not accepted. AE, MC, V. No lunch. Closed Thanksgiving–Easter.*

$–$$ ✕ **Cafe Luna.** Right on the marina in Oak Bluffs, Cafe Luna is a great late-night spot. Downstairs, order thin-crust pizza, focaccia sandwiches, and other delicacies. Upstairs is a funky tapas, wine, and espresso bar that works hard to maintain its cool vibe, which gets easier and easier later and later at night. ⊠ *Oak Bluffs Harbor,* ☎ *508/693–8078. Reservations not accepted. AE, MC, V.*

$$$ 🏠 **Oak House.** The wraparound veranda of this Victorian (1872) faces
★ across a busy street to the wide strand of beach beyond. Several rooms have private terraces. The decor centers on well-preserved woods—some rooms have oak wainscoting from top to bottom—choice antique furniture, and nautical-theme accessories. ⊠ *Sea View Ave., Box 299, 02557,* ☎ *508/693–4187,* 𝔽𝔸𝕏 *508/696–7385. 8 rooms, 2 suites. Continental breakfast and afternoon tea included. AE, D, MC, V. Closed mid-Oct.–mid-May.*

$$ 🏠 **Sea Spray Inn.** Separated from the beach road by a grassy park is this porch-wrapped summer house with an open, breezy feel. The simple and restful decor is highlighted by cheerful splashes of color, including pastel-painted furniture and floors. The Honeymoon Suite has lace-draped bay windows with views of the park; the Garden Room has a king-size bed with gauze canopy and a private porch. ⊠ *2 Nashawena Park, Box 2125, 02557,* ☎ *508/693–9388. 5 rooms with bath, 2 rooms share bath. CP. MC, V. Closed mid-Nov.–mid-Apr.*

Nightlife and the Arts

NIGHTLIFE

The **Ritz Café** (⊠ Circuit Ave., ☎ 508/693–9851) has live blues and jazz on weekends, more often in season. At **David's Island House** restaurant (⊠ Circuit Ave., ☎ 508/693–4516), renowned pianist David Crohan and special guests entertain dinner and lounge patrons with popular and classical music in summer. The **Atlantic Connection** (⊠ 124 Circuit Ave., ☎ 508/693–7129) has comedy and karaoke nights in summer, with live and DJ dance music year-round.

THE ARTS

Children's Theatre (⊠ At Sailing Camp Park, Barnes Rd., ☎ 508/693–4060) has weekday classes for children in summer.

Outdoor Activities and Sports

BIKING

Paths run along the coast road from Oak Bluffs to Edgartown, inland from Vineyard Haven to Edgartown, and from Edgartown to South Beach; all connect with scenic paths that weave through the state forest. Rent bikes at **De Bettencourt's** (⊠ Circuit Ave. Ext., ☎ 508/693–0011).

FISHING

Rent gear, book charters, and hire beach or boat guides at **Dick's Bait and Tackle** (⊠ New York Ave., ☎ 508/693–7669). The party boat **Skipper** (☎ 508/693–1238) leaves from Oak Bluffs Harbor in season.

GOLF

Farm Neck Golf Club (⊠ Farm Neck Way, ☎ 508/693–3057) is a semiprivate club with 18 holes and a driving range. **Dockside Minigolf** (⊠ Dockside Marketplace, Oak Bluffs harbor, ☎ 508/696–7646) offers a less serious version of the game.

WATER SPORTS

Vineyard Boat Rentals (⊠ Dockside Marina, ☎ 508/693–8476) rents 13- and 17-foot Boston Whalers, Bayliners and Jet Skis.

Shopping

Book Den East (⊠ New York Ave., ☎ 508/693–3946) sells out-of-print, antiquarian, and paperback books in an old barn. **The Secret Garden** (⊠ 148 Circuit Ave., ☎ 508/693–4759) has lace curtains, Crabtree & Evelyn fragrances, baby gifts, stationery, children's and local-interest books, wicker furniture, and island watercolors.

Edgartown

㉒ *6 mi from Oak Bluffs.*

Edgartown is tidy and polished, with upscale boutiques, elegant sea captains' houses, well-manicured lawns, and photogenic flower gardens. Two of the finest examples of Greek Revival architecture are on Main Street, between Pease's Point Way and Church Street: the **Old Whaling Church,** built in 1843 and now an arts center, with a 92-foot clock tower; and the roofwalk-topped **Dr. Daniel Fisher House** (1840) next door, now housing offices.

In back of the Fisher House is the oldest dwelling on the island: the 1672 **Vincent House,** a weathered-shingle farmhouse, is of architectural interest and is maintained as a museum of island life. Most of the original wide-board floors, glass, brick, and hardware remain; parts of walls are exposed to reveal construction techniques. Each room is furnished to represent one century in the history of the island, including the Colonial and whaling periods. Guided tours are offered. ⊠ *Main St.,* ☎ *508/627–8017.* ▨ *$3; price can be combined with Fisher House and Whaling Church tours for $5.* ☉ *May–Sept., weekdays 11–4. Call 508/627–8619 for off-season hrs.*

At the corner of Cooke Street (Edgartown's oldest) is a complex of buildings belonging to the **Dukes County Historical Society.** Built in 1765 with raised-wood paneling, wide-board floors, and great hearths, the Thomas Cooke House is a museum documenting the island's history through furniture, tools, costumes, and ship models. It is open in summer only, for docent-guided tours. Accessible year-round are a small whaling-oriented museum, a library, a collection of antique vehicles, a brick tryworks, and the 1,000-prism, 1854 Fresnel lens from the Gay Head Lighthouse. ⊠ *Cooke and School Sts., Edgartown,* ☎ *508/627–4441.* ▨ *$5; reduced admission off-season.* ☉ *July 5–Labor Day, Tues.–Sat. 10–4:30, Sun. noon–4:30; off-season, Wed.–Fri. 1–4, Sat. 10–4.*

Felix Neck Wildlife Sanctuary, 3 miles out of Edgartown, is managed by the Massachusetts Audubon Society, and comprises 350 acres, including 6 miles of trails traversing marshland, fields, woods, seashore, and a pond rich in wildfowl. It offers a full schedule of events all led by naturalists, an exhibit center, and a gift shop. ⊠ *Off Edgar-*

town–Vineyard Haven Rd., ☎ *508/627–4850.* ✉ *$3.* ⊙ *Daily 8–4.*
Closed Mon. Nov.–May.

Beach

South Beach, the island's largest and most popular, is a 3-mile ribbon
of sand on the Atlantic, with strong surf and occasional riptides. From
Edgartown, take the bike path or the trolley. For day-to-day information on beach access for four-wheel-drive vehicles, call the Beach Re-
striction Hotline (☎ 508/693–5966).

Dining and Lodging

$$$ ✗ **Andrea's.** In a restored whaling captain's house, Andrea's serves so-
phisticated meals of fresh fish, pasta, and such dishes as grilled veal
chop and sirloin *cardinale* (with green-and-black-peppercorn sauce).
You can sit in the main room, the glassed-in porch, a semiprivate
room, the rose garden, or the downstairs bistro. ✉ *137 Upper Main
St.,* ☎ *508/627–5850. AE, MC, V. No lunch. Closed Nov.–Apr.*

$$$ ✗ **Savoir Fare.** President Clinton doesn't have to dine here or William
★ Styron to love it for you to call for a reservation. It is simply one of
the most thoughtful and innovative culinary experiences on the island.
A two-chef team has an astonishing way of combining ingredients, such
as: potato gnocchi with fresh porcini mushrooms, duck confit, and dried
cherries; or honey-glazed grilled salmon served with chanterelle risotto
and a Barolo wine reduction. To keep your feet on the ground, surroundings are rather casual, and the attentive service may be slightly
rough. ✉ *14 Church St. (in courtyard opposite Main St.'s Town Hall),*
☎ *508/627–9864. Reservations essential. AE, MC, V. Closed Nov.–Apr.*

$$$$ ✗▥ **Charlotte Inn.** Built in the 1860s, the Charlotte has grown into a
★ five-building complex of meticulously maintained guest accommodations and is one of the finest inns in New England. The inn's popular
restaurant, L'Étoile, is set in a glass-enclosed, conservatory-like room,
with English antiques and gilt-frame oil paintings. The contemporary
French menu highlights imaginative native seafood and shellfish as well
as game. Characteristic dishes from the prix-fixe dinner or Sunday-brunch
menu include grilled swordfish with ginger, lime, and cilantro butter;
or assiette of lobster, littlenecks, and scallops with a lobster, sweet pepper, and basil sauce. The rooms at the Charlotte are elegantly furnished
with English antiques and reproductions; some have fireplaces. The beautifully landscaped grounds include an English garden. ✉ *27 S. Summer
St., inn* ☎ *508/627–4751,* ℻ *508/627–4652; restaurant* ☎ *508/627–
5187. 22 rooms, 3 suites. Restaurant (reservations essential; no lunch;
closed Jan.–mid-Feb. and weekdays off-season). CP. AE, MC, V.*

$$$$ ▥ **Harbor View Hotel.** This 1891 resort hotel has a Victorian theme,
from the airy, elegant dining room to individual rooms done with pastel carpeting and walls, painted wicker, pickled-wood armoires, and
pastel floral drapes—plus telephones, air-conditioning, cable TV, minirefrigerators, and wall safes. Other buildings have rooms and suites with
cathedral ceilings, private decks, or kitchens. In a residential neighborhood
just minutes from town, the hotel has views of Edgartown Lighthouse
and the harbor. Walk on the ¾-mile beach or catch bluefish from the
jetty. ✉ *131 N. Water St., 02539,* ☎ *508/627–7000 or 800/225–
6005,* ℻ *508/627–7845. 124 rooms and suites. Restaurant, bar, pool,
golf privileges, tennis courts, baby-sitting, children's programs, laundry service, concierge, business services. AE, DC, MC, V.*

$$$ ▥ **Daggett House.** The flower-bordered lawn that separates the main
house (1750) from the harbor makes a great retreat after a day of ex-
ploring the town, which is just a minute away. The fine restaurant pre-
serves much of the tavern that it once was. This and two other buildings

are decorated with wallpapers, antiques, and reproductions. The Widow's Walk Suite has a private roof-walk, a full kitchen, a hot tub, and a superb water view. All rooms have phones. No smoking. ⊠ *59 N. Water St., Box 1333, 02539,* ☎ *508/627–4600 or 800/946–3400,* FAX *508/627–4611. 21 rooms, 4 suites. AE, MC, V.*

$$$ 🖭 **Mattakesett.** This community of three- and four-bedroom homes and condominiums is within walking distance of South Beach. Each unit is individually owned and decorated; some are superior, some just average. All have full kitchens, washers and dryers, decks, and cable TV; some have whirlpools or wood-burning stoves. The staff is extremely attentive. ⊠ *Katama Rd., R.F.D. 270, 02539,* ☎ *508/627–4432. 92 units. Pool, tennis courts, aerobics, bicycles, children's program. No credit cards. Closed Columbus Day–Memorial Day.*

Nightlife

A mix of live R&B and reggae and DJ-spun music energizes the crowd at the seasonal **Hot Tin Roof** (⊠ At the airport, ☎ 508/693–9320).

Outdoor Activities and Sports

BIKING

Paths run along the coast road from Oak Bluffs to Edgartown, inland from Vineyard Haven to Edgartown, and from Edgartown to South Beach; all connect with scenic paths that weave through the State Forest. **R. W. Cutler Bike** (⊠ 1 Main St., ☎ 508/627–4052), rents and delivers bikes.

FISHING

Big Eye Charters (☎ 508/627–3649) offers charters for fishing. Rent gear, book charters, and hire beach or boat guides at **Larry's Tackle Shop** (⊠ 141 Main St., ☎ 508/627–5088), which also offers fishing instruction.

Shopping

ART AND CRAFTS

Edgartown Scrimshaw (⊠ Main St., ☎ 508/627–9439) has antique and new scrimshaw, Nantucket lightship baskets, hand-carved whales and decoys, and jewelry. **Edgartown Art Gallery** (⊠ 20 S. Summer St., ☎ 508/627–8508), across from the Charlotte Inn, has 19th- and 20th-century oils and watercolors, plus English antiques and sporting prints. **Soulagnet Collection** (⊠ Colonial Inn Shops, ☎ 508/627–7759) specializes in reproductions of American folk art and also has furniture and local photographs and prints.

BOOKS

Bickerton & Ripley Books (⊠ Main St. at S. Summer St., ☎ 508/627–8463) offers a wide selection of new books as well as a line of cards created by island artists, and sponsors writers' events such as brunches and book-signings.

GIFTS

The Fligors (⊠ 27 N. Water St., ☎ 508/627–8811) has varied offerings, including preppy clothing and gift items.

Chappaquiddick Island

㉓ *6¼ mi by land (via Katama Beach) from Edgartown.*

A sparsely populated area with a great number of nature preserves, the island makes a pleasant day trip from the Vineyard on a sunny day. If you are interested in covering a lot of the island, cycling is an excellent way to save time getting from point to point. Chappaquiddick Island is actually connected to the Vineyard by a long sand spit from South Beach in Katama—a spectacular 2¾-mile walk if you have the energy.

At the end of Dyke Road is the **Dyke Bridge,** infamous as the scene of the 1969 accident in which a young woman was killed in a car driven by Ted Kennedy.

Cape Poge Wildlife Refuge and Wasque Reservation, across the inlet from Dyke's Beach, is a 709-acre wilderness of dunes, woods, salt marshes, ponds, and barrier beach that is an important migration stopover or nesting area for many bird species. Surf casting is best at Wasque Point. ☎ *508/627–7260 or 508/627–3599 for Jeep tours.* ☞ *$3 cars, $3 individuals in season.*

East Beach is a spectacular beach with good swimming. It is accessible only on foot or by four-wheel-drive vehicle from the Wasque Reservation entrance or by boat; it offers heavy surf, good bird-watching, and relative isolation in a lovely setting.

A ferry (☞ Getting Around *in* Martha's Vineyard A to Z, *below*) shuttles passengers between Edgartown and Chappaquiddick Island.

West Tisbury

㉔ *15 mi west of Edgartown.*

The west end of the Vineyard—known as Up-Island, from the nautical expression of going "up" in degrees of longitude as you sail west—is more rural than the east. West Tisbury occupies the center of the island, including most of the 4,000-acre **state forest,** several farms, and a small New England village, complete with an 1859 agricultural hall and **Alley's General Store** (⊠ State Rd., ☎ 508/693–0088), purveyor since 1858 of everything from hammers to dill pickles.

Cedar Tree Neck, 300 hilly acres of unspoiled West Tisbury woods, has wildlife, freshwater ponds, brooks, low stone walls, and wooded trails ending at a stony but secluded North Shore beach where swimming and fishing are prohibited. The guided nature walk, although designed for children, is interesting for all ages. ⊠ *Follow Indian Hill Rd., off State Rd., for 2 mi, then a rough dirt road downhill to right for 1 mi to parking lot at the end.* ☎ *508/693–5207.* ☞ *Free.* ☼ *Daily 8:30–5:30.*

Not far from West Tisbury, **Long Point** nature area has 633 acres of grassland, dense heath, dunes, freshwater and saltwater ponds, and a mile of South Beach, with swimming and surf fishing. ⊠ *In season, turn left onto dirt road ³⁄₁₀ mi west of airport on Edgartown–West Tisbury Rd.; at end, follow signs to parking lot. Off-season, follow unpaved Deep Bottom Rd. (1¹⁄₁₀ mi west of airport) for 2 mi to lot.* ☎ *508/693–3678.* ☞ *$6 cars, $3 adults (in season).* ☼ *Daily 10–6.*

Dining and Lodging

$$$ ✕🏠 **Lambert's Cove Country Inn.** This 1790 farmhouse is set in an apple
★   orchard and approached through pine woods. The restaurant is cozy and romantic, with soft lighting and music, and fine Continental cuisine. The daily selection of six or seven entrées may include cioppino or herb-crusted halibut with the chef's choice of fresh vegetable. In summer a lavish Sunday brunch is served on the deck overlooking the orchard. Some rooms are cheerful, others are a bit tired; all have a rustic, homey feel, with firm beds and country-style furnishings. Public areas include a library with fireplace. ⊠ *Lambert's Cove Rd. (R.R. 1, Box 422, Vineyard Haven 02568),* ☎ *508/693–2298,* ℻ *508/693–7890. 15 rooms. Restaurant (reservations essential; BYOB; closed weekdays off-season; no lunch), tennis courts, beach. CP. AE, MC, V.*

$ ⊞ **Manter-Memorial AYH-Hostel.** The only budget, roof-over-your-head alternative in season, this hostel is one of the country's best. Morning chores are required in summer, and there's an 11 PM curfew June–August. It is near a bike path but 7 miles from the beach. The Island Shuttle makes a stop out front. ⊠ *Edgartown–West Tisbury Rd., Box 158, 02575,* ☎ *508/693–2665. 78 beds. MC, V. Closed daily 10– 5 and Nov.–Apr.*

Outdoor Activities and Sports

HORSEBACK RIDING

Misty Meadows Horse Farm (⊠ Old County Rd., ☎ 508/693–1870) has a large indoor riding area and offers trail rides and lessons. **South Shore Stables** (⊠ Across from the airport, ☎ 508/693–3770) gives English riding lessons and has indoor and outdoor rings, a hunt course, and trails.

Shopping

ART AND ANTIQUES

Granary Gallery at the Red Barn Emporium (⊠ Old County Rd., ☎ 508/693–0455 or 800/472–6279) has country antiques and a gallery, showcasing island artists, with photographs by Alfred Eisenstaedt. **Hermine Merel Smith Fine Art** (⊠ 548 Edgartown Rd., ☎ 508/693–7719) specializes in paintings and drawings by contemporary American impressionists and realists. **Chilmark Pottery** (⊠ Off State Rd., ☎ 508/693–7874) is a workshop and gallery of stoneware, raku, and porcelain.

FARMER'S MARKET

The West Tisbury **Farmer's Market** (⊠ Agricultural Hall, South Rd.), held Saturday 9–noon, mid-June through Columbus Day, and Wednesday 3–6, late June through early September, is the largest in the state.

Chilmark

㉕ *2 mi southeast of Menemsha.*

Chilmark is a rustic wooded area with scenic ocean-view roads and two beautiful (residents-only) beaches.

A **flea market** is held on the grounds of the Chilmark Community Church (⊠ Menemsha Cross Rd., ☎ 508/645–9216) Wednesday and Saturday in season from about 8 AM until 2:30 or 3.

Menemsha

㉖ *4 mi east of Gay Head.*

Along with the fishing shacks and fish markets in the little fishing village of Menemsha, on Vineyard Sound, there are also a few summer boutiques and restaurants, a beach, and good fishing from the jetties. The fishing harbor is a great place to catch a sunset.

Beach

Menemsha Public Beach, backed by dunes, is pebbly and has gentle surf.

Dining and Lodging

$$–$$$ ✕ **Home Port.** You'll either love or hate this bland and boiled classic New England shore cooking. Your best bet is to bring along beer or a killer bottle of wine (some intense German riesling or a rich California pinot blanc), park yourself on the patio and order boiled lobster ONLY. Refuse all appetizers and concentrate your efforts on the lobster at hand. A local favorite is the Back Door at the Home Port: it's decent take-out, and the beach is right there. Some feel that the food, however, isn't worth the price. ⊠ *At the end of North Rd.,* ☎ *508/645–*

2679. Reservations required (2–3 wks in advance July–Aug.). MC, V. BYOB. Closed mid-Oct.–mid-Apr. No lunch.

$$$$ 🏠 **Beach Plum Inn.** The main draws of this 10-acre retreat are the woodland setting, the panoramic view of Vineyard Sound and Menemsha harbor, and the romantic gourmet restaurant with spectacular sunset views. The renovated 1890 Main House is surrounded by cottages; rooms on the second floor of the house have the best views. Both the cottages and the inn rooms have New England country furnishings. The inn provides passes to Chilmark's beautiful private beaches. ⊠ *Beach Plum La., off North Rd., 02552,* ☎ *508/645–9454 or 800/528–6616. 5 inn rooms, 4 cottages. Restaurant, tennis courts, croquet, bicycles, babysitting. Full breakfast included; MAP available. AE, D, MC, V. Closed mid-Oct.–mid-May.*

Outdoor Activities and Sports
North Shore Charters (☎ 508/645–2993) charters fishing boats.

Shopping
Soulagnet Collection (⊠ Basin Rd., ☎ 508/645–3735) specializes in reproductions of American folk art and also has furniture, local photographs, and prints.

Gay Head

㉗ *15 mi southwest of North Tisbury.*

Gay Head is windswept and strikingly beautiful. The **Gay Head Cliffs,** dramatically striated walls of red clay, are the island's major tourist site, and a National Historic Landmark. The approach to the overlook— you can see the Elizabeth Islands across Vineyard Sound—is lined with Native American crafts and food shops. Gay Head is an official Wampanoag Indian township.

Beach
Moshup Beach is a long, beautiful stretch of sand below and left of the Gay Head Cliffs (from the cliffs' pricey parking lot, it's a five-minute walk). Negotiating large boulders and strong surf can make swimming tiring; a nude beach is under the cliffs.

Lodging
$$$$ 🏠 **Outermost Inn.** Built by Hugh Taylor (brother of James) as his year-
★ round home, this serene retreat by the Gay Head Cliffs has spacious rooms with polished light-wood floors, white walls, local art, white-and-black tile baths, TVs (on request), and picture windows giving spectacular views of the lighthouse, the ocean, and surrounding moorland; two rooms have private decks, and one has a hot tub. It's a five-minute walk to the beach. ⊠ *Off Lighthouse Rd., R.R. 1, Box 171, 02535,* ☎ *508/645–3511,* FAX *508/645–3514. 6 rooms, 1 suite. Restaurant (in season; open to public; BYOB). Full breakfast included. AE, D, MC, V.*

Martha's Vineyard A to Z

Arriving and Departing

BY FERRY

If you plan to take a car to the island in summer or on popular weekends, you *must* reserve as far ahead as possible; spaces are often sold out months in advance. If you're without a reservation, get there very early, and be prepared to wait.

From Falmouth: The *Island Queen* (Falmouth Harbor, ☎ 508/548–4800) makes the 40-minute trip to Oak Bluffs from late May through Columbus Day. ☒ *One-way: $6 adults, $3 children under 13, $3 bicycles; round-trip: $10 adults, $5 children, $6 bicycles.*

From Hyannis: Hy-Line (Ocean St. dock, ☎ 508/778–2600 for information; 508/778–2602 for reservations; on the Vineyard ☎ 508/693–0113) makes the 1¾-hour run to Oak Bluffs from late May through October. ☒ *One-way: $11 adults, $5.50 children 5–12, $4.50 bicycles.*

From Nantucket: Hy-Line (☎ 508/228–3949; on the Vineyard, ☎ 508/693–0112) makes 2¼-hour runs to and from Oak Bluffs mid-June–mid-September. ☒ *One-way: $11 adults, $5.50 children 5–12, $4.50 bicycles.*

From New Bedford: The *Schamonchi* (☎ 508/997–1688; on the Vineyard, ☎ 508/693–2088) makes the 1½-hour trip between Billy Wood's Wharf and Vineyard Haven from mid-May to mid-October. ☒ *One-way: $9 adults, $4.50 children under 12, $2.50 bicycles; round-trip same day: $16 adults, $7.50 children, $5 bicycles.*

From Woods Hole: The **Steamship Authority** (☎ 508/477–8600 for information, 508/540–2022 for auto reservations; on the Vineyard, 508/693–0125 for information, 508/693–9130 for auto reservations) operates the only car ferries, which make the 45-minute trip to Vineyard Haven year-round and to Oak Bluffs from late May through mid-September. (Guaranteed standby service for vehicles may be available in summer.) ☒ *One-way: $4.75 adults, $2.40 children 5–12, $3 bicycles. Cars: $38 mid-May–mid-Oct.; $24 mid-Mar.–mid-May and mid-Oct.–Nov.; $18 Dec.–mid-Mar.*

BY PLANE

Martha's Vineyard Airport is in West Tisbury, about 5 miles west of Edgartown (☎ 508/693–7022). **Cape Air** (☎ 508/771–6944 or 800/352–0714) connects the Vineyard with Boston, Hyannis, Nantucket, and New Bedford year-round.

Getting Around

BY BICYCLE AND MOPED

For details on rentals and trails, *see* Biking entries. Most of the bike-rental shops also rent mopeds, as does **Ride-On Mopeds** (⊠ Hy-Line Dock, Oak Bluffs, ☎ 508/693–2076). A standard driver's license is required.

BY BUS AND TROLLEY

From mid-May to mid-October, shuttles operate between Vineyard Haven, Oak Bluffs, and Edgartown daily 7:30 AM–11:30 PM in high season, 7:30–7 other times. Cost one-way: $1.50–$4. Call the shuttle hot line, 508/693–1589, for schedules. Buses from Edgartown to Gay Head run frequently in July and August. Cost one-way: $1–$5. Call the Martha's Vineyard Transit Authority at 508/627–7448 for information. Trolleys around Edgartown (25¢), running from mid-May to mid-September, and from Edgartown to South Beach ($1.50), running from mid-June to mid-September, can be hailed anywhere along their route. For information, call 508/627–9663.

BY FERRY

The three-car **On Time** ferry (⊠ Dock St., Edgartown, ☎ 508/627–9427) makes the five-minute run to Chappaquiddick Island every day, 7:30 AM–midnight June–mid-October, less frequently off-season. ☒ *Round-trip: $4.50 car and driver, $2.50 bicycle and rider, $3.50 moped or motorcycle and rider, $1 individual.*

BY TAXI

Companies serving the island include **All Island** (☎ 508/693–3705), **Marlene's** (☎ 508/693–0037), and **Up Island** (☎ 508/693–5454).

Contacts and Resources

CAR RENTALS

Rentals can be booked through a courtesy phone at Woods Hole ferry terminal, or at the airport desks of **Budget** (☎ 508/693–1911) and **Hertz** (☎ 508/693–2402). **Adventure Rentals** (⊠ Beach Rd., Vineyard Haven, ☎ 508/693–1959) rents cars, mopeds, and dune buggies.

EMERGENCIES

Martha's Vineyard Hospital (⊠ Linton La., Oak Bluffs, ☎ 508/693–0410). **Vineyard Medical Services** (⊠ State Rd., Vineyard Haven, ☎ 508/693–6399).

GUIDED TOURS

Three bus companies (☎ 508/693–1555, 508/693–4681, or 508/693–0058), under one ownership, have two-hour narrated tours of the island, with a stop at Gay Head Cliffs. Buses meet ferries in season; call at other times. ⊠ *$11.50 adults, $3 children.*

Day, sunset, and overnight sails to Nantucket or Cuttyhunk on the 54-foot ketch *Laissez Faire* (☎ 508/693–1646) are offered in season out of Vineyard Haven. Sunset cruises on the motor tour boat *Skipper* (☎ 508/693–1238), out of Oak Bluffs, allow glimpses of celebrities' homes (weather permitting).

PHARMACY

Leslie's Drug Store (⊠ Main St., Vineyard Haven, ☎ 508/693–1010) has pharmacists on 24-hour call.

RESERVATION AGENCIES

Martha's Vineyard and Nantucket Reservations (⊠ Box 1322, 73 Lagoon Pond Rd., Vineyard Haven 02568, ☎ 508/693–7200 or 800/649–5671 in MA) and **Accommodations Plus** (⊠ R.F.D. 273, Edgartown 02539, ☎ 508/696–8880) book bed-and-breakfasts, condominiums, cottages, hotels, and inns. **DestINNations** (☎ 800/333–4667) will arrange any and all details of a visit.

NANTUCKET

Updated by
Dorothy
Antczak

Thirty miles southeast of Hyannis, in the open Atlantic Ocean, lies Nantucket. Settled in the mid-17th century by Quakers and others retreating from the repressive religious authorities of mainland Massachusetts, this 14- by 3-mile island became the foremost whaling port in the world during the golden age of whaling, in the early to mid-19th century. Shipowners and sea captains built elegant mansions that today remain remarkably unchanged, thanks to a very strict code regulating any changes to structures within the town of Nantucket, an official National Historic District. In addition, more than a third of the island's acreage is under protection from development.

Visitors on a day trip usually browse in the downtown's many art galleries, crafts shops, and boutiques, enjoy the architecture and historical museums, and sample the wealth of gourmet restaurants. Those who stay longer appreciate the breezy openness of the island. Its moors—swept with fresh salt breezes and scented with bayberry, wild roses, and cranberries—and its miles of clean, white-sand beaches make Nantucket a respite from the rush and regimentation of life elsewhere. Most shops stay open until Christmas.

Numbers in the margin correspond to points of interest on the Nantucket map.

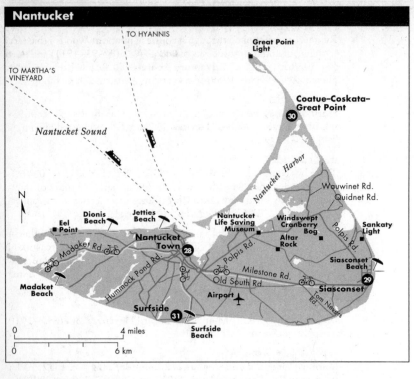

Nantucket Town

28 *30 mi southeast of Hyannis.*

The historical district is in Nantucket Town, which is the center of activity on the island. In high season, the town's sidewalks resemble Fifth Avenue's, as shoppers, strollers, and merrymakers crowd the main drag.

The **Peter Foulger Museum,** on Broad Street in the Nantucket Historical Association (NHA) research center, features changing historical exhibits such as Nantucket and the China Trade. It is run by the historical association, which sells a visitor's pass allowing a single visit to all 14 NHA properties. The pass is available at any of the sites for $8 adults, $4 children 5–14. ✉ *Broad St.,* ☎ *508/228–1894.* ✏ *$5 or NHA Visitor's Pass.* ☉ *Summer, daily 10–5.*

The **Whaling Museum** built in 1846, traces Nantucket's whaling past. The building was originally the Hadwen and Barney factory for refining spermaceti (waxy whale-oil product) and making candles. On exhibit is a fully-rigged whale boat, portraits of sea captains, a large scrimshaw collection, the skeleton of a 43-foot finback whale, and the original 16-foot-high glass prism from the Sankaty Light. Lectures on whaling history are given daily; call for tour times. ✉ *Broad St.,* ☎ *508/228–1736.* ✏ *$5 or NHA Visitor's Pass.* ☉ *Mid-June–Labor Day, daily 10–5; call for spring and fall hrs.*

Built in 1818, the **Pacific National Bank,** at the corner of Main and Fair streets, is a monument to the Nantucket whaling ships it once financed. Above the old-style teller cages, murals show the town as it was in its whaling heyday. At 93–97 Main Street are the well-known **"Three Bricks,"** identical redbrick mansions with columned Greek Revival porches at their front entrances. They were built between 1836 and 1838 by whaling merchant Joseph Starbuck for his three sons.

Two white, porticoed Greek Revival mansions built in 1845–46 stand across the street from the "Three Bricks." One of the buildings, called the **Hadwen House,** is now a museum that reflects the affluence of Nantucket's whaling era. A guided tour points out the grand circular staircase; fine plasterwork; carved Italian marble fireplace mantels; and Regency, Empire, and Victorian furnishings. ✉ *96 Main St.,* ☎ *508/228–1894.* ⌸ *$2 or NHA Visitor's Pass.* ☉ *Mid-June–Labor Day, daily 10–5; call for spring and fall hrs.*

On Milk Street you'll find the **Old Gaol,** an 1805 jailhouse in use until 1933. Walls, ceilings, and floors are bolted with iron, and furnishings consist of rough-plank bunks and open privies. Don't feel too sympathetic, though: Most prisoners were allowed out at night to sleep in their own beds. ✉ *15R Vestal St.,* ☎ *508/228–1894.* ⌸ *Free.* ☉ *Mid-June–Labor Day, daily 10–5; call for spring and fall hrs.*

The **Old Mill,** on South Mill Street, is an octagonal, 1745 Dutch-style windmill, built with lumber from shipwrecks. A spar and wheel rotate the top of the mill and turn the sails into the wind; wood gears and wind power grind cornmeal in season. ☎ *508/228–1894.* ⌸ *$2 or NHA Visitor's Pass.* ☉ *Daily 10–5 in season, weather permitting; call for spring and fall hrs.*

The tower of the **First Congregational Church** provides the best view of Nantucket—for those who climb the 92 steps. Rising 120 feet, the tower is capped by a weathervane depicting a whale catch. Peek in at the church's 1850 trompe-l'oeil ceiling. ✉ *62 Centre St.* ⌸ *$1.50.* ☉ *Mid-June–mid-Oct., Mon.–Sat. 10–4.*

Aptly named, the **Oldest House,** a 1686 saltbox also called the Jethro Coffin House, is the oldest house on the island. Its most striking feature is the massive central brick chimney with a giant brick horseshoe adornment. The sparsely furnished interior has leaded-glass windows and enormous hearths. Cutaway panels reveal 17th-century construction techniques. ✉ *Sunset Hill,* ☎ *508/228–1894.* ⌸ *$3 or NHA Visitor's Pass.* ☉ *Mid-June–Labor Day, daily 10–5; call for spring hrs.*

Maria Mitchell Aquarium displays local marine life. ✉ *28 Washington St., near Commercial Wharf,* ☎ *508/228–5387.* ⌸ *$1.* ☉ *Mid-June–Labor Day, Tues.–Sat. 10–4.*

Beaches

Children's Beach, a calm harbor beach suited to small children, is an easy walk from town. It has a park and playground, lifeguard, food service, and rest rooms. **Jetties Beach,** a short bike or shuttle ride from town, is the most popular beach for families because of its calm surf, lifeguards, bathhouse, snack bar, water-sports rentals, and tennis. **Madaket Beach** is known for great sunsets. Reached by a 6-mile bike path, Madaket has heavy surf, a lifeguard, rest rooms, and food nearby.

Dining and Lodging

$$$–$$$$
★
✕ **Club Car.** Superior Continental cuisine is served in a candlelit dining room with a wall of small-pane windows; a cozy piano bar sits in an attached old railway car. The menu, often featuring seafood, changes with the seasons and includes game in fall. The rack of lamb glazed with honey mustard and herbs is highly recommended. ✉ *1 Main St.,* ☎ *508/228–1101. MC, V. Closed early Dec.–mid-May; Tues.–Wed. mid-May–June and mid-Sept.–early Dec.*

$$-$$$ ✕ **American Seasons.** The menu is organized based on U.S. regions—New England, Down South, Wild West, and Pacific Coast—with specialties from each. Recent favorites are the Maine golden littlenecks and the Hudson Valley foie gras with wild rice. The wine list showcases only American wines (as it should). Folk-art murals and tables hand-painted with decorative game boards are part of the decor. It's very easy to recommend American Seasons to those who want a little adventure. ⊠ *80 Centre St.,* ☎ *508/228–7111. Reservations essential. No smoking. AE, MC, V. No lunch. Closed mid-Dec.–early Apr.*

$$ ✕ **The Brotherhood of Thieves.** Long lines are a fixture outside this very old-English pub restaurant. Inside is a dark, cozy room with low ceilings, a fireplace, and exposed brick and beams; much of the seating is at long, tightly packed tables. Dine on chowder and soups, fried fish and seafood, burgers, jumbo sandwiches, and shoestring fries. A convivial atmosphere prevails, thanks partly to the vast menu of spirits—ales, coffee drinks, brandies, mixed concoctions, etc. ⊠ *23 Broad St., no phone. Reservations not accepted. No credit cards.*

$$ ✕ **The Hearth at the Harbor House.** This island favorite tends to draw a somewhat older clientele. Dine inside or on an outdoor patio on simply prepared New England fare. A lavish Sunday brunch buffet includes a raw bar. The four-course "sunset special" is an excellent deal, and children under 13 dine free when accompanied by their parents. ⊠ *S. Beach St.,* ☎ *508/228–1500. Reservations essential for Sun. brunch. AE, DC, MC, V. No breakfast or lunch in off-season.*

$-$$ ✕ **Off Centre Cafe.** Owner Liz Holland has found her niche: quality
   ★   food, attention to detail, and almost-cheap prices that are a welcome blessing. The style is very cross-cultural, with breakfast faves like huevos rancheros and fresh fruit popovers contrasting with dinnertime Vietnamese spring rolls and smoked-salmon dumplings. The café sells its exceptionally good pastries to other restaurants and shops. The place is small—only 24 seats—but the patio is open in season. ⊠ *29 Centre St.,* ☎ *508/228–8470. No credit cards. No lunch in season.*

$$$$ ▥ **White Elephant.** Long a hallmark of service and style on the island,
   ★   this hotel has a choice location right on the harbor (boat slips are available). From the pool, set on a lawn landscaped with roses, and from most rooms, guests enjoy the comings and goings of boats that moor just offshore. The Breakers is the hotel's ultraluxury arm, with coolly elegant rooms in sumptuous fabrics, half-canopy beds, and window walls or French doors opening onto private harborfront decks (plus minibars and minirefrigerators). Main-inn rooms are done in English country style, with stenciled-pine armoires and florals. All rooms have phones, air-conditioning, and cable TV. ⊠ *Easton St., Box 1139, 02554,* ☎ *508/228–2500 or 800/475–2637,* ℻ *508/325–1195. 48 rooms, 32 cottages (some with kitchens). Restaurant, bar, pool, croquet, children's program, concierge, business services. AE, D, DC, MC, V. Closed mid-Sept.–Memorial Day.*

$$$-$$$$ ▥ **Century House.** Fans of the TV show *Wings* will recognize this gray-shingle 1870s sea captain's home in a residential neighborhood a few minutes' walk from town. The inn beckons its guests home for afternoon ice tea and snacks on the porch or cocktails in front of the fire. Most of the cheery rooms with country furnishings have canopy beds and down comforters; artwork is by former guests. Highlights of the breakfast buffet are homemade granola, fresh-baked breads, and cinnamon coffee. The owners also rent two cottages on the island: one on Nantucket harbor, the other by 'Sconset's beach. ⊠ *10 Cliff Rd., 02554,* ☎ *508/228–0530. 14 rooms, 12 with bath. CP. MC, V.*

$$$-$$$$ ⊞ **Jared Coffin House.** This complex of four buildings is a longtime favorite with many visitors. The main building—a three-story, cupola-top brick mansion built in 1845—has a historic feeling that the others don't have. It is beautifully furnished with Oriental carpets, lace curtains, and antiques (the other buildings have reproductions); rooms across the street are larger. All rooms have phones; some have cable TV and minirefrigerators. Small, less expensive single rooms are also available. ⊠ *29 Broad St., Box 1580, 02554,* ☎ *508/228–2400, or 800/248– 2405,* FAX *508/228–8549. 60 rooms. Restaurant, bar. Full breakfast included. AE, D, DC, MC, V.*

$$$ ⊞ **Centerboard.** White walls (some with pastel murals of moors and sky), natural or mauve-washed light woods, white furniture, and white lacy linens and comforters on featherbeds create a cool, dreamy atmosphere at this bed-and-breakfast. Antique quilts and stained glass add touches of color. The Victorian suite is a stunner, including fine antiques, a working fireplace, and a green-marble bath with whirlpool. ⊠ *8 Chester St., Box 456, 02554,* ☎ *508/228–9696. 4 rooms, 1 suite, 1 studio. CP. AE, MC, V.*

$$-$$$ ⊞ **76 Main Street.** Built in 1883, this inn carefully blends antiques and
★ reproductions, Oriental rugs, handmade quilts, and fine woods. Room 3, originally the dining room, has wonderful woodwork, a carved-wood armoire, and twin four-posters; spacious Room 1 has large windows, massive redwood pocket doors, and an eyelet-dressed canopy bed. Both are on the first floor. The motel-like annex rooms have low ceilings and are a bit dark, but they are large enough for families and have color TVs and refrigerators. No smoking. ⊠ *76 Main St., 02554,* ☎ *508/228– 2533. 18 rooms. CP. AE, D, MC, V.*

$$ ⊞ **18 Gardner Street.** This B&B is set in two antique buildings and features good-sized rooms with elegant satin wallcoverings, white eyelet sheets, and handmade quilts; most rooms have working fireplaces and queen-size beds. All have air-conditioning and cable TV. The 1835 main house has 9-foot ceilings, wide-board floors, and a large fireplace in the common room; a two-bedroom apartment has a kitchen and living and dining areas. No smoking. ⊠ *18 Gardner St., 02554,* ☎ *508/228–1155 or 800/435–1450. 14 rooms (2 share bath), 3 suites. Full breakfast included. AE, D, MC, V.*

Nightlife and the Arts

NIGHTLIFE

The Hearth (⊠ 5 Beach St., ☎ 508/228–1500), the Harbor House hotel's restaurant, has dancing to live music (country, folk, oldies) weekends year-round in its fireplaced lounge, with sports TV, darts, games, and a fun, light menu. **The Regatta at the White Elephant** (⊠ Easton St., ☎ 508/228–2500), a formal hotel restaurant lounge—proper dress advised—has a harbor view and a pianist playing show tunes. **The Box** (⊠ 6 Dave St., ☎ 508/228–9717), a year-round club, has people of all ages up and dancing to live rock and reggae and to recorded music. **The Muse** (⊠ 44 Atlantic Ave., ☎ 508/228–6873 or 508/228–8801) sells pizza to hungry patrons young and old who crowd the dance floor of this club 12 months a year.

THE ARTS

Nantucket Chamber Music Center (⊠ Coffin School, Winter St., ☎ 508/228–3352) gives year-round choral and instrumental concerts as well as instruction. In July and August, the **Nantucket Musical Arts Society** (☎ 508/228–3735) offers Tuesday-evening concerts featuring internationally acclaimed musicians at the First Congregational Church (⊠ 62 Centre St.; concerts accessible to people who use wheelchairs).

Noonday Concerts, with vocal and instrumental music sometimes featuring an 1831 Goodrich organ, are held at the Unitarian Church (✉ 11 Orange St., ☎ 508/228–5466) Thursday at noon.

Actors Theatre of Nantucket (✉ Methodist Church, Centre and Main Sts., ☎ 508/228–6325) presents several plays each season (May–Oct.), plus children's matinees. **Theatre Workshop of Nantucket** (✉ Bennett Hall, Congregational Church, 62 Centre St., ☎ 508/228–4305) stages community theater year-round.

Outdoor Activities and Sports

BIKING
Scenic and well-maintained bike paths lead to Madaket, 'Sconset, and Surfside beaches. **Nantucket Cycling Club** (☎ 508/228–1164) holds open races most of the year.

FISHING
Bluefish and bass are the main catches. **Barry Thurston's Fishing Tackle** (✉ Harbor Sq., ☎ 508/228–9595) and **Bill Fisher Tackle** (✉ 14 New La., ☎ 508/228–2261) rent equipment. Charters leave from Straight Wharf every day in season.

HEALTH AND FITNESS
Club N.E.W. (✉ 10 Young's Way, ☎ 508/228–4750) has aerobics, dance, and yoga classes, exercise machines and free weights, and personal trainers.

TENNIS
Town courts (☎ 508/325–5334; ⊙ Year-round, weather permitting) are at Jetties Beach. **Brant Point Racquet Club** (✉ N. Beach St., ☎ 508/228–3700; closed mid-Oct.–mid-May) has nine clay courts, lessons, and a pro shop.

WATER SPORTS
Indian Summer Sports (✉ Steamboat Wharf, ☎ 508/228–3632) and **Force 5** (✉ Jetties Beach, ☎ 508/228–5358; ✉ 37 Main St., ☎ 508/228–0700) rent all kinds of equipment and give lessons. **The Sunken Ship** (✉ Corner of Broad and S. Water Sts., ☎ 508/228–9226) offers scuba lessons and rents equipment for diving and other sports.

Shopping

ART AND ANTIQUES
Robert Wilson Galleries (✉ 34 Main St., ☎ 508/228–6246) carries fine contemporary American art, most of it traditional and representational. **Sailor's Valentine Gallery** (✉ 40 Centre St., ☎ 508/228–2011) has folk and contemporary art and exquisite sailor's valentines (intricate shell designs in glass boxes).

Forager House (✉ 20 Centre St., ☎ 508/228–5977) specializes in folk art and Americana, including whirligigs, maps and charts, and postcards. **Nina Hellman Antiques** (✉ 48 Centre St., ☎ 508/228–4677) carries scrimshaw, ship models, nautical instruments, and other marine antiques and Nantucket memorabilia. **Tonkin of Nantucket** (✉ 33 Main St., ☎ 508/228–9697) has four floors of fine English antiques, including furniture, china, art, and marine and scientific instruments. **Janis Aldridge** (✉ 50 Main St., upstairs, ☎ 508/228–6673) sells beautifully framed antique prints, including many botanicals. **Paul La Paglia** (✉ 38 Centre St., ☎ 508/228–8760) has moderately priced antique prints, including Nantucket scenes and fish.

BOOKS
Mitchell's Book Corner (✉ 54 Main St., ☎ 508/228–1080) offers the best selection of books on Nantucket; write for a brochure. **Museum**

Shop (✉ Broad St., ☎ 508/228–5785) has island-related books, antique whaling tools, toys, reproduction furniture, and local jellies.

CLOTHING

Murray's Toggery Shop (✉ 62 Main St., ☎ 508/228–0437) is the home of the Nantucket Reds, a collection of cotton clothing for men, women, and children. This shop also carries top-name traditional clothing and footwear for all. **The Peanut Gallery** (✉ 8 India St., ☎ 508/228–2010) has a discriminating collection of children's clothing. **Zero Main** (✉ 0 Main St., ☎ 508/228–4401) stocks stylishly classic women's clothing, shoes, and accessories.

CRAFTS

Four Winds Craft Guild (✉ 6 Straight Wharf, ☎ 508/228–9623), specializing in authentic lightship baskets and collector's scrimshaw, is the oldest shop in Nantucket.

JEWELRY

The Golden Basket (✉ 44 Main St., ☎ 508/228–4344) sells miniature lightship baskets in gold or silver, some with precious stones and pearls, as well as other fine jewelry.

Siasconset

㉙ *6 mi east of Nantucket town.*

The beach community of Siasconset (called 'Sconset)—first a fishing village, then an actors' colony—today offers an unhurried lifestyle in beautiful surroundings. Here you'll find pretty little streets lined with rose-covered cottages with driveways of crushed white shells, a post office, a general store, a few restaurants, and a beach.

☾ Kids and young-at-heart adults will enjoy **J. J. Clammp's** (✉ Nobadeer Farm and Sun Island Rds., off Milestone Rd., ☎ 508/228–8977), an 18-hole miniature golf course, with access to the Milestone Road bike path. There's a free shuttle from town, at Visitors' Services on Federal Street, in season.

Beach

Siasconset Beach, at the end of a 7-mile bike path, is an uncrowded sandy beach with sometimes heavy surf and a lifeguard; rest rooms and food are nearby.

Dining and Lodging

$$$–$$$$ ✕ **Chanticleer.** At this renowned restaurant in a rose-covered cottage in 'Sconset, owner-chef Jean-Charles Berruet has for two decades created sumptuous classic French fare using fresh island ingredients. Prix-fixe menus are offered at dinner (à la carte also available), which is served in the formal French manor-style dining room with trompe l'oeil painting, in the greenhouse room, or in the grill room with fireplace upstairs. The wine cellar is legendary, with 1,500 choices among 38,000 bottles. Lunch in the rose garden is heavenly. ✉ *9 New St.,* ☎ *508/257–6231. Jacket required. AE, MC, V. Closed Mon. and Columbus Day–Mother's Day.*

$$$$ ▦ **Summer House.** Across from 'Sconset Beach, these one- and two-bedroom rose-covered cottages are furnished in a blend of unfussy beach style and romantic English country; most have marble baths with hot tubs. Some have fireplaces or kitchens. ✉ *Ocean Ave., Box 880, 02564,* ☎ *508/257–4577. 8 cottages. 2 restaurants, bar, pool. CP. AE, MC, V. Closed Nov.–late Apr.*

Outdoor Activities and Sports

Siasconset Golf Club (⌧ Milestone Rd., ☎ 508/257–6596) is a public nine-hole course.

En Route A scenic drive along Polpis Road takes you past the precariously perched **Sankaty Light,** built in 1849, and large areas of open moorland. The entrance to the 205-acre **Windswept Cranberry Bog,** open to walkers and bike riders, is also on Polpis, between Quidnet Road and Wauwinet Road.

Coatue–Coskata–Great Point

③⓪ *12¾ mi from Town to Great Point Light, 11 mi from 'Sconset.*

Wauwinet Road takes you to the gateway of Coatue–Coskata–Great Point, an unpopulated spit of sand comprising three cooperatively managed wildlife refuges and entered only on foot or by four-wheel-drive over-sand vehicle (☎ 508/228–2884 for information). Its beaches, dunes, salt marshes, and stands of oak and cedar provide a major habitat for such birds as marsh hawks, oystercatchers, terns, and herring gulls. Because of frequent dangerous currents and riptides and the lack of lifeguards, swimming is strongly discouraged, especially around the **Great Point Light.**

Dining and Lodging

$$$–$$$$ ✕🏨 **Wauwinet.** A superb location (8 mi from town, surrounded by
★ ocean and harbor beaches) sets the exclusive Wauwinet resort apart from all the rest. The restaurant, Topper's, reflects the inn's casual sophistication: hand-painted floors, fine wood paneling, oil paintings. Topper's serves new American cuisine, including sautéed lobster with citrus, wild mushrooms, and roasted peppers in a Chardonnay beurre blanc. The patio overlooking the water is a pleasant place for lunch or drinks, especially at sunset. Fine furnishings and extensive services and amenities make this mid-19th-century property a luxurious perch. Each guest room—decorated in country style, with pine antiques—has a phone, air-conditioning, and TV with VCR; the more expensive rooms have spectacular views of the sunset over the water. ⌧ *120 Wauwinet Rd., Box 2580, 02584,* ☎ *508/228–0145 or 800/426–8718, restaurant 508/228–8768,* 𝖥𝖠𝖷 *508/228–6712. 25 rooms, 5 cottages. Restaurant (reservations essential; closed mid-Dec.–mid-May), bar, tennis courts, croquet, boating, business services. Full breakfast and afternoon port and cheese included. AE, DC, MC, V. Closed Nov.–May.*

En Route The **Nantucket Life Saving Museum,** on the road back to town from Great Point, is housed in a re-creation of an 1874 Life Saving Service station. The station honors the men who valiantly lived by the service's motto: "You have to go out, but you don't have to come back." Exhibits include original rescue equipment and boats, photos, and accounts of daring rescues. ⌧ *Polpis Rd.,* ☎ *508/228–1885.* 💲 *$3.* ☉ *Mid-June–mid-Sept., Tues.–Sun., 9:30–5.*

Surfside

③① *2½ mi south of Nantucket town.*

Surfside Beach is easily reached by shuttle bus or bicycle, and draws a college-age crowd. To the west of Surfside is the **Nantucket Vineyard** (⌧ 3 Bartlett Farm Rd., ☎ 508/228–9235), which offers tastings of its wines.

Lodging

$ 🏨 **Hosteling International–Nantucket.** In a former lifesaving station in a great location at Surfside Beach, this hostel is the island's only budget accommodation (no camping is allowed on Nantucket). There's a group kitchen and common areas. ⊠ *31 Western Ave., 02554,* ☎ *508/228–0433. 49 beds. MC, V. Closed mid-Oct.–mid-Apr.*

Outdoor Activities and Sports

Miacomet Golf Club (⊠ 12 W. Miacomet Rd., ☎ 508/228–8987) is a public nine-hole course abutting Miacomet Pond; an 18-hole course is in the works.

Shopping

The island specialty is Nantucket lightship baskets. These woven baskets of oak or cane, with covers adorned with scrimshaw or rosewood, were first made on lightships by crew members between chores, and are now used as preppy purses. **The Lightship Shop** (⊠ 20 Miacomet Ave., ☎ 508/228-4164) has lightship baskets, a lightship basket repair service, and supplies and molds available for rent to make your own basket.

Nantucket A to Z

Arriving and Departing

BY FERRY

If you plan to take a car to the island in summer or on popular weekends, you *must* reserve as far ahead as possible; spaces are often sold out months in advance.

The **Steamship Authority** (on Nantucket, ☎ 508/228–3274; on the Cape, ☎ 508/477–8600) runs car-and-passenger ferries to the island from Hyannis year-round. The trip takes 2¼ hours. ☺ *One-way: $10 adults, $5 children 5–12, $5 bicycles. Cars: $90 mid-May–mid-Oct., $70 mid-Oct.–Nov. 30 and mid-Mar.–mid-May, $50 Dec.–mid-Mar.*

Hy-Line (on Nantucket, ☎ 508/228–3949; in Hyannis, ☎ 508/778–2600) carries passengers from Hyannis from early May through October. The trip takes 1¾ to 2 hours. Cost one-way: $11 adults, $5.50 children 5–12, $4.50 bicycles. There is also service from Oak Bluffs on Martha's Vineyard (☎ 508/693–0112) early June to mid-September; that trip takes 2¼ hours and costs the same.

BY PLANE

Nantucket Memorial Airport (☎ 508/325–5300) is about 3½ miles southeast of town via Old South Road; cars and jeeps may be rented at airport desks.

Cape Air (☎ 508/771–6944 or 800/352–0714) connects the island with Boston, Hyannis, Martha's Vineyard, and New Bedford year-round.

Getting Around

BY BICYCLE AND MOPED

Bikes and mopeds can be rented near Steamboat Wharf from **Young's Bicycle Shop** (☎ 508/228–1151; also cars), and on Steamboat Wharf or Straight Wharf from the **Nantucket Bike Shop** (☎ 508/228–1999; in season).

BY BUS

In season **Barrett's Tours** (⊠ 20 Federal St., ☎ 508/228–0174) runs shuttles to 'Sconset, Surfside, and Jetties beaches.

BY TAXI

Year-round taxi companies include **A-1 Taxi** (☎ 508/228–3330 or 508/228–4084), **All Points Taxi** (☎ 508/228–5779), and **Atlantic Cab** (☎ 508/228–1112).

Contacts and Resources

Rent cars at the airport desks of **Budget** (☎ 508/228–5666), **Hertz** (☎ 508/228–9421), and **Nantucket Windmill** (☎ 508/228–1227), which also has jeeps. Ask about ferry pick-up service.

Nantucket Cottage Hospital (✉ 57 Prospect St., ☎ 508/228–1200) has a 24-hour emergency room.

For guided four-wheel-drive trips to remote areas for surf casting (including gear rental), contact **Whitney Mitchell** (☎ 508/228–2331).

BY BUS: Barrett's Tours (✉ 20 Federal St., ☎ 508/228–0174), conducted by third-generation Nantucketers, and **Nantucket Island Tours** (✉ Straight Wharf, ☎ 508/228–0334) give 1½-hour narrated bus tours of the island, spring through fall; buses meet ferries.

BY CARRIAGE: Carried Away (☎ 508/228–0218) takes people on narrated carriage rides through the town's historic district in season, and on 19th century-style picnics, complete with home-baked goods.

BY FOOT: Roger Young's historic walking tours (☎ 508/228–1062; in season) of the town center are entertaining and leisurely.

BY VAN: Gail's Scenic Rides (☎ 508/257–6557) has sixth-generation Nantucketer Gail Johnson narrating a lively, 1½-hour van tour.

Nantucket Accommodations (✉ Box 217, ☎ 508/228–9559) and **Martha's Vineyard and Nantucket Reservations** (✉ Box 1322, Lagoon Pond Rd., Martha's Vineyard, ☎ 508/693–7200 or 800/666–4678 in MA) book inns, hotels, bed-and-breakfasts, and cottages. **DestIN-Nations** (☎ 800/333–4667) will arrange any and all details of a visit.

Chamber of Commerce (✉ Pacific Club Bldg., 48 Main St., ☎ 508/228–1700; ☉ Weekdays 9–5). **Nantucket Information Bureau** (✉ 25 Federal St., ☎ 508/228–0925; ☉ Year-round, call for hrs).

Nantucket Whalewatch (✉ Hy-Line dock, Straight Wharf, ☎ 508/283–0313 or 800/942–5464) runs naturalist-led excursions in season.

THE NORTH SHORE

Updated by
Anne
Merewood

The slice of Atlantic coast known as the North Shore extends past grimy docklands, through Boston's well-to-do northern suburbs, to the picturesque Cape Ann region, and beyond the Cape to Newburyport, just south of New Hampshire. It takes in historic Salem, which thrives on a history of witches, millionaires, and maritime trade; Gloucester, the oldest seaport in America; quaint little Rockport, crammed with crafts shops and artists' studios; Newburyport with its redbrick center and rows of clapboard Federal mansions; and miles of sandy beaches. Bright and busy in the short summer season, the North Shore calms some between November and June.

Numbers in the margin correspond to points of interest on the North Shore map.

The North Shore

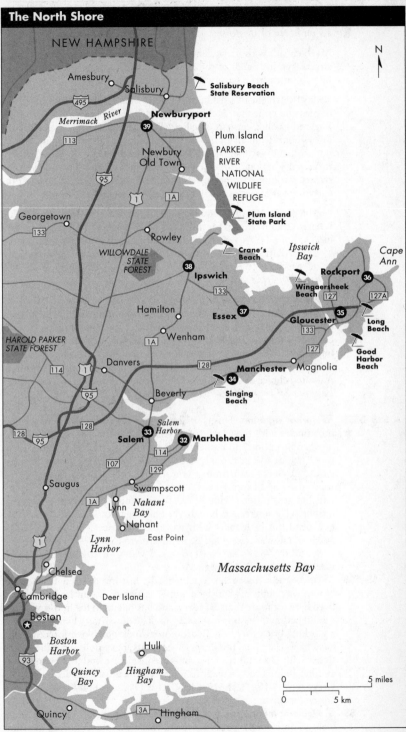

NEW HAMPSHIRE

Amesbury

Salisbury

☂ Salisbury Beach
State Reservation

495

Merrimack River

Newburyport

113

39

Newbury
Old Town

Plum Island

PARKER

RIVER

NATIONAL

WILDLIFE

REFUGE

95

1

1A

Georgetown

☂ Plum Island
State Park

133

Rowley

Crane's
Beach

Ipswich
Bay

Cape
Ann

WILLOWDALE
STATE
FOREST

38

Wingaersheek
Beach

Rockport

36

Ipswich

133

127

127A

Hamilton

37

Essex

Gloucester

35

HAROLD PARKER
STATE FOREST

Wenham

133

Long
Beach

1A

128

127

114

1

Danvers

128

Magnolia

Good
Harbor
Beach

Beverly

Manchester

95

128

Singing
Beach

34

128

Salem
Harbor

33

32 **Marblehead**

95

Salem

114

107

129

Saugus

Swampscott

1A

Nahant
Bay

Lynn

Nahant

1

Lynn
Harbor

East Point

Massachusetts Bay

Chelsea

Cambridge

Deer Island

Boston

★

93

Boston
Harbor

Hull

Quincy
Bay

Hingham
Bay

0   5 miles

0   5 km

Quincy

3A Hingham

Marblehead

③ *15 mi north of Boston.*

Marblehead, with its ancient clapboard houses and narrow, winding streets, retains much of the character of the village founded in 1629 by fishermen from Cornwall and the Channel Islands.

Today, Marblehead's fishing fleet pales in comparison to the armada of pleasure craft that anchors in the harbor: This town is one of New England's sailing capitals, and Race Week (usually the last week of July) draws boats from all along the eastern seaboard. But merchant sailors, not weekend yachtsmen, made Marblehead prosper in the 18th century; many of their impressive Georgian mansions still line downtown streets. Parking is notoriously difficult; try the 30-car public lot at the end of Front Street or along the street in metered areas.

Marblehead's Victorian municipal building, **Abbott Hall** (circa 1876), is unremarkable except for the fact that it houses A. M. Willard's painting *The Spirit of '76*, one of America's treasured patriotic icons, depicting three Revolutionary veterans with fife, drum, and flag. ⊠ *Washington St.,* ☎ *617/631–0528.* ☉ *June–Oct., Mon., Tues., and Thurs. 8–5; Wed. 2:30–8:30; Fri. 8–6.*

Dining and Lodging

$$$ ✕ **The Landing.** Right on Marblehead harbor and still in the historic district, this pleasant, small restaurant offers outdoor dining on a balcony over the sea. Inside are wood chairs and tables and lots of hanging plants. The chef prepares lobster, scallops primavera, seafood scampi, Atlantic sole Florentine, Ipswich clams, and seafood kabob. A limited choice of steak and chicken dishes are also served. ⊠ *Clark's Landing off Front St.,* ☎ *617/631–6268. AE, D, DC, MC, V.*

$$$–$$$$ 🏨 **Harbor Light Inn.** This is the best place to stay in Marblehead, and
★   it competes with the Clark Currier Inn in Newburyport as one of the most comfortable and authentic inns on the North Shore. Special features include five in-room hot tubs, skylights, rooftop decks, and spacious, modern bathrooms. Traditional touches are found in the four-poster and canopy beds, carved arched doorways, sliding (original) Indian shutters, wide-board floors, and antique mahogany furnishings. The innkeepers bought the building next door and added eight big, beautiful bedrooms with working fireplaces, four-poster beds, and painted-wood paneling. ⊠ *58 Washington St., 01945,* ☎ *617/631–2186,* 𝔽𝔸𝕏 *617/631–2216. 20 rooms, 2 suites. Breakfast room, pool, meeting room. CP. AE, MC, V.*

$$–$$$ 🏨 **Harborside House.** In Marblehead's historic district, Harborside House was built in 1850 by a ship's carpenter. Susan Livingston has lived here for more than 30 years, and has operated the house as a successful bed-and-breakfast since 1985. The downstairs living room has a working brick fireplace. Bedrooms, two of which overlook Marblehead harbor with its hundreds of sailboats, have polished wide-board floors with Oriental rugs. Susan is a considerate and interesting host, and her home is convenient to all of Marblehead's attractions. ⊠ *23 Gregory St., 01945,* ☎ *617/631–1032. 3 rooms. Breakfast room. CP. No credit cards.*

$$ 🏨 **Pleasant Manor Inn.** Off the main road between Salem and Marblehead and ⅛ mile from the beach, this rambling Victorian mansion has large guest rooms (some with pineapple four-poster beds) and a carved mahogany staircase. The atmosphere is relaxed and welcoming, and manager Lorraine Hanley offers very reasonable rates. Amelia Earhart stayed in Room 32 in 1923, when the building first became

an inn. ⊠ *Rte. 114, 264 Pleasant St., 01945,* ☎ *617/631–5843. 12 rooms with bath. Air-conditioning, tennis court. CP. No credit cards.*

Salem

★ ③③ *15 mi from Boston, 4 mi from Marblehead.*

Don't be put off by the industrial surroundings; the setting may be tarnished, but Salem is a gem, full of compelling museums, trendy waterfront stores and restaurants, a traffic-free shopping area, and a wide open common with a children's playground and jogging path. Settled in 1630, the town is known for the witchcraft hysteria of 1692, a rich maritime tradition, and the architectural splendor of its Federal homes. The frigates of Salem opened the Far East trade routes and provided the wealth that produced America's first millionaires. Numbered among its native sons are Nathaniel Hawthorne, the navigator Nathaniel Bowditch, and the architect Samuel McIntire.

One way to take in Salem's sights is to follow the **Heritage Trail** (a red line painted on the sidewalk) around the town. If you prefer to ride, the **Salem Trolley** (☞ Guided Tours *in* Contacts and Resources, *below*) gives narrated tours of the city.

Salem unabashedly calls itself "Witch City." Decorations featuring witches astride broomsticks enhance the police cars; witchcraft shops, memorials, and at least one resident witch commemorate the city's infamous witchcraft trials of 1692, when religious zeal ran out of control and resulted in the hangings of 19 alleged witches. Visitors can see the infamous happenings retold in wax at the **Salem Wax Museum** (⊠ 288 Derby St., ☎ 508/740–2929), and by actors at the **Witch Dungeon Museum** (⊠ 16 Lynde St., ☎ 508/741–3570). But if you only have the time or stomach for one version of the witchcraft story, head for the multisensory presentation at the **Salem Witch Museum,** which stages a reenactment of the events using 13 different sets and life-size models. ⊠ *Washington Sq. N,* ☎ *508/744–1692.* ☜ *$4.* ☉ *Daily 10– 5 (until 7 July–Aug.).*

No witch ever lived at **Witch House,** but more than 200 accused witches were questioned here. Authentic late 17th-century decor reflects the era when the trials were held. ⊠ *310½ Essex St.,* ☎ *508/744–0180.* ☜ *$5.* ☉ *Mid-Mar.–Dec. 1, daily 10–4:30 (until 6 July–Aug.).*

Putting its macabre past behind, Salem went on to become a major seaport, with a thriving overseas trade. **Salem Maritime,** a National Historic Site operated by the National Trust, is just beside Derby Wharf. Tours take in the Customs House, made famous in Nathaniel Hawthorne's *Scarlet Letter*; the Government Warehouse; and historic shipowners' homes. ⊠ *174 Derby St.,* ☎ *508/740–1680.* ☜ *Free.* ☉ *Daily 8:30–5.*

Many exotic spoils brought back by Salem's merchant ships are housed in the **Peabody and Essex Museum,** the oldest continuously operating museum in America. It also has exhibits on New England's whaling and fishing past and documents from the witch trials. For an additional fee, you can tour several historic mansions that belonged to shipowners and other wealthy merchants. ⊠ *East India Sq.,* ☎ *508/745– 1876.* ☜ *$7.* ☉ *May–Nov., Mon.–Sat. 10–5, Sun. noon–5; closed Mon. Nov.–May.*

The House of the Seven Gables, immortalized by Nathaniel Hawthorne in his book of the same name, should not be missed. Tour highlights are a secret staircase discovered during 1886 renovations and a garret with a model of the house. This house once belonged to Hawthorne's cousin; the house in Salem where Hawthorne was born in 1804 has been moved next door and is included in the tour. ⊠ *54 Turner St.,* ☎ *508/744–0991.* ⊡ *$7.* ☉ *July–Oct., daily 9:30–6; Nov.–June, daily 10–4:30. Closed 1st wk in Jan.*

☾ **Pioneer Village and Forest River Park,** Salem, re-create the Salem of the 1630s, when this town was the state capital. Costumed interpreters wander among replicas of thatched cottages, dugout homes, and wigwams. ⊠ *Jct. Rtes. 1A and 129,* ☎ *508/745–0525.* ⊡ *$4.50.* ☉ *Mid-May–Oct., Mon.–Sat. 10–5, Sun. noon–5.*

☾ **Salem Willows Park** (at the eastern end of Derby St.), Salem, has picnic grounds, beaches, food stands, amusements, games, boat rentals, and fishing bait.

The **Rebecca Nurse Homestead** was the home of aged, pious Rebecca, a regular churchgoer whose accusation as a witch caused shock waves. Her trial was a mockery (she was pronounced innocent, but the jury was urged to change its verdict), and she was hanged in 1692. Her family took her body afterward and buried her in secret on the grounds of this house. It has period furnishings and is gradually being developed as a model 18th-century farm. ⊠ *149 Pine St.,* ☎ *508/774–8799.* ⊡ *$3.50.* ☉ *June 15–Labor Day, Tues.–Sun. 1–4:30; Labor Day–Oct., weekends 1–4:30; or by appointment. Closed Nov.–Apr.*

Dining and Lodging

$$ ✕ **Chase House.** This restaurant on Pickering Wharf overlooks the harbor and is extremely busy in summer. The main dining room has low ceilings and exposed-brick walls. The menu lists steak, squid, flounder, and "old-fashioned seafood dinners" of clams, scallops, shrimp, fish, and lobster with onion rings. ⊠ *Pickering Wharf,* ☎ *508/744–0000. AE, D, DC, MC, V.*

$$$ ✕⊡ **Hawthorne's Hotel.** The only full-service hotel in Salem is an imposing redbrick structure conveniently situated on the green just a short walk from the commercial center and most attractions. Decorated in brown and beige, guest rooms are appointed with reproduction antiques, armchairs, and desks—business clients are numerous. The formal restaurant, Nathaniel's, serves lobster, swordfish in mustard cream, prime rib, and poached sole on spinach with champagne cream sauce. ⊠ *On-the-Common, 01970,* ☎ *508/744–4080,* FAX *508/745–9842. 83 rooms, 6 suites. Restaurant, bar, exercise room, meeting rooms. AE, D, DC, MC, V.*

$$$ ⊡ **The Inn at Seven Winter St.** Built in 1870, this conveniently located inn with a deck has been accurately restored to re-create the Victorian era. Rooms, although a little dark, are spacious and well furnished, with heavy mahogany and walnut antiques, working marble fireplaces, and Oriental rugs on polished hardwood floors. Two suites with eat-in kitchens are perfect for families. ⊠ *7 Winter St., 01970,* ☎ *508/745–9520. 7 rooms with bath, 2 suites, 1 studio. CP. MC, V.*

$$–$$$ ⊡ **Amelia Payson Guest House.** This Greek Revival house, built in 1845,
★ has been tastefully converted into a bright, airy bed-and-breakfast inn near the common and all of Salem's historic attractions. Pretty rooms are decorated with floral-print wallpaper, brass and canopy beds, nonworking marble fireplaces, and white wicker furnishings. The downstairs parlor has a grand piano. ⊠ *16 Winter St., 01970,* ☎ *508/744–8304. 3 rooms with bath, 1 studio. CP. AE, MC, V.*

Nightlife and the Arts

Salem is not famed for nightlife, but downstairs at **Roosevelt's** restaurant (⊠ 300 Derby St., ☎ 508/745–9608) you can watch local rock bands playing Wednesday–Saturday nights.

The **North Shore Music Theatre** (⊠ 62 Dunham Rd., Beverly, ☎ 508/922–8500) is a professional company that, from May through December, performs popular and modern musicals as well as children's theater. If you like your meal spiced with intrigue, the **Mystery Cafe** (⊠ At the Village Green restaurant, Danvers, ☎ 617/524–2233 or 800/697–2583; Sat. only), an eight-year-old Boston dinner show, features costumed actors who double as waiters, playing out a mystery that evolves around your table.

Shopping

Salem is the center for a number of offbeat shops with a distinct relationship to the city's witchcraft history. The best known supernatural store is **Crow Haven Corner** (⊠ 125 Essex St., ☎ 508/745–8763), where Laurie Cabot, Salem's "official" witch, presides over a fabulous selection of crystal balls, herbs, tarot decks, healing stones, and books about witchcraft. **The Broom Closet** (⊠ 3 and 5 Central St., ☎ 508/741–3669) stocks 250 varieties of fresh dried herbs, aromatic oils, candles, tarot cards, and New Age music. The friendly, knowledgeable staff is happy to educate shoppers about their wares. **Pyramid Books** (⊠ 214 Derby St., ☎ 508/745–7171) stocks New Age and metaphysical books.

Somewhat more conventional than Salem's witchcraft stores are the waterside gift shops on sparkling, restored **Pickering Wharf,** which also has moorings for private boats, a slew of bars and restaurants, and the **Pickering Wharf Antique Gallery** (☎ 508/741–3113) where five rooms house 50 dealers.

Manchester

🚳 *28 mi from Boston, 9 mi from Salem.*

Many Bostonians day trip here in summer, drawn by the long and lovely Singing Beach, so called because of the noise the wind creates blowing against the sand. This fine beach has lifeguards, food stands, and rest rooms but no parking: Non-residents must pay $15 on summer weekends or $8 on weekdays to use a private lot beside Manchester railroad station—a half-mile walk from the sand.

Lodging

$–$$ 🏨 **Old Corner Inn.** Built in 1865, and once used as the Danish Embassy, the Old Corner Inn has bedrooms with bird's-eye maple floors, four-poster beds, brass gaslight fixtures, feather mattresses, and claw foot tubs; some have working fireplaces. The low rates reflect the fact that, although the country location is attractive, it's a mile's walk to the village center and a mile from the nearest beach. ⊠ *2 Harbor St., 01944, ☎ 508/526–4996. 6 rooms with bath, 3 rooms share 2 baths. CP. AE, MC, V.*

Gloucester

🚳 *37 mi from Boston, 8 mi from Manchester.*

On Gloucester's fine seaside promenade is the famous statue of a man at a ship's wheel—eyes on the horizon—dedicated to those "who go down to the sea in ships." The statue was commissioned by the residents in 1923 in celebration of the seaport's 300th anniversary. The oldest seaport in the nation, Gloucester is today a workaday town, a major fishing port, and home to **Rocky Neck,** the oldest working artists' colony in America.

Gloucester also has some of the best beaches on the North Shore. **Wingaersheek Beach** (⊠ Exit 13 off Rte. 128) is a picture-perfect, well-protected cove of white sand and dunes, with the white Annisquam lighthouse in the bay. **Good Harbor Beach** (⊠ Signposted from Rte. 127A) is a huge, sandy, dune-backed beach with a rocky islet just off-shore. Parking on Gloucester beaches costs $10 on weekdays and a hefty $15 on weekends, when the lots often fill by 10 AM. Just north of Good Harbor, **Long Beach** (⊠ Off Route 127A on the Gloucester-Rockport town line) is an excellent place for sunbathing; parking here costs just $5 (because half the beach is in Rockport!).

The **Hammond Castle Museum,** just south of Gloucester, is a massive re-creation of a medieval stone castle, complete with drawbridge, brooding gloomily over the ocean. It was built in 1926 by the inventor John Hays Hammond, Jr., who patented, among some 800 inventions, the remote control and the gyroscope. Inside are medieval furnishings and paintings, and an impressive organ with 8,600 pipes and 126 stops in the Great Hall. Visible from the castle is **Norman's Woe Rock,** made famous by Longfellow's poem "The Wreck of the Hesperus." ⊠ *80 Hesperus Ave., Gloucester,* ☎ *508/283–2080.* ⊠ *$5.50.* ☉ *May–Oct., Wed.–Sun. 10–5; Nov.–Apr., weekends 10–5.*

Dining and Lodging

$$$ ✕ **White Rainbow.** The dining room in this excellent restaurant is in
★   the basement of a west-end store downtown, and candlelight sets a romantic mood. Specialties include Maui onion soup, grilled beef with a Zinfandel wine sauce, and lobster *estancia* (with tomatoes, artichoke hearts, olives, scallions, wine, and herb butter). ⊠ *65 Main St.,* ☎ *508/281–0017. AE, D, DC, MC, V. No lunch. Closed Mon.*

$$ ✕ **Evie's Rudder.** Quaint and quirky, as befits its ramshackle exterior and artists' colony location, Evie's has been dishing up good food and entertainment, under the same ownership, for almost four decades. The building dates from the 1890s, when it was used for fish packing, and has low ceilings, heavy beams, uneven floors, and shingle walls. You can sit on a wharfside deck to feast on seafood, chicken, steak, and, as the menu puts it, "clam chowder New England–style—whoever heard of adding tomatoes? Manhattan-style? Do you see any skyscrapers out there???" Entertainment includes an invisible flaming baton twirling act by the owner's daughter and a retelling of *Pinderella and the Cince* by Evie herself. Don't miss it! ⊠ *Rocky Neck,* ☎ *508/283–7967. D, MC, V. Closed Nov.–Mar., and Mon.–Wed., Apr. and Oct.*

$$$ ⌂ **Bass Rocks Ocean Inn.** This oceanfront manor house, built in 1899 as a wedding present for a bride who subsequently refused to live in such an isolated location, is listed on the National Registry of Historic Places. It contains a game room with a billiard table, a library, a rooftop sundeck, and a sunporch for breakfast and afternoon tea. Large guest rooms, all with sea views, are in the adjacent modern two-story building; each has either a patio or a balcony. ⊠ *107 Atlantic Rd., 01930,* ☎ *508/283–7600. 48 rooms. Pool, bicycles, recreation room. AE, D, DC, MC, V. Closed Nov.–Apr.*

$$$ ⌂ **Best Western Back Shore Motor Lodge.** All guest rooms, perched on a rocky headland, have sea views and sliding doors that lead to decks at the front of the building. Furnishings are good-quality motor-lodge style, with some reproductions. ⊠ *85 Atlantic Rd., East Gloucester 01930,* ☎ *508/283–1198. 23 rooms. Pool. No credit cards.*

$$–$$$ ⊡ **Cape Ann Motor Inn.** This friendly, wood-shingle, three-story motel is as close to the sands as they come, right on Long Beach on the Glouces-ter-Rockport border. Some of the smallish rooms have kitchenettes, and all have balconies and superb views over beach, sea, and the twin lights of Thatcher's Island. The suite has modern furnishings and a whirlpool tub. ⊠ *33 Rockport Rd., 01930,* ☎ *508/281–2900. 29 rooms, 1 suite. AE, D, MC, V.*

Nightlife and the Arts

NIGHTLIFE

The Rhumb Line (⊠ 40 Railroad Ave., ☎ 508/283–9732) offers good food and live entertainment six nights a week in the bar, with rock-and-roll Friday and Saturday, and jazz on Sunday.

THE ARTS

The magnificent organ at the **Hammond Castle Museum** (⊠ 80 Hes-perus Ave., ☎ 508/283–2080) is used for organ concerts year-round, and in summer pops concerts are added to the schedule. The **Glouces-ter Stage Company** (⊠ 267 E. Main St., Gloucester, ☎ 508/281–4099) is a nonprofit professional group staging new plays and revivals May–September.

Outdoor Activities and Sports

FISHING

Gloucester has a great fishing tradition, and many fishermen in the town's busy working harbor offer fishing trips. Try **Captain Bill's Deep Sea Fishing** (⊠ 9 Traverse St., ☎ 508/283–6995) for full- and half-day excursions.

Rockport

  36 *41 mi from Boston, 4 mi from Gloucester.*

Rockport, at the very tip of Cape Ann, derives its name from its gran-ite formations, and many a Boston-area structure is made of stone from the town's long-gone quarries. Today, Rockport is a mecca for sum-mer tourists attracted by its hilly rows of colorful clapboard houses, historic inns, artists' studios, and its beach (albeit rather small).

In summer, parking in town is impossible; leave your car at the Tourist Information Center lot on Route 127 and take the **Cape Ann Trolley,** which leaves roughly once an hour daily in July and August, making 17 stops in and around town. While known primarily as a tourist haunt, Rockport has not gone overboard on T-shirt emporia and the other accoutrements of a summer economy: Shops sell crafts, clothing, and cameras, not trashy souvenirs, and restaurants serve quiche, seafood, or home-baked cookies rather than fast food. From downtown, walk out to the end of **Bearskin Neck** for an impressive view of the open Atlantic and the nearby lobster shack affectionately known as "Motif No. 1" because of its popularity as a subject for artists.

Dining and Lodging

$$$ ✕ **Peg Leg Inn.** Lobster thermidor, lobster Newburg, lobster pie, lob-
★ ster salad, and lobsters boiled, baked, or broiled—take your pick and enjoy this excellent restaurant. The flagstone floor and open kitchen create a comforting, "grandma's house" atmosphere, which is com-plemented by the traditional dress and friendliness of the staff. Also available: pasta, chicken pie, and steak. ⊠ *18 Beach St.,* ☎ *508/546–3038. AE, DC, MC, V. BYOB. Closed Nov.–Apr.*

$$ ✕ **Brackett's Oceanview Restaurant.** A big bay window in this homey
★ restaurant allows an excellent view across the beach. The menu includes

scallop casserole, fish cakes, and other seafood dishes. ⊠ *27 Main St.,* ☎ *508/546–2797. AE, D, DC, MC, V. BYOB. Closed Nov.–Mar.*

$$ ✕ **My Place by the Sea.** The only place to eat outdoors in Rockport is at this restaurant right at the end of Bearskin Neck. The lower deck perches on rocks over the ocean, and the menu includes New England seafood specialties such as lobster, sole fillet stuffed with lobster, and haddock fillet with a savory clam stuffing, as well as steaks, pasta, salads, and sandwiches. ⊠ *Bearskin Neck,* ☎ *508/546–9667. AE, D, DC, MC, V. Closed Nov.–Mar.*

$ ✕ **Portside Chowder House.** This great little hole-in-the-wall restaurant is one of the few in Rockport that's open year-round. Chowder is the house specialty; also offered are lobster and crab plates, salads, burgers, and sandwiches. ⊠ *Bearskin Neck, no phone. No credit cards. No dinner Oct.–Apr.*

$$$$ ✕▥ **Yankee Clipper Inn.** The imposing Georgian mansion that forms the main part of this impressive, perfectly set compound sits surrounded by gardens on a rocky point jutting into the sea. Built as a private home in the 1930s, it's been managed as an inn by one family for 50 years. Most rooms are spacious and have ocean views; all are furnished with antiques and four-poster or canopy beds. In the Quarterdeck building, contemporary rooms have fabulous sea views. The nearby 1840 Greek Revival Bullfinch house is appointed with tasteful antiques but has less of a view. ⊠ *96 Granite St., 01966,* ☎ *508/546–3407. 26 rooms, 6 suites. Restaurant, pool. Full breakfast included. AE, D, MC, V. Closed Dec. 20–Mar. 1.*

$$$ ▥ **Seacrest Manor.** This distinctive inn is surrounded by large gardens on a hill overlooking the sea. Two elegant sitting rooms are furnished with antiques and leather chairs; the hall and staircase are hung with paintings by local artists. Guest rooms vary in size and character and have a combination of traditional and antique furnishings—upstairs, two have large private decks with sea views. ⊠ *131 Marmion Way, 01966,* ☎ *508/546–2211. 8 rooms, 2 share bath. Dining room. Full breakfast included. No credit cards. Closed Dec.–Mar.*

$$–$$$ ▥ **Addison Choate Inn.** This lovely, white clapboard inn sits incon-
★ spicuously among private homes, just a minute's walk from the center of town. The spacious rooms, with large bathrooms, are beautifully decorated. The navy and white captain's room has a dark-wood four-poster bed with a net canopy, handmade quilts, and Oriental rugs. Other rooms—all with polished pine floors—have Hitchcock rockers and headboards, spool or filigree brass beds, local seascape paintings, and antiques. The two luxuriously appointed duplex carriage-house apartments have skylights, cathedral ceilings, and exposed wood beams. ⊠ *49 Broadway, 01966,* ☎ *508/546–7543 or 800/245–7543,* ℻ *508/546–7638. 7 rooms with bath, 2 apartments. Pool. CP. D, MC, V.*

$$ ▥ **Inn on Cove Hill.** This Federal building on a picturesque hillside dates
★ back to 1792, when it was reportedly constructed with money from a cache of pirates' gold. Some guest rooms are small, but all are cheerfully appointed with bright, flowery print paper, patchwork quilts, and old-fashioned beds—some are brass, others are canopy four-posters. Rooms have polished wide-board floors, iron latches, wood bathroom fixtures, and pastel-tone Oriental rugs. ⊠ *37 Mt. Pleasant St., 01966,* ☎ *508/546–2701. 9 rooms with bath, 2 rooms share bath. CP. MC, V. Closed late Oct.–Mar.*

$$ ▥ **Sally Webster Inn.** Sally Webster was a member of Hannah Jumper's
★ so-called hatchet gang, which smashed up the town's liquor stores in 1856 and turned Rockport into the dry town it remains today. Sally lived in this house for much of her life. Guest rooms contain rocking

chairs, nonworking brick fireplaces, pine wide-board floors with Oriental rugs, and pineapple four-poster, brass, canopy, or spool beds. Bonnets and wickerwork hang on the walls; most rooms have candle-lanterns that can be lit in the evening. ⊠ *34 Mt. Pleasant St., 01966,* ☎ *508/546–9251. 8 rooms. Breakfast room. Full breakfast included. D, MC, V. Closed Dec. 20–Jan.*

Shopping

ART AND CRAFTS

An artist's colony, Rockport has a tremendous concentration of artists' studios and galleries selling work by local painters. *The Rockport Fine Arts Gallery Guide*, available from the Rockport Chamber of Commerce (☞ Visitor Information, *see* The North Shore A to Z, *below*) lists about 30 reputable galleries in town.

BOOKSTORES

Toad Hall Bookstore (⊠ 51 Main St., ☎ 508/546–7323) has a range of reading material for children and adults.

CLOTHING

The **Madras Shop** (⊠ 37 Main St., ☎ 508/546–3434) is a typical small-town clothing store, stocking everything from kids' mittens to women's lingerie to men's sneakers. The **John Tarr Store** (⊠ 53 Main St., ☎ 508/546–6524) offers a wide variety of traditional clothing for men, women, and children in a friendly, old-fashioned atmosphere. For children the **Small Fry Shop** (⊠ 18 Bearskin Neck, ☎ 508/546–9354) has dressy outfits, caps and hats, sweaters, and dresses at reasonable prices.

Essex

㊲ *31 mi from Boston, 12 mi from Rockport.*

Surrounded by salt marshes, Essex has many antiques stores and more than 15 seafood restaurants. The movie version of Arthur Miller's *The Crucible,* starring Winona Rider and Daniel Day-Lewis, was filmed in Essex and on nearby Hog Island.

The **Essex Shipbuilding Museum** displays exhibits from the 19th century, when the town was an important shipbuilding center; more twin-mast ships were built here than in any other locale. ⊠ *Rte. 133,* ☎ *508/768–7541.* ☞ *$3.* ☉ *Mid-May–mid-Oct., Thurs.–Mon. 11–4, Sun. 1–4.*

Dining

$$ ✕ **Jerry Pelonzi's Hearthside.** This 250-year-old converted farmhouse epitomizes coziness. Four small dining rooms have open fireplaces and exposed beams: The first is low-ceilinged with stencils on the walls; the others have cathedral ceilings with rough-panel walls and small windows. Entrées include baked stuffed haddock, seafood casserole, sirloin steak, lobster, and chicken. ⊠ *Rte. 133,* ☎ *508/768–6002 or 508/768–6003. AE, MC, V.*

$ ✕ **Woodman's of Essex.** This large wood shack with unpretentious booths is *the* place for seafood in the rough. The menu includes lobster, a raw bar, clam chowder, and, its specialty, fried clams. ⊠ *Rte. 133,* ☎ *508/768–6451. No credit cards.*

Outdoor Activities and Sports

CANOEING

Try the **Ipswich** and **Parker** rivers for freshwater canoeing and the **Essex River Estuary** for saltwater canoeing.

Ipswich

38 *36 mi from Boston, 6 mi from Essex.*

Settled in 1633 and famous for its clams, Ipswich has more 17th-century houses standing and occupied than any other place in America; more than 40 homes in town were built before 1725. Information and walking maps are available at the **Visitor Information Center** (⊠ S. Main St., ☎ 508/356–8540; ☉ Daily 10–4).

New England Alive is a petting farm and nature study center with wild animals, farm animals, and reptiles. ⊠ *189 High St. (Rtes. 1A and 133),* ☎ *508/356–7013.* ☜ *$6.* ☉ *Apr.–Nov., weekdays 10–5, weekends 9:30–6.*

Nightlife and the Arts

Castle Hill (⊠ Argilla Rd. ☎ 508/356–7774) holds an annual festival, July 4 through mid-August, of pop, folk, and classical music, plus a jazz ball.

Outdoor Activities and Sports

FISHING

You can fish in the **Parker and Ipswich rivers,** which are both stocked with trout each spring.

HIKING

Ipswich, with its miles of unique salt marshes, is probably the best place to hike on the North Shore. The Massachusetts Audubon's **Ipswich River Wildlife Sanctuary** (☎ 508/887–9264) has a variety of trails through marshland hills, where there are remains of early Colonial settlements, as well as abundant wildlife. Get a self-guiding trail map from the office (closed Mon.).

Newburyport

39 *38 mi from Boston, 12 mi from Ipswich.*

Newburyport's High Street is lined with some of the finest examples of Federal mansions in New England. You'll notice widow's walks perched atop many houses, most of which were built for prosperous sea captains in this city that was once a leading port and shipbuilding center.

While Newburyport's maritime significance ended with the demise of the clipper ships (some of the best of which were built here), an energetic downtown renewal program has breathed new life into the town's redbrick center. Renovated buildings now house restaurants, taverns, and shops selling everything from nautical brasses to antique Oriental rugs. Massachusetts's smallest city is best seen on foot, and there's all-day free parking down by the water. A stroll through the **Waterfront Park and Promenade** gives a super view of the harbor and the fishing and pleasure boats that moor here. The Classic Revival **Custom House Maritime Museum** (circa 1835) contains exhibits on maritime history, models, tools, and paintings. The audiovisual show is presented hourly. ⊠ *25 Water St.,* ☎ *508/462–8681.* ☜ *$3.* ☉ *Apr.–Dec., Mon.–Sat. 10–4, Sun. 1–4.*

OFF THE   **PARKER RIVER NATIONAL WILDLIFE REFUGE** – A causeway leads from
BEATEN PATH   Newburyport to Plum Island, a narrow spit of land with a long, steeply
                 descending public beach at one end and the Parker River National
                 Wildlife Refuge at the other. The refuge has 4,662 acres of salt marsh,
                 freshwater marsh, beaches, and dunes; it is one of the few natural bar-
                 rier beach dune–salt marsh complexes left on the Northeast coast. The

bird-watching, surf fishing, plum and cranberry picking, and swimming are wonderful. The refuge is popular in summer: On weekends, cars begin lining up outside for the limited parking spaces before 7 AM. ☎ *508/465–5753.* ⌸ *$5 per car, $1 for walkers and bicyclists.* ⊙ *½ hr before sunrise–½ hr after sunset.*

Dining and Lodging

$$$ ✕ **Scandia.** This restaurant is well known locally for its fine cuisine:
★ House specialties include rack of lamb, lobster ravioli, and scallop and shrimp dishes. The dining room is small and narrow and dimly lighted with candles on the tables and candle chandeliers. ✉ *25 State St.,* ☎ *508/462–6271. AE, D, DC, MC, V.*

$$–$$$ ✕⌂ **Garrison Inn.** This four-story Georgian redbrick building is set back from the main road on a small square. Guest rooms vary in size; all have handsome replicas. The best rooms are the top-floor suites. The two restaurants, David's and Downstairs at David's, are under separate management; both are top of the line for both food and service. If you dine upstairs, in a room furnished with chandeliers and white linen, an entrée such as sautéed lobster with sea scallops and mushrooms in anise cream can be yours. Downstairs at David's is less formal, with exposed brick arches, a bar, and a lighter menu of steak, burgers, and fish. An advantage of these restaurants is their child-care facility, where, for a nominal fee, kids can play and eat while parents enjoy their own meals in peace. ✉ *11 Brown Sq., 01950,* ☎ *508/465–0910,* FAX *508/465–4017. 18 rooms, 6 suites. 2 restaurants (*☎ *508/462–8077), bar. Inn: AE, DC, MC, V. Restaurants: AE, D, MC, V. Dinner only.*

$$–$$$ ⌂ **Clark Currier Inn.** One of the best inns on the North Shore, the Clark
★ Currier has guest rooms that are spacious and furnished with antiques—some have pencil-post beds, one has a reproduction sea captain's bed complete with drawers below, and another has a glorious sleigh bed dating from the late 19th century. There's a Federal "good morning" staircase (so called because two small staircases join at the head of a large one, permitting family members to greet each other on their way down to breakfast). ✉ *45 Green St., 01950,* ☎ *508/465–8363. 8 rooms with bath. CP. AE, D, MC, V.*

Nightlife

Blues and rock bands play downstairs at **The Grog** (✉ 13 Middle St., ☎ 508/465–8008) Thursday–Sunday nights.

Outdoor Activities and Sports

FISHING

In Newburyport surf casting is the most popular style of fishing. Bluefish, pollock, and striped bass can be taken from the ocean shores of Plum Island; permits to remain on the beach after dark are free for anyone entering the refuge with fishing equipment in the daylight. You don't need a permit to fish from the public beach at Plum Island, and the best spot to choose is around the mouth of the Merrimac River. For deep-sea fishing try **Newburyport Whale Watch** (✉ 54 Merrimac St., ☎ 508/465–9885).

HIKING

At the **Parker River National Wildlife Refuge** (✉ Plum Island, ☎ 508/465–5753), deer and rabbits share space with 25,000 ducks and 6,000 geese. The 2-mile Hellcat Swamp trail cuts through the marshes and sand dunes, taking in the best of the sanctuary. There are trail maps at the office.

The North Shore A to Z

Getting Around

BY BOAT

A boat leaves Boston for Gloucester daily between May 30 and
Labor Day, at 10 AM; return boat leaves Gloucester at 3 PM. The three-
hour trip costs $18 for adults, $10 for children under 12. Contact
A. C. Cruise Lines (✉ 290 Northern Ave., Boston, ☎ 617/261–6633
or 800/422–8419).

BY BUS

From Boston to the North Shore, buses run less frequently than trains,
but **The Coach Company** (☎ 800/874–3377) offers service along Route
1 and an express commuter service from Boston to Newburyport.
The **Cape Ann Transportation Authority** (CATA) (☎ 508/283–7916)
covers the Gloucester/Rockport region.

BY CAR

The primary link between Boston and the North Shore is Route 128,
which breaks off from I–95 and follows the coast northeast to Gloucester. If you stay on I–95, you'll reach Newburyport. A less direct route,
but a scenic one once north of Lynn, is Route 1A, which leaves Boston
via the Callahan Tunnel. Beyond Beverly, Route 1A goes inland toward
Ipswich and Essex; at this point, switch to Route 127, which follows
the coast to Gloucester and Rockport.

BY TRAIN

Massachusetts Bay Transportation Authority (MBTA) (☎ 617/722–3200)
trains leave Boston's North Station for Salem, Beverly, Gloucester,
Rockport, and Ipswich.

Contacts and Resources

EMERGENCIES

Beverly Hospital (✉ Herrick St., Beverly, ☎ 508/922–3000).

GUIDED TOURS

The **Salem Trolley** (✉ Trolley Depot, 191 Essex St., Salem, ☎ 508/744–
5469) gives one-hour narrated tours of the city. Tours depart from the
Trolley Depot daily every hour from 10–4, April through December,
and cost $8 for adults, $3 for children, and $7 for senior citizens.

Essex River Cruises (✉ 35 Dodge St., Essex Marina, Essex, ☎ 508/768–
6981 or 800/748–3706) offers an interesting way to see local wildlife
and explore part of the extensive salt marshes that make up much of
the North Shore. April through October, the *Essex River Queen* takes
visitors to look for wildlife along the saltwater estuary; clambake and
sunset cruises are also available.

A whale-watching trip is a terrific way to spend the day from May to
October, when four breeds of whale feed off the North Shore. Their
abundance is such that you're practically guaranteed to see a half-dozen—
on ideal days you may see 40. Reputable operations include **Cape Ann
Whale Watch** (✉ 415 Main St., Gloucester, ☎ 508/283–5110), **Captain Bill's Whale Watch** (✉ 9 Traverse St., Gloucester, ☎ 508/283–
6995), **Newburyport Whale Watch** (✉ 54 Merrimac St., Newburyport,
☎ 508/465–9885 or 800/848–1111), and **Yankee Fleet/Gloucester
Whale Watch** (✉ 75 Essex Ave., Gloucester, ☎ 508/283–0313).

LATE-NIGHT PHARMACY

Walgreen's (✉ 201 Main St., Gloucester, ☎ 508/283–7361) is open
until 9 weeknights, 6 on weekends.

STATE PARKS

Of the numerous parks in the area, the following have particularly varied facilities: **Halibut Point State Park** (⊠ Rte. 127 to Gott Ave., Rockport, ☎ 508/546–2997), **Parker River National Wildlife Refuge** (⊠ Plum Island, off Rte. 1A, Newburyport, ☎ 508/465–5753), **Plum Island State Reservation** (⊠ Off Rte. 1A, Newburyport, ☎ 508/462–4481), **Salisbury Beach State Reservation** (⊠ Rte. 1A, Salisbury, ☎ 508/462–4481), and the **Willowdale State Forest** (⊠ Linebrook Rd., Ipswich, ☎ 508/887–5931).

VISITOR INFORMATION

The umbrella organization for the region is the **North of Boston Visitors and Convention Bureau** (⊠ 248 Cabot St., Box 642, Beverly 01915, ☎ 508/921–4990; ⊙ Weekdays 9–5). **Cape Ann Chamber of Commerce** (⊠ 33 Commercial St., Gloucester 01930, ☎ 508/283–1601; ⊙ Weekdays 8–5 and, May–Oct., Sat. 10–6 and Sun. 10–4). **Greater Newburyport Chamber of Commerce and Industry** (⊠ 29 State St., Newburyport 01950, ☎ 508/462–6680; ⊙ Weekdays 9–5, Sat. 10–4, Sun. noon–4). **National Park Service Visitor Information** (⊠ 2 New Liberty St., Salem 02642, ☎ 508/740–1650; ⊙ Daily 9–5). **Rockport Chamber of Commerce** (⊠ Box 67, 3 Main St., Rockport 01966, ☎ 508/546–6575; ⊙ May–Oct., Mon.–Sat. 9–5, Sun. 1–5; Nov.–Apr., weekdays 10–4). **Rockport Chamber of Commerce Information Booth** (⊠ Rte. 127; ⊙ May 21–Oct. 16, Mon.–Sat. 11–5, Sun. noon–5). **Salem Chamber of Commerce and Visitor Information** (⊠ 32 Derby Sq., Salem 01970, ☎ 508/744–0004; ⊙ Weekdays 9–5). **Salisbury Chamber of Commerce** (⊠ Town Hall, Beach Rd., Salisbury 01952, ☎ 508/465–3581; ⊙ Weekdays 9–4).

THE PIONEER VALLEY

Updated by Anne Merewood

The Pioneer Valley, a string of historic settlements along the Connecticut River from Springfield in the south up to the Vermont border, formed the western frontier of New England from the early 1600s until the late 18th century. The fertile banks of the river first attracted farmers and traders; later it became a source of power and transport for the earliest industrial cities in America.

Today, the northern regions of the Pioneer Valley remain rural and tranquil; farms and small towns have typical New England architecture. Farther south, the cities of Holyoke and Springfield are more industrial.

Educational pioneers came to this region as well—to form America's first college for women and four other major colleges, as well as several well-known prep schools.

Numbers in the margin correspond to points of interest on the Pioneer Valley map.

Northfield

⓸ *97 mi from Boston.*

Just south of the Vermont border, this remote little country town is known mainly as a center for hikers, campers, and lovers of the outdoors.

The **Northfield Mountain Recreation Center** has 29 miles of varied hiking trails and rents out canoes and rowboats from the large campground at Barton Cove. From here you can paddle to the Munn's Ferry campground, accessible only by canoe. The center also runs sightseeing tours of the Pioneer Valley, along a 12-mile stretch of the Connecticut River between Northfield and Gill on the *Quinnetukut II* riverboat. Ex-

The Pioneer Valley

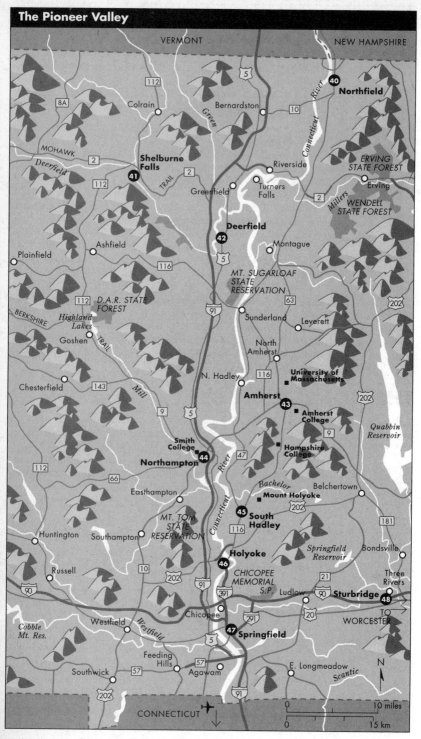

VERMONT

NEW HAMPSHIRE

112

5

10

River

40 **Northfield**

8A

Colrain

Bernardston

Connecticut

ERVING STATE FOREST

MOHAWK

2

Shelburne Falls

Green

Riverside

Erving

Deerfield

41

TRAIL

2

Turners Falls

2

Millers

WENDELL STATE FOREST

112

Greenfield

202

Plainfield

Ashfield

116

Deerfield

42

Montague

BERKSHIRE

112

D.A.R. STATE FOREST

MT. SUGARLOAF STATE RESERVATION

5

Highland Lakes

91

63

Leverett

Goshen

TRAIL

Sunderland

202

Chesterfield

143

Mill

North Amherst

9

5

N. Hadley

116

University of Massachusetts

Quabbin Reservoir

Amherst

43

■ **Amherst College**

202

Smith College

9

44

■ **Hampshire College**

Northampton

River

47

112

66

Bachelor

Belchertown

Easthampton

■ **Mount Holyoke**

45 **South Hadley**

Connecticut

202

181

Huntington

MT. TOM STATE RESERVATION

116

Springfield Reservoir

Bondsville

Southampton

Holyoke

46

Russell

10

202

CHICOPEE MEMORIAL S.P.

21

90

Three Rivers

90

Sturbridge **48**

391

Ludlow

20

TO

Cobble Mt. Res.

Chicopee

291

WORCESTER

Westfield

Westfield

47 **Springfield**

5

Feeding Hills

57

E. Longmeadow

N

Southwick

57

Agawam

Scantic

202

91

CONNECTICUT

0   10 miles

0   15 km

cursions last 1½ hours, and commentary covers geographical, natural, and historical features of the region. You can also take free bus tours up the mountain and visit inside the mountain, to see a large underground power station at work. ⊠ *99 Miller's Falls Rd.,* ☎ *413/659–3714.* ⌑ *Riverboat tour $7; June–early Oct., Wed.–Sun.*

Lodging

$$ ⊞ **Northfield Country House.** Truly remote, this big English manor
★ house is amid thick woodlands on a small hill. A wide staircase leads to the bedrooms, some of which have fireplaces. The smallest rooms are in the former servants' quarters; larger rooms have antiques, several with brass beds. The present owner has considerably renovated this 100-year-old house and has planted hundreds of tulip and daffodil bulbs in the gardens. ⊠ *181 School St., 01360,* ☎ *413/498–2692. 3 rooms with bath, 4 rooms share 2 baths. Pool. Full breakfast included. MC, V.*

Shelburne Falls

❹ *106 mi from Boston.*

Shelburne Falls, straddling the Deerfield River, is a near–perfect example of small-town Americana. A sprinkling of antiques shops and the excellent Copper Angel restaurant overlooking the river make the village a good place to spend the morning. The **Bridge of Flowers** (☎ 413/625–2544) is an arched, 40-foot abandoned trolley bridge transformed by Shelburne Fall's Women's Club into a unique gardened promenade bursting with colors. In the riverbed just downstream from the town are 50 immense **glacial potholes** ground out of the granite during the last ice age.

Dining

$ ✕ **Copper Angel Café.** Perched between the river and Shelburne Falls' main street, the Copper Angel specializes in vegetarian cuisine but also has poultry and fish. Menu items include lentil cutlets with vegetarian gravy, tofu stir-fry with peanut sauce, stuffed chicken breast with garlic mashed potatoes, and scallops wrapped with turkey ham in a maple mustard sauce. Hosts of angels watch over diners, and a copper angel weathervane guards the restaurant from the roof. ⊠ *2 State St.,* ☎ *413/625–2727. Reservations not accepted. MC, V. Closed Mon.–Tues.*

Outdoor Activities and Sports

RAFTING

You can raft along the Deerfield River at Charlemont, on the Mohawk Trail. One-day raft tours over 10 miles of class II–III rapids run daily April through October. ⊠ *Zoar Outdoor, Mohawk Trail, Charlemont 01339,* ☎ *413/339–4010.*

Shopping

The **Salmon Falls Artisans Showroom** (⊠ Ashfield St., ☎ 413/625–9833), carries art, sculpture, pottery, glass, and furniture by 175 local artisans.

Skiing

Berkshire East. Despite its name, Berkshire East is at the head of the Pioneer Valley, 8 miles from Shelburne Falls and 30 miles from the Berkshires. This ski area attracts mostly a regional college crowd and loyal families and youngsters interested in the area's racing program. ⊠ *Box 727, South River Rd., Charlemont 01339,* ☎ *413/339–6617.*

DOWNHILL

The 1,200-foot vertical was once considered more difficult than that of neighboring ski areas. Recent blasting, widening, and sculpting tamed many of the steeper trails, but you can still find steep pitches toward the top. Wide, cruisable intermediate slopes are plentiful, as is beginner terrain. One triple, three double chairlifts and one surface lift serve the 36 trails that are all covered by snowmaking. There's night skiing Wednesday, Friday, and Saturday, 4–10 PM.

CHILD CARE

The nursery takes children from infants through 8 years on weekends; children under 6 ski free. For older children the ski school offers instructional classes. Aspiring racers 5–18 can train on Saturday and Sunday.

Deerfield

★ ㊷ *102 mi from Boston, 10 mi from Shelburne Falls.*

Settled by Native Americans 8,000 years ago, Deerfield was originally a Pocumtuck village—deserted after deadly epidemics and a disastrous war with the Mohawks all but wiped out the tribe. Pioneers eagerly settled in this frontier outpost surrounded by rich farmlands in the 1660s and 1670s, but two bloody massacres at the hands of the Indians and the French caused the village to be abandoned until 1707, when construction began on the buildings that remain today.

Historic Deerfield, a one-street village, now basks in a genteel aura as the site of the prestigious **Deerfield Academy** preparatory school. **"The Street,"** a tree-lined avenue of 50 18th- and 19th-century houses, is protected and maintained as a museum site, with 14 of the preserved buildings open to the public year-round. Some homes contain antique furnishings and decorative arts; other buildings exhibit collections of textiles, silver, pewter, or ceramics. The **Barnard Tavern** has a ballroom with a fiddlers' gallery and several hands-on displays. The whole village is an impressive reflection on 18th- and 19th-century American life. ⊠ *The Street,* ☎ *413/774–5581.* ☜ *1-wk admission to all houses $10; single-house admission $5.* ☉ *Daily 9:30–4:30.*

Dining and Lodging

$$$–$$$$ ✕🏠 **Deerfield Inn.** This inn is in the center of Historic Deerfield and
★ is superbly run by friendly, helpful owner-managers. Guest rooms are decorated with period wallpapers designed for the inn, which was built in 1884. Rooms have antiques and replicas, sofas and bureaus; some have four-poster or canopy beds. Two beds are so high that ladders are provided! The large, sunny dining room is elegantly decorated; specialties include venison and rack of lamb with Dijon mustard and garlic. ⊠ *The Street, 01342,* ☎ *413/774–5587,* 𝔽𝔸𝕏 *413/773–8712. 23 rooms. Restaurant, bar, coffee shop. AE, DC, MC, V. Full breakfast included.*

$$ ✕🏠 **The Whately Inn.** Guest rooms with sloping old wood floors are furnished simply with antiques and four-poster beds. Two are located over the restaurant, which can be noisy. The dining room has exposed beams, tables on a raised stage at one end, and some booths. The room is dimly lighted, with candles on the tables. Roast duck, baked lobster with shrimp stuffing, and rack of lamb all come with salad, appetizer, and dessert. The restaurant is very busy on weekends. ⊠ *Chestnut Plain Rd., Whately Center 01093,* ☎ *413/665–3044 or 800/942–8359. 4 rooms. Restaurant (no lunch except Sun.). AE, MC, V.*

$$ 🏠 **Sunnyside Farm Bed and Breakfast.** Country-style guest rooms of varying sizes are appointed with maple antiques and family heirlooms. All rooms, which are hung with fine art reproductions, have views across the fields, and some overlook the large strawberry farm next door. Guests share a small library. Breakfast is served family-style in the dining

room. The farm is about 8 miles south of Deerfield. ⊠ *11 River Rd., Whately (Box 486, S. Deerfield 01373),* ☎ *413/665–3113. 5 rooms share 2 baths. Pool. Full breakfast included. No credit cards.*

Amherst

43 *14 mi from Deerfield, 8 mi from Northampton.*

Three of the Pioneer Valley's five major colleges—the University of Massachusetts (UMass), Amherst College, and Hampshire College—are in small but lively Amherst with its large "village green." Not surprisingly, the area has a youthful bias, reflected in its numerous bookstores, bars, and cafés.

The poet Emily Dickinson was born and spent most of her life in Amherst; the **Emily Dickinson Homestead** (⊠ 280 Main St., ☎ 413/542–8161, ☞ $3), now owned by Amherst College, offers afternoon guided tours by appointment.

The **Amherst History Museum at the Strong House,** built in the mid-1700s, has an extensive collection of furniture, china, and clothing that reflects the changing styles of interior decoration. ⊠ *67 Amity St.,* ☎ *413/256–0678.* ☞ *Free.* ☉ *May–Oct., Wed.–Sat. 12:30–3:30; Oct.–May, Thurs. 12:30–3:30.*

NEED A BREAK?

Stop into **Café Mediterranean** (⊠ 1 E. Pleasant St., ☎ 413/549-7122) for an afternoon nosh on the fresh, innovative light lunch fare, or try one of the delicious pastries.

The **Hitchcock Center for the Environment** is a nonprofit organization situated in the Larch Hill Conservation Area. It has self-guided nature trails, a resource library that focuses on environmental issues, and natural history programs and workshops for adults and children. ⊠ *525 Pleasant St.,* ☎ *413/256–6006.* ☞ *Free.* ☉ *Wed.–Sat. 9–4.*

The Arts

Major ballet and modern dance companies appear in season at the **UMass Fine Arts Center** (☎ 413/545–2511). The **William D. Mullens Memorial Center** (☎ 413/545–0505), at the University of Massachusetts, showcases concerts, theatrical productions, and other entertainment.

Dining and Lodging

$$ ✕ **Judie's.** A glassed-in porch where students crowd around small tables creates the atmosphere of a cheerful street café. Cuisine is Continental and imaginative American; specialties are salads, sandwiches, popovers, and a selection of gourmet chocolate cakes. ⊠ *51 N. Pleasant St.,* ☎ *413/253–3491. Reservations not accepted. AE, D, MC, V.*

$$$ ✕▥ **Lord Jeffery Inn.** This gabled brick inn with green shutters sits right
★ on the green between the town center and the Amherst College campus. Many bedrooms have light floral decor; others are less formal, with simple cream walls, stencils, and pastel woodwork. The large, elegant dining room has an open fireplace, heavy drapery, and white-painted wood beams. The menu offers a variety of dishes, including veal Madeira, salmon fillet, and grilled garlic and herb New York sirloin. Boltwood's Tavern wraps around the main dining room and serves sandwiches, salads, and other light dishes. ⊠ *30 Boltwood Ave., 01002,* ☎ *413/253–2576,* ☎ *413/256–6152. 40 rooms, 8 suites. Restaurant, bar. AE, DC, MC, V.*

$$ 🏨 **The Allen House.** This inn, honored with a Historic Preservation
★ Award from the Amherst Historical Commission, is a rare find: Restored with historic precision and attention to every last detail, it's a glorious reproduction of the Aesthetic period of the Victorian era. Antiques include a burled walnut bedhead and dresser set, wicker "steamship" chairs, pedestal sinks, screens, carved golden oak and brass beds, goose down comforters, painted wooden floors, and clawfoot tubs. It's a short walk from the center of Amherst, and rates are reasonable. ⊠ *599 Main St., 01002,* ☎ *413/253–5000. 5 rooms with bath. Full breakfast and afternoon tea included. AE, MC, V.*

$$ 🏨 **Campus Center Hotel.** Literally atop the UMass campus, this modern hotel has spacious rooms with large windows that allow excellent views over campus and countryside. The decor is exposed cinderblock, with simple, convenient furnishings. Guests can use university exercise facilities with prior reservation, and the campus status means no tax is charged for accommodations. ⊠ *Murray D. Lincoln Tower, Univ. of Mass., 01003,* ☎ *413/549–6000,* FAX *413/545–1210. 116 rooms, 6 suites. 2 indoor pools, 3 tennis courts, exercise room. AE, D, DC, MC, V.*

Outdoor Activities and Sports

BIKING

The **Norwottuck Rail Trail,** a paved 8½-mile path that links Amherst with Northampton, runs along the old Boston & Maine Railroad bed and is great for pedaling, blading, jogging, and cross-country skiing. **Valley Bicycles** (⊠ 319 Main St., ☎ 413/256–0880) in Amherst is a source of advice and rentals.

FISHING

A massive cleanup program of the Connecticut River has resulted in the return of shad and even salmon to the purer waters, and in fact the river now supports 63 species of fish. The privately owned **Red-Wing Trout Hatchery** raises trout; for a fee visitors may fish in the ponds, paying for fish they catch. ⊠ *500 Sunderland Rd., Amherst, 01002,* ☎ *413/367–9494.* 🎫 *$2; $5 family.*

Shopping

ART AND CRAFTS

The **Leverett Arts Center** (Montague Rd., Leverett, ☎ 413/548–9070), houses 20 resident artists in jewelry, ceramics, glass, and textiles, and an art gallery.

BOOKS

College students and tourists alike enjoy both the well-stocked **Atticus/Albion Bookshop** (⊠ 8 Main St.) and the **Jeffery Amherst Bookshop** (⊠ 55 South Pleasant St.). **Food for Thought** (⊠ 106 N. Pleasant St.) has a huge selection of political, environmental, and social-commentary works.

FOOD

Atkins Farms and Fruit Bowl (⊠ Rte. 116, South Amherst, ☎ 413/253–9528), surrounded by a sea of apple orchards and gorgeous views of the Holyoke Ridge, is an institution in the Pioneer Valley. Sample from its many varieties of apples and other fresh produce, and don't miss the famous cider doughnuts!

Northampton

  ④④ *19 mi from Springfield.*

Small, bustling Northampton was first settled in 1654 and is listed on the National Register of Historic Places. Today it's famous as the site of **Smith College,** the nation's largest liberal arts college for women, founded in 1871. Stroll through the redbrick quadrangles—they're strongly reminiscent of the women's colleges at Cambridge University, England, which were built around the same period. Worth visiting are the **Lyman Plant House** and the **botanic gardens.** The **College Art Museum** (⊠ Rte. 9, ☎ 413/584–2700) has more than 18,000 paintings and is open Tuesday through Sunday afternoons.

You can trace Northampton's history at **Historic Northampton,** an organization that maintains three houses representing its cultural heritage: Parsons House (1730), Shepherd House (1798), and Damon House (1813). ⊠ *46 Bridge St.,* ☎ *413/584–6011.* ⌸ *$2.* ☾ *Tours Mar.–Dec., Wed.–Sun. noon–4.*

The folks who brought us the infamous Teenage Mutant Ninja Turtles have opened the **Words and Pictures Museum,** a repository of sequential art where you can see the latest comic books and graphic novels and create your own. ⊠ *140 Main St.,* ☎ *413/586–8545.* ⌸ *$3.* ☾ *Tues.–Sun. noon–5.*

Northampton was also the Massachusetts home of the 30th U.S. president, Calvin Coolidge. He practiced law here and served as mayor from 1910 to 1911. The **Coolidge Room** at the Forbes Library (⊠ 20 West St., ☎ 413/584–8399) contains a collection of his papers and memorabilia.

Look Memorial Park (⊠ 300 N. Main St., Florence, ☎ 413/584–5457) maintains a small zoo, wading pool, and children's playgrounds.

Dining and Lodging

$$–$$$ ✕ **Eastside Grill.** One of the dining rooms here is a glassed-in porch, the other is wood-paneled with comfortable wood and leather booths; a place at one of the stools lined up before the busy bar is a coveted commodity. The menu changes seasonally but often includes a blackened fish of the day and fresh oysters on the half shell. ⊠ *19 Strong Ave.,* ☎ *413/586–3347. AE, MC, V.*

$$ ✕ **Paul and Elizabeth's.** This classy natural-foods restaurant serves such seasonal specials as butternut-squash soup, home-baked corn muffins, and Indian pudding, as well as Japanese tempura and innovative fish entrées. Rooms are airy with lots of plants and trelliswork, and fans hang from the high ceiling. ⊠ *150 Main St.,* ☎ *413/584–4832. MC, V.*

$ ✕ **Northampton Brewery.** The Pioneer Valley's own microbrewery serves quality pub food like burgers, pizza, and Bourbon St. Stout steak, as well as exotic home brews: old brown dog, Hoover's porter, pale ale, and holiday spiced ale in season. You can sit outdoors to sup in the warmer months. ⊠ *11 Brewster Ct.,* ☎ *413/584–9903. D, MC, V.*

$ ✕ **Sylvester's Restaurant.** Although few people have heard of Dr. Sylvester Graham, a onetime Northampton resident, most Americans are familiar with the graham cracker, which was named after him. Graham believed in eating natural foods and exercising, unpopular ideas in the 1830s: Emerson called him "the poet of bran bread and pumpkins." His former home has been converted into this fitting healthy restaurant, offering homemade breads and healthy soups. ⊠ *111 Pleasant St.,* ☎ *413/586–5343. MC, V. No lunch Mon., Tues.*

$$$–$$$$ ✕☳ **Hotel Northampton.** Antique and reproduction furnishings and open fires in the parlor, lounge, and dining rooms of this hotel in the town center. The porch has a piano and wicker chairs and guest rooms have Colonial reproductions, heavy curtains, and some four-poster beds; some have balconies that overlook a busy street. Service can be substandard.

The Wiggins Tavern specializes in such New England dishes as Yankee cider pot roast, chicken potpie, and Boston scrod. Fires burn in three dimly lighted, "Old World" dining rooms, where heavy exposed beams support low ceilings and antique kitchen appliances decorate every available space. ✉ *36 King St., 01060,* ☎ *413/584–3100,* FAX *413/584–9455. 77 rooms, 5 suites. Restaurant (no lunch; closed Mon., Tues.), bar, café. AE, D, DC, MC, V.*

$$ 🏨 **The Knoll Bed and Breakfast.** A spacious, old-fashioned private home, this B&B sits well away from the busy road and backs onto steep woodlands. There's a sweeping staircase and Oriental rugs on polished wood floors; guest rooms are furnished with a mixture of antiques and hand-me-downs, and some have high four-poster beds. ✉ *230 N. Main St., Florence 01060,* ☎ *413/584–8164. 4 rooms share 2 baths. Library. Full breakfast included. No credit cards.*

$$ 🏨 **Twin Maples Bed and Breakfast.** Seven miles northwest of Northampton near the village of Williamsburg, this 200-year-old, restored farmhouse is surrounded by fields and woods. Inside are exposed beams, brick fireplaces, and wood stoves. Colonial-style antique and reproduction furnishings decorate the small guest rooms, which have restored brass beds and quilts. ✉ *106 South St., Williamsburg 01096,* ☎ *413/268–7925,* FAX *413/268–7243. 3 rooms share bath. Full breakfast included. AE, MC, V.*

Nightlife and the Arts

NIGHTLIFE

The **Iron Horse** (✉ 20 Center St., ☎ 413/584–0610), offering a variety of folk, blues, jazz, Celtic, and alternative music seven nights a week, is a popular spot for students. **Pearl Street** (✉ 10 Pearl St., ☎ 413/584–7771) is the area's largest dance club, with frequent dance parties, gay nights, and live music several nights a week.

THE ARTS

The **Northampton Center for the Arts** (✉ 17 New South St., ☎ 413/584–7327) provides performance space for theater, dance, and musical events, and houses two galleries for the visual arts.

Outdoor Activities and Sports

HIKING

At the **Mount Tom State Reservation** (☞ State Park, *in* Pioneer Valley A to Z, *below*), a 3.3-mile round-trip hike will take you to the summit with its impressive sheer basalt cliffs, formed by volcanic activity 200 million years ago. From the top there are excellent views over the Pioneer Valley and the Berkshires.

At the wide place in the Connecticut River known as the Oxbow, the Massachusetts Audubon Society's **Arcadia Nature Center and Wildlife Sanctuary** (✉ 127 Combs Rd., Easthampton, ☎ 413/584–3009) is open Tuesday–Sunday dawn–dusk (office open 9–3); for hiking and nature trails, as well as regularly scheduled canoe trips.

Shopping

The **Antique Center of Northampton** (✉ 9½ Market St., ☎ 413/584–3600) covers 8,000 square feet and houses 60 dealers. For crafts, try the **Ferrin Gallery at Pinch Pottery** (✉ 179 Main St., ☎ 413/586–4509), which exhibits contemporary ceramics, jewelry, and glass. **Thorne's Marketplace** (✉ 150 Main St. ☎ 413/584–5582) is a funky, four-floor indoor mall converted from an old department store.

South Hadley

45 *10 mi from Amherst, 6 mi from Holyoke.*

Mount Holyoke College, founded in 1837 as the first women's college in the United States, dominates the small village of South Hadley. Among its famous alumnae are Emily Dickinson and Wendy Wasserstein. The handsome wooded campus was landscaped by Frederick Law Olmsted. The **College Art Museum** (☎ 413/538–2245) has exhibits of Asian, Egyptian, and classical art and is open Tuesday–Friday 11–5, weekends 1–5.

Nightlife
Katina's (✉ Rte. 9, Hadley, ☎ 413/586–4463) specializes in rock and blues bands Thursday through Saturday nights, and runs singles dances.

Outdoor Activities and Sports
BOATING

Canoes can be rented during summer and early fall from **Sportsman's Marina Boat Rental Company** (✉ Rte. 9, Hadley, ☎ 413/586–2426).

Shopping
The **Odyssey Bookstore** (✉ 29 College St., ☎ 413/534–7307) has a large, excellent selection. The **Hadley Antique Center** (✉ Rte. 9, ☎ 413/586–4093) contains more than 70 different stores. **Eastern Mountain Sports** (✉ Hampshire Mall, Rte. 9, Hadley, ☎ 413/584–3554) sells hiking gear, maps, and books.

Holyoke

46 *7 mi from Northampton, 8 mi from Springfield.*

A downtrodden town of crumbling redbrick factories and murky canals, Holyoke has little to interest the visitor—apart from an imaginatively restored, industrial but historic city center.

The **Heritage State Park** tells the story of this papermaking community, the nation's first planned industrial city, which has been hard hit by recession. The park is the starting point for the **Heritage Park Railroad** and its antique steam train, which is designed to take visitors on a two-hour ride through the valley, but runs sporadically, depending on financing and demand. ✉ *Heritage State Park, 221 Appleton St.,* ☎ *413/534–1723.* ⚏ *Free.* ☉ *Tues.–Sun. noon–4:30.*

☾ Right beside Heritage Park is the **Children's Museum,** housed in a converted mill by the canal. Packed with hands-on games and educational toys, the museum has a TV station, water guns, and a sand pendulum. ✉ *444 Dwight St.,* ☎ *413/536–5437.* ⚏ *$3.* ☉ *Tues.–Sat. 9:30–4:30, Sun. noon–5.*

The **Volleyball Hall of Fame** is a one-room tribute to the sport and to William Morgan, who invented it here in 1895. ✉ *444 Dwight St.,* ☎ *413/536–0926.* ⚏ *Free.* ☉ *Tues.–Sat. 9:30–4:30, weekends noon–5.*

☾ The **Mt. Tom ski area** (Rte. 5, ☎ 413/536–0516) offers summer amusements with particular appeal for children, including a wave pool and two water slides.

Dining and Lodging

$$–$$$ ✕⌂ **Yankee Pedlar Inn.** This attractive, sprawling inn stands at a busy
★   crossroads near I–91. Rooms are superbly furnished with antiques and four-poster or canopy beds. The Victorian bridal suite is elaborate with lots of lace and curtains while the carriage house has beams, rustic furnishings, and simple canopy beds. The dining room has exposed beams

and antique wood paneling; candle chandeliers provide the lighting. Try baked Boston scrod, prime rib of beef, or New England boiled dinner. ⊠ *1866 Northampton St., 01040,* ☎ *413/532–9494,* ℻ *413/536–8877. 28 rooms, 11 suites. Restaurant, nightclub, meeting rooms. CP. AE, D, DC, MC, V.*

$$ 🏨 **Holiday Inn.** This typical Holiday Inn property is 5 miles from the Mt. Tom ski area. Samuel's Restaurant and Bar is inside, and the huge Ingleside shopping mall and movie theaters are next door. ⊠ *Exit 15 off I–91 (mailing address: Whiting Farms Rd., Holyoke 01040),* ☎ *413/534–3311,* ℻ *413/533–8443. 219 rooms. Restaurant, bar. AE, D, DC, MC, V.*

Shopping
Holyoke Mall, at Ingleside (⊠ Exit 15 off I–91), has nearly 200 stores, including JCPenney, Sears, Filene's, and Lord & Taylor. Factory stores and mill shops stocking paper products and furniture are everywhere; try the **City Paper Co.** (⊠ 390–394 Main St., ☎ 413/532–1352) for wholesale and retail paper and plastic disposables. The **Becker Jean Factory** (⊠ 323 Main St., ☎ 413/532–5797) carries Becker as well as Lee and Levi jeans for men, women, and children.

Skiing
Mt. Tom. Just minutes from Holyoke, Springfield, and several colleges, Mt. Tom attracts skiers for day and night skiing and offers a five-week series of ski-lesson packages for children and adults. In addition, the area holds races and special events for local groups. There is a restaurant, cafeteria, and ski and rental shop. ⊠ *Rte. 5, Holyoke 01041,* ☎ *413/536–0516, ski school 413/536–1575.*

DOWNHILL
Slopes and trails at Mt. Tom tend to be extra wide, if not long, off the vertical of 680 feet. The trails are mostly for intermediates and beginners, with a few steeper pitches. Serving the 15 trails are four double chairlifts and two surface lifts.

CHILD CARE
In addition to daily group lessons on weekends, day camps provide an entire day of instruction for children 6–14. During vacation periods in December and February, five-day lesson programs are offered. Mt. Tom also has midweek instruction programs for schoolchildren.

Springfield
🟠 *101 mi from Boston.*

Springfield is the largest city in the Pioneer Valley—an industrial town where modern skyscrapers rise between grand historic buildings. Although few people would stop to see the city itself, it does have some unusual museums.

Much of Springfield's early development was due to the **Springfield Armory,** the country's first arsenal. Established in 1779 and closed in 1968, the armory made small arms for the U.S. military. It holds one of the most extensive firearms collections in the world. ⊠ *1 Armory Sq. (off State St.),* ☎ *413/734–8551.* 🎟 *Free.* ☉ *Daily 10–5; closed Mon. Labor Day–Memorial Day.*

Perhaps Springfield's greatest claim to fame is that Dr. James Naismith invented basketball here in 1891. The **Naismith Memorial Basketball Hall of Fame** has a cinema, a two-story basketball fountain, and a moving walkway from which visitors can shoot baskets into 20 different-sized hoops. ⊠ *W. Columbus Ave. at Union St.,* ☎ *413/781–6500.* 🎫 *$8.* ☉ *Daily 9–5 (until 6 July–Labor Day).*

Four museums are situated at the museum quadrangle near downtown. The **Connecticut Valley Historical Museum** (☎ 413/263–6895) commemorates the history of the Pioneer Valley. The **George Walter Vincent Smith Art Museum** (☎ 413/263–6894) contains a private collection of Japanese armor, ceramics, and textiles. The **Museum of Fine Arts** (☎ 413/263–6885) has paintings by Gauguin, Renoir, Degas, and Monet. The **Springfield Science Museum** (☎ 413/263–6875) has an "Exploration Center" of touchable displays, a planetarium, and dinosaur exhibits. 🎫 *$4; valid for all museums.* ☉ *Wed.–Sun. noon–4.*

☾ If you're looking for somewhere to let the kids run wild, try **Forest Park** (☎ 413/733–2251), with its many recreational facilities and a children's zoo.

☾ **Riverside Park,** just outside Springfield, is the largest amusement park in New England and has a giant roller coaster and picnic facilities. ⊠ *1623 Main St., Agawam,* ☎ *413/786–9300 or 800/370–7488.* 🎫 *$19.99.* ☉ *Apr. 3–Memorial Day and Labor Day–Oct. 31, weekends 11–11; Memorial Day–Labor Day, Sun.–Thurs. 11–6, weekends 11–11.*

Dining and Lodging

$$ ✕ **Student Prince and Fort Restaurant.** Established in 1935, this restaurant in downtown Springfield serves classic German food, including bratwurst, schnitzel, and sauerbraten, as well as American and seafood dishes. ⊠ *8 Fort St.,* ☎ *413/734–7475. AE, D, DC, MC, V.*

$$ ✕ **Theodores'.** There's saloon-style dining at booths near the bar or in a small adjacent dining room. The 1930s are re-created with period furniture and framed advertisements for such curious products as foot soap. Brass lights date from 1897. Theodores' serves burgers, sandwiches, chicken, and seafood, and hosts live entertainment Thursday through Saturday evenings. ⊠ *201 Worthington St.,* ☎ *413/736–6000. AE, D, DC, MC, V.*

$$$$ 🏨 **Marriott Hotel.** Conveniently located in the middle of downtown, this hotel opens onto the large Baystate West shopping mall. Rooms at the front overlook the river, and all are comfortably decorated with oak furniture and Impressionist prints. ⊠ *1500 Main St., 01115,* ☎ *413/781–7111 or 800/228–9290,* 🗋 *413/731–8932. 264 rooms, 2 suites. Restaurant, bars, indoor pool, 2 saunas, exercise room, meeting rooms. AE, D, DC, MC, V.*

$ 🏨 **Cityspace.** The Springfield YMCA offers high-quality, motel accommodations. The big advantage over other budget motels is that visitors can use all the sports and fitness facilities at the Y for free. Cityspace is close to I–91, near downtown, and a five-minute walk from the Amtrak station. ⊠ *275 Chestnut St., 01104,* ☎ *413/739–6951. 124 rooms with bath. Restaurant, indoor pool, massage, sauna, steam room, exercise room, racquetball, squash. MC, V.*

Nightlife and the Arts

NIGHTLIFE

Theodores' (⊠ 201 Worthington St., ☎ 413/736–6000) has national and local bands and acts Thursday through Saturday evenings.

THE ARTS

The **Berkshire Ballet** performs twice a year at Springfield's American International College—usually in fall and spring. Call the college (☎ 413/737–7000) for details.

A variety of concerts are hosted fall through spring at the **Paramount Performing Arts Center** (⊠ 1700 Main St., 01103, ☎ 413/734–5874) and the **Springfield Civic Center** (⊠ 127 Main St., 01103, ☎ 413/787– 6610). The **Springfield Symphony Orchestra** (⊠ 75 Market Pl., 01103, ☎ 413/733–2291) performs October through May at Symphony Hall, and mounts a summer program of concerts in the Springfield area.

StageWest (⊠ 1 Columbus Center, ☎ 413/781–2340) is the only resident professional theater company in western Massachusetts. The schedule includes a series of plays and musicals October through May.

Sturbridge

48 *55 mi from Boston, 31 mi from Springfield.*

★ It's not technically in the Pioneer Valley, but don't miss the star attraction of central Massachusetts—**Old Sturbridge Village,** one of the country's finest period restorations. The village is a model of an early 1800s New England town with more than 40 buildings on a 200-acre site. Working exhibits include a 200-year-old newspaper printing press and a blacksmith and forge. A wool carding mill and a sawmill beside the duck pond are both powered by water wheels, and down the lane—you can travel there in a horse-drawn carriage or cart—is a pioneer farm complete with cattle and sheep. Some of the village houses are furnished with canopy beds and elaborate decoration; in the simpler, single-story cottages interpreters wearing period costume demonstrate such home-based crafts as spinning, weaving, shoe-making, and cooking. Local schoolchildren often take field-trip lessons in the old schoolroom, and the village store contains an amazing variety of goods necessary for everyday life in the 19th century. ⊠ *1 Old Sturbridge Village Rd., 01566,* ☎ *508/347–3362.* ☑ *$15, valid for 2 consecutive days.* ☉ *Late Apr.–late Oct., daily 9–5; off-season, Tues.–Sun. 10–4; Jan., weekends 10–4.*

The **Quabbin Reservoir,** which provides drinking water for the whole of the greater Boston area, was created in 1939 by flooding the Swift River valley. Buildings in five towns were razed to the ground on April 28, 1938. Even the bodies in the towns' churchyards were exhumed and reburied elsewhere. The only traces of the settlements are a few cellar holes and overgrown lanes that disappear eerily beneath the water. Today the Quabbin is a quiet spot of beauty, with facilities for fishing, cycling, hiking, and picnicking. The two great dams that hold back 400 billion gallons of water can be viewed at the south end, near the visitor's center, which contains pictures of the drowned villages. ⊠ *Quabbin Park Visitor's Center, 485 Ware Rd. (off Rte. 9), Belchertown,* ☎ *413/323–7221.* ☑ *Free.* ☉ *Weekdays 8:30–4:30, weekends 9–5.*

Dining and Lodging

$ ✕ **Rom's.** This has become something of a local institution—after humble beginnings as a sandwich stand, the restaurant was extended to seat about 700 people. The six dining rooms have an Early American decor, with wood paneling and beam ceilings. Now serving Italian and American cuisine ranging from pizza to roast beef, Rom's attracts the crowds with a classic formula: good food at low prices. The veal Parmesan is very popular. ⊠ *Rte. 131,* ☎ *508/347–3349. AE, MC, V.*

$$–$$$$ ✕▨ **Sturbridge Country Inn.** The facade of this one-time farmhouse on Sturbridge's busy Main Street is imposing; the atmosphere is somewhere between that of an inn and a plush business hotel. Guest rooms— all with working gas fireplaces and hot tubs—have reproduction antiques. The best is the top-floor suite; avoid the first-floor rooms—

they're comparably priced but small and noisy (with gurgles from the upstairs plumbing!). The barn adjoining the inn has been converted into the Fieldstone Tavern restaurant: The high-ceilinged, post and beam structure serves traditional New England dinners like hearty stews, grilled chicken, and roast beef. Between mid-June and November, the inn hosts professional live repertory theater in the loft of the barn. ⊠ *530 Main St. (Box 60), 01566,* ☎ *508/347–5503, restaurant 508/347–7603,* FAX *508/347–5319. 8 rooms, 1 suite. Restaurant, bar, hot tubs. CP. AE, D, MC, V. No lunch weekdays.*

$$–$$$ ✕🖾 **Publick House and Col. Ebenezer Crafts Inn.** Rooms in the Pub-
  ★   lick House, which dates to 1771, are Colonial in design, with uneven wide-board floors; some have canopy beds. The neighboring Chamberlain House consists of larger suites, and the Country Motor Lodge has more modern rooms. The Crafts Inn, just over a mile away, has a library, lounge, and guest rooms with four-poster beds, and painted wood paneling. The popular restaurant is big, bustling, and very busy on weekends. The high cathedral ceilings in the main dining room are supported by wood beams and hung with enormous period chandeliers. Food served includes lobster pies, double-thick loin lamb chops, followed by Indian pudding, pecan bread pudding, and apple pie. ⊠ *Rte. 131, On-the-Common, 01566,* ☎ *508/347–3313,* FAX *508/346–1246. 118 rooms, 12 suites. Restaurant, bar, pool, tennis courts, jogging, shuffleboard, playground, meeting rooms. CP at Crafts Inn. AE, DC, MC, V.*

$$$$ 🖾 **The Sturbridge Host.** Ideally located just across the street from Old Sturbridge Village on Cedar Lake, this inn has luxuriously appointed bedrooms with Colonial decor and reproduction furnishings. ⊠ *Rte. 20, 01566,* ☎ *508/347–7393,* FAX *508/347–3944. 241 rooms, 9 suites. 2 dining rooms, bars, indoor pool, miniature golf, tennis courts, sauna, basketball, exercise room, health club, racquetball, boating, fishing, meeting rooms. AE, D, DC, MC, V.*

Pioneer Valley A to Z

Getting Around
BY BUS
Peter Pan Bus Lines (☎ 413/781–2900 or 800/237–8747) links Boston, Springfield, Holyoke, Northampton, Amherst, and South Hadley. Local bus companies with regular service are the **Pioneer Valley Transit Authority** (☎ 413/781–7882) and **Greenfield Montague Transportation Area** (☎ 413/773–9478).

BY CAR
Interstate–91 runs north–south through the entire valley, from Greenfield to Springfield; I–90 links Springfield to Boston; and Route 2 connects Boston with Greenfield in the north.

BY TRAIN
Amtrak (☎ 800/872–7245) serves Springfield from New York City, stopping in New Haven and Hartford, Connecticut, along the way. The *Lake Shore Limited* between Boston and Chicago calls at Springfield once daily in each direction, and three more trains run between Boston and Springfield every day.

Contacts and Resources
ANTIQUES
For a list of members of the **Pioneer Valley Antique Dealers Association,** which guarantees the honest representation of merchandise, write to Maggie Herbert, Secretary, 201 N. Elm St., Northampton 01060.

CAMPING

A list of private campgrounds throughout Massachusetts can be obtained free from the **Commonwealth of Massachusetts Office of Tourism** (✉ 100 Cambridge St., Boston 02202, ☎ 617/727–3201).

EMERGENCIES

Cooley Dickenson Hospital (✉ 30 Locust St., Northampton, ☎ 413/582–2000 or TTY 413/586–8866). **Holyoke Hospital** (✉ 575 Beech St., Holyoke, ☎ 413/534–2500). **Baystate Medical Center** (✉ 759 Chestnut St., Springfield, ☎ 413/784–0000).

RESERVATION SERVICE

Berkshire Bed-and-Breakfast Service (✉ Box 211, Williamsburg, ☎ 413/268–7244, FAX 413/268–7243) provides information and makes reservations at a wide range of area accommodations.

STATE PARKS

Of the 29 state parks and forests in the Pioneer Valley, the following have a wide variety of facilities for outdoor recreation: **Chicopee Memorial State Park** (✉ Burnett Rd., Chicopee), **D.A.R. State Forest** (✉ Rte. 9, Goshen), **Erving State Forest** (✉ Rte. 2A, Erving), **Granville State Forest** (✉ S. Hartland Rd., Granby), **Hampton Ponds State Park** (✉ Rte. 202, Westfield), **Mohawk Trail State Forest** (✉ Rte. 2, Charlemont), **Mount Sugarloaf State Reservation** (Deerfield), **Mount Tom State Reservation** (✉ Rte. 5, Holyoke), and **Wendell State Forest** (✉ Wendell Rd., Wendell).

VISITOR INFORMATION

The **Amherst Area Chamber of Commerce** (✉ 11 Spring St., ☎ 413/253–0700; ☉ Weekdays 9–3:30) and the **Greater Northampton Chamber of Commerce** (✉ 62 State St., ☎ 413/584–1900; ☉ Weekdays 9–5) supply information on these two towns and the surrounding area. The **Greater Springfield Convention and Visitors Bureau** (✉ 34 Boland Way, Springfield 01103, ☎ 413/787–1548; ☉ Weekdays 8:30–5) provides information about the entire Pioneer Valley area.

THE BERKSHIRES

Updated by
Anne
Merewood

More than a century ago, wealthy families from New York and Boston built "summer cottages" in western Massachusetts's Berkshire hills—great country estates that earned Berkshire County the nickname "inland Newport." Although most of those grand houses have since been converted into schools or hotels, the region is still popular, for obvious reasons. Occupying the entire far western end of the state, the area is only about a 2½-hour drive directly west from Boston or north from New York City, yet it lives up to the storybook image of rural New England, with its wooded hills, narrow winding roads, and compact charming villages. Summer offers an astonishing variety of cultural events, not the least of which is the Tanglewood festival in Lenox; fall brings a blaze of brilliant foliage; in winter, it's a popular ski area; and springtime visitors can enjoy maple-sugaring. Keep in mind, however, that the Berkshire's popularity often goes hand-in-hand with high prices and crowds, especially on weekends.

En Route Many visitors will approach the Berkshires along Route 2 from Boston and the East Coast. The **Mohawk Trail,** a 67-mile stretch, follows the former Native American path that ran along the Deerfield River through the Connecticut Valley to the Berkshire hills. Just beyond the town of Charlemont stands **Hail to the Sunrise,** a 900-pound bronze statue of an Indian facing east, with arms uplifted, dedicated to the five Native American nations who lived along the Mohawk Trail. A hand-

The Berkshires

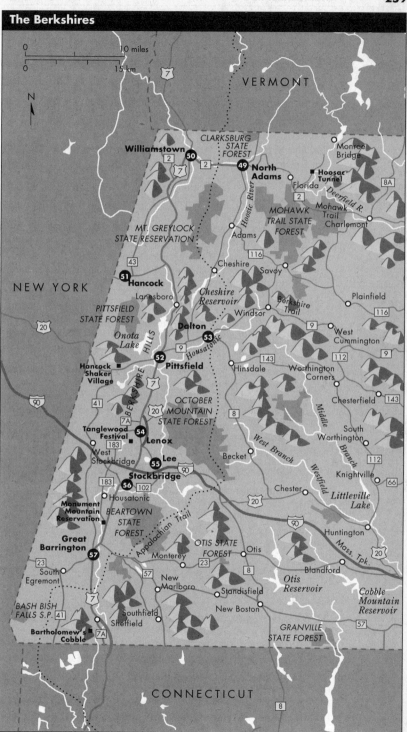

VERMONT

0   10 miles
0   15 km

N

Williamstown
2 50 2
49 North Adams
CLARKSBURG STATE FOREST
Monroe Bridge
Hoosac Tunnel
Florida
2
8A
Mohawk Trail
Charlemont
Deerfield R.
MOHAWK TRAIL STATE FOREST
Hoosic River
MT. GREYLOCK STATE RESERVATION
Adams
116
Cheshire
Savoy
43
51 Hancock
Lanesboro
Cheshire Reservoir
Berkshire Trail
Plainfield
NEW YORK
PITTSFIELD STATE FOREST
Onota Lake
Dalton
53
Windsor
9
West Cummington
116
20
BERKSHIRE HILLS
9
Housatonic
112
9
52 Pittsfield
143
Hinsdale
Worthington Corners
Chesterfield
143
Hancock Shaker Village
41
OCTOBER MOUNTAIN STATE FOREST
20
8
South Worthington
Middle Branch
90
7
West Branch
Westfield Branch
112
Tanglewood Festival
183
7A
54 Lenox
Becket
Knightville
66
West Stockbridge
55 Lee
Littleville Lake
Stockbridge
90
Chester
183 56 102
Housatonic
Monument Mountain Reservation
BEARTOWN STATE FOREST
Appalachian Trail
20
Huntington
Mass. Tpk.
20
90
Great Barrington
57
OTIS STATE FOREST
Monterey
Otis
Blandford
23
South Egremont
57
New Marlboro
23
8
Standisfield
Otis Reservoir
Cobble Mountain Reservoir
7
BASH BISH FALLS S.P. 41
Southfield
Sheffield
New Boston
GRANVILLE STATE FOREST
57
Bartholomew's Cobble
7A

CONNECTICUT
8

ful of somewhat tacky "Indian trading posts" on the highway carry
out the Mohawk theme. Also along the road are many antiques stores
and flea markets.

Bypassing the entrance to the **Hoosac railway tunnel** (which took 24
years to build and, at 4.7 miles, was the longest in the nation when it
was completed in 1875), the road begins a steep ascent to Whitcomb
Summit, the highest point on the trail, then continues to the spectacular Western Summit, with excellent views, before dropping through
a series of hairpin turns into North Adams.

*Numbers in the margin correspond to points of interest on the Berk-
shires map.*

North Adams

⑭ *130 mi from Boston.*

Once a railroad boomtown and a thriving industrial city, North Adams
is still industrial but no longer thriving—the dilapidated mills and row
houses are reminiscent of northern industrial England. It's not really
worth stopping here unless you're intrigued by the ghosts of the Industrial Revolution or are a railway buff, in which case visit the **Western Gateway Heritage State Park,** housed in the restored freight-yard
district. It tells the story of the town's past successes, including the construction of the Hoosac tunnel. The freight-yard district also contains
a number of specialty stores and restaurants. ⊠ *9 Furnace St., Bldg.
4,* ☎ *413/663–6312.* ☜ *Free.* ⊙ *Daily 10–5.*

The only natural bridge in North America caused by water erosion is
the marble arch at **Natural Bridge State Park.** It crosses a narrow 500-
foot chasm with numerous faults and fractures lining the walls. ⊠ *Rte.
8N,* ☎ *413/663–6392.* ☜ *$2 per car.* ⊙ *Memorial Day–Columbus
Day, daily 10–6.*

Williamstown

⑮ *140 mi from Boston, 10 mi from North Adams.*

When Colonel Ephraim Williams left money to found a free school in
what was then known as West Hoosuck, he stipulated that the name
be changed to Williamstown. Williams College opened in 1793, and
even today the town revolves around it. Gracious campus buildings
like the Gothic cathedral, built in 1904, line the wide main street and
are open to visitors. The **Williams College Museum of Art** contains works
emphasizing American, modern, and contemporary art. ⊠ *Main St.,*
☎ *413/597–2429.* ☜ *Free.* ⊙ *Tues.–Sat. 10–5, Sun. 1–5.*

Formerly a private collection, the **Sterling and Francine Clark Art Institute** is now one of the nation's outstanding small art museums. Its
famous works include more than 30 paintings by Renoir, as well as
canvases by Monet, Pissarro, and Degas. ⊠ *225 South St.,* ☎ *413/458–
9545.* ☜ *Free.* ⊙ *Tues.–Sun. 10–5.*

The **Chapin Library of Rare Books and Manuscripts** at Williams College contains the Four Founding Documents of the United States, as
well as 35,000 other books, manuscripts, and illustrations dating
from the 9th to the 20th centuries, including a copy of the Declaration of Independence that had been owned by one of the signers. ⊠
Stetson Hall, Main St., ☎ *413/597–2462.* ☜ *Free.* ⊙ *Weekdays 10–
noon and 1–5.*

Dining and Lodging

$$$ ✕ **Le Jardin.** Set on a hillock above the road just west of Williamstown, this French restaurant has the feel of an inn (there are guest rooms on the upper floor). The two dining rooms are paneled and candlelit, and a fire burns in the hall in season. On offer are snails in garlic butter, oysters baked with spinach and Pernod, sole Florentine, filet mignon, and rack of lamb. ✉ *777 Cold Spring Rd. (Rte. 7),* ☎ *413/458–8032. AE, D, MC, V. Closed Tues. and Dec.–Mar.*

$$$ ✕ **Taconic Restaurant.** The cozy dining room in this yellow clapboard building with green trim has an open fireplace lit in season. Specialties include veal *ticatta* (medallions of veal with prosciutto, capers, and artichoke hearts with lemon sauce), steak-stuffed shrimp, and peppered steak, flamed tableside. ✉ *1161 Cold Spring Rd.,* ☎ *413/458–9499. AE, D, DC, MC, V. Lunch Sun. only.*

$$ ✕ **Four Acres.** On the commercial strip of Route 2 just east of Williamstown, this pleasant restaurant has two dining rooms: One is casual, decorated with street signs, paneling, and mirrors; the other is more formal, with collegiate insignia and modern paintings on the walls. American and Continental cuisine includes sautéed calves' liver glazed in applejack, veal cutlet sautéed in butter and topped with a Newburg of lobster and asparagus, and pork tenderloin with cognac and walnut sauce. ✉ *Rte. 2,* ☎ *413/458–5436. AE, MC, V. Closed Sun.*

$$$$ 🛏 **Williams Inn.** The spacious guest rooms in this modern inn have good-quality, modern furnishings, with floral-print drapes and bedspreads. The lounge has an open fireplace and is comfortable—the atmosphere is collegiate. The inn allows pets for a $5 fee; children under 14 stay free in their parents' room. ✉ *On-the-Green, 01267,* ☎ *413/458–9371,* ℻ *413/458–2767. 103 rooms. Bar, coffee shop, dining room, indoor pool, hot tub, sauna, nightclub (Fri. and Sat. nights). AE, D, DC, MC, V.*

$$$ 🛏 **Field Farm Guest House.** Built in 1948 on 254 acres, the house, which
★ resembles a modern museum, has large guest rooms with big windows and expansive views of the grounds and pond. Three rooms have private decks, and two have working fireplaces decorated with tiles depicting animals, birds, and butterflies. Much of the furniture was handmade by the owner-collector, and there are sculptures in the garden as well as a private graveyard. Cross-country ski trails begin at the door of this unusual B&B. ✉ *554 Sloan Rd. (off Rte. 43), Williamstown 01267,* ☎ *413/458–3135. 5 rooms with bath. Dining room, pool, tennis courts. No credit cards.*

$$ 🛏 **Berkshire Hills Motel.** This excellent motel is housed in a two-story
★ brick-and-clapboard building about 3 miles south of Williamstown. All guest rooms are furnished in Colonial style—each with a rocking chair and reproduction furniture. The lounge has an open fireplace, a piano, and a teddy bear collection. Outside, the pool is across a brook amid 2½ acres of woodland and landscaped gardens. ✉ *Rte. 7, 01267,* ☎ *413/458–3950. 20 rooms with bath. Pool. CP. D, MC, V.*

$$ 🛏 **River Bend Farm.** This farmhouse, constructed in 1770 by one of the founders of Williamstown, has been restored with complete authenticity. Guests enter through a kitchen with an open range stove and an oven hung with dried herbs. Upstairs some bedrooms have wideplank walls, curtains of unbleached muslin, and four-poster beds with canopies or rope beds with feather mattresses. All rooms are sprinkled with antique pieces—chamberpots, washstands, wing chairs, and spinning wheels. For visitors in search of another era, River Bend Farm is the perfect spot. ✉ *643 Simonds Rd., 01267,* ☎ *413/458–5504. 5 rooms share 2 baths. Full breakfast included. No credit cards.*

Nightlife and the Arts

NIGHTLIFE

The Williams Inn (☎ 413/458–9371) has live entertainment on weekends, with jazz on Saturday night.

THE ARTS

The **Williamstown Theatre Festival** presents well-known theatrical works on the Main Stage, and contemporary works on the Other Stage. ⊠ *Adams Memorial Theatre, Williams College Campus,* ☎ *413/597–3400 (box office) or 413/458–3200. July–Aug.*

Outdoor Activities and Sports

Waubeeka Golf Links (⊠ Rte. 7, ☎ 413/458–5869) has 18 holes.

En Route   South of Williamstown, Mt. Greylock, at 3,491 feet, is the highest point in Massachusetts. The 10,327-acre **Mt. Greylock State Reservation** (⊠ Rockwell Rd., Lanesboro, ☎ 413/499–4262/3), provides facilities for cycling, fishing, horseback riding, hunting, and snowmobiling. Walkers can find trail maps for a wide variety of hikes at higher elevations, including a stretch of the Appalachian Trail. Many treks start from the parking lot at the summit of Mt. Greylock, where there's also accommodation May through October.

Hancock

⑤ *15 mi from Williamstown.*

Hancock comes into its own in the winter ski season as the closest village to the big Jiminy Peak ski resort. In summer, the ski resort has an alpine slide, putting course, tennis, swimming, and trout fishing.

Dining and Lodging

$$ ✕ **The Springs.** This restaurant sits in the shadow of Brodie Mountain and its ski resort. A fireplace in the lobby, exposed-brick walls, and wood ceiling (from which hangs the biggest chandelier in the Berkshires) make for a country-lodge atmosphere. On the menu are lobster blended with mushrooms in cream sauce, duckling flambé in cherry sauce, and steak Diane. ⊠ *Rte. 7, New Ashford,* ☎ *413/458–3465. AE, D, DC, MC, V.*

$$$–$$$$ ✕⌸ **The Country Inn at Jiminy Peak.** The massive stone fireplaces in the lobby and lounge give this year-round hotel a ski-lodge atmosphere. All rooms are modern, condo-style suites, and have neat kitchenettes—separated from the living area by a bar and high stools—that are supplied with crockery, electric range, dishwasher, and refrigerator. Rooms at the rear of the building overlook the slopes. ⊠ *Corey Rd., 01237,* ☎ *413/738–5500,* FAX *413/738–5513. 105 suites. Restaurant, bar, pool, 2 hot tubs, 2 saunas, miniature golf, 7 tennis courts, exercise room, meeting rooms. AE, D, DC, MC, V.*

$$$ ✕⌸ **Hancock Inn.** The inn dates to the late 1700s and provides cozy
★ Old World accommodations a mile from Jiminy Peak. Two small dining rooms have stained-glass windows and candles on the tables; specialties include duckling in port wine with figs, honey mustard lamb chops, and veal and shrimp Dijon. ⊠ *Rte. 43, 01237,* ☎ *413/738–5873. 6 rooms with bath. Restaurant, 2 bars, 2 dining rooms. Full breakfast included. AE, MC, V. No lunch.*

$$ **Best Western Springs Motor Inn.** A good choice for skiers, this pleasant motel overlooks the Brodie Mountain slopes from across Route 7 and is convenient to Jiminy Peak as well. Rooms have modern furnishings; those on the second tier are larger, with better views and furnishings. Some rooms have refrigerators; all have coffeemak-

ers. ✉ *Rte. 7, New Ashford 01237,* ☎ FAX *413/458–5945 or 800/528–1234 . 40 rooms with bath. Restaurant, bar, coffee shop, pool, recreation room. AE, D, DC, MC, V.*

Nightlife

Ruby's (✉ Rte. 8, Cheshire Rd., Lanesboro, ☎ 413/499–3993) has dancing to top-40 hits spun by a DJ on Thursday, Friday, and Saturday nights. In winter, the **Blarney Room** (☎ 413/443–4752), on the top floor of the main lodge at the Brodie ski area, has entertainment nightly and live music weekends and Sunday afternoon. **Kelly's Irish Pub,** also at Brodie, has Irish entertainment on weekends.

Shopping

Amber Springs Antiques (✉ 29 S. Main St., Rte. 7, Lanesboro ☎ 413/442–1237), in a shop behind a fine old white-clapboard house, shows an eclectic assortment of American furnishings from the 19th to mid-20th centuries: Tools, pottery, and country store items are the house specialties.

Skiing

Brodie. The snow can be green, the beer is often green, and the decor is *always* green here. Yet there's more here than an Irish ambience to attract young crowds to its weekend and night skiing: The base lodge has a restaurant and bar with live entertainment, lodging is within walking distance of the lifts, and RV trailers can be accommodated on the grounds. ✉ *U.S. 7, New Ashford 01237,* ☎ *413/443–4752, snow conditions 413/443–4751.*

DOWNHILL

Almost all the 28 trails are beginner and intermediate despite the black diamonds, which designate steeper (not expert) runs. They are served by four double chairlifts and two surface lifts, off 1,250 feet of vertical.

CROSS-COUNTRY

The area's cross-country skiing covers 25 kilometers (16 mi) of trails, half of which are groomed daily.

OTHER ACTIVITIES

A sports center (Brodie Racquet Club, ☎ 413/458–4677), 1 mile from the ski area, has five indoor courts for tennis and five for racquetball, an exercise room, and a cocktail lounge.

CHILD CARE

The nursery takes infants through age 8 by the hour, half day, or full day. There are afternoon, weekend, and holiday ski-instruction programs for children.

Jiminy Peak. This area has all the amenities of a major mountain resort just 2½ hours from New York City and three hours from Boston. Condominiums and an all-suites country inn are within walking distance of the ski lifts; more condominium complexes are nearby; and two restaurants and bars are at the slopes. These services attract nearby residents, as well as families, for day and night skiing. Rentals are available on a nightly or weekly basis. Jiminy Peak is a popular choice for conference and convention business because of its self-contained nature and Berkshire location. ✉ *Corey Rd., Hancock 01237,* ☎ *413/738–5500, snow conditions 413/738–7325.*

DOWNHILL

With a vertical of 1,140 feet, Jiminy can claim big-time status. The steeper black-diamond sections are toward the top of the mountain, and there is enough good intermediate terrain to satisfy most skiers. A quad chair—dubbed "Q1" because it was the first in Massachusetts—serves

Jiminy's slopes. The area also has one triple and three double chairlifts and one surface lift for its 28 trails. Night skiing is an option every night of the week.

OTHER ACTIVITIES
Jiminy has a snowboard park and an old-fashioned ice rink.

CHILD CARE
The nursery takes children from 6 months. Children 4–12 can take daily SKIwee lessons; those ages 6–15 can take a series of eight weekends of instruction with the same teacher. There's a kid's ski area with its own lift.

Pittsfield

52 *22 mi from Williamstown.*

The county seat and geographic center of the Berkshires, Pittsfield is not particularly pretty, but it has a lively small-town atmosphere. The **Berkshire Museum** especially appeals to children, with its aquarium, animal exhibits, and glowing rocks. A local repository with a "bit of everything," the museum also contains works of art and historical relics. ⊠ *39 South St.,* ☎ *413/443–7171.* ▣ *$3.* ☉ *Tues.–Sat. 10–5, Sun. 1–5.*

The **Herman Melville Memorial Room** (☎ *413/499–9486*) at the **Berkshire Athenaeum** (⊠ Berkshire Public Library, 1 Wendell Ave.), houses a collection of books, letters, and memorabilia of the author of *Moby-Dick.* **Arrowhead,** the house Melville purchased in 1850, is just outside Pittsfield; the somewhat underwhelming tours include the study in which *Moby-Dick* was written. ⊠ *780 Holmes Rd.,* ☎ *413/442–1793.* ▣ *$5.* ☉ *Memorial Day–Labor Day, daily 10–5; Labor Day–Oct., Fri.–Mon. 10–5.*

★ The **Hancock Shaker Village** was founded in the 1790s, the third Shaker community in America. At its peak in the 1840s, the village had almost 300 inhabitants who made their living from farming, selling seeds and herbs, making medicines, and producing crafts. The religious community officially closed in 1960, its 170-year life span a small miracle considering its vows of celibacy—they took in orphans to maintain their constituency. In 1961 the site opened as a museum. Many examples of the famous Shaker ingenuity are visible at Hancock today: The **Round Stone Barn** with its labor-saving devices and the **Laundry and Machine Shop** with its water-powered instruments are two of the most interesting buildings. ⊠ *Rte. 20, 5 mi west of Pittsfield,* ☎ *413/443–0188.* ▣ *$10.* ☉ *Apr.–Memorial Day and late Oct.–Nov., daily 10–3 (guided tours only); Memorial Day–late Oct., daily 9:30–5.*

Dining and Lodging

$$ ✕ **Dakota.** Moose and elk heads watch over diners at this large restaurant decorated like a rustic hunting lodge. A canoe swings overhead, and Native American artifacts hang on the walls. A broiler stocked with Texan mesquite wood is used for specialties, which include swordfish steaks, shrimp, sirloin, and grilled chicken. ⊠ *Rtes. 7 and 20,* ☎ *413/499–7900. AE, D, DC, MC, V. No lunch Mon.–Sat.*

$$–$$$ ✕▥ **Berkshire Hilton Inn.** The upgraded rooms of this typically comfortable, sophisticated Hilton have the best views over the town and mountains. The large swimming pool, beneath a glass dome, is surrounded by two tiers of rooms, which are great for families. The small, classy restaurant on the second floor serves steak, chicken, and seafood dishes, and a delicious white-chocolate chimichanga for dessert. ⊠ *Berkshire Common, South St., 01201,* ☎ *413/499–2000 or 800/445–*

8667, FAX 413/442–0449. 175 rooms. Restaurant, bars, indoor pool, hot tub, sauna, exercise room, nightclub, meeting rooms. AE, D, DC, MC, V.

Nightlife and the Arts

NIGHTLIFE

On weekends in winter, the **Tamarack Lounge** (☎ 413/442–8316) in the Bousquet ski area's base lodge, has weekend dancing to DJ-spun tunes.

THE ARTS

Berkshire Public Theatre (✉ 30 Union St., ☎ 413/445–4634), the county's only year-round repertory company, performs a variety of modern and traditional pieces. The **Berkshire Ballet** (✉ Koussevitzky Arts Center, Berkshire Community College, West St., ☎ 413/445–5382) performs classical and contemporary works year-round.

Outdoor Activities and Sports

BIKING

The gently rolling Berkshire hills are excellent cycling terrain. Mountain bike trails can be found at the Mt. Greylock State Reservation (☎ 413/499–4262). **Plaine's Cycling Center** (✉ 55 W. Housatonic St., Pittsfield, ☎ 413/499–0294) rents bikes and sells equipment.

BOATING

The **Housatonic River** (the Native American name means "river beyond the mountains") flows south from Pittsfield between the Berkshire hills and the Taconic Range toward Connecticut. You can rent canoes, rowboats, and small motorboats from the **Onota Boat Livery** (✉ 463 Pecks Rd., ☎ 413/442–1724), which also provides dock space on Onota Lake and sells fishing tackle and bait. **Quirk's Marine** (✉ 1249 North St., Rte. 7, ☎ 413/447–7512) sells and services small crafts.

GOLF

The **Pontoosuc Lake Country Club** (✉ Kirkwood Dr., ☎ 413/445–4217) has 18 holes and welcomes non-members.

Skiing

Bousquet Ski Area. In 1935, when skiing was a novelty sport, the installation of a state-of-the-art rope tow at Bousquet made it a true destination resort. Ski trains from New York City brought skiers by the hundreds throughout the winter. In 1936 a group of engineers from General Electric devised a way to light the slopes for night skiing, which further propelled Bousquet into the heady modern era of skiing. Today, while other areas have entered an era of glamour and high prices, Bousquet remains an economical, no-nonsense place to ski. Three members of the U.S. Ski Team (twins Kim and Krista Schmidinger and Heidi Voelker) started racing here, and gate-bashing is still a big part of life. Bousquet remains a fixture in Pittsfield with its same-price-every-day lift-ticket policy and night skiing Monday–Saturday. ✉ *Dan Fox Dr., Pittsfield 01201, ☎ 413/442–8316, snow conditions 413/442–2436.*

DOWNHILL

There are 21 trails at Bousquet, but that's counting every change in steepness, cutoff, and merging slope. There is, however, a good selection of beginner and intermediate runs, with a few steeper pitches, off a 750-foot vertical drop. The area has two double chairlifts and two surface lifts.

OTHER ACTIVITIES

A center across the road has four handball courts, six indoor tennis courts, saunas, and a whirlpool.

CHILD CARE

Bous-Care Nursery watches toddlers and up. This is child care by the hour and reservations are suggested. Ski instruction classes are offered twice daily on weekends and holidays for ages 5 and up.

Dalton

❺❸ *3 mi from Pittsfield.*

Dalton is the home of paper manufacturers Crane and Co., a business started by Zenas Crane in 1801 and now the major employer in town. The **Crane Museum of Paper Making,** housed in the Old Stone Mill (1844), has been beautifully restored with oak beams, Colonial chandeliers, and wide oak floorboards. Exhibits trace the history of American papermaking from Revolutionary times to the present. ✉ *Off Rte. 9, Dalton,* ☎ *413/684–2600.* ▣ *Free.* ☉ *June–mid-Oct., weekdays 2–5.*

Lodging

$$–$$$ 🏠 **Dalton House.** This bed-and-breakfast has a sunny breakfast room with pine chairs and tables at the front of the 170-year-old house, and deluxe rooms in the carriage house. Guests share a split-level sitting room; the average-size bedrooms in the main house are cheerful, with floral-print drapes and wallpaper and white wicker chairs. The spacious carriage house rooms are more impressive, with exposed beams, period furnishings, and quilts. Ski packages including dinner are offered in season. ✉ *955 Main St., 01226,* ☎ *413/684–3854. 9 rooms, 2 suites, all with bath. Pool. CP. AE, MC, V.*

Outdoor Activities and Sports

GOLF

The **Waconah Country Club** (✉ Orchard Rd., ☎ 413/684–2864)) has 18 holes.

Lenox

❺❹ *146 mi from Boston, 5 mi from Pittsfield.*

In the thick of the "summer cottage" region, rich with old inns and majestic buildings, the wealthy village of Lenox epitomizes the Berkshires.

A typical Berkshire cottage is **The Mount,** former summer home of novelist Edith Wharton. The house and grounds were designed and built under Wharton's direction in 1902. An expert in the field of design, Wharton used the principles set forth in her book *The Decoration of Houses* (1897) to plan The Mount for a calm, well-ordered lifestyle. ✉ *Plunkett St.,* ☎ *413/637–1899.* ▣ *$6.* ☉ *Late May–Oct. Tues.–Sun. 10–3.*

★ **Tanglewood,** summer home of the Boston Symphony, is just outside Lenox. The 200-acre estate attracts thousands every summer to hear concerts featuring world-famous performers (☞ The Arts, *below*). One of the most popular ways to experience Tanglewood is to take a blanket and picnic on the grounds while listening to the performance from the lawn.

☺ **The Railway Museum,** in the center of Lenox, is a restoration of the 1902 Lenox station, containing period exhibits and a large working model railway. It's also the starting point for the **Berkshire Scenic Railway,** which operates vintage railroad cars over a portion of the historic New Haven Railway's Housatonic Valley Line. ✉ *Willow Creek Rd.,* ☎ *413/637–2210.* ▣ *Fares vary according to destination.* ☉ *June–late Oct., weekends and holidays.*

The Arts

MUSIC

The best-known music festival in New England is the **Tanglewood** concert series, when the Boston Symphony Orchestra (BSO) takes up residence near Lenox from June through September. The main shed hosts concerts and seats 5,000; the new Seiji Ozawa Hall (named for the BSO conductor) seats approximately 1,200 for recitals and chamber music. Leave your name and address to get a schedule, or order tickets by calling **Symphonycharge** (☎ 617/266–1200).

The **Berkshire Performing Arts Theater** (✉ 70 Kemble St., ☎ 413/637–1800) attracts top-name artists in jazz, folk, rock, and blues.

THEATER

Shakespeare and Company (✉ Plunkett St., ☎ 413/637–3353) performs the works of Shakespeare and Edith Wharton throughout the summer at The Mount.

Dining and Lodging

$$ ✕ **Church St. Cafe.** A well-established, popular Lenox restaurant, the stylish café serves excellent food at reasonable prices. The walls are covered with original art, tables are surrounded by ficus trees, and classical music plays in the background. Specialties include roast duck with thyme and Madeira sauce, rack of pork with wild mushrooms, and crab cakes. ✉ *69 Church St.,* ☎ *413/637–2745. MC, V. Closed Sun.–Mon., Nov.–Apr.*

$ ✕ **Sophia's Restaurant and Pizza.** This unpretentious establishment serves up pizza, generous Greek salads, pasta dishes, and grinders (the Massachusetts equivalent of a submarine sandwich). Seating is in booths with imitation-leather seats. ✉ *Rtes. 7/20,* ☎ *413/499–1101. AE, D, MC, V. Closed Mon.*

$$$$ ✕⊞ **Blantyre.** The competition in Lenox is tough, but Blantyre has to
★ be the best inn in town. If its unique, castlelike Tudor architecture, the sheer size of its public rooms, and its 85 acres of beautifully maintained grounds are not impressive enough, guest rooms in the main house are also fabulous: huge and lavishly decorated, with hand-carved four-poster beds, overstuffed chaise longues, chintz chairs, boudoirs, walk-in closets, and Victorian bathrooms. Although rooms in the carriage house and the cottages are well appointed, they can't compete with the formal grandeur of the main house. The stylishly prepared, three-course evening meal is superb. Of course, all this finery costs a small fortune. ✉ *16 Blantyre Rd. (off Rte. 20), 01240,* ☎ *413/298–3806,* FAX *413/637–4282. 13 rooms with bath, 10 suites. Restaurant, pool, hot tub, sauna, tennis courts, croquet, hiking. CP. AE, DC, MC, V.*

$$$$ ✕⊞ **Wheatleigh.** Wheatleigh was constructed in 1893 as a wedding present for a New York heiress who married a Spanish count. Based on a 16th-century Florentine palace, it's awe-inspiring, with a breathtaking entrance hall and guest rooms that range from medium-size to enormous. Rooms have elegant furnishings and high ceilings; some have working fireplaces with grand marble surrounds. The inn has an excellent, expensive restaurant. ✉ *Hawthorne Rd., 02140,* ☎ *413/637–0610,* FAX *413/637–4507. 17 rooms with bath. Restaurant, bar, 2 dining rooms, pool, tennis courts, meeting rooms. AE, DC, MC, V.*

$$$–$$$$ ⊞ **Cliffwood Inn.** This striking classic Colonial Revival building sits un-
★ expectedly on a quiet residential street in Lenox. Six of the seven guest rooms have fireplaces (one in a bathroom!); four more fireplaces give a glow to the common room, hall, and formal dining room downstairs. Much of the furniture comes from Europe; most guest rooms have canopy

beds. ⊠ *25 Cliffwood St., 01240,* ☎ *413/637–3330,* ⒻⒶⓍ *413/637–0221. 7 rooms with bath. Dining room, pool. CP in summer and on winter weekends. No credit cards.*

$$$–$$$$ 🖼 **Whistler's Inn.** The antiques decorating the parlor of this English
★   Tudor mansion are ornate with a touch of the exotic—some are in the Louis XVI style, others the innkeepers brought back from various travels abroad. Bedrooms are decorated with designer drapes and bedspreads, and some have working fireplaces. The inn is surrounded by pretty landscaped gardens and spruce trees. ⊠ *5 Greenwood St., 01240,* ☎ *413/637–0975. 12 rooms with bath. Badminton, croquet, library. Full breakfast included. AE, D, MC, V.*

$$–$$$$ 🖼 **The Garden Gables.** On 5 acres of wooded grounds a two-minute walk from the center of Lenox, this 250-year-old "summer cottage" has been an inn since 1947. Rooms come in a wide variety of shapes, sizes, and colors; some have brass beds, others have pencil four-posters. There are sloping ceilings, fireplaces, whirlpool baths, and woodland views; one room has a deck and its own entrance close to the 72-foot pool. Breakfast is served buffet-style in the big, airy dining room with wide-board floors, and guests have access to the kitchen and fridge. The long, narrow living room has a Steinway piano, antique writing desks, and painted wooden beams. ⊠ *135 Main St., Box 52, 01240,* ☎ *413/637–0193,* ⒻⒶⓍ *413/637–4554. 18 rooms. Dining room, pool. Full breakfast included. AE, D, MC, V.*

$$–$$$ 🖼 **Apple Tree Inn.** On a hillside across the street from Tanglewood's main gate, the Apple Tree Inn is perfect for summer concertgoers. You don't even need a ticket—the music wafts right across the front lawn! The parlor contains a grand piano, velvet couches, hanging plants, and German nutcracker decorations. Guest rooms have four-poster or brass beds, Victorian washstands, and wicker; some have working fireplaces. Avoid Room No. 5 because it's hot, noisy, and over the kitchen. The 21 rooms in the lodge next door have more modern, motel-style furnishings. ⊠ *334 West St., 01240,* ☎ *413/637–1477. 32 rooms, 30 with bath; 2 suites. Restaurant, bar, pool. AE, D, MC, V. Closed mid-Nov.–Apr.*

$$–$$$ 🖼 **Cranwell Resort and Hotel.** This 100-year-old Tudor mansion with Colonial-style furniture sits on 380 acres. The golf course is groomed in winter for cross-country skiing; in summer, guests can rent mountain bikes. The resort's three restaurants are open to the public: The Wyndhurst is elegant; the Music Room is more of a lounge, with a bar and fireplace; and Sloane's Tavern serves pub fare. ⊠ *55 Lee Rd., 02140,* ☎ *413/637–1364 or 800/272–6935,* ⒻⒶⓍ *413/637–4364. 65 rooms with bath. 3 restaurants, pool, driving range, 18-hole golf course, 2 tennis courts, bicycles. CP. AE, D, DC, MC, V.*

$$ 🖼 **Eastover.** An antidote to the posh atmosphere prevailing in most of Lenox, this resort was opened by an ex-circus roustabout, and the tradition of noisy fun and informality continues with gusto. Guest rooms are functional and vary from dormitory to motel-style; although the period wallpapers are stylish, some rooms with four or more beds resemble hospital wards with their metal rails and white bedspreads. The dining room is vast, but period decor and furnishings temper the absolute informality. The grounds are huge and home to a herd of buffalo. Facilities are extensive, and rates include all meals and activities. ⊠ *East St. (off Rte. 7), Box 2160, 01240,* ☎ *413/637–0625,* ⒻⒶⓍ *413/637–4939. 120 rooms with bath, 75 rooms share baths. Dining room, indoor and outdoor pools, sauna, driving range, tennis courts, badminton, exercise room, horseback riding, volleyball, cross-country skiing, downhill skiing. AE, D, DC, MC, V. Closed weekdays, Labor Day–July.*

Outdoor Activities and Sports

BIKING

Main Street Sports and Leisure (⊠ 48 Main St., ☎ 413/637–4407) rents mountain and road bikes and provides maps and route suggestions.

CANOEING

Main Street Sports and Leisure (⊠ 48 Main St., ☎ 413/637–4407) rents canoes and leads canoe trips on the Housatonic and local lakes.

Shopping

Along Route 7 just north of Lenox are two factory-outlet malls, **Lenox House Country Shops** and **Brushwood Farms.**

Lee

55 *140 mi from Boston, 6 mi from Lenox.*

Lee is dominated by the slew of gas stations, convenience stores, and strip motels that go with its exit from the Massachusetts turnpike. Heavy traffic rumbles through town constantly—best avoid it and head north for Lenox or south to Stockbridge. The town does have many places to stay—try to find something away from the main road.

The Arts

Jacob's Pillow Dance Festival, the oldest in the nation, happens over 10 weeks each summer. Performers vary from well-known classical ballet companies to Native American dance groups and contemporary choreographers. Before the main events, free showings of works-in-progress are staged outdoors. Visitors can picnic on the grounds or eat at the Pillow Café. ⊠ *Rte. 20, Becket (mailing address: Box 287, Lee, 01238),* ☎ *413/637–1322, box office 413/243–0745.* ☉ *June–Sept.*

Dining and Lodging

$$$ ✕ **Cork 'n Hearth.** A large stone fireplace separates the long dining room into two: On one side, wood beams show off all kinds of brassware; on the other, the beams are hung with bundles of dried herbs. Picture windows overlook Laurel Lake, which practically laps against the side of the building. The menu is traditional, offering steak, seafood, chicken Kiev, and veal cordon bleu. ⊠ *Rte. 20,* ☎ *413/243–0535. AE, MC, V. No lunch. Closed Mon.*

$–$$ ✕▥ **Oak n' Spruce Resort.** Unaffected by the noise and bustle of Lee, this resort is surrounded by miles of rolling countryside. Rooms in the main lodge are like high-quality motel rooms; large rooms in the building next door have modern furniture, kitchen units, and sliding doors onto the spacious grounds surrounding this former farm. The lodge lounge is a converted cow barn built around the original brick silo. ⊠ *Meadow St. (Box 237), South Lee 01260,* ☎ *413/243–3500 or 800/424–3003, FAX 413/243–4431. 58 rooms, 131 condos. Restaurant, bar, indoor and outdoor pools, hot tub, sauna, tennis courts, badminton, basketball, health club, hiking, horseshoes, shuffleboard, volleyball, cross-country skiing, nightclub. AE, MC, V.*

$–$$$ ▥ **The Morgan House.** Most guest rooms in this inn, which dates to 1817, are small, but the rates reflect that. Some are very narrow and have scrubbed boards and brightly painted wood furniture; others have four-poster beds, stenciled walls, and well-worn antiques. The lobby is papered with pages from old guest registers; among the signatures are those of George Bernard Shaw and Ulysses S. Grant. ⊠ *33 Main St., 01238,* ☎ *413/243–0181. 14 rooms, 2 with bath. Bar, 3 dining rooms. Full breakfast included. AE, D, DC, MC, V.*

Stockbridge

56 *149 mi from Boston, 7 mi from Lenox.*

Christmas-card perfect, Stockbridge typifies small town New England. It has a history of literary and artistic inhabitants, including sculptor Daniel Chester French, writers Norman Mailer and Robert Sherwood, and, fittingly enough, that champion of small town Americana, painter Norman Rockwell, who lived here from 1953 until his death in 1978.

The **Norman Rockwell Museum** displays 150 of Rockwell's paintings—the largest collection of Rockwell originals in the world. The museum also mounts exhibits by other artists. Its vast grounds are great for hiking and picnicking. ⊠ *Rte. 183 (2 mi from Stockbridge),* ☎ *413/298–4100.* ☒ *$8.* ⊙ *Weekdays 11–4, weekends 10–5.*

Chesterwood was for 33 years the summer home of Daniel Chester French, who is best known for his statues of the Minute Man in Concord and of Abraham Lincoln at the Lincoln Memorial in Washington, DC. ⊠ *Williamsville Rd. (off Rte. 183),* ☎ *413/298–3579.* ☒ *$6.50.* ⊙ *May–Oct., daily 10–5.*

The **Berkshire Botanical Gardens,** at the intersection of Routes 102 and 183, blanket 15 acres of land laced with pretty landscapes: historic perennial, rose, and herb gardens; greenhouses, ponds, and nature trails. Picnicking is encouraged and tours are available. ☎ *413/298–3926.* ☒ *$5.* ⊙ *May–late Oct., daily 10–5.*

Naumkeag, a Berkshire cottage that provides an informative perspective on the gracious living of the "gilded era" of the Berkshires, sits on top of Prospect Hill. The 26-room gabled mansion, designed by Stanford White, is decorated with furniture and art that spans three centuries, including an outstanding collection of Chinese export porcelain. The meticulously kept formal gardens are worth a visit in themselves. ⊠ *Prospect Hill,* ☎ *413/298–3239.* ☒ *$6.50.* ⊙ *Memorial Day–Columbus Day, Tues.–Sun. 10–4:15.*

Dining and Lodging

$$ ✕ **Hoplands.** In this restaurant a mile north of Stockbridge, diners can eat downstairs around the bar or upstairs in a simply furnished room with polished wood chairs and tables and thick carpeting. The menu features scallops, roast chicken, and pork chops. ⊠ *Rte. 102,* ☎ *413/243–4414. AE, MC, V. Closed Tues. and Mar.*

$$$$ ✕🏠 **The Williamsville Inn.** A couple of miles south of West Stockbridge,
★   this inn re-creates the late 1700s, when it was built. Guest rooms have wide-board floors, embroidered chairs, and four-poster or canopy beds; several have country furnishings and working fireplaces; and four rooms in the converted barn have wood-burning stoves. The main dining room has gray Colonial-style wallpaper and a fireplace of unpolished, locally hewn marble. Entrées include veal chops, venison medallions with Juniper berry–sage sauce, and a nightly fish special. ⊠ *Rte. 41, Williamsville 01266,* ☎ *413/274–6118,* 𝔽𝔸𝕏 *413/274–3539. 13 rooms with bath, 1 suite, 2 cottages. Restaurant, bar, pool, tennis courts, badminton, croquet, horseshoes, volleyball. Full breakfast included. AE, MC, V.*

$$$–$$$$ ✕🏠 **The Red Lion Inn.** An inn since 1773, the Red Lion is a massive place, with guest rooms in the main building and in several annexes on the property. It's a well-known landmark and gets plenty of tour-bus traffic. Many guest rooms are small: In general, the annex houses are more appealing. Rooms have floral-print wallpaper and country curtains (from the mail-order store Country Curtains, owned by the innkeepers and operated out of the inn). All are furnished with antiques and hung with Rockwell prints; some have Oriental rugs. The dining rooms are filled with antiques. New England specialties include award-winning clam chowder; broiled scallops prepared with sherry, lemon, and paprika; and steamed or stuffed lobster. ⊠ *Main St., 02162,* ☎ *413/298–5545,* 𝖥𝖠𝖷 *413/298–5130. 75 rooms with bath, 23 rooms share 8 baths, 10 suites. Restaurant (jacket and tie), bar, pool, massage, exercise room, meeting rooms. AE, D, DC, MC, V.*

$$–$$$ ▥ **The Golden Goose.** This friendly, informal place 5 miles south of Lee is cluttered with antiques and bric-a-brac, including dozens of geese in various shapes and sizes—many gifts from guests. Bedrooms are Victorian in style, with quilts and stenciled walls or floral wallpaper. Guests' names are chalked up on the little welcome board on each door. A studio apartment with kitchen and private entrance is perfect for families. ⊠ *123 Main Rd. (Box 336), Tyringham 01264,* ☎ *413/243–3008. 5 rooms with bath, 2 rooms share bath, 1 studio. Dining room. CP. AE, D, MC, V.*

$$ ▥ **Historic Merrell Inn.** This is a genuine old New England inn, built
★ as a stagecoach stopover around 1792. Despite its age, it has some good-size bedrooms—several with working fireplaces. Innkeepers Charles and Faith Reynolds upgraded this already excellent inn, adding new rugs, linens, and vanities as well as curtains and rustic framed prints; thankfully, they retained the authentic, unfussy style that makes it stand out among its peers. These new touches complement the inn's polished wide-board floors, painted plaster walls, and wood antiques. The breakfast room has an open fireplace and contains the only complete "birdcage" Colonial bar in America. ⊠ *1565 Pleasant St. (Rte. 102), South Lee 01260,* ☎ *413/243–1794 or 800/243–1794,* 𝖥𝖠𝖷 *413/243–2669. 9 rooms with bath. Breakfast room. Full breakfast included. MC, V.*

Nightlife and the Arts

NIGHTLIFE

The emphasis in the Berkshires is definitely on classical entertainment, but the most popular of the region's few nightclubs is the **Lion's Den** (☎ 413/298–5545) downstairs at the Red Lion Inn. It has live jazz, folk, or blues every evening.

THE ARTS

The **Berkshire Theatre Festival** stages nightly performances in summer at the century-old theater in Stockbridge. Children's plays, written by local schoolchildren, are performed weekends during the day. ⊠ *Box 797,* ☎ *413/298–5536, box office 413/298–5576.*

The **Robbins-Zust Family Marionettes** have been performing puppet shows for children and families in Pittsfield, Lenox, and Great Barrington since 1971. Each year they mount a varied program, which always includes the old favorite Punch and Judy and other classic fairy-tale stories. ⊠ *East Rd., Richmond 01254,* ☎ *413/698–2591.* 🎫 *$3.50.* ☉ *Late June–late Aug.; call for performance schedule.*

Shopping

UTE Stebich Gallery (⊠ 104 Main St., ☎ 413/637–3566) specializes in international folk art and contemporary art. **Sawyer Antiques** (⊠ Depot St., West Stockbridge ☎ 413/232–7062) sells Early American furniture and accessories in a large, spare, clapboard structure that was once a Shaker mill. **Le Petit Musée** (⊠ 137 Front St., Housatonic ☎ 413/274–1200) is a gallery for small contemporary and vintage works of art. **Spazi** (⊠ 3rd Floor, Barbieri's Lumber Mill, Rte. 183, near

Housatonic, ☎ 413/274–3805) focuses on contemporary painting, sculpture, and photography.

Great Barrington

57 *7 mi from Stockbridge.*

Great Barrington is the largest town in the southern Berkshires and noted as the site of the last attempt by the British to hold court in the country, as well as for the freeing of the first slaves under due process of law. It was also the birthplace of W. E. B. Du Bois, the civil rights leader, author, and educator. Today, the town is a mecca for antiques hunters, as are the nearby villages of South Egremont and Sheffield.

Bartholomew's Cobble (⊠ Rte. 7A, ☎ 413/229–8600), south of Great Barrington, is a natural rock garden beside the Housatonic River. The 277-acre reservation is filled with trees, ferns, wildflowers, and hiking trails.

At **Bash Bish Falls** (⊠ Rte. 23, ☎ 413/528–0330), 16 miles southwest of Great Barrington on the New York State border, Bash Bish Brook (say that 10 times, fast) flows through a gorge and over a 50-foot waterfall into a clear natural pool.

The Arts

The **Berkshire Opera Company** (⊠ 314 Main St., ☎ 413/528–4420) performs two operas in Great Barrington during July and August: one from the standard repertoire and one 20th-century work in English.

Dining and Lodging

$$$ ✕ **Boiler Room Café.** In a turn-of-the-century clapboard house, three
★   comfortable dining rooms are painted in warm colors accented by arches with white moldings and whimsical wood sculptures. Owner Michèle Miller serves an eclectic, sophisticated menu that may include delicious, light New England seafood stew, mouthwatering grilled baby back ribs, or osso bucco Piedmontese. For starters there are outstanding fresh salads, tapas, and chèvre soufflé. ⊠ *405 Stockbridge Rd.,* ☎ *413/528–4280. MC, V. No lunch. Closed Sun. and Mon. except holidays.*

$$$ ✕ **Stagecoach Hill Inn.** This restaurant, constructed in the early 1800s as a stagecoach stop, has a decidedly English character—there are numerous pictures of the British royal family and several hunting scenes on the walls, and there's steak and kidney pie on the menu and British ale on tap. Other menu items include pasta, steak au poivre, and chicken al forno. ⊠ *Rte. 41, Sheffield* ☎ *413/229–8585. AE, D, DC, MC, V.*

$ ✕ **20 Railroad St.** The exposed brick and subdued lighting lend atmosphere to this bustling restaurant, which has a 28-foot mahogany bar taken from the Commodore Hotel in New York City in 1919. Small wood tables are packed together in the long, narrow room. Specialties include sausage pie, beef stew, burgers, and sandwiches. ⊠ *20 Railroad St.,* ☎ *413/528–9345. MC, V.*

$$–$$$ ✕🏠 **The Egremont Inn.** The public rooms in this 1780 inn are enormous—the main lounge, with its vast open fireplace and coffee table made from an old door, is worth a visit in itself. There's a wraparound porch with white wicker chairs; some bedrooms have four-poster beds and clawfoot baths, although they're on the small side. There are three dining rooms; the largest has windows around two sides, uneven, polished pine floors, and a huge brick fireplace. Specialties include rack of venison with sun-dried cherries and salmon with fennel seed and Pernod butter. ⊠ *Old Sheffield Rd. (Box 418), South Egremont 01258,* ☎ *413/528–2111,* FAX *413/528–3284. 22 rooms with bath. Restau-*

rant (reservations essential weekends in season), bar, pool, tennis courts. CP. AE, D, MC, V.

$$$$ 🛏 **Turning Point Inn.** Just ½-mile east of Butternut Basin, this 200-year-old inn used to be the Pixie Tavern, a stagecoach stop. Guests share a sitting room and a living room, with two fireplaces and a piano, as well as a kitchen area. Antiques-filled bedrooms, with uneven, wide-board floors, are of varying sizes, and several have sloping roofs. Breakfasts are a specialty—the hosts are natural-foods advocates and serve up multigrain hot cereals, frittatas with fresh garden vegetables, buckwheat pancakes, eggs, and home-baked muffins or cakes. The barn has been converted into a two-bedroom cottage, which has modern furnishings, a full kitchen, living room, and winterized porch. ⊠ *Rte. 23 and Lake Buel Rd., R.D. 2 (Box 140), 01230,* ☎ *413/528–4777. 4 rooms with bath, 2 rooms share bath, 1 cottage. Cross-country skiing. Full breakfast included (except in cottage). AE, MC, V.*

$$$ 🛏 **Ivanhoe Country House.** The Appalachian Trail runs right across the property of this bed-and-breakfast. The house was originally built in 1780, but various wings were added later. The antiques-furnished guest rooms are generally spacious; several have private porches or balconies, and all have excellent country views. The large sitting room has antique desks, a piano, and comfortable couches. The owners raise golden retrievers in the large grounds and, being a canine-friendly family, they accept guests' pets. ⊠ *254 South Undermountain Rd. (Rte. 41), Sheffield, 01257,* ☎ *413/229–2143. 9 rooms, 2 suites with kitchen. Refrigerators, pool. CP. No credit cards.*

$$–$$$ 🛏 **Weathervane Inn.** The open fireplace and beehive oven in the lounge of this friendly, family-run inn date to the 1760s, when the original building was constructed. The more formal parlor has striking reproduction wallpaper, and guest rooms are decorated with stencils, country curtains, wreaths, Norman Rockwell prints, and rocking chairs. At one point the inn served as a dog kennel—one of the guest bathrooms has inherited an original dog-size bathtub! ⊠ *Box 388, Rte. 23, South Egremont 01258,* ☎ *413/528–9580,* ℻ *413/528–1713. 11 rooms with bath. 2 dining rooms, bar, pool. Full breakfast included; MAP available. Closed Dec. 20–26. AE, MC, V.*

$$–$$$$ 🛏 **Mountain View Motel.** This motel, just 1 mile west of Butternut ski area, has pleasant accommodations, in-room coffee and Norman Rockwell prints on the walls. ⊠ *304 State Rd. (Rte. 23E), 01230,* ☎ *413/528–0250,* ℻ *413/528–0137. 16 rooms with bath, 1 suite, 1 efficiency. AE, MC, V.*

Outdoor Activities and Sports

HIKING

Three miles north of Great Barrington, you can leave your car in a parking lot beside Route 7 and climb Squaw Peak on **Monument Mountain.** The 2.7-mile circular hike (a trail map is displayed in the parking lot) takes you up 900 feet, past glistening white quartzite cliffs, from where Native Americans are said to have leapt to their deaths to placate the gods. From the top there are excellent views of the surrounding mountains.

Shopping

The Great Barrington area, including the small Southern Berkshires towns of Sheffield and South Egremont, has the greatest concentration of antiques stores in the Berkshires. For a list of storekeepers who belong to the **Berkshire County Antiques Dealers Association,** send a SASE to R.D. 1, Box 1, Sheffield 01257.

Coffman's Country Antiques Market (⊠ Rte. 7, Jennifer House Commons, ☎ 413/528–9282) houses 100 quality antiques dealers on three floors, selling furniture, quilts, baskets, and silverware from the 16th century to the 1940s. **Corashire Antiques** (⊠ Rtes. 23 and 7 at Belcher Sq., ☎ 413/528–0014), a shop in a red barn, carries American country furniture and accessories, including the occasional rare Shaker piece. **Mullin-Jones Antiquities** (⊠ 525 S. Main St., Rte. 7, ☎ 413/528–4871) has 18th- and 19th-century country French antiques: armoires, buffets, tables, chairs, and gilded mirrors.

Red Barn Antiques (⊠ Rte. 23, South Egremont, ☎ 413/528–3230) has a wide selection of antique lamps and 19th-century American furniture, glass, and accessories. **The Splendid Peasant** (⊠ Rte. 23 and Old Sheffield Rd., South Egremont, ☎ 413/528–5755) sells 18th- and 19th-century American and European painted country furniture, and has three galleries of museum-quality American folk art.

Bradford Galleries (⊠ Rte. 7, Sheffield, ☎ 413/229–6667) holds monthly auctions of furniture, paintings and prints, china, glass, silver, and Oriental rugs. A tag sale of household items is open daily. **Darr Antiques and Interiors** (⊠ 28 S. Main St., Rte. 7, Sheffield, ☎ 413/229–7773) displays elegant 18th- and 19th-century American, English, Continental, and Oriental furniture and accessories in impressive, formal room settings in a fine Colonial house. A second store houses another 1,600 square feet of antiques. **Dovetail Antiques** (⊠ Rte. 7, Sheffield, ☎ 413/229–2628) shows American clocks, pottery, and country furniture in a small, friendly shop. **Good & Hutchinson Associates** (⊠ Rte. 7, Sheffield, ☎ 413/229–8832) specializes in American, English, and Continental furniture, paintings, fine pottery, and china "for museums and antiquarians."

Antiques at the Buggy Whip Factory (⊠ Main St., Rte. 272, Southfield, ☎ 413/229–3576) provides space for approximately 75 dealers to show American antiques, including formal and country furniture, jewelry, glass, china, sterling, books, and 19th-century fabrics. The factory also houses an artisan's gallery, a few outlet stores, and a café.

Skiing

Butternut Basin. Friendly Butternut Basin has good base facilities, pleasant skiing, and tasty food in the base lodge. Skiers from New York's Long Island and Westchester County and Connecticut's Fairfield County continue to flock to the area. ⊠ *Great Barrington 01230,* ☎ *413/528–2000, ski school 413/528–4433, snow conditions 800/438–7669.*

DOWNHILL

Only a steep chute or two interrupts the mellow intermediate terrain. There are slopes for beginners and something for everyone off the area's 1,000-foot vertical. One new quad, one triple, and four double chairlifts, plus two surface lifts keep skier traffic spread out.

CROSS-COUNTRY

Butternut Basin has 7 kilometers (4 mi) of groomed cross-country trails.

CHILD CARE

The nursery takes children ages 2½–6 daily for indoor activities, and younger toddlers or infants by appointment. The ski school's SKIwee program is for children 4–12. During midweek, youngsters can get group lessons.

The Berkshires A to Z

Getting Around

BY BUS
Peter Pan Bus Lines (☎ 413/442–4451 or 800/237–8747) serves Lee and Pittsfield from Boston and Albany. **Bonanza Bus Lines** (☎ 800/556–3815) connects points throughout the Berkshires with Albany, New York City, and Providence.

BY CAR
The Massachusetts Turnpike (I–90) connects Boston with Lee and Stockbridge, and continues into New York, where it becomes the New York State Thruway. To reach the Berkshires from New York City, take either I–87 or the Taconic State Parkway.

Within the Berkshires the main north–south road is Route 7. The scenic Mohawk Trail (Rte. 2) runs from the northern Berkshires to Greenfield at the head of the Pioneer Valley, and continues across Massachusetts into Boston.

BY TRAIN
Amtrak (☎ 800/872–7245) runs the *Lake Shore Limited,* which stops at Pittsfield once daily in each direction on its route between Boston and Chicago.

Contacts and Resources

ARTS LISTINGS
The daily *Berkshire Eagle* covers the area's extensive summer arts festivals; June through Columbus Day the *Eagle* also publishes *Berkshires Week,* the summer bible for events information. The *Williamstown Advocate* has general arts listings, and the *Boston Globe* publishes news of major concerts on Thursdays.

CANOEING
Suggested canoe trips in the Berkshires include Lenox–Dalton (19 mi), Lenox–Stockbridge (12 mi), Stockbridge–Great Barrington (13 mi) and, for experts, Great Barrington–Falls Village (25 mi). Information about these and other trips can be found in *The AMC River Guide to Massachusetts, Rhode Island, and Connecticut* (AMC, ⊠ 5 Joy St., Boston, 02198).

EMERGENCIES
Fairview Hospital (⊠ 29 Lewis Ave., Great Barrington, ☎ 413/528–0790). **Hillcrest Hospital** (⊠ 165 Tor Ct., Pittsfield, ☎ 413/443–4761). **North Adams Regional Hospital** (⊠ Hospital Ave., North Adams, ☎ 413/663–3701).

GUIDED TOURS
Balloon tours over the Berkshires are offered twice daily year-round (weather permitting) by **American Balloon Works, Inc.** (⊠ East Nassau, NY 12062, ☎ 518/766–5111).

Berkshire Hiking Holidays offers a variety of guided hiking tours: Less ambitious walkers can combine easy hikes with visits to Tanglewood and Berkshire towns; the more experienced trekker can tackle mountain trails. "Hike, bike, and canoe" combines three ways to experience the Berkshires. Overnight accommodation is provided in Berkshire inns. ⊠ *Box 2231, Lenox, 01240,* ☎ *413/499–9648.*

New England Hiking Holidays organizes guided hiking vacations through the Berkshires, with overnight stays at country inns. Hikes vary from 5 to 9 miles per day. ⊠ *Box 1648, North Conway, NH 03860,* ☎ *603/356–9696 or 800/869–0949.*

HIKING

For information on trails and hiking, contact **Berkshire Region Headquarters** (⊠ 740 South St., Pittsfield, 01202, ☎ 413/442–8928).

RESERVATION SERVICES

The **Lenox Chamber of Commerce** (☎ 413/637–3646 or 800/255–3669) and the **Southern Berkshires Chamber of Commerce** (☎ 413/528–4006) have lodging referral services.

SMOKING

Many Berkshires towns are working toward "smoke-free" policies. In Lenox, smoking is forbidden in all restaurants and many inns; Great Barrington, Lee, Stockbridge, and West Stockbridge also have many smoke-free establishments.

STATE PARKS

There are 19 state parks and forests in the Berkshires. Those with camping include **Beartown State Forest** (⊠ Blue Hill Rd., Monterey, ☎ 413/528–0904), **Clarksburg State Forest** (⊠ Middle Rd., Clarksburg, ☎ 413/664–8345), **Mt. Greylock State Reservation** (⊠ Rockwell Rd., Lanesboro, ☎ 413/499–4262/3), **October Mountain State Forest** (⊠ Woodland Rd., Lee, ☎ 413/243–1778), **Otis State Forest** (⊠ Rte. 23, Otis, ☎ 413/528–0904), **Pittsfield State Forest** (⊠ Cascade St., Pittsfield, ☎ 413/442–8992), **Sandisfield State Forest** (⊠ West St., Sandisfield, ☎ 413/229–8212), **Savoy Mountain State Forest** (⊠ 260 Central Shaft Rd., Florida, ☎ 413/663–8469), **Tolland State Forest** (⊠ Rte. 8, Otis, ☎ 413/269–6002), and **Windsor State Forest** (Windsor, ☎ 413/442–8928).

VISITOR INFORMATION

Berkshire Visitor's Bureau (⊠ Berkshire Common, Pittsfield 01201, ☎ 413/443–9186 or 800/237–5747; ◷ Weekdays 8:30–4:30). The **Southern Berkshires Chamber of Commerce** (⊠ 362 Main St., ☎ 413/528–1510; ◷ Weekdays 9:30–4:30, Sat. 9:30–5:30). **Lenox Chamber of Commerce** (⊠ Lenox Academy Building, 75 Main St., 01240, ☎ 413/637–3646; ◷ June, Sept., and Oct., Tues.–Sat. 10–6; July and Aug., Mon.–Sat. 10–5, Sun. 10–2; Oct.–May, Tues.–Sat. 10–5). **Mohawk Trail Association** (⊠ Box 722, Charlemont 01339, ☎ 413/664–6256).

MASSACHUSETTS A TO Z

Arriving and Departing

By Bus

Greyhound (☎ 800/231–2222) and **Peter Pan Bus Lines** (☎ 800/237–8747) connect Boston and other major cities in Massachusetts with cities throughout the United States. **Bonanza** (☎ 800/556–3815) serves Boston and the eastern part of the state from Providence with connecting service to New York.

By Car

Boston is the traffic hub of New England, with interstate highways approaching it from every direction and every major city in the northeast. New England's chief coastal highway, I–95, skirts Boston, while I–90 leads west to the Great Lakes and Chicago. Interstate–91 brings visitors to the Pioneer Valley in western Massachusetts from Vermont and Canada in the north and Connecticut and New York to the south.

By Plane

Boston's **Logan International Airport,** the largest airport in New England, has scheduled flights by most major domestic and foreign carriers.

Bradley International Airport, in Windsor Locks, Connecticut, 18 miles south of Springfield on I–91, has scheduled flights by major U.S. airlines.

Hyannis's **Barnstable Municipal Airport** is Cape Cod's air gateway, with flights from **Business Express/Delta Connection** (☎ 800/345–3400), **Cape Air** (☎ 800/352–0714), **Nantucket Airlines** (☎ 508/790–0300 or 800/635–8787), and **Northwest Airlink** (☎ 800/225–2525). **Provincetown Municipal Airport** is served by **Cape Air.**

Martha's Vineyard Airport is served by **Cape Air** and **Continental Express** (☎ 800/525–0280). **Nantucket Memorial Airport** is served by all the above-mentioned airlines, as well as **Island Airlines** (☎ 508/775–6606 or 800/248–7779) and **Nantucket Airlines** (☎ 508/790–0300 or 800/635–8787).

By Train
Amtrak's Northeast Corridor service (☎ 800/872–7245) links Boston with principal cities between it and Washington, DC. The *Lake Shore Limited,* which stops at Springfield and the Berkshires, carries passengers from Chicago to Boston. On summer weekends, Hyannis is served by the *Cape Codder* from New York, with connecting service to Washington, DC, Philadelphia, and other points.

Contacts and Resources
Visitor Information
Massachusetts Office of Travel and Tourism (✉ 100 Cambridge St., Boston 02202, ☎ 617/727–3201 or 800/447–6277).

5 Vermont

Southern Vermont has farms, freshly starched New England towns, quiet back roads, bustling ski resorts, and strip-mall sprawl. Central Vermont's trademarks include marble quarries north of Rutland and pastures that create the patchwork of the Champlain Valley. The heart of the area is the Green Mountains. The state's largest city (Burlington) and the nation's smallest state capital (Montpelier) are in northern Vermont, as are some of the most remote areas of New England. Much of the state's logging, dairy farming, and skiing take place here.

By Mary H.
Frakes and
Tara Hamilton,
with an
introduction by
William G.
Scheller

Updated by
Anne Peracca

EVERYWHERE YOU LOOK AROUND VERMONT, the evidence is clear: This is not the state it was 25 years ago.

That may be true for the rest of New England as well, but the contrasts between the present and recent past seem all the more sharply drawn in the Green Mountain State, if only because an aura of timelessness has always been at the heart of the Vermont image. Vermont was where all the quirks and virtues outsiders associate with up-country New England were supposed to reside. It was where the Yankees were Yankee-est and where there were more cows than people.

Not that you should be alarmed, if you haven't been here in a while; Vermont hasn't become southern California, or even, for that matter, southern New Hampshire. This is still the most rural state in the Union (meaning that it has the smallest percentage of citizens living in statistically defined metropolitan areas), even if there are, finally, more people than cows. It's still a place where cars occasionally have to stop while a dairy farmer walks cows across a secondary road; and up in Essex County, in what George Aiken dubbed the Northeast Kingdom, there are townships with zero population. And the kind of scrupulous, straightforward, plainspoken politics practiced by Governor (later Senator) Aiken for 50 years has not become outmoded in a state that still turns out on town-meeting day.

How has Vermont changed? In strictly physical terms, the most obvious transformations have taken place in and around the two major cities, Burlington and Rutland, and near the larger ski resorts, such as Stowe, Killington, Stratton, and Mt. Snow. Burlington's Church Street, once a paradigm of all the sleepy redbrick shopping thoroughfares in northern New England, is now a pedestrian mall complete with chic bistros; outside the city, suburban development has supplanted dairy farms in towns where someone's trip to Burlington might once have been an item in a weekly newspaper. As for the ski areas, it's no longer enough simply to boast the latest in chairlift technology. Stratton has an entire "Austrian Village" of restaurants and shops, while a hillside adjacent to Bromley's slopes has sprouted instant replica Victorians for the second-home market. The town of Manchester, convenient to both resorts, is awash in designer-fashion discount outlets.

But the real metamorphosis in the Green Mountains has to do more with style, with the personality of the place, than with the mere substance of development. The past couple of decades have seen a tremendous influx of outsiders—not just skiers and "leaf peepers," but people who've come to stay year-round—and many of them are determined either to freshen the local scene with their own idiosyncrasies or to make Vermont even more like Vermont than they found it. On the one hand, this translates into the fact that one of the biggest draws to the tiny town of Glover each summer is an outdoor pageant that promotes leftist political and social causes; on the other, it means that sheep farming has been reintroduced into the state, largely to provide a high-quality product for the hand-weaving industry.

This ties in with another local phenomenon, one best described as Made in Vermont. Once upon a time, maple syrup and sharp cheddar cheese were the products that carried Vermont's name to the world. The market niche that they created has since been widened by Vermonters—a great many of them refugees from more hectic arenas of commerce—offering a dizzying variety of goods with the ineffable cachet of Ver-

mont manufacture. There are Vermont wood toys, Vermont apple
wines, Vermont chocolates, even Vermont gin. All of it is marketed with
the tacit suggestion that it was made by Yankee elves in a shed out back
on a bright autumn morning.

The most successful Made in Vermont product is the renowned Ben
& Jerry's ice cream. Neither Ben nor Jerry comes from old Green
Mountain stock, but their product has benefited immensely from the
magical reputation of the place where it is made. Along the way, the
company (which started in Burlington under the most modest circumstances in 1979) has become the largest single purchaser of Vermont's still considerable dairy output. Proof that the modern and the
traditional—wearing a red-plaid cap and a Johnson Woolen Mills
hunting jacket—can still get along very nicely in Vermont.

Pleasures and Pastimes

Biking

Vermont is great bicycle-touring country, especially the often-deserted
roads of the Northeast Kingdom that seem to regularly bring yet another more-beautiful-than-the-last vista. A number of companies lead
weekend tours and weeklong trips that travel throughout the state. If
you'd like to go it on your own, most chambers of commerce have
brochures highlighting good cycling routes in their area, including
Vermont Life's "Bicycle Vermont" map and guide, and many bookstores sell *25 Bicycle Tours in Vermont* by John Freidin.

Dining

Vermont restaurants have not escaped common efforts in the Northeast to adapt traditional New England fare to the ways of nouvelle cuisine. The New England Culinary Institute, based in Montpelier, has
trained a number of Vermont chefs who have now turned their attention to such native New England foods as fiddlehead ferns (available
only for a short time in the spring); maple syrup (Vermont is the largest
U.S. producer); dairy products, especially cheese; native fruits and
berries that are often transformed into jams and jellies; "new Vermont"
products such as salsa and salad dressings; and venison, quail, pheas-
ant, and other game.

Your chances of finding a table for dinner vary dramatically with the
season: Many restaurants have lengthy waits during peak seasons
(when it's always a good idea to reserve ahead) and then shut down
during the slow months of April and November. Some of the best dining is found in country inns.

CATEGORY	COST*
$$$$	over $35
$$$	$25–$35
$$	$15–$25
$	under $15

*average cost of a three-course dinner, per person, excluding drinks, service,
and 7% sales tax*

Fishing

Central Vermont is the heart of the state's warm-water lake and pond
fishing. Harriman and Somerset reservoirs have both warm- and cold-
water species; Harriman has a greater variety. Lake Dunmore produced
the state-record rainbow trout; Lakes Bomoseen and St. Catherine are
good for rainbows and largemouth bass. In the east, Lakes Fairlee and
Morey feature bass, perch, and chain pickerel, while the lower part of
the Connecticut River contains small-mouth bass, walleye, and perch;
shad are returning via the fish ladders at Vernon and Bellows Falls.

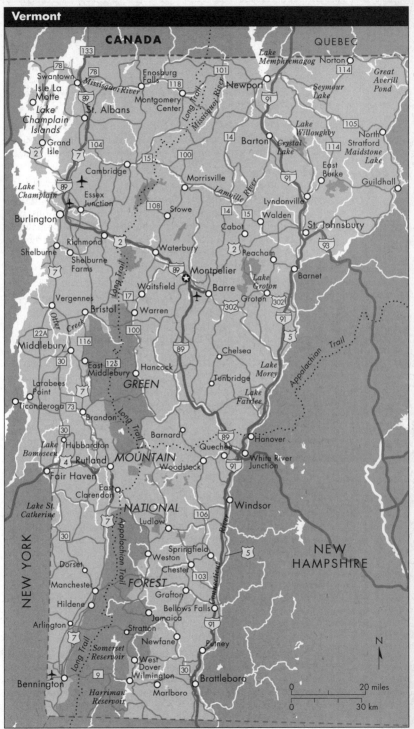

Vermont

CANADA

QUEBEC

133

78
Swantown
Isle La
Motte
Lake
Champlain
Islands
78
Missisquoi River
89
St. Albans

Enosburg
Falls
118
Montgomery
Center
Long Trail
101
Missisquoi River
Newport

Lake
Memphremagog
Norton
114
Great
Averill
Pond
Seymour
Lake
105

2
Grand
Isle
104
7

Cambridge
15
100
14
Barton
Crystal
Lake
Lake
Willoughby
North
Stratford
Maidstone
Lake
114

Lake
Champlain
89
Essex
Junction
108
Stowe
Morrisville
Lamoille River
14
15
Walden
Lyndonville
91
East
Burke
Guildhall

Burlington
Shelburne
Richmond
2
Shelburne
Farms
7
Long Trail
Waterbury
Waitsfield
89
Montpelier
Barre
Cabot
2
Peacham
Lake
Groton
Groton
302
St. Johnsbury
93
Barnet

Vergennes
Bristol
Otter Creek
17
Warren
100
302
91
5

22A
Middlebury
116
30
East
Middlebury
125
Hancock
GREEN
Chelsea
Tunbridge
Lake
Morey
Lake
Fairlee
Appalachian Trail

Larabees
Point
Ticonderoga
7
73
Brandon
Long Trail
MOUNTAIN
Barnard
Quechee
89
Hanover
White River
Junction

Lake
Bomoseen
30
Hubbardton
Rutland
4
Fair Haven
Woodstock
91

East
Clarendon
NATIONAL
106
Windsor

Lake St.
Catherine
30
7
Appalachian Trail
Ludlow
Weston
Springfield
5
Chester
103

NEW
YORK
30
Dorset
FOREST
Grafton
Bellows Falls
91
Connecticut River

Manchester
Hildene
Stratton
Jamaica
Newfane
Putney

Arlington
7
Long Trail
Somerset
Reservoir
West
Dover
Wilmington
30
Brattleboro

Bennington
9
Harriman
Reservoir
Marlboro

NEW
HAMPSHIRE

N

0   20 miles
0   30 km

In Northern Vermont, rainbow trout inhabit the Missisquoi, Lamoille, Winooski, and Willoughby rivers, and there's warm-water fishing at many smaller lakes and ponds. Lakes Seymour, Willoughby, and Memphremagog and Great Averill Pond in the Northeast Kingdom are good for salmon and lake trout. The Dog River near Montpelier has one of the best wild populations of brown trout in the state. Good news is that landlocked Atlantic salmon are returning to the Clyde River because of a breech in the dam.

Lake Champlain, stocked annually with salmon and lake trout, has become the state's ice-fishing capital; walleye, bass, pike, and channel catfish are also taken. Ice fishing is also popular on Lake Memphremagog.

Lodging

Vermont's largest hotels are in Burlington and near the major ski resorts. There's an odd dearth of inns and B&Bs in Burlington, although a plethora of chain hotels provides dependable accommodations. Elsewhere you'll find a variety of inns, bed-and-breakfasts, and small motels. Rates are highest during foliage season, from late September to mid-October, and lowest in late spring and November, when many properties close. Many of the larger hotels offer package rates. Some antiques-filled inns discourage bringing children.

The Vermont Chamber of Commerce publishes the *Vermont Travelers' Guidebook,* which is an extensive list of lodgings, and additional guides to country inns and vacation rentals. The Vermont Travel Division has a brochure that lists lodgings at working farms.

CATEGORY	COST*
$$$$	over $150
$$$	$100–$150
$$	$60–$100
$	under $60

All prices are for a standard double room during peak season, with no meals unless noted, and excluding service charge.

National Forests

The 355,000 acres of Green Mountain National Forest extend down the center of the state, providing scenic drives, picnic areas, lakes, and hiking and cross-country ski trails. Grout Pond Recreation Area and Somerset Reservoir are two idyllic boating and hiking destinations— it's worth the wear on your car's struts and shocks driving dirt roads (closed in winter) to get to them. There are also trail heads for the Appalachian and Long trails here, and the trail to the waterfalls at the Lye Brook Wilderness Area is popular.

Skiing

The Green Mountains run through the middle of Vermont like a bumpy spine, visible from almost every point in the state; generous accumulations of snow make the mountains an ideal site for skiing. Recent increased snow-making capacity and improved, high-tech computerized equipment at many areas virtually assures a good day on the slopes. Vermont has 21 alpine ski resorts with nearly 900 trails and some 4,000 acres of skiable terrain. Combined, the resorts operate some 175 lifts and have the capacity to carry a total of more than 200,000 skiers per hour. In addition, the state offers a wide variety of accommodations and dining options, from inexpensive dormitories to luxurious inns, at the base of most ski mountains or within an easy drive. Though grooming is sophisticated at all Vermont areas, conditions usually range from hard pack to icy, with powder a rare luxury. The best advice for skiing in Vermont is to keep your skis well tuned.

Route 100 is well known as the "Skier's Highway," passing by 13 of the state's ski areas. Vermont's major resorts are Stowe, Jay Peak, Sugarbush, Killington, Okemo, Mt. Snow, and Stratton. Midsize, less hectic areas to consider include Ascutney, Bromley, Bolton Valley, Smugglers' Notch, Pico, Mad River Glen, and Burke Mountain.

Exploring Vermont

Vermont is divided into three regions: the southern part is flanked by Bennington and Brattleboro and played an important role in the formation of Vermont's statehood; the central part is characterized by its mountains and its marble; northern Vermont is the site of the state's capital and largest city yet also is home to its most rural area, the Northeast Kingdom.

Great Itineraries

Although Vermont is a small state, there is much to see and do within its perimeters. Distances are relatively short yet there are mountains and many back roads to contend with, which will slow a traveler's pace. You can take advantage of Vermont's beauty in a variety of ways—skiing or hiking its mountains, biking or driving its back roads, fishing or sailing its waters, shopping for local products, visiting its museums and sites, or simply finding the perfect inn and never leaving the front porch. A stay of at least seven days would allow you to indulge in many of these activities. If your visit must be shorter, you will have to be more selective.

Numbers in the text correspond to numbers in the margin and on the maps.

IF YOU HAVE 3 DAYS

Spend a few hours in historic **Bennington** ⑥, then travel north to see **Hildene** and stay in ⊞ **Manchester** ⑦. The next day, take Route 100 through Weston, north through the Green Mountains to Route 125 where you turn west to explore ⊞ **Middlebury** ㉖. Enter the Champlain Valley the following day, which has views of the Adirondack Mountains to the west. Stop at **Shelburne Farms,** and carry on to **Burlington** ㉟, where you should make a point to watch a sunset from the waterfront and take a walk on Church Street.

IF YOU HAVE 5 DAYS

You can make several side trips off Route 100. After visiting **Bennington** ⑥, **Hildene,** and ⊞ **Manchester** ⑦, spend a day walking around the small towns of **Chester** ⑪ and ⊞ **Grafton** ⑫. Then head north to explore **Woodstock** ⑳ and ⊞ **Quechee** ⑲, making sure to stop at either the Billings Museum or the Vermont Institute of Natural Science. Spend the next day driving leisurely to ⊞ **Middlebury** ㉖, along one of Vermont's most inspiring mountain drives, Route 125 west of Route 100. Driving from Hancock to Middlebury, you'll pass nature trails and the picnic spot at Texas Falls Recreation Area, then traverse a moderately steep mountain pass. Spend your last day in **Burlington** ㉟.

IF YOU HAVE 7 DAYS

Spend a day and two nights in ⊞ **Manchester.** After visiting **Bennington** ⑥ and **Hildene,** and staying overnight in ⊞ **Manchester** ⑦, take the next day to explore the Southern Vermont Arts Center. In the morning, drive to the small towns of **Chester** ⑪ and ⊞ **Grafton** ⑫. Then head north to **Woodstock** ⑳ and ⊞ **Quechee** ⑲. Spend the next day driving leisurely to ⊞ **Middlebury** ㉖, along one of Vermont's most inspiring mountain drives, Route 125 west of Route 100. Spend the afternoon and night in ⊞ **Burlington** ㉟. Then head east to **Waterbury** ㉙ and then north to ⊞ **Stowe** ㉛ and Mount Mansfield for a full day. Begin your last day with a few hours in **Montpelier** ㉘ on your way to **Peacham** ㊵, **St. Johnsbury** ㊴, 🖼 **Lake Willoughby** ㊲, and the serenity and back roads of the Northeast Kingdom. Especially noteworthy are Routes 5, 5A, and 14.

When to Tour Vermont

The number of tourists and the rates for lodging reach their peaks along with the color of the leaves during foliage season, from late September to mid-October. But if you have never seen a kaleidoscope of autumn colors, it is worth braving the slow-moving traffic and paying the extra money. Rates are lowest in late spring and November, although many properties close during these times.

SOUTHERN VERMONT

The Vermont tradition of independence and rebellion began in southern Vermont. Many towns founded in the early 18th century as frontier outposts or fortifications were later important as trading centers. In the western region the Green Mountain Boys fought off both the British and the claims of land-hungry New Yorkers—some say their descendants are still fighting. In the 19th century, as many towns turned to manufacturing, the eastern part of the state preserved much of its farms and orchards.

The first thing you'll notice upon entering the state is the conspicuous lack of billboards along the highways and roads. The foresight back in the 1960s to prohibit their proliferation has made for a refreshing lack of aggressive visual clutter; their absence allows travelers unencumbered views of working farmland, freshly starched New England towns, and quiet back roads, but doesn't hide the reality of abandoned dairy barns, bustling ski resorts, and strip-mall sprawl.

The towns are listed in circular order. We begin in the east, south of the junction of I–91 and Route 9 in Brattleboro, and follow the southern boundary of the state toward Bennington then north up to Manchester and Weston and south back to Newfane.

Numbers in the margin correspond to points of interest on the Southern Vermont map.

Brattleboro

❶ *60 mi south of White River Junction.*

Its downtown bustling with activity, Brattleboro is the center of commerce for southeastern Vermont. At the confluence of the West and Connecticut rivers, this town of about 13,000, originated as a frontier scouting post and became a thriving industrial center and resort town in the 1800s. More recently, the area has become a haven for left-leaning political activists and those pursuing one form of alternative lifestyle or another.

A former railroad station, the **Brattleboro Museum and Art Center** has replaced locomotives with art and historical exhibits as well as an Estey organ from the days when the city was home to one of the world's largest organ companies. ⊠ *Vernon and Main Sts.,* ☎ *802/257–0124.* 🖾 *$2.* ☉ *Mid-May–late-Oct., Tues.–Sun. noon–6.*

Larkin G. Mead, Jr., a Brattleboro resident, stirred 19th-century America's imagination with an 8-foot snow angel he built at the intersection of Routes 30 and 5. **Brooks Memorial Library** has a replica of the angel as well as rotating art exhibits. ⊠ *224 Main St.,* ☎ *802/254–*

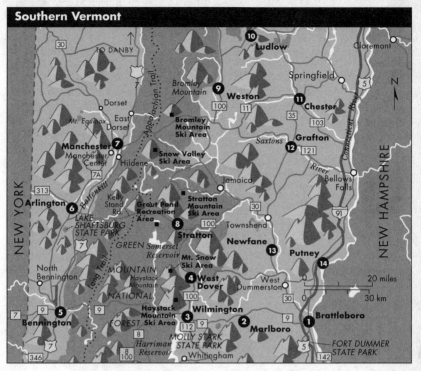

Southern Vermont

5290. ⊙ *Mon.–Wed. 9–9, Thurs. and Fri. 9–6, Sat. 9–5; Memorial Day –Labor Day, Mon.–Sat. 9–noon.*

Dining and Lodging

$ ✕ **Common Ground.** The political posters and concert fliers that line the staircase make you conscious of Vermont's strong progressive element as you ascend into the loft-like, rough-hewn dining rooms. Owned cooperatively by the staff, this vegetarian restaurant serves the likes of cashew burgers, veggie stir-fries, curries, hot soup and stew, and the "humble bowl of brown rice." A chocolate cake with peanut butter frosting and other desserts (sans white sugar, of course) will lure confirmed meat-eaters. ⊠ *25 Elliot St.,* ☎ *802/257–0855. No credit cards. Closed Tues.*

$ ✕ **Mole's Eye Cafe.** Built in the 1930s as the tavern for the long-gone Brooks Hotel, the Mole's Eye is an institution. The appeal of this cozy basement gathering place is its neighborly hospitality—not to mention the home-baked turkey melts, Mexican munchies, and hearty, home-made soups and desserts. ⊠ *High St.,* ☎ *802/257–0771. Reservations not accepted. MC, V.*

$–$$ ✕🏨 **Latchis Hotel.** This grand downtown Art Deco landmark has black-and-white-check bathroom tiles, painted geometric borders along the ceiling, multicolored patterns of terrazzo on the lobby floor. All deluxe rooms come with a refrigerator and movie passes. Odd-numbered rooms have views of the Connecticut River and Main Street. The Latchis Grille is home to the Windham Brewery and serves rich ales and lagers, as well as an eclectic array of pub grub—grilled chicken and fish sandwiches, fried calamari, burgers, salads, and the like. ⊠ *50 Main St., 05301,* ☎ *802/254–6300,* 🖷 *802/254–6304. 30 rooms with bath. Restaurant (closed Mon.). CP. AE, MC, V.*

$$$$ 🏠 **Naulakha.** In 1892, Rudyard Kipling came to southern Vermont and was captivated by the area. He bought 11 acres high in a long and thin protected meadow and built Naulakha (which means "jewel beyond price") so that every room would have a view across woods and farmland to distant hills. Kipling completed *The Jungle Book* here and had intended to stay permanently but sold the house in 1902. Restored by Britain's Landmark Trust, Naulakha has five bedrooms and sleeps eight comfortably. There's a dishwasher, washing machine, wood-burning stove, and a collection of books that would have made Kipling proud. A minimum three-night stay is required. *Information:* ✉ *The Landmark Trust USA, R.R.1, Box 510, 05301,* ☎ *802/254–6868. Reservations:* ✉ *The Landmark Trust, Shottesbrooke, Maidenhead, Berkshire, England SL6 3SW,* ☎ *011/44–1628–825925.*

Nightlife and the Arts

NIGHTLIFE

Mole's Eye Cafe (✉ High St., ☎ 802/257–0771) has live bands: acoustic or folk on Wednesday; open mike on Thursday; danceable R&B, blues, or reggae on weekends (cover charge Fri.–Sat.). **Common Ground** (✉ 25 Elliot St., ☎ 802/257–0855) often has folk or performance art on weekends.

THE ARTS

New England Bach Festival (✉ Brattleboro Music Center, ☎ 802/257–4523), with a chorus under the direction of Blanche Moyse, is held in fall. **Vermont Symphony Orchestra** (☎ 802/864–5741) performs in Bennington and Arlington in winter, in Manchester and Brattleboro in summer.

Outdoor Activities and Sports

CANOEING

Connecticut River Safari (✉ Rte. 5, ☎ 802/257–5008) has guided and self-guided tours as well as canoe rentals.

Shopping

BOOKS

The Book Cellar (✉ 120 Main St., ☎ 802/254–6026), with two floors of volumes, has a large selection of travel books.

CRAFTS

Vermont Artisan Design (✉ 115 Main St., ☎ 802/257–7044), one of the state's best crafts shops, displays contemporary ceramics, glass, wood, and clothing.

Marlboro

❷ *10 mi west of Brattleboro.*

Marlboro is a tiny town that draws musicians and audiences from around the world each summer to the Marlboro Music Festival, founded by Rudolf Serkin and joined for many years by Pablo Casals. Perched high on a hill just off Route 9, **Marlboro College** is the center of musical activity. The demure white-frame buildings have an outstanding view of the valley below, and the campus is studded with apple trees.

The Arts

Marlboro Music Festival (✉ Marlboro Music Center, ☎ 802/254–2394 or, Sept.–June, 215/569–4690) presents a broad range of classical music in weekend concerts in July and August.

Wilmington

❸ *8 mi west of Marlboro.*

Wilmington is the shopping and dining center for the Mt. Snow ski area to the north. Strolling up and down Main Street's cohesive assemblage of 18th- and 19th-century buildings—many of them listed on the National Register of Historic Places—is made more interesting and educational by picking up a copy of the walking-tour guide from the Chamber of Commerce (✉ E. Main St., Box 3, Wilmington 05363, ☎ 802/464–8092).

North River Winery occupies a converted farmhouse and barn and produces such fruit wines as Green Mountain Apple. ✉ *Rte. 112, 6 mi south of Wilmington,* ☎ *802/368–7557.* ◙ *Free.* ◷ *Memorial Day–Dec., daily 10–5; Jan.–Memorial Day, Fri.–Sun. 11–5.*

OFF THE BEATEN PATH — To begin a scenic (though well-traveled) 35-mile circular tour that affords panoramic views of the region's mountains, farmland, and abundant cow population, drive west on Route 9 to the intersection with Route 8. Turn south and continue to the junction with Route 100; follow Route 100 through Whitingham (the birthplace of the Mormon prophet Brigham Young), and stay with the road as it turns north again and takes you back to Route 9.

Dining and Lodging

$$$–$$$$ ✕🖫 **The Hermitage.** Staying in this 19th-century inn is like visiting an
★ English country manor in hunting season. English setters prance about the grounds amid various collections of decoys, while game birds roam the fields near a duck pond—don't get too attached to the birds, however; you'll probably have one for dinner. The most formal rooms are in the Colonial-style main inn and the Wine House, where every room has a fireplace; and about ½ mile down the road is the Brook Bound Lodge, which has most modest rooms and is much less expensive. Furnishings in all are simple turn-of-the-century New England: muslin curtains, white shutters. Beds are four-poster or have towering oak headboards. The restaurant has a traditional Continental menu that specializes in home-raised game birds and venison—and a 2,000-label wine list. ✉ *Coldbrook Rd., Box 457, 05363,* ☎ *802/464–3511. 25 rooms with bath, 4 share 2 baths. Restaurant, pool, sauna, tennis courts, cross-country skiing, snowmobiling. MAP. AE, DC, MC, V.*

$$$–$$$$ ✕🖫 **The White House of Wilmington.** The grand staircase in this Federal-style mansion leads to spacious rooms with antique bathrooms, brass wall sconces, and mah-jongg sets. The newer section has more contemporary plumbing; some rooms have fireplaces, whirlpool tubs, and lofts. A description of the public rooms—heavy velvet drapes, tufted leather wingchairs—suggests formality, yet the atmosphere is casual and comfortable. Although it's just a 10-minute drive to Mt. Snow–Haystack, the White House is primarily a cross-country ski touring center, with a rental shop and 45 kilometers (about 29 miles) of trails. Instruction is also available. ✉ *Rte. 9, 05363,* ☎ *802/464–2135 or 800/541–2135,* 🖷 *802/464–5222. 23 rooms with bath. Restaurant, bar, indoor and outdoor pools, sauna, cross-country skiing. Full breakfast included; MAP available. AE, DC, MC, V.*

$$$ 🖫 **Trail's End.** Bill and Mary Kilburn have taken what was once a barebones ski dorm and created a warm, user-friendly, four-season lodge. The inn's centerpiece is the cathedral-ceiling living room with catwalk loft seating, and an immense, 21-foot fieldstone fireplace. Guest rooms are comfortable, if somewhat simple, though two suites have fireplaces and whirlpool tubs. The real draw is the Kilburns themselves, whose enthusiasm and genuine interest will have you talking over coffee all morning. Breakfast is served at one of three immense round pine tables. ⊠ *Smith Rd., 05363,* ☎ *802/464–2727 or 800/859–2585. 15 rooms with bath. Pool, tennis court, fishing. MAP. MC, V.*

Outdoor Activities and Sports

WATER SPORTS

Lake Whitingham (Harriman Reservoir) is the largest lake in the state; there are boat launch areas at Wards Cove, Whitingham, Mountain Mills, and the Ox Bow. **Green Mountain Flagship Company** (⊠ Nearly 2 mi west of Wilmington on Rte. 9, ☎ 802/464–2975) runs a cruise boat on the lake and rents canoes, kayaks, and sailboats from May through late October.

Shopping

Wilmington Flea Market (⊠ Rtes. 9 and 100 S, ☎ 802/464–3345), open weekends from Memorial Day to mid-October, is a cornucopia of leftovers and never-solds.

West Dover

❹ *6 mi north of Wilmington.*

West Dover is a small, classic New England village with many churches dating back to the 1700s. The year-round population of about 1,000 swells on winter weekends as skiers flock to Mt. Snow/Haystack Ski Resort. There are many condos, lodges, and inns at the base of the mountain to accommodate them.

Dining and Lodging

$$$ ✕ **Doveberry Inn.** The red carpet sets the tone in the two candlelit, intimate dining rooms for the authentic Northern Italian cuisine, including rack of venison with caper and fresh tomato demi-glace served over polenta, wood-grilled veal chop with wild mushrooms, and pan-seared salmon with herbed risotto. ⊠ *Rte. 100,* ☎ *802/464–5652 or 800/722–3204. AE, MC, V.*

$$$ ✕🏠 **Deerhill Inn.** Up on a ridge, this English Country inn has public areas with a wall of west-facing windows with views of the valley below and the ski slopes across the way. A huge fireplace and a garden-scene mural dominate the living room, while English hand-painted yellow wallpaper, an emerald green carpet, and collections of antique plates accent the dining rooms. Each guest room has an endearing quality: One has an Oriental bedroom set, another has a hand–painted mural on the wall, and four have fireplaces. The four balcony rooms are the most spacious and have great views. The fare is upscale comfort food and might include sliced grill chicken breast with onion and pepper chutney, veal medallion with wild mushrooms in a lemon cream sauce, or a black pepper sirloin steak. ⊠ *Valley View Rd., Box 136, 05356,* ☎ *802/464–3100 or 800/993–3379. 13 rooms with bath, 2 suites. Pool. Full breakfast included; MAP available. AE, MC, V.*

Nightlife

The **Snow Barn** (⊠ Near the base of Mt. Snow, ☎ 802/464–3333) has live entertainment five days a week during the ski season. **Deacon's Den Tavern** (⊠ Rte. 100, ☎ 802/464–9361) and the **Sitzmark** (⊠ Rte. 100, ☎ 802/464–3384) have live bands on weekends. At **Poncho's Wreck** (⊠ Wilmington, ☎ 802/464–9320) acoustic jazz or mellow rock is the standard lineup on weekends.

It helps to be pushy in airports.

Introducing the revolutionary new TransPorter™ from American Tourister® It's the first suitcase you can push around without a fight. TransPorter's™ exclusive four-wheel design lets you push it in front of you with almost no effort–the wheels take the weight. Or pull it on two wheels if you choose. You can even stack on other bags and use it like a luggage cart.

Stable 4-wheel design.

TransPorter™ is designed like a dresser, with built-in shelves to organize your belongings. Or collapse the shelves and pack it like a traditional suitcase. Inside, there's a suiter feature to help keep suits and dresses from wrinkling. When push comes to shove, you can't beat a TransPorter™ For more information on how you can be this pushy, call 1-800-542-1300.

Shelves collapse on command.

Making travel less primitive.®

Use your MCI Card® for the easy way to call when traveling.

MCI✦   Calling Card

415 555 1234 2244
J.D. SMITH

Convenience on the road

- Your MCI Card® number is your home number, guaranteed.

- Pre-programmed to speed dial to your home.

- Call from any phone in the U.S.

MCI

1 - 8 0 0 - 7 5 4 - 8 9 4 1

http://www.mci.com

Shopping

Anton of Vermont Quilts (⊠ Rte. 100, 9 mi north of Mt. Snow) has a rich collection of hand-crafted fabrics and quilts.

Skiing

Mt. Snow/Haystack Ski Resort. Currently unpretentious, Mt. Snow, established in the 1950s, has come a long way since the 1960s, when its dress-up-and-show-off ski scene earned it the nickname Mascara Mountain. Purchased in 1977 by SKI, Ltd., which also owns Killington (90 minutes away) and Haystack (2½ miles away), Mt. Snow's service and facilities reveal its parent's highly professional management—from the parking lot and ticket booths to the day-care center and ski-rental area. You will probably encounter crowds at the ski lifts, but Mt. Snow knows how to handle them. One lift ticket lets you ski at Mt. Snow, Killington, and Haystack.

At Mt. Snow, both the bustling Main Base Lodge and the Sundance Base Lodge have food service and other amenities. The Carinthia Base Lodge is usually the least crowded and most easily accessible from the parking lot.

Haystack—the southernmost ski area in Vermont—is much smaller than Mt. Snow, but offers a more personal atmosphere. A modern base lodge is close to the lifts. A free shuttle connects the two ski areas. ⊠ *400 Mountain Rd., Mt. Snow 05356,* ☎ *802/464–3333, lodging 800/245–7669, snow conditions 802/464–2151.*

DOWNHILL

Mt. Snow is a remarkably well-formed mountain. From its 1,700-foot vertical summit, most of the trails down the face are intermediate, wide, and sunny. Toward the bottom and in the Carinthia section are the beginner slopes; most of the expert terrain is on the North Face, where there's a bounty of excellent fall-line skiing. In all, there are 84 trails, of which about two-thirds are intermediate. The trails are served by two quad, six triple, and eight double chairlifts, plus two surface lifts. The ski school's EXCL instruction program is designed to help advanced and expert skiers.

Most of the 43 trails at Haystack are pleasantly wide with bumps and rolls and straight fall lines—good cruising, intermediate runs. There's also a section with three double-black-diamond trails—very steep but short. A beginner section, safely tucked below the main-mountain trails, provides a haven for lessons and slow skiing. Three triple and two double chairlifts and one T-bar service Haystack's 1,400 vertical feet.

CROSS-COUNTRY

Four cross-country trail areas within 4 miles of the resort provide more than 150 kilometers of varied terrain. The Hermitage (⊠ Coldbrook Rd., ☎ 802/464–3511) and the White House (⊠ Rtes. 9 and 100, ☎ 802/464–2135) both have 50 kilometers of groomed trails. Timber Creek (⊠ Rte. 100, just north of Mt. Snow entrance, ☎ 802/464–0999) is appealingly small with 16 kilometers of thoughtfully groomed trails. Sitzmark (⊠ East Dover Rd., Wilmington 05363, ☎ 802/464–3384) has 40 kilometers of trails, with 12 kilometers of them machine tracked.

OTHER ACTIVITIES

Sleigh rides and winter nature walks head the list of nonskiing winter activities at Mt. Snow. Adams Farm (⊠ Higley Hill, ☎ 802/464–3762) has three double-traverse sleighs drawn by Belgian draft horses. Rides include a narrated tour and hot chocolate; call for reservations. The Memorial Park Skating Rink (☎ 802/257–2311) in Brattleboro has rentals.

CHILD CARE

The lively, well-organized child care center (reservations necessary) takes children ages 6 weeks through 12 years in three separate sections: a nursery for those under 18 months, a playroom complex for toddlers up to 30 months, and, adjacent, an even bigger room for older kids. Each has age-appropriate toys and balances indoor play—including arts and crafts—with trips outdoors. Most youngsters sign up for full- or half-day sessions of the ski school–sponsored SKIwee program, designed for those between 4 and 12.

Bennington

5 *21 mi west of Wilmington.*

Bennington, the state's third-largest city and the commercial focus of Vermont's southwest corner lies at the edge of the Green Mountain National Forest. It has retained much of the industrial character it developed in the 19th century, when paper mills, grist mills, and potteries formed the city's economic base. It was in Bennington, at the Catamount Tavern, that Ethan Allen organized the Green Mountain Boys, who helped capture Ft. Ticonderoga in 1775. Here also, in 1777, American general John Stark urged his militia to attack the Hessians across the New York border: "There are the Redcoats; they will be ours or tonight Molly Stark sleeps a widow!"

A chamber of commerce brochure describes an interesting, self-guided walking tour of **Old Bennington,** a National Register Historic District just west of downtown, where impressive white-column Greek Revival and sturdy brick Federal homes stand around the village green. In the graveyard of the **Old First Church,** at the corner of Church Street and Monument Avenue, the tombstone of the poet Robert Frost proclaims, "I had a lover's quarrel with the world."

The **Bennington Battle Monument,** a 306-foot stone obelisk with an elevator to the top, commemorates General Stark's victory over the British, who attempted to capture Bennington's stockpile of supplies. The battle, which took place near Walloomsac Heights in New York State, helped bring about the surrender two months later of the British commander, "Gentleman Johnny" Burgoyne. ⊠ *15 Monument Ave.,* ☎ *802/447–0550.* 🎫 *$1.* ☉ *Mid-Apr.–late Oct., daily 9–5.*

The **Bennington Museum**'s rich collections of early Americana include vestiges of rural life, a good percentage of which are packed into towering glass cases. The decorative arts are well represented; one room is devoted to early Bennington pottery. Two rooms cover the history of American glass and contain fine Tiffany specimens. Devotees of folk art will want to see the largest public collection of the work of Grandma Moses, who lived and painted in the area. Among the 30 paintings and assorted memorabilia is her only self-portrait and the famous painted caboose window. Here you'll also find the only surviving automobile of Bennington's Martin company, a 1925 Wasp. ⊠ *W. Main St. (Rte. 9),* ☎ *802/447–1571.* 🎫 *$5.* ☉ *Daily 9–5.*

NEED A BREAK?

Pop into **Alldays and Onions** (⊠ 519 E. Main St., ☎ 802/447–0043) for scrumptious sandwiches on homemade bread or for desserts, which are baked on the premises.

Contemporary stone sculpture and white-frame neo-Colonial dorms, surrounded by acres of cornfields, punctuate the green meadows of **Bennington College**'s deceptively placid campus. The small coeducational liberal arts college, one of the most expensive in the country, is noted for its progressive program in the arts, as well as a controversial faculty upheaval that sent shockwaves through academia nationwide. ⊠ *Take Route 67A off Route 7 and look for stone entrance gate.*

The Arts

Vermont Symphony Orchestra (☎ 802/864–5741) performs in Bennington and Arlington in winter, in Manchester and Brattleboro in summer.

Oldcastle Theatre Co. (☎ 802/447–0564) performs from April to October.

Dining and Lodging

$$–$$$ ✕ **Main Street Café.** This small 1860 storefront with polished hardwood floors, tin ceilings, candlelit tables, and fresh flowers draws raves for its Northern Italian cuisine that is well worth the few minutes' drive from downtown Bennington. Favorites include the grilled chicken and portobello mushroom with red wine green peppercorn sauce over angel hair pasta, and the homemade sausage with rock shrimp, sweet peppers, mushrooms, garlic, and Romano cheese served over rigatoni. The look is casual chic, like that of a Manhattan loft transplanted to a small town. ⊠ *Rte. 67A, North Bennington,* ☎ *802/442–3210. AE, DC, MC, V. No lunch. Closed Mon.*

$$ ✕ **The Brasserie.** The Brasserie's fare is some of the city's most creative, featuring classic pâtés, omelets, and sandwiches as well as seasonal salads, hearty stews, and soups that are filling enough for a meal. The restaurant uses mostly local produce and organic foods; desserts and bread are always homemade. The decor is clean-lined and contemporary. ⊠ *324 County St. (in the Potters Yard),* ☎ *802/447–7922. MC, V. Closed Tues.*

$ ✕ **Blue Benn Diner.** Breakfast is served all day in this authentic diner.
★ The eats include turkey hash and breakfast burritos that wrap scrambled eggs, sausage, and chiles in a tortilla. Pancakes, of all imaginable varieties, are a favorite. There can be a long wait, especially on weekends. ⊠ *Rte. 7N,* ☎ *802/442–5140. No credit cards. No dinner Sat.–Tues.*

$$–$$$ 🏨 **South Shire Inn.** Canopy beds in lushly carpeted rooms, ornate plaster moldings, and a dark mahogany fireplace in the library create turn-of-the-century grandeur; fireplaces and hot tubs in some rooms add warmth. Furnishings are antique except for the reproduction beds that provide contemporary comfort. The inn is in a quiet residential neighborhood within walking distance of the bus depot and downtown stores. Breakfast is served in the peach-and-white wedding cake of a dining room. ⊠ *124 Elm St., 05201,* ☎ *802/447–3839. 9 rooms with bath. Full breakfast included. AE, MC, V.*

$$ 🏨 **Molly Stark Inn.** This gem of a B&B will make you so comfortable
★ you'll feel like you're staying with an old friend. Tidy blue plaid wallpaper, gleaming hardwood floors, antique furnishings, and a woodburning stove in a brick alcove of the sitting room add country charm to this 1860 Queen Anne Victorian. Molly's Room, at the back of the building, gets less noise from Route 9; the attic suite is most spacious. A secluded cottage with a 16-foot ceiling, a king-size brass bed, and a two-person whirlpool bath surrounded by windows with views of the woods is as romantic as it gets. The innkeeper's genuine hospitality and quirky charisma delight guests, as does the full country breakfast that's been known to feature cinnamon-apple cheddar cheese quiche. ⊠ *1067 E. Main St., 05201,* ☎ *802/442–9631 or 800/356–3076. 6 rooms, 2 with bath. Full breakfast included. AE, D, MC, V.*

Outdoor Activities and Sports

BIKING

Cutting Edge (⊠ 160 Benmont Ave., ☎ 802/442–8664) offers rentals and repairs and sells various types of outdoor equipment.

Shopping

ART AND ANTIQUES

Four Corners East (⊠ 307 North St., ☎ 802/442–2612) has Early American antiques.

CRAFTS

Bennington Potters Yard (⊠ 324 County St., ☎ 802/447–7531) has seconds from the famed Bennington Potters. Prepare to get dusty digging through the bad stuff to find an almost-perfect piece at a modest discount. The complex of buildings also houses a glass factory outlet and sells John McLeod woodenware.

Arlington

❻ *15 mi north of Bennington.*

Don't be surprised to see familiar-looking faces among the roughly 2,200 people of Arlington. The illustrator Norman Rockwell lived here for 14 years, and many of the models for his portraits of small-town life were his neighbors. Settled first in 1763, Arlington was called Tory Hollow for its Loyalist sympathies—even though a number of the Green Mountain Boys lived here, too. Smaller than Bennington and more down-to-earth than upper-crust Manchester to the north, Arlington exudes a certain Rockwellian folksiness. It's also known as the home of Dorothy Canfield Fisher, a novelist popular in the 1930s and 1940s.

There are no original paintings at the **Norman Rockwell Exhibition.** Instead, the exhibition rooms are crammed with reproductions, arranged in every way conceivable: chronologically, by subject matter, and juxtaposed with photos of the models—some of whom work here. ⊠ *Rte. 7A, Arlington, ☎ 802/375–6423. ⌨ $1. ☉ May–Oct., daily 9–5; Nov.–Apr., daily 10–4.*

The Arts

Vermont Symphony Orchestra (☎ 802/864–5741) performs in Bennington and Arlington in winter, in Manchester and Brattleboro in summer.

Dining and Lodging

$$$–$$$$ ✕🏨 **West Mountain Inn.** This romantic inn has a llama ranch on the
   ★   property, African violets and quilted bedspreads in the rooms, and a front lawn with a spectacular view of the countryside. This former farmhouse of the 1840s sits on 150 acres, seemingly a world apart from civilization. Rooms 2, 3, and 4 in the front of the house overlook the front lawn; the three small nooks of room 11 resemble railroad sleeper berths and are perfect for kids. A low-beamed, paneled, candlelit dining room is the setting for six-course prix-fixe dinners featuring such specialties as veal chops topped with sun-dried tomatoes and Asiago cheese. Aunt Min's Swedish rye and other toothsome breads, as well as desserts, are all made on the premises. Tables by the windows are front row to the glorious view of the mountains. ⊠ *Rte. 313, 05250, ☎ 802/375–6516, FAX 802/375–6553. 18 rooms with bath, 4 suites. Restaurant, bar, hiking, skiing. MAP. AE, D, MC, V.*

$$–$$$ ✕🏨 **Arlington Inn.** The Greek Revival columns at the entrance to this
   ★   railroad magnate's home of 1848 give it an imposing presence, yet the inn is more welcoming than forbidding. The charm is created by linens that coordinate with the Victorian-style wallpaper, clawfoot tubs in some

bathrooms, and the house's original moldings and wainscoting. The carriage house, built at the turn of the century, has country French and Queen Anne furnishings. The restaurant, where local produce and meats are favored, serves French Continental dishes like roast duck. Polished hardwood floors, green tablecloths and rose walls, and soft candlelight complement the food; so might a bottle of wine from the extensive collection. ⊠ *Rte. 7A, 05250,* ☎ *802/375–6532 or 800/443–9442. 15 rooms with bath, 3 cottages. Restaurant, bar, tennis courts. Full breakfast included. AE, D, MC, V.*

$$ 🏠 **Hill Farm Inn.** This homey inn still has the feel of the country farmhouse it used to be. The surrounding farmland was deeded to the Hill family by King George in 1775 and is now protected from development by the Vermont Land Trust. The beefalo that roam the 50 acres, the fireplace in the informal living room, the mix of sturdy antiques, the spinning wheel in the upstairs hallway—all convey a relaxed, friendly atmosphere. Room 7 has a beamed cathedral ceiling, and from its porch you can see Mt. Equinox. The rooms in the 1790 guest house are very private, the cabins are rustic and fun. ⊠ *Just off Rte. 7, Box 2015, 05250,* ☎ *802/375–2269 or 800/882–2545. 6 rooms with bath, 5 doubles share 3 baths, 2 suites, 4 cabins in summer. Full breakfast included; MAP available. AE, D, MC, V.*

Outdoor Activities and Sports
CANOEING

Battenkill Canoe, Ltd. (⊠ Rte. 7A, Arlington, ☎ 802/362–2800) has rentals and day trips on the Battenkill and can arrange custom inn-to-inn tours.

Shopping
FOOD AND DRINK

Equinox Nursery (⊠ Rte. 7A, between Arlington and Manchester, ☎ 802/362–2610) carries a wide selection of Vermont-made products, including ice cream from a local dairy.

SHOPPING DISTRICT

Candle Mill Village's (⊠ Old Mill Rd., off Rte. 7A, East Arlington, ☎ 802/375–6068 or 800/772–3759) shops specialize in community cookbooks from around the country, bears in all forms, music boxes, and, of course, candles. The nearby waterfall makes a pleasant backdrop for a picnic.

Manchester

★ ❼ *9 mi north of Arlington.*

Manchester, where Ira Allen proposed financing Vermont's participation in the American Revolution by confiscating Tory estates, has been a popular summer retreat since the mid-19th century. Manchester Village's tree-shaded marble sidewalks and stately old homes reflect the luxurious resort lifestyle of a century ago, while Manchester Center's upscale factory outlets appeal to the affluent 20th-century ski crowd drawn by nearby Bromley and Stratton mountains. Warning: The town has become extremely popular with the shopping-inclined in recent years and can take on the overwhelming feel of a crowded New Jersey mall the weekend before Christmas.

Hildene, the summer home of Abraham Lincoln's son Robert, is a 412-acre estate that the former chairman of the board of the Pullman Company built for his family and their descendants; Mary Lincoln Beckwith, Robert's granddaughter, lived here as recently as 1975. With its Georgian Revival symmetry, gracious central hallway, and grand curved staircase, the 24-room mansion is unusual in that its rooms are not roped off. When the 1,000-pipe Aeolian organ is played, the music emanates from the mansion's very bones. Tours include a short film on the owner's life and a walk through the elaborate formal gardens. ⊠ *Rte. 7A,* ☎ *802/362–1788.* ☞ *$7.* ⊙ *Mid-May–late Oct., daily 9:30–4.*

If you've been swept up by the recent passionate fly-fishing resurgence or have been fishing for years, stop by the **American Museum of Fly Fishing,** which displays more than 1,500 rods, 800 reels, 30,000 flies, and the tackle of such celebrities as Bing Crosby, Winslow Homer, and Jimmy Carter. Its 2,500 books on angling comprise the largest public library devoted to fishing. ⊠ *Rte. 7A,* ☎ *802/362–3300.* ☞ *$3.* ⊙ *May–Oct., daily 10–4; Nov.–Apr., weekdays 10–4.*

The **Southern Vermont Art Center**'s 10 rooms are set on 375 acres dotted with contemporary sculpture. A popular retreat for local patrons of the arts, the nonprofit educational center has a permanent collection, changing exhibits, and a serene botany trail that passes by a 300-year-old maple tree. The graceful Georgian mansion is also the frequent site of concerts, dramatic performances, and films (call for current programs). ⊠ *West Rd., Box 617,* ☎ *802/362–1405.* ☞ *$3.* ⊙ *Mid-May–Oct. 22, Tues.–Sat. 10–5, Sun. noon–5; Dec.–early Apr., Mon.–Sat. 10–4.*

☭ You may want to keep your eye on the temperature gauge of your car as you drive the 5-mile toll road to the top of 3,825-foot **Mt. Equinox.** Remember to look out the window periodically for views of the Battenkill trout stream and the surrounding Vermont countryside. Picnic tables line the drive, and there's an outstanding view down both sides of the mountain from a notch known as "the Saddle." ⊠ *Rte. 7A,* ☎ *802/362–1114.* ☞ *$6.* ⊙ *May–Oct., daily 8 AM–dark.*

Dining and Lodging

$$$–$$$$ ✕ **Chantecleer.** Five miles north of Manchester, intimate dining rooms have been created in a converted dairy barn with a large fieldstone fireplace. The menu reflects the chef's Swiss background: The appetizers include *Bündnerfleisch* (air-dried Swiss beef) and frogs' legs in garlic butter; chateaubriand and veal chops are typical entrées. ⊠ *Rte. 7A, East Dorset,* ☎ *802/362–1616. Reservations essential. AE, DC, MC, V. No lunch. Closed Mon. and Tues in winter, Tues. in summer.*

$$$ ✕ **Bistro Henry's.** Just outside of town, this restaurant attracts a devoted clientele for its authentic Mediterranean fare and attention to detail. The dining room is spacious and open, and a bar sits off in a corner. Recently on the menu were an Alsatian onion tart, eggplant and mushroom terrine Provençal, and sweetbreads with wild mushrooms. There's an extensive, award-wining wine list. Breakfast, lunch, and Sunday brunch are also served. ⊠ *Rte. 11/30,* ☎ *802/362–4982. AE, D, DC, MC, V. Closed Mon.*

$–$$ ✕ **Quality Restaurant.** Gentrification has reached the down-home neighborhood place that was the model for Norman Rockwell's *War News* painting. The Quality now has Provençal wallpaper and polished wood booths, and the sturdy New England standbys of grilled meat loaf and hot roast beef or turkey sandwiches have been joined by tortellini Alfredo with shrimp and smoked salmon. Breakfast is popular. ⊠ *Main St.,* ☎ *802/362–9839. AE, DC, MC, V.*

$$$$ ✕🏠 **Barrows House.** Jim and Linda McGinniss's 200-year-old Federal-★ style inn is a longtime favorite with those who wish to escape the commercial hustle of Manchester (Bromley is about 8 miles away). Originally built as the home of Dorset's minister, it has always been a focal point of town. Carrying on this tradition, the superb dining now draws people from surrounding communities. The deep-red woodwork and li-

brary theme of the pub room makes it an intimate venue in which to sample the elegant country fare, while the greenhouse room, embellished with terra-cotta and deep blue hues, is a pleasant summer eating spot. In addition to the 12 guest rooms in the main building, there are rooms in carriage houses that have easy access to the pool and tennis courts. ⊠ *Rte. 30, Dorset (6 mi north of Manchester) 05251,* ☎ *802/867–4455 or 800/639–1620,* FAX *802/867–0132. 18 rooms with bath, 10 suites. Pool, sauna, tennis courts, bicycles, cross-country skiing. MAP. AE, D, DC, MC, V.*

$$$$ ✕ 🎦 **The Equinox.** This grand white-column resort was a fixture even before Abe Lincoln's family began summering here; it's worth a look around even if you don't stay here. Dining in the Marsh Tavern, you can feel like you're sitting in the middle of a Ralph Lauren Polo ad: spiral-based floor lamps accompany rich, supple upholstered settees and stuffed arm chairs; high bow-back chairs sit around tables with fluted columns; and several fireplaces create a dreamy glow. The food is equally aesthetically pleasing: Devonshire shepherd's pie, and the woodland supper of roast duck, venison sausage, and wild mushrooms are popular; a grains, greens, and beans entrée is offered as well. The Colonnade, where jackets are requested, is as elegant as dining can be. The resort is often the site of large conferences. Guests can take lessons at the falconry school on the premises. ⊠ *Rte. 7A, Manchester Village 05254,* ☎ *802/362–4700 or 800/362–4747,* FAX *802/362–4861. 119 rooms with bath, 27 suites, 10 3-bedroom town houses. 2 restaurants, bar, indoor and outdoor pools, sauna, steam room, health club, golf, tennis courts. AE, D, DC, MC, V.*

$$$–$$$$ ✕ 🎦 **Reluctant Panther.** Spacious bedrooms have goose-down duvets and Pierre Deux linens; they are colored in soft, elegant grays and peaches and styled with an eclectic mix of antique, country, and contemporary furnishings. Ten rooms have fireplaces, and all suites have whirlpools. The best views are from rooms B and D. In Wildflowers, the restaurant long known for its sophisticated cuisine, a huge fieldstone fireplace dominates the larger of the two dining rooms; the other is a small greenhouse with five tables. Glasses and silver sparkle in the candlelight, the service is impeccable, and the menu, which changes daily, might include rack of venison with an herbed cornmeal crust or grilled veal chop with ragout of shiitake and wild mushrooms. ⊠ *West Rd., Box 678, 05254,* ☎ *802/362–2568 or 800/822–2331,* FAX *802/362–2586. 16 rooms with bath, 4 suites. Restaurant (reservations required; closed Tues. and Wed.), bar, meeting room. MAP. AE, MC, V.*

$$$$ 🎦 **The Inn at Ormsby Hill.** This large Federal-style inn was built around 1760 and served as a hideout for Ethan Allen when he was pursued by British soldiers, and later for slaves heading north on the Underground Railroad. Chris and Ted Sprague are gracious hosts (they hold a reception every evening), and Chris is a renowned chef. Breakfasts are a sumptuous affair in the sunlit conservatory, which was built to resemble a ship. Guests arriving Friday night will have the option of a buffet supper that includes hearty soups and stews; on Saturday evenings a four-course dinner is served. Furnished with antiques and canopied or four-poster beds, many of the rooms have a view of either the Green or Taconic Mountains; most have fireplaces and whirlpool tubs. ⊠ *Rte. 7A, R.R.2, Box 3264, 05255,* ☎ *802/362–1163,* FAX *802/362–5176. 10 rooms. Full breakfast included. AE, MC, V.*

$$$ 🎦 **1811 House.** The atmosphere of an elegant English country home can be enjoyed without crossing the Atlantic. A pub-style bar that serves 49 kinds of single-malt scotches and is decorated with horse brasses; the Waterford crystal in the dining room; equestrian paintings; and the English floral landscaping of 3 acres of lawn all make this an inn wor-

thy of royalty. The rooms contain period antiques; six have fireplaces, and many have four-poster beds. Bathrooms are old-fashioned but serviceable, particularly the Robinson Room's marble-enclosed tub. ✉ *Rte. 7A, 05254,* ☏ *802/362–1811 or 800/432–1811,* ℻ *802/362–2443. 11 rooms with bath, 3 cottages. Bar. AE, D, MC, V.*

$$–$$$ ⊡ **Manchester Highlands Inn.** Almost all the guest rooms in this 1898
   ★   inn have at least one rocking chair—a detail that reflects innkeepers Patricia and Robert Eichorn's intention to make relaxing their guests' foremost pastime. There are five sitting rooms, including an amiable pub downstairs and a plant-filled sun room where you can look out over the pool and the mountains beyond. Lots of woodwork, including several sets of original pocket doors between rooms downstairs, contributes to the warm atmosphere. Rooms in the main inn are spacious and light, and all rooms have delicate lace curtains and featherbeds; the Turret and Tower rooms are especially romantic. Rooms in the carriage house are good for skiers and families. ✉ *Highland Ave., 05255,* ☏ *802/362–4565 or 800/743–4565,* ℻ *802/362–4028. 15 rooms with bath. Pool, croquet, recreation room. Full breakfast included. AE, MC, V.*

Nightlife and the Arts

NIGHTLIFE

Avalanche (☏ 802/362–2622) has a little of everything—country, blues, soft rock—on weekends in winter. The **Marsh Tavern** (☏ 802/362–4700) at the Equinox Hotel has more subdued cabaret music and jazz Tuesday through Saturday in summer and on weekends in winter. **Mulligan's** (☏ 802/362–3663) is a popular hang-out spot; it has American cuisine as well as DJs and live bands in the late afternoon and on weekends.

THE ARTS

Vermont Symphony Orchestra (☏ 802/864–5741) performs in Bennington and Arlington in winter, in Manchester and Brattleboro in summer. **Dorset Playhouse** (☏ 802/867–5777) hosts a community group in winter and a resident professional troupe in summer.

Outdoor Activities and Sports

BIKING

The 20-mile Dorset–Manchester trail runs from Manchester Village north on West Street to Route 30, turns west at the Dorset village green onto West Road, and heads back south to Manchester. **Battenkill Sports** (✉ Rte. 7, at Rte. 11/30, ☏ 802/362–2734) in Manchester rents bikes.

FISHING

The Orvis Co. (✉ Manchester Center, ☏ 802/235–9763) hosts a nationally known fly-fishing school on the Battenkill, the state's most famous trout stream, with three-day courses given weekly, April–October. **Battenkill Anglers** (☏ 802/362–3184) teaches the art and science of fly fishing. They have both private and group lessons. **Strictly Trout** (☏ 802/869–3116) will arrange a fly-fishing trip on any Vermont stream or river.

HIKING

One of the most popular segments of the Long Trail starts at Route 11/30 west of Peru Notch and goes to the top of Bromley Mountain (4 hrs). About 4 miles east of Bennington, the Long Trail crosses Route 9 and runs south to the summit of Harmon Hill (2–3 hrs). On Route 30 about 1 mile south of Townshend is Townshend State Park; from here the hiking trail runs to the top of Bald Mountain, passing an alder swamp, a brook, and a hemlock forest (2 hrs).

The **Mountain Goat** (⊠ Rte. 7A just south of Rte. 11/30, Manchester, ☎ 802/362–5159) sells hiking, backpacking, and climbing equipment; it also offers rock and ice-climbing clinics.

Shopping
ART AND ANTIQUES
Carriage Trade (⊠ North of Manchester Center on Rte.7, ☎ 802/362–1125) contains room after room of Early American antiques and has especially fine collections of clocks and ceramics. **Danby Antiques Center** (⊠ ⅛ mi off Rte. 7, 13 mi north of Manchester, ☎ 802/293–9984) has 11 rooms and a barn filled with furniture and accessories, folk art, textiles, and stoneware. **Tilting at Windmills Gallery** (⊠ Rte. 11/30, ☎ 802/362–3022) displays paintings from many well-known artists.

BOOKS
Northshire Bookstore (⊠ Main St., ☎ 802/362–2200) has a large inventory of travel and children's books.

CLOTHING
Orvis Sporting Gifts (⊠ Union St., ☎ 802/362–6455), housed in what was Orvis's shop in the 1800s, carries the outdoor clothing and home furnishings featured in its popular mail-order catalogue and has relatively good bargains. Anne Klein, Liz Claiborne, Donna Karan, Esprit, Giorgio Armani, and Jones New York are among the shops on Routes 11/30 and 7 South in Manchester—a center for **designer factory stores.**

FISHING GEAR
Orvis Retail Store (⊠ Rte. 7A, ☎ 802/362–3750) is one of the largest suppliers of fishing gear in the Northeast.

MALLS AND MARKETPLACES
Manchester Commons (⊠ Rtes. 7 and 11/30, ☎ 802/362–3736), the largest and spiffiest of three large factory-direct minimalls, has such big-city names as Joan and David, Coach, Boston Trader, Ralph Lauren, and Cole-Haan. Not far from the Commons are **Factory Point Square** (Rte. 7) and **Battenkill Place** (Rte. 11).

Skiing
Bromley Mountain. Venerable Bromley's first trails were cut in 1936. Today, Bromley attracts families who enjoy its friendly attitude as well as experienced skiers who seek their skiing roots. The area has a comfortable red-clapboard base lodge, built when the ski area first opened more than 50 years ago, with a large ski shop and a condominium village adjacent to the slopes. ⊠ *Box 1130, Manchester Center 05255., ☎ 802/824–5522 for snow conditions, 802/865–4786 or 800/865–4786 for lodging.*

DOWNHILL
While most ski areas are laid out to face the north or east, Bromley faces south, making it one of the warmer spots to ski in New England. About 36% of its 39 trails are beginner and 35% intermediate; the 29% that has some surprisingly good advanced-expert terrain is serviced by the Blue Ribbon quad chair on the east side. The vertical drop is 1,334 feet. Five double chairlifts, one quad lift, a J-bar, and two surface lifts for beginners provide transportation. A reduced-price, two-day lift pass is available. Kids are still kids (price-wise) up to age 14, but they ski free with a paying adult on nonholiday weekdays. Eighty-four percent of the area is covered by snowmaking.

CROSS-COUNTRY

The Nordic Inn (⊠ Landgrove, ☎ 802/824–6444) grooms all 26 kilometers of its trails and is an intimate, idyllic setting for the sport. It has rental gear and provides lessons.

OTHER ACTIVITIES

Karl Pfister Sleigh Rides (⊠ Landgrove, ☎ 802/824–6320) has a 12-person Travis sleigh with bench seats; call for reservations.

CHILD CARE

Bromley was one of the first ski areas to have a nursery, and it has maintained its reputation as one of the region's best places to bring children. Besides a nursery for children from one month to age 6, there is ski instruction for children ages 3–14.

Stratton

❽ *18 mi southeast of Manchester.*

Stratton has a self-contained town center, with an entire "Austrian village" of shops, restaurants, and lodging, which has grown along with its famous ski resort.

Dining and Lodging

$$$$ ✕🏨 **Windham Hill Inn.** In the converted, turn-of-the-century dairy barn, two rooms share an enormous deck that overlooks the West River Valley. Rooms in the main building are more formal. Personal touches abound throughout the inn: Guest rooms have cherry pencil-post canopy beds made by a local artisan, and there's a restored Steinway piano for guests to try their hand. Near Stratton, this is a perfect place to foster one's craving for the genteel after a reckless day of abandon on the slopes. The restaurant serves classical French fare and a has a prix-fixe menu. ⊠ *West Townshend (10 mi east of Stratton Mountain), 05359, ☎ 802/874–4080 or 800/944–4080, ℻ 802/874–4702. 18 rooms with bath. Restaurant, bar, pool, pond, tennis court, ice-skating, cross-country skiing. AE, D, MC, V. Closed in early spring and Nov. 27–Dec. 26.*

$$$ ✕🏨 **Stratton Mountain Inn and Village Lodge.** The complex includes a 120-room inn—the largest on the mountain—and a 91-room lodge with studio units. Ski packages that include lift tickets bring down room rates. ⊠ *Stratton Mountain Rd., 05155, ☎ 802/297–2500 or 800/777–1700, ℻ 802/297–1778. 211 rooms with bath. 2 restaurants, pool, 2 hot tubs, sauna, golf course, tennis courts, racquetball. AE, D, DC, MC, V.*

Nightlife and the Arts

Mulligan's (☎ 802/297–9293) is a popular hang-out spot; it has American cuisine and DJs and live bands in the late afternoon and on weekends. **Haig's** (☎ 802/297–1300) in Bondville, 5 miles from Stratton, has a unique indoor simulated golf course for those who can't wait for summer. **The Red Fox Inn** (☎ 802/297–2488), also 5 miles from Stratton, has a DJ and occasional live music in the tavern.

Outdoor Activities and Sports

RECREATION AREA

Summertime facilities at **Stratton Mountain** (☎ 800/842–6867) include 15 outdoor tennis courts, 27 holes of golf, horseback riding, and mountain biking (rentals, guided tours, and accessories are available). Instruction programs in tennis and golf are also offered. The area hosts a summer entertainment series as well as an LPGA golf tournament and the Women's Hardcourt Tennis Championships.

Skiing

Stratton Mountain. Recently bought by Intrawest, the owners of Black-comb and Mont Tremblant, Stratton has a new master plan that includes the only high-speed six passenger lift in New England and a 1,000-seat summit lodge complete with cafeteria and five-star restaurant. Since its creation in 1961, Stratton has undergone several physical transformations and upgrades, yet the area's sophisticated character has been retained. It has been the special province of well-to-do families and, more recently, young professionals from the New York–southern Connecticut corridor. Since the mid-80s, an entire village, with a covered parking structure for 700 cars, has arisen at the base of the mountain: Adjacent to the base lodge are a condo-hotel, restaurants, and about 25 shops lining a pedestrian mall. Stratton is 4 miles up its own access road off Route 30 in Bondville, about 30 minutes from Manchester's popular shopping zone. ⊠ *R.R. 1, Box 145, Stratton Mountain 05155,* ☎ *802/297–2200 or 800/843–6867, snow conditions 802/297–4211, lodging 800/787–2886.*

DOWNHILL

Stratton's skiing is in three sectors. The first is the lower mountain directly in front of the base lodge-village-condo complex; a number of lifts reach mid-mountain from this entry point, and practically all skiing is beginner or low-intermediate. Above that, the upper mountain, with a vertical drop of 2,000 feet, has a high-speed, 12-passenger gondola, *Starship XII.* Down the face are the expert trails, while on either side are intermediate cruising runs with a smattering of wide beginner slopes. The third sector, the Sun Bowl, is off to one side with two quad chairlifts and two expert trails, a full base lodge, and a lot of intermediate terrain. Stratton is home to the U.S. Open Snowboarding championships; its snowboard park has a 380-foot halfpipe. A Ski Learning Park with 10 trails and five lifts has its own Park Packages available for novice skiers. In all, Stratton has 92 slopes and trails served by the gondola; a six-passenger lift; four quad, one triple, three double chairlifts; and two surface lifts.

CROSS-COUNTRY

The Stratton area has more than 30 kilometers of cross-country skiing and two Nordic centers: Sun Bowl and Country Club.

OTHER ACTIVITIES

The area's sports center has two indoor tennis courts, three racquetball courts, a 25-meter indoor swimming pool, a hot tub, a steam room, a fitness facility with Nautilus equipment, and a restaurant.

CHILD CARE

The day-care center takes children ages 6 weeks through 5 years for indoor activities and outdoor excursions. The ski school has programs for ages 4–12; both run all day with lunch. SKIwee instruction programs are also available for ages 4–12. A junior racing program and special instruction groups are aimed at more experienced young skiers.

Weston

➒ *20 mi northeast of Manchester.*

Weston is perhaps best known for the **Vermont Country Store,** which may be more a way of life than a shop. For years the retail store and its mail-order catalogue have carried such nearly forgotten items as Lilac Vegetal aftershave, Monkey Brand black tooth powder, Flexible Flyer sleds, pickles in a barrel, and tiny wax bottles of colored syrup. Nostalgia-invoking implements dangle from the store's walls and ceiling. ⊠ *Rte. 100,* ☎ *802/824–3184.* ⊘ *Mon.–Sat. 9–5.*

The **Mill Museum** just down the road has numerous hands-on displays depicting the engineering and mechanics of one of the town's mills. ⊠ *Rte. 100,* ☎ *802/824–8190. Donations accepted.* ⊘ *Late May–early Sept., daily 11–4; Sept.–mid-Oct., weekends 11–4.*

The Arts
Weston Playhouse (☎ 802/824–5288) is the oldest professional summer theater in Vermont.

Dining and Lodging
$$–$$$ ✕⊡ **The Highland House.** There's cross-country skiing right on the property, Bromley Mountain is just 10 minutes away by car, and Stratton and Okemo are also nearby. Guest rooms in this inn on 32 acres are simple, with reproduction furniture, dried-flower wall ornaments, and quilts. In the evenings the six-table dining area becomes a candlelit room where duck with a ginger or raspberry sauce is popular. ⊠ *Rte. 100, Londonderry (5 mi south of Weston) 05148,* ☎ *802/824–3019,* ℻ *802/824–3657. 17 rooms with bath. Restaurant (closed Mon. and Tues.), pool, tennis courts, cross-country skiing. Full breakfast included. AE, MC, V.*

Shopping
CRAFTS
Weston Bowl Mill (⊠ Rte. 100, ☎ 802/824–6219) has finely crafted wood products at mill prices.

FOOD AND DRINK
Vermont Country Store (⊠ Rte. 100, ☎ 802/824–3184) sets aside one room of its old-fashioned emporium for Vermont Common Crackers and bins of fudge and other candy.

En Route   From Weston you might head south on Route 100 through Jamaica and then down Route 30 through Townshend to Newfane, all pretty hamlets typical of small-town Vermont. Just south of Townshend, near the Townshend Dam on Route 30, is the state's longest single-span covered bridge, now closed to traffic.

Ludlow

🔟 *9 mi northeast of Weston.*

Ludlow is a former mill town that now relies on business from Okemo Mountain Ski Resort to fill its shops and restaurants. Black River Academy, where Calvin Coolidge went to school, is located here, and there is a town green with a beautiful, often photographed, historic church.

Dining and Lodging
$$$ ✕⊡ **Okemo Mountain Lodge.** All guest rooms in this three-story, brown-clapboard building have balconies and fireplaces, and the one-bedroom condominiums clustered around the base of the ski lifts are close to restaurants and shops. Also available are Kettle Brook and Winterplace slopeside condominiums, run by Okemo Mountain Lodging Service. ⊠ *Rte. 100, R.F.D. 1, Ludlow 05149,* ☎ *802/228–5571, 802/228–4041, or 800/786–5366;* ℻ *802/228–2079. 76 rooms with bath. Restaurant, bar. AE, D, MC, V.*

Skiing
Okemo Mountain. An ideal ski area for families with children, Okemo has evolved into a popular major resort. The main attraction is a long, broad, gentle slope with two beginner lifts just above the base lodge.

All the facilities at the bottom of the mountain are close together, so family members can regroup easily during the ski day. The net effect of the village area is efficient and attractive—it even boasts today's obligatory clock tower. The Solitude Village Area, under construction at press time, will include a triple chairlift, two new trails, and lodging. ⊠ *R.R. 1, Box 106, Ludlow 05149,* ☎ *802/228–4041, lodging 800/786–5366, snow conditions 802/228–5222.*

DOWNHILL

Above the broad beginner's slope at the base, the upper part of Okemo has a varied network of trails: long, winding, easy trails for beginners; straight fall-line runs for experts; and curving, cruising slopes for intermediates. The 85 trails are served by an efficient lift system of seven quads, three triple chairlifts, and two surface lifts; 92% are covered by snowmaking. From the summit to the base lodge, the vertical drop is 2,150 feet. The ski school offers a complimentary Ski Tip Station, where intermediate or better skiers can get an evaluation and a free run with an instructor. There are innovative snowboard instructional programs for riders of all ages.

CROSS-COUNTRY

Fox Run (⊠ Fox Lane, R.S.D. 1, Box 123, Ludlow 05149, ☎ 802/228–8871) has 26 kilometers of trails, all groomed.

OTHER ACTIVITIES

Brickyard Farm (⊠ South Hill, ☎ 802/228–5032) is the place for sleigh rides in the area with its large 12- to 14-passenger traveler and smaller 4-person sleigh; call to reserve.

CHILD CARE

Penguin Playground Day Care Center, the area's nursery for children 6 weeks–8 years, has a broad range of indoor activities and supervised outings. Children 3 and up can get brief introduction-to-skiing lessons; those ages 4–8 can take all-day or half-day SKIwee lessons.

Chester

⑪ *11 mi east of Weston.*

In Chester, gingerbread Victorians frame the town green. Look for the **stone village** on North Street on the outskirts of town—two rows of buildings constructed from quarried stone, built by two brothers and said to have been used during the Civil War as stations on the Underground Railroad. The **National Survey Charthouse** (⊠ Main St. ☎ 802/875–2121) is a map-lover's paradise: It's good for a rainy-day browse even if maps aren't your passion. The local pharmacy down the street has been in continuous operation since the 1860s.

In Chester's restored 1872 train station you can board the **Green Mountain Flyer** for a 26-mile two-hour round-trip to Bellows Falls, on the Connecticut River at the eastern edge of the state. The journey, in superbly restored cars that date from the golden age of railroading, travels through scenic countryside past covered bridges and along the Brockway Mills gorge. A six-hour tour is also offered, in fall only. ⊠ *Depot St. off Bridge St. (Rte. 12),* ☎ *802/463–3069.* ☞ *2-hr trip $11.* ☺ *Mid-June–early Sept., Tues.–Sun.; early Sept.–mid Oct., daily. Train departs at 11, 12:10, 2; call to confirm.*

Dining and Lodging

$$$ ✗▥ **Inn at Long Last.** An army of toy soldiers fills a glass case beside the enormous fieldstone fireplace in the pine-floor lobby of this Victorian inn, where guests gather for after-dinner drinks before the fire. Bookshelves in the large wood-panel library/pub hold volumes in lit-

erature, science, biography, music, history, and labor economics; one
entire shelf is devoted to George Orwell. Rooms are named after people, places, and things important to innkeeper Jack Coleman, former
president of Haverford College in Pennsylvania, and are decorated simply with personal memorabilia. Some bathrooms are fairly small. The
quietest section of the inn is at the back. Although its atmosphere is
not overly warm, this grand old inn musters respect—characteristics
curiously reflected in the innkeeper as well. ⊠ *Main St., Box 589, 05143,*
☎ *802/875–2444. 30 rooms, 1 with bath in hall. Restaurant, 2 tennis courts. MAP. MC, V.*

Outdoor Activities and Sports
BIKING

A 26-mile loop out of Chester follows the Williams River along Route
103 to Pleasant Valley Road north of Bellows Falls. At Saxtons River,
turn west onto Route 121 and follow along the river to connect with
Route 35. When the two routes separate, follow Route 35 north back
to Chester.

Grafton

★ ⑫ *8 mi south of Chester.*

Grafton is the almost-too-picturesque village that got a second lease
on life when the Windham Foundation provided funds for its restoration: It's now one of the best-kept in the state. Grafton's **Historical Society** documents the change and has other exhibits. ⊠ *Townshend Rd.,*
☎ *802/843–2255. ☜ $1. ☉ Memorial Day–Columbus Day, Sat.
1:30–4; July–Aug., Sun. 1:30–4.*

Dining and Lodging

$$–$$$$ ✕🏠 **The Old Tavern at Grafton.** The white-column porches on both
stories of the main building wrap around this commanding inn that
dates to 1801 and has hosted Daniel Webster and Nathaniel Hawthorne.
There are 14 rooms in the main building, 22 rooms in two houses across
the street, and 30 rooms in several other buildings in town. The rooms
in the older part of the inn are furnished in antiques and evoke New
England's 18th-century frontier days. Two dining rooms, one with for-
mal Georgian furniture and oil portraits, the other with rustic panel-
ing and low beams, serve such hearty traditional New England dishes
as venison stew or grilled quail; cheeses, made just down the road, show
up in some dishes. A popular gathering spot is the Phelps Barn Bar,
which is filled with authentic English pub furniture. ⊠ *Rte. 35, 05146,*
☎ *802/843–2231 or 800/843–1801, FAX 802/843–2245. 66 rooms with
bath. Restaurant, bar, pond, tennis courts, cross-country skiing, recre-
ation room. MC, V. Closed Apr.*

$$ 🏠 **Eaglebrook of Grafton.** A mix of antiques and abstract art give this
★ small country inn an air of city sophistication. The cathedral-ceilinged
sun room, built overlooking the Saxtons River, the seven fireplaces with
soapstone mantels, and the watercolor stencils in the hallways warrant this elegant retreat's feature in a glossy interior-design magazine.
Blue-checked fabric gives one of the three bedrooms a French provincial air; another leans toward American country; the third has a Victorian flavor. Outside, the landscaped stone terrace is a perfect place
to sit with a bottle of wine on a summer evening. The lush furnishings
and care extended by the innkeepers toward their guests assure an indulgent stay. ⊠ *Main St., 05146,* ☎ *802/843–2564. 1 room with bath,
2 rooms share bath. Full breakfast included. MC, V.*

Shopping

Gallery North Star (✉ Townshend Rd., ☎ 802/843–2465) focuses on oils, watercolors, and lithographs by Vermont artists.

Newfane

🔞 *15 mi south of Grafton.*

Newfane is an attractive small town, with crisp white buildings surrounding its village green. The 1939 **First Congregational Church** and the **Windham County Court House,** with its 17 green-shuttered windows and rounded cupola, are often open. The building with the four-pointed spire is **Union Hall,** built in 1832.

Dining and Lodging

$$$–$$$$ ✕☷ **The Four Columns.** Erected 150 years ago for a homesick southern bride, the majestic white columns of the Greek Revival mansion are more intimidating than the Colonial-style rooms inside. Room 1 in the older section has an enclosed porch overlooking the town common; three rooms and a suite are annexed. All rooms have antiques, brass beds, and quilts; some have fireplaces. The third-floor room in the old section is the most private. In the classy restaurant, chef Greg Parks has introduced such nouvelle American dishes as Vermont-raised pheasant with blood-orange ginger sauce and a sauté of scallops and shrimp with coconut lemongrass sauce. ✉ *West St., Box 278, 05345,* ☎ *802/365–7713 or 800/787–6633. 15 rooms with bath. Restaurant (closed Tues., weekdays Apr. and early Dec.), hiking. Full breakfast included; MAP in foliage season. AE, MC, V.*

Shopping

ART AND ANTIQUES

Newfane Antiques Center (✉ Rte. 30, south of Newfane, ☎ 802/365–4482) displays antiques from 20 dealers on three floors.

CRAFTS

Newfane Country Store (✉ Rte. 30, ☎ 802/365–7916) has an immense selection of quilts (which can also be custom ordered) and homemade fudge.

FLEA MARKET

The **Newfane Flea Market** (✉ Rte. 35, 802/365–7771) happens every weekend during summer and fall and is the selling venue for collectible dealers from all over the state.

Putney

🔞 *7 mi east of Newfane, 9 mi north of Brattleboro.*

☖ In Putney, **Harlow's Sugar House** (✉ Rte. 5, 2 mi north of Putney, ☎ 802/387–5852) has horse-drawn sleigh or wagon rides into the sugar bush to watch the maple sugaring in spring, berry picking in summer, and apple picking in autumn. You can buy the fruits of these labors in the gift shop. Crafts aficionados will want to visit **Basketville** (✉ Main St., Box 710, ☎ 802/387–5509), to witness the traditional production methods employed in constructing the incredible number of baskets that are for sale. At **Green Mountain Spinnery,** you can purchase yarn and items knit from local wool and mohair. ✉ *Depot Rd., at Exit 4 of I–91,* ☎ *802/387–4528.* 🎫 *Tours $2.* ☉ *Tours of yarn factory at 1:30 on the 1st and 3rd Tues. of each month.*

Dining and Lodging

$$–$$$ ✕☷ **The Putney Inn.** The main building of this inn dates from the 1790s and was part of a farming estate. It later became a seminary—the present-

day pub was once the chapel. Two fireplaces dominate the lobby, while Wedgwood blue and mahogany hues complement the hand-hewn post-and-beam structure of the sitting areas. The guest rooms have Queen Anne mahogany reproductions. The exterior of the adjacent building is disheartening, but the rooms are spacious and modern and are 100 yards from the banks of the Connecticut River. Guests dine in what was once the attached barn, where massive original beams are also part of the charm. The cuisine is regionally inspired, with innovative flourishes, and includes New England potpies, wild game mixed grill, and burgers with Vermont cheddar. ⊠ *Depot Rd., 05346,* ☎ *802/387–5517 or 800/653–5517,* FAX *802/387–5211. 25 rooms with bath. Full breakfast included. AE, MC, V.*

$–$$ 🔲 **Hickory Ridge House.** The unusually spacious guest rooms of this stately 1808 Federal mansion reflect the original owner's fortune. They have a country-farmhouse decor that is simple yet comfortable; four have fireplaces. Rag rugs cover pine floors, white lace curtains hang at the windows, and walls are cheerful pastels; bathrooms have large tubs. Putney was once a focus of the back-to-the-land movement; traces of that ethos are reflected in the vegetarian breakfasts that might include stuffed pumpkin pancakes or an inspired soufflé. ⊠ *Hickory Ridge Rd., R.D. 3, Box 1410, 05346,* ☎ *802/387–5709. 3 rooms with bath, 4 rooms share 2 baths. Full breakfast included. MC, V.*

Shopping
FOOD AND DRINK

Allen Bros. (⊠ Rte. 5 north of Putney, ☎ 802/722–3395) bakes apple pies, cider doughnuts, and an array of Vermont foods.

Southern Vermont A to Z

Getting Around
BY BUS

Vermont Transit (☎ 802/864–6811, 800/451–3292, or, in VT, 800/642–3133) links Bennington, Manchester, Brattleboro, and Bellows Falls.

BY CAR

In the south the principal east–west highway is Route 9, the Molly Stark Trail, from Brattleboro to Bennington. The most important north–south roads are Route 7; the more scenic Route 7A; Route 100, which runs through the state's center; I–91; and Route 5, which runs along the state's eastern border. Route 30 from Brattleboro to Manchester is a scenic drive. All routes are heavily traveled during peak tourist seasons.

Contacts and Resources
CANOEING

The Connecticut River between Bellows Falls and the Massachusetts border, interrupted by one dam at Vernon, is relatively easy. A good resource is *The Complete Boating Guide to the Connecticut River,* available from **CRWC Headquarters** (⊠ 125 Combs Rd., Easthampton, MA 01027, ☎ 413/584–0018).

EMERGENCIES

Brattleboro Memorial Hospital (⊠ 9 Belmont Ave., ☎ 802/257–0341).

STATE PARKS

The following state parks have camping sites and facilities as well as picnic tables. **Emerald Lake State Park** (⊠ Rte. 7, 9 mi north of Manchester, ☎ 802/362–1655; 430 acres) has a marked nature trail, an onsite naturalist, boat and canoe rentals, and a snack bar. The hiking trails at **Fort Dummer State Park** (⊠ S. Main St., 2 mi south of Brattleboro, ☎ 802/254–2610; 217 acres) afford views of the Connecticut River Valley. **Lake Shaftsbury State Park** (⊠ Rte. 7A, 10½ mi north of Bennington, ☎ 802/375–9978; 101 acres) is one of a few parks in Vermont with group camping; it has a swimming beach, self-guided nature trails, and boat and canoe rentals. **Molly Stark State Park** (⊠ Rte. 9, east of Wilmington, ☎ 802/464–5460; 158 acres) has a hiking trail to a vista from a fire tower on Mt. Olga. **Townshend State Park** (⊠ 3 mi north of Rte. 30, between Newfane and Townshend, ☎ 802/365–7500; 856 acres), the largest in southern Vermont, is popular for the swimming at Townshend Dam and the stiff hiking trail to the top of Bald Mountain. **Woodford State Park** (⊠ Rte. 9, east of Bennington, ☎ 802/447–4169; 400 acres) has an activities center on Adams Reservoir, a playground, boat and canoe rentals, and marked nature trails.

VISITOR INFORMATION

Bennington Area Chamber of Commerce (⊠ Veterans Memorial Dr., Bennington 05201, ☎ 802/447–3311). **Brattleboro Chamber of Commerce** (⊠ 180 Main St., Brattleboro 05301, ☎ 802/254–4565). **Chamber of Commerce, Manchester and the Mountains** (⊠ 2 Main St., R.R. 2, Box 3451, Manchester 05255, ☎ 802/362–2100). **Mt. Snow/Haystack Region Chamber of Commerce** (⊠ E. Main St., Box 3, Wilmington 05363, ☎ 802/464–8092).

CENTRAL VERMONT

Service jobs in tourism and recreation have increased while those in manufacturing have dwindled in central Vermont. Although some industry is still found, particularly in the west around Rutland, the state's second-largest city, it is the southern tip of Lake Champlain—as well as many other, smaller lakes—and several major ski resorts, that really make the area economically viable. Local trademarks include the state's famed marble quarries, just north of Rutland, and large dairy herds and pastures that create the quilted patchwork of the Champlain Valley. The heart of the area is the Green Mountains, running up the state's spine, and the surrounding wilderness of the Green Mountain National Forest, which offers countless opportunities for outdoor recreation and soulful pondering of the region's intense natural beauty—even for those inclined not to venture beyond the confines of their vehicles.

Our tour begins in Windsor, on Route 5 near I–91, at the eastern edge of the state, winds westward toward Route 100, up along the spine of the Green Mountains, and crosses over the ridge at two points, both inspiring passes.

Numbers in the margin correspond to points of interest on the Central Vermont map.

Windsor

⓯ *50 mi north of Brattleboro, 42 mi east of Rutland, 69 mi south of Montpelier.*

Windsor was the delivery room for the birth of Vermont. An interpretive exhibit on Vermont's constitution, the first to prohibit slavery and to establish a system of public schools, is housed in the **Old Constitution House.** The site where, in 1777, grant holders declared Vermont an independent republic contains 18th- and 19th-century furnishings, American paintings and prints, and Vermont-made tools, toys, and kitchenware. ⊠ *Rte. 5,* ☎ *802/674–3773.* ⌐ *$1.* ⊙ *Late May–mid-Oct., Wed.–Sun. 10–4.*

The firm of Robbins & Lawrence became famous for applying the "American system" (the use of interchangeable parts) to the manufacture

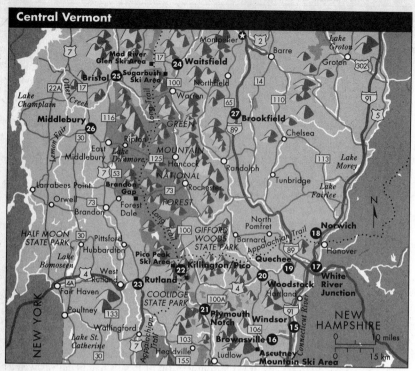

of rifles. Although the company no longer exists, the **American Precision Museum,** in the restored 1846 Windsor House, extols the Yankee ingenuity that created a major machine-tool industry here in the 19th century. The museum contains the largest collection of historically significant machine tools in the country. The **Vermont State Crafts Center** (☎ 802/674–6729), also in the Windsor House, is a gallery of juried, skillfully made Vermont crafts. ⊠ *196 Main St.,* ☎ *802/674–5781.* ▨ *$5.* ⊘ *Weekdays 9–5, weekends and holidays 10–4.*

The **covered bridge** just off Route 5 that spans the Connecticut River between Windsor and Cornish, New Hampshire, is—at 460 feet—the longest in the state.

Dining and Lodging

$$ ✕ **Windsor Station.** This converted main-line railroad station serves such main-line entrées as chicken Kiev, filet mignon, and prime rib. The booths, with their curtained brass railings, were created from the high-back railroad benches in the depot. ⊠ *Depot Ave.,* ☎ *802/674–2052. AE, MC, V. No lunch.*

$$–$$$ ✕▥ **Juniper Hill Inn.** An expanse of green lawn with Adirondack chairs and a garden of perennials sweeps up to the portico of this Greek Revival mansion, built at the turn of the century and now on the National Register of Historic Places. The central living room, with its hardwood floors, oak paneling, Oriental carpets, and thickly upholstered wing chairs and sofas, has a stately feel. Spacious bedrooms have antiques; some have fireplaces. The four-course dinners served in the candlelit dining room may include roast pork glazed with mustard and brandy sauce. The inn is just 7 miles from Mt. Ascutney. ⊠ *Juniper Hill Rd., Box 79, 05089,* ☎ *802/674–5273 or 800/359–2541,* ⅎⅅⅹ

802/674–5273. 16 rooms with bath. Restaurant, pool, hiking. Full breakfast included; MAP available. MC, V.

Brownsville

⑯ *5 mi west of Windsor.*

Brownsville is a small village at the foot of Ascutney Mountain. It has everything a village needs: country store, post office, town hall, and an historic grange building. For further amenities, head to the Ascutney Mountain ski area, which is a self-contained four-season resort.

Dining and Lodging

$$–$$$$ ✕🏨 **Ascutney Mountain Resort Hotel.** One of the big attractions of this five-building resort hotel–condo complex is that the lift is literally outside the main door. The comfortable, well-maintained hotel suites come in different configurations and sizes—some with kitchen, fireplace, and deck. Slope-side multilevel condos have three bedrooms, three baths, and private entries. The Ascutney Harvest Inn, an attractive restaurant serving Continental and traditional cuisine, is within the complex. ⊠ *Box 699, 05037,* ☎ *802/484–7711 or 800/243–0011,* FAX *802/484–3117 or 800/243–0011. 240 suites and condos. Restaurant, 2 bars, health club, billiards. AE, MC, V.*

$–$$ 🏨 **Millbrook Bed and Breakfast.** This Victorian farmhouse, built in 1880, is directly across from the Ascutney ski slopes. Making après-ski idleness easy are the five sitting rooms, eclectically decorated with antiques and contemporary furnishings. ⊠ *Rte. 44 (Box 410), 05037,* ☎ *802/484–7283. 3 rooms with bath, 2 suites. Hot tub. Full breakfast and afternoon tea included. MC, V.*

Nightlife and the Arts

Crow's Nest Club (⊠ Ascutney Mountain Resort Hotel, ☎ 802/484–7711) has live entertainment on weekends. **Destiny** (☎ 802/674–6671) has rock entertainment with live bands during the week and a DJ on Sunday.

Skiing

Ascutney Mountain Resort. Rescued by an extraordinary auction, Ascutney launched its 1993–94 season after being closed for several years due to bankruptcy. It's now owned by the Plausteiner family, whose patriarch, John, was instrumental in operations at Mt. Snow, in Vermont, and White Face Mountain, in Lake Placid, New York. Now with a low debt load, Ascutney's future is much brighter, with its real estate development—once its downfall—now its centerpiece. There's a resort village in five buildings, with hotel suites and condominium units spread throughout. ⊠ *Rte. 44 (right off I–91; Box 699), Brownsville 05037,* ☎ *802/484–7711, lodging 800/243–0011.*

DOWNHILL

Thirty-one trails with varying terrain are covered by nearly 80% snowmaking. Like a stereotypical ski mountain cutout, this one reaches a wide peak, and gently slopes to the bottom. Beginner and novice skiers stay toward the base, while intermediates enjoy the band that wraps the midsection; and for experts there are tougher black diamond runs topping the mountain. One disadvantage to Ascutney, however, is that there is no easy way down from the summit, so novice skiers should not make the trip. For intermediate and advanced skiers, though, the Summit Chair is an enjoyable ride up. Trails are serviced by one double and three triple chairs. Ascutney is popular with families because it offers some of the least expensive junior lift tickets in the region.

CROSS-COUNTRY

There are 32 kilometers (18 miles) of groomed cross-country trails at the resort; lessons, clinics, and rentals are provided.

OTHER ACTIVITIES

Ascutney Mountain Resort Hotel has its own sports and fitness center with full-size indoor and outdoor pools, racquetball, aerobics facilities and classes, weight training, and massage, as well as ice-skating on the pond.

CHILD CARE

Day care is available for children ages 6 months to 6 years, with learn-to-ski options and rental equipment available for toddlers and up (children 6 and under ski free). There are half- and full-day instruction programs for children 3–6 and a Young Olympians program for children 6–14.

White River Junction

17 *14 mi north of Windsor.*

The industrial town of White River Junction, on the Connecticut River, is the home of the **Catamount Brewery,** one of the state's several microbreweries. Catamount has become immensely popular in the Northeast; it brews golden ale, pale ale, a British-style amber, a dark porter, and such seasonal specialties as a hearty Christmas ale. Samples are available at the tour's conclusion and at the company store. ⊠ *58 S. Main St.,* ☎ *802/296–2248.* ☞ *Free.* ☼ *Mon.–Sat. 9–5, Sun. 1–5. July–Oct., 3 tours Mon.–Sat., 2 tours Sun.; Nov.–June, 3 tours Sat. only.*

Norwich

18 *6 mi north of White River Junction.*

Norwich is just across the river from Dartmouth College. There are historic photographs of flour being delivered by horsecart in the **King Arthur Flour Baker's Store** (⊠ Rte. 5, ☎ 802/649–3361), a retail outlet for all things baking-oriented, including baking tools and hard-to-find grains and specialty flours. The company has been in business since 1790.

The **Montshire Museum of Science** has numerous hands-on exhibits that explore space, nature, and technology; there are also living habitats, several aquariums, many children's programs, and a maze of trails to investigate its 100 acres of pristine woodland. One of the finest museums in New England, it's an ideal destination for a rainy day. ⊠ *Montshire Rd., Box 770,* ☎ *802/649–2200.* ☞ *$5.* ☼ *Daily 10–5.*

NEED A
BREAK?

Jasper Murdock's Alehouse (⊠ Main St., ☎ 802/649–1143), America's smallest brewery, serves hearty fare in addition to its home-brewed stouts, porters, and ales in the 1797 Norwich Inn. Closed Monday.

The Arts

Opera North (⊠ Across the Connecticut river from Norwich, in Hanover, NH ☎ 603/643–1946) performs three operas annually at locations throughout Vermont.

Quechee

19 *6 mi west of White River Junction.*

Quechee is perched astride the Ottauquechee River. **Quechee Gorge,** 165 feet deep, is impressive, though overrun by tourists. You can see the mile-long gorge, carved by a glacier, from Route 4, but many visitors picnic nearby or scramble down one of several descents for a closer look. More than a decade ago **Simon Pearce** set up an eponymous glassblowing factory in an old mill by the bank of a waterfall here, using the water power to drive his furnace. The glass studio produces exquisite wares and houses a pottery workshop, a shop, and a restaurant; visitors can watch the artisans at work. ⊠ *Main St.,* ☎ *802/295–2711.* ☉ *Store daily 9–9, workshops weekdays 10–5.*

Dining and Lodging

$$$ ✕ **Simon Pearce.** Candlelight, sparkling glassware from the studio downstairs, contemporary dinnerware, exposed brick, and large windows that overlook the roaring Ottauquechee River create an ideal setting. Sesame-crusted tuna with noodle cakes and wasabi and roast duck with mango chutney sauce are specialties of the house; more than 700 choices on the wine list assure finding that perfect vintage. Ask about the monthly wine tastings. ⊠ *Main St.,* ☎ *802/295–1470. AE, D, DC, MC, V.*

$$–$$$ ✕🏠 **Parker House.** The spacious peach-and-blue rooms of this 1857
★ Victorian mansion are named for former residents: Emily has a marble fireplace and an iron-and-brass bed, Walter is the smallest room, and Joseph has a spectacular view of the Ottauquechee River. All rooms on the third floor are air-conditioned. Lace window panels, highback chairs, and traditional wall stenciling contribute to the dining room's elegant atmosphere. American comfort food is served in the dining room; in warm weather, you can dine on the terrace with its spectacular river view. All guests are welcome to use the facilities of the Quechee Country Club—first-rate golf course, tennis courts, indoor and outdoor pool, and cross-country as well as downhill skiing. ⊠ *16 Main St., Box 0780, 05059,* ☎ *802/295–6077. 7 rooms with bath. Full breakfast included; MAP available. MC, V.*

$$–$$$ 🏠 **Quechee Bed and Breakfast.** Dried herbs hang from the beams in
★ the living room, where a wood settee sits before a floor-to-ceiling fireplace that dates to the original structure of 1795. In the guest rooms, handwoven throws cover the beds and soft pastels coordinate linens and decor. Jessica's Room is the smallest; the Bird Room, with its exposed beams, is one of four that overlook the Ottauquechee River. Rooms at the back are farther from busy Route 4. The wide front porch is adorned with seasonal decorations such as luminarias and cornstalks, and the inn is within walking distance of Quechee Gorge. ⊠ *Rte. 4, 05059,* ☎ *802/295–1776. 8 rooms with bath. Air-conditioning. Full breakfast included. MC, V.*

Outdoor Activities and Sports

FISHING
The Vermont Fly Fishing School/Wilderness Trails (⊠ Quechee Inn, Clubhouse Rd., 05059, ☎ 802/295–7620) leads workshops, rents fishing gear and bicycles, and arranges canoe trips.

POLO
Quechee Polo Club (⊠ Dewey's Mill Rd., ½ mi off Rte. 4, ☎ 802/295–7152) draws several hundred spectators on summer Saturdays to its matches near the Quechee Gorge. Admission is $3 adults, $1 children, or $5 per car.

Shopping

ANTIQUES

The **Hartland Antiques Center** (✉ Rte. 4, ☎ 802/457–4745) has inventory from 48 dealers, including furniture and collectibles such as jewelry and sports and military items.

Quechee Gorge Village (✉ Rte. 4, ☎ 802/295–1550) is an antiques and crafts mall that shows wares from more than 350 dealers in an immense reconstructed barn. A small-scale working railroad will take the kids for a ride, when weather permits, while Mom and Dad browse.

CLOTHING

Scotland by the Yard (✉ Rte. 4, ☎ 802/295–5351) has authentic Scottish kilts, kilt pins in imaginative designs, and jewelry bearing traditional Scottish emblems and symbols.

Woodstock

★ ⓴ *4 mi east of Quechee.*

Woodstock realizes virtually every expectation of a quaint New England town (except for the crowds). Perfectly preserved Federal houses surround the tree-lined village green, and streams flow around the town center, which is anchored by a covered bridge. The town owes much of its pristine appearance to the Rockefeller family's keen interest in historic preservation and land conservation.

Other town shapers include the 19th-century forerunner to modern environmentalism, George Perkins Marsh, who is credited largely with the creation of the Smithsonian Institute in Washington, DC, and Frederick Billings, for whom the **Billings Farm and Museum** is named. Exhibits in the reconstructed Queen Anne farmhouse, school, general store, workshop, and former Marsh homestead demonstrate the lives and skills of early Vermont settlers. Splitting logs doesn't seem nearly so quaint when you've watched the effort that goes into it! ✉ *Rte. 12, ½ mi north of Woodstock,* ☎ *802/457–2355.* ☞ *$6.* ☉ *May–late Oct., daily 10–5; Nov.–Dec., weekends 10–4.*

Period furnishings of the Woodstock Historical Society fill the rooms of the white clapboard **Dana House** (circa 1807). Exhibits include the town charter, furniture, maps, and locally minted silver. The elaborate sleigh once owned by Frederick Billings, displayed in the barn, conjures up visions of romantic rides through the snow. The converted barn also houses the **Canaday Gallery**, which has seasonal exhibits. ✉ *26 Elm St.,* ☎ *802/457–1822.* ☞ *Free.* ☉ *May–late Oct., Mon.–Sat. 10–5, Sun. 2–5. Tours by appointment in winter.*

The **Raptor Center** of the **Vermont Institute of Natural Science** houses 26 species of birds of prey, among them a bald eagle, a peregrine falcon, and the 3-ounce saw-whet owl. All the caged birds have been found injured and unable to survive in the wild. This nonprofit, environmental research and education center is on a 77-acre nature preserve with self-guided walking trails. ✉ *Church Hill Rd.,* ☎ *802/457–2779.* ☞ *$5.* ☉ *May–Oct., daily 10–4; Nov.–Apr., Mon.–Sat. 10–4.*

Dining and Lodging

$$$–$$$$ ✕ **The Prince and the Pauper.** Here is a romantically candlelit Colo-
★   nial setting, a prix-fixe menu, and modern French and American fare with a Vermont accent. The grilled duck breast might have an Oriental five-spice sauce; homemade lamb and pork sausage in puff pastry with a honey-mustard sauce is another possibility. ✉ *24 Elm St.,* ☎ *802/457–1818. D, MC, V. No lunch.*

$$–$$$ ✕ **Bentley's.** Antique silk-fringed lamp shades, long lace curtains, and a life-size carving of a kneeling, winged knight lend a tongue-in-cheek Victorian air to burgers, chili, homemade soups, and entrées like duck in raspberry puree, almonds, and Chambord. You'll find jazz or blues here on weekends. ⊠ *3 Elm St.,* ☎ *802/457–3232. AE, MC, V.*

$$$$ ✕🏨 **Twin Farms.** At the center of this exclusive 235-acre resort stands the 1795 farmhouse where Sinclair Lewis and Dorothy Thompson lived. Rooms and cottages have original watercolors, ample bookshelves, fireplaces, and wood-and-stone furniture. One avant-garde studio has huge arch windows, a cathedral-ceiling living room done in spare classical furnishings, and a king-size bed in a loft overhead. Chef Neil Wigglesworth prepares a prix-fixe menu of rich contemporary cuisine that draws on local recipes. Guests are free to help themselves from an open bar. ⊠ *Stage Rd., off Rte. 12, 8 mi north of Woodstock (Box 115, Barnard, 05031),* ☎ *802/234–9999 or 800/894–6327,* ℻ *802/234–9990. 4 rooms with bath, 8 cottages. 2 bars, dining room, exercise room, boating, bicycles, ice-skating, cross-country and downhill skiing, recreation room, meeting rooms. MAP. AE, MC, V.*

$$$–$$$$ ✕🏨 **Kedron Valley Inn.** Max and Merrily Comins have renovated
★ what, in the 1840s, had been the National Hotel. Many rooms have either a fireplace or a Franklin stove, and each has a quilt. Two rooms have private decks, another has a private veranda, and a fourth has a private terrace overlooking the stream that runs through the inn's 15 acres. Exposed-log walls make the motel units in back more rustic than the rooms in the main inn, but they're decorated similarly. The classically trained chef creates such French masterpieces as fillet of Norwegian salmon stuffed with herb seafood mousse in puff pastry and shrimp, scallops, and lobster with wild mushrooms sautéed in shallots and white wine and served with a Fra Angelico cream sauce. The decor here, too, is striking; a terrace with views of the grounds is open in summer. ⊠ *Rte. 106, 05071,* ☎ *802/457–1473 or 800/836–1193,* ℻ *802/457–4469. 27 rooms with bath. Restaurant, bar, pond, beach. MAP. AE, D, MC, V. Closed Apr. and 10 days before Thanksgiving.*

$$$–$$$$ ✕🏨 **Woodstock Inn and Resort.** The hotel's lobby, with its massive wood-beam mantel and floor-to-ceiling fieldstone fireplace, embodies the spirit of New England. It comes as no surprise to learn that the resort is owned by the Rockefeller family. Modern ash furnishings are high-quality institutional, enlivened by patchwork quilts: The inoffensive decor is designed to please the large clientele of corporate conference attendees. The dinner fare is nouvelle New England; the menu changes seasonally and may include such entrées as salmon steak with avocado beurre blanc, beef Wellington, and prime rib. The wall of windows gives diners a view over the inn's putting green. ⊠ *Rte. 4, 05091,* ☎ *802/457–1100 or 800/448–7900,* ℻ *802/457–6699. 146 rooms with bath. Restaurant, bar, indoor and outdoor pools, saunas, golf, tennis courts, croquet, health club, racquetball, squash, cross-country and downhill skiing, meeting rooms. AE, MC, V.*

$$–$$$ 🏨 **The Woodstocker.** Just a short stroll from the covered bridge and the village green, this 1830s B&B offers the grace and elegance you'd expect in a town like Woodstock. The rooms are large and light, and furnished with a hodgepodge of antiques, like brass and iron four-poster beds and mahogany highboys. The cheerful grandfather clock, a year-round holiday tree that's decorated differently each season, and an intriguing piece with fake drawers carved into the front panel are centerpieces of the common areas. Breakfast might include bananas

Foster, French toast, or an egg strada. ⊠ *61 River St. (Rte. 4), 05091,* ☎ *802/457–3896 or 800/457–3896. 9 rooms with bath. MC, V.*

$–$$ ★ ⊞ **The Winslow House.** This farmhouse built in 1872 once presided over a dairy farm that reached down to the banks of the Ottauquechee River. Although this B&B has only four guest rooms and the common area is small, the two upstairs quarters are uncommonly spacious and have separate sitting rooms: Room 3 is dominated by mahogany furnishings, while the English oak bed, armoire, and mission desk in Room 4 transport you to a more luxurious era. A comfortable, unpretentious place with great cross-country skiing and golf nearby, this B&B is just far enough outside of town to feel secluded. ⊠ *38 Rte. 4, 05091,* ☎ *802/ 457–1820. 4 rooms with bath. D, DC, MC, V.*

Nightlife and the Arts

NIGHTLIFE

Bentleys (⊠ 3 Elm St., ☎ 802/457–3232), a popular restaurant, also has live jazz and blues on weekends.

THE ARTS

Vermont Symphony Orchestra (☎ 802/864–5741) performs in Rutland and, during the summer, in Woodstock. The **Pentangle Council on the Arts** (☎ 802/457–3981) organizes performances of music, theater, and dance at the Town Hall Theater.

Outdoor Activities and Sports

BIKING

Visit **Cyclery Plus** (⊠ 36 Rte. 4W, West Woodstock, ☎ 802/457–3377) for a free touring map of several local rides. They rent equipment and will help plan an extended trip in the area.

GOLF

Robert Trent Jones designed the 18-hole course at **Woodstock Country Club** (⊠ South St., ☎ 802/457–2112), run by the Woodstock Inn.

HORSEBACK RIDING

Kedron Valley Stables (⊠ Rte. 106, South Woodstock, ☎ 802/457–2734 or 800/225–6301) gives lessons and guided trail rides.

RECREATION AREA

At **Suicide Six** (☎ 802/457–6661) outdoor tennis courts, lighted paddle courts, croquet, and an 18-hole golf course are available in the summer.

Shopping

ART AND ANTIQUES

North Wind Artisans' Gallery (⊠ 81 Central St., ☎ 802/457–4587) has contemporary—mostly Vermont-made—craftwork with sleek, jazzy designs.

CLOTHING

Who Is Sylvia? (⊠ 26 Central St., ☎ 802/457–1110), located in the old firehouse, stocks vintage clothing and antique linens, lace, and jewelry.

FOOD AND DRINK

The Village Butcher (⊠ Elm St., ☎ 802/457–2756) is an emporium of Vermont comestibles.

MARKETPLACE

The Marketplace at Bridgewater Mills (⊠ Rte. 4, west of Woodstock, ☎ 802/672–3332) houses several shops and attractions in a three-story converted woolen mill. There's an antiques and crafts center and **The Mountain Brewers**, which produces Long Trail Ale and gives tours and tastings. **Sample Vermont** stocks gourmet foods and gifts from all over the state.

Skiing

Suicide Six. Site of the first ski tow in the United States (1934), this resort is owned and operated by the Woodstock Inn and Resort. The inn, in lovely Woodstock Village, 3 miles from the ski area, offers package plans that are remarkably inexpensive, considering the high quality of the accommodations. March Madness ushers in spring skiing with drastically reduced ticket prices. In addition to skiers interested in exploring Woodstock, the area attracts students and racers from nearby Dartmouth College. ✉ *Woodstock 05091,* ☎ *802/457–6661, lodging 800/448–7900, snow conditions 802/457–6666.*

DOWNHILL
Despite Suicide Six's short vertical of only 650 feet, there is challenging skiing here: There are several steep runs down the mountain's face and intermediate trails that wind around the hill. Beginner terrain is mostly toward the bottom. The 19 trails are serviced by two double chairlifts and one surface lift.

CROSS-COUNTRY
The ski touring center (☎ 802/457–2114) has 60 kilometers (37 miles) of trails. Equipment and lessons are available.

OTHER ACTIVITIES
There's a snowboard area with a halfpipe. A sports center at the Woodstock Inn and Resort (☎ 802/457–1100) has an indoor lap pool; indoor tennis, squash, and racquetball courts; whirlpool, steam, sauna, and massage rooms; and exercise and aerobics rooms.

CHILD CARE
Although the ski area has no nursery, baby-sitting can be arranged through the Woodstock Inn if you're a guest; lessons for children are given by the ski-school staff. There's a children's ski-and-play park for those ages 3–7.

Plymouth Notch

㉑ *14 mi southwest of Woodstock.*

Former U.S. President Calvin Coolidge was born and buried in Plymouth Notch, a town that shares his character: low-key and quiet. The small cluster of state-owned buildings looks more like a large farm than a town; in addition to the homestead there's the general store once run by Coolidge's father, a visitor center, an operating cheese factory, a one-room schoolhouse, and the former summer White House. Coolidge's grave is in the cemetery across Route 100A. ✉ *Rte. 100A, 6 mi south of Rte. 4, east of Rte. 100,* ☎ *802/672–3773.* 🎫 *$4.50.* ☉ *Memorial Day–mid-Oct., daily 9:30–5:30.*

Killington/Pico

㉒ *11 mi (Pico) and 15 mi (Killington) east of Rutland.*

The intersection of Routes 4 and 100 is the heart of central Vermont's ski country, with the Killington, Pico, and Okemo resorts nearby. The Killington access road is characterized by strip development, but the spectacular views from the top of the mountain are worth the drive.

Dining and Lodging

$$$–$$$$ ✗🏨 **Cortina Inn.** This large luxury lodge and miniresort is very comfortable and the location is prime. About ⅔ of the rooms have private balconies, although the views aren't spectacular. Horseback riding, sleigh rides, ice-skating, and guided snowmobile tours are some off-the-slopes activities. The New England Culinary Institute is in residence and provides an excellent breakfast buffet. ✉ *Rte. 4, Mendon 05751,* ☎ *802/773–3333 or 800/451–6108,* FAX *802/775–6948. 98 rooms with bath. Restaurant, bar, indoor pool, outdoor hot tub, sauna, 8 tennis courts, health club. Full breakfast included. AE, D, DC, MC, V.*

$$$ ✕🏠 **Summit Lodge.** This rambling, rustic two-story country lodge on an access road, just 3 miles from Killington Peak, caters to a varied crowd of ski enthusiasts who are warmly met by the lodge's mascots—a pair of Saint Bernards. Country decor and antiques blend with modern conveniences to create a relaxed atmosphere. Two restaurants allow both formal and informal dining. ✉ *Killington Rd., 05751,* ☎ *802/422–3535 or 800/635–6343,* FAX *802/422–3536. 45 rooms with bath, 2 suites. 2 restaurants, bar, pool, pond, hot tub, massage, sauna, racquetball, ice-skating, nightclub, recreation room. AE, DC, MC, V.*

$$ ✕🏠 **The Inn at Long Trail.** This 1938 lodge popular with skiers and hikers is just ¼ mile from the Pico ski slopes and even closer to the Appalachian/Long Trail. The unusual decor (e.g., massive boulders—inside the inn!), has nature as a prevailing theme. Gaelic charm is on hand with Irish music, darts, and Guinness always on tap. The Irish hospitality is extended particularly toward end-to-end hikers who get a substantial break in the rates. Dinner is served from Thursday to Sunday. ✉ *Rte. 4 (Box 267), 05751,* ☎ *802/775–7181 or 800/325–2540,* FAX *802/747–7034. 17 rooms with bath, 5 suites. Full breakfast included; MAP on winter weekends. AE, MC, V.*

Nightlife

Inn at Long Trail (✉ Rte. 4, ☎ 802/775–7181) has a comfortable pub that hosts Irish music on weekends. **The Pickle Barrel** (✉ Killington Rd., ☎ 802/422–3035), a favorite with the après-ski crowd, presents up-and-coming acts and can get pretty rowdy. Try the hot, spicy chicken wings to warm up after skiing at **Casey's Caboose** (✉ Halfway up Killington access road, ☎ 802/422–3795). The **Wobbly Barn** (☎ 802/422–3392), with dancing to blues and rock, is open during ski season.

Outdoor Activities and Sports

ICE SKATING

Cortina Inn (☎ 802/773–3333) has an ice-skating rink with rentals and offers sleigh rides from 6–9 PM; you can also skate on **Summit Pond** (☎ 802/422–4476).

Skiing

Killington. "Megamountain," "Beast of the East," and just plain "huge" are appropriate descriptions of Killington. Despite its extensive facilities and terrain, lift lines on weekends (especially holiday weekends) can be downright dreadful. It has the longest ski season in the East and some of the best package plans anywhere. With a single telephone call skiers can select price, date, and type of ski week they want; choose accommodations; book air or railroad transportation; and arrange for rental equipment and ski lessons. ✉ *400 Killington Rd., Killington 05751,* ☎ *802/422–3333, lodging 800/621–6867, snow conditions 802/422–3261.*

DOWNHILL

It would probably take a skier a week to test all 165 trails on the six mountains of the Killington complex, even though everything interconnects. About 64% of the 935 acres of skiing can be covered with machine-made snow, and that's still more snowmaking than any other area in the world can manage. Transporting skiers to the peaks of this complex are a 2½-mile gondola plus seven quads, four triples, and five double chairlifts, as well as two surface lifts. That's a total of 19 ski lifts, a few of which reach the area's highest elevation, at 4,220 feet off Killington Peak, and a vertical drop of 3,150 feet to the base of the gondola. Ride the new Skyeship, the world's fastest and first heated 8-passenger lift, complete with piped-in music and several luxury signature cabins that can be rented for an entire day. The Skyeship base station has a rotisserie, food court, and a coffee bar. The range of skiing includes everything from Outer Limits, one of the steepest and most challenging trails anywhere in the country, to the 10-mile-long, super-gentle Juggernaut Trail. The new "Fusion Zones" are the management's attempt to create a backcountry experience by thinning wooded terrain.

CHILD CARE

Nursery care is available for children from 6 weeks to 8 years old. There's a one-hour instruction program for youngsters 3–8; those 6–12 can join an all-day program, with a break for lunch.

Pico Ski Resort. Although it's only 5 miles down the road from Killington, venerable Pico has long been a favorite among people looking for uncrowded, wide-open cruiser skiing. When modern lifts were installed and a village square was constructed at the base, some feared that friendly patina would be threatened, but the condo-hotel, restaurants, and shops have not altered the essential nature of Pico. ⌗ *2 Sherburne Pass, Rutland 05701, ☎ 802/775–4346, snow conditions 802/775–4345, lodging 800/848–7325.*

DOWNHILL

From the area's 4,000-foot summit, most of the trails are advanced to expert, with two intermediate bail-out trails for the timid. The rest of the mountain's 2,000 feet of vertical terrain is mostly intermediate or easier. The lifts for these slopes and trails are two high-speed quads, two triples, and three double chairs, plus three surface lifts. The area has 85% snowmaking coverage. Snowboarders are welcome and have their own area, Triple Slope. For instruction of any kind, head to the Alpine Learning Center.

CROSS-COUNTRY

Mountain Meadows (☎ 802/775–7077) has 40 kilometers of groomed trails and 10 kilometers of marked outlying trails; Mountain Top (☎ 802/483–6089) is mammoth with 120 kilometers of trails, 80 of which are groomed.

OTHER ACTIVITIES

A sports center (☎ 802/773–1786) at the base of the mountain has fitness facilities, a 75-foot pool, whirlpool tub, saunas, and a massage room.

CHILD CARE

The nursery takes children from 6 months through 6 years old and provides indoor activities and outdoor play. The ski school has full- and half-day instruction programs for children 3–12 and makes use of the Kids Fun Park.

Rutland

32 mi south of Middlebury, 31 mi west of Woodstock, 47 mi west of White River Junction.

In Rutland, there are strips of shopping centers and a seemingly endless row of traffic lights, and the homes of blue-collar workers vastly outnumber the mansions of the marble magnates who made the town famous. Rutland's traditional economic ties to railroading and marble, the latter an industry that supplied stone to such illustrious structures as the central research building of the New York Public Library in New York City, have been rapidly eclipsed by the growth of the Pico and Killington ski areas to the east.

The **Chaffee Center for the Visual Arts** (⊠ 16 S. Main St., ☎ 802/775–0356) exhibits and sells the work of more than 200 Vermont artists who work in a variety of media.

OFF THE BEATEN PATH

VERMONT MARBLE EXHIBIT – Four miles north of Rutland, in Proctor, is the highlight of the area. Visitors can not only watch the sculptor-in-residence transform stone into finished works of art, but can also choose first-hand the marble they want to use for their custom-built kitchen counter. The gallery illustrates various industrial applications of marble—note the hall of presidents and the replica of Leonardo da Vinci's *Last Supper* in marble—and depicts the industry's history via exhibits and slide shows. You can buy factory seconds and both foreign and domestic marble items here, too. ⊠ 62 Main St., Proctor (follow signs off Rte. 3), ☎ 802/459–2300. ☞ $3.50. ☉ Memorial Day–Oct., daily 9–5:30; Nov.–Memorial Day, Mon.–Sat. 9–4.

The Arts

Crossroads Arts Council (☎ 802/775–5413) presents music, opera, dance, jazz, and theater events. **Vermont Symphony Orchestra** (☎ 802/864–5741) performs in Rutland in the winter and, during the summer, in Woodstock.

Dining and Lodging

$$–$$$ ✕ **Royal's 121 Hearthside.** This Rutland institution has an open hearth with hand-painted tiles, behind which the staff prepares mesquite-grilled chicken with basil, tomato, and mushrooms; roast prime rib; and lamb chops grilled with ginger and rosemary. ⊠ 37 N. Main St., ☎ 802/775–0856. AE, MC, V.

$$ ✕ **Back Home Cafe.** Wood booths, black-and-white linoleum tile, and
★ exposed brick give this second-story café with an outdoor patio the air of a hole-in-the-wall in New York City. Dinner might be baked stuffed fillet of sole with spinach, mushrooms, feta cheese, and tarragon sauce, or any of a number of Italian specialties. Daily lunch specials offer soup, entrée, and dessert for less than $5. The large bar in the back of the restaurant is the site of live weekend entertainment. ⊠ 21 Center St., ☎ 802/775–9313. AE, MC, V.

$–$$ ⛱ **The Inn at Rutland.** There *is* an alternative to motel and hotel chain accommodations in Rutland—at this renovated Victorian mansion. The ornate oak staircase lined with heavy embossed gold and leather wainscoting leads to rooms that blend modern bathrooms with turn-of-the-century touches: botanical prints, elaborate ceiling moldings, frosted glass, and pictures of ladies in long white dresses. Second-floor rooms are larger than those on the third (once the servants' quarters). ⊠ 70 N. Main St., 05701, ☎ 802/773–0575 or 800/808–0575, FAX 802/775–3506. 11 rooms with bath. Hot tub. Full breakfast included. D, DC, MC, V.

Shopping

BOOKS

Tuttle Antiquarian Books (⊠ 28 S. Main St., ☎ 802/773–8229) is a major publisher of books on Asia, particularly Asian art. In addition to its own publications, Tuttle carries rare and out-of-print books, genealogies, and local histories.

CRAFTS

East Meets West (⊠ North of Rutland on Rte. 7 at Sangamon Rd., Pittsford, ☎ 802/443–2242 or 800/443–2242) shows carvings, masks, statues, textiles, pottery, baskets, and other crafts of native peoples from around the world.

Waitsfield

㉔ *55 mi north of Rutland, 32 mi northeast of Middlebury, 19 mi southwest of Montpelier.*

Although in close proximity to Sugarbush and Mad River Glen ski areas, the Mad River Valley towns of Waitsfield and Warren have maintained a decidedly low-key atmosphere. The gently carved ridges cradling the valley and the swell of pastures and fields lining the river seem to keep further notions of ski-resort sprawl at bay. Pick up a map from the Sugarbush Chamber of Commerce and investigate the back roads that spur off Route 100 for some exhilarating valley views.

Dining and Lodging

$$–$$$ ✕ **Chez Henri.** Tucked in the shadows of Sugarbush ski area, this romantic slope-side bistro has garnered a year-round following with traditional French dishes such as cheese fondue, rabbit in red wine sauce, and fillet of beef with peppercorns. Locals frequent the congenial bar and dine alfresco next to a tumbling stream. ⊠ *Sugarbush Village,* ☎ *802/583–2600. AE, MC, V.*

$ ✕ **Richard's Special Vermont Pizza (RSVP).** Walk through the door, and you're immediately transported through time (to the 1950s) and space (to anywhere but Vermont). The pizza—legendary around these parts with its paper-thin crust and toppings like cilantro pesto, cob-smoked bacon, pineapple, and sautéed spinach—has become known for transport as well: Richard will send a pie almost anywhere in the world overnight delivery. And there are plenty of takers. Salads and sandwiches are also available, and there's an RSVP gourmet food store next door for prepared foods to go. ⊠ *Bridge St.,* ☎ *802/496–7787. MC, V.*

$$ ✕▥ **Lareau Farm Country Inn.** Surrounded by 67 acres of pastures and
★ woodland, and just an amble away from Mad River, this collection of old farm buildings (the oldest part dates from 1790) appeals to outdoor enthusiasts as well as to those simply seeking a rejuvenating retreat in the country. There's a lot of history here—the original settler is buried on the property—which innkeepers Susan and Dan Easley love to share; you can explore it yourself on a mile-long stroll, with the help of a detailed walking guide they've put together. The furnishings in the inn are an eclectic mix of Victorian sofas and Oriental rugs. Susan made the quilts in each of the guest rooms, and Dan often plays the piano that was made in Burlington. The many-windowed dining room, the most inviting room in the house, is where the family-style breakfast is served at one of the four massive oak and cherry tables. Sit on the covered porch in an Adirondack chair that faces horses grazing in pastures out back, explore the large jazz collection, swim in the river, take a horse or sleigh ride, or stroll in the beautiful gardens. American Flatbread, the restaurant in the barn, is a recommended experience. ⊠ *Rte. 100, Box 563,* ☎ *802/496-4949 or 800/833–0766. 11 rooms with bath, 2 share bath. Restaurant. D, MC, V.*

$$ ✕▥ **Tucker Hill Lodge.** Attempts to maintain its 1940s-ski-lodge ambience have succeeded. Pine-paneling and otherwise simple furnishings suffice as most guests here are more interested in skiing all day than in Victorian frills. Georgio's Café occupies two dining rooms: one upstairs, with red tablecloths and a deep blue ceiling; and one downstairs, with a bar, open stone oven, and fireplace. Both have a warm Mediterranean feel. *Pettini alla Veneziana* (stone-seared scallops with raisins and pine nuts), and *saltimbocca alla Valdostana* (roulades of beef with fontina cheese and prosciutto) are two specialties. Fondue, pasta dishes, and pizza round out the menu. ⊠ *Rte. 17, 05673,* ☎ *802/496–3983 or 800/543–7841,* 𝔽𝔸𝕏 *802/496–3203. 16 rooms with bath, 6 rooms share bath. Restaurant, pool, tennis court, hiking. Full breakfast included; MAP available. AE, MC, V.*

$$$–$$$$ 📷 **The Inn at the Round Barn Farm.** Art exhibits have replaced cows in the big round barn here (one of only eight in the state), but the Shaker-style building still dominates the farm's 85 acres. The inn's guest rooms are in the 1806 farmhouse, where books line the walls of the cream-color library. The rooms are sumptuous and elegant, with eyelet-trimmed sheets, elaborate four-poster beds, rich-colored wallpapers, and brass wall lamps for easy bedtime reading. Breakfast is served in a cheerful solarium that overlooks landscaped ponds and rolling acreage. ⊠ *E. Warren Rd., R.R. 1, Box 247, 05673,* ☎ *802/496–2276,* 𝔽𝔸𝕏 *802/496–8832. 11 rooms with bath. Indoor pool, cross-country skiing, game room. Full breakfast included; MAP available. AE, MC, V.*

$$ 📷 **Beaver Pond Farm Inn.** A peaceful drive down a country lane lined
★   with sugar maples leads to this small 1840 farmhouse overlooking rolling meadows, a golf course, and cross-country ski trails. Guest rooms are decorated simply, and bathrooms are ample. The focal point of the inn is the huge deck, where, after active days, guests gaze at the mountains and meadows. A full breakfast might include orange-yogurt pancakes. The inn is next door to the Robert Trent Jones–designed Sugarbush Golf Course, which has a 180-yard driving range and is less than a mile from Sugarbush Ski Area. ⊠ *R.D. Box 306, Golf Course Rd., 05674,* ☎ *802/583–2861,* 𝔽𝔸𝕏 *802/583–2860. 4 rooms with bath, 2 share bath. Dining room. Full breakfast included; MAP available Tues., Thurs., Sat. MC, V.*

Nightlife and the Arts

NIGHTLIFE

Giorgio's Café (⊠ Tucker Hill Lodge, Rte. 17, ☎ 802/496–3983) is a cozy spot to warm by the fire to the sounds of soft folk and jazz on weekends. **Gallaghers** (⊠ Rtes. 100 and 17, ☎ 802/496–8800) is a popular spot, with danceable local bands. **The Back Room at Chez Henri** (⊠ Sugarbush Village, ☎ 802/583–2600) has a pool table and is popular with the après-ski and late-night dance crowd.

THE ARTS

Green Mountain Cultural Center (⊠ Inn at the Round Barn, E. Warren Rd., ☎ 802/496–7722), a nonprofit organization, brings concerts and art exhibits, as well as educational workshops, to the Mad River Valley. **The Valley Players** (⊠ Rte. 100, ☎ 802/496–3485) presents a year-round mix of musicals, dramas, follies, and holiday shows.

Outdoor Activities and Sports

BIKING

The popular 14-mile Waitsfield–Warren loop begins when you cross the covered bridge in Waitsfield. Keep right on East Warren Road to the four-way intersection in East Warren; continue straight, then bear right, riding down Brook Road to the village of Warren; return by turning right (north) on Route 100 back toward Waitsfield. **Mad River Bike Shop** (⊠ Rte. 100, ☎ 802/496–9500) offers rentals, mountain bike tours, and maps.

GOLF

Spectacular views and challenging play are the trademarks of the Robert Trent Jones–designed 18-hole course at **Sugarbush Resort** (⊠ Golf Course Rd., ☎ 802/583–2722).

The town of Waitsfield has a skating rink (☎ 802/496–9199) and intends to put a lid on it soon for skating year-round.

Lareau Farm (✉ Rte. 100, Waitsfield, ☎ 802/496–4949) has a 100-year-old sleigh that cruises along the Mad River.

Shopping
Luminosity (✉ Rte. 100, ☎ 802/496–2231) is in a converted church and, fittingly, specializes in stained glass.

All Things Bright and Beautiful (✉ Bridge St., ☎ 802/496–3997) is a 12-room Victorian house jammed to the rafters with stuffed animals of all shapes, sizes, and colors. They have spilled over into the Cape house next door and increased their inventory to include folk art, prints, and collectibles. **Warren Village Pottery** (✉ 5 mi south of Waitsfield, Main St., Warren, ☎ 802/496–4162) sells unique, handcrafted wares from its home-based retail shop.

Green Mountain Coffee Roasters (✉ Mad River Green, ☎ 802/496–5470), utopia for coffee lovers, has beans from all over the world that are roasted in Waterbury.

Skiing
Mad River Glen. Ever wanted to own a ski area? Now you can! In 1995, Mad River Glen became the first ski area to be owned by a cooperative formed by the skiing community. The maximum amount of shareholders rests at 2,000, with no one person owning more than four shares; each shareholder has one vote. To make any changes to the ski area, there has to be a ⅔ majority with at least ½ of the owners voting. This is a group of dedicated knowledgeable skiers devoted to keeping skiing what it used to be—a pristine alpine experience. The ski area was developed in the late 1940s and has changed relatively little since then; the single chairlift may be the only lift of its vintage still carrying skiers. There is an unkempt aura about this place that for 40 years has attracted a devoted group of skiers from wealthy families in the East as well as rugged individualists looking for a less-polished terrain. Remember that most of Mad River's trails (85%) are covered only by natural snow. The apt area motto is "Ski It If You Can." ✉ *Rte. 17, Waitsfield 05673, ☎ 802/496–3551, Cooperative office 802/496–6742 or 800/850–6742, snow conditions 802/496–2001 or 800/696–2001.*

Mad River is steep with natural slopes that follow the contours of the mountain. Terrain changes constantly on 33 interactive trails, of which 75% are intermediate to superexpert. Intermediate and novice terrain are regularly groomed. Four chairs (including the famed single) service the mountain's 2,037-foot vertical. There is no snowboarding on the mountain.

The nursery (☎ 802/496–2123) takes children 6 weeks to 8 years, while the ski school has classes for children 4–12. Junior racing is available weekends and during holiday periods.

Sugarbush. The buzz these days in the ski world surrounds the massive capital improvement plan at Sugarbush. The resort, bought in 1994 by LBO Holdings, which also owns Sunday River in Maine and Attitash in New Hampshire, is determined to become the ultimate skiing destination in Vermont. In the early 1960s Sugarbush had the reputation of being an outpost of an affluent and sophisticated crowd from New York. While that reputation has faded, Sugarbush has spent $28 million to stay on the cutting edge. Skiers familiar with the shuttle bus between the north and south areas can rejoice over the new Slide Brook Express, a quad that connects the two mountains. Snowmaking has increased to 80% coverage, with the installation of a new state-of-the-art, computer-controlled system that the resort has fought long and hard for: Environmental restrictions, land-use permits, and the fact that part of the resort is on National Forest land, have made acquiring the snow-making capacity enjoyed by other major resorts difficult. The base of the mountain has a village of condominiums, restaurants, shops, bars, and a sports center. ✉ *Box 350, Warren 05674,* ☎ *802/583–2381, lodging 800/537–8427, snow conditions 802/583–7669.*

DOWNHILL

Sugarbush is two distinct, now connected, mountain complexes. The Sugarbush South area is what old-timers recall as Sugarbush Mountain: With a vertical of 2,400 feet, it is known for formidable steeps toward the top and in front of the main base lodge. Sugarbush North offers what South has in short supply—beginner runs. North also has steep fall-line pitches and intermediate cruisers off its 2,600 vertical feet. There are 111 trails in all: 23% beginner, 48% intermediate, 29% expert. Lift-capacity is unbelievable. The resort now has 18 lifts: seven quads (including four high-speed versions), three triples, four doubles, and four surface lifts.

CROSS-COUNTRY

More than 25 kilometers (15 miles) of groomed cross-country trails are adjacent to the Sugarbush Inn. Blueberry Lake cross-country ski area (✉ Plunkton Rd., Warren, ☎ 802/496–6687) has 23 kilometers (14 miles) of groomed trails through thickly wooded glades. Ole's (✉ Airport Rd., Warren, ☎ 802/496–3430) runs a cross-country center out of the tiny Warren airport; it has 64 kilometers (40 miles) of trails—42 groomed—that span out into the surrounding woods from the open fields of the landing strips.

OTHER ACTIVITIES

Sugarbush Sports Center (☎ 802/583–2391), near the ski lifts, has Nautilus and Universal equipment; tennis, squash, and racquetball courts; whirlpool, sauna, and steam rooms; and two indoor pools. The Pavilion, a smaller sports center, (☎ 802/538–2605) has all the activities listed above save the racquet sports.

CHILD CARE

The Sugarbush Day School accepts children ages 6 weeks through 6 years; older children have indoor play and outdoor excursions. There's half- and full-day instruction available for children ages 4–11. Kids have their own magic carpet lift, and Sugarbear Forest, a terrain garden, has fun bumps and jumps to test their skiing agility.

En Route   Route 17 from Waitsfield to Bristol winds westward up and over the Appalachian Gap, one of Vermont's most panoramic mountain passes: The views from the top and on the way down the other side toward the quiet town of Bristol are a just reward for the challenging drive.

Bristol

㉕ *20 mi west of Waitsfield.*

The **Lake Champlain Maritime Museum** commemorates the days when steamships sailed along the coast of northern Vermont carrying logs,

In case you want to see the world.

At American Express, we're here to make your journey a smooth one. So we have over 1,700 travel service locations in over 120 countries ready to help. What else would you expect from the world's largest travel agency?

do more

AMERICAN EXPRESS

Travel

http://www.americanexpress.com/travel

In case you want to be welcomed there.

We're here to see that you're always welcomed at establishments everywhere. That's why millions of people carry the American Express® Card – for peace of mind, confidence, and security, around the world or just around the corner.

do more

In case you're running low.

We're here to help with more than 118,000 Express Cash locations around the world. In order to enroll, just call American Express before you start your vacation.

do more

Express Cash

And just in case.

We're here with American Express® Travelers Cheques
and Cheques *for Two*.® They're the safest way to carry
money on your vacation and the surest way to get a
refund, practically anywhere, anytime.
Another way we help you...

do more

AMERICAN
EXPRESS

Travelers
Cheques

livestock, and merchandise bound for New York City. The exhibits housed here in a one-room stone schoolhouse, circa 1818, include historic maps, nautical prints, and a collection of small crafts. ⊠ *Basin Harbor Rd. (14 mi west of Bristol, 6 mi west of Vergennes),* ☎ *802/475–2022.* ⌨ *$5.* ⊗ *Early May–late Oct., daily 10–5.*

Dining

$$$ ✕ **Mary's at Baldwin Creek.** One of the most inspired eating experiences in the state, Mary's is in a 1790 farmhouse on the outskirts of town. The "summer kitchen," with a blazing fireplace and rough-hewn barn-board walls, and the lighter, pastel-colored main room provide breathing room; secluded corner tables abound. The innovative, ever-changing cuisine includes a legendary garlic soup, Vermont rack of lamb with a rosemary-mustard sauce, duck cassis smoked over applewood, and Mako shark with a banana salsa. For dessert, the raspberry gratin is a favorite. Sunday brunch is a local ritual. ⊠ *Rte. 116, north of Bristol,* ☎ *802/453–2432. AE, MC, V. Closed Mon., lunch served only in summer.*

Outdoor Activities and Sports

BIKING

A challenging 32-mile ride starts in Bristol: Take North Street from the traffic light in town and continue north to Monkton Ridge and on to Hinesburg; to return, follow Route 116 south through Starksboro and back to Bristol. The **Bike and Ski Touring Center** (⊠ 74 Main St., Middlebury, ☎ 802/388–6666) offers rentals.

Shopping

CRAFTS

Folkheart (⊠ 18 Main St., ☎ 802/453–4101) carries an unusual selection of jewelry, toys, and crafts from around the world.

FOOD AND DRINK

Bristol Market (⊠ 28 North St., ☎ 802/453–2448), open since the early 1900s, proffers gourmet health foods and local products.

Middlebury

★ ㉖ *34 mi south of Burlington.*

In the late 1800s Middlebury was the largest Vermont community west of the Green Mountains: an industrial center of river-powered wool, grain, and marble mills. Otter Creek, the state's longest river, traverses the town center. Still a cultural and economic hub amid the Champlain Valley's serene pastoral patchwork, the town and countryside beckon a day of exploration.

This is Robert Frost country; Vermont's late poet laureate spent 23 summers at a farm just east of Ripton. The mustard-color buildings of Middlebury College's Breadloaf Campus are home of the renowned writer's conference begun by Frost; go a mile further to hike the easy ¾-mile **Robert Frost Interpretive Trail,** which winds through quiet woodland. Plaques along the way bear quotations from Frost's poems. There's a picnic area across the road from the trailhead.

Smack in the middle of town, **Middlebury College** (☎ 802/388–3711), founded in 1800, was conceived as an accessible alternative to the more worldly University of Vermont—although the two schools have since traded reputations. The provocative contrast of early 19th-century stone buildings against the postmodern architecture of the Fine Arts Building and sports center make for an opinion-provoking campus stroll. The **Middlebury College Museum of Art** has a permanent collection of paintings and sculpture that includes work by Rodin and Hiram Powers. ⊠ *Fine Arts Bldg.,* ☎ *802/388–3711, ext. 5235.* 🎫 *Free.* ⊙ *Tues.–Fri. 10–5, weekends noon–5.*

The **Vermont Folklife Center** is in the basement of the restored 1801 home of Gamaliel Painter, the founder of Middlebury College. The rotating exhibits explore all facets of Vermont life using means as diverse as contemporary photography, antiques, paintings by folk artists, and manuscripts. ⊠ *2 Court St.,* ☎ *802/388–4964.* 🎫 *Donations accepted.* ⊙ *Weekdays 9–5 and, May–Oct., Sat. noon–4.*

Take the guided tour at the **Sheldon Museum,** an 1829 marble-merchant's house whose period rooms contain furniture, toys, clothes, kitchen tools, and paintings that span from Colonial times to the early 20th century. ⊠ *1 Park St.,* ☎ *802/388–2117.* 🎫 *$1.50.* ⊙ *June–Oct., Mon.–Sat. 10–5; Nov.–May, weekdays 10–5.*

NEED A
BREAK?   **Calvi's** (⊠ Merchants Row) has an old-fashioned marble-counter soda fountain and an extensive menu of ice-cream dishes.

More than a crafts store, the **Vermont State Craft Center at Frog Hollow** is a juried display of the work of more than 250 Vermont artisans. The center sponsors classes with some of those artists. ⊠ *Mill St.,* ☎ *802/388–3177.* ⊙ *Jan.–May, Mon.–Sat. 9:30–5; June–Dec., Mon.–Sat. 9:30–5, Sun. noon–5.*

The Morgan horse—the official state animal—has an even temper, good stamina, and legs that are a bit truncated in proportion to its body. The University of Vermont's **Morgan Horse Farm,** about 2½ miles from Middlebury, is a breeding and training farm where, in summer, you can tour the stables and paddocks. ⊠ *Follow sign off Rte. 23,* ☎ *802/388–2011.* 🎫 *$3.50.* ⊙ *May–Oct., daily 9–4:30; Nov.–Apr., weekdays 9–4:30, Sat. 9–noon.*

The Arts

Middlebury College (☎ 802/388–3711) sponsors music, theater, and dance performances throughout the year at Wright Memorial Theatre.

Dining and Lodging

$$$ ✕ **Woody's.** In addition to cool jazz, diner-deco light fixtures, and ab-
★   stract paintings, Woody's has a view of Otter Creek just below. There are nightly specials; the seafood mixed grill is very popular. ⊠ *5 Bakery La.,* ☎ *802/388–4182. AE, DC, MC, V.*

$$–$$$ ✕🏨 **Swift House Inn.** The white-panel wainscoting, elaborately carved
★   mahogany and marble fireplaces, and cherry paneling in the dining room give this Georgian home of a 19th-century governor and his philanthropist daughter a formal elegance. Rooms—each with Oriental rugs and nine with fireplaces—have such antique reproductions as canopy beds, swag curtains, and clawfoot tubs. Some bathrooms have double whirlpool tubs. Rooms in the house by the road suffer from street noise. In the dining room, the adventurous menu might include rack of lamb roasted with hazelnut and baby red lentils in port wine sauce, or grilled filet mignon with onion marmalade. ⊠ *25 Stewart La., 05753,* ☎ *802/388–9925,* 📠 *802/388–9927. 21 rooms with bath. Restaurant, pub, sauna, steam room. CP; MAP available. AE, D, MC, V.*

$$–$$$ ✕🏨 **Waybury Inn.** The Waybury Inn may look familiar—it appeared as the "Stratford Inn" on television's *Newhart.* Guest rooms, some of which have the awkward configuration that can result from the conversion of a building of the early 1800s, have quilted pillows, antique furnishings, and middle-age plumbing. Comfortable sofas around the fireplace create a homey living room, and the pub, which serves more than 100 different kinds of beer, is a favorite local gathering spot. ⊠ *Rte. 125, 05740,* ☎ *802/388–4015 or 800/348–1810. 14 rooms with bath. Restaurant, pub. Full breakfast included. D, MC, V.*

Outdoor Activities and Sports

BOATING

Otter Creek Canoes (⊠ New Haven, ☎ 802/388–6159) has maps, guides, and rents gear. They will deliver canoes to the site of your choice. Rent boats from **Chipman Point Marina** (⊠ Rte. 73A, Orwell, ☎ 802/948–2288), where there is dockage for 60 boats.

FISHING

Yankee Charters (⊠ 34 North St., Vergennes, 05491, ☎ 802/877–3318) rents gear and sets up half-day or full-day trips on Lake Champlain from April to October.

HIKING

Several day hikes in the vicinity of Middlebury take in the Green Mountains. About 8 miles east of Brandon on Route 73, one trail starts at Brandon Gap and climbs steeply up **Mt. Horrid** (1 hr). On Route 116, about 5½ miles north of East Middlebury, a U.S. Forest Service sign marks a dirt road that forks to the right and leads to the start of the hike to **Abbey Pond,** which has a fantastic beaver lodge and dam in addition to a view of Robert Frost Mountain (2–3 hrs).

South of Lake Dunmore on Route 53, a large turnout marks a trail to the **Falls of Lana** (2 hrs). Four other trails—two short ones of less than a mile each and two longer ones—lead to the old abandoned Revolutionary War fortifications at **Mt. Independence;** to reach them, take the first left turn off Route 73 west of Orwell and go right at the fork. The road will turn to gravel and once again will fork; take a sharp left hand turn toward a small marina. The parking lot is on the left at the top of the hill.

Shopping

CRAFTS

Holy Cow (⊠ 52 Seymour St., ☎ 802/388–6737) is where Woody Jackson creates and sells his infamous Holstein cattle-inspired T-shirts and memorabilia.

MARKETPLACE

Historic Marble Works (☎ 802/388–3701), a renovated marble manufacturing facility, is a collection of unique shops set amid quarrying equipment and factory buildings.

Brookfield

㉗ *15 mi south of Montpelier.*

Crossing the **floating bridge at Brookfield** (⊠ Rte. 65 off I–89 and follow signs) feels like driving on water. The bridge, supported by almost 400 barrels, sits at water level and is the scene of the annual ice harvest festival in January (the bridge is closed in winter).

Dining and Lodging

$$–$$$ ✕🏠 **Autumn Crest Inn.** This inn is in the middle of nowhere, atop a knoll with a nearly 180-degree view of a 46-acre work-horse farm and the surrounding valley. One could spend the whole day on the Queen Anne–style porch that graces the front of the 1790 inn. Early risers can see the sunrise in the winter. The overall feel of the inn is casual, like relaxing in a friend's living room. Guest rooms in the older part of the house have more character. The newer section feels a bit too motel-like, although the suites are spacious and comfortable. The creative din-

ner menu is seasonal country gourmet. Breakfast might be peach-schnapps French toast or gingerbread pancakes. ⊠ *R.F.D. 1, Clark Rd., Box 150, Williamstown 05679,* ☎ *802/433–6627 or 800/339–6627. 18 rooms with bath. Restaurant (closed Mon., Tues.), pond, horseback riding, cross-country skiing, sleigh rides. Full breakfast included; MAP available. AE, MC, V.*

$$–$$$
★ ✕🎬 **Green Trails Inn.** This inn comprises 1790 and 1830 farmhouses that are the focal point of a sleepy, yet stubborn town that has voted several times to keep the village roads dirt and the nation's only wooden floating bridge still floating. Everything about this place is an expression of the friendliness of the innkeepers: The massive fieldstone fireplace that dominates the living and dining area of the inn is symbolic of the stalwart, down-to-earth hospitality. The rooms are furnished simply with quilts and a spattering of early American antiques. One two-room suite has a fireplace, another has a whirlpool tub. The dining is gourmet and might include rock cornish game hen with Cumberland sauce. Taking a walk down a tree-shaded country road was never so pleasant. ⊠ *Main St., 05036,* ☎ *802/276–3412 or 800/243–3412. 14 rooms, 8 with bath. Cross-country skiing, ski shop, sleigh rides. Full breakfast included; MAP available in winter. MC, V.*

Central Vermont A to Z

Getting Around

BY BUS

Vermont Transit (☎ 802/864–6811, 800/451–3292, or, in VT, 800/642–3133) links Rutland, White River Junction, Burlington, and many smaller towns.

BY CAR

The major east–west road is Route 4, which stretches from White River Junction in the east to Fair Haven in the west. Route 125 connects Middlebury on Route 7 with Hancock on Route 100; Route 100 splits the region in half along the eastern edge of the Green Mountains. Route 17 travels east–west from Waitsfield over the Appalachian Gap through Bristol and down to the shores of Lake Champlain. I–91 and the parallel Route 5 follow the eastern border; Routes 7 and 30 are the north–south highways in the west. I–89 links White River Junction with Montpelier to the north.

Contacts and Resources

EMERGENCIES

Rutland Medical Center (⊠ 160 Allen St., Rutland, ☎ 802/775–7111). **Porter Medical Center** (⊠ South St., Middlebury, ☎ 802/388–7901).

GUIDED TOURS

Country Inn Along the Trail (⊠ R.R. 3, Box 3265, Brandon 05733, ☎ 802/247–3300) leads skiing, hiking, and biking trips from inn to inn in Central Vermont. **The Icelandic Horse Farm** (⊠ Common Rd., Waitsfield, ☎ 802/496–7141) offers year-round guided riding expeditions on easy-to-ride Icelandic horses. Full-day and half-day rides, weekend tours, and inn-to-inn treks are available.

LODGING REFERRAL SERVICES

The **Woodstock Area Chamber of Commerce** (☎ 802/457–2389) and **Sugarbush Reservations** (☎ 800/537–8427) provide lodging referral services.

STATE PARKS

The following state parks have camping and picnicking facilities: **Ascutney State Park** (⊠ Rte. 5, 2 mi north of I–91, Exit 8, ☎ 802/674–

2060) has a scenic mountain toll road and snowmobile trails. **Coolidge State Park** (⊠ Near Woodstock, Rte. 100A, 2 mi north of Rte. 100, ☎ 802/672–3612), in Calvin Coolidge National Forest, includes the village where Calvin Coolidge was born and is great for snowmobiling. **Gifford Woods State Park**'s Kent Pond (⊠ Near Rutland, Rte. 100, ½ mi north of Rte. 4, ☎ 802/775–5354) is a terrific fishing hole. **Half Moon State Park**'s principal attraction is Half Moon Pond (⊠ Town Rd., 3½ mi off Rte. 30, west of Hubbardton, ☎ 802/273–2848). The park has approach trails, nature trails, and a naturalist, as well as boat and canoe rentals.

VISITOR INFORMATION

The following offices are open weekdays 9–5. **Addison County Chamber of Commerce** (⊠ 2 Court St., Middlebury 05753, ☎ 802/388–7951). **Quechee Chamber of Commerce** (⊠ Box 106, Quechee 05059, ☎ 802/295–7900 or 800/295–5451). **Rutland Region Chamber of Commerce** (⊠ 256 North Main St., Rutland 05701, ☎ 802/773–2747). **Sugarbush Chamber of Commerce** (⊠ Rte. 100, Box 173, Waitsfield 05673, ☎ 802/496–3409). **Windsor Area Chamber of Commerce** (⊠ Main St., Box 5, Windsor 05089, ☎ 802/674–5910). **Woodstock Area Chamber of Commerce** (⊠ 18 Central St., Box 486, Woodstock 05091, ☎ 802/457–3555).

NORTHERN VERMONT

Both the state's largest city (Burlington) and the nation's smallest state capital (Montpelier) are in this region, as are some of the most rural and remote areas of New England. Much of Vermont's logging and dairy farming take place in the northern stretches of the state, where the most snow falls (hence the profusion of ski areas—Jay, Burke, Bolton, Smugglers' Notch, and Stowe). Cradled between the population centers of Burlington and Montpelier to the south and the border with Canada to the north, the Northeast Kingdom stretches vast and untamed, where moose sightings and the harsh reality of rural life are much more common than microbreweries and hip cafés (Budweiser and diners are more the norm). With Montréal only an hour from the border, the Canadian influence is strong, and Canadian accents and currency common (the closer you get to the border, the more bilingual signs you'll encounter).

You'll find plenty to do in the region's cities (Burlington, Montpelier, St. Johnsbury, and Barre), in the bustling resort area of Stowe, in the Lake Champlain islands, and in the wilds of the Northeast Kingdom.

Our tour begins in the state capital, Montpelier, and moves west towards Waterbury, Stowe, and Burlington. Then we travel north through the Champlain Islands and turn east again, following the boundary with Canada toward Jay Peak and Newport. Turning south into the heart of the Northeast Kingdom, we eventually reach St. Johnsbury, and complete the circle in Barre.

Numbers in the margin correspond to points of interest on the Northern Vermont map.

Montpelier

28 *38 mi east of Burlington, 115 mi north of Brattleboro.*

The Vermont legislature anointed Montpelier as the state capital in 1805. Today, with fewer than 10,000 residents, the city is the country's least populous seat of government. The intersection of State and Main streets is the city hub, bustling with the activity of state and city workers during the day. It's an endearing place to spend an afternoon browsing in the local shops; in true, small-town Vermont fashion, the streets become deserted at night.

Built in 1859, following its predecessor's destruction (the first time by the legislators themselves, the second time by fire), the current **Vermont State House**—with its gleaming gold dome and granite columns 6 feet in diameter (plucked from the ground right next door in Barre)—is quite impressive for a city this size. The interior of the building had a facelift in 1994, but most of the original furnishings are still in place and continue to reflect the intimacy of the state's citizen legislature. ⊠ *115 State St.,* ☎ *802/828–2228.* 🎟 *Free.* ☉ *Weekdays 8–4; tours July–mid-Oct. every ½ hr 10–3:30, Sat. 11–3.*

Perhaps you're wondering what the last panther shot in Vermont looked like? Why New England bridges are covered? What a niddy-noddy is? Or what Christmas was like for a Bethel boy in 1879? ("I skated on my new skates. In the morning Papa and I set up a stove for Gramper.") The **Vermont Museum,** on the ground floor of the Vermont Historical Society offices in Montpelier, satisfies the curious with intriguing and informative exhibits. ⊠ *109 State St.,* ☎ *802/828–2291.* 🎟 *$3.* ☉ *Tues.–Fri., 9–4:30, Sat. 9–4, Sun. noon–4.*

Dining and Lodging

$$$ ✕ **The Chef's Table.** Nearly everyone working here is a student at the
★   New England Culinary Institute. Although this is their training ground, the quality and inventiveness are anything but beginner's luck. The menu changes daily. The atmosphere is more formal than that of its sister operation downstairs, the **Main Street Bar and Grill.** Tips are *verboten!* ⊠ *118 Main St.,* ☎ *802/229–9202 or 802/223–3188 for Grill. MC, V. Closed Sun.*

$$$–$$$$ ✕🏠 **The Inn at Montpelier.** This spacious inn built in the early 1800s was renovated with the business traveler in mind; yet the architectural detailing, antique four-poster beds, Windsor chairs, stately upholstered wing chairs, and the classical guitar on the stereo attract non-business folks. The formal sitting room has a Federal feel to it, and the wide wraparound Colonial Revival porch is perfect for reading a good book or watching the town go by. The rooms in the annex across the street are equally elegant. There's also an outstanding restaurant. ⊠ *147 Main St., 05602,* ☎ *802/223–2727,* 📠 *802/223–0722. 19 rooms with bath. Restaurant, meeting rooms. CP. AE, MC, V.*

Shopping

ANTIQUES

Great American Salvage (⊠ 3 Main St., ☎ 802/223–7711) supplies architectural detailing: moldings, brackets, stained-glass and leaded windows, doors, and trim retrieved from old homes.

BOOKS

Bear Pond Books (⊠ 77 Main St., ☎ 802/229–0774) is an inviting store with a comfy browsing area and comprehensive selections.

CLOTHING

Vermont Trading Company (⊠ 2 State St., ☎ 802/223–2142) has natural-fiber clothing and funky accessories.

Waterbury

㉙ *12 mi northwest of Montpelier.*

Waterbury holds one of Vermont's best-loved attractions: **Ben & Jerry's Ice Cream Factory,** the mecca, nirvana, and Valhalla for ice-cream

Northern Vermont

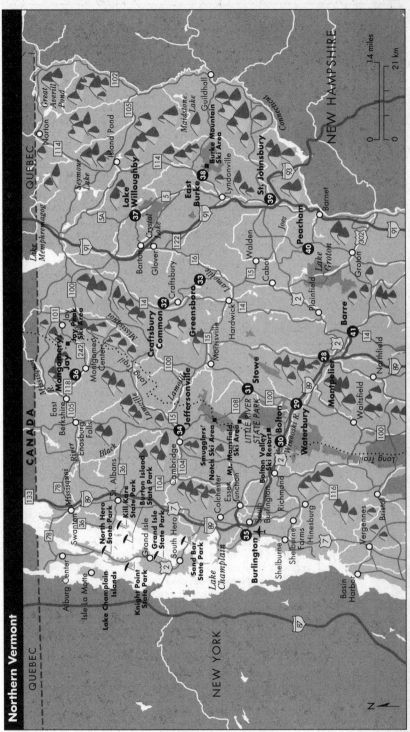

QUEBEC

NEW HAMPSHIRE

14 miles
21 km

Great Averill Pond

Norton

102

105

114

Island Pond

Maidstone Lake

Guildhall

Burke Mountain Ski Area

QUEBEC

Lake Memphremagog

91

Seymour Lake

Lake Willoughby

37

Crystal Lake

Barton

5A

5

East Burke

38

Lyndonville

91

St. Johnsbury

39

93

Barnet

Connecticut

Joes

Peacham

40

Lake Groton

Groton

302

91

Glover

122

Craftsbury

14

Craftsbury Common

32

16

Greensboro

33

Walden

Cabot

Plainfield

2

Barre

41

14

Northfield

89

100

101

Jay Peak Ski Area

Jay

Mississquoi

Montgomery Center

242

36

Montgomery

118

East Berkshire

105

Enosburg Falls

Missisquoi River

Black

78

89

Swanton

36

St. Albans

North Hero State Park

Kill Kare State Park

Grand Isle

Grand Isle State Park

Burton Island State Park

South Hero

2

7

Sand Bar State Park

Knight Point State Park

Alburg Center

Isle La Motte

Lake Champlain Islands

133

78

Long Trail

Hazen's Notch

Lamoille

Jeffersonville

34

Cambridge

104

Smugglers' Notch Ski Area

Mt. Mansfield Ski Area

Essex Junction

Colchester

Richmond

South Burlington

Burlington

35

Shelburne

Shelburne Farms

Hinesburg

7

116

Vergennes

Bristol

Basin Harbor

Lake Champlain

87

NEW YORK

Morrisville

15

Hardwick

14

Wolcott

15

Stowe

31

108

Little River State Park

Bolton Valley Ski Resort

Bolton

30

Waterbury

Winooski R.

29

100

89

Waitsfield

Montpelier

28

2

CANADA

Trout River

100

Long Trail

Long Trail

N

lovers. Ben and Jerry, who began selling ice cream from a renovated gas station in Burlington in the 1970s, have created a business that has become one of the most influential voices in community-based activism in the country. Their social and environmental consciousness have made the company a model of corporate responsibility. Fifty percent of tour proceeds go to Vermont community groups. The plant tour is a bit self-congratulatory and only skims the surface of the behind-the-scenes goings-on that many would no doubt like to learn more about—a flaw forgiven when the free samples are offered. ⌧ *Rte. 100, 1 mi north of I–89,* ☎ *802/244–5641.* ☎ *Tour $1.* ☉ *Daily 9–6 (till 9 in summer and fall); tours every ½ hr.*

Dining and Lodging

$$–$$$ ✕🏨 **Thatcher Brook Inn.** There were once two sawmills across the street from this 1899 mansion, which was the residence for the sawyers and their families—it's hard now to picture their lives, with the hub of activity centered around Ben & Jerry's ice cream factory next door. Twin gazebos are poised on either end of the front porch, and stands of giant white pines bolster the inn, defining its space on busy Route 100. Comfortable guest rooms have modern bathroom fixtures and floral wallpaper. Some have fireplaces and whirlpool tubs. The pine paneling, fireplace, framed *Life* magazine covers, and tables with backgammon boards painted right on them make the pub a popular socializing spot. Classic French cuisine is served in the dining room where dark green walls and mauve linens accent original woodwork. The inn's central location makes it a perfect base for exploring some of the state's most popular tourist attractions. ⌧ *Rte. 100, 05676,* ☎ *802/244–5911 or 800/292–5911,* ℻ *802/244–1294. 25 rooms with bath. Pub. Full breakfast included; MAP available. AE, D, DC, MC, V.*

Outdoor Activities and Sports

HIKING

Mount Mansfield State Forest and **Little River State Park** (⌧ Rte. 2, 1½ mi west of Waterbury) have extensive trail systems, including one that reaches the site of the Civilian Conservation Corps unit that was here in the 1930s.

Shopping

FOOD AND DRINK

Cabot Creamery Annex (⌧ Rte. 100, 2½ mi north of I–89, Waterbury, ☎ 802/244–6334) is the retail store and tasting center for Vermont's king of cheese. **Cold Hollow Cider Mill** (⌧ Rte. 100, Waterbury Center, ☎ 802/244–8771 or 800/327–7537) sells cider, baked goods, and Vermont produce, and offers tastes of the fresh-pressed cider. **Green Mountain Chocolate Co.** (⌧ Rte. 100, Waterbury, ☎ 802/244–1139) greets you with cases and cases of hand-rolled truffles, cakes, cookies, and umpteen-zillion types of candies.

Bolton

🌑 *20 mi east of Burlington, 20 mi west of Montpelier.*

Bolton attracts cross-country and alpine skiers in the winter and mountain bikers and hikers in the summer. There isn't much of a town per se, but the Bolton Valley Resort is always bustling with activity.

Dining and Lodging

$$$ ✕🏨 **Bolton Valley Resort.** Like the ski area, this self-contained resort is geared to families. Hotel units are ski-in, ski-out, and have either a fireplace or a kitchenette; condominium units have as many as four bedrooms. Children under 6 ski and stay free. Ask about ski packages. ⌧ *Mountain Rd., 05477,* ☎ *802/434–2131 or 800/451–3220,* ℻

804/434–4547. 143 rooms with bath. 7 restaurants, deli, pub, indoor and outdoor pools, sauna, 9 tennis courts, health club. AE, D, DC, MC, V.

$–$$ ✕▣ **Black Bear Inn.** Within the walls of this mountaintop country inn
★ are 24 guest rooms; each has a quilt made by the innkeeper, in-room movies (a different one each night), and—you guessed it—bears! Be sure to ask for a room with a balcony, many of which overlook the Green Mountains and ski trails. ⊠ *Mountain Rd., 05477,* ☎ *802/434– 2126 or 800/395–6335,* ℻ *802/434–5761. 24 rooms with bath. Restaurant, pool. MC, V.*

Nightlife

Bolton Valley Resort's **James Moore Tavern** (☎ 802/434–2131) has live entertainment.

Skiing

Bolton Valley Resort. Although some skiers come for the day, most people who visit this resort stay at one of the hotels or condominium complexes at the base of the mountain. Because of this proximity and the relatively gentle skiing, Bolton attracts more beginners and family groups than singles. The mood is easygoing, the dress and atmosphere casual; there is a ski shop, a country store, deli, post office, eight restaurants and lounges, sports club, and meeting and convention space. ⊠ *Box 300, Bolton 05477,* ☎ *802/434–2131, lodging 800/451– 3220, condos 800/451–5025.*

DOWNHILL

Many of the 48 interconnecting trails on Bolton's two mountains, each with a vertical drop of 1,625 feet, are rated intermediate and novice. However, some 23% is expert terrain. In fact, as a note of credibility, the DesLauriers brothers of Warren Miller–movie fame ski and work here. Timberline Peak trail network, with a vertical of 1,000 feet, is where you'll find some of the wider slopes and more challenging terrain. Serving these trails are one quad chair, four doubles, and one surface lift—enough to prevent long lift lines on all but the most crowded days. Top-to-bottom trails are lit for night skiing 4–10 PM every evening except Sunday. Bolton also has a halfpipe, snowboard park, and 70% snowmaking coverage.

CROSS-COUNTRY

Bolton Valley, with its more than 100 kilometers (62 miles) of cross-country trails, 20 kilometers (12 miles) of which are machine tracked, is a favorite of Vermonters. Lessons and rentals (including telemark) are available.

OTHER ACTIVITIES

The sports center has an indoor pool, whirlpool, sauna, one indoor tennis court, and an exercise room. Weekly events and activities include sleigh rides and races.

CHILD CARE

The child care center has supervised play and games, indoors and outdoors, for infants and children up to 6 years old. Child care is also available three nights per week. For children who want to learn to ski, there are programs for ages 5–15.

Stowe

★ ③①   *8 mi north of Waterbury, 22 mi northwest of Montpelier, 36 mi northeast of Burlington.*

To many, Stowe rings a bell as the place the von Trapp family, of *Sound of Music* fame, chose to settle after fleeing Austria. Set amid acres of pastures that fall away dramatically and allow for wide-angle panoramas of the mountains beyond, the **Trapp Family Lodge** (⊠ Luce Hill Rd., ☎ 802/253–8511) is the site of a popular outdoor music series in summer and an extensive cross-country ski trail network in winter.

For more than a century the history of Stowe has been determined by the town's proximity to **Mt. Mansfield,** the highest elevation in the state. As early as 1858, visitors were trooping to the area to view the mountain whose shape suggests the profile of the face of a man lying on his back. If hiking to the top isn't your idea of a good time, in summer you can take the 4½-mile **toll road** to the top for a short scenic walk and a magnificent view. ⊠ *Mountain Rd., 7 mi from Rte. 100,* ☎ *802/253–3000.* ⊇ *$12.* ☉ *Late May–early Oct., daily 10–5.*

An alternative means of reaching Mt. Mansfield's upper reaches is the eight-seat **gondola** that shuttles continuously up to the area of "the Chin," which has a small restaurant (dinner reservations required). ⊠ *Mountain Rd., 8 mi from Rte. 100,* ☎ *802/253–3000 or 800/253–4754.* ⊇ *$9.* ☉ *June–early Oct., daily 10–5; Dec.–Apr., daily 8:30–4 for skiers; Oct.–Nov. and May, weekends 10–5.*

When you tire of shopping on Stowe's Main Street and on Mountain Road (most easily accomplished by car), head for the town's **recreational path** that begins behind the Community Church in the center of town and meanders for 5⅓ miles along the river valley. There are many entry points along the way; whether you're on foot, ski, bike, or in-line skates, it's a tranquil means of enjoying the outdoors.

Dining and Lodging

$$ ✕ **Foxfire Inn.** A restored Colonial building might seem an unusual place in which to find such superb Italian delicacies as veal rollatini, steak saltimbocca, and *tartufo* (vanilla and chocolate gelato in a chocolate cup with a raspberry center). However, this old farmhouse a couple of miles north of Stowe proper blends the two well, and its popularity with locals proves it's worth the short drive. ⊠ *Rte. 100,* ☎ *802/253–4887. AE, D, MC, V.*

$$ ✕ **Villa Tragara.** A farmhouse has been carved into intimate dining nooks
★ where romance reigns over such specialties as ravioli filled with four cheeses and served with a half-tomato, half-cream sauce. The tasting menu is a five-course dinner for $35 (plus $15 for coordinating wines). ⊠ *Rte. 100, south of Stowe,* ☎ *802/244–5288. AE, MC, V.*

$$$–$$$$ ✕⊞ **Topnotch at Stowe.** This resort, built in the 1970s, just 3 miles from the base of the mountain, is one of the state's most posh. Floor-to-ceiling windows, a freestanding circular stone fireplace, and cathedral ceilings make the lobby an imposing setting. Rooms have thick rust-color carpeting, a small shelf of books, and perhaps a barn-board wall or an Italian print. ⊠ *Mountain Rd., 05672,* ☎ *802/253–8585 or 800/451–8686,* 𝔽𝔸𝕏 *802/253–9263. 92 rooms with bath, 14 2–3 bedroom town homes, 8 suites. 2 restaurants, bar, indoor and outdoor pools, 14 tennis courts, health club, horseback riding, cross-country skiing, sleigh rides. AE, D, MC, V.*

$$$ ✕⊞ **Edson Hill Manor.** This French Canadian–style manor built in 1940 sits atop 225 acres of rolling hills. Oriental rugs accent the dark wide-board floors and a tapestry complements the rich, burgundy-patterned sofas that face the huge stone fireplace in the living room. The comfortable guest rooms are pine paneled, and have fireplaces, canopy beds, and down comforters. The dining room is really the heart of the place: The walls of windows allowing contemplation of the inspiring view compete for diners' attention with paintings of wildflowers, an ivy-covered stone arch, and vines climbing to the ceiling. The highly

designed, sculpted food is coined "eclectic American" and is served on handpainted plates. ⊠ *1500 Edson Hill Rd., 05672,* ☎ *802/253–7371 or 800/621–0284,* FAX *802/253–4036. 25 rooms with bath. Restaurant (no lunch; closed Sun.–Thurs. in Apr. and May), pool, hiking, cross-country skiing, horseback riding. Full breakfast included; MAP available. AE, D, MC, V.*

$$ ✕⌷ **The Gables Inn.** The converted farmhouse is a rabbit warren of charming, antiques-filled rooms. The four rooms in the carriage house have cathedral ceilings, fireplaces, TVs, and whirlpool tubs. There is a porch with comfortable chairs on which you can enjoy the view of Mt. Mansfield. The tiny plant-filled sunroom is perfect for lazy mornings, and the generous breakfasts are legendary. ⊠ *Mountain Rd., 05672,* ☎ *802/253–7730 or 800/422–5371,* FAX *802/253–8989. 17 rooms with bath, 2 suites. Dining room, pool, hot tub. Full breakfast included; MAP available. AE, D, MC, V.*

$$ ⌷ **The Inn at the Brass Lantern.** Home-baked cookies in the afternoon, a basket of logs by your fireplace, and stenciled hearts along the wainscoting reflect the care taken in turning this 18th-century farmhouse into a place of welcome. You'll find no pretentions here. All rooms have quilts and country antiques; most are oversize and some have fireplaces and whirlpool tubs. And although the inn (really a B&B) is precariously close to the Grand Union supermarket next door, the breakfast room (and some guest rooms) has a terrific view of Mt. Mansfield. ⊠ *Rte. 100, ½ mi north of Stowe, 05672,* ☎ *802/253–2229 or 800/729–2980,* FAX *802/253–7425. 9 rooms with bath. Breakfast room. AE, MC, V.*

Nightlife and the Arts

NIGHTLIFE

The **Matterhorn Night Club** (☎ 802/253–8198) has live music and dancing; **BK Clark's** (☎ 802/253–9300) also has live music. Other options include the lounges at **Topnotch at Stowe** (☎ 802/253–8585), for live weekend entertainment, and the less-expensive **Stoweflake Inn** (☎ 802/253–7355).

THE ARTS

Stowe Performing Arts (☎ 802/253–7792) sponsors a series of classical and jazz concerts during July in the Trapp Family Concert meadow. **Stowe Stage Co.** (⊠ Stowe Playhouse, Mountain Rd., ☎ 802/253–7944) performs musical comedy in July and August.

Outdoor Activities and Sports

BIKING

The junction of Routes 100 and 108 is the start of a 21-mile tour with scenic views of Mt. Mansfield; the course takes you along Route 100 to Stagecoach Road, to Morristown, over to Morrisville, and south on Randolph Road. The **Mountain Bike Shop** (⊠ Mountain Rd., ☎ 802/253–7919) supplies equipment and offers guided tours.

CANOEING

Umiak Outdoor Outfitters (⊠ 849 S. Main St., ☎ 802/253–2317) specializes in canoes and kayaks and rents them for day trips; they also lead guided overnight excursions.

FISHING

The **Fly Rod Shop** (⊠ Rte. 100, 3 mi south of Stowe, ☎ 802/253–7346) rents and sells equipment.

HIKING

For the climb to **Stowe Pinnacle,** go 1½ miles south of Stowe on Route 100 and turn east on Gold Brook Road opposite the Nichols Farm Lodge; turn left at the first intersection, continue straight at an intersection by a covered bridge, turn right after 1.8 miles, and travel 2.3 miles to a parking lot on the left. The trail crosses an abandoned pasture and takes a short, steep climb to views of the Green Mountains and Stowe Valley (2 hrs).

ICE SKATING

Jackson Arena (☎ 802/253–6148) is a public ice-skating rink that rents skates.

SLEIGH RIDES

Charlie Horse Carriage and Sleigh Rides (☎ 802/253–2215) is open daily 11–4; evening group rides are by reservation.

TENNIS

The **Stowe Area Association** (☎ 802/253–7321), which hosts a grand prix tennis tournament in early August, can recommend nearby public courts.

Shopping

The **Mountain Road** is lined with shops from town up toward the ski area.

BOOKS

Bear Pond Books (⊠ Main St., ☎ 802/253–8236) is an inviting store with a comfy browsing area. There is a large selection of Vermont and regional books.

CRAFTS

Vermont Rug Makers (⊠ Main St., ☎ 802/253–6288) weaves imaginative rugs and tapestries from fabrics, wools, and exotic materials; custom orders are a specialty.

Skiing

Stowe Mountain Resort. To be precise, the name of the village is Stowe and the name of the mountain is Mt. Mansfield, but to generations of skiers, the area, the complex, and the region are just plain Stowe. The resort is a classic that dates to the 1930s, when the sport of skiing was a pup. Even today the area's mystique attracts more serious skiers than social skiers. In recent years, on-mountain lodging, improved snowmaking, new lifts, and free shuttle buses that gather skiers from lodges, inns, and motels along the Mountain Road, have added convenience to the Stowe experience. Yet the traditions remain: the Winter Carnival in January, the Sugar Slalom in April, ski weeks all winter. So committed is the ski school to improvements that even noninstruction package plans include one free ski lesson. Three base lodges provide plenty of essentials, including two on-mountain restaurants. ⊠ *5781 Mountain Rd., Stowe 05672,* ☎ *802/253–3000, lodging 800/253–4754, snow conditions 802/253–3600.*

DOWNHILL

Mt. Mansfield, with a vertical drop of 2,360 feet, is one of the giants among Eastern ski mountains. It was the only area in the East featured in Warren Miller's 1995 film, *Endless Winter.* Its symmetrical shape allows skiers of all abilities long, satisfying runs from the summit. The famous Front Four runs (National, Liftline, Starr, and Goat) are the intimidating centerpieces for tough, expert runs, yet there is plenty of mellow intermediate skiing and one long beginner trail from the top that ends at the Toll House, where there is easier terrain. Mansfield's satellite sector is a network of intermediate and one expert trail off a basin served by a gondola. Spruce Peak, separate from the main mountain, is a teaching hill and a pleasant experience for intermediates and beginners. In addition to the new high-speed, eight-passenger gondola, Stowe has one quad, one triple, and six double chairlifts, plus one handle tow and poma, to service its 45 trails. Night skiing has been added on a trial basis; trails are accessed by the gondola. The resort has 73% snowmaking coverage.

CROSS-COUNTRY

The resort has 35 kilometers (22 miles) of groomed cross-country trails and 40 kilometers (25 miles) of back-country trails. There are four interconnecting cross-country ski areas with more than 150 kilometers (93 miles) of groomed trails within the town of Stowe.

CHILD CARE

The child care center takes children ages 2 months through 12 years. Children's Adventure Center on nonthreatening Spruce Peak is headquarters for all children's programs, ages 3–12. Extremely Teen is a program for ages 13–16.

En Route Northwest of Stowe is an exciting and scenic, although indirect, route to Burlington: **Smugglers' Notch,** the narrow pass between Mt. Mansfield and Madonna Peak that is said to have sheltered 18th-century outlaws in its rugged, bouldered terrain. Weaving around the huge stones that shoulder the road, you'd hardly know you're on state highway Route 108. There are parking spots and picnic tables at the top. The notch road is closed in winter.

The junction of Routes 15 and 108 presents some intriguing choices: Head east on Route 15 for a pleasant antiques-store-dotted drive through the towns of Johnson (home of Johnson Woolen Mills) and Morrisville and loop back toward Stowe; continue farther east on Route 15, turning north 4 miles outside of Morrisville toward Craftsbury Common or north on Route 126 in Hardwick toward Greensboro, two idyllic towns with long histories as vacation destinations; or turn west in Jeffersonville on Route 15 toward Burlington and attractions to the southwest.

Craftsbury Common

③② *27 mi northeast of Stowe.*

Craftsbury Common is a picturesque village perched on a hill. It has the requisite large town green surrounded by crisp white buildings.

Dining and Lodging

$$–$$$ ✕⚏ **Craftsbury Inn.** Just down the road from Craftsbury Common's traditional New England green, this 1850 Greek Revival country inn with a two-tiered porch is a well-situated base for outdoor enthusiasts and those in search of real respite. Antiques, Oriental rugs, leaded floor-to-ceiling windows, and dark blue and mauve accents create a warm ambience; two bird's eye maple hutches, gleaming pine floors, and embossed tin ceilings embellish the sitting rooms. Guest rooms have custom-made quilts and either brass, iron, or canopy beds. The wood-burning stove, bright yellow wallpaper, and picture windows in the dining room herald the inn's exceptional fare, which includes butternut-squash-and-apple soup, poached salmon with cucumber caper sauce, and rack of lamb with Roquefort sauce. ⊠ *Main St., 05826,* ☎ *802/586–2848 or 800/336–2848. 10 rooms, 6 with bath. Restaurant (closed Mon., Tues.), bar, cross-country skiing. Full breakfast included; MAP available. MC, V.*

Greensboro

③③ *10 mi southeast of Craftsbury Common.*

Greensboro is an idyllic small town with a long history as a vacation destination.

Wiley's Store (⊠ Main St., ☎ 802/533–2621), with wooden floors and tin ceilings that boast of its old-time authenticity, warrants attentive exploration; you never know what you might find in this packed-to-the-rafters emporium.

Dining and Lodging

$$$–$$$$ ×⊞ **Highland Lodge.** Tranquility defined: An 1860 house that over-looks a pristine lake, with 120 acres of rambling woods and pastures laced with hiking and skiing trails (ski rental available). Widely touted as having one of the best front porches in the state, this quiet family resort is part refined elegance, of the preppy New England sort, and part casual country, of the summer camp sort. Comfortable guest rooms have Victorian-style furnishings and most have views of the lake; cottages are more private, simply furnished, and great for families. The dinner menu is fairly traditional and might include entrées such as roasted Vermont leg of lamb and grilled Black Angus sirloin. ⊠ *Caspian Lake, 05841,* ☎ *802/533–2647,* ℻ *802/533–7494. 11 rooms with bath, 11 cottages. Restaurant, lake, tennis court, hiking, boating, cross-country skiing, recreation room. MAP. D, MC, V. Closed mid-Mar.–late May, mid-Oct.–mid-Dec.*

Jeffersonville

③④ *18 mi north of Stowe, 28 mi northeast of Burlington.*

Jeffersonville's activities are closely linked with those of Smuggler's Notch Ski Resort.

Dining and Lodging

$$$$ × **Le Cheval D'Or.** Easily one of the most renowned restaurants in the state, this institution carries the requisite attitude that goes along with such a reputation. A world-famous chef, incredible classic French cuisine, elegant atmosphere, and jackets, please! ⊠ *Main St. (Box 426),* ☎ *802/644–5556. Reservations essential. Jacket and tie. AE, D, MC, V. Closed Wed.*

$$$–$$$$ ×⊞ **Smugglers' Notch Resort.** This large year-round resort has con-temporarily furnished condos, most with fireplaces and decks. Rates include lift tickets and ski lessons. ⊠ *Rte. 108, 05464,* ☎ *802/644–8851 or 800/451–8752,* ℻ *802/644–1230. 375 condos. 3 restaurants, bar, indoor pool, hot tub, sauna, 10 tennis courts, exercise room, baby-sitting, ice-skating, recreation room, children's programs, nursery, playground. AE, DC, MC, V.*

$$ ⊞ **The Highlander Motel.** Although most of the rooms are motel-style, the Highlander also has three inn-style, antiques-filled units that have views of the mountain. No matter what configuration you choose, you won't be far from Smugglers' Village, 2½ miles away. You can enjoy breakfast by the fire. ⊠ *Rte. 108 S, 05464,* ☎ *802/644–2725 or 800/367–6471,* ℻ *802/644–2725. 15 rooms with bath. Restaurant (breakfast only), recreation room. MC, V.*

Nightlife

In the Smugglers' area, most après-ski action centers around the afternoon bonfires and nightly live entertainment in the **Meeting House** (☎ 802/644–8851) or **Smugglers' Lounge** (⊠ Village Restaurant, ☎ 802/644–2291). Sleigh rides, fireworks, and torch-light parades occur twice weekly.

Shopping

ANTIQUES

The Buggy Man (⊠ Rte. 15, 7 mi east of Jeffersonville, ☎ 802/635–2110) and **Mel Siegel** (⊠ Rte. 15, 7 mi east of Jeffersonville, ☎ 802/635–7838) both have affordable, quality antiques.

CLOTHING

Johnson Woolen Mills (⊠ Main St., Johnson, 9 mi east of Jefferson-ville, ☎ 802/635–2271) is an authentic factory store with great deals on woolen blankets, yardgoods, and the famous Johnson outerwear.

CRAFTS

Vermont Rug Makers (⊠ Route 100C, East Johnson, 10 mi east of Jeffersonville, ☎ 802/635–2434) weaves imaginative rugs and tapestries from fabrics, wools, and exotic materials; custom orders are a specialty. **By Vermont Hands** (⊠ Rte. 15, Johnson, 8 mi east of Jeffersonville, ☎ 802/635–7664) displays furniture, pottery, jewelry, rugs, quilts, and other works by more than 90 Vermont artisans in a farmhouse that dates back to the late 1700s.

Skiing

Smugglers' Notch Resort. Most everything you might need is at the base of the lifts. Most skiers stay at the resort. Smugglers' has long been respected for its family programs and, therefore, attracts such clientele. The Family Snowmaking Learning Center, opened in 1995 on the Meadowlark trail, shows skiers the processes of state-of-the-art computer-controlled snowmaking and teaches them about weather and snow crystals. ⊠ *Smugglers' Notch 05464,* ☎ *802/644–8851 or 800/451–8752.*

DOWNHILL

Smugglers' has three mountains. The highest, Madonna, with a verti-cal drop of 2,610 feet, is in the center and connects with a trail net-work to Sterling (1,500-foot vertical). The third mountain, Morse (1,150-foot vertical), is more remote, but you can visit all three with-out removing your skis. The wild, craggy landscape lends a pristine, wilderness feel to the skiing. The tops of each of the mountains have expert terrain—a couple of double black diamonds make Madonna memorable—while intermediate trails fill the lower sections. Morse spe-cializes in beginner trails. The 56 trails are served by five double chair-lifts, including the Mogul Mouse Magic Lift, and one surface lift. There is now top-to-bottom snowmaking on all three mountains, al-lowing for 61% coverage.

CROSS-COUNTRY

The area has 37 groomed and tracked kilometers (23 miles) of cross-country trails.

OTHER ACTIVITIES

Management committed itself to developing an activities center long be-fore the concept was adopted by other ski resorts. The self-contained village has ice-skating, sleigh rides, and horseback riding. Vermont Horse Park (☎ 802/644–5347) also offers rides on authentic horse-drawn sleighs. For indoor sports, there are hot tubs, tennis courts, and a pool.

CHILD CARE

The child care center is a spacious facility that takes children from 6 weeks through 6 years old. Children ages 3–17 have ski camps that have instruction, and movies, games, and story-time for the little ones.

Burlington

★ ③ *76 mi south of Montreal, 393 mi north of New York City, 223 mi northwest of Boston.*

Vermont's largest population center, Burlington was recently named one of the country's "Dream Towns" by *Outside* magazine. A criterion was where you can find it all: a real job, a real life, and the big outdoors. It seems many agree with this characterization: The city is growing rapidly as housing complexes now heavily outnumber family farms. Burlington was founded in 1763 and had a long history as a trade center following the growth of shipping on Lake Champlain in the 19th century. More recently, energized by the roughly 20,000 students from the area's five colleges, including the University of Vermont, and an abundance of culture-hungry, transplanted urban dwellers, Burlington draws an eclectic element. It was for years the only city in America with a socialist mayor—now the nation's sole socialist congressional representative. The **Church Street Marketplace**—a pedestrian mall of funky shops, intriguing boutiques, and an appealing menagerie of sidewalk cafés, food and crafts vendors, and street performers—is an animated downtown focal point. Burlington's festive town center is where most people in central and northern Vermont are drawn at least occasionally to do errands or see a show.

Crouched on the shores of Lake Champlain, which shimmers in the shadows of the Adirondacks to the west, Burlington's revitalized **waterfront** teems with outdoor enthusiasts in summer who stroll along its recreation path and ply the waters in sailboats and motorcraft. A replica of an old Champlain paddlewheeler, *The Spirit of Ethan Allen,* takes people on narrated cruises on the lake and, in the evening, dinner and moonlight dance sailings that drift by the Adirondacks and the Green Mountains. ✉ *Burlington Boat House,* ☎ *802/862–9685.* 🎫 *$8.* ☉ *Cruises June–mid-Oct., daily 10–9.*

Part of the waterfront's revitalization and still a work-in-progress, the ☙ **Lake Champlain Basin Science Center** is in the perfect location to fulfill its mission to educate the public about the ecology, history, and culture of the lake region. The hands-on focus of the Secrets of the Lake exhibit will have you looking eye to eye with a turtle, touching fossils, learning how and why a fish moves, and seeing the direct influence on the lake of non-native species such as the zebra mussel. From looking at plankton through a "kidscope" to dragging a net off UVM's research boat docked on the property, there are activities here for the whole family. ✉ *One College St.,* ☎ *802/864–1848.* 🎫 *$2.* ☉ *Memorial Day–Labor Day, daily 11–5; fall and winter, weekends and school vacations 11–4.*

NEED A BREAK?
Stop by **Uncommon Grounds** (✉ 42 Church St.) for a cup o' joe and biscotti and to look at the rotating art exhibits.

Ethan Allen, Vermont's famous early settler, is a figure of some mystery. The visitor center at the **Ethan Allen Homestead** by the Winooski River answers questions about his flamboyant life and raises some you may not have thought of. The house, about 70% original, has such frontier hallmarks as nails pointing through the roof on the top floor, rough saw-cut boards, and an open hearth for cooking. ✉ *North Ave., off Rte. 127, north of Burlington,* ☎ *802/865–4556.* 🎫 *$3.50.* ☉ *Mid-May–mid-June, Tues.–Sun. 1–5; mid-June–Oct. 19, Mon.–Sat. 10–5, Sun. 1–5.*

A few miles south of Burlington, the Champlain Valley gives way to fertile farmland, affording chin-dropping views of the rugged Adirondacks across the lake. Five miles from the city, one could trace all New
★ England history simply by wandering the 45 acres of the **Shelburne Museum,** whose 37 buildings seem an anthology of individual museums. The large collection of Americana contains 18th- and 19th-century period homes and furniture, fine and folk art, farm tools, more than 200 carriages and sleighs, Audubon prints, even a private railroad car from the days of steam. And an old-fashioned jail. And an assortment of duck decoys. And an old stone cottage. And a display of early toys. And the *Ticonderoga,* an old sidewheel steamship, curiously misplaced, grounded amid lawn and trees. ⊠ *Rte. 7, 5 mi south of Burlington,* ☎ *802/985–3346.* ⊑ *$17.50 (2 consecutive days).* ☉ *Mid-May–mid-Oct., daily 10–5; call ahead for limited winter hrs.*

★ ☙ **Shelburne Farms** has a history of improving the farmer's lot by developing new agricultural methods. Founded in the 1880s as a private estate, the 1,400-acre property is now an educational and cultural resource center. Here you can see a working dairy farm, milk a cow and get up close to many other farm animals at the Children's Farmyard, listen to nature lectures, or simply stroll the immaculate grounds on a scenic stretch of Lake Champlain waterfront. The original landscaping, designed by Frederick Law Olmsted, the creator of Central Park and Boston's Emerald Necklace, gently channels the eye to expansive vistas and aesthetically satisfying views of such buildings as the five-story, 2-acre Farm Barn. ⊠ *West of Rte. 7 at the junction of Harbor and Bay Rds., 6 mi south of Burlington,* ☎ *802/985–8686.* ⊑ *$6.50.* ☉ *Visitor center and shop daily 9:30–5; tours Memorial Day–mid-Oct., last tour at 3:30.*

☙ A multi-colored silo jutting out of a building marks the **Vermont Teddy Bear Company.** Another example of the success of Vermont-made products, Vermont Teddy Bear is out to make fun in addition to bears. On their tour you'll hear more bear puns than you ever thought possible while learning how a few homemade bears, sold from a cart on Church Street, has turned into a multi-million-dollar business. In summer, there is a children's play tent set up outdoors, and you can wander the beautiful 57-acre property. ⊠ *2236 Shelburne Rd., Shelburne,* ☎ *802/985–3001,* ⊑ *Tour $1.* ☉ *Tours Mon.–Sat. 10–4, Sun. 11–4; store Mon.–Sat. 9–6, Sun. 10–5.*

At the 6-acre **Vermont Wildflower Farm,** the display along the flowering pathways changes constantly: violets in the spring, daisies and black-eyed Susans for summer, and fall colors that rival the trees' foliage. You can buy wildflower seeds, crafts, and books here. ⊠ *Rte. 7, 5 mi south of the Shelburne Museum,* ☎ *802/425–3500.* ⊑ *$3.* ☉ *Early May–late Oct., daily 10–5.*

OFF THE BEATEN PATH **GREEN MOUNTAIN AUDUBON NATURE CENTER –** Bursting with great things to do, see, and learn, this is a wonderful place to orient yourself to Vermont's outdoor wonders. The center's 300 acres of diverse habitats are a sanctuary for all things wild, and the 5 miles of trails beg you to explore and understand the workings of differing natural communities. The center offers such events as dusk walks, wildflower and birding rambles, nature workshops, and educational activities for both kids and adults. ⊠ *18 mi southeast of Burlington, Huntington-Richmond Rd., Richmond,* ☎ *802/434-3068.* ⊑ *Donations accepted.* ☉ *Grounds dawn–dusk; center weekdays 8–4:30.*

LAKE CHAMPLAIN ISLANDS – Samuel de Champlain's claim on the islands dotting the northern expanses of Lake Champlain is represented on Isle La Motte by a granite statue that looks south toward the site of the first French settlement and its shrine to St. Anne. Today the Lake Champlain Islands are a center of water recreation in summer, and ice fishing in winter. North of Burlington, the scenic drive through the islands on Route 2 begins at I–89 and travels north through South Hero, Grand Isle, and Isle La Motte to Alburg Center, 5 miles from the Canadian border. Here Route 78 will take you east to the mainland.

MISSISQUOI NATIONAL WILDLIFE REFUGE – The 5,800 acres of federally protected wetlands, meadows, and woods provide a beautiful setting for bird-watching, canoeing, or walking nature trails. ⊠ *Swanton, 36 mi north of Burlington,* ☎ *802/868–4781.*

Dining and Lodging

$$–$$$ ✕ **Isabel's.** In part of an old lumber mill, this eclectic, inspired American-cuisine restaurant notable for its artful presentation has high ceilings, exposed-brick walls, and knockout views spanning west from its Lake Champlain frontage. The menu changes weekly and has included salmon stuffed with spinach and feta wrapped in a phyllo pastry with béchamel sauce, and lamb loin with basil walnut pesto. Lunch and weekend brunch are popular; outdoor patio dining beckons on warm days. ⊠ *112 Lake St.,* ☎ *802/865–2522. AE, DC, MC, V. No dinner Mon., Tues.*

$$ ✕ **The Daily Planet.** Contemporary plaid oilcloth, an old jukebox playing Aretha Franklin, a solarium, and a turn-of-the-century bar add up to one of Burlington's hippest restaurants. This is Marco Polo cuisine—basically Mediterranean with Oriental influences: lobster risotto with peas, braised lamb loin with polenta and chutney, various stir-fries. ⊠ *15 Center St.,* ☎ *802/862–9647. AE, DC, MC, V.*

$–$$ ✕ **Sweet Tomatoes.** The wood-fired oven of this bright and boisterous trattoria sends off a mouth-watering aroma. With hand-painted ceramic pitchers, bottles of dark olive oil perched against a backdrop of exposed brick, and crusty, bull-headed bread that comes with a bowl of oil and garlic for dunking, this soulful eatery beckons you to Italy's countryside. The selections on the extensive, exclusively Italian wine list have been thoroughly tested—vineside—by the owners. The menu includes *caponata* (roasted eggplant with onions, capers, olives, parsley, celery, and tomatoes), *cavatappi* (pasta with roasted chicken and sautéed mushrooms, peas, and walnuts in a pecorino-Romano-carbonara sauce), and an extensive selection of pizzas. ⊠ *83 Church St.,* ☎ *802/660–9533. MC, V.*

$$$–$$$$ ✕▥ **The Inn at Shelburne Farms.** This is storybook land: Built at the turn of the century as the home of William Seward and Lila Vanderbilt Webb, the Tudor-style inn perches on Saxton's Point overlooking Lake Champlain, the distant Adirondacks, and the sea of pastures that make up this 1,000-acre working farm. Each guest room is different, from the wallpaper to the period antiques. The two dining rooms define elegance. A seasonal menu includes home-grown products that might include loin of pork with an apple-cider–sundried-cranberry chutney, or rack of lamb with spinach-and-roasted-garlic pesto. The inn's profits help support the farm's environmental education programs for local schools. ⊠ *Harbor Rd., Shelburne 05482,* ☎ *802/985–8498,* ℻ *802/985–8123. 24 rooms, 17 with bath. Restaurant, lake, tennis courts, hiking, boating, fishing, recreation room. AE, DC, MC, V. Closed mid-Oct.–mid-May.*

$$$ ✕⊞ **Inn at Essex.** This Georgian-style hotel that sits back from the suburban sprawl encircling Burlington—about 10 miles from downtown—is a state-of-the-art conference center dressed in country-inn clothing. Attentive staff, rooms with flowered wallpaper, and library books on the reproduction desks lend character. The two restaurants—the refined Butler's and the more casual Birchtree Cafe—are run by the New England Culinary Institute. Students are coached by an executive chef and rotate through each position, from sous-chef to waiter—these are great chefs in the making. The updated New England style shows off sweet dumpling squash with ginger-garlic basmati rice, and lobster in yellow corn sauce with spinach pasta at Butler's; chicken potpie and seafood stew with saffron risotto in the café. ⊠ *70 Essex Way, off Rte. 15, Essex Junction 05452,* ☏ *802/878–1100 or 800/288–7613,* FAX *802/878–0063. 97 rooms with bath. 2 restaurants, pool, library. AE, D, DC, MC, V.*

$$$ ✕⊞ **Radisson Hotel–Burlington.** This sleek corporate giant is the hotel closest to downtown shopping, and it faces the lakefront. Odd-numbered rooms have an incredible view of the Adirondack Mountains. The hotel's restaurant serves traditional, yet inspired, Continental fare. ⊠ *60 Battery St., 05401,* ☏ *802/658–6500 or 800/333–3333,* FAX *802/658–4659. 255 rooms with bath. Restaurant, bar, indoor pool, exercise room, airport shuttle. AE, D, DC, MC, V.*

Nightlife and the Arts

NIGHTLIFE

Vermont Pub and Brewery (⊠ College and St. Paul Sts., ☏ 802/865–0500) makes its own beer and fruit seltzers and is arguably the most popular spot in town. It serves lunch and dinner, and folk musicians play here regularly. **Last Elm Cafe** (⊠ N. Winooski Ave., no phone), a good old-fashioned coffeehouse, is a good bet for folk music. **Club Metronome** (⊠ 188 Main St., ☏ 802/865–4563) stages an eclectic musical mix that ranges from the newest in cutting edge to funk, blues, reggae, and the occasional big name. **Nectar's** (⊠ 188 Main St., ☏ 802/658–4771) is always jumping to the sounds of local bands.

THE ARTS

Flynn Theatre for the Performing Arts, a grandiose old structure, is the cultural heart of Burlington; it schedules the Vermont Symphony Orchestra, theater, dance, big-name musicians, and lectures. ⊠ *153 Main St.,* ☏ *802/863–8778 for information, 802/863–5966 for tickets.*

Burlington City Arts (☏ 802/865–7166 or 802/865–9163 for 24-hr Artsline) is a wealth of up-to-date information on anything arts-related in the city.

Vermont Symphony Orchestra (☏ 802/864–5741) performs at the Flynn Theatre in winter and outdoors at Shelburne Farms in summer. The **UVM Lane Series** (☏ 802/656–4455 for programs and times, 802/656–3085 for box office) sponsors classical as well as folk music concerts in the Flynn Theatre, Ira Allen Chapel, and the UVM Recital Hall.

St. Michael's Playhouse (☏ 802/654–2281) is the state's old equity theater company. The **Lyric Theater** (☏ 802/658–1484) puts on musical productions year-round.

Outdoor Activities and Sports

BIKING

A recreational path runs 9 miles along Burlington's waterfront. South of Burlington, a moderately easy 18½-mile trail begins at the blinker on Rte. 7, Shelburne, and follows Mt. Philo Road, Hinesburg Road, Route 116, and Irish Hill Road. **Earl's** (⊠ 135 Main St., ☏ 802/862–

4203) and **North Star Cyclery** (✉ 100 Main St., ☎ 802/863–3832) rent equipment and provide maps.

Marina services are available north and south of Burlington. **Malletts Bay Marina** (228 Lakeshore Dr., Colchester, ☎ 802/862–4077) and **Point Bay Marina** (✉ Thompson's Point, Charlotte, ☎ 802/425–2431) both provide full service and repairs.

Sailworks (✉ 189 Battery St., ☎ 802/864–0111) sells marine outerwear and gives windsurfing lessons at Sand Bar State Park in summer. **Burlington Community Boathouse** (✉ Foot of College St., Burlington Harbor, ☎ 802/865–3377) has sailboard and boat rentals (some captained) and lessons. **Chiott Marine** (✉ 67 Main St., ☎ 802/862–8383) caters to all realms of water sports with two floors of hardware, apparel, and accessories. **Marble Island Resort** (✉ Colchester, ☎ 802/864–6800) rents sailboats, canoes, paddle boats, and aquacycles from April through June.

Shopping

Architectural Salvage Warehouse (✉ 212 Battery St., ☎ 802/658–5011) has clawfoot tubs, stained-glass windows, mantels, andirons, and the like. The large rhinoceros head bursting out of the **Conant Custom Brass** (✉ 270 Pine St., ☎ 802/658–4482) storefront will lure you in to see the custom work; the store specializes in decorative lighting and bathroom fixtures. There is also a smattering of antique collectibles.

Chassman & Bem Booksellers (✉ 1 Church St., ☎ 802/862–4332), probably the best bookstore in Vermont, has more than 40,000 titles, with a discriminating selection of children's books and a large magazine rack.

April Cornell (✉ 97 Church St., ☎ 802/862–8211) carries a fun collection of casual yet indulgent women's clothing; it also sells rich, hand-dyed linens and colorful stoneware. **Vermont Trading Company** (✉ 66 Church St., ☎ 802/864–3633) has natural-fiber clothing and funky accessories.

At the **Shelburne Country Store** (✉ Village Green, Shelburne, ☎ 802/985–3657), step back in time as you walk past the potbellied stove and take in the aroma emanating from the fudge neatly piled behind huge antique glass cases. Candles, weather vanes, glassware, and Vermont food products are its specialties.

Bennington Potters North (✉ 127 College St., ☎ 802/863–2221) has, in addition to its popular pottery, interesting gifts, glassware, furniture, and other housewares. **Vermont State Craft Center** (✉ 85 Church St., ☎ 802/863–6458) is an elegant gallery displaying contemporary and traditional crafts by more than 200 Vermont artisans. **Yankee Pride** (✉ Champlain Mill, Winooski, ☎ 802/655–0500) has a large inventory of quilting fabrics and supplies as well as Vermont-made quilts.

Church Street Marketplace (✉ Main St.–Pearl St., ☎ 802/863–1648), a pedestrian thoroughfare, is lined with boutiques, cafés, and street vendors. **Burlington Square Mall** (✉ Church St.) has Porteous (the city's major department store) and some 50 shops. **The Champlain Mill** (✉ Rte. 2/7, northeast of Burlington, ☎ 802/655–9477), a former woolen mill on the banks of the Winooski River, has three floors of stores. Built to resemble a ship, the funky **Wing Building** (⊠ Next to ferry dock on waterfront) houses several boutiques, a café, and an art gallery.

En Route The top of the mountain pass on Route 242 in Montgomery Center and the Jay Peak area affords vast views of Canada to the north and of Vermont's rugged Northeast Kingdom to the east.

Montgomery/Jay

③⑥ *51 mi northeast of Burlington.*

Montgomery is a small village near Jay Peak ski resort.

Dining and Lodging

$$–$$$ ✕⊞ **The Black Lantern.** Built in 1803 as a hotel for mill workers, the inn has been providing bed and board ever since. Though the feeling is country, little touches of sophistication abound: Provençal print wallpaper in the dining room, a subtle rag-roll finish in the rooms in the renovated building next door. All suites have whirlpools and most have fireplaces. The restaurant's menu includes pan-seared salmon served with a red pepper sauce and grilled lamb Margarite. ⊠ *Rte. 118, Montgomery Village, 05470,* ☎ *802/326–4507 or 800/255–8661,* 𝖥𝖠𝖷 *802/326–4077. 10 rooms with bath, 6 suites. Restaurant. Full breakfast included. AE, D, MC, V.*

$$$ ✕⊞ **Hotel Jay & Condominiums.** Ski-lodge simplicity sets the tone in the hotel, with wood paneling in the rooms, built-in headboards, and vinyl wallpaper in the bathroom. Right at the lifts, it's very convenient for people who plan to spend most of their time on the slopes. Rooms on the southwest side have a view of Jay Peak, those on the north overlook the valley, and upper floors have balconies. The 120 condominiums (most slope-side) have one to three bedrooms and modern kitchens, washers and dryers, and spacious living areas with fireplaces. A minimum two-night stay is required. In winter, lift tickets and some meals are included in the rates. In summer, rates are very low. ⊠ *Rte. 242, 05859,* ☎ *802/988–2611 or 800/451–4449,* 𝖥𝖠𝖷 *802/988–4049. 48 rooms with bath, 120 condos. Restaurant, bar, pool, sauna, tennis courts, recreation room. MAP in winter. AE, D, DC, MC, V.*

$$ ✕⊞ **The Inn on Trout River.** The wood-burning stove is often the center of attention in the two-tiered living and dining area of this 100-year-old inn, although the piano, the library, the pub with a U-shaped bar, or the pool table down in the recreation room could equally draw your attention. Guest rooms are decorated in the English country cottage style and all have down quilts and flannel sheets in winter; the largest has a Franklin potbelly stove, a dressing area, and a clawfoot tub. The back lawn rambles down to the river, and llama treks are offered in warm months. The restaurant serves American and Continental fare. ⊠ *Main St., Montgomery Center, 05471,* ☎ *802/326–4391 or 800/338–7049. 10 rooms with bath. Restaurant, pub, recreation room, library. Full breakfast included; MAP available. AE, D, MC, V.*

Skiing

Jay Peak. The most natural snow of any ski area in the East falls at Jay Peak. Sticking up out of the flat farmland, Jay catches an abundance of precipitation from the maritime provinces of Canada. Its proximity to Québec attracts Montréalers and discourages Eastern seaboarders; hence, some bargain packages. At press time, building was underway for a double chairlift and accompanying beginner trail. ⊠ *Rte. 242, Jay 05859,* ☎ *802/988–2611 or 800/451–4449.*

DOWNHILL

Jay Peak is in fact two mountains with 62 trails, the highest reaching nearly 4,000 feet with a vertical drop of 2,153 feet, served by a 60-passenger tram (the only one in Vermont). The area also has a quad, a triple, and two double chairlifts, and two T-bars. The smaller mountain has more straight-fall-line, expert terrain, while the tram-side peak has many curving and meandering trails perfectly suited for intermediate and beginning skiers. Jay is known for its glade skiing and now has 13 gladed trails. Every morning at 9 AM the ski school offers a free tour, from the tram down one trail. The area has 80% snowmaking coverage.

CROSS-COUNTRY

A touring center at the base of the mountain has 20 kilometers (12 miles) of groomed cross-country trails. A network of 200 kilometers (124 miles) of trails is in the vicinity.

CHILD CARE

The child care center for youngsters 2–7 is open from 9 to 4. Guests of Hotel Jay or the Jay Peak Condominiums get this nursery care free, as well as free skiing for children 6 and under, evening care, and supervised dining at the hotel. Children 5–12 can participate in an all-day SKIwee program, which includes lunch.

En Route The descent from Jay Peak on Route 101 leads to Route 100, which can be the beginning of a scenic loop tour of routes 14, 5, 58, and back to 100, or take you east to the city of **Newport** on Lake Memphremagog. The waterfront is the dominant view of the city, which is built on a peninsula. The grand hotels of the last century are gone, yet the buildings still drape dramatically along the lake's edge and climb the hills behind.

You will encounter some of the most unspoiled areas in all Vermont on the drive south from Newport on either Route 5 or I–91 (I–91 is faster, Route 5 is prettier). This region, the Northeast Kingdom, is named for the remoteness and stalwart independence that has helped to preserve its rural nature.

Lake Willoughby

③⑦ *7 mi northeast of Barton, 28 mi north of St. Johnsbury.*

On the northern shore of Lake Willoughby the cliffs of surrounding Mts. Pisgah and Hor drop to water's edge and give this glacially carved, 500-foot-deep lake a striking resemblance to a Norwegian fjord; some also compare the landscape to Lucerne's or Scotland's. In any case, Lake Willoughby is stunning. The lake is popular for both summer and winter recreation, and the trails to the top of Mt. Pisgah reward hikers with glorious views.

The **Bread and Puppet Museum** is an unassuming, ramshackle barn that houses a surrealistic collection of props used in past performances by the world-renowned Bread and Puppet Theater. The troupe, whose members live communally on the surrounding farm, have been performing social and political commentary with the towering (they're supported by people on stilts), eerily expressive puppets for about 30 years. ⊠ *South of Lake Willoughby, Rte. 122, Glover, 1 mi east of Rte. 16,* ☎ *802/525–3031.* ⊡ *Donations accepted.* ⊙ *Call for hrs.*

Dining and Lodging

$$ ✕⊞ **WillowVale.** The best thing about this inn is its location. The guest rooms are somewhat uninspired—furnished with functional reproductions—but the comfortable pub with its long, attractive bar and the huge veranda bedecked with rockers and Adirondack chairs are appealing gathering places. The popular, elegant dining room, with its polished wood floor, black bow-back chairs, and green linens, has windows on three sides, so watching the sun set is often an integral part of dinner. The cuisine is traditional Continental. ⊠ *Rte. 5A, Box 404, Westmore 05860,* ☎ *802/525–4123 or 800/541–0588. 7 rooms with bath, 4 cottages. Restaurant (closed Mon.–Thurs. in winter), pub. CP. AE, MC, V.*

$$ ▦ **Fox Hall Inn.** Throughout this 1890 Cottage Revival, listed on the
★ National Register of Historic Places, furnishings and rooms are embellished by moose miscellany—a response to northern Vermont's passionate interest in these once-scarce creatures. The generous wraparound veranda overlooking Lake Willoughby is dotted with swinging seats and comfortable chairs and is perfect for a summer evening spent listening to the loons. The two corner turret rooms are the most distinctive and spacious, and have lake views; the other rooms are also bright and furnished with wicker and quilts. ⊠ *Rte. 16, 05822,* ☎ *802/525–6930. 9 rooms, 4 with bath. Hiking, boating, cross-country skiing, snowmobiling. Full breakfast and afternoon snacks included. MC, V.*

En Route If it's a moose sighting you're after, head north on Route 114 toward **Island Pond,** an outpost of a town, where the beasts are all but common.

East Burke

㊳ *17 mi south of Lake Willoughby.*

If a taste of real Vermont is what you're after, head to the twin towns of East Burke and West Burke, where a jam-packed general store, a post office, and a couple of great places to eat are about all you'll find.

Dining and Lodging
$–$$ ✕ **The Pub Outback.** A huge copper bar with rough-hewn beams and rafters overhead set the tone in this casual, friendly restaurant. Appealing to both the après-ski crowd and families, it serves the likes of black bean cakes, burgers, and shrimp and chicken piccata. ⊠ *Rte. 114,* ☎ *802/626–5187. D, MC, V.*

$–$$ ✕ **River Garden Café.** Eat outdoors on the enclosed porch or the patio and enjoy the perennial gardens that rim the grounds; the café is bright and cheerful on the inside as well. The healthful fare includes roasted rack of lamb, Vermont smoked trout, bruschetta, pastas, and stir-fries. ⊠ *Rte. 114,* ☎ *802/626–3514. MC, V. Closed Mon.*

$–$$ ✕▦ **Old Cutter Inn.** Only ½ mile from the Burke Mountain base lodge is this small converted farmhouse that will fulfill your quest for the quaint-inn experience. The restaurant serves fare that reflects the Swiss chef/owner's heritage, as well as other superb Continental cuisine. ⊠ *R.R. 1 (Box 62), 05832,* ☎ *802/626–5152. 10 rooms, 5 with bath. Restaurant, bar, pool. MAP available. MC, V. Closed Apr., Nov.*

$–$$$ ▦ **Burke Mountain Resort.** A variety of modern accommodations are available at this resort, from economical to luxurious, fully furnished slopeside town houses and condominiums with kitchens and TVs. Some have fireplaces, others have wood-burning stoves. Two-night minimum stay is required. ⊠ *Box 247, 05832,* ☎ *800/541–5480,* ⒻⒶⓍ *802/626–3364. AE, D, MC, V.*

Nightlife
The **Pub Out Back** (⊠ East Burke, ☎ 802/626–5187) is a congenial gathering place, its oval copper bar a welcome sight to Burke Mountain skiers and moose seekers.

Outdoor Activities and Sports

SLEIGH RIDES

The Wildflower Inn (✉ Darling Hill Rd., ☎ 800/627–8310) has 15-passenger sleighs drawn by Belgian draft horses.

Shopping

COUNTRY STORE

Baily's Country Store (✉ Rte. 114, East Burke, ☎ 802/626–3666), a veritable institution, supplies locals and visitors alike with baked goods, wine, clothing, and other sundries.

Skiing

Northern Star. In 1995, Burke was purchased by Northern Star Ski Corp. and renamed Northern Star. The resort has a reputation for being a low-key, family mountain that draws most of its skiers from Massachusetts and Connecticut. In addition to having plenty of terrain for tenderfeet, intermediate skiers, experts, racers, telemarkers, and snowboarders are stimulated here on the time-honored New England narrow trails that the resort has endeavored to preserve. Many of Northern Star's packages are significantly less expensive than those at other Vermont areas. Burke Mt. Academy has contributed a number of notable racers to the U.S. Ski Team, including Olympians Diann Roffe-Steinrotter, Julie Parisien, Matt Grosjean, and Casey Puckett. ✉ *Mountain Rd., Box 247, East Burke 05832,* ☎ *802/626–3305, lodging 800/541–5480, snow conditions 800/922–2875.*

DOWNHILL

With a 2,000-foot vertical drop, Northern Star is something of a sleeper among the larger eastern ski areas. Although there is limited snowmaking (35%), the mountain's northern location and exposure assure plenty of natural snow. It has one quad, one double chairlift, and two surface lifts. Lift lines, even on weekends and holidays, are light to nonexistent.

CROSS-COUNTRY

Northern Star Ski Touring Center has more than 60 kilometers (37 miles) of trails (54 groomed); some lead to high points with scenic views.

CHILD CARE

The nursery here takes children ages 6 months to 6 years. SKIwee lessons through the ski school are available to children ages 4–16.

St. Johnsbury

39 *39 mi east of Montpelier.*

St. Johnsbury is the southern gateway to the Northeast Kingdom. Though chartered in 1786, St. Johnsbury's identity was not firmly established until 1830, when Thaddeus Fairbanks invented the platform scale, a device that revolutionized weighing methods that had been in use since the beginning of recorded history. Because of the Fairbanks family's philanthropic bent, this city with a distinctly 19th-century industrial feel has a strong cultural and architectural imprint.

Opened in 1891, the **Fairbanks Museum and Planetarium** attests to the Fairbanks family's inquisitiveness about all things scientific. The red-brick building in the squat Romanesque architectural style of H. H. Richardson houses eclectic collections of Vermont plants and animals and an intimate 50-seat planetarium. Especially bizarre are the intricate "bug" paintings created by an amateur entomologist and inventor that worked with Thomas Edison. ✉ *Main and Prospect Sts.,* ☎ *802/748–2372.* ☞ *$4.* ☉ *July–Aug., Mon.–Sat. 10–6, Sun. 1–5;*

Sept.–June, Mon.–Sat. 10–4, Sun. 1–5. Planetarium shows July–Aug., daily at 11 and 1:30; Sept.–June, weekends at 1:30.

The **St. Johnsbury Athenaeum,** with its dark rich paneling, polished Victorian woodwork, and ornate circular staircases that rise to the gallery around the perimeter, is a tiny gem. The gallery at the back of the building has the overwhelming *Domes of Yosemite* by Albert Bierstadt and a lot of sentimental 19th-century material. ⊠ *30 Main St.,* ☎ *802/748–8291.* ⌹ *Free.* ⊙ *Mon., Wed. 10–8; Tues., Thurs., Fri. 10–5:30; Sat. 9:30–4.*

OFF THE
BEATEN PATH

CABOT CREAMERY COOPERATIVE – The biggest cheese producer in the state has a visitor center with an audiovisual presentation about the state's dairy and cheese industry, tours of the plant, and—best of all—samples. ⊠ *3 mi north of Route 2, midway between Barre and St. Johnsbury, Cabot,* ☎ *802/563–2231 or 800/639–4031 for orders only.* ⌹ *$1.* ⊙ *June–Oct., daily 9–5; Nov.–May, Mon.–Sat. 9–4. Closed Jan.*

The Arts

Catamount Arts (⊠ 60 Eastern Ave., ☎ 802/748–2600) brings avant-garde theater and dance performances to the Northeast Kingdom as well as classical music and daily film screenings.

Dining and Lodging

$$$–$$$$ ✕⊡ **Rabbit Hill Inn.** In the formal, Federal parlor, mulled cider is served from the fireplace crane on chilly afternoons. The low wooden beams of the Irish pub next door are a casual contrast to the rest of the inn. Rooms are each as stylistically different as they are consistently indulgent: The Loft, with its 8-foot Palladian window, king canopy bed, double whirlpool bath, and corner fireplace, is one of the most requested. Rooms toward the front of the inn get views of the Connecticut River and New Hampshire's White Mountains. Eclectic, regional cuisine is served in the low-ceiling dining room—perhaps grilled sausage of Vermont pheasant with pistachios or smoked chicken and red lentil dumplings nestled in red pepper linguine. Meat and fish are smoked on the premises, and the herbs and vegetables often come from gardens out back. ⊠ *Rte. 18, Lower Waterford 05848,* ☎ *802/748–5168 or 800/762–8669,* ℻ *802/748–8342. 16 double rooms with bath, 5 suites. Restaurant, pub, boating, hiking, cross-country skiing. MAP and afternoon tea. AE, MC, V. Closed 1st 3 wks in Apr. and 1st 2 wks in Nov.*

$$–$$$ ✕⊡ **Wildflower Inn.** Nearly every room in the inn's four buildings gets
★ a piece of the 500 acres of incredible views. This rambling complex of old farm buildings—which date from 1796—was a working dairy farm until 1985. Guest rooms in the restored Federal-style main house, as well as in the carriage houses, are decorated simply with both reproductions and contemporary furnishings. The most spacious rooms are the suites called the Meadows, which are in what used to be the blacksmith shop. In warm weather, the inn is family-oriented in every respect: There's a petting barn, planned children's activities, a kid's swimming pool; the inn quiets down a bit in winter when it caters more to cross-country skiers. Meals feature hearty, country-style food with homemade breads and vegetables from the garden. ⊠ *North of St. Johnsbury on Darling Hill Rd., Lyndonville 05851,* ☎ *802/626–8310 or 800/627–8310,* ℻ *802/626–3039. 15 rooms with bath, 7 suites. Restaurant, pool, pond, hot tub, sauna, tennis court, fishing, ice-skating, cross-country skiing, sleigh rides, recreation room. Full breakfast and afternoon snacks included. MC, V. Closed Apr. and Nov.*

Outdoor Activities and Sports

Village Sport Shop (⊠ Lyndonville, north of St. Johnsbury, ☎ 802/626–8448) rents canoes and kayaks for plying the Connecticut and Passumpsic rivers or Lake Willoughby.

Groton Pond (⊠ Rte. 302, off I–91, 20 mi south of St. Johnsbury, near Peacham, ☎ 802/584–3829) is a popular spot for trout fishing; boat rentals are available.

Peacham

40 *10 mi southwest of St. Johnsbury.*

Peacham is a tiny hamlet whose stunning scenery and 18th-century charm have made it a favorite for urban refugees and artists seeking solitude and inspiration, as well as for movie directors looking for the quintessential New England village. The largely ignored, yet laudable *Ethan Frome*, starring Liam Neeson, was filmed here.

NEED A BREAK?   Stop at the **Peacham Store** (⊠ Main St.) for a quirky combination of Yankee Vermont sensibility and Hungarian eccentricity. Transylvanian goulash, stuffed peppers, and lamb-and-barley soup are among the take-out specialties. Browse through the locally made crafts while waiting for your order. In the spring of 1995, the store was converted into a diner to film *c/o Spitfire Grill*, starring Ellen Burstyn.

Barre

41 *7 mi east of Montpelier, 35 mi south of St. Johnsbury.*

Barre has been famous as the source of Vermont granite ever since two men began working the quarries in the early 1800s; the large number of immigrant laborers attracted to the industry made the city prominent in the early years of the American labor movement. Although the town itself may lack charm and appeal to visitors, it's a classic example of real working-class New England life.

The attractions of the **Rock of Ages granite quarry** range from the awe-inspiring (the quarry resembles the Grand Canyon in miniature) to the absurd (the company invites you to consult a directory of tombstone dealers throughout the United States). The view from the artisan center, which you pass on the drive to the visitor center, seems like a scene out of Dante's *Inferno*: A dusty, smoky haze hangs above the acres of people at work, with machines screaming as they bite into the rock. The process that transfers designs to the smooth stone and etches them into it is fascinating. ⊠ *Exit 6 off I–89, follow Rte. 63,* ☎ *802/476–3115.* ☞ *$2.* ☉ *Quarry and visitor center May–mid-Oct., daily 8:30–5; artisan center weekdays 8–3:30. Quarry shuttle bus tour weekdays 9:30–3:30.*

The Arts

Barre Opera House (⊠ City Hall, Main St., ☎ 802/476–8188) hosts music, opera, theater, and dance performances.

Northern Vermont A to Z

Getting Around

Lake Champlain Ferries (☎ 802/864–9804), in operation since 1826, operates three ferry crossings during the summer months and one in winter through thick lake ice. Ferries leave from the King Street Dock in Burlington. This is a convenient means of getting to and from New York, as well as a pleasant way to spend an afternoon. Call for the current schedule.

BY BUS

Vermont Transit (☎ 802/864–6811, 800/451–3292, or, in VT, 800/642–3133) links Burlington, Stowe, Montpelier, Barre, St. Johnsbury, and Newport.

BY CAR

In north-central Vermont, I–89 heads west from Montpelier to Burlington and continues north to Canada. Interstate 91 is the principal north–south route in the east, and Route 100 runs north–south through the center of the state. North of I–89, Routes 104 and 15 provide a major east–west transverse. From Barton, Routes 5 and 122 south are beautiful drives. Strip-mall drudge bogs down the section of Route 5 around Lyndonville.

BY TRAIN

The *Sugarbush Express* runs between Middlebury and Burlington with stops in Vergennes and Shelburne. Relax in coach cars, dating to 1917, as you contemplate the views of Lake Champlain, the valley farmlands, and surrounding mountains. There are two departures from each terminus during the week, and three on weekends. ⊠ *Box 350, Warren 05674.* ☎ *802/583–2381.* 🎟 *$8.* ☉ *Mid-June–Columbus Day.*

Contacts and Resources

BEACHES

Some of the most scenic Lake Champlain beaches are on the Champlain islands. **North Hero State Park** (☎ 802/372–8727) has a children's play area nearby. **Knight Point State Park** (⊠ North Hero, ☎ 802/372–8389) is the reputed home of "Champ," Lake Champlain's answer to the Loch Ness monster. **Sand Bar State Park** (⊠ Milton) is near a waterfowl preserve. Arrive early to beat summer crowds. 🎟 *$1.* ☉ *Mid-May–Oct.*

The **North Beaches** are on the northern edge of Burlington: North Beach Park (⊠ North Ave., ☎ 802/864–0123), Bayside Beach (⊠ Rte. 127 near Malletts Bay), and Leddy Beach, which is popular for sailboarding.

EMERGENCIES

Fletcher Allen Health Care (⊠ Colchester Ave., Burlington, ☎ 802/656–2345). For 24-hour medical health care information, call ☎ 802/656–2439.

GUIDED TOURS

Cold Hollow Llamas (⊠ R.D. 1, Box 1019, Belvedere 05442 ☎ 802/644–5846) is run by a couple that are also foresters; they lead trips through the countryside and can answer questions about Vermont's natural history. The gourmet picnic lunches are a highlight.

Watch spectacular sunsets over the Adirondack Mountains while floating in a sea kayak with **True North Kayak Tours** (⊠ Burlington, ☎ 802/860–1910). You can rent sea kayaks, take natural history tours, and arrange custom multi-day trips.

HIKING

Stop into the headquarters of the **Green Mountain Club** (⊠ Rte. 100, R.R. 1, Box 650, 1 mi north of Waterbury Center, 05677, ☎ 802/244–7037), which maintains the Long Trail—the north–south border-to-border footpath that runs the length of the spine of the Green

Mountains—as well as other trails nearby. The club sells maps and guides, and experts dispense advice.

A lodging referral service can be reached at ☎ 800/247–8693.

The following have camping and picnicking facilities. **Burton Island State Park** (⊠ Follow directions to Kill Kare Park, St. Albans, ☎ 802/524–6353; 253 acres) is accessible only by ferry or boat; at the nature center a naturalist discusses the island habitat. There's a 100-slip marina with hookups and 20 moorings, and a snack bar. **Grand Isle State Park** (⊠ Rte. 2, 1 mi south of Grand Isle, ☎ 802/372–4300; 226 acres) has a fitness trail and a naturalist. **Kill Kare State Park** (⊠ Rte. 36, 4½ mi west of St. Albans Bay, then south on town road 3½ mi, ☎ 802/524–6021; 17.7 acres) is popular for sailboarding; there is ferry service to Burton Island. **Little River State Park** (⊠ Little River Rd., 3½ mi north of Rte. 2, 2 mi east of Rte. 100, ☎ 802/244–7103; 12,000 acres) has marked nature trails for hiking on Mt. Mansfield and Camel's Hump, boat rentals, and a ramp. **Smugglers' Notch State Park** (⊠ Rte. 108, 10 mi north of Mt. Mansfield, ☎ 802/253–4014; 25 acres) is good for picnicking and hiking on wild terrain among large boulders.

The following offices are open weekdays 9–5. **Greater Newport Area Chamber of Commerce** (⊠ The Causeway, Newport 05855, ☎ 802/334–7782). **Lake Champlain Regional Chamber of Commerce** (⊠ 60 Main St., Suite 100, Burlington 05402, ☎ 802/863–3489) is also open on summer weekends 10–2. **St. Johnsbury Chamber of Commerce** (⊠ 30 Western Ave., St. Johnsbury 05819, ☎ 802/748–3678). **Smugglers' Notch Area Chamber of Commerce** (⊠ Box 3264, Jeffersonville 05464, ☎ 802/644–2239). The **Stowe Area Association** (⊠ Main St., Box 1320, Stowe 05672, ☎ 802/253–7321 or 800/247–8693) is also open November–March, weekdays 9–9, Saturday 10–5, Sunday 10–5.

VERMONT A TO Z

Arriving and Departing

By Bus
Vermont Transit (☎ 802/864–6811, 800/451–3292, or, in VT, 800/642–3133) connects Bennington, Brattleboro, Burlington, Rutland, and other Vermont cities and towns with Boston, Springfield, Albany, New York, Montréal, and cities in New Hampshire. **Bonanza** (☎ 800/556–3815) connects New York City with Bennington twice daily.

By Car
Interstate–91, which stretches from Connecticut and Massachusetts in the south to Québec (Hwy. 55) in the north, reaches most points along Vermont's eastern border. I–89, from New Hampshire to the east and Québec (Hwy. 133) to the north, crosses central Vermont from White River Junction to Burlington. Southwestern Vermont can be reached by Route 7 from Massachusetts and Route 4 from New York.

By Plane
Burlington International Airport (☎ 802/863–2874) has scheduled daily flights on Continental, Delta, United, and USAir. West of Bennington and convenient to southern Vermont, **Albany–Schenectady County Airport** in New York State is served by 10 major U.S. carriers.

By Train

Amtrak's (☎ 800/872–7245) new *Vermonter,* a daytime service linking Washington, DC, with Brattleboro, Bellows Falls, Claremont, White River Junction, Montpelier, Waterbury, Essex Junction, and St. Albans, replaces the *Montrealer.* The *Adirondack,* which runs from Washington, DC, to Montréal, serves Albany, Ft. Edward (near Glens Falls), Ft. Ticonderoga, and Plattsburgh, allowing relatively convenient access to western Vermont.

Getting Around

By Car

The official speed limit in Vermont is 50 mph, unless otherwise posted; on the interstates it's still 65 mph. You can get a state map, which has mileage charts and enlarged maps of major downtown areas, free from the Vermont Travel Division. *The Vermont Atlas and Gazetteer,* sold in many bookstores, shows nearly every road in the state and is great for driving on the back roads.

By Plane

Aircraft charters are available at Burlington International Airport from **Inotech Aviation** (☎ 802/658–2200) and **Valet Air Services** (☎ 802/863–3626). **Southern Vermont Helicopter** (✉ West Brattleboro, ☎ 802/257–4354) provides helicopter transportation throughout New England.

Contacts and Resources

B&B Reservation Agencies

American Country Collection of Bed and Breakfasts (✉ 1353 Union St., Schenectady, NY 12308, ☎ 518/370–4948) and **American–Vermont Bed and Breakfast Reservation Service** will help you find lodging (✉ Box 1, E. Fairfield 05448, ☎ 802/827–3827). You can also try calling the chambers of commerce in many ski areas.

Emergencies

Vermont State Police (☎ 800/525–5555), Vermont's **Medical Health Care Information Center** (☎ 802/864–0454), and **Telecommunications Device for the Deaf** (TDD) (☎ 802/253–0191) have 24-hour hot lines.

Foliage Hot Line

Call (☎ 802/828–3239) for tips on peak viewing locations and times.

Guided Tours

BIKING

The first bike tour operator in the United States and one of the most respected, **Vermont Bicycle Touring** (✉ Box 711, Bristol 05443, ☎ 802/453–4811 or 800/245–3868) operates numerous tours throughout the state. **Bicycle Holidays** (✉ Box 2394, Munger St., Middlebury, ☎ 802/388–2453) creates custom-designed bike trips and will help you put together your own inn-to-inn tour by providing route directions and booking your accommodations.

CANOEING

Umiak Outdoor Outfitters (✉ 849 S. Main St., Stowe 05672, ☎ 802/253–2317) has shuttles to nearby rivers for day excursions as well as customized overnight trips. **Vermont Canoe Trippers/Battenkill Canoe, Ltd.** (✉ Box 65, Arlington 05250, ☎ 802/362–2800) organizes canoe tours (some are inn-to-inn) and fishing trips.

HIKING

North Wind Touring (✉ Box 46, Waitsfield 05673, ☎ 802/496–5771 or 800/496–5771) offers guided walking tours through Vermont's countryside. **Hiking Holidays** (✉ Box 750, Bristol 05443, ☎ 802/453–4816 or 800/245–3868) leads guided walks with lodging in country inns. **Walking Tours of Southern Vermont** (✉ R.R. 2, Box 622, Arlington, ☎ 802/375–1141 or 800/588–9255) specializes in inn-to-inn tours, some of which include yoga and massage. Canoe tours are also organized.

HORSEBACK RIDING

Kedron Valley Stables (✉ Box 368, South Woodstock 05071, ☎ 802/457–1480 or 800/225–6301) has one- to six-day riding tours with lodging in country inns.

Hiking

The **Green Mountain Club** (✉ Rte. 100, Box 650, Waterbury Center 05677, ☎ 802/244–7037) publishes a number of helpful hiking maps and guides. The club also manages the Long Trail, the north–south trail that traverses the entire state.

National Forest

For information about the Green Mountain National Forest, contact the **Forest Supervisor, Green Mountain National Forest** (✉ 231 N. Main St., Rutland 05701, ☎ 802/747–6700) or the **U.S. Forest Service** (✉ Rte. 11/30, east of Manchester, ☎ 802/362–2307).

Visitor Information

Vermont Travel Division (✉ 134 State St., Montpelier 05602, ☎ 802/828–3236 or 800/837–6668) is open weekdays 7:45–4:30. **Vermont Chamber of Commerce** (✉ Box 37, Montpelier 05601, ☎ 802/223–3443) is open weekdays 8:30–5.

There are **information centers** on the Massachusetts border at I–91, the New Hampshire border at I–89, the New York border at Route 4A, and the Canadian border at I-89.

6 New Hampshire

Portsmouth, star of New Hampshire's 18-mile coastline, has great restaurants, theater, and an impressive historic district; Exeter is an enclave of Revolutionary War history. The lakes region, rich with historic landmarks, also has good restaurants, hiking trails, and antiques shops. People come to the White Mountains to hike, ski, and photograph vistas and vibrant foliage. Mt. Washington's peak claims the harshest winds and lowest temperatures ever recorded. Western and central New Hampshire are the unspoiled heart of the state.

By Paula J.
Flanders and
Michelle
Seaton, with
an introduction
by William G.
Scheller

WHEN GENERAL JOHN STARK coined the expression "Live Free or Die," he knew what he was talking about. Stark had been through the Revolutionary War battles of Bunker Hill and Bennington—where he was victorious—and was clearly entitled to state the choice as he saw it. It was, after all, a choice he was willing to make. But Stark could never have imagined that hundreds of thousands of his fellow New Hampshire men and women would one day display the same fierce sentiment as they traveled the streets and roads of the state: Live Free or Die is the legend of the New Hampshire license plate, the only state license plate in the Union to adopt a sociopolitical ultimatum instead of a tribute to scenic beauty or native produce.

The citizens of New Hampshire are a diverse lot who cannot be tucked neatly into any pigeonhole. To be sure, a white-collar worker in one of the high-tech industries that have sprung up around Nashua or Manchester is no mountaineer defending his homestead with a muzzle-loader, no matter what it says on his license plate.

Yet there is a strong civic tradition in New Hampshire that has variously been described as individualistic, mistrustful of government, even libertarian. This tradition manifests itself most prominently in the state's long-standing aversion to any form of broad-based tax: There is no New Hampshire earned-income tax, nor is there a retail sales tax. Instead, the government relies for its revenue on property taxes, sales of liquor and lottery tickets, and levies on restaurant meals and lodgings—the same measures that other states use to varying degrees. Nor are candidates for state office likely to be successful unless they declare themselves opposed to sales and income taxes.

Another aspect of New Hampshire's suspiciousness of government is its limitation of the gubernatorial term of service to two years: With the running of the reelection gauntlet ever imminent, no incumbent is likely to take the risk of being identified as a proponent of an income or a sales tax—or any other similarly unpopular measure.

And then there's the New Hampshire House of Representatives. With no fewer than 400 members, it is the most populous state assembly in the nation and one of the largest deliberative bodies in the world. Each town with sufficient population sends at least one representative to the House, and he or she had better be able to give straight answers on being greeted—on a first-name basis—at the town hardware store on Saturday.

Yankee individualism, a regional cliché, may or may not be the appropriate description here, but New Hampshire does carry on with a quirky, flinty interpretation of the Jeffersonian credo that the government governs best that governs least. Meanwhile, visitors to New Hampshire see all those license plates and wonder whether they're being told that they've betrayed General Stark's maxim by paying an income tax or a deposit on soda bottles—still another indignity the folks in the Granite State have spared themselves.

Pleasures and Pastimes

Beaches

New Hampshire makes the most of its 18-mile coastline, and several good beaches (e.g., Hampton Beach, Hampton, and Rye) await visitors. Those who prefer warm lake waters to the bracing Atlantic can

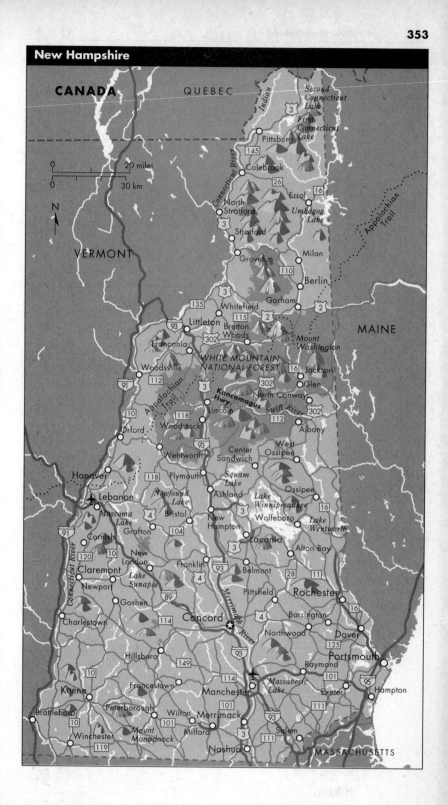

New Hampshire

choose among some of the finest lakes in New England, such as Lake Winnipesaukee, Lake Sunapee, and Newfound Lake.

Beaches tend to be crowded on weekends, with the sun worshipers arriving in droves around 10. The state maintains some metered parking spaces, but these are scarce; private lots charge around $5 a day along the coast.

Biking
A safe and scenic route along New Hampshire's seacoast is the bike path along Route 1A, for which you can park at Odiorne Point and follow the road 14 miles south to Seabrook. Some bikers begin at Prescott Park and take Route 1B into Newmarket, but beware of the traffic. Another pretty route is from Newington Town Hall to the Great Bay Estuary. The volume of traffic on the major roads on the seacoast makes cycling difficult and dangerous for people unfamiliar with the area: Avoid Routes 1, 4, and 101.

Not surprisingly, the best way to cycle in the White Mountains is on a mountain bike. You'll find excellent routes detailed in the mountain-bike guide map "20 Off Road and Back Road Routes in Mt. Washington Valley," sold at area sports shops. There's also a bike path in Franconia Notch State Park, at the Lafayette Campground.

Dining
New Hampshire's visitors need not live on boiled dinners alone. The state is home to some of the best seafood in the country, and not just lobster: salmon pie, steamed mussels, fried clams, seared tuna steak. Each region has its share of country French dining rooms and nouvelle American kitchens, but the best advice is to eat where the locals do. That can be anywhere from a local greasy-spoon diner to an out-of-the-way inn whose chef builds everything—including the home-churned butter—from scratch. And while it's still in vogue to stop by country stores for fudge and penny candy, roadside farmstands and small gourmet groceries—stocking the likes of cranberry chutneys and hot pepper jellies—are growing in popularity. Because restaurants around the lakes serve throngs of visitors in summer, be sure to call for reservations. In peak season, everything is booked. Off-season, whole communities seem to close for the winter.

CATEGORY	COST*
$$$$	over $35
$$$	$25–$35
$$	$15–$25
$	under $15

*per person for a three-course meal, excluding drinks, service, and 8% tax

Fishing
You'll find lake trout and salmon in Winnipesaukee, trout and bass in the smaller lakes, and trout in various streams all around the area. Alton Bay has an "Ice Out" salmon derby in spring. In winter, on all the lakes, intrepid ice fishers fish from huts known as "ice bobs." In the Sunapee region, you can fish for brook, rainbow, and lake trout; smallmouth bass; pickerel; and horned pout. In the Monadnock region, there are more than 200 lakes and ponds, most of which offer good fishing. Here you'll find rainbow trout, brown trout, smallmouth and largemouth bass, some northern pike, white perch, golden trout, pickerel, and horned pout.

Hiking
Some of the East's most spectacularly scenic hiking trails, including several that lead to Mt. Washington's summit, are in the White Moun-

tains. Mt. Monadnock, in the southwestern part of the state, is believed
to be the second most climbed mountain in the world after Japan's Mt.
Fuji. Other state parks and privately maintained recreation areas have
trails along lake shores, through forests, and within sight and sound
of the crashing Atlantic Ocean.

Lodging

New Hampshire has long been a mecca for summer vacationers. In the
mid-19th century, wealthy Bostonians would pack up and move to their
grand summer homes in the countryside for two- or three-month
stretches. Today many of these homes have been restored and converted
into country inns, offering the truest local experience. An occupa-
tional hazard of innkeepers is that they invariably know—and feel com-
pelled to tell you—where to find the best off-the-beaten-track restaurant,
secluded hiking trail, and heretofore undiscovered antiques shop. Inns
vary greatly in size and feel. The smallest have only a couple of rooms;
typically, they're done in period style. The largest let more than 30 rooms
and offer private baths, fireplaces, even hot tubs. A few of the grand
old resorts still stand, with their world-class cooking staffs and their
tradition of top-notch service. And for those who prefer cable TV to
precious antiques, the hotel chains are well represented in the larger
cities and along major highways. In Manchester and Concord, as well
as along major highways, chain hotels and motels dominate the lodging scene. But in the Monadnock region, dozens of colorful inns are
tucked away in small towns and on back roads.

CATEGORY	COST*
$$$$	over $190
$$$	$145–$190
$$	$100–$145
$	under $100

*All prices are for a standard double room during peak season, with no
meals unless noted, and excluding service charge and 8% tax.*

National and State Parks and Forests

New Hampshire parklands vary widely, even within a region. The White
Mountain National Forest covers 770,000 acres in northern New
Hampshire. Major recreation parks are at Franconia Notch, Crawford
Notch, and Mt. Sunapee. Rhododendron State Park, in Monadnock,
has a singular collection of wild rhododendrons; Mt. Washington Park
is on top of the highest mountain in the Northeast. In addition, 23 state
recreation areas provide vacation facilities that include camping, picnicking, hiking, boating, fishing, swimming, bike trails, winter sports,
and food services.

Shopping

ANTIQUES AND CRAFTS

Outside the state's outlet meccas, shopping revolves around antiques
and local crafts. Dozens of galleries and open studios along roads are
marked by blue New Hampshire state signs. The lake region's crafts
shops, galleries, and boutiques are all geared to the summer influx of
tourists—the wares tend toward T-shirts and somewhat tacky trinkets.
Many close in the off-season (late Oct.–mid-Apr.). Summertime fairs,
such as the League of New Hampshire Craftsmen's, at Mt. Sunapee
State Park, and Hospital Day, in New London, showcase some of the
area's best juried arts and crafts.

Antiques shops are plentiful throughout New Hampshire, with the dens-
est concentrations along Route 4, between Route 125 and Concord;
along Route 119, from Fitzwilliam to Hinsdale; along Route 101,
from Marlborough to Wilton; and in the towns of North Conway, North

Hampton, Hopkington, Hollis, and Amherst. In the lakes region, most antiques shops are along the eastern side of Winnipesaukee near Wolfeboro and around Ossipee. Particularly in the Monadnock region, dealers abound in barns and home stores that are strung along back roads and "open by chance or by appointment." Also, don't ignore the flea markets and yard sales rampant during the summer—deals are just waiting to happen.

MALLS

Because New Hampshire steadfastly refuses to institute a sales tax, border towns, like Salem and Nashua, have developed into shopping meccas for visitors from neighboring states. Good-sized malls and strings of chain specialty shops abound in these locations.

OUTLET STORES

North Conway, once of interest primarily to skiers and foliage viewers, now finds itself a year-round destination for bargain hunters who arrive in droves to visit its more than 150 outlet stores. New Hampshire's other, albeit smaller, concentrations of outlet stores are in North Hampton and Lincoln.

Skiing

Scandinavian settlers who came to New Hampshire's high, handsome, rugged peaks in the late 1800s brought their skis with them. Skiing got its modern start in the Granite State in the 1920s, with the cutting of trails on Cannon Mountain.

Today there are about 20 ski areas in New Hampshire, ranging from the old, established slopes (Cannon, Cranmore, Wildcat) to the most contemporary (Attitash, Loon, Waterville Valley). Whatever the age of the area, traditional activities—carnivals, races, ski instruction, family services—are important aspects of the skiing experience. On the slopes, skiers encounter some of the toughest runs in the country alongside some of the gentlest, and the middle range is a wide one.

The New Hampshire ski areas participate in a number of promotional packages allowing a sampling of different resorts. There's Ski 93 (referring to resorts along I–93), Ski New Hampshire, Ski the Mt. Washington Valley, and more.

Exploring New Hampshire

New Hampshire's 18-mile coastline's main attraction is Portsmouth, a historic city and cultural center with great dining; a bit inland is Exeter, home of the eponymous prep school and an enclave of Revolutionary War history. The lakes region, rich with historic landmarks, also has good restaurants, hiking trails, and antiques shops. People come to the White Mountains to hike, ski, and photograph vistas and vibrant foliage. Western and central New Hampshire are the unspoiled heart of the state.

Great Itineraries

Numbers in the text correspond to numbers in the margin and on the maps.

IF YOU HAVE 3 DAYS

Drive along Route 1A to see the coastline or take a boat tour of the Isles of Shoals before exploring ⊡ **Portsmouth** ⑧, New Hampshire's liveliest city. The next day, explore New Hampshire's largest inland body of water, Lake Winnipesaukee. ⊡ **Wolfeboro** ㉓, on the edge of the lake, makes a good overnight stop. The following day, drive across the scenic Kangamagus Highway from **Conway** ㉘ to **Lincoln** ㉗ to see the granite ledges and mountain streams for which the White Mountains are famous. Interstate 93 will take you to Route 101 to return to Portsmouth or straight south to the border with Massachusetts.

IF YOU HAVE 5 DAYS

After visiting **Portsmouth** ⑧ and **Wolfeboro** ㉓, extend your exploration of the lakes region to include quieter Squam and Ossipee Lakes and the charming towns that surround them: **Moultonborough** ㉑, **Center Harbor** ⑱, and **Tamworth** ㉒. Spend your third night in the charming White Mountain town of **Jackson** ㉚. This town is equally beautiful in the winter, when some of the finest cross-country skiing trails in the country are available, and in the summer, when hiking is the main activity. After crossing the Kangamagus Highway to **Lincoln** ㉗, continue to explore the western part of the White Mountain National Forest by following Route 112 to Route 110. Take Route 25 to 25B and follow Route 10 south through the upper Connecticut River valley. **Hanover** ㊹, home of Dartmouth College, is a good overnight stop. Interstate 89 will bring you back to Interstate 93 via **Newbury** ㊷ and the Lake Sunapee region.

IF YOU HAVE 8 DAYS

By spending two nights in **Portsmouth** ⑧, you'll have time to visit Strawbery Banke Museum and soak up more of the restaurant and cultural scene. After exploring **Wolfeboro** ㉓ and **Jackson** ㉚, continue north on Route 16 through spectacular Pinkham Notch to Mount Washington, where you can hike or drive to the top. Return to Route 302 and Route 3 to **Franconia** ㊲, home of Franconia Notch State Park, which has interesting geological features like the Flume and the Old Man of the Mountain. Drive along Route 112 to Route 110 and take Route 25 to 25B; follow Route 10 south through the upper Connecticut River valley where the scenery is straight out of Currier & Ives. After exploring **Hanover** ㊹, home of Dartmouth College, and the Shaker Community at **Enfield** ㊸, take either Route 12A along the Connecticut River or Route 10 south to **Keene** ㊽. Route 119 East leads to Rhododendron State Park in **Fitzwilliam** ㊾. Nearby is Mt. Monadnock, the most-climbed mountain in the United States; in Jaffrey, take the trail to the top. Dawdle along back roads on your way to the preserved villages of **Harrisville, Dublin,** and **Hancock**; then continue east along Route 101 to return to the coast.

When to Tour New Hampshire

New Hampshire is truly a year-round destination. In summer, visitors flock to seaside beaches, mountain hiking trails, and lake boat ramps. In the cities, festivals, like Portsmouth's Prescott Park Arts Festival, bring music and theater to the forefront. Fall brings leaf-peepers, especially to the White Mountains and along the Kancamagus Trail. Skiers take to the slopes and the cross-country trails in winter when Christmas lights and winter carnivals brighten the long, dark nights. April's mud season, the black fly season in late May, and unpredictable weather keep visitors away. Spring does have its joys, though, not the least of which is the appearance of New Hampshire's state flower. From mid-May through early June, the purple lilac decorates the state in shades of lavender.

THE COAST

The first VIP to vacation on the New Hampshire coast was George Washington, in 1789. By all accounts he had a pretty good time, although a bizarre fishing accident left him with a nasty black eye. President Washington couldn't have had nearly as much fun as today's traveler. Accompanied as he was by 14 generals (all in full dress uniform), he couldn't walk barefoot along the sandy beaches, or picnic at Odiorne Point overlooking the ocean. He probably did get a nice look at the homes of John Paul Jones and John Langdon, however, both of which still stand.

Today's visitor will find swimming, boating, fishing, and water sports amid the beaches and state parks of New Hampshire's 18-mile coastline. Hampton Beach has a 1940s-style boardwalk, complete with arcade and nightly entertainment. Portsmouth has it all: the shopping, the restaurants, the music, the theater, and one of the best historic districts in the nation. In Exeter, New Hampshire's enclave of Revolutionary War history, visitors can take a walking tour that explores the 18th- and early 19th-century homes clustered around Phillips Exeter Academy. If President Washington could do it all again, he would probably leave the generals at home and enjoy a leisurely dinner at a quiet seaside inn.

A tour of the coast can take a Sunday afternoon or last for several days. This section begins with Seabrook, the town closest to the Massachusetts border; follows the coast to Portsmouth; and circles inland to Newington, Durham, and Exeter.

Numbers in the margin correspond to points of interest on the New Hampshire Coast map.

Seabrook

❶ *2 mi north of the Massachusetts border, 16 mi south of Portsmouth, 55 mi southeast of Concord.*

Although once known mainly as the inspiration for Al Capp's *Li'l Abner* comic strip, the town has become synonymous with Seabrook Station, one of New England's eight nuclear power plants, which looms large on the Atlantic.

At the **Seabrook Science & Nature Center,** adjacent to Seabrook Station nuclear power plant, you can tour extensive exhibits on the science of power, see control-room operators in training and walk through a replica of a cooling tunnel. In addition, you can pedal a bike to create electricity and use interactive computer games to learn about nuclear power. On the nature side, the center maintains the ¾-mile Owascoag nature trail, a touch pool for kids, and several large aquariums of local sea life. ⊠ *Lafayette Rd.,* ☎ *800/338–7482.* 🖼 *Free.* ☉ *Weekdays 10–4.*

Lodging

$$ 🏨 **Hampshire Inn.** This modern motel has one-, two-, and three-room suites with microwaves and refrigerators. An exercise room, added in 1995, offers treadmills, weight machines, and StairMasters. The lobby, although small, is light and airy; breakfast is served here in the morning, replaced by hot drinks and cookies in the afternoon. ⊠ *Rte. 107, 03874,* ☎ *603/474–5700 or 800/932–8520,* 🖷 *603/474–2886. 35 rooms with bath. In-room modem lines, indoor pool, exercise room. CP. AE, D, DC, MC, V.*

Hampton Falls

❷ *2 mi north of Seabrook, 14 mi south of Portsmouth.*

Although rapidly becoming more suburban, the town still retains some of the rural flavor that once characterized all the small towns on New Hampshire's coast. Consequently, one of its pleasures during the summer and fall is buying fresh fruits and vegetables at a local farm. For a real back-to-nature experience, look for signs that say "PYO" (pick your own). If produce doesn't catch your fancy, do your picking from the many antiques shops lining Route 1.

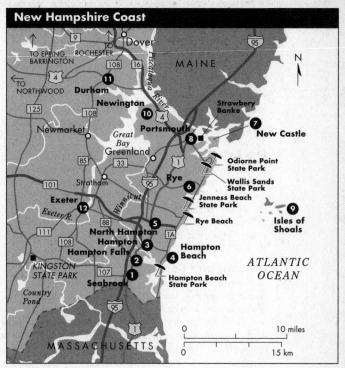

At **Applecrest Farm Orchards,** you can pick your own apples and berries or buy fresh fruit pies and cookies from the bakery. Fall brings cider pressing, hay rides, pumpkins, and music on weekends. In winter you can follow a cross-country ski trail through the orchard. ⊠ *Rte. 88,* ☎ *603/926–3721.* ⊙ *Daily 10–dusk.*

The **Raspberry Farm** has eight varieties of pick-your-own berries, including blackberries, strawberries, and blueberries. There are generally two picking seasons for strawberries and raspberries: summer and fall. The shop sells fresh baked goods, jams, and sauces. ⊠ *3 mi inland on Rte. 84,* ☎ *603/926–6604.* ⊙ *Early June–late Oct., weekdays noon–5, weekends 9–5. Call for picking conditions.*

Lodging

$ ▦ **Hampton Falls Motor Inn.** Intricate Burmese wall hangings and leather furniture decorate the lobby of this modern motel. Although the rooms are typical of those found in chain motels, they were refurbished in 1996 and many have a view of the neighboring farm, unusual on Route 1. An enclosed porch by the indoor pool looks out over the woods and fields. ⊠ *11 Lafayette Rd. (Rte. 1), 03844,* ☎ *603/926–9545,* ℻ *603/926–4155. 33 rooms with bath, 15 suites. Restaurant (no dinner), indoor pool. AE, D, DC, MC, V.*

Shopping

Antiques shops line Route 1 in Hampton Falls, including **Antiques New Hampshire** (☎ 603/926–9603), a group shop with 35 dealers. **Antiques One** (☎ 603/926–5332) carries everything but furniture, including a wide selection of books and maps. **Antiques at Hampton Falls** (☎ 603/926–1971) has silver, jewelry, and collectibles. The **Barn at Hampton Falls** (☎ 603/926–9003) is known for its American and European furniture.

Hampton

❸ *2 mi north of Hampton Falls, 12 mi south of Portsmouth.*

One of New Hampshire's first towns, Hampton was settled in 1638 with the name Winnacunnet, which means "beautiful place of pines." The center of the early town was **Meeting House Green,** where today 42 stones represent the founding families. **Tuck Museum,** across from Meeting House Green, contains displays on the town's early history. ✉ *40 Park Ave.,* ☎ *603/929–0781.* 🎫 *Free.* ⏲ *June–Sept., Wed.–Fri. and Sun. 1–4 PM; and by appointment (☎ 603/926–2543).*

The Arts

From July through September, the **Hampton Playhouse** brings familiar Hollywood and New York theater faces to the seacoast with its summer theater. Matinees are Wednesday and Friday at 2:30; children's shows are Saturday at 11 and 2. Schedules and tickets are available at the box office or at the Chamber of Commerce Sea Shell on Ocean Boulevard in Hampton Beach. ✉ *357 Winnacunnet Rd., Rte. 101E, 03842,* ☎ *603/926–3073.*

Lodging and Camping

$$ **Victoria Inn.** Built as a carriage house in 1875, this romantic bed-and-breakfast is done in the style Victorians loved best: wicker, chandeliers, and lace. One room is completely lilac; the honeymoon suite has white eyelet coverlets and a private sunroom. Innkeepers Bill and Ruth Muzzey have named one room in honor of Franklin Pierce, the former U.S. president who for years summered in the home next door. Breakfast includes unusual dishes such as broiled grapefruit and orange French toast. ✉ *430 High St. (½ mi from Hampton Beach), 03842,* ☎ *603/929–1437. 6 rooms, 3 with bath. Full breakfast included. MC, V.*

$ **The Curtis Field House.** This small B&B is situated on 5 acres between Exeter and Hampton. The Cape-style house is decorated in the Federal style, and guest rooms have four-poster beds, comfortable chairs, and private baths. Relaxing on the sundeck with a good book and enjoying the fragrant gardens is a favorite pastime. ✉ *735 Exeter Rd., 03842,* ☎ *603/929–0082. 3 rooms with bath. Full breakfast included. No credit cards. Closed Nov.–May.*

$ **Tidewater Campground.** There are 200 sites, a large playground, a pool, and a basketball court here. ✉ *160 Lafayette Rd., 03842,* ☎ *603/926–5474.*

$ **Tuxbury Pond Camping Area.** ✉ *W. Whitehall Rd., South Hampton 03842,* ☎ *603/394–7660.*

Hampton Beach

❹ *2 mi east of Hampton, 14 mi south of Portsmouth.*

An estimated 150,000 people visit this town on the 4th of July alone. If you like fried dough, loud music, arcade games, palm readers, parasailing, and tens of thousands of bronzed bodies, don't miss it. The 3-mile boardwalk looks like it was snatched out of the 1940s; here kids can play games and see how saltwater taffy is made. Free outdoor concerts are held many evenings along with a once-a-week fireworks display. There are talent shows and karaoke performances in the Seashell Stage, right on the beach.

Each summer locals crown a Miss Hampton Beach, hold a children's festival, and celebrate the end of the season with a huge seafood feast the weekend after Labor Day. For a quieter time, stop by for a sunrise stroll, when only seagulls and the odd jogger interrupt the serenity.

Dining and Lodging
$$–$$$ ✕🏨 **Ashworth by the Sea.** This hotel was built across the street from Hampton Beach in 1912; most rooms have private decks, and the furnishings vary from period to contemporary. The beachside rooms have a breathtaking ocean view, while the others look out onto the pool or the quiet street. ✉ *295 Ocean Blvd., 03842,* ☎ *603/926–6762 or 800/345–6736,* 🖷 *603/926–2002. 105 rooms with bath. 3 restaurants, pool. AE, D, DC, MC, V.*

Nightlife
The **Hampton Beach Casino Ballroom** has been bringing name entertainment to the Hampton Beach area for more than 30 years. Tina Turner, the Monkees, Jay Leno, and Loretta Lynn have all played here. Expect a crowd of as many as 2,500 people. ✉ *Ocean Beach Blvd.,* ☎ *603/ 926–4541.* ☺ *Apr.–Oct.*

North Hampton
❺ *3 mi north of Hampton, 11 mi southwest of Portsmouth.*

Factory outlets along Route 1 coexist in this town with the mansions lining Route 1A.

Gardeners will want to visit the **Fuller Gardens.** Designed in 1939, these Colonial-revival estate gardens bloom all summer long with 2,000 rosebushes of every shade and type, a Hosta display garden, and a serenity-inspiring groomed Japanese garden. ✉ *10 Willow Ave.,* ☎ *603/ 964–5414.* 🎟 *$4.* ☺ *Early May–mid-Oct., daily 10–6.*

Shopping
The **North Hampton Factory Outlet Center** (✉ Lafayette Rd., Rte. 1, ☎ 603/964–9050) has tax-free goods and discounts on such brand names as Famous Footwear and American Tourister. The center has a diverse group of stores including the Leather Outpost and the Sports Outpost. Bass has its own factory outlet there as well.

En Route On Route 1A as it winds through North Hampton and Rye sits a group of immodest mansions known as **Millionaires' Row.** Because of the way the road curves, the drive south along this route is even more breathtaking than the drive north.

Rye
❻ *5 mi north of North Hampton, 6 mi south of Portsmouth.*

In 1623 the first European settlers landed at Odiorne Point in what is now Rye, making it the birthplace of New Hampshire. The main reasons for visiting Rye are the quality of its beaches and the spectacular view from Route 1A. There are actually three towns—Rye, Rye Beach, and Rye North Beach—clustered along the coast. While locals may appreciate the nuances, visitors are unlikely to notice as they move from one to the other.

☺ You'll find **Odiorne Point State Park** north of Wallis Sands State Park on Route 1A. The park encompasses more than 350 acres of protected land. You can pick up an interpretive brochure on any one of the nature trails or simply stroll and enjoy the beautiful vistas of the nearby Isles of Shoals. The tidal pools here are considered the best in New England and show off crabs, periwinkles, and sea anemones. Don't miss the recently expanded **Seacoast Science Center,** located within the park. The Science Center, which also organizes lectures, guided bird walks, and interpretive programs, has exhibits on the area's natural history and traces the social history of Odiorne Point back to the Ice

Age. Kids love the two-pool touch tank and the 1,000-gallon Gulf of Maine deepwater aquarium. ⊠ *Rte. 1A, Rye,* ☎ *603/436–8043.* ⌨ *$1 to Science Center, $2.50 for parking in summer and fall and on weekends.* ⊙ *Daily 11–5.*

Beaches

Good for swimming and sunning, **Jenness Beach** (Rte. 1A) is a favorite with locals. Facilities include a bathhouse, life guards, and parking. **Wallis Sands State Park** (Rte. 1A) is another swimmers' beach with bright white sand, bathhouse, and ample parking.

Lodging

$$ 🏠 **Rock Ledge Manor.** Built out on a point and offering a 270° ocean view from a full wraparound porch, this mid-19th-century mansion was once part of a resort colony and just predates the houses along Millionaire's Row. It is the only area inn directly on the ocean, and all rooms have water views. The owners speak French and English and serve a huge breakfast each morning in the sunny dining room overlooking the Atlantic. ⊠ *1413 Ocean Blvd. (Rte. 1A), 03870,* ☎ *603/431–1413. 4 rooms, 2 with bath. Full breakfast included. No credit cards. Closed Nov.–May.*

New Castle

❼ *5 mi north of Rye, 1 mi south of Portsmouth.*

The small island of New Castle, just east of Portsmouth, was once known as Great Island, although it's made up of just a single square mile of land. The narrow roads lined with pre-Revolutionary houses make the island perfect for walking.

The old **Wentworth By The Sea,** which was the last of the great seaside resorts, is impossible to miss when approaching New Castle. It sits empty today and overlooks a golf course; it was the site of the signing of the Russo-Japanese Treaty in 1905, a fact that attracts many Japanese tourists.

Ft. Constitution was originally Ft. William and Mary, a British stronghold overlooking Portsmouth Harbor. Rebel patriots raided the fort in 1774 in one of the first overt acts of defiance against the King of England. The rebels later used the stolen munitions against the British at the Battle of Bunker Hill. Interpretive panels throughout the park further explain its history. ⊠ *Ft. Constitution, Great Island.* ⊙ *Mid-June–Labor Day, daily 9–5; Labor Day–mid-June, weekends 9–5.*

Portsmouth

❽ *1 mi north of New Castle, 45 mi southeast of Concord.*

Portsmouth, the largest city in the state, is the cultural epicenter of the coast: Here you will find restaurants of every stripe and in every price range, plus theater, music, art galleries, and an excellent historic district. Originally settled in 1623 as Strawbery Banke, it became a prosperous port prior to the Revolutionary War.

The **Portsmouth Trail** passes many homes in the Historic District that were built prior to 1776. The trail breaks the city into three sections that can be done separately or linked together. Purchase a walking tour guide and map from the information kiosk on Market Square, the Chamber of Commerce, or from any of the houses offering tours, many of which are within walking distance of one another.

Although the walking trail can be enjoyed year-round, seven houses along the way offer tours to visitors during the summer and fall. One of the most interesting is the **John Paul Jones House**, home of the **Portsmouth Historical Society** (often featured in Sears paint commercials). The yellow, hip-roofed Colonial contains costumes, glass, guns, portraits, and documents of the late 18th century. ✉ *43 Middle St.,* ☎ *603/436–8420.* 🎫 *$4.* ⏲ *Mid-May–mid-Oct., Mon.–Sat. 10–4, Sun. noon–4.*

Lining the hall staircase of the **Warner House** are the earliest known painted murals in the United States, dating from 1718. ✉ *150 Daniel St.,* ☎ *603/436–5909.* 🎫 *$4.* ⏲ *Mid-May–mid-Oct., Mon.–Sat. 10–4, Sun. noon–4.*

Also on the Portsmouth Trail, the **Moffatt-Ladd House**, built in 1763, tells the story of Portsmouth's merchant class through portraits, letters, and fine furnishings. ✉ *154 Market St.,* ☎ *603/436–8221.* 🎫 *$4.* ⏲ *Mid-May–mid-Oct., Mon.–Sat. 10–4, Sun. noon–4.*

NEED A BREAK?

Gourmet coffee shops abound in Portsmouth. **Breaking New Grounds** (✉ 16 Market St., ☎ 603/436–9555) serves cappuccino, espresso, and all the hybrids, along with cheesecake and cookies. The **Ceres Bakery** (✉ 51 Penhallow St., ☎ 603/436–6518) has elaborate tarts and tortes, as well as soups and light lunches.

The first English settlers named the area around what's now called Portsmouth for the abundant wild strawberries they found along the shore of the Piscataqua River. Today **Strawbery Banke** is a 10-acre outdoor museum with period gardens and more than 40 buildings that date from 1695 to 1820. The district was slated for urban renewal in the late 1950s, but a group of concerned residents successfully fought to preserve it. The museum is now a study in the evolution of a neighborhood, with nine furnished homes representing several different time periods.

For example, the **Drisco House**, built in 1795, was first used as a dry-goods store, and one room still depicts this history; the living room, on the other hand, is decorated just as it was in the 1950s. The boyhood home of Thomas Bailey Aldrich (author of *The Story of a Bad Boy*) is still called **Nutter House**, the name he gave it in that novel—it's been restored to just as it was when he wrote about it, right down to the wallpaper and hanging bookshelves. In the **Wheelwright House** you can see daily demonstrations of 18th-century cooking. ✉ *Marcy St.,* ☎ *603/433–1100 or 603/433–1106.* 🎫 *$10; tickets good for 2 consecutive days.* ⏲ *May–Oct., daily 10–5; weekend after Thanksgiving, 10–4; 1st 2 weekends in Dec., 3:30–8:30.*

Picnicking is popular in historic **Prescott Park,** which is on the waterfront between Strawbery Banke and the Piscataqua River. A large formal garden with lively fountains is the perfect place to while away an afternoon. The park also contains **Point of Graves**, Portsmouth's oldest burial ground, and two historic warehouses that date from the early 17th century. The **Sheafe Museum**, was the warehouse where John Paul Jones outfitted the **USS *Ranger*,** one of the U.S. Navy's earliest ships. ✉ *Prescott Park, Marcy St.,* ☎ *603/431–8748.* ⏲ *Sheafe Museum Memorial Day–Labor Day, Wed.–Sun. 8–4.*

At the **Children's Museum of Portsmouth,** hands-on exhibits explain such subjects as lobstering, geography, computers, recycling, and outer space. Some programs require advance reservations. ✉ *280 Marcy St.,* ☎ *603/436–3853.* 🎫 *$3.50.* ⏲ *Tues.–Sat. 10–5, Sun. 1–5. Also Mon. 10–5 in summer and during school vacations.*

Now a state historic home, the **Wentworth-Coolidge Mansion** was originally the residence of Benning Wentworth, New Hampshire's first Royal Governor. Notable among the period furnishings is the carved pine mantelpiece in the council chamber; also notice Wentworth's own imported lilac trees, which bloom each May. ⊠ *Little Harbor Rd. at South Street Cemetery,* ☎ *603/436–6607.* ☉ *Mid-June–Labor Day, daily 10–5.*

The **Port of Portsmouth Maritime Museum,** in Albacore Park, is home of the **USS Albacore,** which was built here in 1953 as a prototype submarine—a floating laboratory assigned to test a new hull design, dive brakes, and sonar systems for the Navy. The nearby Memorial Garden and its reflecting pool are a memorial to those lost in submarine service. ⊠ *600 Market St.,* ☎ *603/436–3680.* 🖃 *$4.* ☉ *May–Columbus Day, daily 9:30–5:30; Columbus Day–Apr., daily 9:30–4.*

Dining and Lodging

Portsmouth's restaurants draw local patrons as well as tourists and people who travel from as far away as Concord and Manchester. Consequently, Thursday through Sunday nights, year-round, tend to be busy, so reservations are wise.

$$$ ✕ **Library at the Rockingham House.** This Portsmouth landmark was once a luxury hotel and the site of the press signing of the Russo-Japanese Treaty in 1905. Most of the building has been converted to condominiums, but the restaurant retains the original atmosphere, with hand-carved Spanish mahogany paneling and bookcases on every wall. Here even the dividers between booths are stacked with old tomes, and the wait staff presents each bill in the pages of a vintage bestseller. The food, too, seems to belong in a social club of another century. Don't miss the roasted Long Island duckling with a maple-bourbon glaze, or the filet mignon with bérnaise sauce. ⊠ *401 State St.,* ☎ *603/431–5202. AE, DC, MC, V.*

$$ ✕ **Blue Mermaid World Grill.** The stately, 1810 exterior of the Nutter-
★   Rhymes house belies the hot, Jamaican-style dishes that come from the Blue Mermaid's wood-burning grill. Specialties include smoked scallop chowder and whole fire-roasted bass with flaming herbs. In the summer, you may eat lunch on the deck overlooking the 13 other houses, dating from 1720 to 1830, that are grouped in this area called The Hill. There's live entertainment every Thursday and Friday. ⊠ *The Hill,* ☎ *603/427–2583. AE, D, DC, MC, V.*

$$ ✕ **Porto Bello.** Owner Yolanda Desario and her mother have brought
★   the tastes of Naples to downtown Portsmouth. In this second-story dining room overlooking the harbor, you can enjoy daily antipasto specials ranging from grilled portobello mushrooms to stuffed calamari. Pastas include spinach gnocchi and homemade ravioli filled with eggplant, walnuts, and Parmesan and Romano cheeses. A house specialty is veal *carciofi*—a 4-ounce cutlet served with artichokes. The tastes are so simple and the ingredients so fresh, you won't have trouble finishing four courses. ⊠ *67 Bow St., 2nd floor,* ☎ *603/431–2989. D, MC, V. Closed Sun. No dinner Mon.; no lunch Sun.–Tues.*

$–$$ ✕ **B.G.'s Boathouse Restaurant.** A local favorite, this place looks like an old fisherman's shack but serves the best seafood in town and plenty of it. Many customers arrive by boat. ⊠ *Rte. 1B,* ☎ *603/431–1074. Reservations not accepted. AE, D, MC, V.*

$–$$ ✕ **Karen's.** Pass through the purple door and into the restaurant that locals would like to keep secret. Sautés, stir-frys, pasta, and sandwiches, such as open-face blackened swordfish, are on the lunch menu. The dinner menu changes completely every few days, but house specialties are light, simple seafood dishes prepared to perfection. For Sunday brunch look for the eggs Sardou or the eggnog French toast specials. ✉ *105 Daniel St.,* ☎ *603/431–1948. Reservations not accepted. AE, D, MC, V. No smoking. No lunch Sun.–Wed.*

$–$$ ✕ **Portsmouth Brewery & Restaurant.** You can watch the brewing process of 15 different kinds of ale at this restaurant's in-house brewery. The upscale pub-style fare includes spicy shrimp, stir-fry combinations, burritos, fresh tuna steak au poivre, and fish-and-chips. There's live entertainment Wednesday through Saturday. ✉ *56 Market St.,* ☎ *603/431–1115. AE, D, MC, V.*

$$–$$$ ✕▥ **Sheraton Portsmouth Hotel.** Portsmouth's only luxury hotel, this five-story redbrick building offers a nice harbor view, a central location, and recently renovated guest rooms. The hotel houses the area's main conference center, making it a perfect choice for business travelers. Suites have full kitchens and living rooms. The main restaurant features fresh seafood and American cuisine. The Krewe Orleans restaurant and bar serves Cajun specialties. ✉ *250 Market St., 03801,* ☎ *603/431–2300 or 800/325–3535,* ℻ *603/433–5649. 148 rooms with bath, 29 suites. 2 restaurants, bar, indoor pool, health spa, nightclub. AE, D, DC, MC, V.*

$$$ ▥ **Sise Inn.** If you can't decide between a hotel and a small inn with
★ period decor, stay at this Queen Anne town house in Portsmouth's historic district, which captures the best of both worlds. Each room is individually decorated with special fabrics, rubbed woods, and antique reproductions, but all have cable TV and some rooms have whirlpool baths as well. Victorian style meets postmodern, with a Continental breakfast thrown in. The inn is close to the Market Square area and within walking distance of the theater district and several restaurants. ✉ *40 Court St., 03801,* ☎ ℻ *603/433–1200 or 800/267–0525. 34 rooms with bath. Fans, in-room VCRs. CP. AE, DC, MC, V.*

$$ ▥ **Governor's House B&B.** This 1917 Georgian mansion was for more
★ than 30 years home to New Hampshire's governor, Charles Dale. Innkeepers Nancy and John Grossman reopened it in 1992 as a bed-and-breakfast and have fully restored the four rooms with period antiques—right down to the canopy beds. Nancy's fanciful, hand-painted-tile murals in the bathrooms justify a visit, as does the folk-art mural by New York artist Edward Leight in the sitting room. Guests enjoy a gourmet, low-fat breakfast each morning. ✉ *32 Miller Ave., 03801,* ☎ *603/431–6546,* ℻ *603/427–0803. 4 rooms with bath. Air-conditioning, tennis. Full breakfast included. AE, MC, V.*

$$ ▥ **Martin Hill Inn.** Set in two buildings downtown, this charming inn is within walking distance of the historic district and waterfront; quiet rooms are comfortably furnished with antiques. ✉ *404 Islington St.,* ☎ *603/436–2287. 4 rooms with bath, 3 suites. MC, V.*

Nightlife and the Arts

NIGHTLIFE

The **Portsmouth Gaslight Co.** (✉ 64 Market St., ☎ 603/430–8582) is a popular brick-oven pizzeria and restaurant by day. But on summer nights, this place transforms itself into a party. That's when the management opens up the back courtyard, brings in live local rock bands, and serves a special punch in plastic sandpails. By midnight, not only is the courtyard full, but the three-story parking garage next door has become a makeshift auditorium. People come from as far away as Boston and Portland to hang out at the **Press Room** (✉ 77 Daniel St., ☎ 603/431–5186) for folk, jazz, blues, and bluegrass performances. Tuesday in this old, three-story brick building, is open-mike night; on Sunday the jazz starts at 7.

Music in Market Square (☎ 603/436–9109) is a summer series of free concerts given Friday at noon. Classical musicians, both vocal and instrumental, perform inside the North Church in Market Square. **Prescott Park Arts Festival** (✉ 105 Marcy St., ☎ 603/436–2848) kicks off with the Independence Day Pops concert and continues for eight weeks with the works of more than 100 regional artists, as well as music, dance, and an outdoor theater production four nights a week. Don't miss the Chowder Festival or the Sunday jazz picnic.

Beloved for its acoustics, the **Music Hall** (✉ 28 Chestnut St., ☎ 603/436–2400) is the 14th oldest operating theater in the country (circa 1878). Its mission is to bring the best touring events to the seacoast—from classical and pop to dance and theater. The hall also hosts an ongoing art-house film series. The **Seacoast Repertory Theatre** (✉ 125 Bow St., ☎ 603/433–4472 or 800/639–7650) is one of the area's top regional theaters. The Portsmouth Academy of Performing Arts and the Portsmouth Youth Theatre combine to fill its calendar with musicals, classic dramas, and new works by upcoming playwrights. The **Player's Ring** (✉ 105 Marcy St., ☎ 603/436–8123) also brings a variety of touring theatrical groups to the seacoast. The **Pontine Movement Theater** (✉ 135 McDonough St., ☎ 603/436–6660) is housed in a renovated warehouse that seats only 75 people, so tickets to dance performances may be difficult to acquire.

Outdoor Activities and Sports

The **Urban Forestry Center** (✉ 45 Elwyn Rd., ☎ 603/431–6774) has marked trails appropriate for short hikes.

Shopping

Market Square, in the center of town, has gift and clothing boutiques, card shops, and exquisite crafts stores. The **Museum Shop at the Dunaway Store** (✉ Marcy St., ☎ 603/433–1114) stocks reproduction and contemporary furniture, quilts, crafts, candy, gifts, postcards, and books about the area's history. **N. W. Barrett** (✉ 53 Market St., ☎ 603/431–4262) specializes in fine art and crafts from both local and nationally acclaimed artists. The second floor showcases furniture in every price range, including affordable steam-bent oak pieces and one-of-a-kind lamps and rocking chairs. On the first floor, you can browse through the leather, jewelry, pottery, and fiber displays. **Pierce Gallery** (✉ 105 Market St., ☎ 603/436–1988) sells reasonably priced prints and paintings of both the Maine and New Hampshire coasts. **Tulips** (✉ 19 Market St., ☎ 603/431–9445) was Portsmouth's first crafts gallery and still specializes in wood crafts and quilts.

Portsmouth has several funky consignment shops and antiquarian bookstores near Market Square. **The Portsmouth Bookshop** (✉ 1 Islington St., ☎ 603/433–4406) carries a huge selection of old and rare books and maps. Look for classic and vintage clothing at **Mad Lydia's Waltz** (✉ 20 Market St., 2nd floor, ☎ 603/433–7231).

Alie Jewelers (✉ 1 Market St., ☎ 603/436–0531) carries gold, silver, and gemstone jewelry designed by New England artisans.

Isles of Shoals

❾ Ten miles off the coast lie nine small islands (eight at high tide): the Isles of Shoals. Many, like Hog Island, Smuttynose, and Star Island, retain the earthy names given them by the transient fishermen who first visited in the early 17th century. A colorful history of piracy, murder, and ghosts surrounds the archipelago, long populated by an independent lot who, according to one writer, hadn't the sense to winter on the mainland. Not all of the islands lie within the New Hampshire border: After an ownership dispute between Maine and New Hampshire, they were divvied up between the two states (five went to Maine, four to New Hampshire). For information on visiting these islands, *see* Guided Tours *in* Contacts and Resources, *below.*

Celia Thaxter, a native islander, romanticized these islands with her poetry in *Among the Isles of Shoals,* published in 1873. In her time, **Appledore Island** became an offshore retreat for her coterie of writers, musicians, and artists. The island is now used by the Marine Laboratory of Cornell University. **Star Island** houses a non-denominational conference center, but is open to tours.

Newington

⑩ *2 mi northwest of Portsmouth.*

With the closing of Pease Air Force Base and the conversion of that space to public lands and private industry, Newington is undergoing a transformation. The region's only malls are here, and from the highway this seems like simply a commercial town. The original town center, hidden away from the traffic and the malls, retains an old-time New England feel.

One attraction that will appeal to visitors is the **Red Hook Ale Brewery** in the Pease International Tradeport, visible from Route 4. Although still under construction at press time, the facility is on schedule to open in the fall of 1996. Visitors will be able to tour the brewery, taste brews in the beer garden and pub, and browse for souvenirs in the gift shop. At press time, the admission price was estimated at $1.

Dining and Lodging

$$ ✕ **Newick's Lobster House.** Newick's might serve the best lobster roll on the New England coast, but regulars cherish the onion rings, too. This casual lobster shack serves seafood and atmosphere in heaping portions. Picture windows allow terrific views over Great Bay. ✉ *431 Dover Point Rd., Dover,* ☎ *603/742–3205. AE, D, MC, V.*

$ 🏠 **Moody Parsonage Bed and Breakfast.** The first things guests notice about this red-clapboard Colonial are the original paneling, beautiful old staircases, and wide pine floors. With a fire crackling on chilly evenings and a spinning wheel in the living-room corner, some think they've stepped back in time. The house was built in 1730 for John Moody, the first minister of Newmarket, and if he came back today, he'd recognize it inside and out. Innkeeper Debbie Reed serves summer breakfasts on the front porch, which has a golf-course view. ✉ *15 Ash Swamp Rd., 03857,* ☎ *603/659–6675. 1 room with bath, 3 share bath. CP. No credit cards. No children under 8.*

Shopping

Country Curtains (✉ 2299 Woodbury Ave., ☎ 603/431–2315), on the Old Beane Farm, sells curtains, bedding, furniture, and folk art. Sunday flea markets are held in the **Star Center** (✉ 25 Fox Run Rd., ☎ 603/431–9403). **Fox Run Mall** (✉ Fox Run Rd., ☎ 603/431–5911) is huge and generic, as a mall should be. This one houses Filene's, Jordan Marsh, JCPenney, Sears, and 100 other stores.

GREAT BAY ESTUARY – Bird-watchers will love the Great Bay Estuary. Here, among the 4,471 acres of tidal waters, mud flats, and about 48 miles of inland shoreline, visitors can see the great blue heron, osprey, and the snowy egret, all of which are especially conspicuous during their spring and fall migrations. The area is most famous, however, for having New Hampshire's largest concentration of winter eagles. Several area towns have recreation areas along the bay. Hikers will find trails at **Adam's Point** (in Durham) and at **Sandy Point** (in Greenland), and canoeists can put in at **Chapman's Landing** (Rte. 108, Stratham) on the Squamscott River. Access to the Great Bay is a bit tricky and parking limited, but the Fish and Game Department's **Sandy Point Discovery Center** (✉ Depot Rd. off Rte. 101, Greenland, ☎ 603/778–0015) distributes maps and information, and has displays about the estuary.

Durham

⑪ *7 mi northwest of Newington.*

Settled in 1635 and home of General John Sullivan, Revolutionary War hero and three-time New Hampshire governor, Durham was where Sullivan and his band of rebel patriots stored the gunpowder they stole from Fort William and Mary (☞ Fort Constitution *in* New Castle, *above*). Easy access to Great Bay via the Oyster River made Durham a center of maritime activity in the 19th century. Today's attractions center around the water; the University of New Hampshire, which occupies much of the town's center; and a selection of farms that welcome visitors.

The University of New Hampshire Art Gallery occasionally exhibits items from a permanent collection of about 1,100 pieces, but generally uses its space to host traveling exhibits that showcase both contemporary and historic art. Noted items in the permanent collection include 19th-century Japanese woodblock prints and late 19th- and early 20th-century American landscape paintings. ✉ *Paul Creative Arts building,* ☎ *603/862–3712.* ⊙ *Sept.–May, Mon.–Wed. 10–4, Thurs. 10–8, weekends 1–5.*

Emery Farm sells fruits and vegetables during in summer (including pick-your-own raspberries, strawberries, and blueberries), pumpkins in the fall, and Christmas trees in December. The farm shop carries breads and pies, as well as local crafts. Children enjoy petting the resident goats, sheep, and other furry critters. ✉ *Rte. 4,* ☎ *603/742–8495.* ⊙ *May–Dec., daily.*

At **Little Bay Buffalo Farm,** overlooking the water, David Langley raises a herd of about 30 bison. In addition to selling bison meat and gift items in the farm's shop, he offers tours through the Isles of Shoals Steamship Company (☞ Guided Tours, *in* Contacts and Resources, *below*). ✉ *50 Langley Rd., 03824,* ☎ *603/868–3300.*

At **Misty Meadows Farm,** Wendy and Clyde Fogg maintain large herb and perennial gardens. Wendy operates the farm's herb shop and conducts wild plant identification walks in the summer and fall. The farm also has more than 3 miles of trails for walking and cross-country skiing. Hayrides and sleighrides take place in season. ✉ *185 Wednesday Hill Rd., off Rte. 155,* ☎ *603/659–2436.* ▣ *Free.* ⊙ *Trails: year-round, daily, dawn–dusk. Shop: Mar.–Dec., Wed.–Sat. 10–5, Sun. noon–5; Jan., Sat. 11–4; Feb., Fri.–Sat. 10–5, Sun. noon–5.*

The Arts

The University of New Hampshire stages many musical and theatrical performances throughout the year. The **Celebrity Series** (☎ 603/862–

3227) brings world-class music, theater, and dance to Durham. **The UNH Department of Theater and Dance** puts on a number of well-staged shows each year (☎ 603/862–2919).

Dining and Lodging

$–$$ ✕🖳 **New England Center Hotel.** In a lush wooded area on the campus of the University of New Hampshire, this hotel is large enough to be a full-service conference center, but quiet enough to feel like a retreat. You'll find larger rooms in the new wing, each with two queen-size beds. Decor is typical of most chain hotels. ✉ *15 Strafford Ave., 03824,* ☎ *603/862–2800,* FAX *603/862–4351. 115 rooms with bath. 2 restaurants, bar, exercise room. AE, DC, MC, V.*

$ 🖳 **Hickory Pond Inn.** Among the amenities at this inn is a nine-hole, par-three golf course. Guest rooms have fresh, flowered wallpaper and individualized color schemes. The common areas are spiffy as well and include a charming breakfast room and a reading nook with a wood-stove. ✉ *One Stagecoach Rd., 03824,* ☎ *603/659–2227 or 800/658–0065,* FAX *603/659–7910. 8 rooms with bath, 8 rooms share 2 baths. No smoking. 9-hole golf course. CP. AE, MC, V.*

$ 🖳 **The Pines Guest House.** This stately yellow farmhouse has remained in the same family for five generations: The period antiques that fill the guest rooms and the china and silver you'll use at breakfast are all family heirlooms. Owner Roger Jaques hopes to eventually verify a family story that Lafayette stayed in the house in 1825 when he stopped to visit General John Sullivan's daughter, who owned the house at that time. ✉ *47 Dover Rd., 03824,* ☎ *603/868–3361. 5 rooms with bath. CP. No credit cards.*

Outdoor Activities and Sports

HIKING

Take a picnic to **Wagon Hill Farm** (✉ Rte. 4, across from Emery Farm), overlooking the Oyster River. The old farm wagon, sitting by itself on the top of a hill above Route 4, is one of the most photographed spots in New England. The farm is town-owned and open to the public, so don't stop on dangerous Route 4 to take your photos. Instead, park in the designated area next to the farmhouse and follow the walking trails to the wagon and through the woods to the picnic area by the water. Sledding and cross-country skiing are popular winter activities.

Shopping

Salmon Falls Pottery & Stoneware (✉ Oak St. Engine House, Dover, ☎ 603/749–1467 or 800/621–2030) produces handmade, salt-glaze stoneware, using a method that was popular among early American potters. Potters are on hand if you want to place a special order or just watch them work.

Exeter

12 *13 mi south of Durham, 8 mi west of Hampton Beach.*

In 1638 the town's first settlers built their homes around the falls where the freshwater Exeter River meets the salty Squamscott. During the Revolutionary War, Exeter was the state capitol, and it was here that the first state constitution and the first declaration of independence from Great Britain were put to paper.

Phillips Exeter Academy opened its doors in 1783 and is still one of the nation's most esteemed prep schools. The **American Independence Museum,** in the Ladd-Gilman House (adjacent to Phillips Exeter Academy), celebrates the birth of our nation. Built by Nathaniel Ladd as the first brick house in town, it was eventually converted into a governor's mansion for John Taylor Gilman. The story of the revolution unfolds during each guided tour, which shows off drafts of the U.S. Constitution and the first Purple Heart. ⊠ *1 Governor's La.,* ☎ *603/772–2622.* ▣ *$4.* ☉ *May–Oct., Wed.–Sun. noon–5.*

Beach

For freshwater swimming, try **Kingston State Park** (☎ 603/642–5471) at Kingston on Great Pond (not to be confused with Great Bay).

Dining, Lodging, and Camping

$$ ✕ **Vincent's String Bridge Cafe.** Centrally located in the heart of Exeter, Vincent's serves up a variety of Italian specialties: everything from veal scallopine to chicken marsala. Specials, like shrimp in a garlic sherry sauce, combine the best of fresh local ingredients. At lunch, try soup or a salad, served with an individual loaf of bread still warm from the oven. ⊠ *69 Water St.,* ☎ *603/778–8219. MC, V.*

$ ✕ **Loaf and Ladle.** This understated café serves hearty chowders, soups, stews, and huge sandwiches on homemade bread—all cafeteria-style. Check the blackboard for the ever-changing rotation of stews, breads, and desserts. Overlooking the river, the café is handy to the shops, galleries, and historic houses along Water Street. ⊠ *9 Water St.,* ☎ *603/778–8955. Reservations not accepted. AE, D, DC.*

$$$ ✕▣ **Exeter Inn.** This three-story brick, Georgian-style inn on the campus of Phillips Exeter Academy is furnished lavishly with antique and reproduction pieces but possesses every modern amenity. It's been the choice of visiting parents for the past half century. The dining room's house specialty is the chateaubriand served on an oaken plank with duchess potatoes and a béarnaise sauce, although the chef also boasts of a showstopping veal culinaire, the preparation of which changes daily. On Sunday, the line forms early for a brunch (reservations not accepted) of more than 60 delicious options. The big, bright sunporch's centerpiece is a live fig tree. ⊠ *90 Front St., 03833,* ☎ *603/772–5901 or 800/782–8444,* ℻ *603/778–8757. 50 rooms with bath. Restaurant, exercise room. AE, D, DC, MC, V.*

$–$$ ▣ **Inn by the Bandstand.** This 1809 Federal town house in the town center, listed in the National Register of Historic Places, has been lovingly restored by owners George and Muriel Simmons. Six rooms have working fireplaces; all have private baths. After a day of sightseeing, relax in the parlor with a complimentary glass of sherry. ⊠ *4 Front St., 03833,* ☎ *603/772–6352. Air-conditioning. CP. AE, MC, V.*

$ ⛺ **Exeter Elms Family Campground.** This campground has riverfront sites, a swimming pool, and canoes for rent. ⊠ *188 Court St., 03833,* ☎ *603/778–7631.*

Shopping

Exeter League of New Hampshire Craftsmen (⊠ 61 Water St., ☎ 603/778–8282) showcases original jewelry, woodworking, and pottery produced by select, juried members. **A Picture's Worth a Thousand Words** (⊠ 65 Water St., ☎ 603/778–1991) sells antique and contemporary prints and frames them in-house. You can also choose from a wonderful collection of old maps, town histories, and rare books. **Starlight Express** (⊠ 103 Water St.) sells clocks with elaborate, hand-painted faces, picture frames, candles, and other accessories for the house.

The Coast A to Z

Arriving and Departing

BY BUS

C&J (☎ 603/742–5111), **Concord Trailways** (☎ 800/639–3317), **Peter Pan Bus Lines** (☎ 603/889–2121), and **Vermont Transit** (☎ 603/228–3300 or 800/451–3292) all provide bus service to New Hampshire's coast from other regions.

BY CAR

The main route to New Hampshire's coast from other states is I–95, which stretches from the border with Maine to the border with Massachusetts.

Getting Around

BY BUS

Coast (☎ 603/862–2328), originally designed for the students at the University of New Hampshire, now serves many of the towns in New Hampshire's coastal section.

BY CAR

For coastal scenery, follow Route 1A, which shows off the water, the beaches, and some breathtaking summer estates. For convenience, follow Route 1, which wends slightly inland. Route 1B tours the island of Newcastle, and Route 4 connects Portsmouth with Dover, Durham, and Rochester. Route 108 links Durham and Exeter. The quick route along the coast is I–95.

Contacts and Resources

BOATING

Between April and October, deep-sea fishermen head out for cod, mackerel, and bluefish. There are rentals and charters aplenty, offering half- and full-day cruises, as well as some night fishing at Hampton, Portsmouth, Rye, and Seabrook piers. Try **Eastman Fishing & Marine** (Seabrook, ☎ 603/474–3461), **Atlantic Fishing Fleet** (Rye Harbor, ☎ 603/964–5220), **Al Gauron Deep Sea Fishing** (Hampton Beach, ☎ 603/926–2469), and **Smith & Gilmore** (Hampton Beach, ☎ 603/926–3503).

EMERGENCIES

New Hampshire State Police (☎ 603/679–3333 or 800/852–3411). **Portsmouth Regional Hospital** (⊠ 333 Borthwick Ave., ☎ 603/436–5110 or 603/433–4042). **Exeter Hospital** (⊠ 10 Buzzell Ave., ☎ 603/778–7311).

FARM PRODUCE

Farm products, such as homemade jams and pickles, are available at **Tuttle's Farm** (⊠ Dover Point Rd., Dover, ☎ 603/742–4313); *also see* Hampton Falls *and* Durham, *above.* **Calef's Country Store** (⊠ Rte. 9, Barrington, ☎ 603/664–2231) carries a wide variety of gifts and farm products.

GUIDED TOURS

In Portsmouth, **Insight Tours** offers walking tours and one- to three-hour bus tours focusing on the history and architecture of this town. ⊠ *579 Sagamore Ave., Portsmouth, 03801,* ☎ *603/436–4223 or 800/745–4213.*

Clip-clop your way through Colonial Portsmouth and Strawbery Banke with **Portsmouth Livery Company** (☎ 603/427–0044), which gives narrated horse-and-carriage tours. Look for carriages in Market Square.

The **Isles of Shoals Steamship Company** runs island cruises, whale-watching expeditions, and river trips. Captain Bob Whittaker hosts these voyages aboard the **M/V Thomas Laighton,** a replica of a Victorian steamship, on which he regales passengers with tall tales. Breakfast, lunch, and light snacks are available on board, or you can bring your own. Some trips include a stopover and historic walking tour on Star Island. Trips on Great Bay include foliage excursions and tours of the Little Bay Buffalo Farm in Durham. ⊠ *Barker Wharf, 315 Market St., Portsmouth,* ☎ *603/431–5500 or 800/441–4620.* ☉ *Tour cruises mid-June–Labor Day, Oct.; whale-watching cruises May–Oct.*

New Hampshire Seacoast Cruises offers both narrated tours of the Isles of Shoals and whale-watching expeditions from June to Labor Day out of Rye Harbor State Marina. ⊠ *Rte. 1B, Rye, 03870,* ☎ *603/964–5545 or 800/734–6488.*

Portsmouth Harbor Cruises offers tours of Portsmouth Harbor, trips to the Isles of Shoals, foliage trips on the Cocheco River, and sunset cruises aboard the M/V *Heritage.* ⊠ *Ceres Street Dock, Portsmouth,* ☎ *603/436–8084 or 800/776–0915.* ☉ *Tour cruises June–Oct.*

HIKING

In addition to hiking opportunities mentioned throughout this section, an excellent 1-mile trail reaches the summit of **Blue Job Mountain** (⊠ Crown Point Rd. off Rte. 202A, 1 mi from Rochester), where there is a fire tower with a good view. The **Bureau of Trails** (☎ 603/271–3254) keeps up the Rockingham Recreation Trail, which wends 27 miles from Epping to Manchester and is open to hikers, bikers, snowmobilers, and cross-country skiers.

VISITOR INFORMATION

Hours are generally Monday through Friday, 9–5. **Seacoast Council on Tourism** (⊠ 235 West Rd., Suite 10, Portsmouth 03801, ☎ 603/436–7678 or 800/221–5623) serves the entire coastal area. **Exeter Area Chamber of Commerce** (⊠ 120 Water St., Exeter 03833, ☎ 603/772–2411). **Greater Dover Chamber of Commerce** (⊠ 299 Central Ave., Dover 03820, ☎ 603/742–2218). **Greater Portsmouth Chamber of Commerce** (⊠ 500 Market St. Ext., Portsmouth 03801, ☎ 603/436–1118). **Hampton Beach Area Chamber of Commerce** (⊠ 836 Lafayette Rd., Hampton 03842, ☎ 603/926–8717).

LAKES REGION

Lake Winnipesaukee, a Native American name for "Smile of the Great Spirit," is the largest of the dozens of lakes scattered across the eastern half of central New Hampshire. In fact, with 283 miles of shoreline, it's the largest in the state. Dotted as it is with so many islands, some claim Winnipesaukee has an island for every day of the year. In truth, there are 274 of them, which fails this speculation by about three months.

Unlike Winnipesaukee, which hums with activity all summer long, the more secluded Squam Lake, with a dearth of public-access points, seems to shun visitors. Perhaps it was this tranquillity that attracted producers of the 1981 film *On Golden Pond;* several scenes of this Oscar-winning film were shot here. Nearby Lake Wentworth is named for the first Royal Governor of the state, who, in building his country manor here, established North America's first summer resort.

This region is rich with historic landmarks, including some well-preserved Colonial and 19th-century villages. Eating and recreational opportunities abound, too: There are dozens of good restaurants, several golf courses, hiking trails, and good antiquing along the way. But to experience the Lakes Region to its fullest, you'll want to enjoy some form of water play, whether it be swimming, fishing, sailing, or just sitting on an old dock dangling your toes in any of these icy lakes.

The towns in this section begin with Alton Bay, at Lake Winnipesaukee's southernmost tip, and move clockwise around the lakes, starting on Route 11.

Numbers in the margin correspond to points of interest on the New Hampshire Lakes map.

Alton Bay

⑬ *35 mi northeast of Concord, 41 mi northwest of Portsmouth.*

Neither quiet nor secluded, Lake Winnipesaukee's southern shore is alive with tourists from the moment the first flower blooms until the last maple has shed its leaves. Two mountain ridges hold 7 miles of Winnipesaukee in Alton Bay, the name of both the inlet and the town at its tip. Aside from the lake's cruise boats, which dock here, there are a dance pavilion, miniature golf, a public beach, and a Victorian-style bandstand for summer concerts.

Dining

$$$$ ✕ **Crystal Quail.** This restaurant's namesake dish is now served year-round, but this tiny restaurant, in an 18th-century farmhouse, is worth the drive even if you don't prefer quail. The prix-fixe menu may include saffron-garlic soup, a house pâté, quenelle-stuffed sole, or duck in crisp potato shreds. You're welcome to bring your own alcohol since the Crystal Quail doesn't have a liquor license. As seating is for just 12 patrons, this is the most intimate dining experience in New Hampshire. ⊠ *Pitman Rd., Center Barnstead (12 mi south of Alton Bay),* ☎ *603/269–4151. Reservations essential. No credit cards. BYOB. No lunch. Closed Mon., Tues.*

Gilford

⑭ *18½ mi northwest of Alton Bay.*

One of the larger public beaches on Lake Winnipesaukee is in Gilford, a resort community. When incorporated in 1812, the town asked its oldest resident to name it. A veteran of the Battle of the Guilford Courthouse, in North Carolina, he borrowed that town's name—though apparently he didn't know how to spell it. The town today is as quiet and peaceful as it must have been then. Commercial development has been shunned here; you couldn't buy a T-shirt or piece of pottery if you tried.

☾ The **Gunstock Recreation Area** is a sprawling four-season recreation park with an Olympic-size pool, a children's playground, hiking and mountain biking trails, horses, paddleboats, and a campground with 300 tent and trailer sites. A major downhill-skiing center (☞ Skiing, *below*), it once claimed the longest tow rope in the country—an advantage that helped local downhill skier and Olympic silver medalist Penny Pitou perfect her craft. ⊠ *Route 11A,* ☎ *603/293–4341.*

The Arts

New Hampshire Music Festival (⊠ 88 Belknap Mountain Rd., 03246, ☎ 603/524–1000) brings award-winning professional orchestras to the Lakes Region each summer from early July through mid-August.

Beach

Ellacoya State Beach (⊠ Rte. 11) covers just 600 feet along the southwestern shore of Lake Winnipesaukee with views of the Ossipee and Sandwich mountain ranges.

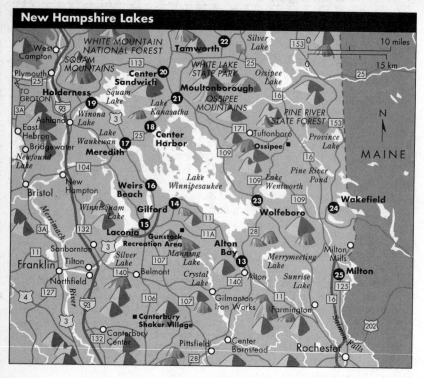

New Hampshire Lakes

Dining and Lodging

$$–$$$ ✕⌂ **B. Mae's Resort Inn.** All the rooms in this resort and conference center are large; some one-bedroom condominiums have kitchens. ⌂ *Rte. 11A, 03246,* ☎ *603/293–7526 or 800/458–3877,* FAX *603/293– 4340. 82 rooms with bath. Restaurant, bar, indoor pool, exercise room, recreation room. AE, D, DC, MC, V.*

$$–$$$ ✕⌂ **Gunstock Country Inn.** This country-style resort and motor inn about a minute's drive from the Gunstock recreation area has rooms of various sizes furnished with American antiques and with views of the mountains and Lake Winnipesaukee. ⌂ *580 Cherry Valley Rd. (Rte. 11A), 03246,* ☎ *603/293–2021 or 800/654–0180,* FAX *603/293–2050. 27 rooms with bath. Restaurant, indoor pool, health club. AE, MC, V.*

Shopping

Pepi Hermann Crystal (⌂ 3 Waterford Pl., ☎ 603/528–1020) sells hand-cut crystal chandeliers and stemware; you can also take a tour and watch the artists at work.

Skiing

Gunstock. High above Lake Winnipesaukee, the pleasant, all-purpose ski area of Gunstock attracts some skiers for overnight stays and others—many from Boston and its suburbs—for day skiing. Gunstock allows skiers to return lift tickets for a cash refund for any reason—weather, snow conditions, health, equipment problems—within an hour and 15 minutes of purchase. That policy plus a staff highly trained in customer service give class to an old-time ski area; Gunstock dates to the 1930s. ⌂ *Box 1307, Laconia, 03247, Rte. 11A,* ☎ *603/293–4341 or 800/486–7864.*

DOWNHILL

Clever trail cutting, along with trail grooming and surface sculpting three times daily have made this otherwise pedestrian mountain an interesting place for intermediates. That's how most of the 45 trails are rated, with a few more challenging runs and designated sections for slow skiers and learners. Lower Ramrod trail is specially set up for snowboarding. The 1,400 feet of vertical has one quad, two triple, and two double chairlifts and two surface tows. Gunstock has the third largest night-skiing facility in New England, with 13 trails lit for night and five lifts operating.

CROSS-COUNTRY

For the cross-country crowd, Gunstock has 40 kilometers (25 miles) of cross-country trails. Fifteen kilometers (9⅓ miles) are rated for advanced skiers, and there are backcountry trails as well.

CHILD CARE

The nursery takes children from 6 months; the ski school teaches the SKIwee system to children 3–12.

Laconia

⑮ *5 mi southwest of Gilford.*

When the railroad reached Laconia—then called Meredith Bridge—in 1848, the formerly sleepy community became a manufacturing and trading center. Today, the **Belknap Mill,** the oldest unaltered, brick-built textile mill in the United States, contains a knitting museum devoted to the textile industry. ⊠ *Mill Plaza,* ☎ *603/524–8813.* ☉ *Weekdays 9–5, Sat. 9–1.*

The Arts

The **Belknap Mill Society** (⊠ Mill Plaza, ☎ 603/524–8813) is a year-round cultural center housed in a 19th-century textile mill. The society sponsors concerts, exhibits, a lecture series, and workshops in arts and crafts and on history.

Beaches

Two of the area's public beaches are in Laconia: **Bartlett Beach** (⊠ Winnisquam Ave.) and **Opechee Park** (⊠ N. Main St.).

Dining and Lodging

$$ ✕ **Le Chalet Rouge.** This yellow house with a modestly decorated dining room is not unlike the country bistros of France. Neither the decor nor the menu is flashy, which most diners find refreshing. To start, try the wonderful house pâté, escargots, or steamed mussels. Steak au poivre is tender and well-spiced and the duckling is prepared with seasonal sauces: rhubarb in spring, raspberry in summer, orange in fall, creamy mustard in winter. ⊠ *385 W. Main St., Tilton (10 mi west of Laconia),* ☎ *603/286–4035. Reservations essential. AE.*

$–$$ ✕⊡ **Hickory Stick Farm.** The 200-year-old Cape-style inn has two
★ large, old-fashioned guest rooms with cannonball beds, stenciled wallpaper, and lace curtains. Breakfast is on the sunporch and might include such goodies as peach-and-cream-cheese-stuffed French toast. The specialty of this nearly half-century old restaurant is roast duckling with country herb stuffing and orange-sherry sauce, which you order by portion—the quarter, half, or whole duck. Also consider the beef tenderloin, rack of lamb, or a vegetarian casserole. ⊠ *60 Bean Hill Rd., Belmont (4 mi from Laconia), 03246,* ☎ *603/524–3333. 2 rooms with bath. Restaurant (no lunch). Full breakfast included. AE, D, MC, V. Call for winter hrs.*

Shopping

Strictly New England (⊠ 569 Main St., ☎ 603/524–7589) sells a variety of local crafts including Laconia pottery, birdhouses made in

Meredith, and lap robes in New Hampshire's official tartan. The **Belk-nap Mall** (☎ 603/524–5651), on Route 3, has boutiques, crafts stores, and a New Hampshire state liquor store.

OFF THE
BEATEN PATH

CANTERBURY SHAKER VILLAGE – This outdoor museum has crafts demonstrations, a large shop with fine Shaker reproductions, and a restaurant that serves Sunday brunch, lunch daily, and candlelight dinners before the 7 PM tour on Friday and Saturday nights. Most visitors spend the better part of a day here. Tours last 90 minutes and visit half of the 24 restored buildings on the property. This religious community flourished in the 1800s and practiced equality of the sexes and races, common ownership, celibacy, and pacifism. Shakers were known for the simplicity and integrity of their designs, especially in household furniture; they are also the inventors of such items as the clothespin and the flat broom. ⊠ *288 Shaker Rd., 7 mi from Exit 18 off I–93, Canterbury, ☎ 603/783–9511. ⊐ $8. ⊙ May–Oct., daily 10–5; Apr., Nov., Dec., Fri.–Sun. 10–5 (Fri. and Sat., dinner and 7 PM tour; reservations essential).*

Weirs Beach

🅰 *7½ mi north of Laconia.*

Weirs Beach—dubbed New Hampshire's Coney Island—is Lake Winnipesaukee's center for arcade activity. Anyone who loves souvenir shops, fireworks, bumper cars, and hordes of children will be right at home. Several cruise boats (☞ Guided Tours *in* Contacts and Resources, *below*) depart from the town dock for tours of the lake.

The period cars of the **Winnipesaukee Railroad** carry passengers along the lake's shore on an hour-long ride; boarding is at Weirs Beach or Meredith. ⊠ *Box 9, Lincoln 03251 (mail), ☎ 603/279–5253. ⊐ 1-hr trip $7.50, 2-hr trip $8.50. ⊙ July–mid-Sept., daily; weekends only Memorial Day–late June and late Sept.–mid-Oct. Call for hrs for special Santa trains in Dec.*

ℭ There's a giant **Water Slide** (☎ 603/366–5161) overlooking the lake.
ℭ For a more extensive summer water slide experience, try **Surf Coaster** (☎ 603/366–4991): Seven different slides, a wave pool, and an extensive area for young children, combine to keep the whole family busy. You can spend all day or night working your way through the miniature golf course, 20 lanes of bowling, and more than 500 games at
ℭ **Funspot** (☎ 603/366–4377).

NEED A
BREAK?

Kellerhaus (⊠ Daniel Webster Hwy., ☎ 603/366–4466), just north of Weirs Beach and overlooking the lake, is an alpine-style building that has been selling homemade chocolates, hard candy, and ice cream since 1906. Kids love the ice-cream smorgasbord, which has a great variety of toppings. Fortunately, the price is based not on the number of scoops but on the size of the dish.

Nightlife

M/S Mount Washington (☎ 603/366–2628) has moonlight dinner-and-dance cruises Tuesday–Saturday evenings, with two bands and a different menu each night.

Outdoor Activities and Sports

BOATING

You'll find pontoon boats, power boats, and personal watercraft for rent at **Thurston's Marina** (☎ 603/366–4811) in Weirs Beach.

Meredith

⑰ *6 mi north of Weirs Beach.*

Meredith, on Route 3 at the western extremity of Lake Winnipesaukee, has a fine collection of crafts shops and art galleries, and two museums. An information center is across from the Town Docks.

The town has become well known as the home of **Annalee's Doll Museum.** Visitors can view a vast collection of the famous felt dolls and learn about the woman behind their creation. ⊠ *Rte. 104,* ☎ *603/279–4144.* ➤ *$2.*

On rainy days you can visit the **Children's Museum and Shop,** where kids can make bubbles and play instruments. ⊠ *28 Lang St.,* ☎ *603/279–1007 or 800/883–2377.* ➤ *$5.* ⊙ *Tues.–Sat. 9:30–5, Sun. noon–5.*

The Arts
The **Lakes Region Summer Theatre** (⊠ Interlakes Auditorium, Rte. 25, 03253, ☎ 603/279–9933) has Broadway musicals six nights a week.

Beach
Wellington State Beach (⊠ Off Rte. 3A, Bristol), on the western shore of Newfound Lake, is one of the most beautiful area beaches. You can swim or picnic along the ½-mile sandy beach or take the scenic walking trail.

Lodging and Camping
$ **Nutmeg Inn.** This white Cape-style house with black shutters was built in 1763 by a sea captain who obtained the dwelling's timber by dismantling his ship. An 18th-century ox yoke is bolted to the wall over a walk-in-size fireplace, and the wide-board floors are original. All the rooms, two of which have fireplaces, are named after spices and decorated accordingly. The inn is on a rural side street off Route 104, the main link between I–93 and Lake Winnipesaukee. ⊠ *80 Pease Rd., 03253,* ☎ *603/279–8811. 8 rooms with bath, 2 rooms share bath, 1 suite. Pool, meeting rooms. Full breakfast included. D, MC, V. Closed late Oct.–May.*

$ **Clearwater Campground.** This is a wooded, tent and RV campground on Lake Pemigewasset. ⊠ *Rte. 104, 03253,* ☎ *603/279–7761.*

$ **Meredith Woods.** Here are year-round camping and RV facilities and an indoor heated pool. ⊠ *Rte. 104, 03253,* ☎ *603/279–5449 or 800/848–0328.*

Outdoor Activities and Sports
BOATING
You can rent power boats from **Meredith Marina and Boating Center** (⊠ Bay Shore Dr., ☎ 603/279–7921).

Shopping
At the **Old Print Barn** (⊠ Winona Rd., look for "Lane" on the mailbox, ☎ 603/279–6479), choose from 1,000 rare prints from around the world. This is the largest print gallery in northern New England. The **Meredith League of New Hampshire Craftsmen** (⊠ Rte. 3, ½ mi north of the junction of Rtes. 3 and 104, ☎ 603/279–7920) sells the juried work of area artisans. **Mill Falls Marketplace** (☎ 603/279–7006), on the bay in Meredith, contains nearly two dozen shops, as well as restaurants and an inn.

Center Harbor

(18) *6 mi northeast of Meredith.*

The town of Center Harbor, set on the middle of three bays at the northern end of Winnipesaukee, also borders Lakes Squam, Waukewan, and Winona.

Dining and Lodging

$–$$ ✕🏠 **Red Hill Inn.** The large bay window in the common room of this rambling inn overlooks "Golden Pond." Furnished with Victorian pieces and country furniture, many rooms have fireplaces, and some have whirlpool baths; one has a mural of nursery-rhyme characters. Chef Elmer Davis loves dessert. The wait staff recites close to a dozen choices, including his famous vinegar pie (which is sweeter than it sounds) and Kentucky high pie. But before you get that far, try baked brie wrapped in phyllo, and any one of two dozen entrées, including lamb and duck. ✉ *R.D. 1, Box 99M (Rte. 25B), 03226,* ☎ *603/279–7001 or 800/573–3445,* ℻ *603/279–7003. 21 rooms with bath. Restaurant, bar. Full breakfast included. AE, D, DC, MC, V.*

Outdoor Activities and Sports

HIKING

Red Hill, a trail on Bean Road off Route 25, northeast of Center Harbor, really does turn red in autumn. The reward at the end of the trail in any season is a beautiful view of Squam Lake and the mountains.

Shopping

Keepsake Quilting & Country Pleasures (✉ Senter's Marketplace on Rte. 25, mailing address: Box 1459, Meredith 03253, ☎ 603/253–4026) calls itself America's largest quilt shop and proves it with 5,000 bolts of fabric, hundreds of quilting books, and countless supplies.

Holderness

(19) *15 mi northwest of Meredith.*

Routes 25B and 25 lead to the town of Holderness, perched between Squam and Little Squam lakes. The Katharine Hepburn and Henry Fonda movie, *On Golden Pond,* was filmed on Squam and its quiet beauty attracts nature lovers.

🦢 The **Science Center of New Hampshire,** on the shores of Squam Lake, is a 200-acre nature center. The center maintains several trails, including a ¾-mile trail where you might encounter black bears, bobcats, otter, and snowy owls. Trailside exhibits provide plenty of hands-on activities for kids. The center also sponsors educational events, including an "Up Close to Animals" series in July and August in which visitors can study such species as the red shouldered hawk. ✉ *Jct. Rtes. 113 and 25,* ☎ *603/968–7194.* 🎫 *$7.* 🕙 *May–Oct., daily 9:30–4:30.*

Dining, Lodging, and Camping

$$$$ ✕🏠 **Manor on Golden Pond.** Built in 1903, this dignified inn has well-
★   groomed grounds, clay tennis courts, a swimming pool, and a private dock with canoes, paddle boats, and a boathouse. Guests can stay in the main inn, the carriage-house suites, or one of the four housekeeping cottages. Ten rooms have wood-burning fireplaces; three have two-person whirlpool baths. Guests feast on a five-course prix-fixe dinner with such specialties as rack of lamb, filet mignon, and nonpareil apple pie. ✉ *Rte. 3, 03245,* ☎ *603/968–3348 or 800/545–2141,* ℻ *603/968–2116. 17 rooms in main house, 6 rooms in carriage house, and 4 2-bedroom housekeeping cottages, all with bath. Restaurant, pub. AE, MC, V.*

$–$$ 🏨 **Inn on Golden Pond.** This informal country home, built in 1879 and set on 50 wooded acres, is just across the road from Squam Lake. Visitors have lake access and can stroll among the property's many nature trails. Rooms have a traditional country decor of hardwood floors, braided rugs, easy chairs, and calico-print bedspreads and curtains; the quietest are in the rear on the third floor. You may savor homemade rhubarb jam at breakfast, from rhubarb grown on the property. ✉ *Rte. 3, Box 680, 03245,* ☎ *603/968–7269. 8 rooms with bath. Full breakfast included. AE, MC, V.*

$ ⚠ **Squam Lakeside Camp Resort and Marina.** Open year-round, this campgroud has full hookups and cable TV. ✉ *Rte. 3, 03245,* ☎ *603/968–7227.*

$ ⚠ **Yogi Bear's Jellystone Park.** This area is especially good for families. ✉ *Rte. 32, N. Ashland 03217,* ☎ *603/968–9000.*

Center Sandwich

⑳   *12 mi northeast of Holderness.*

With Squam Lake to the west and the Sandwich Mountains to the north, Center Sandwich enjoys one of the prettiest settings of any town in the Lakes region; and the village center has charming 18th- and 19th-century buildings. So inspiring is the town and its views that John Greenleaf Whittier used the Bearcamp River as the inspiration for his poem "Sunset on the Bearcamp." The town attracts artisans, so crafts shops abound.

The **Historical Society Museum** of Center Sandwich traces the history of the town largely through the faces of its inhabitants. Mid-19th-century portraitist and town son Albert Gallatin Hoit has eight works here; they are hung alongside a local photographer's exhibit portraying the town's mothers and daughters. ✉ *Maple St.,* ☎ *603/284–6269;* ☉ *June–Sept., Tues.–Sat. 11–5.*

Dining and Lodging

$ ✕🏨 **Corner House Inn.** The three comfortable, old-fashioned rooms upstairs in this quaint Victorian inn display original paintings and quilted wall hangings by local artists. Before you get to the white chocolate cheesecake with Key-lime filling, served in a converted barn, you may want to try the chef's lobster-and-mushroom bisque or mouthwatering crab cakes. Exposed beams mix with candlelight and the whimsical touches of local arts and crafts. Come by on Thursday to hear storytellers perform in the glow of the woodstove. ✉ *Rtes. 109 and 113, 03227,* ☎ *603/284–6219,* FAX *603/284–6220. 3 rooms with bath. Restaurant. Full breakfast included. AE, D, MC, V. Closed Mon. and Tues. Nov.–mid-June.*

Shopping

Sandwich Home Industries (✉ Rte. 109, ☎ 603/284–6831), the 65-year-old grandparent of the League of New Hampshire Craftsmen, was formed to foster cottage crafts. There are crafts demonstrations in July and August and sales of home furnishings and accessories mid-May–October. **Ayottes' Designery** (☎ 603/284–6915, ☉ Thurs.–Sat. 10–5 or by appointment) is the handweaving business of Robert and Roberta Ayotte. In addition to selling weaving supplies, they weave rugs, wall hangings, and placemats.

Moultonborough

㉑ *5 mi south of Center Sandwich.*

Moultonborough claims 6½ miles of shoreline on Lake Kanasatka, as well as a small piece of Squam.

People love to browse in the **Old Country Store and Museum.** The store has been selling everything including handmade soaps, antiques, maple products, aged cheeses, and penny candy since 1781. The museum displays antique farming and forging tools. ⊠ *Moultonborough Corner,* ☎ *603/476–5750.*

The town's best-known attraction is the **Castle in the Clouds.** Construction began in 1911 on this odd, elaborate stone mansion and went on for three years; owner Thomas Gustave Plant pumped $7 million into this dwelling, which, amazingly, was built without nails. It has 16 rooms, eight bathrooms, and doors made of lead. Unfortunately, Plant spent the bulk of his huge fortune on this project and died penniless in 1946. Castle Springs water is now bottled on the property. ⊠ *Rte. 171,* ☎ *603/476–2352 or 800/729–2468.* ☜ *$10 with tour, $4 without tour.* ☉ *Mid-June–mid-Oct., daily 9–5; mid-May–mid-June, weekends 10–4.*

The Loon Center at the **Frederick and Paula Anna Markus Wildlife Sanctuary** on the northwestern shore of Lake Winnipesaukee is the headquarters of the Loon Preservation Committee, an Audubon Society project. Loons, one of New Hampshire's most popular birds, are threatened by lake traffic, poor water quality, and habitat loss. At the center, you can learn about the black and white birds whose calls haunt New Hampshire lakes. In addition, two nature trails wind through the 200-acre property. Vantage points on the Loon Nest Trail overlook the spot that resident loons sometimes occupy in June. ⊠ *Lees Mills Rd., 03254 (follow signs from Rte. 25 to Blake Rd. to Lees Mills Rd.),* ☎ *603/476–5666.* ☉ *July 4–Columbus Day, daily 9–5; rest of yr., Mon.–Sat. 9–5.*

Dining

$$–$$$ ✕ **The Woodshed.** This 1860s former barn has farm implements and antiques hanging on the walls. Eat from the raw bar or try the New England section of the menu, which includes clam chowder, scrod, and Indian pudding. Diners love the Denver chocolate pudding, a dense pudding-cake served warm with vanilla ice cream. ⊠ *Lee's Mill Rd.,* ☎ *603/476–2311. AE, D, DC, MC, V. Closed Mon.*

$$ ✕ **Sweetwater Inn.** Chef and owner Mike Love makes eveything from scratch, right down to the home-churned blackberry-honey butter. He makes the pasta daily for the lobster ravioli (with a pepper-vodka sauce) and the fettuccine jambalaya (with chicken, scallops, andouille sausage, and Cajun spices). Paellas and pollo con gambas (chicken breast and shrimp sautéed with brandy) add to the mix. No salt is used in any dish. The decor is as eclectic as the menu: The formality of linen tablecloths and effusive service is tempered by the woodstoves and proliferation of local art. ⊠ *Rte. 25,* ☎ *603/476–5079. AE, DC, MC, V.*

Tamworth

㉒ *11 mi northeast of Moultonborough.*

President Grover Cleveland summered here. His son, Francis, returned to stay and founded the Barnstormers Theater. Tamworth also has a clutch of villages within its borders. At one of them—Chocorua—the view through the birches of Chocorua Lake has been so often photographed that you may get a sense of having been here before. Don't miss the tiny South Tamworth post office—this charming building looks like a children's playhouse.

NEED A
BREAK? The **Country Handcrafters & Tea Room** is a great place to stop for ice cream, coffee, or tea and scones. Take time to go upstairs and browse through room after room of handcrafted items. Rooms are arranged thematically, right down to the stenciling on the walls, with a Christmas room, a bride's room, and a children's room. ⊠ *Rte. 16, Chocorua 03817,* ☎ *603/323-8745.* ⊙ *Daily 10-5.*

The Arts

Arts Council of Tamworth (☎ 603/323–7793) produces concerts—soloists, string quartets, revues, children's programs—from September through June, followed by a summer arts show the last weekend in July. **Barnstormers** (⊠ Main St., ☎ 603/323–8500), New Hampshire's oldest professional theater, performs Equity summer theater in July and August. The box office opens in June; before June, call the Tamworth Inn (☞ Dining and Lodging, *below*) for information.

Dining and Lodging

$$ ✕🅃 **Tamworth Inn.** Although the Barnstormer Theater has moved
★ across the street, they still rehearse at the inn. Summer guests never miss a performance, unless they're hiking the trails in the nearby Hemenway State Forest. Every room has 19th-century American pieces and handmade quilts. In the dining room, try the provolone-and-pesto terrine and the pork tenderloin with apple-walnut cornbread stuffing and an apple cider sauce. Warning: The profiterole Tamworth is big enough for two. There's also a pub that offers lighter fare. Sunday brunch is a summer favorite. ⊠ *Main St., Box 189, 03886,* ☎ *603/323–7721 or 800/642–7352,* 𝖥𝖠𝖷 *603/323–2026. 15 rooms with bath. Restaurant (closed Sun.–Mon. in summer, Sun.–Tues. in winter), pub, pool. Full breakfast included; MAP available. MC, V.*

Outdoor Activities and Sports

White Lake State Park (⊠ Rte. 16, 03886, ☎ 603/323–7350) has a 72-acre stand of native pitch pine, which is a National Natural Landmark. The park also has hiking trails, a sandy beach, trout fishing, canoe rentals, two separate camping areas, a picnic area, and swimming.

En Route Between Ossipee and West Ossipee, Route 16 passes sparkling Lake Ossipee, known for fine fishing and swimming. Among these hamlets you'll also find several antiques shops and galleries. At Tramway Artisans (⊠ Rte. 16, West Ossipee, 03890–0748, ☎ 603/539–5700) you can choose from the work of more than 100 different artisans, many local. Jewelry, turned wooden bowls, pewter goblets, and glassware are just a few of the items for sale.

Wolfeboro

❷❸ *28 mi south of Tamworth, 15 mi southeast of Moultonborough.*

Wolfeboro's downtown area is right on Winnipesaukee, attracting droves of tourists all summer long: The Chamber of Commerce estimates that the population increases tenfold each June. Wolfeboro has been a resort since John Wentworth, the first Royal Governor of the state, built his summer home on the shores of Lake Wentworth in 1763.

Governor Wentworth's house burned in 1820, but you can see some salvaged items at the **Libby Museum** along with an unusual natural-history collection. ⊠ *Rte. 109,* ☎ *603/569–1035.* ⊙ *Memorial Day–Labor Day, Tues.–Sun. 10–4.*

The **Clark House Historical Exhibit and Museum** takes a conventional look at the town's history; one exhibit re-creates a late 19th-century fire station, complete with a red fire engine. ⊠ *S. Main St.,* ☎ *603/569–4997.* ⏱ *July–Aug., Mon.–Sat. 10–4.*

Wolfeboro is headquarters to the **Hampshire Pewter Company** (⊠ 40 Mill Rd., ☎ 603/569-4944), where artisans still use 17th-century techniques to make pewter hollowware and accessories. Shop tours begin on the hour, weekdays in summer; less often off-season.

Beach

Wentworth State Beach (Rte. 109) has good swimming and picnicking areas, and a bath house.

Dining and Lodging

$$ ✕ The Bittersweet. This converted barn has an eclectic display of old quilts, pottery, sheet music, and china. Although it may feel like a cozy crafts shop, it's really a restaurant that locals love for the nightly specials that range from seafood to Chateaubriand. The upper level has antique tables and chairs and candlelight dining, while the lower level post-and-beam lounge, decorated with Victorian wicker furniture, serves lighter fare. ⊠ *Rte. 28,* ☎ *603/569–3636. AE, D, MC, V.*

$$ ✕🖼 Wolfeboro Inn. This white-clapboard house was built nearly 200 years ago but has 19th- and 20th-century additions, which extend to the waterfront of Wolfeboro Bay. Rooms have polished cherry and pine furnishings, armoires (to hide the TVs), stenciled borders, and country quilts. More than 45 brands of beer are available at Wolfe's Tavern, where food is cooked in a fireplace. Try the veal Wolfeboro, a delicious combination of sautéed veal, lobster, and shrimp topped with a cream sauce. The main dining room serves a very popular twin-lobster special. ⊠ *90 N. Main St., 03894,* ☎ *603/569–3016 or 800/451–2389,* 𝖥𝖠𝖷 *603/569–5375. 44 rooms with bath, 5 suites. 2 restaurants, bar, beach, boating. CP. AE, D, MC, V.*

Outdoor Activities and Sports

HIKING

A few miles north of town on Route 109 is the trailhead to **Abenaki Tower.** A short (¼-mile) hike to the 100-foot post-and-beam tower, followed by a more rigorous climb to the top, rewards you with a vast view of Winnipesaukee and the Ossipee mountain range.

WATER SPORTS

The Lake Winnipesaukee is teeming with boats in summer. Look for waterskiing regulations at every marina. Scuba divers can explore a 130-foot-long cruise ship that sunk in 30 feet of water off Glendale in 1895. **Dive Winnipesaukee Corp.** (⊠ 4 N. Main St., ☎ 603/569–2120) runs charters out to this and other wrecks and offers instruction, rentals, repairs, and scuba sales. It also offers lessons in waterskiing and windsurfing.

Shopping

Dow's Corner Shop (⊠ Rte. 171, Tuftonboro Corner, ☎ 603/539–4790) has not one but two of everything. So crowded with historic memorabilia, this antiques shop could pass as a museum.

Wakefield

㉔ *18 mi east of Wolfeboro, 26 mi southeast of Tamworth.*

East of Winnipesaukee lie several villages that lack the lake's tourism bustle and combine to form **Wakefield.** The town itself has 10 lakes. **Wakefield Corner,** on the Maine border, is a registered historic district, with a church, houses, and an inn looking just as they did in the 18th century.

  The charming **Museum of Childhood** displays a one-room schoolhouse from 1890, model trains, antique children's sleds, and 3,000 dolls. ✉ *Off Rte. 16 in Wakefield Corner,* ☎ *603/522–8073.* 🎟 *$3.* 🕐 *Memorial Day–Columbus Day, Mon. and Wed.–Sat. 11–4, Sun. 1–4.*

Lodging

$ 🏨 **Wakefield Inn.** The restoration of this 1804 stage-coach inn, in
★ Wakefield's historic district, has been handled with an eye for detail. The dining room windows retain the original panes and Indian shutters, but the centerpiece of the building is the free-standing spiral staircase that rises three stories. Rooms are named for famous guests (such as John Greenleaf Whittier) or past owners. The large guest rooms have wide pine floors, big sofas, and handmade quilts. Guests can make their own quilt in one weekend with the Quilting Package course offered in late fall and early spring. ✉ *2723 Wakefield Rd., 03872,* ☎ *603/522–8272 or 800/245–0841. 7 rooms with bath. Full breakfast included. MC, V.*

Milton

  ㉕ *15½ mi south of Wakefield.*

Milton stretches out alongside the Salmon Falls River, Town House Pond, Milton Pond, and Northeast Pond; all of which flow together to create a seemingly endless body of water.

The **New Hampshire Farm Museum** is a collection of farm implements and tools and a living museum with weekend events demonstrating farm-related crafts. In yellow buildings trimmed with green, you'll find blacksmith and cobbler shops, a country store, and a furnished farmhouse. There are numerous special events throughout the summer. ✉ *Rte. 125,* ☎ *603/652–7840.* 🎟 *$5.* 🕐 *Mid-June–Columbus Day, Tues.–Sat. 10–4, Sun. noon–4.*

Lakes Region A to Z

Arriving and Departing

BY CAR

Most people driving into this region arrive via I–93 to Route 3 in the west or by the Spaulding Turnpike to Route 11 in the east.

BY PLANE

The nearest airports serviced by major commercial carriers are both about an hour outside the Lakes region. You can fly into **Manchester Airport** (☎ 603/624–6556), the state's largest, which has scheduled flights from USAir, Delta, Continental, Northwest Airlink, United, and TWA.

Getting Around

BY BUS

Concord Trailways (☎ 800/639–3317) has daily stops in Tilton, Laconia, Meredith, Center Harbor, Moultonborough, and Conway.

BY CAR

On the western side of the Lakes region, I–93 is the principal north–south artery. Exit 20 leads to Route 11 and the southwestern side of Lake Winnipesaukee. Take Exit 23 to Route 104 to Route 25 and the northwestern corner of the region. From the coast, Route 16 stretches to the White Mountains, with roads leading to the lakeside towns.

Moultonborough Airport Charter (⊠ Rte. 25, Moultonborough, ☎ 603/476–8801) offers chartered flights and tours.

Contacts and Resources

BOATING
The **Lakes Region Association** (⊠ Box 589, Center Harbor 03226, ☎ 603/253–8555) gives boating advice.

EMERGENCIES
Lakes Region General Hospital (⊠ 80 Highland St., Laconia, ☎ 603/524–3211).

FISHING
For up-to-date fishing information, call the **New Hampshire Fish and Game** office (☎ 603/744–5470).

GOLF
There are a number of 18-hole golf courses in the lakes region. A few to try are **White Mountain Country Club** (⊠ N. Ashland Rd., Ashland, ☎ 603/536–2227), **Kingswood Golf Course** (⊠ Rte. 28, Wolfeboro, ☎ 603/569–3569), and **Waukewan Golf Course** (⊠ Off Rtes. 3 and 25, Center Harbor, ☎ 603/279–6661).

GUIDED TOURS
The **M/S *Mount Washington*** (⊠ Box 5367, 03247, ☎ 603/366–2628 or 603/366–5531) is a 230-foot craft that makes three-hour cruises of Lake Winnipesaukee. Departures are mid-May through mid-October, from Weirs Beach, Wolfeboro, Center Harbor, and Alton Bay.

The **M/V *Sophie C.*** (☎ 603/366–2628) has been the area's floating post office for more than a century. It even has its own cancellation stamp. The boat departs Weirs Beach with both mail and passengers Saturday and Sunday from May 20 to June 11 and Monday through Saturday June 12 to September 2.

See the Lakes region by air with **Sky Bright** (Laconia Airport, ☎ 603/528–6818), which offers airplane and helicopter tours and instruction on aerial photography.

The Golden Pond Boat Tour visits filming sites of the movie *On Golden Pond* aboard the *Lady of the Manor*, a 28-foot pontoon craft. ⊠ *Manor Resort*, ☎ 603/279–4405. ⊡ *$10.* ☻ *Memorial Day–late Oct.*

Squam Lake Tours takes up to 20 passengers on a two-hour pontoon tour of "Golden Pond." Their boat can also be chartered for guided fishing trips and private parties. ⊠ *Box 185, 03245,* ☎ *603/968–7577.* ☻ *Late May–Oct.*

HIKING
The Lakes region is full of beautiful trails. Contact the Alexandria headquarters of the **Appalachian Mountain Club** (☎ 603/744–8011) or the **Laconia Office of the U.S. Forest Service** (☎ 603/528–8721) for advice and information.

VISITOR INFORMATION
Hours are generally weekdays 10–5. **Lakes Region Association** (⊠ Box 589, Center Harbor 03226, ☎ 603/253–8555). **Laconia Chamber of Commerce** (⊠ 11 Veterans Sq., Laconia 03246, ☎ 603/524–5531 or 800/531–2347). **Wolfeboro Chamber of Commerce** (⊠ Railroad Ave., Wolfeboro 03894, ☎ 603/569–2200).

THE WHITE MOUNTAINS

Sailors approaching East Coast harbors frequently mistake the pale peaks of the White Mountains—the highest range in the northeastern United States—for clouds. It was 1642 when explorer Darby Field could no longer contain his curiosity about one mountain in particular. He set off from his Exeter homestead and became the first man to climb what would eventually be called Mt. Washington, king of the Presidential range. More than a mile high, Mt. Washington must have presented Field with a slew of formidable obstacles—its peak claims the harshest winds and lowest temperatures ever recorded.

A few hundred years after Field's climb, curiosity about the mountains has not abated. People come here by the tens of thousands to hike and climb in spring and summer, to photograph the dramatic vistas and the vibrant sea of foliage in autumn, and to ski in winter. In this four-season vacation hub, many year-round resorts (some of which have been in business since the mid-1800s) are destinations in themselves, with golf, tennis, swimming, hiking, cross-country skiing, and renowned restaurants.

This section begins in Waterville Valley, off I–93, continues to Lincoln, across the Kangamagus Highway to North Conway, and circles north on Routes 16 and 302 back to the northern reaches of I–93. There is some backtracking involved because the mountains limit the number of roads.

Numbers in the margin correspond to points of interest on the White Mountains map.

Waterville Valley

㉖ *63 mi from Concord.*

In 1835, visitors began arriving in this valley—a 10-mile-long cul-de-sac cut by one of New England's Mad Rivers and circled by mountains—and they have come in increasing numbers ever since. First a summer resort, then essentially a ski area, and now a year-round resort, Waterville Valley has been developed (with taste and regard for the New England sensibility) to resemble a small town: There are inns, lodges, and condominiums; restaurants, cafés, taverns; shops, conference facilities, a grocery store, and a post office.

In winter, those who don't ski can ice skate, snowboard, or snowshoe, or amuse themselves in the sports center with tennis, racquetball, squash, a 25-meter indoor pool, jogging track, exercise equipment and classes, whirlpools, saunas, steam rooms, and a games room. In summer, hiking and mountain biking are popular.

Lodging

$$$–$$$$ 🏨 **Golden Eagle Lodge.** Waterville's premier condominium property is reminiscent of the grand hotels of an earlier era. This full-service complex, which opened in 1989, has a two-story lobby and a very capable front-desk staff. ⊠ *Snow's Brook Rd., 03215,* ☎ *603/236–4600 or 800/910–4499,* 𝖥𝖠𝖷 *603/236–4947. 139 suites. Kitchenettes, indoor pool, sauna, recreation room. AE, D, DC, MC, V.*

$$–$$$$ 🏨 **Black Bear Lodge.** This all-suite hotel has one- and two-bedroom units with full kitchens. Each unit in this family-oriented lodge is individually owned and decorated. Children's movies are shown every night in season, and there's bus service to the slopes. ⊠ *Village Rd. (Box 357), 03215,* ☎ *603/236–4501 or 800/349–2327,* 𝖥𝖠𝖷 *603/236–*

The White Mountains

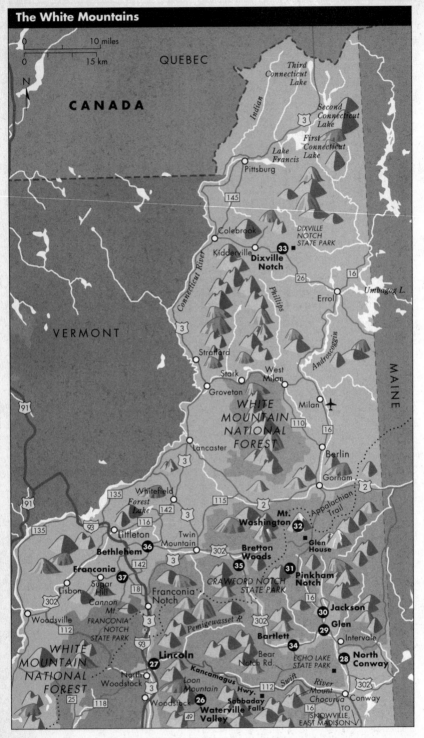

0 10 miles
0 15 km

N

QUEBEC

CANADA

Third
Connecticut
Lake

Second
Connecticut
Lake

First
Connecticut
Lake

Indian

3

Lake
Francis

Pittsburg

145

DIXVILLE
NOTCH
STATE PARK

Colebrook

Kidderville

Dixville
Notch   33

26   16

Phillips

Errol

Umbagog L.

VERMONT

Connecticut River

3

Strafford

Stark

Groveton

West
Milan

WHITE
MOUNTAIN
NATIONAL
FOREST

Milan

110

16

Androscoggin

MAINE

91

Lancaster

Berlin

Gorham

Appalachian Trail

2

3

Whitefield

135

Forest
Lake

116

91

135

93

Littleton

Bethlehem   36

Franconia   37

Lisbon

302

Woodsville

112

WHITE
MOUNTAIN
NATIONAL
FOREST

Sugar
Hill

Cannon
Mt.

FRANCONIA
NOTCH
STATE PARK

142

Twin
Mountain

3

18

Franconia
Notch

3

93

142

115

2

302

Mt.
Washington

32

Bretton
Woods   Glen
House

35

CRAWFORD NOTCH
STATE PARK

302

31   Pinkham
     Notch

16

30   Jackson

29   Glen

Intervale

Pemigewasset R.

Bartlett

34

Bear
Notch Rd.

ECHO LAKE
STATE PARK

28   North
     Conway

25

118

Lincoln   27

North
Woodstock

3

Woodstock

49

Kancamagus Hwy.

Loon
Mountain

26

Sabbaday Falls

Waterville
Valley

112   Swift

Mount
Chocorua

16
TO
SNOWVILLE,
EAST MADISON

River

Conway

302

2

4114. 107 suites. Indoor-outdoor pool, sauna, steam room, exercise room. AE, D, DC, MC, V.

$-$$$ ☎ **Snowy Owl Inn.** The fourth-floor bunk-bed lofts at this cozy, intimate inn are ideal for families; first-floor rooms are suitable for couples who want a quiet getaway. There is an atrium lobby with a three-story central fieldstone fireplace and many prints and watercolors of snowy owls. Four restaurants are within walking distance. ⊠ Village Rd. (Box 407), 03215, ☎ 603/236–8383 or 800/766–9969, FAX 603/236–4890. 80 rooms with bath. Indoor pool, sauna. CP. AE, D, DC, MC, V.

Nightlife and the Arts

NIGHTLIFE
The **Common Man** (☎ 603/236–8885), overlooking Corcoran's Pond, is known for a zesty cheese dip. Weekend and holiday entertainment can be found at **Legends 1291** (☎ 603/236–4678), Waterville's only year-round disco.

THE ARTS
At the **Waterville Valley Music Festival** (☎ 603/236–8371 or 800/468–2553), performers of every ilk of music, from folk to country to blues, play on the Concert Pavilion in the Town Square Saturday night from July through Labor Day.

Skiing
Waterville Valley. This resort was founded by former U.S. ski-team star Tom Corcoran and designed with families in mind, with broad, well-groomed trails. The main village is about a mile from the slopes, but a shuttle makes a car unnecessary. ⊠ Waterville Valley 03215, ☎ 603/236–8311, snow conditions 603/236–4144, lodging 800/468–2553.

DOWNHILL
Mt. Tecumseh, a short shuttle ride from the Town Square and accommodations, has been laid out with great care and attention to detail. This ski area has hosted more World Cup races than any other in the East, so most advanced skiers will be adequately challenged. The bulk of the 54 trails are intermediate: straight down the fall line, wide, and agreeably long. A new tree-skiing area adds variety. The lifts serving the 2,020 feet of vertical rise include one high-speed, detachable quad, three triple and four double chairlifts, and four surface lifts. A second mountain, Snow's, about 2 miles away from Mt. Tecumseh, is open on weekends and holidays for snowboarders only. It has five natural snow trails and one double chairlift off a 580-foot vertical with rails, funboxes, table tops, and quarter pipes.

CROSS-COUNTRY
The Waterville Valley Cross-country network, with the ski center in the Town Square, has 105 kilometers (62 miles) of trails, 70 (43½) of them groomed.

CHILD CARE
The nursery takes children 6 months through 4 years old. There are SKIwee lessons and other instruction for children ages 3–12. The Kinderpark, a children's slope, has a slow-running lift and special props to hold children's attention. Children under 6 ski free anytime; midweek, those under 13 ski and stay free with a parent on five-day packages.

Lincoln

㉗ At Exit 32 off I–93; 30 mi from Waterville Valley.

Lincoln, at the western end of the Kangamagus Highway, is a center for ski activity and is one of the state's liveliest resort towns. Festivals, like the New Hampshire Scottish Highland Games in mid-September, keep Lincoln swarming with visitors year-round.

For scenic views of the Pemigewasset River and the White Mountain National Forest, take a narrated ride on the **Hobo Railroad.** ⊠ *Rte. 112,* ☎ *603/745–2135.* 🎟 *$8.* ☼ *June–Labor Day daily; May, Sept., Oct. weekends.*

ℭ **Loon Mountain Park** offers summer fun as well as winter skiing. In the summer and fall, you can ride the gondola ($8) to the summit for a panoramic view of the White Mountain National Forest. Self-guiding nature walks from the summit lead to glacial caves. Other recreational opportunities include horseback riding, mountain biking, and in-line skating. ⊠ *Kangamagus Hwy., 03251,* ☎ *603/745–8111.*

ℭ At the **Whale's Tale Water Park,** you can float on an inner tube along a gentle river or careen down a giant waterslide. ⊠ *Rte. 3, North Lincoln,* ☎ *603/745–8810.* 🎟 *$14.95 for 47" and taller, $12.95 for under 47".* ☼ *July and Aug., daily 10–8:30. Call for early and late season hrs.*

Dining and Lodging

$$–$$$ ✕🏠 **Mountain Club on Loon.** This first-rate, slope-side resort hotel has an assortment of accommodations, such as suites that sleep as many as eight, studios with Murphy beds, and 70 units with kitchens. Guest rooms are within walking distance of the lifts, and condominiums are both on-slope and nearby. There's live entertainment in the lounge most winter weekends. Take Exit 32 from I–93 (Kancamagus Highway). ⊠ *Rte. 112, 03251,* ☎ *603/745–2244 or 800/229–7829,* ℻ *603/745–2317. 234 rooms with bath. Restaurant, bar, indoor pool, massage, sauna, aerobics, health club, racquetball, squash. AE, D, MC, V.*

$$ ✕🏠 **Indian Head Resort.** Views across the 180 acres of this resort motel near Cannon Mountain ski area are of Indian Head Rock, the Great Stone Face, and the Franconia Mountains. ⊠ *Rte. 3, North Lincoln 03251,* ☎ *603/745–8000 or 800/343–8000,* ℻ *603/745–8414. 98 rooms with bath. Restaurant, indoor pool, outdoor pool, lake, sauna, tennis court, fishing, ice-skating, recreation room. AE, D, DC, MC, V.*

$–$$ ✕🏠 **Mill House Inn.** This hotel on the western edge of the Kancamagus Highway has country-inn style and free transportation to Loon Mountain during ski season. Nearby there's shopping, a cinema, and the North Country Center for the Performing Arts. ⊠ *Box 696, 03251,* ☎ *603/745–6261 or 800/654–6183,* ℻ *603/745–6896. 74 rooms with bath, 22 suites. Restaurant, indoor and outdoor pools, hot tub, sauna, tennis court, exercise room, nightclub. AE, D, DC, MC, V.*

Nightlife and the Arts

NIGHTLIFE

Thunderbird Lounge (⊠ Indian Head Resort, North Lincoln, ☎ 603/745–8000) has nightly entertainment year-round. Skiers love the **Granite Bar** at the Mountain Club at the Loon Mountain Resort (☎ 603/745–8111). You can also dance at the **Loon Saloon** at the ski area. **Dickens** (☎ 603/745–2278), in the Village of Loon, has live musical entertainment.

THE ARTS

North Country Center for the Arts (⊠ Mill at Loon Mountain, ☎ 603/745–2141) presents concerts, children's theater, and art exhibitions from July through September.

Outdoor Activities and Sports

HIKING

A couple of short hiking trails off the Kancamagus offer great rewards for relatively little effort. The parking and picnic area for **Sabbaday**

Falls, about 20 miles east of Lincoln, is the trailhead for an easy ½-mile trail to the falls, a multilevel cascade that plunges through two potholes and a flume. **Russell Colbath Historic House** (circa 1831), 2 miles east of Sabbaday Falls, is now a U.S. Forest Service information center that marks the beginning of the **Rail 'N River Forest Trail,** a gentle ½-mile self-guided tour of White Mountains logging and geological history. It's wheelchair- and stroller-accessible. At **Lost River Reservation** (North Woodstock, ☎ 603/745–8031; ⊙ May–Oct.), you can tour the gorge and view such geological wonders as the Guillotine Rock and the Lemon Squeezer.

Shopping

Lincoln Square Outlet Stores (⊠ Rte. 112, ☎ 603/745–3883) stock predominantly factory seconds including London Fog, Van Heusen, and Bass. **Millfront Marketplace, Mill at Loon Mountain** (⊠ I–93 and the Kancamagus Hwy., ☎ 603/745–6261), a former paper factory, has become a full-service shopping center and inn, with restaurants, boutiques, a bookstore, a pharmacy, and a post office.

Skiing

Loon Mountain. A modern resort on the Kancamagus Highway and the Pemigewasset River, Loon Mountain opened in the 1960s and saw serious development in the 1980s. In the base lodge and around the mountain are a large number of food services and lounge facilities. ⊠ *Kancamagus Hwy., 03251, ☎ 603/745–8111, snow conditions 603/745–8100, lodging 800/227–4191.*

DOWNHILL

Wide, straight, and consistent intermediate trails prevail at Loon. Beginner trails and slopes are set apart, so faster skiers won't interfere. Most advanced runs are grouped on the North Peak section farther from the main mountain. The vertical is 2,100 feet; a four-passenger gondola, one high-speed detachable quad (with a second scheduled to follow in 1996), two triple and three double chairlifts, and one surface lift serve the 43 trails and slopes.

CROSS-COUNTRY

The touring center at Loon Mountain has 35 kilometers (22 miles) of cross-country trails.

CHILD CARE

The nursery takes children as young as 6 weeks. The ski school runs several programs for children of different age groups. Children 5 and under ski free every day, while those 6–12 ski free midweek during non-holiday periods when parents participate in a five-day ski week.

En Route Although traveling at Mach One along I–93 is the fastest way to the White Mountains, it's hardly the most scenic. From Lincoln, you can latch onto the **Kancamagus Highway** for classic White Mountains vistas and follow it nearly all the way to North Conway. This 34-mile trek erupts into fiery color each fall, when photo-snapping drivers can really slow things down. Prepare yourself for a leisurely pace, and enjoy the four scenic overlooks and picnic areas (all well marked).

North Conway

㉘ *68 mi north of Concord, 42 mi east of Lincoln.*

North Conway is a shopper's paradise, with more than 150 outlet stores ranging from Anne Klein to Joan & David. Most of them lie along Route 16.

Nonshoppers may wish to spend an afternoon on the **Conway Scenic Railroad,** which offers several trips of different durations in vintage trains pulled either by steam or diesel engines. The five-hour trip through Crawford Notch winds through some of the finest scenery in the Northeast. Lunch is available in the dining car. The Victorian train station has displays of railroad artifacts, lanterns, and old tickets and timetables. ⊠ *Rtes. 16 and 302, (Main St.),* ☎ *603/356–5251 or 800/232–5251.* ☞ *$7.50.* ⊙ *Mid-May–late Oct., daily 9–6; Apr.–mid-May and Nov.–late Dec., weekends 9–6. Reserve early during foliage season.*

At **Echo Lake State Park,** you needn't be a rock climber to glimpse views from the 1,000-foot **White Horse** and **Cathedral** ledges. From the top you'll see the entire valley in which Echo Lake shines like a diamond. An unmarked trailhead another ⁷⁄₁₀-mile on West Side Road leads to **Diana's Baths,** a spectacular series of waterfalls. ⊠ *Off Rte. 302,* ☎ *603/356–2672.* ☞ *$2.50.*

Dining and Lodging

$$ ✕ **Scottish Lion.** Although this restaurant-pub serves more than Scotch, ★   it is its specialty—you can choose from 50 varieties. In the tartan-carpeted dining rooms, you can find scones and Devonshire cream at breakfast, game and steak-and-mushroom pies at lunch and dinner. The "rumpldethump" potatoes (mashed potatoes mixed with cabbage and chives then baked au gratin) are deservedly famous. ⊠ *Rte. 16,* ☎ *603/356–6381. AE, D, DC, MC, V.*

$$–$$$ ✕▥ **Darby Field Inn.** After a day of outdoor activity in the White Mountain National Forest (which borders the property), you can warm yourself before the living room's fieldstone fireplace or by the woodstove in the bar. Most of the rooms in this unpretentious 1826 converted farmhouse have mountain views and queen-size beds. The restaurant's prix-fixe menu usually offers the inn's signature dish, chicken marquis (a sautéed breast of chicken with mushrooms, scallions, tomatoes, and white wine), or roast Wisconsin duckling glazed with Chambord or Grand Marnier. Don't leave without trying the dark chocolate pâté with white-chocolate sauce or the famous Darby cream pie. ⊠ *Bald Hill Rd., Conway 03818,* ☎ *603/447–2181 or 800/426–4147,* ℻ *603/447–5726. 15 rooms, 14 with bath, 1 suite. Restaurant, bar, pool, cross-country skiing. Jan.–Mar. rates are MAP. AE, DC, MC, V. Closed Apr.*

$$–$$$ ✕▥ **Hale's White Mountain Hotel and Resort.** This hotel with Victorian flair, which stands alone in a meadow, has guest rooms with spectacular mountain views. Proximity to the White Mountain National Forest and Echo Lake State Park makes guests feel farther away from civilization (and the nearby outlet malls) than they actually are. And the presence of a serene nine-hole golf course and 17 miles (30 kilometers) of cross-country ski trails helps, too. ⊠ *Box 1828, West Side Rd., 03860,* ☎ ℻ *603/356–7100 or* ☎ *800/533–6301. 80 rooms with bath, 11 suites. Restaurant, bar, pool, 9-hole golf course, tennis court, health club, hiking, cross-country skiing. AE, D, MC, V.*

$$–$$$ ✕▥ **Snowvillage Inn.** Journalist Frank Simonds built the main gam-★   brel-roof house in 1916. To complement the tome-jammed bookshelves found in the inn, guest rooms are named after the likes of Faulkner, Hemingway, and Twain. Of course, the nicest of the rooms, with 12 windows that look out over the Presidential Range, is a tribute to native son Robert Frost. Each of the two additional buildings—the carriage house and the chimney house—has a library, too. The innkeepers take guests on gourmet-picnic hikes up the mountains. The candlelit dining room with views of the mountains offers the specialties of French chef Alain Ginestet. Try the mouthwatering grilled shrimp with roasted red pepper puree, and leave plenty of room for dessert, when you'll have to choose between apple strudel and French silk pie. ✉ *Box 68, Stuart Rd., 03849,* ☎ *603/447–2818 or 800/447–4345. 18 rooms with bath. Restaurant (reservations essential), sauna, cross-country skiing. Full breakfast included, MAP available. AE, D, DC, MC, V. Closed Apr.*

$$ ✕⊞ **Best Western Red Jacket Mountain View.** This motor inn-cum-resort has many of the amenities of a fine hotel. Most rooms are spacious and have balconies or decks overlooking the White Mountains. The cozy public rooms have deep chairs and plants, and the 40-acre grounds are neatly landscaped. ✉ *Rte. 16, Box 2000, 03860,* ☎ *603/356–5411 or 800/752–2538,* FAX *603/356–3842. 152 rooms with bath, 12 town houses. Restaurant, indoor pool, outdoor pool, sauna, 2 tennis courts, recreation room, children's program in summer, playground. AE, D, DC, MC, V.*

$$ ✕⊞ **Purity Spring Resort.** In the late 1800s, Purity Spring was a farm and sawmill on a private lake. Since 1944 it's been a four-season resort with two Colonial inns, a series of lakeside cottages, and a ski lodge. In winter, families take advantage of the King Pine Ski Area, located on the property. You have a choice between hotel-style rooms in the ski area or inn-style rooms in the main lodge. ✉ *Rte. 153 (mailing address: HQ 63, Box 40, East Madison 03849),* ☎ *603/367–8896 or 800/373–3754,* FAX *603/367–8664. 74 rooms, 61 with bath. Restaurant, indoor pool, lake, hot tub, tennis court, hiking, volleyball, fishing. Rates are MAP or AP. AE, D, MC, V.*

$ ✕⊞ **Eastern Slope Inn Resort and Conference Center.** This elegant National Historic Site on 35 acres near Mt. Cranmore has been an operating inn for more than a century. The inn's restaurant serves traditional American fare in a glassed-in courtyard and has nightly entertainment. ✉ *Main St., 03860,* ☎ *603/356–6321 or 800/258–4708,* FAX *603/356–8732. 125 rooms with bath. Restaurant, pub, indoor pool, hot tub, sauna, tennis courts, recreation room. AE, D, MC, V.*

$ ⊞ **Cranmore Inn.** This authentic country inn, not a converted summer home or farmhouse, is at the foot of Mt. Cranmore. It opened in 1863, and the decor reflects this history with furnishings that date back to the mid-1800s. It is within easy walking distance of North Conway Village. ✉ *Kearsarge St., 03860,* ☎ *603/356–5502 or 800/526–5502,* FAX *603/356–6052. 18 rooms with bath. Restaurant, pool. Full breakfast included. AE, MC, V.*

Nightlife and the Arts

The **Best Western Red Jacket Mountain View** (☎ 603/356–5411) has weekend and holiday entertainment. **Horsefeather's** (✉ Main St., ☎ 603/356–6862) hops on the weekends. **Mt. Washington Valley Theater Company** (✉ Eastern Slope Playhouse, ☎ 603/356–5776) has musicals and summer theater from July through September, as well as a local group called the Resort Players, who give pre- and post-season performances. On Tuesday, the tavern in the **New England Inn** (Intervale, ☎ 603/356-5541) hosts a high-quality open-mike session that locals call "hoot night."

Shopping

ANTIQUES

Antiques & Collectibles Barn (✉ Rte. 16/302, 3425 Main St., ☎ 603/356–7118), 1½ miles north of the village, is a 35-dealer colony with everything from furniture and jewelry to coins and other collectibles. **North Country Fair Jewelers** (✉ Main and Seavy Sts., ☎ 603/356–5819) carries diamonds, antique and estate jewelry, silver, watches, coins, and accessories. **Richard M. Plusch Fine Antiques** (✉ Rte. 16/302, ☎ 603/356–3333) deals in period furniture and accessories, including glass, sterling silver, Oriental porcelains, rugs, and paintings. **Sleigh Mill Antiques** (✉ Snowville, off Rte. 153, ☎ 603/447–6791), an old sleigh and carriage mill 6 miles south of Conway, specializes in 19th-century oil lighting and early gas and electric lamps.

CRAFTS
The **Basket & Handcrafters Outlet** (✉ Kearsarge St., ☎ 603/356–5332) is perfect for those looking for gift baskets, dried-flower arrangements, and country furniture. **Handcrafters Barn** (✉ Rte. 16, ☎ 603/356–8996), a one-stop shopping emporium, sells the work of 350 area artists and artisans, and has a shipping area to send your purchases home. **League of New Hampshire Craftsmen** (✉ Main St., ☎ 603/356–2441) sells wares made by the area's best juried artisans.

FACTORY OUTLETS
More than 150 factory outlets huddle around Route 16, where you'll find the likes of Timberland, Pfaltzgraff, London Fog, Anne Klein, and Reebok. You can call the Mount Washington Valley Chamber of Commerce (✉ Box 2300, North Conway 03860, ☎ 603/356–3171) for a guide to the outlets.

SPORTSWEAR
Popular stores for skiwear include **Chuck Roast** (✉ Rte. 16, ☎ 603/356–5589), **Joe Jones** (✉ Rte. 16, ☎ 603/356–6848), and **Tuckerman's Outfitters** (✉ Norcross Circle, ☎ 603/356–3121). You'll wait about a year for made-to-order **Limmer Boots** (✉ Intervale, ☎ 603/356–5378), but believers say they're worth the wait and the price.

Skiing
King Pine Ski Area at Purity Spring Resort. King Pine, a little more than 9 miles from Conway, has been a family-run ski area for more than 100 years. The Hoyt family offers many ski-and-stay packages throughout the winter season, including free skiing to midweek resort guests. There's an indoor pool and fitness complex, ice-skating, and dogsledding. *✉ Rte. 153, E. Madison, 03849, ☎ 603/367–8896 or 800/367–8897; ski information 800/373–3754.*

DOWNHILL
King Pine's gentle slopes make it an ideal area for families just learning to ski. Because most of the terrain is geared for beginner and intermediate skiers, experts won't be challenged here except for a brief pitch on the Pitch Pine trail. Sixteen trails are serviced by a triple chair, double chair, and two J-bars. There's night skiing on Tuesday, Friday, Saturday, and holidays.

CROSS-COUNTRY
King Pine has 27 kilometers (15½ miles) of cross-country skiing. Sixty-five kilometers (40 miles) of groomed cross-country trails weave through North Conway and the countryside along the Mount Washington Valley Ski Touring Association Network (✉ Rte. 16, Intervale, ☎ 603/356–9920).

CHILD CARE
Children up to 6 years old are welcome (8:30–4) at the nursery on the second floor of the base lodge. Lessons are offered to children ages 4 and up.

Mt. Cranmore. This ski area, on the outskirts of North Conway, came into existence in 1938. An aggressive mountain-improvement program has been under way for several years, and because of a recent merger with nearby Attitash Bear Peak (☞ Bartlett, *below*), tickets are good at both ski areas. A fitness center completes the "new" Cranmore with an indoor climbing wall, tennis courts, exercise equipment, and pool. ⊠ *Box 1640, 03860,* ☎ *603/356–5543, snow conditions 800/786–6754, lodging 800/543–9206.*

DOWNHILL

The mountain's 32 trails are well laid out and fun to ski. Most of the runs are naturally formed intermediates that weave in and out of glades. Beginners have several slopes and routes from the summit, while experts must be content with a few short but steep pitches. One high-speed quad, two triples and two double chairlifts carry skiers to the top. There is night skiing Thursday through Saturday and during holiday periods. There's also outdoor skating and a halfpipe for snowboarders.

CHILD CARE

The nursery takes children 1 year and up. There's instruction for children 4–12.

Glen

㉙ *6 mi north of North Conway.*

Glen is hardly more than a crossroads between North Conway and Jackson, but its central location has made it the home of a few noteworthy attractions and dining and lodging options.

That cluster of fluorescent buildings on Route 16 is **StoryLand,** a theme park with life-size storybook and nursery-rhyme characters, a flume ride, Cinderella's castle, a Victorian-theme river-raft ride, a farm-family variety show, and a simulated voyage to the moon. The kids will want to stay all day. ⊠ *Rte. 16,* ☎ *603/383–4293.* ▩ *$15.* ☉ *Mid-June–Labor Day, daily 9–6; Labor Day–Columbus Day, weekends 10–5.*

A trip to **Heritage New Hampshire,** next door to StoryLand, is as close as you may ever come to experiencing time travel. Theatrical sets, sound effects, and animation usher you aboard the *Reliance* and carry you from a village in 1634 England over tossing seas to the New World. You will saunter along Portsmouth's streets in the late 1700s and applaud a speech by George Washington. ⊠ *Rte. 16,* ☎ *603/383–9776.* ▩ *$15.* ☉ *Mid-May–mid-Oct., daily 9–5.*

Dining and Lodging

$ ✕ **Margaritaville.** The authentic Mexican food served here is enhanced by the tart, locally renowned margaritas. Guests enjoy exceptional service in this family-run establishment. You can dine outdoors in summer. ⊠ *Rte. 302,* ☎ *603/383–6556. MC, V.*

$–$$ ✕▣ **Bernerhof.** This Old World hotel is right at home in its alpine setting. Rooms eschew the lace-and-doily decor of many Victorian inns, opting instead for hardwood floors with hooked rugs, antique reproductions, and large, plain windows. The fanciest four rooms have brass beds and spa-size bathtubs; one suite has a Finnish sauna. Stay three days, and you'll be served a champagne breakfast in bed. In the restaurant, one side of the menu lists such Swiss specialties as fondue and wiener schnitzel, while the other side is rife with classic French and new American dishes. The wine list favors French and Austrian labels. Ask about the Taste of the Mountains, a hands-on cooking school hosted by some of the region's top chefs. ⊠ *Rte. 302, 03838,* ☎ *603/383–4414 or 800/548–8007,* ℻ *603/383–0809. 9 rooms with bath. Restaurant, pub. Full breakfast included. AE, D, MC, V.*

$–$$ ✕▣ **Best Western Storybook Resort Inn.** On a hillside near Attitash, this family-owned, family-run motor inn is well suited to—what else?—

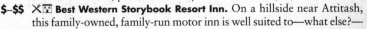

families, particularly because of its large rooms. Copperfield's Restaurant has gingerbread, sticky buns, farmer's omelets, and a children's menu. ⊠ *Box 129, Glen Junction 03838,* ☎ *603/383–6800,* FAX *603/383–4678. 78 rooms with bath. Restaurant, indoor and outdoor pools, sauna. AE, DC, MC, V.*

Nightlife
The **Bernerhof Inn** (☎ 603/383–4414) is the setting for an evening of fondue and soft music by the fireside. **Red Parka Pub** (☎ 603/383–4344) is a hangout for barbecue lovers. The crowd swells to capacity on the weekends.

Jackson

30 *4 mi north of Glen.*

While North Conway has given over much of the town to outlet malls and traffic, the village of Jackson, just north of Glen on Route 16, has retained its storybook New England character. Art and antiques shopping, tennis, golf, fishing, and hiking to the area's many waterfalls round out summer and fall activities. When the snow flies, Jackson becomes the state's cross-country skiing capital and is rated as one of the top four areas in the country for enjoying the sport.

Dining and Lodging

$$$
★ ✕⌂ **Inn at Thorn Hill.** This Victorian house, designed in 1895 by Stanford White, has frilly decor with polished dark woods, rose-motif papers, and plenty of lace, fringe, and knickknacks. Guests are just a few steps away from beautiful cross-country trails and Jackson Village itself. The four-course prix-fixe menu changes frequently and may include the *duck á deux* (a sautéed breast of duck with blackberry sauce and confit of duck leg) or a pounded tenderloin with apples, Calvados, cream, and Stilton cheese. Desserts include cappuccino crème caramel, dark-chocolate torte, and saffron-poached pears with raspberry coulis. The owners, from California, maintain an extensive wine list. ⊠ *Thorn Hill Rd., 03846,* ☎ *603/383–4242 or 800/289–8990,* FAX *603/383–8062. 20 rooms with bath. Restaurant (reservations essential), pub, pool. MAP. AE, DC, MC, V. Closed Sun.–Thurs. in Apr.*

$$–$$$ ✕⌂ **Christmas Farm Inn.** Despite its winter-inspired name, this 200-year-old village inn is an all-season retreat. Rooms in the main inn and the saltbox next door are all done with Laura Ashley prints. In the cottages, log cabin, and dairy barn, suites have beam-ceilings and fireplaces and more rustic Colonial furnishings. These rooms are better suited to families. Some standbys in the restaurant include vegetable-stuffed chicken, shrimp scampi, and New York sirloin; the list of homemade soups and desserts varies nightly. Also served are "heart-healthy" dishes approved by the American Heart Association. ⊠ *Box CC, Rte. 16B, 03846,* ☎ *603/383–4313 or 800/443–5837,* FAX *603/383–6495. 34 rooms with bath, 5 with whirlpool tub. Restaurant, pub, pool, sauna, volleyball, recreation room, playground. MAP. AE, MC, V.*

$$ ✕⌂ **Eagle Mountain House.** This country estate, which dates from 1879, is a showplace. Since it's close to Wildcat Mountain ski area and Attitash Bear Peak, you can also cross-country ski right from the door. The public rooms are rustically elegant, in keeping with the period of tycoon roughing-it; the bedrooms are large and furnished with period pieces. On a warm day, nurse a drink from a rocking chair on the wraparound deck. ⊠ *Carter Notch Rd., 03846,* ☎ *603/383–9111 or 800/966-5779,* FAX *603/383–0854. 93 rooms with bath. Restaurant, pool, hot tub, sauna, 9-hole golf course, 2 tennis courts, health club, playground. AE, D, DC, MC, V.*

$–$$ ✗⊞ **Wentworth.** This resort, built in 1869, still retains a Victorian look, although there are such European touches as French provincial antiques. All rooms have TVs and telephones; some have working fireplaces and whirlpool tubs, too. Although the superb cuisine in the dining room— New England regional with fresh ingredients from the local area—is innovative, take at least one snack in the more casual lounge, where you can order raclette and Swiss or chocolate fondue. ⊠ *Rte. 16A, 03846,* ☎ *603/383–9700 or 800/637–0013,* ℻ *603/383–4265. 60 rooms with bath in summer, 40 in winter. Restaurant, bar, air-conditioning, pool, golf, tennis, ice-skating, cross-country skiing, sleigh rides. MAP available. AE, D, DC, MC, V.*

$ ✗⊞ **Wildcat Inn & Tavern.** After a day of skiing, collapse on a comfy sofa by the fire in this small 19th-century tavern in the center of Jackson Village. The fragrance of home-baking permeates into guest rooms, which are full of interesting furniture and knickknacks. The tavern, which often has musical entertainment, is a lodestone for skiers in nearby condos and bed-and-breakfasts. ⊠ *Rte. 16A, 03846,* ☎ *603/383–4245 or 800/228–4245,* ℻ *603/383–6456. 12 rooms, 10 with bath. Restaurant, bar. Full breakfast included. AE, DC, MC, V.*

$–$$$ ⊞ **Nordic Village Resort.** The light wood and white walls of these deluxe condos near Black Mountain and Attitash Bear Peak are as Scandinavian as the snowy views. The Club House has pools and spa, and there is a nightly bonfire at Nordic Falls. Larger units have fireplaces, full kitchens, and whirlpool baths. ⊠ *Rte. 16, Jackson 03846,* ☎ *603/383–9101 or 800/472–5207,* ℻ *603/383–9823. 140 condominiums. Indoor and outdoor pools, spa, steam room, ice-skating, sleigh rides. D, MC, V.*

$$ ⊞ **Ellis River House.** Some rooms in this converted farmhouse on the
★ Ellis River have fireplaces, two-person whirlpool baths, or private balconies. Each is beautifully decorated with period antiques and has views of the White Mountains or the river. In winter, a snow bridge across the river connects you with the Ellis River Trail and Jackson's renowned cross-country trail system. Inn guests can enjoy a candle-lit dinner in the elegant dining room. The pony, Blaze, who trots to the edge of his paddock whenever guests arrive, fancies himself the welcoming committee. ⊠ *Rte. 16 (Box 656), 03846,* ☎ *603/383–9339 or 800/233– 8309,* ℻ *603/383–4142. Dining room, outdoor pool, sauna, spa. Full breakfast included. AE, D, DC, MC, V.*

$–$$ ⊞ **Inn at Jackson.** This Victorian inn, built in 1902 from a design by Stanford White, has spacious rooms—six with fireplaces—with oversize windows and an open, airy feel. Other than an imposing grand staircase in the front foyer, the house is unpretentious: The hardwood floors, braided rugs, smattering of antiques, and beautiful mountain views are sure to make you feel at home. The hearty breakfast will fill you up for the entire day. ⊠ *Thornhill Rd., 03846,* ☎ *603/383–4321 or 800/289–8600,* ℻ *603/383–4085. 14 rooms with bath. Air-conditioning, hot tub, cross-country skiing. AE, D, DC, MC, V.*

Nightlife
The **Shannon Door Pub** (⊠ Rte. 16, ☎ 603/383–4211) is the place to enjoy a Greek salad, Guinness on draft, and the area's best British musicians. The **Shovel Handle Pub** in Whitneys' Village Inn (☎ 603/383– 8916) is the après-ski bar adjacent to Black Mountain's slopes.

Shopping
The **Jack Frost Shop** is a popular store for skiwear (Main St., ☎ 603/383–4391.)

Outdoor Activities and Sports

ICE-SKATING

Nestlenook Farm (⊠ Dinsmore Rd., ☎ 603/383–0845) offers romantic sleigh rides and maintains an outdoor ice-skating rink complete with music and a bonfire. You can rent skates here or get yours sharpened.

Skiing

Black Mountain. Here the setting is 1950s and the atmosphere is friendly and informal—skiers have fun here. There's a country feeling at the big base building, which resembles an old farmhouse, and at the skiing facilities, which generally have no lines. Black has the essentials for families and singles who want a low-key skiing holiday. The Family Passport allows two adults and two juniors to ski at discounted rates. Midweek rates here are usually the lowest in Mt. Washington Valley. ⊠ *Rte. 16B, 03846,* ☎ *603/383–4490 or 800/475–4669.*

DOWNHILL

The bulk of the terrain is easy to middling, with intermediate trails that wander over the 1,150-vertical-foot mountain. Devil's Elbow on the Black Beauty trail—once a real zinger—has been expanded and is no longer as difficult to ski. There are a triple and a double chairlift and two surface tows. Most of the skiing is user-friendly, particularly for beginners. The southern exposure adds to the warm atmosphere. In addition to ski trails, snowboarders can use the halfpipe to practice their freestyle stunts.

CHILD CARE

The nursery takes children up to 6 years old. The ski school has instruction for ages 3–12.

Pinkham Notch

31 *9 mi north of Jackson.*

Although not a town per se, this scenic area covers the eastern side of Mount Washington and includes several spectacular ravines including Tuckerman's Ravine, famous for spring skiing. The Appalachian Mountain Club maintains a visitors' center here.

Skiing

Great Glen Trails at Mount Washington. There are 18 kilometers (11 miles) of cross-country trails here (with an additional 25 kilometers planned by 1997) and access to more than 50 acres of backcountry. You can even ski the lower half of the Mount Washington Auto Road. Trees shelter most of the trails, so Mount Washington's famous weather shouldn't be a concern. ⊠ *Rte. 16, Pinkham Notch (Box 300, Gorham 03581),* ☎ *603/466–2333.*

OTHER ACTIVITIES

At Great Glen Trails you can go skating or snowshoeing, or try the Scandinavian sport of kicksledding.

Wildcat. Although Wildcat has been working hard to live down its reputation of being a difficult mountain, its runs include some spectacular double black diamond trails. The 2.75-mile-long Polecat is where skiers who can hold a wedge should head, while experts can be found zipping down the Lynx, a run constantly voted by patrons of a local bar as the most popular in the Mt. Washington Valley. On a clear day, there is no better view than that of Mt. Washington from here. Tuckerman's Ravine, where skiers trek in spring to hike up and ski down, can also be seen. Trails are classic New England—narrow and winding. ⊠ *Pinkham Notch (Rte. 16, Jackson 03846),* ☎ *603/466–3326, snow conditions 800/643–4521, lodging 800/255–6439.*

DOWNHILL

Wildcat's expert runs deserve their designations and then some. Intermediates have mid-mountain-to-base trails, and beginners will find gentle terrain and a broad teaching slope. The 39 runs with a 2,100-foot vertical drop, are served by a two-passenger gondola and one double and four triple chairlifts.

CHILD CARE

The child care center takes children 18 months and up. All-day SKI-wee instruction is offered to children 5–12. A separate slope is used for teaching children to ski.

Mount Washington

㉜ *15 mi north of Glen.*

Yes, you can drive to the top of Mt. Washington, the highest mountain (6,288 feet) in the northeastern United States and the spot where weather observers have recorded 231-mile-per-hour winds (the strongest in the world), but you'll have to endure the **Mt. Washington Auto Road** to get here. This toll road opened in 1861 and is said to be the nation's first manufactured tourist attraction. The road, which is closed in inclement weather, begins at **Glen House,** a gift shop and rest stop 15 miles north of Glen. Allow two hours round-trip and check your brakes first. Cars with automatic transmissions that can't shift down into first gear aren't allowed on the road at all. A better option is to hop into one of the vans at Glen House for a 1½-hour guided tour. Up top, visit the **Sherman Adams Summit Building,** which contains a museum of memorabilia from each of the three hotels that have stood on this spot. There's also a nice display of native plant life and alpine flowers, as well as a glassed-in viewing area where you can hear the roar of that record-breaking wind. ☎ *603/466–3988.* 🎫 *$14 car and driver, $5 adult passengers; van fare $18 adults.* ☉ *Daily mid-May–late Oct.*

Dixville Notch

㉝ *60 mi north of Mount Washington.*

Not everyone will want to venture this far north; but if you want to really get away from it all, Dixville Notch is the place to go. Just 12 miles from the Canadian border, this tiny community is known for only two things. It's the home of the Balsams Grand Resort Hotel, one of the oldest and most esteemed resorts in New Hampshire. Perhaps more important, Dixville Notch is also the first election district in the nation to vote in the presidential elections. Long before the sun rises on election day, the 34 or so voters gather in the little meeting room beside the hotel bar to cast their ballots and make national news.

Dining and Lodging

$$$$ ✕⊞ **Balsams Grand Resort Hotel.** At this resort, founded in 1866, guests
★   will find many nice touches: valet parking, gourmet meals, dancing and entertainment nightly, cooking demonstrations, and other organized recreational activities. Families particularly enjoy magic shows and late-night games of broomball. The Tower Suite, with its 20-foot conical ceiling, is in a Victorian-style turret and offers 360° views. Standard rooms have views of the 15,000-acre estate and the mountains beyond as well as overstuffed chairs and soft queen-size beds. In summer the buffet lunch is heaped upon a 100-foot-long table. Given this awesome amount of food, it's amazing that anyone has room left for the stun-

ning dinners—but they do. A starter might be chilled strawberry soup spiked with Grand Marnier, followed by poached fillet of salmon with golden caviar sauce and chocolate hazelnut cake. ☎ 603/255–3400 or 800/255–0600, in NH, 800/255–0800, FAX 603/255–4221. 232 rooms with bath. Restaurant (reservations essential, jacket and tie), pool, golf, tennis, hiking, boating, mountain bikes, ice-skating, cross-country skiing, downhill skiing, children's programs. Rates are AP in summer, MAP in winter, and include sports and entertainment. AE, D, MC, V. Closed late March–mid-May, mid-Oct.–mid-Dec.

$$ ⊞ **The Glen.** This rustic lodge, with stick furniture, fieldstone, and pine, is on First Connecticut Lake, surrounded by log cabins, seven of which are right on the water. The cabins are best for families and come equipped with efficiency kitchens and mini refrigerators—not that you'll need either because rates include meals in the lodge restaurant. ✉ Box 77, Rte. 3, 03592, ☎ 603/538-6500 or 800/445–4536. 8 rooms, 10 cabins, all with bath. Restaurant, dock. Rates are AP. No credit cards. Closed mid-Oct.–mid-May.

Outdoor Activities and Sports
Dixville Notch State Park (✉ Rte. 26, ☎ 603/788–3155), the northernmost notch in the White Mountains, has picnic areas, a waterfall, and a hiking trail to Table Rock.

Skiing
Balsams. Skiing was originally provided as an amenity for hotel guests at the Balsams, but the area has since become popular with day-trippers as well. ✉ £203576, ☎ 603/255–3400 or 800/255–0600, in NH 800/255–0800, snow conditions 603/255–3951, FAX 603/255–4221.

DOWNHILL
Sanguinary, Umbagog, Magalloway are the tough-sounding slope names that are really only moderately difficult, leaning toward intermediate. There are trails from the top of the 1,000-foot vertical drop for every skill level. One double chairlift and two T-bars carry skiers up the mountain.

CROSS-COUNTRY
Balsams has 76 kilometers (45 miles) of cross-country skiing, tracked and also groomed for skating (a cross-country ski technique), with natural-history markers annotating some trails; there's also telemark and backcountry skiing.

CHILD CARE
The nursery takes children up to age 6 at no charge to hotel guests. There are lessons for children 3 and up.

OFF THE BEATEN PATH

PITTSBURG – Just north of the White Mountains, Pittsburg contains the four Connecticut Lakes and the springs that form the Connecticut River. In fact, the entire northern tip of the state—a chunk of about 250 square miles—lies within its town borders, the result of a border dispute between the United States and Canada in the early 19th century. The international border not yet fixed, the inhabitants of this region declared themselves independent of both countries in 1832 and wrote a constitution providing for an assembly, council, courts, and militia. They named their nation the Indian Stream Republic, after the river that passes through the territory—the capital of which was Pittsburg. In 1835 the feisty, 40-man Indian Stream militia invaded Canada—with only limited success. The Indian Stream war ended more by common consent than surrender; in 1842 the Webster-Ashburton Treaty fixed the international boundary. Indian Stream was incorporated as Pittsburg, making it the largest township in New Hampshire. Favorite uses of the land today are canoeing and photography; the pristine wilderness brims with moose. Contact the **Colebrook-Pittsburg Chamber of Commerce** (Colebrook 03576, ☎ 603/237-8939) for information about the region.

Bartlett

❸④ *7 mi southwest of Glen.*

Bear Mountain to the south, Mount Parker to the north, Mount Cardigan to the west, and the Saco River to the east combine to create an unforgettable setting for the village of Bartlett, incorporated in 1790. Also in Bartlett, Bear Notch Road has the only midpoint access to the Kancamagus (closed winter).

☾ From Glen, Route 302 follows the Saco River to Bartlett and the **Attitash Ski Area** ⊠ Rte. 302, ☎ 603/374-2368), which has a dry alpine slide, a water slide, a driving range, and a chairlift to the White Mountain Observation Tower, which delivers 270° views of the Whites.

Dining, Lodging, and Camping

$$$ ✕🏨 **Attitash Mountain Village.** This condo-motel complex—just across the street from the mountain via a tunnel under the road—has a glass-enclosed pool and units that will accommodate 2–14 people. Quarters with fireplaces and kitchenettes are especially good for families. The style is Alpine-contemporary; the staff, young and enthusiastic. ⊠ *Rte. 302, 03812-0358,* ☎ *603/374-6501 or 800/862-1600,* 𝖥𝖠𝖷 *603/374-6509. 250 rooms with bath. Restaurant, pub, indoor pool, sauna, recreation room. AE, D, MC, V.*

$ ⛺ **Dry River Campground.** This campground in Crawford Notch State Park has 30 tent sites and is a popular base for hiking the White Mountain National Forest. ⊠ *Rte. 302, Harts Location,* ☎ *603/374-2272.*

Skiing

Attitash Bear Peak. A savvy management has directed the resort's appeal to active young people and families. New ownership in 1995 brought additional money to expand the resort. There are five new trails, expanded snow making, and updated lifts. Keeping a high and busy profile, the area hosts many race camps and equipment demo days. Lodging at the base of the mountain is available in condominiums and motel-style units a bit away from the hustle of North Conway. Attitash Bear Peak has a computerized lift-ticket system that is also good at its sister resort Mt. Cranmore, about 10 minutes away; skiers now go through turnstiles on their way to the lifts. In essence, the Smart Ticket allows you to pay by the run. Skiers can share the ticket, which is good for two years (including summer when it can be used on the slides). ⊠ *Rte. 302, 03812,* ☎ *603/374-2368.*

DOWNHILL

Enhanced with massive snowmaking (98%), the trails now number 45. There are expert pitches at the top of the mountain, but the bulk of the skiing is geared to advanced intermediates and below, with wide fall-line runs from mid-mountain. Beginners have a share of good terrain on the lower mountain. Serving the 23 kilometers (14½ miles) of trails and the 1,750-foot vertical drop are one high-speed quad, one six-grip quad, two triple, four double chairlifts, and two surface tows.

CHILD CARE

Attitots Clubhouse takes children ages 6 weeks through 5 years. Other children's programs accommodate those up to 16 years of age.

En Route   Route 302 passes through **Crawford Notch State Park** (⌧ Rte. 302, Harts Location, ☎ 603/374–2272), where you can stop for a picnic and a short hike to Arethusa Falls or the Silver and Flume cascades.

Bretton Woods

35 *20 mi northwest of Bartlett.*

Bretton Woods is known as the home of the Mount Washington Hotel, one of the nation's few remaining grand hotels. Early in this century, as many as 50 private trains a day brought the rich and famous from New York and Philadelphia to the hotel. In July 1944 the World Monetary Fund Conference convened here and established the American dollar as the basic unit of international exchange.

In 1858, when Reverend Thompson asked the state legislature for permission to build a steam railway up Mt. Washington, one legislator responded that he'd have better luck building a railroad to the moon. In spite of such skeptic views, the **Mt. Washington Cog Railway** opened in 1869 and has since been giving tourists a thrilling alternative to driving or climbing to the top. Allow three hours round-trip. ⌧ *Rte. 302, 6 mi northeast of Bretton Woods,* ☎ *603/846–5404; outside NH, 800/922–8825, ext. 7.* ⌧ *Round-trip $35. Reservations advised.* ☉ *May weekends, limited schedule; June–Oct., daily 8:30–4:30, weather permitting.*

Dining and Lodging

$$$$ ✕▥ **Mount Washington Hotel.** The 1902 construction of this leviathan was one of the most ambitious projects of its day. It quickly became one of the nation's favorite grand resorts, most notable for its 900-foot-long veranda, which affords a full view of the Presidential range. With its stately public rooms and its large, Victorian-style bedrooms and suites, the atmosphere still courts a turn-of-the-century formality; jacket and tie are expected in the dining room at dinner and in the lobby after 6. This 2,600-acre property has an extensive recreation center. ⌧ *Rte. 302, 03575,* ☎ *603/278–1000 or 800/258–0330,* ⓕⒶⓍ *603/278–3457. 195 rooms with bath. 2 restaurants, indoor and outdoor pools, sauna, golf, tennis, hiking, horseback riding, bicycles, children's programs. MAP. AE, MC, V. Closed mid-Oct.–mid-May.*

$–$$ ✕▥ **Bretton Woods Motor Inn.** Rooms have contemporary furnishings, a balcony, and views of the Presidential Range. Darby's Restaurant has a circular fireplace around which it serves Continental cuisine. The bar is a hangout for après skiers. The motor inn, across the road from the Mount Washington Hotel, shares its facilities in summer. ⌧ *Rte. 302, 03575,* ☎ *603/278–1000 or 800/258–0330,* ⓕⒶⓍ *603/278–3457. 50 rooms. Restaurant, bar, indoor pool, sauna, recreation room. AE, D, MC, V.*

Skiing

Bretton Woods. This area has an attractive three-level, open-space base lodge, a convenient drop-off area, easy parking, and an uncrowded setting. On-mountain town houses are available with reasonably priced packages. The spectacular views of Mt. Washington itself are worth the visit; the scenery is especially beautiful from the Top o' Quad restaurant. ⌧ *Rte. 302, 03575,* ☎ *603/278–5000, information 800/232–2972, lodging 603/278–1000.*

DOWNHILL

The skiing on the 30 trails is mostly gentle, with some intermediate pitches near the top of the 1,500-foot vertical, and a few expert runs. One quad, one triple, and two double chairlifts, and one T-bar service the trails. The area has night skiing Friday, Saturday, and holidays. A limited lift-ticket policy helps keep lines short.

CROSS-COUNTRY

The large cross-country ski center at Bretton Woods has 90 kilometers (51 miles) of groomed and double-track trails.

CHILD CARE

The nursery takes children ages 2 months through 5 years. The ski school has an all-day program for ages 3–12, using progressive instructional techniques. Rates include lifts, lessons, equipment, lunch, and supervised play.

Bethlehem

36 *25 mi west of Bretton Woods.*

In the 1920s the quiet town of Bethlehem, on Route 302, was known for only one thing: hay-fever relief. The crisp air at this elevation (1,462 feet) boasts a blissfully low pollen count. In the days before antihistamines, hay-fever sufferers arrived by the busload. The town also became home to a group of Hasidic Jews who established a kosher resort in the Arlington and Alpine hotels.

Dining and Lodging

$$–$$$ ✕🏨 **Adair.** In 1927 attorney Frank Hogan built this three-story Geor-
★ gian Revival home as a wedding present for his daughter Dorothy Adair. Walking paths on this luxury country inn's 200 acres offer magnificent mountain views. Each of the guest rooms has a mountain view and is elegantly decorated with a variety of period antiques and antique reproductions. There is no smoking allowed on the property. ⊠ *Old Littleton Rd., 03574,* ☎ *603/444–2600 or 800/441–2606,* 𝔽𝔸𝕏 *603/444–4823. 8 rooms with bath, 1 suite. Restaurant (no credit cards), tennis court, billiards. Full breakfast included. AE, MC, V.*

Outdoor Activities and Sports

RECREATION AREA

Bretzfelder Park, a 77-acre nature and wildlife park, has a picnic shelter.

Franconia

37 *10 mi south of Bethlehem.*

Travelers first came to Franconia because the notch of the same name provided a north-south route through the mountains. Both the town, which is north of the notch, and the notch itself are worth visiting. Famous literary visitors include Washington Irving, Longfellow, and Nathaniel Hawthorne, who wrote a short story about the Old Man of the Mountain.

The Frost Place, Robert Frost's home from 1915 to 1920, is where the poet wrote his most remembered poem, "Stopping by Woods on a Snowy Evening." To be sure, the mountain views from this house would inspire any writer. Two rooms contain memorabilia and a few signed editions of his books. Outside, you can follow a short trail marked with lines of Frost's poetry. The house is lived in by poets-in-residence and is the sight of occasional poetry readings. ⊠ *Ridge Rd. (off Rte. 116; follow signs),* ☎ *603/823–5510.* 🎟 *$3.* ☉ *Memorial Day–June, weekends 1–5; July–Columbus Day, Wed.–Mon. 1–5.*

Franconia Notch State Park, just south of Franconia, contains a few of New Hampshire's best-loved attractions. **Cannon Mountain Aerial Tramway** will lift you 2,022 feet for one more sweeping mountain vista.

It's a five-minute ride to the top, where marked hiking trails lead from the observation platform. ⊠ *Cannon Mountain Ski Area,* ☎ *603/823–5563.* ⊡ *$9.* ⊙ *Memorial Day–3rd weekend in Oct., daily 9–4.*

The **New England Ski Museum,** just north of Cannon Mountain at the foot of the tramway, has old trophies, skis and bindings, boots, and ski apparel dating from the late 1800s, as well as a collection of photos. ☎ *603/823–7177.* ⊙ *Dec.–Apr., Thurs.–Tues. noon–5; Memorial Day–Columbus Day, daily noon–5.*

No one should leave the White Mountains without seeing the granite profile of the **Old Man of the Mountain,** the icon of New Hampshire. Nathaniel Hawthorne wrote about it; New Hampshire resident Daniel Webster bragged about it; P. T. Barnum wanted to buy it. The two best places to view the giant stone face are the highway parking area on Route 3 or along the shores of Profile Lake.

The **Flume** is an 800-foot-long natural chasm discovered at about the same time as the Old Man by a local woman en route to her favorite fishing hole. Today the route through the flume has been built up with a series of boardwalks and stairways. The narrow walls give the gorge's running water a deeply eerie echo. ⊠ *Exit 1 off I–93,* ☎ *603/745–8391.* ⊡ *$6.* ⊙ *May–Oct., daily 9–5.*

Dining, Lodging, and Camping

$$–$$$$ ✗▥ **Sugar Hill Inn.** The old carriage on the lawn and wicker chairs on the wraparound porch contribute to the Colonial charm of this converted 1789 farmhouse. Because the building has tilted and sagged over the years, not a single room is square or level. Many rooms have hand-stenciled walls, a view of Franconia Notch, and rippled antique windows; all contain antiques. Afternoon tea includes scones and tea breads. The restaurant serves hearty New England fare that includes lamb and beef dishes, homemade chowders and soups (try the mushroom-dill soup), and delicious desserts. There are 10 rooms in the inn and six in three country cottages (some with fireplaces). This is a no-smoking property. ⊠ *Rte. 117, 03580,* ☎ *603/823–5621 or 800/548–4748,* ℻ *603/823–5639. 16 rooms with bath. Restaurant, pub, cross-country skiing. Full breakfast included, MAP available (required during foliage season). MC, V. Closed Apr., Christmas week.*

$–$$$ ✗▥ **Franconia Inn.** This resort has every manner of recreation for all seasons. You can golf next door at Sunset Hill's nine-hole course, play tennis, ride horseback, swim in the pool or sit in the hot tub, order your lunch to go for a day of hiking—even try soaring from the inn's own airstrip. Movies are shown evenings in the lounge. Rooms have designer chintzes, canopy beds, and country furnishings; some have whirlpool baths or fireplaces. At meals, children choose from a separate menu, while adults stick to medallions of veal with apple-mustard sauce or filet mignon with sun-dried tomatoes. ⊠ *Easton Rd., 03580,* ☎ *603/823–5542 or 800/473–5299,* ℻ *603/823–8078. 34 rooms with bath. Restaurant, pool, hot tub, tennis, croquet, horseback riding, bicycles, ice-skating, cross-country skiing, sleigh rides. Full breakfast included, MAP available. Closed Apr.–mid-May. AE, MC, V.*

$–$$ ✗▥ **Hilltop Inn.** Guests declare staying with innkeepers Mike and Meri Hern is just like staying at Grandma's house—they even welcome pets. The rooms are done in a quirky mix of antiques with handmade quilts, Victorian ceiling fans, piles of pillows, and big, fluffy towels. The TV room, downstairs, has hundreds of movies on tape. The inn serves dinner in the fall, but you'll be lucky to get a table. Even the locals fight for the chance to try Meri's specialty: duck glazed with sauces such as poached pear, raspberry port, and curried apple-and-Vidalia-onion. The large country breakfast includes homemade jams and pancakes made with homegrown berries, cheese soufflés, and smoked bacon or salmon. ⊠ *Rte. 117, Main St., Sugar Hill 03585,* ☎ *603/823–5695 or 800/770–5695,* FAX *603/823–5518. 3 rooms with bath, 3 suites, 1 2-bedroon cottage. Restaurant (fall only; reservations essential), bar, library. Full breakfast included, MAP available in fall. D, MC, V.*

$ ✕🖭 **Horse and Hound Inn.** Off the beaten path yet convenient to the Cannon Mountain tram, this traditional inn is on 8 acres surrounded by the White Mountain National Forest. Antiques and assorted collectibles provide a cheery atmosphere, and on the grounds are 10 kilometers (6 miles) of cross-country ski trails. Pets are welcome. ⊠ *205 Wells Rd., 03580,* ☎ *603/823–5501 or 800/450–5501. 10 rooms, 8 with bath. Restaurant, bar, cross-country skiing. Full breakfast included. AE, D, DC, MC, V. Closed Apr. and Nov.*

$ ⚠ **Lafayette Campground.** This campground, in Franconia Notch State Park, has hiking and biking trails, 97 tent sites, showers, a camp store, and easy access to the Appalachian Trail. Reservations are not accepted. ⊠ *Franconia Notch State Park, 03580,* ☎ *603/823–9513.*

Nightlife

Hillwinds (⊠ Main St., ☎ 603/823–5551) has live entertainment on weekends.

Shopping

The **Franconia Marketplace** (⊠ Main St., ☎ 603/823–5368) only sells products made in Franconia. Stores in the complex include the **Grateful Bread Quality Bakery** and **Tiffany Workshop**, which sells clothing and crystal jewelry.

Skiing

Cannon Mountain. Nowhere is the granite of the Granite State more pronounced than here. One of the first ski areas in the United States, the massif has retained the basic qualities that make the sport unique— the camaraderie of young people who are there for challenge and family fun. The New England Ski Museum (☞ Franconia, *above*) is adjacent to the base of the tramway. Cannon, which is owned and run by the state, gives strong attention to skier services, family programs, snowmaking, and grooming. ⊠ *Franconia Notch State Park, 03580,* ☎ *603/823–5563, snow conditions 603/823–7771 or 800/552–1234.*

DOWNHILL

The tone of this mountain's skiing is reflected in the narrow, steep pitches off the peak of the 2,146 feet of vertical rise. Some trails marked intermediate may seem more difficult because of the sidehill slant of the slopes (rather than the steepness). Under a new fall of snow, Cannon has challenges not often found at modern ski areas. There is an 70-passenger tramway to the top, one quad, one triple, and two double chairlifts, and one surface lift.

CHILD CARE

Cannon's Peabody Base Lodge takes children 1 year and older. All-day and half-day SKIwee programs are available for children 4–12, and season-long instruction can be arranged.

Franconia Village Cross-Country Ski Center (☎ 603/823–5542) has 65 kilometers (40 miles) of groomed trails and 20 kilometers (12 miles) of backcountry trails. One popular trail leads to Bridal Veil Falls, a great spot for a picnic lunch. Nordic skiing is also available on a 13-kilometer (8-mile) bicycle path through Franconia Notch State Park.

The White Mountains A to Z

Arriving and Departing

BY CAR

Access to the White Mountains is from I–93 via the Kangamagus Highway or Route 302. From the seacoast, Route 16 is the popular choice.

BY PLANE

The nearest airport served by major commercial carriers is about an hour outside the White Mountains region. **Manchester Airport** (☎ 603/624–6556), the state's largest, has scheduled flights from USAir, Delta, Continental, Northwest Airlink, United, and TWA.

Getting Around

BY BUS

Concord Trailways (☎ 800/639–3317) stops in Chocorua, Conway, and Jackson. **Greyhound Lines** (☎ 800/231–2222) serves 37 New Hampshire towns.

BY CAR

I–93 and Route 3 bisect the White Mountain National Forest, running north from Massachusetts to Québec. To the east, Route 16 brings visitors north from the New Hampshire coast. The Kancamagus Highway (Route 112), the east–west thoroughfare through the White Mountain National Forest, is a scenic drive but is often impassable in winter. Route 302, a longer, more leisurely east–west path, connects Lincoln to North Conway.

BY PLANE

Franconia Airport & Soaring Center (✉ Easton Rd., Franconia, ☎ 603/823–8881) and **Mt. Washington Regional Airport** (✉ Airport Rd., Whitefield, ☎ 603/837–9532) both take charters and private planes.

Contacts and Resources

CAMPING

White Mountain National Forest (✉ 719 N. Main St., Laconia 03246, ☎ 603/528–8721) has 20 campgrounds with more than 900 campsites spread across the region; only some take reservations. All sites are subject to a 14-day limit.

CANOEING

River outfitter **Saco Bound Canoe & Kayak** (✉ Box 119, Center Conway 03813, ☎ 603/447–2177 or 603/447–3801) leads gentle canoeing expeditions, guided kayak trips, white-water rafting on seven rivers, lessons, equipment, and transportation.

CROSS-COUNTRY SKIING

Contact the nonprofit **Jackson Ski Touring Foundation** (✉ Box 216, Jackson Village 03846, ☎ 603/383–9355 or 800/866–3332) for information about its 156 kilometers (94 miles) of trails that wind through Jackson Village, along the Ellis River, and up into the backcountry.

EMERGENCIES

Memorial Hospital (✉ Intervale Rd., North Conway, ☎ 603/356–5461).

FISHING

For trout and salmon fishing, try the **Connecticut Lakes,** though any clear stream in the White Mountains will do. Many are stocked, and there are 650 miles of them in the national forest alone. **Conway Lake** is the largest of the area's 45 lakes and ponds; it's noted for smallmouth bass and—early and late in the season—good salmon fishing. The

New Hampshire Fish and Game Office (☎ 603/788–3164) has up-to-date information on fishing conditions.

The **North Country Angler** (✉ N. Main St., ☎ 603/356–6000) schedules intensive guided fly-fishing weekends.

HIKING

With 86 major mountains in the area, the hiking possibilities seem endless. Innkeepers can usually point you toward the better nearby trails; some inns schedule guided daytrips for their guests. The **White Mountain National Forest** (✉ U.S. Forest Service, 719 N. Main St., Laconia 03247, ☎ 603/528–8721 or 800/283–2267) has information on hiking opportunities.

The **Appalachian Mountain Club** (✉ Box 298, Gorham 03581, ☎ 603/466–2721, 603/466–2725 for trail information, 603/466–2727 for reservations or for the free AMC guide to the huts and lodges) headquarters at Pinkham Notch offers lectures, workshops, slide shows, and movies June–October. Accommodations include a 100-bunk main lodge and eight rustic cabins. The club's hut system provides reasonably priced meals and dorm-style lodging on several different trails throughout the Whites.

New England Hiking Holidays (✉ Box 1648, North Conway 03860, ☎ 603/356–9696 or 800/869–0949) offers inn-to-inn, guided hiking tours that include two, three, or five nights in country inns.

LLAMA TREKKING

Snowvillage Inn (✉ Snowville 03849, ☎ 603/447–2818 or 800/447–4345) conducts a guided trip up Foss Mountain. Your elegant picnic will include gourmet food from the inn's kitchen along with champagne. Luckily you don't have to carry the food, the fine china, or the silverware—llamas do that for you. Reservations are essential.

White Mountain Llamas at the Stag Hollow Inn (✉ Jefferson 03583, ☎ 603/586–4598) will introduce you to llama trekking, with one- to four-day hikes on beautiful, secluded trails. The hiking trips include picnic foods, but the primary focus is on the surrounding nature.

RESERVATION SERVICES

Mt. Washington Valley has more than 100 hotels, lodges, and motels, many of which can be reached through the **Mount Washington Valley Chamber of Commerce Travel and Lodging Bureau** (☎ 800/223–7669). The **Mt. Washington Valley Visitors Bureau** (☎ 603/356–3171 or 800/367–3364), **Country Inns in the White Mountains** (☎ 603/356–9460 or 800/562–1300), and the **Jackson Resort Association** (☎ 800/866–3334) are also reservation services.

VISITOR INFORMATION

Hours are generally weekdays 9–5. **Mt. Washington Valley Visitors Bureau** (✉ Box 2300, North Conway 03860, ☎ 603/356–5701 or 800/367–3364). **White Mountain Attractions Association** (✉ Kangamagus Highway, Lincoln 03251, ☎ 603/745–8720).

WESTERN AND CENTRAL NEW HAMPSHIRE

Here is the unspoiled heart of New Hampshire. While the beaches to the east attract sun worshipers, and the resort towns to the north keep the skiers and hikers beating a well-worn path up I–93, Western and Central New Hampshire has managed to keep the water slides and the outlet malls at bay. In the center of New Hampshire you'll see the pris-

tine town green 50 times over. Here each village has its own historical society, a tiny museum filled with odd bits of historical memorabilia: a cup from which George Washington took tea, a piano that
belonged to the Alcotts. The town of Fitzwilliam remembers Amos J.
Parker. He was not a famous man, but a 19th-century lawyer whose
belongings and papers survived him. His home has become a museum
and a window into his era.

Beyond the museums and picture-perfect greens, this area offers the
shining waters of Lake Sunapee and the looming presence of Mt. Monadnock, the second-most-climbed mountain in the world. When you're
done climbing and swimming and visiting the past, look for the wares
and small studios of area artists. The region has long been an informal artists' colony where people come to write, paint, and weave in
solitude.

The towns in this section, beginning with Concord, the state's capitol,
are listed in counterclockwise order. From Concord, you can take I–89
through the Lake Sunapee region to Hanover, follow the Connecticut
River south to Keene, and then meander through the Monadnock region to Manchester.

*Numbers in the margin correspond to points of interest on the Dart-
mouth–Lake Sunapee map.*

Concord

③⑧ *40 mi north of the Massachusetts border via I–93, 20 mi north of Manchester, 45 mi northwest of Portsmouth.*

New Hampshire's capital is a quiet, conservative town (population
38,000) that tends to the state's business but little else. The residents
joke that the sidewalks roll up promptly at 6. Aside from shopping in
the boutiques on Main Street, you may want to follow the **Coach and
Eagle** walking trail through Concord's historic district. Get trail maps
from the Chamber of Commerce (⊠ 244 N. Main St.) or from stores
along the marked trail. The tour includes the Greek Revival home that
was the **residence of Franklin Pierce** until he moved to Washington to
become our nation's 14th president. ⊠ *14 Penacook St., no phone.*
⊡ *$2.* ⊙ *Mid-June–Labor Day, weekdays 11–3.*

You can walk through the gilt-domed **State House**, the oldest such building in which a legislature still meets. ⊠ *107 N. Main St.,* ☎ *603/271–
1110.* ⊙ *Weekdays 8–4:30.*

Visit the **Museum of New Hampshire History** (⊠ 6 Eagle Sq., ☎
603/226–3189) to see an original Concord Coach. During the 19th
century, when more than 3,000 of them were built in Concord, this
was about as technologically perfect a vehicle as you could find—many
say it's the coach that won the West. Other exhibits provide an overview
of New Hampshire's history, from the Abenaki Indians to the settlers
of Portsmouth up to current times.

⟳ The **Christa McAuliffe Planetarium,** one of the world's most advanced,
was named for the teacher who was killed in the *Challenger* space-shut-
tle explosion in 1986. There are shows on the solar system, constella-
tions, and space exploration that use computer graphics, sound
equipment, and views through the 40-foot dome telescope. Children
especially love seeing the tornado tubes, magnetic marbles, and other
hands-on exhibits. ⊠ *3 Institute Dr., New Hampshire Technical Institute,* ☎ *603/271–7827.* ⊡ *Exhibit free, show $6.* ⊙ *Tues.–Thurs.
9–4, Fri. 9–7, Sat. noon–5, Sun. noon–4. Call for show times.*

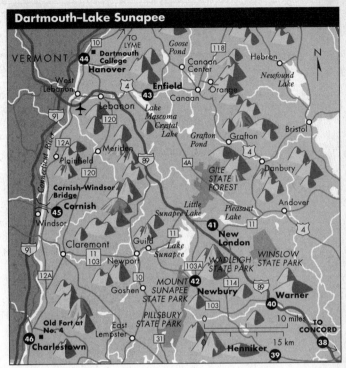

Dartmouth–Lake Sunapee

Dining

$$–$$$ ✕ **Vercelli's.** If you can resist the homemade bread and olive butter (good luck), you might have room for one of the generous Italian entrées on the extensive menu. The many veal specialties and seafood are stellar. ⊠ *11 Depot St.,* ☎ *603/228–3313. MC, V.*

$$ ✕ **Hermanos Cocina Mexicana.** On the weekends the line to get in forms ★ at 5 sharp; if you're not in it, don't bother. This restaurant's popularity has spawned a gift shop next door. The food is standard Mexican, raised to a higher level by fresh ingredients and the cook's ability to resist gloppy sauces. ⊠ *11 Hills Ave.,* ☎ *603/224–5669. Reservations not accepted. MC, V.*

Outdoor Activities and Sports

CANOEING

Hannah's Paddles, Inc. rents canoes for use on the Merrimack River. ⊠ *15 Hannah Dustin Dr.,* ☎ *603/753–6695.* ☉ *June–Oct., daily; spring and fall, weekends.*

Shopping

The **League of New Hampshire Craftsmen** (⊠ 36 N. Main St., ☎ 603/228–8171) offers a vast array of juried crafts in many mediums. **Mark Knipe Goldsmiths** (⊠ 2 Capitol Plaza, Main St., ☎ 603/224–2920) will turn your antique stones into rings, earrings, and pendants. The **New Hampshire Antiquarian Society** (⊠ Main St., Hopkinton, ☎ 603/746–3825) holds silent auctions. **Steeplegate Mall** (⊠ 270 Loudon Rd., ☎ 603/224–1523), has more than 70 stores, including chain department stores and some smaller crafts shops.

Henniker

39 *20 mi west of Concord via Route 202 or I–89 and Route 202.*

Once a mill town producing such things as bicycle rims, Henniker reinvented itself after a 1936 flood damaged the factories. New England College was established in the following decade, bringing a college flavor to this old town, where residents delight in being "the only Henniker in the world." Governor Wentworth named the town in honor of his friend, Juhn Henniker, a London merchant and member of the British Parliament. One of the area's covered bridges can be found on campus.

Dining and Lodging

$$ ✕⊞ **Colby Hill Inn.** The cookie jar is always full in this Federal Colonial farmhouse, where guests are greeted warmly by a pair of Great Danes. There is no shortage of relaxing activities: You can curl up with a book by the parlor fireplace, stroll through the gardens and 5 acres of meadow, ice-skate out back in winter, or play badminton in summer. Rooms in the main house contain antiques, Colonial reproductions, and such frills as lace curtains and Laura Ashley prints. In the carriage-house rooms, plain country furnishings, white walls, and exposed beams are the norm. The innovative breakfast might include scrambled eggs and Boursin on a puff pastry or raspberry-stuffed French toast. The dining menu is excellent: Try the chicken Colby Hill (breast of chicken stuffed with lobster, leeks, and Boursin) or the New England seafood pie. ⊠ *The Oaks, 03242,* ☎ *603/428–3281 or 800/531–0330,* ℻ *603/428–9218. 16 rooms with bath. Dining room, air-conditioning, pool, ice-skating, recreation room. Full breakfast included. No children under 7. AE, D, DC, MC, V.*

$ ✕⊞ **Meeting House Inn & Restaurant.** This quiet, cozy 200-year-old farmhouse, located conveniently at the base of Pat's Peak, considers itself a lovers' getaway. The old barn has become a restaurant that specializes in leisurely, romantic dining; and guests enjoy breakfast in bed, which is served in a picnic basket. ⊠ *Rte. 114 (Flanders Rd.), 03242,* ☎ *603/428–3228,* ℻ *603/428–6334. 6 rooms with bath. Restaurant, hot tub, sauna. Full breakfast included. AE, D, MC, V.*

Shopping

The **Fiber Studio** (⊠ 9 Foster Hill Rd., ☎ 603/428–7830) sells beads, hand-spun natural-fiber yarns, spinning equipment, and looms.

Skiing

Pat's Peak. Near Boston and the coastal metropolitan region, Pat's Peak is geared to families. Base facilities are rustic, and friendly personal attention is the rule. ⊠ *Rte. 114, 03242.* ☎ *603/428–3245, snow conditions 800/742–7287.*

DOWNHILL

Despite its size of only 710 vertical feet, with 20 trails and slopes, Pat's Peak has something for everyone: New skiers are well served with a wide slope, chairlift, and several short trails; intermediates have wider trails from the top; and advanced skiers have a couple of real thrillers. One triple and two double chairlifts, 1 T-bar, and two surface lifts serve the runs.

CHILD CARE

The nursery takes children ages 6 months through 5 years. Special nursery ski programs for children ages 4–12 are offered on weekends and during vacations. All-day lessons for self-sufficient skiers ages 4–12 are scheduled throughout the season.

Warner

40 *18 mi north of Henniker.*

Three New Hampshire governors were born in this quiet, agricultural town just off I–89. Buildings dating from the late 1700s and early 1800s, and a charming library gives the town's main street a welcoming feel.

Mount Kearsarge Indian Museum is a moving monument to Native American culture. You'll find incomparable artistry, including moose-hair embroidery, a tepee, quillwork, and basketry, and you'll learn of the bond between the region's Native American population and nature. Self-guided walks lead through gardens of vegetables and through "medicine woods" of herbs and healing plants. ⊠ *Kearsarge Mountain Rd., 03278,* ☎ *603/456–2600.* ⊠ *$6.* ⊙ *May–mid-Dec., Mon.–Sat. 10–5, Sun. 1–5.*

A scenic auto road at **Rollins State Park** (⊠ off Rte. 103, Warner) snakes nearly 3,000 feet up the southern slope of Mt. Kearsarge, where you can then tackle on foot the ½-mile trail to the summit.

Lodging

$ ▤ **English House Bed & Breakfast.** Afternoon tea is a must at this Edwardian inn. The British owners have furnished the large, sunny bedrooms with English and American antiques and watercolors by innkeeper Gillian Smith's mother and uncle, both well known in Britain. Smith offers occasional classes in jewelry making. The full English breakfast includes homemade yogurt. ⊠ *Main St., Andover 03216,* ☎ *603/735–5987. 7 rooms with bath. Cross-country skiing. Full breakfast and afternoon tea included. MC, V.*

New London

41 *12 mi northwest of Warner, 10 mi west of Andover.*

New London, the home of Colby-Sawyer College (1837), is a good base for exploring the Lake Sunapee region. Be sure to visit the 10,000-year-old **Cricenti's Bog,** just off Business Route 11 (Business Route 11 goes right through town; Route 11 goes around town). A short trail, maintained by the local conservation commission, shows off the shaggy mosses and fragile ecosystem of this ancient pond.

OFF THE BEATEN PATH
ANDOVER – In the small town of Andover is the **Andover Historical Society Museum,** housed in a beautiful and ornamental mid-19th-century railway station. Museum exhibits include an original Western Union telegraph office, a dugout canoe, and—on the tracks outside—an old caboose. ⊠ *Potter Pl.,* ☎ *603/735-5950.* ⊙ *Sat. 10-3, Sun. 1-3.*

The Arts

The **New London Barn Playhouse** (☎ 603/526–4631), a converted barn on Main Street, has been putting on non-equity Broadway-style and children's plays every summer.

Dining, Lodging, and Camping

$$ ✕▤ **New London Inn.** This rambling 1792 country inn in the center of town has two porches overlooking Main Street. Rooms have mostly Victorian pieces; those in the front of the house overlook the pretty campus of Colby-Sawyer College. The nouvelle-inspired menu starts with items like pan-smoked Atlantic salmon cakes with roasted red pepper aioli, and includes such entrées as smoked mozzarella and basil ravioli served with caramelized onions, balsamic vinegar, and fresh tomato. ⊠ *140 Main St., 03257,* ☎ *603/526-2791 or 800/526-2791,* FAX

603/526–2749. 30 rooms with bath. Restaurant (no lunch; closed Sun., Mon. off-season). Full breakfast included. AE, MC, V.

$–$$ ⊡ **Follansbee Inn.** Built in 1840, this quintessential country inn on the shore of Lake Kezar is a perfect fit in the 19th-century village of North Sutton, about 4 miles south of New London. Common rooms and bedrooms alike are loaded with collectibles and antiques. You can ice-fish on the lake as well as ski across it in the winter and swim or boat from the inn's pier in the summer. ⊠ *Rte. 114, North Sutton 03260,* ☎ *603/927–4221 or 800/626–4221. 23 rooms, 11 with bath. Dining room (guests only), lake, boating, fishing, ice-skating, cross-country skiing, tobogganing. Full breakfast included. MC, V.*

$ ⊡ **Pleasant Lake Inn.** This quiet, family-run property is aptly named for its location and ambience. The herbs, preserves, and other yummy things found on the dining table were grown on the property; all the baked goods come from the inn's kitchen. The original farmhouse dates from 1790, and that early country look has been maintained with sparse furnishings and a fireplace. ⊠ *125 Pleasant St., Box 1030, 03257,* ☎ *603/526–6271 or 800/626–4907. 11 rooms with bath. Dining room (guests only). No children under 6. Full breakfast included. MC, V.*

$ ⚠ **Otter Lake Camping Area.** ⊠ *Otterville Rd., 03257,* ☎ *603/763–5600.*

Outdoor Activities and Sports
FISHING
Pleasant Lake, off Route 11 in Elkins, has salmon, brook trout, and bass.

Shopping
Artisan's Workshop (⊠ Edgewood Inn, 186 Main St., ☎ 603/526–4227) carries jewelry, hand-blown glass, and other local handcrafts.

Skiing
Norsk Cross Country Ski Center. There are several scenic cross-country ski trails here, which are perfect for hiking in the warmer months. ⊠ *Rte. 11,* ☎ *603/526–4685.*

Newbury

㊷   *10 mi south of New London, on the edge of Mt. Sunapee State Park.*

In the distance you can see the sparkle of Lake Sunapee. Beyond it, Mt. Sunapee rises to an elevation of nearly 3,000 feet. Together they are the region's outdoor recreation center. **Mt. Sunapee State Park** (⊠ Rte. 103, ☎ 603/763–2356) has 130 acres of hiking and picnic areas, a beach, and a bath house. You can rent canoes at the beach, take a narrated cruise on the lake, or a chairlift to the summit. In winter the mountain becomes a downhill ski area and host to national ski competitions. In summer the park holds the League of New Hampshire Craftsmen's Fair, a Fourth of July flea market, the Antique and Classic Boat Parade, and the Gem and Mineral Festival. The **Lake Sunapee Association** (⊠ Box 400, Sunapee 03782, ☎ 603/763–2495) has information on local events.

Camping
$ ⚠ **Crow's Nest Campground.** This campground is open year-round. ⊠ *Rte. 10, Newport 03773,* ☎ *603/863–6170.*

$ ⚠ **Northstar Campground.** This campground is open May to October. ⊠ *278 Coonbrook Rd., Newport 03773,* ☎ *603/863–4001.*

Outdoor Activities and Sports

FISHING

Lake Sunapee has brook and lake trout, salmon, smallmouth bass, and pickerel.

Shopping

Dorr Mill Store (☒ Rte. 11/103, Guild, ☎ 603/863–1197), the yarn and fabric center of the Sunapee area, draws droves of rug hookers, knitters, and quilters to browse the huge collection of fiber.

Skiing

Sunapee. Without glitz or glamour, state-run Sunapee remains popular among locals and skiers from Boston, Hartford, and the coast for its low-key atmosphere and easy skiing (although a new black diamond slope raised the total number of expert slopes to six in 1995). Two base lodges supply the essentials. ☒ *Mt. Sunapee State Park, Rte. 103, 03772, ☎ 603/763–2356, snow conditions 603/763–4020, lodging 603/763–2495 or 800/552–1234.*

DOWNHILL

This mountain is 1,510 vertical feet, the highest in southern New Hampshire, and has 19 miles of gentle-to-moderate terrain with a couple of pitches that could be called steep. A nice beginner's section is beyond the base facilities, well away and well protected from other trails. Three triple and three double chairlifts and one surface lift transport skiers.

CHILD CARE

The Duckling Nursery takes children from 12 months through 5 years of age. Little Indians ski instruction gives ages 3 and 4 a taste of skiing, while SKIwee lessons are available for ages 5–12.

Enfield

43 *35 mi north of Newbury.*

In 1782, two Shaker brothers from Mount Lebanon, New York, arrived at a community on the northeastern side of Mascoma Lake. Eventually, they formed Enfield, the ninth of 18 Shaker communities in this country, and moved it to the lake's western shore.

The Museum at Lower Shaker Village preserves the legacy of the Enfield Shakers. A self-guided walking tour leads through 13 of the buildings that remain. The museum preserves and explains many Shaker artifacts, and skilled artisans demonstrate Shaker artisanry. There are numerous special events each year. ☒ *Rte. 4A, 03748, ☎ 603/632–4346. ☒ $3.50. ☉ June–mid-Oct., Mon.–Sat. 10–5, Sun. noon–5; mid-Oct.–May, Sat. 10–4, Sun. noon–4.*

Outdoor Activities and Sports

FISHING

In **Lake Mascoma,** you can fish for rainbow trout, pickerel, and horned pout.

Shopping

West Lebanon, just west of Enfield on the Vermont border, has a busy commercial section. The owners of the **Mouse Menagerie of Fine Crafts** (☒ West Lebanon, ☎ 603/298–7090) have created a collector's series of toy mice in every profession and sport, and they also sell furniture, wind chimes, and hundreds of other gifts. The **Powerhouse** (☒ Rte. 12A, 1 mi north of Exit 20 off I–89, West Lebanon, ☎ 603/298–5236), a onetime power station, comprises three adjacent buildings of specialty stores, boutiques, and restaurants decorated with freestanding sculpture and with picture-window views of the Mascoma River.

Hanover

44 *12 mi west of Enfield via Route 120 from Lebanon.*

Eleazer Wheelock founded Hanover's **Dartmouth College** in 1769 to educate Native American youth. Daniel Webster graduated in 1801. Robert Frost spent part of a brooding freshman semester on this campus before giving up on college altogether. Today Dartmouth is the northernmost Ivy League school and the cultural center of the region. The buildings that cluster around the green include the **Baker Memorial Library**, which houses a number of literary treasures, including a collection of 17th-century editions of Shakespeare. If the towering arcade at the entrance to the **Hopkins Center** (☎ 603/646–2422) appears familiar, it's probably because it resembles the project that architect Wallace K. Harrison completed just after designing it: New York City's famed Metropolitan Opera House at Lincoln Center. In addition to the exhibits on African, Asian, European, and American art, the **Hood Museum of Art** owns Picasso's Vollard etchings, Paul Revere's silver, and paintings by Winslow Homer. Rivaling the collection's force is the museum's architecture: a series of a austere redbrick buildings with copper roofs arranged around a small courtyard. Free guided tours are given on some weekend afternoons. ⊠ *Wheelock St.,* ☎ *603/646–2808.* ☉ *Tues.–Sat. 10–5 (Wed. until 9), Sun. noon–5.*

Dining and Lodging

$$$–$$$$
★ ✗⊞ **Hanover Inn.** Owned and operated by Dartmouth College, this Georgian brick house rises four white-trimmed stories and is the oldest continuously operating business in New Hampshire. The building was converted to a tavern in 1780 and has been open ever since. Rooms have Colonial reproductions, pastels, Audubon prints, and large sitting areas. The highly acclaimed and very formal Daniel Webster Room serves such regional American dishes as soy-seared tuna steak with shrimp dumplings. The contemporary Ivy Grill offers a lighter menu. ⊠ *The Green, Box 151, 03755,* ☎ *603/643–4300 or 800/443–7024,* ℻ *603/646–3744. 92 rooms with bath. 2 restaurants. AE, D, DC, MC, V.*

Nightlife and the Arts

NIGHTLIFE

Peter Christian's Tavern (⊠ 39 S. Main St., ☎ 603/643–2345) has live folk and jazz performances Tuesday and Thursday evenings.

THE ARTS

Hopkins Center (⊠ Dartmouth College, ☎ 603/646–2422) has a 900-seat theater for film and music, a 400-seat theater for plays, and a black-box theater for new plays and the Dartmouth Symphony Orchestra. Each summer, the Big Apple Circus performs here.

Outdoor Activities and Sports

CANOEING

The Connecticut River is generally considered safe after June 15, but canoeists should always use caution. This river is not for beginners. **Ledyard Canoe Club of Dartmouth** (☎ 603/643–6709), on the Connecticut River, provides canoe and kayak rentals and classes.

Shopping

Goldsmith Paul Gross, of **Designer Gold** (⊠ 3 Lebanon St., ☎ 603/643–3864), designs settings for color gemstones and opals—all one-of-a-kind or limited-edition. He also carries some silver jewelry by other American artisans. **Partridge Replications** (⊠ 53 S. Main St., ☎ 603/643–1660), which also has a shop in Peterborough, specializes in reproductions of Colonial furniture and decorative accessories, including sconces, chandeliers, ironware, mirrors, and trivets.

Cornish

㊺ *18 mi south of Hanover on Route 12A.*

The village of Cornish is best known today for its four covered bridges, one of which is the longest in the United States: The **Cornish-Windsor Bridge** was built in 1866 and rebuttressed in 1988–89. It spans the Connecticut River, connecting New Hampshire with Vermont.

At the turn of the century Cornish was known primarily as the home of Winston Churchill (no relation to the British prime minister), then the country's most popular novelist. His novel *Richard Carvell* sold more than a million copies. Churchill was such a celebrity that he hosted Teddy Roosevelt during the president's 1902 visit. At that time the town was an enclave of artistic talent. Painter Maxfield Parrish lived and worked here, and sculptor Augustus Saint-Gaudens (1848–1907) set up his studio and created the heroic bronzes for which he is known. Today the **Saint-Gaudens National Historic Site,** Saint-Gaudens's house with original furnishings, studio, gallery, and 150 acres of gardens can now be toured. Scattered throughout are full-size replicas of the sculptor's work, as well as sketches and casting molds. Sunday afternoon at 2, you can sit on the lawn and enjoy chamber music. ⊠ *Off Rte. 12A,* ☎ *603/675–2175.* 🎫 *$2.* ☉ *Memorial Day weekend–Oct., daily 8:30–4:30; grounds open until dusk.*

The Arts

The beautifully restored 19th-century **Claremont Opera House** (⊠ Tremont Sq., Claremont, ☎ 603/542–4433) hosts plays and musicals from September through May.

Lodging

$$–$$$ 🏨 **Home Hill Country Inn.** This restored 1800 mansion set back from the river on 25 acres of meadow and woods is a tranquil place. The chef-owner, from Brittany, has given the inn a French influence with 19th-century patrician antiques and collectibles. A suite in the guest house is a romantic hideaway. The dining room serves classic and nouvelle French cuisine. ⊠ *River Rd., Plainfield 03781,* ☎ *603/675–6165. 9 rooms with bath, 2 suites, 1 seasonal cottage. Pool, 9-hole golf course, tennis court, cross-country skiing. CP. MC, V.*

$–$$ 🏨 **Chase House Bed & Breakfast Inn.** This is the birthplace of Salmon
★ P. Chase, who was Abraham Lincoln's secretary of the treasury, a chief justice of the United States, and a founder of the Republican Party. It's been restored to 19th-century elegance with Colonial furnishings and Waverly fabrics throughout. Ask for a room with a canopy bed or one with a view of the Connecticut River valley and Mt. Ascutney. The innkeeper will give you the history of the house and can point out all of the area's historical landmarks. Breakfast often includes pancakes made from an Amish friendship bread starter. ⊠ *Rte. 12A (1½ mi south of Cornish-Windsor covered bridge), R.R. 2, Box 909, 03745,* ☎ *603/675–5391 or 800/401–9455,* FAX *603/675–5010. 7 rooms with bath. Boating. Full breakfast included. No smoking. No children under 12. MC, V.*

Outdoor Activities and Sports

CANOEING

The Connecticut River is generally considered safe after June 15, but canoeists should always use caution: This river is not for beginners. **Northstar Canoe Livery** (⊠ Rte. 12A, Balloch's Crossing, ☎ 603/542–5802) rents canoes for half- or full-day trips on the Connecticut River.

Charlestown

⓸⓺ *20 mi south of Cornish.*

Charlestown has the state's largest historic district: Sixty-three homes of Federal, Greek Revival, and Gothic Revival architecture are clustered about the center of town; 10 of them predate 1800. Several merchants on Main Street distribute brochures that outline an interesting walking tour of the district.

Ⓒ Just 1½ miles north of Charlestown, you'll find the **Fort at No. 4,** which in 1747 was an outpost on the lonely periphery of Colonial civilization. That year it withstood a massive attack of 400 French soldiers, which changed the course of New England history. Today it is the only living-history museum from the era of the French and Indian War. Costumed interpreters cook dinner over an open hearth and demonstrate weaving, gardening, and candlemaking. Each year the museum holds full reenactments of militia musters and battles from the French and Indian War era. ⊠ *Rte. 11W, Springfield Rd.,* ☎ *603/826–5700.* 🎫 *$6.* ☉ *Late May–mid-Oct., Wed.–Mon. 10–4 (weekends only 1st 2 wks of Sept.).*

On a bright, breezy day you may want to detour to the **Morningside Flight Park** (⊠ Rte. 12/11, ☎ 603/542–4416), not necessarily to take hang-gliding lessons, although you could. Safer to watch the bright colors of the gliders as they swoop over the school's 450-foot peak.

Numbers in the margin correspond to points of interest on the Monadnock Region and Central New Hampshire map.

Walpole

⓸⓻ *12 mi south of Charlestown.*

Walpole is a town that has yet another perfect town green. This one is surrounded by homes built about 1790, when the town constructed a canal around the Great Falls of the Connecticut River and brought commerce and wealth to the area. The town now has 3,200 inhabitants, more than a dozen of whom are millionaires.

James Michener visited and wrote here, as did Louisa May Alcott, author of *Little Women.* The **Old Academy Museum** (⊠ Main St., ☎ 603/756–3449; ☉ Sun. 2–4) contains the original piano mentioned in that novel; it had been a gift to the Alcott sisters.

OFF THE
BEATEN PATH

Around here, maple-sugar season is the first harbinger of spring, occurring about the first week in March. The days now are a bit warmer but the nights are still frigid; this is when a drive along maple-lined backroads reveals thousands of taps and buckets catching the fresh but labored flow of unrefined sap. Plumes of smoke rise from nearby sugarhouses—the residue of furiously boiling down this precious liquid in a process called sugaring off. Many sugarhouses are open to the public; after a short tour and demonstration, you can sample the syrup with traditional unsweetened doughnuts and maybe a pickle—or taste hot syrup over fresh snow, a favorite confection. Open to the public are **Bacon's Sugar House** (⊠ 72 Dublin Rd., Jaffrey Center, ☎ 603/532–8836); **Bascom's** (⊠ Mt. Kingsbury, Rte. 123A, Alstead, ☎ 603/835–2230), which serves maple pecan pie and maple milkshakes; **Clark's Sugar House** (⊠ off Rte. 123A, Alstead, ☎ 603/835–6863); **Old Brick Sugar House** (⊠ Summit Rd., Keene, ☎ 603/352–6812); **Parker's Maple Barn** (⊠ Brookline Rd., Mason, ☎ 603/878–2308), where a restaurant serves a whole grain–pancake breakfast any time of day

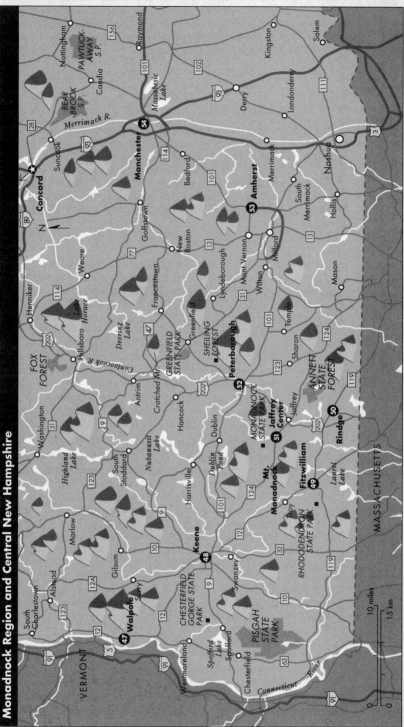

Monadnock Region and Central New Hampshire

along with less maplely items; and **Stuart & John's Sugar House & Pan-cake Restaurant** (⊠ Rtes. 12 and 63, Westmoreland, ☎ 603/399–4486), which offers a tour and pancake breakfast. Always call ahead for hours and to see that the sap is running.

Keene

48 *18 mi southeast of Walpole.*

Keene is the largest city in the southwest corner, and the proud locus of the widest main street in America. On that tree-lined street is **Keene State College,** hub of the local arts community. Its **Arts Center on Brickyard Pond** (☎ 603/358–2168) has three theaters and eight art studios. The **Thorne-Sagendorph Art Gallery** (☎ 603/358–2720) houses George Ridci's *Landscape,* alongside traveling exhibits from museums around the country. Concerts are given here by nationally known rock and folk stars as well as local musicians and chamber groups. The **Putnam Art Lecture Hall** (☎ 603/358–2160) shows art films and international films.

NEED A
BREAK?

Timoleans (⊠ 25–27 Main St., ☎ 603/357–4230) is a classic diner. You won't get a seat any time during the rush between noon and 1, but it's perfect for early and late lunches or the best pie in town.

The Arts

The **Apple Hill Chamber Players** (E. Sullivan, ☎ 603/847–3371) produce summer concert series. The **Arts Center at Brickyard Pond** (☎ 603/358–2168) has year-round music, theater, and dance performances. The **Colonial Theatre** (⊠ 95 Main St., ☎ 603/352–2033) opened in 1924 as a vaudeville stage. It still hosts some folk and jazz concerts and has the largest movie screen in town. The **Moving Company Dance Center** (⊠ 76 Railroad, ☎ 603/357–2100) holds theme dances on Friday and Saturday nights, which range from swing to line dancing to Latin ballroom.

Dining, Lodging, and Camping

$–$$ ✕ **Henry David's.** The ambience is that of a greenhouse, especially up-
★   stairs, with hundreds of plants hanging from and perched upon the exposed beams of this airy restaurant that was once a private home. Start with the crab bisque or tomato cheddar soup. The house sandwiches, though named for area towns and villages, are thinly veiled versions of such popular standbys as Reubens and turkey clubs. A nice light lunch or dinner can be made of the sweet pea spinach salad served with a variety of breads. ⊠ *81 Main St.,* ☎ *603/352–0608. DC, MC, V.*

$–$$ ✕ **One Seventy Six Main.** Similar in quality to Henry David's, this restaurant distinguishes itself with a pub serving a vast selection of international beers. On offer are seafood, burgers, pasta, and a delightfully spicy summer gazpacho. ⊠ *176 Main St.,* ☎ *603/357–3100. AE, D, MC, V.*

$$$ ✕🏠 **Chesterfield Inn.** Surrounded by gardens, the inn sits on a rise above
★   Route 9, the main Brattleboro–Keene road. Rooms, which are quite spacious, are tastefully decorated with armoires, fine antiques, and period-style fabrics, and smack of luxury with air-conditioning, refrigerators, and telephones in the bathroom. The dining room entrance leads through the kitchen, allowing a sneak preview of what's to come. Favorites include country pâté and duck with mango chutney. ⊠ *Rte. 9, West Chesterfield 03466,* ☎ *603/256–3211 or 800/365–5515,* 𝐅𝐀𝐗 *603/256–6131. 11 rooms with bath, 2 suites. Restaurant. Full breakfast included. AE, D, DC, MC, V.*

$ 🏠 Carriage Barn Guest House. The Main Street location across from Keene State College puts major sights within walking distance. The house is furnished with antiques and quilts, most of which were made locally: The nightstands, for example, are fashioned out of antique desks from a local school. In the warmer months, breakfast is served in a summerhouse out under a willow tree. ⊠ *358 Main St., 03431,* ☎ *603/357–3812. 4 rooms with bath. CP. No credit cards.*

$ ⛺ Surry Mountain Camp Ground. This campground is north of Keene and east of Walpole. ⊠ *271 Rte. 12A, Surry 03431,* ☎ *603/352–9770.*

Outdoor Activities and Sports
FISHING

In the Monadnock region there are more than 200 lakes and ponds, most of which offer good fishing. You'll find rainbow trout, smallmouth and largemouth bass, and some northern pike in Chesterfield's **Spofford Lake. Goose Pond** (West Canaan, just north of Keene) has smallmouth bass and white perch.

Shopping
ANTIQUES

For some interesting antiquing, check out **The Antique Shops** (Rte. 12, Westmoreland, ☎ 603/399–7039), where 40 dealers sell a little bit of everything.

BOOKS

The best used bookstore in the region, the **Homestead Bookshop** (⊠ Jct. of Rtes. 101 and 124, Marlborough, ☎ 603/876–4213) carries an extraordinary collection of town histories, biographies, and cookbooks.

MARKETPLACE

Colony Mill Marketplace (⊠ 222 West St., ☎ 603/357–1240) was an old mill building but has been converted into a shopping center of specialty stores and boutiques, including **Autumn Woods** (☎ 603/352–5023), which sells fine Shaker-style furniture and Colonial reproductions in birch, maple, and pine; **Country Artisans** (☎ 603/352–6980), which showcases the stoneware, textiles, prints, and glassware of regional artists; the **Toadstool Bookshop** (☎ 603/352–8815), which has a huge selection of children's books, and also carries good reading material on regional travel and history; and **Ye Goodie Shoppe** (☎ 603/352–0326), dating from 1931 and specializing in handmade chocolates and confections.

Fitzwilliam

㊾ *16 mi south of Keene.*

A well-preserved historic district of Colonial and Federal houses has made the town of Fitzwilliam, on Route 119, the subject of thousands of picture postcards—particularly views of its landscape in winter, when a fine white snow settles on the oval common. Town business is still conducted in the 1817 meeting house. The **Fitzwilliam Historical Society** (⊠ Village Green, ☎ 603/585–7742) maintains a museum and country store in the **Amos J. Blake House** (🕐 Late May–mid-Oct., Sat. 10–4, Sun. 1–4). Blake's law office looks much as it did when he used it. The rest of the museum displays period antiques and artifacts.

More than 16 acres of wild rhododendrons burst into bloom in mid-July at **Rhododendron State Park.** This is the largest concentration of *Rhododendron maximum* north of the Alleghenies. Bring a picnic lunch and sit in a nearby pine grove, or follow the marked footpaths through the flowers. ⊠ *Off Rte. 12, 2½ mi northwest of the common.*

Dining and Lodging

$$–$$$　✕🏠 **Inn at East Hill Farm.** At this 1830 farmhouse inn, children are not only allowed, they are expected. In fact, if you don't have kids, you may be happier elsewhere. Children collect the eggs for the next day's breakfast; milk the cows; feed the animals; and participate in arts and crafts, storytelling, hiking, and games. Three meals are included in the room rate, all served family-style. The innkeepers schedule weekly sleigh rides or hay rides, and can whip up a picnic lunch for families who want to spend the day away. ⊠ *Monadnock St., Troy 03465,* ☎ *603/242–6495 or 800/242–6495,* FAX *603/242–7709. 42 rooms with bath. Restaurant, indoor pool, 2 outdoor pools, sauna, tennis, horseback riding, boating, waterskiing, fishing, baby-sitting. AP required. D, MC, V.*

$　✕🏠 **Fitzwilliam Inn.** Vermont Transit buses from Boston's Logan Airport stop at the door, just as the stagecoach once did. Indoors, too, much remains as it was in 1796. Upstairs, the furniture is a hodgepodge of early and late hand-me-downs. Locals dally in the tavern, and the restaurant serves spiced-up Yankee cooking like pork medallions with a mustard cream sauce and fresh venison. There's a Sunday concert series here in winter. ⊠ *The Green, 03447,* ☎ *603/585–9000,* FAX *603/585–3495. 28 rooms, 15 with bath. Restaurant, bar, pool, cross-country skiing. D, MC, V.*

$　🏠 **Amos Parker House.** The garden of this old Colonial B&B is the
★　most spectacular in town, complete with lily ponds, Oriental stone benches, and Dutch waterstones. Two rooms have garden views, although any guest is welcome to sit on the deck and listen to the birds. ⊠ *Rte. 119, Box 202, 03447,* ☎ *603/585–6540. 4 rooms with bath. Full breakfast included. No credit cards.*

$　🏠 **Hannah Davis House.** This 1820 Federal house has, despite a full refurbishment and conversion into a B&B, lost none of its original elegance. The view of a nearby bog is marred only by the natural flaws in the antique windows. The original beehive oven still sits in the kitchen, and one suite has two Count Rumford fireplaces. The inn is just two buildings off the village green, and your host has the scoop on area antiquing. There's cable TV and a VCR in the common area. ⊠ *186 Depot Rd., 03447,* ☎ *603/585–3344. 6 rooms with bath. Full breakfast included. D, MC, V.*

Outdoor Activities and Sports

FISHING

You can find rainbow and golden trout, pickerel, and horned pout in **Laurel Lake** (Fitzwilliam). There are rainbow and brown trout in the **Ashuelot River.**

Shopping

Fitzwilliam Antique Center (⊠ Rtes. 12 and 119, ☎ 603/585–9092) always has refinished cupboards in stock, along with other antique furnishings.

Rindge

🔟 *8 mi east of Fitzwilliam on Route 119.*

In the village of Rindge, you can spend a quiet moment at the **Cathedral of the Pines,** an outdoor church and a memorial to the American women, both civilian and military, who sacrificed their lives in service to their country. There's an inspiring view of Mt. Monadnock and Mt. Kearsarge from the church's **Altar of the Nation,** which is composed of rock from every U.S. state and territory. All faiths hold services here, with organ meditations at midday, Monday through Thursday. The

Memorial Bell Tower, with its carillon of international bells, is built of native stone; Norman Rockwell designed the bronze tablets over the four arches. Flower gardens, an indoor chapel, and a museum of military memorabilia share the hilltop. ⊠ *Cathedral Rd., off Rte. 119,* ☎ *603/899–3300.* ⊙ *May–Oct., dawn–sunset.*

Jaffrey Center

⑤ *7 mi north of Rindge.*

Novelist Willa Cather came to the historic village of Jaffrey Center in 1919 and stayed in the Shattuck Inn, which now stands empty on Old Meeting House Road. She pitched a tent not far from here in which she wrote several chapters of her signature work, *My Antonia.* She returned here nearly every summer thereafter until her death, and now she is buried here in the Old Burying Ground according to her last wishes. **Amos Fortune Forum,** near Old Burying Ground, brings nationally known speakers to the 1773 meeting house on summer evenings.

The drawing card of **Monadnock State Park** is, of course, **Mt. Monadnock.** The oft-quoted statistic about Mt. Monadnock is that it's the most climbed mountain in America—second in the world to Japan's Mt. Fuji. Whether this is true or not, locals agree that it's never lonely at the top. Some days more than 400 people crowd its bald peak. Monadnock rises to 3,165 feet, and on a clear day the hazy Boston skyline is visible from its summit. The park maintains picnic grounds and some tent campsites and sells a trail map for $2. Five trailheads branch into more than two dozen trails of varying difficulty that wend their way to the top. Some are considerably shorter than others, but you should allow between three and four hours for any round-trip hike. A visitor center has a small museum documenting the mountain's history. ⊠ *2½ mi north of Jaffrey Center, off Rte. 124, 03452,* ☎ *603/532–8862.* ⊙ *Year-round.*

OFF THE
BEATEN PATH

HARRISVILLE – This perfectly preserved mill town was founded in 1774 by Abel Twitchell. The **Harris Mill,** an old woolen mill, still stands in the heart of town. The combination of red brick and blue sky reflecting off **Harrisville Pond** is worth at least one picture. **Harrisville Designs** (⊠ Mill Alley, ☎ 603/827–3333) operates out of a historic building and sells hand-spun and hand-dyed yarn sheared from local sheep, as well as looms for the serious weaver. The shop also hosts classes in knitting and weaving.

Outdoor Activities and Sports

FISHING

Gilmore Pond in Jaffrey has several types of trout.

Shopping

Sharon Arts Center (⊠ Rte. 123, Sharon, ☎ 603/924–7256) is not just a gallery of local pottery, fabric, and woodwork, but a learning center with classes on everything from photography to paper marbling.

Peterborough

㉒ *8 mi north of Jaffrey.*

In Peterborough, you'll find the nation's first free public library, which opened here in 1833. The **MacDowell Colony** (⊠ 100 High St., ☎ 603/924–3886 or 212/966–4860) was founded by the composer Edward MacDowell in 1907 as an artists' retreat. Willa Cather wrote part of *Death Comes for the Archbishop* here. Thornton Wilder was in residence when he wrote *Our Town*; Peterborough's resemblance to fic-

titious Grover's Corners is no coincidence. Artists reside here in solitude, so only a small portion of the colony is open to visitors.

At **Twelve Pine** (✉ 1 Summer St., ☎ 603/924–6140), you can stock
your picnic basket with chicken burritos—famous throughout the region—or one of the special pasta salads. The store even sells leftovers
out of the fridge for a reduced price. Don't expect to linger: There are
no tables in this tiny place, just room enough for the line to form.

Dining and Lodging

$$$ ✕ **Boilerhouse at Noone Falls.** A mid-19th-century woolen mill has been
converted into offices, shops, a café, and this upscale restaurant, which
manages a diverse menu that includes everything from venison to
pasta. Dinner entrées include gravlax of Norwegian salmon (cured on
the premises with salt, sugar, dill, and vodka, then served with Bermuda
onions, capers, and caviar) or veal with forest mushrooms in a brandy-
Madeira cream sauce. Popular lunch entrées are tricolor tortellini with
red pepper, and the lemon chicken with pine nuts and capers. A dish
of homemade ice cream tops things off nicely. ✉ *Rte. 202,* ☎ *603/924–
9486. D, MC, V.*

$–$$ ✕ **Latacarta.** Put a New Age restaurant in an old movie theater and
you get the essence of Peterborough. The low-fat, low-cholesterol
menu, which changes daily, emphasizes foods from a variety of cultures. Salt-free and reduced-calorie dishes are available. You won't believe that the incredible desserts—Indian pudding, pear crisp—are all
sugar-free. ✉ *6 School St.,* ☎ *603/924–6878. AE, MC, V. Closed Mon.*

$$–$$$ ✕🏠 **Inn at Crotched Mountain.** This 1822 Colonial inn has nine fire-
places, four of which are in private rooms. The other five spread cheer
among several common areas, which makes this a particularly romantic place to stay when the snow is falling on Crotched Mountain.
Rooms are furnished with early Colonial reproductions. The chef splits
the menu between such Eastern specialties as Indonesian charbroiled
swordfish with a sauce of ginger, green pepper, onion, and lemon and
more regional dishes such as cranberry-port pot roast. ✉ *Mountain
Rd., Francestown 03043,* ☎ *603/588–6840. 13 rooms, 8 with bath.
Restaurant, bar, pool, tennis, cross-country skiing. Full breakfast included. MAP required weekends. No credit cards.*

$$ ✕🏠 **Hancock Inn.** This Federal inn dates from 1789 and is the pride
of the historically preserved town for which it's named. Common
areas possess the warmth of a tavern, with fireplaces, big wing chairs,
couches, dark-wood paneling, and murals. Rooms are done in the tra-
ditional Colonial style with high four-poster antique beds. The dining
room serves traditional Yankee fare by candlelight; the rubbed natural
woodwork gives an intimate feel. ✉ *Main St., Hancock 03447,* ☎
603/525–3318 or 800/525–1789, ℻ *603/525–9301. 11 rooms with
bath. Restaurant, bar. AE, D, MC, V.*

$ ✕🏠 **Birchwood Inn.** Thoreau slept here, probably on his way to climb
Monadnock or to visit Jaffrey or Peterborough. Country furniture
and handmade quilts outfit the bedrooms, as they did in 1775 when
the house was new and no one dreamed it would someday be listed in
the National Register of Historic Places. In the dining room, she-crab
soup and roast duckling are two Saturday-night specials, and if you're
really lucky you might find cream-cheese pecan pie or one of the fresh
fruit cobblers on the blackboard dessert menu. Everything is cooked
to order, so allow time for lingering. ✉ *Rte. 45, Temple 03084,* ☎
603/878–3285. 7 rooms, 5 with bath. Restaurant (reservations essential;

BYOB; no lunch; closed Sun., Mon.). Full breakfast included. No credit cards.

Nightlife and the Arts

NIGHTLIFE

Folkway (⊠ 85 Grove St., ☎ 603/924–7484), a restaurant and coffeehouse, has become a New England institution, with such artists as the Story, Greg Brown, Trout Fishing in America, and dozens of local musicians. The best seats are saved for those who have dinner (reservations advised). The crafts shop, upstairs, has a great selection of folk tapes and CDs, and carries the work of local artisans and weavers.

THE ARTS

Monadnock Music (☎ 603/924–7610) produces a summer series of concerts from mid-July to late August, with solo recitals, chamber music, and orchestra and opera performances by renowned musicians. Concerts usually take place evenings at 8 and Sunday at 4; many are free. The **Peterborough Players** (⊠ Stearns Farm, Middle Hancock Rd., ☎ 603/924–7585) have been taking summer stock theater to a new level for more than 60 seasons. The plays are held in a converted barn. The **Temple Town Band** (☎ 603/878–2829) was founded in 1799 and is believed to be the oldest band in the nation, although they have not been in continuous existence. Members range from teenagers to septuagenarians. The band plays a selection of patriotic songs, traditional marches, and show tunes at the Jaffrey Bandstand, the Sharon Arts Center, and local festivals and events.

Outdoor Activities and Sports

FISHING

Go to **Dublin Pond** (Dublin) for several types of trout.

Shopping

ANTIQUES AND GALLERIES

Peterborough Antiques (⊠ 76 Grove St., Peterborough, ☎ 603/924–7297) sells English and Continental paintings, jewelry, and accessories. **North Gallery at Tewksbury's** (⊠ Rte. 101, ☎ 603/924–3224) has a wide selection of thrown pots, sconces, candlestick holders, and woodworkings. **Partridge Replications** (⊠ 83 Grove St., ☎ 603/924–3002) specializes in reproductions of Colonial furniture and decorative accessories, including sconces, chandeliers, ironware, and mirrors.

SPORTS/OUTDOORS GEAR

The corporate headquarters and retail outlet of **Eastern Mountain Sports** (⊠ 1 Vose Farm Rd., ☎ 603/924–7231) not only sells everything from tents to skis to hiking boots, but also gives hiking and camping classes, and kayaking and canoeing demonstrations.

En Route If you travel from Peterborough to Amherst via Route 101, you'll pass **Temple Mountain** (☎ 603/924–6949), a wintertime cross-country and downhill ski area that's perfect for beginners. **Miller State Park** (☎ 603/924–3672), also off Route 101, has an auto road that takes you almost 2,300 feet up Mt. Pack Monadnock.

Amherst

➌ *30 mi east of Peterborough via Route 101.*

Amherst is known for both its town green and the dawn-to-dusk flea market held Sunday on the western outskirts of town. It operates April through October and attracts dealers and decorators from all over New England.

The Arts

American Stage Festival (⊠ Rte. 13 N, Milford, ☎ 603/673–4005) is the state's largest professional theater. The season runs from early June through Labor Day and includes five Broadway plays and one new work, as well as a children's theater series.

Dining

$$$ ✕ **Colonel Shepard House.** This Colonial house dates to 1757. Its four dining rooms evoke romance and intimacy, with dark-wood wainscoting, Oriental rugs, and candlelight flickering off the gilt-frame prints. The meat-intensive dishes include filet mignon, veal, and rack of lamb, complemented by nightly seafood specials and an extensive wine list. Attentive service and a French chef who makes pan sauces to order for each entrée keep diners coming back. ⊠ 29 Mt. Vernon St., Milford, ☎ 603/672–2527. AE, D, MC, V. No lunch. Closed Mon.

$$ ✕ **Ram in the Thicket.** The inviting prix-fixe menu changes monthly; all courses are always delicious. A first course might be artichoke hearts and mushrooms in brie served warm over French bread, or perhaps a kalamata-olive paste on polenta. Do try the filet mignon, the rack of lamb, or the pork tenderloin. The late 19th-century house has a screened-in porch that's perfect for summer dining. ⊠ Off Rte. 101, ½ mi from Wilton, ☎ 603/654–6440. AE. Closed Mon., Tues. No lunch.

Manchester

🔢 10 mi northeast of Amherst.

Manchester is New Hampshire's largest city, with just over 100,000 residents. The town grew around the power of the Amoskeag Falls on the Merrimack River, which fueled several small textile mills through the 1700s. By 1828, a group of investors from Boston had bought the rights to the river's water power and built on its eastern bank the **Amoskeag Textile Mills.** At its peak in 1906, the mills employed 17,000 people and churned out more than 4 million yards of cloth per week. They formed the entire economic base of Manchester, and when they closed in 1936, the town was devastated. As part of an economic recovery plan, the mill buildings have been converted into warehouses, classrooms, restaurants, and office space. You can wander among these huge blood-red buildings; contact the **Manchester Historic Association** (⊠ 129 Amherst St., ☎ 603/622–7531) for a map.

The **Currier Gallery of Art,** in a Beaux Arts building downtown, has a permanent collection of paintings, sculpture, and decorative arts from the 13th through the 20th centuries. Don't miss the Zimmerman House, designed by Frank Lloyd Wright in 1950. A response to the Depression, Wright called this sparse, utterly functional living space "Usonian." It's one of only five Wright houses in the Northeast and New England's only Wright-designed residence open to the public. ⊠ 192 Orange St., 03104, ☎ 603/669–6144. ⊠ $4; free Fri. 1–9; Zimmerman House $6 and reservations required. ⊙ Mon., Wed., Thurs., weekends 11–5; Fri. 11–9.

The Arts

The **Palace Theatre** (⊠ 80 Hanover St., ☎ 603/668–5588) is the state's performing arts center—home to the state symphony and opera and the New Hampshire Philharmonic. It also hosts national tours and musical acts.

Dining and Lodging

$$$–$$$$ ✕🛏 **Bedford Village Inn.** This luxurious Federal-style inn, just minutes from Manchester, was once a working farm and still shows horsenuzzle marks on its old beams; gone, however, are the hayloft and the

old milking room, which have been converted into lavish suites, complete with king-size beds, imported marble in the whirlpool baths, and three telephones. The tavern has seven intimate dining rooms, each with original wide pine floors and huge fireplaces. The menu, which often includes such New England favorites as lobster and Atlantic salmon with a chardonnay beurre blanc, changes every two weeks. ✉ *2 Old Bedford Rd., Bedford 03110,* ☎ *603/472–2001 or 800/852–1166,* FAX *603/472–2379. 12 suites, 2 apartments. Restaurant, meeting rooms. AE, DC, MC, V.*

Shopping

Try **Bell Hill Antiques** (✉ Rte. 101 at Bell Hill Rd., Bedford, ☎ 603/472–5580) for country furniture, glass, and china. The enormous **Mall of New Hampshire** (✉ S. Willow St., Exit 1, ☎ 603/669–0433) has every conceivable store and is anchored by Sears, Filene's, and Lechmere.

Western and Central New Hampshire A to Z

Arriving and Departing

BY CAR

Most people who travel up from Massachusetts do so on I–93, which passes through Manchester and Concord before cutting a path through the White Mountains. I–89 connects Concord to the Merrimack Valley and continues on to Vermont. Farther south, Route 101 connects Keene and Manchester, then continues to the seacoast.

BY PLANE

Manchester Airport (☎ 603/624–6556), the state's largest, has scheduled flights from USAir, Delta, Continental, Northwest Airlink, United, and TWA.

Getting Around

BY BUS

Concord Trailways (☎ 800/639–3317) runs from Concord to Berlin and from Littleton to Boston. **Advance Transit** (☎ 802/295–1824) services towns in the upper valley.

BY CAR

Routes 12 and 12A are picturesque but slow-moving. Route 4 crosses the region, winding between Lebanon and the seacoast. Other pretty routes include 101, 202, and 11.

Contacts and Resources

BIKING

For information on organized bike rides in southern New Hampshire contact the **Granite State Wheelmen** (✉ 16 Clinton St., Salem, no phone). **Monadnock Bicycle Touring** (✉ Box 19, Keene Rd., Harrisville 03450, ☎ 603/827–3925) has inn-hopping bicycle tours of the region. **Eastern Mountain Sports** (☞ Peterborough, *above*) and the **Greater Keene Chamber of Commerce** (✉ 8 Central Sq., Keene 03431, ☎ 603/352–1303) have maps and information on local bike routes.

EMERGENCIES

Dartmouth Hitchcock Medical Center (✉ 1 Medical Ctr. Dr., Lebanon, ☎ 603/650–5000). **Cheshire Medical Center** (✉ 580 Court St., Keene, ☎ 603/352–4111). **Monadnock Community Hospital** (✉ 452 Old Street Rd., Peterborough, ☎ 603/924–7191). **Elliot Hospital** (✉ 1 Elliot Way, Manchester, ☎ 603/669–5300 or 800/235–5468). **Concord Hospital** (✉ 250 Pleasant St., Concord, ☎ 603/225–2711). **Nashua Memorial Hospital** (✉ 8 Prospect St., Nashua, ☎ 603/883–5521).

Monadnock Mutual Aid (☎ 603/352–1100) responds to any emergency, from a medical problem to a car fire.

FISHING

For word on what's biting where, contact the **Department of Fish and Game** in Keene (☎ 603/352–9669).

RESERVATION SERVICE

There's a **lodging reservation service** in the Sunapee region (☎ 603/763–2495 or 800/258–3530).

STATE PARKS

In addition to those state parks mentioned earlier, **Bear Den Geological Park** (Gilsum) is a 19th-century mining town surrounded by more than 50 abandoned mines. In **Curtiss Dogwood State Reservation** (⌧ Lyndeborough, off Rte. 31), namesake blossoms are out in early May. Bring hiking boots, a mountain bike, a fishing pole, or skis to enjoy the 13,000 acres of **Pisgah State Park** (⌧ Off Rte. 63 or Rte. 119), the largest wilderness area in the state.

VISITOR INFORMATION

Hours are generally weekdays 9 to 5. **Concord Chamber of Commerce** (⌧ 244 N. Main St., Concord 03301, ☎ 603/224–2508). **Hanover Chamber of Commerce** (⌧ Box A–105, Hanover 03755, ☎ 603/643–3115). **Lake Sunapee Business Association** (⌧ Box 400, Sunapee 03782, ☎ 603/763–2495 or, in New England, 800/258–3530). **Manchester Chamber of Commerce** (⌧ 889 Elm St., Manchester 03101, ☎ 603/666–6600). **Monadnock Travel Council** (⌧ 48 Central Sq., Keene 03431, ☎ 603/352–1303). **Peterborough Chamber of Commerce** (⌧ Box 401, Peterborough 03458, ☎ 603/924–7234). **Southern New Hampshire Visitor & Convention Bureau** (⌧ Box 115, Windham 03087, ☎ 800/932–4282).

NEW HAMPSHIRE A TO Z

Arriving and Departing

By Bus
Greyhound (☎ 800/231–2222) and its subsidiary **Vermont Transit** (☎ 603/228–3300 or 800/451–3292) link the cities of New Hampshire with major cities in the eastern United States. **Peter Pan Bus Lines** (☎ 800/237–8747) also serves the state.

By Car
I–93 is the principal north–south route through Manchester, Concord, and central New Hampshire. To the west, I–91 traces the Vermont–New Hampshire border. To the east, I–95, which is a toll road, passes through the coastal area of southern New Hampshire on its way from Massachusetts to Maine. I–89 travels from Concord to Montpelier and Burlington, Vermont.

By Plane
Manchester Airport (☎ 603/624–6556), the state's largest, has scheduled flights by USAir, Delta, Continental, Northwest Airlink, United, and TWA. **Keene Airport**'s (☎ 800/272–5488) Colgan Air offers flights to Rutland, Vermont, and Newark, New Jersey. **Lebanon Municipal Airport** (☎ 603/298–8878), near Dartmouth College, is served by Delta Business Express and USAir.

Getting Around

By Bus

Coast (Durham, ☎ 603/862–2328), **C&J** (☎ 603/742–5111), **Concord Trailways** (☎ 800/639–3317), and **Vermont Transit** (☎ 603/228–3300 or 800/451–3292) provide bus service between the state's cities and towns.

By Car

The official state map, available free from the Office of Travel and Tourism Development (☞ Visitor Information, *below*), has directories for each of the tourist areas.

By Plane

Small local airports that handle charters and private planes are **Berlin Airport** (☎ 603/449–7383) in Milan, **Concord Airport** (☎ 603/224–4033), **Jaffrey Municipal Airport** (☎ 603/532–7763), **Laconia Airport** (☎ 603/524–5003), **Nashua Municipal Airport** (☎ 603/882–0661), and **Sky Haven Airport** (☎ 603/332–0005) in Rochester.

Contacts and Resources

Biking

Bike & Hike New Hampshire's Lakes (☎ 603/968–3775), **Bike the Whites** (☎ 800/933–3902), **Great Outdoors Hiking & Biking Tours** (☎ 603/356–3271 or 800/525–9100), **Monadnock Bicycle Touring** (✉ Box 19, Harrisville 03450, ☎ 603/827–3925), **New England Hiking Holidays** (☎ 603/356–9696 or 800/869–0949), and **Sunapee Inns Hike & Bike Tours** (☎ 800/662–6005) organize bike tours.

Bird-Watching

Audubon Society of New Hampshire (✉ 3 Silk Farm Rd., Concord 03301, ☎ 603/224–9909) schedules monthly field trips throughout the state and a special fall bird-watching tour to Star Island and others of the Isles of Shoals.

Camping

New Hampshire Campground Owners Association (✉ Box 320, Twin Mountain 03595, ☎ 800/822–6764) will send you a list of all private, state, and national-forest campgrounds.

Visitor Information

New Hampshire Office of Travel and Tourism Development (✉ Box 1856, Concord 03302, ☎ 603/271–2343). **Events, foliage, and ski conditions** (☎ 800/258–3608 or 800/262–6660). **New Hampshire State Council on the Arts** (✉ 40 N. Main St., Concord 03301, ☎ 603/271–2789).

7 Maine

Due to overdevelopment, Maine's southernmost coastal towns won't give you the rugged, "downeast" experience, but the Kennebunks will: classic town-scapes, rocky shorelines, sandy beaches, and quaint downtown districts. Purists hold that the Maine coast begins at Penobscot Bay. Acadia National Park is Maine's principal tourist attraction for some, while others prefer the Casco Bay Islands coupled with Portland's plethora of restaurants and nightlife. Freeport has become a mecca for shoppers who thrive on the discount prices offered at outlets in the shadow of the famous outfitter L. L. Bean. The vast north woods is a destination for outdoors enthusiasts.

By David
Laskin, with an
introduction by
William G.
Scheller

Updated by
Dale Northrup

N THE MAINE–NEW HAMPSHIRE BORDER is a welcome sign that plainly announces the philosophy of the region: WELCOME TO MAINE: THE WAY LIFE SHOULD BE. Local folk say too many cares are on the road when you can't make it through the traffic signal on the first try. Romantics luxuriate upon the feeling of a down comforter on an old, yellowed pine bed or in the orange glow of a fieldstone fireplace. Families love the unspoiled beaches and safe inlets dotting the shoreline. Hikers and campers are revived by the exalting and exhausting climb to the top of Mount Katahdin. All this is ample reason the sun rises first over Maine as it embraces America each day.

Maine is by far the largest state in New England. At its extremes it measures 300 miles north to south and 200 miles across; all five other New England states could fit within its perimeters. There is an expansiveness to Maine, a sense of real distance between places that hardly exists elsewhere in the region, and along with the sheer size and spread of the place there is a tremendous variety of terrain. One speaks of "coastal" Maine and "inland" Maine, as though the state could be summed up under the twin emblems of lobsters and pine trees. Yet the state's topography and character are a good deal more complicated.

Even the coast is several places in one. South of the rapidly gentrifying city of Portland, such resort towns as Ogunquit, Kennebunkport, and Old Orchard Beach (sometimes called the Québec Riviera because of its popularity with French Canadians) predominate along a reasonably smooth shoreline. Development has been considerable; north of Portland and Casco Bay, secondary roads turn south off Route 1 onto so many oddly chiseled peninsulas that it's possible to drive for days without retracing your route and to conclude that motels, discount outlets, and fried-clam stands are taking over the domain of presidents and lobstermen. Freeport is an entity unto itself, a place where a bewildering assortment of off-price, name-brand outlets has sprung up around the famous outfitter L. L. Bean.

Inland Maine likewise defies characterization. For one thing, a good part of it is virtually uninhabited. This is the land Henry David Thoreau wrote about in *The Maine Woods* 150 years ago; aside from having been logged over several times, much of it hasn't changed since Thoreau and his Native American guides passed through. Ownership of vast portions of northern Maine by forest-products corporations has kept out subdivision and development; many of the roads here are private, open to travel only by permit. The north woods' day of reckoning may be coming, however, for the paper companies plan to sell off millions of acres in a forested belt that reaches all the way to the Adirondacks in New York State. State governments and environmental organizations are working to preserve as much as possible of the great silent expanses of pine.

Logging the north created the culture of the mill towns, the Rumfords, Skowhegans, Millinockets, and Bangors that lay at the end of the old river drives. The logs arrive by truck today, but Maine's harvested wilderness still feeds the mills and the nation's hunger for paper.

Our hunger for potatoes has given rise to an entirely different Maine culture, in one of the most isolated agricultural regions of the country. Northeastern Aroostook County is where the Maine potatoes come from, and this place, too, is changing. In what was once called the Potato Empire, farmers are as pressed between high costs and low

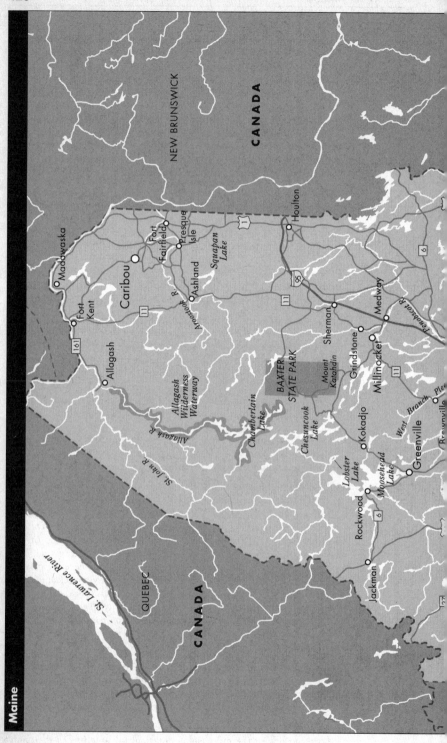

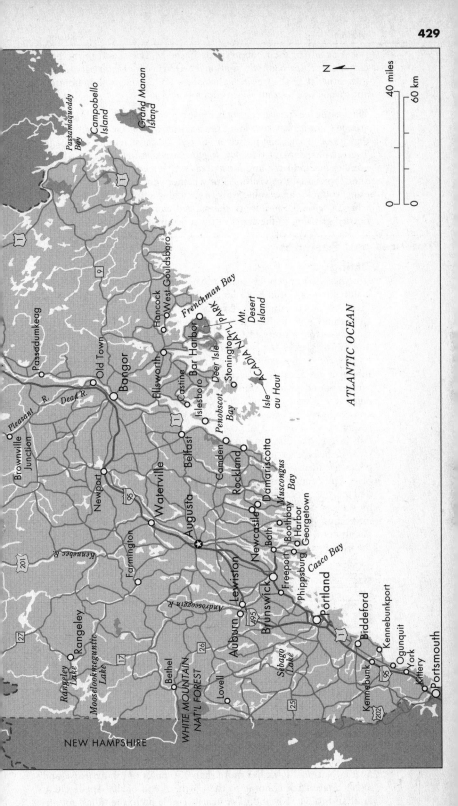

N

40 miles
60 km

Passamaquoddy Bay

Campobello Island

Grand Manan Island

Passadumkeag

Brownville Junction

Old Town

Bangor

Dead R.

Pleasant R.

Ellsworth

West Gouldsboro

Hancock

Frenchman Bay

Bar Harbor

ACADIA NAT'L PARK

Mt. Desert Island

Castine

Islesboro

Deer Isle

Stonington

Isle au Haut

Penobscot Bay

Belfast

Camden

Rockland

Damariscotta

Muscongus Bay

Newcastle

Bath

Boothbay Harbor

Georgetown

Augusta

Waterville

Newport

Farmington

Kennebec R.

Androscoggin R.

Lewiston

Auburn

Brunswick

Freeport

Phippsburg

Casco Bay

Portland

Sebago Lake

Rangeley

Rangeley Lake

Mooselookmeguntic Lake

Bethel

Lovell

WHITE MOUNTAIN NAT'L FOREST

Biddeford

Kennebunkport

Ogunquit

York

Kittery

Kennebunk

Portsmouth

NEW HAMPSHIRE

ATLANTIC OCEAN

prices as any of their counterparts in the Midwest; add to the bleak economic picture a growing national preference for Idaho baking potatoes rather than the traditional small, round Maine boiling potatoes, and Aroostook's troubles are compounded.

The visitor seeking an untouched fishing village with locals gathered around a pot-bellied stove in the general store may be sadly disappointed; that innocent age has passed in all but the most remote of villages. Tourism has supplanted fishing, logging, and potato farming as Maine's number one industry, and most areas are well equipped to receive the annual onslaught of visitors. But whether you are stepping outside a motel room for an evening walk or watching a boat rock at its anchor, you can sense the infinity of the natural world. Wilderness is always nearby, growing to the edges of the most urbanized spots.

Pleasures and Pastimes

Dining

Whether your appetite is ready for home cooking at a country inn, a clambake on a Casco Bay island, lobster and coleslaw on the dock in Freeport, or something more refined such as a honeymoon dinner at Kennebunk's White Barn Inn, you find it in Maine. The coast in York County—from Kittery to Old Orchard Beach—is wedged with clam and lobster shacks. As a general rule, the closer you are to a working harbor, the fresher your lobster will be. Aficionados eschew ordering lobster in restaurants, preferring to eat them "in the rough" at classic lobster pounds, where you select your lobster swimming in a pool and enjoy it at a waterside picnic table. Shrimp, scallops, clams, mussels, and crab are also caught in the cold waters off Maine, and the better restaurants in Portland and the coastal resort towns prepare the shellfish in creative combinations with lobster, haddock, salmon, and swordfish. Blueberries are grown commercially in Maine, and Maine cooks use them generously in pancakes, muffins, jams, pies, and cobblers. Full country breakfasts of fruit, eggs, breakfast meats, pancakes, and muffins are commonly served at inns and bed-and-breakfasts. Almost every nook and cranny of Portland's Old Port Exchange houses interesting little restaurants and coffeehouses. Head Down East to Penobscot Bay as well to sample the local catch or venture to one of the islands in that bay.

CATEGORY	COST*
$$$$	over $35
$$$	$25–$35
$$	$15–$25
$	under $15

average cost of a three-course dinner, per person, excluding drinks, service, and 7% restaurant sales tax

Hiking

From seaside rambles to backwoods hiking, Maine has a walk for everyone. This state's beaches are mostly hard packed and good for walking. Many coastal communities, like York, Ogunquit, and Bar Harbor, have shoreside paths for people who want to keep sand out of their shoes yet enjoy the sound of the crashing surf and the clifftop views of inlets and coves. And those who like to walk in the woods will not be disappointed: Ninety percent of the state is forested land. Acadia National Park has more than 150 miles of hiking trails, and Baxter State Park is home to the northern end of the Appalachian Trail and to Mt. Katahdin, at nearly 1-mile high, the tallest mountain in the state.

Lodging

The beach communities in the south beckon visitors with their weathered look. You're apt to find a room with an ocean view in these parts. More stately digs are the classic inns of Kennebunkport. Bed-and-breakfasts and Victorian inns furnished with lace, chintz, and mahogany have joined the family-oriented motels of Ogunquit, Boothbay Harbor, Bar Harbor, and the Camden-Rockport region. Camden sports more than a dozen high caliber inns, each with a rich history. Although accommodations tend to be less luxurious away from the coast, Bethel, Center Lovell, and Rangeley also have sophisticated hotels and inns. Portland delivers a cornucopia of establishments: a landmark hotel built in 1927, a romantic country inn in the city, and an old armory turned fine hotel. The Acadia area provides a myriad of dining and lodging opportunities with atmospheres to suit a couple on their honeymoon or a family on their annual pilgrimage. Bar Harbor still welcomes the celebrity trade and politicos to its grand homes and waterfront hotels; it has the greatest concentration of accommodations on Mount Desert Island. Much of this lodging has been converted from elaborate 19th-century summer cottages. In Western Maine, Bethel has the largest concentration of inns and bed-and-breakfasts. Greenville and Rockwood offer the largest selection of restaurants and accommodations in the North Woods region. At some of Maine's larger hotels and inns with restaurants, Modified American Plan (MAP; rates include breakfast and dinner) is either an option or required during the peak summer season.

CATEGORY	COST*
$$$$	over $100
$$$	$80–$100
$$	$60–$80
$	under $60

Prices are for a standard double room during peak season, excluding 7% lodging sales tax.

Skiing

Weather patterns that create snow cover for Maine ski areas may come from the Atlantic or from Canada, and Maine may have snow when other New England states do not—and vice versa. In recent years ski-area operators in Maine have embraced snowmaking with a vengeance, and they now have the capacity to cover thousand-foot-plus mountains. In turn, more skiers have discovered Maine skiing, yet in most cases this has still not resulted in crowds, hassles, or lines. Ski-area acquisition wars produced positive results: S-K-I Inc., which owns a number of ski areas in New England, including Killington in Vermont, became part owner of Sugarloaf/USA and immediately put in a new high-speed quad chairlift and announced plans for new trails. This should enable this granddaddy of Maine resorts to compete with Sunday River, which has become a huge, well-managed attraction and one of New England's most popular ski destinations.

Further good news for Maine ski areas is the building of more and better lodging; best news of all is that skiers generally find lower prices here for practically every component of a ski vacation or a day's outing: lift tickets, accommodations, lessons, equipment, and meals. A further result of the ski acquisition wars is that Sugarloaf/USA and Sunday River skiers now can buy lift ticket packages good for these areas as well as their sister resorts in New Hampshire and Vermont.

Exploring Maine

Lying in the southernmost region of the state, York County has a coastline with many small beach communities such as York, Ogunquit, and Kennebunkport. Portland has nightlife and a distinguished art museum; the Portland International Jetport provides good access. Portland is a good hub for adventuring to both the southern coastal communities and for sampling areas a bit father north, such as Freeport and Boothbay Harbor. More than a dozen windjammer sailing vessels depart from Penobscot Bay and the towns of Rockland, Camden, Belfast, and Castine, Down East. Hikers and outdoors enthusiasts will appreciate the Acadia National Park region and Bar Harbor—bring along your mountain bike or rent one. Travelers primarily interested in Acadia or the North Woods regions might elect to fly into Bangor to make their way to Moosehead Lake or Baxter State Park.

Great Itineraries

Numbers in the text correspond to numbers in the margin and on the maps.

IF YOU HAVE 2 DAYS

On your first day, explore ⛟ **Portland** ⑧–⑯, wandering the streets of the Old Port Exchange and cruising to one of the Casco Bay Islands. The next day, head south to **Kennebunkport** ⑥ and ⛟ **Ogunquit** ③ to stroll the Marginal Way of Perkins Cove and picnic on the beach.

IF YOU HAVE 4 DAYS

After ⛟ **Portland** ⑧–⑯, stay two nights in the ⛟ **Kennebunks** ⑤–⑥. Shoppers will want to converge on two prime outlet centers—one in **Kittery** ①, 40 miles south of Portland and the other in **Freeport** ⑰, 17 miles to the north. ⛟ **Camden** ㉕ is a good place to overnight. Hikers and cyclists should concentrate their efforts on **Acadia National Park** ㉞–㊷.

IF YOU HAVE 8 DAYS

Inch your way up the southern coast from **Kittery** ① to ⛟ **Ogunquit** ③ to ⛟ **Kennebunkport** ⑥, planning your days according to how much lobster you need to ingest or how many PTHs (peak tanning hours) are required on the beach. Spend three nights in ⛟ **Portland** ⑧–⑯, exploring the growing number of brew pubs and coffeehouses, cruising Casco Bay, and shopping in the Old Port. Have dinner in Freeport ⑰ and shop till you drop at L. L. Bean—at 3 AM if you'd like! Board a ferry or cruiser in ⛟ Boothbay Harbor and take a day cruise to the artists colony on **Monhegan Island** ㉓. Spend your last two days in ⛟ **Bar Harbor** ㉞ and **Acadia National Park** ㉞–㊷.

When to Tour Maine

Summer is the choicest time for a vacation in Maine. The weather is warmest in July and August although September is less crowded. In warm weather, the arteries along the coast are clogged with out-of-state license plates, campgrounds are filled to capacity, and hotel rates are high. In July and August, consider coming during the week when Route 1 is not lined bumper-to-bumper. Lodging places usually charge less Sunday through Thursday.

If fall foliage is your interest don't get here too early. Early October is best for the region south of Boothbay Harbor to Kittery and late September for areas farther north. Inland towns often experience colder weather earlier than the coastal regions (that's what turns the leaves). In southern Maine one can usually count on October 5–10 as prime viewing dates. In September and October the days are sunny and the nights crisp. September is good for visiting a country fair and October is harvest time for potatoes in northern Maine and pumpkins all over. Roadside stands sell vegetables and apples and cider.

In winter, the coastal towns in southern Maine almost completely close down—some take in phone booths and, if the sidewalks could be rolled up, they probably would. Maine's ski areas have increased their snow-making capabilities, allowing for good skiing in early December. Lift tickets and lodging cost less during the week, and lift lines are shorter. Lobsters cost a bit more in winter, but they have hard shells (in summer they have soft shells and tend to be weighted down more by water).

Springtime is mud season here, as in most rural areas of New England. Mud season is followed by spring flowers and the start of wildflowers in meadows along the roadsides.

YORK COUNTY COAST

Maine's southernmost coastal towns, most situated in York County, won't give you the rugged, windbitten "downeast" experience, but they are easily reached from the south, and most have the sand beaches that all but vanish beyond Portland.

These towns are most popular in summer, an all-too-brief period. As a result, crowds converge and gobble up rooms and dinner reservations at prime restaurants. Still, even day-trippers who come for a few fleeting hours to southern Maine can appreciate the magical warmth of the sand along this coast. You can easily stop in for a singular "shore" dinner when time is too precious to spend a day or two.

North of Kittery, the Maine coast has long stretches of hard-packed white-sand beach, closely crowded by nearly unbroken ranks of beach cottages, motels, and oceanfront restaurants. The summer colonies of York Beach, Ogunquit, and Wells Beach have the crowds and the ticky-tacky shorefront overdevelopment. Farther inland, York's historic district is on the National Register.

More than any other region south of Portland, the Kennebunks—and especially Kennebunkport—offer the complete Maine coast experience: classic townscapes where white-clapboard houses rise from manicured lawns and gardens; rocky shorelines punctuated by sandy beaches; quaint downtown districts packed with gift shops, ice-cream stands, and tourists; harbors where lobster boats bob alongside yachts; lobster pounds and well-appointed dining rooms.

These towns are best explored on a leisurely holiday of two days—more if one requires a fix of solid beach time. The Maine Turnpike (I–95) allows you to skip the shoreline as you wish or you may envelop everything to follow on these pages by staying on Route 1.

Numbers in the margin correspond to points of interest on the Southern Maine Coast map.

Kittery

❶ *55 mi north of Boston, 5 mi north of Portsmouth, NH.*

Kittery, which lacks a large sand beach of its own, hosts a complex of factory outlets that makes it more popular, or at least better known with tourists, than the true summer beach communities.

Kittery, which is just across the New Hampshire border, has about 200 **outlet stores.** Here along a several-mile stretch of Route 1 you can find just about anything you want, from hardware to underwear. Noteworthy names you'll encounter are Crate & Barrel, Eddie Bauer, Dansk, Ralph Lauren, Tommy Hilfiger, DKNY, Bose, Old Navy, Yankee Candle, J. Crew, and many, many more.

When you've had it with shopping (or if you want to skip the shopping altogether, for that matter), and decide a little history or seashore is needed,

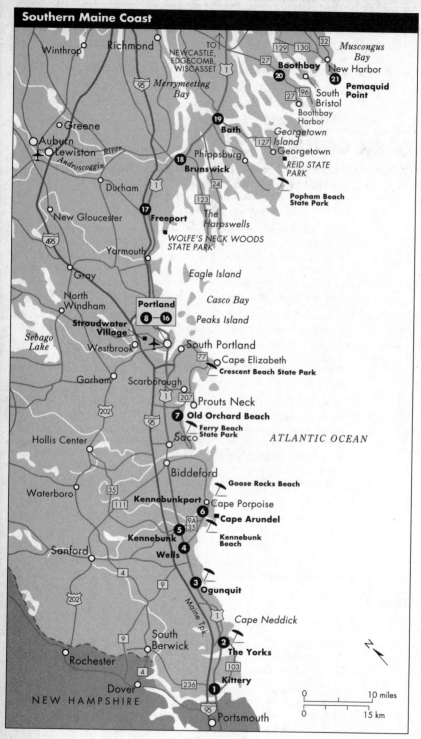

Southern Maine Coast

Winthrop
Richmond
TO
NEWCASTLE,
EDGECOMB,
WISCASSET
129   130   32
*Muscongus
Bay*
27   **Boothbay**
New Harbor
20
21
**Pemaquid
Point**
*Merrymeeting
Bay*
95
27   96   South
Bristol
Boothbay
Harbor
Greene
19   **Bath**
*Georgetown
Island*
Auburn
Lewiston
127   Georgetown
**REID STATE
PARK**
River
Phippsburg
Androscoggin
18   **Brunswick**
**Popham Beach
State Park**
Durham
24
123
New Gloucester
17   **Freeport**
*The
Harpswells*
495
Yarmouth
**WOLFE'S NECK WOODS
STATE PARK**
Gray
Eagle Island
North
Windham
Casco Bay
Portland
8   16
Peaks Island
**Stroudwater
Village**
*Sebago
Lake*
Westbrook
South Portland
77   *Cape Elizabeth*
Crescent Beach State Park
Gorham
Scarborough
1
207   **Prouts Neck**
202
95
7   **Old Orchard Beach**
**Ferry Beach
State Park**
ATLANTIC OCEAN
Hollis Center
Saco
Waterboro
Biddeford
Goose Rocks Beach
35
Kennebunkport   *Cape Porpoise*
111
6   **Cape Arundel**
9A
35
5
**Kennebunk
Beach**
Kennebunk
Sanford
4
Wells
9
3   **Ogunquit**
Cape Neddick
1
Maine Tpk.
9
**South
Berwick**
2
The Yorks
236
Rochester
103
4
Kittery
1
NEW HAMPSHIRE
Dover
95
Portsmouth

N

0   10 miles
0   15 km

drive north of the outlets and go east on Route 103 for a peek at the hidden Kittery most tourists miss. Along this winding stretch are two **forts**: Ft. Foster (1872), an active military installation until 1949, and Ft. McClary (1690), staffed during five wars. There are also hiking and biking trails, and, best of all, great views of the water.

The Arts

Hamilton House (⊠ Vaughan's La., South Berwick, ☎ 603/436–3205), the Georgian home featured in Sarah Orne Jewett's *The Tory Lover*, presents "Sundays in the Garden," a series of six free summer concerts ranging from classical to folk music in July and August. Concerts begin at 4; the grounds are open noon until 5 for picnicking. ☒ *$5.*

Dining and Lodging

$–$$ ✕ **Warren's Lobster House.** A local institution, this waterfront restaurant offers reasonably priced boiled lobster, first-rate scrod, and a huge salad bar. You can dine outdoors overlooking the water in season. ⊠ *Rte. 1,* ☎ *207/439–1630. AE, MC, V.*

$–$$ 🏠 **Deep Water Landing.** This comfortable, turn-of-the-century New England frame house welcomes guests to the three rooms on its third floor. Fruit trees and flower beds border the lawns, and the breakfast room has water views. ⊠ *92 Whipple Rd., 03904,* ☎ *207/439–0824. 3 rooms share bath. Full breakfast included. No credit cards.*

The Yorks

2 *4 mi north of Kittery.*

The Yorks are typical of small-town coastal communities found in New England and are smaller than most. Many of their nooks and crannies can be explored in a few hours.

The **York Village Historic District** has a number of 18th- and 19th-century buildings that are maintained by the Old York Historical Society. Most of the buildings are clustered along York Street and Lindsay Road; some charge admission. You can buy an admission ticket for all the buildings at the **Jefferds Tavern** (⊠ Rte. 1A and Lindsay Rd.), a restored late 18th-century inn. The **Old York Gaol** (1720) was once the King's Prison for the Province of Maine; inside are dungeons, cells, and the jailer's quarters. The 1731 **Elizabeth Perkins House** reflects the Victorian style of its last occupants, the prominent Perkins family. The historical society offers tours with guides in period costumes, crafts workshops, and special programs in summer. ☎ *207/363–4974.* ☒ *$6. ☉ Mid-June–Sept., Tues.–Sat. 10–5, Sun. 1–5.*

Get your camera ready for a photo of the essence of Maine. If you drive down Nubble Road from Route 1A and go to the end of Cape Neddick you can park and gaze out at the **Nubble Light** (1879), which sits on a tiny island just offshore. The keeper's house is a tidy Victorian cottage with pretty gingerbread woodwork and a red roof.

Beaches

York's **Long Sands Beach** has free parking and Route 1A running right behind it; the smaller **Short Sands Beach** has meter parking. Both beaches have commercial development.

Dining and Lodging

$$–$$$ ✕ **Cape Neddick Inn.** This restaurant and art gallery has an airy ambience, with tables set well apart, lots of windows, and art everywhere. The New American menu has included a lobster macadamia tart (shelled lobster sautéed with shallots, macadamia nuts, sherry, and cream and served in pastry), breaded pork tenderloin, and such appe-

tizers as spicy sesame chicken dumplings and gravlax with Russian pepper vodka. The menu changes every six weeks. ✉ *Rte. 1, Cape Neddick,* ☎ *207/363–2899. AE, MC, V. No lunch. Closed Mon. and Tues. Columbus Day–May 31.*

$$–$$$ ✕ **York Harbor Inn.** The dining room of this inn has country charm
★ and great ocean views. For dinner, start with Maine crab cakes, a classic Caesar salad, or a creamy seafood chowder, and then try the lobster-stuffed chicken breast with Boursin sauce or the angel-hair pasta with shrimp and scallops. Just save room for the crème caramel or any of the other wonderful desserts. ✉ *Rte. 1A (Box 573), York Harbor 03911,* ☎ *207/363–5119 or 800/343–3869. AE, DC, MC, V. No lunch off-season.*

$$–$$$$ ✕ **Dockside Guest Quarters and Restaurant.** On an 8-acre private island in the middle of York Harbor, the Dockside promises water views, seclusion, and quiet. Rooms in the Maine House, the oldest structure on the site, have Early American antiques, marine artifacts, and nautical paintings and prints. Four modern cottages tucked among the trees have less character but bigger windows on the water, and many have kitchenettes. Entrées in the esteemed dining room may include scallop-stuffed shrimp Casino, broiled salmon, and roast stuffed duckling. There's also a children's menu. ✉ *York Harbor off Rte. 103, Box 205, York 03909,* ☎ *800/270–1977 or 207/363–2868,* FAX *207/363–1977. 22 rooms, 20 with bath; 5 suites. Restaurant (*☎ *207/363–2722; closed Mon.), badminton, croquet, dock, boating, bicycles. MC, V. Closed late Oct.–Apr.*

Ogunquit

❸ *68 mi north of Boston, 39 mi southwest of Portland.*

Probably more than any other south coast community, Ogunquit combines coastal ambience, style, and good eating. Shore Road passes the 100-foot **Bald Head Cliff,** which allows a view up and down the coast. On a stormy day the surf can be quite wild here. Shore Road will take you right into downtown Ogunquit. This coastal village became a resort in the 1880s and gained fame as an artists' colony. Like a mini Provincetown, Ogunquit's gay population swells in summer with inns and small clubs catering to a primarily gay clientele. Families love the protected beach area and friendly environment.

Perkins Cove, a neck of land connected to the mainland by Oarweed Road and a pedestrian drawbridge draws visitors to its jumble of sea-beaten fish houses. These have largely been transformed by the tide of tourism to shops and restaurants. When you've had your fill of browsing and jostling the crowds at Perkins Cove, stroll out along the **Marginal Way,** a mile-long footpath that hugs the shore of a rocky promontory known as Israel's Head. Benches along the route give walkers an opportunity to stop and appreciate the open sea vistas, flowering bushes, and million-dollar homes.

Ogunquit Museum of American Art, in a low-lying concrete building overlooking the ocean, is set amid a 3-acre sculpture garden. Inside are works by Henry Strater, Marsden Hartley, William Bailey, Gaston Lachaise, Walt Kuhn, and Reginald Marsh. The huge windows of the sculpture court command a view of cliffs and ocean. ✉ *Shore Rd.,* ☎ *207/646–4909.* ▣ *$3.* ☉ *July–Sept., Mon.–Sat. 10:30–5, Sun. 2–5.*

Beaches

The 3 miles of wide sand beach have snack bars, boardwalk, rest rooms, and changing areas at the Beach Street entrance. The less crowded section to the north is accessible by footbridge and has portable rest rooms, all-day paid parking, and trolley service. The ocean beach, backed by the Ogunquit River, is ideal for children because it is sheltered and waveless. There is a parking fee.

Dining and Lodging

$$$–$$$$ ✕ **Arrows.** Elegant simplicity is the hallmark of this 18th-century farmhouse, 2 miles up a back road. The menu changes daily, offering such entrées as fillet of beef glistening in red and yellow sauces, grilled salmon and radicchio with marinated fennel and baked polenta, and Chinese-style duck glazed with molasses. Appetizers, like Maine crabmeat mousse and lobster risotto, and desserts, such as strawberry shortcake with Chantilly cream and steamed chocolate pudding, are also beautifully executed and presented. ⊠ *Berwick Rd.,* ☎ *207/361–1100. MC, V. Closed Mon. and Thanksgiving–May.*

$$–$$$$ ✕ **Hurricane.** Don't let its weather-beaten exterior deter you—this
★ small, comfortable seafood bar-and-grill offers first-rate cooking and spectacular views of the crashing surf. Start with lobster chowder, napoleon of smoked salmon, grilled chicken satay, or the house salad (assorted greens with pistachio nuts and roasted shallots). Entrées include fresh lobster-stuffed pasta shells, baked salmon and brie baklava, and shrimp scampi served over fresh pasta. Be sure to save room for the classic crème brûlée. ⊠ *Perkins Cove,* ☎ *207/646–6348. AE, D, DC, MC, V.*

$$ ✕ **Ogunquit Lobster Pound.** Select your lobster live, then dine under the trees or in the rustic dining room of this log cabin. The menu includes steamed clams, steak, and chicken; and there's a children's menu. ⊠ *Rte. 1,* ☎ *207/646–2516. Reservations not accepted. AE, MC, V. Closed late Oct.–mid-May.*

$$–$$$ ▨ **The Colonial: A Resort by the Sea.** This complex of accommodations in the middle of Ogunquit includes a large white Victorian inn, modern motel units, and efficiency apartments. Inn rooms have flowered wallpaper, Colonial reproduction furniture, and white ruffle curtains. Efficiencies are popular with families. One-third of the rooms have water views. ⊠ *Shore Rd., Box 895, 03907,* ☎ *207/646–5191. 80 units, 44 with bath; 36 suites. Restaurant, pool, hot tub, shuffleboard, playground, laundry service. AE, D, MC, V. Closed Nov.–Apr.*

$–$$$ ▨ **West Highland Inn.** A century-old white-clapboard house set back behind shrubs and lawn in the center of town, the West Highland is homey and close to the beach. Rooms are furnished with odds and ends of country furniture; breakfast is served in the dining room or on an enclosed sunporch. ⊠ *14 Shore Rd., Box 1221, 03907,* ☎ *207/646–2181. 15 units, 11 with bath; 4 efficiency suites. CP. MC, V. Closed Nov.–mid-May.*

Nightlife and the Arts

NIGHTLIFE
Much of the nightlife in Ogunquit revolves around the precincts of Ogunquit Square and Perkins Cove, where visitors stroll, often enjoying an after-dinner ice cream cone or espresso. The colorful **Front Porch** (⊠ Ogunquit Square at Main St. and Shore Rd., ☎ 207/646–3976), marked by yellow awnings, has a popular piano bar and attracts a mostly gay clientele. **Le Club** (⊠ 13 Main St., ☎ 207/646–6655) is a dance club that caters to gay patrons.

THE ARTS
Ogunquit Playhouse (⊠ Rte. 1, ☎ 207/646–5511), one of America's oldest summer theaters, mounts plays and musicals with name entertainment from late June to Labor Day.

Outdoor Activities and Sports
Finestkind (⊠ Perkins Cove, ☎ 207/646–5227) has cruises to Nubble Light, cocktail cruises, and lobstering trips.

Shopping
Ogunquit's shopping ranges from T-shirt shops and gift and beachwear boutiques to a delectable candy shop, bakery, and ice cream parlor. Local artists display their work in a number of shops along Shore Road.

Wells

❹ *5 mi north of Ogunquit, 35 mi southwest of Portland.*

This family-oriented beach community consists of several densely populated miles of shoreline interspersed with trailers and summer and year-round homes.

Wells Reserve sprawls over 1,600-acres and consists of meadows, orchards, fields, salt marshes, and an extensive trail network, as well as two estuaries and 9 miles of seashore. The visitor center features an introductory slide show and five rooms of exhibits. In winter, cross-country skiing is permitted on the premises. ⊠ *Laudholm Farm Rd., Laudholm (3 mi from Wells),* ☎ *207/646–1555.* ☞ *Free; parking $5.* ☉ *Grounds daily 8–5; visitor center May–Oct., Mon.–Sat. 10–4, Sun. noon–4; Nov.–Apr., weekdays only.*

☾ A must for motor fanatics as well as youngsters, the **Wells Auto Museum** has 70 vintage cars, antique coin games, and a restored Model T you can ride in. ⊠ *Rte. 1,* ☎ *207/646–9064.* ☞ *$3.50.* ☉ *Mid-June–Sept., daily 10–5; Memorial Day–Columbus Day, weekends 10–5.*

Dining and Lodging
$$–$$$ ✕ **The Grey Gull.** This charming century-old Victorian inn has views of the open sea and rocks on which seals like to sun themselves. In the evening, try any of the excellent seafood dishes, chicken breast rolled in walnuts and baked with maple syrup, Yankee pot roast, or soft-shell crabs almondine. Breakfast is popular here in the summer: Blueberry pancakes, ham-and-cheese strata, or eggs McGull served on crabcakes with hollandaise sauce are good choices. ⊠ *475 Webhannet Dr., at Moody Point,* ☎ *207/646–7501. AE, D, MC, V.*

$$ ✕ **Billy's Chowder House.** As the crowded parking lot suggests, this simple restaurant in a salt marsh is popular with locals and tourists alike. For a generous lobster roll or haddock sandwich (not to mention chowders), Billy's is hard to beat. ⊠ *Mile Rd.,* ☎ *207/646–7558. AE, MC, V. Closed mid-Dec.–mid-Jan.*

Outdoor Activities and Sports
Rachel Carson National Wildlife Refuge (⊠ Rte. 9) is a mile-long loop through a salt marsh bordering the Little River and a white-pine forest where migrating birds and waterfowl of many varieties are regularly spotted.

Shopping
Several factory outlet stores along Route 1 from Kittery to Wells sell clothing, shoes, glassware, and other products from top-of-the-line manufacturers.

Kenneth & Ida Manko (⊠ Seabreeze Dr., ☎ 207/646–2595) displays and sells folk art, rustic furniture, paintings, and a large selection of 19th-century weather vanes. From Route 1 head east on Eldridge Road for a half-mile, then turn left on Seabreeze Drive. **R. Jorgensen**

(✉ Rte. 1, ☎ 207/646–9444) has an eclectic selection of 18th- and 19th-century formal and country period antiques from the British Isles, Europe, and the United States. **Douglas N. Harding Rare Books** (✉ Rte. 1, ☎ 207/646–8785) has a huge stock of old books, maps, and prints.

Kennebunk

❺ *5 mi north of Wells, 27 mi southwest of Portland.*

The archly New England look of historic Kennebunk is evidenced by shuttered white-clapboard homes the size of a fraternity house or a glamorous country inn. Route 1 becomes Main Street in Kennebunk. For a sense of the area's history and architecture one must only stroll the sidewalks of this community.

The cornerstone of the **Brick Store Museum,** a block-long preservation of early 19th-century commercial buildings, is **William Lord's Brick Store.** Built as a dry-goods store in 1825 in the Federal style, the building has an open-work balustrade across the roof line, granite lintels over the windows, and paired chimneys. Walking tours of Kennebunk's National Historic Register District depart from the museum on Friday at 1 and on Wednesday at 10, June through October. ✉ *117 Main St.,* ☎ *207/985–4802.* ☐ *$3.* ⏲ *Tues.–Sat. 10–4:30. Closed Sat. in winter.*

Beaches

Gooch's Beach, Middle Beach, and **Kennebunk Beach** (also called Mother's Beach) are the three areas of **Kennebunk Beach.** Beach Road, with its cottages and old Victorian boardinghouses, runs right behind them. Gooch's and Middle beaches attract lots of teenagers; Mother's Beach, which has a small playground and tidal puddles for splashing, is popular with moms, dads, and kids. For parking permits (fee charged in summer), go to the Kennebunk Town Office (✉ 1 Summer St., ☎ 207/985–2102).

Dining

$$ ✕ **The Impastable Dream.** If it's pasta you crave, head to this cozy restaurant set in an old Cape Cod cottage on Main Street. Tables are small and close together and the decor is simple, but the food is reasonably priced, plentiful, and very good. ✉ *17 Main St.,* ☎ *207/985–6039. Reservations not accepted. D, MC, V. Closed Sun.*

Shopping

J. J. Keating (✉ Rte. 1, ☎ 207/985–2097) deals in antiques, reproductions, estate furnishings, and auctions. **Marlow's Artisans Gallery** (✉ 39 Main St., ☎ 207/985–2931) carries a large and eclectic collection of crafts. **Chadwick's** (✉ 10 Main St., ☎ 207/985–7042) carries a selection of women's casual clothing.

Kennebunkport

❻ *27 mi southwest of Portland, 10 mi northeast of Ogunquit.*

When George Bush was president, Kennebunkport was best known as the summer White House, as Bush maintains his family's summer home here. World leaders dropped in for a little lobster and a speed boat ride to complement their summit talks. But long before Bush came into the public eye, tourists were coming to Kennebunkport to soak up the local salt air, seafood, and sunshine. This is a picture-perfect town with manicured lawns, elaborate flower beds, freshly painted homes, and small-town wholesomeness.

Tourists flock to Kennebunkport mostly in summer; some come in early December when the **Christmas Prelude** is celebrated on two weekends. Santa arrives by fishing boat and the Christmas trees are lighted as carolers stroll the sidewalks. This is also an opportune time to receive end-of-the-year bargains from shopkeepers.

The **Wedding Cake House,** on Summer Street (Rte. 35) has long been a local landmark for the Kennebunks. The legend behind this confection in fancy wood fretwork is that its sea-captain builder was forced to set sail in the middle of his wedding, and the house was his bride's consolation for the lack of a wedding cake. The home, built in 1826, is not open to the public but there is a gallery and studio in the attached carriage house.

Route 35 merges with Route 9 in Kennebunk and takes you right into Kennebunkport's **Dock Square,** the busy town center, which is lined with shops and galleries and draws crowds in the summer. When you stroll the square, walk onto the drawbridge to admire the tidal Kennebunk River.

The very grand **Nott House,** known also as White Columns, is an imposing Greek Revival mansion with Doric columns that rise the height of the house. It is a gathering place for village walking tours, which are given Wednesday and Friday in July and August. ⊠ *Maine St.,* ☎ *207/967–2751.* ☒ *$3.* ☉ *June–late Oct., Wed.–Sat. 1–4.*

Ocean Avenue follows the Kennebunk River from Dock Square to the sea and winds around the peninsula of **Cape Arundel.** Parson's Way, a small and tranquil stretch of rocky shoreline, is open to all. As you round Cape Arundel, look to the right for the entrance to George Bush's summer home at Walker's Point.

☺ The **Seashore Trolley Museum** displays a century of streetcars (1872–1972) and includes trolleys from major metropolitan areas and world capitals—Boston to Budapest, New York to Nagasaki, and San Francisco to Sydney, Australia—all beautifully restored. Best of all, you can take a trolley ride for nearly 4 miles over the tracks of the former Atlantic Shoreline trolley line, with a stop along the way at the museum restoration shop, where trolleys are transformed from junk into gems. ⊠ *Log Cabin Rd.,* ☎ *207/967–2800.* ☒ *$6.* ☉ *May–mid-Oct., daily 10–5:30; reduced hrs in spring and fall.*

☺ At the **Maine Aquarium,** live sharks, seals, penguins, a petting zoo, a tidal pool, snack bar, and gift shop make a busy stop on a rainy day. Seals are fed at 11 AM and 1:30 and 3 PM, and penguins at 10 and 2. The aquarium lies about 20 minutes north of Kennebunkport's Dock Square in Saco. ⊠ *Rte. 1, Saco,* ☎ *207/284–4511.* ☒ *$6.50.* ☉ *Daily 9–5.*

Beach

Goose Rocks, a few minutes' drive north of town, is the largest beach in the Kennebunk area and the favorite of families with small children. For a parking permit (fee charged), go to the Kennebunkport Town Office (⊠ Elm St., ☎ 207/967–4244; ☉ Weekdays 8–4:30) or the police department (⊠ Rte. 9, ☎ 207/967–2454; ☉ 24 hrs).

Dining and Lodging

$$$–$$$$ ✕ **Windows on the Water.** This restaurant overlooks Dock Square and the working harbor of Kennebunkport. Try the California lobster ravioli or the gorgonzola-stuffed mignon. The "A Night on the Town" special, a five-course dinner for two, including wine, tax, and gratuity, for $74, is a good value if you have a healthy appetite. ⊠ *Chase Hill Rd.,* ☎ *207/967–3313. Reservations essential. AE, D, DC, MC, V.*

$$$–$$$$ ✕⚏ **Cape Arundel Inn.** Were it not for the rocky shore beyond the picture windows, the pillared porch with wicker chairs, and the cozy parlor (with fireplace and backgammon boards) that you pass through en route to the dining room, you might well think you were dining at a major Boston restaurant. Entrées include marlin with sorrel butter; coho salmon with mushrooms, white wine, and lemon; and pecan chicken with peaches and crème fraîche. The inn has 14 guest rooms, seven in the Victorian-era converted summer "cottage" and six in a motel facility adjoining. There's also a carriage-house apartment. ⊠ *Ocean Ave., 04046,* ☎ *207/967–2125. Restaurant (no lunch). AE, MC, V. Closed mid-Oct.–mid-May.*

$$$–$$$$ ✕⚏ **White Barn Inn.** This is probably Maine's best restaurant. The rustic
★ but elegant dining room of this inn serves regional New England cuisine. The fixed-price menu changes weekly and may include steamed Maine lobster nestled on fresh fettuccine with carrots and ginger in a Thai-inspired honey and sherry vinegar sauce or grilled veal chop with baby carrots, wild rice cakes, sorrel, and lemon grass in a curry sauce. The lovely rooms have luxurious baths and are expensively appointed with a blend of hand-painted pieces and period furniture. ⊠ *Beach St., Box 560C, 04046,* ☎ *207/967–2321. 24 rooms with bath. Jacket required for dinner. Restaurant, outdoor pool, bicycles. CP. AE, MC, V.*

$$$$ ⚏ **Old Fort Inn.** This no-smoking inn at the crest of a hill on a quiet road off Ocean Avenue has a secluded, countryish feel. The front half of the former barn is an antiques shop (specializing in Early American pieces); the rest of the barn is the reception area and parlor decorated with grandfather clocks, antique tools, and funny old canes. Guest rooms are in a long, low fieldstone-and-stucco carriage house. Rooms are not large, but the decor is witty and creative: There are quilts on the four-poster beds; wreaths, primitive portraits, and framed antique bodices hang on the walls; and the loveseats are richly upholstered. Superior rooms and suites have whirlpools. ⊠ *Old Fort Ave., Box M, 04046,* ☎ *207/967–5353, ᶠᴬˣ 207/967–4547. 14 rooms with bath, 2 suites. Air-conditioning, minibars, pool, tennis courts. CP. AE, D, MC, V. Closed mid-Dec.–mid-Apr.*

$$$–$$$$ ⚏ **Bufflehead Cove.** On the Kennebunk River at the end of a winding dirt road, the friendly gray-shingle bed-and-breakfast affords the quiet of country fields and apple trees only five minutes from Dock Square. Guest rooms in the main house are dollhouse-pretty, with white wicker and flowers painted on the walls. The Hideaway Suite, with a two-sided gas fireplace, king-size bed, and large whirlpool tub, overlooks the river, while the Garden Studio offers a fireplace and the most privacy. ⊠ *Gornitz La., Box 499, 04046,* ☎ *207/967–3879. 3 rooms with bath, 3 suites. Dock. AE, D, MC, V. Closed midweek Jan.–Mar.*

$$$–$$$$ ⚏ **Captain Jefferds Inn.** The three-story white-clapboard sea captain's mansion with black shutters, built in 1804, has been filled with the innkeeper's collections of majolica, and American and Sienese pottery. Most rooms have Laura Ashley fabrics and wallpapers, and many have been furnished with a wide variety of antiques and collections from all over the world. ⊠ *Pearl St., Box 691, 04046,* ☎ *207/967–2311. 13 rooms with bath; 4 suites in carriage house, 2 with kitchenettes. Croquet. Full breakfast included. MC, V. Closed Dec.–Apr.*

$$$–$$$$ ⚏ **The Seaside.** The modern motel units, all with cable TVs and sliding glass doors opening onto private decks or patios (half with ocean views), are appropriate for families; so are the cottages, which have from one to four bedrooms. The four bedrooms in the inn, furnished with antiques, are more suitable for adults. ⊠ *Gooch's Beach, 04046,* ☎ *207/967–4461. 26 rooms with bath, 10 cottages. Beach, play-*

*ground, laundry service. CP for inn and motel guests. MC, V. Inn rooms
closed Labor Day–June; cottages closed Nov.–Apr.*

Outdoor Activities and Sports
BIKING
Cape-Able Bike Shop (✉ Townhouse Corners, ☎ 207/967–4382)
rents bicycles ($8–$25) and gives away free maps of the area.

FISHING
Cape Arundel Cruises (✉ Performance Marine, Rte. 9, ☎ 207/967–
5595) has half-day and full-day trips on its deepwater fishing boat. Passengers take 1½-hour narrated cruises down the Kennebunk River and
out to Cape Porpoise.

Chick's Marina (✉ 75 Ocean Ave., ☎ 207/967–2782) offers sightseeing
and fishing cruises for up to six people.

WHALE-WATCHING
The *Indian* (✉ Ocean Ave., ☎ 207/967–5912) offers half-day trips to
view the whale migrations. The ***Nautilus*** (Cape Arundel Cruises, ✉ Performance Marine, Rte. 9, ☎ 207/967–5595), goes on whale-watching cruises from May through October daily at 10 AM.

Shopping
Boutiques, T-shirt shops, a Christmas store, a decoy shop, and restaurants encircle Kennebunkport's Dock Square. The best bargains often
are had during December. Many shops close for the winter.

Old Fort Inn and Antiques (✉ Old Fort Ave., ☎ 207/967–5353) stocks
a small but choice selection of primitives, china, and country furniture
in a converted barn adjoining an inn. **Kennebunk Book Port** (✉ 10 Dock
Sq., ☎ 207/967–3815 or 800/382–2710), housed in a rum warehouse
built in 1775, has a wide selection of titles and specializes in local and
maritime subjects. **The Wedding Cake Studio** (✉ 104 Summer St., ☎
207/985–2818) sells faux finishes, trompe l'oeil, decorative painting,
hand-painted clothing, and original artwork.

Old Orchard Beach
❼ *18 mi south of Portland, 25 mi northeast of Portsmouth.*

Old Orchard Beach, a 7-mile strip of sand beach with an amusement
park reminiscent of a mini Coney Island, is only a few miles north of
Biddeford on Route 9 and borders Scarborough to its south. Despite
the summertime crowds and fried-food odors, the carnival atmosphere
can be infectious. During the 1940s and 50s, in the heyday of the Big
Band era, the pier had a dance hall where name entertainers performed. Fire claimed the end of the pier but booths housing games and
candy concessions still line both sides. In summer the town sponsors
fireworks (usually Thursday night).

There are many, many places to stay here from cheap little motels to
cottage colonies to full-service seasonal hotels. This area is popular from
July 4 through Labor Day with the Québecois who come to soak up
the summer sun.

Palace Playland (☎ 207/934–2001) on Old Orchard Street has an array
of rides and booths, including a carousel and a Ferris wheel with dizzying ocean views. There is no free parking anywhere in town, but ample
lots are situated on almost every block. ☉ *June–Labor Day.*

Dining and Lodging

$$$$ ✕▥ **Black Point Inn.** At the neck of the peninsula that juts into the ocean at Prouts Neck, 12 miles south of Portland and about 10 miles north of Old Orchard by road (but only a few strokes by canoe across the marsh from the tip of Pine Point), stands one of the stylish old-time resorts of Maine. This English-style country house has a sunporch and a music room with a grand piano. In the guest rooms are mahogany bedsteads, Martha Washington bedspreads, and white-ruffle Priscilla curtains. Older guests prefer the main inn; families choose from the four cottages. The extensive grounds offer beaches, hiking, a bird sanctuary, and sports. The dining room has a menu strong in seafood. ✉ *510 Black Point Rd., Scarborough 04074,* ☎ *207/883–4126 or 800/258–0003,* ℻ *207/883–9976. 80 rooms with bath, 6 suites. Restaurant, bar, indoor and outdoor pools, hot tub, golf, tennis courts, croquet, volleyball, boating, bicycles. AE, MC, V. Closed Dec.–Apr.*

Outdoor Activities and Sports

BIRD-WATCHING

Biddeford Pool East Sanctuary (✉ Rte. 9, Biddeford) is a nature preserve where shorebirds congregate. Be sure to bring your binoculars.

CANOEING

The **Maine Audubon Society** (✉ Rte. 9, Scarborough, ☎ 207/781–2330 or 207/883–5100 mid-June–Labor Day) offers daily guided canoe trips and canoe rentals in **Scarborough Marsh,** the largest salt marsh in Maine. Programs at Maine Audubon's Falmouth headquarters include nature walks and a discovery room for children. Call ahead for information.

York County Coast A to Z

Arriving and Departing

BY CAR

Route 1 from Kittery is the shopper's route north, while other roads hug the coastline. Interstate–95 should be faster for travelers headed for specific towns north of Ogunquit. The exit numbers can be confusing: As you go north from Portsmouth, Exits 1–3 lead to Kittery and Exit 4 leads to the Yorks. After the tollbooth in York, the Maine Turnpike begins, and the numbers start over again, with Exit 2 for Wells and Ogunquit and Exit 3 (and Route 35) for Kennebunk and Kennebunkport. Route 9 goes from Kennebunkport to Cape Porpoise and Goose Rocks.

BY PLANE

The closest airport is the Portland International Jetport, 35 miles northeast of Kennebunk, with service from Continental Express, Delta, USAir, United, and other commuter services.

Getting Around

BY CAR

Parking is tight in Kennebunkport in peak season. Possibilities include the municipal lot next to the Congregational Church ($2/hr, May–Oct.), the Consolidated School on School Street (free, June 25–Labor Day), and, except on Sunday morning, St. Martha's Church (free year-round) on North Street.

BY TROLLEY

A trolley circulates among the Yorks from June to Labor Day. Eight trolleys serve the major tourist areas and beaches of Ogunquit, including four that connect with Wells from mid-May through mid-October. The trolley from Dock Square in Kennebunkport to Kennebunk Beach runs from late June to Labor Day. ▥ *$1–$3.*

Contacts and Resources

EMERGENCIES

Maine State Police (Gray, ☎ 207/793–4500 or 800/482–0730). **Kennebunk Walk-in Clinic** (✉ Rte. 1N, ☎ 207/985–6027). **Southern Maine Medical Center** (✉ 1 Medical Center Dr., Biddeford, ☎ 207/283–7000; emergency room 207/283–7100).

VISITOR INFORMATION

Off-season, most chambers of commerce are open weekdays 9–5; the hours below are for summer only.

Kennebunk-Kennebunkport Chamber of Commerce (✉ 173 Port Rd., Kennebunk, ☎ 207/967–0857; ⊙ Mon.–Thurs. 9–6, Fri. 9–8, Sat. 10–6, Sun. 11–4). **Kittery-Eliot Chamber of Commerce** (✉ 191 State Rd., Kittery, ☎ 207/439–7545; ⊙ Weekdays 10–5). **Maine Publicity Bureau** (✉ Rte. 1 and I–95, Kittery, ☎ 207/439–1319; ⊙ Daily 8–6). **Ogunquit Chamber of Commerce** (✉ Box 2289, Ogunquit, ☎ 207/646–2939 or 207/646–5533, mid-May–mid-Oct.; ⊙ Daily 9–5, later Fri. and Sat.). **Wells Chamber of Commerce** (✉ Box 356, Wells 04090, ☎ 207/646–2451; ⊙ Daily 9–5, Fri. and Sat. until 6). The **Yorks Chamber of Commerce** (✉ Box 417, York, ☎ 207/363–4422; ⊙ Daily 9–6; extended hrs on weekends).

PORTLAND TO PEMAQUID POINT

Maine's largest city, Portland, is small enough to be seen in a day or two. It continues to undergo a cultural and economic renaissance: New inns, renewed hotels, and a bright but struggling performing arts center have joined the neighborhoods of historic homes. The Old Port Exchange, perhaps the finest urban renovation project on the East Coast, balances modern commercial enterprise with a salty waterfront character in an area bustling with restaurants, shops, and galleries. The piers of Commercial Street abound with opportunities for water tours of the harbor and excursions to the Calendar Islands.

Freeport, north of Portland, is a town made famous by the L. L. Bean store, whose success led to the opening of scores of other clothing stores and outlets. Brunswick is best known for Bowdoin College. Bath has been a shipbuilding center since 1607, and the Maine Maritime Museum preserves its history.

The Boothbays—the coastal areas of Boothbay Harbor, East Boothbay, Linekin Neck, Southport Island, and the inland town of Boothbay—attract hordes of vacationing families and flotillas of pleasure craft. The Pemaquid peninsula juts into the Atlantic south of Damariscotta and just east of the Boothbays, and near Pemaquid Beach one can view the objects unearthed at the Colonial Pemaquid Restoration.

This south mid-coast area gives visitors a fisheye's overview of Maine: a little bit city, a little more coastline, and a nice dollop of history and architecture. The towns are arranged in such a manner as to easily drive to a selection of spots and return to Portland in a single day or to make an overnight in the Boothbay Region.

Portland

105 mi northeast of Boston, 320 mi northeast of New York, 215 mi southwest of St. Stephen, New Brunswick.

Portland's first home was built on the peninsula now known as Munjoy Hill in 1632. When the Civil War broke out in 1861, Maine was asked to raise only a single regiment to fight, but the state raised 10 and sent the 5th Maine Regiment into the war's first battle at Bull Run. Not long after, much of Portland was destroyed on July 4 in the Great Fire of 1866 when a boy threw a celebration firecracker into a pile of wood shavings; 1,500 buildings burned to the ground. Poet Henry Wadsworth Longfellow said at the time his city reminded him of the ruins of Pompeii. The Great Fire started not far from where tourists now wander the streets of the Old Port Exchange. Portland offers many aspects of a large city without big city problems. Its restaurants flourish, even during hard times, and the endearing mood of the city, its people, and its nightlife make it the state's most popular region.

Numbers in the margin correspond to points of interest on the Southern Maine Coast and Portland maps.

Congress Street, Portland's main street, runs the length of the peninsular city from alongside the Western Promenade in the southwest to the Eastern Promenade on Munjoy Hill in the northeast, passing through the small downtown area. A few blocks southeast of downtown, the bustling Old Port Exchange sprawls along the waterfront. Just below Munjoy Hill is India Street where the city's Great Fire of 1866 started.

8 One of the notable homes on Congress Street is the **Neal Dow Memorial,** a brick mansion built in 1829 in the late Federal style by General Neal Dow, a zealous abolitionist and prohibitionist. The library has fine ornamental ironwork, and the furnishings include the family china, silver, and portraits. Don't miss the grandfather clocks and the original deed granted by James II. ⊠ *714 Congress St.,* ☎ *207/773–7773.* ⊡ *Free.* ⊙ *Tours weekdays 11–4.*

⑨ Touching is okay at the **Children's Museum of Maine,** where little ones can pretend they are fishing for lobster, or are shopkeepers or computer experts. Camera Obscura, on the third floor, charges a separate admission fee ($2). ⊠ *142 Free St.,* ☎ *207/828–1234.* ⊡ *$4.* ⊙ *Mon., Wed., Thurs. 10–5, Fri. 10–8, Tues. and Sun. noon–5.*

⑩ The distinguished **Portland Museum of Art** has a strong collection of seascapes and landscapes by such masters as Winslow Homer, John Marin, Andrew Wyeth, and Marsden Hartley. Homer's *Pulling the Dory* and *Weatherbeaten,* two quintessential Maine coast images, are here. The Joan Whitney Payson Collection includes works by Monet, Picasso, and Renoir. The strikingly modern Charles Shipman Payson building was designed by Harry N. Cobb, an associate of I. M. Pei, in 1983. ⊠ *7 Congress Sq.,* ☎ *207/775–6148 or 207/773–2787.* ⊡ *$6; free Thurs. evenings 5–9.* ⊙ *Tues.–Sat. 10–5 (Thurs. until 9), Sun. noon–5. Call for winter hrs.*

NEED A
BREAK?

Congress Square is the center of the burgeoning arts district. A perfect pre- or post-concert stop is **Coffee By Design** (⊠ 620 Congress St., ☎ 207/772–5533). It's opposite the State Theater and has its own revolving art show lining the walls.

⑪ The **Wadsworth Longfellow House** of 1785, the boyhood home of the poet and the first brick house in Portland, is worth a special stop. The late Colonial-style structure sits back from the street and has a small portico over its entrance and four chimneys surmounting the hip roof. Most of the furnishings are original to the house. Christmas is celebrated with special tours of the house to highlight a particular period in the history of the poet. ⊠ *485 Congress St.,* ☎ *207/879–0427.* ⊡ *$4.* ⊙ *June–Oct., Tues.–Sun. 10–4.*

Portland

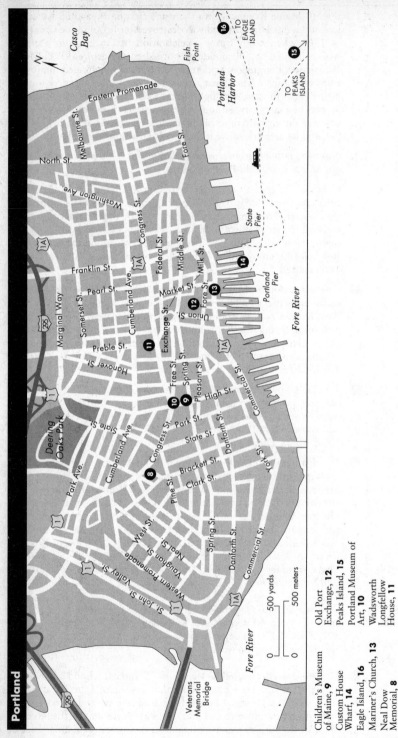

Casco Bay

Fish Point

Eastern Promenade

Melbourne St.

North St.

Washington Ave.

Congress St.

Fore St.

Franklin St.

1A

Pearl St.

Cumberland Ave.

Federal St.

Middle St.

Milk St.

State Pier

14

Portland Pier

13

Portland Harbor

16 TO EAGLE ISLAND

15 TO PEAKS ISLAND

Somerset St.

Marginal Way

295

Preble St.

Hanover St.

Market St.

Exchange St.

Union St.

Fore St.

12

11

Fore River

1

Free St.

Spring St.

10 9

Pleasant St.

High St.

Commercial St.

Deering Oaks Park

State St.

Cumberland Ave.

Congress St.

Park St.

State St.

Danforth St.

York St.

Park Ave.

8

Brackett St.

Pine St.

Clark St.

1

West St.

Vaughan St.

Neal St.

Western Promenade

Spring St.

Danforth St.

St. John St.

Valley St.

1

1A

Commercial St.

Fore River

295

Veterans Memorial Bridge

N

0   500 yards
0   500 meters

Children's Museum of Maine, **9**
Custom House Wharf, **14**
Eagle Island, **16**
Mariner's Church, **13**
Neal Dow Memorial, **8**

Old Port Exchange, **12**
Peaks Island, **15**
Portland Museum of Art, **10**
Wadsworth Longfellow House, **11**

⑫ The **Old Port Exchange,** the primary reason to visit downtown Portland, bridges the gap between yesterday and today. Allow a couple of hours to wander at leisure on Market, Exchange, Middle, and Fore streets. Like the Customs House, the brick buildings and warehouses of the Old Port Exchange were built following the Great Fire of 1866 and were intended to last for ages. When the city's economy slumped in the middle of the present century, however, the Old Port declined and seemed slated for demolition. Then artists and craftspeople began opening shops here in the late 1960s, and in time restaurants, chic boutiques, bookstores, and gift shops followed. The Old Port Festival is celebrated annually in June when street vendors and performers fill each block. You can park your car either at the city garage on Fore Street (between Exchange and Union streets) or opposite the U.S. Customs House at the corner of Fore and Pearl streets.

⑬ The **Mariner's Church** (⊠ 376 Fore St.) has a fine facade of granite columns. The **Elias Thomas Block** on Commercial Street, between Custom House Wharf and DiMillo's Marina, demonstrates the graceful use of bricks in commercial architecture. Inevitably the salty smell of the sea will
⑭ draw you to one of the wharves off Commercial Street; **Custom House Wharf** retains some of the older, rougher waterfront atmosphere.

OFF THE
BEATEN PATH
STROUDWATER VILLAGE – This village was spared the devastation of the fire of 1866 and thus contains some of the best examples of 18th- and early 19th-century architecture in the region. Here are the remains of mills, canals, and historic homes, including the **Tate House.** Portland's oldest house was built in 1755 with paneling from England. It overlooks the old mast yard where George Tate, Mast Agent to the King, prepared tall pines for the ships of the Royal Navy. *Tate House, ⊠ 1270 Westbrook St., Stroudwater Village (3 mi west of Portland), ☎ 207/774–9781. ⊠ $3. ☉ July–Sept. 15, Tues.–Sat. 10–4, Sun. 1–4.*

Beaches
Crescent Beach State Park (⊠ Rte. 77, Cape Elizabeth, ☎ 207/767–3625; ⊠ $2.50 late Apr.–mid-Oct. or $1 off-season), about 8 miles south from Portland, has a sand beach, picnic tables, seasonal snack bar, and bathhouse. **Ferry Beach State Park** (⊠ Follow signs off Rte. 9 in Saco, ☎ 207/283–0067; ⊠ $2 late Apr.–mid-Oct.), has picnic facilities with grills and extensive nature trails.

Dining and Lodging
$$$–$$$$ ✕ **Back Bay Grill.** Mellow jazz, a 28-foot mural, an impressive wine
★   list, and good food make this simple, elegant restaurant a popular spot. Appetizers such as black-pepper raviolis with red Swiss chard, pancetta, and Fontina cheese in chicken broth are followed by grilled chicken, halibut, oysters, salmon, trout, veal chops, or steak. Don't miss the desserts—the crème brûlée is legendary. Call ahead for winter hours. ⊠ *65 Portland St., ☎ 207/772–8833. AE, D, DC, MC, V. Closed Sun.*

$$–$$$ ✕ **Cafe Always.** White linen tablecloths, candles, and Victorian-style murals by local artists set the mood for innovative cuisine. Begin with Pemaquid Point oysters seasoned with pink peppercorns and champagne, or grilled duck, before choosing from vegetarian dishes, pasta, or more substantial entrées, such as grilled tuna with a fiery Japanese sauce or leg of lamb with goat cheese and sweet peppers. ⊠ *7 Middle St., ☎ 207/774–9399. MC, V. Closed Sun., Mon.*

$$–$$$ ✕ **Seamen's Club.** Built just after Portland's Great Fire of 1866, and an actual sailors' club in the 1940s, this restaurant has become an Old Port Exchange landmark, with its Gothic windows and carved medallions. Seafood is an understandable favorite—moist, blackened tuna, salmon, and swordfish prepared differently each day and lobster fet-

tuccine are among the highlights. ✉ *375 Fore St.,* ☎ *207/772–7311. AE, DC, MC, V.*

$$–$$$ ✕ **Street and Co.** You enter through the kitchen, with all its wonderful
★ aromas, and dine amid dried herbs and shelves of staples on one of a
dozen copper-topped tables (so your waiter can place a skillet of steam-
ing seafood directly in front of you). In one dining room is a beer and
wine bar. Begin with lobster bisque or grilled eggplant—vegetarian
dishes are the only alternatives to fish. Choose from an array of superb
entrées, ranging from calamari, clams, or shrimp served over linguine,
to blackened, broiled, pan-seared, or grilled seafood. The desserts are
top-notch. ✉ *33 Wharf St.,* ☎ *207/775–0887. AE, MC, V. No lunch.*

$$ ✕ **Katahdin.** Somehow, the painted tables, flea-market decor, mis-
matched dinnerware, and log pile bar work together here. The cuisine,
large portions of home-cooked New England fare, is equally unpre-
tentious and fun: Try the chicken potpie, fried trout, crab cakes, or the
nightly Blue Plate special—and save room for the fruit cobbler. ✉ *106
High St.,* ☎ *207/774–1740. Reservations not accepted. D, MC, V.*

$$$ ✕🏠 **Inn By The Sea.** Situated on Greater Portland's most prime real
estate, this all-suite inn is set back from the shoreline and has views of
the ocean—Crescent Beach and Kettle Cove in particular. The dining
room, open to the public, serves fine seafood and other regional cuisine. The architecture throughout is typically New England: One-bed-
room units are decorated in pine and wicker; two-bedroom suites have
Chippendale furnishings. ✉ *40 Bowery Beach Rd., Cape Elizabeth (7
mi south of Portland) 04107,* ☎ *207/799–3134 or 800/888–4287.
Restaurant, pool, tennis, croquet. AE, D, MC, V.*

$$$$ 🏠 **Pomegranate Inn.** Clever touches such as faux marbling on the moldings and mustard-colored rag-rolling in the hallways give this bed-and-
breakfast a bright, postmodern air. Most guest rooms are spacious and
bright, accented with original paintings on floral and tropical motifs;
four of the rooms have fireplaces. Telephones and televisions make this
a good choice for businesspeople. The location on a quiet street in the
city's Victorian Western Promenade district ensures serenity. ✉ *49 Neal
St., 04102,* ☎ *207/772–1006 or 800/356–0408. 7 rooms with bath,
1 suite. Full breakfast included. AE, D, MC, V.*

$$$–$$$$ 🏠 **Portland Regency Hotel.** The only major hotel in the center of the Old
Port Exchange, the Regency building was Portland's armory in the late
19th century. Rooms have four-poster beds, tall standing mirrors, flo-
ral curtains, and loveseats. The health club is the best in the city. ✉ *20
Milk St., 04101,* ☎ *207/774–4200 or 800/727–3436,* 🖷 *207/775–2150.
95 rooms with bath, 8 suites. Restaurant, massage, sauna, steam room,
aerobics, health club, nightclub, meeting rooms. AE, D, DC, MC, V.*

$$$–$$$$ 🏠 **Radisson Eastland.** This 1927 hotel has a prime location in Port-
land's up-and-coming arts district. In 1945 the hotel refused to admit
President Roosevelt's dog Fala so Mrs. Roosevelt took the canine and
headed to nearby Yarmouth for the night. The staff must be more ac-
commodating now because most of the rock bands performing at the
nearby Cumberland County Civic Center stay here. Rooms in the
tower section have floor-to-ceiling windows; higher floors have har-
bor views. ✉ *157 High St., 04101,* ☎ *207/775–5411 or 800/777–
6246,* 🖷 *207/775–2872. 204 rooms with bath. 2 restaurants, 2 bars,
sauna, exercise room, meeting rooms. AE, D, DC, MC, V.*

Nightlife and the Arts

NIGHTLIFE

For dancing, head to **Granny Killam's** (✉ 55 Market St., ☎ 207/761–
2787). The college crowd also beats feet to **Zootz Nightclub** (✉ 31 For-

est Ave. ☎ 207/773–8187), which is open weekends until 3 AM. **The Pavillion** (✉ 188 Middle St., ☎ 207/773–6422) is a dance club located in a former bank. The gay crowd goes to the **Underground** (✉ 3 Spring St., ☎ 207/773–3315).

Gritty McDuff's—Portland's Original Brew Pub (✉ 396 Fore St., ☎ 207/772–2739) serves fine ales, brewed on the premises, along with British pub fare and local seafood dishes. **Khalidi's Creative Seafoods** (✉ 36 Market St., ☎ 207/871–1881) has a good selection of Maine microbrewery beers on draft. **Three Dollar Dewey's** (✉ 241 Commercial St., ☎ 207/772–3310), long a popular night spot, is an English-style ale house. **Top of the East** (✉ Radisson Eastland Hotel, 157 High St., ☎ 207/775–5411) has a view of the city and live entertainment—jazz, piano, and comedy.

THE ARTS

Portland Performing Arts Center (✉ 25A Forest Ave., ☎ 207/774–0465) hosts music, dance, and theater performances. The **State Theatre** (✉ 609 Congress St., ☎ 207/879–1112) has come a long way from its days as a porn-film house—it's now one of the star attractions in Portland's up-and-coming arts district. The struggling theater has gone nonprofit in an effort to make ends meet. Among the numerous events hosted here are film premieres and concerts by nationally known artists. **Cumberland County Civic Center** (✉ 1 Civic Center Sq., ☎ 207/775–3458) hosts concerts, sporting events, and family shows in a 9,000-seat auditorium.

Portland Symphony Orchestra (✉ 30 Myrtle St., ☎ 207/773–8191) gives concerts October through August.

Mad Horse Theatre Company (✉ 955 Forest Ave., ☎ 207/797–3338) performs contemporary and original works. **Portland Stage Company** (✉ 25A Forest Ave., ☎ 207/774–0465), a producer of national reputation, mounts six productions, from October through May, at the Portland Performing Arts Center.

Outdoor Activities and Sports

BASEBALL

The new stadium at Hadlock Field (✉ 271 Park Ave.,) is the site of home games for the **Portland Seadogs** (☎ 207/879–9500), a farm team of the Florida Marlins. During their initial year in Portland, the team received unprecedented support and sells out nearly all its 71 home games in advance. The season begins in mid-April and goes to about Labor Day. Ticket prices range from $2 to $6.

BOAT TRIPS

For tours of the harbor, Casco Bay, and the nearby islands, try **Bay View Cruises** (✉ Fisherman's Wharf, ☎ 207/761–0496), **The Buccaneer** (✉ Long Wharf, ☎ 207/799–8188), **Casco Bay Lines** (✉ Maine State Pier, ☎ 207/774–7871), **Eagle Tours** (✉ Long Wharf, ☎ 207/774–6498), or **Old Port Mariner Fleet** (✉ Long Wharf, ☎ 207/775–0727).

DEEP-SEA FISHING

Half- and full-day fishing charter boats are operated out of Portland by **Devils Den** (✉ DiMillo's Marina, ☎ 207/761–4466).

HOCKEY

Portland is home to the **Portland Pirates** (☎ 207/828–4665), the farm team of the Washington Capitals. The Pirates play 40 home games at the Cumberland County Civic Center (✉ 85 Free St., 04101) each season, beginning in October and running into April, depending upon whether they make the playoffs. ☞ *$8–$13.*

Shopping

ART AND ANTIQUES

The **Pine Tree Shop & Bayview Gallery** (⊠ 75 Market St., ☎ 207/773–3007 or 800/244–3007) has original art and prints by prominent Maine painters. **Stein Glass Gallery** (⊠ 20 Milk St., ☎ 207/772–9072) specializes in contemporary glass, both decorative and utilitarian. **Abacus** (⊠ 44 Exchange St., ☎ 207/772–4880) has unusual gift items in glass, wood, and textiles, plus fine modern jewelry.

F. O. Bailey Antiquarians (⊠ 141 Middle St., ☎ 207/774–1479), Portland's largest retail showroom, carries antique and reproduction furniture and jewelry, paintings, rugs, and china.

BOOKS

Carlson and Turner (⊠ 241 Congress St., ☎ 207/773–4200) is an antiquarian book dealer with an estimated 50,000 titles. **Raffles Cafe Bookstore** (⊠ 555 Congress St., ☎ 207/761–3930) carries an impressive selection of fiction and nonfiction, plus the best selection of periodicals north of Boston. Coffee and a light lunch are served, and there are frequent readings and literary gatherings.

BOUTIQUES

The best boutique shopping in Portland is at the **Old Port Exchange,** where many shops are concentrated along Fore and Exchange streets.

CLOTHING

Joseph's (⊠ 410 Fore St., ☎ 207/773–1274) has elegant tailored designer clothing for men and women.

MALL

Those who require mall shopping with national brand stores should go 5 miles south of Portland to the **Maine Mall** (⊠ Maine Mall Rd., South Portland, ☎ 207/774–0303), which has 145 stores and is anchored by Sears, Filenes, JCPenny, Jordan Marsh, and Lechmere.

Casco Bay Islands

The islands of Casco Bay are also known as the Calendar Islands because there seems to be one for every day of the year. The brightly painted ferries of Casco Bay Lines are the lifeline to the Calendar Islands of Casco Bay, which realistically number about 140, depending on the tides and how one defines an island. There is frequent service to the most populated ones including Peaks, Long, Little Diamond, and Great Diamond. In summer, one of Maine's quintessential experiences is taking a Casco Bay Cruise—if even only to Peaks Island for a hour or two of walking about.

⑮ **Peaks Island,** nearest Portland, is the most developed, and some residents commute to work in Portland. Yet you can still commune with the wind and the sea on Peaks, explore an old fort, and ramble along the alternately rocky and sandy shore. This trip by boat is particularly enjoyable at or near sunset. Take the boat to the island and order a lobster sandwich or cold beer on the outdoor deck of **Jones' Landing** restaurant, steps from the dock. A circle trip without stops takes about 90 minutes. On the far side of the island you can stop on the rugged shoreline and have lunch. A small museum with Civil War artifacts is maintained in the **Fifth Maine Regiment** building.

⑯ The 17-acre **Eagle Island,** owned by the state and open to the public for day trips in summer, was the home of Admiral Robert E. Peary, the American explorer of the North Pole. Peary built a stone-and-wood house on the island as a summer retreat in 1904, then made it his permanent residence. The house remains as it was when Peary was here with his stuffed Arctic birds and the quartz he brought home and set into the fieldstone fireplace. The *Kristy K.*, departing from Long Wharf, makes a four-hour narrated tour and also offers tours of Portland Headlight and seal-watching cruises on the *Fish Hawk.* ⊠ *Long Wharf,* ☎ *207/774–6498.* 🖼 *Excursion tour $15, Headlight tour $8.* ☉ *Departures mid-June–Labor Day, daily beginning 10* AM.

Chebeague Island measures about 5 miles long and is less than 2 miles across at its widest. Service to the island is via **Casco Bay Lines** (☎ 207/774–7871) from Portland or via the **Chebeague Transportation Company** (☎ 207/846–3700) from the dock on Cousins Island, north of Portland and accessible by car. You can take along your bicycle or plan to stay overnight at the **Chebeague Island Inn** (☎ 207/846–5155), open April through October.

Lodging

$$ 🖬 **Keller's B&B.** This turn-of-the-century home provides rustic accommodations with deck views of Casco Bay, the boat landing, and the Portland skyline. Guest rooms are in a motel-like addition. The small private beach is just steps from your room. Guests select breakfast from a menu. ⊠ *20 Island Ave., Peaks Island,* ☎ *207/766–2441. 4 rooms with bath. Full breakfast included. No credit cards.*

Outdoor Activities and Sports

SEA KAYAKING

Maine Island Kayak Co. (⊠ 70 Luther St., Peak's Island, ☎ 800/796–2373) provides instruction, expeditions, and tours along the Maine coast.

Freeport

⑰ *17 mi northeast of Portland, 10 mi southwest of Brunswick.*

Freeport, on Route 1, northeast of Portland, has charming back streets lined with old clapboard houses and a small harbor on the Harraseeket River, but the overwhelming majority of visitors come to shop—L. L. Bean is the store that put Freeport on the map. Besides the shops that conform to strict local building guidelines, the town has many historical buildings and lovely New England architecture.

Dining and Lodging

$–$$ ✕ **Freeport Cafe.** This small restaurant south of Freeport's shopping district serves creative homemade food, including soups, salads, sandwiches, and dinner entrées. Breakfast is available all day. ⊠ *Rte. 1,* ☎ *207/865–3106. AE, D, DC, MC, V.*

$ ✕ **Harraseeket Lunch & Lobster Co.** This no-frills, bare-bones, genuine lobster pound and fried-seafood place is beside the town landing in South Freeport. Seafood baskets and lobster dinners are what it's all about; you can eat outside at picnic tables in good weather. ⊠ *Main St., South Freeport,* ☎ *207/865–4888. Reservations not accepted. No credit cards.* ☉ *May 1–Oct. 15.*

$$$–$$$$ ✕🖬 **Harraseeket Inn.** This gracious 1850 Greek Revival home, just two blocks from the biggest retailing explosion ever to hit Maine, includes a three-story addition that looks like an old New England inn but is in fact a steel and concrete structure with elevators, whirlpools, and modern fireplaces. Despite these modern appointments, the Harraseeket gives its visitors a country-inn experience, with afternoon tea served in the mahogany drawing room. Guest rooms have reproductions of Federal canopy beds. The formal, no-smoking dining room, serving New England–influenced Continental cuisine, is a simply decorated, airy space with picture windows facing the inn's garden courtyard. The Broad Arrow Tavern appears to have been furnished by L.

L. Bean, with fly rods, snowshoes, and moose heads; the hearty fare includes ribs, burgers, and charbroiled skewered shrimp and scallops. ⊠ *162 Main St., 04032,* ☎ *207/865–9377 or 800/342–6423,* FAX *207/865–1684. 48 rooms, 2 suites. Restaurant (collar shirt at dinner), bar, croquet. AE, D, DC, MC, V.*

Outdoor Activities and Sports

BOAT TRIPS

Atlantic Seal Cruises (⊠ South Freeport, ☎ 207/865–6112) has daily trips to Eagle Island, where you can tour Admiral Peary's museum home, and evening seal and osprey watches on the *Atlantic Seal* and *Arctic Seal.*

NATURE WALKS

Wolfe's Neck Woods State Park has self-guided trails along Casco Bay, the Harraseeket River, and a fringe salt marsh, as well as walks led by naturalists. There are picnic tables and grills, but no camping. ⊠ *Wolfe's Neck Rd. (follow Bow St. opposite L. L. Bean off Rte. 1),* ☎ *207/865–4465.* 🎫 *Memorial Day–Labor Day $2; $1 off-season.*

Shopping

Freeport's name is almost synonymous with shopping: L. L. Bean and the 70 **factory outlets** that opened during the 1980s are here. Outlet stores are in the **Fashion Outlet Mall** (⊠ 2 Depot St.) and the **Freeport Crossing** (⊠ 200 Lower Main St.), and many others crowd **Main Street** and **Bow Street.** The *Freeport Visitors Guide* (⊠ Freeport Merchants Association, Box 452, Freeport 04032, ☎ 207/865–1212) has a complete listing.

Founded in 1912 as a small mail-order merchandiser of products for hunters, guides, and fisherfolk, **L. L. Bean** now attracts some 3.5 million shoppers a year to its giant store in the heart of Freeport's shopping district. Here you can still find the original hunting boots, along with cotton, wool, and silk sweaters; camping and ski equipment; comforters; and hundreds of other items for the home, car, boat, or campsite. Across the street from the main store, a Bean factory outlet has seconds and discontinued merchandise at discount prices. ⊠ *Rte. 1,* ☎ *800/341–4341.* 🕐 *24 hrs.*

Harrington House Museum Store (⊠ 45 Main St., ☎ 207/865–0477) is a restored 19th-century merchant's home owned by the Freeport Historical Society; all the period reproductions that furnish the rooms are for sale. In addition, you can buy books, rugs, jewelry, crafts, Shaker items, toys, and kitchen utensils.

DeLorme's Map Store (⊠ Rte. 1, ☎ 207/865–4171) carries an exceptional selection of maps and atlases of Maine, New England, and the rest of the world; nautical charts; and travel books.

Brunswick

⑱ *10 mi north of Freeport, 11 mi west of Bath.*

Brunswick is best known for its lovely brick or clapboard homes and the stately ivy league Bowdoin College. Poet Henry Wadsworth Longfellow attended Bowdoin and a plaque is displayed outside his window. Another literary notable, Harriet Beecher Stowe came to Brunswick and wrote *Uncle Tom's Cabin.*

In the center is Brunswick's business district, Pleasant Street, and—at the end of Pleasant Street—**Maine Street,** which claims to be the widest (198 feet across) in the state. Friday from May through October sees a fine **farmer's market** on the town mall, between Maine Street and Park Row.

Maine Street takes you to the 110-acre campus of **Bowdoin College,** an enclave of distinguished architecture, gardens, and grassy quadrangles in the middle of town. Campus tours (☎ 207/725–3000) depart every day but Sunday from the admissions office in Chamberlain Hall. Nathaniel Hawthorne and Henry Wadsworth Longfellow are counted among the alumni. Among the historic buildings are Massachusetts Hall, a stout, sober, hip-roofed brick structure dating from 1802, which once housed the entire college. Hubbard Hall, an imposing 1902 neo-Gothic building is home to Maine's only gargoyle. In addition, it houses the **Peary-MacMillan Arctic Museum.** The museum contains photographs, navigational instruments, and artifacts from the first successful expedition to the North Pole, in 1909, by two of Bowdoin's most famous alumni, Admiral Robert E. Peary and Donald B. MacMillan. ☎ 207/ 725–3416. ⊠ Free. ☉ Tues.–Sat. 10–5, Sun. 2–5.

Don't miss the **Bowdoin College Museum of Art,** in a splendid Renaissance Revival style building, with seven galleries radiating from a rotunda. Designed in 1894 by Charles F. McKim, the building stands on a rise, its facade adorned with classical statues and the entrance set off by a triumphal arch. The collections encompass Assyrian and Classical art and that of the Dutch, Italian, French, and Flemish old masters; a superb gathering of Colonial and Federal paintings, notably the Gilbert Stuart portraits of Madison and Jefferson; and a Winslow Homer Gallery of engravings, etchings, and memorabilia (open summer only). The museum's collection also includes 19th- and 20th-century American painting and sculpture, with works by Mary Cassatt, Andrew Wyeth, and Robert Rauschenberg. ⊠ Walker Art Bldg., ☎ 207/725–3275. ⊠ Free. ☉ Tues.–Sat. 10–5, Sun. 2–5.

OFF THE
BEATEN PATH

THE HARPSWELLS – A side trip from Bath or Brunswick on Route 123 or Route 24 takes you to the peninsulas and islands known collectively as the Harpswells. The numerous small coves along Harpswell Neck shelter the boats of local lobstermen, and summer cottages are tucked away amid the birch and spruce trees.

The Arts

Bowdoin Summer Music Festival (⊠ Bowdoin College, ☎ 207/725–3322 for information or ☎ 207/725–3895 for tickets) is a six-week concert series featuring performances by students, faculty, and prestigious guest artists. **Maine State Music Theater** (⊠ Pickard Theater, Bowdoin College, ☎ 207/725–8769) stages musicals from mid-June through August with celebrity performers. **Theater Project of Brunswick** (⊠ 14 School St., ☎ 207/729–8584) performs from late June through August.

Beach

Popham Beach State Park (Phippsburg, ☎ 207/389–1335; ⊠ $2; $1 Nov.–Apr.), at the end of Route 209, south of Bath, has a good sand beach, a marsh area, and picnic tables.

Dining and Lodging

$–$$ ✕ **The Great Impasta.** This small, storefront restaurant is a great spot for lunch, tea, or dinner. Try the seafood lasagna, or match your favorite pasta and sauce to create your own dish. ⊠ 42 Maine St., ☎ 207/729–5858. Reservations not accepted. AE, D, DC, MC, V.

$$$–$$$$ ✕⊞ **Captain Daniel Stone Inn.** This Federal inn overlooks the Androscoggin River. While no two rooms are furnished identically, all offer executive-style comforts and many have whirlpool baths and pullout sofas in addition to queen-size beds. A guest parlor, 24-hour breakfast room, and excellent service in the Narcissa Stone Restaurant make this

an upscale escape from college-town funk. ⊠ *10 Water St., 04011,* ☎ FAX *207/725–9898. 32 rooms with bath. Restaurant (no lunch Sat.). CP. AE, DC, MC, V.*

$$$–$$$$ ✕⊡ **Stowe House.** This lovely New England inn was where Harriet Beecher Stowe wrote *Uncle Tom's Cabin.* Commendable rooms and a fine dining room specializing in regional Maine cuisine attract many natives from as far away as Portland. ⊠ *63 Federal St., 04086,* ☎ *207/725–5543,* FAX *207/725–9813. 18 rooms and suites with bath. Restaurant. CP. AE, DC, MC, V.*

$$$–$$$$ ⊡ **Harpswell Inn.** The stately dormered white clapboard Harpswell Inn is surrounded by spacious lawns and neatly pruned shrubs. The living room has a view of Middle Bay and Birch Island from its position on Lookout Point. Half the rooms also have water views. The carriage house in back has two luxury suites, one with a whirlpool. The 1761 no-smoking inn welcomes children over 10. ⊠ *141 Lookout Point Rd., S. Harpswell, 04079,* ☎ *207/833–5509 or 800/843–5509. 13 rooms, 6 with bath; 2 suites. MC, V.*

Outdoor Activities and Sports

SEA KAYAKING

H2Outfitters (⊠ Orr's Island, ☎ 207/833–5257) offers instruction, rentals, and half-day through multi-day trips.

Bath

⑲ *11 mi east of Brunswick, 38 mi northeast of Portland.*

Bath, east of Brunswick on Route 1, has been a shipbuilding center since 1607. Today, the Bath Iron Works turns out guided-missile frigates for the U.S. Navy and merchant container ships.

The **Maine Maritime Museum and Shipyard** in Bath has ship models, journals, photographs, and other artifacts to stir the nautical dreams of old salts and young. The 142-foot Grand Banks fishing schooner *Sherman Zwicker,* one of the last of its kind, is on display when in port. You can watch boatbuilders wield their tools on classic Maine boats at the restored Percy & Small Shipyard and Boat Shop. The outdoor shipyard is open May–November; during these months visitors may take scenic tours of the Kennebec River on the *Summertime.* During off-season, the Maritime History Building has indoor exhibits, videos, and activities. ⊠ *243 Washington St.,* ☎ *207/443–1316.* ◱ *$7.50.* ☉ *Daily 9:30–5.*

The huge rotting hulls of the schooners *Hester* and *Luther Little* rest in Wicasset, testaments to the town's once-busy harbor. Those who appreciate both music and antiques will enjoy a visit to the **Musical Wonder House** to see and hear the vast collection of antique music boxes from around the world. ⊠ *18 High St., Wiscasset (10 mi northeast of Bath),* ☎ *207/882–7163.* ◱ *1-hr presentation on main floor $10; 3-hr tour of entire house $30 or $50 for 2 people.* ☉ *May 15–Oct. 15, daily 10–6. Last tour usually 4 PM; call ahead for 3-hr tours.*

Travel from Wiscasset to Newcastle in restored 1930s coaches on the ☝ **Maine Coast Railroad.** ⊠ *Rte. 1, Wiscasset,* ☎ *207/882–8000.* ◱ *$10.*

The Arts

Chocolate Church Arts Center (⊠ 804 Washington St., ☎ 207/442–8455) offers changing exhibits by Maine artists in a variety of mediums, including textiles, photography, painting, and sculpture. The center also hosts folk, jazz, and classical concerts; theater productions; and performances for children, including puppet shows and

Portland Symphony Orchestra Kinderkonzerts. Sign up for classes and workshops in visual and performing arts.

Beach

Reid State Park (☎ 207/371–2303; ☒ $2.50 late Apr.–mid-Oct.), on Georgetown Island, off Route 127, has 1½ miles of sand on three beaches. Facilities include bathhouses, picnic tables, fireplaces, and snack bar. Parking lots fill by 11 AM on summer Sundays and holidays.

Dining and Lodging

$$ ✕ **Kristina's Restaurant & Bakery.** This frame house-turned-restaurant, with a front deck built around a huge maple tree, turns out some of the finest pies, pastries, and cakes on the coast. A satisfying dinner of New American cuisine, may include fresh seafood and grilled meats. All meals can be packed to go. ☒ *160 Centre St.,* ☎ *207/442–8577. D, MC, V. No dinner Sun. Closed Jan. Call ahead in winter.*

$$$ ⊞ **Fairhaven Inn.** This cedar-shingle house built in 1790 is set on 17 acres of pine woods and meadows sloping down to the Kennebec River. Guest rooms are furnished with handmade quilts and mahogany pineapple four-poster beds. The home-cooked breakfast offers such treats as peach soup, blintzes, and apple upside-down French toast. ☒ *R. R. 2, Box 85, N. 04530,* ☎ *207/443–4391. 8 rooms, 5 with bath. Hiking, cross-country skiing. Full breakfast included. AE, MC, V.*

Shopping

The **Wiscasset Bay Gallery** (☒ Water St., Wiscasset, ☎ 207/882–7682) specializes in 19th- and 20th-century American and European artists.

Boothbay

⑳ *60 mi northeast of Portland, 50 mi southwest of Camden.*

When Portlanders want to take a brief respite from what they know as city life, many come north to the Boothbay Region, which is comprised of Boothbay proper, East Boothbay, and Boothbay Harbor. This part of the near mid-coast shoreline is a craggy stretch of inlets where pleasure crafts anchor alongside trawlers and lobster boats. Commercial Street, Wharf Street, the By-Way, and Townsend Avenue are lined with shops, galleries, and ice-cream parlors. Excursion boats (☞ Outdoor Activities and Sports, *below*) leave from the piers off Commercial Street. From the harbor visitors may elect to catch a boat to Monhegan Island or be content visiting the little shops, waterfront restaurants, and inns.

At the **Boothbay Railway Village,** about a mile north of Boothbay, you can ride 1½ miles on a narrow-gauge steam train through a re-creation of a turn-of-the-century New England village. Among the 24 village buildings is a museum with more than 50 antique automobiles and trucks. ☒ *Rte. 27,* ☎ *207/633–4727.* ☒ *$6.* ☉ *Memorial Day–mid-Oct., weekends 9:30–5; June 10–Columbus Day, daily 9:30–5; special Halloween schedule. Closed Columbus Day–Memorial Day.*

Dining and Lodging

$$–$$$ ✕ **Black Orchid.** The classic Italian fare includes fettuccine alfredo with fresh lobster and mushrooms, and *petit filet à la diabolo* (fillets of Angus steak with marsala sauce). The upstairs and downstairs dining rooms have a Roman-trattoria ambience, with frilly leaves and fruit hanging from the rafters and little else in the way of decor. In the summer there is a raw bar outdoors. ☒ *5 By-Way, Boothbay Harbor,* ☎ *207/633–6659. AE, MC, V. No lunch. Closed Nov.–Apr.*

$$ ✕ **Andrew's Harborside.** The seafood menu is typical of the area—lobster, fried clams and oysters, haddock with seafood stuffing—but the harbor view makes it memorable. Lunch features lobster and crab rolls; children's and senior citizens' menus are available. You can dine outdoors on a harborside screened porch in summer. ⊠ *8 Bridge St, Boothbay Harbor,* ☎ *207/633–4074. Dinner reservations accepted for 5 or more. MC, V. Closed mid-Oct.–mid-May.*

$$$–$$$$ ⊞ **Fisherman's Wharf Inn.** All rooms overlook the water at this Colonial-style motel built 200 feet out over the harbor. The large dining room has floor-to-ceiling windows, and several day-trip cruises leave from this location. ⊠ *42 Commercial St., Boothbay Harbor 04538,* ☎ ℻ *207/633–5090, ext. 602 or 800/628–6872. 54 rooms with bath. Restaurant. AE, D, DC, MC, V. Closed late Oct.–mid-May.*

$$$ ⊞ **Anchor Watch.** This country Colonial on the water overlooks the outer harbor and lies within easy walking distance of town. Guest rooms are decorated with quilts and stenciling and are named for the Monhegan ferries that ran in the 1920s. Breakfast includes apple puff pancake, muffins, fruit, omelets, blueberry blintzes, and more. The owners also operate the *Balmy Days* motorcraft to Monhegan. ⊠ *3 Eames Rd., Boothbay Harbor 04538,* ☎ *207/633–7565. 4 rooms with bath. Dock. Full breakfast included. MC, V. Closed Jan.*

$$–$$$ ⊞ **Kenniston Hill Inn.** The oldest inn in Boothbay (circa 1786), this classic center-chimney Colonial with its white clapboards and columned porch offers comfortably old-fashioned accommodations on 4 acres of land only minutes from Boothbay Harbor. Five guest rooms have fireplaces, some have four-poster beds, rocking chairs, and gilt mirrors. ⊠ *Rte. 27, Box 125, 04537,* ☎ *207/633–2159. 10 rooms with bath. Full breakfast included. D, MC, V.*

$$ ⊞ **The Pines.** Families seeking a secluded setting with lots of room for little ones to run will be interested in this motel on a hillside a mile from town. Rooms have sliding glass doors opening onto private decks, two double beds, and small refrigerators. ⊠ *Sunset Rd., Box 693, Boothbay Harbor 04538,* ☎ *207/633–4555. 29 rooms with bath. Pool, tennis, playground. D, MC, V. Closed mid-Oct.–early May.*

Nightlife and the Arts

NIGHTLIFE
McSeagull's Gulf Dock (⊠ Boothbay Harbor, ☎ 207/633–4041) draws young singles with live music and a loud bar scene.

THE ARTS
Carousel Music Theater (⊠ "The Meadows," Boothbay Harbor, ☎ 207/633–5297) mounts musical revues from Memorial Day to Columbus Day. **Round Top Center for the Arts** (⊠ Business Rte. 1, Damariscotta, ☎ 207/563–1507) has exhibits, concerts, shows, and classes.

Outdoor Activities and Sports

BOAT TRIPS
Appledore (☎ 207/633–6598), a 66-foot windjammer, departs from Pier 6 at 9:30, noon, 3, and 6 for voyages to the outer islands. **Argo Cruises** (☎ 207/633–2500) runs the *Islander* for morning cruises, Bath Hellgate cruises, whale watching, and the popular Cabbage Island Clambake; the *Islander II* for 1½-hour trips to Seal Rocks; the *Miss Boothbay*, a licensed lobster boat, for lobster-trap hauling trips. Biweekly evening cruises feature R&B or reggae. Departures are from Pier 6. **Balmy Day Cruises** (☎ 207/633–2284 or 800/298–2284) has day trips to Monhegan Island and tours of the harbor and nearby lighthouses. **Cap'n Fish's Boat Trips** (☎ 207/633–3244) offers sightseeing cruises throughout the region, including puffin cruises, lobster-haul-

ing and whale-watching rides, trips to Damariscove Harbor, Pemaquid Point, and up the Kennebec River to Bath, departing from Pier 1. **Eastward** (☎ 207/633–4780) is a Friendship sloop with six-passenger capacity that departs from Ocean Point Road in East Boothbay for full- or half-day sailing trips. Itineraries vary with passengers' desires and the weather.

Shopping

BOOTHBAY HARBOR

Boothbay Harbor, and Commercial Street in particular, is chockablock with gift shops, T-shirt shops, and other seasonal emporia catering to visitors. One may purchase a Maine souvenir from a street vendor or buy gourmet coffee at another cart. A host of snacks and other treats are sold in summer—from freshly squeezed lemonade to hot pretzels from the **Pretzelogic** vendor on Main St. **Maine Trading Post** (✉ 80 Commercial St., ☎ 207/633–2760) sells antiques and fine reproductions that include rolltop desks able to accommodate personal computers, as well as gifts and decorative accessories. **House of Logan** (✉ Townsend Ave., ☎ 207/633–2293) sells clothing for men and women; children's clothes can be found next door at the **Village Store.**

DAMARISCOTTA

Maine Coast Book Shop (✉ Main St., ☎ 207/563–3207) carries a good selection of books and magazines and often hosts author signings. **Franciska Needham Gallery** (✉ Water St., ☎ 207/563–1227) has contemporary paintings and sculpture by Maine and New York artists.

EDGECOMB

Edgecomb Potters (✉ Rte. 27, ☎ 207/882–6802) sells glazed porcelain pottery and other crafts at rather high prices. Some discontinued items or seconds may be purchased for less. These potters have an excellent reputation and have a store in Freeport if you miss this one. **Sheepscot River Pottery** (✉ Rte. 1, ☎ 207/882–9410) has original hand-painted pottery as well as a large collection of American-made crafts including jewelry, kitchenware, furniture, and home accessories. The **Gil Whitman Gallery** (✉ Rte. 1, N. Edgecomb, ☎ 207/882–7705) exhibits the work of bronze sculptor Gil Whitman in a barn gallery and an outdoor sculpture garden, where giant metal flowers bloom amidst the real thing. The studio and workshop areas also are open to visitors.

En Route On the way to Pemaquid Point from the Boothbay region, you'll have to pass through Damariscotta, an appealing shipbuilding town on the Damariscotta River. The buildings and homes here evoke that New England charm probably so familiar to you by now: clapboard, stone foundations, brick, and stately chimneys.

Pemaquid Point

㉑ *15 mi south of Damariscotta.*

Here's a good spot to have a reliable Maine coast map handy—not because getting to Pemaquid Point is so difficult, it's just nice to have a confirmation that the circuitous route you're taking really is getting you somewhere. After all, this is a region filled with river outlets, rocky inlets, and peninsulas. Navigation is a breeze coming from Boothbay or Wiscasset. Follow Route 27 out of Boothbay or Route 1 north from Wiscasset into Damariscotta, then head south on Route 129 and 130 into Pemaquid Point.

At the **Colonial Pemaquid Restoration,** on a small peninsula jutting into the Pemaquid River, English mariners established a fishing and trading settlement in the early 17th century. The excavations at **Ft. William**

Henry, begun in the mid-1960s, have turned up thousands of artifacts from the Colonial settlement, including the remains of an old customs house, tavern, jail, forge, and homes, and from even earlier Native American settlements. The state operates a museum displaying many of the artifacts. ⊠ *Rte. 130,* ☎ *207/677–2423.* 🎟 *$1.50.* ☉ *Memorial Day–Labor Day, daily 9:30–5.*

Route 130 terminates at the **Pemaquid Point Light,** which looks as though it sprouted from the ragged, tilted chunk of granite that it commands. The former lighthouse-keeper's cottage is now the **Fishermen's Museum,** with photographs, models, and artifacts that explore commercial fishing in Maine. Here, too, is the **Pemaquid Art Gallery,** which mounts changing exhibitions from July 1 through Labor Day. ⊠ *Rte. 130,* ☎ *207/677–2494.* 🎟 *Donation requested.* ☉ *Memorial Day–Columbus Day, Mon.–Sat. 10–5, Sun. 11–5.*

Dining and Lodging

$$$–$$$$ ✕🏨 **Bradley Inn.** Within walking distance of the Pemaquid Point lighthouse, beach, and fort, the 1900 Bradley Inn began as a rooming house for summer rusticators and alternated between abandonment and operation as a B&B until its complete renovation in the early 1990s. Rooms are comfortable and uncluttered; ask for one of the cathedral-ceiling, waterside rooms on the third floor, which deliver breathtaking views of the sun setting over the water. The Ship's Restaurant has a frequently rotating menu, including a variety of fresh seafood dishes; there's light entertainment in the pub on weekends. ⊠ *Rte. 130, H. C. 61, Box 361, New Harbor 04554,* ☎ *207/677–2105,* 📠 *207/677–3367. 12 rooms with bath, 1 cottage, 1 carriage house. Restaurant, pub, croquet, bicycles. CP. AE, D, MC, V. Closed Jan.–Mar.*

$$$$ 🏨 **Newcastle Inn.** The white-clapboard house, vintage mid-19th century, has a romantic living room with a fireplace, loveseat, plenty of books, and river views. It also has a sunporch with white wicker furniture and ice-cream-parlor chairs. Guest rooms have been carefully appointed with unique beds—an old spool bed, wrought-iron beds, a brass-pewter bed, a sleigh bed, and several canopy beds—and rabbits are everywhere: stuffed, wooden, ceramic. Breakfast is a gourmet affair that might include scrambled eggs with caviar in puff pastry, ricotta cheese pie, or a frittata. The five-course dinner served nightly brings people back again and again. ⊠ *River Rd., Newcastle, 04553,* ☎ *207/563–5685 or 800/832–8669. 15 rooms with bath. 2 dining rooms, pub. Full breakfast included; MAP available. AE, MC, V.*

Portland to Pemaquid Point A to Z

Getting Around

BY BUS

Greater Portland's **Metro** (☎ 207/774–0351) runs seven bus routes in Portland, South Portland, and Westbrook. The fare is $1 for adults, 50¢ for senior citizens and people with disabilities, and children (under 5 free); exact change ($1 bills accepted) is required. Buses run from 5:30 AM to 11:45 PM.

BY CAR

The Congress Street exit from I–295 takes you into the heart of Portland. Numerous city parking lots have hourly rates of 50¢ to 85¢; the Gateway Garage on High Street, off Congress, is a convenient place to leave your car while exploring downtown. North of Portland, I–95 takes you to Exit 20 and Route 1, Freeport's Main Street, which continues on to Brunswick and Bath. East of Wiscasset you can take

Route 27 south to the Boothbays, where Route 96 is a good choice for further exploration.

Contacts and Resources

CAR RENTAL

Alamo (✉ Rear 9 Johnson St., ☎ 207/775–0855 or 800/327–9633, Portland). **Avis** (✉ Portland International Jetport, ☎ 207/874–7501 or 800/331–1212). **Budget** (✉ Portland International Jetport, ☎ 207/772–6789 or 800/527–0700). **Hertz** (✉ 1049 Westbrook St., Portland International Jetport, ☎ 207/774–4544 or 800/654–3131). **Thrifty** (✉ 1000 Westbrook St., Portland International Jetport, ☎ 207/772–4628 or 800/367–2277).

EMERGENCIES

Maine Medical Center (✉ 22 Bramhall St., Portland, ☎ 207/871–0111). **Mid Coast Hospital** (✉ 1356 Washington St., Bath, ☎ 207/443–5524; ✉ 58 Baribeau Dr., Brunswick, ☎ 207/729–0181). **St. Andrews Hospital** (✉ 3 St. Andrews La., Boothbay Harbor, ☎ 207/633–2121).

VISITOR INFORMATION

Off-season, most information offices are open weekdays 9–5; the hours below are for summer only.

Boothbay Harbor Region Chamber of Commerce (✉ Box 356, Boothbay Harbor, ☎ 207/633–2353; ⊙ Weekdays 9–5, Sat. 11–4, Sun. noon–4). **Chamber of Commerce of the Bath Brunswick Region** (✉ 45 Front St., Bath, ☎ 207/443–9751; ✉ 59 Pleasant St., Brunswick, ☎ 207/725–8797; ⊙ Weekdays 8:30–5). **Convention and Visitors Bureau of Greater Portland** (✉ 305 Commercial St., ☎ 207/772–5800; ⊙ June 1–Columbus Day, weekdays 8–6, weekends 10–6). **Freeport Merchants Association** (✉ Box 452, Freeport, ☎ 207/865–1212; ⊙ Weekdays 9–5). **Greater Portland Chamber of Commerce** (✉ 145 Middle St., Portland, ☎ 207/772–2811; ⊙ Weekdays 8–5). **Maine Publicity Bureau** (✉ Rte. 1, Exit 17 off I–95, Yarmouth, ☎ 207/846–0833; ⊙ Daily 9–5).

PENOBSCOT BAY

Purists hold that the Maine coast begins at Penobscot Bay, where the vistas over the water are wider and bluer, the shore a jumble of broken granite boulders, cobblestones, and gravel punctuated by small sand beaches, and the water numbingly cold. Port Clyde in the southwest and Stonington in the southeast are the outer limits of Maine's largest bay, 35 miles apart across the bay waters but separated by a drive of almost 100 miles on scenic but slow two-lane highways. From Pemaquid Point at the western extremity of Muscongus Bay to Port Clyde at its eastern extent, it's less than 15 miles across the water, but it's 50 miles for the motorist, who must return north to Route 1 to reach the far shore.

Rockland, the largest town on the bay, is Maine's major lobster distribution center and the port of departure for several bay islands. The Camden Hills, looming green over Camden's fashionable waterfront, turn bluer and fainter as one moves on to Castine, the elegant small town across the bay. In between Camden and Castine is the Mayberryesque town of Belfast and the flea-market mecca of Searsport. Because both communities are less glitzy than other bay towns, they offer value dining and lodging. Deer Isle is connected to the mainland by a slender, high-arching bridge, but Isle au Haut, accessible from Deer Isle's fishing town of Stonington, can be reached by passenger ferry only: More than half of this steep, wooded island is wilderness, the most remote section of Acadia National Park.

Penobscot Bay

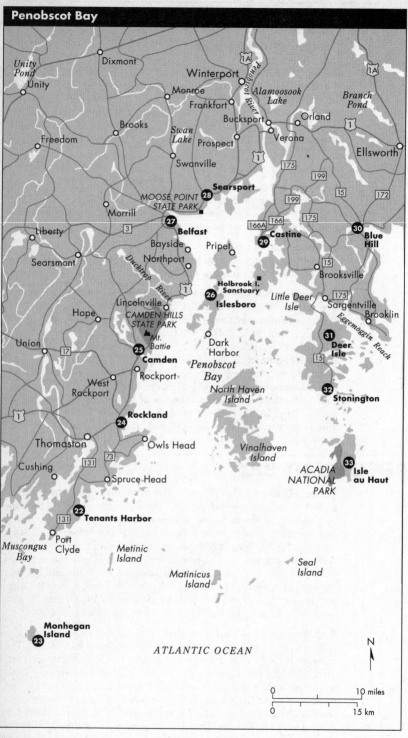

ATLANTIC OCEAN

N

| 0 | | 10 miles |
| 0 | | 15 km |

The most promising shopping areas are Main and Bay View streets in Camden, Main Street in Blue Hill, and Main Street in Stonington. Antiques shops are clustered in Searsport and scattered around the outskirts of villages, in farmhouses and barns; yard sales abound in summertime.

Numbers in the margin correspond to points of interest on the Penobscot Bay map.

Tenants Harbor

㉒ *13 mi south of Thomaston.*

In and around Tenant's Harbor you'll see waterside fields, spruce woods, ramshackle barns, and trim houses. Tenants Harbor is a quintessential Maine fishing town, its harbor dominated by lobster boats, its shores rocky and slippery, its center a scattering of clapboard houses, a church, a general store. The fictional Dunnet Landing of Sarah Orne Jewett's classic book, *The Country of the Pointed Firs,* is based on this region.

Dining and Lodging

$$–$$$ ✕⌂ **East Wind Inn & Meeting House.** On a knob of land overlooking the harbor and the islands, the East Wind offers simple hospitality, a wraparound porch, and unadorned but comfortable guest rooms, each furnished with an iron bedstead, flowered wallpaper, and a heritage bedspread. The dinner menu features seafood supreme, prime rib, boiled lobster, and baked stuffed haddock. ⌸ *Rte. 131 (10 mi off Rte. 1), Box 149, 04860,* ☎ *207/372–6366,* ℻ *207/372–6320. 23 rooms, 9 with bath; 3 suites. Restaurant (no lunch). CP. AE, MC, V.*

Monhegan Island

㉓ *East of Pemaquid Point, south of Port Clyde.*

Tiny, remote Monhegan Island, with its high cliffs fronting the open sea, was known to Basque, Portuguese, and Breton fishermen well before Columbus "discovered" America. About a century ago Monhegan was discovered again by some of America's finest painters, including Rockwell Kent, Robert Henri, and Edward Hopper, who sailed out to paint the savage cliffs, the meadows, the wild ocean views, and the shacks of fisherfolk. Tourists followed, and today Monhegan is overrun with visitors in summer.

Port Clyde, a fishing village at the end of Route 131, is the point of departure for the *Laura B.* (☎ 207/372–8848 for schedules), the mailboat that serves Monhegan Island. The *Balmy Days* (☎ 207/633–2284 or 800/298–2284) sails 16 miles from Boothbay Harbor to Monhegan on daily trips in summer.

Visitors land at the dock served by boats from Boothbay Harbor and Port Clyde and usually come for a few hours, and that's just about all the time you need unless you plan to do some painting and stay overnight—with advance reservation because choices are limited.

The **Monhegan Museum,** contained in an 1824 lighthouse, has wonderful views of Manana Island and the Camden Hills in the distance. Inside are displays depicting island life and local flora and birds. The volunteer on duty at the door does not charge admission, although a donation is appreciated and suggested. ☉ *July–mid-Sept.*

Islanders will direct you to **Cathedral Woods,** a forested area where children and adults build miniature houses of small branches and

other natural material for the woodland fairies. Part of the tradition
is for an existing house to be returned to its natural condition—providing parts for others to make their own houses.

Beach

Swim Beach, a five minute walk from the ferry, is rather rocky but rarely
has more than a few sunworshippers in sight, a few with kids in tow.

Outdoor Activities and Sports

WALKING

Everyone who comes to Monhegan comes to either paint or walk the
half dozen trails around the island. In all, there are 17 miles crisscrossing
the island, each interspersed with weathered homes doubling as artist's
studios.

Rockland

②④ *27 mi south of Belfast, 53 mi northeast of Brunswick.*

Rockland earned its reputation as a large fishing port and the commercial hub of the coast, with working boats moored alongside a
growing flotilla of cruise schooners. Although Rockland retains its working-class flavor, the expansion of the Farnsworth Museum, combined
with additional boutiques, restaurants, and bed-and-breakfasts has made
it a good stop for coastal travelers. This also is the point of departure
for popular day trips to Vinalhaven, North Haven, and Matinicus islands. The outer harbor is bisected by a nearly mile-long granite break-
water, which begins on Samoset Road and ends with a lighthouse that
was built in 1888.

In downtown Rockland is the **William A. Farnsworth Library and Art
Museum.** Here are oil and watercolor landscapes of the coastal areas
you have just seen, among them N. C. Wyeth's *Eight Bells* and Andrew Wyeth's *Her Room.* Jamie Wyeth is also represented in the collections, as are Winslow Homer, Rockwell Kent, and the sculptor
Louise Nevelson. Next door is the Farnsworth Homestead, a handsome
Greek Revival dwelling furnished in the Victorian style. (For admission information, *see* Olson House, *below.*)

OFF THE
BEATEN PATH
CUSHING – The William A. Farnsworth Library and Art Museum also op-
erates the **Olson House,** which was made famous by Andrew Wyeth's
painting, *Christina's World.* ✉ *352 Main St., Cushing (14 mi southwest
of Rockland),* ☎ *207/596–6457.* ☞ *Museum and homestead $5;
Olson House $3.* ☉ *Museum Mon.–Sat. 10–5, Sun. 1–5, closed Mon.
Oct.–May; Olson House Wed.–Sun. 11–4, closed Oct.–May.*

☺ **Owls Head Transportation Museum,** displays antique aircraft, cars, and
engines and stages weekend air shows. ✉ *Rte. 73, Owls Head (2 mi
south of Rockland),* ☎ *207/594–4418.* ☞ *$6.* ☉ *May–Oct., daily 10–
5; Nov.–Apr., weekdays 10–4, weekends 10–3.*

Dining and Lodging

$$
★
✗ **Jessica's.** Perched on a hill at the extreme southern end of Rock-
land, Jessica's occupies four cozy dining rooms in a tastefully renovated
Victorian home. Billed as a European bistro, this restaurant lives up
to its Continental label with creative entrées that include veal Zurich,
paella, and pork Portofino; other specialties of the Swiss chef are fo-
caccia with a selection of toppings and a half-dozen pastas and risot-
tos. ✉ *2 S. Main St. (Rte. 73),* ☎ *207/596–0770. D, MC, V. Closed
Tues. in winter.*

$$$–$$$$ ▣ **Limerock Inn.** You can walk to the Farnsworth and the Shore Village museums from this magnificent Queen Anne–style Victorian on a quiet residential street. Meticulously decorated rooms include Island Cottage, with a whirlpool tub and doors that open onto a private deck overlooking the backyard garden, and Grand Manan, which has a fireplace, whirlpool tub, and a four-poster king-size bed. ⊠ *98 Limerock St., 94841,* ☎ *207/594–2257 or 800/546–3762. 8 rooms with bath, 2 can be suites. Croquet, boating, bicycles. Full breakfast included. MC, V.*

$$$–$$$$ ▣ **Samoset Resort.** Next to the breakwater, on the Rockland–Rockport town line, is this sprawling oceanside resort with excellent facilities. ⊠ *Warrenton St., Rockport,* ☎ *207/594–2511; outside ME, 800/341–1650;* FAX *207/594-0722. 132 rooms, 18 suites. Restaurant, indoor and outdoor pools, golf, tennis, racquetball, fitness center. AE, D, DC, MC, V.*

Outdoor Activities and Sports

BOAT TRIPS

North End Shipyard Schooners (⊠ Box 482, ☎ 800/648–4544) operates three- and six-day cruises on the schooners *American Eagle, Isaac H. Evans,* and *Heritage.* **Vessels of Windjammer Wharf** (⊠ Box 1050, ☎ 207/236–3520 or 800/999–7352) organizes three- and six-day cruises on the *Pauline,* a 12-passenger motor yacht, and the *Stephen Taber,* a windjammer. **Timberwind** (⊠ Box 247, ☎ 207/236–0801 or 800/759–9250) is a 100-foot windjammer that sails out of Rockport harbor on three- and six-day trips. **Bay Island Yacht Charters** (⊠ 120 Tillison Ave., ☎ 207/236–2776 or 800/421–2492) offers bareboat and charters, daysailer rentals, and sailing lessons.

DEEP-SEA FISHING

The 42-foot *Henrietta* (☎ 207/594–5411) departs the Rockland Landings Marina (end of Sea St.) at 7:30 daily, returning at 5, from late May to September, weather permitting. Bait and tackle are provided, alcohol is prohibited, reservations are essential.

Shopping

The **Personal Bookstore** (⊠ 78 Main St, Thomaston, ☎ 207/354–8058 or 800/391–8058) is a book lover's treasure. Maine authors frequently do book-signings; browsers will find some autographed copies on the shelves. **Reading Corner** (⊠ 408 Main St., ☎ 207/596–6651) carries an extensive inventory of cookbooks, children's books, Maine titles, best-sellers, and one of the area's best newspaper and magazine selections. **The Store** (⊠ 435 Main St., ☎ 207/594–9246) has top-of-the-line cookware, table accessories, and an outstanding card selection.

Camden

②   *8 mi north of Rockland, 19 mi south of Belfast.*

Camden, "Where the mountains meet the sea"—an apt description, as you will discover when you step out of your car and look up from the harbor. Camden is famous not only for geography but for the nation's largest fleet of windjammers—relics and replicas from the age of sail. At just about any hour during the warmer months you're likely to see at least one windjammer tied up in the harbor, and windjammer cruises are a superb way to explore the ports and islands of Penobscot Bay.

NEED A   **Ayer's Fish Market** (⊠ 43 Main St. ☎ 207/236–3509) has the best fish
BREAK?   chowder in town; take a cup to the pleasant park at the head of the harbor when you're ready for a break from the shops on Bay View and Main streets.

The entrance to the 5,500-acre **Camden Hills State Park** (☎ 207/236–3109) is 2 miles north of Camden on Route 1. If you're accustomed to the Rockies or the Alps, you may not be impressed with heights of not much more than 1,000 feet, yet the Camden Hills are landmarks for miles along the low, rolling reaches of the Maine coast. You can see them from Monhegan Island. The park contains 20 miles of trails, including the easy Nature Trail up Mount Battie. The 112-site camping area, open mid-May through mid-October, has flush toilets and hot showers. ☞ *Trails and auto road up Mount Battie $2.*

Dining and Lodging

$$ ✕ **Waterfront Restaurant.** A ringside seat on Camden Harbor can be had here; the best view is from the outdoor deck, open in warm weather. The fare is primarily seafood: boiled lobster, scallops, bouillabaisse, steamed mussels, Cajun barbecued shrimp. Lunchtime highlights include Tex-Mex dishes, lobster and crabmeat salads, and tuna niçoise. ⊠ *Bay View St.,* ☎ *207/236–3747. Reservations not accepted. AE, MC, V. Closed winter.*

$$$$ ✕🏠 **Whitehall Inn.** One of Camden's best-known inns, just north of town on Route 1, is an 1843 white-clapboard, wide-porch ship-captain's home with a turn-of-the-century wing. Just off the comfortable main lobby with its faded Oriental rugs, the Millay Room preserves memorabilia of the poet Edna St. Vincent Millay, who grew up in the area. Rooms are sparsely furnished, with dark-wood bedsteads, white bedspreads, and clawfoot bathtubs. Some rooms have ocean views. The dining room, serving traditional and creative American cuisine, is open to the public. Dinner entrées include salmon in puff pastry and swordfish grilled with roasted red pepper sauce. ⊠ *52 High St. (Rte. 1), Box 558, 04843,* ☎ *207/236–3391 or 800/789–6565,* 🅵🅰🆇 *207/236–4427. 44 rooms with bath. Restaurant (no lunch), golf privileges, tennis courts, shuffleboard. MAP. AE, MC, V. Closed mid-Oct.–late May.*

$$$$ 🏠 **Inn at Sunrise Point.** For comfort and location, you can't beat this fine B&B perched on the water's edge, with magnificent views over Penobscot Bay. Travel-writer Jerry Levitin built his dream getaway here. Three rooms in the main house and four cottages are simply, but tastefully decorated. Each room has a television and VCR, fireplace, terrycloth robes, and telephone. The cottages also have whirlpool tubs and private decks. A full breakfast is served in the solarium; guests take high tea in the paneled library with stone fireplace. ⊠ *Box 1344, 04843,* ☎ *207/236–7716 or 800/435–6378. 7 rooms with bath. Closed winter.*

$$$$ 🏠 **Norumbega.** This stone castle, built in 1886 amid Camden's ele-
★   gant clapboard houses, was obviously the fulfillment of a fantasy. The public rooms have gleaming parquet floors, oak and mahogany paneling, richly carved wood mantels over four fireplaces on the first floor alone, gilt mirrors, and Empire furnishings. At the back of the house, several decks and balconies overlook the garden, the gazebo, and the bay. The view improves as you ascend; the penthouse suite has a small deck, private bar, and a skylight in the bedroom. On arrival, guests are welcomed with complimentary aperitifs. ⊠ *61 High St., 04843,* ☎ *207/236–4646,* 🅵🅰🆇 *207/236–0824. 12 rooms with bath. Full breakfast included. AE, MC, V.*

$$$–$$$$ 🏠 **Windward House.** A choice bed-and-breakfast, this 1854 Greek Revival house of 1854 is at the edge of downtown. Rooms have fishnet lace canopy beds, cherry highboys, curly-maple bedsteads, and clawfoot mahogany dressers; two have fireplaces. Guests are welcome to the three common rooms: the library where complimentary sherry, cof-

fee, and tea are served, the living room with a soapstone fireplace, and the dining room. A game room is outfitted with board games for quiet evenings. Breakfasts may include quiche, apple puff pancakes, peaches-and-cream French toast, or soufflés. A pleasant, private deck in back overlooks extensive English cutting gardens. ⊠ *6 High St., 04843,* ☎ *207/236–9656,* FAX *207/230–0433. 7 rooms with bath, 1 suite. Full breakfast included. AE, MC, V.*

$$$ **Camden Maine Stay.** Within walking distance to shops and restau-
★ rants, this 1802 clapboard inn is on the National Register of Historic Places. The grounds are classic and inviting, from the waving flag and colorful flowers lining the granite walk in summer to the snow-laden bushes in winter. Rooms are equally colorful and fresh with lots of East-lake furniture. One room has been converted to a luxury suite. ⊠ *22 High St., 04842,* ☎ *207/236–9636. 7 rooms, 5 with bath; 1 suite. Breakfast included. AE, MC, V.*

Nightlife and the Arts

NIGHTLIFE

Peter Ott's Tavern (⊠ 16 Bay View St., ☎ 207/236–4032) is a steak-house with a lively bar scene. **Sea Dog Tavern & Brewery** (⊠ 43 Mechanic St., ☎ 207/236–6863) is a popular brew pub offering locally made lagers and ales in a retrofitted woolen mill.

THE ARTS

Bay Chamber Concerts (⊠ Rockport Opera House, Rockport, ☎ 207/236–2823) offers chamber music every Thursday night and some Friday nights during July and August; concerts are given once a month September through May.

Outdoor Activities and Sports

BIKING

Maine Sport (⊠ Rte. 1, Rockport, ☎ 207/236–8797) rents bikes, camping and fishing gear, canoes, kayaks, cross-country skis, ice skates, and skis.

BOAT TRIPS

Windjammers create a stir whenever they sail into Camden harbor, and a voyage around the bay on one of them, whether for an afternoon or a week, is unforgettable. The season for the excursions is June through September. Excursion boats, too, provide a great opportunity for getting afloat on the waters of Penobscot Bay. Eggemoggin Reach is a famous cruising ground for yachts, as are the coves and inlets around Deer Isle and the Penobscot Bay waters between Castine and Camden.

Angelique (⊠ Yankee Packet Co., Box 736, ☎ 207/236–8873 or 800/282–9989) makes three- and six-day trips. *Appledore* (⊠ 0 Lily Pond Dr., ☎ 207/236–8353 or 800/233–7437) has two-hour day sails as well as private charters. *Betselma* (⊠ 35 Pearl St., ☎ 207/236–4446) offers two two-hour excursions and eight one-hour trips from Camden's Public Landing every day between June and October. No reservations needed. **Maine Windjammer Cruises** (⊠ Box 617, ☎ 207/236–2938 or 800/736–7981) has three two-masted schooners making two-, four-, and six-day trips along the coast and to the islands. *Roseway* (⊠ Box 696, ☎ 207/236–4449 or 800/255–4449) takes three-, four-, and six-day cruises.

Indian Island Kayak Co. (⊠ 16 Mountain St., ☎ 207/236–4088) gives one- and multi-day kayaking tours. **Maine Sport** (⊠ Rte. 1, Rockport, ☎ 207/236–8797), the best sports outfitter north of Freeport, rents sailboards and organizes whitewater-rafting and sea-kayaking expeditions, starting at the store.

Shopping

Maine's Massachusetts House Galleries (⊠ Rte. 1, Lincolnville, ☎ 207/789–5705) has a broad selection of regional art, including bronzes, carvings, sculptures, and landscapes and seascapes in pencil, oil, and watercolor. The **Pine Tree Shop & Bayview Gallery** (⊠ 33 Bay View St., ☎ 207/236–4534) specializes in original art, prints, and posters— almost all with Maine themes. The **Owl and Turtle Bookshop** (⊠ 8 Bay View St., ☎ 207/236–4769) sells a thoughtfully chosen selection of books, CDs, cassettes, and cards, including Maine-published works. The two-story shop has special rooms devoted to marine books and children's books. The **Windsor Chairmakers** (⊠ Rte. 1, Lincolnville, ☎ 207/789–5188 or 800/789–5188) sells custom-made, handcrafted beds, chests, china cabinets, dining tables, highboys—and, of course, chairs.

Skiing

Camden Snowbowl. No other ski area can boast a view over island-studded Penobscot Bay. ⊠ *Box 1207, Camden 04843,* ☎ *207/236–3438.*

DOWNHILL

In a Currier & Ives setting there's a 950-foot-vertical mountain, a small lodge with cafeteria, a ski school, and ski and toboggan rentals. Camden Snowbowl has 11 trails accessed by one double chair and two T-bars. It also has night skiing.

CROSS-COUNTRY

There are 16 kilometers (10 mi) of cross-country skiing trails at the **Camden Hills State Park** (☎ 207/236–9849), and 20 kilometers (12½ mi) at the **Tanglewood 4-H Camp** in Lincolnville (☎ 207/789–5868), about 5 miles away.

OTHER ACTIVITIES

Camden Snowbowl has a small lake that is cleared for ice-skating and a 400-foot toboggan run that shoots sledders out onto the lake.

En Route The lovely community of **Bayside,** a section of Northport that is off Route 1 on the way to Belfast, is dotted with 150-year-old Queen Anne cottages that have freshly painted porches and exquisite architectural details. Some of these homes line the main one-lane thoroughfare of George Street; others are clustered on bluffs with water views around town greens complete with flagpoles and swings; yet others are on the shore.

Islesboro

㉖ *4 mi east of Lincolnville.*

Islesboro, reached by car-and-passenger ferry (Maine State Ferry Service, ☎ 207/734–6935 or 800/491–4883) from Lincolnville Beach, on Route 1 north of Camden, has been a retreat of wealthy, very private families for more than a century. The long, narrow, mostly wooded island has no real town to speak of; there are scatterings of mansions as well as humbler homes at Dark Harbor (where celebrity couples Kirstie Alley and Parker Stevenson and John Travolta and Kelly Preston live) and at Pripet near the north end. Since the amenities on Islesboro are quite spread out, you don't want to come on foot. If you plan to spend the night here, you should make a reservation well in advance.

NEED A
BREAK?
Dark Harbor Shop (⊠ Main Rd., ☎ 207/734–8878; ☉ Memorial Day–Labor Day) on Islesboro is an old-fashioned ice cream parlor where folks gather for sandwiches, newspapers, gossip, and gifts.

Dining and Lodging

$$$$ ✕⊞ **Dark Harbor House.** The yellow-clapboard, 1896 neo-Georgian summer "cottage" has a stately portico and a dramatic hilltop setting. An elegant double staircase curves from the ground floor to the spacious bedrooms; some have balconies, five have fireplaces, two have four-poster beds. The dining room, open to the public for dinner by reservation, emphasizes seafood. ⊠ *Main Rd., Box 185, 04848,* ☎ *207/734–6669. 10 rooms with bath. Restaurant. MC, V. Closed mid-Oct.–mid-May.*

Belfast

㉗ *46 mi east of Augusta, 27 mi north of Rockland.*

Belfast has a lively waterfront and a charming Main Street beckoning architectural buffs to do the 1-mile self-guided walking tour of period sea captain's homes, reminders of the town's heyday in the 1800s. Belfast was once home to more sea captains than any other port in the world. You can also take a train ride along the water or through fall foliage; take a bay excursion on a former Mississippi riverboat; or explore the galleries of this town that has an active artistic community.

☾ **Belfast & Moosehead Lake Railroad,** one of the oldest railroads in the country, has two narrated scenic rail trips in Waldo County. A diesel train leaves from Belfast's waterfront and runs along an inland river. The other railhead is in Unity, 35 miles inland, where a steam locomotive passes over Unity Pond and by working farmlands and small villages. A staged train robbery is fun for children, as is the pre-ride demonstration of turning the engine around at Unity station. Both locations have dining facilities and offer seating in first-class, coach, or open-air cars, which are the most fun in good weather. There are special fall foliage tours that are longer than the usual 1½-hour excursions; and there's a discount if you ride both the railroad and Belfast's riverboat, **Voyageur.** ⊠ *One Depot Sq., Unity 04988,* ☎ *207/948–5500 or 800/392–5500.* ☲ *$14.* ⊙ *May–Oct. Call for schedule information and directions.*

The Arts

The Belfast Maskers (⊠ Railroad Theater, Box 1017, ☎ 207/338–9668) deserve their strong regional reputation. This group, which has received celebrity support from the likes of Ali McGraw and Liv Ullmann, present both modern and classic works year-round.

Dining and Lodging

$–$$ ✕ **90 Main.** This family-run restaurant with an outdoor patio in the back is helmed by young chef and owner Sheila Costello. Using Pemaquid oysters, Maine blueberries, organic vegetables grown on a nearby farm, and other fresh, local ingredients, Costello creates flavorful dishes that delight all the senses. Choose from a chalkboard full of specials that always includes a macrobiotic option, or start with the smoked seafood and pâté sampler or the spinach salad topped with sautéed chicken, sweet peppers, hazelnuts, and a warm raspberry vinaigrette. Entrées include ribeye steak and seafood linguine fra Diablo. ⊠ *90 Main St.,* ☎ *207/338–1106. AE, MC, V.*

$ ✕ **Weathervane.** Because this small northeastern chain has cut out the middleman—buying directly from fishermen and self-distributing their goods—an average meal of very fresh raw, grilled, fried, broiled, or sautéed seafood costs under $10. Shellfish like littleneck clams and the ubiquitous Maine lobster, tender rings of calamari, and fish from smelt to swordfish are available in combination platters. There are also token non-seafood items like sirloin and chicken tenders. This location has outdoor waterfront seating. ⊠ *Main St.,* ☎ *207/338–1774. Reservations not accepted. MC, V.*

$$ 🏠 **The Inn on Primrose Hill.** Built in 1812 and once the home of a navy admiral, this 14-room inn near the waterfront is the most elegant in town. The inn's Ionic columns belie its original Federal architecture. The 2 acres that surround it have formal gardens, a terrace with wrought-iron furniture, and both horseshoes and a boccie court; a porch swing is an agreeable addition. Owners Pat and Linus Heinz have taken great care to keep and restore authentic details such as ornate Waterford chandeliers, a mahogany dining set, and a black marble fireplace. There are several spacious public rooms including double parlors, a library with a large-screen cable TV, and a sunny conservatory with wicker and plump upholstered furniture. Guest rooms have either partial bay views or garden views. ⊠ *100 High St.,* ☎ *207/338–6982. 3 rooms with bath, 1 room shares bath. Boccie, horseshoes. Full breakfast and afternoon tea included. No credit cards.*

$–$$ 🏠 **Thomas Pitcher House.** Easygoing hosts Fran and Ron Kresge run a cheerful bed-and-breakfast that's one block from Belfast's Main Street. Bright common areas include a small library, a formal dining room with Chippendale furnishings, and a parlor with a marble fireplace and Victorian touches. Upstairs, carefully decorated guest rooms have supremely comfortable beds and floral, paisley, and/or striped accents. Ron is a master breakfast chef—beg for his ham and cheese soufflé. No children under 12 accepted. ⊠ *5 Franklin St.,* ☎ *207/338–6454. 4 rooms with bath. Full breakfast included. No credit cards.*

Outdoor Activities and Sports

BOATING

The 150-passenger **Voyageur** (☎ 800/392–5500) leaves Belfast twice daily in season for 1½-hour narrated tours of the bay. Sightings of seals and cormorants are common; dolphins show themselves more rarely. This former Mississippi riverboat has both open and enclosed decks and food-and-beverage service. Sailing schedules coordinate with that of the Belfast & Moosehead Lake Railroad; a discount applies if you travel on both.

Belfast Kayak Tours (⊠ R. R. 1, Box 715, Freedom, ☎ 207/382–6204) guides paddlers of all levels by the hour in sturdy double kayaks.

Chance Along (⊠ 140 High St., ☎ 207/338–6003 or, in ME, 800/286–6696) offers sailing instructions and outings, sailboat rentals and bareboat charters, and boat repairs and storage.

FLIGHTSEEING

Ace Aviation (⊠ Belfast Municipal Airport, ☎ 207/338–2970) takes up to three people at approximately $25 per 15 minutes, for panoramic views of the jagged coastline, lighthouses, and islands. Planes are available for charter.

STATE PARKS

Moose Point State Park (Rte. 1, between Belfast and Searsport, ☎ 207/548–2882) is ideal for easy hikes and picnics overlooking Penobscot Bay; there are no camping facilities.

Shopping

J. S. Ames Fine Art (⊠ 68 Main St., ☎ 207/338–1558) carries contemporary art in all mediums. **The Good Table** (⊠ 72 Main St., ☎ 207/338–4880) sells an imaginative array of gifts and gourmet items.

Searsport

28 *11 mi north of Belfast, 57 mi east of Augusta.*

Searsport, Maine's second-largest deepwater port (after Portland)—claims to be the antiques capital of Maine. The town's stretch of Route 1 has many antiques shops and a large weekend flea market in season.

Searsport preserves a rich nautical history at the **Penobscot Marine Museum,** where eight historic and two modern buildings document the region's seafaring way of life. Included are display photos of 284 sea captains, artifacts of the whaling industry (lots of scrimshaw), hundreds of paintings and models of famous ships, navigational instruments, and treasures collected by seafarers. ⊠ *Church St.,* ☎ *207/548–2529.* ⌂ *$5.* ⊙ *June–mid-Oct., Mon.–Sat. 10–5, Sun. noon–5.*

Lodging

$–$$ ▦ **Hichborn Inn.** A Victorian Italianate on the National Register for Historic Places, this inn was originally the home of N.G. Hichborn, a cousin of Paul Revere. Small and romantic, the Hichborn is just north of Searsport, off Route 1, in a quiet neighborhood one door down from a classic white-steepled New England church. Public areas include a music room with a piano; a cheery sunporch with tables for two set for breakfast; and a parlor with maroon walls, a fireplace, and a tray of brandy, sherry, and cordials for self-service. Of the three guest rooms, one has a brass bed, one a sleigh bed, and the other an ornate Victorian carved walnut bed. Finishing touches include marble-top dressers and robes. Your hosts might serve fruit soup and Belgian waffles for breakfast. Eight friendly, protective ghosts have been spotted here over the years. Children are not accepted. ⊠ *Church St. (Box 115), Stockton Springs, 04981,* ☎ *207/567–4183. 2 rooms with bath, 1 room shares bath. Full breakfast included. No credit cards.*

Shopping

Billing itself the antiques capital of Maine, Searsport hosts a massive weekend **flea market** on Route 1 during the summer months. Indoor shops, most of them in old houses and barns, are also on Route 1, in Lincolnville Beach as well as in Searsport. Shops are open daily during the summer months, by chance or by appointment from mid-October through the end of May.

Castine

29 *16 mi south of Bucksport.*

Historic Castine, over which the French, the British, the Dutch, and the Americans fought from the 17th century to the War of 1812, has two museums and the ruins of a British fort, but the finest aspect of Castine is the town itself: the lively, welcoming town landing, the serene Federal and Greek Revival houses, and the town common. Castine invites strolling, and you would do well to start at the town landing, where you can park your car, and walk up Main Street past the two inns and on toward the white Trinitarian Federated Church with its tapering spire.

The town common is ringed by a collection of white-clapboard buildings that includes the Ives House (once the summer home of the poet Robert Lowell), the Abbott School, and the Unitarian Church, capped by a whimsical belfry that suggests a gazebo. This makes an ideal walk in summer or fall and it takes on a special glow at Christmas.

Dining and Lodging

\$\$–\$\$\$ ✕ **Chez Michel.** This unassuming restaurant, serving up a fine rabbit pâté, mussels marinière, steak au poivre, and poached salmon, might easily be on the Riviera instead of Lincolnville Beach. Chef Michel Hetuin creates bouillabaisse as deftly as he whips up New England fisherman chowder, and he welcomes special requests. ⊠ *Rte. 1, Lincolnville Beach,* ☎ *207/789–5600. Reservations accepted for 6 or more. D, MC, V. Closed Nov.–mid-Apr.*

\$\$\$\$ ✕▥ **The Pentagoet.** The rambling, pale-yellow Pentagoet, a block from Castine's waterfront, has been a favorite stopping place for more than a century. The porch wraps around three sides of the inn and has two charming "courting swings." Decor in guest rooms includes hooked rugs, a mix of Victorian antiques, and floral wallpapers. Dinner in the deep-rose-and-cream formal dining room is an elaborate affair; entrées always include lobster creatively prepared. Complimentary hors d'oeuvres are served evenings in the library-cum-music room, where there is often live chamber music. Inn guests can choose from a hearty breakfast or a lighter breakfast buffet. ⊠ *Main St., 04421,* ☎ *207/326–8616 or 800/845–1701. 16 rooms with bath. Restaurant (reservations essential, no lunch). MAP. MC, V. Closed Nov.–late May.*

\$\$–\$\$\$\$ ✕▥ **The Castine Inn.** Light, airy rooms, upholstered easy chairs, and
★   fine prints and paintings are typical of the guest-room furnishings here. One room has a pineapple four-poster bed. The third floor has the best views: the harbor over the handsome formal gardens on one side, the village on the other. The dining room, decorated with a wraparound mural of Castine and its harbor, is open to the public for breakfast and dinner; the menu includes traditional New England fare—Maine lobster, crabmeat cakes with mustard sauce, and chicken-and-leek potpie—plus such creative entrées as sweetbreads with hazelnut butter and roast duck with peach chutney. In the snug, English-style pub off the lobby are small tables, antique spirit jars over the mantel, and a fireplace. ⊠ *Main St., Box 41, 04421,* ☎ *207/326–4365,* 🅵🅰🆇 *207/326–4570. 17 rooms with bath, 3 suites. Restaurant, pub. Full breakfast included. MC, V. Closed Nov.–mid-Apr.*

Nightlife and the Arts

NIGHTLIFE

Dennett's Wharf (⊠ Sea St., ☎ 207/326–9045) draws a crowd every lunchtime for a terrific view and every evening for drinking and dancing. It's open from May to October.

THE ARTS

Cold Comfort Productions (⊠ Box 259, no phone), a community theater, mounts plays in July and August.

Shopping

Chris Murray Waterfowl Carver (⊠ Upper Main St., ☎ 207/326–9033) sells award-winning wildfowl carvings and offers carving instruction.

Blue Hill

㉚ *19 mi southeast of Bucksport.*

Castine may have the edge over Blue Hill in charm, for its Main Street is not a major thoroughfare and it claims a more dramatic perch over its harbor, yet Blue Hill is certainly appealing and has a better selection of shops and galleries. Blue Hill, renowned for its pottery, has two good shops in town.

The Arts

Kneisel Hall Chamber Music Festival (⊠ Kneisel Hall, Rte. 15, ☎ 207/374–2811) has concerts on Sunday and Friday in summer. **Left Bank Bakery and Cafe** (⊠ Rte. 172, ☎ 207/374–2201) rates a gold star for bringing notable musical talent from all over the country to sleepy Blue Hill.

Dining and Lodging

$$–$$$ ✕ **The Firepond.** The Firepond attracts customers from all over the re-
★ gion. The upstairs dining room has the air of an English country house's library, with built-in bookshelves, antiques, and Oriental carpets; a street-level dining area increases the seating capacity to 120. The kitchen delivers old favorites like lobster Firepond—with three cheeses, served over pasta—and veal, pork, and scallop specialties. ⊠ *Main St.,* ☎ *207/374–9970. AE, MC, V. Closed Jan.–Apr.*

$$ ✕ **Jonathan's.** The downstairs room has captain's chairs, linen tablecloths, and local art; in the post-and-beam upstairs, there's wood everywhere, plus candles with hurricane globes and high-back chairs. The ever-changing menu may include pan-seared medallions of venison with sweet-potato pancakes and several fresh-fish entrées. The wine list has 200 selections from French and California vineyards as well as from the Bartlett Maine Estate Winery in Gouldshore. ⊠ *Main St.,* ☎ *207/374–5226. MC, V. Closed winter.*

$$$$ 🏠 **John Peters Inn.** The John Peters is unsurpassed for the privacy of
★ its location and the good taste in the decor of its guest rooms. The living room has two fireplaces, books and games, a baby grand piano, and Empire furniture. Oriental rugs are everywhere. Huge breakfasts in the light and airy dining rooms include the famous lobster omelet, served complete with lobster-claw shells as decoration. The Surry Room has a king-size bed, a fireplace, curly-maple chest, gilt mirror, and six windows. The large rooms in the carriage house, a stone's throw down the hill from the inn, have dining areas, cherry floors and woodwork, wicker and brass accents, and a modern feel. ⊠ *Peters Point, Box 916, 04614,* ☎ *207/374–2116. 7 rooms with bath and 1 suite in inn; 6 rooms with bath in carriage house. Pool, pond, boating. Full breakfast included. MC, V. Closed Nov.–Apr.*

Outdoor Activities and Sports

BOATING

The **Phoenix Centre** (⊠ Rte. 175, Blue Hill Falls, ☎ 207/374–2113) gives sea-kayaking tours of Blue Hill Bay and Eggemoggin Reach.

STATE PARK

Holbrook Island Sanctuary (⊠ Penobscot Bay, Brooksville, ☎ 207/326–4012) has a gravelly beach with a splendid view and hiking trails through meadow and forest; no camping facilities.

Shopping

Old Cove Antiques (⊠ Rte. 15, Sargentville, ☎ 207/359–2031) has folk art, quilts, hooked rugs, and folk carvings. **Leighton Gallery** (⊠ Parker Point Rd., ☎ 207/374–5001) shows oil paintings, lithographs, watercolors, and other contemporary art in the gallery, and sculpture in its garden. **Handworks Gallery** (⊠ Main St., ☎ 207/374–5613) carries unusual crafts, jewelry, and clothing. **North Country Textiles** (⊠ Main St., ☎ 207/374–2715) specializes in fine woven shawls, placemats, throws, baby blankets, and pillows in subtle patterns and color schemes.

Rackliffe Pottery (⊠ Rte. 172, ☎ 207/374–2297) is famous for its vivid blue pottery, including plates, tea and coffee sets, pitchers, casseroles, and canisters. **Rowantrees Pottery** (⊠ Union St., ☎ 207/374–5535) has an extensive selection of styles and patterns in dinnerware, tea sets, vases, and decorative items.

En Route   The scenic Route 15 south from Blue Hill passes through Brooksville and on to the graceful suspension bridge that crosses Eggemoggin Reach to Deer Isle. The turnout and picnic area at Caterpillar Hill, 1 mile south of the junction of routes 15 and 175, commands a fabulous view of Penobscot Bay, the hundreds of dark green islands, and the Camden Hills across the bay, which from this perspective look like a range of mountains dwarfed and faded by an immense distance—yet they are less than 25 miles away.

Deer Isle

③   *8 mi south of Blue Hill.*

Deer Isle has a mostly sparsely settled landscape of thick woods opening to tidal coves, shingled houses with lobster traps stacked in the yards, and dirt roads that lead to summer cottages.

Haystack Mountain School of Crafts attracts internationally renowned glassblowers, potters, sculptors, jewelers, blacksmiths, printmakers, and weavers to its summer institute. You can attend evening lectures or visit the studios of artisans at work (by appointment only). *⊠ South of Deer Isle Village on Rte. 15, turn left at Gulf gas station and follow signs for 6 mi,* ☎ *207/348–2306.* ⊡ *Free.* ☉ *June–Sept.*

Dining and Lodging

$$$$ ✕🏠 **Pilgrim's Inn.** The bright red, four-story, gambrel-roof house dat-
★   ing from about 1793 overlooks a mill pond and harbor in Deer Isle Village. The library has wing chairs and Oriental rugs; a downstairs taproom has a huge brick fireplace and pine furniture. A generous array of hors d'oeuvres is served before dinner each evening. Guest rooms have English fabrics and carefully selected antiques. The dining room is in the attached barn, an open space both rustic and elegant, with farm implements, French oil lamps, and tiny windows. The five-course, single-entrée menu changes nightly; it might include rack of lamb or fresh local seafood, scallop bisque, asparagus and smoked salmon, and poached pear tart for dessert. *⊠ Rte. 15A, 04627,* ☎ *207/348–6615. 13 rooms, 8 with bath, 1 seaside cottage. Restaurant (reservations essential, no lunch), bicycles. Full breakfast included; MAP available. MC, V. Closed mid-Oct.–mid-May.*

$$–$$$ ✕🏠 **Goose Cove Lodge.** The heavily wooded property at the end of a back road has a fine stretch of ocean frontage, a sandy beach, a long sandbar that leads to the Barred Island nature preserve, and nature trails. Cottages and suites are in either secluded woodlands or on the shore; some are attached, some have a single large room while others have one or two bedrooms. All but two units have fireplaces. The restaurant's prix-fixe four-course repast (always superb and always including at least one vegetarian entrée) is preceded by complimentary hors d'oeuvres. Friday night, there's a lobster feast on the inn's private beach. *⊠ Box 40, Sunset 04683,* ☎ *207/348–2508,* 𝖥𝖠𝖷 *207/348–2624. 11 cottages, 12 suites. Restaurant (reservations essential, no lunch), hiking, volleyball, beach, boating. MAP. MC, V. Closed mid-Oct.–mid-May. One wk minimum stay in July and Aug.*

Shopping

Old Deer Isle Parish House Antiques (⊠ Rte. 15, Deer Isle Village, ☎ 207/348–9964) is a place for poking around in the jumbles of old kitchenware, glassware, books, and linen. **Blue Heron Gallery & Studio** (⊠ Church St., Deer Isle Village, ☎ 207/348–6051) sells the work of the Haystack Mountain School of Crafts faculty. **Deer Isle Artists Association** (⊠ Rte. 15, Deer Isle Village, no phone) has group exhibits of prints, drawings, and sculpture from mid-June through Labor Day.

Stonington

32 *7 mi south of Deer Isle.*

Stonington is an emphatically ungentrified community that tolerates summer visitors but makes no effort to cater to them. Main Street has gift shops and galleries, but this is a working port town, and the principal activity is at the waterfront, where fishing boats arrive with the day's catch. The high, sloped island that rises beyond the archipelago of Merchants Row is Isle au Haut (accessible by mailboat from Stonington), which contains sections of Acadia National Park.

Lodging

$–$$ ☷ **Captain's Quarters Inn & Motel.** Accommodations, as plain and unadorned as Stonington itself, are in the middle of town, a two-minute walk from the Isle au Haut mailboat. You have your choice of motel-type rooms and suites or efficiencies, and you can take your breakfast muffins and coffee to the sunny deck overlooking the water. ⊠ *Main St., Box 69, 04681,* ☎ *207/367–2420 or 800/942–2420,* FAX *207/367–5165. 13 units with bath. AE, D, MC, V.*

Outdoor Activities and Sports

BOAT TRIPS

Palmer Day IV (☎ 207/367–2207) departs Stonington Harbor each day at 2 between July 1 and Labor Day for a two-hour excursion. Each Thursday morning, a special four-hour cruise stops at North Haven and Vinalhaven Islands.

Isle au Haut

33 *7 mi south of Stonington.*

Isle au Haut thrusts its steeply ridged back out of the sea south of Stonington. Accessible only by passenger mailboat (☎ 207/367–5193), the island is worth visiting for the ferry ride alone, a half-hour cruise amid the tiny, pink-shore islands of Merchants Row, where you may see terns, guillemots, and harbor seals. More than half the island is part of **Acadia National Park**: 17½ miles of trails extend through quiet spruce and birch woods, along cobble beaches and seaside cliffs, and over the spine of the central mountain ridge. From late June to mid-September, the mailboat docks at **Duck Harbor** within the park. The small campground here, with five Adirondack-type lean-tos (☉ Mid-May–mid-Oct.), fills up quickly; reservations are essential, and they can be made only after April 1 by writing to Acadia National Park (⊠ Box 177, Bar Harbor 04609).

Dining and Lodging

$$$–$$$$ ☷ **The Keeper's House.** This converted lighthouse-keeper's house, set on a rock ledge surrounded by thick spruce forest, has its own special flavor. There is no electricity, but every guest receives a flashlight at registration; guests dine by candlelight on seafood or chicken and read in the evening by kerosene lantern. Trails link the historic inn with Acadia National Park's Isle au Haut trail network, and you can walk to the village. The innkeepers are happy to pack lunches for anyone who wants to spend the day exploring the island. The five guest rooms are spacious, airy, and simply decorated with painted wood furniture and local crafts. A separate cottage, the Oil House, has no indoor plumbing. Access to the island is via the daily (except Sunday and holidays) mailboat from Stonington—a scenic, 40-minute trip. ⊠

Box 26, 04645, ☎ 207/367–2261. 5 rooms share bath, 1 cottage. Dock, bicycles. AP, BYOB. No credit cards. No Sun. check-in. Closed Nov.–Apr.

Penobscot Bay A to Z

Getting Around

BY CAR

Route 1 follows the west coast of Penobscot Bay, linking Rockland, Rockport, Camden, Belfast, and Searsport. On the east side of the bay, Route 175 (south from Rte. 1) takes you to Route 166A (for Castine) and Route 15 (for Blue Hill, Deer Isle, and Stonington). A car is essential for exploring the bay area.

Contacts and Resources

B&B RESERVATION AGENCY

Camden Accommodations, (⊠ 77 Elm St., Camden, ☎ 207/236–6090 or 800/236–1920, 𝔽𝔸𝕏 207/236–6091) provides assistance for reservations in and around Camden.

EMERGENCIES

Blue Hill Memorial Hospital (⊠ Water St., Blue Hill, ☎ 207/374–2836). **Island Medical Center** (⊠ Airport Rd., Stonington, ☎ 207/367–2311). **Penobscot Bay Medical Center** (⊠ Rte. 1, Rockport, ☎ 207/596–8000). **Waldo County General Hospital** (⊠ 56 Northport Ave., Belfast, ☎ 207/338–2500).

VISITOR INFORMATION

Belfast Area Chamber of Commerce (⊠ Box 58, Belfast 04915, ☎ 207/338–5900; information booth ⊠ 31 Front St., ☉ May–Oct., daily 10–6). **Blue Hill Chamber of Commerce** (⊠ Box 520, Blue Hill 04614, no phone). **Castine Town Office** (⊠ Emerson Hall, Court St., Castine 04421, ☎ 207/326–4502). **Rockland–Thomaston Area Chamber of Commerce** (⊠ Harbor Park, Box 508, Rockland 04841, ☎ 207/596–0376; ☉ Daily 8–5 in summer, weekdays 9–4 in winter). **Rockport-Camden-Lincolnville Chamber of Commerce** (⊠ Public Landing, Box 919, Camden 04843, ☎ 207/236–4404; ☉ Summer weekdays 9–5, Sat. 10–5, Sun. 12–4; winter weekdays 9–5, Sat. 10–4). **Searsport Chamber of Commerce** (⊠ East Main St., Searsport 04974, ☎ 207/548–6510).

BAR HARBOR AND ACADIA

East of Penobscot Bay, Acadia is the informal name for the area that includes Mount Desert Island (pronounced "dessert") and its surroundings: Blue Hill Bay; Frenchman Bay; and Ellsworth, Hancock, and other mainland towns. Mount Desert, 13 miles across, is Maine's largest island, and it harbors most of Acadia National Park, Maine's principal tourist attraction with more than 4 million visitors a year. The 40,000 acres of woods and mountains, lake and shore, footpaths, carriage roads, and hiking trails that make up the park extend to other islands and some of the mainland. Outside the park, on Mount Desert's east shore, Bar Harbor has become a busy tourist town. An upper-class resort town of the 19th century, Bar Harbor serves park visitors with a variety of inns, motels, and restaurants.

Numbers in the margin correspond to points of interest on the Acadia map.

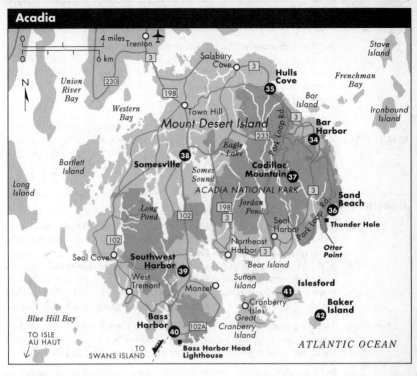

Acadia

Acadia

0 ___ 4 miles
0 ___ 6 km

N

Trenton

Union River Bay

Western Bay

Town Hill

Mount Desert Island

Bartlett Island

Long Island

Somesville

Somes Sound

Eagle Lake

Salsbury Cove

Hulls Cove ③⑤

Bar Island

Park Loop Rd.

Bar Harbor ③④

Stave Island

Frenchman Bay

Ironbound Island

Cadillac Mountain ③⑦

ACADIA NATIONAL PARK

Long Pond

Jordan Pond

Seal Harbor

Sand Beach ③⑥

Thunder Hole

Otter Point

Seal Cove

Southwest Harbor ③⑨

West Tremont

Manset

Bass Harbor ④⓪

Bass Harbor Head Lighthouse

Northeast Harbor

Bear Island

Sutton Island

Cranberry Isles

Great Cranberry Island

Islesford ④①

Baker Island ④②

ATLANTIC OCEAN

Blue Hill Bay

TO ISLE AU HAUT

TO SWANS ISLAND

Bar Harbor

③④ *160 mi northeast of Portland, 22 mi southeast of Ellsworth. Coastal Route 1 passes through Ellsworth, where Route 3 turns south to Mount Desert Island and takes you into Bar Harbor.*

Most of Bar Harbor's grand mansions were destroyed in a mammoth fire that devastated the island in 1947, but many of the surviving estates have been converted to attractive inns and restaurants. Motels abound, yet the town retains the beauty of a commanding location on Frenchman Bay. Shops, restaurants, and hotels are clustered along Main, Mt. Desert, and Cottage streets.

Bar Harbor Historical Society Museum, on the lower level of the Jesup Memorial Library, displays photographs of Bar Harbor from the days when it catered to the very rich. Other exhibits document the great fire of 1947. ✉ *34 Mt. Desert St.,* ☎ *207/288–4245.* ✎ *Free.* ☉ *Mid-June–mid-Oct., Mon.–Sat. 1–4 or by appointment.*

Acadia Zoo has pastures, streams, and woods that shelter about 40 species of wild and domestic animals, including reindeer, wolves, monkeys, and a moose. A barn has been converted to a rain-forest habitat for monkeys, birds, reptiles, and other Amazon creatures. ✉ *Rte. 3, Trenton, north of Bar Harbor,* ☎ *207/667–3244.* ✎ *$5.* ☉ *May–Nov., daily 9:30–dusk.*

Mount Desert Oceanarium has exhibits in three locations on the fishing and sea life of the Gulf of Maine, as well as hands-on exhibits such as a "touch tank." ✉ *Clark Point Rd., Southwest Harbor,* ☎ *207/244–7330;* ✉ *Rte. 3, Thomas Bay, Bar Harbor,* ☎ *207/288–5005;* ✉ *Lobster Hatchery at 1 Harbor Pl., Bar Harbor,* ☎ *207/288–2334. Call* *for admission fees (combination tickets available for all 3 sites).* ⊙ *Mid-May–mid-Oct., Mon.–Sat. 9–5; hatchery evenings July–Aug.*

Jackson Laboratory, a center for research in mammalian genetics, studies cancer, diabetes, heart disease, AIDS, muscular dystrophy, and other diseases. ✉ *Rte. 3, 3½ mi south of Bar Harbor,* ☎ *207/288–3371.* ⊙ *Free audiovisual presentations, mid-June–mid-Sept., Tues. and Thurs. at 3.*

OFF THE BEATEN PATH

BARTLETT MAINE ESTATE WINERY – Enjoy tours, tastings, and gift packs. Wines are produced from locally grown apples, pears, blueberries, and other fruit. ✉ *Rte. 1, Gouldsboro, north of Bar Harbor (via Ellsworth),* ☎ *207/546–2408.* ⊙ *June–mid-Oct., Tues.–Sat. 10–5, Sun. noon–5.*

Acadia National Park

③⑤ The **Hulls Cove** approach to Acadia National Park is 4 miles northwest of Bar Harbor on Route 3. Even though it is often clogged with traffic in summer, the **Park Loop Road** provides the best introduction to the park. At the start of the loop at Hulls Cove, the **visitor center** shows a free 15-minute orientation film. Also available at the center are books, maps of the hiking trails and carriage roads in the park, the schedule for naturalist-led tours, and cassettes for drive-it-yourself park tours.

En Route Traveling south on the Park Loop Road, you'll reach a small ticket booth where you pay the $5-per-vehicle entrance fee to Acadia National Park. Take the next left to the parking area for Sand Beach.

③⑥ **Sand Beach** is a small stretch of pink sand backed by the mountains of Acadia and the odd lump of rock known as The Beehive. The **Ocean Trail,** which parallels the Park Loop Road from Sand Beach to the Otter Point parking area, is a popular and easily accessible walk with some of the most spectacular scenery in Maine: huge slabs of pink granite heaped at the ocean's edge, ocean views unobstructed to the horizon, and **Thunder Hole,** a natural seaside cave into which the ocean rushes and roars.

③⑦ **Cadillac Mountain,** at 1,532 feet, is the highest point on the eastern seaboard. From the smooth, bald summit you have a 360-degree view of the ocean, islands, jagged coastline, and the woods and lakes of Acadia and its surroundings. You can drive, as well as hike, to the summit.

On completing the 27-mile Park Loop Road, you can continue your auto tour of the island by heading west on Route 233 for the villages on Somes Sound, a true fjord—the only one on the East Coast—which almost bisects Mount Desert Island. **Somesville,** the oldest settlement on the island (1621), is a carefully preserved New England village of white-clapboard houses and churches, neat green lawns, and bits of blue water visible behind them.

③⑨ Route 102 south from Somesville takes you to **Southwest Harbor,** which combines the rough, salty character of a working port with the refinements of a summer resort community. From the town's Main Street (Rte. 102), turn left onto Clark Point Road to reach the harbor.

NEED A BREAK?

At the end of Clark Point Road in Southwest Harbor, **Beal's Lobster Pier** serves lobsters, clams, and crab rolls in season at dockside picnic tables.

En Route From Southwest Harbor, continue south on Route 102, following Route 102A where the road forks and passing through the communities of Manset and Seawall on your way to Bass Harbor.

Bass Harbor

40 *4 mi south of Southwest Harbor.*

The Bass Harbor Head **lighthouse,** which clings to a cliff at the eastern entrance to Blue Hill Bay, was built in 1858. The tiny lobstering village of Bass Harbor has cottages for rent, inns, a restaurant, a gift shop, and the Maine State Ferry Service's car-and-passenger ferry to **Swans Island.** ☎ *207/244–3254. 5 daily runs June–Nov.; fewer trips rest of yr.*

Island Excursions

Off the southeast shore of Mount Desert Island at the entrance to Somes Sound, the five **Cranberry Isles**—Great Cranberry, Islesford (or Little Cranberry), Baker Island, Sutton Island, and Bear Island—escape the hubbub that engulfs Acadia National Park in summer. Great Cranberry and Islesford are served by the **Beal & Bunker passenger ferry** (☎ 207/244–3575) from Northeast Harbor and by **Cranberry Cove Boating Company** (☎ 207/244–5882) from Southwest Harbor. Baker Island is reached by the summer cruise boats of the **Islesford Ferry Company** (☎ 207/276–3717) from Northeast Harbor; Sutton and Bear islands are privately owned.

41 **Islesford** comes closest to having a village: a collection of houses, a church, a fishermen's co-op, a market, and a post office near the ferry dock. The **Islesford Historical Museum,** run by Acadia National Park, has displays of tools, documents relating to the island's history, and books and manuscripts of the writer Rachel Field (1894–1942), who summered on Sutton Island. ⊠ *Islesford Historical Museum,* ☎ *207/288–3338.* 🎫 *Free.* ☉ *Mid-June–Labor Day, Tues.–Sat. 10:30–noon, 12:30–4:30.*

42 The 123-acre **Baker Island,** the most remote of the group, looks almost black from a distance because of its thick spruce forest. The Islesford Ferry cruise boat from Northeast Harbor offers a 4½-hour narrated tour, during which you are likely to see ospreys nesting on a sea stack off Sutton Island, harbor seals basking on ledges, and cormorants flying low over the water. Because Baker Island has no natural harbor, the tour boat ties up off-shore, and you take a fishing dory to get to shore.

Dining, Lodging, and Camping

$$$ ✕ **The Porcupine Grill.** Named for a cluster of islets in Frenchman Bay, this two-story restaurant has earned culinary fame for its cornbread-stuffed pork chops, crabmeat terrine made with local goat cheese, salmon with citrus relish, fresh pastas, and a Caesar salad tossed with Reggiano Parmesan and fried shrimp. Soft green walls, antique furnishings, and Villeroy & Boch porcelain create an ambience that complements the cuisine. ⊠ *123 Cottage St., Bar Harbor,* ☎ *207/288–3884. AE, DC, MC, V. No lunch. Closed Mon.–Thurs. Jan.–June.*

$$–$$$ ✕ **George's.** Candles, flowers, and linens grace the tables of the four
★ small dining rooms in this old house. The menu shows a distinct Mediterranean influence in the phyllo-wrapped lobster; the lamb and wild game entrées are superb. ⊠ *7 Stephen's La., Bar Harbor,* ☎ *207/288–4505. AE, D, DC, MC, V. No lunch. Closed late Oct.–mid-June.*

$$ ✕ **Jordan Pond House.** Oversize popovers (with homemade strawberry jam) and tea are a century-old tradition at this rustic restaurant in the park, where in fine weather you can sit on the terrace or the lawn and admire the views of Jordan Pond and the mountains. Take tea or stay for a dinner of lobster stew, seafood thermidor, or fisherman's stew.

⌧ *Park Loop Rd., Bar Harbor,* ☎ *207/276–3316. Reservations essential. AE, D, MC, V. Closed late Oct.–May.*

$$$$ ✕⌧ **Claremont Hotel.** Built in 1884 and operated continuously as an inn, the Claremont calls up memories of long, leisurely vacations of days gone by. The yellow-clapboard structure commands a view of Somes Sound, croquet is played on the lawn, and cocktails and lunch are served at the Boat House in midsummer. The rooms in the main inn evoke a bygone era. There are also two guest houses on the property and 12 cottages, some with water views. These have not been updated as much as the rooms, and their facilities have garnered some complaint. The large, old-style dining room, open to the public for breakfast and dinner, is awash in light streaming through the picture windows. The menu changes weekly and always includes fresh fish and at least one vegetarian entrée. ⌧ *Off Clark Point Rd., Box 137, Southwest Harbor 04679,* ☎ *207/244–5036 or 800/244–5036,* ⛶ *207/244–3512. 24 rooms with bath, 12 cottages, 2 guest houses. Restaurant ($$, reservations essential, jacket required for dinner, no lunch), tennis court, croquet, dock, boating, bicycles. MAP. No credit cards. Hotel and restaurant closed mid-Oct.–mid-June. Cottages closed Nov.–late May.*

$$$–$$$$ ✕⌧ **Le Domaine.** This inn, on 100 acres 9 miles east of Ellsworth, has
★   seven rooms done in French country style, with chintz and wicker, simple desks, and window seats; five of them have balconies or porches over the gardens. The elegant but not intimidating dining room has polished wood floors; copper pots hanging from the mantel; and silver, crystal, and linen on the tables. A screened-in dining area overlooks the gardens in back. Owner Nicole Purslow, trained at Cordon Bleu in her native France, prepares such specialties as *lapin pruneaux* (rabbit in a rich brown sauce), sweetbreads with lemon and capers, and coquilles St. Jacques. ⌧ *Rte. 1, Box 496, Handcock 04640,* ☎ *207/422–3395, 207/422–3916, or 800/554–8498;* ⛶ *207/422–2316. 7 rooms with bath. Restaurant (no lunch), badminton, hiking, boating, fishing. MAP. AE, D, MC, V. Closed Nov.–mid-May.*

$$$$ ⌧ **Holbrook House.** Built in 1876 as a summer home, the lemon-yellow Holbrook House stands right on Mt. Desert Street, the main access route through Bar Harbor. The downstairs public rooms include a lovely, formal sitting room with bright, summery chintz on chairs and framing windows and a Duncan Phyfe sofa upholstered in white silk damask. The guest rooms and two separate cottages are all furnished with lovingly handled family pieces in the same refined taste as the public rooms. ⌧ *74 Mt. Desert St., Bar Harbor 04609,* ☎ *207/288–4970 or 800/695–1120. 10 rooms with bath in inn, 2 cottage suites with private patios and hammocks. Croquet. Full breakfast and afternoon refreshments included. MC, V. Closed late Oct.–May.*

$$$$ ⌧ **Inn at Canoe Point.** Seclusion and privacy are bywords of this snug,
★   100-year-old Tudor-style house on the water at Hulls Cove, 2 miles from Bar Harbor and ¼ mile from Acadia National Park's Hulls Cove Visitor Center. The Master Suite, a large room with a fireplace, is a favorite for its size and for its French doors, which open onto a waterside deck. The inn's large living room has huge windows on the water, a granite fireplace, and a waterfront deck where a full breakfast is served on summer mornings. ⌧ *Box 216, Rte. 3, Bar Harbor 04609,* ☎ *207/288–9511. 3 rooms with bath, 2 suites. Full breakfast included. No credit cards.*

$$$–$$$$ ⌧ **Cleftstone Manor.** Attention, lovers of Victoriana! This inn was made in high Victorian heaven expressly for you. Ignore the fact that it is set amid sterile motels just off Route 3, the road along which traffic roars into Bar Harbor. Inside this rambling brown house, a deeply plush mahogany-and-lace world awaits. The parlor is cool and richly furnished with red velvet and brocade-trim sofas with white doilies, grandfather and mantel clocks, and oil paintings hanging on powder-blue walls. Guest rooms are similarly ornate, and five rooms have fireplaces. ⊠ *Rte. 3, Eden St., Bar Harbor 04609,* ☎ *207/288–4951 or 800/962–9762. 14 rooms with bath, 2 suites. Full breakfast and afternoon and evening refreshments included. D, MC, V. Closed Nov.–late Apr.*

$$–$$$ 🏠 **The Island House.** This sweet B&B on the quiet side of the island has simply decorated bedrooms in the main house as well as a carriage house suite, complete with sleeping loft and kitchenette. Rate includes full breakfast. ⊠ *Box 1006, Southwest Harbor 04679,* ☎ *207/244–5180. 4 rooms share 3 baths, 1 suite. No credit cards.*

$$–$$$ 🏠 **Wonder View Inn.** Although the rooms here are standard motel accommodations, with two double beds and nondescript furniture, this establishment is distinguished by its extensive grounds, an imposing view of Frenchman Bay, and a convenient location opposite the Bluenose Ferry Terminal. The woods muffle the sounds of traffic on Route 3. The gazebo-shaped dining room—the Rinehart Dining Room—has picture windows overlooking the bay and is open to the public for breakfast and dinner. ⊠ *Rte. 3, Box 25, Bar Harbor 04609,* ☎ *207/288–3358 or 800/341–1553,* 🖷 *207/288–2005. 80 rooms with bath. Dining room, pool. AE, D, MC, V. Closed late Oct.–mid-May.*

$ ⛺ **Blackwoods and Seawall.** In Acadia National Park, **Blackwoods** (⊠ Rte. 3, Northeast Harbor, ☎ 800/365–2267), open year-round, and **Seawall** (⊠ Rte. 102A, Northeast Harbor, ☎ 207/244–3600), open late May to late September, fill up quickly during the summer season, even though they have a total of 530 campsites. Space at Seawall is allocated on a first-come, first-served basis, starting at 8 AM. Between mid-May and mid-October, reserve a Blackwoods site within eight weeks of a visit. No reservations are required off-season.

$ ⛺ **Lamoine State Park.** Off Mount Desert Island, but convenient to it, this campground is open mid-May–mid-October; the 55-acre park has a splendid front-row seat on Frenchman Bay. ⊠ *Rte. 84, Lamoine,* ☎ *207/667–4778.*

Nightlife and the Arts

NIGHTLIFE
Acadia has relatively little nighttime activity. A lively boating crowd frequents the lounge at the **Moorings Restaurant** (⊠ Shore Rd. Manset, ☎ 207/244–7070), which is accessible by boat and car, and stays open until after midnight from mid-May through October.

THE ARTS
Arcady Music Festival (☎ 207/288–3151) schedules concerts (primarily classical) at a number of locations around Mount Desert Island, as well as at selected off-island sites, from mid-July through August. **Bar Harbor Festival** (⊠ 59 Cottage St., Bar Harbor, ☎ 207/288–5744) programs recitals, jazz, chamber music, string-orchestra, and pops concerts by up-and-coming young professionals from mid-July to mid-August. **Pierre Monteux School for Conductors and Orchestra Musicians** (⊠ Rte. 1, Hancock, ☎ 207/422–3931) presents public concerts by faculty and students during the term (late June–late July). Symphonic concerts are Sunday at 5 and chamber-music concerts are Wednesday at 8—all held in the Pierre Monteux Memorial Hall.

Outdoor Activities and Sports

BIKING
The network of carriage roads that wind through the woods and fields of Acadia National Park is ideal for biking and jogging when the

ground is dry and for cross-country skiing in winter. The Hulls Cove Visitor Center has a carriage-road map.

Bikes can be rented at **Acadia Bike & Canoe** (⊠ 48 Cottage St., Bar Harbor, ☎ 207/288–9605), **Bar Harbor Bicycle Shop** (⊠ 141 Cottage St., ☎ 207/288–3886), and **Southwest Cycle** (⊠ Main St., Southwest Harbor, ☎ 207/244–5856).

BOATING

Harbor Boat Rentals (⊠ Harbor Pl., 1 West St., ☎ 207/288–3757) has 13- and 17-foot Boston whalers and other powerboats. **Manset Yacht Service** (⊠ Shore Rd., ☎ 207/244–4040) rents sailboats.

For canoe rentals and guided kayak tours, try **Acadia Bike & Canoe** (☞ Biking, *above*) or **National Park Canoe Rentals** (⊠ 137 Cottage St., Bar Harbor, ☎ 207/288–0342, or Pretty Marsh Rd., Somesville, at the head of Long Pond, ☎ 207/244–5854).

CARRIAGE RIDES

Wildwood Stables (⊠ Park Loop Rd., near Jordan Pond House, ☎ 207/276–3622) gives romantic tours in traditional horse-drawn carriages on the 51-mile network of carriage roads designed and built by philanthropist John D. Rockefeller, Jr. There are three two-hour trips and three one-hour trips daily, including a "tea-and-popover ride" that stops at Jordan Pond House (☞ Dining and Lodging, *above*) and a sunset ride to the summit of Day Mountain.

CRUISES

Acadian Whale Watcher (⊠ Golden Anchor Pier, West St., Bar Harbor, ☎ 207/288–9794 or 800/421–3307) runs 3½-hour whale-watching cruises June–mid-October. **Chippewa** (⊠ Bar Harbor Inn Pier, ☎ 207/288–4585 or 207/288–2373) is a 65-foot classic motor vessel that cruises past islands and lighthouses three times a day (including sunset) in summer. **Natalie Todd** (⊠ Bar Harbor Inn Pier, ☎ 207/288–4585 or 207/288–2373) offers two-hour cruises on a three-masted windjammer mid-May–mid-October. **Frenchman Bay Company** (⊠ Harbor Place, Bar Harbor, ☎ 207/288–3322 or 800/508–1499) operates the windjammer *Bay Lady,* the nature/sightseeing cruise vessel *Acadian,* and the 300-passenger *Whale Watcher* in summer.

Bass Harbor Cruises (⊠ Bass Harbor Ferry Dock, Bass Harbor, ☎ 207/244–5365) operates two-hour nature cruises (with an Acadia naturalist) twice daily in summer.

Blackjack (⊠ Town Dock, Northeast Harbor, ☎ 207/276–5043 or 207/288–3056), a 33-foot Friendship sloop, makes four trips daily, mid-June–mid-October.

HIKING

Acadia National Park maintains nearly 200 miles of foot and carriage paths, ranging from easy strolls along flatlands to rigorous climbs that involve ladders and handholds on rock faces. Among the more rewarding hikes are the Precipice Trail to Champlain Mountain, the Great Head Loop, the Gorham Mountain Trail, and the path around Eagle Lake. The Hulls Cove Visitor Center has trail guides and maps.

Shopping

Bar Harbor in summer is prime territory for browsing for gifts, T-shirts, and novelty items; for bargains, head for the outlets that line Route 3 in Ellsworth, which have good discounts on shoes, sportswear, cookware, and more.

Marianne Clark Fine Antiques (Main St., Southwest Harbor, ☎ 207/244–9247) has an eclectic array of formal and country furniture, American paintings, and accessories from the 18th and 19th centuries.

BOOKS
Port in a Storm Bookstore (✉ Main St., Somesville, ☎ 207/244–4114) is a book lover's nirvana on a rainy day (or even a sunny one) on Mount Desert Island.

CRAFTS
Acadia Shops (5 branches: ✉ 45 and 85 Main St., Bar Harbor; ✉ Inside the park at Cadillac Mountain summit; ✉ Thunder Hole on Ocean Dr.; ✉ Jordan Pond House on Park Loop Rd.) sell crafts and Maine foods and books. **Island Artisans** (✉ 99 Main St., Bar Harbor, ☎ 207/288–4214) is a crafts cooperative. **The Lone Moose–Fine Crafts** (✉ 78 West St., Bar Harbor, ☎ 207/288–4229) has ship models, art glass, and works in clay, pottery, wood, and fiberglass. The **Eclipse Gallery** (✉ 12 Mt. Desert St., Bar Harbor, ☎ 207/288–9048) carries hand-blown glass, ceramics, art photography, and wood furniture.

Bar Harbor and Acadia A to Z

Getting Around
BY CAR
North of Bar Harbor, the scenic 27-mile Park Loop Road takes leave of Route 3 to circle the eastern quarter of Mount Desert Island, with one-way traffic from Sieur de Monts Spring to Seal Harbor and two-way traffic between Seal Harbor and Hulls Cove. Route 102, which serves the western half of Mount Desert, is reached from Route 3 just after it crosses onto the island or from Route 233 west from Bar Harbor. All of these island roads pass in, out, and through the precincts of Acadia National Park.

Contacts and Resources
CAR RENTAL
Avis (✉ 99 Godfrey Blvd., Bangor International Airport, ☎ 207/947–8383 or 800/331–1212). **Budget** (✉ Hancock County Airport, ☎ 207667–1200 or 800/527–0700). **Hertz** (✉ 299 Godfrey Blvd., Bangor International Airport, ☎ 207/942–5519 or 800/654–3131). **Thrifty** (✉ 357 Odlin Rd., Bangor International Airport, ☎ 207/942–6400 or 800/367–2277).

EMERGENCIES
Mount Desert Island Hospital (✉ 10 Wayman La., Bar Harbor, ☎ 207/288–5081). **Maine Coast Memorial Hospital** (✉ 50 Union St., Ellsworth, ☎ 207/667–5311). **Southwest Harbor Medical Center** (✉ Herrick Rd., Southwest Harbor, ☎ 207/244–5513).

GUIDED TOURS
Acadia Taxi and Tours (☎ 207/288–4020) conducts half-day historic and scenic tours of the area.

National Park Tours (☎ 207/288–3327) operates a 2½-hour bus tour of Acadia National Park, narrated by a local naturalist. The bus departs twice daily, May–October, across from Testa's Restaurant at Bayside Landing on Main Street in Bar Harbor.

Acadia Air (☎ 207/667–5534), on Route 3 in Trenton, between Ellsworth and Bar Harbor at Hancock County Airport, offers aircraft rentals and seven different aerial sightseeing itineraries, from spring through fall.

VISITOR INFORMATION
Acadia National Park (✉ Box 177, Bar Harbor 04609, ☎ 207/288–3338; the **Hulls Cove Visitor Center,** off Rte. 3, at start of Park Loop Rd., ☉ May–June and Sept.–Oct., daily 8–4:30; July and Aug. until 6 PM). **Bar Harbor Chamber of Commerce** (✉ 93 Cottage St., Box 158, Bar Harbor 04609, ☎ 207/288–3393, 207/288–5103, or 800/288–5103; ☉ Summer weekdays 8–5, winter weekdays 8–4:30). There's also an information office in **Bluenose Ferry Terminal** (✉ Rte. 3, Eden St., ☉ July–early Oct., daily 8 AM–11 PM; mid-May–July and early Oct.–mid-Oct., daily 9–5).

WESTERN LAKES AND MOUNTAINS

Fewer than 20 miles northwest of Portland and the coast, the lakes and mountains of western Maine begin their stretch north along the New Hampshire border to Québec. In winter this is ski country; in summer the woods and waters draw vacationers to recreation or seclusion in areas less densely populated than much of Maine's coast.

The Sebago–Long Lake region has antiques stores and lake cruises on a 42-mile waterway. Kezar Lake, tucked away in a fold of the White Mountains, has long been a hideaway of the wealthy. Children's summer camps dot the region like fireflies on a warm summer's night. Bethel, in the Androscoggin River valley, is a classic New England town, its town common lined with historic homes. The far more rural Rangeley Lake area brings long stretches of pine, beech, spruce, and sky—and stylish inns and bed-and-breakfasts with easy access to golf, boating, fishing, and hiking.

Numbers in the margin correspond to points of interest on the Western Maine map.

Sebago Lake

㊺ *17 mi northwest of Portland.*

Sebago Lake, which provides all the drinking water for Greater Portland, is Maine's best-known lake after Moosehead. Many camps and year-round homes surround Sebago, resulting in its popularity for water sports. At the north end of the lake, the **Songo Lock** (☎ 207/693–6231), which permits the passage of watercraft from Sebago Lake to Long Lake, is the one surviving lock of the Cumberland and Oxford Canal. Built of wood and masonry, the original lock dates from 1830 and was expanded in 1911; today it sees heavy traffic in summer.

The 1,300-acre **Sebago Lake State Park** on the north shore of the lake provides opportunities for swimming, picnicking, camping with 250 campsites, boating, and fishing (salmon and togue). ☎ *207/693–6613, June 20–Labor Day; other times, 207/693–6231.*

OFF THE
BEATEN PATH

SABBATHDAY LAKE SHAKER MUSEUM – Established in the late 18th century, this is the last active Shaker community in the United States. Members continue to farm crops and herbs, and visitors are shown the meetinghouse of 1794—a paradigm of Shaker design—and the ministry shop with 14 rooms of Shaker furniture, folk art, tools, farm implements, and crafts of the 18th to early 20th centuries. There is a small gift shop on the premises but don't expect to find a selection of furniture and other large Shaker items for sale. On the busy road out front, a farmer usually has summer and fall vegetables for sale at the barn. In autumn, he sells cider and apples and pumpkins too. On Sunday, the Shaker day of prayer, the community is closed to visitors. ✉ *Rte. 26, New Glouces-*

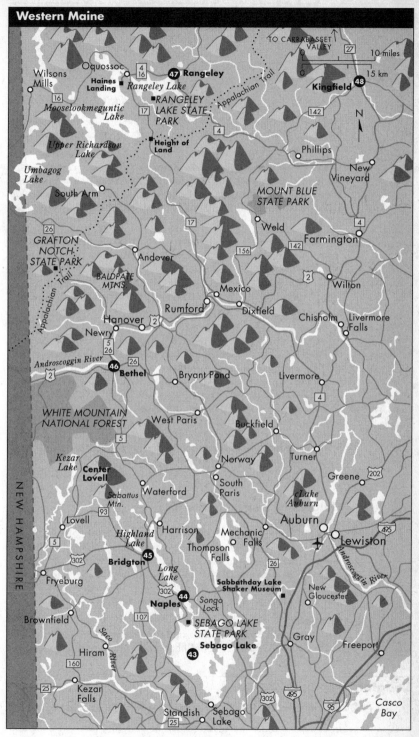

Western Maine

Wilsons
Mills

Oquossoc

Haines
Landing

4
16

47 **Rangeley**

Rangeley Lake

*Mooselookmeguntic
Lake*

17

RANGELEY
LAKE STATE
PARK

*Upper Richardson
Lake*

■ Height of
Land

*Umbagog
Lake*

South Arm

26

GRAFTON
NOTCH
STATE PARK

*BALDPATE
MTNS.*

Andover

TO CARRABASSET
VALLEY

27

10 miles

0

15 km

Kingfield **48**

N

142

Phillips

New
Vineyard

MOUNT BLUE
STATE PARK

Weld

142

4

Farmington

156

Appalachian Trail

4

Appalachian Trail

Hanover

Newry

5
26

Androscoggin River

2

26

46 **Bethel**

Mexico

Rumford

Dixfield

Chisholm

2

Wilton

Livermore
Falls

Bryant Pond

Livermore

4

WHITE MOUNTAIN
NATIONAL FOREST

West Paris

Buckfield

5

*Kezar
Lake*

Center
Lovell

*Sabattus
Mtn.*

93

Lovell

Norway

South
Paris

Turner

Greene

202

*cLake
Auburn*

5

*Highland
Lake*

Waterford

Harrison

Mechanic
Falls

Auburn

495

45

302

Bridgton

Fryeburg

*Long
Lake*

Thompson
Falls

26

Lewiston

Androscoggin River

Brownfield

302

44

Naples

107

*Songo
Lock*

Sabbathday Lake
Shaker Museum ■

New
Gloucester

Gray

Freeport

Saco River

Hiram

160

■ SEBAGO LAKE
STATE PARK

43

Sebago Lake

302

495

Casco
Bay

25

Kezar
Falls

Standish

25

Sebago
Lake

95

NEW HAMPSHIRE

ter (20 mi north of Portland, 12 mi east of Naples), ☎ 207/926–4597.
🎫 Tour $4, extended tour $5.50. ☉ Memorial Day–Columbus Day,
Mon.–Sat. 10–4:30.

Naples

④ *16 mi northwest of North Windham, 32 mi northwest of Portland.*

Naples is mostly a summer community that swells with seasonal residents and visitors and enjoys an enviable location between Long Lake
and Sebago Lake.

The **Naples Historical Society Museum** has a jailhouse, a bandstand, a
Dodge 1938 fire truck, a coach, and information about the Cumberland and Oxford Canal and the Sebago–Long Lake steamboats. ⊠ *Village Green, Rte. 302,* ☎ 207/693–6364. 🎫 *Free.* ☉ *July–Aug.; call
for hrs.*

🕭 **Songo River Queen II,** a 92-foot stern-wheeler, takes passengers on hour-long cruises on Long Lake and longer voyages down the Songo River
and through Songo Lock. ⊠ *Rte. 302, Naples Causeway,* ☎ 207/693–
6861. 🎫 *Songo River ride $9, Long Lake cruise $6.* ☉ *July–Labor
Day, 5 trips daily; June and Sept., weekends.*

Lodging

$$$–$$$$ 🏨 **Inn at Long Lake.** This three-story inn, built in 1900, is far enough
off the main road to ensure quiet, yet it is within walking distance of
the Naples Causeway for boating trips on Long Lake. The rooms, named
after barges, all have television and air-conditioning, and some have a
lake view. ⊠ *Lake House Rd., Box 806, 04055,* ☎ 207/693–6226 *or
800/437–0328. 14 rooms with bath, 2 suites. CP. AE, D, MC, V.*

$$–$$$ 🏨 **Augustus Bove House.** Built as the Hotel Naples in 1850, the brick
bed-and-breakfast at the crossroads of Routes 302 and 114 has lake
views from the front rooms and is convenient to shops. It has been restored to show off its gracious charm: Each wallpapered room is a different color and is furnished with antiques. ⊠ *R.R. 1, Box 501, 04055,*
☎ 207/693–6365. 11 rooms, 7 with bath. Full breakfast included. AE,
D, MC, V.

Outdoor Activities and Sports

WATER SPORTS

Route 302 cuts through Naples and in the center at the Naples Causeway are rental craft for fishing or cruising. Sebago, Long, and Rangeley lakes are popular areas for sailing and motorboating. For rentals,
try **Long Lake Marina** (⊠ Rte. 302, ☎ 207/693–3159), **Naples Marina** (⊠ Rtes. 302 and 114, ☎ 207/ 693–6254; motorboats only), or
Sun Sports Plus (⊠ Rte. 302, ☎ 207/693–3867).

Shopping

Cry of the Loon Shop Fine Gifts and Crafts Art Gallery (⊠ Rte. 302,
South Casco, ☎ 207/655–5060) has crafts, gifts, gourmet foods, and
two galleries.

Bridgton

⑤ *8 mi north of Naples, 16 mi east of Fryeburg, 30 mi south of Bethel.*

In and around the rather drab town of Bridgton, between Long and
Highland Lakes, are antiques shops, a museum, and the Shawnee Peak
ski resort.

The **Bridgton Historical Society Museum** is in a former fire station that
was built in 1902. On display are artifacts of the area's history and

materials on the local narrow-gauge railroad. ✉ *Gibbs Ave.,* ☎ *207/647–3699.* 🎫 *$2 admission.* ⊙ *July–Aug., Tues.–Fri. 10–4.*

Dining and Lodging

$–$$ ✕ **Black Horse Tavern.** In this Cape Cod cottage, more than 200 years old, is a country-style restaurant with a shiny bar, horse blankets and stirrups for decor, and an extensive menu of steak and seafood specialties. A predominantly young crowd dines here on pan-blackened swordfish or sirloin, scallop pie, and ribs. Starters include nachos, buffalo wings, and chicken and smoked-sausage gumbo. ✉ *8 Portland St.,* ☎ *207/647–5300. Reservations not accepted. D, MC, V.*

$$$$ ✕🏨 **Quisisana.** Music lovers will think they've found heaven on earth at this delightful resort on Kezar Lake about 14 miles northwest of Bridgton. After dinner, the staff, students and graduates of some of the finest music schools in the country, perform at the music hall—everything from Broadway revue to concert piano. White cottages have pine interiors and cheerful decor. One night you might have a typical New England dinner of clam chowder, lobster, and blueberry pie; the next night you might have a choice of saddle of lamb with a black olive tapenade or salmon and leek roulade with a roasted red pepper sauce. All meals and activities are included in the rates (except for a nominal fee for use of the motorboats). Most of the season, a one-week stay beginning Saturday is required. ✉ *Pleasant Point Rd., Center Lovell, 04016,* ☎ *207/925–3500,* 🖷 *207/925–1004 in season. 16 rooms with bath in 2 lodges, 38 cottages. Restaurant, 3 tennis courts, windsurfing, boating, waterskiing. MAP. Closed Sept.–mid-June.*

$$$ 🏨 **The Waterford Inne.** This gold-painted house on a hilltop provides a good home base for trips to local lakes, ski trails, and antiques shops. The bedrooms, each with its own theme in furnishings, have lots of nooks and crannies. Nicest are the Nantucket Room, with whale wallpaper and a harpoon, and the Chesapeake Room, with private porch and fireplace. A converted woodshed has five additional rooms, and though they have slightly less character than the inn rooms, four have the compensation of sunny decks. ✉ *Chadbourne Rd., Box 149, Waterford, 04088,* ☎ *207/583–4037. 9 rooms, 6 with bath; 1 suite. Badminton, ice-skating, cross-country skiing. Full breakfast included. AE. Closed Apr.*

$$–$$$ 🏨 **Noble House.** On a hill on a quiet tree-lined street overlooking Highland Lake and the White Mountains, this stately B&B with a wide porch dates from the turn of the century. The parlor is dominated by a grand piano and fireplace; in the dining room beyond, hearty breakfasts are served family-style on china and linen. The honeymoon suite, a single large room, has a lake view, a whirlpool bath, and white wicker furniture. ✉ *37 Highland Rd., Box 180, 04009,* ☎ *207/647–3733. 9 rooms, 6 with bath; 2 suites. Croquet, dock, boating. Full breakfast included. Reservations essential in winter. AE, MC, V.*

Outdoor Activities and Sports

CANOEING

Two scenic routes on the Saco River (near Fryeburg) are the gentle stretch from Swan's Falls to East Brownfield (19 mi) and from East Brownfield to Hiram (14 mi). For rentals, try **Canal Bridge Canoes** (✉ *Rte. 302, Fryeburg Village,* ☎ *207/935–2605)* or **Saco River Canoe and Kayak** (✉ *Rte. 5, Fryeburg,* ☎ *207/935–2369).*

Skiing

Shawnee Peak. On the New Hampshire border, Shawnee Peak draws many skiers from the North Conway, New Hampshire (18 mi), area and from Portland (45 mi). Management has set goals to maintain its popularity with families while upgrading facilities. ⌧ *Box 734, Rte. 302, Bridgton 04009,* ☎ *207/647–8444.*

DOWNHILL

Shawnee Peak has a 1,300-foot vertical, and perhaps the most night-skiing terrain in New England. Most trails are pleasant cruisers for intermediates, with some beginner slopes, and a few pitches suitable for advanced skiers. One triple and three double chairlifts service the 31 ski runs.

CHILD CARE

The area's nursery takes children from 6 months through 6 years. The SKIwee program is for children 4–6; those 7–12 also have a program. Children under 8 ski free when accompanied by a parent. The Youth Ski League has instruction for aspiring racers.

En Route   From Bridgton, the most scenic route to Bethel is along Route 302 west, across Moose Pond to Knight's Hill Road, turning north to Lovell and Route 5, which will take you on to Bethel. It's a drive that lets you admire the jagged crests of the White Mountains outlined against the sky to the west and the lush, rolling hills that alternate with brooding forests at roadside. At Center Lovell you can barely glimpse the secluded Kezar Lake to the west, the retreat of wealthy and very private people; Sabattus Mountain, which rises behind Center Lovell, has a public hiking trail and stupendous views of the Presidential range from the summit.

Bethel

46   *66 mi north of Portland, 22 mi east of Gorham, NH.*

Bethel is pure New England, a town with white-clapboard houses and white-steeple churches and a mountain vista at the end of every street. In winter this is ski country: Sunday River is in Bethel, and Ski Mt. Abram is nearby. Sunday River's warmer-months facilities include two tennis courts, a volleyball court, and a mountain bike park with lift-accessed trails.

A stroll in Bethel should begin at the **Moses Mason House and Museum,** a Federal home of 1813. On the town common, across from the sprawling Bethel Inn and Country Club, the Mason Museum has nine period rooms and a front hall and stairway wall decorated with murals by Rufus Porter. You can also pick up materials for a walking tour of Bethel Hill Village, most of which is on the National Register of Historic Places. ⌧ *14 Broad St.,* ☎ *207/824–2908.* ⌧ *$2.* ☉ *July–Labor Day, Tues.–Sun. 1–4; day after Labor Day–June, by appointment.*

The **architecture** of Bethel is something to behold. The **Major Gideon Hastings House** on Broad Street has a columned-front portico typical of the Greek Revival style. The severe white **West Parish Congregational Church** (1847), with its unadorned triangular pediment and steeple supported on open columns is on Church Street, around the common from the Major Gideon Hastings House.

The campus of **Gould Academy** (⌧ *Church St.,* ☎ *207/824–7700*), a preparatory school, opened its doors in 1835; the dominant style of the school buildings is Georgian, and the tall brick main campus building is surmounted by a white cupola.

Dining and Lodging

$$ ✕ **Mother's Restaurant.** This gingerbread house furnished with wood-stoves and bookshelves is a cozy place to enjoy the likes of Maine crab cakes, broiled trout, and a variety of pastas. There's outside dining in summer. ⊠ *Upper Main St.,* ☎ *207/824–2589. Reservations accepted only for large groups. MC, V. Closed Wed. in summer.*

$$–$$$ ✕🖼 **Bethel Inn and Country Club.** Bethel's grandest accommodation
★ is a full-service resort with extensive facilities, including 36 kilometers (22 miles) of cross-country skiing. Although not very large, guest rooms in the main inn, sparsely furnished with Colonial reproductions, are the most desirable: The choice rooms have fireplaces and face the mountains that rise over the golf course. All 40 two-bedroom condos on the fairway face the mountains; they are clean, even a bit sterile. A formal dining room, serves elaborate dinners of roast duck, prime rib, lobster, and swordfish. The MAP plan is a good value. ⊠ *Village Common, Box 49, 04217,* ☎ *207/824–2175 or 800/654–0125,* 🅵🅰🅷 *207/824–2233. 57 rooms with bath, 40 condo units. Restaurant, bar, pool, golf, tennis, health club, cross-country skiing, conference center. MAP available. AE, D, DC, MC, V.*

$$–$$$ ✕🖼 **Sudbury Inn.** The classic white-clapboard inn on Main Street offers good value, basic comfort, and a convenient location. The lobby's redbrick fireplace and pressed-tin ceiling are warm and welcoming and the dining room (upholstered booths and square wood tables) has a country charm; the dinner menu runs to prime rib, sirloin au poivre, broiled haddock, and lasagna. The pub, with a large-screen TV and a larger selection of microbrews, is a popular hangout. A huge country breakfast includes omelets, eggs Benedict, pancakes, and homemade granola. ⊠ *151 Main St., Box 369, 04217,* ☎ *207/824–2174 or 800/395–7837,* 🅵🅰🅷 *207/824–2329. 17 rooms with bath, 7 suites. Restaurant, pub. Full breakfast included. MC, V.*

$$–$$$ ✕🖼 **Summit Hotel and Conference Center.** This condominium hotel, an instant hit with Sunday River skiers, has 700 slope-side units, most with kitchenettes. An 800-seat ballroom and conference facilities give a great excuse to combine business and skiing for groups of 10–400. ⊠ *Box 450, 04217,* ☎ *207/824–3000 or 800/543–2754,* 🅵🅰🅷 *207/824–2111. 230 units with bath. Restaurant, pool, tennis, health club, baby-sitting, meeting rooms. AE, D, MC, V.*

$ ✕🖼 **Sunday River Inn.** On the Sunday River ski-area access road, this modern chalet has private rooms for families and dorm rooms (bring your sleeping bag) for groups and students, all within easy access of the slopes. Hearty meals are served buffet-style, and the comfy living room is dominated by a stone hearth. The inn operates a ski touring center. ⊠ *Sunday River Rd., R.F.D. 2 (Box 1688), 04217,* ☎ *207/824–2410,* 🅵🅰🅷 *207/824–3181. 16 rooms share baths, 2 rooms with bath, 5 dorms, 1 apartment chalet with 4 rooms. Hot tub, sauna, cross-country skiing. MAP. AE, MC, V. Closed Apr.–Thanksgiving.*

National Forest and State Park

White Mountain National Forest straddles New Hampshire and Maine. Although the highest peaks are on the New Hampshire side, the Maine section has magnificent rugged terrain, camping and picnic areas, and hiking opportunities from hour-long nature loops to a 5½-hour scramble up Speckled Mountain—with open vistas at the summit. ⊠ *Evans Notch Visitation Center, 18 Mayville Rd., 04217,* ☎ *207/824–2134.* ⊙ *Weekdays 8–4:30.*

Grafton Notch State Park (☎ 207/824–2912), on Route 26, 14 miles north of Bethel on the New Hampshire border, offers unsurpassed mountain scenery, picnic areas, gorges to explore, swimming holes, and camping. You can take an easy nature walk to Mother Walker Falls or Moose Cave and see the spectacular Screw Auger Falls; or you can hike to the summit of Old Speck Mountain, the state's third-highest peak. If you have the stamina and the equipment, you can pick up the Appalachian Trail here, hike over Saddleback Mountain, and continue on to Katahdin. The **Maine Appalachian Trail Club** (⊠ Box 283, Augusta 04330) publishes a map and trail guide.

Nightlife

At Sunday River, nightlife is spread out between the mountain and downtown Bethel. At the mountain, try **Bumps Pub** (☎ 207/824–3000) for après-ski and evening entertainment—Tuesday night is comedy night, ski movies are shown on Wednesday, and bands play weekends and holidays. **Sunday River Brewery** (☎ 207/824–4253) on Route 2 has pub fare and live entertainment—usually progressive rock bands—on weekends. The **Sudbury Inn** (☎ 207/824–2174) also is popular for après-ski and has music that tends toward the blues. For a quiet evening, head to the piano bar at the **Bethel Inn** (☎ 207/824–2175).

Outdoor Activities and Sports

DOG-SLEDDING

Mahoosuc Guide Service (⊠ Bear River Rd., Newry, ☎ 207/824–2073) leads day and multiday, fully-outfitted dog-sledding expeditions on the Maine–New Hampshire border.

Shopping

The Lyons' Den (⊠ Rte. 2, Hanover, near Bethel, ☎ 207/364–8634), a great barn of a place, carries glass, china, tools, prints, rugs, hand-wrought iron, and some furniture. **Bonnema Potters** (⊠ 146 Lower Main St., ☎ 207/824–2821) sells plates, lamps, tiles, and vases in colorful modern designs.

Skiing

Ski Mt. Abram. This ski area has a friendly, rustic Maine feeling and is known for its snow grooming, home-style cooking, and family atmosphere. Skiers here prefer its low-key, friendly attitude and wallet-friendly rates compared to the much bigger Sunday River, nearby. Many skiers choose to stay in reasonably priced condominiums on the mountain road. ⊠ *Rte. 26, Box 120, Locke Mills 04255,* ☎ *207/875–5003.*

DOWNHILL

The mountain reaches just over 1,000 vertical feet, the majority of its terrain intermediate, with fall-line steep runs and two areas for beginning and novice skiers. The area has two double chairlifts and three T-bars. In addition to learn-to-ski classes, there are regular improvement clinics for all ability levels and age groups. Management has a plan that includes 100-percent snowmaking coverage (80% is already covered), new lift capacity and base facilities. Already in place are a children's terrain garden, a half-pipe for snowboarders, a snowboard park, two expert trails, and expanded snowmaking.

CHILD CARE

The Ski Mt. Abram's Day Care Center takes children from 6 months through 6 years. The ski school offers class lessons on weekends and during vacation weeks to children 3–6 who are enrolled in the nursery. For juniors 6–16 there are individual classes plus a series of 10 two-hour lessons on weekends.

Sunday River. In the 1980s, Sunday River was a sleepy little ski area with minimal facilities. Today it is among the best managed, forward-looking ski areas in the East; in fact, expansion could be the resort's middle name. A ski train operates between Portland and Bethel in season. Spread throughout the valley are three base areas, a condominium hotel, trailside condominiums, town houses, and a ski dorm that provide the essentials. Sunday River is home to the Maine Handicapped

Skiing program, which provides lessons and services for skiers with disabilities. ✉ *Box 450, Bethel 04217,* ☎ *207/824–3000; snow conditions, 207/824–6400; reservations, 800/543–2754.*

DOWNHILL

White Heat has gained fame as the steepest, longest, widest lift-served trail in the East; but skiers of all abilities will find plenty of suitable terrain, from a 5-kilometer (3-mi) beginner run to newly cut glades. Oz is a peak with 70 acres of tree islands, cliffs, and rolls in the terrain flanked by glades. The area has 120 trails, the majority in the intermediate range. Expert and advanced runs are grouped from the peaks, and most beginner slopes are near the base of the area. Trails spreading down from eight peaks have a total vertical descent of 2,340 feet and are served by eight quads, five triples, and two double chairlifts.

OTHER ACTIVITIES

Within the housing complexes are indoor pools, outdoor heated pools, saunas, and hot tubs. Sunday River also has a snowboard park.

CHILD CARE

Sunday River operates two licensed day-care centers for children ages 6 weeks through 6 years. Coaching for children ages 3 to 18 is available in the Children's Center at the South Ridge base area.

En Route   The routes north from Bethel to the Rangeley district are all scenic, particularly in the autumn when the maples are aflame. In the town of Newry, make a short detour to the **Artist's Bridge** (turn off of Rte. 26 onto Sunday River Rd. and drive about 3 mi), the most painted and photographed of Maine's eight covered bridges. Route 26 continues on to **Grafton Notch State Park,** about 12 miles from Bethel. Here you can hike to stunning gorges and waterfalls and into the Baldpate Mountains. Past the park, Route 26 continues to Errol, New Hampshire, where Route 16 will return you east around the north shore of Mooselookmeguntic Lake, through Oquossoc, and into Rangeley. A more direct route (if marginally less scenic) from Bethel to Rangeley still allows a stop in Newry. Follow Route 2 north and east from Bethel to the twin towns of Rumford and Mexico, where Route 17 continues north to Oquossoc, about an hour's drive. When you've gone about 20 minutes beyond Rumford, the signs of civilization all but vanish and you pass through what seems like untouched territory; in fact, the lumber companies have long since tackled the virgin forests, and sporting camps and cottages are tucked away here and there. The high point of this route is **Height of Land,** about 30 miles north of Rumford, with its unforgettable views of range after range of mountains and the huge, island-studded blue mass of Mooselookmeguntic Lake directly below. Turnouts on both sides of the highway allow you to pull over for a long look. **Haines Landing** on Mooselookmeguntic Lake lies 7 miles west of Rangeley. Here you can stand at 1,400 feet above sea level and face the same magnificent scenery you admired at 2,400 feet from Height of Land on Route 17. Boat and canoe rentals are available at Mooselookmeguntic House.

Rangeley

47 *39 mi northwest of Farmington.*

Rangeley, north of Rangeley Lake on Route 4/16, has lured fisherfolk, hunters, and winter-sports enthusiasts for a century to its more than 40 lakes and ponds, and 450 square miles of woodlands. Rangeley has a rough, wilderness feel to it—indeed some of its best parts, including the choice lodgings, are tucked away in the woods, around the lake, and along the golf course.

On the south shore of Rangeley Lake, **Rangeley Lake State Park** (☎ 207/864–3858) has superb lakeside scenery, swimming, picnic tables, a boat ramp, showers, and camping.

OFF THE BEATEN PATH **SANDY RIVER & RANGELEY LAKES RAILROAD** – Ride a mile through the woods in a restored narrow-gauge railroad on a century-old train drawn by a replica of the Sandy River No. 4 locomotive. ✉ *Rte. 4, Phillips (20 mi southeast of Rangeley),* ☎ *207/639-3352.* *$3.* *May–Oct., 1st and 3rd Sun. each month; rides at 11, 1, and 3.*

The Arts

Rangeley Friends of the Arts (✉ Box 333, ☎ 207/864–5364) sponsors musical theater, fiddlers' contests, rock and jazz, classical, and other summer fare, mostly at Lakeside Park.

Dining, Lodging, and Camping

$–$$ ✕ **Oquossoc House.** Stuffed bears and bobcats keep you company as you dine on lobster, prime rib, filet mignon, or pork chops. The lunch menu promises chili, fish chowder, and lobster roll. ✉ *Rtes. 17 and 4, Oquossoc,* ☎ *207/864–3881. Reservations essential on summer weekends. No credit cards. Closed weekdays Nov.–mid-May.*

$$$$ ✕ **Country Club Inn.** This retreat, built in the 1920s on the Mingo Springs Golf Course, enjoys a secluded hilltop location and sweeping lake and mountain views. The inn's baronial living room has a cathedral ceiling, a fieldstone fireplace at each end, and game trophies. Guest rooms downstairs in the main building and in the motel-style wing added in the 1950s are cheerfully if minimally decorated with wood paneling or bright wallpaper. The glassed-in dining room—open to nonguests by reservation only—has linen-draped tables set well apart. The menu includes roast duck, veal, fresh fish, and filet mignon. ✉ *Box 680, Mingo Loop Rd., 04970,* ☎ *207/864–3831. 19 rooms with bath. Restaurant, pool. MAP. AE, MC, V. Closed Apr.–mid-May, mid-Oct.–Dec. 25.*

$$–$$$ ✕ **Rangeley Inn and Motor Lodge.** From Main Street you see only the massive, three-story, blue inn building (circa 1907), but behind it the newer motel wing commands Haley Pond, a lawn, and a garden. The traditional lobby and a smaller parlor have 12-foot ceilings, a jumble of rocking and easy chairs, and polished wood. The inn's sizable guest rooms have iron and brass beds and subdued wallpaper; some have clawfoot tubs while others have whirlpool tubs. Motel units contain Queen Anne reproduction furniture and velvet chairs. Gourmet meals are served in the spacious dining room with the Williamsburg brass chandeliers. ✉ *Main St., Box 160, 04970,* ☎ *207/864–3341 or 800/666–3687,* FAX *207/864–3634. 36 rooms with bath, 15 motel units with bath. Restaurant, bar, meeting room. MAP available. AE, D, MC, V. Closed Sun.-Wed. winters.*

$$$–$$$$ **Hunter Cove on Rangeley Lake.** These lakeside cabins, which sleep two to six people, offer all the comforts of home in a rustic setting. The interiors are unfinished knotty pine and include kitchens, screened porches, full baths, and comfortable, if plain, living rooms. Cabin No. 1 has a fieldstone fireplace and all others have wood-burning stoves for backup winter heat. Cabins No. 5 and No. 8 have hot tubs. Summer guests can take advantage of a sand swimming beach, boat rentals, and a nearby golf course. In winter, snowmobile right to your door or ski nearby (cross-country and downhill). ✉ *Mingo Loop Rd.,* ☎ *207/864–3383. 8 cabins with bath. Beach. AE.*

$–$$$ **Town & Lake Motel.** This complex of efficiencies, motel units, and cottages alongside the highway and on Rangeley Lake is just down the road from the shops and restaurants of downtown Rangeley. Two-bedroom cottages with well-equipped kitchens are farther from the highway, and some face Saddleback. Pets are welcome. ⊠ *Rte. 16, 04970,* ☎ *207/864–3755. 16 motel units with bath, 10 cottages. Boating. AE, MC, V.*

$ ⚠ **Rangeley Lake State Park.** This park has 50 campsites spread well apart in a spruce and fir grove on the south shore of the lake. They should be booked in advance, especially for peak summer dates. ⊠ *South shore of Rangeley Lake,* ☎ *207/864–3858.*

Outdoor Activities and Sports

BOATING

Rangeley and Mooselookmeguntic lakes are good for scenic canoeing, sailing, and motorboating. For rentals call **Mooselookmeguntic House** (⊠ Haines Landing, Oquossoc, ☎ 207/864–2962), **Rangeley Region Sport Shop** (⊠ Main St., ☎ 207/864–5615), or **Mountain View Cottages** (⊠ Rte. 17, Oquossoc, ☎ 207/864–3416).

FISHING

Freshwater fishing for brook trout and salmon is at its best in May, June, and September; the Rangeley area is especially popular with those who fly-fish. Nonresident freshwater anglers over the age of 12 must have a fishing license. The **Department of Inland Fisheries and Wildlife** (⊠ 284 State St., Augusta 04333, ☎ 207/287–2871) can provide further information.

If you'd like a fishing guide, try **Clayton (Cy) Eastlack** (⊠ Mountain View Cottages, Oquossoc, ☎ 207/864–3416) or **Grey Ghost Guide Service** (⊠ Box 24, Oquossoc, ☎ 207/864–5314).

SNOWMOBILING

This is a popular mode of winter transportation in the Rangeley area, with more than 100 miles of maintained trails linking lakes and towns to wilderness camps. **Maine Snowmobile Association** (⊠ Box 77, Augusta 04330) has information on Maine's nearly 8,000-mile Interconnecting Trail System.

Skiing

Saddleback Ski and Summer Lake Preserve. A down-home, laid-back atmosphere prevails at Saddleback, where the quiet and the absence of crowds, even on holiday weekends, draw return visitors—many of them families. The base area has the feeling of a small community for the guests at trailside homes and condominiums. With recent expansion and plans for more, Saddleback is becoming a major resort. ⊠ *Box 490, Rangeley 04970,* ☎ *207/864–5671; snow conditions, 207/864–3380; reservations, 207/864–5364.*

DOWNHILL

The expert terrain is short and concentrated at the top of the mountain; an upper lift makes the trails easily accessible. The middle of the mountain is mainly intermediate, with a few meandering easy trails; the beginner or novice slopes are toward the bottom. Two double chairlifts and three T-bars carry skiers to the 40 trails on the 1,830 feet of vertical.

CROSS-COUNTRY

Forty kilometers (25 mi) of groomed cross-country trails spread out from the base area and circle Saddleback Lake and several ponds and rivers.

CHILD CARE

The nursery takes children ages 6 weeks through 8 years. There are ski classes and programs for children of different levels and ages, through the teen years.

Kingfield

48 *33 mi east of Rangeley, 15 mi west of Phillips, 21 mi north of Farmington.*

In the shadows of Mt. Abraham and Sugarloaf Mountain, Kingfield has everything a "real" New England town should have: a general store, historic inns, and a white-clapboard church. Don't ignore Sugarloaf in summer: The resort has an 18-hole golf course and six tennis courts for public use in warmer months.

The **Stanley Museum** houses a collection of original Stanley Steamer cars built by the Stanley twins, Kingfield's most famous natives. ⌂ *School St.,* ☎ *207/265–2729.* 🎫 *$2.* ☉ *Tues.–Sun. 1–4. Closed Apr. and Nov.*

Dining and Lodging

$$–$$$$ ✕🏨 **Sugarloaf Inn Resort.** This lodge provides ski-on access to Sugarloaf/USA, a complete health club, and rooms that range from king-size on the fourth floor to dorm-style (bunk beds) on the ground floor. A greenhouse section of the Seasons restaurant affords views of the slopes and offers "ski-in" lunches. At breakfast the sunlight pours into the dining room, and at dinner you can watch the snow-grooming machines prepare your favorite run. Adult alpine and Nordic lessons are available. ⌂ *R.R. 1 (Box 5000), 04947,* ☎ *207/237–2000 or 800/843–5623,* 🖷 *207/237–3773. 37 rooms with bath, 4 dorm-style rooms. Restaurant, health club, meeting rooms. AE, MC, V.*

$$–$$$$ ✕🏨 **Sugarloaf Mountain Hotel.** This six-story brick structure at the base of the lifts on Sugarloaf combines a New England ambience with European-style service. Oak and redwood paneling in the main rooms is enhanced by contemporary furnishings. Valet parking, ski tuning, lockers, and mountain guides are available through the concierge. ⌂ *R.R. 1, Box 2299, Carrabassett Valley 04947,* ☎ *207/237–2222 or 800/527–9879,* 🖷 *207/237–2874. 100 rooms with bath, 26 suites. Restaurant, pub, hot tub, massage, sauna, spa. AE, D, DC, MC, V.*

$$$–$$$$ 🏨 **Inn on Winter's Hill.** This Georgian Revival mansion, which was designed in 1895, was the first home in Maine to have central heating. The mansion's four rooms are eclectically furnished, with pressed-tin ceilings and picture windows overlooking an apple orchard and the mountains beyond; the renovated barn's 16 rooms are simply and brightly furnished. The inn has a restaurant renowned for its New England dinners and its wine tastings. Try the beef Wellington or duck with blueberry-apple sauce, and the crêpes suzette for dessert. ⌂ *R.R. 1, Box 1272, 04947,* ☎ *207/265–5421 or 800/233–9687,* 🖷 *207/265–5424. 20 rooms with bath. Pool, tennis, hot tub, cross-country skiing. AE, D, DC, MC, V.*

$ 🏨 **Lumberjack Lodge.** Only a half mile from Sugarloaf's access road, this Tyrolean-style building contains eight efficiency units, each with living and dining area, kitchenette, full bath, and bedroom, but no phone or TV. Units sleep up to eight people. A free shuttle to the lifts operates during the peak season. ⌂ *Rte. 27, 04947,* ☎ *207/237–2141. 8 units. Sauna, recreation room. AE, MC, V.*

Nightlife

At Sugarloaf, nightlife is concentrated at the mountain's base village, with frequent entertainment in the base lodge at **Widowmaker's**

Lounge (☎ 207/237–6845). Also in the base lodge is **Gepetto's** (☎ 207/237–2953), a popular après-ski hangout that serves American-style food. Get there early to get a seat in the greenhouse, which overlooks the mountain. Monday night is blues night at the **Bag & Kettle** (☎ 207/237–2451), which is the best choice for pizza and burgers. A microbrewery on the access road called the **Sugarloaf Brewing Company** (☎ 207/237–2211) pulls in revellers who come for après-ski brews.

Outdoor Activities and Sports

DOG-SLEDDING

T.A.D. Dog Sled Services (✉ Rte. 27, Carrabassett Valley, ☎ 207/246–4461) offers short 1½-mile rides near Sugarloaf/USA. Sleds accommodate up to two adults and two children.

Skiing

Sugarloaf/USA. This is now a major ski resort, with two sizable hotels, a condominium complex, and a village cluster of shops, restaurants, and meeting facilities. Sugarloaf likes to refer to itself as the "Snowplace of the East" because of the abundance of natural snow it usually receives, plus its ability to manufacture 20 tons of snow per minute. S-K-I Inc. has acquired partial ownership of Sugarloaf, giving it the capital it needs to upgrade snowmaking even further, add new lifts, and expand terrain. ✉ *R.R. 1, Box 5000, Kingfield 04947,* ☎ *207/237–2000; snow conditions, 207/237–2000.*

DOWNHILL

With a vertical of 2,820 feet, Sugarloaf is taller than any other New England ski peak, except Killington in Vermont. The advanced terrain begins with the steep snowfields on top, wide open and treeless. Coming down the face of the mountain, there are black-diamond runs everywhere, often blending into easier terrain. A substantial number of intermediate trails can be found down the front face, and a couple more come off the summit. Easier runs are predominantly toward the bottom, with a few long, winding runs that twist and turn from higher elevations. Serving the resort's 116 trails are a high-speed quad, Maine's only gondola, two quads, one triple, eight double chairlifts, and one T-bar.

CROSS-COUNTRY

The Sugarloaf Ski Touring Center has 100 kilometers (62 miles) of cross-country trails that loop and wind through the valley. Trails connect to the resort.

OTHER ACTIVITIES

Snowboarders will find two snowboard parks and a half-pipe, the largest in the Northeast. The Sugarloaf Sports and Fitness Club (☎ 207/237–6946) has an indoor pool, six indoor and outdoor hot tubs, racquetball courts, full fitness and spa facilities, and a beauty salon. Use of club facilities is included in all lodging packages.

CHILD CARE

A nursery takes children from 6 weeks through 6 years. Once they reach 3, children are allowed to try ski equipment for free. A night nursery is open on Wednesday and Saturday, 6–10 PM by reservation. Instruction is provided on a half-day or full-day basis for ages 4–14. Nightly activities are free.

Western Lakes and Mountains A to Z

Getting Around

BY CAR

A car is essential to a tour of the western lakes and mountains. Of the variety of routes available, the itinerary in Exploring, above, takes Route 302 to Route 26 to Route 2 to Route 17 to Route 4/16 to Route 142.

BY PLANE

Mountain Air Service (⊠ Rangeley, ☎ 207/864–5307) provides air access to remote areas.

Contacts and Resources

CAMPING

The **Maine Campground Owners Association** (⊠ 655 Main St., Lewiston 04240, ☎ 207/782–5874) has a statewide listing of private campgrounds.

EMERGENCIES

Bethel Area Health Center (⊠ Railroad St., Bethel, ☎ 207/824–2193). **Rangeley Regional Health Center** (⊠ Main St., Rangeley, ☎ 207/864–3303).

GUIDED TOURS

Naples Flying Service (⊠ Naples Causeway, ☎ 207/693–6591) offers sightseeing flights over the lakes in summer.

RESERVATION SERVICES

Condominium lodging at Shawnee Peak is available through the **Bridgton Group** (☎ 207/647–2591). Bethel's **Chamber of Commerce** (☎ 207/824–3585 or 800/442–5826) has a reservations service.

VISITOR INFORMATION

Off-season, most chambers are open weekdays 9–5; the hours below are for summer only.

Bethel Area Chamber of Commerce (⊠ Box 439, Bethel, 04217, ☎ 207/824–2282; ☉ Mon.–Sat. 9–5). **Bridgton–Lakes Region Chamber of Commerce** (⊠ Box 236, Bridgton, 04009, ☎ 207/647–3472; ☉ July and Aug., daily 10–4). **Rangeley Lakes Region Chamber of Commerce** (⊠ Box 317, Rangeley, 04970, ☎ 207/864–5571; ☉ Mon.–Sat. 9–5, Sun. in July and Aug. 10–2).

THE NORTH WOODS

Maine's north woods, a vast area of the north central section of the state, is best experienced by canoe or raft, hiking trail, or on a fishing or hunting trip. The driving tour below takes in three great theaters for these activities—Moosehead Lake, Baxter State Park, and the Allagash Wilderness Waterway—as well as the summer resort town of Greenville, dramatically situated Rockwood, and the no-frills outposts that connect them. Here, exploring is an adventure. For much of what to see and do in this region consult Outdoor Activities and Sports; for outfitters, *see* Contacts and Resources.

Numbers in the margin correspond to points of interest on The North Woods map.

Rockwood

49 *180 mi north of Portland, 20 mi north of Greenville.*

Rockwood, on Moosehead Lake's western shore, is a good starting point for a wilderness trip or a family vacation on the lake. Moosehead Lake,

The North Woods

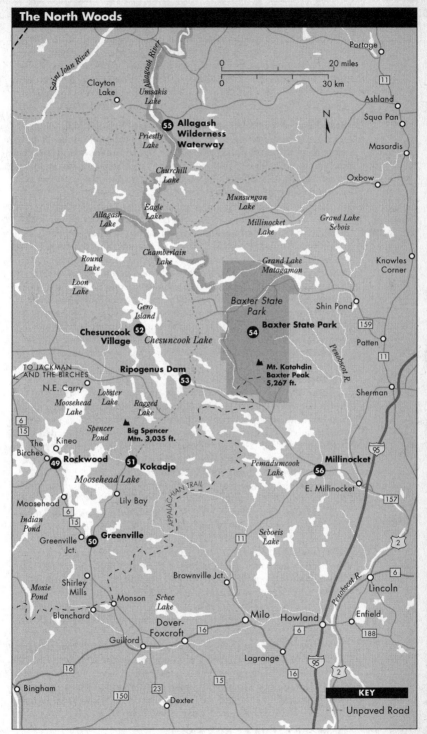

Portage

Saint John River

Allagash River

Clayton Lake

Umsakis Lake

0   20 miles

0   30 km

11

Ashland

55 **Allagash Wilderness Waterway**

Priestly Lake

Squa Pan

N

Masardis

Churchill Lake

Munsungan Lake

Oxbow

Eagle Lake

Allagash Lake

Millinocket Lake

Grand Lake Sebois

Knowles Corner

Round Lake

Chamberlain Lake

Grand Lake Matagamon

Loon Lake

Gero Island

Baxter State Park

Shin Pond

159

52 **Chesuncook Village**

Chesuncook Lake

54 **Baxter State Park**

Patten

Penobscot R.

11

TO JACKMAN AND THE BIRCHES

Ripogenus Dam

53

▲ Mt. Katahdin Baxter Peak 5,267 ft.

Sherman

N.E. Carry

Lobster Lake

Ragged Lake

6
15

Moosehead Lake

Spencer Pond

▲ Big Spencer Mtn. 3,035 ft.

95

The Birches

Kineo

49 **Rockwood**

51 **Kokadjo**

Pemadumcook Lake

56 **Millinocket**

Moosehead Lake

APPALACHIAN TRAIL

E. Millinocket

157

Moosehead

Lily Bay

6

Indian Pond

15

Seboeis Lake

2

Greenville Jct.

50 **Greenville**

11

Penobscot R.

6

Lincoln

Moxie Pond

Shirley Mills

Brownville Jct.

Enfield

Monson

Sebec Lake

Blanchard

Milo

Howland

188

Guilford

Dover-Foxcroft

16

6

95

Bingham

16

Lagrange

2

150

23

Dexter

15

16

KEY

– – Unpaved Road

Maine's largest, offers more in the way of rustic camps, restaurants, guides, and outfitters than any other northern locale. Its 420 miles of shorefront, three-quarters of which is owned by paper manufacturers, is virtually uninhabited. While not offering much in the way of amenities, Rockwood has the most striking location of any town on Moosehead: The dark mass of **Mt. Kineo,** a sheer cliff that rises 789 feet above the lake and 1789 feet above sea level, looms just across the narrows (you get an excellent view just north of town on Rte. 6/15).

East Outlet of the Kennebec River, a popular Class II and III whitewater run for canoeists and whitewater rafters is accessible about 10 miles from Rockwood on Route 6/15 south. You'll come to a bridge with a dam to the left. The outlet ends at the Harris Station Dam at Indian Pond, headwaters of the Kennebec. This is a scenic area to view even if you have no plans to raft.

OFF THE
BEATEN PATH

KINEO – Once a thriving summer resort, the original Mount Kineo Hotel (built in 1830 and torn down in the 1940s) was accessed primarily by steamship. Although an effort to renovate the remaining buildings in the early 1990s failed, Kineo makes a pleasant day trip from Rockwood. Visitors may rent a motor boat from Rockwood and make the trek across the lake in about 15 minutes. There's a small marina on the shore, in the shadow of Mt. Kineo, and a half dozen buildings dot the land—some are for sale and others are being restored, but there is no real town here. A tavern sells cold libations for in-house consumption or to take with you in case you plan to explore the mountain for the day. A walkway laces the perimeter of the mountain for less vigorous visitors.

Dining and Lodging

$$ ✕ **The Birches Resort.** This family-oriented resort offers the full north-country experience: Moosehead Lake, birch woods, log cabins, and boats for rent. The turn-of-the-century main lodge has four guest rooms, a lobby with trout pond, and a living room dominated by a fieldstone fireplace. There are 15 cottages that have wood-burning stoves or fireplaces and sleep from two to 15 people. The dining room overlooking the lake is open to the public for breakfast and dinner; the fare is pasta, seafood, and steak. ⊠ *Off Rte. 6/15, on Moosehead Lake, Box 41, 04478,* ☎ *207/534–7305 or 800/825–9453,* FAX *207/534–8835. 4 lodge rooms share bath, 15 cottages. Dining room (closed weekdays Nov.–Apr.), hot tub, sauna, boating. AE, D, MC, V.*

$$$$ **Attean Lake Lodge.** This lodge, about an hour west of Rockwood, has been owned and operated by the Holden family since 1900. The 18 log cabins (sleeping two to six) offer a secluded, island environment. A tastefully decorated central lodge has a library and games. ⊠ *Birch Island, Box 457, Jackman 04945,* ☎ *207/668–3792. 18 cabins with bath. Beach, boating, recreation room, library. AP. AE, MC, V. Closed Oct.–May.*

$–$$ **Rockwood Cottages.** These eight white cottages with blue trim, on Moosehead Lake off Route 15 and convenient to the center of Rockwood, are ideal for families. The cottages, which have screened porches and fully equipped kitchens, sleep two to seven. There is a one-week minimum stay in July and August. ⊠ *Rte. 15, Box 176, 04478,* ☎ *207/534–7725. 8 cottages. Sauna, dock, boating. D, MC, V.*

Outdoor Activities and Sports
BOATING
Mt. Kineo Cabins (⊠ Rte. 6/15, ☎ 207/534–7744) rents canoes and larger boats on Moosehead Lake for the trip to Kineo.

Rent a boat or take a shuttle operated by **Rockwood Cottages** (☎ 207/534–7725) or **Old Mill Campground** (☎ 207/534–7333) and hike one of the trails to the summit of Mt. Kineo for a picnic lunch and panoramic views of the region.

CRUISES
Jolly Roger's Moosehead Cruises (☎ 207/534–8827 or 207/534–8817) has scheduled scenic cruises, mid-May through mid-October, aboard the 48-foot *Socatean* from Rockwood. Reservations are advised for the 1½-hour moonlight cruise, which runs only eight evenings in summer. Charters are also available.

Greenville

50 *160 mi northeast of Portland, 75 mi northwest of Bangor.*

Greenville, the largest town on Moosehead Lake, has a smattering of shops, restaurants, and hotels. Greenville is home to the Squaw Mountain ski area, which, in summer, runs a recreation program for children midweek, and has two tennis courts, hiking, and lawn games.

Moosehead Marine Museum has exhibits on the local logging industry and the steamship era on Moosehead Lake, plus photographs of the Mount Kineo Hotel. ⊠ *Main St.,* ☎ *207/695–2716.* 🎫 *Free.* ☉ *Late May–early Oct., Tues.–Sun. 9–5.*

The Moosehead Marine Museum offers 2½-hour, six-hour, and full-day trips on Moosehead Lake aboard the *Katahdin,* a 1914 steamship (now diesel). The 115-foot *Katahdin* (fondly called the *Kate*), carried passengers to Kineo until 1942 and then was used in the local logging industry until 1975. ⊠ *Main St., (boarding is on the shoreline by the museum),* ☎ *207/695–2716.* 🎫 *$15–$22.* ☉ *Late May–Sept.*

Dining and Lodging

$ ✕ **Kelly's Landing.** This casual, family-oriented restaurant on the Moosehead shorefront has both indoor and outdoor seating, excellent views, and a dock for visiting boaters. The fare includes sandwiches, burgers, lasagna, seafood dinners, and prime rib. ⊠ *Rte. 6/15, Greenville Junction,* ☎ *207/695–4438. MC, V.*

$ ✕ **Road Kill Cafe.** The motto here is "Where the food used to speak for itself." It's not for everyone, but if you don't mind a menu with items such as the chicken that didn't make it across the road, Bye-Bye Bambi Burgers, Brake and Scrape sandwiches, and Mooseballs, this fun-loving spot is for you. The staff takes pride in its borderline-rude attitude, but it's all in fun. Tables on the rear deck have a view of the water. ⊠ *Rte. 15, Greenville Junction,* ☎ *207/695–2230. D, MC, V.*

$$–$$$ ✕🏠 **Greenville Inn.** Built more than a century ago as the retreat of a wealthy lumbering family, this rambling blue, gray, and white structure is a block from town, on a rise over Moosehead Lake. The ornate cherry and mahogany paneling, Oriental rugs, and leaded glass create an aura of masculine ease. Cottages have mountain and lake views, and some have decks overlooking the lake. Two of the dining rooms have water views; a third dining room, with dark-wood paneling, has a subdued, gentlemanly air. The menu, revised daily, reflects the owners' Austrian background: shrimp with mustard dill sauce, salmon marinated in olive oil and basil, veal cutlet with mushroom cream sauce; popovers accompany the meal. ⊠ *Norris St., Box 1194, 04441,* ☎ *207/695–2206. 6 rooms, 4 with bath; 1 suite in carriage house; 6 cottages. Restaurant (reservations essential; no lunch). Full breakfast included. D, MC, V. Closed Nov. and Apr.*

$$$$ 🏨 **Lodge at Moosehead Lake.** This mansion overlooking Moosehead
★   Lake is about as close to luxury as it gets in the north woods. All rooms
have whirlpool baths, fireplaces, and hand-carved four-poster beds; most
have lake views. The restaurant, where breakfast is served year-round
and dinner is served in the off-season, has a spectacular view of the
lake. ⊠ *Lily Bay Rd., 04441,* ☎ *207/695–4400,* 🅵🅰🆇 *207/695–2281.
5 rooms with bath. Restaurant, bar, hot tub. D, MC, V.*

$$ 🏨 **Chalet Moosehead.** Just 50 yards off Route 6/15, the efficiencies—
which have two double beds, a living room with sofabed, and a kitch-
enette—motel room, and cabin are right on Moosehead Lake and
have picture windows to capture the view. The attractive grounds lead
to a private beach and dock. ⊠ *Rte. 6/15, Box 327, Greenville Junc-
tion 04442,* ☎ *207/695–2950 or 800/290–3645. 8 efficiencies, 7
motel rooms with bath, 1 cabin with bath. Horseshoes, beach, dock,
boating. AE, D, MC, V.*

$–$$ 🏨 **Sawyer House Bed & Breakfast.** The convenient in-town location
across the street from the lake makes it easy to tour Greenville on foot
from this comfortable B&B. The two upstairs rooms are on the small-
ish side, but the room on the first floor is huge. Guests have use of a
family room with television, where a full breakfast is served. ⊠ *Lake-
view St., Box 521, 04441,* ☎ *207/695–2369,* 🅵🅰🆇 *207/695–3087. 3
rooms with bath. D, MC, V.*

$ 🏨 **Squaw Mountain Resort.** From the door of the resort you can ski
to the slopes and to cross-country trails. The motel-style units and dorm
rooms have picture windows opening onto the woods or the slopes,
and Katahdin and Moosehead Lake (6 miles away) can be seen from
the lawn. The restaurant serves hearty family meals, and there's usually entertainment on the weekends. ⊠ *Rte. 15, 04441,* ☎ *207/695–
1000. 58 rooms with bath. Restaurant, cafeteria, tennis courts, ski shop,
playground. AE, MC, V.*

$ ⛺ **Lily Bay State Park.** This state park, 8 miles northeast of Greenville,
has a wooded, 93-site campground with a good swimming beach and
two boat-launching ramps. ⊠ *Lily Bay Rd.,* ☎ *207/695–2700.*

Outdoor Activities and Sports

FISHING

Togue, landlocked salmon, and brook and lake trout lure thousands of
fisherfolk to the region from ice-out in mid-May through September;
the hardiest return between January 1 and March 30 for the ice fishing. For up-to-date information on water levels, call 207/695–3756.

RAFTING

The Kennebec and Dead rivers, and the West Branch of the Penobscot
River, offer thrilling white-water rafting (guides strongly recommended).
These rivers are dam-controlled also, so trips run rain or shine daily
from May through October (day trips and multi-day trips are offered).
Most guided raft trips on the Kennebec and Dead rivers leave from
The Forks, southwest of Moosehead Lake, on Route 201; Penobscot
River trips leave from either Greenville or Millinocket. Many rafting
outfitters offer resort facilities in their base towns.

Shopping

The Corner Shop (⊠ Rte. 6/15, ☎ 207/695–2142) has a selection of
books, gifts, and crafts. **Sunbower Pottery** (⊠ Scammon Rd., ☎
207/695–2870) has local art and pottery, specializing in moose mugs.
Indian Hill Trading Post (⊠ Rte. 6/15, ☎ 207/695–2104) stocks just
about anything you might possibly need for a north woods vacation,
including sporting and camping equipment, canoes, casual clothing, shoes,
hunting and fishing licenses; there's even an adjacent grocery store.

Skiing

Big Squaw Mountain Resort. Remote but pretty, this resort has stumbled along in recent years, with frequent changes in management. It appears to be stabilizing, though, and this should bode well for skiers. It is best to call for up-to-date information before visiting. A hotel at the base of the mountain, integrated into the main base lodge, has a restaurant, bar, and other services. ⊠ *Box D, Greenville 04441,* ☎ *207/695–1000.*

DOWNHILL

Trails are laid out according to difficulty, with the easy slopes toward the bottom, intermediate trails weaving from midpoint, and steeper runs high up off the 1,750-vertical-foot peak. The 22 trails are served by one triple and one double chairlift and one surface lift.

CHILD CARE

The nursery takes children from infants through age 6. The ski school has daily lessons and racing classes for children of all ages.

Kokadjo

⑤ *22 mi northeast of Greenville.*

Northeast of Greenville lies the outpost of Kokadjo, population "not many." Kokadjo is easily recognizable by the sign: KEEP MAINE GREEN. THIS IS GOD'S COUNTRY. WHY SET IT ON FIRE AND MAKE IT LOOK LIKE HELL?

En Route As you leave Kokadjo, bear left at the fork and follow signs to Baxter State Park. Five miles along this road (now dirt) brings you to the Bowater/Great Northern Paper Company's Sias Hill checkpoint, where June–November you'll sign in and pay a user fee ($8 per car for non-residents, valid for 24 hours) to travel the next 40 miles of this road. Access is through a working forest where you're likely to encounter logging trucks (yield right of way), logging equipment, and work in progress. At the bottom of the hill after you pass the checkpoint, look to your right—there's a good chance you'll spot a moose.

Chesuncook Village

⑤ *25 min north by float plane from Kokadjo.*

Chesuncook Lake lies at the end of the logging road on your left. Chesuncook Village, at its far end, is accessible only by boat or seaplane in summer. This tiny wilderness settlement has a church (open in summer), a few houses, a small store, and a spectacularly remote setting (it's home to two sporting camps).

Lodging

$$ 🏠 **Chesuncook Lake House.** Guests can gain access to this lodge only by boat or floatplane, or in winter, they can drive to within 3 miles and come in by snowmobile or cross-country skis. Chesuncook Lake House, listed on the National Register as a historical site, has been an oasis of civilization in otherwise rugged wilderness since 1864. French-born Maggie McBurnie, who operates the sporting camp with her husband, Bert, cooks all the meals—solid New England fare with a French touch. ⊠ *Rte. 76, Box 656, 04441,* ☎ *207/745–5330 or 207/695–2821, for Folsom's Air Service. 4 rooms in main house share 2 baths; 3 housekeeping cottages. MAP for rooms in main house. Boating. No credit cards.* ⊙ *Year-round.*

Ripogenus Dam

53 *20 mi northeast of Kokadjo, 25 min southeast of Chesuncook Village by float plane.*

Ripogenus Dam and the granite-walled Ripogenus Gorge are on Ripogenus Lake, east of Chesuncook Lake. The gorge is the jumping-off point for the famous 12-mile West Branch of the Penobscot River whitewater rafting trip and the most popular put-in point for Allagash canoe trips. The Penobscot River drops more than 70 feet per mile through the gorge, giving rafters a hold-on-for-your-life ride. The best spot to watch the Penobscot rafters is from Pray's Big Eddy Wilderness Campground, overlooking the rock-choked **Crib Works rapid** (a Class V rapid). To get here, follow the main road northeast and turn left on Telos Road; the campground is about 10 yards after the bridge.

En Route From the Pray's Big Eddy Wilderness Campground, take the main road (here called the Golden Road for the amount of money it took the Great Northern Paper Company to build it) southeast toward Millinocket. The road soon becomes paved. After you drive over the one-lane Abol Bridge and pass through the Bowater/Great Northern Paper Company's Debsconeag checkpoint, bear left to reach Togue Pond Gatehouse, the southern entrance to Baxter State Park.

Baxter State Park

54 *24 mi northwest of Millinocket.*

Few places in Maine are as remote, or as beautiful some will say, as Baxter State Park and the Allagash. Baxter State Park (☎ 207/723–5140), a gift from Governor Percival Baxter, is the jewel in the crown of northern Maine, a 201,018-acre wilderness area that surrounds **Katahdin,** Maine's highest mountain (5,267 feet at Baxter Peak) and the terminus of the Appalachian Trail.

OFF THE BEATEN PATH   **LUMBERMAN'S MUSEUM –** This museum comprises 10 buildings filled with exhibits depicting the history of logging, including models, dioramas, and equipment. ⊠ *Shin Pond Rd. (Rte. 159), Patten (22 mi southeast of Baxter State Park),* ☎ *207/528-2650.* 🎟 *$2.50.* ☽ *Memorial Day–Sept., Tues.–Sat. 9–4, Sun. 11–4.*

Camping

⚠ **Baxter State Park.** This park is open for camping from May 15 to October 15, and it's important that you reserve in advance by mail (phone reservations not accepted) if you plan to camp here. Reservations can be made beginning January 1, and some sites are fully booked for midsummer weekends soon after that. The state also maintains primitive backcountry sites that are available without charge on a first-come, first-served basis. ⊠ *Baxter State Park Authority, 64 Balsam Dr., Millinocket 04462.*

Outdoor Activities and Sports

HIKING

Katahdin, in Baxter State Park, draws thousands of hikers every year for the daylong climb to the summit and the stunning views of woods, mountains, and lakes from the hair-raising Knife Edge Trail along its ridge. Since the crowds can be formidable on clear summer days, those who seek greater solitude might choose instead to tackle one of the 45 other mountains in the park, all accessible from a 150-mile trail network. South Turner can be climbed in a morning (if you're fit), and it affords a great view of Katahdin across the valley. On the way you'll pass Sandy Stream Pond, where moose are often seen at dusk. The Owl, the Brothers, and Doubletop Mountain are good day hikes.

The Allagash Wilderness Waterway

55 *22 mi north of Ripogenus Dam.*

The Allagash is a 92-mile corridor of lakes and rivers that cuts across 170,000 acres of wilderness, beginning at the northwest corner of Baxter and running north to the town of Allagash, 10 miles from the Canadian border.

Outdoor Activities and Sports

CANOEING

The Allagash rapids are ranked Class I and Class II (very easy and easy), but that doesn't mean the river is a piece of cake; river conditions vary greatly with the depth and volume of water, and even a class I rapid can hang your canoe up on a rock, capsize you, or spin you around. On the lakes, strong winds can halt your progress for days. The Allagash should not be undertaken lightly or without advance planning; the complete 92-mile course requires seven to 10 days. The canoeing season along the Allagash is mid-May through October, although it's wise to remember that the black-fly season ends about July 1. The best bet for a novice is to go with a guide; a good outfitter will help plan your route and provide your craft and transportation.

The Mount Everest of Maine canoe trips is the 110-mile route on the St. John River from Baker Lake to Allagash Village, with a swift current all the way and two stretches of Class III rapids. Best time to canoe the St. John is between mid-May and mid-June, when the river level is high.

Those with their own canoe who want to go it alone can take Telos Road north from Ripogenus Dam, putting in at Chamberlain Thoroughfare Bridge at the southern tip of Chamberlain Lake, or at Allagash Lake, Churchill Dam, Bissonnette Bridge, or Umsaskis Bridge. One popular and easy route follows the Upper West Branch of the Penobscot River from Lobster Lake (just east of Moosehead Lake) to Chesuncook Lake. From Chesuncook Village you can paddle to Ripogenus Dam in a day.

The Aroostook River from Little Munsungan Lake to Fort Fairfield (100 mi) is best run in late spring. More challenging routes include the Passadumkeag River from Grand Falls to Passadumkeag (25 mi with Class I–III rapids); the East Branch of the Penobscot River from Matagamon Wilderness Campground to Grindstone (38 mi with Class I–III rapids); and the West Branch of the Pleasant River from Katahdin Iron Works to Brownville Junction (10 mi with Class II–III rapids).

Millinocket

56 *90 mi northwest of Greenville, 19 mi southeast of Baxter State Park.*

Millinocket, with a population of 7,000, is a gateway to Baxter State Park.

OFF THE
BEATEN PATH

KATAHDIN IRON WORKS – For a worthwhile day trip from Millinocket, take Route 11 west to a trailhead just north of Brownville Junction. Follow the trail to Katahdin Iron Works, the site of a once-flourishing mining operation that employed nearly 200 workers in the mid-1800s; a deteriorated kiln, a stone furnace, and a charcoal-storage building are all that remain. The trail continues over fairly rugged terrain into **Gulf Hagas,** the

Grand Canyon of the east, with natural chasms, cliffs, a 3-mile gorge, waterfalls, pools, exotic flora, and natural rock formations.

Dining and Lodging

$–$$ ✕ **Scootic Inn and Penobscot Room.** This informal restaurant and lounge offers lunches and dinners daily, with a varied menu of steak, seafood, pizza, and sandwiches. A large-screen TV is usually tuned to sports. ⊠ *70 Penobscot Ave.,* ☎ *207/723–4566. AE, D, MC, V.*

$$ 🏨 **Atrium Motel.** Off Route 157 next to a shopping center, this motor inn has a large central atrium with facilities that make up for its unappealing location and standard motel furnishings. ⊠ *740 Central Ave., 04462,* ☎ FAX *207/723–4555. 72 rooms with bath, 10 suites. Indoor pool, hot tub, health club. CP. AE, D, DC, MC, V.*

North Woods A to Z

Getting Around

BY CAR

A car is essential to negotiate this vast region but may not be useful to someone spending a vacation entirely at a wilderness camp. While public roads are scarce in the north country, lumber companies maintain private roads that are often open to the public (sometimes by permit only). When driving on a logging road, always give lumber company trucks the right of way. Be aware that loggers often take the middle of the road and will neither move over nor slow down for you.

BY PLANE

Charter flights, usually by seaplane, from Bangor, Greenville, or Millinocket to smaller towns and remote lake and forest areas can be arranged with flying services, which will transport you and your gear and help you find a guide: **Currier's Flying Service** (⊠ Greenville Junction, ☎ 207/695–2778), **Folsom's Air Service** (⊠ Greenville, ☎ 207/695–2821), **Jack's Air Service** (⊠ Greenville, ☎ 207/695–3020), **Katahdin Air Service** (⊠ Millinocket, ☎ 207/723–8378), **Scotty's Flying Service** (⊠ Shin Pond, ☎ 207/528–2626).

Contacts and Resources

CAMPING

Reservations for state park campsites (excluding Baxter State Park) can be made from January until August 23 through the **Bureau of Parks and Lands** (☎ 207/287–3824 or 800/332–1501 in ME). Make reservations as far ahead as possible (at least 7 days in advance), because sites go quickly. **Maine Sporting Camp Association** (⊠ Box 89, Jay 04239, no phone) publishes a list of its members, with details on the facilities available at each camp.

Camping and fire permits are required for many areas outside of state parks. The **Bureau of Parks and Lands** (⊠ State House Station 22, Augusta 04333, ☎ 207/287–3821) will tell you if you need a camping permit and where to obtain one. The **Maine Forest Service, Department of Conservation** (⊠ State House Station 22, Augusta 04333, ☎ 207/287–2791) will direct you to the nearest ranger station, where you can get a fire permit (Greenville Ranger Station: ☎ 207/695–3721). **North Maine Woods** (⊠ Box 421, Ashland 04732, ☎ 207/435–6213) maintains 500 primitive campsites on commercial forest land and takes reservations for 20 of them; early reservations are recommended. **Maine Publicity Bureau** (⊠ 325B Water St., Box 2300, Hallowell 04347, ☎ 207/623–0363 or, outside ME, 800/533–9595) publishes a listing of private campsites and cottage rentals. The **Maine Campground Owners Association (MECOA)** (⊠ 655 Main St., Lewiston

04240, ☎ 207/782–5874) publishes a helpful annual directory of its members; a dozen are located in the Katahdin/Moosehead area, and 20 are in the Kennebec and Moose River Valleys.

Most canoe rental operations will arrange transportation, help plan your route, and provide a guide. Transport to wilderness lakes can be arranged through the flying services listed under Getting Around the North Woods by Plane, *above*.

The **Bureau of Parks and Lands** (✉ State House Station 22, Augusta 04333, ☎ 207/287–3821) has a list of outfitters that arrange Allagash trips and also provides information on independent Allagash canoeing and camping. We list some outfitters below.

Allagash Canoe Trips (✉ Box 713, Greenville 04441, ☎ 207/695–3668) offers guided trips on the Allagash Waterway, plus the Moose, Penobscot, and St. John rivers. **Allagash Wilderness Outfitters/Frost Pond Camps** (✉ Box 620, Greenville 04441, ☎ 207/695–2821) provides equipment, transportation, and information for canoe trips on the Allagash and the Penobscot rivers. **Mahoosuc Guide Service** (✉ Bear River Rd., Newry 04261, ☎ 207/824–2073) offers guided trips on the Penobscot, Allagash, and Moose rivers. **North Country Outfitters** (✉ Box 41, Rockwood 04478, ☎ 207/534–2242 or 207/534–7305) operates a white-water canoeing and kayaking school, rents equipment, and sponsors guided canoe trips on the Allagash Waterway and the Moose, Penobscot, and St. John rivers. **North Woods Ways** (✉ R.R. 2 Box 159-A, Guilford 04443, ☎ 207/997–3723) organizes wilderness canoeing trips on the Allagash, as well as on the Moose, Penobscot, St. Croix, and St. John rivers. **Willard Jalbert Camps** (✉ 6 Winchester St., Presque Isle, 04769, ☎ 207/764–0494) has been sponsoring guided Allagash trips since the late 1800s.

Charles A. Dean Memorial Hospital (✉ Pritham Ave., Greenville, ☎ 800/260–4000 or 207/695–2223). **Mayo Regional Hospital** (✉ 75 W. Main St., Dover-Foxcroft, ☎ 207/564–8401). **Millinocket Regional Hospital** (✉ 200 Somerset St., Millinocket, ☎ 207/723–5161).

Hunting and fishing guides are available through most wilderness camps, sporting goods stores, and canoe outfitters. For assistance in finding a guide, contact **North Maine Woods** (☞ Visitor Information, *below*). A few well-established guides are **Gilpatrick's Guide Service** (✉ Box 461, Skowhegan 04976, ☎ 207/453–6959), **Maine Guide Fly Shop and Guide Service** (✉ Box 1202, Main St., Greenville 04441, ☎ 207/695–2266), and **Professional Guide Service** (✉ Box 346, Sheridan 04775, ☎ 207/435–8044).

Northern Maine Riding Adventures (✉ Box 16, Dover-Foxcroft 04426, ☎ 207/564–3451 or 207/564–2965), owned by Registered Maine Guides Judy Cross-Strehlke and Bob Strehlke, offers one-day, two-day, and weeklong pack trips (10 people maximum) through various parts of Piscataquis County. A popular two-day trip explores the Whitecap–Barren Mountain Range, near Katahdin Iron Works (☞ Off the Beaten Path, *above*).

The following outfitters are among the more than two dozen that are licensed to lead trips down the Kennebec and Dead rivers and the West Branch of the Penobscot River: **Crab Apple Whitewater** (✉ Crab Apple

Acres Inn, The Forks 04985, ☎ 207/663–2218), **Eastern River Expeditions** (✉ Box 1173, Greenville 04441, ☎ 800/634–7238), **Maine Whitewater, Inc.** (✉ Box 633, Bingham 04920, ☎ 207/672–4814 or 800/345–6246), **Northern Outdoors** (✉ Box 100, The Forks 04985, ☎ 207/663–4466 or 800/765–7238), and **Unicorn Expeditions** (✉ Box T, Brunswick 04011, ☎ 207/725–2255 or 800/864–2676).

VISITOR INFORMATION

Baxter State Park Authority (✉ 64 Balsam Dr., Millinocket 04462, ☎ 207/723–5140). **Millinocket Area Chamber of Commerce** (✉ 1029 Central St., Millinocket 04462, ☎ 207/723–4443; ☉ Memorial Day–Sept., daily 8–5; Oct.–Memorial Day, weekdays 9–noon.) **Moosehead Lake Region Chamber of Commerce** (✉ Rtes. 6 and 15, Box 581, Greenville 04441, ☎ 207/695–2702; ☉ Memorial Day–Columbus Day, daily; call for hrs). **North Maine Woods** (✉ Box 421, Ashland 04732, ☎ 207/435–6213), a private organization, publishes maps, a canoeing guide for the St. John River, and lists of outfitters, camps, and campsites.

MAINE A TO Z

Arriving and Departing

By Boat

Marine Atlantic (☎ 207/288–3395 or 800/341–7981) operates a car-ferry service year-round between Yarmouth (Nova Scotia) and Bar Harbor. **Prince of Fundy Cruises** (☎ 800/341–7540 or, in ME, 800/482–0955) operates a car ferry between Portland and Yarmouth, May through October.

By Bus

Vermont Transit (☎ 207/772–6587), a subsidiary of **Greyhound,** connects towns in southwestern Maine with cities in New England and throughout the United States. **Concord Trailways** (☎ 800/639–3317) has daily year-round service between Boston and Bangor (via Portland), with a coastal route connecting towns between Brunswick and Searsport.

By Car

Interstate–95 is the fastest route to and through the state from coastal New Hampshire and points south, turning inland at Brunswick and going on to Bangor and the Canadian border. Route 1, more leisurely and scenic, is the principal coastal highway from New Hampshire to Canada.

By Plane

Both of Maine's major airports, **Portland International Jetport** (☎ 207/774–7301) and **Bangor International Airport** (☎ 207/947–0384), have scheduled daily flights by major U.S. carriers.

Hancock County Airport (☎ 207/667–7329), in Trenton, 8 miles northwest of Bar Harbor, is served by Colgan Air (☎ 207/667–7171 or 800/272–5488). **Knox County Regional Airport** (☎ 207/594–4131), in Owls Head, 3 miles south of Rockland, has flights to Boston on Colgan Air (☎ 207/596–7604 or 800/272–5488).

By Train

Amtrak (☎ 800/872–7245) service between Boston and Portland is not anticipated until at least 1997; call for an update.

Getting Around

By Boat

Casco Bay Lines (☎ 207/774–7871) provides ferry service from Portland to the islands of Casco Bay, and **Maine State Ferry Service** (☎ 207/596–2202 or 800/491–4883) provides ferry service from Rockland, Lincolnville, and Bass Harbor to islands in Penobscot and Blue Hill bays.

By Car

In many areas a car is the only practical means of travel. The *Maine Map and Travel Guide,* available for a small fee from offices of the Maine Publicity Bureau, is useful for driving throughout the state; it has directories, mileage charts, and enlarged maps of city areas.

By Plane

Regional flying services, operating from regional and municipal airports (☞ Arriving and Departing, *above*), provide access to remote lakes and wilderness areas as well as to Penobscot Bay islands.

By Train

During the ski season, **Sunday River Ski Resort** operates the *Sunday River Silver Bullet Ski Express* (☎ 207/824–7245) through scenic terrain between Portland and Bethel. No reservations are necessary for the once-a-day run; lift tickets can be purchased aboard the train.

Contacts and Resources

Guided Tours

Golden Age Festival (✉ 5501 New Jersey Ave., Wildwood Crest, NJ 08260, ☎ 609/522–6316 or 800/257–8920) offers a four-night bus tour geared to senior citizens, with shopping at Kittery outlets and L. L. Bean, a Boothbay Harbor boat cruise, and stops at Kennebunkport, Mount Battie in Camden, and Acadia National Park. Tours operate May to mid-October.

Visitor Information

Maine Publicity Bureau (✉ 325B Water St., Box 2300, Hallowell 04347, ☎ 207/623–0363 or, outside ME, 800/533–9595; FAX 207/623–0388). **Maine Innkeepers Association** (✉ 305 Commercial St., Portland 04101, ☎ 207/773–7670) publishes a statewide lodging and dining guide.

8 Portraits of New England

"A Solo Sojourn on Cape Cod's Beaches," by Anthony Chase

Books and Videos

A SOLO SOJOURN ON CAPE COD'S BEACHES

WHEN YOU RIDE a motorcycle slowly across the Newport Bridge on a fair, windless Saturday morning in early May, it comes as a bit of a shock to realize that there are sea gulls at your elbows. They glide without moving their wings, a few feet from the handlebars. Several hundred yards below, the sea is a silent blue-green diamond field, full of sparkling whitecap flaws. If you are on your way north, to the outer dunes of Cape Cod, the gulls will stay there, like feather guides, wild and discrete, nearby, in the bright droning of the north Atlantic surf.

I am spending the better part of a week walking the lower Cape, from Chatham to Provincetown, staying the night at different inns in different towns along the way, relishing the clean sheets and hot showers, setting off again early the next morning. A small rucksack reduces my worldly possessions to about seven pounds. The landscape is the journey's rationale: forest, wetlands, ponds, and ocean a movable spa. I want to swim in the surf and the kettle holes, eat seafood caught nearby, hang my shabby body out in the wind to dry, like a threadbare rug after a long winter.

Spending a week outdoors in New England—preferably in the spring or fall, when milder breezes and empty beaches make walking a delight—nevertheless invites a tormented relationship with the weather, and so I plan on constantly changing plans. If long stretches of beach walking become too grueling, I'm prepared to find a road that winds along the coast; a storm could restrict me to the same town for three days; head winds might send me into the forest for shelter. I will rely on that fascinating state of mind we tend to abandon as we fumble through middle age: serendipity.

Henry David Thoreau made three trips to Cape Cod in the middle of the 19th century and published his journal descriptions in book form in 1865. In a piece called "Walking," originally published in *The Atlantic* in 1862, he remarks: "I have met with but one or two persons in the course of my life who understood the art of Walking, that is, of taking walks—who had a genius, so to speak, for *sauntering*: which word is beautifully derived 'from idle people who roved about the country, in the middle Ages . . . under pretense of going *à la Sainte Terre,*' to the Holy Land, till the children exclaimed, 'There goes a *Sainte-Terrer,*' a Saunterer, a Holy-Lander . . . Some . . . would derive the word from *sans terre,* without land or home, which . . . will mean, having no particular home, but equally at home everywhere. For this is the secret of successful sauntering . . . no more vagrant than the meandering river, which is all the while sedulously seeking the shortest course to the sea."

Thoreau is known for his eccentricities: living as a hermit in a cabin at Walden Pond, paddling down Concord rivers in a rowboat, or exploring the remote forests of northern Maine in the company of Native American guides. But in fact, he was as sane, and almost as suburban, as anyone. He taught in a secondary school, he worked as a surveyor, and he took an active interest in his family's pencil-manufacturing business. One legacy of Thoreau's life and work is his understanding that there can be no appreciation of solitude without society's presence; there can be no healthy arrangement of human affairs without the surrounding energies of the natural world.

The year's first contact with the ocean is always startling. In the fading afternoon light the water shines more brightly than the sky, in Caribbean shades, with lime-green shallows and blue depths offshore, as if lit by an underwater sun: The sand is free of people, but there are a dozen terns out fishing. They lift off and fly upstream, land, settle their feathers, and drift gently past again.

At low tide, a beach walk is a pleasant stroll on hard sand, with playful surf cooling your ankles. At high tide, the same walk becomes a grueling trudge through ankle-deep, shifting grains. T. E. Lawrence knew. Tide is everything. It is a short climb up to the summit of the Chatham Bar itself. Turning back, I can see the shingled homes and white steeples, the New England Thoreau knew.

Ten yards down the beach's outer slope, every trace of human presence disappears. It is not being on the beach by myself that is so exhilarating; it is being in the company of the shorebirds, the horseshoe crabs, and the striped bass swimming in schools offshore. The spring waves crumble and boom. Long hollow green-and-yellow tunnels rise, slide, tower, and fall along the scalloped ridges at the bottom of the tier of dunes. The sky is cloudless and blue, without any trace of high summer's humid haze. It is low tide and the gulls are fishing.

Every mile or so I stop to remove a piece of clothing. Long pants, sweater, T-shirt, socks, and sneakers all end up in the rucksack, and, after a three-hour walk up the Nauset beaches, I arrive at the green lawn, the oasis of the Nauset Knoll, with a sunburn on the back of my knees.

I sit watching the light easing, the cool gray mists rolling in. I fall asleep when my breathing synchronizes with the waves arriving from the ocean, the water snoring.

I study the wrinkled map. A route runs through Orleans to the old Cape Cod railroad bed, which the astute citizens have transformed into a bike trail. It leads quietly through an enormous marsh, through a pine wood, and past freshwater kettle ponds with beautiful names.

As I walk out into the marsh, the wind begins veering from the north. A mackerel sky appears. Everything seethes: water and grasses, even last year's unraked oak leaves. The railroad bed passes straight through the marsh in a way a road never would. I head out onto the cattail territory, the nesting red-winged blackbirds watching me go. Turtles are basking, but as the clouds send shadows like wind gusts across the water, I watch them one by one plop and swim down. As I reach the edge of the black kettle pond, a marsh hawk begins to wheel and cry. Something about the bird screaming and the haunting impression made by the visible sky is simultaneously startling and reassuring; a brief experience of the world, a Zen telephone call.

Hours pass. As the features of the world glide by, I can identify them on the map. This is satisfying; just reading off the names tells a traveler what the inhabitants thought about the place he's in: Ireland Land, Mean Tide Way, Winterberry Road.

OUT HERE the boundaries dissolve: bird/human, man/nature, mudflat/bay. This is "land" because there are acres and acres of cattails waving, but it is sea as well, because the water fumes a few feet from the trail. And the misty atmosphere clings to the fibers of your sweater, drips gently from your eyebrows, mingling with the sweat above your eyes.

After a 3-mile crossing of the marsh, in the shelter of the first woods on the northern side, I notice a tiny sand crescent at the edge of Herring Pond. I settle under a young maple and spread a cloth for a picnic lunch. Testing the shallow, transparent water, I think, why not, and quickly wade in. Standing waist deep, just about to plunge, I notice a fur head paddling a few yards offshore: A muskrat is diving and reappearing after long fishing trips to the bottom. The raw wind and the May chill of the pond quickly transform my idea of a leisurely swim into a quick splash and a sprint back to shore for a towel.

After I cross the lowlands and have my picnic and my swim, I stop briefly in an ancient cemetery and browse among the gravestones the way you'd wander the aisles of a bookstore, looking for titles, other lives. Bright orange and yellow lichen stand out on the wet black tilted graves. Some of the stones are so old the writing has been worn to an illegible carved wrinkle, haiku epitaphs faded like the bones they identify.

Cold water and the shadows of the pine trees on the gold needles at their feet make me think of the first Pilgrim expeditions to this territory. By walking through a landscape and stopping to swim the waters, a traveler can sense the world in a way earlier generations did. I can trace the roots of our current ecological crises back to the First Encounter Beach, a mile from where I am hiking along and musing. That "first encounter" between European and native civilizations was an exchange of weapons fire. The European conception of land as property displaced a native understanding of the natural realm as common bounty. If you cannot own an ocean, or a cloud, or the sunlight, how can you own a hill, a meadow, a salt marsh, a beach?

In the imagination of everyone who grew up in New England, there is a kind of Ur-Town, and I was convinced that no such place remained. Wellfleet changes my mind. There is a forested bay and an estuary ringed by the hardwoods and the quiet town. The white steeple leans away into the changing clouds. The few streets wind among the watermen's houses, and the children still run barefoot in the picket fence backyards. A dog yelps, a slow car putters by, the ships in the harbor ride their algae moorings, and a walker sidles effortlessly in.

I eat a plate of pasta with oyster sauce and drink a glass of wine at a place called Aesop's Tables, and for the only time in my week outdoors the sky pours, and just as the world grows absolutely black, the lightning bolts of the passing squall make the candles on every table tremble and fade. Ancient Taoist philosophers in China said that hunger makes the best sauce; it's also true that a thunderstorm makes a room cozy and a dinner by a ship captain's hearth even more delightful.

THE NEXT MORNING, after an hour spent winding among small hardwood thickets and low watery ferns, for the first time out of earshot of the sea, I get that little uh-oh feeling that usually means, "You are completely lost."

The world and the map no longer coincide. I choose the world. I make the week's most valuable mistake, turning left at an unsigned intersection. The road gives way to a sandy trail, and I find myself in one of those beautiful lost valleys where the wealthy hide. A woman mowing in a pasture explains a different route to the water, and in half an hour I reach a dune paradise—long, deep, surging ridges, grassy bowls, sheltered valleys entirely without footprints. It is only the swarm of hungry mosquitoes that starts me sprinting toward the coast, where the onshore wind will keep them away. The bay is a different body of water altogether; it is pacific, with transparent green and blue gradations, quite shallow, with visible stones and ran-

domly strewn kelp drawings on the bottom. I wade in and swim. The ocean here is warmer and as quiet as a pond. No matter how hot I am, the cool is instant, total, and as I sit eating my market picnic, alone in all directions, even my thoughts are clean.

The next few miles of walking are effortless. Here along Ryder Beach the heather rolls up toward the forest and the land itself begins to swell. It is bare without being barren, somewhat wistfully austere. Edward Hopper built himself a house in Truro in the 1930s, and the clear light he gave his life to is still here. Up in the warm meadows, there is toe-soft loam producing flowers, twitching gently in the early afternoon; coiled streams and estuaries are set in beside the land. I'm trying not to exaggerate, but you can't tell if what you're seeing is a painting or a dream.

The morning of the final day, I wake to a room full of chilly fog. Having left both windows open, I am literally wrapped in weather. On the Highland Road to the Cape Cod Lighthouse for the final leg, my footsteps have a new reluctance.

One of the most remarkable aspects of this week outdoors is the experience of the ocean on its own terms; what seems recreational and tame among the tilted umbrellas and radios and Frisbee-chasing dogs becomes altogether unfamiliar after a few hours alone. Water rises and falls, wrapping an entire globe as it rockets through outer space, centrifugally whirling as it goes. The water speaks in tongues, and after several days you begin to listen.

My hands are actually cold, my knuckles frozen. I'm playing Guess the Season. In a world of sand and water and wind, there are fewer clues. The wind booms, the ocean's humming, and the loud waves build and fall and shake the gravel I'm on as the last wave hisses and recedes into the next.

After several days of steady traveling up the coast, walking and thinking fuse, the ordinary divisions of mind and body lose their boundaries. The easygoing motion of my limbs seems to belong to the Cape dunes and riverbeds, the way the ebbing and flooding tides, the piled clouds, the crying birds, do. Toward the end of his life Thoreau made an unobtrusive entry in his journal: "All I can say is that I live and breathe and have my thoughts." Out here that short list of attributes seems plenty.

The harbor side streets are empty as I go searching for a room. It is strange to have touched a long stretch of geography with your feet. You feel a friendship toward the roaming world out there; contact has given you calm.

A lighthouse blinks every four seconds. A white lobster boat is mooring in the last light. I find a room in a house by the water. As New England weather will, the sky changes while I'm at the front desk checking in. Up on the third floor, I can look off into the sunset's afterglow. The sky clears, turning cheddar gold.

— *Anthony Chase*

BOOKS AND VIDEOS

NEW ENGLAND has been home to some of America's classic authors, among them Herman Melville, Edith Wharton, Mark Twain, Robert Frost, and Emily Dickinson. Henry David Thoreau wrote about New England in *Cape Cod, The Maine Woods,* and his masterpiece, *Walden.*

Melville's *Moby-Dick,* set on a 19th-century Nantucket whaler, captures the spirit of the whaling era; Gregory Peck starred in the 1956 screen version under John Huston's direction. Nathaniel Hawthorne portrayed early New England life in his novels *The Scarlet Letter* (the 1995 movie stars Demi Moore) and *The House of the Seven Gables* (the actual house, in Salem, is open to the public). Newburyport native Henry James's books include *The Bostonians, Daisy Miller,* and *Portrait of a Lady.* The beautiful 1994 screen adaptation of Louisa May Alcott's classic, *Little Women,* casts Winona Ryder as Jo and Susan Sarandon as Marmee. Visitors are welcome at Alcott's house (look for shots of it in the movie) in Concord. A historian tells the fascinating story of the Alcotts in *The World of Louisa May Alcott,* which has more than 200 photographs. Hog Island, near Essex, Massachusetts, was a 1995 location for the filming of *The Crucible,* Arthur Miller's 1953 play about the Salem witch trials. It stars Daniel Day-Lewis and Winona Ryder, again in a New England-based film (although much of *Little Women* was shot in Vancouver).

Among books written about the Maine islands are Philip Conkling's *Islands in Time,* Bill Caldwell's *Islands of Maine,* and Charlotte Fardelmann's *Islands Down East.* Kenneth Roberts set a series of historical novels, beginning with *Arundel,* in the coastal Kennebunk region during the Revolutionary War. Ruth Moore's *Candalmas Bay, Speak to the Winds,* and *The Weir;* and Elisabeth Ogilvie's "Tide Trilogy" books capture both the romanticism and hardships of coastal life. Carolyn Chute's 1985 best seller, *The Beans of*

Egypt, Maine, offers a fictional glimpse of the hardships of contemporary rural life. After a limited theatrical release in 1994, the movie version of the book, starring Martha Plimpton, is in video stores with the title, *Forbidden Choices.*

Charles Morrissey's *Vermont: A History* delivers just what the title promises. *Without a Farmhouse Near,* by Deborah Rawson, describes the impact of change on small Vermont communities. *Real Vermonters Don't Milk Goats,* by Frank Bryan and Bill Mares, looks at the lighter side of life in the Green Mountain state. Both books and movies, *Peyton Place* and *Ethan Frome* have links to Vermont.

Visitors to New Hampshire may enjoy *The White Mountains: Their Legends, Landscape, and Poetry,* by Starr King, and *The Great Stone Face and Other Tales of the White Mountains,* by Nathaniel Hawthorne. New Hampshire was also blessed with the poet Robert Frost, whose first books, *A Boy's Way* and *North of Boston,* are set here. It's commonly accepted that the Grover's Corners of Thornton Wilder's *Our Town* is the real-life Peterborough; Willa Cather wrote part of *Death Comes for the Archbishop* while residing in Peterborough. The 1981 movie, *On Golden Pond,* was partially filmed on Squam Lake.

Sloan Wilson's novel *The Man in the Gray Flannel Suit* renders the life of a Connecticut commuter (Cary Grant in the movie version) in the 1950s. Julia Roberts's first movie, the charming *Mystic Pizza,* focuses on a group of young Mystic women and their romances. In *Theophilus North,* Thornton Wilder portrays Newport, Rhode Island, in its social heyday.

Also published by Fodor's, *New England's Best Bed & Breakfasts* has more than 300 reviews; *National Parks and Seashores of the East* covers many New England destinations; and *Where Should We Take the Kids? The Northeast* provides ideas on what to do with the little ones while in New England.

INDEX

Escape to ancient cities and

journey to  *exotic islands with*

CNN Travel Guide, a wealth of valuable advice. Host

Valerie Voss will take you to

all of your favorite destinations,

 *including those off the beaten*

path. Tune-in to your passport to the world.

CNN TRAVEL GUIDE
SATURDAY 12:30 PMET   SUNDAY 4:30 PMET

Fodor's Travel Publications

Available at bookstores everywhere, or call 1–800–533–6478, 24 hours a day.

Gold Guides

U.S.

Alaska

Arizona

Boston

California

Cape Cod, Martha's Vineyard, Nantucket

The Carolinas & the Georgia Coast

Chicago

Colorado

Florida

Hawai'i

Las Vegas, Reno, Tahoe

Los Angeles

Maine, Vermont, New Hampshire

Maui & Lāna'i

Miami & the Keys

New England

New Orleans

New York City

Pacific North Coast

Philadelphia & the Pennsylvania Dutch Country

The Rockies

San Diego

San Francisco

Santa Fe, Taos, Albuquerque

Seattle & Vancouver

The South

U.S. & British Virgin Islands

USA

Virginia & Maryland

Washington, D.C.

Foreign

Australia

Austria

The Bahamas

Belize & Guatemala

Bermuda

Canada

Cancún, Cozumel, Yucatán Peninsula

Caribbean

China

Costa Rica

Cuba

The Czech Republic & Slovakia

Eastern & Central Europe

Europe

Florence, Tuscany & Umbria

France

Germany

Great Britain

Greece

Hong Kong

India

Ireland

Israel

Italy

Japan

London

Madrid & Barcelona

Mexico

Montréal & Québec City

Moscow, St. Petersburg, Kiev

The Netherlands, Belgium & Luxembourg

New Zealand

Norway

Nova Scotia, New Brunswick, Prince Edward Island

Paris

Portugal

Provence & the Riviera

Scandinavia

Scotland

Singapore

South Africa

South America

Southeast Asia

Spain

Sweden

Switzerland

Thailand

Tokyo

Toronto

Turkey

Vienna & the Danube

Fodor's Special-Interest Guides

Caribbean Ports of Call

The Complete Guide to America's National Parks

Family Adventures

Gay Guide to the USA

Halliday's New England Food Explorer

Halliday's New Orleans Food Explorer

Healthy Escapes

Kodak Guide to Shooting Great Travel Pictures

Net Travel

Nights to Imagine

Rock & Roll Traveler USA

Sunday in New York

Sunday in San Francisco

Walt Disney World, Universal Studios and Orlando

Walt Disney World for Adults

Where Should We Take the Kids? California

Where Should We Take the Kids? Northeast

Worldwide Cruises and Ports of Call

Special Series

Affordables

Caribbean
Europe
Florida
France
Germany
Great Britain
Italy
London
Paris

Fodor's Bed & Breakfasts and Country Inns

America
California
The Mid-Atlantic
New England
The Pacific Northwest
The South
The Southwest
The Upper Great Lakes

The Berkeley Guides

California
Central America
Eastern Europe
Europe
France
Germany & Austria
Great Britain & Ireland
Italy
London
Mexico
New York City
Pacific Northwest & Alaska
Paris
San Francisco

Compass American Guides

Arizona
Canada
Chicago
Colorado
Hawaii
Idaho
Hollywood
Las Vegas

Maine
Manhattan
Montana
New Mexico
New Orleans
Oregon
San Francisco
Santa Fe
South Carolina
South Dakota
Southwest
Texas
Utah
Virginia
Washington
Wine Country
Wisconsin
Wyoming

Fodor's Citypacks

Atlanta
Hong Kong
London
New York City
Paris
Rome
San Francisco
Washington, D.C.

Fodor's Español

California
Caribe Occidental
Caribe Oriental
Gran Bretaña
Londres
Mexico
Nueva York
Paris

Fodor's Exploring Guides

Australia
Boston & New England
Britain
California
Caribbean
China
Egypt
Florence & Tuscany
Florida

France
Germany
Ireland
Israel
Italy
Japan
London
Mexico
Moscow & St. Petersburg
New York City
Paris
Prague
Provence
Rome
San Francisco
Scotland
Singapore & Malaysia
Spain
Thailand
Turkey
Venice

Fodor's Flashmaps

Boston
New York
San Francisco
Washington, D.C.

Fodor's Pocket Guides

Acapulco
Atlanta
Barbados
Jamaica
London
New York City
Paris
Prague
Puerto Rico
Rome
San Francisco
Washington, D.C.

Mobil Travel Guides

America's Best Hotels & Restaurants
California & the West
Frequent Traveler's Guide to Major Cities
Great Lakes
Mid-Atlantic

Northeast
Northwest & Great Plains
Southeast
Southwest & South Central

Rivages Guides

Bed and Breakfasts of Character and Charm in France
Hotels and Country Inns of Character and Charm in France
Hotels and Country Inns of Character and Charm in Italy
Hotels and Country Inns of Character and Charm in Paris
Hotels and Country Inns of Character and Charm in Portugal
Hotels and Country Inns of Character and Charm in Spain

Short Escapes

Britain
France
New England
Near New York City

Fodor's Sports

Golf Digest's Best Places to Play
Skiing USA
USA Today The Complete Four Sport Stadium Guide

Fodor's Vacation Planners

Great American Learning Vacations
Great American Sports & Adventure Vacations
Great American Vacations
Great American Vacations for Travelers with Disabilities
National Parks and Seashores of the East
National Parks of the West

WHEREVER YOU TRAVEL, *H*ELP IS NEVER FAR AWAY.

From planning your trip to providing travel assistance along the way, American Express® Travel Service Offices are always there to help.

New England

CONNECTICUT
American Express Travel Service
Stamford
203/359-4244

MAINE
American Express Travel Service
Portland
207/772-8450

MASSACHUSETTS
American Express Travel Service
Boston
617/439-4400

American Express Travel Service
Cambridge
617/868-2600

NEW HAMPSHIRE
Griffin Travel Service (R)
Manchester
603/668-3730

RHODE ISLAND
American Express Travel Service
Cranston
401/943-4545

VERMONT
Milne Travel (R)
Brattleboro
802/254-8844

American-International Travel (R)
Burlington
802/864-9827

Travel

http://www.americanexpress.com/travel

American Express Travel Service Offices are located throughout New England. For the office nearest you, call 1-800-YES-AMEX.